PROFILES IN CARDIOGY

EDITORS:

J. WILLIS HURST, M.D.,

C. RICHARD CONTI, M.D.,

W. BRUCE FYE, M.D., M.A.

Published by The Foundation for Advances in Medicine and Science, Inc., Mahwah, N.J.

Overleaf: Laënnec at a patient's bedside—using his stethoscope.

DEDICATION

*To our heroes past and present who have contributed
to our knowledge of the heart and circulation and,
with it all, lived interesting lives worth telling.*

TABLE OF CONTENTS

PREFACE

Most medical progress is due to the extension of the knowledge created by our predecessors. Because that is true it is possible to study the evolution of an idea over a period of time and determine whether the next step is a wise one or not. This approach to medical history is absolutely necessary else we continue to reinvent the wheel or move in the wrong intellectual direction. For example, the invention of an electrical pacemaker made sense because the workers of the past identified the conduction system of the heart. They also taught us how electricity travels from the atrioventricular node, through the bundle of His, and down the conduction system of the two ventricles. Knowing that, it was only a matter of time until someone harnessed electricity so that the ventricles could be stimulated using an artificial pacemaker.

In addition, the lives of those who create new ideas, or perform necessary tasks in a scholarly manner, also deserve our attention. First, it is always interesting and worthwhile to study the lives of creative people. Second, it is useful to appreciate the obstacles our predecessors faced when they tried to teach the profession what they had discovered. For example, Forssmann pushed on with cardiac catheterization when his supervisors proclaimed he was foolish and demanded that he stop immediately. He chose to persevere, which, from his own writing, brings spice and merriment to anyone who reads his account of his actions.

There are several excellent books on the history of cardiology. The following quotations are from three of them. The authors support the concept that a knowledge of the history of cardiology is not only fascinating, but that it plays an essential role in the struggle for advancement.

The following passage is from the Preface of *Cardiac Classics* edited by Willius and Keys:

> One cannot read and contemplate the classics without being aroused by a desire to express apologies to the old masters, for there are many moderns who have written certain lines, believed to be original, only to find that the same observations and thoughts were expressed many years before. It is reasonable to conclude that the classics of medical antiquity form the basis of modern medicine and the physician of today relinquishes many cultural advantages when [he] avoids acquaintance with his distinguished predecessors.[1]

The following passage is from the Foreword of *Circulation of the Blood: Men and Ideas* edited by Fishman and Richards:

> The primary objective in its design has been to provide a study of the origins, discovery, and progress of certain of the great ideas of this branch of science, and to bring to life, insofar as possible, the great men who made these discoveries and achieved this progress.[2]

The following passage is from the introduction of *The History of Cardiology* by Acierno:

> This level of excellence did not emerge *de novo*. As in all human endeavors, it rests upon concepts established in the past and contributed by researchers from various countries throughout the world, but especially from those of the western civiliza-

tion. Furthermore, no matter how novel each new concept or technique may appear to be, it is, in reality, but an extension or refinement of an earlier contribution.[3]

The birth of this first edition of the book *Profiles in Cardiology* came about as follows. In 1985 one of the editors (JWH) of the journal *Clinical Cardiology* suggested to the publisher that a short profile of a contributor to the field of cardiology should be included in each issue of the journal. The plan for production included asking various physicians to write the profiles, but also to accept unsolicited profiles written by interested individuals. The profiles were to be short and would include contributors from the present as well as from the distant past. The content of the profiles would be a mixture of the scientific contributions and the lives and personae of the individuals who did the work. Three profiles were published in 1985 and since 1986 a profile has appeared in *Clinical Cardiology* each month.

There is no end in sight as to the number of profiles that must be written about the many past contributors to the field of cardiology. In addition, there are many current workers in the field whose profiles must be included in future issues of the journal. This first book is a collection of the profiles that have already been published in the journal *Clinical Cardiology*. The second edition, to be published some 10 years from now, will include the profiles of other contributors from the distant past as well as profiles of individuals who are currently making significant discoveries.

So, with this preamble in mind, we the editors hope you enjoy and profit from reading the profiles of the individuals who gave you— almost imperceptibly—a lot of the knowledge that makes your work possible. The editors wish to thank the authors for the interesting vignettes (profiles) they have provided *Clinical Cardiology* for the last 15 years. We thank all of the secretaries, especially Carol Miller who keeps order in the office of JWH. We also thank the first-rate publishing team of *Clinical Cardiology* for its eagerness to publish the biographical sketches of the contributors to cardiology that bring spice to our lives.

J. Willis Hurst, M.D.
C. Richard Conti, M.D.
W. Bruce Fye, M.D., M.A.

References

1. Willius FA, Keys TE: *Cardiac Classics*. St. Louis: The C.V. Mosby Company, 1941:xi
2. Fishman AP, Richards DW: *Circulation of the Blood: Men and Ideas*. New York: Oxford University Press, MCMLXIV:ix
3. Acierno LJ: *The History of Cardiology*. London: The Parthenon Publishing Group, 1994:vii

Antonio di Paolo Benivieni

W. Bruce Fye, M.D., M.A.

Department of Cardiology, Marshfield Clinic, Marshfield, Wisconsin, USA

Antonio di Paolo Benivieni (Fig. 1) was born in Florence, Italy, on November 3, 1443, at the dawn of the Italian Renaissance.[1,2] He was a boy when German printer Johann Gutenberg published the first book using moveable type and a middle-aged man when Christopher Columbus discovered America. Antonio's father, a nobleman and notary, was a member of a prominent and wealthy Florentine family, so he had extraordinary educational opportunities. Young Benivieni studied medicine at the Universities of Pisa and Siena after being educated in Florence by tutors.

After completing his medical studies, Benivieni returned to Florence where he practiced medicine for more than three decades. His peers considered him a skilled diagnostician and praised his ability to treat difficult cases. As Benivieni's reputation spread, some of Florence's most influential families became his patients or sought his opinion on specific problems. Eventually, he cared for many prominent Florentines, including the Medicis.

Benivieni's most enduring contribution was his book *De abditis nonnullis ac mirandis morborum et sanationum causis* (On some hidden and remarkable causes of disease and recovery). Published posthumously in 1507 by Benivieni's brother Girolamo and the physician-philosopher Giovanni Rosati, it contained 111 chapters that included about 200 brief case reports. Girolamo explained in his preface to the book that his brother had jotted down the fragments during more than 32 years of active medical practice. The original manuscript, rediscovered in 1855 by Italian historian Francesco Puccinotti, reveals that Benivieni's brother and the publisher (Filippo Giunti) omitted several dozen case reports from the printed book.

British historian Charles Singer translated Benivieni's book into English in 1954, making the text more accessible to physicians and historians.[3] The book provides useful insight into the context and content of medical practice of urban Italian medical and surgical practice in the late fifteenth century.[4–6]

Like other European physicians of his time, Benivieni was a Galenist. His anatomical concepts and his therapeutic approaches reflected the teachings of the ancient Greek physician.[7] Medical treatments included the administration of various herbs and phlebotomy using lancets or leeches. In his book, Benivieni briefly described several surgical procedures

FIG. 1 Antonio di Paolo Benivieni, 1443–1502. From Ref. 3 with permission.

such as operating on a baby with an imperforate anus, cauterizing an artery to prevent exsanguination in a man wounded during a fight, and removing a bladder stone that had caused anuria.

Although Benivieni was primarily a clinician, many medical historians have considered him a founder of pathology. His book includes summaries of twenty autopsies he performed in an attempt to clarify the clinical findings and the cause of death. Benivieni was not the first Renaissance doctor to perform autopsies for this purpose, however. By the late fifteenth century, there was increasing interest in dissection and clinico-pathologic correlation as some physicians began to question Galen's teachings.

Benivieni briefly described the pathologic findings in patients found at autopsy to have had intestinal perforation, gall stones, urinary obstruction due to bladder cancer, and syphilis (which had recently appeared in Europe). Some of Benivieni's case reports related to patients on whom he had operated. At the time, surgery was limited mainly to the treatment of superficial disorders and fractures, however. The great Italian pathologist Giovanni Battista Morgagni (1682–1771) cited several of Benivieni's cases in his own classic collection of clinico-pathologic correlations *De sedibus et causis morborum per anatomen indagatis*, published in 1761.

Historians have held different opinions about Benivieni's significance and that of his book. American medical historian Ralph Major characterizes him as a "pathfinder in medicine who blazed a new path which physicians waited for more than two centuries to follow" (quote p. 749).[8] But British historian of science Lynn Thorndike argues that Benivieni's case reports "merely continue the tradition long established by the more elaborate *Consilia* of physicians of the preceding two centuries" (quote p. vol. 4. p. 586).[9] Thorndike also disputes the claim that Benivieni was a pioneer in performing autopsies in an attempt to discover the etiology of his patients' symptoms and the cause of their death. He explains that the importance of Benivieni's little book "appears to have been exaggerated by past historians of medicine; partly perhaps because it was more accessible in print, easier to read, and better known than earlier and more elaborate works in manuscript" (quote p. 590).[9]

Benivieni died in Florence in 1502. Although it may be unjustified to term him the father of pathologic anatomy, he surely helped to establish the tradition of clinico-pathologic correlation that led eventually to many important discoveries.

References

1. Franceschini P: Antonio Benivieni. In *Dictionary of Scientific Biography* (Ed. Gillispie CC). New York:Charles Scribner's Sons, 1970:1, 611–612
2. Long ER: Antonio Benivieni and his contribution to pathological anatomy. In Benivieni A: *De abditis nonnullis ac mirandis morborum et sanationum causis. The Hidden Causes of Disease* (Ed. Singer C). Springfield:Charles C Thomas, 1954:17–56
3. Benivieni A: *De abditis nonnullus ac mirandis et sanationum causis. The Hidden Causes of Disease* (Ed. Singer C). Springfield: Charles C Thomas, 1954
4. Castiglioni A: *Italian Medicine*. New York:Paul B. Hoeber, 1932
5. Siraisi NG: *Medieval & Early Renaissance Medicine*. Chicago: University of Chicago, 1990
6. Gordon BL: *Medieval and Renaissance Medicine*. New York:Philosophical Library, 1959
7. Temkin O: *Galenism: Rise and Decline of a Medical Philosophy*. Ithaca:Cornell University Press, 1973
8. Major RH: Antonio di Paolo Benivieni. *Bull Hist Med* 1935;3: 739–755
9. Thorndike L: *A History of Magic and Experimental Science. 1923-1958*. New York:Columbia University Press, 1923:4:586–592

Jean François Fernel

W. Bruce Fye, M.D., M.A.

Department of Cardiology, Marshfield Clinic, Marshfield, Wisconsin, USA

Jean François Fernel (Fig. 1), one of the greatest physicians of the Renaissance, wrote the earliest systematic treatises on physiology and pathology (and coined both terms). Fernel was born in Montdidier, France, about 1497.[1] As a student at the Collège de Sainte Barbe in Paris, he studied mathematics, astronomy, and philosophy. Fernel completed his medical training at the University of Paris in 1530 and was appointed Professor of Medicine at the university four years later. His fame spread rapidly. By the middle of the sixteenth century, he was France's most prominent physician.

For Fernel and other Renaissance physicians, physiology was based on observation and description rather than on experimentation.[2] The experimental tradition in physiology began with William Harvey's publication of his discovery of the circulation in 1628.[3] Fernel, however, was a skilled anatomist and a keen observer of the natural history of disease. He performed many autopsies and emphasized the value of clinicopathologic correlation.

Fernel's book on physiology, *De naturali parte medicinae* (On the Natural Parts of Medicine), was published in Paris in 1542. When the book appeared, Fernel was already a prominent physician with a busy practice and a popular lecturer. The book enhanced his reputation further. Based mainly on Galenic theory and humoral medicine, it described the functions of the healthy body as Fernel and his contemporaries interpreted them. Fernel's book on physiology "remained *the* treatise on its subject" for more than a century, according to neurophysiologist Charles Sherrington, his biographer.[4a]

Written more than 80 years before William Harvey described the circulation, Fernel's book reflected Galenic teachings about the functions of the heart, the liver, and the blood vessels.[5] For Fernel and his contemporaries, the heart was not the principal organ that it became following Harvey's discovery of the circulation. Like Galen, Fernel believed that the liver was the source of the entire venous system. He thought the liver produced blood (as well as bile), and that this new blood was carried from the organ to all parts of the body through the vena cava and its branches. This traditional Galenic view did not recognize the pumping function of the heart. Rather, blood simply flowed outward from the veins as it was needed by the various parts of the body.

Fernel portrayed the heart as two-chambered because the atria were not recognized as a discrete part of the organ. Still, Fernel's description of the heart's structure represented an advance. He believed that the active phase of the cardiac cycle was dilatation or diastole, when blood was drawn into the heart; so, in diastole, the heart functioned as a suction pump. Fernel made another observation that represented an original contribution to cardiac physiology. He argued that the arteries increased in size when the ventricles shrank during systole. This contradicted the traditional teaching that the arteries increased in diameter at the same time the heart expanded in diastole. Fernel attributed the expansion of the arteries to ventricular systole, an event that moved a mixture of blood and compressed spirit from the heart into the arteries.

In 1554 Fernel published *Medicina*, his most important book. It was a systematic survey of what was then known about human disease. In addition to a revised version of the physiology portion of *De naturali parte medicinae*, Fernel's new book included major sections on pathology and therapeutics. He coined the term pathology in this book which, according to Sherrington, "in several ways broke new ground."[4b] Rather than a collection of random case reports, it was a methodical study of disorders, arranged by the organ system. On the basis of this book, Fernel is often called "the father of pathology." Historian of pathology Esmond Long contrasted Fernel with Antonio Benivieni whose pioneering book on pathologic anatomy appeared in 1507. Whereas Benivieni "was a brave pioneer groping his way in the dark, Fernel was a full-fledged pathologist."[6]

In *Medicini*, Fernel classified diseases as general or special. The special diseases were localized to a particular organ whereas the general diseases were not. He also emphasized the importance of symptoms and signs and focused on abnormalities of the pulse and urinary secretion. Internist and historian Saul Jarcho commented recently,

> The clear, systematic arrangement of Fernel's textbook, its extensive reference to clinical experience, and the repeated recourse to autopsy compel the admiration of the modern reader. It is not surprising that Fernel was regarded as a leading physician of the Renaissance.[7a]

Fernel included a brief description of heart disease and described various cardiac symptoms, notably syncope and palpitation which, according to him, were the most prominent cardiac symptoms. He explained:

FIG. 1   Jean François Fernel, 1497–1558. Source: From the collection of the author.

Syncope is a swift collapse of the forces. The pulse is either nil or extremely rare and indistinct. The upper most parts are cold; the temples, neck, and thorax are soaked in cold sweat; the face is pale; the whole body lies as if without sinews; and the mind and all sensation are absent.[7b]

Fernel's *Medicini* also contained original descriptions of pathologic conditions, including what is probably the earliest report of endocarditis.

Fernel was appointed physician-in-chief to the King of France in 1556. Two years later, after developing a fever, he died in Fontainebleau. Fernel's writings were reprinted frequently for several decades after his death, reflecting the profound influence he had on sixteenth century medicine. Guillaume Plancy, Fernel's pupil and biographer, observed shortly after his death: "It was his first object to teach how the signs of a disease can be recognized with certainty, and, that done, how the disease is to be overcome."[4c]

References

1. Granit R: Jean François Fernel. In *Dictionary of Scientific Biography* (Ed. Gillispie CC), Vol. 4, p. 584–586. New York: Charles Scribner's Sons, 1971
2. Rothschuh KE: *History of Physiology*. Huntington, N.Y.: Robert E. Krieger, 1973
3. Frank RG Jr: *Harvey and the Oxford Physiologists: A Study of Scientific Ideas*. Berkeley and Los Angeles: University of California Press, 1980
4. Sherrington C: *The Endeavour of Jean Fernel with a List of the Editions of His Writings*. (a) p. 1; (b) p. 101; (c) p. 161 (Plancy). Cambridge: Cambridge University Press, 1946
5. Harris CRS: *The Heart and the Vascular System in Ancient Greek Medicine from Alcmaeon to Galen*. London: Oxford University Press, 1973
6. Long ER: *A History of Pathology*, p. 38. New York: Dover Publications, Inc., 1965
7. Jarcho S: *The Concept of Heart Failure from Avicenna to Albertini*. (a) p. 27; (b) 25. Cambridge, Mass.: Harvard University Press, 1980

Realdo Colombo

W. Bruce Fye, M.D., M.A.

Cardiovascular Division, Mayo Clinic, Rochester, Minnesota, USA

Realdo Colombo (Fig. 1), born in Cremona, Italy, between 1510 and 1515, published the first definitive description of the pulmonary circulation.[1, 2] The son of an apothecary, he received his preliminary education in Milan, then began to study medicine as an apprentice to Giovanni Antonio Lonigo, a prominent Venetian surgeon. After seven years in Venice with Lonigo, he moved to Padua to continue his studies at the university, a leading center for medical education. He arrived at Padua at an exciting time. Andreas Vesalius was writing and preparing the illustrations for his monumental anatomical work, *De humani corporis fabrica libri septum.*

A superior student and talented anatomist, Colombo became Vesalius's assistant in 1541. He substituted for him during the 1542 term, when Vesalius was in Switzerland overseeing the printing of his book to appear the following year. Their friendship ended soon, however, when Colombo criticized Vesalius publicly. After teaching anatomy in Pisa from 1545 to 1548, Colombo moved to Rome where he hoped to collaborate with Michelangelo on an illustrated anatomical textbook that would compete with Vesalius's atlas. He began teaching at the Sapienza and spent the rest of his life in Rome.

During the the sixteenth century, anatomical dissection grew in popularity in Paris and northern Italy, and Colombo flourished in this milieu. He lived at a time when a few anatomists were beginning to challenge Galen's teachings. Galen had dominated medical thought for almost 1400 years. But Colombo, like Vesalius, was not bound by tradition. Both preferred to extend knowledge by direct observation, and performed countless autopsies, dissections, and vivisections during the 1540s and 1550s.

Colombo's book, *De re anatomica*, incorporated his original observations and synthesized contemporary anatomical thought. The book of 15 chapters, was completed just before his death in 1559. Michelangelo had died five years earlier, so their planned collaboration did not come to fruition. The only illustration in Colombo's book is an elaborate engraving that depicts him performing a dissection. According to twentieth century scholars Robert Moes and C. D. O'Malley, the book was popular and influential. Because "the language was uncomplicated and the descriptions succinct," they thought it likely that most contemporaries "paid lip-service to the massive *Fabrica* [of Vesalius] and read *De re anatomica*."[3]

This rare book includes Colombo's original description of the pulmonary circulation based on hundreds of dissections and vivisections. This sets Colombo apart from two individuals who earlier described the pulmonary circulation: the thirteenth century Arabic physician Ibn al-Nafis of Damascus and the Spanish biologist and philosopher Michael Servetus, whose description appeared in a theological book in 1553. Historian Leonard Wilson concluded that Colombo arrived at his conclusions about the pulmonary circulation independently.[4] There was no printed version of Ibn al-Nafis's observations; they were passed on in Arabic manuscripts. Almost all copies of Servetus's book were destroyed the year it was published—when he was burned at the stake in Geneva for heresy. A comparison of their writings demonstrates that Colombo's understanding of the pulmonary circulation was more sophisticated than that of the other two writers.

Galen completed his influential treatise on the usefulness of the parts of the body around 175 A.D. It included detailed discussions of the anatomy and physiology of the cardiovascular system. Galen believed that blood circulated from the right to the left ventricle through invisible pores in the interventricular septum.[5] His notion of the heart's anatomy and physiology came under increasing scrutiny as Renaissance anatomists began to perform vivisections and dissect human cadavers. In the second (1555) edition of his anatomy, Vesalius rejected Galen's teaching that blood passed through the interventricular septum, although he did not propose an alternate route. Several contemporaries, most of whom embraced Galen's teachings, protested.

Colombo went further than his former colleague Vesalius:

> Between these ventricles there is a septum through which almost everyone believes there opens a pathway for the blood from the right ventricle to the left, and that the blood is rendered thin so that this may be done more easily for the generation of vital spirits. But they are in great error, for the blood is carried through the pulmonary artery to the lung and is there attenuated; then it is carried, along with air, through the pulmonary vein to the left ventricle of the heart. Hitherto no one has noticed this or left it in writing, and it especially should be observed by all.[6]

So Colombo's classic observations came amid growing controversy over Galen's teachings of cardiac anatomy and physiology. Recently, historian Jerome Bylebyl summarized the status of the ancient Greek physician's views about the cardiovascular system during the time of Vesalius and Colombo:

> In the Galenic physiology of the sixteenth century, the right cardiac ventricle was thought to receive blood from

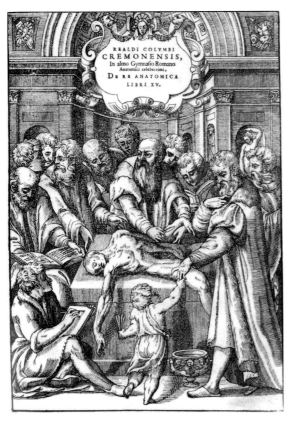

FIG. 1   Realdo Colombo (1510/1515–1559). (From the collection of W. Bruce Fye.)

the vena cava and to send it into the pulmonary artery to nourish the lungs. The left ventricle was supposed to ventilate the innate heat of the heart by breathing in and out through the pulmonary vein ...the left ventricle was thought to receive blood from the right ...through minute pores in the intervening septum. From this blood and from some of the air received from the lungs, the left ventricle generated vital spirits and arterial blood . . . distributed to the entire body through the arteries to preserve life.[1(a)]

Colombo disproved the Galenic teaching that the pulmonary artery and vein[s] contained different amounts of blood and air (or spirit). Based on many dissections of humans and vivisections of living animals, the Italian anatomist argued that the pulmonary vein[s], like all other veins in the body, contained blood rather than just air. He proposed that blood mixed with air in the lungs rather than in the heart itself. In his discussion of the function of the lungs Colombo stated that air

. . . is carried by means of the trachea through the whole lung, but the lung mixed the air together with that blood which is carried from the right ventricle of the heart through the pulmonary artery. For this pulmonary artery, in addition to the fact that it carries blood for its nutrition, is so broad that it could carry it for the sake of another purpose as well. Blood of this kind is agitated on

account of the unceasing movement of the lungs, it is rendered thin and it is mixed together with the air, and in this collision and breaking up it is prepared so that mixed blood and air are taken up at the same time through the pulmonary vein and finally are carried through its trunk to the left ventricle of the heart.[4(a)]

Colombo also understood the function of the cardiac valves, which further undermined the traditional Galenic view of the heart's structure and function. Speaking of the four valves, he explained,

. . . two of them have been constructed so that they carry [blood] inwardly to the heart, that is, when the heart is dilated [in diastole]; but the other two carry [blood] outward when the heart is constricted [in systole]. Therefore when it is dilated, and those membranes are loosened and yield ingress, the heart receives blood from the vena cava into the right ventricle, and also prepared blood from the pulmonary vein, as we said, along with air into the left ventricle. And when the heart is compressed [in systole], these valves are closed lest the vessels receive anything regressing along the same path; and at the same time the valves of both the aorta and the pulmonary artery are opened; they permit the passage of the outgoing spirituous blood which is diffused through the whole body and of the natural blood which is carried to the lungs; and it is always thus when the heart is dilated, as we noted before: [that the] other [valves] open and then shut. And so you will find that the blood which has entered the right ventricle is unable to return to the vena cava.[6(a)]

Colombo's book and its clear articulation of the pulmonary circulation had a profound effect on English physician William Harvey, who published his description of the circulation of the blood in 1628. Harvey had used Colombo's book when he prepared his 1616 lectures on anatomy for the College of Physicians of London. Gweneth Whitteridge, a leading Harvey scholar, showed that he owed his understanding of cardiac systole and diastole as well as the pulmonary circulation to Colombo.[7] The pioneering Italian anatomist died in 1559 in Rome, just as his book was about to be published.

References

1. Bylebyl JJ: Realdo Colombo. In *Dictionary of Scientific Biography* (Ed. Gillespie CC), p. 354–357. New York: Charles Scribner's Sons, 1971;(a) p. 356
2. Ekoynan G, De Santo NG: Realdo Colombo (1516–1559): A reappraisal. *Am J Nephrol* 1997;17:261–268
3. Moes RJ, O'Malley CD: Realdo Colombo: On those things rarely found in anatomy. An annotated translation from his *De Re Anatomica* (1559). *Bull Hist Med* 1960;34:508–528
4. Wilson LG: The problem of the discovery of the pulmonary circulation. *J Hist Med Allied Sci* 1962;17:229–244;(a) p. 243
5. Harris CRS: *The Heart and Vascular System in Ancient Greek Medicine*. London: Oxford University Press, 1973
6. Coppola ED: The discovery of the pulmonary circulation: A new approach. *Bull Hist Med* 1957;21:44–77;(a) p. 65
7. Whitteridge G: *William Harvey and the Circulation of the Blood*. London: Macdonald, 1971

Andreas Vesalius and *De Humani Corporis Fabrica*

MARK E. SILVERMAN, M.D.

Department of Cardiology, Emory University School of Medicine, and Piedmont Hospital, Atlanta, Georgia, USA

They ought to be grateful to me as the first who has dared to attack man's false opinions, to lay bare the extraordinary frauds of the Greeks, and to provide our contemporaries with an unusual opportunity for searching out the truth.

> —Andreas Vesalius
> *Letter on the China Root, 1546*

Andreas Vesalius was the beacon who guided medicine out of its dark ages. His revolutionary book, *De Humani Corporis Fabrica,* ushered in a renaissance in anatomy that liberated medical innovation from the second century dogma of Claudius Galen and eventually made possible the seventeenth century discovery of the circulation of blood by William Harvey.[1-5]

Vesalius was born in Brussels in 1514 or 1515, the son of the imperial apothecary to Margaret of Austria and Charles V. Several ancestors were prominent court physicians.[1-6] Because his father was frequently absent, the young Vesalius was greatly influenced by his mother who encouraged him to read the extensive family collection of ancient medical treatises. Little is known of his childhood until age 15, when he entered the University of Louvain where he studied Greek, Latin, Hebrew, rhetoric, and philosophy, and displayed a precocious interest in anatomy by dissecting mice, moles, rats, and dogs.

In 1533 Vesalius enrolled at the medical school of the University of Paris, where he learned anatomy under the tutelage of John Guinter and the celebrated Jacobus Sylvius. Their teaching was based on animal and infrequent human dissections using the medieval approach—barber surgeons, often unskilled, performed the dissection while the instructor, sitting above, read from the writings of Galen whose teachings were held to be divine and indisputable.[2,3] Frustrated by limited access to human material, Vesalius made unauthorized trips to charnel houses outside the walls of Paris to obtain skeletal material and bodies of executed criminals left hanging for dissolution. From these remains, he became so expert on osseous anatomy that he could identify each bone when blindfolded.[2] These human dissections led to a growing realization that the anatomy of Galen was based primarily on monkeys and dogs. His anatomical prowess was recognized by his instructors, who gave him the unusual opportunity to perform a public anatomy where he displayed skills that far surpassed the usual dissector. Vesalius was later described by Guinter as "... a young man, by Hercules, of great promise, possessing an extraordinary knowledge of medicine, learned in both languages (Greek and Latin), and very skilled in dissection of bodies."[1]

The outbreak of the Franco-German war in 1536 forced Vesalius, an enemy-alien, to leave Paris before finishing his medical degree. He returned to the University of Louvain where he continued his countryside forays and was able to procure an almost completely articulated skeleton.[2] His growing reputation led to an invitation to conduct the first public anatomy in Louvain in 18 years, at which time he performed both the lecture and the dissection. His first book, *Paraphrase on the Ninth Book of Rhazes,* which deals with illness from head to foot, was published in 1537.[5,7] A public dispute arose between Vesalius and Jeremiah Drevère, his instructor and an influential teacher, over the proper method to perform a venesection. Drevère vociferously supported the medieval practice that blood must be drawn from a vein opposite the affected side; Vesalius strongly argued the classical view that the vein on the same side should be chosen. In defending himself, Vesalius revealed his contempt for Drevère, his loyalty to his Paris professors, and his belief in Galen.

Having finished his baccalaureate, Vesalius moved to the famous University of Padua near Venice where he received his Doctor of Medicine with honors in 1537. Shortly thereafter, at the age of only 23, he was appointed to the chair of surgery and anatomy (Fig. 1).[1-3] Padua was the recognized center of intellectual discourse and the rebirth of the humanistic spirit where opportunities for original thought and experiment could flourish. In his role as Professor of Surgery and Anatomy, Vesalius had the opportunity to perform public dissections. These events consisted of detailed human and animal dissections demonstrated daily over several weeks in front of a large audience who paid fees to attend. These dissections were enlivened by Vesalius through the novel use of accurate drawings. Prior to Vesalius, illustrations were felt to detract from the printed word. With the artistic help of John Stephen van Calcar, Vesalius assembled a set of anatomical plates for the aid of his students—The Tabulae Anatomicae Sex—published in 1538. The same year he revised Guinter's *Institutiones Anatomicae* to be used as a text to accompany his lectures and demonstrations. The revision included the following insight into the motion of heart:

FIG. 1   Andreas Vesalius. (Reproduced courtesy of the New York Academy of Medicine Library.)

FIG. 2   Title page of *De Humani Corporis Fabrica*. (Reproduced courtesy of the New York Academy of Medicine Library.)

When [the heart] is dilated it draws spirit from the lung by way of the pulmonary vein for the sake of refrigeration, and blood from the vena cava; when it is contracted it expels the sooty vapors through the pulmonary vein, blood into the lungs through the pulmonary artery, and spirit through the aorta into the whole body. For the heart is the source and origin of native heat, pulsation, and the animal faculty. Therefore it is proper to inquire whether the pulse is the same in the heart and in the arteries: that is, whether the transmission of material from the heart occurs on its contraction, and the introduction of material on its distention.

In 1539, Vesalius published his views on bloodletting in the "Venesection letter."[7] Although the letter indicates his continuing support for the authority of Galen, he also incorporates his opinion that a scientific approach based on dissection merits respect.

Over the next several years Vesalius labored over the production of his magnum opus, *De Humani Corporis Fabrica* (On the Structure of the Human Body).[8] The expository Latin text and the accompanying magnificent illustrations represent the fruition of his anatomic experience, his willingness to present anatomy with an unbiased eye, and the independent spirit of an undaunted man who was willing to challenge the ancient dogma of Galen despite the acerbic opposition of his

teachers and other authorities. Prior to *De Fabrica*, anatomical illustrations were crude, with the notable exception of Da Vinci (1452–1519), whose sketches lay unavailable for centuries. The 227 woodcut engravings in *De Fabrica* were precise, accurate, and closely incorporated into the verbose text of 659 pages.[5] The spirit of the Renaissance, which taught that art is a reflection of nature, is represented by background countryside landscape seen in the renowned "muscle-men series."[5,8] The true identity of the artist has never been determined; the major considerations include van Calcar, Titian, artists supervised by Titian, or Vesalius himself.[1–6] Published in 1543 by Operinus of Basil, the final work is a masterpiece, referred to by Osler as "the full flower of the Renaissance. . .a sumptuous tone. . .the chef d'oeuvre of any medical library"[4] and by others as the foundation of modern anatomy.[1,3] One of the more interesting and controversial aspects of the work is the title page (Fig. 2) depicting Vesalius in the center performing a dissection in front of an excited crowd of students, clergy, officials, and laymen who are pressing forward to glimpse the human dissection. Animals at the extreme sides and barber surgeons placed under the dissecting table indicate symbolically that the medieval approach is no longer suitable.[1] An articulated skeleton, serving for reference and as a symbol of death, hangs over the female cadaver. A compact version for beginners, *The Epitome*, was also published in 1543.

The significance of *De Fabrica* lies in its insistence that anatomy must be based on findings verified by human observation, not on the teaching of Galen and other ancient authorities.[1] Many of the errors of Galen are corrected and new information is picturesquely provided about structures not previously discussed in detail. For example, in his description of the cardiac valves, he provides a name for the left atrioventricular valve by suggesting that it resembles a bishop's mitre (head dress). While correcting the anatomy of Galen, Vesalius does not dispute Galenic physiology. According to Galen, chyle was transformed into blood in the intestine and then transported to the liver by a dynamic process of attraction inherent in the fibers of all vessels.[9] A "natural spirit," necessary for organ function, was added in the liver. A portion of this enhanced blood was then attracted into the vena cava and traveled to the right ventricle where impurities were carried off to the lung to be expelled. A small portion of the blood also moved through invisible pores in the ventricular septum into the left ventricle where it combined with inspired "pneuma" and formed the "vital spirit." The vital spirit was drawn into the aorta and arterial system to be distributed throughout the body. Vesalius considered the heart to be a two-chambered structure; the right atrium was an expansion of the superior and inferior venae cavae and the left atrium a part of the pulmonary vein. He was dubious about the existence of pores in the ventricular septum. In the revised edition he expresses further doubts:

> In presenting reasons for the construction of the heart and the use of the parts I have in large degree fitted my discourse to the teachings of Galen, not because I believe them to be in entire agreement with the truth but because I am yet hesitant to present a completely new use and function for those parts.

The book is not without significant error; at times Vesalius inexplicably depends upon animal anatomy.[1]

The reaction to *De Fabrica* was severe, especially from Sylvius, his former teacher and an ardent Galenist, who said, "Let no one give heed to that very ignorant and arrogant man who, through his ignorance, ingratitude, impudence, and impiety denies everything his deranged or feeble vision cannot locate." Bitter over the acrimonious reception, Vesalius burned his notes for a manuscript on Galen and other works. In 1546, in "The letter on the China Root," he brilliantly defended his criticisms of Galen.[1–3] Despite his stunning achievement at the age of only 29 and a revision of *De Fabrica* in 1555, Vesalius contributed very little else of importance. While he was away from Padua attending to the publication of *De Fabrica,* Realdus Columbus, his former pupil, joined with others in criticizing him and replaced him as lecturer in anatomy. Dispirited and frustrated over the turn of events, Vesalius left academic life and became physician to Charles V, the Emperor of Spain. As an imperial physician, he traveled extensively and gained further fame for his ability to drain empyema and to prognosticate.[1] After the abdication of Charles V to his son Phillip II of Spain in 1559, Vesalius moved to Madrid where he served in the imperial court despite jealousies shown to him by the Spanish physicians.

In 1564 he embarked on a pilgrimage to Jerusalem. The reasons for his trip are uncertain. He may simply have tired of imperial life and the envy of the Spanish physicians or desired to return to Padua where the chair of anatomy was vacant following the death of Fallopius. There is also an unconfirmed and probably erroneous story that he began a dissection only to discover that the person, a nobleman, was still alive. It is conjectured that he consented to a pilgrimage to expiate the Inquisition. After traveling to Jerusalem, where he learned that he could return to his former position at Padua, he apparently became ill during an extended stormy voyage in which food and water supplies were depleted. He died of an unknown cause October 15, 1564, at the age of 50, shortly after reaching the island of Zante, near Greece. A contemporary wrote,

> But what shall I say of the great Vesalius, so excellent and unusual for our times?. . .He was a very great philosopher and physician, but in matters of anatomy so rare and singular that it can deservedly be said that he was almost the founder, and marvelously illustrated and brought that very noble science to perfection.[1]

References

1. O'Malley CD: *Andreas Vesalius of Brussels*. University of California Press, Berkeley (1964)
2. Ball JM: *Andreas Vesalius, the Reformer of Anatomy*. Medical Science Press, St. Louis (1910)
3. Cushing HW: *A Bio-bibliography of Andreas Vesalius*. Schuman, New York (1943)
4. Osler W: *The Evolution of Modern Medicine*. Yale University Press, New Haven (1921)
5. Saunders JB de CM, O'Malley CD: *The Illustrations from the Works of Andreas Vesalius of Brussels*. The World Publishing Co., Cleveland (1950)
6. Lambert SW, Wiegand W, Ivins WM Jr: *Three Vesalian Essays*. The Macmillan Company, New York (1952)
7. Saunders JB de CM, O'Malley CD: *Andreas Vesalius Bruxellensis: The Bloodletting Letter of 1539*. H. Schuman, New York (1947)
8. Vesalius A: *De Humani Corporis Fabrica Libre Septem*. Operinus, Basil (1543)
9. Cournand A: Air and blood. In *Circulation of the Blood: Men and Ideas*. (Eds. Fishman AP, Richards DW). American Physiological Society, Bethesda (1982)

Andrea Cesalpino

W. Bruce Fye, m.d., m.a.

Department of Cardiology, Marshfield Clinic, Marshfield, Wisconsin, USA

Andrea Cesalpino (Andreas Caesalpinus) (Fig. 1) was born in Arezzo, Italy, on June 6, 1519.[1] Although he is best remembered for his many contributions to botany, Cesalpino made important observations on the anatomy and physiology of the heart more than 50 years before William Harvey published his theory of the circulation. While a medical student at the University of Pisa, Cesalpino studied under Realdo Colombo, an anatomist who described the pulmonary circulation in his 1559 book *De re anatomica*. Cesalpino was appointed director of the Botanical Garden of Pisa shortly after he received his doctorate in 1551. Between 1569 and 1591, he was ordinary professor of medicine at his alma mater.

In 1571 Cesalpino published *Peripateticarum quaestionum libri quinque*, a wide-ranging book that reflected his admiration for Aristotle. In this 128-page monograph, Cesalpino proposed that blood flows continuously from the vena cava into the heart from which it travels through the pulmonary vessels to the aorta.[2, 3] This theme recurs in several of his later books. Historian and Harvey scholar Walter Pagel claimed that Cesalpino's "statement of the 'continuous motion of the blood through the veins into and through the arteries away from the heart' marks a breakaway from Galen and a stepping stone for Harvey."[4]

Cesalpino recognized something that earlier writers failed to appreciate: that blood in the great veins flowed in only one direction—toward the heart. Pagel points out that for more than three decades Cesalpino "consistently and at prominent places in his books reiterated that there is 'a perpetual motion of blood from the veins into the heart and from the heart into the arteries.' "[4] This contradicted Galen's concept that blood ebbed and flowed from the heart, a belief that had influenced medical theory and practice since the second century.[5]

Beginning with Giovanni Nardi in 1655, some authors (mostly Italians) have claimed that Cesalpino, not Harvey, deserves credit for discovering the circulation. John Arcieri, professor of the history of medicine at the University of Rome, articulated this view in a controversial 1945 book.[6] The following year, English historian Charles Singer, himself the author of a book on the discovery of the circulation, attacked Arcieri's methods and his motivation in a caustic review. After praising Harvey's use of experimentation to prove that the blood circulates through a closed system of arteries and veins, Singer commented that Cesalpino included in his "gaseous and difficult volumes . . . passages on the circulation [that] are essentially philosophical disquisitions."[7]

Fig. 1 Engraving of Andrea Cesalpino (1519-1603). (From the collection of W. Bruce Fye, M.D.)

Gweneth Whitteridge, a leading 20th century Harvey scholar, argued that some of Cesalpino's champions had misinterpreted his meaning. "The whole controversy," she wrote, "would seem to have arisen from the fact that when he does describe correctly the manner in which the blood enters and leaves the heart, he uses the word *circulatio*." She continued, Cesalpino "is not applying the word *circulation* to the movement of the blood in the vessels, but to the action of cooling the hot blood from the heart." When he used the term circulation it had "nothing to do with the physiological circulation described by Harvey."[8] Clinician historian Sigismund Peller agreed, noting that Cesalpino "employed the term circulation long before there was any thought of the movement of blood in a closed circuit."[9]

Although Cesalpino recognized that the blood in the great veins flowed toward the heart, he did not appreciate that blood in all of the veins returned only to the heart. He assumed that some venous blood was drawn into the arteries. Accepting Galen's teaching that there were invisible anastomoses between the arteries and veins in the lungs and throughout the body, Cesalpino thought that arteries could "draw on the contents of the veins at any point in their course," according to Pagel.[10] He did not understand that blood flowed in only one direction between the arteries and veins.

Although Cesalpino cannot be credited with the discovery of the circulation, he did provide "remarkable and unprecedented insight into the relationship of the heart, arteries, and veins to each other," according to historian and Harvey scholar Jerome Bylebyl.[11] Cesalpino's discovery of the direction of blood flow in the great veins set the stage for a comprehensive theory of the circulation. He did not speculate on what happened to the blood propelled into the aorta and the arteries, however. This would be part of William Harvey's seminal contribution; he was the first person to prove that the heart pumped blood continuously through a closed circuit.

In 1592 Cesalpino moved to Rome where he served as physician to Pope Clement VIII and taught medicine at the Sapienza. He died on February 23, 1603.

References

1. Mägdefrau K: Andrea Cesalpino. In *Dictionary of Scientific Biography* (Ed. Gillispie CC), XV p. 80–81. New York: Charles Scribner's Sons, 1978

2. Cesalpino A: *Peripateticarum quaestionum libri quinque.* Venice: Guinta, 1571

3. Clark ME, Nimis SA, Rochefort GR: Andreas Cesalpini, *Quaestionum peripateticarum libri V, liber V, quaestio IV. J Hist Med Allied Sci* 1978;33:185–213

4. Pagel W: *William Harvey's Biological Ideas: Selected Aspects and Historical Background,* p. 169, 171. New York: S. Karger, 1967

5. Harris CRS: *The Heart and the Vascular System in Ancient Greek Medicine from Alcmaeon to Galen.* London: Oxford University Press, 1973

6. Arcieri JP: *The Circulation of the Blood and Andrea Cesalpino of Arezzo.* New York: S. F. Vanni, 1945

7. Singer C: Review of John P. Arcieri, The circulation of the blood and Andrea Cesalpino of Arezzo. *Bull Hist Med* 1946;19:122–124

8. Whitteridge G: *William Harvey and the Circulation of the Blood,* p. 66–67. New York: American Elsevier, Inc., 1971

9. Peller S: Harvey's and Cesalpino's role in the history of medicine. *Bull Hist Med* 1949;23:213–235

10. Pagel W: The philosophy of circles—Cesalpino—Harvey: A penultimate assessment. *J Hist Med Allied Sci* 1957;12:140–157

11. Bylebyl JJ: Cesalpino and Harvey on the portal circulation. In *Science, Medicine and Society in the Renaissance: Essays to Honor Walter Pagel* (Ed. Debus AG), 2, p. 39–52. New York: Science History Publications, 1972

The Botallo Mystery

SVEN-GÖRAN FRANSSON, M.D., PH.D.

Department of Thoracic Radiology, University Hospital, Linköping, Sweden

In several dictionaries the name of Botallo appears as eponym for three cardiovascular anatomical structures: the foramen ovale, the ductus arteriosus, and the ligamentum arteriosum, and in an anatomical atlas based on international nomenclature it is still linked to both the ductus arteriosus and its corresponding ligament.[1–4] Some, however, claim that the Botallo eponym for the ductus arteriosus is erroneous, and that his original description in 1564 is only a note and remains just a short passage in his book *Opera Omnia*, a Leiden edition not printed until 1660. The structures he described were already known, and the word rediscovery is sometimes used in connection with Botallo.[2, 5–8]

Leonardo Botallo

Botallo was an Italian surgeon working at the French royal court and was doctor to several prominent people (Fig. 1). As an army surgeon he opposed the current theory that shot-wounds were poisonous, and he advocated a milder treatment than was customary although he was a strong believer in bloodletting. Both these issues are illustrated on a title page of the *Opera Omnia*. The poor prognosis of chest wounds at that time led Botallo to conclude that all wounds involving the lung were beyond cure.[6, 8–10] In 1560 he published *De curandis vulneribus sclopettorum*, to be followed by several new editions. He published the first description of hay fever in *De catarrho commentarius* and commented on medical ethics and on the treatment of syphilis. He opposed the astrological influence on medical thought.[2, 6, 8, 10]

Botallo was born in Asti, Italy, but there is disagreement about his birthdate, 1519 or 1530, with 1530 sometimes given as the year of his graduation.[2, 3, 8, 10] According to other sources, Botallo graduated doctor of medicine at the Italian university of Pavia in 1543. He then studied under Fallopio, the successor of Vesalius at Padua. A year later he joined the French military forces as a surgeon. In his final years he was probably afflicted by malaria. The place and year of death are uncertain, 1587/88 or 1600, and his burial place is unknown.[6–8, 10]

Cardiovascular Discoveries

Botallo repudiated the openings in the intraventricular septum described by Galen. Instead, he aimed to show that blood passed by means of a "duct" between the right and left atria, which he claimed to have discovered. He called it *vena arteriarum nutrix*, nourishing arteries and vital spirit. He claimed that this passage varied in humans, but was always patent in calves, swine, and dogs. His account was first published as a short note in 1564, added to *De catarrho*, reprinted the year after, and once more in 1641. According to others, Botallo's duct corresponds to the foramen ovale, and had also been described in the second century by Galen in his *De Usu Partium*. Canalis was Botallo's name for the ductus arteriosus.[2, 5–7, 9, 11]

Perhaps because of a too superficial interpretation of Botallo's text, his name became attached to certain anatomical structures of the heart already described before him. In his 1660 edition of the *Opera Omnia,* van Horne inserted Botallo's short version but also a long footnote and an illustration, probably his own, of the heart (Fig. 2). Van Horne also mentions Galen's description. There is no evidence that Botallo's original note was accompanied by any illustration. Furthermore, Botallo's interpretation of Galen's and Colombo's concept of the circulation is said to be incomplete.[7, 11]

Even the great men of science William Harvey and later Albrecht von Haller are supposed to have prolonged the misconception by referring to Botallo. Although Galen knew of the existence of the foramen ovale and its normal closure, Botallo seems have been the first to describe a persistent foramen ovale after birth, but without understanding its function in the fetal state. A persistent ductus arteriosus after birth was described much later in 1757 by the German Reinmann.[8, 11, 12] In 1786, the Swedish surgeon Hagströmer described a patent foramen ovale in a deceased 40-year-old woman; the report is to be found in the proceedings of the Swedish Royal Academy of Science (Fig. 3). At this time, a number of case reports of patent foramen ovale in the adult were known, and Hagströmer refers to Bartholin, von Haller, Vieussens, and Morgagni, among others, but not to Botallo or earlier sources.

FIG. 1 The dates of Botallo's birth and death are given variously as 1519 or 1530, and 1587, 1588, or 1600, respectively. This photograph was published in *Botallo Leonardo: Astese, medico regio* by Prof. Dott. Leonardo Carerj (Asti, Italy: Casa Editrice Arethusa, 1954). The legend shown below the photograph indicates that Botallo's name was erroneously spelled Botali rather than Botallo in the figure. The author and publisher wish to thank Dr. Louis Acierno of the University of Central Florida and Dr. Frabboni of Bologna for their help in locating the photograph.

Hagströmer presents correct knowledge of the physiology of the fetal circulation including the function of both the foramen ovale and ductus arteriosus. He strongly refutes a contemporary idea that divers with a patent foramen ovale ought to perform better due to longer survival without air; on the contrary, a patent foramen ovale can predispose to decompression sickness and other forms of paradoxical embolism or arterial desaturation.[13, 14]

The ductus arteriosus is derived from the sixth left bronchial arch. It usually closes functionally within hours af-

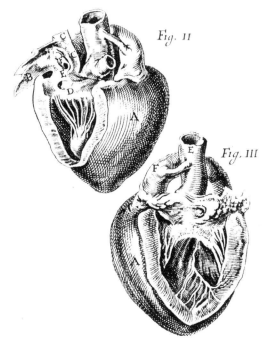

FIG. 2 Illustration probably inserted by van Horne relating to Botallo's description of cardiac anatomy. *Opera Omnia* 1660, from Uppsala University Library, the Waller collection.

FIG. 3 Title page to the 1786 proceedings of the Swedish Royal Academy of Science, containing Hagströmer's description of a persistent foramen ovale in an adult.

ter birth and permanently during the following weeks. This muscular constriction of the ductus is stimulated by a high level of blood oxygenation. In the African and South American lungfish, however, a ductus similar to the ductus arteriosus of mammals acts in a cyclic fashion depending on the animal's phase of immersion or air breathing. The lungfish is able to breathe by way of lungs or, to a lesser extent, gills.[5, 15]

In 1564, another Italian physician, Julio Cesare Aranzio, pupil of Vesalius at Padua and subsequently professor of anatomy at Bologna, described both the fetal foramen ovale and the ductus arteriosus, but modestly claimed only to elaborate in detail on Galen's earlier descriptions. Both these anatomical structures were supposed to nourish the heart and lungs with venous and arterial blood, respectively.[2, 7, 16] According to other sources, Aranzio was the true discoverer of the ductus arteriosus; he also mentions the postnatal closure of the ductus arteriosus and foramen ovale. Another discovery in connection with Aranzio and the heart is the *corpora Arantii* or nodules of the semilunar aortic valve.[1–3, 6, 16] In 1561, both Fallopio and Vesalius also mentioned the ductus arteriosus and the foramen ovale.[2, 11, 12]

Much later, in 1875, the Viennese pathologist Karl Rokitansky described in detail congenital heart disorders derived from defects in the atrial and ventricular septa.[17] In 1938, Robert Gross, working in Boston, performed the first successful surgical closure of a persistent ductus arteriosus. This operation was soon to be taken up by Scandinavian surgeons, and pioneer work on the arteriographic depiction of the ductus arteriosus followed in Sweden.[12] This, of course, was many centuries after the discovery of this anatomical structure sometimes still named after Botallo, who actually described the foramen ovale.

References

1. *Dorland's Illustrated Medical Dictionary*. Philadephia: W.B. Saunders Co., 1988
2. Norman JM: *Morton's Medical Bibliography*. Aldershot: Scolar Press, 1991
3. *International Dictionary of Medicine and Biology*. New York, Chichester, Brisbane, Toronto, Singapore: John Wiley & Sons, Inc., 1986
4. Feneis H: *Pocket Atlas of Human Anatomy*. Stuttgart: Georg Thieme Publishers, 1976
5. Baue AE, Geha AS, Hammond GL, Laks H, Naunheim KS: *Glenn's Thoracic and Cardiovascular Surgery*. Norwalk, San Mateo: Appleton & Lange, 1991
6. Castiglione A: *A History of Medicine*. New York: Jason Aronson Inc., 1975
7. French RK: The thorax in history, 5. Discovery of the pulmonary transit. *Thorax* 1978;33:555–564
8. Gillispie CC: *Dictionary of Scientific Biography*. New York: Charles Scribner's Sons, 1970
9. Hurt R: *The History of Cardiothoracic Surgery*. New York, London: The Parthenon Publishing Group, Inc., 1996
10. Walton JN, Beeson PB, Scott RB, Owen SG, Rhodes P: *The Oxford Companion to Medicine*. Oxford, New York, Toronto: Oxford University Press, 1986
11. Franklin KJ: Ductus venosus (*Arantii*) and ductus arteriosus (*Botalli*). *Bull Hist Med* 1941;9:580–584
12. Gøtzsche H: *Congenital Heart Disease*. Copenhagen: Published by the author, 1952
13. Wilmhurst PT, de Belder MA: Patent foramen ovale in adult life. Editorial. *Br Heart J* 1994;71:209–212
14. Hagströmer AJ: Foramen ovale in sept. auricular. Cordis funnet öpet hos en ålderstigen menniska; jämte anmärkningar därom, p. 45–49 (in Swedish). *Swedish Royal Academy of Science*, 1786
15. Fishman AP, DeLaney RG, Laurent P: Circulatory adaptation to bimodal respiration in the dipnoan lungfish. *J Appl Physiol* 1985; 59:285–294
16. Acierno LJ: *History of Cardiology*. New York: The Parthenon Publishing Group Inc., 1994
17. Fejfar Z, Hlaváčková L: Profiles in cardiology. Karl Rokitanski. *Clin Cardiol* 1997;20:816–818

William Harvey and the Discovery of the Circulation of Blood

M. E. SILVERMAN, M.D.

Department of Medicine, Division of Cardiology, Emory University School of Medicine and Piedmont Hospital, Atlanta, Georgia, USA

The discovery of the circulation of blood by William Harvey in the 17th century ranks as one of the greatest achievements in science, the beginning of modern cardiology, and the introduction of experimental observation. Although others before him, notably Servetus, Columbus, Cesalpino, and Fabricius, had glimpsed parts of the puzzle, Harvey's genius was to fit it together and provide undeniable scientific proof based on quantitative analysis and extensive animal experimentation.

William Harvey was born April 1, 1578 in Folkestone, England, the son of a former mayor of the city. At the age of 10, he went to Kings College, Canterbury and five years later to Caius College, Cambridge. Following graduation in 1597 at age 19, he enrolled in the famous medical school at the University of Padua in Italy, where he studied anatomy and physiology under Fabricius, whose discovery of the venous valves and their orientation provided Harvey with his initial insight into the circulation of the blood. He was also influenced by his predecessors at Padua: Andreas Vesalius, who wrote *De Humani Corporis Fabrica*, which repudiated the human anatomy and undermined the pervasive influence of Galen on medicine; Realdus Columbus, who stated that the pulmonary vein contained blood (not air as had been taught) and that the heart was active in systole; and Andreas Cesalpino, the first person to use the term "circulation."

Harvey graduated from Padua with high honors in 1602 and returned to London where he developed a large family practice. He married in 1604, and became the chief physician at St. Bartholomew's Hospital in 1609. In 1615 he was appointed to be the Lumleian lecturer of the Royal College of Physicians, a position which gave him the opportunity to demonstrate anatomy and physiology to the college members.

For over 1400 years prior to Harvey's discovery, the teachings of Claudius Galen, a revered second century Greek physician, were virtually unchallenged. Galen and his successors taught that ingested food was continuously transformed into blood by the liver. A natural spirit promoting growth and nutrition was added in the liver and carried throughout the body by the veins. In the right ventricle, impurities in the

blood were expelled into the pulmonary artery and then exhaled. He taught that purified blood crossed invisible pores in the ventricular septum to enter the left heart. "Pneuma," inspired from the air into the lungs, was transported through the pulmonary veins to the left heart where it combined with the purified blood to form the "vital spirit." By a process of active dilatation, the vital spirit entered the arteries and traveled to the organs to provide bodily function. Respiration cooled the overheated blood and helped to force blood from the heart into the vessels. Animal spirit was added in the brain and sent via hollow nerves for the purpose of sensation, motion, and higher function.

Between the time that Harvey returned to England and became the Lumleian lecturer, he had dissected and observed more than 80 species of animals. Although he initially exclaimed that he almost believed that "the motion of the heart was to be understood by God alone," he persisted in his experiments until he formulated his concept of the circulation. His theories and experiments can be summarized as follows:

> …the chief function of the heart is the transmission and pumping of the blood through the arteries to the extremities of the body. Thus the pulse which we feel in the arteries is nothing else than the impact of blood from the heart.

In order to dispel the Galenic idea that active arterial dilatation attracted blood from the heart, Harvey needed to prove that the heart provided the propulsive force behind the circulation. He noted that with contraction the heart became thicker and smaller as if to expel its contents. As the ventricles became smaller, the pulmonary artery and aorta became dilated. The arterial pulse would cease if the heart stopped beating. With each cardiac contraction, blood would spurt from a cut artery or an incised ventricle.

> In the more perfect warm-blooded adult animals, as man, the blood passes from the right ventricle of the heart through the pulmonary artery to the lungs, from there through the pulmonary vein into the left auricle, and then into the left ventricle.

Harvey postulated, but was unable to provide direct evidence, that the blood travels from the right heart through the

This article introduced the new department "Profiles in Cardiology" which features clinicians who have made a significant contribution to the study of cardiovascular disease. The department is edited by J. Willis Hurst, Co-editor of Clinical Cardiology.

William Harvey. (Photograph supplied courtesy of the U.S. National Library of Medicine).

lungs and then to the left heart. He reasoned that the right ventricle produces a force capable of pushing blood through the porous substance of the lungs. The absence of pores in the ventricular septum is vehemently stated—"But, damn it, no such pores exist, nor can they be demonstrated!" The similar size of the pulmonary artery and aorta suggested to him that they share a similar function, while the orientation of the cardiac valves allows only for a transit of blood flow into the lungs and then through the left heart into the aorta. His dissections showed that the lungs provide the only possible route for the blood found in the pulmonary veins and left heart. Although not mentioned until a letter written in 1651, Harvey subsequently proved that when the pulmonary artery is ligated and the right ventricle is injected forcefully with water, no fluid can cross the ventricular septum into the left heart. When fluid is injected into the pulmonary artery, it returns to the left ventricle.

> But suppose even the smallest amount of blood be transmitted through the lungs and heart at a single beat, a greater quantity would eventually be pumped into the arteries and the body than could be furnished by the food consumed, unless by constantly making a circuit and returning.

Harvey was the first to use quantitative analysis to prove that blood is not continuously formed in the liver. He estimated that approximately half an ounce is forced out of the heart with each contraction.

When this amount is multiplied by the number of heart beats in a half hour, the total greatly exceeds the quantity that could possibly be supplied from the food or contained within the veins and arteries. Furthermore, when an artery is cut, the animal will exsanguinate and the heart beat will eventually cease; the faster the heart rate, the more rapidly this will occur. Therefore, he reasoned, blood must be a fixed quantity.

> …it is obvious that blood enters a limb through the arteries and returns through the veins, that the arteries are the vessels carrying blood from the heart and the veins the channels returning it to the heart…

Harvey demonstrated that when the aorta is compressed, the heart turns purple and becomes distended until the compression is released. A very tight ligature on the arm blocks the arterial pulsation below the ligature, causing the hand to turn cool. Following release of the ligature, the hand and veins become swollen. If the ligature is made moderately tight, the arterial pulsation is diminished, but not abolished, while the veins below the ligature become distended. He noted that the orientation of the venous valves allows blood to flow only toward the heart and shows that a probe inserted into a vein can pass easily in the direction of the heart but not away from it. The blood in a superficial arm vein can be stripped only toward the heart. When the vein leading to the heart is pinched, the heart becomes pale and empty; with release the normal size and color returns. By these critical experiments, Harvey proved that blood circles from the heart to the arteries and then to the veins and back to the heart. Harvey assumed a connection "porosities" between arteries and veins but did not have the means available to demonstrate it. In 1661, using the newly discovered microscope, Malpighi described the capillary circulation and provided the missing link to Harvey's circle.

After marshalling all of his evidence, Harvey proposed his idea of the circulation of the blood:

> It has been shown by reason and experiment that blood by the beat of the ventricles flows through the lungs and heart and is pumped to the whole body. There it passes through pores in the flesh into the veins through which it returns from the periphery everywhere to the center, from the smaller veins into the larger ones, finally coming to the vena cava and right auricle. This occurs in such an amount, with such an outflow through the arteries, and such a reflux through the veins, that it cannot be supplied by the food consumed. It is also much more than is needed for nutrition. It must therefore be concluded that the blood in the animal body moves around in a circle continuously, and that the action or function of the heart is to accomplish this by pumping. This is the only reason for the motion and beat of the heart.

He initially presented his concept at the Lumleian lecture in 1616; however, *Exercitatio Anatomica De Motu Cordis et Sanguinis in Animalibus* was not published until 1628 when it was released as a poorly bound, cheap, paper edition from Frankfurt, containing many printing errors. Anticipating an adverse reaction to his heretical views, Harvey wrote:

> What remains to be said on the quantity and source of this transferred blood, is, even if carefully reflected

upon, so strange and undreamed of, that not only do I fear danger to myself from the malice of a few, but I dread lest I have all men as enemies, so much does reverence for ambiguity influence all men. But now the die is cast; my hope is in the love of truth and in the integrity of intelligence.

DeMotu Cordis did precipitate great criticism as well as praise. Although his practice apparently suffered, Harvey became very active in the Royal College of Physicians, where he served as treasurer and on committees to maintain ethical practice and oppose malpractice and quackery. As the physician to Charles I, he experienced the vicissitudes of politics during the Civil War of 1642 when he was forced to flee to Oxford and his valuable notes on comparative anatomy were destroyed by Puritan forces. In a masterpiece of understatement, Harvey commented,

Let gentle minds forgive me, if recalling the irreparable injuries I have suffered, I here give vent to a sigh.

In 1651, at the age of 73, he published *Exercitationes de Generatione Animalium*, a compilation of his views on embryology and comparative anatomy that was well received and was a forerunner of modern embryology. By the late 1650s, his reputation was fully re-established and he became venerated by his colleagues and honored by the public. He suffered from severe gout and had to decline the presidency of the Royal College of Physicians in 1654. At the age of 79, he suffered a stroke and died on June 3, 1657.

Although we know little about William Harvey as a person, he was described as short, roundfaced, with an olive complexion, black hair, dark eyes, a diminutive beard, and a shaggy mustache. He was known to be hotheaded on occasion, free of bigotry, practical, and to enjoy fine arts and reading the classics. As a practicing physician, consultant, teacher, and leader in his community and professional organization, Harvey set an example for the physicians of his time.

But as an investigator in search of unbiased truth, he eclipsed those who preceded him and provided the model for those who followed.

References

Bean WB: William Harvey. *Arch Intern Med* 1958;102:149

Bendiner E: The revolutionary physician of kings: William Harvey. *Hosp Pract* November, 1978;129

Comroe JH: Harvey's 1651 perfusion of the pulmonary circulation of man. *Circulation* 1982;65:1

Cournand A: Air and blood. In *Circulation of the Blood: Men and Ideas* (Eds. Fishman AP, Richards DW). American Physiological Society, 1982

Fishman AP: The pulmonary circulation. *J Am Med Assoc* 1978;239:1299

Frank RG Jr: The image of Harvey in commonwealth and restoration England. In *William Harvey and His Age* (Ed. Bylebyl JJ). Baltimore: The Johns Hopkins University Press, 1979

Garrison FH: *An Introduction to the History of Medicine*, 4th Edition, p. 246–249. Philadelphia: W. B. Saunders Company, 1948

Harvey W: *Exercitatio Anatomica de Motu Cordis et Sanguinis in Animalibus.* (Translated by Leake CD). Springfield: Charles C Thomas, 1970

Herrick JB: *A Short History of Cardiology*, p. 23–30. Springfield: Charles C Thomas, 1942

Jarcho S: William Harvey described by an eyewitness (John Aubrey). *Am J Cardiol* 1958;2:381

Key JD, Keys TE, Callahan JA: Historical development of concept of blood circulation. *Am J Cardiol* 1979;43:1026

Keynes G: *The Personality of William Harvey—the Linacre Lecture Delivered at St. John's College.* Cambridge: Cambridge University Press, 1949

Osler W: *The Evolution of Modern Medicine*, p 163–173. New Haven: Yale University Press, 1921

Prieur GO: William Harvey. *Histor Bull Calgary Clin* 1952;17:21

Sigerist HE: *The Great Doctors.* Garden City: Doubleday, 1958

Wells LA: William Harvey and the convergence of medicine and science. *Mayo Clin Proc* 1978;53:234

Willius FA, Dry TJ: *A History of the Heart and the Circulation*, p. 294–298. Philadelphia: W. B. Saunders Company, 1948

Zeman FD: The old age of William Harvey. *Arch Intern Med* 1963;111:829

René Descartes

W. Bruce Fye, M.D., M.A.

Cardiovascular Division, Mayo Clinic, Rochester, Minnesota, USA

René Descartes was born in La Haye, Touraine, France, on March 31, 1596 (Fig. 1). He was a pioneer of physiology, and he contributed an early and very important response to William Harvey's theory of the circulation of the blood. Although there are many facets to Descartes' career, this paper will focus on his controversy with Harvey.[1, 2] In addition to Descartes' many significant contributions to mathematics, physics, and philosophy, he also wrote the first book devoted to human physiology. This classic work, *De homine figuris*, was published posthumously in Latin in 1662, in French in 1664, and in English in 1972.[3] Although Descartes completed the manuscript in 1632, he decided not to have it printed because he feared he would be subjected to an inquisition such as Galileo faced when his controversial book *Dialogue Concerning the Two Chief World Systems* appeared that same year. Meanwhile, in the fall of 1632, Descartes read Harvey's *De motu cordis*, which had been published four years earlier. Descartes' reading of this small but significant book led him to formulate an alternate theory of the heart's function.

Today, we take for granted many aspects of cardiac physiology that were unknown until William Harvey published his revolutionary theory of the circulation in 1628. We also accept the fact that discoveries are made and new interpretations of experimental observations are articulated constantly as researchers study the mechanisms of disease and clinical investigators seek more effective treatments. It is important to acknowledge, however, that researchers make choices when they develop their hypotheses, design their experiments, interpret their data, and publish their findings. Although based on astute observations and vivisections, Harvey framed his theory of the circulation in a way that reflected his vitalism and the lingering influence of Aristotle.[4] Descartes, on the other hand, wanted to adapt certain aspects of Harvey's discovery to his own unique goal of uniting physiology with philosophy and certain other intellectual traditions, something that has been called Cartesian anthropology.[5]

Although several of Harvey's contemporaries rejected his novel theory of the circulation, Descartes was surely one his most influential critics. Descartes' theory of the heart's function, which he elaborated in 1637 in his book *Discours de la Methode*, was one factor that stimulated Harvey to perform additional experiments that he reported in 1649.[6] Descartes' book also caused some of Harvey's supporters to publish their views on the matter.[7] Peter Anstey's recent essay, "Descartes' Cardiology and Its Reception in English Physiology," provides valuable insight into Descartes' challenge of certain aspects of Harvey's theory.[8]

Descartes respected Harvey and accepted the English physician's theory that blood circulated through the body in a closed system of arteries and veins. Both men rejected Galen's view that blood simply moved forward and backward through the same vessels. The teachings of this ancient Greek physician had dominated Western medical thought for almost 1,400 years, so it is not surprising that new explanations of physiological phenomena met with resistance.[9] Descartes challenged Harvey's assertion that the heart was fundamentally a muscular pump that propelled blood throughout the body and back to the heart. He also disputed Harvey's explanation of the nature of systole and diastole, phenomena they both had studied without the aid of any instruments of precision.

Harvey and Descartes approached the problem of the circulation from different perspectives. Descartes' concept of physiology reflected his dedication to constructing a unified philosophical system that embraced physics, mathematics, psychology, cosmology, epistemology, and certain aspects of religion. He viewed the body in a mechanistic way, that is, that the human body was basically a machine and that its various functions could be reduced to mechanical models similar to the workings of a clock, or machines that were based upon levers and pulleys. Although Descartes (who was not a physician) performed dissections and a few vivisections as he sought to elucidate the functions of the body, he was not an experimentalist; Harvey was.

Despite his mechanistic tendencies, Descartes rejected Harvey's notion that the heart was simply a pump that propelled blood through the body. In part, this reflected Descartes' belief that all muscles were controlled by the will. Although Descartes acknowledged that some muscular actions, such as scratching, could result from a reflex action, he rejected the notion of involuntary muscular contraction. In 1648, two years before his death, he was working on a book on the human body that he never finished. Parts of the manuscript, entitled *La description du Corps Humain*, were published posthumously in 1664. A recent translation of a passage from this text demonstrates Descartes' conviction that the mind and the body were critically linked: "If we suppose that the heart beats the way Harvey describes it, we would have to imagine some faculty causes this motion, and the nature of this faculty

FIG. 1 René Descartes (March 31, 1596–February 11, 1650). From the collection of Dr. W. Bruce Fye.

would be much more difficult to understand than what it claims to explain."[10]

Descartes argued that the heart was not a pump, but a furnace. The heart heated small particles in the blood, causing them to expand or "rarefy" almost instantaneously. This dynamic and sudden expansion of the blood within the heart caused the organ to swell, forced the atrioventricular valves to close, and pushed the semi-lunar valves open. When the heated blood was released into the arteries it caused them to expand, something that was visible to the naked eye and could be felt by the fingers. Descartes explained that as the blood cooled it took less space, and the arteries and veins collapsed—as did the heart itself. He agreed with Harvey that blood returned to the heart through a system of veins, but it was the heated blood that animated the system rather than the heart itself.

When the cooled blood returned from various parts of the body to the heart, Descartes explained, it mixed with a small amount of blood that remained in the heart. This residual blood, according to Descartes, possessed a yeast-like property that caused the returning blood to expand in the ventricles, thereby starting the process over once again. So, Descartes compared the heart to a furnace; he did not think of it as a muscle: its motion was not the result of an involuntary muscular contraction as Harvey believed. Rather, the heart changed size and shape because the blood within it expanded quickly as it was heated and was forced out into the vascular system where it would cool off rapidly as it circulated through the body.

Descartes explained his reasoning in a detailed letter to Dutch physician and anatomist Johan van Beverwijck in 1643:

Although to be sure I am in full agreement with Harvey in regard to the circulation of the blood . . . yet in regard to the motion of the heart I am in entire disagreement with him. For he will have it, if my memory serves me, that the heart in the diastole by expanding permits blood to enter and in the systole forces it out by contracting. Now my explanation of the whole process is as follows. When the heart is empty, new blood of necessity flows into the right ventricle through the vena cava and into the left ventricle through the pulmonary veins.

Next, Descartes describes his theory of how blood moved through the heart to circulate through the body. He explained that as a little blood flowed into each ventricle,

. . . finding there more heat than in the veins from which it flowed, of necessity it expands and wants much more room than before. . . . Now when blood in the heart expands in this way, it suddenly and forcibly pushes out the walls of the ventricles in all directions. This causes the valves . . . which are at the openings of the pulmonary artery and great artery to open. . . . they are necessarily opened and closed respectively merely by this expansive force of the blood; and this expansion of the blood causes the diastole of the heart.[11]

William Harvey felt compelled to respond to Descartes' theory because it challenged a critical part of his concept of the circulation: that the heart was a pump that contracted actively and regularly to propel blood through the body. Both men were products of the Renaissance; although they shared certain beliefs about physiology, they used different approaches to attempt to interpret and explain the functions of the heart. Harvey was an experimentalist who measured things and used mathematics to quantify the heart's output. Despite his sophistication in mathematics, Descartes was more of an empiricist who sought to frame the heart's motion in terms of his larger philosophical views about the relationship of bodily functions and the will.

Harvey's position was strengthened as some of his defenders published essays that refuted critical portions of Descartes' theory. For example, Kenelm Digby, an English natural philosopher, included a detailed refutation of Descartes' theory of the circulation in his 1644 book, *Two Treatises*. Dutch physician James de Back criticized Descartes in a 1648 essay, "Dissertatio de Corde," that was appended to the 1648 Rotterdam edition of Harvey's book on the circulation. De Back's paper was translated into English and was appended to the first English translation of Harvey's book, published in 1653.

Descartes died in Stockholm on February 11, 1650, presumably of pneumonia. Harvey, who died seven years later, is remembered mainly for his discovery of the circulation of the blood. Descartes' role in stimulating Harvey to undertake further research on the circulation and in encouraging the English physician's supporters to articulate their views has been largely forgotten. Descartes is remembered mainly for his contributions to philosophy, mathematics (especially geometry), and physics. He influenced many prominent seventeenth century scientists such as Nicholas Steno, Robert Hooke, Thomas Willis, and Giovanni Borelli. The active scholarly enterprise that focuses on Descartes at the beginning of the twenty-first century reflects his lingering and significant influence in several important areas of learning and thought.[12]

References

1. Gaukroger S: *Descartes: An Intellectual Biography*. New York: Oxford University Press, 1995
2. Carter RB: *Descartes' Medical Philosophy: The Organic Solution to the Mind-Body Problem*. Baltimore: The Johns Hopkins University Press, 1983
3. Descartes R: *Treatise of Man*. French text with translation and commentary by Thomas Steele Hall. Cambridge: Harvard University Press, 1972
4. Pagel W: *William Harvey's Biological Ideas*. New York: S. Karger, 1967
5. Bitbol-Hespériès A: Cartesian physiology. In *Descartes' Natural Philosophy* (Ed. Gaukroger S, Schuster J, Sutton J), p. 349–382. New York: Routledge, 2000
6. Harvey W: *De circulatione sanguinis*. Cambridge: Roger David, 1649
7. Weil E: The echo of Harvey's De Motu Cordis (1628). *J Hist Med Allied Sci* 1957;12:167–174
8. Anstey P: Descartes' Cardiology and Its Reception in England. In *Descartes' Natural Philosophy* (Ed. Gaukroger S, Schuster J, Sutton J), p. 420–444. New York: Routledge, 2000
9. Harris CRS: *The Heart and the Vascular System in Ancient Greek Medicine*. London: Oxford University Press, 1973
10. Shea WR: *The Magic of Numbers and Motion: The Scientific Career of René Descartes*, p 308. Canton Mass.: Science History Publications, 1991
11. Lindeboom GA: *Descartes and Medicine*, p. 106–107. Amsterdam: Rodopi, 1979
12. Gaukroger S, Schuster J, Sutton J (eds): *Descartes' Natural Philosophy*. New York: Routledge, 2000

Giovanni Alfonso Borelli

W. Bruce Fye, M.D., M.A.

Department of Cardiology, Marshfield Clinic, Marshfield, Wisconsin, USA

Giovanni Alfonso Borelli (1608–1679) (Fig. 1) is remembered mainly for his pioneering attempt to explain muscle function in terms of mathematical and physical principles.[1] One modern historian believes that "his importance to the advance of physiology may be likened to that of Galileo to physics."[2] Born in Naples in 1608, Borelli was influenced profoundly by natural philosopher Tommaso Campanella and mathematician Benedetto Castelli. Between 1627 and 1635, he studied with Castelli at the University of Rome. Born at the close of the Renaissance, Borelli lived in an era not only of great intellectual ferment, but of religious persecution.[3–5] His mentor Campanella spent many years in prison after he was denounced to the Inquisition for heresy.

From 1635 to 1656, Borelli was lecturer in mathematics at the Studium in Messina, Sicily. He then moved to Pisa where, in 1659, he helped organize the Accademia del Cimento, a group of intellectuals whose shared interest was research in the physical and natural sciences. Prince Leopold provided them with a laboratory and scientific instruments. Shortly after arriving in Pisa, Borelli established a private anatomical laboratory in his home where he performed research and taught. His students included the microscopist Marcello Malpighi and the physiologist Lorenzo Bellini. By the time Borelli arrived in Pisa, he had become especially interested in the structure and function of muscles; this would be a major focus of his research for the next two decades.

Borelli was an early proponent of what came to be known as the myogenic theory of the heartbeat. Based on observations he had made on excised frog hearts, he told his friend Malpighi in 1661,

> When the left ventricle has stopped beating, the left auricle continues to beat; that when this has also stopped moving, the right ventricle nevertheless goes on beating; that when the right ventricle ceases, the beating of the right auricle persists for some time; and that when this too has stopped, a certain movement of the contained blood may finally be seen there.[6]

Borelli was one of the founders of an important intellectual movement known as iatromechanism, which framed physiologic events in terms of mathematical and physical principles. Historian Thomas Hall explains,

For Borelli, living bodies are machines. The life of the machine is the totality of movements exhibited by the moving parts and by the machine as a whole. The whole machine is an assemblage of smaller component machines, and these of still smaller ones.[7]

The advocates of iatromechanism (including Robert Boyle in England, René Descartes in France, and Niels Stensen in Denmark) espoused experimentation and careful observation as the chief methods for studying the structure and functions of living organisms and their component parts. In 1663, a group of men in Naples who embraced the iatromechanism viewpoint created the Accademia degli Investiganti. Borelli was attracted to this academy whose members shared his interest in research. In 1667, he demonstrated several experiments on the muscular motion of animals that he had performed in Pisa a few years earlier.[8]

Borelli summarized the results of nearly two decades of experiments and observations on the muscles in his two-volume book *De motu animalium*, which was published in Rome in 1680–1681.[9, 10] Historian of science Howard Adelmann calls the work a "masterpiece." He explains that the book was

> . . . a rigidly mechanical, mathematical and physical analysis of various animal functions…[which] became the bible of the iatromathematical or iatromechanical school that was developed by Borelli's students and successors.[6]

This classic book, the first thorough study of muscle physiology, reveals Borelli's extensive experience with dissection and vivisection and reflects his conviction that biological functions could be explained in terms of physical and mathematical principles.

The first volume consists of 23 chapters on the skeletal muscles responsible for the "external motions of animals" and on the forces that these muscles generate. The second volume includes 21 chapters on the "internal motions of animals and their immediate causes." A series of detailed copper engravings amplifies the text. In the three chapters on the heart and circulation, Borelli attempted to describe the contraction of the organ in terms of accepted mathematical and geometric principles.

FIG. 1   Giovanni Alfonso Borelli (1608–1679). (Image from the collection of W. Bruce Fye, M.D.)

Supporting Niels Stensen's view that the heart was a muscle similar to other muscles in the body, Borelli argued that

> . . . both are made of the same components, bundles of fleshy fibres and a tendinous substance, contractile, of the same shape, arranged and bound in the same way, similarly penetrated by nervous ramifications, similarly irrigated by blood from arteries.[10]

He pointed out that while the heart contracted much like other muscles, it was different in that it was not attached to any limb. The purpose of cardiac contraction was to propel blood into the arterial circulation. Borelli theorized that the heart's cavities were compressed as a result of the lateral walls coming closer together, not as a result of a foreshortening of the ventricles. He supported this and his many propositions by experiments and mathematical equations.

A prolific author, Borelli published several books dealing with physics, mathematics, hydraulics, and astronomy.[11] During the closing years of his life he was plagued by ill health and political tensions. He died a few months before the first volume of *De motu animalium* appeared in 1680.

References

1. Settle TB: Giovanni Alfonso Borelli. In *Dictionary of Scientific Biography,* Vol. 2, p. 306–314. New York: Charles Scribner's Sons, 1973
2. Bastholm E: *The History of Muscle Physiology from the Natural Philosophers to Albrecht von Haller,* p.174. Copenhagen: Ejnar Munksgaard, 1950,
3. Wightman WPD: *Science and the Renaissance: An Introduction to the Study of the Emergence of the Sciences in the Sixteenth Century.* New York: Hafner Publishing Co., 1962
4. Sarton G: *Six Wings: Men of Science in the Renaissance.* Bloomington: Indiana University Press, 1957
5. Webster C. (Ed.):*The Intellectual Revolution of the Seventeenth Century.* London: Routledge & Kegan Paul, 1974
6. Adelmann HB: *Marcello Malpighi and the Evolution of Embryology,* Vol.1, p. 192. Ithaca: Cornell University Press, 1966
7. Hall TS: *Ideas of Life and Matter: Studies in the History of General Physiology, 600 B.C.–1900 A.D.,* p. 347–348. Chicago: University of Chicago Press, 1969
8. Fisch MH: The Academy of the Investigators. In *Science Medicine and History, Essays on the Evolution of Scientific Thought and Medical Practice Written in Honour of Charles Singer* (Ed. Underwood EA), Vol. 1, p. 521–523. London: Oxford University Press, 1953
9. Borelli GA: *De motu animalium.* Rome: Angelo Bernabo, 1680–1681
10. Borelli GA: *On the Movement of Animals (Translated by Paul Maquet),* p. 281. New York: Springer-Verlag, 1989
11. Armitage A: "Borelli's hypothesis" and the rise of celestial mechanics. *Ann Sci* 1950;6:268–292

Olof Rudbeck

SVEN-GÖRAN FRANSSON, M.D., PH.D.

Department of Thoracic Radiology, University Hospital, Linköping, Sweden

Olof Rudbeck the Elder

This Swedish man of science (Fig. 1) is best known for his discovery of the lymphatic system and for the dispute concerning priority over the Dane Thomas Bartholin who, in 1653, published his findings on the same subject just before Rudbeck. In Uppsala one year earlier, the 22-year-old Rudbeck, with his teacher, Professor Olaus Stenius, performed an anatomical demonstration of his results on a dog in the presence of Queen Christina of Sweden.[1, 2]

The Circulation

In 1652, Rudbeck, however, made another important but less well known contribution to Swedish medical science with his first dissertation, *De circulatione sanguinis*, namely, the introduction of the modern concept of the circulation of blood as described by William Harvey. This dissertation embraced experimental methods in medical research. It was printed in Västerås and defended at Uppsala University. Just as Harvey had dedicated his work on the circulation to King Charles I, Rudbeck dedicated his work to the Swedish queen. The purpose of this first paper was probably to prepare and facilitate the reception of his second and greater discovery—that of the lymphatic system—completing the physiology of the circulation. Harvey promoted his new ideas in lectures from the beginning of 1616, but his thesis was not printed until 1628. Its acceptance was slow, but grew steadily on the European continent, mainly in the Netherlands, Germany, and Denmark. This was the premise for Rudbeck's studies on the circulation.[1–4]

Rudbeck's findings were based on a number of animal dissections (he mentions cat, eel, crayfish, and fish) and experiments proving the existence of anastomoses between arteries and veins. He described the heart in systole and diastole, and the function of the valves. He observed and probed with his finger the beating hearts of different animals, and by ligatures proved the direction of the blood flow. An anatomical description of the arterial system of the body, including the coronary arteries, is also included. His results regarding circulation of the blood were concentrated into 26 statements in the first dissertation. He not only confirmed Harvey's results, but he also widened Harvey's views regarding the arterial pulse,

refuted the notion that the liver was a blood-forming organ, and rebutted ancient, lingering Galenic doctrines by repudiating the production of "vital spirits" in the heart.[1, 2]

Like Harvey, Rudbeck calculated the amount of blood pumped from the human left ventricle, but a too-low approximation of the left ventricular volume ejected into the aorta resulted in underestimation of the cardiac output. His calculations were based on a heart rate of 4,000 beats per hour (67 beats per minute) and a volume of half a drachm (1.8 g) per systole or 20 libras per hour (7,126 g). According to some authors, Harvey underestimated both heart rate (33 beats per minute) and the left ventricular volume ejected (3.9 g or 500 ounces in one half hour), although he calculated with different sets of figures.[1–3, 5–7]

Apart from Harvey, Rudbeck also quotes the German Hermann Conring, at one time physician to Queen Christina and the Dutch scientist Johannes Walaeus (Jan De Wale). Both were early supporters of Harvey's ideas, and Walaeus, too, made calculations regarding cardiac output with an assessment close to that of Harvey. Conring repeated Harvey's experiments, confirming and publishing the new idea in 1640, and was the first in Germany to acknowledge the Harveyan doctrine. In 1641 in Leyden, Walaeus published the results of animal experiments, further confirming Harvey's theories. He also stimulated Thomas Bartholin during his studies in Leyden to introduce Harvey's concept in Denmark. Thomas Bartholin became a professor in Copenhagen, and revised and illustrated new editions of the popular book on anatomy that his father, Caspar Bartholin the Elder, had published. Some of Rudbeck's own illustrations resemble those in Thomas Bartholin's book and were also inspired by Harvey's thesis on the circulation. Another illustration derives from a Dutch work on bloodletting[1, 2, 7, 8] or is possibly a modification of a figure in *Filactirion della Flebotomia et Arteriotomia...*by Giovanni Maria Castellani, printed in 1619.[9]

Biography

Olof Rudbeck was born in 1630 in the Swedish city of Västerås, the son of Bishop Johannes Rudbeckius. After medical studies at Uppsala beginning in 1648, and after publishing his two medical dissertations, Olof Rudbeck spent the years 1653 and 1654 at the University of Leyden with the sup-

Fig. 1   Olof Rudbeck, 1630–1702. Painting from Uppsala University Art Collections.

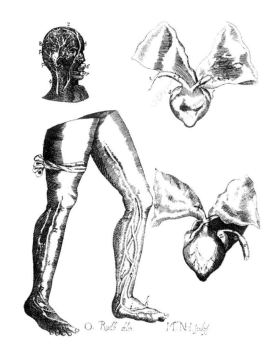

Fig. 2   Illustrations from Rudbeck's thesis on the circulation.[11] The drawings are by Rudbeck and the copper engravings by Magnus Nicolai Helsingius.

port of the Swedish queen. Beginning in 1655, he served for five years as a lecturer at Uppsala University and was then appointed professor, a post he held until 1691 when he was succeeded by his son, Olof Rudbeck the Younger. Together with his colleague, Professor Petrus Hoffvenius, Rudbeck the Elder modernized medical education at Uppsala University. Both Rudbeck and Hoffvenius were strong defenders of modern ideas in science based on Cartesian philosophy, and Rudbeck's teacher, Stenius, initially professor of astronomy and later of medicine, may have been the first Swedish Cartesian. The French man of science René Descartes (Cartesius) was another protagonist of Harvey; he died in 1650 after brief service at the Swedish court under Queen Christina.[1–3]

Apart from anatomy, Rudbeck lectured on chemistry, physics, mathematics, astronomy, and botany. Although his interest in medical education waned, he was active within many other fields, such as architecture and construction, mechanics, archaeology, and industrial enterprises. For a time he was the despotic administrator of the university. He also built an anatomical theatre at Uppsala University between 1662 and 1663, founded and financed a botanical garden at Uppsala, and fulfilled various governmental assignments. He had remarkable skills in drawing and music.[2, 10]

In the 1670s he started work on *Campus Elysii*, a monumental edition of botanical illustrations in 12 volumes that aimed to describe all known plants in the world. In 1702, after completing two volumes, most of his personal belongings, including several thousand wood carvings, were lost in a disastrous fire; he died that same year. Another project of characteristically heroic dimensions was the publication of

his *Atlantica* in four volumes between 1679 and 1702. This work, identifying Sweden as the mythical Atlantis, was a mixture of historical knowledge and pure speculation in a truly patriotic spirit. It met with considerable interest on the European continent.[1, 2, 10] Rudbeck is buried in Uppsala Cathedral.

References

1. Hagelin O: *Rare and Important Books in the Library of the Karolinska Institute*. Stockholm: Contributions from the Karolinska Institute Library and Museum Collections, Vol III, 1992
2. Rudbeck O: *Disputatio Anatomica de Circulatione Sangvinis*. Facsimile reprint (foreword in English) Stockholm: Rediviva Publishing House, 1977
3. Lindroth S: Harvey, Descartes, and Young Olaus Rudbeck. *J History Med Allied Sci* 1957;XII:209–219
4. Bayon HP: William Harvey, physician and biologist: His precursors, opponents and successors. Part II. *Ann Sci* 1938;3:83–118
5. Kilgour FG: William Harvey. *Sci Amer* 1952;186:58–62
6. Kilgour FG: William Harvey's use of the quantitative method. *Yale J Biol Med* 1954;26:410–421
7. Pagel W: *New Light on William Harvey*. Basel: S. Karger, 1976
8. Gotfredsen E: The reception of Harvey's doctrine in Denmark. *Acta Med Scand* 1952;(suppl 266):75–86
9. Castellani GM: *Filactirion della Flebotomia et Arteriotomia* 1619. Louise M. Darling Biomedical Library (biomedref@library.ucla.edu) under "Bloodletting."
10. Lindroth S: *Svensk lärdomshistoria*. Stormaktstiden (in Swedish). Norstedts, 1975
11. Minnesskrift utgifen å tvåhundraårs-dagen av Olof Rudbeck den äldres död (in Swedish). Stockholm: P.A. Norstedt & Söner, 1902

Richard Lower

W. Bruce Fye, M.D., M.A.

Department of Cardiology, Marshfield Clinic, Marshfield, Wisconsin, USA

Nobel laureate André Cournand considered Richard Lower's 1669 book *Tractatus de corde* to be one of the most important texts in the history of physiology because of "the nature of the observations, the rigor of the experimental design and demonstrations, [and] the simple and convincing form of the presentation."[1] Lower's book is the most important contribution to circulatory physiology after William Harvey's *De motu cordis* which was published in 1628, three years before Lower's birth.

Born into an affluent family in Tremeer, Cornwall, England, in 1631, Lower received undergraduate and medical degrees from Oxford. In the 17th century England was the intellectual center of medical and scientific research. In the stimulating atmosphere of Oxford Lower came under the influence of Thomas Willis, Robert Boyle, Robert Hooke, and Christopher Wren.[2, 3, 4] For several years he served as Willis's assistant—they collaborated informally until Willis's death in 1675.

At Oxford, Lower began, with Robert Hooke, a series of experiments that he continued in London when he entered medical practice there in 1666, when the metropolis was just recovering from the Great Plague and would be soon devastated by a massive fire. Lower survived these catastrophes, and his pioneering experiments on the heart and circulation were reported in his monograph *Tractatus de corde item de motu & colore sanguinis* published in 1669.[5]

This 220-page book included his important observations on the structure of cardiac muscle, studies in which Lower boiled the hearts of various animals in order to carefully dissect the various layers of the myocardium. He was impressed by the complex arrangement of the muscular fibers in the heart and felt their unique arrangement was responsible for the contraction of the ventricular cavity in systole that propelled blood into the vascular system. The illustrations in Lower's book depict the scroll-like structure of the left ventricular muscle.

Lower rejected the opinion of French philosopher and scientist René Descartes and others that blood left the heart because it fermented and simply spilled out. Lower's experiments were designed to refute this theory that ignored the critical role of muscular contraction in ejecting blood from the heart. He showed that an animal's heart continued to beat after it was excised and after it was emptied of blood. Moreover, Lower demonstrated that small pieces of excised heart muscle continued to beat as well. It would, however, be another 250 years before the myogenic theory of the heartbeat was proved conclusively.[6]

Other experiments described in Lower's book dealt with the quantity of blood in the vascular system, the velocity of blood flow, and the aeration of blood. In a series of experiments performed with Robert Hooke, Lower showed that the red color of arterial blood was due to its contact with "fresh air" in the lungs. He claimed that the red color of blood in the arterial circulation was "entirely due to the penetration of particles of air into the blood."

Lower's book also contained observations on the technique and safety of blood transfusion, a procedure he first attempted in 1665. Two years later he showed that transfusion could be

Fig. 1 Richard Lower 1631–1691. Engraving from the collection of W. Bruce Fye, M.D.

safely carried out in humans. Lower declared, "while *Harvey* first taught that the blood by its *circulation* within its own vessels ensures life to the body, we also revealed that it could be *transferred* outside the confine of its own body for the health of a second."[7]

When it appeared in 1669, Lower's book received praise from British and Continental physicians and scientists. It helped establish his reputation as William Harvey's successor as the leading investigator on the anatomy and physiology of the circulation. His London practice thrived, which limited the time Lower could devote to his experimental work. Lower's accomplishments were acknowledged by his election to Fellowship in the Royal College of Physicians. When he died in 1691, Lower was hailed as one of England's greatest contributors to medical science.

References

1. Fishman AP, Richards DW: *Circulation of the Blood: Men and Ideas*. Oxford University Press, New York (1964)
2. Franklin KJ: The work of Richard Lower (1631–1691). *Proc Royal Soc Med* 25, part 1, 113-118 (1932)
3. Hoff EC, Hoff PM: The life and times of Richard Lower, physiologist and physician (1631–1691). *Bull Hist Med* 3, 517–535 (1936)
4. Frank RG Jr: *Harvey and the Oxford Physiologists: Scientific Ideas and Social Interaction*. University of California Press, Berkeley and Los Angeles (1974)
5. Franklin KJ (trans.): *A facsimile edition of Tractatus de corde item de motu & colore sanquinis et chyli in eum transitu*. Oxford University Press, London and Oxford (1932)
6. Fye WB: The origin of the heart beat: A tale of frogs, jellyfish and turtles. *Circulation* 76, 493–500 (1987)
7. Quote from Franklin, note 5 (no page number in original).

Niels Stensen

W. Bruce Fye, m.d., m.a.

Department of Cardiology, Marshfield Clinic, Marshfield, Wisconsin, USA

Niels Stensen (Nicolaus Steno) (Fig. 1) was born in Copenhagen, Denmark, in 1638.[1–3] When he was 18, Stensen entered the University of Copenhagen where he studied under Thomas Bartholin, one of the seventeenth century's leading anatomists, and Ole Borch, a prominent chemist. After graduation, Stensen continued his education in Amsterdam, Paris, and Leyden. He became a leading participant in an intellectual movement known as iatromechanism (also termed iatrophysics or iatromathematics).[4] Arising from the ferment of the Scientific Revolution, iatromechanism represented a new paradigm that framed physiologic events in terms of physical and mathematical principles.[5, 6] Disciples of iatromechanism, such as Santorio Santorio, Giovanni Borelli, and René Descartes, championed experimentation and careful observation as the chief methods for studying the structure and functions of living organisms and their component parts.[7]

Stensen made his first important discovery in 1660, while studying under anatomist Gerhard Blaes (Blasius) at Amsterdam. While dissecting a sheep's head, Stensen identified the duct that carries saliva from the parotid gland to the mouth. Soon, he became increasingly interested in the function of muscles and the heart. William Harvey had published his revolutionary theory of the circulation just 32 years earlier. In his classic book *De motu cordis*, the English physician and anatomist argued that the heart was a pump which propelled the blood through a circuit of arteries and veins.[8] Many of Harvey's contemporaries, however, continued to embrace certain of Galen's and Aristotle's teachings, including the belief that the heart was the primary source of "innate heat" and the "vital spirit."[9]

Shortly after Harvey died in 1657, Stensen proposed that the heart was a muscle—and nothing more. The 24-year-old medical scientist told his mentor Bartholin in 1662, "I think I am able to prove that there exists nothing in the heart that is not found in a muscle, and that there is nothing missing in the heart which one finds in a muscle."[3] It was known already that skeletal muscles contained arteries, veins, and nerves in addition to muscle fibers; but Stensen found that the heart contained these same elements. By structural analogy, he concluded that the organ was a muscle and only a muscle.

In 1664, Stensen explained in his classic book, *De musculis et glandulis observationum specimen*, that

Fig. 1 Niels Stensen (1683–1686). (Photograph from the collection of W. Bruce Fye, M.D.)

The heart has been considered the seat of natural warmth, as the throne of the soul and even as the soul itself. Some have greeted the heart as the sun, others as the king; but if you examine it more closely, one finds it to be nothing more than muscle.[10, 11]

By describing the heart in this way, Stensen was doing more than simply summarizing conclusions he had drawn from a series of ingenious experiments and careful dissections; he was challenging beliefs that physicians had held for centuries.[12]

Stensen published additional observations on muscles in a 1667 book that anticipated a concept that came to be called the myogenic theory of the heartbeat.[13] He explained that "the heart, extracted from the body, is moved with repeated beats, although neither new blood flows into its vessels nor does new spirit enter it through the nerves from the brain."[14, 15] Although William Harvey had identified the atrium as the origin of the heartbeat in 1651, he thought its movement was "excited by the blood."

Stensen's new book incorporated the results of additional experiments he had performed and summarized discussions on the structure and function of muscles he had had in 1665 and 1666 with Dutch scientist Jan Swammerdam and English anatomist William Croone. It also included a novel mathematical and geometrical framework that Stensen had elaborated to explain muscle contraction. This theory has been characterized recently as a "turning point in the history of muscle physiology."[16] In addition to Stensen's classic work on the anatomy and physiology of muscle, he also made important contributions to neuroanatomy, embryology, comparative anatomy, and geology. He died in Germany in 1686.

References

1. Cioni R: *Niels Stensen: Scientist-Bishop*. New York: P.J. Kennedy & Sons, 1962
2. Poulsen JE, Snorrason E (Eds.): *Nicolaus Steno, 1638–1686: A Reconsideration by Danish Scientists*. Gentofte, Denmark: Nordisk Insulinlaboratorium, 1986
3. Scherz G: Niels Stensen. In *Dictionary of Scientific Biography*. New York: Charles Scribner's Sons, 1976:13, 30–35
4. Brown TM: The College of Physicians and the acceptance of iatromechanism in England, 1665-1695. *Bull Hist Med* 1970;44: 12–30
5. Hall TS: *Ideas of Life and Matter: Studies in the History of General Physiology, 600 B.C.–1900 A.D.* Chicago: University of Chicago Press, 1969
6. Webster C (Ed.): *The Intellectual Revolution of the Seventeenth Century*. London: Routledge & Kegan Paul, 1974
7. Shea WR: *The Magic of Numbers and Motion: The Scientific Career of René Descartes*. Canton, Mass.: Science History Publications, 1991
8. Harvey W: *Exercitatio Anatomica. De Motu Cordis et Sanguinis in Animalibus* (1628) (Ed. Leake CD). Springfield, Ill.: Charles C Thomas, 1928
9. Whitteridge G: *William Harvey and the Circulation of the Blood*. New York: American Elsevier, Inc., 1971
10. Stensen N: *De musculis et glandulis observationum specimen cum epistolis duabus anatomicis*. Copenhagen: Matthias Godicchen, 1664
11. Miller WS: Niels Stensen. *Johns Hopkins Hosp Bull* 1914;25: 44–51
12. Harris CRS: *The Heart and the Vascular System in Ancient Greek Medicine from Alcmaeon to Galen*. London: Oxford University Press, 1973
13. Fye WB: The origin of the heart beat: A tale of frogs, jellyfish and turtles. *Circulation* 1987;76:493–500
14. Stensen N: *Elementorum myologiae specimen, seu musculi descriptio geometrica*. Florence: Stellae, 1667
15. Fulton JF, Wilson LG: *Selected Readings in the History of Physiology*. 2nd ed. Springfield, Ill.: Charles C Thomas, 1966
16. Bastholm E: *The History of Muscle Physiology from the Natural Philosophers to Albrecht von Haller*. Copenhagen: Ejnar Munksgaard, 1950

Lorenzo Bellini

W. Bruce Fye, M.D., M.A.

Department of Cardiology, Marshfield Clinic, Marshfield, Wisconsin, USA

Lorenzo Bellini (Fig. 1) was born in Florence, Italy, on September 3, 1643.[1] He was a pioneer in iatromechanism, a theoretic system that framed physiologic events such as the circulation of the blood in terms of mathematical and physical principles.[2] Bellini studied philosophy, mathematics, and medicine at the University of Pisa where he came under the influence of Giovanni Alfonso Borelli, a founder of iatromechanism.[3] A brilliant student, Bellini was just 20 years old when he was appointed professor of theoretical medicine at his alma mater. Five years later, he was selected to fill the university's chair of anatomy.

For Borelli, Bellini, and other disciples of iatromechanism, "living bodies are machines," according to historian Thomas Hall. Hall explains that

The life of the machine is the totality of movements exhibited by the moving parts and by the machine as a whole. The whole machine is an assemblage of smaller component machines, and these of still smaller ones, and so on until we reach the corpuscular level.[4]

With other proponents of iatromechanism (including Robert Boyle in England, René Descartes in France, and Niels Stensen in Denmark), Bellini and his mentor Borelli embraced experimentation and careful observation as the chief methods for studying the structure and functions of living organisms and their component parts.

Precocious and ambitious, Bellini published his first book when he was just 19 years old. *Exercitatio anatomica de usu renum* (1662) was a pioneering work on the anatomy and physiology of the kidneys. Bellini rejected Galenic theories about renal structure and function that had dominated Western medical thought for almost 1,500 years. With the aid of a magnifying glass, he made observations that led him to conclude that the kidney was not composed of solid fibrous strands; rather, it contained vast numbers of hollow tubes or canaliculi that extended radially from the papillae to the renal cortex.[5]

Bellini proposed a physical theory of urinary secretion that reflected the tenets of iatromechanism. He argued that the small arteries of the kidney discharged blood into spaces in the renal parenchyma where it was separated into two parts: the aqueous portion drained off into the tubules he had identified to form urine while the more solid portion returned to the circulatory system via the renal vein. The size and configuration of the particles in the blood determined which route they took.[6] Bellini's mechanical explanation of the formation of urine "came remarkably close to the process of glomerular filtration; the only component he had failed to observe was the glomerulus," according to nephrologist Leon Fine.[7]

Bellini's most important book, *De urinis et pulsibus et missione sanguinis*, was published in Bologna in 1683. Now very rare, this 606 page volume represented the first significant attempt to frame medical theory in terms of iatromechanism. In some respects, it was an extension of Borelli's *De motu animalium*, published 3 years earlier.[8]

William Harvey's theory of the circulation was of fundamental importance to Bellini and other proponents of iatromechanism.[9] Bellini asserted that good health depended on optimal function of the circulation of the blood, and that disease was a manifestation of an inefficient circulation. Rejecting ancient humoral pathology, he viewed blood as a physical fluid with specific properties that could be interpreted in terms of mathematical and physical principles. He also emphasized the importance of analyzing the chemical composition of the urine.

Bellini emphasized that disease was often due to alterations in the elasticity or "tone" of the solids, or in the density of the fluids which hindered their motion. This, in turn, could cause local congestion or stagnation. Bellini's enthusiastic support of therapeutic bleeding reflected this pathophysiologic concept. He tried to prove that this phlebotomy increased the velocity of the circulation, thereby washing away "morbid matter" and restoring health.[10]

In the section of his 1683 book that dealt with disorders of the chest, Bellini described several examples of heart disease. Syncope, orthopnea, and other cardiac symptoms were discussed and interpreted. He also made early observations on the coronary circulation. According to historian Joshua Leibowitz, Bellini proposed that coronary calcification could reduce coronary blood flow. Leibowitz also notes that Bellini reported the case of a patient who died with a clinical picture consistent with ischemic heart disease as we now understand it, "in whose coronary arteries he found a 'stone'." Leibowitz concluded that Bellini had observed a coronary occlusion at autopsy.[11]

Italian physician and anatomist Marcello Malpighi affirmed on the imprimatur leaf of *De urinis et pulsibus et mis-*

Fɪɢ. 1 Lorenzo Bellini, 1643–1704. Photograph from the collection of W. Bruce Fye, M.D.

sione sanguinis that he considered the book an important achievement. He applauded the fact that medicine was "treated solidly and ingeniously by a new method."[12] The most vocal champion of Bellini's theories was the Scottish physician and mathematician Archibald Pitcairne, lecturer on theoretical medicine at the University of Leyden.[13] Bellini's works were also admired by Hermann Boerhaave of Leyden, the most prominent medical teacher of the early eighteenth century.

Pitcairne thought Bellini's general theory of disease was an important innovation and urged him to expand his approach beyond the organ-based focus that he had used in his book on the kidney and in *De urinis.* Bellini responded by publishing *Opuscula aliquot* in 1695, which he dedicated to Pitcairne. His interpretation of iatromechanism was developed most fully in this book which was structured as a series of postulates, theorems, and corollaries dealing with a wide range of medical topics.

Bellini's theories were championed in England during the early eighteenth century by George Cheyne and Richard Mead, but his influence declined in the mid-eighteenth century as iatromechanism came to be viewed as an oversimplification that ignored chemical phenomena and other factors that influenced health and disease.

After a decade of failing health, Bellini died in 1704.

References

1. Brown TM: *Lorenzo Bellini. Dictionary of Scientific Biography*, 1, p. 592–594. New York: Charles Scribner's Sons, 1970

2. Brown TM: The College of Physicians and the acceptance of iatromechanism in England, 1665–1695. *Bull Hist Med* 1970; 44:12–30

3. Settle TB: *Giovanni Alfonso Borelli. Dictionary of Scientific Biography*, 2, p. 306–314. New York: Charles Scribner's Sons, 1973

4. Hall TS: *Ideas of Life and Matter: Studies in the History of General Physiology, 600 B.C.–1900 A.D.*, p. 347–348. Chicago: University of Chicago Press, 1969

5. Murphy LJT: *The History of Urology*, p. 57–58. Springfield, Ill: Charles C Thomas, 1972

6. Foster M: *Lectures on the History of Physiology during the Sixteenth, Seventeenth and Eighteenth Centuries.* Cambridge: Cambridge University Press, 1901

7. Fine L: Evolution of renal physiology from earliest times to William Bowman. In *Renal Physiology: People and Ideas* (Eds. Gottschalk CW, Berliner RW, Giebisch GH), p. 1–30. Bethesda: American Physiological Society, 1987

8. Borelli GA: *De motu animalium.* Rome: Angelo Bernabo, 1680

9. Harvey W: *Exercitatio anatomica. De motu cordis et sanguinis in animalibus [1628]* (Ed. Leake CD). Springfield, Ill.: Charles C Thomas, 1928

10. Withington ET: *Medical History from the Earliest Times: A Popular History of the Healing Art.* London: The Scientific Press, Ltd., 1984

11. Leibowitz JO: *The History of Coronary Heart Disease.* London: Wellcome Institute of the History of Medicine, 1970

12. Adelmann HB: *Marcello Malpighi and the Evolution of Embryology.* 5 vols, 1, p. 462. Ithaca: Cornell University Press, 1966

13. King LS: *The Philosophy of Medicine: The Early Eighteenth Century.* Cambridge: Harvard University Press, 1978

Giovanni Maria Lancisi, 1654–1720

W. B. Fye, M.D., M.A.

Cardiology Department, Marshfield Clinic, Marshfield, Wisconsin, USA

Giovanni Maria Lancisi, perhaps the greatest Italian clinician of his generation, made numerous important contributions to cardiology. He was born in Rome on October 26, 1654.[1,2] Following preliminary training he entered the Collegio Romano where he studied philosophy and liberal arts. He also briefly studied theology, but became progressively interested in natural history. Finally, he turned his attention to medicine and enrolled in the senior college of the Sapienza at Rome. There, Lancisi studied chemistry, botany, and astronomy in addition to medicine.[3] He gained practical experience in the hospitals of Rome where he saw patients and participated in numerous autopsies. In 1672, at the age of 18, he was awarded the degree of Doctor of Philosophy and Medicine from the Sapienza. Four years later Lancisi was elected assistant physician in the San Spirito Hospital in Sassia under Giovanni Tiracorda, former physician to Pope Innocent X.

It was at the San Spirito that Lancisi's powers of observation and clinical acumen matured. In the words of his contemporary, Assalto, Lancisi "showed the greatest industry and constantly attended at the bedsides of the patients, carefully noted their signs and symptoms, used his skill to try to explore the causes of their diseases, and was present to observe the issue."[4] After two years, Lancisi left San Spirito Hospital to obtain additional medical training at the Picentine College of our Saviour in Lauro. There he spent five years reading the works of classical and contemporary medical authors.

In 1684, Lancisi was appointed Public Professor of Anatomy in the Senior College of the University of Sapienza in Rome. During the 13 years he held that position, his reputation as a teacher and lecturer grew steadily. He was interested in anatomical research and collaborated with Marcello Malpighi in studies on the embryology of the heart. Lancisi's popularity and influence within the institution led the Rector to refurbish and expand the anatomical theater where Lancisi lectured and dissected.

At the age of 34, Lancisi was selected by Pope Innocent XI to be the Pontiff's personal physician. When the Pope died in 1689, Lancisi returned to private practice and teaching. A decade later, Lancisi was again called to serve the Vatican. This time he was consulted in the case of Innocent XII for whom he cared until the Pontiff's death. His successor, Clement XI, appointed Lancisi to the prestigious position of Physician to the Pontiff. An erudite man, Pope Clement sought Lancisi's assistance in improving the health of Rome's inhabitants. Among the reforms Lancisi urged were measures designed to reduce air pollution.

Lancisi's interest in sudden death can be traced to an epidemic of unexpected deaths that occurred in Rome in 1705. At the request of Clement XI, Lancisi made a thorough study of the matter and conducted autopsies on many of the victims. His observations and conclusions were published in a monograph *De subitaneis mortibus* in 1707.[5,6] Lancisi explained that various theories had been put forth by laymen to explain the deaths:

> They blamed in their ignorance no less than in their rashness, at one moment the rotten quality of the tobacco, and at another the fetid exhalations from past earthquakes, then again the abuse of chocolate, and finally an unknown virus within their surroundings.[7]

Lancisi sought to explain the deaths in terms of contemporary medical theory and noted there were three "major fluids" and three "major solids" necessary for life. The fluids were air, blood, and nervous "fluid," while the solids were the respiratory system, the cardiovascular system, and the nervous system. Sudden death could result from a major disorder of any of these.[8] In order to support his belief that these solids and liquids were vital for life Lancisi presented examples including asphyxiation due to coal gas inhalation and exsanguination due to hemorrhage. He argued that sudden death occurred most frequently when a combination of disorders affecting the liquids and solids was present.

Lancisi emphasized that sudden death could result from structural abnormalities of the heart or great vessels. Reflecting his sophisticated understanding of cardiac physiology, he claimed that sudden death could result from disorders that impaired either systolic or diastolic function of the heart. The former might be due to disturbances that "weaken the structure of the heart" while the latter might result "from causes that compress it most violently, such as contraction or swelling of the heart, of the pericardium, or of adjacent parts."[9]

Although a clear description of angina pectoris would not appear for more than half a century, when William Heberden published his classic description of this distressing symptom,

FIG. 1   Giovanni Maria Lancisi, 1654–1720.

Lancisi described complaints which surely represented this entity. He wrote,

> ...internal pains of the chest, accompanied at one moment by difficulty of breathing, especially when ascending hills, and at another by a strangling sensation of the heart and frequently by an uneven pulse... are apt to kill out of time, particularly if the patients subject themselves to violent exertions and glut themselves with unwholesome food.[10]

Although not specific for heart disease, some patients with these symptoms undoubtedly had angina pectoris, and Lancisi felt they were at risk for sudden death. He also identified recurrent syncope as a predictor of sudden death in some patients. Some of Lancisi's case reports include descriptions of pathologic findings that suggest cardiac disease was responsible for some, but not all, of the sudden deaths he described.

Another subject that interested Lancisi throughout his life was cardiac enlargement and aneurysms of the great vessels. His classic work, *De Motu Cordis et Aneurysmatibus*, in which Lancisi summarized his views on diseases of the cardiovascular system, was published posthumously in 1728.[11,12] In this important work he discussed the various conditions that might lead to enlargement of the heart and the symptoms that resulted from disorders of cardiac structure and function. Lancisi also demonstrated the relationship of syphilis to the development of aortic aneurysms. He emphasized the significance of cardiac dilatation and showed that neck vein distension was a useful sign in predicting the presence of right heart enlargement.

Lancisi died in 1720 after a brief illness. Physician and historian Saul Jarcho claimed recently Lancisi deserves to be considered "the true founder of cardiovascular pathology and one of the founding fathers of clinical cardiology."[13]

References

1. Assalto P: Vita (of Lancisi) by Assalto (1720). In *De Aneurysmatibus, Opus Posthumum, Giovanni Maria Lancisi, 1654–1720. Aneurysms, the Latin Text of Rome, 1745*. Revised, with Translation and Notes by Wilmer Cave Wright. Macmillan Co., New York (1952) ix-xxi
2. Foote J: Giovanni Maria Lancisi (1654–1720). *Int Clin* 2, 292 (1917)
3. Castiglioni A: *Italian Medicine*. Paul B. Hoeber, New York (1932)
4. Ref. 1, xiii
5. Lancisi GM: *De subitaneis mortibus*. Francisci Buagni, Rome (1707)
6. White PD, Boursy AV: *Translation of De subitaneis mortibus (On Sudden Deaths)*. St. John's University Press, New York (1971)
7. Ref. 6, xix
8. King LS: *The Medical World of the Eighteenth Century*. University of Chicago Press, Chicago (1958)
9. Ref. 6, 24
10. *Ibid.*, 52
11. Lancisi GM: *De Motu Cordis et Aneurysmatibus*. J.M. Salvioni, Rome (1728)
12. Lancisi GM: *De Aneurysmatibus, Opus Posthumum... Aneurysms, the Latin Text of Rome, 1745*. Revised, with Translation and Notes by Wilmer Cave Wright. Macmillan Co., New York (1952)
13. Jarcho S: *The Concept of Heart Failure*. Harvard University Press, Cambridge (1980) 274

Antonio Maria Valsalva

SVEN-GÖRAN FRANSSON, M.D., PH.D., AND ANDREA RUBBOLI, M.D., FESC*

Department of Thoracic Radiology, University Hospital, Linköping, Sweden; *Section of Cardiology, Maggiore Hospital, Bologna, Italy

The Italian Valsalva (Fig. 1) described the aortic sinuses of Valsalva in his *Opera*, which was not published until 1740. Giulio Cesare Arantius was professor of anatomy at Bologna and a predecessor to Valsalva. He had described the cartilaginous nodules of the aortic valve, that is, *noduli Arantii*. The role of the eddy currents in the sinus of Valsalva and the closure of this valve have regained much interest since the time of Leonardo da Vinci's experimental glass model combined with an excised valve specimen in 1513. According to one dictionary of medical eponyms, the name Valsalva is associated with another three descriptions, namely, the Valsalva antrum of the ear, the Valsalva maneuver as a test of circulatory function, and the otological Valsalva test. Still other anatomic structures bearing his name are Valsalva's muscle and *taeniae Valsalvae*.[1-8]

Valsalva, who was born in Imola in 1666, came from a distinguished family and was well educated in the humanities, mathematics, and natural sciences. His father was a goldsmith, and the name of Valsalva was derived from a castle in the possession of the family. After studies of the liberal arts, he entered the faculty of medicine and philosophy in Bologna. He was a pupil of Marcello Malpighi, founder of microscopic anatomy, and graduated from the medical school in 1687. In 1705, he was appointed professor of anatomy at Bologna and eventually president of the Academy of the Sciences. He attended several hospitals, but especially Sant'Orsola. Valsalva, in turn, was the teacher of the famous Giovanni Battista Morgagni who edited Valsalva's complete writings published posthumously in 1740; in the same year he also published a biography on Valsalva. Like Malpighi, he was named a fellow of the Royal Society of London. Mutual admiration was expressed in the relationships between Valsalva and his teacher and between Valsalva and his pupils. He was much appreciated among contemporary colleagues, a generous man, a dedicated scientist and according to Morgagni: "He had a high and broad forehead, black and very lively eyes . . . his face was calm, but not without gravity; he was not of large size, but of fine figure, of strength adapted to endure hard labours; his hand was steady . . ." In 1709, he married Elena Lisi, the daughter of a noble Bolognese family.[1, 4–6, 8, 9]

Despite impaired health, Valsalva maintained his devotion to teaching, science, and medical practice within the fields of anatomy, physiology, surgery, and even psychiatry. At a young age, Valsalva had successfully removed a dog's kidney. He was an opponent of cauterization in the treatment of wounds and advocated methods in the cure of aneurysm and in some causes of deafness. He recommended humanitarian treatment of mentally ill patients. Still, his main interest was the anatomy and function of the middle and internal ear, including the muscles of the external ear and the pharyngeal muscles even in the fetus and the newborn. He also described the function of and named the Eustachian tube with its muscle, demonstrated the communication between the mastoid cells and the tympanic cavity, and made observations on physiologic and pathologic processes of the ear. The publication of *De aure humana* in 1704 followed numerous dissections and years of intense work, including animal experiments. It also contains a description of the Valsalva maneuver and patency test of the auditory tubes. He deteriorated in health, lost his sense of smell, and also recognized the prodromal symptoms, in the form of dyslalia, of the disease that would eventually cause his death from apoplexy in 1723. He had also noted the connection between hemiplegia and the contralateral location of the causative cere-

ANTON MARIA VALSALVA
DAL MEDAGLIONE MARMOREO NELL'ARCHIGINNASIO BOLOGNESE

FIG 1. Portrait of Valsalva (1666–1723), Archiginnasio Palace, Bologna (from P. Capparoni: Profili bio-bibliografici di medici e naturalisti . . . Instituto Nazionale Medico Farmacologico, Rome, 1925).

bral lesion. Valsalva is buried in the church of San Giovanni in Monte, Bologna, and the old university building Archiginnasio holds a marble medallion with his portrait.[4, 8, 9]

The Valsalva family donated a collection of dried anatomical specimens to be used for educational purposes to the Institute of Sciences founded in 1711. The wear of this material that followed possibly inspired the work of the Bolognese school of wax modeling and the artists Ercole Lelli and the Manzolini family. This new anatomic collection includes models of the heart and lungs and is today presented at the Museum of Anatomy.[4, 8–10] Valsalva lived during the baroque period and also the foundation of scientific academies in Rome, London, Paris, and in Germany. He was the contemporary of great men such as Newton, the composer Bach, and Molière, who ridiculed the medical profession in his writings. Valsalva was truly a great man himself, described as a skillful surgeon and excellent physician, a meticulous anatomist with high scientific integrity, and a man of great kindness. Morgagni wrote "... there is nobody of those times who goes ahead of him, very few who are his equals."[9]

References

1. Acierno LJ: *History of Cardiology*. New York: The Parthenon Publishing Group Inc., 1994
2. Walton J, Barondess J, Lock S: *The Oxford Medical Companion*. Oxford, New York, Tokyo: Oxford University Press, 1994
3. Wiley J: *International Dictionary of Medicine and Biology*. New York, Chichester, Brisbane, Toronto, Singapore: John Wiley & Sons, Inc., 1986
4. Gillispie CC: *Dictionary of Scientific Biography*. New York: Charles Scribner's Sons, 1970
5. Castiglione A: *A History of Medicine*. New York: Jason Aronson Inc., 1975
6. Norman JM: *Morton's Medical Biography*. Aldershot: Scolar Press, 1991
7. Robicsek F: Leonardo da Vinci and the Sinuses of Valsalva. *Ann Thorac Surg* 1991;52:328–335
8. Firkin BG, Whitworth JA: *Dictionary of Medical Eponyms*. Carnforth, Park Ridge: The Parthenon Publishing Group, 1987
9. Castiglione A: Antonio Maria Valsalva. *Medical Life* 1932;39: 83–107
10. Maraldi NM, Mazzotti G, Cocco L, Manzoli FA: Anatomical waxwork modeling: The history of the Bologna Anatomy Museum. *Anat Rec* 2000;261:5–10

Johann and Daniel Bernoulli

W. Bruce Fye, M.D., M.A.

Cardiovascular Division, Mayo Clinic, Rochester, Minnesota, USA

Johann Bernoulli (Fig. 1) and his son Daniel (Fig. 2) made pioneering contributions to the fields of hemodynamics and muscle mechanics. Johann Bernoulli was born in Basel, Switzerland, on August 6, 1667, and was educated at the university there.[1] His studies focused on mathematics and medicine. Bernoulli's inaugural dissertation on the movement of muscles, published in 1694, is important for several reasons, including the fact that it represents the first application of the principles of differential calculus to a biological problem.[2]

As a student of mathematics and medicine, he was influenced by the so-called iatromechanism school, led by Giovanni Borelli.[3] Johann was among the first to embrace and extend the emerging field of differential calculus, and his writings propelled him to the front ranks of mathematics, along with Gottfried Wilhelm Leibnitz and Isaac Newton. After Newton died in 1727, Johann's many important publications and his other academic activities led to a consensus that he was Europe's leading mathematician.

Johann's second son, Daniel, was born on February 8, 1700, in Groningen, The Netherlands, where his father was then teaching.[4] The family moved to Basel five years later when Johann was appointed to the chair of mathematics at the University of Basel. Not long after entering the university to study philosophy, young Daniel displayed special aptitude for mathematics. He received his medical degree in 1720 with a dissertation on the physiology of respiration. It was already evident, however, that his main interest was mathematics. When he was just 24 years old, he published an influential treatise on this subject that enhanced greatly his reputation among academics.

A prolific theorist and author, Daniel published dozens of papers on physics and mathematics, while several publications and lectures dealt with physiology. Two of his most important physiologic writings were treatises on muscular mechanics (1728) and the mechanical work done by the heart (1737). At this early stage of his career—and at a time when university positions were scarce—Daniel was a peripatetic teacher and scholar. Between 1725 and 1733 he taught at the Imperial Academy of Science in St. Petersburg, Russia. While there, he worked with Leonhard Euler and began writing his classic monograph on hydrodynamics, *Hydrodynamica, sive de viribus et motibus fluidorum*, published in 1738.[5] It reflects the influence of the iatromechanism tradition of Giovanni Borelli.

Daniel Bernoulli's book on hydrodynamics reveals his sophistication in physics and mathematics and provides ample evidence that he was helping to define a new field of scientific endeavor. Although others had written on hydraulics (the motion of fluids) and hydrostatics (the pressures and various equilibria of stagnant fluids), Bernoulli believed that it was important to unite these subjects.[6] In the process he coined the term hydrodynamics and helped launch a new area of physical and physiologic research.

Bernoulli's book is primarily a treatise on physics, but it contains many complex mathematical equations necessary to support his theories and explain his observations. In it he describes the behavior of fluids in a wide variety of circumstances, some of which were quite common in eighteenth century Europe. For example, he describes mathematically the flow of water through pipes from reservoirs to homes and the principles that explained the function of fountains—then, as now, a prominent feature of many European cities. Other sections deal with theoretical problems that did not have a distinct parallel in contemporary everyday life.

Although the book does not address the circulation directly, there are several portions that are relevant to future investigations of blood flow. Chapters deal with the equilibrium of standing fluids, the velocities of fluids flowing out of a vessel, the motion of water flowing from containers that are kept constantly full (such as fountains), the motion of fluids within the walls of vessels, the motion of homogeneous and heterogeneous fluids through vessels of irregular shape, and the motion of fluids that are pushed forward not by their own weight but by some external force, among others.

Daniel developed several experimental techniques that were critical for the future development of hydrodynamics and circulatory physiology. His text includes many experiments that he devised and performed to better understand and describe the behavior of fluids in different circumstances. According to Hunter Rouse, who was responsible for the first English translation of Bernoulli's book on hydrodynamics, the European scientist was "the first to connect manometers to piezometric openings in the walls of vessels, to consider the establishment with time of flow in a long conduit, and to attempt to predict conduit pressure in terms of the velocity."[7a]

Although this classic monograph on hydrodynamics does not include an explicit formulation of the so-called Bernoulli equation, it sets the stage for the eventual elabora-

FIG. 1 Johann Bernoulli (1667–1748). From the National Library of Medicine. Reproduced with permission.

FIG. 2 Daniel Bernoulli (1700–1782). From the National Library of Medicine. Reproduced with permission.

tion of that formula. A principle that Bernoulli proved and used throughout his book was that "the velocities of fluids are everywhere reciprocally proportional to the areas of the vessels."[7b]

Daniel Bernoulli's father, Johann, also contributed significantly to the fields of hydrodynamics and muscle mechanics, but controversy surrounded some of his later work. In 1732, four years after Daniel published his classic book on hydraulics, Johann published a book on the same subject. Although it contained some new and important observations, most of the elder Bernoulli's contemporaries (and subsequent generations of scholars) considered it to be largely plagiarized from his son.

Daniel Bernoulli's important contributions were acknowledged in various ways during his lifetime. For example, he won ten prizes from the Paris Academy of Sciences for essays he submitted. They dealt with a wide variety of subjects such as gravity, tides, ocean currents, astronomy, and magnetism. He belonged to many of the leading scientific societies of Europe, including those of Berlin, Bern, Bologna, London,

Paris, and Zurich. His father died on January 1, 1748, and Daniel died on March 17, 1782.

References

1. Fellman EA, Fleckenstein JO: Johann Bernoulli. In *Dictionary of Scientific Biography* (Ed. Gillispie CC), p. 51–55. New York: Charles Scribner's Sons, 1973

2. Bernoulli J: *Dissertation on the Mechanics of Effervescence and Fermentation and on the Mechanics of the Movement of the Muscles*. (Eds. Manquet P, Ziggelaar A). Philadelphia: American Philosophical Society, 1997

3. Brown T: *The Mechanical Philosophy and the "Animal Oeconomy."* New York: Arno Press, 1981

4. Straub H: Daniel Bernoulli. In *Dictionary of Scientific Biography* (Ed. Gillespie CC), p. 36–46. New York: Charles Scribner's Sons, 1973

5. Bernoulli D: *Hydrodynamica*. Strassburg: Johann Reingold, 1738

6. Rouse H, Ince S: *History of Hydraulics*. New York: Dover Publications, 1957

7. Bernoulli D: *Hydrodynamics & Hydraulics* by J. Bernoulli, (a) p. xii; translated from the Latin by T. Carmody and H. Kobus. Preface by H. Rouse; (b) p. 159. New York: Dover Publications, 1968

Giorgio Baglivi

W. Bruce Fye, M.D., M.A.

Mayo Clinic, Rochester, Minnesota, USA

Seventeenth century physician and medical scientist Giorgio Baglivi (Fig. 1) published the first clinical description of pulmonary edema and made classic observations on the histology and physiology of muscle. Although some biographers claim that Baglivi was born in Ragusa, Sicily, the most authoritative writers conclude that he was born in Dubrovnik, Croatia, on September 8, 1668.[1, 2] His birth name was Duro Armeno. Orphaned at the age of two, he was raised by an uncle. When Duro was 15, he and his younger brother were adopted by Pietro Angelo Baglivi, a prominent physician of Lecce, Italy. Renamed Giorgio Baglivi, the ambitious young man served as an apprentice to his adoptive father and attended medical lectures at Naples. Thereafter, he worked in hospitals in several Italian cities including Florence, Padua, Pisa, and Venice.

In 1691, Giorgio moved to Bologna where he studied with the leading Italian physician and microscopist Marcello Malpighi. Eventually becoming Malpighi's assistant, Baglivi came into contact with several leading Italian physicians and medical scientists of the day. Many letters to and from Baglivi survive, and his extensive correspondence with Lorenzo Bellini, Marcello Malpighi, Francesco Redi, and others reveals much about his life and research interests.[3] When Malpighi moved to Rome in 1692, he invited Baglivi to join him. They lived and worked together until Malpighi died two years later.

Baglivi rapidly joined the ranks of Rome's elite physicians and medical scientists. Within four years of his arrival in that ancient city, he was appointed second physician to the Pope and elected professor of anatomy at the Sapienza. In 1696, he was appointed physician-in-chief of practical medicine at the institution. In addition to his active practice, Baglivi continued his work in experimental physiology and microscopy. As a result of this unusual combination of practical clinical experience and research, his writings reveal an unusually sophisticated understanding of the structure and function of various organs, especially the lungs. Nevertheless, he lived at a time when medical theory and practice were still dominated by the ancient authorities Hippocrates and Galen. Baglivi's books attempted to reconcile his clinical observations and research findings with their teachings.

Baglivi was an influential member of an important intellectual movement in European medicine, termed iatromechanics, founded in the middle of the seventeenth century. Several prominent medical scientists such as René Descartes in France, Robert Boyle in England, Niels Stensen in Denmark, and Giovanni Borelli in Italy embraced iatromechanics, also known as the iatrophysics or iatromathematics school. They framed physiologic events in terms of mathematical and physical principles and advocated experimentation and careful observation as the chief methods for studying and understanding the structure of the body and the functions of its component parts.[4]

In 1696, Baglivi published an important book on medical practice, *De praxi medica*, which was translated into English eight years later.[5] This book includes descriptions of several vivisections and experiments that he performed, some of which were designed to study cardiac innervation. Like Borelli, Baglivi was an early supporter of the myogenic theory of the heartbeat, something not proved convincingly until the end of the nineteenth century by William Gaskell. Baglivi reported in *De praxi medica*, "If you take out the Heart of a Frog and lay it upon a Table, 'twill beat with a regular Systole and Diastole for half an hour after, and sometimes for a whole hour, especially if it be expos'd to the heat of the Sun."[5a] This suggested that the heart beat independently of vagal or other innervation.

Baglivi's most significant scientific observations resulted from his sophistication in microscopy, which he owed mainly to his mentor Malpighi. In his classic monograph *De fibra motrice*, published in 1700, Baglivi first differentiated smooth from striated muscle.[6, 7] He used a compound microscope to study isolated muscle fibers he had obtained by soaking muscle in a solution of water, alcohol, and vinegar. Reflecting his deep commitment to iatromechanism, Baglivi proposed a theory of muscle contraction that revealed his advanced understanding of the structure of muscle fibers. He concluded that heart muscle contracted spontaneously as demonstrated by its behavior following excision of the organ, which resulted in its denervation. Baglivi also emphasized the fundamental importance of the fiber as a structure that helped to determine the function of various organs. In contrast to the traditional emphasis placed on the body's fluids, he argued that all physiologic functions and pathologic processes should be framed in terms of these fibers.

An astute clinician, Baglivi left masterful descriptions of what later was termed cardiac asthma. In his classic study of the early history of heart failure, twentieth century clinician-historian Saul Jarcho credits Baglivi with publishing "the first

Fig. 1   Giorgio Baglivi, 1669–1707. Photograph from the collection of W. Bruce Fye, M.D., M.A.

acceptable clinical portrayal of pulmonary edema."[8] Baglivi's 1696 book also includes a classic description of paroxysmal nocturnal dyspnea. The following quotation is taken from the 1704 English translation of Baglivi's book:

If in the Night time, especially after three or four hours Sleep, the Patient awakes of a sudden, with a violent Asthma and Suffocation Fits upon him, and presently runs to the Windows in quest of the free Air; you may rest assur'd that he has a Dropsy in his Breast especially if his Hands or Feet begin to swell; and the face loses its wonted color; and above all, if he observes a heavy Numness, or a beginning Palsy in his Arm.[5b]

In the first collected edition of his works, published in 1704, Baglivi extended his earlier observations on [cardiac] asthma and added a chapter on "rare affections of the lungs."[9] This section includes Baglivi's description of signs and symptoms that are consistent with heart failure and pulmonary edema. He does not attribute the complaints and findings to cardiac dysfunction, but he characterizes the condition as a "dangerous disease." His classic description of "suffocative catarrh" is worth quoting:

It is caused chiefly by stagnation and sudden coagulation of blood in the lungs and about the precordium. . . . the patient has . . . a pain in the chest, and difficulty in breathing; also interrupted speech, anxiety, cough, stertor, a widely spaced slow pulse, foam at the mouth, and the like.

Baglivi explains that "the foam at the mouth is caused by impaired circulation of blood about the lungs and consequent impairment of the circulation of lymph in the upper parts of the

body near the face; hence the lymph is forced out in the shape of foam."[9a] Although bloodletting was used regularly for a wide variety of complaints, it surely helped patients with acute pulmonary edema. Baglivi writes, "An instant remedy for this disease during the paroxysm is repeated bloodletting."[9b]

Baglivi also wrote about the structure of medical practice and the state of medical education. He proposed a degree of specialization in medicine that has yet to develop. In 1696 he advocated the creation of "Colleges of Physicians" to improve the practice of medicine. He recommended that these colleges be divided into two parts: one devoted to "reading the Books that contain Observations, and the other for making and setting down new Observations."[5c] More than 300 years ago, and more than two centuries before cardiology began to emerge as a specialty, he wrote, "Let every fellow of this Literate Society have one Disease allotted him for the task of his whole Life, which he ought to pursue. . ." For a given disease Baglivi recommended that after the physician had read all of the descriptions of the disorder he should investigate all aspects of it. He specifically encouraged study of the

. . . Nature or Idea of the Disease in general, their Diagnosticks and Prognosticks, the Cautions and general Precepts, the most accurate Methods of Cure, the choicest and most specifick Remedies, the mutual Transmutations of Symptoms and Diseases, with the measure of their duration, the Efforts, Method, and Order of Nature in expelling the morbisick Matter.[5d]

Baglivi was a leading physician of his time who contributed much to our understanding of muscle structure and function and published classic descriptions of a wide variety of disorders such as pulmonary edema. He also had many interests beyond medicine, including geology, mineralogy, oceanography, and zoology. This prominent physician, inspired researcher, and prolific author died in Rome on June 15, 1707, at the young age of 38.

References

1. Grmek MD: Georgius Baglivi. In *Dictionary of Scientific Biography* (Ed. Gillespie CC), p. 391–393. New York: Charles Scribner's Sons, 1970
2. Stenn F: Georgio Baglivi. *Ann Med Hist* 1941; 3rd ser., 3:183–194
3. Schullian DM, ed.: The *Baglivi Correspondence from the Library of Sir William Osler*. Ithaca: Cornell University Press, 1974
4. Brown T: *The Mechanical Philosophy and the "Animal Oeconomy."* New York: Arno Press, 1981
5. Baglivi G: *The Practice of Physick*, (a) p. 459; (b) p. 91; (c) p. 231; (d) p. 232. London: Andrew Bell, 1704
6. Baglivi G: *De fibra motrice, et morbosa*. Perusiae: Apud Constantinum, 1700
7. Bastholm E: *The History of Muscle Physiology*. Copenhagen: Ejnar Munksgaard, 1950
8. Jarcho S: Giorgio Baglivi on the practice of medicine (1700, 1704). *In The Concept of Heart Failure from Avicenna to Albertini* (Ed. Jarcho S), p. 228–236, quote from p. 229. Cambridge: Harvard University Press, 1980
9. Baglivi G: *Opera Omnia Medico-Practica, et Anatomica*, (a) translated in Jarcho, op. Cit. p. 229–230; (b) p. 230. Lugduni: Anisson and Posuel, 1704

Stephen Hales: Theologian, Botanist, Physiologist, Discoverer of Hemodynamics

W. D. HALL, M.D.

Division of Hypertension, Emory University School of Medicine, Atlanta, Georgia, USA

Stephen Hales was born on September 17, 1677, in the village of Bekesbourne in Kent. He was the sixth and last son of Thomas and Mary Hales, one of the oldest and most distinguished families in Kent.[1,2]

Following early education in private schools, Hales attended Bene't College (Corpus Christi) in Cambridge at age 19 to study theology and become an Anglican priest. He received his Bachelor of Arts degree at age 22 (1699). At age 26 (1703), he became a Fellow of the College, received his Master of Arts degree, and was ordained as deacon of a local parish in Bugden.

It was in Cambridge about 1708 that Hales apparently conducted his initial animal experiments on the pressure, flow, and resistance of the circulation. By current standards it is somewhat unusual that a recently ordained priest should initiate invasive studies on the nature of the circulation. However, his seven years of college had provided a very liberal education in classics, mathematics, and science, in addition to theology and philosophy. Moreover, his keen interest in science was obviously kindled by a remarkable pre-med student, William Stukeley, who arrived in Cambridge in 1704.[3] Together they studied anatomy, attended the physics lectures of William Whiston and the chemistry lectures of Vagagni. They made a variety of dog and frog dissections in the laboratory space vacated by Sir Isaac Newton who had recently accepted a new position in London. Hales, a disciple of Newtonian physical science and the order and balance of the universe, became fascinated with the quantitative aspects of pressure and flow in living plants and animals;[4] this contrasted with the earlier and more classical focus on anatomy.

Experiments on the arterial (crural artery) and venous (jugular vein) pressure were apparently first made about 1708 on a few dogs. Stukeley completed his M.D. degree and left Cambridge in 1708, and Hales left in 1709 to accept an appointment as clergyman in charge of the parish (i.e., curate) of Teddington in Middlesex. Teddington was a rural community about 15 miles outside of London and with a population of less than 500. One might speculate that Hales was seeking a farm environment where he could keep animals, one that was small enough that he could fulfill his theological responsibilities yet have time to pursue scientific interests. He received his Bachelor of Divinity degree three years after his arrival in Teddington.

About 1714, six years after the initial dog experiments in Cambridge, Hales conducted additional studies in Teddington using three horses, one sheep, one doe, and about 20 dogs. One of the most classic (Experiment III) of his 25 detailed animal experiments was conducted in the cold of December on an elderly mare (aged 10–14) which was otherwise to be killed as unfit for service.[5] This was apparently the third and last horse studied by Hales. With the mare restrained in the right lateral decubitus position, he exposed the left carotid artery and inserted a brass cannula with a 1/7 inch bore (Fig. 1). The cannula was then connected to an excised windpipe of a goose to allow pliancy of the measurement apparatus as the unanesthetized horse would strain or struggle. The goose windpipe was connected to a glass tube 12 ¾ feet high. When Hales released the carotid artery ligature, blood spurted to a height of 9 ½ feet (114 inches, or 289.6 cm) above the level of the left ventricle, rising and falling rhythmically to different levels during contraction and relaxation of the heart. This 9′6″ height of the blood pressure compared favorably with the 9′8″ and 8′3″ heights recorded in two previous horses. In these experiments, Hales determined that the peak levels of pressure correlated with the output of the heart, whereas the lowest levels of blood pressure were associated with a resistance to flow caused by the rest of the circulatory system. Hales was thus the first to measure arterial and venous blood pressure as well as the first to recognize the concept of cardiac output and total peripheral resistance. Subsequent experiments demonstrated that the output of the heart and the heart rate varied with stress and physical exertion, that the workload imposed on the left ventricle was related to blood pressure and the surface area of the ventricle, and that a variety of substances altered the degree of constriction or dilatation of small blood vessels.

Although there was apparently little public reaction to Hales's animal experimentation, he was not enamoured by the animal work or the experimental facilities, commenting that he ". . . did not then pursue the Mater any further, being discouraged by the Disagreeableness of Anatomic Dissections." In subsequent years he turned his attention to the dynamics of the pressure and flow of sap in plants, using many of the same techniques applied earlier to animals. More than a century passed before the first intra-arterial pressure was recorded accurately in man (Faivre in 1856).[6,7]

FIG. 1   Experiment III. From *Medical Times* 72, 11 (1944). Reproduced with permission of the publisher.

The animal experiments conducted by Hales in 1708 and 1714 were submitted to the Royal Society of London in 1725. His results were read before the Society over several years and the work was published in 1733. Hales had already been recognized by the scientific community by election to Fellowship in the Royal Society in 1718.

Stephen Hales was not only a theologist, botanist, and physiologist, but also a man of community service. For example, he designed a water supply system for the village of Teddington and a ventilation system for crowded prisons and hospitals.[8] He fought publicly against "gin-drunkenness" in urban and suburban London. As a co-founder of the Royal Society of Arts, he helped award grants to promising young artists. In 1732, he, along with James Oglethorpe, was elected one of the original 17 Trustees for the American colony of Georgia.[9] A flowering tree native to Georgia was named in his honor (Halesia).

Hales was awarded a Doctor of Divinity degree from Oxford in 1733. In 1739, for experiments on the solubility of kidney stones, he received the distinguished Copley Medal of the Royal Society. In 1753, he was honored as one of only eight foreign associates of the French Academy of Science.

During his retirement years in Teddington, Hales was known at age 80 to continue his pursuit of plant experiments.

He died suddenly on January 4, 1761, at age 83. Today, the Stephen Hales Award is given by the American Society of Plant Physiologists for outstanding contributions in botany. In Westminster Abbey, a monument stands in his honor. In each of our offices is a blood pressure cuff.

References

1. Burget GE: Stephen Hales (1677-1761). *Ann Med Hist* 7, 109 (1925)
2. Cohen IB: Stephen Hales. *Sci Am* 234, 98 (1976)
3. Clark-Kennedy AE: Stephen Hales, DD, FRS. *Br Med J* 2, 1656 (1977)
4. Editorial: Stephen Hales—father of hemodynamics. *Med Times* 72 (11), 315 (1944)
5. Hales S: Statical essays: containing haemastaticks. An account of some hydraulick and hydrostatical experiments made on the blood and blood vessels of animals. Volume 2, Royal Society of London (1733)
6. Faivre J: Études expérimentales sur les lésions organiques du coeur. *Gaz Méd de Paris*, 727 (1856)
7. Major RH: The history of taking the blood pressure. *Ann Med Hist* 2, 47 (1930)
8. Geist DC: An English clergyman and environmental health. *Arch Environ Health* 24, 373 (1972)
9. Wilber JA: The founding of Georgia and the discovery of blood pressure. *J Med Assoc Ga* 70 (5), 332 (1981)

Giovanni Battista Morgagni and the Foundation of Modern Medicine

HECTOR O. VENTURA, M.D.

Section of Cardiology, Department of Medicine, Tulane University Hospital and Clinic, New Orleans, Louisiana, USA

Introduction

Rudolf Virchow[1] epitomized Giovanni Battista Morgagni's influence on the development of modern medicine when he wrote, "The full consequences of what he worked out were harvested in London and Paris, in Vienna and in Berlin. And thus we can say that, beginning with Morgagni and resulting from his work, the dogmatism of the old schools was completely shattered, and that with him the new medicine begins." This "new medicine"[2] began with the publication of Morgagni's masterpiece known as *De Sedibus et Causis Morborum per Anatomen Indagatis Libri Quinque* or "*The Seats and Causes of Disease Investigated by Anatomy in Five Books.*" Although the title of the book speaks for itself, this work contained seven hundred case reports with a detailed clinical history followed by a report of the pathology found at autopsy. Clinical symptoms are in the author's words, "the cry of the suffering organs," thus creating the anatomical concept of diseases. The latter implied that there was a correlation between the symptoms that the patients experienced and the pathologic findings found at autopsy. In addition to Vesalius' *Fabrica* and Harvey's *De Motu Cordis*, *De Sedibus* was the final vinculum by which the old medicine was to be buried perpetually. The extent of Morgagni's accomplishments for future generations of physicians can be summarized in the words of W.T. Gairdner,[3] the president of the Glasgow Pathological and Clinical Society. In 1874, a century after the publication of the *De Sedibus*, he told an audience of leaders of Scottish medicine:

> All more eminent moderns, and even the men of our own time, although they work with new means and appliances, amid a flood of new light from physiology and histological anatomy, and amid a science of organic chemistry … are all of them successors and legitimate heirs of Morgagni's labours and method … For it is this method and this spirit that make the essential distinction of the modern-minded physician or surgeon and that separate him … from the man whom Molière has depicted for us in outrageous caricature …

Life and Medical Career

Giovanni Battista Morgagni (Fig. 1) was born on February 25, 1682, in Forli, a small town 35 miles southeast of Bologna, Italy.[4] He was a precocious student, already manifesting in his teenage years an intense interest in such diverse subjects as poetry, philosophy, and medicine. Throughout his life, he was to maintain his interest in philosophy and literature along with history and archaeology. This interest generated many papers on archaeological findings in the vicinity of Ravenna and Forli; letters to Lancisi on "The Manner of Cleopatra's Death"; and commentaries on Celsus, Sammonicus, and Varro. At the age of sixteen he went to Bologna to study medicine and philosophy, soon coming under the patronage of Antonio Maria Valsalva, the great anatomist who had been a pupil of Malpighi. Upon receiving his degree with distinction in 1701, Morgagni became Valsalva's assistant for six years. During that time he published his first work on anatomy, *Adversaria Anatomica Prima*, which was presented before the Academia Inquietorum of which he had just been elected president. He left Bologna for a postgraduate study in anatomy at Padua and Venice, and upon completion of these studies he left academia to return to Forli to become a practicing physician. Soon he became a successful practitioner and married Paola Verazeri, the daughter of a noble family of Forli. Together they raised twelve daughters and three sons, eight of the girls becoming nuns and one of the boys entering the priesthood. According to Dr. Nuland's[2] description of Morgagni, he was a tall, robust person with an engaging personality. His peers and students admired him not only for his scientific achievements but also for his nobility of character. Dr. Nuland[2] writes,

> His years were characterized by regularity of habits and consistency of devotion to his scientific work, to his large family, and to the religious principles that guided both his search for the truth and the stability of his spirit. As one reads the descriptions of his personality that have come down to us, the image that emerges is that of a serene scholar, much admired by his students of many nationalities and by his friends, among whom were included several of the most powerful figures of the day, such as Pope Benedict XIV and the Holy Roman Emperor Joseph II. He enjoyed warm professional relationships with some of the great medical thinkers of his time, including Hermann Boerhaave of Leyden, Albrecht von Haller of Berne, Johann Meckel of Göttingen, and Richard Mead of London, a group whose spectrum of interests reflected Morgagni's own interests, ranging from education to research to the care of the sick.

FIG. 1 Giovanni Battista Morgagni (1682–1771). Photograph courtesy of Clendening History of Medicine Library, Kansas University Medical Center.

In 1711, he was appointed professor of practical medicine at the University of Padua, and four years later, the University authorities, on the advice of Lancisi, appointed him professor of anatomy. In an address delivered after receiving this appointment he remarked that he was overwhelmed by the thought of holding the same chair that had been filled by, among others, Vesalius and Falloppio. He soon became a popular teacher, attracting not only Italian students but also foreigners, particularly Germans, who came in large numbers to attend his lectures and demonstrations. The second volume of *Adversaria Anatomica* appeared in 1717, and his *Adversaria Anatomica Omnia* in 1719. These works established his reputation as an anatomist, a scholar of great intellectual capacity, and a master of Latin prose. It was, however, *De Sedibus et Causis Morborum per Anatomen Indagatis*, a book published in 1761, when Morgagni was 79 years old, that inscribed his name among the greatest in the history of medicine. He has justly received the title of the "Father of Pathology." It would be a mistake, however, to consider Morgagni solely a pathologist. He also carried out many physiologic experiments and was active as a practitioner of medicine and a clinical consultant. In 1935, for the first time, his *Consulti Medici* was published in Bologna by Enrico Benassi, who found 12 large volumes of unpublished manuscript written by Morgagni in the library at Parma. These consultations, 100 in number, record Morgagni's advice on the diagnosis and treatment of pateints referred by other physicians or often advice based on the physicians' letters regarding patients he did not see personally. These consultations reveal Morgagni as a clear and cogent reasoner. He died at age 89, in the house to which he had brought his family, at 3003 Via S. Massimo. A memorial plaque may still be seen bearing the sentence "Giamb. Morgagni, after founding pathological anatomy, died here on Dec. 6, 1771."

Contributions to the Field of Medicine and Cardiology

The number of pathologic observations described by Morgagni, many of them for the first time, is enormous. His observations are included in the *De Sedibus et Causis Morborum per Anatomen Indagatis Libri Quinque* or *The Seats and Causes of Disease Investigated by Anatomy in Five Books*, which was published in 1761, when Morgagni was 79 years old. Prior to the publication of *De Sedibus*, the first attempt to correlate premortem symptoms with postmortem findings was described in a book named the *Sepulchretum Sive Anatomica Practica.*[2, 4] Theophilus Bonetus published this treatise first in 1679, and an enlarged second edition appeared in 1700. It included almost 3,000 cases in which clinical histories were correlated with autopsy reports and commentary. There were several deficiencies in the *Sepulchretum*, which made the work virtually useless to scholars. These included misquotations, misinterpretations, inaccurate observations, and the lack of a proper index. The idea for *De Sedibus* was generated in 1740, while Morgagni was involved in a discussion of the deficiencies of Theophilus Bonetus' encyclopedic compilation. At the time, Morgagni had agreed to write a series of letters to a young friend, which were to resolve the various questions that were unsatisfactorily answered by Bonetus. These letters would be written in the course of the years on the basis of Morgagni's own personal observations at the autopsy table. It took 20 years to complete the task and the resultant 70 letters, included in 5 books, represent the core of *De Sedibus*. Each book dealt with a different category: (1) Diseases of the Head, (2) Diseases of the Thorax, (3) Diseases of the Abdomen, (4) Diseases of a General Nature and Disease requiring Surgical Treatment, and (5) Supplement. The importance of *De Sedibus* was previously commented upon, but it is important to emphasize that Morgagni's correlation between symptoms and structural organ changes removed pathology from the anatomical museum halls to the realm of the practicing physician. Morgagni devoted several letters of the *De Sedibus* to a study of the diseased heart, in which he accurately described the principal cardiac lesions which he found after the death of the patients. He included a description of angina pectoris, he suggested that dyspnea and asthma were the result of diseases of the heart, and he also suggested a relationship between syphilis and aneurysm. He described the rupture of the heart, vegetative endocarditis, pericardial effusion, adhesions, and calcifications. In addition, he described cyanotic congenital cardiac defects. Perhaps Morgagni's best classical descriptions included mitral stenosis, heart block, calcareous stenosis of the aortic valve with regurgitation, coronary sclerosis, and aneurysm of the aorta. Few passages of some of these descriptions are important to illustrate the significance of Morgagni's contributions to cardiology.[4] The ninth letter describes heart block: "... he was in his sixty-eight year, of a habit moderately fat ... when he was first seiz'd with the epilepsy, which left behind in the greatest slowness of pulse, and in a like manner a coldness of the body ... the disorder often returned." This clinical narration was to become the Stokes-Adams syndrome, when these two physicians from the Irish school correlated the slow pulse with heart disease. In the 24th letter, he writes,

… the pulse has been weak and small, but not intermittent, when on account of an incarcerated hernia … he was brought to the hospital at Padua … whether the pulse had been in that state before this disorder came on, or whether it was rather brought on by this disease, join'd with an inflammation of the intestines, to such a degree, that a speedy death prevented any method of cure to be attempted … As I examined the internal surface of the heart, the left coronary artery appeared to have been changed into a bony canal from its very origin to the extent of many fingers breadth, where it embraces the greater part of the base. And part of that very long branch, also, which it sends down upon the anterior surface of the heart, was already become bony to so great space as could be covered by three fingers place transversely.

This letter clearly describes coronary artery disease due to atherosclerosis and perhaps its association with sudden death.

The 26th letter named "Treats of sudden death, from a disorder of the sanguiferous vessels, specially those lie in the thorax" narrates a patient with an aortic aneurism. He writes

A man who had too much given to the exercise of tennis and the abuse of wine, was in consequence of both these irregularities, seized with a pain in the right arm, and soon after of the left, joined with a fever. After these there appeared a tumour on the upper part of the sternum, like a large boil: by which appearance some vulgar surgeon being deceived, and either not having at all observed, or used to bring these tumors to suppuration; and these applications were of the most violent kind. As the tumour still increased, other applied emollient medicines, from which it seemed to them to be diminished; … only soon recovered its former magnitude, but even was, plainly, seen to increase every day … when the patient came into the Hospital of Incurables, at Bologna … it was equal in size to a quince; and what was much worse, it began to exude blood in one place… he was ordered to keep himself still and to think seriously and piously of his departure from this mortal life, which was near at hand, and inevitable … this really happened on the day following, from the vast profusion of blood that had been foretold, though not soon expected by the patient … and there was a large aneurism, into which the anterior part of the curvature of the aorta itself being expanded, and partly consumed the upper part of the sternum, the extremities of the clavicles which lie upon it … and where the bones had been consumed or affected with caries, there not the least traces of the coats of the artery remained … the deplorable exit of this man teaches in the first place, how much care ought to be taken in the beginning, that an internal aneurism may obtain

to increase: and in the second place, if, either by ignorance of the persons who attempt their cure, or the disobedience of the patient, or only by the force of the disorder itself, they do at length increase …

This observation exemplifies the reason why *De Sedibus* was such an important vinculum to the foundation of modern medicine. One can witness, first, the meticulous clinical description of a disease process that correlates with anatomopathologic findings; second, the judicious interpretation of the findings; and finally the attempt to describe a prognosis and a therapeutic strategy. Morgagni's ability to integrate and synthesize information was paramount to accomplish progress in medicine, either in the diagnosis or the treatment of diseases.

Conclusion

Dr. John Morgan, one of the original faculty of the College of Philadelphia, an institution that was to become America's first medical school, visited Morgagni in 1764. He wrote in his diary:[5] "Went to pay my Respects to the celebrated Morgagni to whom I had letters from Dr Serrati of Bologna. He received me with the greatest Politeness imagineable, and shew'd me with abundant Civilities with a very good grace. He is now 82 years of age, yet reads without spectacles and is alert as a Man of 50." He also wrote[5] *De Sedibus* was "in ye highest Estimation throughout all Europe, and all ye Copies of the last [third] Edition already bought up." It is interesting to note that Morgan received a gift from the old master, a copy of *De Sedibus*, which he left in the American College of Physicians in Philadelphia. Its presence at the College should remind the present and future generations of physicians of something very consequential to the learning and practice of medicine. When, during a clinical pathologic conference, we attempt to make a diagnosis from a clinical history and our conclusions are confirmed or denied by the pathologist's report of the autopsy, operation, or biopsy, we are reproducing the pages of the *De Sedibus*. The use of the clinical pathologic conference is and will be one of the most useful methods to teach medicine. This may be Giovanni Battista Morgagni's indelible legacy to medicine.

References

1. Virchow R: Morgagni and the anatomic concept. *Bull Hist Med* 1929;7:975–990
2. Nuland S: Doctors. *The New Medicine, the Anatomical Concept of Giovanni Morgagni*, p 145–170. New York: Random House Inc., 1988
3. Gairdner WT: The progress of pathology. *Br Med J* 1874;2:515–517
4. Acierno LJ: *History of Cardiology (Panoramic View of Cardiology)*, p 51–54. New York: Parthenon Publishing Group Ltd., 1994
5. Morgan J: *The Journal of Dr. John Morgan*. Philadelphia: Lippincott, 1907

Jean-Baptiste de Sénac

CHARLES F. WOOLEY, M.D.

Department of Internal Medicine, The Ohio State University, Division of Cardiology, Columbus, Ohio, USA

Historians of medicine advise caution when accepting sequence in discovery. However, when Jean Baptiste de Sénac (Fig. 1) repeated the earlier experiments of William Harvey and Richard Lower and verified their observations on circulatory physiology, he extended their approach to reducing theory to factual data and established experimental sequence beyond question. It is possible then to speak of the Harvey-Lower-Sénac Cascade without the censure of the historians.

Sénac blended his clinical and experimental observations with the collective wisdom, explored the anatomy, physiology, and clinical aspects of the cardiovascular system, and eventually gathered these materials in his monumental work, *The Tractus*, frequently referred to as the first comprehensive cardiology text in the Western world.

Sénac's early history is a blank page. We know that he lived from 1693 to 1770, that his degree was from Montpellier, and that he came to Paris when he was about 30 years of age. He was an associate member of the Academy of Sciences in 1723, moved to Versailles in 1733 where he was physician at the Royal Hospital of Versailles, and was appointed as chief physician to Louis XV in 1752.[1]

His fame in cardiology is based upon his *Traité de la Structure du Coeur, de son Action, et de ses Maladies,* a work published in 1749 when he was 56 years old. This was a four-book treatise of more than 1,200 pages, and "offered a synthesis what was known about the cardiovascular system in the middle of the eighteenth century."[1] A second edition was published after his death, and his text remained influential throughout the eighteenth century.

Sénac's text was a systematic treatment of anatomy, physiology, the circulation of the blood, and diseases of the heart. His observations included detailed descriptions of the structure of the heart and the orientation of the cardiac muscle fibers, the increased incidence of heart disease with age, the relationship of pericarditis to inflammation of the lungs and the mediastinum, and the association of hydrothorax with heart failure. Writing before the works by Auenbrugger, Corvisart, and Laennec, the early masters of cardiovascular and pulmonary diagnosis, Sénac verified his clinical observations with the cardiovascular lesions observed at autopsy, establishing a precedent for French cardiology in the nineteenth century.

FIG. 1 Jean Baptiste de Sénac (1693-1770). Digitized line drawing from a print provided by the National Library of Medicine.

Palpitation: A Classification

When Sir John McMichael analyzed the history of atrial fibrillation in 1982,[2] he began with William Harvey's establishment of the origin of the heart beat in the right atrium and progressed to Sénac's views and physiologic ideas about cardiac function which were "much in advance of his time."

When Sénac repeated Harvey's and Lower's experiments, he analyzed them critically and then "asked many difficult questions."[2] He stood firm on the right atrial origin of the heart beat, as established by Harvey, and also concluded that the nerves of the heart were important in the precipitation of palpitation.

It was McMichael's view that Sénac established the irritability of the heart with his experimental studies, described atrial fibrillation in his experimental animal studies, and understood the role of mitral valve disease in the causation of palpitation. Sénac noted that "the causes of palpitation are not the causes of the natural heart-beat," hinting at their ectopic origin.[2]

Sénac discussed palpitations as the most common problem and classified palpitations into major clinical categories. Palpitations which occurred with fever, exercise, or mental stress were neither indicators of heart disease nor dangerous. Other types of palpitations were associated with specific organic cardiac lesions. Sénac wrote that palpitations that were irregular and linked to mitral valve disease, "the long and rebellious palpitations," were related to distension and strain of the atria with increased atrial volumes. According to McMichael,

De Sénac's remarkable insights into the correlations of mitral disease with gross pulse irregularities were based on his own observations on cardiac muscle irritability and the atrial origin of the heart beat as established by William Harvey and expanded by de Sénac's own meticulous observations.[2]

Palpitations Treated with Quinine "Mixed with a Little Rhubarb"

Sénac recommended therapy of "rebellious palpitations" with cinchona, or Peruvian bark, given as "quinquina mixed with a little rhubarb."[3] According to Bowman, Sénac, the author of an earlier book on malaria, "was likely familiar with the use of quinine in the treatment of malaria."[1] The use of quinine by Sénac for treatment of "rebellious palpitations" was an outgrowth of the use of "stomachic" remedies in the treatment of palpitations. The rationale involved the causative role of stomach derangements in the pathogenesis of palpitations. Sénac observed that,

Of all the stomachic remedies the one whose effects have appeared to me the most constant and the most prompt in many cases, is Quinine mixed with a little rhubarb. Long and rebellious palpitations have ceded to this febrifuge, seconded with a light purgative.[3]

As McMichael notes, "De Sénac advanced understanding to its very limits in his day in exemplary observation and deep critical thought."[2] Harvey's observations about atrial origin of cardiac rhythm were confirmed, Lower's ideas about palpitations were examined, and Sénac extended the work of both of these seventeenth century figures into the mid-eighteenth century.

The associations of palpitations with mitral valve disease, distended atria, and gross pulse irregularities were remarkable insights. Concepts about palpitations in terms of altered cardiac physiology, correlations with cardiac physiology, and recognizable clinical phenomena were major advances in understanding palpitations.

The use of a medication for treatment of "long and rebellious palpitations" with a putative therapeutic rationale was an equally important contribution, particularly since the choice of quinine resulted in the introduction of a drug that would evolve into quinidine, a therapy for cardiac arrhythmias that persists until the present.

That clinical recognition of palpitations was possible, that palpitations could be classified, and that treatment of certain types of palpitations was feasible, were ideas "a century and a half ahead of his time."[2]

There is a great deal more to the Sénac story than the Harvey-Lower-Sénac lineage and Sénac's contributions to the recognition, classification, and treatment of palpitations.[1] Yet it is in these areas of mutual interest that twentieth century cardiologists may reflect on Sénac's contributions to our heritage as thoughtful observers, experimental physiologists, and students of the natural history of cardiac disease, as we anticipate the twenty-first century.

References

1. Bowman IA: Jean-Baptiste Sénac and his treatise on the heart. *Texas Heart Inst J* 14, 4–11 (1987)
2. McMichael J: History of atrial fibrillation 1628-1819, Harvey—de Sénac—Laennec. *Br Heart J* 48, 193–197 (1982)
3. Willius FA, Keys TE: *Classics of Cardiology*. Robert E. Krieger Publishing Company, Malabar, Florida. (1983) 1, 159–163

Albrecht von Haller

W. BRUCE FYE, M.D., M.A.

Department of Cardiology, Marshfield Clinic, Marshfield, Wisconsin, USA

Eighteenth century physiologist Albrecht von Haller (Fig. 1) made many important contributions to our knowledge of the structure and function of the heart. Medical historian Heinrich Buess considered Haller the founder of modern hemodynamics and claimed that most physiologic research performed before the mid-19th century was based upon his work.[1] Haller was born in Bern, Switzerland, on October 16, 1708.[2, 3] A prodigy, he became interested in literature and languages as a child. By the age of 15, Haller had mastered Latin, Greek, and Hebrew and had written several poems and other literary works.

Haller began his medical studies at Tübingen in 1724. The following year he moved to Leiden, then one of the world's centers for medical training. There he studied with Hermann Boerhaave, Bernhard Siegfried Albinus, and Frederik Ruysch. After receiving his medical degree from Leiden at the age of 18, Haller traveled to France, Belgium, and England for additional training in medicine and anatomy.

After returning to Switzerland in 1728 and studying mathematics with Johann Bernoulli at Basel, Haller entered medical practice in Bern. There he inaugurated a series of anatomical investigations, began assembling a collection of botanical specimens, and pursued a wide variety of other interests. In 1736, Haller became professor of anatomy, surgery, and medicine at the newly founded University of Göttingen. Haller spent two decades at Göttingen and published his classic physiology text *Primae Lineae Physiologiae* there in 1747.[4]

Haller's observations on the heart beat were his most significant contribution to cardiovascular physiology.[5] When he excised hearts from animals Haller found that they continued to beat despite the lack of any connection to the nervous system. Based on these experiments, he proposed that the heart muscle had intrinsic irritability that was stimulated by blood flowing over the organ's walls. American physiologist William Howell claimed in 1905 that Haller thus "formulated a clear-cut myogenic hypothesis which served to mark the beginning of a new discussion lasting until the present day."[6]

Haller published two classic monographs on cardiovascular physiology. His 1754 book was translated into English three years later as *A Dissertation on the Motion of the Blood, and on the Effects of Bleeding*.[7] A supplementary volume described 235 vivisections Haller performed to investigate the structure and function of the heart and vascular system.[8] Haller employed many techniques in his experiments on the

FIG. 1 Albrecht von Haller, 1708–1777. (Engraving provided from the private collection of W. Bruce Fye, M.D.).

cardiovascular system including microscopy, vascular injection, desiccation, vascular puncture, and ligation. He was the first to produce experimental thrombosis and used a microscope to document the process in the mesenteric vein of the frog. Haller also made important observations on the relationship between atrial and ventricular contraction, the effect of respiration on venous return and pulmonary blood flow, and the structure of the cardiac valves.

Haller's books on the cardiovascular system included concepts that he first advanced in a 1753 essay on the sensible and irritable parts of animals. Historian Owsei Temkin characterized this monograph as a "landmark in the history of physiology."[9] In it, Haller distinguished between the nerve impulse (sensibility) and muscular contraction (irritability). These concepts influenced two generations of doctors and medical scientists.[10] Haller's many important contributions to physiology were summarized in his massive eight-volume monograph *Elementa Physiologia* published in Lausanne between 1757 and 1766.[11]

Haller's contributions were not limited to medicine and physiology. He is widely viewed as a founder of the science of botany. One of the most prolific authors of all times, Haller published several books and hundreds of papers on anatomy, physiology, embryology, botany, and medicine.[12, 13] He first described pericardial calcification in his 1755 book *Opuscula Pathologicae*. Haller's anatomical atlas *Icones Anatomicae*, published in parts between 1743 and 1756, is especially notable for its superb illustrations of the blood vessels and viscera. Medical historian Fielding Garrison noted that Haller was "the principal founder of medical and scientific bibliography."[14] He compiled a series of exhaustive bibliographies on medicine, surgery, anatomy, and botany that today provide unique insight into the early history of these fields. Frail throughout much of his life, Haller suffered from a wide variety of medical problems and became addicted to opiates during his final years. He died on December 12, 1777.

References

1. Buess H: William Harvey and the foundation of modern haemodynamics by Albrecht von Haller. *Med Hist* 14, 175–182 (1970)

2. Hintzsche E: (Victor) Albrecht von Haller. In *Dictionary of Scientific Biography*. Charles Scribner's Sons, New York (1972) 61–67

3. Klotz O: Albrecht von Haller (1708-77). *Ann Med Hist* n.s. 8, 10–26 (1936)

4. Haller A: *Primae Lineae Physiologiae in Usum Praelectionum Academicarum*. A. Vandenhoeck, Göttingen (1747)

5. Fye WB: The origin of the heart beat: A tale of frogs, jellyfish and turtles. *Circulation* 76, 493–500 (1987)

6. Howell WH: The cause of the heart beat. *Harvey Lectures* series 1905-06, 305–337 (1906) Quote from 307.

7. Haller A: *A Dissertation on the Motion of the Blood, and on the Effects of Bleeding*. J. Whiston and B. White, London (1757)

8. Haller A: *A Second Dissertation on the Motion of the Blood, and Effects on Bleeding*. J. Brown, London (1757)

9. Haller A: A dissertation on the sensible and irritable parts of animals. Introduction by Owsei Temkin. *Bull Hist Med* 4, 651–699 (1936)

10. Roe S.A. (ed.): *The Natural Philosophy of Albrecht von Haller*. Arno Press, New York (1981)

11. Buess H: Albrecht von Haller and his *Elementa Physiologiae* as the beginning of pathological physiology. *Med Hist* 3, 123–131 (1959)

12. Lundsgaard-Hansen-von-Fischer S: *Verzeichnis der gedruckten Schriften Albrecht von Hallers*. Paul Haupt, Bern (1959)

13. Willius FA, Dry TJ: *A History of the Heart and Circulation*. W.B. Saunders Co., Philadelphia (1948)

14. Garrison FH: *An Introduction to the History of Medicine*. W.B. Saunders, Philadelphia (1929) Quote from 318.

William Heberden and Some Account of a Disorder of the Breast

MARK E. SILVERMAN, M.D.

Department of Medicine, Emory University School of Medicine and Piedmont Hospital, Atlanta, Georgia, USA

But there is a disorder of the breast marked with strong and peculiar symptoms, considerable for the kind of danger belonging to it, and not extremely rare, which deserves to be mentioned more at length. The seat of it, and sense of strangling, and anxiety with which it is attended, may make it not improperly be called angina pectoris. They who are afflicted with it, are seized while they are walking, (more especially if it be up hill, and soon after eating) with a painful and most disagreeable sensation in the breast, which seems as if it would extinguish life, if it were to increase or to continue; but the moment they stand still, all this uneasiness vanishes.

—William Heberden (1802)

On July 21, 1768, William Heberden presented his paper, "Some Account of a Disorder of the Breast," to his fellow members of the Royal College of Physicians of London (Bedford, 1968). This classic report, based initially on a clinical analysis of only 20 patients, is remarkable for its detailed observations, clarity, and poetic style—"in a manner so graphic and complete as to compel the admiration and envy of all subsequent authors" (Osler) (Bedford, 1968). The report was published in 1772 in the *Transactions of the Royal College*, and contains the essential features of angina pectoris as we understand it today. Without the benefit of autopsies, Heberden conjectured that the disorder was due to a cramp and/or ulcer (Heberden, 1802). Because he had noted that the pulse was not always altered in his patients, a finding thought to be a necessary accompaniment of heart disease, he discounted the heart as the likely source of the discomfort (Bedford, 1968; Pruitt, 1983). An opportunity for an autopsy was eventually afforded Heberden in 1772 when an "unknown" person recognized that he suffered the symptoms as described in Heberden's report and willed that, upon his death, an autopsy should be performed (Cohen, 1962; Kligfield, 1981; Liebowitz, 1970). Heberden enlisted the aid of John Hunter, the great anatomist and pathologist; however, little of etiologic importance was found. According to a later account by Jenner, the coronary arteries were probably not examined (Rolleston, 1933). The paucity of pathology was nonetheless encouraging to Heberden who commented (Proudfit, 1983):

Since it was not due owing to any malconformation, or morbid destruction of parts necessary to life, we need not despair of finding a cure.

In addition to describing the symptoms and prognosis, Heberden also provided a name—*angina pectoris*—which would allow physicians to diagnose, communicate about, and study this disorder. The label "angina" was appropriated by Heberden from its association with sore throat or quinsy (Vincent's angina) where it meant strangling and anxiety (Osler, 1897; Rolleston, 1939). Edward Jenner, a close friend of Heberden, was the first to suggest that coronary artery disease (ossification) was the cause of angina pectoris (Liebowitz, 1970; Pruitt, 1983). Out of consideration for John Hunter, his colleague, who suffered from recurrent angina, Jenner refrained from publishing his theory. In 1799, the coronary artery theory is credited to Jenner by Caleb Parry in his book *An Inquiry into the Symptoms and Causes of Syncope Anginosa, commonly called Angina Pectoris* (Liebowitz, 1970).

William Heberden was born in London in 1710, one of six children to Richard and Elizabeth Cooper Heberden (Buller, 1899; Cohen, 1962; Macmichael, 1830). At the age of 7, the year in which his father died, he attended St. Saviours grammar school in Southwark. In 1724, at the age of 14, he entered St. John's College, Cambridge, where he subsequently received a Bachelor of Arts degree in 1728, Fellow of the College in 1730, Master of Arts in 1732, and medical degree in 1739. As an undergraduate, he became a scholar in Greek and Hebrew literature, contributing a paper to a literary society "A Letter from Cleander to Alexias on Hippocrates and the State of Physic in Greece."

Heberden practiced medicine in Cambridge for 10 years and also taught a course on materia medica in which he drew upon his knowledge of the classics to enrich his lectures. His first important article, "Antitheriaca: An Essay on Mithridotium and Theriaca," was published in 1745 and served to undermine and eventually to dispel the use of an ancient concoction used as a universal antidote (Paulshack, 1982). In 1748 he moved to London where he married Elizabeth Martin and developed a large practice. His wife died after only two years of marriage, leaving him one son. From his second marriage in 1760 to Mary Wollaston, Heberden had eight more children, including William Jr., who subsequently became physician to George III and published his father's *Commentaries on the History and Cure of Diseases* in 1802. Although he did not associate with a hospital, as did most physicians at that time, he soon became an esteemed leader of English medicine in an era ornamented by such great physicians as John and William Hunter, William Withering, Ed-

FIG. 1 William Heberden (1710–1801). (Photograph supplied courtesy of the U.S. National Library of Medicine.)

ward Jenner, Caleb Parry, David Pitcairn, and John Fothergill (Chaplin, 1919; Macmichael, 1830). He was also friendly with Benjamin Franklin who induced Heberden to publish a booklet on prevention of smallpox for use in the American colonies (Rolleston, 1933).

Heberden was an active participant in many professional societies and was elected Fellow of the Royal Society of Physicians (1746), Fellow of the Royal Society of Medicine (1749), Fellow of the Society of Antiquaries (1770), honorary member of the Royal Society of Medicine in Paris (1778), and vice president of the Royal Humane Society (1787). As a member of the Royal College of Physicians, he delivered the Goulstonian Lectures (1749), the Harveian Oration (1750), and the Croonian Lectures (1760) (Buller, 1879; Cohen, 1962). He was sympathetic to the cause of the licentiates of the Royal College of Physicians, members who could not be elected to fellowship because they did not hold a degree from Oxford or Cambridge. He played a major role in establishing the *Medical Transactions of the Royal College,* a method by which members could report personal observations on their patients for discussion (Rolleston, 1933). His paper on angina pectoris was published in the medical *Transactions* in 1772 and attracted wide attention. In 1761 he tactfully declined the request of George III to become physician to Queen Charlotte because he was "apprehensive it might interfere with those communications of life which he had now formed." He was a patron of literary works, an ardent supporter of many charitable and professional societies, a botanist, and a classical scholar (Bedford, 1968). His attitude toward his patients conveyed tenderness, cheerfulness, and wisdom. In a letter to Chief Justice Lord Kenyon, W.C. Wells said (Rolleston, 1933):

> Dr Heberden, my Lord, stands in a manner alone in his profession. No other person, I believe, either in this or any other country, has ever exercised the art of medicine with the same dignity or has contributed so much to raise it in the estimation of mankind.

He retired from practice in 1782, at the age of 73 (Cohen, 1962),

> . . . before my presence of thought, judgement and recollection was so impaired, that I could not do justice to my patients. It is more desirable for a man to do this a little too soon than a little too late, for the chief danger is on the side of not doing it soon enough."

His popular *Commentaries on the History and Cure of Diseases,* completed in 1782 but published posthumously in 1802 by his son, contains his meticulous notes recorded in Latin at the bedside then updated monthly for 40 years as he assiduously observed the course of disease (Herrick, 1928-1935). Heberden believed that accurately written observations were the essence of learning (Rolleston, 1933).

> The exercise of composition opens and enlarges the mind and improves the taste . . . if men of letters could be obliged to write always with a view to publishing though without ever doing so, they would be perhaps the happiest of men.

He was aware that many diseases were transient and was scornful of new therapy saying, "New medicines, and new methods of cure, always work miracles for a while" (Rolleston, 1933). Unlike his contemporaries, he rarely prescribed bleeding, purging, or sweating. In addition to his description of angina pectoris, the book contains original descriptions of arthritic nodules (Heberden's nodes), tuberculosis of the hip, biliary dyspepsia, ringworm, visual disturbances in migraine, purpura, night blindness, and the difference between chickenpox and smallpox (Herrick, 1928–1935). His writing was concise and reveals a pragmatic approach in which he relied upon his personal observations and analysis while rejecting the dogma and systems of ancient authorities. Hypothesis and conjecture were avoided while common sense and clinical experience were emphasized.

He remained alert, cheerful, and serene until his death May 17, 1801, at the age of 91. Throughout his long life, he enjoyed great respect and admiration from his friends and colleagues who described him as modest, dignified, meticulous, and deeply religious (Buller, 1879, Crummer, 1928; Davidson, 1922; Herrick, 1928–1935; Macmichael, 1830). Referring to Heberden's classical scholarship, William Osler called him "the English Celsius" while Samuel Johnson described him as "ultimum Romanorum, the last of our learned physicians" (Cohen, 1962). As a consummate bedside observer, Heberden revived the tradition of Sydenham and set the stage for Addison and Bright who would follow (Chaplin, 1919). His account of angina pectoris has stood the test of time and is, perhaps, clinical observation at its finest.

References

Bedford DE: William Heberden's contribution to cardiology. *J Roy Coll Phys Lond* 2, 127 (1968)

Buller AC: *The Life and Works of Heberden*. Bradbury Agnew & Co., London, 1879

Chaplin A: *Medicine in England During the Reign of George III: The Fitzpatrick Lectures of the Royal College of Physicians, 1917-1918*. Published by the author, London, 1919

Cohen, HC: William Heberden. *Ann Rheum Dis* 21(1), 1 (1962)

Crummer L: Prefatory essay to an introduction to the study of physic by William Heberden, M.D. *Ann Med Hist* 10, 226 (1928)

Davidson PB: William Heberden, M.D., FRS. *Ann Med Hist* 4, 336 (1922)

Heberden W: *Commentaries on the History and Cure of Diseases*. London (1802)

Herrick JB: William Heberden. *Bull Soc Med Hist Chicago* 4, 30 (1928-1935)

Kligfield P: The frustrated benevolence of "Dr. Anonymous." *Am J Cardiol* 47, 185 (1981)

Leibowitz JO: *The History of Coronary Heart Disease*. University of Calif Press, Berkeley and Los Angeles, 1970

Macmichael W: *Lives of British Physicians*. J Haddon, London, 1830

Osler W: *Lectures on Angina Pectoris and Allied States*. D. Appleton & Company, New York, 1897

Paulshock BZ: William Heberden, M.D. and the end of Theriac. *New York State J Med* 82, 1612 (1982)

Proudfit WL: Origin of concept of ischaemic heart disease. *Br Heart J* 50, 209 (1983)

Pruitt RD: Symptoms, signs, signals, and shadows. The pathophysiology of angina pectoris—a historical perspective. *Mayo Clin Proc* 58, 394 (1983)

Rolleston H: The two Heberdens. *Ann Med Hist* 5, 409 (1933)

Rolleston H: The history of angina pectoris. *Glasgow Med J* 9, 205 (1937)

John Hunter (1728–1793)

Mimi C. Skandalakis, John E. Skandalakis, M.D., Ph.D., F.A.C.S.

Centers for Surgical Anatomy and Technique, Emory University, Atlanta, Georgia, USA

John Hunter (Fig. 1) was born in 1728, near the village of East Kilbride in Scotland, to John and Agnes Hunter. Of his nine brothers and sisters, only two survived far into adulthood: his brother William, 10 years his senior and a noted physician and scientist, and a sister Dorothea who was the mother of Matthew Baillie, another distinguished physician.

Though Hunter was born in an age that still saw the practice of bloodletting, he endeavored to bring medicine into the modern era of scientific reasoning. At age 20, he began studying medicine at William's anatomy school in London, where he had 10 years of intensive anatomical training. From 1749 to 1750 he also held a post at Chelsea Hospital under the direction of William Cheselden, noted physician and anatomist.

Hunter's apprenticeship with his brother ended in 1759 due to nonspecific health reasons, and the following year Hunter joined the army as a staff surgeon, traveling to Belleisle and Portugal. During this tenure, Hunter developed his surgical skills and collected information for his subsequent book, *A Treatise on the Blood, Inflammation, and Gun-Shot Wounds*.[1] In 1763, he returned to London and was appointed to the staff of St. George's Hospital. At this time he became a fellow of the Royal Society and a member of the Company of Surgeons, later the Royal College of Surgeons.

In 1771, Hunter, now 43, married Anne Home after a seven-year engagement (Anne, a poet of some renown, contributed lyrics to many of Joseph Haydn's works while he lived in London). In the same year, Hunter published his first book, *The Natural History of the Human Teeth*.[2] The couple had four children, but only two lived into adulthood.

Hunter's contributions to science and medicine are so monumental that volumes have recounted them, and his contributions to cardiology are significant. Hunter studied congenital abnormalities of the heart such as septal defects, dextroposition of the aorta, pulmonary stenosis, and ductus arteriosus.[3,4] As early as 1764 he described bicuspid aortic valves.[3] He was familiar with valvular heart disease, pericarditis, endocarditis, cardiac enlargement, arrhythmia, and cardiac function. He performed three autopsies in cases of ischemic heart disease,[4] and in one case in 1770, he stated that the coronary artery was ossified. Five years later he found another ossified coronary artery.

The first episode of Hunter's own coronary disease took place in 1773. The severe epigastric pain lasted 45 minutes, and within two hours he was asymptomatic. In the spring of

1777 he suffered another episode, and Edward Jenner, former pupil and long-time friend, who went on to discover the importance of vaccination and to develop the coronary artery theory of angina pectoris, diagnosed the attack as angina pectoris. In 1785 he experienced another prolonged episode of pain with angina that raised the concerns of Jenner, though he never reported his suspicions to his friend and teacher.[4] Since he had performed autopsies on patients who had died from angina pectoris, Hunter probably knew about his disease. His symptoms worsened in 1789, and he reported episodes of severe pain. Hunter's attacks were not only exertional, but also emotional in precipitation.[5] He once was quoted as saying,

FIG. 1 Sir Joshua Reynolds' portrait of John Hunter. Reproduced with permission of the President and Council of the Royal College of Surgeons of England.

"My life is at the mercy of any rogue who chooses to provoke me."[6]

On October 16, 1793, Hunter attended a board meeting at St. George's Hospital. It is generally believed that a statement made by Hunter was disputed vehemently by one of the other attendants at the meeting and Hunter's then famous temper overtook him. He ran choking with anger from the room where he expired in the hands of one of the attendant physicians.

The autopsy, performed by Hunter's brother-in-law Everard Home, revealed atherosclerosis with calcification in the coronary arteries and ossified internal carotid and vertebral arteries. The general consensus is that Hunter's illness was a nonspecific atherosclerosis which resulted in his death.

Hunter was buried on October 22, 1793, in the crypt of the Church of St. Martin-in-the-Fields in London, with only a few friends and associates attending. In 1859, Frank Buckland, a nineteenth century natural history authority, led an exhaustive but successful search for Hunter's coffin, and his body was reinterred in Westminster Abbey, attesting to the imperishable splendor of his work and his rightful place in history with England's great men and women.

References

1. Hunter J: *A Treatise on the Blood, Inflammation, and Gun-shot Wounds.* Printed by John Richardson, for George Nicol, Bookseller to his Majesty, Pall-Mall, London (1794)

2. Hunter J: *The Natural History of the Human Teeth.* Printed for J. Johnson, No. 72, St. Paul's Church-Yard (1771)

3. Keele KD: John Hunter's contribution to cardiovascular pathology. *Ann R Coll Surg Engl* 39(4), 248–259 (1966)

4. Proudfit WL: John Hunter: On heart disease. *Br Heart J* 56, 109–114 (1986)

5. Kligfield P: John Hunter, angina pectoris and medical education. *Am J Cardiol* 45, 367–369 (1980)

6. Kobler J: *The Reluctant Surgeon. A Biography of John Hunter.* Doubleday, New York (1960) 204–209

Lazzaro Spallanzani*

W. B. Fye, M.D., M.A.

Cardiology Department, Marshfield Clinic, Marshfield, Wisconsin, USA

Lazzaro Spallanzani (Fig. 1) was a leading eighteenth century scientist who made classic observations on the physiology of the circulation. He was born in the village of Scandiano in northern Italy on January 12, 1729.[1–3] After receiving preliminary education at home, Spallanzani enrolled in the Jesuit Seminary at Reggio Emilia at the age of 15, where he demonstrated proficiency in rhetoric, ancient and modern languages, and philosophy. In response to the urgings of his father Gianniccolo, a successful lawyer, Lazzaro enrolled in the University of Bologna to study jurisprudence in 1749.

At Bologna, Spallanzani came under the influence of his cousin Laura Bassa who was professor of mathematics and physics at the ancient university. With Bassa's encouragement, Spallanzani turned his attention to the sciences and mathematics. After receiving a doctorate from Bologna in 1754, Spallanzani joined the faculty of the College of Reggio where he taught logic, metaphysics, and Greek. He soon became deeply interested in nature and, reflecting this new orientation, accepted a call to the University of Modena to hold the chair of natural philosophy.

In 1761, Spallanzani participated in a scientific expedition to the Reggian Apennines and to Lake Ventasso. During this journey he made important observations on the nature of mountain springs. This work brought him into contact with Antonio Vallismeri the younger. Through Vallismeri, Spallanzani became interested in the works of the French naturalist Georges Buffon and his sometime collaborator John Needham, the English microscopist. In this era there was great interest in the theory of spontaneous generation, and Needham's observations on this subject intrigued Spallanzani. On the basis on several hundred experiments which he performed to study the problem, Spallanzani disproved Needham's theory of spontaneous generation.[4,5] These experiments stimulated Spallanzani's deep interest in microscopy.

During the 1760s, Spallanzani began a series of observations and experiments on the circulation. These studies were stimulated by observations made by the Swiss physiologist Albrecht von Haller. Haller had recently published two monographs on the circulation that summarized his experiments on the origin of the heartbeat, the velocity of blood flow, and other circulatory phenomena.[6,7]

Spallanzani shared Haller's belief that experimentation was superior to simple observation and classification as a method to gain insight into the nature of living organisms. The results of Spallanzani's preliminary studies on the circulation were reported in 1768.[8] Five years later he published a detailed summary of more than 300 experiments on the circulation.[9] This classic monograph was translated into English in 1801.[10] His book included the results of 337 experiments designed to study the embryologic development of the circulatory system, the influence of gravity on blood flow, the effects of wounds on blood flow, the relationship of the brain and heart, and other phenomena.

Like Haller, Spallanzani used a microscope in his studies of the circulation. The Italian scientist, however, used a more sophisticated instrument that had recently been developed by the Dutch entomologist Pierre Lyonet. Lyonet's dissecting microscope used refracted light, which improved the visualization of the blood vessels and the flow of blood within them.[11] Spallanzani studied the circulation in various species including the water salamander, frogs, lizards, and kittens. His observations on the development of the circulation were performed on chick embryos.

Through experimentation, Spallanzani disproved Haller's claim that the ventricle emptied completely during systole. Although he acknowledged that there was variation between species, Spallanzani argued that, in general, some blood remained in the ventricle at end systole. The configuration of the heart during systole and diastole had long been a subject of controversy. On the basis of visual observations made in salamanders, lizards, frogs, and toads, Spallanzani concluded that the heart shortened during systole and lengthened in diastole in these species. When he found that some pericardial fluid was always present in healthy animals, Spallanzani concluded that its presence did not indicate disease.

Spallanzani, reflecting his sophistication in physics and mathematics, applied the principles of hydraulics to his studies of the flow of blood through arteries and veins. Based on his investigations, he claimed that the velocity of blood was constant throughout the vascular system and was independent of the size of the vessels through which it flowed or its distance from the heart. He was intrigued by the phenomenon of arterial pulsation and tried to determine whether this rhythmic expansion of the vessels was caused by the motion of blood through them in systole or was a local phenomenon. Among

*This paper is adapted from an essay prepared for the Classics of Cardiology Library, Gryphon Editions (Birmingham).

FIG. 1 Lazzaro Spallanzani, 1729–1798. Photograph from private collection of W. Bruce Fye, M.D.

the hypotheses that had been put forth to explain the flow of blood through the circulation—and that Spallanzani sought to disprove—was that

> The contraction of the arteries, the attraction of the capillary vessels, a *vibratory* or *oscillatory* action in the vascular coats arising from the stimulus of the blood. and, in short, the air contained in the arteries and veins rarefied by the heat of this fluid, have each in their turns been supposed powerfully to second the action of the heart.[12]

On the basis of his experiments and observations, Spallanzani refuted these theories and concluded that the circulation of the blood was due entirely to cardiac systole.

Spallanzani's fame grew in response to his popular lectures and many publications. In 1769, he was selected as professor of natural history at the University of Pavia, a chair he held for three decades. This ancient university, long a center of scientific learning, had recently benefited from the patronage of the Empress Maria Theresia. Spallanzani thrived at Pavia where he taught, served as curator of the museum of natural history,

and continued his various investigations. He made major contributions to many areas of science, and, as his monograph on the circulation demonstrates, was a pioneer of the experimental method. His interests were not limited to the life sciences but extended to physics, chemistry, meteorology, and geology.

Acknowledged by his peers as a scientific leader, Spallanzani received numerous honors. He was elected to many of Europe's most prestigious scientific societies. Hailer was so impressed by Spallanzani's studies on the circulation and his other investigative work that he facilitated the Italian scientist's election to the Royal Society of Sciences of Göttingen. Spallanzani became ill in February 1798 with abdominal pain and urinary retention. He died a few days later following a stroke. Arturo Castiglioni, a prominent Italian medical historian, characterized Spallanzani as a "tireless investigator, deep thinker, experienced traveller, and brilliant conversationalist [who was] one of the finest scientific figures of the [eighteenth] century . . . who perhaps even more than Hailer determined new directions for physiology."[13]

References

1. Dolman C: Lazzaro Spallanzani. In *Dictionary of Scientific Biography*. Vol. 12 (Ed. Gillespie CC). Charles Scribner's Sons, New York (1975) 553-567
2. Burget GE: Lazzaro Spallanzani (1729-1799). *Ann Med Hist* 6, 177 (1924)
3. Tourdes J: A sketch of the life of the author. *In Spallanzani, Abbe. Experiments upon the Circulation of the Blood, throughout the Vascular System: On Languid Circulation: On the Motion of the Blood, Independent of the Action of the Heart: And on the Pulsations of the Arteries. With Notes, and a Sketch of the Literary Life of the Author.* Translated into English, and Illustrated with Additional Notes; by R. Hall, M.D., J. Ridgway, London (1801) 1-118
4. Needham J: *A History of Embryology* 2nd ed. Ableard-Schuman, New York (1959)
5. Meyer A: *The Rise of Embryology*. Stanford University Press, Stanford (1939)
6. von Haller A: *A Dissertation on the Motion of the Blood, and on the Effects of Bleeding*. J Whiston & B White, London (1757)
7. Fye WB: The origin of the heart beat: A tale of frogs, jellyfish, and turtles. *Circulation* 76, 493 (1987)
8. Spallanzani L: *Dell'azione del cuore ne 'vasi sanguigni. Nuove osservazioni*. Modena (1768)
9. Spallanzani L: *De'fenomeni della circolazione . . . dissertazioni quattro*. Modeno (1773)
10. Spallanzani A[L]: *Experiments upon the Circulation of the Blood, throughout the Vascular System: On Languid Circulation: On the Motion of the Blood, Independent of the Action of the Heart: And on the Pulsations of the Arteries. With Notes, and a Sketch of the Literary Life of the Author by J. Tourdes.* Translated into English, and Illustrated with Additional Notes; by R. Hall, M.D. J. Ridgway, London (1801)
11. Clay R, Court T: *The History of the Microscope*. Holland Press, London (1975)
12. Spallanzani L: *Experiments*. 271
13. Castiglioni A: *A History of Medicine*. Alfred A. Knopf, New York (1941) 613, 612

William Withering and An Account of the Foxglove

M. E. Silverman, M.D.

Department of Medicine (Cardiology), Emory University School of Medicine; Department of Cardiology, Piedmont Hospital, Atlanta, Georgia, USA

After all, in spite of opinion, prejudice, or error, Time will fix the real value upon this discovery, and determine whether I have imposed upon myself and others, or contributed to the benefit of science and mankind.

—William Withering
An Account of the Foxglove[1]

The role of the heart in causing an accumulation of fluid or difficulty in breathing was little understood prior to the nineteenth century. Symptoms that, in retrospect, may have been due to heart failure were referred to as "suffocative catarrh," " dropsy" of the lung or thorax, and "asthma," and often attributed to dysfunction in the lung, throat, or neck.[2] The responsibility of the heart in the development of the symptoms of heart failure can be traced to the writings of Raymond Vieussens (1635?–1715) and Giovanni Lancisi (1654–1720).[2] Before 1785, treatment of these diagnoses was confined to bleeding, purgatives, blistering, garlic, "medicinal" intake of wine or good ale, and the removal of ascitic fluid. It was William Withering who introduced and described the first effective drug for the treatment of dropsy—the foxglove.[1]

William Withering was born in March 1741 at Wellington in Shropshire, England.[3–8] The only son of a successful apothecary and the nephew of two physicians, Withering received ample encouragement from his family to study medicine. At the age of 21 years, he entered the esteemed medical school at the University of Edinburgh. Here he was considered a diligent student and was a member of the Latin club and the Masonic Order. He read a number of papers to the student medical society (including one on dropsy), and learned from his Scottish associates how to play the bagpipe and golf.[3] After graduation in 1766, he toured Europe, returning to assist his father until an opportunity to practice became available in the nearby village of Stafford. In Stafford he married Helena Cooke, an artist whose specialty was botanical arrangements, and who had been one of his first patients. Although Withering had expressed a disinterest in botany as a medical student, under the influence of his new wife he soon became an avid collector of plants, cones, fruits, rocks, and minerals. These studies culminated in his first book, *A Botanical Arrangement of All the Vegetables Naturally Growing in Great Britain with Descriptions of the Genera and Species According to Linnaeus*. Published in 1776, this book was the first to provide a complete description of the flora of Great Britain and to use the Linnaean binomial nomenclature.[3,8] The book, which Withering considered his most important work, established him as a leading botanist and continued in print over 100 years through 14 editions.[8] His multifarious activities in Stafford also included bowling on the green, performing on the flute and bagpipe at musical gatherings, participating in amateur dramatic productions of Shakespeare, reading poetry, and keeping a meteorological journal.[3]

To increase his income, which had not exceeded 100 pounds a year in Stafford, Withering moved to the thriving, industrial city of Birmingham in 1775 at the urging of Erasmus Darwin, the grandfather of Charles Darwin.[4] His medical practice prospered and his income soon reached 1,000 pounds a year, exceeding his entire income in eight years at Stafford. He was also able to devote time to chemistry and mineralogy, pioneering in the analysis of the waters of famous English springs, investigating the solubility of salts, Peruvian bark, and urinary stones, discovering barium carbonite (later named "witherite"), and publishing several scientific papers.[3,6] He became a valued member of the famous Lunar Society, a group of intellectuals who gathered monthly at the time of the full moon. Among the group's members were James Watt, the inventor of the steam engine; Josiah Wedgwood, the pottery maker; Erasmus Darwin; Joseph Priestley, the discoverer of oxygen; and many famous guests such as Benjamin Franklin.[3,4,6] Withering soon enjoyed the highest esteem of his colleagues, friends, and patients. He was said to be a charitable man of an affectionate and domestic nature, devoted to his family as well as to his many interests.[3] His virtues included patience, common sense, sincerity, kindness, an affable manner with a touch of reserve, and an attractive appearance.[3] His good judgment and willingness to offer advice led to his appointment as referee in settling many delicate matters. A vigorous intelligence, an ability to pursue one interest at a time until he was satisfied with the results, a lively curiosity, and meticulous habits of recording were the basis for his success as a scientist.[9] As a physician, he was interested in the psychodynamics as well as the disease in his patients and objected to the common practice of purging and bleeding. A deeply religious man with strong political convictions, Withering opposed dueling, slavery, the use of liquor, and sympathized with the ideals of the French Revolution.[3]

FIG. 1 William Withering (1741–1799). (Photograph provided by the National Library of Medicine, Bethesda, Maryland.)

From 1776 until his death in October 1799, Withering suffered recurrent hemoptysis and increasing shortness of breath as a result of tuberculosis.[3] Nevertheless, for many years he maintained a practice, said to be the largest outside of London, held a daily clinic for the poor where he treated several thousand patients a year at no charge, traveled widely by horse-drawn vehicles on bad country roads to see consults, and published *An Account of the Scarlet Fever and Sore Throat or Scarlatina Anginosa, Particularly as It Appeared in Birmingham in 1778*, which described in detail the epidemic of scarlet fever and postulated that it was infectious in etiology.[3]

Each winter took its toll on his precarious health. In 1792 he was forced to resign from the hospital staff and travel to Portugal to convalesce and avoid the inclement English weather. Although he was able to finish the third edition of his widely read book on botany in 1796, he became increasingly short of breath. His debilitation left him unable to write or carry on a conversation and subject to repeated episodes of pleurisy and hemoptysis. He died October 6, 1799, at the age of 58.[3,6]

Withering lived during the tumult of the American and French Revolutions, a time of Mozart, Beethoven, Voltaire,

Franklin, Paine, Washington, Pitt, and Burke.[3] His medical and scientific contemporaries included Jenner, Parry, Heberden, Hunter, Priestley, Lavoisier, and Linnaeus. In this illustrious company of luminaries, Withering stood near the front in reputation and achievement. At the time of his death, a friend wrote that "The flower of English physicians is indeed Withering."[3]

Although Withering is often credited with the discovery of digitalis, the medicinal use of the drug can be traced back to the thirteenth century. Until its toxic effects refuted its value as a medicinal therapy, digitalis had been a recommended treatment for headaches, spasm, epilepsy, sores, goiter, skin disease, vertigo, and as an emetic and purgative.[8] Leonard Fuchs, a Bavarian physician, coined the word digitalis in 1542 because the plant resembled a "fingerhut," the German word for fingerstall (referring to the thimblelike configuration of the flower).[4]

The English "foxglove" is a tall wildflower with eye-catching purple bells that blooms from June until the end of July throughout the mid and western counties of England where Withering practiced.[3] During Withering's travels through the countryside to see patients, he learned that a certain herbal tea was effective for treating dropsy.

> In the year 1775 my opinion was asked concerning a family receipt for the cure of the dropsy. I was told that it had long been kept a secret by an old woman in Shropshire who had sometimes made cures after the more regular practitioners had failed. I was informed also, that the effects produced were violent vomiting and purging; for the diuretic effects seemed to have been overlooked. This medicine was composed of twenty or more different herbs; but it was not very difficult for one conversant in these subjects to perceive, that the active herb could be no other than the Foxglove.[1]

Withering's clinical instincts as a physician, combined with his knowledge and experience as a botanist and chemist, stimulated him to study the effects of the foxglove on his patients. His book, *An Account of the Foxglove*, is based on the careful compilation of 163 case studies, including his own and others sent to him over a period of 10 years. First he explains how to prepare and use the drug:

> I still continue to prefer the leaves. These should be gathered after the flowering stem has shot up, and about the time that the blossoms are coming forth. The leaf-stalk and mid-rib of the leaves should be rejected, and the remaining part should be dried, either in the sunshine, or on a tin pan or pewter dish before a fire. If well dried, they readily rub down to a beautiful green powder, which weighs something less than one-fifth of the original weight of the leaves. . . . I give to adults from one to three grains of this powder twice a day.[1]

Withering then provides detailed case reports from which he draws the following conclusions:

The Foxglove when given in very large and quickly-repeated doses, occasions sickness, vomiting, purging, giddiness, confused vision, objects appearing green or yellow; increased secretion of urine, with frequent motions to part with it, and sometimes in ability to retain it; slow pulse, even as slow as 35 in a minute, cold sweats, convulsions, syncope, death.

When given in a less violent manner, it produces most of these effects in a lower degree; and it is curious to observe, that the sickness, with a certain dose of the medicine, does not take place for many hours after its exhibition has been discontinued.

Let the medicine therefore be given in the doses, and at the intervals mentioned above:—let it be continued until it either acts on the kidneys, the stomach, the pulse, or the bowels; let it be stopped upon the first appearance of any one of these effects, and I will maintain that the patient will not suffer from its exhibition, nor the practitioner be disappointed in any reasonable expectation.[1]

Withering continues by describing the types of patients in whom the drug may or may not have a favorable effect, noting that it is not helpful in ascites but works best in those patients whom we would recognize today to have advanced heart failure or atrial fibrillation.

On the contrary, if the pulse be feeble or intermitting, the countenance pale, the lips livid, the skin cold, the swollen belly soft and fluctuating, or the anasarcous limbs readily pitting under the pressure of the finger, we may expect the diuretic effect to follow in a kindly manner.[1]

At the beginning of the book, Withering cautions the reader to be aware that the cases presented are "the most hopeless and deplorable that exist" and that no general deductions can be gathered. At the conclusion of the book he warns the reader not to have too high an expectation of the drug but at the same time he offers the following as inferences:[1]

I. That the Digitalis will not universally act as a diuretic.
II. That it does do so more generally than any other medicine.
III. That it will often produce this effect after every other probable method has been fruitlessly tried.
IV. That if this fails, there is but little chance of any other medicine succeeding.
V. That in proper doses, and under the management now pointed out, it is mild in its operation, and gives less disturbance to the system, than squill, or almost any other active medicine.
VI. That when dropsy is attended by palsy, unfound viscera, great debility, or other complication of disease, neither the Digitalis, nor any other diuretic can do more than obtain a truce to the urgency of the symptoms; unless by gaining time, it may afford opportunity for other medicines to combat and subdue the original disease.
VII. That the Digitalis may be used with advantage in every species of dropsy, except the encysted.
VIII. That it may be made subservient to the cure of diseases, unconnected with dropsy.
IX. That it has a power over the motion of the heart, to a degree yet unobserved in any other medicine, and that this power may be converted to salutary ends.

An Account of the Foxglove was published in 1785; it cost five shillings and contained 207 pages. A beautiful colored picture of the purple foxglove plant served as frontispiece.[3] The book received good reviews, widespread acceptance, and, for over two centuries, has continued to be regarded as the inception of clinical pharmacology and a classic model for scientific investigation.[4,9]

References

1. Withering W: *An Account of the Foxglove and Some of Its Medical Uses.* M. Swinney, Birmingham (1785) (The Classics of Medicine Library, Special Edition, 1979)
2. Jarcho S: *The Concept of Heart Failure: From Avicenna to Albertini.* Harvard University Press, Cambridge, MA (1980)
3. Roddis LH: *William Withering: The Introduction of Digitalis into Medical Practice.* Paul B. Hoeber, Inc., New York (1936)
4. Krikler DM: The foxglove, "the old woman from Shropshire" and William Withering. *J Am Coll Cardiol* 5 (suppl A), 3 (1985)
5. Somberg J, Greenfield D, Tepper D: Digitalis: 200 years in perspective. *Am Heart J* 111, 615 (1986)
6. Peck TW, Wilkinson KD: *William Withering of Birmingham.* John Wright & Sons, Ltd., Bristol (1950)
7. Rahimtoola SH: Digitalis and William Withering, the clinical investigator. *Circulation* 52, 969 (1975)
8. Wray S, Eisner DA, Allen DG: *Two Hundred Years of the Foxglove* in *The Emergence of Modern Cardiology.* (Eds. Bynum WF, Lawrence C, Nutton V). Wellcome Institute for the History of Medicine, London (1985) 132–150
9. Fisch C: William Withering: An account of the foxglove and some of its medical uses 1785–1985. *J Am Coll Cardiol* (suppl A), 1 (1985)

Alessandro Volta

CLYDE PARTIN, M.D., FACP

Emory University School of Medicine, Atlanta, Georgia, USA

Born into nobility, but rather harsh financial circumstances, on February 18, 1745, in Como, Italy, Alessandro Volta (Fig. 1) would come to electrify the world with his intellect and accomplishments. His father would die in debt and had so squandered the patrimony that his family lived in poverty, which later prompted Volta to conclude, "I was actually poorer than poor."[1] His intellectual capacity was initially suspect as he was mute until age four, when he vigorously uttered "NO" to register his dissenting opinion on a planned family activity. His household soon recognized that they had a real intellectual jewel in their midst. From this most inauspicious genesis, Volta was feted in his lifetime as "one of the greatest leaders of thought, not alone in electricity, but in all departments of the physical sciences."[1]

Curiously, the founding fathers of electricity were mostly clergymen. Though extremely religious, Volta was one of the first nonclerical pioneers to devote his life to electricity and the associated physical sciences. Poverty so penetrated his existence that his education was secured only through the fortuitous clerical positions of his uncles and the Jesuit Colleges' fee structure. One uncle was a canon, the other an archdeacon of the Cathedral, and the college required no tuition, subsisting on support from foundations. His uncles and the Jesuit priests provided living expenses. This juxtaposition of religion and education was a strong influence on Volta's formative years, extending the theme of the role of the church in the early days of electrical evolution. In the sixth decade of his life, Volta felt moved to pen an eloquent confession of faith that provided an imposing rebuttal to the notion that one "cannot be a great scientist and firm believer in religion."[1]

By age seven, Volta's academic promise was evident. Family friends provided assistance to obtain mundane items such as copybooks for school. As was not too unconventional in the tenor of the times, his college education was essentially completed at age 16. He had a tendency to daydream in school and was frequently distracted. As a "mere boy he often asked questions with regard to natural phenomena that were puzzlers to his masters, and sometimes complained of their lack of knowledge."[1] He proved to be a quick study, impatient with those who had less talent. He was fluent in six languages, was a seeker of knowledge, and developed a love of the classics with a particular fondness for poetry. He penned a poem, in Latin, of about five hundred verses concerning the life and work of Joseph Priestly, the discoverer of oxygen. He briefly

flirted with a notion to enter the Jesuit Order, a plan nixed by his family. His uncles removed him from the Jesuit school and sent him to the Seminary at Benzi. There he acquiesced to his family's wishes, abandoning the route to priesthood. He briefly studied law; then he exerted his will and devoted himself to the study of the natural sciences.

Again, the role of the men of cloth played a hand in the fate of the electrical sciences. Father Gattoni, a canon at the Cathedral of Como, had been a student with Volta and shared his fascination with the natural sciences. Gattoni, being well off and recognizing Volta's potential as a brilliant experimenter, provided both the emotional and financial spark that allowed them both to carry out their investigations. It was here on the shores of Lake Como that the experimental groundwork for modern electrical science blossomed. Volta was an intense and devoted investigator, foregoing sleep, food, and companionship once he became engrossed in a problem. Friends found him an unusual travel companion, so distracted was he by his work and constantly preoccupied with reconciling his theories with experimental proof.

Volta published his first paper on electricity at age 24 in 1769. However, a letter he wrote at age 19 to Abbe Nollet, the day's leading scientist on electricity, showed that Volta already had a firm theoretical grasp of electrical phenomena. He presciently postulated that all bodies had electrical substance within them in a state of equilibrium. A perturbation of this equanimity, representing some interaction between a proposed electrical essence and matter, led to an electrical event. Working steadily, by 1775 he announced the development of the electrophorus. Prior to the electrophorus, students of electricity were hindered by the ephemeral existence of the subject under scrutiny, garnering their data on the basis of fleeting static discharges. The electrophorus acted as a reservoir, providing a more lasting source of subject matter. Of an exceedingly careful nature, Volta wrote to Joseph Priestly before announcing his invention. Joseph Priestly, known to most as the father of modern chemistry, was the author of a respected work on the complete history of electricity. Volta wished to know if his machine was "novel in the domain of electrical advance."[1]

A steady current of useful inventions followed, including the condensing electroscope, which allowed the measurement of minute amounts of electricity; the electrical pistol, which assisted in the study of inflammable gases; the eudiometer, a contraption for measuring oxygen levels. Besides the practical

ALEXANDER . VOLTA .
IN . RE . ELECTRICA . PRINCEPS .
VIM . RAIAE . TORPEDINIS . MEDITATVS .
NATVRAE INTERPRES ET . AEMVLVS

From Volta, "L'Identità del Fluido Elettrica", 1814.

FIG. 1 Alessandro Volta (1745–1827). Source: Dibner B: *Ten Founding Fathers of the Electrical Science.* Burndy Corporation, Norwalk, Conn. 1954.

benefits accrued from these innovations, they elevated the status of university physics departments to a more respectable realm. In light of these successes, Volta began his academic career at the College of Como in 1774, serving as professor of experimental physics. In 1779, he began a 40-year career at the University of Pavia, where he initially concentrated on the study of gases. Some of his observations were instrumental in the establishment of Charles' law. In 1786, Volta sojourned throughout Europe, discoursing with the great minds of science.[1]

In 1791, Volta received a copy of a paper from Luigi Galvani, a professor of anatomy at the University of Bologna. Galvani had serendipitously noted the muscles of some dissected frog legs he was studying contracted when a nearby electrostatic generator unexpectedly discharged. He and his assistants also observed that the touch of a scalpel produced a similar result. Galvani's explanation for the muscular movement was an ethereal and miasmic substance he called "animal electricity," a school of thought that became known as Galvanism. Volta, intrigued by Galvani's work but not one to jump to conclusions, instituted his own series of experiments. In a series of ingenious studies, Volta's "incredulity" changed to doubt. Maintaining his "methodological rule of keeping strictly to the facts, without transcending them in bold theoretical constructs. [sic] This led him to adopt very severe and prudent criteria for selecting hypothesis and explanations."[2] Volta concluded that the "muscle twitchings were not due to the presence of animal electricity, but due to the fact that the metals touching the different portions of the moist nerve muscle preparation really set up minute currents of ordinary electricity."[1] While reams would come to be written about the competing theories of Galvani and Volta, suffice it to say that Volta's

demonstrations showed how "thoroughly empirical were his methods and how modern his scientific spirit," conclusively refuting Galvanism.

Volta's studies not only laid the groundwork for electrochemistry but also led him to develop the Voltaic pile—so called because of the way he stacked metal discs on top of each other—better known today as the battery. This invention, announced in 1800, garnered him world acclaim. The French Academy of Sciences invited him to Paris to demonstrate his findings. Napoleon was a patron of the sciences and, in astute recognition of the practical aspects of Volta's work, awarded him 6,000 lire and an annual stipend of 3,000 lire. Shocked by Napoleon's gift, Volta would not accept the money until the decree was approved by the Pope. Fame and numerous honors followed. At the International Electrical Congress in Paris in 1881, the term "volt" was advanced as a measure of electrical force, thus formally and eponymically enshrining Volta into perpetuity.

Volta lived a simple and unpretentious life, dedicated to the church and revered by loyal servants and his neighbors for his humanitarian and endearing demeanor. He became known in the community as "*Il mago benefico*" (the beneficent magician), a reflection of the love and respect the townspeople had for him.

Fortunately, "after the Galvani-Volta debates had ended the life sciences would no longer be driven by the animal-spirits paradigm of the past."[3] Recent reflections on Galvani and Volta's careers have pointed out several misconceptions and even claimed both were right.[4–6] Galvani deserves more credit for his original groundwork in electrophysiology, even if it was Volta who more correctly elucidated Galvani's findings. Furthermore, Volta should be looked upon not as a mere physicist, but as a multifaceted scientist whose work had great relevance for electrochemistry and the physiology of neuroscience. Neither did any work in cardiac electrophysiology but others, building on the accomplishments of Volta and Galvani, would usher in the age of electrocardiography. We would do well to remember the words of Arago, who, in his eulogy of Volta, who died at the age of 82, proclaimed the electric battery as "the most marvelous instrument created by the mind of man, not excluding even the telescope or steam engine."[7]

References

1. Potamian B, Walsh JJ: *Makers of Electricity.* New York: Fordham University Press, 1909
2. Pera M: *The Ambiguous Frog: The Galvani-Volta Controversy on Animal Electricity.* Translated by Jonathon Mandelbaum. Princeton, N.J.: Princeton University Press, 1992
3. Finger S: *Minds Behind the Brain: A History of the Pioneers and Their Discoveries.* New York: Oxford University Press, 2000
4. Piccolino M: Luigi Galvani and animal electricity: Two centuries after the foundation of electrophysiology. *Trends Neurosci* 1997;20(10):443–448
5. Piccolino M: The bicentennial of the Voltaic battery (1800–2000): The artificial electric organ. *Trends Neurosci* 2000;23(4):147–151
6. Hellman H: *Great Feuds in Medicine.* New York: John Wiley & Sons, Inc., 2001
7. Dibner B: *Ten Founding Fathers of the Electrical Science.* Norwalk, Conn: Burndy Corporation, 1954

Edward Jenner

W. Bruce Fye, M.D., M.A.

Department of Cardiology, Marshfield Clinic, Marshfield, Wisconsin, USA

Edward Jenner was born in Berkeley, Gloucestershire, England on May 17, 1749.[1–3] Best known for introducing vaccination in 1798, Jenner also made important observations on the relationship between coronary artery disease and angina pectoris. This brief biographical sketch will focus on Jenner's contribution to our understanding of the pathophysiology of angina. In his landmark history of coronary heart disease, medical historian Joshua Leibowitz claimed that "among the authors who furthered the coronary theory of angina pectoris, Edward Jenner has quite a prominent place."[4]

At the age of 13, Jenner began studying medicine as an apprentice to Abraham Ludlow, a surgeon in the village of Sodbury. Jenner's formal medical training began in 1770 when he went to London and enrolled as a student at William Hunter's Great Windmill Street school of anatomy. He also served as John Hunter's house pupil at St. George's Hospital. Jenner first became interested in angina while he was Hunter's assistant. A brilliant surgeon and physiologist, Hunter greatly admired Jenner, and the two became close friends.

Angina pectoris was first described in 1768 by British physician William Heberden. That year he presented a paper "Some Account of a Disorder of the Breast" at a meeting of the Royal College of Physicians of London. Published 4 years later, Heberden's paper is an acknowledged classic of clinical medicine.[5] Although his description of angina pectoris is masterful, Heberden did not speculate on the pathophysiology of the disorder.

Shortly after he published his observations on angina, Heberden received an anonymous letter from a physician who thought he suffered from the condition. The doctor requested that Heberden perform an autopsy on him upon his death. When this anonymous physician died 3 weeks later, Heberden asked John Hunter to perform the postmortem examination. Jenner helped Hunter perform the autopsy and later recalled that it represented the first case of angina he had seen. Because there was no recognition of the association of coronary artery disease and angina at the time, it is not surprising that Hunter and Jenner did not pay special attention to these vessels. They found no obvious abnormalities in the heart or other organs that explained the man's death.[6, 7]

After 2 years as Hunter's assistant, Jenner returned to Gloucestershire to begin his career as a country doctor. Once in practice, he saw a few more patients with angina. After visiting John Hunter in Bath in 1785, Jenner concluded that his friend and mentor was having attacks of angina. This further stimulated Jenner's interest in the condition.

In 1786, Jenner told William Heberden that he had witnessed three autopsies of patients who had attacks of angina. While the first two autopsies "[threw] but little light upon the subject," the postmortem on a third patient led Jenner to conclude that the symptoms were due to coronary artery disease.[8] He explained that the most recent autopsy revealed "a kind of firm fleshy tube, formed within the [coronary] vessel, with a considerable quantity of ossific matter dispersed irregularly through it." Jenner proposed that this pathologic finding had been overlooked in patients who had suffered from angina because the coronary arteries were often covered by epicardial fat.

In his letter to Heberden, Jenner made an assertion that is today acknowledged as the first explicit statement linking disease of the coronary arteries to angina pectoris. He explained, "the importance of the coronary arteries, and how much the heart must suffer from their not being able to perform their functions, (we cannot be surprised at the painful spasms) is a subject I need not enlarge upon, therefore shall only just remark that it is possible that all the symptoms may arise from this one circumstance." Jenner also revealed to Heberden his reluctance to share this concept with John Hunter because "it may deprive him of the hopes of a recovery" as there was no known remedy for the coronary artery lesions he thought caused angina pectoris.

Beginning in 1788, Jenner met with a few of his medical colleagues three times a year at the Fleece Inn at Rodborough to discuss cases and other matters of mutual interest.[9] Caleb Parry, a member of this small group known formally as the Gloucestershire Medical Society and informally as the Medico-convivial, claimed that "in that society the influence of the heart on the animal oeconomy had often been the subject of discussion."[10] In the introduction to his classic 1799 monograph on angina pectoris, Parry credited Jenner with suggesting that "Angina

Fig. 1 Edward Jenner (1749–1823). (Photograph from the collections of W. Bruce Fye, M.D.)

Pectoris arose from some morbid change in the structure of the heart."[10a]

Parry found Jenner's observations interesting and compelling. Jenner told Parry that, while he was carefully dissecting the heart of a patient he had seen with angina, his "knife struck something so hard and gritty, as to notch it." At first Jenner thought a piece of ceiling plaster had fallen into the dissecting field, but on closer inspection he discovered that the "coronaries were become [sic] bony canals." This case led Jenner to conclude that angina was caused by "malorganization" of the coronary arteries.[11]

Parry accepted Jenner's hypothesis that angina pectoris was a disease of the heart related to a disorder of the coronary arteries. Although Parry first published the coronary theory of angina pectoris, he gave full credit to his friend Jenner for proposing the concept. Jenner told Parry, who

cared for Hunter when the surgeon was in Bath for health reasons, "At this very time, my valued friend, Mr. John Hunter, began to have the symptoms of Angina Pectoris too strongly marked upon him; and this circumstance prevented any publication of my ideas on the subject, as it must have brought on an unpleasant conference between Mr. Hunter and me." Jenner continued, "I mentioned both to Mr. Cline and Mr. Home my notions of the matter at one of Mr. Hunter's Sunday night meetings; but they did not seem to think much of them. When, however, Mr. Hunter died [in 1793], Mr. Home very candidly wrote to me, immediately after the dissection, to tell me I was right."[11]

Jenner's fame rests mainly upon his 1798 book on vaccination which "caused a revolution in medical thought and practice."[11] His pioneering observations on the relationship of coronary artery disease and angina pectoris are less well known. As Parry claimed in his 1799 monograph *Syncope Anginosa,* Jenner's findings and his conclusions were a crucial step toward understanding the pathophysiology of angina. After a brief illness, Jenner died in 1823.

References

1. Baron J: *The Life of Edward Jenner, M.D.* Henry Colburn, London (1827)
2. Saunders P: *Edward Jenner: The Cheltenham Years, 1795–1823.* University Press of New England, Hanover, N.H. (1982)
3. Fisher RB: *Edward Jenner, 1749–1823.* André Deutsch, London (1991)
4. Leibowitz JO: *The History of Coronary Heart Disease.* , Wellcome Institute of the History of Medicine, London (1970). Quote from p. 93.
5. Heberden W: Some account of a disorder of the breast. *Medical Transactions, College of Physicians of London* 2, 59–67 (1772)
6. Kligfield P: The early pathophysiologic understanding of angina pectoris. *Am J Cardiol* 50, 1433–1435 (1982)
7. Segall HN: The first clinico-pathological history of angina pectoris. *Bull Hist Med* 18, 102–108 (1945)
8. Jenner to Heberden, 1778 [1786]. Quoted in Baron (Ref. 1) p. 39
9. Proudfit WL: The Fleece Medical Society. *Br Heart J* 46, 589–594 (1981)
10. Parry CH: *An Inquiry into the Symptoms and Causes of the Syncope Anginosa Commonly Called Angina Pectoris.* R. Cruttwell, Bath, England (1799); (a) 3–5
11. LeFanu W: *A Bibliography of Edward Jenner.* St. Paul's Bibliographies, Winchester, England (1985)

Antonio Scarpa

W. BRUCE FYE, M.D., M.A.

Department of Cardiology, Marshfield Clinic, Marshfield, Wisconsin, USA

Anatomist and surgeon Antonio Scarpa (Fig. 1) was born on May 19, 1752, in Motta di Livenza, Italy.[1, 2] Although he made many significant contributions, Scarpa is included in the profiles series because of his classic observations on aneurisms and his original description of the cardiac nerves. After being tutored by his uncle, Canon Paulo Scarpa, he entered the University of Padua in 1766. There, he was taught by Leopoldo Caldani, a celebrated anatomist, and Giovanni Morgagni, generally acknowledged as the founder of pathologic anatomy. Morgagni, in his mid-eighties when Scarpa arrived at Padua, was very impressed by the young man and invited him to be his assistant and personal secretary.

Although Morgagni died shortly after Scarpa received his degree in 1770, the eminent pathologist catalyzed the young medical graduate's career. Scarpa was just 20 years old when Morgagni helped him obtain his first academic post (professor of anatomy and clinical surgery at the University of Modena). Scarpa's skill as an anatomist and his manual dexterity as a surgeon won him many admirers at Modena. Soon, he was also appointed chief surgeon at the city's military hospital.

The Duke of Modena, hoping to improve medical education at the university, sent Scarpa to France and England to visit several hospitals in 1781. During his trip, Scarpa performed many autopsies and worked with several prominent surgeons. In Paris, he assisted Baron Michael de Wenzel and other prominent French surgeons. In London, he attended lectures delivered by John and William Hunter and assisted Percival Pott, then England's leading surgeon. Impressed by William Hunter's enormous anatomical museum, Scarpa hoped to develop a similar facility at Modena.

In 1783, shortly after his return to Modena, Scarpa was offered the chair of anatomy at the University of Pavia, one of Italy's oldest universities.[3] Scarpa's anatomical researches and teaching at Pavia benefited from the order of Emperor Joseph II that resulted in the transfer of bodies of patients who had died at the hospital to the medical school for dissection. Because dissection was permitted in Pavia, Scarpa's courses included anatomical demonstrations and he encouraged his students to dissect cadavers. His anatomical course was very popular and attracted students from throughout Europe. Soon, Scarpa was overseeing the construction of an anatomical museum and an anatomical amphitheater to replace the sixteenth century facility built by Gabriele Cuneo.

Scarpa made many anatomical discoveries as a result of his painstaking dissections. He made several original observa-

FIG. 1 Antonio Scarpa, 1752–1832. Photograph from the collection of W. Bruce Fye.

tions on the anatomy of the nervous system, especially the structure of the sensory organs. For example, he first described the vestibule and the membranous labyrinth of the ear. His 1801 monograph on ophthalmology was translated into several languages and was the standard text for many years. Published in 1809 and illustrated with magnificent copper engravings, Scarpa's book on hernias reflected his talents as an anatomist, artist, and surgeon.

In 1794, Scarpa published his greatest work, *Tabulae neurologicae ad illustrandam historian cardiacorum nervorum*. This magnificent atlas included seven spectacular life-size copper engravings created by Faustino Anderloni after Scarpa's own drawings.[4] Two of the plates illustrate the innerva-tion of the heart. Although it was already known that nerves accompanied the coronary arteries, Scarpa first showed (in this work) that these nerves connected directly to the cardiac muscle fibers. Speaking of the plates in this massive volume, British physician and historian Benjamin Ward Richardson claimed he had never seen more beautiful medical illustrations.[5]

Scarpa's classic monograph on aneurysms, *Sull'Aneurisma. Riflessioni ed osservazione anatomico-chirurgiche*, was published in Pavia in 1804. In it, Scarpa described the normal and pathologic aspects of the arteries and showed that earlier concepts about the pathophysiology of aneurysms were incorrect. He argued that an aneurysm was not simply a dilated segment of a normal artery. Rather, it was the result of localized disease of the arterial wall. After carefully studying healthy and diseased arteries, he concluded that the most common precursor of an aneurysm was an ulcerated atheromatous plaque. In this book, Scarpa also first distinguished between true and false aneurysms and showed that arteriosclerosis began in the intima of arteries. Like his other publications, it was illustrated with spectacular copper engravings based on his own drawings.

Reflecting his interest and experience in surgery, Scarpa published *Memoria sulla legatura delle principali arterie degli arti con una appendice all'opera sull'aneurisma* in 1817. It included a summary of his experience with ligatures in the treatment of aneurysms. Scarpa also reported his important observations on the collateral circulation of the limbs, based on animal experiments and many dissections.

Among the subjects that Scarpa studied experimentally was the effect of blood transfusions in animals. He showed that animals that had been exsanguinated could be revived with blood transfusions. Scarpa was not only a productive scientist who made many anatomical and physiologic observations, he was also an innovative and skillful surgeon who became wealthy as a result of his successful practice. After retiring from the chair of anatomy at Pavia at the age of 66, Scarpa held the post of rector of the medical faculty at the institution. He died on October 30, 1832, at the age of 87.

References

1. Franceschini P: Antonio Scarpa. In *Dictionary of Scientific Biography*, Vol. 12, p. 136–139. New York: Charles Scribner's Sons, 1975

2. Monti A: *Antonio Scarpa in Scientific History and His Role in the Fortunes of the University of Pavia.* New York: Vigo Press, 1957

3. Castiglioni A: *Italian Medicine.* New York: Paul B. Hoeber, 1932

4. Mann RJ: Scarpa, Hodgson, and Hope, artists of the heart and great vessels. *Mayo Clin Proc* 1974;49:889–892

5. Richardson BW: Antonio Scarpa, F.R.S., and surgical anatomy. In *Disciples of Aesculapius*, p. 143–157. London: Hutchinson & Co.,1900

Sir Dominic John Corrigan

J. STONE, M.D.

Department of Medicine (Cardiology), Emory University School of Medicine, Atlanta, Georgia, USA

Within the universe of medical eponyms, those associated with aortic regurgitation (AR) must surely rank among the most history laden. Consider the following, for example (Rolleston, 1940):

1. Duroziez's "double intermittent" murmur over the femoral arteries
2. Traube's sign: the "pistol-shot" sound over the femoral arteries
3. De Musset's sign: the jerking nodlike movement of the head with each systole: De Musset named this sign after his famous poet-novelist brother, Alfred De Musset, who displayed the sign probably as a result of syphilitic involvement of the aorta
4. Austin Flint presystolic mitral rumble associated with AR
5. Quincke's "capillary pulse" in the nailbeds
6. Muller's alternating blanch/flush of the uvula.

In addition to these, there is, of course, the collapsing quality of the pulse in AR, often called (interchangeably and *incorrectly*) a "water-hammer" pulse and "Corrigan's pulse." Of the pulse abnormalities, there will be more to say presently. Suffice it to say at this point that Corrigan's name leads all the others in this eponymic hierarchy. Indeed, so inextricably is Corrigan's name associated with AR that Trousseau, the great French physician, called aortic regurgitation "Maladie de Corrigan" (Willius and Keys, 1941).

There is, always, a certain quirkiness, though, in what history chooses to store up in its memory—or perhaps it is the human brain, with its propensity to oversimplify and "pigeonhole" that is at fault here. In any event, the contributions of Dominic John Corrigan were far broader than his clinical description of this single valvular lesion, as the intuitive reader will know already.

A Brief Life History and Context

Corrigan was born in Dublin, Ireland, in 1802. His father was a successful farmer and merchant of agricultural tools; his mother is described as intelligent and beautiful. Corrigan's early education was excellent: it was done at the lay College at Maynooth, one of the first Catholic educational institutions.

There he studied Latin, Greek, and French, together with physical science and natural philosophy. There, too, he came under the influence of a Dr. O'Kelly, the college physician, to whom Corrigan was apprenticed for several years. O'Kelly was largely responsible for Corrigan's decision to study medicine at the University of Edinburgh (from which he received his M.D. degree in 1825). The subject of his thesis was "Scrofula": clearly, tuberculosis was still ubiquitous (Williamson, 1925).

Corrigan's classmates at Edinburgh included William Stokes (Cheyne-Stokes respirations and Stokes-Adams attacks), also a Dubliner. Another colleague was James Hope, from London, who was later to quarrel with Corrigan over which of them should receive historical priority in the clinical recognition of AR (Mulcahy, 1961).

After graduation, Corrigan returned to Dublin and began his practice, which was slow initially; but in time he became one of Europe's most famous physicians. Corrigan's great contemporaries in Dublin included the physicians Graves, Marsh, and Stokes and the surgeons Colles, Carmichael, Cusack, and Adams (obituary, *British Medical Journal*, 1980). Among these great figures, Corrigan was to hold his own very well indeed.

About 1830, Corrigan was appointed physician to the Jervis Street Hospital, where he was allotted only six beds. But this relatively small number was sufficient for one who was as industrious and observant as Corrigan. Even prior to the Jervis Street appointment (while he worked at a dispensary and in the Cork Street Fever Hospital) (Mulcahy, 1961), Corrigan began to make observations, to experiment, and to write. Between late 1828 and 1830, he wrote four papers: the first, "Aneurism of the Aorta," appeared in the February 7, 1829 issue of *The Lancet*. After 1830, there was a veritable torrent of papers from Corrigan's pen: his bibliography numbers more than 100 papers and monographs on a wide variety of topics (editorial, *Journal of the American Medical Association*, 1962). His areas of interest and publication range from the clinical and experimental (early on) to those concerned with social-medical-political issues of the day (in later life).

All his life, Corrigan seems to have been an outspoken person: this trait became particularly evident during the great Potato Famine in Ireland from about 1845–1847. During the famine (which was caused by a plant fungus), some 750,000 people died of starvation or disease; thousands more emigrat-

FIG. 1 Sir Dominic Corrigan, 1802–1880. Courtesy National Library of Medicine.

ed from Ireland. In fact, Corrigan's attacks upon "the authorities" during this crisis resulted in his being "black-balled" (in 1847) when he stood for election to the King's and Queen's College of Physicians. But this was a temporary setback only: eight years later, he was elected a Fellow and from 1858 to 1863 served as President of the College (Mulcahy, 1961).

Honors were heaped on Corrigan with great frequency. He received an honorary M.D. degree from the University of Dublin (1849), served as Physician-in-Ordinary in Ireland to Queen Victoria (1870), and became Vice Chancellor of the Queen's University (1871). In 1866, he was made a baronet: he was one of only eight physicians in the history of Ireland to receive this honor. Corrigan was gifted in many areas: he was one of the founders of the Dublin Pathological Society in 1838; in 1870, at the age of 68, Sir Dominic was elected to represent Dublin in the House of Commons, a seat he held for four years. Nor was his fame limited to Ireland or the British Isles. He served as President not only of the Royal Irish Academy and the Royal Zoological Society of Ireland, but also as President of the Harveian Society of London and the Academy of Medicine in Paris (Willius and Keys, 1941), a startling record indeed.

In Corrigan's mature years, he was troubled by attacks of gout and by personal tragedies which included the deaths of all three of his sons prior to Corrigan's own death, in 1880, following a severe stroke. The medical journals of the day bear eloquent testimony to his accomplishments in their obituaries (*The Lancet* and *British Medical Journal,* 1880).

Contributions to Medicine

As noted, Corrigan's very first paper was in the area of cardiology: "Aneurism of the Aorta" appeared in 1829. In fact, three of his first four papers dealt with cardiac topics—the fourth was concerned with "epidemic fever in Ireland." Of Corrigan's many contributions to the medical literature, four seem to stand out and are worthy of at least brief mention.

1. "On Permanent Patency of the Mouth of the Aorta, Or Inadequacy of the Aortic Valves" (1832) *Edinburgh Medical and Surgical Journal* 37, 225-245 (his most famous paper, about which more later)
2. "On Cirrhosis of the Lung" (1838) *Dublin Journal of Medical Science,* XIII, 266. In this paper, Corrigan distinguished "cirrhosis of the lung" (fibrotic disease of the lung) from tubercular "phthisis"; the paper dealt not only with clinical, but also with pathological features and natural history of the disease process (Agnew, 1965).
3. "On Aortitis as One of the Causes of Angina Pectoris" (1837) *Dublin Journal of Medical Science,* XII, No. 25. This paper anticipated by 70 years the later description, by Sir Clifford Allbutt, of the pathogenetic mechanisms of aortitis in the etiology of angina.
4. "Lectures on the Nature and Treatment of Fever" (1853), a monograph published in Dublin. In it, Corrigan confirmed earlier poorly accepted accounts stressing the difference between typhus and typhoid fever.

But it was Corrigan's paper of 1832 on aortic regurgitation that made him famous.

"On Permanent Patency of the Mouth of the Aorta…": Corrigan's Paper of 1832

In the capriciousness of history, as it happens, a number of early descriptions dealing with AR preceded Corrigan's 1832 paper. The most noteworthy of these are the following (Rolleston, 1940):

1. William Cowper (1705): described the pulse in AR as "intermittent"
2. Raymond de Vieussens (1715): described the collapsing quality of the pulse
3. James Douglas (1715): description of a young man with a loud murmur audible several feet from the bedside, together with necropsy findings consistent with AR
4. R. J. Bertin (1824): description in French of "retroversion of aortic valves"
5. Thomas Hodgkin (1828-1829): account of "retroversion of the valves of the aorta," which recognized many of the clinical findings in AR. Of some interest is the fact that Hodgkin has been partially overlooked not only in regard to aortic valve disease, but also in the very disease, "lymphadenoma," that bears his name ("Hodg-

kin's disease"): his insights into that disease lay in historical oblivion until their merit was recognized years later by Samual Wilks

6. James Hope (1831): Hope, Corrigan's classmate at Edinburgh, published a short account of aortic valve disease and later quarreled with Corrigan as to which of them should receive attribution in history.

But Corrigan's description of AR in 1832 eclipsed all the others, primarily because of its comprehensive nature. It included the following sections (Willius and Keys, 1941):

Pathology. A description of four major abnormalities of the valves: 'cribriform' defects; rupture of a valve cusp; shortening/thickening of the leaflets; and gross dilatation of the aortic ring.

Symptoms. Primarily those of heart failure, especially dyspnea, cough, orthopnea, but also 'oppression across the chest.'

Signs. Corrigan described the 'bruit de soufflet' (the 'bellows murmur') and 'frémissement' (or thrill over the carotid/subclavian arteries). In Corrigan's paper, he was clearly preoccupied with *systolic* events, though he did describe a 'double bruit' in severe cases. In part, Corrigan's lack of attention to diastole may reflect the less-than-adequate stethoscopes of the day.

The Pulse in AR. Corrigan's description of the pulse in AR was primarily *visual* in nature: 'the arterial trunks of the head, neck, and superior extremities immediately catch the eye by their singular pulsation,' he writes. He did, however, note that the pulse in AR was 'invariably full,' in contrast to that of aortic stenosis (in which it was 'small and contracted'). Corrigan also makes the interesting observation that elevation of the extremities by the patient produced a marked accentuation of the fullness of the arterial pulse. It was *not* Corrigan, however, who described the pulse in AR as 'water-hammer' in type. A 'water-hammer' was a 'chemical toy' of the time: it consisted of a glass tube partially filled with water in a vacuum—inverting the tube caused the water to rush to the other end, where it landed with a shock and a short hard knocking sensation. Thomas Watson, in lectures given in 1836 and 1837, appears to have been the first person to compare the collapsing pulse of AR to this toy: thus the term 'water-hammer pulse' rightfully ought to bear Watson's, not Corrigan's, name (Dock, 1934).

Experiments and therapeutics. Elsewhere in his paper Corrigan describes some experiments in which he was able to generate sounds ('murmurs') in tubing as a result of turbulent flow. He stresses the fact that patients with aortic regurgitation may live for many years and, in any event, are not predisposed to sudden death.

Corrigan insisted, furthermore, that the therapy of heart disease in his time was not physiologic in nature and tended to be 'harrassing' (*sic*) in nature. He decried contemporary methods, which included frequent phle-

botomies and a starvation diet. He prescribed as follows: (1) a generous diet; (2) abstinence from alcohol; (3) normal activities on the part of the patient; and (4) reassurance of the patient that sudden death was 'never' seen in aortic regurgitation (in contrast, for example, to aneurysm).

Corrigan himself displayed considerable physiological sophistication: he deplored the use of digitalis, saying that it slowed the pulse and prolonged diastole, which resulted in an increase in the amount of aortic regurgitation. He also clearly felt that the marked hypertrophy present in some hearts was a natural response of the heart to overload (and not part of the disease itself). He advocated the use of 'opiate' in cases with profound shortness of breath.

Other Medical Interests of Corrigan

As noted, Corrigan's contributions outside of cardiology were great indeed. Of historical interest are two papers dealing with noncardiac subjects, which in themselves may be surprising. Corrigan described in 1846 what has become known as "Corrigan's Button" (Widdess, 1967). The "button" was a piece of thick iron wire, two inches long with a wooden handle. The button was heated in a flame, then touched rapidly over "the affected part" producing a series of red circles (not blisters) that served as a form of "counterirritation." The button was used, e.g., in cases of rheumatism, lumbago, and neuralgia; the concept of counterirritation was that a second sensation (such as the heat produced by application of the button) diminished the primary irritation causing the patient's symptoms.

Corrigan also became interested for a time in the problem of enuresis in childhood. His approach (in the case of boys, at least) was to apply a thin layer of collodion over the prepuce of the penis (or over the edges of the urethra): as the collodion dried, it drew the edges together and "thus the exit for the escaping urine is closed" (Corrigan, 1977).

Corrigan the Man

Corrigan's impact was exerted not only by the force of his writing. His personality also had a great influence on those around him. A couple of personal characteristics may suffice to give some flavor to the reader. For example, he tried never to show haste in front of a patient and "was careful never to allow a patient to see him looking at his watch" (Mulcahy, 1961). As a further example, one paper on Corrigan includes the following story (Williamson, 1925):

Once, when attending a lady of rank in fever, when he entered her room, accompanied by her anxious husband, he said to the latter: "She is better." The visit completed, when they left the patient, the husband asked him how he knew at a glance and without examination that the patient was better. "I knew it," said Sir Dominic, "by an infallible symptom—I saw the handle of a looking-glass peeping from under her pillow!" He was right. The lady was better and made an excellent recovery.

Thus, Corrigan went about his medical duties. Over a hundred years later, contemporary physicians continue to make observations such as the above, all the while standing in debt to this great figure of nineteenth century medicine.

References

Agnew RAL: The achievement of Dominic John Corrigan. *Med Hist* 9, 230 (1965)

Corrigan DJC: On the treatment of incontinence of urine in childhood and youth by collodion (paper of 1871). Quoted in *Pediatrics* 60, 476 (1977)

Dock G: Dominic John Corrigan: I. His place in the development of our knowledge of cardiac disease and, 11. The Water-hammer pulse. *Ann Med Hist* 5, 381 (1934)

Editorial: Sir Dominic John Corrigan. *JAMA* 180, 146 (1962)

Mulcahy R: Sir Dominic John Corrigan. *Irish J Med Sci* 430, 454 (1961)

Obituary of Corrigan, DJC: *Br Med J* 1, 227 (1880)

Obituary of Corrigan, DJC: *The Lancet* 1, 268 (1880)

Rolleston Sir H: History of aortic regurgitation. *Ann Med Hist* 2, 271, third series (1940)

Widdess JDH: Corrigan's button. *Irish J Med Sci* 495, 137 (1967)

Williamson RT: Sir Dominic Corrigan. *Ann Med Hist* 7, 354 (1925)

Willius FA, Keys TE: Sir Dominic John Corrigan. In *Classics of Cardiology*, Vol. 2, Dover Publications, New York, (1941) 419

Jean-Nicolas Corvisart

J. D. CANTWELL, M.D.

Preventive Medicine Center, Cardiac Rehabilitation, and the Internal Medicine Training Program, Georgia Baptist Medical Center, Atlanta, Georgia, USA

Upon the muscular efficacy of the heart depends life itself.
—Corvisart

He was one of Napoleon's physicians, which alone would have marked him for historical significance. His contributions to medicine and cardiology went far beyond that, however, for he was one of the most brilliant physicians in the first half of the nineteenth century.[1–12]

Jean-Nicolas Corvisart (Fig. 1) was born in the Ardennes region of France in 1755, in the small village of Dricourt. He was expected to follow in the footsteps of his father, a lawyer with the parliament under Louis XV. However, he found the study of law rather dull compared with what he saw on visits to the wards and lecture rooms of the Hôtel Dieu, Paris's largest hospital, where he rented a room while attending law school.

Early Years

Corvisart became an outstanding medical student at the Faculté de Médecine, noted for his work ethic, powers of observation, and independent spirit. He was stocky in build, vigorous in manner, and rather outspoken, not afraid to deviate with tradition. Upon graduation from medical school in 1782 he applied for a job at the new Hôpital des Paroisses, which had been financed by French Minister of Finance Necker. His application was denied by Madame Necker, probably because Corvisart refused to don a powdered wig.

His early practice of medicine was conducted among the poor of Saint-Sulpice. At the Hôpital de la Charité, a large teaching center, he came under the influence of the noted physician, Dubois de Rochefort. His first published work was a eulogy to this fine teacher, in 1789, the same year that the revolution began in France.

The quality of medical education in France deteriorated for several years after the revolution, but in 1794 the young French Republic initiated a new system. Corvisart became professor of medicine at La Charité, where his reputation as a skilled diagnostician and excellent teacher grew. He gained considerable experience with Auenbrugger's technique of percussion, studying it in both patients and cadavers. As Robinson stated, "before Corvisart, percussion was the secret of a few; after Corvisart, percussion became the property of the profession."[8]

In 1797, Corvisart translated into French Maximillian Stoll's book on fevers. He became professor of clinical medicine at the Collège de France. He typically taught students (including Dupuytren, Bayle, Laennec, Cuvier, and Bretonneau) in the mornings and saw private patients in the afternoons. His lectures were noted for ". . . elegance of form and exactness of logical thought."[2] In his spare time he edited the *Journal de Médecine, Chirurgie et Pharmacie*.

Textbook on Heart Disease

In 1806, Corvisart published his best known work, *Essay on the Diseases and Organic Lesions of the Heart and Large Vessels*. It was a significant advance since Senac's textbook of cardiology (1749), placing additional emphasis on clinical aspects, yet still emphasizing anatomical and necropsy findings.

The book was based on Corvisart's clinical lectures, assembled by one of his students, C. N. Horeau. It classified heart disease on the basis of the anatomical tissues involved, such as the pericardium, muscle, and fibrous and tendinous structures. Corvisart distinguished between cardiac hypertrophy and dilatation (using the terms "active" and "passive" aneurysms). He considered cardiac disorders to be organic and functional, and believed that temperament played a role in heart disease.

Corvisart was one of the first to emphasize the importance in cardiac examination of palpable precordial thrills, especially in mitral stenosis. He described the clinical symptoms, along with the postmortem findings, in tricuspid stenosis. Disorders of the pericardium were discussed, including fibrinous pericarditis, tubercles of the pericardium, and the concept of pancarditis. He believed that valvular vegetations could become dislodged, with resultant symptoms of dyspnea, fever, and palpitations. In retrospect, he was probably describing instances of bacterial endocarditis.

Curiously, angina pectoris was not mentioned, even though Heberden had written of it nearly a quarter of a century earlier. Digitalis was also omitted, although Withering published his findings in 1785. Herrick speculated that war between England and France, slowing transmission of medical news between these countries—or possibly national pride—may have been a factor in the omission.

Fig. 1 Jean-Nicolas Corvisart (1755–1821). Reproduced with permission from the National Library of Medicine.

Translation of Auenbrugger's Book

Corvisart did the second French translation of Auenbrugger's book on percussion in 1808, a year before Auenbrugger's death. The title was *New Method for Recognizing the Internal Disorders of the Chest*. He added his own experience with this diagnostic technique, but gave full credit to Auenbrugger, writing:

I might easily have elevated myself to the rank of an author, if I had elaborated anew the doctrine of Auenbrugger and published an independent work on percussion. In this way, however, I should have sacrificed the name of Auenbrugger to my own vanity, a thing which I am unwilling to do. It is he, and the beautiful invention which of right belongs to him, that I desire to recall to life.[3]

In the preface to his translation, Corvisart stated: "I declare from experience, that this sign of which I treat is one of the greatest importance, not only in detecting disease, but also in curing it, and therefore merits first place after exploration of the pulse and respiration."[1] When his student, Laennec, introduced the stethoscope and the technique of auscultation, the methods of modern cardiac physical diagnosis—inspection, palpation, percussion, and auscultation—became complete.

Personal Physician to Napoleon Bonaparte

According to one source, Napoleon suffered from symptoms of respiratory distress and was told of Corvisart, a spe-

cialist in disorders of the chest. The latter subsequently "tapped the imperial thorax with his finger-tips,"[8] beginning a relationship that lasted from 1804 until Napoleon's fall from power in 1815.

Napoleon was a difficult patient, demanding satisfactory explanations of every symptom and each therapeutic step, and often obstinately refusing to take prescribed medications. "I do not believe in medicine," he once said, "but I do believe in Corvisart."[11] This vote of confidence may have related more to the physician's general medical skills than to his cardiopulmonary expertise. During the Italian campaign, Napoleon developed a severe itching syndrome, which he subsequently transmitted to his wife, Josephine. He "cursed and reviled" several physicians who unsuccessfully tried various ointments and potions.[4] Corvisart was summoned, and cured the scabies without knowing the etiology, using a mixture of alcohol, olive oil, and powdered cevadilla (the latter containing the drug, veratrine). Another time Corvisart found the emperor enraged, managed to calm him, and discovered the cause of his great discomfort—part of a toothpick was stuck between two of his teeth.

Later Years: and Laennec's Tribute

With the fall of Napoleon, Corvisart's own health began to fail. He severed all political ties, turned down the advances of the new government, and retired. In 1820, the year before his death, he did meet with the Academie Royale de Médecine, which included the most prominent physicians in France, more than half of whom had been his students.

His most famous student, Rene Laennec, had a high regard for Corvisart, and also for Bayle. In his preface to *A Treatise on the Diseases of the Chest*, Laennec wrote:

If I have occasionally differed from these distinguished authors, I trust that no one will misinterpret my motives. No one can be more sensible of their merits both as men and physicians, than myself. At the very time I question their opinions, I most willingly confess my great obligations to them: It is much easier to improve a field already cultivated, than to reclaim a wild and barren soil.[7]

He went on to say of Corvisart's writings,

. . . it is to be regretted that those of them published by others, are far from giving a just idea of the author's merits. The uncertainty of the signs of diseases, and the vagueness of description in these, appear particularly striking to those who, like myself, were his pupils, and habitual witnesses of the boldness and precision of his diagnostics. This defect, no doubt, partly depends on the incommunicable tact of the physician, which forms so great a part of the art, and which M. Corvisart possessed in the highest degree.[7]

Unfortunately for Napoleon, his physicians on St. Helena lacked Corvisart's bedside skills, and misdiagnosed his perforated peptic ulcer and peritonitis. He died in 1821, the same year as the physician who had gained his confidence and esteem, initially by percussing his chest and later curing his itch.

References

1. Corvisart JN: *An Essay on the Organic Diseases and Lesions of the Heart and Great Vessels.* (Translated from the French by J. Gates, with an introduction by D.W. Richards). Hafner Publishing Co., New York (1962)
2. Castiglioni A: *A History of Medicine.* (Translated from the Italian, Ed. E.B. Krumbhaar.) Alfred A. Knopf, New York, (1941)
3. Corvisart JN: *Nouveau Méthode pour reconnaître les maladies internales de la poitrine.* Paris, 1808.
4. Dale PM: *Medical Biographies. The Ailments of Thirty-three Famous Persons.* University of Oklahoma Press, Norman, OK (1952)
5. Herrick JB: *A Short History of Cardiology.* Charles C Thomas, Springfield (1942)
6. Holmes WR: The illness and death of Napoleon. *J Med Assoc Ga* 72 (1983) 201–204
7. Laennec RTH: *A Treatise on the Diseases of the Chest, in Which They are Described According to Their Anatomical Characters, and Their Diagnosis Established on a New Principle by Means of Acoustic Instruments.* (Translated by John Forbes.) Underwood, London (1921)
8. Robinson V: *The Story of Medicine.* Tudor Publishing Co., New York (1931)
9. Roth N: *Medtronic News* (Summer 1986)
10. Selwyn-Brown A: *The Physician Throughout the Ages.* Capehart-Brown Co., Inc., New York (1928)
11. Siegrist HE: *The Great Doctors.* W. W. Norton & Co., New York (1933)
12. Willius FA, Dry TJ: *A History of the Heart and the Circulation.* W.B. Saunders Co., Philadelphia (1948)

Caleb Hillier Parry

W. Bruce Fye, m.d., m.a.

Department of Cardiology, Marshfield Clinic, Marshfield, Wisconsin, USA

Caleb Hillier Parry was born on October 21, 1755, at Cirencester, Gloucester, England.[1–3] The son of a Presbyterian minister, he was the eldest of ten children. Following preliminary education at Cirencester and Warrington, Parry enrolled in Edinburgh University where he studied medicine under William Cullen. At this time Edinburgh was a leading center of medical education.[4] Parry received his medical degree from the ancient university in 1778. His Edinburgh education was supplemented by an apprenticeship to Thomas Denman at the Middlesex Hospital in London.

Parry married in 1778 and, after a tour of Holland, Flanders, and France, settled in Bath where he remained for the rest of his life. Initially his practice grew slowly, but Parry was reassured by his former teacher Denman: "I am not surprised to find your receipts come in slowly at present, but all young practitioners think, when they set up their standard, that the world should immediately flock to it, and they are generally disturbed when they find the contrary. But all business is progressive, and the steps now taken may be so calculated as to produce their effect ten years hence.[2]

As Denman predicted, Parry's reputation and practice grew. Eventually many members of the British nobility sought consultations with him. A contemporary biographer wrote of Parry, "As a practitioner, he was distinguished by a clear insight into the nature of various maladies, by promptness and decision in their treatment, and by a marked humanity and kindness to his patients."[2] Parry also cared for thousands of indigent patients in Bath. An energetic and inquisitive physician, he consistently recorded the details of interesting cases he saw. His large clinical experience, combined with a curious and orderly mind, made it possible for Parry to make important contributions to the medical literature.

A prolific author, Parry wrote a number of papers and several books. His classic monograph on angina pectoris was published in Bath in 1799.[5] It had been nearly three decades since William Heberden published the first description of angina.[6] His observations stimulated several British physicians to study angina during the closing years of the eighteenth century.[7] Among them was Parry's childhood friend and schoolmate Edward Jenner, best known for introducing vaccination. Parry credited Jenner with elaborating the theory that "ossification" or calcification of the coronary arteries was responsible for angina pectoris.

Parry's book on angina was based on a presentation he made before a medical society in Gloucestershire in 1788. He expressed surprise that the distressing symptom had only recently been described: "Although there can be no reason to doubt that mankind must have been subject to this disorder from the remotest antiquity, it is somewhat extraordinary that so many ages should have elapsed without any notice of its existence either as a distinct disease, or as a variety of one commonly known."[5]

In addition to presenting his own experience with patients suffering from attacks of angina, Parry included a comprehensive summary of earlier case reports. When his book appeared in 1799, Parry concluded from a thorough review of the literature that only ten essays on angina pectoris had been published and only nine patients with anginal attacks had undergone autopsy. Parry's case reports were remarkably detailed and included the relevant pathological findings. He practiced in an era when there was growing emphasis on clinico-pathological correlation.

Angina pectoris, Parry noted, tended to occur in obese males over the age of fifty. "The first symptom is an uneasy sensation, which has been variously denominated a stricture, an anxiety, or a pain, extending generally from about the middle of the sternum across the left breast and, in certain stages of the disorder, usually stretching into the left arm a little above the elbow." Parry found that angina was usually precipitated by exertion, "such as walking, particularly up hill or up stairs, against the wind, or in a quick pace," and was relieved by rest.[5]

Although very few cases had been published in which an association between calcified coronary arteries and angina pectoris had been demonstrated, Parry concluded "that there is an important connection between the rigid and obstructed state of these vessels and the disease in question [angina pectoris]."[5] Although he acknowledged that degenerative changes of the aortic valve could "cooperate" with ossification of the coronary arteries to cause angina, Parry rejected the theory that aortic valve disease alone could cause this complaint.

Thus, Parry attributed angina pectoris to "induration" and "ossification" of the coronary arteries. Addressing the consequences of these degenerative changes of the coronary arteries, he claimed, "we can suppose that the coronaries may be so obstructed as to intercept the blood, which should be the prop-

FIG 1   Caleb Hillier Parry, 1755–1822

er support of the muscular fibres of the heart that [the] organ must become thin and flaccid, and unequal to the task of circulation."[5] As one would expect from the title of his book, Parry included an extensive chapter on syncope. He attributed many cases of syncope to cardiac disorders that resulted in inadequate cerebral perfusion. This view was supported, Parry believed, by the empiric observation that the common procedure of therapeutic bleeding often resulted in the patient fainting.

To prevent the development of coronary artery disease, Parry urged moderation in eating and drinking. The Bath physician was pessimistic about the willingness of patients to follow this suggestion, however: "It is sufficient for me to have mentioned these means of prevention, little expecting that a knowledge of them will induce mankind to guard against a rare and remote effect, while they are not deterred from habits of intemperance by those fevers, dropsies, and other diseases, which they every day see to be their equally-fatal and more immediate consequences."[5] It seems that human nature has changed little in two centuries. In addition to moderation in diet and the avoidance of "flesh meats," Parry advocated "moderate bodily exercise" as a means of making the development of coronary artery disease less likely.

Parry's monograph on angina pectoris was warmly received and was translated into German in 1801 and French in

1806. His fame and his practice grew steadily during the early years of the 19th century. Although Parry wrote on many other subjects, he maintained his interest in diseases of the cardiovascular system.

Parry first described the phenomenon of bradycardia in response to carotid massage. In 1815, he wrote: "[If] strong pressure is made on one, and more especially on both carotids … the action of the heart will, in many instances, be immediately diminished as to frequency and force."[8] Several papers on disorders of the heart and circulation were included in two volumes of his medical essays that appeared posthumously in 1825.[9]

One of Parry's most important contributions was his classic description of exophthalmic goiter.[10] He saw his first case of the condition in 1786, and his series of eight cases was reported in his posthumous works. He referred to the condition as one of "enlargement of the thyroid gland in connection with enlargement or palpitation of the heart."[9] Parry's description of his first patient provides a vivid picture of what has come to be known as Grave's disease, although Parry's publication preceded that of Robert Graves by a decade.

Parry saw a 37-year-old woman in 1786 who was thought to have had rheumatic fever six years earlier. When she saw Parry she complained of palpitations that were aggravated by exercise. Parry found her pulse to be 156, strong, but irregular. He noted that she "had no cough, tendency to fainting, or blueness of the skin, but had twice or thrice been seized in the night with a sense of constriction and difficulty of breathing, which was attended with a spitting of a small quantity of blood." She also had frequent episodes of severe sharp pain in the lower sternal area.

Three months after delivering a child the patient developed a mass on the right side of her neck that continued to enlarge. When Parry examined her he found an "enormous" thyroid gland occupying both sides of her neck, "protruding forwards before the margin of the lower jaw." Her eyes "protruded from their sockets, and the countenance exhibited an appearance of agitation and distress." The patient deteriorated, developing massive edema, ascites, and oliguria. Parry concluded that she had probably died when her visits to him ceased. On the basis of his eight cases Parry concluded that there was "some connection between the malady of the heart and the bronchocele."[9]

In 1816, Parry published an important monograph on the pulse that included a summary of more than two dozen experiments he had conducted on a variety of mammals.[11] In this book he discussed the pulsatile expansion of the arteries and the importance of collaterals. Parry refuted the theory that arterial pulsation was due to an intrinsic property of the vessels themselves. He attributed their motion to the force given to the blood by ventricular systole.

This book would be Parry's last contribution. He suffered a stroke in 1816 that resulted in hemiplegia and aphasia. Parry died six years later at the age of sixty-seven and was buried in Bath.

References

1. Fye WB: *Caleb Hillier Parry*. Birmingham, AL: Gryphon Editions, Ltd., 1987

2. MacMichael W: "Parry" In *Lives of British Physicians*, 2nd ed., p. 275–304. London: John Murray, 1830

3. Rolleston HD: "Caleb Hillier Parry, M.D., F.R.S." *Ann Med Hist* 1925;7:205–215

4. Risse GB: *Hospital Life in Enlightenment Scotland: Care and Teaching at the Royal Infirmary of Edinburgh*. Cambridge: Cambridge University Press, 1986

5. Parry, CH: *An inquiry into the Symptoms and Causes of the Syncope Anginosa Commonly called Angina Pectoris*. Bath, England: R. Cruttwell, 1799

6. Heberden, W: "Some account of a disorder of the breast." *Medical Transactions Published by the College of Physicians of London* 1772;2:59–67

7. Leibowitz, JO: *The History of Coronary Heart Disease*. London: Wellcome Institute of the History of Medicine, 1970

8. Parry, CH: *Elements of Pathology and Therapeutics. Vol. 1. General Pathology*. London: Underwood, 1815

9. Parry, CH: *Collections from the Unpublished Medical Writings of the Late Caleb Hillier Parry*. 2 vols. London: Underwood, 1825

10. Medvei, VC: *A History of Endocrinology*. Boston: MTP Press Ltd., 1982

11. Parry, CH: *An Experimental inquiry into the Nature, Cause, and Varieties of the Arterial Pulse; and into Certain Other Properties of the Larger Arteries, in Animals with Warm Blood*. London: Underwood, 1816

René-Joseph-Hyacinthe Bertin*

W. Bruce Fye, M.D., M.A.

Cardiology Department, Marshfield Clinic, Marshfield, Wisconsin, USA

One of the pioneers of 19th century cardiology, René-Joseph-Hyacinthe Bertin was born on April 10, 1757, in Gohard, France.[1,2] His father, Exupère-Joseph Bertin, was a prominent physician who is remembered eponymically for his description of invaginated renal cortical tissue, the "columns of Bertin." After studying in Paris the younger Bertin received his medical degree in 1791 from Montpelier, one of Europe's leading medical schools. He gained practical experience as a military physician during the French Revolution and in the Napoleonic wars.

After military service Bertin returned to Paris where he became physician-in-chief to the Cochin Hospital, one of Paris's busiest hospitals. Disorders of the cardiovascular system were of special interest to Bertin and his assistant Jean Baptiste Bouillaud. Their rich clinical experience was reflected in Bertin's 1824 monograph on diseases of the heart and great vessels that was edited by Bouillaud.

During the first half of the 19th century Paris was the world's center for medical education.[3] Ambitious American medical graduates often supplemented their meager training at home with study in the hospitals of Paris. Several leading French medical texts were translated into English by American physicians. Among these were René Théophile Hyacinthe Laennec's book on auscultation, Jean Nicholas Corvisart's work on diseases of the heart, and several of Xavier Bichat's books on pathology. Bertin's monograph on heart disease was translated by Charles Chauncy of Portsmouth, New Hampshire, in 1833.[4]

Although Chauncy acknowledged the significance of Laennec's book on auscultation and diseases of the chest and credited Corvisart with being the first to undertake a serious study of heart disease, he claimed that Bertin's was the most comprehensive book on cardiovascular diseases. Chauncy's enthusiasm for Bertin's monograph was shared by the Royal Academy of Sciences of the Institute of France. A committee of this prestigious society praised the book.

One of the earliest advocates of auscultation, Bertin enthusiastically described the practical value of this new technique and its utility in elucidating cardiovascular disorders. He also emphasized the role of auscultation in elucidating the pathophysiology of cardiac disorders: "The happy discovery of auscultation has diffused, within a few years, more light on the diagnosis of the diseases of the heart than all the other modes of exploration had done for two centuries."[4a]

Bertin possessed unusual insight into the physical principles responsible for heart murmurs associated with valvular stenosis. "Nothing appears to us more easy to be conceived than the mechanism of the sound which accompanies the constriction of the orifices of the heart. The blood being obliged to pass from the cavity of the auricles or of the ventricles, across a very narrow opening, must necessarily produce more or less friction; and it is precisely this friction which produces the murmur."[4b]

One of the chief contributions of physicians of the so-called French school to medical education and to the science and practice of medicine was their emphasis on clinico-pathological correlation. Reflecting this philosophy Bertin was a strong believer in the value of autopsies. He thought that "pathological anatomy and physiology are the great luminaries of medicine" and without them "this science would languish in eternal obscurity."[4c]

Therapeutic bleeding was a mainstay of medical practice in Bertin's era. He reported several cases of patients with symptoms consistent with congestive heart failure who improved in response to bleeding. One patient, a 35-year-old mattress maker who had suffered from progressive dyspnea on exertion for several years, illustrates this point. Repeated bleedings with leeches led to dramatic improvement in his dyspnea, orthopnea, and paroxysmal dyspnea. One dramatic episode was characterized by "violent dyspnoea; almost convulsive contractions of the common respiratory muscles,... impending suffocation, livid face, cold sweats." The patient improved dramatically following the removal of twelve ounces of blood.[4d]

Bertin was especially interested in cardiac hypertrophy and emphasized that earlier authors often confused hypertrophy and dilatation. He acknowledged that these two processes often coexisted but stressed that they also occurred independently. As early as 1811 Bertin had pointed out that "dilatation does not constantly accompany thickening of the walls of the heart; that this thickening may take place while the cavity preserves its natural

*Adapted with permission from an essay prepared for the Classics of Cardiology Library, Gryphon Editions, Delran, NJ.

capacity; that even hypertrophy may coincide with a contracted cavity, as if it had taken place at the expense of the last."[4e]

In 1806, French physician Jean Nicholas Corvisart published the first significant classification of cardiac hypertrophy. Bertin advanced his own scheme in which he distinguished three forms of hypertrophy. He termed them "simple," "eccentric," and "concentric." Simple hypertrophy was isolated thickening of the walls of the heart without chamber dilatation. In eccentric hypertrophy the walls were thickened and the cavities were dilated. Concentric hypertrophy was characterized by thickened walls with small cardiac chamber size.

More than other contemporary medical writers, Bertin recognized the spectrum of ventricular hypertrophy. Without fully comprehending the etiology or significance of his observations, Bertin described conditions that we now recognize as ischemic myocardial damage combined with ventricular hypertrophy and idiopathic hypertrophic subaortic stenosis—he claimed that hypertrophy could be confined to the interventricular septum.

Disturbances of cardiac rhythm did not escape Bertin's notice. He distinguished continuous from intermittent palpitations. In his opinion, intermittent palpitations might be precipitated by the ingestion of alcohol, tea, and coffee, and were commonly associated with "hysteria, hypochondriasis, and melancholy." Bertin thought that "continuous palpitations deserve the most attention...they are most frequently associated with some lesion of the heart."[4f] He recognized that sudden death was often due to diseases of the heart and aorta and emphasized that syncope was not a disease itself, but was a symptom of some underlying abnormality.

Our current aggressive approach to the evaluation and treatment of patients with known or suspected heart disease, encouraged by financial constraints and government regulations, contrasts dramatically with the leisurely pace of medical care in the Napoleonic era. Few patients went to French (or American) hospitals in the 19th century and when they did, their stays were often lengthy. For example, Bertin described the case of a 56-year-old porter who entered the Cochin Hospital on October 25, 1821. "We could not examine him until the month of January, 1822, when he said he had been sick for four months only."[4g]

Bertin's monograph on diseases of the heart and blood vessels is very comprehensive. Widely heralded in its day, it now provides valuable insight into the practice of medicine in the early 19th century. This was a very dynamic era: cardiac diagnosis was advancing dramatically as a result of the introduction of the stethoscope and emphasis on careful clinicopathological correlation. Bertin played an important role in this evolution although he died in 1828, shortly after the publication of his book.

References

1. Dezeimeris J: René-Joseph-Hyacinthe Bertin. In *Dictionnaire Historique de la Médécine Ancienne et Moderne.* Chez Bechet, Paris (1828) 1,372–374
2. Hirsch A: René-Joseph-Hyacinthe Bertin. In *Biographisches Lexicon der hervorragenden Ärzte aller Zeiten und Völker.* 2nd Ed. Urban & Schwarzenberg, Berlin (1929) 1, 505
3. Ackerknecht EH: *Medicine at the Paris Hospital,* 1794–1848. Johns Hopkins Press, Baltimore (1967)
4. Bertin RJ: *Treatise on the Diseases of the Heart and Great Vessels.* Carey, Lea & Blanchard, Philadelphia (1834) (a) xliii; (b) 226; (c) xlix; (d) 109; (e) 282; (f) 417; (g) 97

John Ferriar

W. Bruce Fye, M.D., M.A.

Department of Cardiology, Marshfield Clinic, Marshfield, Wisconsin, USA

British physician John Ferriar (Fig. 1) is included in the Profiles in Cardiology series because he published the first monograph on digitalis after William Withering (1785). Ferriar was the first to suggest that digitalis was beneficial in dropsy (severe congestive heart failure), in part because it appeared to act directly on the heart. He was also one of the first physicians to recognize an association between acute rheumatism and heart disease.

Ferriar was born in Oxnam, Roxburghshire, England, on November 6, 1761.[1,2] He received his M.D. from the University of Edinburgh and practiced briefly in Stockton-on-Tees before moving to Manchester in 1785. A thoughtful and inquisitive physician, Ferriar took notes on interesting cases, and between 1792 and 1813 he published four volumes of essays based on his extensive clinical experience.[3–6]

The first volume of Ferriar's essays included an 86-page article on remedies for dropsy and a paper on dilatation of the heart. The monograph on dropsy included 47 brief case reports and a tabular summary of outcomes. Ferriar compared the outcomes of patients treated with the three main remedies he used: digitalis, cream of tartar, and "tonic pills." He admitted that "On reviewing these observations, which were made without . . . predilection for any remedy, the result appears not highly in favor of the digitalis." Nevertheless, Ferriar concluded, "From what I have seen of its effects, I shall hereafter give it a preference in most cases of dropsy."[3]

Ferriar extended his observations on the treatment of dropsy in 1795. He published case reports on 56 additional patients and summarized their treatments and outcomes in a table. Based on his total experience with 103 patients, Ferriar thought that cream of tartar was more effective than digitalis in the treatment of dropsy. Still, he concluded that the combination was probably the best approach for treating this problematic condition.[4] As Ferriar's experience with digitalis increased, he became more impressed with its value.

Ferriar published *An Essay on the Medical Properties of the Digitalis Purpurea, or Foxglove* in 1799.[7] As in his earlier essays, this small 66-page book provides interesting insight into medical practice of this era. He was impressed with the value of digitalis and credited Withering with teaching physicians how to use it "with safety and success."[7a] Ferriar regarded digitalis "as a remedy of the highest class" and claimed that "its exhibition has become as familiar in my practice, as that of peruvian bark, or opium, with which it de-

serves to be ranked, and I give it with as little dread, (though never without caution) as either of those medicines."[7b]

Ferriar knew that digitalis was a potentially dangerous drug. He encouraged doctors to start therapy with the smallest possible dose and to increase the amount prescribed with "the most scrupulous care."[7c] One effect of foxglove that especially impressed Ferriar was its ability to slow the pulse. He explained, "while [digitalis] lessens the frequency and quickness of the arterial contraction, it often encreases [*sic*], at the same time, the secretion in the kidnies [*sic*]." Based on his experience, he concluded that "the diuretic power of Digitalis does not appear to me a constant and essential quality of the plant; the power of reducing the pulse is its true characteristic."[7d]

Ferriar emphasized the special utility of digitalis in the treatment of palpitations. He felt that it was "strongly indicated" in that condition. "Even in cases depending on organic lesions of the heart, or great blood-vessels," Ferriar claimed, "it has relieved the symptoms, and rendered life not only longer, but more supportable."[7e] His growing enthusiasm for digitalis led him to recommend it for a variety of noncardiac conditions, including pleurisy and other types of active inflammation. But Ferriar acknowledged that he had not been able to verify all of the claims that others had made on behalf of digitalis.

Based on his own experience with digitalis, brief articles published by other physicians, and verbal reports of his colleagues, Ferriar concluded that (1) the medicine was useful in the treatment of active hemorrhage because it retarded the velocity of the circulation; (2) the diuretic action of digitalis was independent of its effects on the velocity of the circulation; (3) digitalis was of benefit in the treatment of tuberculosis; (4) it was effective in the treatment of pleural effusion; (5) it was helpful in chronic cough, spasmodic asthma, and palpitations; (6) it was indicated in "most cases of dropsy" because of its diuretic powers; (7) it must be administrated cautiously if given on a regular basis; and (8) "in simple inflammatory diseases" it might take the place of "repeated bleeding and purging."[7f]

Still, Ferriar conceded that more experience was necessary before it could be concluded confidently that digitalis was of definite benefit in conditions other than dropsy. He proposed what might be considered an antecedent of the controlled clinical trial:

FIG. 1   John Ferriar (1761–1815).

Conclusions of so much moment to the welfare of mankind, cannot be formed from the events of a few weeks or months. They must depend on an estimate of the greater number of results, from many cases, under circumstances nearly similar. This is the foundation of experience with every rational man, not only in medicine, but in all reasoning concerning probable evidence. The mischief of precipitate conclusions is nowhere more sensibly felt, than in medical practice.[7g]

Ferriar was also much interested in literature and wrote essays, poetry, and plays. He formed a large library and wrote an essay on bibliomania, a term applied to collectors whose quest for books becomes a consuming passion. He died in Manchester on February 4, 1815.

References

1. Brockbank EM: *John Ferriar: Public Health Work, Tristram Shandy, other Essays and Verses. William Osler: His Interest in Ferriar, Biographical Notes*. London: William Heinemann Medical Books, 1950

2. Ruhrah J: John Ferriar. *Ann Med Hist* 1921;3:349–353

3. Ferriar J: *Medical Histories and Reflections*, p. 94–95. Warrington: T. Cadell, 1792

4. Ferriar J: *Medical Histories and Reflections*. Volume 2. London: Cadell and Davies, 1795

5. Ferriar J: *Medical Histories and Reflections*. Volume 3. London: Cadell and Davies, 1798

6. Ferriar J: *Medical Histories and Reflections*. Volume 4. London: Cadell and Davies, 1813

7. Ferriar J: *An Essay on the Medical Properties of the Digitalis Purpurea, or Foxglove*, a, p. ii; b, p. iv; c, p. 9; d, p. 13; e, p. 34; f, p. 47–49; g, p. 46–47. Manchester: Cadell & Davies, 1799

Julien Jean César Legallois

W. Bruce Fye, M.D., M.A.

Department of Cardiology, Marshfield Clinic, Marshfield, Wisconsin, USA

Julien Jean César Legallois was a pioneer of vivisection who helped to inaugurate the intellectual tradition of experimental physiology in France continued by Magendie, Bernard, and Brown-Sequard.[1] The son of a Breton farmer, Legallois was born in Cherrueix, near Dol, France, February 1, 1770.[2,3] After completing preliminary courses at the Collège de Dol, he was among the first students at the new Paris School of Medicine.[4]

Shortly after graduation, Legallois inaugurated a series of experiments on the essential functions of the animal organism. He summarized this research in his 1812 book, *Expériences sur le principe de la vie*, which was translated into English the following year.[5] A challenging obstetrical case led Legallois to wonder how long a full-term fetus could survive without breathing after the umbilical cord was cut. In attempting to study this question experimentally, he examined the role of the lungs, the heart, and the nervous system in maintaining life. He was familiar with the earlier experiments of Albrecht von Haller, Francesco Redi, Xavier Bichat, Georg Prochaska, and Charles Bonnet, each of whom contributed to the growing understanding of the complex interrelationships of the organs necessary for life.[6]

Legallois performed a series of experiments to explore the mechanism of respiration. By decapitating animals or otherwise destroying the nervous connections of the brain and spinal cord, he concluded that the accessory nerve of the eighth cranial nerve played a critical role in breathing. Legallois also determined that respiration was controlled by a respiratory center located in the medulla oblongata. According to historians Clark and Hacyna, this was the first time that "an area of brain substance ... having a specific function had been defined accurately by experiment."[7]

Legallois's studies of the heartbeat were also of great significance. Familiar with the experiments of the Swiss physiologist Albrecht van Haller on the irritability of muscular tissues, Legallois hoped to prove that the brain was directly responsible for the control and maintenance of the heartbeat.[8] While he did not reject totally Haller's myogenic theory of the heartbeat, Legallois argued that his belief—that intrinsic muscular irritability was the sole cause of the heartbeat—was wrong. Legallois designed a series of experiments on rabbits to clarify the role of the nervous system in stimulating the heartbeat and maintaining the circulation. He attempted to disrupt the neural influences on the heart in various ways including decapitation, destruction of the spinal cord, and asphyxia by drowning.

Haller and others had shown that the hearts of experimental animals often continued to beat spontaneously for several minutes after they were removed from the body. Legallois found that the denervated heart was not sufficiently strong to propel blood through the blood vessels, however. Legallois emphasized that "nervous power" produced in the brain and the "spinal marrow"

and distributed to the body through the nerves played a significant role in the motion of the heart. Although later investigators disproved some of Legallois's theories, his experiments showed that there was an important relationship between the heart and nervous system.

Legallois developed a primitive isolated heart-lung preparation in rabbits in which he ligated the inferior vena cava, aorta, carotid arteries, and jugular veins and ventilated the lungs through a pewter syringe inserted into the trachea of a decapitated rabbit. In the course of these experiments, he made an observation that anticipated the development of the heart-lung machine nearly 150 years later: "If the place of the heart could be supplied by injection, and if, for the regular continuance of this injection, there could be furnished a quantity of arterial blood, whether natural, or artificially formed ... then life might be indefinitely maintained."[5,10]

Shortly after the appearance of his book, Legallois was appointed physician to the Bicêtre, a large hospital on the outskirts of Paris. This pioneer of experimental physiology died of pneumonia two years later at the age of 44. Through his research and writings, Legallois inspired others to use vivisection to expand knowledge about the structure and functions of living organisms. Unlike his successors, he did not confront the hostility of the organized antivivisectionist movement which arose in the middle of the nineteenth century.[11]

References

1. Lesch JE: *Science and Medicine in France: The Emergence of Experimental Physiology 1790–1855*. Harvard University Press, Cambridge (1984)
2. Fye, WB: *Julien Jean César Legallois*. Gryphon Editions, Birmingham, Ala. (1989)
3. Kruta V: Julien Jean César Legallois. In *Dictionary of Scientific Biography*, Vol. 8. Charles Scribner's Sons, New York (1973) 132–135
4. Ackerknecht E: *Medicine at the Paris Hospital, 1794–1848*. Johns Hopkins University Press, Baltimore (1967)
5. Legallois JJC: *Experiments on the Principle of Life, and Particularly on the Principle of the Motions of the Heart, and on the Seat of this Principle*. Translated by N.C. and J.G. Nancrede. M. Thomas, Philadelphia (1813)
6. Gasking E: *The Rise of Experimental Biology*. Random House, New York (1970)
7. Clarke E, Jacyna LS: *Nineteenth-Century Origins of the Neuroscientific Concepts*. University of California Press, Berkeley and Los Angeles (1987) 246
8. Fye WB: The origin of the heartbeat: A tale of frogs, jellyfish, and turtles. *Circulation* 76, 493–500 (1987)
9. Fye WB: H. Newell Martin and the isolated heart preparation: The link between the frog and open heart surgery. *Circulation* 73, 857–864 (1986)
10. French RD: *Antivivisection and Medical Science in Victorian Society*. Princeton University Press, Princeton (1975)

Marie-François-Xavier Bichat

W. BRUCE FYE, M.D., M.A.

Department of Cardiology, Marshfield Clinic, Marshfield, Wisconsin, USA

Marie-François-Xavier Bichat (Fig. 1) made important observations on the physiology of sudden death. He was born on November 14, 1771, in the village of Thoirette-en-Bas, near Lyons, France.[1,2] He played a major role in establishing Paris as the world's center for medical education and research in the early nineteenth century.[3,4] Bichat's father, Jean-Baptiste, was a graduate of the medical school at Montpelier and practiced in Poncin. After completing his preliminary education in Nantua and Lyon in 1791, Xavier began medical training at the Hôtel Dieu in Lyon where he worked under Marc-Antoine Petit, a famous surgeon.

Bichat entered the medical profession at a time when medicine, like all aspects of French culture, was undergoing dramatic reorganization as a result of the Revolution.[5] After France declared war on Austria in 1792, Bichat served in the military hospitals of Lyon and Bourg. He moved to Paris in 1794 where he studied at the Grand Hôpital de l'Humanité (Hôtel Dieu) under the distinguished surgeon Pierre-Joseph Desault. Recognizing Bichat's abilities and his potential, Desault got the young man an appointment as a *chirurgien-externe* at the hospital and invited him to live with his family. After Desault died in 1795, Bichat edited his mentor's writings with the help of Jean Nicholas Corvisart.

By the end of the century, Bichat was busy teaching private courses in anatomy, physiology, and surgery, and caring for patients at the Grand Hôpital. A pioneer of vivisection in France, he adapted surgical techniques he had learned during the Revolution for his animal experiments. He also used vivisection in his physiology courses.[6] As a founder of the Société Médicale d'Emulation, Bichat (together with Corvisart, Pierre Jean Georges Cabanis, Guillaume Dupuytren, and Philippe Pinel) was recognized as a leader in French medical science.[7,8] This group contributed to the development of hospital-based teaching, the centerpiece of the Paris clinical school during the first half of the nineteenth century.

Bichat was a leading proponent of vitalism, a doctrine that rejected the notion that the principles of physics and chemistry could be applied to organic life and physiologic functions. He believed that animal organisms were imbued with certain "vital properties" that could not be reduced to simple laws of physics and chemistry. The roots of Bichat's vitalism can be traced to a group of influential eighteenth century Montpelier physicians, especially François Boissier de Sauvages (1706–1767).

By 1798 Bichat was working on several books that reflected his deep interest in anatomy and physiology and his enthusiasm for vitalism. Bichat's first book, *Traité des membranes en général et de diverses membranes en particulier*, published in 1799, included his doctrine of tissue pathology. He argued that pathology must be viewed not in terms of whole organs but in terms of the membranes or tissues that make up the organs.

Bichat proposed that just as elementary matter could unite to make more complex compounds in chemistry, the tissues combined to form various organs. He distinguished 21 different tissues according to their gross appearance, texture, and unique properties such as extensibility and contractility. He argued that these tissues were the fundamental components of all organs and bodily structures. During the mid-nineteenth century, European medical scientists such as Rudolf Virchow used the microscope to refine and extend Bichat's approach to create histology and cellular pathology.[9]

Bichat's second book, *Recherches physiologiques sur la vie et la mort*, published in 1800, reveals his passion for physiologic research. In addition to undertaking an extensive series of vivisections in an attempt to confirm his theories of the physiology of life and death, he performed experiments on decapitated humans immediately following execution by the guillotine. The first part of this important book is a theoretical discussion of the differences between animal and organic life. In the second part, Bichat describes a series of observations and experiments he undertook to study the relationships of the brain, heart, and lungs in violent or sudden death. He recognized the critical importance of all three components of the body and emphasized the functional independence of the brain and heart.

Anatomie générale appliqué à la physiologie et à la médecine, published in 1801, incorporated Bichat's vitalist ideas in a systematic discussion of anatomy. In this four-volume work, he extended his description of the tissues in health and disease. In 1801, while teaching a course in pathologic anatomy at the Hôtel-Dieu in Paris, Bichat performed more than 600 autopsies. In addition to his many anatomic observations and physiologic experiments, he contributed to the founding of experimental pharmacology by studying the effects of various drugs on animals. Bichat's final book, *Traité d'anatomie descriptive*, was completed posthumously by a cousin and a former pupil. This five-volume work consisted of a detailed exposition of the various systems of the body.

FIG. 1 Marie-François-Xavier Bichat, 1771–1802. From the collection of W. Bruce Fye, M.D.

Bichat became ill late in 1801 and died of tuberculosis on July 22, 1802. Despite his short life—he was just 30 when he died—Bichat had taught many students and had published several books. He had a profound influence on clinical teaching and medical practice in Europe and America. Johns Hop-kins internist William Sidney Thayer declared in 1902 that Bichat's greatest contribution was the "introduction into anatomy and physiology of methods of accurate, systematic observation and experiment, methods similar to those which distinguished the later clinical schools of Laennec, Louis, and the physiologic studies of Claude Bernard."[10]

References

1. Haigh E: Xavier Bichat and the medical theory of the eighteenth century. *Med Hist* (suppl 4), 1984
2. Canguilhem G: Marie-François-Xavier Bichat. In *Dictionary of Scientific Biography* (Ed. Gillespie CC), p. 122–123. New York: Charles Scribner's Sons, 1973
3. Ackerknecht EH: *Medicine at the Paris Hospital, 1794–1848.* Baltimore: Johns Hopkins Press, 1967
4. Foucault M: *The Birth of the Clinic: An Archaeology of Medical Perception.* New York: Pantheon Books, 1973
5. Vess DM: *Medical Revolution in France 1789–1796.* Gainesville: University Presses of Florida, 1975
6. Rupke NA, ed.: *Vivisection in Historical Perspective.* London: Well-come Institute, 1987
7. Lesch JE: *Science and Medicine in France: The Emergence of Experimental Physiology, 1790–1855.* Cambridge: Harvard University Press, 1984
8. Maulitz RC: *Morbid Appearances: The Anatomy of Pathology in the Early Nineteenth Century.* Cambridge: Cambridge University Press, 1987
9. Long ER: *A History of Pathology.* 2nd ed. New York: Dover Publications, Inc., 1965
10. Thayer WS: Bichat. *Bull Johns Hopkins Hosp* 1903;14:197–201

John Blackall

W. Bruce Fye, m.d., m.a.

Cardiology Department, Marshfield Clinic, Marshfield, Wisconsin, USA

John Blackall (Fig. 1) was born in Exeter, England, on December 24, 1771.[1] After preliminary education at Exeter Grammar School, he entered Balliol College, Oxford. Between 1793 and 1801, he received A.B., A.M., and M.D. degrees and got clinical experience at the Radcliffe Infirmary in Oxford. He also studied under John Latham at St. Bartholomew's Hospital in London.[2, 3] In 1801, he moved to Totnes, about 25 miles south of Exeter, where he rapidly built a large practice. Six years later, he joined the Devon and Exeter Hospital staff.

Blackall became very interested in patients with "dropsy," a term applied to conditions in which serous fluid accumulated in various cavities of the body. Based on his extensive clinical experience, Blackall published a book on the subject, *Observations on the Nature and Cure of Dropsies*, in 1813. An expanded edition was published 2 years later.[4] Various terms had already been introduced to describe localized accumulations of fluid in the body. Blackall discussed many of them in his book: "anasarca" referring to swelling of the entire body that first affected the dependent parts, "ascites" referring to the accumulation of fluid in the abdomen, "hydrothorax," the term applied to the condition we now call pleural effusion, and "dropsy" of the brain referring to hydrocephalus (a term also used in Blackall's day).

Blackall presented several brief case reports of patients with dropsy, including some he had cared for in the Devon and Exeter Hospital. He did not speculate about the causes of his patients' symptoms or physical findings; it would be several decades before physicians routinely concerned themselves with what came to be termed pathophysiology.[5] Blackall emphasized the value of studying the urine in patients with dropsy. Employing chemical techniques that had been described recently by Liverpool physician John Bostock, he used heat together with various acids and alkalies to detect albumin and other protein substances in the urine of his patients.

Blackall's therapeutics reflected the age in which he practiced—heroic treatments based on the humoral theory of disease were the rule. He bled patients with leeches, caused blisters by applying irritating compounds to the skin, and prescribed purgatives. One specific remedy for dropsy was available: British physician William Withering had introduced digitalis for this condition a generation earlier, and Blackall was impressed with its efficacy. He found it especially effective in the treatment of hydrothorax and was convinced that the plant remedy prolonged life in some instances.

Fig. 1 John Blackall, 1771–1860. (From the collection of the author.)

Blackall was also interested in angina pectoris, first reported in 1772 by London physician William Heberden. His book on dropsy included an appendix with several case reports, which represented a major addition to the literature on this condition. Blackall had cared for a 65-year-old sailor in 1798 who was hospitalized because of frequent episodes of angina brought on by minimal exertion and accompanied by dyspnea and anxiety. In the hospital, the patient's anginal attacks became increasingly frequent and prolonged. Blackall examined the man during an attack and found him acutely ill, dyspneic, and with a "very feeble and intermittent" pulse. In less than 3 hours, "whilst using some very slight exercise, [the patient] fell down and expired instantly." It is likely that Blackall's patient had suffered a myocardial infarction, but this clinical syndrome was not recognized until the twentieth century.[6]

In 1798, the relationship between angina pectoris and coronary artery disease was unknown.[7] The following year, Caleb Parry published a classic book on angina in which he stressed the "important connection between the rigid and obstructed state of these [coronary] vessels" and angina.[8] Blackall examined the coronary arteries of a 60-year-old patient who died suddenly in 1807 after a year of progressive angina. At autopsy both the left and right coronary arteries were found to have severe calcific changes. Blackall was struck by the inconsistent relationship between coronary artery disease at autopsy and angina, however. He acknowledged that there were no effective cures for angina. His recommendations focused on dietary measures and a popular form of therapy known as counterirritation. It would be more than half a century before amyl nitrite and nitroglycerin were introduced to treat anginal attacks.[9]

Blackall was elected a Fellow of the Royal College of Physicians in 1815. His book on dropsy went through four editions in London and was reprinted in America in 1820. Blackall's reputation grew and his practice thrived, in large part due to the popularity of his book on dropsy. Continuing in private practice until he was 80, Blackall died in 1860 in Exeter.

References

1. Munk W: John Blackall. In *The Roll of the Royal College of Physicians of London*, 2nd ed. Royal College of Physicians, London (1878) 3, 138–141

2. Robb-Smith AHT: *A Short History of the Radcliffe Infirmary*. United Oxford Hospitals, Oxford (1970)

3. Medvei VC, Thornton JL (eds.): *The Royal Hospital of Saint Bartholomew 1123–1973*. St. Bartholomew's Hospital, London (1974)

4. Blackall J: *Observations on the Nature and Care of Dropsies, and Particularly on the Coagulable Part of the Blood in Dropsical Urine: To Which is Added, an Appendix, Containing Several Cases of Angina Pectoris, With Dissections, &c.* (2nd ed.). Longman, Hurst, Rees, Orme, and Brown, London (1815)

5. Faber K: *Nosography: The Evolution of Clinical Medicine in Modern Times* (2nd ed.). Paul B. Hoeber, New York (1930)

6. Fye WB: The delayed recognition of acute myocardial infarction: It took half a century. *Circulation* 72, 262–271 (1985)

7. Kligfield PD: The early pathophysiologic understanding of angina pectoris. *Am J Cardiol* 50, 1433–1434 (1982)

8. Parry C: *An Inquiry into the Symptoms and Causes of the Syncope Anginosa, Commonly Called Angina Pectoris*. R. Cruttwell, Bath (1799)

9. Fye WB: Nitroglycerin: A homeopathic remedy. *Circulation* 73, 21–29 (1986)

Thomas Young

W. Bruce Fye, M.D., M.A.

Department of Cardiology, Marshfield Clinic, Marshfield, Wisconsin, USA

British natural philosopher and physician Thomas Young (Fig. 1) is remembered mainly for his pioneering observations on physiologic optics.[1,2]

Young's most significant scientific contribution was his undulatory (or wave) theory of light.[3] He is included in the Profiles in Cardiology series because of his 1809 paper, "On the Functions of the Heart and Arteries," recently declared "a milestone in cardiovascular mechanics" by a Dutch physiologist.[4]

Thomas Young was born at Milverton, near Taunton, England, on June 13, 1773. The youngest of ten children, he was a prodigy who was able to read fluently at the age of two. After receiving his preliminary education from tutors and at boarding schools, Young began to study medicine in 1792 at the Great Windmill Street School, London. This private anatomical school, founded by William Hunter, was then operated by William Cruikshank and Matthew Baillie.

Two years later, Young enrolled at Edinburgh University, then the center of medical education in the English-speaking world.[5] Too inquisitive and ambitious to focus on a single discipline, Young spent much of his time at Edinburgh studying several ancient and modern languages, mathematics, and physics—interests he maintained throughout his life. In 1795 Young traveled to the Continent to continue his education at the University of Göttingen, from which he received an M.D. degree the following year.

Shortly after he returned from the Continent, Young enrolled at Cambridge University in order to qualify for licensure by the Royal College of Physicians of London. He moved to London in 1800 to establish a medical practice and to participate in the scientific life of the metropolis. An imposing intellect who had made important observations on the physics of light and sound in his early twenties, Young moved comfortably among London's scientific elite. He had been elected a Fellow of the Royal Society in 1794, a few months after he had presented an important paper on the mechanism of accommodation of the eye to the members of this prestigious organization.

In London, Young combined his medical life with research and writing on a wide range of subjects, especially physics and natural philosophy. In 1801, the Royal Institution hired him as Professor of Natural Philosophy. Meanwhile, he continued his studies at Cambridge and received his medical degrees from the ancient university in 1803 (M.B.) and 1808

(M.D.) But Young's medical practice did not flourish; it would never be his main interest.[6] His publications, circle of friends, and affiliations reflected his focus on physics and mathematics and his interest in a variety of other subjects such as Egyptian hieroglyphics.

As part of the requirement for his Cambridge M.D. degree, Young wrote a dissertation on inflammation, then a subject of special interest to the medical community. Rather than discussing the clinical or pathologic aspects of inflammation, however, Young explored one specific aspect of the problem that many physicians would have viewed as arcane. A scientist more than a clinician, Young was interested in the physical principles that governed the circulation of the blood through the arteries.

Young presented the purely mathematical portion of his studies on hydraulics to the Royal Society in May 1808. After having reviewed contemporary theories about blood flow, Young had concluded that it was necessary to

> investigate minutely and comprehensively the motion of fluid in pipes, as affected by friction, the resistance occasioned by flexure, the laws of the propagation of an impulse through the fluid contained in an elastic tube, the magnitude of a pulsation in different parts of a conical vessel, and the effect of a contraction advancing progressively through the length of a given canal.[7]

Six months later, Young delivered the prestigious Croonian Lecture to the same group. In his address "On the function of the heart and arteries," Young reported the physiologic aspects of his research on hemodynamics. His sophistication in physics and mathematics is evident throughout his brief essay. A reductionist, Young opened his lecture by stating, "The mechanical motions, which take place in an animal body, are regulated by the same general laws as the motions of inanimate bodies." He went on to articulate certain hemodynamic principles that are now taken for granted. Young explained that the circulation of the blood depended "on the muscular and elastic powers of the heart and of the arteries" which, in turn, related directly "to the most refined departments of the theory of hydraulics."[8]

The most significant part of Young's hemodynamic investigations dealt with the elastic properties of the arteries. He explained,

FIG. 1 Thomas Young (1773–1829). Photograph from the collection of W. Bruce Fye, M.D.

We are to consider the blood in the arteries as subjected to a certain pressure, by means of which it is forced into the veins, where the tension is much less considerable; and this pressure, originating from the contractions of the heart, and continued by the tension of the arteries, is almost entirely employed in overcoming the friction of the vessels.[8]

Young estimated the magnitude of the arterial pressure and the "resistance" in the blood vessels. In discussing these concepts, he acknowledged the earlier observations of Stephen Hales on blood pressure and James Keill and Albrecht von Haller on the velocity of blood. Discussing the propagation of the pulse, Young explained that

the successive transmission of the pulsations of the heart, through the length of the arteries, is so analogous to the motion of the waves on the surface of water, or to that of a sound transmitted through the air, that the same calculations will serve for determining the principal affections of all these kinds of motion.[8]

The most important conclusion Young drew from his study of the circulation related to the supposed active role the arter-ies played in propelling the blood through the circulation. He rejected the traditional concept that the arterial walls contributed to the motion of blood. Using sophisticated mathematical and physical formulae, Young showed that "they are much less concerned in the progressive motion of the blood, than is almost universally believed." He explained that the rhythmic expansion of the arteries was due solely to the heart's action in propelling a greater volume of blood through the vessel; the arteries did not actively contract as part of this process as some observers had argued. Young concluded that "in the ordinary state of the circulation, the muscular powers of the arteries have very little effect in propelling the blood."

Although Young was elected physician to St. George's Hospital in 1811, his medical practice was never especially successful. A contemporary biographer noted that Young "was not a popular physician. He wanted that confidence or assurance which is so necessary to the successful exercise of his profession."[9]

Young gave up his medical practice in 1818 to devote his attention to his scientific and antiquarian interests. That year he was appointed Superintendent of the *Nautical Almanac* and Secretary of the Board of Longitude, reflecting his interest in celestial navigation. Young died at the age of 56 having suffered recurrent attacks of "asthma." At autopsy, he was found to have marked left ventricular hypertrophy and advanced atherosclerosis of the aorta.

References

1. Wood A, Oldham F: *Thomas Young, Natural Philosopher: 1773–1829.* Cambridge: Cambridge University Press, 1954
2. Peacock G: *Life of Thomas Young, M.D., F.R.S.* London: John Murray, 1855
3. Morse EW: Thomas Young. In *Dictionary of Scientific Biography* 14, p. 562–572. New York: Charles Scribner's Sons, 1976
4. Laird JD: Thomas Young, M.D. (1773–1829). *Am Heart J* 1980; 100:1–8
5. Rosner L: *Medical Education in the Age of Improvement: Edinburgh Students and Apprentices, 1760–1826.* Edinburgh: Edinburgh University Press, 1991
6. Behrman S: Thomas Young, the physician. *Clio Medica* 1975;10: 277–284
7. *Miscellaneous Works of the Late Thomas Young.* 3 volumes (Eds. Peacock G, Leitch J). London: John Murray, 1855
8. Young T: On the functions of the heart and arteries. *Philo Trans (London)* 1809;1–31
9. Pettigrew TJ: Thomas Young. In *Medical Portrait Gallery: Biographical Memoirs of the Most Celebrated Physicians, Surgeons, etc. etc. Who Have Contributed to the Advancement of Medical Science*, vol. 4, 13, p. 1–24. London: Whittaker and Co., 1840

John Collins Warren

W. Bruce Fye, M.D., M.A.

Cardiovascular Division, Mayo Clinic, Rochester, Minnesota, USA

In 1809, John Collins Warren (Fig. 1) published the first monograph on heart disease in the United States.

Warren was born in Boston, Massachusetts, on August 1, 1778.[1] His father, John Warren, was a surgeon during the Revolutionary War and a founder of the Harvard Medical School. After graduating from Harvard College in 1797, young Warren became his father's apprentice, reflecting the fact that there were no medical schools or hospitals in Boston at the time. In this era, the most ambitious young American doctors went to Europe for formal training. Warren sailed abroad in 1800 to spend two years traveling and studying medicine in London, Edinburgh, Leiden, and Paris.

In London, Warren served as an assistant to William Cooper, a senior surgeon at Guys Hospital. He also performed dissections at Guys and attended lectures delivered by Astley Cooper and other leading London physicians and surgeons. Warren next traveled to Edinburgh, then a magnet for American medical students.[2] There he took courses from Charles and John Bell, Alexander Monro, John Gregory, and other popular medical teachers. On his way to Paris in 1801, Warren journeyed through Holland where he bought a large collection of medical books that included many classic anatomical and surgical texts. Paris was just recovering from the French Revolution, but Warren was pleased with the opportunities it afforded him for medical study. He attended lectures and clinics given by Guillaume Dupuytren, Raphael Sabatier, and other prominent medical professors. Warren also attended Jean Nicholas Corvisart's clinic at the Le Charié Hospital. Corvisart was a pioneer in the study of the diseases of the heart. His lectures on the subject, first published by a pupil in 1806, became the basis of his classic book, *Essai sur les maladies et les lésions organiques du coeur et des gros vaisseaux.*

After returning to Boston, Warren joined his father in medical practice and began seeing as many as 50 patients a day. Young Warren wanted to do more than just practice medicine, and he soon became a member of the medical and academic elite of that growing city. With James Jackson he helped found the *New England Journal of Medicine and Surgery* in 1812, and the Massachusetts General Hospital, which opened in 1821.[3] Warren was also an active participant in the Massachusetts Medical Society. He delivered a paper on organic heart diseases at the February 1809 meeting of the society. Later that year he extended his observations and published the first monograph on heart disease written by an American. Published by Thomas Wait of Boston, the 61 page book reflected Corvisart's influence. The title, *Cases of Organic Diseases of the Heart, with Dissection and Some Remarks Intended to Point out the Distinctive Symptoms of These Diseases,* revealed Warren's interest in pathological anatomy and clinical pathological correlation.[4]

Warren informed his readers that his purpose, in part, was to convince them that

> ...derangements of the primary organ of the circulation cannot exist without producing so great disorder of the functions of that and of other parts, as to be sufficiently conspicuous by external signs; but, as these somewhat resemble the symptoms of different complaints, especially of asthma, phthisis pulmonalis [tuberculosis], and water in the thorax, it has happened, that each of these has been sometimes confounded with the former. The object of the following statement of cases is to shew [sic], that, whatever resemblance there may be in the symptoms of the first, when taken separately, to those of the latter diseases, the mode of connection and degree of those symptoms at least is quite dissimilar; and there are also symptoms, peculiar to organic diseases of the heart, sufficiently characteristic to distinguish them from other complaints.[4] (pp. 1–2)

Warren's monograph included 11 case reports, one of which is of special interest: he described in detail the case of James Sullivan, the Governor of Massachusetts. In 1807, at the age of 63, Sullivan developed a permanently irregular pulse followed by symptoms consistent with an embolus to his right arm. Later that year, he developed a cough and began to complain of palpitations and progressive exertional dyspnea. When Warren examined Sullivan he discovered "the pulsation of the carotid arteries was uncommonly strong; the radial arteries seemed ready to burst from their sheaths; the veins, especially the jugulars, in which there was often a pulsatory motion, were every where turgid with blood." He characterized Sullivan's complexion as "livid." Sullivan also complained of occasional heaviness in his chest and "some nights ... were passed in sitting up in bed, under a fit of asthma, as it was called."[4] (p. 5) Sullivan's dyspnea, orthopnea, and other

FIG. 1 John Collins Warren (1778–1856). From the personal collection of W. Bruce Fye.

symptoms consistent with what we now term heart failure progressed during 1808.

It is noteworthy that Warren described the phenomenon of Cheyne-Stokes respiration a decade before Cheyne's classic paper was published.[5] Warren explained,

> The respiration was so distressing, as to produce a wish for speedy death; the eyes became wild and staring. No sleep could be obtained; for, after dosing [sic] a short time, he started up in violent agitation, with the idea of having suffered a convulsion. During the few moments of forgetfulness, the respiration was sometimes quick and irregular, sometimes slow, and frequently suspended for the space of twenty five, and even so long as fifty seconds.[4] (p. 7)

Sullivan developed progressive edema and eventually anasarca. Warren concluded that he had "an organic disease of the heart" that included aortic valve calcification and probable cardiac enlargement. He felt that his patient would likely succumb to his heart disease within three months. Despite heroic measures that included the use of "much medicine," Sullivan's health declined progressively and he died in December. The autopsy revealed cardiac enlargement, marked left ventricular hypertrophy, aortic stenosis, mitral stenosis, and coronary arteries that were "considerably ossified." James Jackson was impressed with the book and concluded it would "lay before the American public much more knowledge respecting the diseases of the heart, and large vessels, than has hitherto been presented to them."[4] (p. 22)

Warren concluded his book with a summary of the signs and symptoms that suggested the presence of heart disease. He believed that palpitations and an irregular pulse were often the first sign of heart disease. The earliest symptom was often dyspnea, followed by cough and orthopnea. Physical examination, especially of the heart, was still very limited when Warren's book appeared in 1809. Within the next decade, however, Corvisart would popularize percussion of the chest and Laennec would invent the stethoscope. So, Warren relied on the ancient practices of observation and palpation of the pulse. He noted that patients with heart disease often had evidence of venous distention and an irregular pulse. Certain signs and symptoms, if they occurred together, should alert the physician to the possibility of heart disease. For example, Warren explained that in cases of heart disease edema often developed in conjunction with exertional dyspnea and orthopnea. He explained that edema often started in the legs but would progress up to the abdomen, chest, and eventually the face. He emphasized that this was distinct from asthma and hydrothorax, diseases that were often confused with what we now term heart failure.[6]

Warren employed the standard therapeutic approaches of his day and prescribed blisters, cathartics, opium, and a simple diet. He believed that bloodletting was the most effective remedy for dyspnea and was an advocate of the use of digitalis. Warren extended his observations on heart disease in an article that appeared in 1812 in the first volume of the *New England Journal of Medicine and Surgery*. He applauded the recent publication of an English translation of Corvisart's book on heart disease and indicated that he planned to continue to publish interesting case reports of cardiovascular diseases.[7]

Warren was a proponent of clinicopathologic correlation, an approach championed by European physicians, because he was convinced this would lead to a better understanding of the pathophysiology of cardiovascular disease. Near the end of Warren's long and productive career, he performed an operation that would help to transform the practice of surgery. In 1846 he performed the first major operation in which ether anesthesia was used. Warren continued to see patients until two weeks before his death on May 4, 1856.

References

1. Warren E: *The Life of John Collins Warren*, M.D. Boston: Ticknor and Fields, 1860
2. Risse GB: *Hospital Life in Enlightenment Scotland: Care and Teaching at the Royal Infirmary of Edinburgh*. Cambridge: Cambridge University Press, 1986
3. Beecher HK, Altschule MD: *Medicine at Harvard: The First Three Hundred Years*. Hanover, N.H.: University Press of New England, 1977
4. Warren JC: *Cases of Organic Diseases of the Heart*. Boston: Thomas B. Wait, 1809
5. Kelly EC: John Cheyne—William Stokes. *Med Classics* 1939;3: 698–746
6. Jarcho S: *The Concept of Heart Failure from Avicenna to Albertini*. Cambridge, Mass.: Harvard University Press, 1980
7. Warren JC: Cases of organic diseases of the heart and lungs. *N Engl J Med Surg* 1812;1:120–130

Allan Burns*

W. B. FYE, M.D.

Marshfield Clinic, Marshfield, Wisconsin, USA

Allan Burns was born in Glasgow, Scotland, on September 18, 1781.[1,2] His father, John Burns, was a minister, and his older brother John would become a leading anatomist and surgeon at the University of Glasgow. When he was 14, Allan began studying medicine and soon was serving as demonstrator of anatomy for his brother. By 20, Allan Burns was acknowledged as a skilled anatomist and demonstrator.

Although he never received a university degree in medicine, Burns gained clinical experience through attending patients with his brother. Young Burns kept careful records on the clinical features of these cases and attempted to explain the signs and symptoms observed during life by detailed pathologic examination. Indeed, he attempted to anticipate the pathologic findings from the symptoms and physical findings noted during life. His pupil and associate Granville Sharp Pattison recalled that Burns was an unusually skilled and patient dissector.

In 1804, Burns was considering entering the medical service of the army, when he was presented with an unusual opportunity. Russia, under the rule of Alexander I and Catherine, sought greater influence in the affairs of Western Europe, which was becoming increasingly unstable in the face of Napoleon's aggression. Catherine established a hospital in St. Petersburg which she wanted organized along the lines of British hospitals. A British surgeon was, therefore, sought as its director, and Burns was offered the position despite his lack of formal training and limited experience. Burns missed his native Scotland, however, and remained in St. Petersburg for only six months. He returned to Glasgow to assume his brother's lecturing duties at the university.

Diseases of the heart were of special interest to Burns, and when he was 27 he began writing his classic monograph, *Observations on Some of the Most Frequent and Important Diseases of the Heart*, which was published in 1809.[3] This volume on cardiovascular disease is notable not only because it is the first monograph on heart disease in the English language; it contains several important observations on the pathophysiology of congenital and acquired cardiac disorders. Burns was familiar with the writings of the leading anatomists, pathologists, and practitioners of the eighteenth century. In his book he refers frequently to the works of John Hunter,

John Bell, Joseph Lieutaud, Jean Baptiste Senac, and Giovanni Baptiste Morgagni, among others.

Burns's interest in, and familiarity with, the natural history of disease as well as his thorough knowledge of cardiac anatomy and pathology are apparent in his book. It consists of 12 chapters devoted to such subjects as cardiac enlargement, chronic inflammation of the heart, coronary artery disease, valvular heart disease, anomalies and acquired disorders of the great vessels, and congenital heart disease.

It is important to recognize that this monograph was written prior to the introduction of mediate auscultation. Observation and palpitation were employed, but percussion had not yet been widely accepted. Laennec would not publish his treatise on auscultation for another decade. Burns reported cases in which audible murmurs were heard without placing the ear on the chest and denoted this "audible palpation."

The pathologic findings of cardiac dilatation and hypertrophy were of interest to Burns, who believed that hypertrophy was generally more "dangerous" than dilatation. Burns found the right ventricle dilated more often than the left, probably reflecting the greater prevalence of congenital and rheumatic heart disease in this era when the average life span was short and ischemic heart disease relatively less common. Among the congenital abnormalities Burns described in his book are patent ductus arteriosus, patent foramen ovale, and ventricular septal defect.

Burns acknowledged the limitations of contemporary approaches to the treatment of cardiac disorders. Dietary measures were felt to be important in cases of heart disease because they assured proper digestion and elimination. Digitalis had been introduced into medical practice a quarter of a century earlier by William Withering, and Burns advocated its use in a variety of cardiac conditions. He also suggested that tincture of opium, squill, ginger, castor oil, and mercury were efficacious in certain cases of heart disease. Reflecting the therapeutic philosophy of the time, Burns advocated bleeding and the application of blisters for some patients.

From the standpoint of therapy, Burns recognized the limitations of medicine in his era. In discussing mitral stenosis, for example, he characterized it as

> . . . a defect, which it is beyond the power of medicine to remove. To attempt to cure this disease is futile. As I have already stated, we are in most diseases of the heart,

---

*This paper is adapted from an essay prepared for the Classics of Cardiology Library, Gryphon Edition, Birmingham.

called upon rather to prevent positive evil, than to re-move what is already present.

Burns's book appeared in an era when there was great interest in angina pectoris.[4] He was familiar with the writings of William Heberden, Edward Jenner, and Caleb Parry on this subject. Burns believed that angina was due to "some organic lesions of the nutrient vessels of the heart." Indeed, he drew an analogy between coronary artery disease and the ligation of a peripheral artery in order to explain his interpretation of the pathophysiology of angina pectoris. It would be nearly a century before major advances were made in our understanding of what we now term ischemic heart disease, however.[5]

Cardiac resuscitation was described by the Scottish anatomist in the context of the treatment of patients with angina pectoris. If syncope accompanied an attack of angina, Burns advocated applying cold water to the forehead and breast and forcing the patient to inhale ammonia. In cases where

> . . . the cessation of vital action is very complete, and continues long, we ought to inflate the lungs, and pass electric shocks through the chest; the practitioner ought never, if the death has been sudden, and the person not very advanced in life, to despair of success, till he has unequivocal signs of real death.

Burns advised that resuscitative efforts should begin

> . . . as soon as you can reach the place where the patient is laid; and here, as in every case of asphyxia, you will probably be obligated to persist in the use of the necessary means, for a considerable length of time, before you can be certain of either succeeding or failing.

This approach to sudden death preceded the development of modern cardiopulmonary resuscitation by 150 years! Burns claimed that it was occasionally successful.[6]

Burns's book reveals his advanced understanding of the pathophysiology of the formation of intracardiac thrombi. He explained that in some cardiac disorders

> . . . the blood stagnates longer in the heart than it usually does, or ought to do, while here it undergoes changes by the reciprocal action of the blood on the heart, and of the heart, on the blood; new organized matter is deposited, and adheres to the parieties of the cavity in which it is lodged. This concretion slowly increases, the first particle acting as the exciting cause for the deposition of the second, and so on.

It was Burns's belief that the formation of a thrombus within the heart implied a more serious underlying disease of that organ.

It is apparent that Burns had unusual insight into many aspects of the structure and function of the heart in health and disease. This knowledge was not gained from long years of clinical experience or with the aid of diagnostic instruments; it was derived from Burns's thorough knowledge of the medical literature, from his extensive pathologic experience, and from a keen mind. He was aggressive and innovative and declared, somewhat condescendingly, "that a young practitioner seldom ventures to deviate from what he has read in books, or heart at lectures." Burns was not afraid to venture beyond the limits of contemporary knowledge. Although the Scottish anatomist was not always right in his interpretation of the pathophysiology of the heart and circulation, his monograph is a sophisticated summary of contemporary knowledge and includes several important original observations on congenital and acquired cardiac disorders.

Burns was only 28 when he published his valuable monograph on the heart. He was soon preparing his work on the surgical anatomy of the head and neck which included important observations on the anatomy of the great vessels. He soon became ill, however, and for the final three years of his short life he was in declining health. His career as an anatomist, pathologist, teacher, and author was cut short by recurrent gastrointestinal ailments complicated by abscess formation and fatal sepsis, vividly described by his colleague Pattison. Burns died at the age of 31 in 1813 but left the world a great classic of cardiology.

References

1. Pattison GS: A short account of the life of the author. In *Observations on the Surgical Anatomy of the Head and Neck, Illustrated by Cases and Engraving*. F. Lucas, Jr., Baltimore, (1823) vii-xxix

2. Herrick JB: Allan Bums: 1781-1813. Anatomist, surgeon, and cardiologist. *Bull Soc Section Med Hist Chicago* 4, 457 (1935)

3. Burns A: *Observations on Some of the Most Frequent and Important Diseases of the Heart: on Aneurysm of the Thoracic Aorta; on Preternatural Pulsation in the Epigastric Region; and on the Unusual Origin and Distribution of Some of the Large Arteries of the Human Body. Illustrated by Cases*. Thomas Bryce, Edinburgh (1809)

4. Leibowitz JO: *The History of Coronary Heart Disease*. Well-come Institute of the History of Medicine, London (1970)

5. Fye WB: The delayed diagnosis of myocardial infarction: It took half a century! *Circulation* 72, 262 (1985)

6. Fye WB: Ventricular fibrillation and defibrillation: Historical perspectives with emphasis on the contributions of John Mac-William, Carl Wiggers, and William Kouwenhoven. *Circulation* 71, 858 (1985)

René Laënnec

J. STONE, M.D.

Department of Medicine (Cardiology), Emory University School of Medicine, Atlanta, Georgia, USA

"It was the best of times, it was the worst of times"—thus Charles Dickens began his masterpiece set during that period of French history which includes the French Revolution—the end of the 1700s and the beginning of the 1800s. Revolution was in the air: the Industrial Revolution was cranked up, the American Revolution just over. In 1791, the year of *The Magic Flute* and Mozart's death, Beethoven was 21, ready to assume his full revolutionary powers. In France it was the time of the Reign of Terror, of political turmoil and retribution, of *la Guillotine* (invented in 1791 by a physician). According to Webb, by the time a certain young man in Nantes, France, was 15 years old, he "had seen fifty heads fall into the basket under the guillotine outside the windows of his home." That young man was René Théophile Hyacinthe Laënnec.

Laënnec was born in Quimper, in Brittany, in the far west of France, on February 17, 1781. His mother died when he was a few years old. His father was a mediocre lawyer who was afflicted with the writing of much poetry, a combination which led to an improvident situation for his children. When young Laënnec was seven years old, he and his brother were placed in the care of their paternal uncle in Nantes: their uncle was Guillaume Laënnec, a physician who had studied under John Hunter in England. Guillaume largely raised the young boys and was to be a major influence in the life of his young nephew.

Laënnec's early schooling in Nantes was characteristic of the time: religion, grammar, geography, Latin prose and verse. At 11 years of age, Laënnec translated some Virgil into French. The young boy had an affinity for natural history and made collections of flora and fauna. Webb speculates that Laënnec may have been friends with John James Audubon, the naturalist, who lived in Nantes and was about the same age. It was an idyllic time in some ways, one that was to be interrupted in 1789 by the French Revolution. Despite its chaos, Laënnec's education went on. In 1795, at the age of 14½, he began a five-year study of medicine in a hospital in Nantes where his uncle was in charge of 100 beds. His medical studies included anatomy, physiology, pathology, and therapeutics. Moreover, he began a study of Greek and continued his Latin, which he learned to speak fluently. At one point, Laënnec was devoted to playing the flute, which he is said to have practiced six hours a day at times! Under the pseudonym Cenneal (Laënnec spelled backwards), he also found time to write poetry recurrently—probably it was in his genes. But in 1801, he went to Paris in order to continue his study of medicine at L'École de Médecine. His teacher there was to be Jean-Nicolas Corvisart.

Corvisart was the leading figure in French clinical medicine, physician to Napoleon, and the person responsible for reviving Auenbrugger's technique of percussion (described in 1761, it was faltering in terms of actual clinical usage). Laënnec also came under the influence of Bichat and Dupuytren; the latter taught him a special course in anatomy. In Paris, Laënnec's career accelerated greatly. In 1802, he wrote his first paper, a necropsy-based study of ossification of the mitral valve with dilatation of the ventricle. The paper illustrates Laënnec's lifelong bent—the correlation of autopsy results with clinical findings. Shortly after this first excursion into print, he completed a study of peritonitis, described the subdeltoid bursa, and investigated the capsules of the liver, spleen, and kidneys. Throughout this time, Laënnec was virtually penniless, receiving very little financial help from his father; but he persevered and at the age of 22 was awarded first prize in both Medicine and Surgery at L'École de Médecine.

By 1803, Laënnec was writing regularly for *Journal de Médecine;* he wrote on meningitis and bone diseases, and his study of pneumonia was to become a classic. (In time, of course, his name was also to become eponymically associated with atrophic cirrhosis of the liver.) His doctoral thesis, on Hippocrates and his doctrines, was facilitated by his knowledge of Greek. Laënnec was rapidly becoming well known in Parisian medical circles, but his two major contributions, an understanding of tuberculosis and the development of the stethoscope, were still to be realized.

The Tubercle

Late in 1803, Laënnec was able to say that tubercles could be noted in every tissue of the body, including bone. Koch's discovery of the tubercle bacillus was still decades away (1882). But Laënnec was able to bring great order to the contemporary thinking about this disease. An example is a salient point he made in his famous lecture on tuberculosis delivered in March 1804: "phthisis," a term applied to a motley, undifferentiated group of pulmonary diseases, Laënnec maintained, was simply tuberculosis of the lungs. Shortly after this lecture, Laënnec narrowly missed conscription into Napoleon's army for the battle of Austerlitz.

FIG. 1 René T. H. Laënnec, 1781–1826. Courtesy National Library of Medicine.

A Miscellany of Efforts

The years from 1804 to 1816 were, for Laënnec, ones of building a practice, becoming an editor of the *Journal de Médecine,* and of developing his clinical skills. During these years spent in Paris, Laënnec wrote about angina (he is said to have had at least two attacks himself), coming to the conclusion that it was due to "cardiac neuralgia," since he often found no lesions of the coronary arteries at autopsy. In 1816, Laënnec accepted an appointment at the Necker Hospital in Paris, where the denouement of his life's work was to occur and his *magnum opus* was to be written.

The Stethoscope

Inspection, palpation, and percussion were all available to (if not always used by) clinicians of Laënnec's time. And there were even precedents for listening to the heart and lungs by *immediate* means—placing the ear directly on the patient's chest. This technique, spoken of by Hippocrates, Boyle, Double, and Hooke, among others, was in fact not often utilized because of concerns both of modesty and of hygiene. It was Laënnec's genius to adapt, for the purpose of auscultation, the physical principle that sound could be transmitted through a wooden baton (he writes of seeing children at play with such a baton). In his first case, Laënnec used a rolled-up cylinder of paper to examine an obese young woman. Use of the "cornet de papier" appears subsequently in the Necker Hospital records. Modifications in the initial simple wooden baton were then made: a hole was bored down the center (for improved sound reception and, especially, for the appreciation of pectoriloquy); the baton was divided, for portability, into halves which could be screwed together; and a funnel-like insertion was placed on the chest end. Laënnec most often called this new instrument "the cylinder,"

but also called it a "stethoscope." In 1819, Laënnec's famous treatise on *mediate* auscultation *(Traité de l'Auscultation Médiate)* was published; it was translated into English two years later by John Forbes.

1821, the year of Forbes' translation of Laënnec, was the year of John Keats' death from tuberculosis. This great figure, like Laënnec, had spent five years in an apprenticeship in medicine, then trained at Guy's and St. Thomas' Hospitals in London. Finally, though, he made his choice for poetry. The parallels between the two men's lives are striking ones: both studied medicine and loved poetry; their careers diverged, one to medicine, the other to poetry, both to greatness; and both were to die of tuberculosis at an early age.

At first, Laënnec's discovery of the stethoscope was ridiculed, as one might predict. But gradually its utility was recognized, both for examination of the heart and the lungs. His fame became widespread as physicians from all over Europe came to hear him speak and to go on rounds with him (as many as 50 student observers accompanied him on these rounds). He was inducted into the Academy of Medicine; he succeeded his teacher, Corvisart, in the College; and he was made a Knight of the Legion of Honor.

Laënnec's contributions to medical terminology were vast, especially in the area of pulmonary disease: rales; pectoriloquy; egophony; succussion. He accurately described emphysema, pneumothorax, bronchiectasis, and the auscultatory findings in pulmonary edema. He also described cardiac sounds and murmurs, but he related genesis of the second heart sound to atrial systole, which led to inaccuracies. Nevertheless, this new instrument of learning and of prognosis was in the clinician's hands: It was to become, along with the white coat, the very symbol of the profession. And it was to ensure that generations of physicians spent appreciable amounts of their time, not in the library or lecture hall, but at the bedside, as King emphasizes.

In December 1824, Laënnec finally married: the woman was then 44 years old and had been his housekeeper for years. It was a marriage of convenience, one that was to be quite shortlived. Laënnec had suffered from asthma since childhood and was always quite thin. In the early 1820s, by Laënnec's own estimate, fully one-third of the hospitalized patients in Paris were there with tuberculosis. The eventual outcome for this giant of medicine is not hard to predict. In April 1826, as he neared the completion of a second edition of his book, Laënnec developed severe pulmonary symptoms and gradually became emaciated. His course was inexorably downhill and almost certainly caused by tuberculosis, though no autopsy was performed. Death came to one of the greatest physicians of all time on August 13, 1826. He was 45 years old.

Selected references

Dickens C: *Tale of Two Cities* (1859)
King LS: Auscultation in England, 1821-1837. *Bull Hist Med* 33, 446 (1959)
Laënnec RTH: A treatise on the diseases of the chest, in which they are described according to their anatomical characters, and their diagnosis established on a new principle by means of acoustick instruments (translated by John Forbes). Underwood, London (1821)

James Wardrop

W. BRUCE FYE, M.D., M.A.

Department of Cardiology, Marshfield Clinic, Marshfield, Wisconsin, USA

Although James Wardrop (Fig. 1) is now better known for his contributions to ophthalmology, he published important books on heart disease and aneurysms.

Wardrop was born on August 14, 1782, at Torbane-Hill, Linlithgow, Scotland.[1–3] After receiving his preliminary education at Edinburgh, he became an apprentice to his uncle, Andrew Wardrop, a prominent surgeon in that city. When he was nineteen, Wardrop was appointed house surgeon at the Edinburgh Royal Infirmary, one of Europe's leading medical institutions.[4] Wardrop moved to London in 1802, where he attended the lecture courses of John Abernethy and Astley Cooper. He also studied medicine at three of London's leading hospitals: Guy's, St. Thomas's, and St. George's. Wardrop supplemented his training by touring hospitals in Paris, Vienna, and other continental centers of medical education.

After completing his foreign studies, Wardrop returned to Edinburgh where he entered practice. Although he was elected a fellow of the College of Surgeons of Edinburgh, Wardrop concluded that his professional opportunities in the Scottish metropolis were limited, and so he returned to London in 1808. There, his practice and reputation grew steadily, and he was elected a member of the Royal College of Surgeons of London in 1814.

In 1826, Wardrop founded the West London Hospital of Surgery, where he lectured and demonstrated surgical techniques to interested students and practitioners. These practical courses were very popular. Dozens of physicians and surgeons, including several from the continent, attended the weekly demonstrations in the hospital's amphitheater to see Wardrop operate. Eventually, he also lectured on surgery at St. Bartholomew's Hospital and at the Great Windmill Street School of Medicine.

Wardrop published *On Aneurism, and its Cure by a New Operation* in 1828.[5] The book included sections devoted to the pathology of aneurysms, the techniques that Hunter and Brasdor had developed to treat them, and the surgical approach that Wardrop had devised to attempt to cure them. Although Wardrop advocated surgical treatment for aneurysms, he acknowledged that many aneurysms were in locations that were inaccessible. His innovation was to ligate the branches of a diseased vessel distal to the aneurysm in an attempt to reduce the flow of blood through the aneurysm. This, in turn, would favor the development of thrombus within the aneurysm, thereby diminishing the risk of rupture or progressive expansion.

Wardrop published his first book on heart disease in 1837.[6] A greatly expanded second edition entitled *On the Nature and Treatment of the Diseases of the Heart* appeared 14 years later.[7] The first part of Wardrop's book demonstrates his interest in the relation of cardiac function to the respiratory and nervous systems. His conclusions reflect an appreciation of the complex physiologic relationships of the heart, lungs, and brain.

Wardrop emphasized the importance of accurate diagnosis. "The diagnosis of diseases," he wrote, "may be considered as the stepping-stone to their treatment."[7a] Although he was not a strong supporter of auscultation, he thought the procedure could help a physician make the correct diagnosis. At a time when many prominent clinicians still debated the value of the stethoscope (introduced a generation earlier by Laennec), Wardrop told his readers: "Notwithstanding all that may be said against auscultation, we ought not ... deny the utility of the information to be derived from it."[7b]

Wardrop was frustrated with the state of therapeutics and contended that advances in the treatment of heart disease were not "at all commensurate with the progress of physiological and pathological science."[7c] His approaches to treatment reflected a blend of late eighteenth and early nineteenth century views on the pathophysiology of heart disease. Wardrop wrote a book on bloodletting in 1835,[8] and his monograph on heart disease published 16 years later revealed his continued enthusiasm for the practice:

> Bloodletting may be considered one of the most valuable curative means in the treatment of diseases of the heart ... There is almost no malady to which the heart is liable, wherein bloodletting is not useful during at least some period of its progress.[7d]

Although many leading clinicians of Wardrop's era shared his enthusiasm for bloodletting, the popularity of the procedure was declining steadily.

Wardrop discussed diseases of the pericardium, myocardium, and endocardium in his comprehensive 587-page book. With respect to coronary artery disease, he explained,

> When the coats of the coronary arteries are diseased, it must often happen that the heart, not being supplied with its wonted [sic] quantity of blood, its muscles become pale and flaccid, and unfit to carry on vigorously the circula-

FIG. 1 James Wardrop, 1782–1869. From the collection of W. Bruce Fye.

tion; and consequently arise an assemblage of symptoms … to which the name of *angina pectoris* has been given.[7e]

Like his contemporaries, Wardrop did not attribute angina exclusively to coronary artery disease. Although acute myocardial infarction was not recognized as a distinct syndrome until the early twentieth century, Wardrop did link myocardial dysfunction with coronary artery disease.

Wardrop closed his book with an apology: "I have earnestly to express the hope, that the indulgent reader will not reproach me for its numerous imperfections."[7f] Contemporary and more recent reviews of Wardrop's book were mixed. British cardiologist and historian Evan Bedford remarked in 1962 that while Wardrop's book included "much of interest and originality" it was "tedious."[9] A revised edition of his book on heart disease appeared in Edinburgh in 1859. Wardrop died in London on February 13, 1869.

References

1. Pettigrew TJ: James Wardrop. In *Medical Portrait Gallery: Biographical Memoirs of the Most Celebrated Physicians, Surgeons, etc, etc.*, vol. 2, p. 1-16. London: Whittaker & Co., 1840
2. O'Farrell PT: An early Victorian surgeon-cardiologist (James Wardrop, 1782–1869). *Irish J Med Sci* 1956;[issue no. 366]:271–275
3. Power DA: James Wardrop. In *The Compact Edition of the Dictionary of National Biography*, vol. 2, p. 2199. New York: Oxford University Press, 1975
4. Risse GR: *Hospital Life in Enlightenment Scotland: Care and Teaching at the Royal Infirmary of Edinburgh*. Cambridge: Cambridge University Press, 1986
5. Wardrop J: *On Aneurysm, and its Cure by a New Operation*. London: Longman & Co., 1828
6. Wardrop J: *On the Nature and Treatment of Diseases of the Heart; with Some Views on the Physiology of the Circulation*, Part I. London: J. Churchill, 1837
7. Wardrop J: *On the Nature and Treatment of the Diseases of the Heart: Containing also an Account of the Musculocardiac; the Pulmocardiac; and the Venopulmonary Functions*, (a) p. 265; (b) p. 259; (c) p. 286; (d) p. 321; (e) p. 545–546; (f) p. 585. London: John Churchill, 1851
8. Wardrop J: *On Blood-Letting: An Account of the Curative Effects of the Abstraction of Blood*. London: J.-B. Balliere, 1835
9. Bedford DE: The surgeon-cardiologists of the 19th century. *Br Heart J*, 1967;29:461–468

George J. Guthrie

W. Bruce Fye, M.D., M.A.

Department of Cardiology, Marshfield Clinic, Marshfield, Wisconsin, USA

George James Guthrie (Fig. 1) made important contributions to vascular surgery. Born in London on May 1, 1785, Guthrie was just 13 years old when he became an apprentice to John Philips, a Pall Mall surgeon.[1-3] Despite his age, Guthrie was allowed to study medicine at the Mary-le-Bone Infirmary. Two years later, he was appointed assistant surgeon to the 29th Infantry Foot Regiment.

Guthrie's medical career was shaped by his intense military experience. The Peninsular War broke out in 1808 as a result of Napoleon's desire to control Spain and Portugal. Guthrie sailed to Portugal as part of a British naval force of 10,000 men sent to help evict the French troops. As a senior regimental surgeon, he operated on hundreds of wounded soldiers during the next several months. Vascular injuries were common in the Peninsular War, and Guthrie developed a special interest in this serious problem.[4]

After the war, Guthrie returned to London where he entered practice and studied with John Abernethy, a surgeon at St. Bartholomew's Hospital. He also enrolled in the Great Windmill Street School of Anatomy, where he attended lectures delivered by Charles Bell and Benjamin Brodie, surgeons especially interested in aneurysms and other arterial diseases. Although Guthrie's military experience gave him a unique opportunity to study and treat traumatic vascular injuries, he learned about other forms of vascular disease from his teachers and from his experience in civilian practice.

Guthrie published his classic book, *On the Diseases and Injuries of Arteries, with the Operations Required for their Cure*, in 1830.[5] When it appeared, this monograph was the definitive work on the surgical treatment of arterial injuries and diseases. Guthrie also included sections devoted to the pathophysiology, diagnosis, and nonsurgical treatment of vascular diseases; for example, he explained that the arteries in most older persons showed degenerative changes at autopsy. Although "atheromatous" deposits could be identified between the coats of the arteries, their pathogenesis was not understood.

Guthrie presented a clear picture of the progressive changes of arterial degeneration:

> The atheromatous patches sometimes pervade the whole surface of an artery, and are conjoined more frequently with calcareous than other matter, and a thin layer of this earthy deposit is frequently perceived on their surface. These patches are often found to yield by ulceration, by which the internal coat is destroyed, or is torn by the impulse of the blood.[5a]

Much of Guthrie's book dealt with aneurysms, a serious problem that had challenged surgeons for centuries. The signs and symptoms of aneurysms that involved arteries of the axilla, groin, and extremities depended on their location, size, and rate of expansion. It is not surprising that Guthrie, a surgeon whose philosophy toward the management of disease was shaped on the battlefield, favored a direct approach to the treatment of aneurysms of the extremities.

Three types of local treatment for aneurysms had been tried: general compression of the involved limb, direct compression over the affected artery, and ligation of the diseased vessel. The application of ligatures to the affected artery was an ancient operation—it was first described by the 6th century Byzantine physician Aetius of Amida.[6] New techniques for applying ligatures and various other operative approaches had been invented during the seventeenth and eighteenth centuries.

Several British and continental surgeons attempted to refine vascular procedures during the early nineteenth century, and Guthrie described their methods and results in detail.[7] These abridged case reports provide valuable insight into the medical and surgical practices of the era. Guthrie also summarized the animal experiments performed by several surgeons in their attempts to better understand the pathophysiology of aneurysms and their treatment.

Intrathoracic aneurysms were especially dangerous, and they defied surgical intervention. Usually, these aneurysms increased in size gradually, and complications arose as a result of compression and erosion of adjacent structures such as the vertebrae or ribs. Guthrie explained, "After the hard parts have been removed [by erosion and absorption], the progress of the aneurysm is more rapid."[5b] Progressive thinning and distension of the overlying skin or of an adjacent mucous membrane would eventually lead to oozing of blood and, ultimately, fatal rupture. Guthrie also discussed the concept of "dissecting aneurysms," thought to have caused the death of Great Britain's King George II in 1760.

Attempts to treat aneurysms medically were usually ineffective. Guthrie explained that the traditional medical approach included strict bed rest, minimal food intake, daily bleedings with lancets or leeches, the external application of

FIG. 1   George J. Guthrie, 1785–1856. Source: From the collection of W. Bruce Fye, M.D.

cold (ice, snow, or evaporating liquids), and the administration of various medications. Digitalis and preparations of lead

were most often used as they were thought to reduce the action of the heart and arteries.

Guthrie's interests were of broad range. In addition to his valuable book on arterial disease, he wrote important works on military surgery, ophthalmic surgery, hernia, diseases of the genitourinary system, and injuries of the brain. He died in London on May 1, 1856.

References

1. Pettigrew TJ: George James Guthrie. In *Medical Portrait Gallery: Biographical Memoirs of the Most Celebrated Physicians, Surgeons, etc. etc.* 4 vols., 4, p. 1–220. London: Whittaker & Co., 1840
2. Wakley T: Biographical sketch of George James Guthrie. *Lancet* 1850;1:727–736
3. Howell HAL: George James Guthrie. *J Royal Army Med Corps* 1910;14:577–587
4. Cantlie N: A *History of the Army Medical Department.* Edinburgh: Churchill Livingstone, 1974
5. Guthrie GJ: *On the Diseases and Injuries of Arteries, with the Operations Required for Their Cure.* London: Burgess and Hill, 1830; (a) p. 28, (b) p. 57
6. Friedman SG: A *History of Vascular Surgery.* Mount Kisco, NY: Futura Publishing Co., 1989
7. Wells LA: Aneurysm and physiologic surgery. *Bull Hist Med* 1970; 44:411–424

John Forbes

W. BRUCE FYE, M.D., M.A.

Department of Cardiology, Marshfield Clinic, Marshfield, Wisconsin, USA

British physician John Forbes (Fig. 1) is best remembered for popularizing the stethoscope among English-speaking doctors. The stethoscope, medicine's first powerful diagnostic tool, was invented by French physician René Theophile Hyacinthe Laennec in 1816. Laennec reported his early experience with auscultation in a two-volume book published three years later. Forbes translated Laennec's monograph into English in 1821 and published his own book on the subject in 1824.

John Forbes was born in Cuttlebrae, Banffshire, in northeast Scotland in 1787.[1,2] After receiving his preliminary education at Fordyce Academy, Forbes entered Marischal College in Aberdeen at the age of 16. Three years later he matriculated at the University of Edinburgh from which he received a diploma in surgery in 1807. After spending nearly a decade as a surgeon in the Royal Navy, Forbes returned to Edinburgh in 1816 to resume his medical studies. At this time, Edinburgh was a world center of medical education.[3] After receiving a Doctorate of Medicine degree, Forbes entered practice in the village of Penzance, in Cornwall. It was there that he became interested in the new technique of auscultation.

Forbes learned of Laennec's invention of the stethoscope from James Clark, a former classmate at the Fordyce Academy and the University of Edinburgh. Clark published the first description in English of Laennec's technique of auscultation in his 1820 book on the climate, diseases, hospitals, and medical schools of France, Italy, and Switzerland. Forbes was fascinated by Laennec's book on auscultation and acquired one of the first stethoscopes made by the French physician. After using the instrument for a few months, he was convinced of its value as a diagnostic aid. He thought an English translation of Laennec's book would stimulate British physicians to adopt the technique. Forbes's translation of Laennec's monograph on auscultation was first published in London in 1821.[4] It was reprinted in America two years later.

Forbes did not claim that auscultation was simple to learn. Indeed, he thought the stethoscope was unlikely to "ever come into general use, notwithstanding its value … because its beneficial application requires much time, and gives a good deal of trouble both to the patient and the practitioner."[4a] Forbes admitted that his initial attempts to use the stethoscope were "very unsatisfactory" because he had not carefully followed "the directions given for using the instrument."[4b] With "a little practice" Forbes found that the stethoscope provided a great deal of useful information, however. As a result, Forbes became one of his generation's most ardent champions of auscultation.

In 1824, Forbes published *Original Cases with Dissections and Observations Illustrating the Use of the Stethoscope and Percussion*.[5] His earlier prediction that few doctors would use the stethoscope proved accurate. Forbes complained that as far as he knew the only physician in Great Britain using the stethoscope was Andrew Duncan, Jr., of Edinburgh. Although James Clark used the instrument, he practiced in Rome. Forbes was frustrated that his translation of Laennec's book had not inspired English-speaking doctors to use the stethoscope. Still, he acknowledged that many scientific advances were not appreciated when they were first announced. Forbes explained, "innumerable discoveries could be mentioned, which, at the time they were made, seemed of no value, but which eventually proved of the greatest importance."[5a]

British cardiologist and medical book collector Evan Bedford considered Forbes's 1824 book "the earliest English work on the stethoscope."[6] Forbes came to believe that Laennec's large monograph was more than most doctors wanted to read on the subject. He thought they would be more likely to use a concise manual on auscultation and percussion. He hoped that his new book would stimulate others to use the techniques which he knew were of great value in evaluating patients with cardiac or pulmonary disease.

Just as Forbes decried the infrequent use of auscultation by his English-speaking contemporaries, he lamented their failure to appreciate the value of percussion. Leopold Auenbrugger's 1761 Latin treatise on percussion received little attention until 1808 when Jean Nicholas Corvisart translated it into French. Forbes's 1824 book included a brief biographical sketch of Auenbrugger and the first English translation of the Austrian physician's essay on percussion. When medical historian Henry Sigerist reprinted Forbes's translation of Auenbrugger's treatise in 1936, he claimed that it was "a classic which should be in every medical student's hands."[7] In addition to Auenbrugger's essay and brief excerpts from Laennec's monograph on auscultation, Forbes's book included a summary of Paris physician Victor Collin's recent manual on cardiac physical diagnosis.

Fig. 1   John Forbes, M.D. (1787–1861). (Portrait from the collection of W. Bruce Fye, M.D.)

More than half of Forbes's book was devoted to 39 case reports in which auscultation and percussion proved helpful. He selected cases from his own practice because he thought English readers would find them more compelling than simply reading translations of Laennec's cases. Several of Forbes's patients died, and his summaries included a summary of the pathologic findings. Like Laennec, Forbes emphasized the importance of correlating auscultatory and pathologic findings. Only in this way could physicians hope to understand the etiology of the symptoms and physical findings present in a given case. Forbes's book appeared when clinicopathologic correlation was widely heralded as the primary way to advance medical knowledge.[8]

Forbes saw himself as the chief proponent of auscultation and percussion in the English-speaking world. He had come to place great reliance on these new diagnostic techniques and wanted to see his countrymen take advantage of them. Forbes thought auscultation and percussion were useful even in incurable cases because they helped doctors clarify the nature of the underlying disease. This would help the physician render a more accurate prognosis. Forbes argued, "it is of no slight importance to the sufferer from an incurable malady, that the medical attendant understands the nature of it, and knows it to be incurable. This knowledge will, at least, prevent the employment of painful, disagreeable, or merely useless remedies."[5b]

Auscultation was in its infancy when Forbes published his book. The origin of the heart sounds was poorly understood, and no one had distinguished systolic from diastolic murmurs. Experience had shown, in Forbes's opinion, that the absence of expected auscultatory findings could be helpful in certain cases. For example, he knew that pleurisy and pericarditis usual-ly were accompanied by a characteristic harsh sound (later termed a "rub") when the painful area was examined by the stethoscope. If that sound was absent, the physician should consider other diagnostic possibilities to explain the patient's complaint.

European physicians gradually adopted auscultation. American doctors were even slower to employ the technique, however. A Massachusetts physician claimed in 1829, "The use of the Stethoscope has become familiar to many of the most enlightened and distinguished practitioners of Europe. In England it is ordered to be used generally by the army surgeons, who are required to report their observations." This American noted, however, "in this country it still remains a novelty."[9]

Forbes made many other notable contributions to medicine. With John Conolly and Alexander Tweedie, he edited the four-volume *Cyclopaedia of Practical Medicine* between 1831 and 1835. Arranged alphabetically, the work included contributions by 67 prominent physicians and surgeons. Forbes compiled an extensive bibliography to the work which physiologist and historian John Fulton characterized as "the first serious attempt on the part of anyone in the English-speaking world to give a subject classification for medical literature."[10]

Forbes's health began to fail shortly after the appearance of his 1857 book *Of Nature and Art in the Cure of Disease*. He died in November 1861.

References

1. Bishop PJ: The life and writings of Sir John Forbes (1787-1861). *Tubercle* 42, 55–261 (1961)
2. Sakula A: Sir John Forbes (1787-1861)—a bicentenary review. *J R Coll Physicians Lond* 21, 77–81 (1987)
3. Risse GB: *Hospital Life in Enlightenment Scotland: Care and Teaching at the Royal Infirmary of Edinburgh.* Cambridge University Press, Cambridge (1986)
4. Laennec RTH: *A Treatise on the Diseases of the Chest … Translated [by and] with a Preface and Notes by John Forbes.* T. and G. Underwood, London (1821); (a) xix, (b) xxi
5. Forbes J: *Original Cases with Dissections and Observations Illustrating the Use of the Stethoscope and Percussion in the Diagnosis of Diseases of the Chest.* T. and G. Underwood, London (1824); (a) xv; (b) xix
6. *The Evan Bedford Library of Cardiology.* Royal College of Physicians, London (1977) 98
7. Forbes J: On percussion of the chest being a translation of Auenbruger's original treatise entitled "Inventum novum ex percussione thoracis humani, ut signo abstrusos interni pectoris morbos detegendi." [Vienna 1761] Introduction by Henry E. Sigerist. *Bull Hist Med* 4, 373–403 (1936)
8. Maulitz RC: *Morbid Appearances: The Anatomy of Pathology in the Early Nineteenth Century.* Cambridge University Press, Cambridge (1987)
9. Collin M: *A Short Treatise on the Different Methods of Investigating the Diseases of the Chest. Translated by W.N. Ryland … [with] an Explanatory Introduction by a Fellow of the Massachusetts Medical Society.* Benjamin Perkins & Co., Boston (1829), viii
10. Fulton JF: *The Great Medical Bibliographers.* University of Pennsylvania Press, Philadelphia (1951) 64

Jan Evangelista Purkinje (Purkině)

P. SCHWEITZER, M.D.

Division of Cardiology, Department of Medicine, Bronx VA Medical Center, Bronx; Division of Cardiology, Mount Sinai School of Medicine, New York, New York

Jan Evangelista Purkinje (Purkině in Czech) was born on December 17, 1787, in the small Moravian town Libovice which, at that time, was part of the Austro-Hungarian Empire.[1] It is interesting that his Czech origin is not well known. Earlier editions of *Dorland's Medical Dictionary* (prior to 1944) described Purkinje as a Hungarian physiologist, and the North American Society for Pacing and Electrophysiology currently assigns him to Polish ancestry.

Purkinje is well known for his contributions in various fields of anatomy, physiology, and pharmacology, as well as for the development of different instruments (perimeter, goniometer) to be used for his scientific work. Although Purkinje's major interest was not the anatomy and physiology of the cardiovascular system, his name is most frequently associated with the specialized intraventricular conduction system, the so-called "Purkinje fibers or network." In addition to his contributions to anatomy and physiology, Purkinje was a great Czech patriot.[2] He was active in the Czech national movement and a strong advocate of Czech scientific literature. Purkinje was one of the founders of the Czech scientific journal *Krok* (*Step*) which published some of his work.

Purkinje's original intention was to become an educator. To fulfill this aim he entered the Piarist order, where he stayed for three years studying philosophy, physics, and natural sciences. His interest in the latter field was probably central to his decision to leave the order to pursue further study in philosophy and natural sciences. This assumption is supported by his own words: "Next I turned to philosophy, whose teachings had freed my soul. And I had the deep feeling that in natural sciences, about which I had but meager ideas at this time, I might accomplish something worth while." After completing his courses in philosophy in Prague, Purkinje accepted a teaching post in the family of Baron Hildprandt, who was to remain his benefactor and adviser for many years. At the age of 26, Purkinje took up the study of medicine in Prague, which he finished by defending his dissertation "Beitrag zur Kenntniss des Sehens in Subjectiver Hinsicht" (Contribution to the Knowledge of Vision from a Subjective Point of View).

During the next five years, Purkinje worked as an assistant in anatomy and physiology and continued his research in various fields of physiology and pharmacology. At the time, the knowledge of the effect and dosage of various drugs was in its infancy and most of the information originated in experimental animal studies, which Purkinje considered inadequate. For these reasons, Purkinje conducted self-experimentation with different drugs including digitalis and extractum belladonnae.[3] During this period, Purkinje applied for professorships of pharmacology and physiology in Prague and other cities of the Austro-Hungarian Empire and Germany without success. It was not until 1823 that he became Professor of Physiology and Pathology in Breslau in East Prussia (presently Wroclaw in Poland). After 27 years in Breslau, Purkinje was offered the Chair of Physiology in Prague and returned to his native country. Purkinje died on July 28, 1869 a few months before his eighty-second birthday.

There are three areas of cardiology in which Purkinje made important contributions. First and best known is the discovery of the fibers of the specialized intraventricular conduction system, the second is the role of the heart on venous return, and third is the description of the effect of digitalis in humans which has its origin in self-experimentation.

The description of the fibers of the conduction system first appeared in the Annals of the Medical Faculty of Jagellon University in Cracow in 1839. In this article, which was written at the request of two prominent members of the medical faculty in Cracow, Purkinje described the microscopic structure of the fibers of the intraventricular conduction system. According to his theory, these fibers could be seen by the naked eye and were most likely of cartilaginous origin. Six years later, Purkinje published another paper on the same subjects in *Archiv für Anatomie,* which was also translated into English and published in *Medical Gazette* in London. In this second paper, Purkinje suggested that the fibers are muscular in nature. As indicated by its title, "Mikroskopisch-Neurologische Beobachtungen" (Microscopic-Neurologic Observations), this report was not limited to the fibers of the heart but included observations on other anatomical structures.

The second contribution of Purkinje in cardiovascular physiology was his definition of the role of the heart in venous return. Before Purkinje's time, it was believed that the main factors responsible for venous return were dilatation of the heart, elasticity of the great vessels, and atmospheric pressure. Purkinje challenged these assumptions and suggested that the most important mechanism was the increased size of the right atrium secondary to the movement of the tricuspid valve during systole. He presented this idea in a lecture in 1843, and in

FIG. 1   Jan Evangelista Purkinje (1781–1869). From *Jan Evangelista Purkině*, Život a Dîlo. Avicenum, Prague (1986). (Reprinted with permission.)

a publication, "Über die Saugkraft des Herzens" (The Suction Force of the Heart), a few years later in Breslau. In the same paper, Purkinje also suggested that successful research in cardiovascular physiology requires close cooperation between the fields of physiology, physics, and mathematics.

The third contribution of Purkinje is in pharmacology. Purkinje's interest in pharmacology grew out of his medical studies. With the help of a friend whose father was a pharmacist, Purkinje had access to different drugs, including digitalis. By self-administration of extract of the digitalis leaf over four days, Purkinje developed visual and cardiac manifestations that define digitalis toxicity.

In summary, Purkinje is one of the most prominent Czech scientists of the nineteenth century. In appreciation of his contributions to progress in medicine, the society of Czech and Slovak physicians decided to call their association "The Czechoslovak Medical Society of Jan Evangelista Purkině." Perhaps the greatest deference to him is that his name has become part of the vocabulary of basic and clinical electrophysiologists all over the world.

References

1.   Travničková E: *Jan Evangelista Purkině;* Život a dîlo. Avicenum, Prague (1986)
2.   John HJ: *Jan Evangelista Purkině;* Czech Scientist and Patriot 1787–1869. The American Philosophical Society, Independence Square, Philadelphia (1959)
3.   Altman LK: *Who Goes First? The Story of Self-Experimentation in Medicine.* Random House, New York (1986) 92–95

Pierre Mere Latham, 1789–1875*

W. B. FYE, M.D.

Cardiology Department, Marshfield Clinic, Marshfield, Wisconsin, USA

Peter Mere Latham (Fig. 1), born in London in 1789, was the son of John Latham, a leading medical practitioner.[1,2] The younger Latham received his undergraduate and medical education at Oxford. His courses there were complemented by practical work at St. Bartholomew's Hospital, one of London's largest medical institutions.[3] At St. Bartholomew's, Latham was not merely a detached observer—he had significant responsibility for the patients of James Haworth, who had succeeded his father as physician to the hospital. He supplemented this hospital experience with outpatient work with Thomas Bateman in the Public Dispensary on Carey Street.

In 1815, Latham was elected physician to the Middlesex Hospital, a large London institution. Only 26 years old, he found his work there challenging and intellectually stimulating. At this time Latham began a study of the controversial but widely employed practice of bleeding. His study of the effects of bleeding patients with fevers was based on uncontrolled observation and was undertaken before Pierre Louis introduced statistics into medicine. Latham concluded that the procedure was beneficial, and, like most of his contemporaries, he continued to bleed his patients.[4]

Latham's first publication reported the results of an investigation he had made with Peter Mark Roget on an epidemic of scurvy and dysentery affecting the inmates of the penitentiary at Millbank. According to Thomas Watson, Latham's biographer and an astute Victorian physician, this book was "pregnant with evidence of acute and patient research, and of clear cogent reasoning."[5] In addition to his clinical and literary activities, Latham enjoyed teaching. Beginning in the fall of 1816, he delivered courses of lectures on the practice of physic in London.

Following in his father's footsteps, Latham was appointed physician to St. Bartholomew's Hospital in 1824. The quality of education at this distinguished institution had declined in the years recently preceding his appointment. According to one observer, "the practical instruction given in the medical wards at that hospital at the time of Dr. Latham's election as physician was at its lowest point. He at once applied himself to its improvement; he worked in the wards with uncommon diligence and energy, and his clinic was recognized ere long, as the most careful, precise, and painstaking in London."[6]

Diseases of the heart became a subject of special interest to Latham, largely in response to the recent invention of the stethoscope by Laennec. In 1828, Latham published the text of seven lectures entitled "Pathological Essays on Some Disorders of the Heart," in the *London Medical Gazette*. Eight years later he brought out his important work, *Lectures on Subjects Connected with Clinical Medicine*. In this work, Latham placed great emphasis on auscultation, a technique nearly two decades old, but still little used by British physicians.

Latham's book stimulated renewed interest in, and respect for, auscultation.[7] He emphasized the need for practical experience with auscultation: "The sounds which naturally accompany the movements of the healthy heart, can only be learnt by the practice of listening to them. It is useless to describe them." He also claimed, "the ear must be a well-educated and well-practiced ear, or it is not a trustworthy witness."[8] English physicians appreciated Latham's attempts to render Laennec's technical terminology into simpler phrases and words with which they were more familiar.

In 1846 Latham published two volumes of clinical lectures devoted to diseases of the heart. He chose diseases of the heart as the subject of his book because "after all that has been written upon it, something, I have thought, is still wanting to bring it within the easy reach of the medical student."[9] Latham emphasized the relatively limited scope of his work compared with the more comprehensive treatise of James Hope: "Mine is a limited purpose. It is to regard the diseases of the heart only in one point of view, i.e., as they appear in the living man." But this, he informs us, included clinical diagnosis, clinical history, and medical treatment—hardly a modest undertaking.[9] This work was highly regarded when it appeared in 1846. One biographer commented that Latham's volumes left nothing to be desired and were "among the choicest writings of our profession, and will always be admired and valued."[6]

Extensive sections of the book dealt with auscultation. Latham's understanding of the genesis of heart sounds and murmurs was far more sophisticated than Laennec's, and his book reflects the more recent discoveries. Latham recognized the significance of auscultation:

> Now clinical observation, though never blind, was, until lately, always deaf, yet there were always many diseases

---

*This paper has been adapted from an essay prepared for the Classics of Cardiology Library, Gryphon Editions, Birmingham.

FIG. 1   Pierre Mere Latham (1789–1875). From Ref. 8.

which during the life of the patient spoke only to the ear. These could never have been known, or could only have been guessed at, until clinical observation learnt the use and exercise of that sense by which alone they are discerned. Hence auscultation has had the effect of making it appear that *rare* diseases have all at once become stangely multiplied, whereas it has only disclosed what was before hidden, and made that the subject of sure diagnosis which was before hit upon by chance.[9]

Latham's perceptive comments anticipated the clinical significance of the subsequent development of x-rays, electrocardiography, echocardiography, and, more recently, Doppler echocardiography.

From his lectures, we learn something of Latham's practice. During a five-year period he cared for 136 patients with acute rheumatism at St. Bartholomew's Hospital. The heart was affected in nearly two-thirds of these patients—they developed murmurs or pericardial friction rubs. Angina pectoris was a disease that had long interested Latham. One of his case reports of a patient with angina represented "a classic description of a coronary thrombosis" in the opinion of historian Joshua Leibowitz.[10] Although the clinical syndrome of myocardial infarction would not be recognized for more than

half a century, Latham believed that he had detected a new clinical entity because of the brief period between the first episode of chest discomfort and the last during which the patient died. In most of his cases the delay between first symptoms and death was only a few hours to two weeks. The pathophysiology of myocardial infarction was not understood in Latham's time, so it is not surprising that he was unable to explain the significance of his group of patients who died shortly after their anginal symptoms first appeared.[11]

Other chapters of *Lectures on Subjects Connected with Clinical Medicine* were devoted to rheumatism, endocarditis, valvular diseases that resulted from rheumatism, pericarditis, diseases of the heart's muscular structure, myocardial hypertrophy, arterial and venous diseases, dropsy (congestive heart failure), and angina pectoris. Although most remedies Latham advocated have proved ineffective, his descriptions of the clinical symptoms and physical findings in his patients remain interesting and instructive. He was aware of the value of preventive medicine and hoped that advances in understanding of pathophysiology would provide the knowledge necessary to interrupt the development of, or alter the natural history of, heart diseases.

His classic monograph on heart disease enhanced Latham's stature in the English-speaking medical world. A leader in nineteenth century cardiology, he was known as "Heart" Latham to his contemporaries. After a long and productive life Latham died at Torquay at the age of 86.

References

1. Spaulding WB: Peter Mere Latham (1789–1875): A great medical educator. *Can Med J* 104, 1109 (1971)
2. Stone DB: Peter Mere Latham. *Arch Int Med* 110, 516 (1962)
3. Medvei VC, Thornton JL: *The Royal History of St. Bartholomew, 1123-1973.* Royal Hospital of St. Bartholomew, London (1974)
4. Niebyl PH: The English blood-letting revolution. Or modern medicine before 1850. *Bull Hist Med* 51, 464 (1977)
5. Watson T: In Memoriam: Dr. Peter Mere Latham. In *The Collected Works of Dr. P. M. Latham* (Ed. Martin R). 2 vols. New Sydenham Society, London (1876) 1, xx
6. Munk W: *The Roll of the Royal College of Physicians of London, Comprising Biographical Sketches.* 2nd ed., 3 vols. Royal College of Physicians, London (1878) 3, 186, 187
7. Jarcho S: Peter Latham on the uses of cardiac auscultation (1847). *Am J Cardiol* 16, 571 (1965)
8. Bean WB, Ed.: *Aphorisms from Latham.* Prairie Press, Iowa City, Iowa (1962), 83
9. Latham PM: *Lectures on Subjects Connected with Clinical Medicine, Comprising Diseases of the Heart.* 2nd ed., 2 vols. Longman, Brown, Green, and Longmans, London (1846), vi, vii, 100, 101
10. Leibowitz JO: *The History of Coronary Heart Disease.* Wellcome Institute of the History of Medicine, London (1970), 117
11. Fye WB: The delayed diagnosis of myocardial infarction: It took half a century. *Circulation* 72, 262 (1985)

Marshall Hall

W. Bruce Fye, M.D., M.A.

Department of Cardiology, Marshfield Clinic, Marshfield, Wisconsin, USA

Marshall Hall (Fig. 1) was born in Basford, near Nottingham, England, on February 18, 1790.[1,2] After receiving his preliminary education at the Nottingham Academy, he studied anatomy and chemistry at Newark, England. Hall entered the medical school at the University of Edinburgh in 1809. William Prout, a friend of Hall's at Edinburgh, recalled that he was a "remarkably energetic and persevering" student.[3]

After receiving his medical degree in 1812, Hall was appointed Resident Medical Officer at the Edinburgh Royal Infirmary, then one of the world's leading medical institutions.[4] Following the completion of this part of his formal training, Hall spent a year on the Continent where he visited medical schools in Paris, Berlin, and Göttingen. In 1816, after this unusually comprehensive educational experience, Hall established a medical practice in Nottingham.

Hall published a pioneering book on diagnosis in 1817[5] that enhanced his reputation and helped him build a very successful practice. This book challenged a tradition followed by most of Hall's contemporaries: many physicians treated symptoms empirically without focusing on what might be the underlying cause of a patient's complaint. Hall was an early advocate of the stethoscope. In the second edition of his book on diagnosis (1834),[6] he emphasized the value of the recent invention as an aid to diagnosis. By this time, Hall had moved to London where he spent the rest of his professional career.

Although Hall earned his living as a practitioner, he was deeply interested in experimentation. A prolific writer, he wrote 19 books and more than 150 papers. Between 1824 and 1830, Hall published several papers and a book on the consequences of blood-letting. He believed the popular therapeutic technique was overused and harmed some patients.

Many of Hall's peers admired his literary and scientific contributions, and he was elected a Fellow of the Royal Society in 1832 and a Fellow of the Royal College of Physicians nine years later. Thomas Wakley, editor of the *Lancet*, thought Hall's contributions to physiology were among the most important since William Harvey's classic studies on the circulation of the blood in the seventeenth century. But Hall was a controversial figure. His strong personality attracted a few vocal detractors in addition to several supporters.

Hall's most important contribution to circulatory physiology, *A Critical and Experimental Essay on the Circulation of the Blood*, was published in 1831.[7] In his history of the capillary circulation, physiologist Eugene Landis called this scarce book Hall's "outstanding achievement." Hall was the first to distinguish capillaries from arterioles and venules on anatomical grounds. Using a Dollond achromatic microscope, Hall described for the first time the minute arteriolo-venular communications that came to be known as "direct channels or thoroughfare channels."[8]

In an attempt to study the influence of the nervous system on the circulation, Hall performed vivisections in which he destroyed the brains and spinal cords of fishes and frogs. He concluded that the brain and spinal cord influenced the heart's action, but that cardiac muscle "possess[es] a degree of irritability independently of the large masses of the nervous system." He explained, The irritability is doubtless the faculty or property of the muscular fibre; yet it may become extinct without any obvious change in that fibre. Its continuance or renewal depends ultimately upon the masses of the nervous system.[7a,9] After extending his experiments Hall found that

> ...from the moment the whole of the brain and medullae was destroyed, the circulation gradually, progressively, but slowly failed. It cannot, therefore, by any means, be said that the circulation is independent of the brain and spinal marrow.[7b]

Hall felt compelled to defend the emerging science of experimental physiology that was beginning to come under intense scrutiny and criticism by the embryonic antivivisectionist movement.[10] Hall argued, "The whole science of medicine and surgery, indeed, is dependent on physiology. To exclude physiological investigation, would be to erect an utter barrier to the progress of our art."[7c] Anticipating Claude Bernard's comprehensive synthesis of the philosophy of the experimental method first published in 1865, Hall elaborated several principles of experimental physiology:

1. We should never have recourse to experiment, in cases in which observation can afford us the information required.
2. No experiment should be performed without a distinct and definite object.
3. We should not needlessly repeat experiments which have already been performed by physiologists of reputation.
4. Experiments should be performed 'with the least possible infliction of suffering.'
5. Every physiological experiment should be performed under such circumstances as will secure a

<small>Fig. 1</small> Marshall Hall, 1790–1857. From the collection of the author.

due observation and attestation of its results, and so obviate, as much as possible, the necessity for its repetition.[7d, 11]

Hall also urged the formation of societies for physiologic research in which the members would assist each other in the performance and documentation of their experiments. He felt that by following these precepts "the science of physiology will be rescued from the charges of uncertainty and cruelty, and will be regarded by all men, at once as an important and essential branch of knowledge and scientific research."[7e]

Some of Hall's most important experimental work related to his studies of the reflex action in the 1830s. Commenting on Hall's contributions to neurophysiology, neurologist and historian Walther Riese noted, "For the first time in the history of neurology the concept of the reflex arc was adopted as a basic mechanism of nervous disease, and this makes Marshall Hall the father of modern neurology."[12]

Despite all of the time he devoted to his physiologic research, Hall's practice thrived. During the 1830s and 1840s, he lectured at several hospitals and private medical schools in London. Hall spent a year traveling throughout North America in 1853 and 1854. He died in Brighton, England, in 1857.

References

1. Hall C: *Memoirs of Marshall Hall*, M.D. London: Richard Bentley, 1861
2. Clarke E: Marshall Hall. In *Dictionary of Scientific Biography* (Ed. Gillispie CC), 6, p. 59–61. New York: Charles Scribner's Sons, 1972
3. Green JHS: Marshall Hall (1790–1857): A biographical study. *Med Hist* 1958;2:120–133 (quote p. 121)
4. Risse GB: *Hospital Life in Enlightenment Scotland: Care and Teaching at the Royal Infirmary of Edinburgh*. Cambridge: Cambridge University Press, 1986
5. Hall M: *On Diagnosis*. London: Longman and Co., 1817
6. Hall M: *The Principles of Diagnosis*. London: Longman and Co., 1834
7. Hall M: *A Critical and Experimental Essay on the Circulation of the Blood; Especially as Observed in the Minute and Capillary Vessels of the Batrachia and of Fishes*. London: R.B. Seeley and W. Burnside, 1831. (a) p. 127; (b) p. 140–141; (c) p. 8–9, (d) p. 2–7, (e) p. 8
8. Landis EM: The capillary circulation. In *Circulation of the Blood: Men & Ideas* (Eds. Fishman AP, Richards DW), p. 355–406 (quote p. 363). New York: Oxford University Press, 1964.
9. Fye WB: The origin of the heartbeat. *Circulation* 1987;76:493–500
10. French RD: *Antivivisection and Medical Science in Victorian Society*. Princeton: Princeton University Press, 1975
11. Bernard C: *An Introduction to the Study of Experimental Medicine*. New York: Macmillan Co., 1927
12. Riese W: History and principles of classification of nervous diseases. *Bull Hist Med* 1945;18:465–512

Robert Adams—"A Dublin Master of Clinical Expression"

CHARLES F. WOOLEY, M.D.

The Ohio State University, Columbus, Ohio, USA

Members of the nineteenth century "Dublin school" march across the pages of medical history, leaving a series of clinical descriptions and syndromes that resonate in the language of contemporary medicine. Graves disease, Cheyne-Stokes respiration, Colles fascia, Colles fracture, the Corrigan pulse, and Stokes-Adams attacks are clinical fragments that remain as the legacy of a golden era of Irish medicine that began in the 1820s. The dynamics of this renaissance in Irish medicine and the interactions among the participants form the framework for the comprehensive biography of Dominic Corrigan by Eoin O'Brien, Irish cardiologist and author.[1]

Robert Adams (Fig. 1) was Dublin born; his mother was a Miss Filgate, his father was a solicitor. His training as a surgeon began when he was indentured to William Hartigan, a prominent Irish surgeon, after whose death he was transferred to George Stewart, the Surgeon-General for the English army in Ireland, in 1813. He graduated B.A. in the University in 1814, but did not take the M.B. degree until 1842. He became an M.D. in that year, and in 1861 received a newly instituted qualification of Master in Surgery. The greater part of Adams' anatomical studies was prosecuted in the College of Surgeons under Abraham Colles' direction. He was promoted to the Membership of the College in 1818.[2]

Obviously, this is not the usual background for a clinician remembered primarily for his medical and cardiovascular observations. However, Cameron tells us that Adams was both a surgeon and anatomist of the first rank, and a careful reading of his papers on diseases of the heart reveals an astute and thoughtful physical diagnostician with a physiologic bent. Early in the post-Laennec auscultatory era, Adams was a member of an eight-man committee appointed by the British Association for the Advancement of Science in 1835 to investigate the causes of the auditory cardiac phenomena. The committee repeated a number of experiments and reached a series of conclusions about the origins of the heart sounds that served as consensus until recording methods were introduced into the cardiovascular physiology later in the century.[3]

Adams uses a conversational manner in his description of patients with diseases of the heart, published in 1827.[4] In it, the individual patient history and clinical course were correlated with the postmortem dissections of the period. He described "some remarkable examples of derangement of that organ which have occurred to me in practice" accompanied "with such observations only as have naturally arisen in my mind during a painful attendance on these melancholy cases."

Observations on the function of the normal pericardium precede the clinical profiles of patients with acute pericarditis, rheumatic pericarditis, and ossification of the pericardium—"the heart encircled by a zone of bone." One case presentation is a poignant reminder of the clinician's limitations. A young woman aged 16 years died of an obscure febrile illness of only 14 days' duration; acute purulent pericarditis was found at autopsy. Adams' sentiments have been echoed by clinicians who care for individuals with a catastrophic illness, the outcome of which is beyond contemporary medical diagnosis and therapy:

> Thus, while the dissection in this case gave us an instructive and, at the same time, a humiliating lesson, it also afforded a consolation to the medical attendants and friends of the lady by showing that every measure had been resorted to which a better knowledge of the actual seat of her fatal illness could have suggested.[4]

Adams discussed the natural history and possible etiology of patients presenting with congestive heart failure associated with changes affecting the muscular structure of the heart, "active enlargement of the heart without any valvular disease." He commented about one patient "that on different occasions he would have been suffocated had it not been for the timely and decided relief venesection afforded him."[4]

Rupture of the chordae tendineae of the mitral valve in a 34-year-old musician "of a very robust frame . . . seized with a most acute pain" in the left side of the thorax, was accompanied by oppressed breathing which required the patient to sit leaning forward for relief. Within a short time edema appeared; his pulse was 148, unequal, irregular, and indistinct; exercise intolerance was pronounced, accompanied by dyspnea; anasarca and death followed. In sum, Adams noted that "the accident [was] soon followed by a train of the most distressing symptoms, which art can but little alleviate, and which speedily terminated in death."[4]

Patients with mitral stenosis presented with "paroxysms of dyspnoea hemoptysis;" uneasiness in lying in any but one position; irregular palpitations seen underneath the lower extremity of the sternum; strong pulsations in the jugular veins; and on auscultation "a hissing purring noise as it has

FIG. 1 Robert Adams (1791–1875). Computer graphic from a portrait, courtesy of the National Library of Medicine.

been denominated, caused by the transmission of blood through a narrow orifice, is in most cases very evident."[4]

Adams describes a youth of 15 years of age with severe mitral obstruction and pulsatile neck veins. At postmortem, the severe mitral obstruction was accompanied by massive right ventricular enlargement concealing the small left ventricle. Adams reflected on the pulsations seen in the jugular veins which "demand our consideration . . . the cause of this symptom has been much disputed," and concluded that the jugular venous distention and pulsation

> . . . results from the regurgitation of blood from the right ventricle into the auricle, by which the current descending from the jugular veins is repelled back into these vessels during the systole of the ventricle. The pulsations in the jugular veins I have always observed to be synchronous with the action of the heart, even with the pulsations which were not perceptible in the arteries.[4]

A decade later, when T. W. King published his classic tricuspid valve paper—an essay on the safety valve function of the right ventricle—in the *Guy's Hospital Reports*, he acknowledged the earlier paper by Adams and a personal communication from the author.

Adams was aware of the association between apoplexy and the heart when he described "an officer in the revenue, aged 68 years . . . just recovering from the effects of an apoplectic attack . . . and remarkable slowness of the pulse, which generally ranged at the rate of 30 in a minute." The patient had experienced recurrent attacks for 7 years, and died suddenly following an attack. Adams commented on the circumstances "where the heart is slow in transmitting the blood it receives . . . a means of accounting for the lethargy, loss of

memory, and vertigo, which attends these cases." He concluded that "apoplexy must be considered less a disease in itself than symptomatic of one, the organic seat of which was the heart."[4]

Slow pulse with epileptic paroxysms had been described earlier; however, when William Stokes, a leading figure in the Dublin school, published *Observations on Some Cases of Permanently Slow Pulse* in 1846, he extended the clinical spectrum as he described how a slow heart could interfere with consciousness, and returned to Adams' earlier case presentation and pathophysiologic rationale. Resurrecting Adams' earlier report provided the linkage that contributed to the Stokes-Adams eponym. Huchard named the condition "maladie de Stokes-Adams" in his text in 1889. When Osler discussed *On the So-Called Stokes-Adams Disease (Slow Pulse with Syncopal Attacks, etc.)* in 1903, he had the benefit of the observations on heart block made during the intervening years by a number of physiologists, among them Gaskell, Galabin, and Chauveau. Thus, Osler could speak of "various forms" of the Stokes-Adams syndrome which were soon clarified further with developments in understanding the mechanisms of cardiac conduction and electrophysiology.

As were his Dublin school contemporaries, Adams was deeply interested in medical education and was involved in the beginnings of the Peter-Street School of Medicine and the Carmichael School of Medicine. Thirty years after his case reports of patients with heart disease, he published his *Treatise on Rheumatic Gout, or Chronic Rheumatic Arthritis of All the Joints*; the term chronic rheumatic arthritis has been attributed to Adams. He served three terms as President of the Royal College of Physicians of Dublin and was Regius Professor of Surgery at the University of Dublin.

Less has been written about the personal life of Robert Adams than other members of the Dublin school, and there are large gaps in his biographical profiles. Cameron speaks of Adams as a "short, stout man, with a chubby face—fond of horses, and always had a good one to draw his well-known cabriolet."[2] Perhaps the best characterization of Adams is that bestowed by O'Brien when he wrote of Adams as one of the "Dublin masters of clinical expression."[5]

References

1. O'Brien E: *Conscience and Conflict—A Biography of Sir Dominic Corrigan, 1802–1880*. Dublin: The Glendale Press, 1993:107–170
2. Cameron CA: *History of the Royal College of Surgeons in Ireland and of the Irish Schools of Medicine*. Dublin: Fannin & Company, 1886:395–396
3. *Lancet* 1834–1835;2:740
4. Adams R: Cases of Diseases of the Heart. *Dublin Hospital Reports* 1827;4:353–453
5. O'Brien E: Dublin masters of clinical expression. II. Robert Adams (1791–1875). *J Irish Coll Physicians Surgeons* 1974;3:127–129

Ernst, Wilhelm, and Eduard Weber

W. Bruce Fye, M.D., M.A.

Department of Cardiology, Marshfield Clinic, Marshfield, Wisconsin, USA

This biographical essay is unique in the Profiles series because it describes the careers and contributions of three individuals. The brothers Ernst Heinrich Weber (June 24, 1795–January 26, 1878) (Fig. 1), Wilhelm Eduard Weber (October 24, 1804–June 23, 1891) (Fig. 2), and Eduard Friedrich Wilhelm Weber (March 6, 1806–May 18, 1871) (Fig. 1) are included herein because of their important research and publications dealing with hemodynamics and electrophysiology.[1–4] They were born in Wittenberg, Germany (about 60 miles southwest of Berlin), into a family of 12 children. Ernst Weber, the oldest of the brothers, studied medicine at the Universities of Wittenberg and Leipzig. He spent his career at the University of Leipzig where his research and teaching focused initially on anatomy and comparative anatomy. Appointed to the Chair of Anatomy at the ancient university in 1821, Ernst also held the Chair of Physiology there beginning in 1840. When Carl Ludwig created his unique physiologic institute at Leipzig in 1865, Ernst gave up the Chair of Physiology and retired six years later.[5] Wilhelm Weber received his medical degree from the University of Halle in 1826.[6] Five years later he became a professor of physics at University of Göttingen, where he began a long and productive collaboration with the mathematician and physicist Carl Friedrich Gauss. In 1843, Wilhelm became a professor of physics at Leipzig, where his brothers Ernst and Eduard were already on the faculty. Eduard received his medical training at Halle and taught anatomy at Leipzig, where he became a full professor in 1847.

During the first half of the nineteenth century, physiology was transformed in France and Germany from a mainly observational and philosophical pursuit into an experimental science grounded in vivisection. The most influential pioneers of this new experimental physiology were François Magendie and Johannes Evangelista Purkinje.[7] The Weber brothers began their academic careers in this fertile intellectual context. In 1821, Ernst launched a series of experiments on the physics of fluids. His younger brother Wilhelm, just 18 years old at the time, assisted him in these pioneering investigations. Their sophisticated research resulted in the publication in 1825 of *Wellenlehre, auf Experimenten gegründet*, a 575-page monograph on wave theory that included 18 copper plate illustrations. This classic book included the first detailed application of hydrodynamic principles to the study of the circulation of the blood.[8]

The Webers' book was recognized immediately as an important contribution to physics and physiology. It represented one of the earliest and most successful attempts to replace vitalistic physiology with an approach that employed principles from physics and mathematics. Recently, German historian and physiologist Carl Rothschuh described the Webers as pioneers of the what he termed the "physico-mathematical" approach to physiology. This new experimental model was more fully developed in Germany two decades later by Carl Ludwig, Herman von Helmholtz, Emil DuBois Reymond, and Ernst von Brücke. Rothschuh characterized the Webers' 1825 book as a work that "laid the groundwork for a more exact analysis of the undulatory movements occurring in fluids, especially when circulating through cylinders, the true basis for the motions of the blood."[9] During the next quarter century, the Webers and other scientists extended these experiments on the dynamics of wave motion in fixed and elastic tubes.[10]

In 1827, Ernst described the effect of the elasticity of blood vessels in transforming the pulsatile movement of the blood in the aorta into a continuous flow of blood in arterioles and capillaries. Several decades earlier, Swiss physiologist Albrecht Haller had argued that each contraction of the heart caused the entire blood column to move forward en masse from the aortic valve to the capillaries, resulting in the pulse beating simultaneously throughout the body.[11] Ernst showed, however, that the pulse wave traveled at 9.24 meters per second and arrived in the feet a fraction of a second after it reached the jaw. In a series of experiments over three decades, Ernst produced an ever-clearer picture of the role of elasticity and resistance in the vascular system as a determinant of the distribution and rate of flow of blood throughout the body. His pioneering research culminated in the publication of *Ueber die Anwendung der Wellenlehre auf die Lehre vom Kreislauf des Blutes und insbesondere auf die Pulslehre* in 1850.

The Weber brothers' second major contribution to physiology was their discovery of the phenomenon of vagal inhibition of the heartbeat.[12] Ernst and Eduard's important experiments in electrophysiology began as a study of the physiology of muscle and were made possible by Michael Faraday's 1831 invention of the dynamo or electric generator. They connected one pole of an electromagnetic apparatus to the nostril of a frog and connected the other pole to the mid portion of the experimental animal's spinal cord. When they applied electric

FIG. 1 Ernst Heinrich Weber (1795–1878) (right) and Eduard Friedrich Wilhelm Weber (1806–1871) (left). From the collection of W. Bruce Fye.

FIG. 2 Wilhelm Eduard Weber (1804–1891). From the collection of W. Bruce Fye.

current, they noted dramatic slowing and sometimes frank standstill of the heart. Later, they extended their experiments from frogs to warm-blooded mammals such as cats, dogs, and rabbits. The Weber brothers first reported their observations at a scientific congress in Naples, Italy, in 1845 and published them in detail the following year.[13]

Physiologist and historian John Fulton translated the portion of their paper in which vagal inhibition was first described:

> If the medulla oblongata of a frog or the ends of the isolated vagus nerves are excited by the rotation of a fairly strong electro-magnetic machine, the heart suddenly stops beating, but if the end of excitation begins after a short interval to beat again: at first slowly and weakly, then gradually more strongly and more frequently until finally the original beat observed before excitation is restored.

Fulton claimed that the Webers "deserve great credit for finally tracing the pathway of the effect which they observed to the vagus." He concluded that

> …the experiment is a very important milestone in the history of physiology not merely because of its significance to the circulation, but because it brought to light a wholly new kind of nervous action and it formed the beginning of a series of highly significant researches upon the inhibitory processes occurring within the central nervous system.[14]

The diverse and important contributions of the Weber brothers extended well beyond their classic publications on hemodynamics and electrophysiology. They were influential

teachers and mentors to two generations of scientists who continued to expand understanding of the structure and function of the human body and the physical and mathematical principles that governed many aspects of physiology.

References

1. Bueck-Rich U: *Ernst Heinrich Weber (1795–1878) und der Anfang einer Physiologie der Hautsinne*. Zürich: Juris Druck (1970)
2. Dawson PM: Life and work of Ernst Heinrich Weber. *Phi Beta Pi Quarterly* 1928;25:86–116
3. Kruta V: Ernst Heinrich Weber. In *Dictionary of Scientific Biography*, Vol. 14 (Ed. Gillespie CC), p. 199–202. New York: Charles Scribner's Sons, 1976
4. Woodruff AE: Wilhelm Eduard Weber. In *Dictionary of Scientific Biography*, Vol. 14 (Ed. Gillespie CC), p. 203–209. New York: Charles Scribner's Sons, 1976
5. Fye WB: Carl Ludwig and the Leipzig Physiological Institute: A factory of new knowledge. *Circulation* 1986;74:920–928
6. Werner K: *Wilhelm Weber*. Leipzig: B. G. Teubner (1976)
7. Coleman W, Holmes FL (Eds.): *The Investigative Enterprise: Experimental Physiology in Nineteenth-Century Medicine*. Berkeley and Los Angeles: University of California Press (1988)
8. Weber EH, Weber W: *Wellenlehre auf Experiment gegründet oder über die Wellen tropfbarer Flüssigkeiten mit Anwendung auf die Schall- und Lichtwellen*. Leipzig: Gerhard Fleischer (1825)
9. Rothschuh KE: *History of Physiology*, p. 178. Huntington, N.Y.: Robert E. Krieger (1973)
10. Fishman AP, Richards DW (Eds.): *Circulation of the Blood: Men and Ideas*. New York: Oxford University Press (1964)
11. Buess H: William Harvey and the foundation of modern haemodynamics by Albrecht von Haller. *Med Hist* 1970;14:175–182
12. Hoff HE: The history of vagal inhibition. *Bull Hist Med* 1940;8: 461–496
13. Weber E: Muskelbewegung. In *Handwörterbuch der Physiologie* (Ed. Wagner R), p. 1–122. Braunschweig: Friedrich Vieweg, 1846
14. Fulton JF, Wilson LG: *Selected Readings in the History of Physiology*, 2 ed., p. 295–296. Springfield, Ill.: Charles C Thomas, 1966

Jean Baptiste Bouillaud

Barry D. Silverman, M.D.

Department of Cardiology, Northside Hospital, Atlanta, Georgia, USA

The Napoleonic era (1795-1815) introduced a period of great social, economic, political, and scientific change. The spirit of medical science was stimulated by reasoned logical diagnosis and meticulous autopsy control. Morgagni, Boerhaave, Sydenham, Haller, the Hunters, Vieussens, and Senac were foremost in promoting this progress. During the first half of the nineteenth century there was a revolution in the treatment of disease and the development of a new school of medicine. Patients had been bled, blistered, purged, and vomited, frequently dosed with mercury, antimony, and other compounds. In this age, there was growth of a remarkable skeptical spirit; a new school of physicians sought to study rationally and scientifically. France, largely spared from the ravages of war, was the medical Mecca of the world. There, Bichat, Portal, Dupuytren, Corvisart, Louis, and Laennec advanced important new concepts in anatomy, pathology, physical diagnosis, and pathophysiology. Jean Baptiste Bouillaud was one of the most distinguished physicians of this period.[1]

The contributions of Jean Baptiste Bouillaud were especially significant in cardiology. His studies included meticulous measurement of the heart, identification of the endocardium and a description of endocarditis, important contributions in auscultation of the heart and descriptions of new physical signs, statement of his law of coincidence, and cardinal studies in congenital heart disease. In addition, he accomplished pioneering work in neurology. He esteemed the work of Gall in cerebral localization of neurologic deficits and made substantial contributions in this area.[2]

Jean Baptiste Bouillaud was born on September 16, 1796, at Bragette near Angoulème in France. He was educated at the Lycée Angoulème and won awards for excellence and a prize for Latin verse. Latin was especially valuable as it was the language of science and medicine in the nineteenth century. He was encouraged by a physician uncle, a surgeon-major in the army, to study medicine. In 1814, he traveled to Paris for study. However, as a student at the École Polytechnique, he became embroiled in the war and joined a Hussar regiment to resist the allies. Unsuccessful at the Barrière de Clichy, he returned to his studies in 1816.[3]

Bouillaud was a pupil of Dupuytren and attended him in his last illness. He was instructed by the professor to perform his autopsy. He diligently attended the lectures of Corvisart, and was a pupil of Magendie and a disciple of Broussais. His fervent faith in Broussais' views may have resulted in some diminution of Bouillaud's reputation. Broussais was an avid advocate for bleeding. Bouillaud often recommended and encouraged this practice, even after it had fallen into disfavor and was recognized by most practitioners to be harmful.[2]

Bouillaud interned at the Hôpital Cochin under René-Joseph Bertin and assisted him in the preparation of his book on diseases of the heart, published in 1824. He was an active investigator and published several well-received monographs that established his reputation and resulted in his election to the Académie de Médecine in 1826. He was appointed professor of clinical medicine in 1831. He served on the staffs of several hospitals until his appointment to the Hôpital de la Charité. This institution was made famous by Corvisart and Laennec. In 1836, he published his *Nouvelles recherches sur le rhumatisme articulaire aigu* which first stated his law of coincidence. His other important works include *Essai sur la philosophie médicale et sur les généralities de la clinique médicale* published in 1836; *Clinique médicale de l'Hôpital de la Charité* published in three volumes in 1837; *Traîté de nosographique médicale,* which appeared in five volumes in 1846.[3]

Bouillaud was also a respected teacher and a successful and busy practitioner. His patients included celebrities and royalty including Napoeon III. He served as a politician and was elected to the Chamber of Deputies in 1840. He was enthusiastically involved in the development of the profession. He served as Dean of the Paris faculty of medicine in 1848, president of the Academy of Medicine in 1862, and president of the first International Congress of Medicine in 1867.

Bouillaud was the first to describe the endocardium and its inflammation, endocarditis. He comments in the preface to his first edition of *Traîté des maladies du coeur,* "I have given the name of endocardium to the inner lining of this organ and that of endocarditis to its inflammation." In his treatise, he states, "It is of the greatest importance to know thoroughly the anatomic characteristics proper to each of of the periods of endocarditis, if one would comprehend in a clear and precise manner the principal symptoms which it produces in its course." His "law of coincidence" stated: "In severe acute generalized articular rheumatism the coincidence of endocarditis, pericarditis, or endo-pericarditis is the rule, the law, and the non-coincidence the exception." He felt that myocarditis occurred independently of endocarditis and pericarditis.[5]

FIG. 1 Jean Baptiste Bouillaud, 1796–1881. (Photograph from the collection of Dr. Bruce Fye and used with permission).

The first accurate methods of weighing and measuring the heart are the result of Bouillaud's studies. He is credited with creating the topographical anatomy of the heart. Bouillaud recognized the importance of auscultation in diagnosing disorders of the heart. In contrast, Laennec discounted auscultation as helpful in the diagnosis of heart disease. Bouillaud described the split second heart sound and correctly attributed this to aortic and pulmonic closure, the opening snap of mitral steno-

sis, and venous hums in chlorosis; he noted the significance of the murmur of pericarditis, and is credited with describing gallop rhythm. Bouillaud published a treatise on congenital heart disease and suggested that congenital anomalies were caused by both development defects and diseases of the fetus. He commented on abnormalities of cardiac rhythm and studied aortic aneurysm. He was among the first to recognize the importance of chemistry and physics to medicine.[2]

Bouillaud died in his eighty-eighth year in 1881, and a statue was erected in his honor four years later at Angouléme. He was an outstanding clinician, a thoughtful researcher, a prodigious scholar in his studies, a respected teacher, and a leader of the profession; yet, he was criticized and almost forgotten after his death. This may be the result of his resistance to accept changes, especially his insistence on bleeding. Heavy and repeated bleeding was his practice long after it had been widely discredited.

References

1. Osler W: Medicine in the nineteenth century (Chap. XIII). In *Aequanimitas,* 2nd ed., p.227–276, 1906
2. Rolleston JD: Jean Baptiste Bouillaud. *Proc Roy Soc Med (Sect Hist Med)* 1937;24:1253–1262
3. Willius FA, Keys TE: Jean Baptiste Bouillaud (1796–1881) and on the pathology of endocarditis (1835). *Classics of Cardiology,* Vol. II, p. 443–455. Malabar: Robert E. Krieger Co., 1983
4. Herrick JB: A short history of cardiology (Chap. IV). In *Laennec to Virchow, 1819–1845,* p.84–162. Springfield: Charles C Thomas, 1942
5. Willius FA, Dry TJ: *A History of the Heart and the Circulation: The First Half of the Nineteenth Century,* p. 106–146. Philadelphia: W.B. Saunders Co., 1948

James Hope*

W. B. Fye, M.D.

Cardiology Department, Marshfield Clinic, Marshfield, Wisconsin, USA

James Hope (Fig. 1) was born in 1801 in the village of Stockport, near Manchester, England.[1] He studied first at Oxford before beginning his medical studies at the famed Edinburgh University in the Fall of 1820. While there, Hope became active in the affairs of the Royal Medical Society, a spirited organization that sponsored weekly meetings in which currnet medical topics were debated by the members.[2] Laennec's recent invention, the stethoscope, attracted the attention of leading Edinburgh physicians, and Hope heard members of the society discuss its usefulness. The stethoscope led to a resurgence of interest in disorders of the thoracic organs, and Hope chose the subject of heart disease for his first presentation before the Society in 1823.

After five years in Edinburgh, Hope departed for London to study at Saint Bartholomew's Hospital where William Harvey had practiced two centuries earlier. Ambitious British medical graduates of this era routinely supplemented their training with study on the continent. Paris was the acknowledged center of medical education. Perhaps the greatest contribution of French medicine during this era was the encouragement of rigorous and systematic correlation of clinical findings with the postmortem appearance of the various organs.[3]

Hope studied at several of the best hospitals in Paris and took courses with many of the leaders of French medicine. His teachers included Gabriel Andral, Pierre Louis, Alexis Boyer, and August-François Chomel. As a clinical clerk under Chomel at the famed Hôtel Dieu, Hope was in charge of six to ten patients. His responsibilities included taking careful notes on each case, suggesting options for treatment, and performing and recording the results of postmortem examinations.

Following four years of study on the continent, Hope embarked upon his medical practice in London. He soon became physician to Marylebone Infirmary where he was in charge of nearly 100 beds. The patients at this institution were from the lowest classes of British society and often came to the hospital with advanced illnesses. Hope's work at Marylebone increased his already burgeoning clinical experience. An early and ardent supporter of auscultation, Hope regularly used a stethoscope in examining his patients. He sought to prove its usefulness by careful correlation of the history, physical findings, and postmortem results.

Laennec's premature death left the field of auscultation open to other workers. The great French clinician had published many important observations, but several of his conclusions regarding the heart sounds were soon challenged by other advocates of the stethoscope. Vivisection had been used for centuries to study the circulation, and Hope turned to animal experiments to clarify the etiology of the heart sounds. In his research he employed various cold-and warm-blooded animals, including donkeys. After stunning an animal (anesthe-

Fig. 1 James Hope, M.D. 1801–1841. From Grant K (Ed). *Memoir of the Late James Hope, M.D. . . . by Mrs. Hope*. 3rd ed., J. Hatchard & Sons, London (1844).

*This paper has been adapted from an essay prepared for the Classics of Cardiology Library, Gryphon Editions (Birmingham).

sia had not been discovered) and initiating artificial ventilation, Hope opened the chest and placed his stethoscope directly on the animal's heart.[4,5] In this way he was able to make important observations on regurgitant murmurs and the auscultatory features of mitral stenosis.

Hope believed the principles of fluid dynamics could aid him in his attempt to uncover the physiology of the heart sounds. He emphasized the role of turbulence in the production of heart murmurs that were now clearly heard with the stethoscope. Hope's experiments on the heart sounds and murmurs were summarized in his classic volume, *Treatise on the Diseases of the Heart and Great Vessels*, which appeared in 1831.[6] He explained that his conclusions were based on patients he had seen, and his animal experiments. His monograph included several case reports in which a brief clinical sketch was accompanied by a description of the physical findings, autopsy results, and comments.

Unlike Laennec's monograph on diseases of the chest, Hope's work included extensive sections regarding the treatment of diseases of the heart. These comments provide valuable insight into contemporary approaches to the treatment of diseases in general. As was characteristic of this era, Hope advocated "heroic" therapy. For example, for the treatment of acute pericarditis, he advised bloodletting to the verge of syncope. In addition to venesection, leeches were used extensively for this purpose. In cases of valvular heart disease, Hope urged the use of bloodletting in moderation and suggested that this was most useful if employed to relieve dyspnea. He also advocated the use of diuretics and digitalis if edema and decreased urine volume were present.

His book was warmly received by the medical profession. Shortly after the publication of the third edition of his book on the heart in 1839, Hope's health began to fail rapidly. He had been ill for three years and was soon forced to retire from medical practice. Hope died at the age of 40 in May 1841. During his brief life, he left a rich record of his sophisticated research into the origin of the heart sounds and the physiology of the circulation.

References

1. Grant K (ed): *Memoir of the Late James Hope, M.D. . . . by Mrs. Hope*. 3rd ed. J. Hatchard & Sons, London (1844)

2. Guthrie D (ed): *History of the Royal Medical Society, 1737–1937*. Edinburgh University Press, Edinburgh (1952)

3. Ackerknecht E: *Medicine at the Paris Hospital, 1794–1848*. Johns Hopkins Press, Baltimore (1967)

4. Keele KD: The application of the physics of sound to 19th century cardiology: With particular reference to the part played by C. J. B. Williams and James Hope. *Clio Medica* 8, 191 (1973)

5. Bluth I: James Hope and the acceptance of auscultation. *J Hist Med Allied Sci* 25, 202 (1970)

6. Hope J: *A Treatise on the Diseases of the Heart and Great Vessels*. W. Kidd, London (1832)

Karl Rokitanski

ZDENĚK FEJFAR, M.D., AND LUDMILA HLAVÁČKOVA, PH.D.*

*Institute for the History of Medicine, 1st Medical Faculty, Charles University, Prague, Czech Republik

The son of a Czech county officer and an Irish mother, Karl Rokitanski was born February 19, 1804, in Hradec Králové, the cultural center of eastern Bohemia. He was matriculated at the medical faculty of Prague's Charles University at the age of 18. Two years later he left Prague and continued his studies at the medical faculty of Vienna University. In 1827, a year before receiving his M.D. degree, he started work in the dissection lab of the Vienna General Hospital as an unpaid volunteer, and three years later became a paid assistant dissector. In 1832, he was nominated associate professor and custodian of the Museum of Pathology at the medical faculty of Vienna University, and two years later was nominated Chair of Pathology—the first at Vienna University.[1]

Apart from his monumental work in pathology, Rokitanski gave considerable attention to promoting modern teaching at the university. He was elected Dean of the Medical School of Vienna University for four terms (1849–1850, 1856–1857, 1859–1860, 1862–1863) and even became the first freely elected rector of Vienna University during 1852 and 1853. A member of the Academy of Sciences in Vienna since 1848 and elected its President in 1869, Rokitanski led the Academy until his death on July 23, 1878. Beginning in 1863, he worked as a medical referee in the Ministry of Culture and Education and became a member of the Upper Chamber of the Austro-Hungarian Imperial Council in 1874. In the same year, he was raised to nobility by having a baronetcy conferred upon him.

Stimulated by French and English medical literature, Rokitanski's basic principle of work, from the beginning of his involvement in pathology, was "conclusion based on observation," in contrast to the then prevailing German "Naturphilosophie" speculation. An advantage of this intelligent autodidact was the unique situation in Vienna. With only one dissection laboratory and approximately 2,000 autopsies performed a year, Rokitanski learned how to systematize and classify organ lesions from macroscopic observations and identified a great number of diseases. In close cooperation with his clinical colleagues and friends (in internal medicine with Josef Skoda in particular) confrontation with the clinical diagnosis —apart from diagnostic advances in other medical specialties such as surgery, gynecology, obstetrics, ophthalmology, and dermatology—substantially promoted diagnosis of diseases at bedside.

Within a decade, Rokitanski published his fundamental work, *Handbook of Pathological Anatomy*. Volume 2 in 1842 and Volume 3 in 1844 covered descriptions of diseased organs. This handbook is the foundation of pathology as a separate discipline and appeared to instant high acclaim. In fact, pathologic anatomy became the most fundamental part of medicine. Rokitanski became the main star in the so-called second medical school of Vienna, which attracted students and postgraduates from all of Europe as well as from overseas. In 1885, Virchow considered his classification of diseases to be of similar importance for pathology as that of Linné for botany. Chairs of pathology in most universities of the Austro-Hungarian empire were filled by his pupils.

The fate of the first volume on general pathology, published in 1848, was different. As a great number of deaths occurred without macroscopically visible organ lesions, and as it was not possible to localize the disease in specific organs, Rokitanski put forth a hypothesis called "Krasen Lehre"—humoral pathology—with the site of the disease state being somewhere in the blood fluid embracing all organs. The idea was formulated before organic chemistry and biochemistry came into being. Young Rudolph Virchow, then 27, recognized the fallacy of attempts to explain morphology by means of a not yet developed chemistry and took a strong line over the humoral hypothesis. Within a short time, the giant Rokitanski understood, and the second edition of the handbook came out in 1855 without the theory of humoral pathology.[2]

Looking at the problem a hundred years later, it appears that Rokitanski's idea was too advanced to be understood. In the thrombotic theory of atherogenesis proposed by Duguid and Astrup, the latter's description is very clear:

> Rokitanski suggested that fibrinous deposits were produced on the vessel wall by an effect of the exudate released from injured tissue on some components in the blood. This concept was one of the main reasons for Virchow's rejection of Rokitanski's idea, since he thought blood clotting was caused by oxygen. Intuitively, Rokitanski reached views concerning physiological processes which forecast observations made many years later. His concepts were developed before fibrinogen was known as an entity, before thrombin was known,

FIG. 1 Dissection laboratory at Vienna General Hospital. (Source: Ref. No. 2). Reproduced by permission of the Institute for the History of Medicine, University of Vienna.

before the clot promoting effect of the tissue extract was known and more than sixty years before its role as an activator and its difference from thrombin was revealed by Morawitz and Fuld and Spiro.

Rokitanski's swan song was the monograph *The Defects of the Heart Septum*. In this monograph of 56 pages, lavishly illustrated and dedicated to the Society of Physicians in Vienna, the author describes his personal observations of 24 patients with ventricular septal defects and 20 with atrial septal defects. A detailed characterization of various forms of defects is followed by the description of the evolution of chicken embryos (experiments by Lindes) and of the origin of heart malformations, including the various forms of the transposition of the great vessels.[4]

Beginning with his early days as dissector, Rokitanski, by his new approach to pathology as well as by his approach to teaching and research at the University of Vienna, brought fresh air to progress and liberalization. He was the leading spirit in the struggle to overcome the traditional approach of the first Vienna medical school and, as head of young students, he brought new life into the university. In the second half of the century Vienna again became the center of medicine in Europe, and the pathologist Rokitanski, with

FIG. 2 Collegium of professors at Vienna University. Karl von Rokitanski (1804–1878) is seated in the middle holding a book. On his right is Joseph Skoda. Source: Ref. No. 2. Reproduced by permission of the Institute for the History of Medicine, University of Vienna.

the internist Joseph Skoda, were the two most important personalities in attracting students from all over Europe to visit and study in Vienna.

As the first pathologist on our planet, Karl Rokitanski has a place among the most outstanding personalities of medicine in the world, first of all because of his unbelievable performance. His published work is based on personal knowledge of more than 60,000 autopsies performed in his Institute and more than 25,000 forensic autopsies. In addition, he held several important appointments at Vienna University, at the Ministry of Culture and Education, as well as at the Academy of Sciences. Rokitanski's successor, Prof. R. Herschel (1824–1881) compared his contribution to medicine with that of Copernicus to astronomy. It seems that he did not exaggerate.

Karl Rokitanski's particular contribution to cardiology is the idea of the thrombus formation in the wall of the artery as the beginning of atherogenesis, based on the findings of fibri-nous deposits in the pulmonary artery; and, of course, the detailed description and classification of atrial and ventricular septal defects.

References

1. von Rokytanski C: Selbstbiographie und Antrittrede (Ed. Lesky E). Graz, Köln, Vienna: Hermann Böhlauf Nachf., 1960
2. Lesky E: Wiener medizinische Schule im 19. Köln, Vienna, Graz: Jahrhundert, 1965
3. Astrup T: Role of blood coagulation and fibrinolysis in the pathogenesis of arteriosclerosis. In *Connective Tissue, Thrombosis and Atherosclerosis* (Ed. Page IH), p. 223–240. Proceedings of a conference held in Princeton, New Jersey, May 12–14, 1958. New York and London: Academic Press, 1959
4. von Rokitanski C: Die Defekte der Scheidewände des Herzens. Pathologisch-anatomische Abhandlung, p. 1–156. Wien: W. Baumüller Verlag, 1875

William Stokes (1804–1878)

J. D. CANTWELL, M.D.

Preventive Medicine Center, the Cardiac Rehabilitation Program; and the Internal Medicine Residency Program, Georgia Baptist Medical Center, Atlanta, Georgia, USA

Throughout the first half of the nineteenth century, most of Ireland (including the city of Dublin) was in a state of decay. The culmination of this was the potato famine of 1845–1849, wherein over a million Irish men, women, and children died of malnutrition and starvation; countless others, including my great grandfather, emigrated to other countries. In the midst of these most trying of times, a remarkable group of internists, including Stokes, Graves, Corrigan, and Cheyne made the Dublin School of Medicine famous. To paraphrase Herrick, they were not only practical physicians but also men with investigative spirits, gifted lecturers and bedside teachers, authors of now classic articles and books and founders of journals and medical societies. One of the most talented was William Stokes (Fig. 1).[1–8]

Family Background and Early Years

The Stokes family came to Ireland in 1680. William's great grandfather, an engineer, devised a system for supplying piped water to the city of Dublin. Whitley Stokes (William's father) was a physician and initially an ardent member of the United Irishmen. He was eccentric, but very able, and became Regius Professor of Medicine in Trinity College. He helped establish the College Botanical Gardens and the Zoological Gardens, and also published, at his own expense, a translation of the New Testament into Irish.

William was born in Dublin in 1804. His academic beginnings were less than auspicious. He left formal schooling after only one day, "after having drawn blood by sending a slate at his master's head."[5] He initially seemed shy, lazy, and incompetent, and lacked interest in either sports or education, preferring to read the ballads of Sir Walter Scott, lying in a field, his head "propped on the neck of a red cow."[5] Stimulated by his mother's tears, he began to reform. He joined his father on long walks in the woods and developed an interest in the archaeologists, painters, lawyers, and doctors who dropped by his father's study. He was not admitted to Trinity College, perhaps because of his father's nonconformity or prior connections with the United Irishmen, but a tutor helped him learn the essentials of Greek, Latin, and math, and his father instructed him in science. William began working in the laboratories of Trinity College and the Royal College of Surgeons, and walked the wards of Meath Hospital with the students and Dr. Robert Graves. He subsequently attended medical school in Edinburgh, where he spent the days in lectures and the nights making house calls with Professor Alison. He graduated in 1825 and promptly published a 269-page treatise on the use of the stethoscope. This was the first English publication on this new technique. It took William three months to write it, and earned for him the sum of 70 pounds. It also helped establish his academic reputation.

After graduation, Stokes began working in Dublin's General Dispensary. In a subsequent letter to Mary Black (his future wife) he wrote: "In the course of my practice here I meet with instances of want and wretchedness that wring my very heart, and I wish for the fortune of a prince that I might relieve them."[1] In 1826, he joined the staff at the Meath Hospital (a year after John Cheyne was forced to limit his own practice there due to ill health) and became immersed in treating victims of the typhus epidemic.

Events in His Career

Stokes spent 50 years working at Meath Hospital, including 30 years of collaboration with Robert Graves. The latter was eight years older, and died 25 years before Stokes. According to Herrick they were colleagues, but not rivals, unusually effective lecturers and bedside clinicians, prolific writers (and often coauthors), and active participants in medical societies. Of Graves, Stokes wrote, "He was once my teacher, later my colleague, always my friend."[5]

In 1837, Stokes published *A Treatise on the Diagnosis and Treatment of Diseases of the Chest,* the first of his three medical texts. It was considered the best book on the subject since Laennec's. In it he referred to a case described by Cheyne in 1818, a bedridden 60-year-old man who was flushed, speechless, and hemiplegic:

The only peculiarity in the last period of his illness, which lasted only eight or nine days, was in the state of his respiration. For several days, his breathing was irregular; it would entirely cease for a quarter of a minute, then it would become perceptible, though very low, then

FIG. 1   William Stokes, M.D. (1804–1878). Photograph provided by the National Library of Medicine, Bethesda, Maryland.

by degrees it became heaving and quick, and then it would cease again.[3]

Stokes observed this in other cases and linked it to a weakened heart. He commented that in this condition (the apneic phase) "the patient may remain as such a length of time as to make his attendants believe that he is dead . . . ."[8] The condition is now known as Cheyne-Stokes respiration.

In 1845, Stokes became Regius Professor of Medicine at Dublin University. The next year, writing in the *Dublin Quarterly Journal*, he described two of his cases with syncopal episodes and a slow pulse, and mentioned five other case reports, including one that fellow Dubliner Robert Adams (a surgeon) had published in 1827. The latter case was a 68-year-old man who had multiple "apoplectiform seizures'" over a 7-year period. Adams noted "the remarkable slowness of the pulse which generally ranged at the rate of 30 in a minute."[3] The patient subsequently died during a similar attack and the autopsy showed a dilated right ventricle, a soft and thin-walled left ventricle, "specks of bone" in the aortic valve, and fatty changes in the myocardium. Stokes described cannon waves in the neck of his two patients, noting that "the pulsation of veins is of a kind which we have never before witnessed."[3] He mainly wanted to draw attention to the combination of the cerebral and cardiac phenomena, "of which our knowledge is still imperfect."[3] The condition today is recognized as the Adams-Stokes attacks (or Morgagni-Adams-Stokes attacks, for Morgagni had mentioned a prematurely slow pulse in 1760).

Stokes published his second medical book, *Diseases of the Heart and Aorta*, in 1854, aimed at helping the general practitioner and featuring experience gleaned from case histories. This book "carried the renown of the Dublin School throughout Europe and became a classic in United States schools as well."[1] Stokes stressed the importance of a murmur in diagnosis, and the difficulty in distinguishing the existence of functional and organic disease (which can "occasionally baffle the powers of even the most enlightened and experienced physician"[6]). He also cautioned against overreliance on the stethoscope, for "too many depend on it alone to ascertain the disease."[4] He recognized that the efficiency of heart muscle could be improved with graduated exercise: "The symptoms of debility of the heart are often removable by a regulated course of gymnastics, or by pedestrian exercise."[6] He was aware of angina pectoris, but felt that "obstruction of the coronary arteries must be considered as but a remote cause of angina."[3]

Personal Attributes

Stokes had an attractive personality, was modest and courteous, and possessed an "intermittent exuberance of almost childlike spirits."[5]

He had a multitude of interests beyond medicine, including archaeology, music, art, and literature. His closest nonmedical friend was Petrie, an archaeologist and collector of Irish music, whom Stokes memorialized in a biography. The Stokes' home in Merrion Square was open to friends every Saturday evening for fellowship and stimulating conversation. A country home near the seaside provided a brief respite from his large private practice, hospital work, and teaching duties. In his typical day:

I rise early, write until breakfast, then go to the dispensary where I sit in judgement on disease for an hour; then to the hospital, where I go around the wards attended by a crowd of pupils. From the hospital I return home, write again until two, then go around and visit my patients through the various parts of the town attended by a pupil.[5]

As an educator, Stokes believed that medical doctors and surgeons should get the same basic training ("The constitution is one; there is no division of it into a medical and surgical domain").[5] He felt that medicine was not a single science but "an art, depending on all sciences,"[6] and that a liberal education could give a student the moral character so necessary for medicine:

. . . the still prominent evils among us are the neglect of general education, the confounding of instruction with education, and the giving of greater importance to the special training than to the general culture of the student.[6]

This emphasis on the advantages of a liberal education for medical students "was exemplified by his own life."[2] One can see why he was such a popular teacher, for "his great object in teaching medicine was to make his pupils practical men, to stimulate them to original investigations, and to make them feel that he himself was in all cases their fellow-student."[7]

Later Years and Honors

Stokes was elected physician to the Queen in Ireland in 1861. In 1867, he served as President of the British Medical Association. His last book, *Lectures on Fever*, was published in 1871, the same year the University of Dublin established the Diploma in State Medicine (at his urging) for those who wished to emphasize preventive medicine. In 1874, because of his interest in and patronage of the arts, he was elected President of the Irish Academy. In 1875, Stokes resigned as physician to Meath Hospital and as Regius Professor of Medicine. The following year the German government honored him with the Prussian Order of Merit. In November 1877, Stokes had a stroke, and died on January 10, 1878. He was buried at St. Finlans, in Howth.

Thus ended the life of not just an outstanding clinician, teacher, and writer, but of a cultured man and prominent citizen of Dublin, one "ever conscious of the unique position of a doctor in society."[6] His obituary stated it best:

Stokes did not obtain any title. He never coveted any; he never sought any. He was a prince from birth of the aristocracy of intellect. His name is crowned with the triple coronet of the gratitude of the poor, for whom he tenderly and piously cared; the confidence of the public, whose approbation he universally secured; and the love and esteem of his profession, whose honour and interests he unflinchingly upheld.[7]

Acknowledgment

Fay Boyer, Librarian at Georgia Baptist Medical Center, was extremely helpful in obtaining selected references.

References

1. Bendiner E: The Dublin School: From poverty, a rich legacy. *Hosp Prac* 19, 221 (1984)
2. Brian VA: William Stokes. 1804–1878. *Nursing Times* 73, 311 (1977)
3. Herrick JB: *A Short History of Cardiology.* Charles C Thomas, Springfield (1942)
4. Logan P: William Stokes. View of a student. *Irish Med J* 71, 602 (1978)
5. O'Brien B: William Stokes (1804–1878). *Irish Med J* 71, 598 (1978)
6. O'Brien E: William Stokes 1804–78; the development of a doctor. *Br Med J* 2, 749 (1978)
7. Schoenberg DG, Schoenberg BS: Eponym: William Stokes: Stoking the fires of preventive and pathophysiologic patterns. *South Med J* 71, 956 (1978)
8. Timepiece. A Peculiarity of Respiration. *J Cardiovasc Med* 7, 496 (1982)

Joseph Skoda

ZDENĚK FEJFAR, M.D., AND LUDMILA HLAVÁČKOVA, PH.D.

Institute for the History of Medicine, First Medical Faculty, Charles University Prague, Prague, Czech Republic

Joseph Skoda was born in Plzeň, Bohemia (later Czechoslovakia), on May 12, 1805. The third son of a poor locksmith, he had to give private lessons as a teenager in order to graduate from the gymnasium (high school) in Plzeň. There was no money for candles or lamp oil, and the adolescent Skoda spent evenings studying by the light from the kitchen stove flames. In 1825, after graduation and studies in philosophy, he went to Vienna to study medicine. In addition to medicine he studied higher mathematics and physics and he passed the examination so successfully that his teacher, Prof. Baumgartner, urged him to devote his life to mathematics.

The degree of doctor of medicine was conferred on Skoda on July 18, 1831. Because of the cholera epidemic at that time he was obliged, as were other doctors, to work in the so-called cholera districts. Young Skoda, with a fresh medical degree, performed this duty for a year, leaving it in November 1833. On his return, he obtained a job at Vienna General Hospital as a houseman without pay. This started his amazing career as the founding father of modern physical diagnostics. His famous courses on diseases of the chest began in 1834 and soon attracted young colleagues from the Austrian monarchy as well as from other European countries.[1]

Objective observation based on physical diagnosis confirmed or corrected by pathology revolutionized medicine at that time—the generation before Skoda and his friend Rokitansky had attempted to explain diseases by changes in the environment (temperature, barometric pressure, humidity, etc.). Percussion of the chest, introduced by the Austrian L. Auenbrugger in his book, published in 1771 in Latin, remained unnoticed in his country. It was promoted, on the other hand, by J.N. Corvisart (1755–1821) in Paris, and together with auscultation, introduced by R.T.H. Laennec (1748–1822), the French clinicians moved ahead of the old Austrian school. Their diagnostic conclusions, however, were reached intuitively, and percussion or auscultation phenomena were ascribed as typical for specified organ disease (liver, lung tuberculosis, etc.).

Skoda reimported Auenbrugger's use of percussion. His approach—in contrast to that of the French colleagues—was based solely on the objective description of physical signs. To him, the acoustic phenomena produced by percussion were not specific for a given organ, but for the amount of air or fluid; hollow, empty, tympanic, high, deep, clear, dull. Based on acoustic phenomena, Skoda tried to explain the physical changes in an organ and then, from the anatomical and pathologic possibilities, he reached a clinical diagnostic conclusion.

In a similar way, Skoda developed a system of physical diagnosis of the diseases of the heart and pericardium. His classical monograph *Abhandlung über Percussion und Auscultation* was first published in 1839.[2]

Although he was famous abroad and well-known in European intellectual circles, he was not accepted—was even rejected— by older Austrian doctors who could not understand his new diagnostic procedures. Before instituting a new procedure at the Vienna General Hospital, it was necessary to obtain the approval of the director and the chief physician of the hospital. In their absence and thus without their consent, Skoda performed a tracheotomy with his colleague, surgeon Schuh. The procedure was performed correctly; nevertheless, Skoda was in danger of losing his medical license. Fortunately, thanks to his fame, which was recognized in Austria by, among others, the Court Councellor baronet Türckheim, officer in charge of the Court Committee for Studies, Skoda was disciplined only by having to work in an asylum for three months.

Skoda's chief in the medical department allowed him, however, to continue his diagnostic investigations. Nevertheless, Skoda declined to prolong his contract with the Vienna General Hospital that year and, in October 1839, started work as doctor of the poor in St. Ulrich, a suburb of Vienna. The temporary assignment did not stop his increasing fame.

The case of the Duc de Blacas, a resident of Vienna, is an example of Skoda's expertise. Three top Austrian experts diagnosed the severe state of health of the patient as liver disease. The duke's French personal physician was not in agreement with them and asked for a consultation with Dr. Skoda. The latter, using his technique of percussion and auscultation, found a large abdominal aneurysm and predicted an early death of the patient. At autopsy, Skoda, using percussion, again proved that he had outlined the dimensions of the aneurysm correctly.

One of the consultants was Dr. Türckheim, who realized the importance of the new diagnostic approach and followed all of Skoda's activities (e.g., pericardial paracentesis, performed again with Dr. Schuh 1840). He also appreciated the fact that an increasing number of foreign doctors came to Vienna to learn Skoda's diagnostic methods. In 1840, he established the department for diseases of the chest, with Skoda

FIG. 1 Joseph Skoda (1805–1881). Reproduced by permission of the Institute for the History of Medicine, University of Vienna, Vienna, Austria.

in charge. A year later, Skoda was appointed chief physician and the department was expanded to include two wards, for internal and skin diseases. Skoda selected young Dr. F. Hebra from Moravia (1816–1880) to care for patients with skin diseases. The choice was excellent; in a few years, Hebra became another leading physician of Czech origin at the Vienna University and is considered the founding father of classical dermatology.

In September 1846, Skoda was at last given the chair of Professor of Special Pathology and Therapy at the Vienna University and became Ordinarius at the Department of Internal Medicine. Two years later, he became a full member of the Royal Academy of Sciences in Vienna. For reasons of health (he suffered from severe gout for years) Prof. Skoda resigned from all his functions in 1871. The students honored him with a famous torch parade. He died in Vienna 10 years later and was buried in the same cemetery as Hebra and Rokitansky. The three stars of the Vienna second medical school remain together for eternity.[3]

The most famous publication by Skoda was *Percussion and Auscultation* (1st edition 1839), in which the young house physician described the fundamentals of physical diagnostics that are still valid today. In the same year, jointly with the pathologist J. Kolletschka (1803–1847), he published an important paper on the relation between the pathology and in-life diagnosis of pericarditis. The authors presented precise observations in patients and compared them with autopsy results in a way never done before. Diagnosis of the pericardial concrescence in life is the subject of another important paper that utilizes the physiologic approach to describe the influence of the atria and of lung ventilation on function of the heart and on circulation.[4, 5]

Skoda critically evaluated various therapeutic approaches using statistical methods and tried to eliminate those that were ineffective, futile, or harmful (e.g., ungrounded venesection). On the other hand, he treated patients with digitalis, quinine and scilla (squill), started to use chloralhydrate, salicylates, and syringe of Pravaz. The label of "therapeutic nihilist" conferred on him by some of his pupils was unjustified and unjust. Moreover, he insisted on prophylactic hygienic measures (for example, of the drainage and water supply in Vienna) in view of the epidemics of cholera and typhoid, and supported the effort of I.F. Semmelweiss.[1]

Dr. Joseph Skoda died June 13, 1881. He ended his life as a famous and wealthy physician but used the greater part of his possessions for charity and also for financial support of his cousin in Plzeň, the founder of the Skoda automobile factory.

References

1. Lesky E: *Wiener medizinische Schule im 19. Jahrhundert*, p. 1–660. Graz, Cologne, Vienna: Herrmann Böhlauf, 1865

2. Škoda J: *Abhandlung über Perkussion und Auskultation*, p. 1–271. Vienna: J.G.Ritter von Mösle Witwe & Braumüller, 1839

3. von Schrötter L: Josef Skoda. *Wiener klin Wschrft* 1805;18 (50):1–26

4. Škoda J: *Erscheinungen, aus denen sich die Verwachsung des Herzens mit dem Herzbeutel am lebenden Menschen erkennen lässt*. Reprint of the Royal Academy of Sciences (mathematics-natural history class) session, November 1851

5. Skoda J: *Über die Funktion der Vorkammern des Herzens und über den Einfluss der Contractionskraft der Lunge und der Respirationsbewegungen auf die Blutzirkulation*. Reprint of the Royal Academy of Sciences (mathematics-natural history class) session, November 1852

Henry Ingersoll Bowditch

W. Bruce Fye, m.d., m.a.

Department of Cardiology, Marshfield Clinic, Marshfield, Wisconsin, USA

Boston physician Henry Ingersoll Bowditch made several important contributions to medicine and public health during the nineteenth century.[1] His 1846 book *The Young Stethoscopist* signalled "the formal acceptance of physical diagnosis in the United States" according to clinician-historian Saul Jarcho.[2] Born in Salem, Massachusetts, in 1808, Henry was the son of Nathaniel Bowditch, a prominent mathematician best known for his writings on the principles of navigation. After graduating from Harvard College and Harvard Medical School, Henry sailed to Europe in 1832 to study medicine in Paris, then the world's center for medical education.[3] He spent nearly two years there, where his teachers included several leaders of French medicine. Bowditch was especially impressed by the great clinician and pathologist Pierre Louis.[4, 5] After returning to Boston, Bowditch entered medical practice and was appointed admitting physician of the Massachusetts General Hospital.

Bowditch was among the first American physicians to become proficient in the use of the stethoscope invented by French physician René Théophile Hyacinthe Laennec and described in his two volume 1819 book on auscultation. Bowditch's experiences in several Paris hospitals provided him with an excellent opportunity to learn how to use this new diagnostic tool. He hoped that his book on the stethoscope, a concise manual on the instrument and its use, would encourage American physicians and students to use it as a routine part of their examination of patients with symptoms that might be caused by disorders of the heart or lungs. Although he emphasized auscultation in his book, Bowditch also discussed the value of other techniques of physical diagnosis of thoracic diseases. If the issue was heart disease, he urged physicians to use several techniques in sequence: inspection, palpation, percussion, and auscultation.

In this era, stethoscopes were monaural and fashioned out of various types of wood. George Cammann of New York introduced the flexible binaural stethoscope in 1852.[6] This innovation enhanced the value of cardiac auscultation considerably. Between 1820 and 1850, several European and American physicians and medical scientists made observations and performed experiments which helped to clarify the origin of heart sounds and murmurs. While animal research and clinico-pathologic correlations helped to elucidate the significance of various abnormal heart sounds and murmurs, many auscultatory phenomena were poorly understood when Bowditch's book appeared in 1846.

Because the stethoscope gave doctors a powerful tool to hear heart sounds and detect cardiac murmurs, it stimulated interest in valvular heart disease as a clinical problem. For more than a generation, the mere presence of a heart murmur was viewed as an indicator of significant heart disease. By the early twentieth century, it had become clear that some murmurs were "innocent" and did not imply a poor prognosis. When Bowditch's monograph on the stethoscope appeared, medical specialization had not yet evolved; he included subjects that we would not expect to find in a text on auscultation today. In addition to extensive sections on auscultation of the heart and lungs, he discussed obstetric auscultation, cephalic auscultation, and auscultation in other diseases such as fractures. Indeed, in an era when animals were vitally important as a means of transportation or income in America's largely rural economy, Bowditch even included a chapter on veterinary auscultation.

In a review of Bowditch's book and three other contemporary works on cardiac physical diagnosis, Philadelphia physician Alfred Stillé emphasized that even the best book on physical diagnosis was "almost worthless" unless the techniques were illustrated at the bedside. Many physicians had found it difficult to learn auscultation from books—some of them questioned the value of the technique. Stillé wrote,

> Unless the student be told what are the sounds he hears in auscultation, unless one more experienced than himself inform him of the name of every sound, and present to his ear the sound corresponding to every name, the descriptions and definitions of his "Manual" must continue meaningless to him.[7]

Although his book on auscultation was an important contribution, Bowditch published many papers on a wide variety of subjects. His articles on tuberculosis and the technique of thoracentesis were among his most important essays. Bowditch began to practice medicine when "heroic" therapy (consisting of blood-letting, purging, blistering, and the administration of large doses of medicines) was widely accepted. Under the influence of Pierre Louis and other French physicians, Bowditch developed a healthy skepticism of this traditional therapeutic approach. He was impressed with the importance of sanitation in preventing the spread of disease. One of the pioneers of the public health movement in America, Bowditch was a founder and the first president of the Massachusetts State Board of

FIG. 1 Henry Ingersoll Bowditch, 1808–1892.

Health (the first such organization in America).[8] One of the most influential physicians of his generation, he was elected president of the American Medical Association in 1877.

Bowditch died of tuberculosis in 1892 at the age of 84. His many accomplishments were praised in an obituary published in the *Boston Medical and Surgical Journal*. The writer noted that

> …he was one of the earliest advocates of specialties in medicine in the country [and] … was one of the first to believe in women as physicians, and thought it but justice to them, as well as good policy for the communi-

ty, to give them the same advantages of study as to men.[9]

William Osler thought Bowditch "was one of the finest characters I have ever met in the profession."[10]

Due in part to Bowditch's writings and his personal influence, American physicians adopted the stethoscope as an aid to the diagnosis of diseases of the heart and lungs. Gradually, the instrument became the symbol of the physician. Historian Stanley Reiser observed recently,

> Today the stethoscope is the old warrior of medicine. Although it cannot compete with the array of elaborate and expensive technologies for which it paved the way, it clings tenaciously, resisting retirement. Its staying power in modern times is based in part on its giving both physicians and patients a sense of continuity with the past.[11]

References

1. Bowditch VY (ed.): *Life and Correspondence of Henry Ingersoll Bowditch*. Houghton, Mifflin & Co., Boston (1902)
2. Jarcho S: The young stethoscopist. *Academy Bookman* 17, 2–6 (1964)
3. Ackerknecht EH: *Medicine at the Paris Hospital, 1794–1848*. Johns Hopkins University Press, Baltimore (1967)
4. Bollet AJ: Pierre Louis: The numerical method and the foundation of quantitative medicine. *Am J Med Sci* 266, 92–101 (1973)
5. Bowditch HI: *Brief Memories of Louis and Some of His Contemporaries in the Parisian School of Medicine of Forty Years Ago*. John Wilson & Son, Boston (1872)
6. McKusick VA: The history of cardiovascular sound. In *Cardiovascular Sound in Health and Disease*. Williams & Wilkins, Baltimore (1958) 3–54
7. Stille A: Bibliographical notices. *Am J Med Sci* 21, 171–177 (1846)
8. Walking AA: Henry Ingersoll Bowditch. *Ann Med Hist* 5, 428–437 (1933)
9. Henry Ingersoll Bowditch, M.D. *Boston Med Surg J* 126, 67–70 (1892)
10. Osler W: *Bibliotheca Osleriana: A Catalogue of Books Illustrating the History of Medicine and Science*. Oxford University Press, Oxford (1929) 196
11. Reiser SJ: The medical influence of the stethoscope. *Scientific American* 240, 148–156 (1979)

Thomas Bevill Peacock*

W. B. FYE, M.D.

Cardiology Department, Marshfield Clinic, Marshfield, Wisconsin, USA

Thomas Bevill Peacock (Fig. 1) was born on December 21, 1812 in York, England.[1] At the age of sixteen, following preliminary education, he was apprenticed to John Fothergill, a Darlington surgeon. Five years later, Peacock enrolled in the medical school of University College, London. As was characteristic of ambitious British medical graduates of this era, he supplemented his London training with study in Paris—then the world's foremost center for medical education. There, Peacock was exposed to leaders of the "French school" who emphasized clinicopathologic correlation and enthusiastically employed Laennec's recent invention, the stethoscope.[2] This instrument revolutionized the diagnosis of diseases of the chest and led to unprecedented interest in disorders of the cardiac valves.

Completion of his training abroad and additional study at Edinburgh University led to an M.D. degree for Peacock, who then entered medical practice in Chester, England. As part of his practice, Peacock participated in many autopsies. His rich experience in clinicopathologic correlation was reflected in his writings. In 1843, Peacock moved to London where he practiced at several hospitals, but St. Thomas's Hospital soon became the institutional center of his medical life.[3] By now he had earned a reputation as a highly regarded teacher and popular lecturer. Reflecting his interest in pathologic anatomy, Peacock was one of the founders, in 1847, of the Pathological Society of London. A prolific writer, Peacock published many case reports and autopsy notes in the society's transactions. During his long career, he made more than 150 presentations before the society.

Many of Peacock's lectures and papers dealt with anomalies and diseases of the cardiovascular system. His first publication, which appeared in 1843, was a sophisticated study of aortic dissections.[4] Fifteen years later, he wrote a monograph on congenital heart disease considered by Maude Abbott to be the first comprehensive study of the subject.[5-7] The book was well-written, included fine engravings depicting congenital cardiac malformations, and was supplemented by useful bibliographies. In a careful analysis of more than one hundred cases of congenital heart disease for which clinical information was available, Peacock found that three-quarters of the patients had symptoms at birth or shortly thereafter and

half of the remainder became symptomatic during the first year of life.

Peacock's book on congenital heart disease reveals his sophisticated understanding of cardiac physiology. His discussion of cyanotic congenital heart disease is especially noteworthy. In this era before the discovery of x-rays and the invention of the electrocardiogram and other sophisticated diagnostic modalities, Peacock had to rely on symptoms and physical findings in his attempts to characterize the underlying heart defect. Treatment consisted of hygienic measures such as the avoidance of cold, a nutritious diet, and standard therapeutic approaches of the era, including bleeding.

In 1864, Peacock was elected to deliver the prestigious Croonian Lectures of the Royal College of Physicians. These lectures were devoted to valvular heart disease and formed the substance of Peacock's important monograph on the subject published in 1865.[8] This volume was the first significant account of the subject in English. Among the causes of valvular heart disease Peacock identified were congenital malformations, rheumatic fever and other inflammatory conditions, overexertion, and diseases of the kidney. He used the numerical method pioneered by Pierre Louis to evaluate the frequency of these etiologies in his series of patients with valvular heart disease. Peacock believed that rheumatic fever was the most common etiology of valvular lesions in patients with isolated mitral valve disease or combined aortic and mitral valve disease. In Peacock's opinion, isolated aortic valve disease was usually due to a congenital malformation of the valve.

After considering the causes of valvular heart disease and the value of the stethoscope in their detection, Peacock discussed their consequences. He emphasized the pathologic aspects of valvular abnormalities rather than their physiologic consequences. In this era, diseases were viewed primarily as disorders of structure—pathologic anatomy was the focus of most of Peacock's writings. It was not until the end of the 19th century that disordered function—pathologic physiology—was viewed as the explanation of most cardiac symptoms.[9] Despite his emphasis on pathologic anatomy, Peacock had a rather advanced understanding of the hemodynamic consequences of valvular lesions.

Peacock's approach to therapeutics reflected the era in which he practiced. Emphasis was placed on diet, the avoidance of cold, and standard remedies thought to be beneficial

*This paper is adapted from an essay prepared for the Classics of Cardiology Library published by Gryphon editions, Birmingham.

FIG. 1   Thomas Bevill Peacock 1812–1882. Reproduced with permission from the Royal College of Physicians. Source of photograph: Medical History 6, facing 254, 1962.

in diseases of the heart. These included so-called alkalies, tonics, and diuretics. The special role of digitalis in disorders of the heart was well recognized, but Peacock expressed concern that it was used too liberally. This monograph on valvular heart disease, like his other publications, reflected Peacock's familiarity with the historical and contemporary literature of his subject.

A supplementary volume on the prognosis of disorders of the cardiac valves appeared in 1877.[10] Peacock believed that the prognosis was dependent not only upon the specific disorder of the valves but on the state of the myocardium as well. He explained that progressive symptoms, complications, and death in cases of valvular heart disease related to accompanying myocardial dysfunction as well as to thrombosis and em-

bolism. A skilled auscultator, busy clinician, and talented pathologist, Peacock recognized the inconsistent relationship between the intensity of murmurs and the significance of the underlying valvular abnormality. For example, he noted that a loud murmur might result from minimal obstruction while severe obstruction might be accompanied by a soft murmur. Not only were the auscultatory findings variable in Peacock's opinion; the natural history of valvular heart disease was often unpredictable. The presence of a heart murmur did not invariably lead to severe disability or death.

Peacock's two important monographs provided valuable insight into the pathophysiology and consequences of valvular heart diseases and his contemporaries welcomed them. His career would soon come to a close, however. In 1877, Peacock was forced to give up several of his professional activities because of a cerebrovascular accident. After two more attacks he died on May 30, 1882.

References

1. Porter IH: The nineteenth-century physician and cardiologist Thomas Bevill Peacock (1812–1882). *Med Hist* 6, 240 (1962)
2. Ackerknecht E: *Medicine at the Paris Hospital, 1794-1848.* Johns Hopkins Press, Baltimore (1967)
3. McInnes EM: *St. Thomas's Hospital.* George Allen & Unwin, Ltd., London (1963)
4. Jarcho S: Thomas Bevill Peacock on dissecting aneurysm (1843). *Am J Cardiol* 6, 813 (1960)
5. Peacock T: *On Malformations, &c., of the Human Heart with Original Cases.* J. Churchill, London (1858)
6. Abbott M: Congenital cardiac disease. In *Modern Medicine: Its Theory and Practice in Original Contributions by American and Foreign Authors.* (Osler W, Ed). Lea & Febiger, Philadelphia (1908) 327
7. Flaxman N: Peacock and congenital heart disease. Thomas Bevill Peacock (1812-1882). *Bull Hist Med* 7, 1061 (1939)
8. Peacock TB: *On Some of the Causes and Effects of Valvular Disease of the Heart.* John Churchill, London (1865)
9. Maulitz R: Pathologists, clinicians, and the role of pathophysiology. In *Physiology in the American Context, 1850–1940* (Geison GL, Ed). American Physiological Society, Bethesda (1987) 209
10. Peacock TB: *On the Prognosis in Cases of Valvular Disease of the Heart.* J. & A. Churchill, London (1877)

Austin Flint, 1812–1886*

W. B. FYE, M.D.

Cardiology Department, Marshfield Clinic, Marshfield, Wisconsin, USA

Austin Flint (Fig. 1), one of nineteenth century America's most prominent physicians and prolific writers, was born at Petersham, Massachusetts, in 1812.[1–3] He would continue the family tradition of medical practice that dated back to his grandfather, Edward Flint, who served as a medical officer in the Revolutionary War. After studying at Amherst College, Austin Flint entered the Harvard Medical School in 1830. There, he studied under Jacob Bigelow, John C. Warren, and James Jackson, who were all strongly influenced by the French school of medicine with its emphasis on the newer techniques of physical diagnosis and clinicopathologic correlation.[4]

Following graduation from Harvard in 1833 at the age of 21, Flint entered practice in Boston and Northampton. Two years later he married Anne Skillings of Boston. In 1836, shortly after the birth of a son, Austin Jr., the family moved to Buffalo, New York. There, in 1845, he founded the *Buffalo Medical Journal*, and two years later, the Buffalo Medical School. Flint held the chair of medicine at the new school for five years, then he left Buffalo for Kentucky where he held a similar position at the University of Louisville. A peripatetic medical teacher, Flint also taught at Rush Medical College in Chicago and at the New Orleans Medical School early in his career.

During the 1850s, Flint was a frequent contributor to the medical literature. Reflecting the prevalence of infectious diseases in mid-nineteenth century America, many of his early writings dealt with fevers and contagious diseases. His interest in physical diagnosis of the chest and the prevalence of pulmonary disorders led Flint to write valuable papers on the diagnosis of diseases of the lungs using auscultation and percussion. An 1850 article on pericarditis complicating pleuropneumonitis signaled the beginning of Flint's deep interest in cardiac physical diagnosis. He soon produced several notable papers dealing with the origin and significance of abnormal heart sounds and murmurs.

On the eve of the American Civil War, Flint published his classic monograph, *A Practical Treatise on the Diagnosis, Pathology, and Treatment of Diseases of the Heart*. This was the first comprehensive book on heart disease published by an American. Flint wrote this monograph to "meet the wants of the medical student and practitioner."[5] Throughout his life, Flint methodically recorded the details of the cases he saw, and his book on heart disease was based on his own series of approximately 200 cases of patients with cardiac disorders and the published reports of other "trustworthy observers." Among the sources Flint used were case reports and summaries published by representatives of the Irish, British, and French schools of medicine. He acknowledged his indebtedness to William Stokes, James Hope, Walter Walshe, Jean Baptiste Bouillaud, and Charles Forget, among others.

Flint's interest in physical signs of heart disease is apparent throughout his book which appeared prior to the introduction of graphic techniques to study cardiac function and nearly half a century before the invention of the electrocardiogram or the discovery of x-rays. It is not surprising, therefore, that Flint proclaimed, "the diagnosis of cardiac disease is for the most part based on the physical signs."[5] Flint justifiably concluded that his work placed more emphasis on the clinical significance of abnormalities of the heart sounds than any contemporary work on the heart. Several important and original observations regarding the pathophysiology of heart sounds and murmurs are included in his book. Flint was widely acknowledged as a pioneer of cardiac physical diagnosis and has been called the "American Laennec."[6] His description of the murmur of aortic insufficiency that mimics mitral stenosis, for which he is remembered eponymically, appeared in 1862.

Flint's book on the heart consists of 10 chapters devoted to cardiac enlargement, valvular lesions, congenital heart disease, inflammatory disorders with emphasis on pericarditis, functional disorders of the heart and diseases of the aorta, and other subjects. Angina pectoris and disorders of the myocardium are discussed in separate chapters, reflecting the contemporary lack of understanding of the relationship of coronary artery disease to myocardial lesions.[7]

Although treatment is discussed, Flint emphasized diagnosis in his book. Reflecting the growing conservatism which characterized medical practice of this era, Flint advised bleeding only rarely, and cautioned against the excessive use of mercury. Although he was not a therapeutic nihilist, and the therapeutic agents he suggested reflected contemporary teachings, Flint was skeptical of the efficacy of remedies commonly advocated. Speaking of angina pectoris, he declared, "Rational treatment based on knowledge

*This paper has been adapted with permission from an essay prepared for the Classics of Cardiology Library, Gryphon Editions, Birmingham

FIG. 1 Austin Flint 1812–1886. From Atkinson WB (Ed): *The Physicians & Surgeons of The United States*. Charles Robson, Philadelphia, 1878.

of the particular morbid condition or conditions involved in cardiac lesions, on which the affection is immediately dependent, cannot be laid down; for this knowledge is not yet acquired. Nor has clinical experience led to the discovery of the means of striking at the pathological root of this affection. There is no special medication to be pursued in cases of angina, with the hope of effecting a cure."[5] It would be decades before nitroglycerin was introduced into medical practice for the treatment of angina pectoris.[8]

Present-day readers of Flint's book may be surprised to learn that he advocated exercise for many cardiac disorders. He believed that "indolence or inaction" could lead to weakness of the heart and "fatty degeneration" of the heart muscle—the histologic finding we now associate with ischemic damage of the myocardium. Flint advocated a "healthy" diet and advised that patients with a predisposition to fatty degeneration avoid "fatty substances and those readily converted into fat." A contemporary reviewer, almost certainly George Cheyne Shattuck, professor of medicine at Harvard Medical

School and a student with Flint in that institution nearly three decades earlier, claimed that the work "should be in the hands of all practitioners and students. It is a credit to American literature."[9]

Flint moved to New York in 1859. Two years later he helped found the Bellevue Hospital Medical College where he was a professor of medicine until his death. A prolific author, Flint contributed more than 200 articles and several books to the medical literature. Among these were monographs on fevers and diseases of the respiratory system and a popular handbook of auscultation and percussion that went through several editions. In 1866, he published his widely heralded textbook of medicine that American surgeon and medical historian Samuel D. Gross believed was the best medical text written by an American.[10,11]

In addition to his activities as a medical teacher and author, Flint was a successful and highly regarded practitioner. His many accomplishments were acknowledged by his peers. He was elected president of the New York Academy of Medicine in 1873. Eleven years later he served as president of the American Medical Association. When he died of a stroke at the age of 74, he was still fully active in his profession. Flint is best remembered for his contributions to physical diagnosis—a field he pioneered in the United States.

References

1. Shaftel N: Austin Flint, Sr. (1812-1886): Educator of physicians. *J Med Educ* 35, 1122 (1960)
2. Smith DC: Austin Flint and auscultation in America. *J Hist Med Allied Sci* 33, 129 (1978)
3. Evans AS: Austin Flint and his contributions to medicine. *Bull Hist Med* 32, 224 (1958)
4. Ackerknecht EH: *Medicine at the Paris Hospital: 1794-1848*. Johns Hopkins Press, Baltimore (1967)
5. Flint A: *A Practical Treatise on the Diagnosis, Pathology, and Treatment of Diseases of the Heart*. Blanchard & Lea, Philadelphia (1859) v, vii, 265
6. McKusick VA: The history of cardiovascular sound. In *Cardiovascular Sound in Health and Disease*. Williams & Wilkins, Baltimore (1958) 3
7. Fye WB: The delayed diagnosis of myocardial infarction: It took half a century! *Circulation* 72, 262 (1985)
8. Fye WB: Nitroglycerin: A homeopathic remedy. *Circulation* 73, 21 (1986)
9. Shattuck GS: Review. A practical treatise on the diagnosis, pathology, and treatment of diseases of the heart. *Am J Med Sci* ns 40, 141 (1860)
10. Flint A: *A Treatise on the Principles and Practice of Medicine*. Henry C. Lea, Philadelphia (1866)
11. Fye WB: The literature of American internal medicine: A historical view. *Ann Intern Med* 106, 451 (1987)

Claude Bernard

BARRY D. SILVERMAN, M.D., FACP, FACC

Department of Cardiology, Northside Hospital, Atlanta, Georgia, USA

Claude Bernard (1813–1872) (Fig. 1), a French physician and scientist, was responsible for the introduction of scientific methods in the study of living organisms. A contemporary of Louis Pasteur, Bernard's contributions in the experimental laboratory and his writings on the philosophy of science establish him as one of the most important figures of the nineteenth century. He introduced physiology as an important area of medical study. His book, *Introduction to the Study of Experimental Medicine,* is a seminal work in the philosophy of science. The book influenced Emile Zola particularly in his use of "naturalism" in fiction. The work has been compared with Rene Descartes' *Discourse on Method* in its contribution to the philosophy of science. This publication created the foundation for animal experimentation as the method to study health and disease in man.

Bernard published a wide variety of biological and physiologic studies. His most important discoveries were in the areas of pancreatic function in digestion; the glycogenic function of the liver; the action of poisons, especially his study of curare; and muscle physiology and vasomotor nerve function. His studies of the neural control of vascular tone are pivotal to the understanding of the vascular system and these studies are his principal contribution to cardiology.

Claude Bernard was born on July 12, 1813, in the village of Saint-Julien, Canton de Villefranche-sur-Saone, France. Bernard's family had inherited a wine grove, but they were unable to support themselves from the vineyard alone. His father was also the village schoolmaster. Classes were held at his home, as there were no public schools in France at that time. Bernard's schooling began at the age of eight with instruction in Latin. He was described as unfocused, serious, silent, and pensive as a student. He was a poor reader and not an exceptional student.

At 18, Bernard was apprenticed to M. Mille, a pharmacist in the Faubourg de Vaise of Lyons. There his work included periodic visits to the veterinary school, the first of its kind in Europe, where the pharmacy supplied drugs for the sick animals. It was during this time that Bernard developed his skepticism for the empiricism of nineteenth century medicine. A favorite French remedy was "La Thériaque," in great vogue at the time as an effective cure for many illnesses. The nostrum consisted of 60 different ingredients including opium, squills, spikenard, and myrrh. M. Millet took liberties with the formula, often adding drugs which he would otherwise have discarded. This unscientific creation of a medical remedy invoked in Bernard a distrust and disgust for the makeshift nature of drug therapies.

Bernard was allowed one night off a month, and this was usually spent at the Théâtre de Célestins. The theater quickly enveloped him and he yearned to be a playwright. He composed a small vaudeville sketch, *La Rose du Rhône*, and sold it for 100 francs. This inspired him to write a five-act drama. His new direction resulted in considerable inattention at the pharmacy and led to his dismissal in July of 1833. He finished his play, which he titled *Arthur de Bretagne*, and left for Paris to begin his new career. There he procured an introduction to a noted literary critic and professor of literature at the Sorbonne, M. Saint-Marc Girardin. Girardin was unimpressed with the young playwright and allegedly stated, "You have not the temperament of a dramatist, you have done some pharmacy, study medicine."[1a]

Following that advice, Bernard entered medical school in 1834 at the age of 21. He was considered by his contemporaries to be taciturn, awkward, and inattentive at lectures. Nonetheless, he excelled at anatomy and later commented that "anatomy is the basis necessary for all medical investigation…anatomy, in itself, teaches nothing without observation of the living."[1b] Physiology was not a separate science in medical school at this time; metaphysical speculation and vitalism were the predominant concepts. In France, François Magendie (1783–1855) stood alone in experimental physiology. A busy physician and professor of medicine, he was Bernard's most important teacher and mentor. Magendie refused to place any credence in statements that had not been confirmed by experiment; he was a great proponent of animal experimentation.

In 1836, Bernard passed the test to be an externe and in 1839 became an interne. He worked in the services of Falret, Valpeau, and Maisonneuve before joining Magendie at the Hôtel Dieu. He never practiced clinical medicine, entering the laboratory as soon as he completed his medical training. At 32, he married Marie Françoise Maartin, the daughter of a physician. They had four children but only two daughters, Jeanne Henriette and Marie Louise, survived beyond childhood. His marriage was not a happy one and he was separated from his wife at the end of his career. Marie Françoise was a bigoted woman who worked against her husband's activities and was bitter that he would not turn his interests toward a

FIG. 1   Claude Bernard, 1813-1873. (Photograph from the collection of Dr. Bruce Fye, used with permission.)

prosperous medical practice. She did not understand his work and was strenuously opposed to animal experimentation. His closest nonprofessional relationship was with Mme. Raffalovich, a prosperous Russian Jew living in France who was interested in science and philosophy. A confidant and friend, she assisted by translating foreign publications, providing a nonscientific social outlet, and discussing and even collaborating with him on new ideas.

In 1847, Bernard achieved his first academic advancement when he was appointed to the position of substitute lecturer for Magendie. He assumed the responsibility for the summer lecture series and was elected to his first scientific society, the Société Philomathique de Paris, created to keep its members abreast of the latest scientific discoveries. Bernard was a founder of the Société de Biologie in 1848, a society established by a younger group of physicians and naturalists to study phenomena pertaining to the science of life. He was elected "perpetual president" in 1867. It was an active society with weekly meetings, the records of which refer to Bernard at almost every session.

In 1843, Bernard won his doctorate with a dissertation on gastric juice. It was characteristic of his career that once he dealt with a problem he maintained a life-long interest. His studies moved from the digestive juices and the discovery of the glycogenic function of the liver to the nature of diabetes, the phenomenon of animal heat, the function of the blood in regulating body temperature, and the function of vasomotor nerves in the dilatation and constriction of blood vessels. His studies of the vasomotor nervous system led to the under-

standing of the sympathetic nervous system. Most of his discoveries originated in his initial laboratory work from 1843 to 1851. These studies were carried out in a small laboratory in the heart of the Latin Quarter in Paris. His laboratory was a small, dank, unhealthy room in which he carried out studies that were chronically underfunded and often in opposition to a community opposed to vivisection. Early in his studies, Bernard understood the importance of chemistry to his investigations. In 1844, he collaborated with the young chemist M. Barreswill. That collaboration continued for some time and together they published six papers. Additional early collaborators in other studies were Davaine, Rayer, Brown-Séquard, Pelouze, Charcot, and Robin.

An example of Bernard's experimental method is revealed in this description of his study of pancreatic juice. He brought rabbits from market into the laboratory and noted their urine was clear and acid—unusual for this animal, which is a herbivore. He assumed that they were in the state of a carnivore living on their own blood because they had not eaten for some time. He studied the rabbits by repeatedly feeding grass and fasting them, noting the changing nature of the urine. He then repeated the study feeding beef to see whether that had the same effect as fasting, and autopsied the animals to determine whether the beef had been digested. He noted that the lymphatics of the rabbit were white and milky at a point 30 cm below the pylorus, a point much lower than in the dog where the lymphatics turn white and milky just below the pylorus. The difference coincided with the insertion of the pancreatic duct. This led to his recognition that pancreatic juices may be responsible for the emulsion of fat.

In 1849, Bernard received the Legion of Honor medal in recognition of his work on pancreatic digestion and, in 1853, the Academy of Science award for his studies on sympathetic nerve function. He was elected to the prestigious Academy of Science in 1854, and the same year a new chair was created for him in general physiology at the Sorbonne. On Magendie's death in 1855, Bernard was appointed his successor at the College of France. He received many other official honors, including membership in the Imperial Senate.

His published works include *Introduction to the Study of Experimental Medicine* (1865), and the 14 volumes of his published lectures including *Lectures on Experimental Pathology and Lectures on Vital Phenomena Common to Animals and Plants. Introduction to the Study of Experimental Medicine* is more than a scientific treatise on experimental methods; it is an essay on the philosophy of experimental methods and a rationale of scientific discovery. The book is written with clarity and precision. Bernard states,

The observer listens to nature; the experimenter questions nature and forces it to reveal itself…He must observe without preconceived ideas…The experimenter poses his idea like a question, an interpretation anticipating nature with more or less probability, from which he logically deduces consequences which at every moment he confronts with reality by means of experiment.[2]

Unlike Descartes, Bernard understood that the mind does not create scientific facts, but recognizes them from the experience of the external world. Yet, unlike Magendie, he understood that discovery is not produced from mere observation alone but that the mind must participate. Before Bernard, metaphysics believed that there was a certain vital force in living beings which was not subject to the experimental method but understood a priori. Bernard understood that determinism could be applied to the science of life as well as to the inanimate world, although its application to life is more difficult because of its greater variability and complexity.

Claude Bernard was a man of genius who brought the study of life and its processes to medicine. He had an expansive imagination, unique experimental ability, and a logical yet inventive mind.[3] He defined life in a statement written in 1869, three years before his death:

In saying that life is the directing idea and evolutive force of the living being I express merely the idea of a unity in the succession of all the morphological and chemical changes accomplished by the germ from the beginning to the end of life.[1c]

References

1. Olmsted JMD: *Claude Bernard Physiogist,* (a) p 12, (b) p16, (c) p 250. New York and London: Harper and Brothers, 1938
2. Vitanen R: *Claude Bernard and His Place in the History of Ideas,* p 14. Lincoln: University of Nebraska Press, 1960
3. Castiglioni A: *A History of Medicine.* New York: Jason Aronson, Inc., 1975

Carl Ludwig*

W. Bruce Fye, M.D., M.A.

Cardiology Department, Marshfield Clinic, Marshfield, Wisconsin, USA

The pioneering Scottish pharmacologist T. Lauder Brunton claimed nearly a century ago, "More than to anyone else since the time of Harvey, do we owe our present knowledge of the circulation to Carl Ludwig."[1] Carl Friedrich Wilhelm Ludwig (Fig. 1) was born in Witzenhausen, Germany, on December 29, 1816.[2,3] His father, a former officer in the Napoleonic wars, held a municipal position in the city of Hanau, where young Ludwig attended preparatory school. Typical of ambitious students of his day, Carl then studied at several universities including those at Marburg, Erlangen, and Bamburg. Following graduation, he was appointed assistant in anatomy under Ludwig Fick at the University of Marburg where he also worked in Robert Bunsen's chemical laboratory. During a visit to Berlin in 1847, Ludwig met three pupils of Johannes Müller, professor of anatomy and physiology at the University of Berlin. This cohort of four, Emil Du Bois-Reymond, Hermann von Helmholtz, Ernst von Brücke and Ludwig, redefined physiology as an experimental science based on physics and chemistry rather than an empirical field preoccupied with speculation and untested theorizing.[4]

Ludwig published the first volume of his classic textbook of physiology in 1852.[5] This pioneering work challenged traditional scientific theories, suggested new concepts, and proposed what Ludwig believed were the best experimental approaches to investigate the functions of living organisms. After holding faculty positions in Marburg, Zurich, and Vienna, Ludwig was appointed professor of physiology at the University of Leipzig in 1865. He remained there until his death three decades later. With the generous financial support of King Johann of Saxony, Ludwig designed a new physiologic institute at Leipzig which was the most advanced experimental laboratory in the world when it opened in 1869.

Ludwig's institute provided unparalleled opportunities for physiologic research, and his program attracted scientifically oriented medical graduates from Europe, England, Asia, and America. More than 200 advanced pupils were trained by him in physiology during his long career. Among his pupils were several Americans who became leading medical scientists and medical educators during the closing years of the nineteenth century. Ludwig encouraged many of his advanced pupils to investigate the physiology of the heart and circulation, among them Henry P. Bowditch and Henry Sewall from America; Robert Tigerstedt, Hugo Kronecker, Luigi Luciani, Angelo Mosso, Willy Kühne, Karl Ewald Hering, Samuel von Basch, Julius Cohnheim, Adolf Fick, Otto Frank, Heinrich Quincke, and Werner Spalteholz from the continent; and Walter Gaskell, Lauder Brunton, Ray Lankester, William Rutherford, William Stirling, Augustus D. Waller, and Edward Schäfer from Great Britain.

Although generous and consistent government funding were important, Ludwig's scientific ability and personality were the major factors in the success of his Leipzig Physiological Institute. His intellectual generosity and unselfishness in order to further the careers of his pupils is legendary. Ludwig's productivity, and that of the students who worked in his laboratory, was unprecedented. Not only were their papers numerous, a high percentage were important contributions to medical and scientific knowledge.

Throughout his long career, circulatory physiology was a dominant area of research for Ludwig. This interest in the circulatory system led him to develop an instrument to record hemodynamic and other physiologic events accurately. His kymograph, invented in 1846, placed a stylus connected to a mercury manometer in contact with a rotating smoke drum to record physiologic events graphically over time. This instrument permitted the simultaneous recording of several physiologic variables such as blood pressure, pulse rate, and respiratory frequency. The objectivity provided by such recordings allowed Ludwig and his colleagues to identify previously unrecognized physiologic relationships. For example, by simultaneously recording the pulse wave and respiratory pattern, he first described sinus arrhythmia in 1847. Modern hemodynamic monitoring equipment currently used in clinical medicine and research can be traced to Ludwig's kymograph.

Ludwig's brilliant work in cardiovascular physiology was the result of a sustained effort aimed at understanding the physical principles of the circulation. These studies were facilitated by the delicate instruments of precision he devised. With his pupil Adolf Beutner, Ludwig used his kymograph and other apparatus to measure for the first time the pulmonary artery pressure by inserting a cannula into the left pulmonary artery. With Johannes von Dries, Ludwig first measured capillary pressure. Ludwig and another pupil, Johann von Dogiel, measured regional blood flow for the first time in 1867 using a "Stromuhr" or flowmeter they developed. Adolph Fick, one of Ludwig's earliest pupils, extended the principles of measuring blood flow pioneered by his teacher to elaborate his well-known approach to quantitating cardiac output. The principles and techniques of graphic registration developed in animal ex-

---

*This paper is adapted with permission from an essay that appeared in the author's Preludes and Progress series in *Circulation*.

FIG. 1 Carl Friedrich Wilhelm Ludwig (1816–1895). German physiologist who made numerous contributions to cardiovascular physiology and invented the kymograph. (Photograph provided by the National Library of Medicine, Bethesda, MD.)

periments in Ludwig's laboratory were soon applied to humans by Alfred Volkmann in Germany and Étienne Jules Marey in France, who developed techniques to record the pulse waves and apical impulse in humans.

Cardiovascular innervation held a special interest for Ludwig. With his Russian pupil, Elie de Cyon, he discovered the vasomotor reflexes in 1866. Their discovery of the "depressor nerve" represented the first proposal of reflex regulation of the cardiovascular system through afferent nerve endings in the heart. While later studies proved that the afferent nerves were actually located in the great arteries, the concept of autoregulation of the circulation can be traced to their observations. With his American pupil Henry Bowditch, Ludwig discovered two fundamental laws of cardiac physiology, the "all-or-none" law of cardiac muscle and the "Treppe" or staircase phenomenon. The physiology of the peripheral circulation also interested Ludwig. Shortly after Claude Bernard demonstrated the existence of vasodilator and vasoconstrictor nerves, Ludwig began a series of experiments that demonstrated the role of vascular tone in maintaining blood pressure.

Among Ludwig's most important contributions were his discoveries in the area of respiratory physiology. While still at Vienna, he and his Russian colleague Ivan Sechenov invented a mercury blood pump that allowed them to separate the respiratory gasses in blood in vivo. In an extensive series of experiments, Ludwig and his students elucidated the physiology of tissue oxygenation and respiratory gas exchange. In the course of this work Ludwig first measured the oxygen tension in blood. His technique made it possible to measure the saturation of oxygen and carbon dioxide in the blood stream. The results of these experiments led him to conclude that the oxygen uptake of an organ was related to the work it performed.

To evaluate various bodily functions, Ludwig developed or refined techniques to perfuse isolated organs. This made it possible to study the functions of denervated organs that were perfused with blood or solutions containing various compounds. A particularly useful experimental model that he developed was an isolated frog heart preparation in which the organ could be kept beating for days by perfusing it with defibrinated blood. Many of Ludwig's important discoveries in cardiac physiology were made using this isolated frog heart preparation. Eventually, other workers, most notably H. Newell Martin of the Johns Hopkins University, extended and refined Ludwig's technique and developed an isolated mammalian heart preparation. In addition to its value in elucidating myocardial function, this work ultimately led to the development of the heart-lung machine.[6]

Despite his focus on physiology, Ludwig also made important contributions to anatomy. When it was necessary or desirable to have a better understanding of the morphologic aspects of a problem he was studying, Ludwig would not hesitate to turn to the microscope or to enter the dissecting room to explore the structure of an organ. Among his important contributions to anatomy were studies of the structure of the myocardium, the kidney, and the vasculature of the eye and inner ear. In the course of investigations to evaluate the vascular supply of various organs, he refined older techniques of injecting blood vessels and lymphatics with substances that made it easier to study their minute anatomy. Ludwig's skillful correlation of anatomy and physiology facilitated his research and led him to many discoveries regarding the function of various organs.

Although he was an outstanding physiologist who made many significant discoveries, perhaps Ludwig's most important contribution was his role in training two generations of physiologists. They learned philosophy as well as technique, and introduced both into their homelands. Why was Ludwig so influential, and why was the Leipzig Physiological Institute so productive? William Welch, a pioneering American pathologist and medical educator, argued at the turn of the century that Ludwig's institute "exerted the greatest and most fruitful influence" on the field of physiology because of "the general plan of its organization, its admirable equipment, the number and importance of the discoveries there made, its development of exact methods of experimentation, the personal character and genius of its director, and the number of experimenters there trained from all parts of the civilized world."[7]

References

1. Brunton TL: Modern developments of Harvey's work. *Lancet* 2, 893 (1894)
2. Schroer H: *Carl Ludwig, Begründer der messenden Experimentalphysiologie, 1816–1895.* Wissenschaftliche Verlagsgesellschaft M B H, Stuttgart (1967)
3. Fye WB: "Carl Ludwig and the Leipzig Physiological Institute: A factory of new knowledge." *Circulation* 74, 920 (1986)
4. Cranefield PF: The organic physics of 1847 and the biophysics of today. *J Hist Med Allied Sci* 12, 407 (1957)
5. Ludwig C: *Lehrbuch der Physiologie des Menschen.* 2 vols., Akademische Verlagshandlung C. F. Winter, Heidelberg (1852–1856)
6. Fye WB: H. Newell Martin and the isolated heart preparation: The link between the frog and open heart surgery. *Circulation* 73, 857 (1986)
7. Welch WH: The evolution of modern scientific laboratories. *Johns Hopkins Hosp Bull* 7, 19 (1896)

Rudolf Albert von Koelliker

W. Bruce Fye, M.D., M.A.

Department of Cardiology, Marshfield Clinic, Marshfield, Wisconsin, USA

Rudolf Albert von Koelliker made several basic electro-physiologic observations that were important for the subsequent development of electrocardiography. For example, he and Heinrich Müller were the first to record and describe the diphasic action current of cardiac muscle in 1856. Born in Zurich, Switzerland, on July 6, 1817, von Koelliker (Fig. 1) matriculated at the University of Zurich when he was 19.[1,2] Typical of ambitious students of his era, he took additional courses at other European universities. After spending a semester at Bonn in 1838, von Koelliker enrolled at the University of Berlin for three semesters. There, he studied physiology and comparative anatomy with Johannes Müller, microscopy with Jacob Henle, and embryology with Robert Remak. He received his Ph.D. degree from Zurich in 1841 and his M.D. degree the following year from the University of Heidelberg.

Von Koelliker aspired to an academic career in the natural sciences; he never planned to practice medicine. Shortly after Henle was appointed professor of anatomy at Zurich in 1840, he invited von Koelliker to serve as his assistant. Von Koelliker's main research interests were in histology and embryology at this point. An energetic and ingenious investigator, he seemed destined for academic success. Before he was 30, von Koelliker had made several important discoveries, including the fact that nerve fibers originated in and were continuous with nerve cells and that the involuntary nonstriated muscle fibers in the walls of blood vessels were actually elongated nucleated cells. His many contributions to neurohistology (including the description of neuroglia and ganglion cells) were important for the subsequent development of the neurone theory. He made a fundamental contribution to the cell theory by demonstrating the cellular nature of various tissues. This productive researcher also showed that spermatozoa were produced in the tissues of the testicle.

Von Koelliker was appointed professor of physiology, microscopy, and comparative anatomy at the University of Würzburg in 1847. Two years later, he was also chosen to be the professor of anatomy. These areas of teaching and research were often united during the first half of the nineteenth century. They began to emerge as distinct disciplines during the second half of the century as knowledge expanded, more workers entered the fields, new investigative techniques were developed, and more academic positions were created. Indeed, through his research, writing, and teaching, von Koelliker helped to establish histology and cytology as distinct scientific fields.

Although von Koelliker is remembered mainly for his contributions to embryology and histology, he made several important observations in the new field of experimental physiology. Indeed, his demonstration that muscle contraction was accompanied by an electric current was a fundamental discovery that helped set the stage for the rapid development of electrophysiology during the second half of the nineteenth century. von Koelliker's interest in electrophysiology was stimulated, in part, by recent advances in research techniques used to study the physiology of the nervous system and the innervation of muscle. Using an experimental nerve-muscle preparation known as the "rheoscopic frog," Italian physicist Carlo Matteucci (1811–1868) discovered in 1842 that an electrical current accompanied the contraction of all muscles, including cardiac muscle. The following year, German physiologist Emil DuBois-Reymond (1818–1896) extended Matteucci's observations. He recorded a resting electrical current in relaxed muscle and showed that this current diminished when the muscle contracted. DuBois-Reymond termed this negative fluctuation in the current an "action potential."[3]

Von Koelliker and Müller demonstrated in 1856 that these same fluctuations of resting current could be recorded from the spontaneously beating heart. Experimenting on frogs, they placed electrodes connected to a galvanometer on the base and apex of an excised ventricle. They discovered that the galvanometer's needle moved with each contraction, indicating that an electric current accompanied the contraction. Next, they placed the nerve of a nerve-muscle preparation on the ventricular surface of the beating heart and discovered that the frog leg contracted with each cardiac systole. The timing of the contraction was a critical part of their discovery.[4,5] In their history of electrocardiography, Burch and DePasquale explained that these researchers discovered that "the muscle in the nerve-muscle preparation contracted just prior to electric systole and again, with a more feeble twitch, at the beginning of diastole."[6]

The fact that the limb twitched *before* the ventricle contracted suggested that the electrical impulse preceded the contraction of the heart. This led von Koellicker and Müller to conclude that the electrical current might actually cause the heart to contract. They also discovered that this first contraction resulted from a negative variation of the heart's intrinsic

Fig. 1 Rudolf Albert von Koelliker, 1817–1905. From the collection of W. Bruce Fye.

electrical current. The second minute twitch, a positive variation at the beginning of diastole, represented recovery of the ventricles from excitation. Dutch physiologist Willem Einthoven, who invented the electrocardiograph in 1902, termed this second (positive) deflection a T wave in 1895 when he recorded the action potential of the heart using a capillary electrometer. Von Koelliker and Müller's experiments were extended by Franciscus Donders, Theodor Engelmann, John Burdon-Sanderson, Augustus Waller, and others in the 1870s. Their observations were another important part of what might be called the prehistory of electrocardiography.[7]

Von Koelliker spent more than 50 years on the faculty of the University of Würzburg. Acknowledged as one of the greatest medical scientists of the nineteenth century, he received honorary degrees from the universities of Utrecht, Bologna, Glasgow, and Edinburgh. He was a founder and first chair of the German Anatomical Society. A prolific author, von Koelliker published several influential monographs and popular textbooks as well as more than 300 papers. He retired from teaching at the age of 80 although he continued his research. He died in Würzburg in 1905.

References

1. Cameron GR: Rudolf Albert v. Koelliker (1817–1905). *Ann Science* 1955;11,166–172
2. Hintzsche E: Rudolf Albert von Koelliker. In *Dictionary of Scientific Biography* (Ed. Gillispie CC) Vol. 7, p. 437–440. New York: Charles Scribner's Sons, 1973
3. Katz LN, Hellerstein HK: Electrocardiography. In *Circulation of the Blood: Men and Ideas* (Ed. Fishman AP, Richards DW), p. 265–351. New York: Oxford University Press, 1964
4. von Koelliker A, Müller H: Nachweis der negativen Schwankung des Muskelstroms am natürlich sich kontrahierenden Herzen. *Verhandlungen der Physikalisch-Medizinischen Gesellschaft in Würzberg.* 1856;6:528–533
5. Frank RG Jr: The telltale heart: Physiological instruments, graphic methods, and clinical hopes 1854–1914. In *The Investigative Enterprise: Experimental Physiology in Nineteenth-Century Medicine*, p. 211–290. Berkeley and Los Angeles: University of California Press, 1988
6. Burch GE, DePasquale NP: A *History of Electrocardiography with a New Introduction by Joel D. Howell*, 2nd ed., p. 222. San Francisco: Jeremy Norman, 1990
7. Fye WB: A history of the origin, evolution, and impact of electrocardiography. *Am J Cardiol* 1994;73:937–949

Frans C. Donders

FREEK W.A. VERHEUGT, M.D.

Department of Cardiology, University Hospital Nijmegen, Nijmegen, The Netherlands

Professor Frans Cornelius Donders was the first to record heart sounds indirectly. This was an important contribution to cardiology. Born in 1818 in Tilburg, The Netherlands, he attended Medical School in Utrecht and made his thesis in 1840 at Leiden University. At age 27 he became a Member of the Royal Netherlands Academy of Sciences and, in 1847, was appointed Professor of Physiology at the University of Utrecht (Fig. 1). He turned out to be a pluripotent physiologist and was oriented mainly in metabolism, respiration, and ophthalmology; He also became interested in the physiology of the heart muscle, with a special interest in variations in the rhythm of the heart and the influence of the vagal nerve on it.

In the field of cardiovascular physiology, his most important work was on the rhythm of heart sounds. In an 1868 paper,[1] he described the duration of systole and diastole at various heart rates. He registered heart sounds in an indirect way. With his stethoscope he listened to the heart sounds of normal individuals and registered them on a rotating carbonized cylinder with a movement of his hand. First he estimated the error of his method. He used a metronome as the standard of reference of regularity. Listening to the sounds of the metronome, he registered them on the cylinder and calculated the registered differences in regularity on the cylinder in over 1,000 observations. He found that his personal error was 1.25%.

Using his method of registering the rhythm of heart sounds, he detected that the duration of systole was rather constant: between 0.301 and 0.327 s, when the heart rate was between 75 and 100 beats/min. Even in cases of extreme bradycardia (< 30 beats/min), the duration of systole was not increased: it was 0.325 s. Only in tachycardia was the duration of systole shortened, but at heart rates under 100 beats/min the duration of systole was very constant. His findings have frequently been confirmed by direct phonocardiography; therefore, he is considered to be the inventor and first user of phonocardiography.

Using his indirect registration of heart sounds, Donders made interesting observations on the variability of the heart rate during respiration. In his experiments, he registered both respiration directly and heart sounds indirectly on the rotating carbonized cylinder after dissecting the vagal nerve in animals, and thus studied the influence of the vagal nerve on heart rate and respiration for the first time.

Later he developed the "physiological rheoscope." He connected the nerve of a nerve-muscle preparation of a frog with the beating heart of a dog. Just prior to ventricular systole, the frog muscle contracted. He estimated the duration of this time lag at a 1/70 part of a second. By these observations he became the godfather of the pre-ejection period, later described in the

FIG. 1 Professor Frans C. Donders (1818–1891) in his physiologic laboratory at the University of Utrecht. Source: The University Museum Leiden, The Netherlands.

era of systolic time intervals. Finally, with his physiologic rheoscope, he observed a second twitch of the frog muscle just after the end of systole and at the beginning of diastole. This second electrical change in the ventricle was later identified as the T wave in the electrocardiogram; thus, Donders was also the founding father of ventricular repolarization.

Many young investigators visited Donders' laboratory in Utrecht, among them Theodore Engelmann and Willem Einthoven (1860–1927), the developer of electrocardiography, for which he received the Nobel Prize for Medicine in 1924.

Although Donders made some unique observations in the field of cardiovascular physiology, his main experimental and clinical investigations were concentrated on ophthalmology. It is interesting that his most famous pupil, Willem Einthoven, did his thesis on ophthalmology in 1885.

In 1888 Donders suffered a minor stroke and his health deteriorated rapidly. The chair of physiology at Utrecht University was taken over by Theodore Engelmann. Donders died in 1891 in Utrecht at the age of 71. He will be remembered as the founding father of indirect phonocardiography, the pre-ejection period, and ventricular repolarization.

Reference

1. Donders FC: On the rhythm of the sounds of the heart. *Dublin Quarterly Med Sci* 1868;89:225

John Eric Erichsen

W. Bruce Fye, M.D., M.A.

Department of Cardiology, Marshfield Clinic, Marshfield, Wisconsin, USA

John Eric Erichsen (Fig. 1) is included in the *Profiles in Cardiology* series because of his pioneering observations on the consequences of experimental ligation of the coronary arteries and his important book on aneurysms, published more than 150 years ago.[1,2] The son of a successful Danish banker, Erichsen was born in Copenhagen on July 19, 1818; but he also had strong family ties to Great Britain: his mother and paternal grandmother were both English. It is not surprising, therefore, that young John was educated in England. After preliminary schooling at Mansion House, Hammersmith, Erichsen began to study medicine at University College, London. His studies were supplemented by postgraduate work in Paris, then the world's leading center of clinical medicine and medical education.[3]

Shortly after Erichsen returned to London as house surgeon at University College Hospital, he began a series of animal experiments designed to study the effects of coronary occlusion. Although French physician Pierre Chirac studied the effects of ligating the coronary arteries in a dog in 1698, there was little interest in the subject until the nineteenth century.[4] Erichsen wondered what effect blocking the coronary circulation would have on the heart's action. He also hoped to clarify the relationship between abrupt coronary occlusion and sudden death. The results of his innovative experiments were published in an 1842 paper, *On the Influence of the Coronary Circulation on the Action of the Heart*.[5]

Erichsen used silk sutures to ligate the proximal coronary arteries of two anesthetized dogs and six rabbits. In seven of the animals, the average duration of ventricular action following ligation was 23½ min.

Erichsen concluded on the basis of his experiments

…that the arrest of the coronary circulation produces a speedy cessation of the heart's action. Secondly, that an increase in the quantity of blood sent into, or retained in the muscular fibre of the heart, produces a corresponding increase in the activity of that organ.[5]

Erichsen explained,

The bearing of these results on the immediate cause of death in some diseases of the heart is sufficiently obvious. Any circumstances that may interfere with the passage of the blood through the coronary arteries, either directly, as in ossification of the coats of those vessels, or indirectly, by there not being sufficient blood sent out of the left ventricle, as in cases of extreme obstruction or regurgitant disease of the aortal [sic] or mitral valves, may occasion the fatal event.[5]

Erichsen's investigations signaled a new interest in the pathophysiology of the coronary circulation. Several European and American investigators extended his studies during the second half of the nineteenth century.[6] It was not until the early twentieth century, however, that the pathophysiology and clinical features of acute coronary occlusion in humans were clarified by the Russian physicians W. P. Obrastzow and N. D. Straschesko and the American James B. Herrick.[7]

In 1843, Erichsen began to lecture on anatomy and physiology at Westminster Hospital Medical School in London. George James Guthrie, a pioneering military surgeon on the staff of the hospital, had already made important contributions to vascular surgery. He may have further stimulated Erichsen's interest in the cardiovascular system. While at Westminster Hospital, Erichsen published a collection of papers on aneurysms.[8] This valuable 524-page book began with a brief extract from Galen's works and included longer sections from several dozen publications on the subject published between 1542 and 1799.

For his book, Erichsen translated several of the essays into English for the first time. It demonstrated the gradual evolution of understanding about the pathophysiology of aneurysms. The first section of the book dealt with the etiology, symptoms, and pathology of aneurysms, while the second was devoted to treatment. He included 20 works in the first section, among them important monographs by Giovanni Maria Lancisi (1728) and Donald Monroe (1760). Enhanced by Erichsen's annotations, the book provides valuable in-sight into the growth of knowledge about diseases of the blood vessels and the early developments of vascular surgery.

In recognition of his interest in experimental medicine and surgery, Erichsen was elected secretary of the physiologic section of the British Association for the Advancement of Science. In 1848 he was appointed assistant surgeon to University College Hospital in London. It was there, just two years earlier, that one of Erichsen's mentors, Robert Liston, performed the first operation using ether anesthesia in England.[9]

Fig. 1   John Eric Erichsen, 1818–1896. Source: Underwood EA: *Science, Medicine and History*, p. 342. London: Oxford University Press, 1953. Reproduced with permission from the publisher.

Erichsen's colleagues acknowledged his talents and accomplishments, and he advanced through the ranks at University College Hospital. In 1850, at the age of 32, Erichsen was promoted to surgeon at the hospital and Chair of Surgery at University College. The first edition of his widely heralded textbook on surgery appeared three years later.[10] Erichsen's reputation grew rapidly as a result of his many publications, and his clinical judgement was acclaimed by those who consulted him. A popular and respected teacher, Erichsen's pupils included Joseph Lister and Henry Thompson. Erichsen was elected to many professional societies and became Surgeon Extraordinary to Queen Victoria in 1887. He died nine years later at Folkestone, England, the birthplace of William Harvey.

References

1. Dahl-Iversen E: Sir John Erichsen, Bt.: A 19th century heart experimentalist. *Acta Chir Scand* 1961;283(suppl):1–7

2. Power D, Spencer WG, Gask GE: Sir John Eric Erichsen. In *Plarr's Lives of the Fellows of the Royal College of Surgeons of England*, p. 378–380. Bristol, England: John Wright & Sons, 1930

3. Ackerknecht EH: *Medicine at the Paris Hospital, 1794–1848.* Baltimore: Johns Hopkins University Press, 1967

4. Fye WB: Acute coronary occlusion always results in death, or does it? The observations of William T. Porter. *Circulation* 1985;71: 4–10

5. Erichsen JE: On the influence of the coronary circulation on the action of the heart. *London Med Gaz* 1842;2:561–564

6. Leibowitz JO: *The History of Coronary Heart Disease.* London: Wellcome Institute of the History of Medicine, 1970

7. Fye WB: Acute myocardial infarction: A historical summary. In *Acute Myocardial Infarction* (Eds. Gersh BJ, Rahimtoola SH), p. 3–13. New York: Elsevier Science Publishing Co., 1991

8. Erichsen JE: *Observations on Aneurism Selected from the Works of the Principal Writers on that Disease from the Earliest Periods to the Close of the Last Century.* London: Sydenham Society, 1844

9. Merrington WR: *University College Hospital and Its Medical School: A History.* London: William Heinemann, 1976

10. Erichsen JE: The *Science and Art of Surgery.* London: Walton & Maberly, 1853

Rudolph Virchow and Cellular Pathology

HECTOR O. VENTURA, M.D.

Section of Cardiology, Department of Medicine, Tulane University Hospital and Clinic, New Orleans, Louisiana, USA

In the mid-nineteenth century, the fundamental role of the "sick cell" as the essence of all diseases was not known. This concept had to await introduction until the renowned German physician and pathologist Rudolph Virchow[1] published his masterpiece *Cellular Pathology as Based upon Physiological and Pathological Histology*. He wrote that the cell is "the ultimate irreducible form of every living element, and . . . from it emanate all the activities of life both in health and in sickness." He was to become one of the most important physicians of his time. His influence in medicine was to be felt for many years. Utilizing data from the multiple dissections he performed throughout the years, Virchow derived a general theory of the disease processes and subsequently fought for its acceptance.

Life and Medical Career

Rudolph Ludwig Carl Virchow (Fig. 1) was born on October 13, 1821, in Schivelbein, Pomerania. In 1838 he won a scholarship to study medicine at the Friedrich-Wilhelms Institute in Berlin and received his medical degree in 1843.[1] During medical school, Virchow was inspired by the work of Johannes Peter Müller, whose researches in physiology were leading to important new advances in studies of microscopic and pathologic anatomy.

After graduation, Virchow became an intern at Berlin's Charité Hospital, a very important institution in medicine at the time. It was there that Virchow began his lifelong career in pathology. He served as a prosector of pathology, performing dissections for anatomical demonstrations, and in 1847 he became a privadozent, which allowed him to become a teacher. His scientific endeavors enabled him to study the inflammatory theory of atherosclerosis, to describe that pus was made up of white blood cells, and to define leukemia as a disease.[1] Perhaps a more important contribution was the introduction of new methods of research, namely, experimental pathology. With his friend Bruno Reinhardt, he also created a new journal, *Archiv für pathologische Anatomie und Physiologie, und für klinische Medizin*, today known as *Virchow's Archives*. By no means was he detached from the social unrest characteristic of the 1840s. Virchow published a weekly paper, *Die Medizinische Reform*, that had a markedly political orientation, and his editorial comments as well as his articles annoyed the German authorities. He became politically en-

gaged after investigating a typhus epidemic in Upper Silesia, which was the home to an oppressed Polish minority in Prussia. As part of a commission formed by the government following an exposé in the press, Virchow traveled to the region, reported that the essential basis for the epidemic was social, and prescribed "democracy, education, freedom, and prosperity."[2] For his harsh antiroyalist views and his political stance, his salary was cut off and therefore he was effectively removed from the Charité. He left Berlin to occupy the new chair of pathologic anatomy at Würzburg. There, he spent seven years building a reputation as a teacher and researcher. He not only was the author of many papers on pathologic anatomy but also had begun the publication of his monumental *Handbuch der speziellen Pathologie und Therapie*. In addition, during his tenure at Würzburg, he had begun to formulate his now famous theory of cellular pathology. Virchow's importance at Würzburg also can be measured by the increase in attendance at the school and by the students whom he taught. Names such as Friedreich, Haeckel, Rindfleisch, Gegenbaur, and Kussmaul later became prominent physicians.[3]

In 1856, Virchow was recalled to Berlin to become Professor Ordinarius of Pathology, and he dedicated within the great Charité the first institutional building ever solely devoted to study and research in this branch of medicine. Virchow had not been long in Berlin before he established the capital's medical statistics, particularly those related to housing and death rate, infant mortality, and causes of death. The limits of medicine were not enough for this man of tremendous energy and variety; therefore he became a member of the municipal council in 1861 and in 1862 he was elected to the Lower House with "Kulturkampf" as a slogan. In addition to his medical duties at the Charité he gave personal attention to army sanitation from 1866 to 1870 previous to the Franco-Prussian war. In 1870, he took the first hospital train to France and back home; during the remainder of the conflict he fought epidemics among soldiers in the field and prevented other epidemics in the barracks. After the war Virchow played a leading role in the construction of Moabit, Friedrichsheim, and urban city hospitals. In the same year, 1871, he designed the model sanitary system for Berlin. His gradually widening interests led him as far as ancient Troy in 1879, and to Spain and Portugal in 1880 in pursuit of his studies in anthropology and archeology. In 1880, at the age of 60 years, he entered the Reichstag, arraying himself immediately among Bismarck's bit-

Fig. 1 Rudolph Ludwig Carl Virchow, 1821–1902. Source: Photograph reproduced from Ref. No. 2 (public domain).

terest opponents. All these activities and more occurred while he was paving the way to the foundation of modern medicine. Small in stature, he has been described as "an elastic, professional figure, with snappy black eyes, quick in mind and body, with a touch of Slav, something of a martinet in the morgue or lecture room, often transfixing inattention or incompetence with a flash of sarcasm."[4] His working technique was also very impressive. No detail was too insignificant for his personal attention; he possessed a meticulous sense of order and did not know confusion or hurry; indeed, there was practically no time when a humblest research worker, after failing to secure an assistant to look through his microscope, found him inaccessible. His professional activities continued until his eightieth birthday. He was in full possession of all his faculties, able to appreciate and enjoy a national holiday in his honor, commendations from governments or scientific societies around the world, and the great gold medal of science from the Kaiser himself. Three years before his death he dedicated the celebrated pathologic museum to which he had donated his own personally assembled collection of more than 23,000 specimens. His productive life came to an end on September 5, 1902, at age 81. While attempting to board a streetcar in Berlin, he slipped, fell, and fractured his femur. He subsequently died of complications following this accident. The funeral ceremonies were held in the Berlin Rathaus.[3]

Contributions to the Field of Medicine and Cardiology

Virchow's contributions to medicine were numerous. He published an incredible number of studies from 1843 to 1901.

These were assembled by Schwalbe immediately after Virchow's death. Virchow's bibliography required 118 pages and the total number of publications was 2,124. Among the more outstanding of his major contributions to scientific literature, some that molded medical thought for all times must be mentioned: *Archiv*, 1847; *Virchow's Jahresbericht*, 1851; *Handbuch der speziellen Pathologie und Therapie*, 1854; *Die Cellularpathologie*, 1858; *Die Krankhaften Geschwuelste*, 1863, 1865, and 1867; and *Sectionstechnik*, 1876. "Experiment" he wrote, "is the ultimate court of the science of pathologic physiology."[5] He established the study of normal structures as key to understanding pathologic ones. He was the first to develop a necropsy technique that disturbed structural relations to the minimal degree and favored diagnosis to the maximum. Early on in his career, he demonstrated the importance of fibrin in the blood coagulation process and he coined the terms embolism and thrombosis. It was early in the 1850s that he developed the cell doctrine and the fundamental principles of cellular pathology. With the appearance of *Cellular Pathology as Based upon Physiological and Pathological Histology,* modern clinical medicine was founded. "What Virchow accomplished in Cellular Pathology," writes physician and author Sherwin Nuland,[5] "was nothing less than to enunciate the principles upon which medical research would be based for the next hundred years and more." Inspired by Theodore Schwann's cellular theory, Virchow corrected and extended it. He called the cell the fundamental unit of life and hypothesized on the existence of cell division to account for reproduction. He demonstrated that muscle and bone are composed of cells, that connective tissue was mixed with nerve cells in the spinal cord and brain, and he developed a basic classification of cellular tissue. In summary, Virchow formulated what came to be known as the cell doctrine: Ommis cellula e cellula (every cell arises from another cell). He wrote, "Development cannot cease to be continuous, because no particular generation can start a fresh series of developments. We must reduce all tissues to a single simple element, the cell" . . . "the ultimate irreducible form of every living element, and . . . from it emanate all the activities of life both in health and in sickness."[2]

In the field of cardiology, Virchow made a seminal contribution to the understanding of atherosclerosis.[6] Until Virchow's, several theories on the pathogenesis of atherosclerosis had been proposed. The most popular at the time was the thrombogenic theory, championed by Rokitansky in 1841. He proposed that the deposits observed in the inner layer of the arterial wall derived primarily from fibrin and other blood elements rather than being the result of a purulent process. Subsequently, the atheroma resulted from the degeneration of the fibrin and other blood proteins as a result of a preexisting crasis of the blood, and finally these deposits were modified toward a pulpy mass containing cholesterol crystals and fatty globules. This theory came under attack by Virchow with the presentation of his inflammatory theory a few years later. His description of the pathogenesis of atherosclerosis was an indepth study of the histologic characteristics of the atherosclerotic lesion in all its stages. First and foremost, he recognized that the atherosclerotic lesion was situated within or underneath the intimal layer of the vasculature and that the primary deposit occurred by imbibition of certain blood elements. Accordingly, the next stage was due to a softening of the connective tissue matrix at the site of deposition followed by an active proliferation within the intima. A fatty metamorphosis of the connective tissue cells followed, which ultimately led to intimal thickening. In attempting to explain the nature of the process, Virchow utilized the name of "endarteritis deformans." By this he meant that the atheroma was a product of an inflammatory process within the intima and that the fibrous thickening evolved as a consequence of a reactive fibrosis induced by proliferating connective tissue cells within the intima. He maintained that mechanical forces initiated the irritative stimulus and that the endarteritis was part of a repair mechanism. His theory has elements that are acceptable to current thinking, but it also has features that have been invalidated. However, suffice it to say that Virchow's concept of local intima injury as the initiating "irritative" stimulus is still accepted and it has been extended to include other factors besides mechanical factors. In 1864, two years after his pupil Von Recklinghausen described the association of numerous rhabdomyomas of the heart and sclerotic changes in the brain, Virchow reported the case of a child with brain tuberous sclerosis and rhabdomyoma of the heart whose sister died of a cerebral tumor. This was the first hint of the familial nature of the disease.[7]

Another very important contribution to medicine was the instruction of many famous physicians who have carried forward the torch of the master. These names include pathologists such as Von Recklinghausen, Klebs, Cohnheim, Ponfick, Orth, and Grawitz, and chemists such as Hoppe-Seyler and Salkowski. Virchow's conclusions transmitted by his associates and followers were to make every student around the world cell-minded.[3] Here in the United States, the influence of Dr. Welch and Dr. Osler has been paramount in pathology and medicine for many decades. Welch also drew inspiration from Cohnheim, who himself was part of the small group taught by Virchow. Osler was inspired by Virchow when he spent three months at the Charité observing clinics and Virchow himself. He writes in a letter " . . . But it is the master mind of Virchow, and the splendid Pathological Institute which rises like a branch hospital in the grounds of the Charité, that specially attracts foreign students to Berlin."[8a]

Conclusion

Rudolph Virchow created the basis for experimental pathology and made observations in medicine that have stood the passing of time. His life was dedicated not only to the study of medicine but also to patients, since he believed that physicians "ought to be the attorneys for the poor." His contributions to human knowledge went beyond medicine and encompassed other branches of the humanities. In an address about Virchow's life, on the occasion of the celebration of Virchow's seventieth birthday, William Osler wrote about his personal association with " . . . the father of modern pathology." Regarding the importance of Virchow's work, he wrote " . . . The influence of his work has been deep and far reaching, and in one way or another has been felt by each one of us."[8b] Perhaps his life can be best summarized by his biographer at the time of his death, "Germany would complain of having lost four great men at once: her leading pathologist, her leading anthropologist, her leading sanitarian, and her leading liberal."[2]

References

1. Virchow R: *Encyclopaedia Britannica*, 19, p. 150–151, 1974
2. Simmons J: Rudolph Virchow and the cell doctrine. In *The Scientific 100—A Ranking of the Most Influential Scientists, Past and Present*, p. 88–92. New Jersey: Carol Publishing Group, 1996
3. Bartlett W: *A Sketch of Virchow's Life and Time in Lectures on the History of Medicine*. Mayo Foundation Lectures, p. 457–489. Philadelphia: W.B. Saunders, 1933
4. Garrison FH: *An Introduction to the History of Medicine*, p. 569–572. New York: W.B. Saunders, 1929
5. Nuland S: *Doctors. The Fundamental Unit of Life Sick Cells, Microscopes, and Rudolf Virchow*, p. 304–343. New York: Random House Inc., 1988
6. Acierno LJ: *History of Cardiology (Atherosclerosis)*, p. 109–127. New York: Parthenon Publishing Group Ltd., 1994
7. Acierno LJ: *History of Cardiology (Genetics and Cardiovascular Disease)*, p. 399–446. New York: Parthenon Publishing Group Ltd., 1994
8. Cushing H: The Life of Sir William Osler, Vol. 1 (a) p. 110, (b) p. 355. Oxford: Clarendon Press, 1925

Pierre-Carl Potain

JOHN D. CANTWELL, M.D.

Preventive Cardiology and Cardiac Rehabilitation, Georgia Baptist Medical Center, Atlanta, Georgia, USA

Pierre-Carl Potain was one of France's premier physicians, a clinician who was among the first to bring "instruments of precision" to the bedside.[1]

Among the many accomplishments of this Paris physician were the following:

Assistance in development of the sphygmomanometer

Description of the opening snap in mitral stenosis[2]

Analysis of the wave form of the internal jugular vein

A classic description of gallop rhythm and distinction between a split first heart sound and a presystolic gallop; identification of the palpable presystolic precordial distension that may coincide with a fourth heart sound

Identification of the venous hum, and distinction between arterial and venous sounds in the neck

Description of cardiac clicking sounds (which he attributed to pericardial adhesions, but in retrospect could have reflected mitral valve prolapse)

Description of a tambour second heart sound and increased dullness at the upper right sternal border (known today as "Potain's sign") in syphilitic aortitis and aortic dilatation

Description of hepatic pulsations in tricuspid regurgitation

Development of an instrument to count erythrocytes

Design of a thoracentesis apparatus

Background

Pierre-Carl Potain (Fig. 1) was born in Paris on July 19, 1825. Many of his ancestors had practiced medicine and surgery in the town of Saint-Germain, dating back at least to 1662. His father, discouraged by an anatomy course, dropped out of medicine and became the post officer at Saint-Germain. He promised himself that his son would recapture the family tradition. Lacking financial resources to provide for his son's education, he resolved to educate the boy himself. As the son later recalled:

> For 10 years he [the father] consecrated all of his leisure time to this enterprise every day. When his office closed he put my books under my arm and took me into the forest (winter, summer, rain, snow, anytime). There he gave me lessons of grammar, lessons of literature, lessons on everything. My mother, who remembered to fill me with

tenderness and veneration, assisted in accomplishing the task of teaching me German, which my father did not know.[3]

Potain kept a journal as a youth and once accused himself of "frittering away his time,"[3] blaming himself for being interested in too many things (woodworking, composing melodies, designing art, writing poetry).

Upon choosing a career, Potain considered a polytechnical school, given his taste for exact sciences and for mechanics, but "in response to the voice of his father"[3] he decided upon medicine.

He received his medical degree from the University of Paris in 1853 (his inaugural thesis was on vascular murmurs following hemorrhage). Part of his training was at the Hospital Salpêtrière, where he developed cholera. He became the assistant to Jean-Baptiste Bouillaud and eventually became chief of Professor Bouillaud's clinic at la Charité Hospital. He had worked earlier at Hospital St. Antoine and the Hospital Necker (where Laënnec had practiced several decades earlier). In 1861 Potain became adjunct professor in the Faculty of Medicine at the University of Paris. After a brief interlude in 1870, when he enlisted as an infantryman and took part in combat in the Franco-Prussian War, he returned to academic medicine and became professor of clinical medicine in 1876. His students included Louis-Henri Vaquez, Louis-Joseph Teissier, and Scipione Riva-Rocci (the Italian who advanced the development of the sphygmomanometer).

Scientific Contributions

In 1867 Potain described the wave form of the internal jugular vein, combining palpation of the precordium or auscultation with inspection of the veins for the purpose of timing the venous waves. The previous year he had noted that the second heart sound typically split during inspiration and was single during expiration. Also in 1867 he differentiated between arterial and venous murmurs in the neck:

> Two kinds of murmurs are heard in the neck: arterial murmurs and venous murmurs. Arterial murmurs are intermittent; venous murmurs may be continuous, intermittent, or continuous with reinforcements.[4]

FIG. 1 Pierre-Carl Potain (1825–1901). Photograph reproduced from Ref. No. 10.

Of the venous hum he wrote:

The thrill, which is felt by placing the finger lightly above the clavicle over the course of the vessel of the neck, is sometimes continuous and frequently intermittent. It is this last case which interests us above all here. … A light pressure exerted above the point of exploration can make it appear or reinforce it, while a stronger pressure extinguishes it completely, proofs positive. … that we are concerned with a venous phenomenon and that this thrill does not arise at all from an artery.[4]

In 1876 he wrote the classic description of gallop rhythm, a term first used by his professor, Bouillaud. Of the fourth heart sound he wrote:

The formation of the rhythm of which I wish to speak, is as follows: We distinguish here three sounds, namely: the two normal sounds show most frequently their normal characteristics, without any modification. The first especially maintains its normal relationship to the apex heart and to the arterial phase. As to the abnormal sound, it is placed immediately before it, preceding it sometimes by a very short time; always notably larger, however, than that which separates the two parts of a reduplicated sound.[5]

He distinguished the fourth sound from a split first sound:

In the first place, the abnormal sound has, in no way, the timbre or usual characteristics of a valvular sound.… Finally (and this is the unanswerable argument that

makes unnecessary all other reasons), I have heard, in certain patients, successively and in the same cardiac revolution, the 'bruit de gallop' itself and a reduplication of the first heart sound. I mean that after the full sound which constitutes the first part of the gallop rhythm, one noted clearly a doubled first sound, a reduplicated clicking of the usual type.[6]

Potain felt that the fourth heart sound reflected "the abruptness with which the dilation of the ventricle takes place during the presystolic period, a period which corresponds to the contraction of the auricle."[5] The third heart sound he attributed to "sudden cessation of distention of the ventricle in early diastole."[5]

In 1894 Potain described "small, sharp clicking sounds" which he attributed to pericardial adhesions.[7] Although Perloff states that remnants of pericardial rubs may rarely persist,[8] Potain could also have been referring to the systolic clicks of mitral valve prolapse, which were not described until the 1960s.

Potain was mechanically inclined and made important observations with an air sphygmomanometer, an advancement of Marey's aneroid device.[9] He also developed an aspirator with a vacuum attachment (known as Potain's apparatus), which enabled one to do a thoracentesis and to replace the fluid progressively with air to prevent sudden expansion of the lung.[3] In addition, he devised an instrument to count red blood cells.[10]

General Comments

Potain had "a very lean body, was a bit hunched over, [and] had a puny appearance."[3] His face was "long, ascetic, asymmetrical" and he had a "profoundly wrinkled forehead, a sparse beard, a prominent nose which jutted out, a mouth with very slight lips, and a bony cranium as if pounded with a hammer, surrounded by a crown of frizzled hair which fell out the neck."[3] Despite this lack of handsome physical features, he radiated beauties "more precious than beauty herself."[3] He was "gentle to his patients, kind to his pupils at the bedside, and just in the examination of their wisdom and learning."[11] He "never gloried in the renown to which he came, valueing more the service rendered or the solution to a difficult problem. This was his joy."[3] His charity never stopped, it was said, even when his purse was empty. Punctual in his medical functions, he arrived at the hospital at 8:30 A.M. and passed in front of each patient's bed, "responding affectionately to the sick, who seemed to collect advice and encouragement from him."[3]

At night, after dinner, he prepared his lessons and work for the following day and upon finishing enjoyed being with friends and listening to symphonies of the great composers, including Bach, Mozart, and Beethoven. He never went to sleep "without having read some pages from his favorite authors, Blaise Pascal and Paul-Louise Courier."[3] Faithful to the memory of his early classical education "he was always a strong defender of eloquent and ancient literature and of the intellectual culture which he considered necessary for the future of medicine."[3]

Potain became the foremost clinician of his time in Paris, astute at bedside observations and physiologic correlations. He was honored with memberships in the Academy of Science, the Academy of Medicine, and the Institute of France. The French government designated him as a Commander of the Legion of Honor.[11] In collaboration with several other physicians Potain published his clinical and necropsy observations on cardiovascular and pulmonary disorders in a 1,000-page monograph.[12]

Potain retired at the end of December 1900, a profoundly emotional occasion for him. The day of his departure he was unable to speak words of farewell to his colleagues. The tears coursing down his face said it all.

On January 1, 1901, colleagues Teissier and Vaquez visited him at home, reflecting the love and devotion that sons might give to their father. Potain's parting words were prophetic: "When the function is extinguished the organ must disappear."[3]

Several days later "he felt little suffering and simply slept later than usual. Minutes later his servant entered his room and found that he was not breathing. He left discreetly, just as he had come, and the death which he had was more gentle than his life."[3]

We should remember him today the next time we record blood pressures, note inspiratory splitting of the second heart sound, detect gallop rhythms, listen for venous hums and carotid bruits in the neck, study the wave form in the internal jugular vein, and detect the tambour second heart sound in aortic root disease or the opening snap in mitral stenosis.

Acknowledgments

The author thanks Fay Evatt and her library staff for help in locating several references, Rebecca Vanderhorst for translation of Reference No. 3, and Susan Barron for preparation of the manuscript.

References

1. Castiglioni A: *A History of Medicine*. Alfred A. Knopf, New York (1941) 828
2. Wood P: *Diseases of the Heart and Circulation*. Eyre and Spottiswoode, London (1950) 286
3. Vaquex H: Pierre-Carl Potain (1825-1901). Obituary (Fr). *Bull Acad Med Paris* 97, 569–587 (1927)
4. Potain PC: Des mouvements et des bruits qui se passent dans les veines jugulaires. *Bull Mem Soc Med Hop Paris* 4, 3 (1866)
5. Potain PC: Concerning the cardiac rhythm called gallop rhythm. *Bull Mem Soc Med Hop* 12, 137 (1876). In *Physical Examination of the Heart and Circulation,* 2nd Ed. (Ed. Perloff JK). W.B. Saunders Co., Philadelphia (1992) 200–201
6. Potain PC: Concerning the cardiac rhythm called gallop rhythm. *Bull Mem Soc Med Hop* Paris 12, 137 (1876). In *Physical Examination of the Heart and Circulation,* 2nd Ed. (Ed. Perloff JK). W.B. Saunders Co., Philadelphia (1992) 204
7. Potain PC: Clinique médicale de la Charité. Paris. Masson (1894). In *Cardiovascular Sound in Health and Disease* (Ed. McKusick VA). The Williams and Wilkins Co., Baltimore (1958)
8. Perloff JK: *Physical Examination of the Heart and Circulation*, 2nd Ed. W.B. Saunders Co., Philadelphia (1992) 192
9. Lewis WH: The evolutions of clinical sphygmomanometry. *Bull NY Acad Med* 17, 871–881 (1941)
10. Willius FA, Dry TJ: *A History of the Heart and the Circulation*. W.B. Saunders Co., Philadelphia (1948) 163
11. Editorial: Pierre-Carl Potain (1825-1901). Cardiovascular physician. *J Am Med Assoc* 196, 134 (1966)
12. Potain C: *Clinical Observations From la Charité Medical Clinic*. G. Masson, Paris (1894)

Adolph Fick: Mathematician, Physicist, Physiologist

Louis J. Acierno, M.D., FACC

Cardiopulmonary Sciences, Department of Health Professions and Physical Therapy, University of Central Florida, Orlando, Florida, USA

The scion of an architect, and the last to join a family of scholars that eventually counted among eight siblings a professor of anatomy and one of law, Adolph Fick (Fig. 1) made his entry into this world in 1829 in Cassel, Germany. Early in life, Adolph showed a remarkable talent for mathematics and physics. He enrolled at the University of Marburg with the express purpose of acquiring the appropriate academic credentials in these two related disciplines. However, under the prodding of his brother Heinrich, who was professor of law, young Adolph was persuaded to matriculate in medicine, a field that Heinrich felt would certainly benefit from Adolph's expertise in mathematics and physics.[1]

Soon after taking his medical degree, Fick turned his attention to physiology, accepting a prosectorship with Carl Ludwig in Zurich. The year was 1852 and Fick was a mere 23 years of age. He was to remain with Ludwig for 16 years, leaving Zurich to accept the chair of physiology in Würzburg. Throughout his stay at Zurich, Fick made many contributions as a scientist well versed in mathematics, physics, and physiology, as brother Heinrich had already perceived. He was a quiet, scholarly man whose pastimes included pursuit of his marked interest in philosophy and literature.

Fick's first contribution as a physicist was made in 1855 when he was just 26 years old. It consisted of a concept that he developed mathematically from Fourier's theory of heat equilibrium. The resulting statement put forth the physically sound and logical view that diffusion is proportional to concentration gradient. Experimental proof of the view was provided 25 years later.[2]

A year after this distinctive achievement, Fick published a well-rounded monograph entitled *Medical Physics*.[3] Here, for the first time, he introduced his thoughts on certain physiologic problems such as the mixing of air in the lungs, measurement of carbon dioxide output in humans, the heat economy of the body, and the work of the heart. The monograph was a gold mine of information. Aside from a detailed discussion of the mechanics of muscular contraction and the molecular physics of gases and water, optics, color vision, animal heat, and conservation of energy, it dealt with hydrodynamics of the circulation fortified with sound recordings of circulatory events. It was the first book of its kind, and medicine had to wait almost a century before it yielded its landmark status to Otto Glasser's monumental *Medical Physics*.[4]

Throughout his tenure of more than three decades at Würzburg, and in his quiet unassuming manner, Fick contributed a steady and focused stream of information that was always on the cutting edge of knowledge in the three disciplines that he mastered. Although his major field of inquiry was devoted to the physiology of muscular contraction, he utilized the experimental knowledge gained from this activity to elucidate in quantitative terms the calculation of cardiac output. In fact, Fick is immortalized in cardiology because of a brief and obscure publication in 1870 wherein he described how mass balance might be used to measure cardiac output. It was a mathematical concept so pure in its logic that it contained *sui generis* its own intrinsic proof for its validity. The concept was an outgrowth of his mathematical approach to physiologic events.[1]

The concept now known as the Fick principle was published in the brief proceedings of the Würzburg Physikalische Medizinische Gesellschaft for July 9, 1870.[5]

An account of his presentation before the society follows:

> It is astonishing that no one has arrived at the following obvious method by which [the amount of blood ejected by the ventricle of the heart with each systole] may be determined directly, at least in animals. One measures how much oxygen an animal absorbs from the air in a given time, and how much carbon dioxide it gives off. During the experiment one obtains a sample of arterial and venous blood; in both the oxygen and carbon dioxide content are measured. The difference in oxygen content tells how much oxygen each cubic centimeter of blood takes up in its passage through the lungs. As one knows the total quantity of oxygen absorbed in a given time one can calculate how many cubic centimeters of blood passed through the lungs in this time. Or if one divides by the number of heart beats during this time one can calculate how many cubic centimeters of blood are ejected with each beat of the heart. The corresponding calculation with the quantities of carbon dioxide gives a determination of the same value, which controls the first.[5]

It is of interest that the preceding item in the proceedings announces the election of Wilhelm Roentgen to the society.

The physical law that underlies Fick's principle is that matter can neither be created nor destroyed. Thus, the volume of

FIG. 1 Adolph Fick, 1829–1901. *Source*: Fishman AP, Richards DW: *Circulation of the Blood: Men and Ideas*, p. 94. New York: Oxford University Press, 1964. Reproduced with permission.

oxygen taken up by the lungs must be equal to the amount of oxygen used by the tissues. Fick's principle is expressed by the following equation:

$$\text{Cardiac output} = \frac{\text{oxygen consumption}}{\text{arteriovenous oxygen difference}}$$

As usual, Fick did not bother either to advance or investigate the experimental proof for his principle. It was not until Grehant and Quinquad in 1886 that the validity of the Fick principle was demonstrated.[6] Further experimental proof was supplied by Zuntz and Hagemann, just three years before Fick's death.[7] Verification of the Fick principle in humans was initially accomplished in 1930. It was made possible through the daring exploits of Baumann and Grollman[8] at a time when cardiac catheterization had yet to be established as a clinical tool. They obtained samples of mixed venous blood by insert-ing a spinal tap needle just to the right of the sternum that entered the right ventricular chamber by puncturing its wall.[8]

Fick was also an innovator and inventor of sorts. Among the many instruments that he devised, some of those that had an impact on cardiovascular physiology were the plethysmograph, the pneumograph, and his version of the aneroid manometer. These were a reflection of his desire to attain precision in his physiologic experiments.

Fick remained at Würzburg for 31 years during which time he created an institute of physiology that became known as one of the foremost centers of its kind throughout the world. Over the years, in addition to his teaching and research activities, he climbed the academic ladder, finally becoming rector of the university. In turn, his own family continued the scholarly tradition of his father's family. His sons apparently inclined toward their uncle's choice of professions, one becoming an anatomist and the other a jurist.[1]

Fick relinquished his teaching duties on his 70th birthday by declaring that it was time for younger men to carry on this function. Despite his apparent good health he died of apoplexy only a year later. His sons memorialized him through the creation of the Adolph Fick Fund which awards a prize every five years for an outstanding contribution to physiology.

Although errors can occur in applying the Fick principle, as Guyton pointed out in 1930, these errors are small and in no way diminish its value.[9] It is fitting at this point to let it be known that Adolph Fick shall always be remembered as the mathematician and physicist who expanded the horizons of physiology and left a lasting impact on the determination of cardiac output.

References

1. Shapiro E: Adolph Fick—forgotten genius of cardiology. *Am J Cardiol* 1972;30:662–665
2. Fick A: Über Diffusion. *Ann Phys* 1855;94:59
3. Fick A: *Die Medizinische Physik*. Vieweg: Braunschweig, 1856
4. Acierno LJ: *The History of Cardiology*. London, New York: The Parthenon Publishing Group, 1994
5. Fick A: Über die Messung des Blutquantums in den Herzventrikeln. Würzburg: SB-Phys-Med Ges, July 9, 1870
6. Grehant N, Quinquad CE: Recherches expérimentales sur la mesure du volume de sang qui traverse les poumons en un temps donné. *C R Soc Biol Paris* 1886;36:285
7. Zuntz N, Hagemann O: Untersuchungen über den Stoffwechsel des Pferdes bei Ruhe und Arbeit. *Landw Jh* 1898;27 (Ergänz. Bd. 3)
8. Grollman A: The *Cardiac Output in Man in Health and Disease*, p. 11. Springfield, Illinois: Charles C Thomas, 1932
9. Guyton AC: *Cardiac Output and Its Regulation*, p. 30. Philadelphia: W. B. Saunders, 1930

Etienne-Jules Marey: 19th Century Cardiovascular Physiologist and Inventor of Cinematography

MARK E. SILVERMAN, M.D.

Emory University School of Medicine, and Division of Cardiology, Piedmont Hospital, Atlanta, Georgia, USA

If, indeed, graphic expression makes it possible for us to obtain scientific evidence, let us leave eloquent insinuation and flowery language to fulfill other roles; let us plot and compare the curves of the phenomena we investigate and forge ahead like geometricians, whose proofs are never questioned.

—Etienne-Jules Marey
La Méthode Graphique
Manuscript, Collège de France[1]

Etienne-Jules Marey (Fig. 1) was the foremost cardiovascular physiologist in the 19th century and a technical genius whose passion to record and analyze motion led to singular advances in the graphic method and to his invention of cinematography.[1, 2]

Marey was born March 5, 1830, in Beaune, France (Côte d'Or), the only child of a wine manager of the Bouvard winery.[2–4] His interest was engineering; however, his father persuaded him to enter medical school in Paris in 1849, after which he interned at the Hôpital Cochin. He practiced briefly but reversed direction and chose physiology as a career. For the brilliant young Marey the timing was opportune, for the golden period of physiology was just starting to flourish. After the early 17th century discovery of the circulation of blood by William Harvey and the measurement of intra-arterial and venous pressure in the horse by Stephen Hales in 1733, understanding of cardiac physiology had not advanced.[5] The introduction of the stethoscope by Laennec in 1819 had greatly stimulated an interest in auscultation and the heart; however, Laennec confused the understanding of cardiovascular physiology by incorrectly attributing the second heart sound to atrial systole.[6] The invention of the kymograph by Carl Ludwig in Germany in 1847—the graphic method—was the catapult that truly launched physiology as a science.[6] Before the kymograph, experiments were based primarily on visual observation. The kymograph allowed, for the first time, the opportunity to transcribe timed physiologic data on smoked paper that could be accurately analyzed and compared. It has been said that the introduction of the kymograph into physiology resulted in a revolution in science roughly comparable to the effect of the telescope on physics. Claude Bernard (1813–1878), in Paris, led the way by founding experimental physiology and developing a technique for cardiac catheterization.[5, 7] In 1844, he inserted glass thermometers into the cardiac ventricles of a horse via the jugular vein and carotid artery to measure temperature differences, and in 1847, he was the first to measure intracardiac pressures accurately.[7]

Influenced by Bernard and imbued with the desire to record the form and motion of arterial blood, Marey modified the clumsy, multilevered sphyghmograph developed by Karl Vierodt to inscribe the arterial pulse noninvasively.[8] In his doctoral thesis in 1859, which described the velocity and wave form of the arterial pulse, Marey used this instrument.[4] Following this experiment, he developed a pneumatic tambour (the Marey tambour) with Charles Buisson that greatly amplified the transmitting and recording capabilities of his equipment and permitted the recording of two simultaneous pulses—the first polygraph—which he used to estimate external blood pressure semiaccurately for the first time and to study respiratory motion.[1] In 1860, he began an important collaboration with Auguste Chauveau, a professor of veterinary physiology in Lyon.[6, 9] Together they investigated the timing of the apex impulse in the cardiac cycle, an area of controversy that had led to bitter disagreement over the sequence of the cardiac cycle.[6, 10] To prove their thesis that the apex beat was due to the contraction of the ventricle (and not recoil from ventricular ejection), they had to develop a method to measure the rapidly changing intracardiac pressures and the apex beat simultaneously. Their novel double-lumen technique is regarded as the real beginning of intracardiac pressure recordings.[7]

> We felt that it was necessary to record the onset of contraction for each of the heart chambers, as well as the onset of the apex beat, and to do this in a large mammal so that no doubt could remain as to the application of these findings to human physiology. ... In order to identify the moment of contraction for each heart chamber, it became necessary to determine the precise moment when the blood pressure of the heart chambers increased as the direct result of contraction. This was accomplished in the following manner: A double-tubed catheter was inserted into the jugular vein and guided into the heart. One catheter extended to the ventricle, while the other shorter one ended in the atrium.

FIG. 1 Etienne-Jules Marey (1830–1904). Photograph supplied courtesy of the U.S. National Library of Medicine.

Changes in blood pressure were transmitted from the atrium through the catheter to a connected recording device. The same situation existed for the ventricle. … An apparatus which recorded the onset of the apex beat was also put into position.[6]

In further experiments, the two investigators were the first to describe and interpret simultaneous pressures in the right atrium and right ventricle, the left ventricle and aorta, and the pulmonary artery pressure, the atrial influence on the ventricular pressure curve, the isometric phase of ventricular contraction, the chronology of valve motion, and the synchrony of left and right ventricular contraction.[5] Their innovative technique would set the stage for the 20th century contributions by Thomas Lewis and Carl Wiggers to the cardiac cycle and the Nobel prize in 1956 to Forssmann, Cournand, and Richards for cardiac catheterization in the human. Other original work on the heart by Marey included the discovery of the refractory period of heart muscle in 1875, and the first recording in animals of the electrogram of the heart using a capillary electrometer in 1876, preceding the work of Waller who recorded the first human electrogram in 1887.[11] His books, *Circulation of the Blood* (1863 and 1881), *Movement* (1868), and *The Graphic Method* (1878 and 1885) were important and enduring contributions to the basic understanding of cardiac physiology.

In 1881, at the age of 51, not content with pioneering accomplishments in just one field, Marey turned his attention to the field of chronophotography (his term).[2–4] He desired to understand locomotion of all kinds by capturing and scientif-

ically analyzing the slowest and fastest movements in nature. The flight of insects and birds, the racing horse, the movement of fish, the walking and sports motion of humans fascinated him and spurred him on to develop more refined graphic methods.[2, 3] He soon realized that the inertia inherent in his polygraphic technique was ultimately limiting to his experiments. He turned to the new photographic method developed by Muybridge in San Francisco as a better way to refine his studies.[3] Muybridge had famously photographed horses in motion (to show Leland Stanford whether all four legs were off the ground at one time).[3, 4] Instead of 24 cameras lined in a row, the technique used by Muybridge, Marey revolved daguerreotype glass plates behind a single shutter and lens, a gun-like technique borrowed from Janssen's astronomical revolver of 1874. In 1882 he was able to capture birds in flight at an unsatisfying 12 frames per second. He then turned to ribbons of silver bromide impregnated paper that had been developed by Eastman and Balagny. In 1888, he recorded the flight of a pigeon at 60 frames a second on a single strip. This is regarded as the first motion picture and was published in his classic book of 1890: *Le Vol des Oiseaux* in which he paid tribute to Muybridge and Janssen.[3] In 1889, he demonstrated his moving picture to Thomas Edison in Paris, which stimulated Edison's interest in the potential of this new art medium.[2] Marey did not care about the artistic or commercial aspects of his invention, preferring instead to pursue the scientific advantages of this photographic approach in his many studies on locomotion, subsequently published in his popular book, *Le mouvement* (1894). His schematized photographs of body movements displaying a white line outlining the lengths of the limbs against a black body and background directly influenced the famous 1911 painting, *Nude Descending the Staircase* by Marcel Duchamps.[4]

Renowned as an international scientist, Marey left little record of his private life. After his medical training, he lived a Bohemian life in Paris, living in an apartment on rue Cuvier, then moving into an old building of the Comédie Française where he converted an auditorium and backstage into his laboratory and living space.[3, 4] He was appointed assistant professor at the Collège de France in 1867 and was admitted to the Académie de Médécine in 1872 and the Académie de Sciences in 1878.[1, 4] In 1895, he was elected to the presidency of that prestigious institution. A site in the Parc des Princes was given to Marey by the Municipal Council of Paris in 1881 to further his work in physiology and photography.[4] An institute, later named the Institut Marey, was established in 1901 to honor and continue his work. In 1880 he moved to a fashionable house on the boulevard Delessert and also purchased a villa on a beach near Naples, Italy, where he developed his photographic gun and made the first moving pictures of sea waves.[4] From then on he would winter in Naples and live in France the rest of the year. He never married but did adopt a daughter in Italy. He was known to suffer from gallstones and phlebitis.[10] The cause of his death on May 15, 1904, is unstated. He was regarded by friends and colleagues as perfectionistic, affable, generous, and as a supreme physiologist who married the disciplines of physics and engineering into his research. In 1875, he was nominated by Claude Bernard for the physiology prize of the Institute of France. Bernard's nomination speech praised him saying,[2]

> The entire world knows that the objective of the graphic method is to determine and translate into visual terms the variations in a phenomenon by means of the inflections of a geometrical curve. Mr. Marey has solved this difficult problem for physiology and medicine. He has created instruments and equipment by means of which the vital phenomenon is not dependent upon the often impossible or incorrect interpretation of the observer and is instead subjected to the sensitive and rigorous evaluation of a precise instrument because it records itself. By looking at the infinite variety of living phenomena and their enormous complexity, it is possible to appreciate the means and ingenuity it was necessary to apply to make them accessible to graphic recording. At virtually each step of the way, Mr. Marey found himself confronted with all sorts of difficulties which he overcame by means of his intellect and inventive imagination. … Moreover, the most striking proof of Mr. Marey's success is found in the fact that the procedures he has proposed for observing biological phenomena have been introduced in all physiology laboratories in France and abroad and have become working and research tools it will no longer be possible to do without.[2]

His obituary in the *Lancet* of 1904 reads,

> Physiology has lost one of its brightest ornaments, a worker who did much to extend its boundaries and added much to the means whereby man is enabled to analyze the secrets of nature and, above all, to investigate the phenomena of motion as manifested in "organized beings". … Marey, by his character, by his personal attraction, by his work, by his discoveries, and by his modesty, was a man who was beloved by all who had the pleasure of knowing him. His fame will rest on his successful endeavor to apply the graphic method to the investigation of biological science.[10]

References

1. Sonolet J: Etienne Jules Marey: *The Graphic Method and Cardiovascular Research*. Medtronic-France Catalogue of the Exposition, 1980
2. Michaelis AR: E.J. Marey—Physiologist and first cinematographer. *Med Hist* 1966;10:201–203
3. Dagonet F: *Etienne-Jules Marey: A Passion for the Trace*. New York: Zone Books, 1992
4. Snellen HA: *E.J. Marey and Cardiology*. Rotterdam: Kooyker Scientific Publications, 1980
5. Acierno LJ: *The History of Cardiology*. New York: The Parthenon Publishing Group, 1994: 557
6. Espinosa RD, Viletstra RE, Mann RJ: J.B.A. Chauveau, E.J. Marey, and their resolution of the apex beat controversy through intracardiac pressure recordings. *Mayo Clin Proc* 1983;58:197–202
7. Mueller RL, Sanborn TA: The history of interventional cardiology: Cardiac catheterization, angioplasty, and related interventions. *Am Heart J* 1995;129:146–172
8. Lawrence C: Physiologic apparatus in the Wellcome Museum I. The Marey sphygmograph. *Med Hist* 1978;22:196–200
9. Hoff HE, Geddes LA: A historical perspective on physiological monitoring: Chauveau's projecting kymograph and the projecting physiograph. *Cardiovasc Res Center Bull* 1975;14:3–35
10. Obituary: Etienne J. Marey. *Lancet* 1904;I:1530–1531
11. Geddes LA, Hoff HE: The capillary electrometer: The first graphic recorder of bioelectric signals. *Arch Int Hist Sci* 1961;14:275–290

William Henry Broadbent*

W. B. FYE, M.D.

Cardiology Department, Marshfield Clinic, Marshfield, Wisconsin, USA

William Henry Broadbent (Fig. 1), one of Victorian Britain's leading physicians, made several important contributions to our knowledge of heart disease. Broadbent was born on January 23, 1835, in the village of Lindley, near Longwood, England.[1-3] Initially, he seemed destined to join his father's manufacturing business, but he was attracted to medicine by an uncle who practiced in Manchester. Broadbent became his uncle's apprentice while he studied at Owens College and the Royal School of Medicine in Manchester.

A dedicated and energetic student, Broadbent informed his parents in 1856, "I am working very hard now. I get up about seven; read till a quarter past eight; then go to the school and remain there, either attending lectures or dissecting till half-past two. I then go to the surgery to dinner; then back to the school till six, when I return to the surgery and work till ten. I then return to Broughton, and it is generally twelve before I get to bed."[4]

In addition to his apprenticeship, Broadbent gained practical experience at the Manchester Royal Infirmary. An excellent student, he passed the qualifying examination offered by the College of Physicians of London in 1857. Rather than enter practice, Broadbent decided to supplement his Manchester training with postgraduate study in Paris. Although its popularity was beginning to wane, Paris remained a mecca for ambitious medical students in the middle of the nineteenth century.[5] Broadbent walked the wards of the Paris hospitals and attended lectures at the École de Médecine. He was most impressed by Armand Trousseau, physician to the Hôtel Dieu and one of the greatest clinicians of the day.

Broadbent returned to London in 1858 and accepted a position as resident obstetric officer at St. Mary's Hospital, the institution where he would spend the rest of his career. In 1859, Broadbent was selected to fill an unexpected vacancy in the medical resident staff at St. Mary's Hospital. This new appointment represented a pleasant change for Broadbent who noted that he wanted "particularly to study diseases of the chest, and to compare the results of the various methods of treatment."[6] One of the physicians who most influenced Broadbent at St. Mary's was Francis Sibson. Sibson emphasized the importance of clinicopathologic correlation and was especially interested in diseases of the heart. Broadbent often assisted him in performing autopsies on patients who died under their care.

When his term as medical resident at St. Mary's expired, Broadbent entered medical practice in London. He also lectured on comparative anatomy and physiology. In part, he took these teaching posts to supplement his modest income from practice. In addition to his activities in practice and teaching, Broadbent began to publish numerous articles during the 1860s. His first article on cardiac disease appeared in 1866 and dealt with prognosis in heart disease.[7]

Medical research was not rewarded with either prestige or financial support in this era, but Broadbent enthusiastically pursued and encouraged this activity. In 1867, he urged physicians to add to medical knowledge through research or by publishing clinical observations:

> We owe it to our profession to contribute, so far as in us lies, to the common stock of knowledge. The particular stone we have picked up may be small, and the cairn thrown up by thousands who have passed by the same way has reached the dimensions of a mountain. Our pebble may be indistinguishable on the heap, but, so it be our very own, let us add it.[8]

Broadbent's own experiments in this period dealt with the therapeutic effect of drugs. He employed frogs in his research, which was carried out in a back room of his home that served as his study and laboratory. During the 1870s, Broadbent turned his attention increasingly to diseases of the heart and vascular system. He published papers on the heart sounds, hemiplegia associated with valvular heart disease, aneurysms, endocarditis, mitral stenosis, blood pressure, and angina pectoris. A special interest of Broadbent's throughout his career was the pulse. In 1875, he delivered a series of lectures on the pulse at St. Mary's Hospital. The pulse was also the subject of his Croonian Lectures delivered before the Royal College of Physicians in 1887. These lectures formed the basis of a comprehensive monograph published three years later.

This book included a valuable historical survey of the theories of the pulse from ancient times. Broadbent advocated careful and systematic evaluation of the pulse in all cases. Initially, the examiner should note the frequency as well as the regularity (or irregularity) of the beats. Next, the force or

---

*This paper is adapted from an essay prepared for the Classics of Cardiology Library, Gryphon Editions (Birmingham).

FIG. 1 William Henry Broadbent 1835–1907 (Source: *Life of Sir William Broadbent*, London: John Murray, 1909).

strength of the pulse should be noted. The character of the pulse should also be ascertained by noting its rise, duration, and fall. Broadbent explained, "It is impossible to examine with attention a large number of pulses, whether among the healthy or the sick, without being struck by the extraordinary diversity of frequency, size, character, tension, and force met with."[9]

With the publication of his book on the pulse, Broadbent's stature in the English-speaking medical world grew. Leading figures of the day sought consultations with him. The Prince of Wales informed Broadbent in 1892, "There is no one who stands higher in the medical profession in this country than you do, and I am most anxious to ask you to accept the appointment as my physician-in-ordinary, not only on account of the high position you hold, but as some mark of gratitude and appreciation of the services you rendered to our beloved sons during their dangerous illnesses."[10]

By this time Broadbent was at work on a comprehensive monograph on heart disease. One of his goals in publishing the volume was to aid physicians in their attempts to render accurate prognoses in cases of heart disease. In his preface Broadbent explained, "The prognosis of heart disease already engaged my attention when I was house-physician under Sibson at St. Mary's Hospital, and my first paper on this subject was read before the Harveian Society in 1866. Up to that time there had not, so far as I am aware, been any systematic study and exposition of the indications by which the probable course of disease of the heart in different cases might be fore-

seen, and ideas which tended to obscure the interpretation of the symptoms and physical signs were held by physicians of great experience and authority." He continued, "The prognosis of heart disease is worthy of special study, not only on account of its inherent importance, but also because the knowledge which enables the medical man to forecast clearly the course of the disease constitutes the best preparation for its treatment."[11]

Valvular disease is emphasized in Broadbent's book. This reflected the frequency of valvular heart disease in the nineteenth century, as well as the role of the stethoscope in directing the attention of physicians toward this class of cardiac diseases, which were often accompanied by dramatic auscultatory findings. There was little emphasis on what we term ischemic heart disease in this era before the introduction of the electrocardiograph or the recognition of the clinical syndrome of acute myocardial infarction.[12] The book includes a classic description of the physical signs of constrictive pericarditis. Broadbent is remembered eponymically for his observations on this entity. He explained, "Systolic retraction of the lower portions of the posterior or lateral walls of the thorax may indicate the presence of a universally adherent pericardium."[13]

In 1896, Broadbent retired as physician to St. Mary's Hospital. The following year he was elected a Fellow of the Royal Society in acknowledgment of his important scientific contributions. He was also appointed Physician Extraordinary to Queen Victoria, reflecting the esteem in which he was held as a practitioner by the British profession and aristocracy. Broadbent died in 1907 of empyema that complicated a bout of pneumonia. This closed the career of one of the most successful physicians of the Victorian era. His writings on heart disease remain classics and can be read with profit by present day physicians.

References

1. Broadbent ME: *Life of Sir William Broadbent*. John Murray, London (1909)
2. Obituary. Sir William Henry Broadbent. *Lancet* 2, 126 (1907)
3. Obituary, Sir William Henry Broadbent. *Br Med J* 2, 177 (1907)
4. Ref. 1, 19-20
5. Ackerknecht EH: *Medicine at the Paris Hospital, 1794–1848*. Johns Hopkins University Press, Baltimore (1967)
6. Ref. 1, 55
7. Broadbent W (ed): *Selections from the Writings Medical and Neurological of Sir William Broadbent*. Henry Frowde, London (1908)
8. Ref. 1, 108
9. Broadbent WH: *The Pulse*. Cassell and Co., London (1890), 47
10. Ref. 1, 237
11. Broadbent WH and Broadbent JFH: *Heart Disease: With Special Reference to Prognosis and Treatment*. Baillière, Tindall and Cox, London (1897) v
12. Fye WB: The delayed diagnosis of myocardial infarction: It took half a century. *Circulation* 72, 262 (1985)
13. Ref. 11, 221

Portrait of a Contributor: Wilhelm Ebstein (1836–1912)

J. Willis Hurst, M.D.

Division of Cardiology, Emory University School of Medicine, Atlanta, Georgia, USA

It is difficult to label Wilhelm Ebstein because he was a clinician, pathologist, chemist, basic scientist, teacher, and writer (Fig. 1). It is a mystery that so few know him because he was extremely productive and made many significant medical contributions.[1]

Ebstein was born on November 27, 1836, in Jauer (now Jawor) in Schlesien, Prussia (Silesia, Poland). In 1855 he entered the University of Breslau (now Wroclaw, Poland) for a short period of time but transferred to the University of Berlin where he graduated from medical school in 1859. He was influenced by the medical greats of that era, including Moritz Romberg, Emil Du Bois-Reymond, and Rudolf Virchow. He became assistant physician to the all Saints' Hospital in Breslau, but after nine years he left to participate in the Franco-Prussian War. After his return from the war, he became the medical officer to the state's almshouses in Breslau. He became professor of medicine in Göttingen in 1874; as the years passed, he became well known as a keen observer.

Ebstein[2] wrote 237 articles: 72 were about metabolic diseases, 38 dealt with gastrointestinal diseases, 16 were about infectious diseases, 12 were concerned with heart disease, 15 dealt with medical history, and the remainder were about various subjects that interested him.

Nephrologists and urologists should claim him because he wrote about uric acid secretion by the kidney[3] and discussed the cause of kidney stones.[4] The hematologists know him as the originator of the description of Pel-Ebstein fever associated with lymphoma.[5]

He has been called the "forgotten founder of biochemical genetics"[6,7] because he believed that obesity, gout, and diabetes mellitus were inheritable cellular metabolic diseases. His book discussing the use of a low-carbohydrate diet for obesity was popular, and several editions were published.[8]

Infectious disease experts should claim him because he wrote 16 articles on infectious diseases,[2] while orthopedists should know him for his description of trichterbrust (funnel chest).[9] The basic scientists can claim him because of his work showing that damage to the internal ear of a rabbit produced gastric erosions.[10] The cardiologists claim him because he described an unusual type of congenital heart disease. His detailed description of the first patient was undoubtedly influenced by his earlier relationship to Rudolf L.K. Virchow. He published his description of the autopsy in 1866.[11] The diagrams of the heart that accompanied the article were made by Oskar Wyss. The illustrations show the anomalous tricuspid valve that is displaced downward into the right ventricle and a patent foramen ovale.

Schiebler, Gravenstein, and Van Mierop translated Ebstein's original description into English and published it in the *American Journal of Cardiology* in 1968.[12] Their translation is reproduced here with permission from the publisher and authors. Note Ebstein's effort to explain the clinical findings in the case.[12]

> The right side of the heart was opened from the entrance of the superior vena cava along the right border of the right atrium and ventricle to the apex … The Eustachian valve … was normally developed. However, the valve of the coronary sinus, or Thebesian valve … was completely absent. The fossa ovalis … in the atrial septum was not completely closed. In the valve of the foramen ovale there were multiple openings …
>
> … an extremely abnormal appearance of the tricuspid valve. A membrane … originated from a quite normally developed right annulus fibrosus … It … was related to both the anterior … and posterior … walls of the right ventricle and blended with the posterior half of the endocardium of the ventricular septum … This membrane, together with markedly opacified and thickened posterior half of the endocardium of the ventricular septum, formed a sac …
>
> Fifteen mm. below the right annulus fibrosus, and directly under the membranous portion of the ventricular septum, a (malformed) leaflet about the size of a 40 cent piece [?] took its origin from the endocardium.
>
> When the right atrium, during systole, ejected blood into the right ventricle, which was in diastole, the blood ran partly into the cul-de-sac (which was closed by the repeatedly mentioned membrane), and partly through the cleft-like opening into the right conus arteriosus and that part of the right ventricle situated between the outside of the membrane and the inner wall of the right ventricle. A small amount of blood could also flow into the right ventricle through the multiple small openings in the membrane.
>
> During the right ventricular systole the blood caught in the sac of necessity regurgitated into the right atrium … Only a small part of it could, therefore, get into the right conum arteriosus through the slit-like opening. On the other hand, blood located in the right conus arteriosus was expelled during ventricular systole into the pul-

FIG. 1   Wilhelm Ebstein (1836–1912). Ebstein made significant contributions to the understanding of heart diseases, renal diseases, metabolic diseases, and blood diseases. (Photograph provided by the National Library of Medicine, Bethesda, Maryland.)

monary artery. In this manner, despite severe tricuspid valve insufficiency a fairly sizeable amount of blood managed to get into the pulmonary arterial system. At the same time only a portion of the blood in the body of the right ventricle regurgitated into the right atrium during ventricular systole, a circumstance which should not be underestimated as a contributing factor to the relatively long survival of the patient. Regurgitation of blood into the right atrium caused its dilatation and prevented complete closure of the valve of the foramen ovale …

This backing up of blood was transmitted beyond the right atrium into the region of the superior vena cava. Not only was this vein markedly dilated, but at the bedside the jugular veins were seen to pulsate synchronously with the heartbeat … at autopsy we could demonstrate competence of the venous valves in the common jugular veins and subclavian veins, we … explain this … by the fact that such an impulse could be transmitted through the valves into the column of blood distal to the valves …

Note his explanation for the systolic and diastolic murmurs.

(1) The systolic murmur was produced during ventricular systole when the blood regurgitating into the right atrium met the blood flowing in the opposite direction out of the vena cava …

(2) The diastolic murmur occurred secondary to the flowing of blood into the ventricular cavity over the inner surface of the repeatedly mentioned membrane, the surface of which was not quite smooth.

Ebstein's disease of the heart is now recognized more frequently. Its current recognition has improved because of increased awareness of the condition as well as cardiac catheterization and echocardiography.

Let us stand in awe at the contributions of this relatively unknown giant.

Acknowledgment

This article is based on the excellent dissertation by Ruth J. Mann, B.S., and T.T. Lie, M.D., at the Mayo Clinic.[1] I wish to thank them and the publisher for permitting me to abstract their article.

References

1.   Mann RJ, Lie JT: The life story of Wilhelm Ebstein (1836–1912) and his almost overlooked description of a congenital heart disease. *Mayo Clin Proc* 54, 197–204 (1979)
2.   Ebstein E: Wilhelm Ebstein's Arbeiten aus den Jahren 1859–1906. *Dtsch Arch Klin Med* 89, 367–378 (1906)
3.   Ebstein W, Nicolaier A: Ueber die Ausscheidung der Harnsäure durch die Nieren: Eine experimentelle Untersuchung. *Arch Pathol Anat* 143, 337–368 (1896)
4.   Ebstein W, Nicolaier A: Mechanisms of genesis and growth of calculi. *Am J Med* 45, 684–692 (1968)
5.   Ebstein W: Das chronische Rückfallsfieber, eine neue Infectionskrankheit. *Berl Klin Wochenschr* 24, 565–568 (1887)
6.   Ebstein W: Ueber die Stellung der Fettleibigkeit, der Gicht und der Zuckerkrankheit im nosologischen System. *Dtsch Med Wochenschr* 24, 693–697 (1898)
7.   Bartalos M: Wilhelm Ebstein, a forgotten founder of biochemical genetics? *Humangenetik* 1, 396 (1965)
8.   Ebstein W: *Die Fettleibigkeit (Corpulenz) und ihre Behandlung nach physiologischen Grundsätzen.* J.F. Bergmann, Wiesbaden (1883)
9.   Ebstein W: Ueber die Trichterbrust. *Dtsch Arch Klin Med* 30, 411–428 (1882)
10. Ebstein W: Experimentelle Untersuchungen über das Zustandekommen von Blutextravasaten in der Magenschleimhaut. *Arch Exp Pathol* 2, 183 (1874)
11. Ebstein W: Ueber einen sehr seltenen Fall von Insufficienz der Valvula tricuspidalis, bedingt durch eine angeborene hochgradige Missbildung derselben. *Arch Anat Physiol*, 238 (1866)
12. Schiebler GL, Gravenstein JS, Van Mierop LHS: Ebstein's anomaly of the tricuspid valve: Translation of original description with comments. *Am J Cardiol* 22, 867–873 (1968)

Reproduced with permission from *The Emory University Journal of Medicine* (Volume 3, No. 3, July-September, 1989).

Julius Friedrich Cohnheim

W. Bruce Fye, M.D., M.A.

Mayo Clinic, Rochester, Minnesota, USA

Julius Friedrich Cohnheim (Fig. 1), a founder of experimental pathology, made many important contributions to cardiovascular physiology and pathology. His exhaustive monograph on pathology was the second most influential nineteenth century text on the subject (after Rudolf Virchow's classic 1858 book on cellular pathology). Cohnheim was born on July 20, 1839, in Demmin, a small town in the Prussian Province of Pomerania.[1–3] After receiving his preliminary education in Demmin and the ancient city of Prenzau, Cohnheim moved to Berlin in 1856 to study medicine. The following year he moved to Würzburg, where he studied histology with Rudolf Albert von Kölliker, a pioneer of microscopic anatomy. Cohnheim returned to Berlin in 1860 where, after receiving his medical degree, he started his dissertation under the supervision of Rudolf Virchow. Impressed by the young Prussian, Virchow appointed him his chief assistant in 1865.

During the 1860s, Cohnheim focused his research on the mechanism of inflammation, a subject of considerable debate at the time.[4] Cohnheim performed a series of animal experiments in an attempt to gain a better understanding of the complex process of inflammation. He concluded that acute inflammation was the result of leukocytes that circulated to the site of injury and then migrated through capillary walls to form collections of blood cells that contributed to what had long been termed "pus." This theory challenged his mentor Virchow's interpretation of inflammation, but it was an important contribution that set the stage for later work on the subject.

In 1868, at the age of 29, Cohnheim became professor of pathology at the University of Kiel. By then he had become especially interested in the circulation as well as in venous obstruction and arterial embolism. He also studied the role of collateral vessels in the context of arterial obstruction. The following year he worked for two months in Carl Ludwig's laboratory of experimental physiology at the University of Leipzig. Ludwig's laboratory was a factory of new knowledge where several scientists focused on cardiovascular physiology.[5] During the last decades of the nineteenth century, the German universities led the world in research and many budding American medical scientists and academic physicians studied there.[6,7] Cohnheim moved to Breslau in 1872 where he helped create a pathologic institute at the university. That year he published a monograph *Untersuchungen über die em-*

bolischen Processe,[8] that summarized the important research on the circulatory system he had undertaken during the previous four years. This rare book includes Cohnheim's theory that infarction of various organs such as the heart and kidney occurred as a result of occlusion of terminal arteries. He also described his experiments that shed light on the pathophysiology of abscess formation. Cohnheim's classic two-volume work on general pathology, *Vorlesungen über allgemeine Pathologie,*[9] was published between 1877 and 1880; this work was translated into English a decade later.[10] About one-third of the text is devoted to the pathology of the cardiovascular system. By this time Cohnheim's reputation had grown to the point that he attracted students and ambitious young medical scientists from various countries, including William Welch and William Councilman from the United States.

Carl Weigert, who had also trained with Virchow, became Cohnheim's assistant in 1874. Reflecting Virchow's and Cohnheim's interest in thrombosis and embolism, Weigert focused his research on these problems. Cohnheim encouraged Weigert's studies, which culminated in 1880 with the publication of a classic paper on infarcts.[11] Weigert discussed the pathologic appearance of "infarcts" in several organs, including the heart. Based on several years of experiments, he claimed that passive tissue injury was the fundamental mechanism of cellular proliferation in inflammation. He applied his theory to the poorly understood histologic finding of "chronic myocarditis" and concluded that thrombotic or embolic occlusion of the coronary arteries often complicated atherosclerosis in them. If a vessel became occluded slowly and adequate collaterals existed, then the muscle it supplied would be gradually replaced by fibrous tissue. If, on the other hand, the occlusion occurred abruptly, large areas of scar appeared. This paper, based on research that Weigert performed in Cohnheim's pathologic institute, is justly viewed as a milestone in the description of the pathologic aspects of myocardial infarction.[12]

Cohnheim's chapters on the heart reflect his sophisticated understanding of cardiac pathology and physiology. For example, we are now focusing more attention on abnormal diastolic function as a factor in several clinical settings, especially heart failure. Cohnheim characterized diastole as an active process in which the heart acted as a "suction-pump." He described the heart's function in systole as a "force-pump." His text is filled with descriptions of animal experiments that

FIG. 1 Julius Friedrich Cohnheim, July 20, 1839–August 15, 1884. From the collection of W. Bruce Fye, M.D., M.A.

he or his associates and pupils performed to investigate and explain various aspects of cardiovascular physiology or pathology. The subjects that he discussed in detail include the pathophysiology of pericardial effusion, the relationship of coronary embolism and severe coronary atherosclerosis to sudden death and left ventricular dysfunction (as a result of myocardial necrosis), the causes and consequences of ventricular hypertrophy, the pathophysiology of thrombosis and embolism, and arteriosclerosis. Cohnheim's comprehensive and influential monograph on pathology addressed many other subjects in addition to the cardiovascular system.

Cohnheim described the physiology of cardiac contraction in terms of concepts that we usually attribute to Otto Franck (1895) and Ernest Starling (1918). Indeed, Starling's work was influenced by various publications of the Scottish physiologist Charles Roy, who had studied with Cohnheim and worked in his laboratory.[13] Cohnheim explained,

The work done by the heart . . . is determined by the quantity of blood reaching the ventricle during diastole, and the amount of resistance to be overcome by the heart in propelling it into the arteries; and because both factors are normally liable to constant variations, the amount of work done by each contraction is also probably a constantly varying quantity.[10]

Cohnheim was especially interested in the pathophysiology of valvular heart disease and performed a series of experiments to help elucidate the mechanism of left ventricular hypertrophy or dysfunction in cases of aortic stenosis or insufficiency. He recognized that various other pathologic and physiologic abnormalities could cause ventricular hypertrophy. Cohnheim explained that left or right ventricular hypertrophy might result from "diseases of the vascular system, whether of the greater or lesser circulation, that give rise to increase of resistance."[10] He discussed peripheral resistance in great detail.

In 1877, William Welch, a recent American medical graduate studying in Europe, wrote to his father from Breslau and described his impressions of Cohnheim. Welch, who would become the first pathologist at Johns Hopkins and a leader in medical education, was struck by Cohnheim's intense desire to elucidate the mechanisms of the various signs and symptoms of disease:

Cohnheim's interest centers on the explanation of the fact. It is not enough for him to know that congestion of the kidney follows heart disease or that hypertrophy of the heart follows contraction of the kidney, or that atheroma occurs in old age, he is constantly inquiring why does it occur under these circumstances. He is almost the founder and certainly the chief representative of the so-called experimental or physiological school of pathology. . .[14]

Cohnheim moved to Leipzig in 1878 to accept the chair of pathology at the university. But he would live only six more years. Beginning in the early 1870s, Cohnheim began to have recurrent attacks of gout. He died suddenly in Wiesbaden on August 15, 1884. During his brief life, Cohnheim had a tremendous influence on pathology and experimental medicine. Long after his death his influence resonated through his writings and the contributions of his pupils, who established laboratories of experimental pathology modeled after those Cohnheim had developed in Germany.

References

1. Weigert C: Julius Cohnheim. In *Gesammelte Abhandlungen*, Vol. 2 (Ed. Rieder R), p. 729–734. Berlin: Julius Springer, 1906
2. Kühne W: Zur Erinnerung an Julius Cohnheim. In *Gesammelte Abhandlungen von Julius Cohnheim* (Ed. Wagner E), p. vii–li. Berlin: August Hirschwald, 1885
3. Malkin HM: Julius Cohnheim (1839–1884). His life and contributions to pathology. *Ann Clin Lab Sci* 1984;14:335–342
4. Maulitz RC: Rudolf Virchow, Julius Cohnheim and the program of pathology. *Bull Hist Med* 1978;52:162–182
5. Fye WB: Carl Ludwig and the Leipzig Physiological Institute: A factory of new knowledge. *Circulation* 1986;74:920–928
6. Bonner TN: *American Doctors and German Universities: A Chapter in International Intellectual Relations, 1870–1914*. Lincoln: University of Nebraska Press, 1963
7. Fye WB: *The Development of American Physiology: Scientific Medicine in the 19th Century*. Baltimore: Johns Hopkins University Press, 1987
8. Cohnheim J: *Untersuchungen über die embolischen Processe*. Berlin: August Hirschwald, 1872
9. Cohnheim J: *Vorlesungen über allgemeine Pathologie*, 2 volumes. Berlin: August Hirschwald, 1877, 1880
10. Cohnheim J: *Lectures on General Pathology* (translated by McKee AB), Vol. 1, p. 43–65. London: New Sydenham Society, 1889–1890
11. Weigert C: Ueber die pathologischen Gerinnungs-Vorgänge. *Arch Pathol Anat* (Virchow). 1880;79:87–123
12. Fye WB: The delayed diagnosis of myocardial infarction: It took half a century! *Circulation* 1985;72:262–271
13. Chapman CB, Mitchell JH: *Starling on the Heart*. London: Dawsons of Pall Mall, 1965
14. Welch to his father (April 1877). In *William Henry Welch and the Heroic Age of American Medicine* (Eds. Flexner S, Flexner JT), p. 95. New York: Viking Press, 1941

Henry Pickering Bowditch

W. Bruce Fye, M.D., M.A.

Department of Cardiology, Marshfield Clinic, Marshfield, Wisconsin, USA

Henry Pickering Bowditch, America's first full-time physiologist, is remembered for his description of two fundamental characteristics of myocardium: the "Treppe" or staircase phenomenon and the "all-or-none principle."[1,2] While important, these discoveries are not Bowditch's most significant contribution to medical science. As a role model and as an educational reformer, Bowditch contributed greatly to the professionalization of physiology in America. The full-time system in medical education and the emphasis on research among America's academic physicians and medical scientists can be traced to the efforts of Bowditch and a few of his contemporaries.[3]

Bowditch was born in Boston in 1840, the son of Jonathan I. Bowditch, an affluent Boston merchant and Harvard overseer, and the nephew of Henry I. Bowditch, a pioneer of public health and a leading American physician. Following graduation from Harvard College and the Lawrence Scientific School and service in the Civil War, young Bowditch entered the Harvard Medical School. There his interest in experimental medicine was inspired by the peripatetic physiologist Charles-Eduoard Brown-Séquard. Following graduation in 1869, Bowditch went abroad where he studied with Claude Bernard in Paris and Carl Ludwig at the new Leipzig Physiological Institute. Ludwig trained many leaders of experimental medicine during the second half of the 19th century. Elsewhere, I characterized his research institute as a "factor of new knowledge."[4]

While Bowditch was abroad, Charles Eliot was elected president of Harvard and major curricular changes were introduced at the Harvard Medical School.[5] Eliot offered Bowditch the physiology chair at Harvard and invited him "to take part in the good work of reforming medical education." When he returned to Boston in 1872, the young physiologist was imbued with the research ethic and committed to a career in medical science. He brought back sophisticated laboratory apparatus paid for by his father and inaugurated at Harvard a unique program of research and graduate education in advanced physiology.

Although his laboratory was modest at the outset—two attic rooms—Bowditch's appointment represented the beginning of university support for the full-time medical scientist whose role was to combine research with teaching. Bowditch opened his laboratory to colleagues and advanced students who shared his enthusiasm for science and experimental medicine. Papers based on their investigations began to appear regularly in the literature. Responding to the growing demands from faculty and students for modern teaching and research facilities, Harvard constructed a spacious, well-equipped physiological laboratory building in 1883.

This same year Bowditch became a dean of the Harvard Medical School. He held this influential position for a decade. Bowditch's publications reflected his broad interests and included studies of neurophysiology, anthropometry, and medical education. Due in large part to Bowditch and to H. Newell Martin of Johns Hopkins, physiology was emerging as a discipline in America at this time.[6] Bowditch played a crucial role in founding the American Physiological Society in 1887 and served as its first president. This organization represented the formalization of a network of scientists who shared an in-

Fig. 1 Henry Pickering Bowditch 1840–1911. Photograph obtained from and reproduced with permission of Rare Books and Manuscripts Division, Francis A. Countway Library of Medicine, Boston, Massachusetts.

terest in experimental medicine and a fear of the threat posed by the antivivisection movement.

Under Bowditch's direction the Harvard physiology department thrived during the final years of the 19th century. Many ambitious and productive investigators worked there and several of them assumed important positions at other institutions. In 1888 two of Bowditch's mentors expressed their appreciation for what he had accomplished. Brown-Séquard told the Harvard physiologist he was proud of him, and Carl Ludwig exclaimed, "you have founded a physiological institute." When William Townsend Porter arrived in Bowditch's department in 1893 he found a stimulating atmosphere in which to continue the pioneering studies of the coronary circulation that he began a few years earlier in Germany.[7]

By 1900, Bowditch no longer taught physiology and his publications reflected his interest in the reform of medical education. He remained active in the affairs of Harvard, however, and helped the school get a million dollar donation from J. Pierpont Morgan in 1901. This led to a major expansion of the Harvard Medical School and facilitated the introduction of curricular reforms. The closing years of Bowditch's life were marked by progressive disability from Parkinson's disease. He died in 1911. A teacher, investigator, and educational reformer, Henry Bowditch was one of the most influential medical scientists of his generation.

References

1. Fye WB: Why a physiologist? The case of Henry P. Bowditch. *Bull Hist Med* 56, 19–29 (1982)

2. Fishman AP, Richards DW: *Circulation of the Blood: Men and Ideas*. Oxford University Press, New York (1964)

3. Fye WB: The origin of the full-time faculty system: Implications for clinical research. *J Am Med Assoc* 265, 1555–1562 (1991)

4. Fye WB: Carl Ludwig and the Leipzig Physiological Institute: A factory of new knowledge. *Circulation* 74, 920–928 (1986)

5. Ludmerer KM: *Learning to Heal: The Development of American Medical Education*. Basic Books, New York (1985)

6. Fye WB: *The Development of American Physiology: Scientific Medicine in the Nineteenth Century*. The Johns Hopkins University Press, Baltimore (1987)

7. Fye WB: Acute coronary occlusion always results in death, or does it? *Circulation* 71, 4–10 (1985)

J. Milner Fothergill*

W. Bruce Fye, M.D., M.A.

Cardiology Department, Marshfield Clinic, Marshfield, Wisconsin, USA

John Milner Fothergill was born on April 11, 1841, in the village of Morland in northwest England.[1] His father, a physician, urged him to pursue a medical career. When he was 13 years old, Fothergill began to serve as his father's apprentice and "learned to roll pills, spread plaster, make ointments...and brew infusions."[2] Fothergill went on to receive formal medical training at the University of Edinburgh where he studied with several prominent medical teachers.

Fothergill received his M.D. in 1865. His hope of continuing his education was forestalled when he was called home to assist his sick father in his country practice. After his father's death, Fothergill practiced in Morland until he was appointed senior resident medical officer at the Leeds Public Dispensary in 1869. There, he gained valuable clinical experience and wrote a monograph on digitalis that won the Hastings prize of the British Medical Association.

The book appeared at a time when there was substantial debate about the drug's mechanism of action and efficacy. Fothergill characterized himself as an "enthusiast" for digitalis and closed his book with the claim that this "most powerful" cardiac drug could "no longer be overlooked by any one in the profession who regards either his own interests or those of his patients."[3] Edward Waring, a contemporary authority on therapeutics, claimed that Fothergill's book "contains much original research, and forms an interesting contribution to the physiological and therapeutic history of digitalis, especially in relation to heart disease."[4]

After two years of clinical work at Leeds, Fothergill, like many ambitious young physicians of his day, traveled to the continent to improve his chances of obtaining a post in London. He visited leading clinics and hospitals and studied with Karl Rokitansky in Vienna and Ludwig Traube in Berlin, each of whom had a special interest in the cardiovascular system.[5]

From his days at Edinburgh, Fothergill had a special interest in diseases of the heart. In 1872, he published a highly acclaimed monograph, *The Heart and Its Diseases, with Their Treatment*.[6] This comprehensive treatise covered both diagnosis and therapy. While Fothergill emphasized the value of auscultation, "the most beautiful and most perfect means we possess for ascertaining the condition of the heart," he urged physicians not to neglect the patient's history.[6A] With the invention of the stethoscope by French physician René Théophile Hyacinthe Laennec in 1816, doctors tended to emphasize auscultatory findings over symptoms when evaluating patients with suspected heart disease. A contemporary of Fothergill's credited him with having done "excellent service in frequently declaiming against the tendency to employ the stethoscope and other instruments of precision in the search after physical signs, to the neglect of the study of the rational symptoms of disease."[7]

Fothergill thought that the chapter on cardiac hypertrophy was the most important section of his book. He differentiated several forms of cardiac enlargement: simple hypertrophy, simple dilatation, hypertrophy combined with dilatation, and left ventricular hypertrophy combined with right heart dilatation. Fothergill's conclusions regarding the pathophysiology of these various combinations reflected a sophisticated synthesis of classic teachings and recent observations made in continental laboratories and clinics.

Fothergill opened his chapter on myocardial diseases by noting "the difficulty of the subject and the acknowledged imperfection of our observations."[6B] At this time there was great confusion about the condition termed "fatty degeneration" of the myocardium. Many causes were suggested for this pathological finding that we now associate with ischemic heart disease. Along with a few others, Fothergill thought it was in some way related to coronary artery disease:

> Fatty degeneration is at...times connected with ossification of the coronary arteries...It would appear, however, that the calibre of the first portion of the coronary arteries, and the construction of the orifice, by which they are exposed to unusual strain, offer an *a priori* probable clue. The coronary circulation is not, however, itself always equally affected, and some parts are more diseased than others, leading to more and less advanced conditions of degeneration in the muscular walls themselves. The coronary vessels are often obstructed by growths of atheroma in tubercular masses at their orifice, and sudden blocking by a dislodged mass is one cause of sudden death by cardiac syncope.[6C]

A decade later, Julius Cohnheim and his colleagues in Leipzig would publish their important observations on the pathophysiology of myocardial infarction. It would be another 40 years, however, before American physician James B. Herrick would define the syndrome of survival following acute coronary thrombosis leading to myocardial infarction.[8,9]

---

* This paper is adapted (with permission) from a biographical sketch prepared for the Classics of Cardiology Library.

FIG. 1 J. Milner Fothergill: 1841–1888. (Photograph from the collection of W. Bruce Fye, M.D.)

In his chapter on the treatment of heart disease, Fothergill acknowledged the limitations of contemporary remedies but explained, "it must not be taken for granted that all disorders and diseased conditions of the heart are equally removed from the reach of therapeutics."[6D] His approach to therapeutics reflected the growing influence of the new field of pharmacology on medical practice.[10] While Fothergill advocated several traditional remedies for the treatment of cardiac disorders, he was skeptical of the value of many popular medications.

As might be expected from his interest in digitalis, Fothergill advocated this drug for a variety of cardiac disorders including aortic stenosis and heart failure. In his discussion of congestive heart failure and "cardiac asthma," he discussed several traditional measures of dilating the capillaries to "unload the venous centres" and eliminate the need for bleeding, long a mainstay in the treatment of these conditions.[6E, 11]

Fothergill's book was applauded by the medical profession. A reviewer in *The Lancet* characterized it as "a great help to practitioners."[12] An expanded second edition appeared in 1879. As he had hoped, his monograph on heart disease helped Fothergill build a consulting practice in London. Having passed the qualifying examination for membership in the Royal College of Physicians of London, he was appointed assistant physician to the West London Hospital. He was also elected to the staff of the London Hospital for Diseases of the Chest at Victoria Park. Fothergill's fame rested mainly on his publications; however, he achieved only modest success as a clinician. Suprisingly, he never held a teaching position in any of London's medical schools.

Pharmacology and therapeutics interested Fothergill greatly. Aided by grants from the British Medical Association, he undertook investigations of several drugs thought to have therapeutic potential. His study of the cardiac effects of aconite, digitalis, belladonna, and other substances formed the basis of his book *The Antagonism of Remedial Agents; and What it Teaches* that won the Fothergillian Gold Medal of the Medical Society of London in 1878.[13]

Unlike his book on therapeutics, most of Fothergill's writings were summaries of the work of contemporary physicians and medical scientists. He reviewed their experiments and observations and synthesized their opinions in a way popular with practitioners and students. An indefatigable writer, Fothergill wrote several books and countless articles, editorials, and letters dealing with a variety of subjects. One contemporary writer observed that "his pen was always kept active, and the number of his published works and papers during the last 15 years of his life is a rare proof of the enthusiasm and fertility of his mind."[8] Another biographer characterized his literary style as "vigorous and attractive, so that his works are eminently readable as well as practical." Alluding to Fothergill's girth, this writer continued, "It may be said of him, literally and metaphorically, he is 'a man of weight in his profession.'"[1]

American physicians also held Fothergill in high esteem. He was known to them through his books that were reprinted in New York and Philadelphia and from his role as London correspondent to the *Philadelphia Medical Times*. Formal recognition of his influence in America came in the form of an honorary degree from Rush Medical College in Chicago and election as a foreign associate fellow of the College of Physicians of Philadelphia.

Fothergill married in 1880 but had no children. A diabetic, he developed vascular insufficiency complicated by a gangrenous foot and died in a diabetic coma in at the age of 47.

References

1. Leyland J: J. Milner Fothergill, M.D. In *Contemporary Medical Men and their Professional Work*, 2 volumes. Provincial, Leicester (England) (1888) 1, 98–105
2. Fothergill JM: Autobiography of the late J. Milner Fothergill, M.D., London, Eng. *N Engl J Med Monthly* 21, 47–54, 91–98, 135–142 (1902)
3. Fothergill JM: *Digitalis; Its Mode of Action, and Its Use: An Enquiry Illustrating the Effect of Remedial Agents Over Diseased Condition of the Heart.* H. K. Lewis, London (1871)
4. Waring EJ: *Bibliotheca Therapeutica, or Bibliography of Therapeutics*, 2 volumes. New Sydenham Society, London (1878-1879)
5. Neuburger M: *British Medicine and the Vienna School, Contacts and Parallels.* William Heinemann, London (1943)
6. Fothergill JM: *The Heart and Its Diseases: With Their Treatment.* H. K. Lewis, London (1872) (A) 18: (B) 145; (C) 159; (D) 200; (E) 213
7. John Milner Fothergill, M.D.Ed., M.R.C.P.L. *Lancet* 1, 92–93 (1888)
8. Fye WB: The delayed recognition of acute myocardial infarction: It took half a century. *Circulation* 72, 262–271 (1985)
9. Fye WB: Acute coronary occlusion always results in death—or does it? The observations of William T. Porter. *Circulation* 71, 4–10 (1985)
10. Leake Chauncey D: *An Historical Account of Pharmacology to the Twentieth Century.* Charles C Thomas, Springfield, IL (1975)
11. Fye WB: T. Lauder Brunton and amyl nitrite: A Victorian vasodilator. *Circulation* 74, 222–229 (1986)
12. [Review of] The Heart and Its Diseases...by J. Milner Fothergill. *Lancet* 2, 853–854 (1872)
13. Fothergill JM: *The Antagonism of Therapeutic Agents: and What It Teaches.* Macmillan and Co., London (1878)

T. Lauder Brunton, 1844–1916*

W. B. FYE, M.D.

Cardiology Department, Marshfield Clinic, Marshfield, Wisconsin, USA

Thomas Lauder Brunton (Fig. 1), a Scottish physician and medical scientist, is remembered for having introduced the vasodilator amyl nitrite as a remedy for angina pectoris more than a century ago. This is only one of his many contributions, however. Brunton's accomplishments justify considering him the father of modern cardiovascular pharmacology.

Born in Roxburgh, in southeast Scotland, in 1844, Brunton received his medical and scientific training at the University of Edinburgh (B.Sc., 1867; M.D., 1868; D.Sc., 1870).[1,2] It was there that his interest in therapeutics and experimental medicine was stimulated by his teacher Douglas Maclagan. Brunton was frustrated with the empirical approach to therapeutics that characterized medical practice in the middle of the nineteenth century. He sought to advance knowledge of drugs through systematic research. While a medical student, he studied the pharmacology and clinical use of digitalis, which had been introduced into medical practice in 1785 by William Withering. Brunton's observations on digitalis were reported in his graduation thesis for which he was awarded a gold medal by the University of Edinburgh.[3]

Brunton learned of amyl nitrite from faculty members at Edinburgh who were interested in this substance that had been synthesized in 1844 by the French chemist Antoine Balard. London physician Benjamin Ward Richardson discussed possible medical uses of amyl nitrite at meetings of the British Association for the Advancement of Science between 1863 and 1865.[4] Arthur Gamgee, a recent Edinburgh graduate, also studied the physiologic effects of amyl nitrite and encouraged Brunton to continue these investigations when he discovered that inhalation of the substance reduced arterial tension as measured by the sphygmograph.

While a house physician at the Edinburgh Royal Infirmary, Brunton became impressed with the lack of effective treatment for angina pectoris. Although the popularity of therapeutic bleeding had declined by the late 1860s, it was still advocated for the treatment of angina by some authors. When Brunton bled patients with angina some of them seemed to improve. He explained, "As I believe the relief produced by the bleeding to be due to the diminution it occasioned in the arterial tension, it occurred to me that a substance which possesses the power of lessening it in such an eminent degree as nitrite of amyl would probably produce the same effect, and might be repeated as often as necessary without detriment to the patient's health."[5]

Brunton began to study the effects of amyl nitrite on patients in the Edinburgh Royal Infirmary. When it was administered to patients with chest pain thought to represent angina, the discomfort usually disappeared in less than a minute. This was accompanied by facial flushing—an outward sign of the effect of amyl nitrite on the vascular system. Brunton published his observations on the value of amyl nitrite in angina in Lancet in 1867. Amyl nitrite was rapidly accepted by practitioners as an effective agent for angina pectoris.

After graduating from Edinburgh, Brunton went to Europe where he worked with several leaders of physiology and pharmacology, including Ernst von Brücke in Vienna and Willy Kühne in Amsterdam. In 1869, Brunton went to Leipzig where he was one of Carl Ludwig's first pupils in the new Leipzig Physiological Institute. Under Ludwig's direction, the recently graduated Scot studied the effect of amyl nitrite on denervated arterioles. On the basis of these experiments Brunton concluded that the reduced arterial tension that followed the inhalation of amyl nitrite was due to vasodilatation rather than any direct depressant effect on the heart.[6]

Brunton was a dedicated and enthusiastic experimentalist by the time he returned from Ludwig's institute where so many leaders of experimental physiology and pharmacology were trained during the second half of the nineteenth century.[7] However, as opportunities for full-time careers in medical research were virtually nonexistent in this era, Brunton entered medical practice in London. He obtained a teaching appointment as lecturer on therapeutics at St. Bartholomew's Hospital, a venerable London institution, where William Harvey had taught 250 years earlier. Brunton soon organized a small (6 by 12 foot!) laboratory at St. Bartholomew's in which to continue his pharmacologic research.

There, he extended his studies of amyl nitrite and even experimented with nitroglycerin before it was advocated for the treatment of angina pectoris by William Murrell in 1879. Although Brunton observed that nitroglycerin, like amyl nitrite, lowered the blood pressure of his experimental animals, he did not propose the substance as a remedy for angina. He gave up his experiments with nitroglycerin because working with the substance gave him severe headaches.[8,9] Brunton was farsighted in his assessment of the potential value of vasodilators

---

*This essay has been adapted from an article in the Preludes and Progress series published in Circulation.

FIG. 1 Thomas Lauder Brunton: 1844–1916. Photograph reproduced with permission from the Wellcome Institute of the History of Medicine Library, London, England.

in conditions other than angina, however. He believed longer acting vasodilators would be discovered and would be useful in the treatment of hypertension of chronic renal disease, and in heart failure ". . . where the enfeebled ventricle is barely able to overcome the elastic resistance of the arterial walls and force the blood onwards."[10]

Brunton was a prolific author; during the first 20 years of his career he published nearly 50 articles, most based on his own research. He also published several books, including a classic textbook of pharmacology and therapeutics. Like many of his scientifically oriented medical colleagues, Brunton consistently spoke out in defense of animal experimentation. He was deeply concerned about the potential impact of the antivivisectionists on experimental medicine. The passage of the British Cruelty to Animals Act in 1876 interrupted his studies on the toxicology of snake venom.[11,12]

Brunton's discovery of the efficacy of amyl nitrite in the treatment of angina was the result of a combination of deductive reasoning and empiricism. His original conception of the pathophysiology of angina was incorrect but was no less sophisticated than that of his peers. By the time of Brunton's

death in 1916, it was recognized that he had overestimated the significance of elevated blood pressure in causing angina. A writer of one of Brunton's obituaries claimed, "His famous discovery has, therefore, been called the lucky shot, but such hits are made only by persons who have profoundly studied the conditions."[13] François-Franck first suggested that amyl nitrite was a coronary vasodilator in 1903. Brunton accepted the new evidence on the pathophysiology of angina and the proposal that organic nitrates acted directly on the coronary arteries.[14]

Brunton's contributions to the development of cardiovascular pharmacology were remarkable—especially when it is recalled that he was primarily a practitioner who pursued his research on a part-time basis. His long-time friend Mitchell Bruce succinctly summed up his career: "It was the aim of Lauder Brunton's life to leave therapeutics, if possible, as a science instead of merely an art, as he found it."[15] Brunton succeeded in achieving this goal.

References

1. Fye WB: T. Lauder Brunton and amyl nitrite: A Victorian vasodilator. *Circulation* 74, 222 (1986)
2. Obituary: Sir T. Lauder Brunton. *Lancet* 2, 572 (1916)
3. Brunton TL: *On Digitalis: With some Observations on the Urine*. John Churchill and Sons, London (1868)
4. Richardson BW: Report of the physiological action of nitrite of amyl. *Rep Br Assoc Adv Sci* 34, 120 (1864)
5. Brunton TL: On the use of nitrite of amyl in angina pectoris. *Lancet* 2, 97 (1867)
6. Brunton TL: On the action of nitrite of amyl on the circulation. *J Anat Physiol* 5, 92 (1871)
7. Fye WB: Carl Ludwig and the Leipzig Physiological Institute: "A factory of new knowledge." *Circulation* 74, 920 (1986)
8. Brunton TL, Tait ES: Preliminary notes on the physiological action of nitroglycerin [1876]. In: Brunton TL: *Collected Papers on Circulation and Respiration. First Series, Chiefly Containing Laboratory Researches*. Macmillan, London (1907) 474
9. Fye WB: Nitroglycerin: A homeopathic remedy. *Circulation* 73, 21 (1986)
10. Brunton TL, Bokenham TJ: Note on the effect of amyl nitrite. *Pharm J* 19, 491 (1888)
11. French RD: *Antivivisection and Medical Science in Victorian Society*. Princeton University Press, Princeton (1975)
12. Brunton TL: The relationship of physiology, pharmacology, pathology and practical medicine. *Nature* 45, 473 (1897)
13. Allbutt C: Thomas Lauder Brunton. 1844–1916. *Proc R Soc Lond [Biol]* 89, xliv (1916)
14. Brunton TL: *Therapeutics of the Circulation*, ed 2. John Murray, London (1914)
15. Obituary: Sir T. Lauder Brunton. *Lancet* 2, 571 (1916)

H. Newell Martin

W. Bruce Fye, M.D., M.A.

Cardiology Department, Marshfield Clinic, Marshfield, Wisconsin, USA

Henry Newell Martin (Fig. 1), America's leading 19th century cardiac physiologist, was born on July 1, 1848, in Newry, County Down, Ireland.[1–3] The eldest of 12 children of a congregational minister, Martin entered University College London when he was 15.

There he studied under the leading British physiologists William Sharpey and Michael Foster. When Foster went to Cambridge University in 1870 to inaugurate a physiological laboratory he took Martin along as his assistant. Soon, according to historian Gerald Geison, Foster was directing "all of his energies as well as those of his students toward a solution to the problem of the heart beat and its origin."[4] In this environment Martin gained valuable insight into the theories and experimental approaches in the emerging field of cardiac physiology.

Martin was also assistant to Thomas Huxley and helped the leading biologist and educational reformer write his popular textbook of elementary biology that was published in 1875. Huxley was mainly responsible for Martin coming to America the following year to take the chair of biology at Johns Hopkins University. Graduate training and research were to be the focus at the new university in Baltimore. In 1875, Hopkins president Daniel Gilman went to Europe seeking faculty members for the institution that was scheduled to open the following year. Huxley urged Gilman in the strongest terms to hire his protegé Martin.

Immediately after Martin's arrival at Johns Hopkins University the 27-year-old Irishman began to develop an innovative program of advanced instruction and research in biology. Gilman and the trustees of the well-endowed university shared Martin's ambition, and his department thrived. Martin's 1878 marriage to Hetty Cary, widow of a Confederate officer, facilitated his entry into Baltimore society. By the early 1880s, Martin had assembled an outstanding group of productive young scientists at Johns Hopkins. They included William K. Brooks, William T. Sedgwick, Henry Sewall, and William H. Howell.

Shortly after his arrival in America, Martin gave demonstrations to Baltimore medical students and delivered public lectures in biology. Like his mentor Huxley, Martin sought to popularize science. He began teaching a Saturday biology course for school teachers in 1879. Two years later the first of several editions of his popular college textbook *The Human Body* appeared. With Henry Bowditch of Harvard and Horatio Wood of the University of Pennsylvania, Martin served as an American editor of Foster's *Journal of Physiology* when it was inaugurated in 1878. Martin also started a journal, *Studies from the Biological Laboratory of the Johns Hopkins University*, that appeared irregularly beginning in 1879.

Reflecting Foster's influence, the predominant theme of Martin's research was circulatory physiology. In the early 1880s Martin and his colleagues developed the first isolated mammalian heart preparation. Half a century later American physiologist Walter Meek characterized this achievement as "possibly the greatest single contribution ever made from an American physiological laboratory."[5] With his associates William Howell and Frank Donaldson, Jr., Martin used his isolated heart preparation to study a wide range of physiological and pharmacological problems.

Anticipating conclusions drawn several years later by Otto Frank and Ernest Starling, Howell and Donaldson claimed in 1884 that cardiac output was dependent on ventricular diastolic pressure. Five years later Martin published a study on the effects of temperature on the heart beat. This important series of experiments demonstrated that myocardial performance was dependent on adequate coronary perfusion. Eventually, many European and American investigators used Martin's isolated heart preparation and variations of it in their experiments. The isolated heart preparation described by German physiologist Oscar Langendorf in 1895 represented a refinement of Martin's model.

By the age of 40 Martin was a recognized leader in the emerging discipline of experimental physiology. In 1881 George Shrady, editor of the *Medical Record*, declared: "The opportunities for physiological and morphological study and research at [Johns Hopkins] are probably the best in this country. And it is a centre which has already shown evidences of good scientific work. The medical profession should feel gratified that opportunities for such work now exist in this country."[6]

Aided by a group of bright and productive graduate students and associates, Martin made several important contributions to cardiovascular physiology. His accomplishments were acknowledged by his election as a Fellow of the Royal Society of London and his selection as the society's Croonian lecturer in 1883. That year Johns Hopkins recognized Martin's success (and his promise) by erecting a spacious and well-equipped biological laboratory building. When the

FIG. 1 Henry Newell Martin (1848-1896). Reproduced with permission of Bachrach Bros., Baltimore, Maryland and the Ferdinand Hamburger, Jr. Archives of The Johns Hopkins University.

American Physiological Society was founded in 1887, Martin served as secretary-treasurer and, with Henry Bowditch and S. Weir Mitchell, was influential in defining the character of the new organization.[7]

Martin's life and career soon entered a period of dramatic decline, however. When his assistants accepted positions elsewhere, he had to teach introductory courses and oversee much of the routine laboratory work at Johns Hopkins. This limited the time Martin had to devote to research and the supervision of advanced pupils, which caused him great consternation. When his new laboratory opened in 1883 Martin became the target of a malicious and sustained attack by antivivisectionists who objected to the animal experiments undertaken in his laboratory.

A sensitive and temperamental man, Martin was, by 1891, an alcoholic suffering from painful peripheral neuritis that resulted in morphine addiction. His deterioration accelerated the following year when his wife died. As Martin's absences from the university due to alcoholism and its complications became more frequent and prolonged, the officers of Johns Hopkins concluded that he could not play the important role they had envisioned for him in their medical school, scheduled to open in 1893.

After William Osler, who was his physician, urged him to resign, Martin returned to England in the spring of 1894 where he hoped to resume some physiological studies in his friend Edward Sharpey-Schafer's laboratory. Martin never regained his health, however, and died in 1896 at the age of 48 at Burley-in-Wharfdale, Yorkshire.

During his short career Martin made important scientific discoveries and developed the isolated mammalian heart model that became a mainstay of cardiac research. This innovative and productive scientist also played a major role in the professionalization of American physiology. Martin's most important publications were reprinted in a quarto volume published by the Johns Hopkins Press in 1895.[8]

References

1. Fye WB: H. Newell Martin: A remarkable career destroyed by neurasthenia and alcoholism. *J Hist Med Allied Sci* 40, 133–160 (1985)
2. Fye WB: H. Newell Martin and the isolated heart preparation: The link between the frog and open heart surgery. *Circulation* 73, 857–864 (1986)
3. Breathnach CS: Henry Newell Martin (1848-1893) [sic]. A pioneer physiologist. *Med Hist* 13, 271–279 (1969)
4. Geison GL: *Michael Foster and the Cambridge School of Physiology: The Scientific Enterprise in Late Victorian Society*. Princeton University Press, Princeton (1978)
5. Meek WJ: The beginnings of American physiology. *Ann Med Hist* 10, 111–125 (1928)
6. Shrady G: Biological study at the Johns Hopkins University. *Med Rec* 19, 408–409 (1881)
7. Fye WB: *The Development of American Physiology: Scientific Medicine in the 19th Century*. Johns Hopkins University Press, Baltimore (1987)
8. Martin HN: *Physiological Papers*. Johns Hopkins Press, Baltimore (1895)

William Osler

W. B. FYE, M.D., F.A.C.P., F.A.C.C.

Cardiology Department, Marshfield Clinic, Marshfield, Wisconsin, USA

It would be presumptuous and inaccurate to claim that William Osler was a cardiologist. Although he was a generalist and lived in an era when the subspecialties of internal medicine were not yet differentiated, there were several specific areas of medicine that especially interested Osler. The cardiovascular system was one such area. A recent publication emphasizes the magnitude of Osler's writings on diseases of the heart and circulation: nearly one third of his clinical papers and pathologic reports dealt with these subjects.[1] It is appropriate, therefore, that Osler's life and contributions to cardiovascular disease be reviewed in this series of biographical sketches of individuals who have played a major role in the development of cardiology.

William Osler was born in 1849 in the village of Bond Head, Canada, about 40 miles north of Toronto,[2,3] the eighth child of an Anglican clergyman. The Osler family moved to Dundas, Ontario, when William was eight years old. There, under the influence of the Reverend William Johnson of Weston School, young Osler developed an interest in natural history, microscopy, and books. Although Osler originally contemplated a clerical career like his father, he was encouraged to enter medicine by James Bovell, a physician and naturalist who taught at Trinity College and the Toronto Medical School. After studying medicine at Toronto for two years, Osler transferred to McGill Medical College in Montreal where he graduated in 1872.

While a medical student, Osler's hobby of natural history study evolved into an profound interest in pathology.[4] This interest was stimulated by R. Palmer Howard, Osler's professor of medicine, who was also an avid pathologist. Through Howard, Osler became familiar with the works of the great clinicopathologists R. T. H. Laennec, William Stokes, and Robert Graves, whose writings during the first half of the nineteenth century included classic descriptions of heart disease and cardiac pathology.

As was typical of ambitious medical graduates of the day, Osler supplemented his formal medical education with postgraduate training in the clinics and hospitals abroad. Osler spent more than a year and a half working in the physiology laboratory of John Burdon-Sanderson at University College, London. The young Canadian also attended ward rounds and clinics at some of London's leading hospitals. During the winter of 1873–1874, Osler visited several leading medical institutions on the continent, where he studied with Rudolf Virchow, Carl Rokitansky, and other contemporary leaders in the field of pathology.

Although Osler initially planned to become an ophthalmologist, the position he hoped to obtain in Montreal was filled while he was abroad. This led the young medical graduate to accept an appointment as lecturer in the Institutes of Medicine at McGill upon his return to Montreal. Soon, Osler combined his responsibilities as a medical teacher with work in the autopsy room and private practice. His extraordinary productivity as a medical writer was soon evident. Almost immediately upon his return from Europe, Osler began contributing papers to Canadian medical journals. These articles were based on autopsies he had performed or interesting cases he had seen.[5] Several of his pathologic papers described unusual congenital or acquired diseases of the heart or great vessels.

During the first decade of his medical career in Montreal, Osler reported cases of cardiac arrhythmia, unusual auscultatory findings, congenital deformities of the cardiac valves, including his classic observations on the bicuspid aortic valve, and wrote two major papers on "infectious" endocarditis. This last subject would be the topic of Osler's Gulstonian Lecture delivered before the Royal College of Physicians of London in 1885. In this important address Osler emphasized the predisposition of deformed valves to infection. His own microscopic investigations of the hearts from patients who had died of endocarditis revealed microorganisms in the valve tissue in every case. Osler's fascination with endocarditis reflected his interest in heart disease and the "bacteriomania" that was sweeping the medical world in this era of dramatic growth of bacteriology made possible by the discoveries of Louis Pasteur, Robert Koch, and other pioneers of microbiology.

Osler is often thought of as an American physician, but, indeed, he was never an American citizen, and he lived in the United States for only two decades. His American years are generally acknowledged as the most productive period of his life, however. The American period began in 1884 when Osler left Montreal to become Professor of Clinical Medicine at the University of Pennsylvania. In Philadelphia, he continued to combine clinical and pathologic work. In the morning Osler visited patients in the wards of the new Hospital of the University of Pennsylvania, and in the afternoon he performed autopsies with pupils in attendance at the Philadelphia General Hospital or "Blockley."

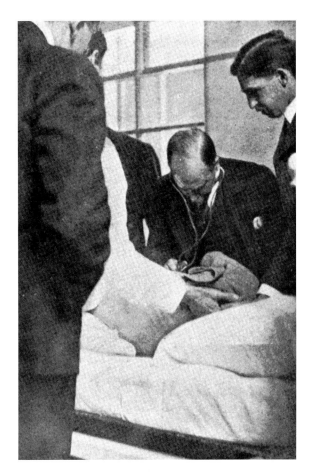

Fig. 1 Osler at the bedside in 1903. From *The Life of Sir William Osler* by W. Cushing, Oxford University Press, 1925. Reproduced with permission of the publisher.

Although Osler spent only five years in Philadelphia, he published several important papers on heart disease during that brief period. Among these was a comprehensive review on diseases of the heart published in 1885 in his friend William Pepper's monumental five-volume system of medicine. The following year, Osler presented a classic paper on the nature and complications of bicuspid aortic valve at the inaugural meeting of the Association of American Physicians. In 1887, Osler reported cases in civilians that resembled the syndrome of "irritable heart" that his friend Jacob M. DaCosta had previously described in soldiers. Osler's patients suffered from chest pain, dypsnea, and palpitations; they tended to be young and predominantly female. Wooley has recently argued that some of these cases probably represented examples of what is now known as the mitral valve prolapse syndrome.[6]

Osler's long-standing interest in diseases of the nervous system and his friendship with S. Weir Mitchell, a pioneering American neurologist, led him to see patients at the Philadelphia Orthopedic Hospital and Infirmary for Nervous Diseases. There, he saw several children with rheumatic fever who were admitted with chorea. Based on this experience, Osler emphasized the importance of careful examination of the heart in children with chorea or rheumatism. In a classic paper published in 1887 he stressed that chronic valvular disease resulted from the valvulitis that often accompanied chorea but was frequently overlooked by contemporary physicians. Osler's interests in pathology and diseases of children were combined in his review of congenital heart disease published in 1889 in John Keating's comprehensive pediatrics textbook.

Osler had visited the Johns Hopkins Hospital during its construction in 1886 and was impressed with the institution and its planned medical school. When he was offered the position of physician-in-chief of the hospital and professor of medicine two years later, Osler promptly accepted. Although overshadowed by his writings on typhoid fever and tuberculosis, diseases that were responsible for enormous morbidity and mortality in this era, Osler continued to write on disorders of the heart and circulatory system during his years in Baltimore. His monumental medical textbook was published in 1892 and included a comprehensive discussion on diseases of the heart. This extensive section included a consideration of the etiology, morbid anatomy, symptoms, diagnosis, and therapy of diseases of the pericardium, substance of the heart, valves, and great vessels, and reflected Osler's broad experience in the autopsy room and at the bedside.

Ischemic heart disease attracted relatively little attention among physicians during most of the nineteenth century. The invention of the stethoscope by Laennec had led physicians to focus their attention on valvular heart disease. During the closing decades of the century, important pathologic and physiologic studies were beginning to shed light on the relationship of coronary stenosis and occlusion to angina pectoris and myocardial infarction, however.[7] Osler followed these developments with interest and delivered a series of lectures on angina pectoris in 1896 that formed the basis of an important monograph that was published the following year. Nearly 15 years later, he chose the subject of angina pectoris for his Lumleian Lecture before the Royal College of Physicians of London. In this address, Osler mentioned coronary artery spasm in addition to fixed coronary stenosis as a possible cause of angina. The syndrome of acute myocardial infarction in man was not addressed, however; it would remain for James Herrick to elucidate the pathophysiology and clinical significance of that event in 1912.

In 1904, at the height of a spectacular career as a teacher, author, and consultant at Johns Hopkins, Osler was informed that he was being considered for the position of Regius Professor of Medicine at Oxford. Although he believed the facilities at Johns Hopkins were "probably unequalled in English-speaking countries," Osler felt that he was "over-worked" and sought a less demanding position.[8] Much to the regret of the American medical profession and his Baltimore colleagues, Osler accepted the Oxford position in 1905. The year following his departure for England, Osler delivered the prestigious Harveian oration before the Royal College of Physicians. The lecture was established and endowed by William Harvey 250 years earlier. Medical history had long been a sincere interest of Osler's, and he chose as his topic the discovery of the circulation of the blood. Although Osler dreaded preparing for the lecture, he was pleased with the result and the reception his presentation received.

During the final decade of his life, Osler wrote on a wide variety of cardiovascular diseases. These included Stokes-Adams disease, peripheral vascular disease, cerebrovascular disease, syphilitic and atherosclerotic aneurysms of the aorta, and hypertension. When Osler died of complications of recurrent bronchopulmonary infections in 1919, he was hailed as one of the world's greatest physicians. His former associate Thomas McCrae claimed that Osler "exercised a deeper and more far-reaching influence on American medicine than any other man."[9] This brief essay, focused on but one aspect of Osler's remarkable contributions to medicine, does not do justice to one of the most influential physicians of his generation. Happily, the reprinting of many of Osler's writings on the cardiovascular system and his literary essays will make it easier for contemporary physicians and medical students to benefit from his wisdom and clinical experience.

References

1. *William Osler's Collected Papers on the Cardiovascular System*: edited with an introduction by W. Bruce Fye, M. D., Gryphon Editions, Ltd., Birmingham (1985)
2. Cushing W: *The Life of Sir William Osler* (2 vols) Oxford University Press, London (1925)
3. Nation EF, Roland CG, McGovern JP: *An Annotated Checklist of Osleriana*. Kent State University Press, Kent, Ohio (1976)
4. Rodin AE: *Oslerian Pathology: An Assessment and Annotated Atlas of Museum Specimens*. Coronado Press, Lawrence, Kansas (1981)
5. Abbott ME (ed): *Classified and Annotated Bibliography of Sir William Osler's Publications*, 2d ed. McGill University Medical Museum, Montreal (1939)
6. Wooley CF: From irritable heart to mitral valve prolapse: The Osler connection. *Am J Cardiol* 53, 870 (1984)
7. Fye WB: The delayed diagnosis of myocardial infarction: It took half a century! *Circulation* 72, 262 (1985)
8. Letter from Osler to John Burdon-Sanderson, 21 June 1904. Published in Cushing, *Life of Osler* (Ref. 2)
9. McCrae T: The influence of William Osler on medicine in America. *Can Med Assoc J* 10, 102 (1920)

Etienne-Louis Fallot: Is It His Tetralogy?

Louis J. Acierno, M.D.

Department of Health Professions and Physical Therapy, Cardiopulmonary Sciences Program, University of Central Florida, Orlando, Florida, USA

The congenital cardiac disturbance characterized by pulmonic stenosis, interventricular septal defect, hypertrophy of the right ventricle, and dextroposition of the aorta carries the eponym "tetralogy of Fallot." The classical paper by Etienne-Louis Fallot (Fig. 1), describing in detail the components of this common cause of "maladie bleu," appeared in 1888 in an obscure French journal.[1, 2] The issue in which it appeared devoted 98 pages to a series of six articles on the pathologic anatomy of congenital heart disease with cyanosis. Fallot's article was titled *Contribution à l'anatomie pathologique de la maladie bleue (cyanose cardiaque)*.[3] Four years later, a paper was presented to the Royal Academy of Medicine in Ireland by Ambrose Birmingham, professor of anatomy in the Cecilia Street School of Medicine. It came to be known as the pentalogy of Fallot since, in addition to the components described by Fallot, Birmingham added a fifth, namely, an interatrial communication.[4] In retrospect, this seems superfluous, since Fallot did also say that "At times, there is an additional entirely accessory defect; namely, patency of the foramen ovale."

The malformations described by Fallot as a cause of blue babies were, however, originally described by Niels Stensen, the discoverer of the parotid duct, as far back as 1671.[5] Indeed, in the two centuries that followed, many notables were to add their descriptions to the malady; these included Eduard Sandifort (1777), William Hunter (1784), Farré (1814), Gintrac (1824), Peacock (1866), Debely (1878), and Roger (1879).

Steno (the latinized surname of this Danish anatomist and theologian) came upon this congenital abnormality in a fetus, describing in accurate detail the multiple cardiac defects as seen at autopsy. A little more than a century later, the Dutch physician, teacher, and linguist, Eduard Sandifort, described in his book *Observationes Anatomico-Pathologicae* what he thought was both a rare and unusual malady of the heart. The patient had cyanosis as an infant and complained of extreme fatigue, headaches relieved with venesection, fainting spells, palpitations, and pedal edema. When the patient died at the age of 12½ years, Sandifort described at postmortem the very same four salient defects that Stensen had originally reported in the fetus in 1671.[6] Hunter's description of the malady seen at autopsy was rather vivid and so typical of the British in their ability to transmit imagery via the written word. Who can fault his description where "the passage from the right ventricle into the pulmonary artery, which should have admitted a finger, was

not so wide as a goose quill; and there was a hole in the partition of the two ventricles, large enough to pass the thumb from one to the other. . . The greatest part of the blood in the right ventricle was driven with that of the left ventricle into the aorta, or great artery, and so lost all the advantage which it ought to have had from breathing."[7]

Fallot's comprehensive account of the malformation, his demonstration that the disease could be readily diagnosed prior to death, and that, among the congenital abnormalities of the heart, these multiple cardiac defects were common rather than rare, were probably the three most important elements responsible for the designation of his name as the marker for the entire syndrome. The eponym persists to this day, despite the fact that Fallot quite candidly acknowledged the contributions of his predecessors. In particular, Fallot referred to the thesis of Debely that had been published just a decade before.[8]

Fallot's paper itself is rather terse and to the point; however, he did manage to include a review of the literature in the decade that followed the publication of Debely's account. Of a total of 55 cases reported during this decade as examples of the "maladie bleu," Fallot pointed out that only 39 of these had the four components characteristic of his own cases. His delineation of the pathogenesis of the multiple defects was similar to that of William Hunter. Both were of the opinion that the multiple defects were a consequence of pulmonary stenosis. Fallot and Hunter were in error, of course; neither one recognized the embryologic nature of the defects.

Fallot had expressly forbidden the publication of any eulogy after his death, and this may be the reason for the scarcity of biographical data. Serendipitously, I was able to find a short biography in a text written by Mattei.[9] All that can be said is that he was born on September 20, or 29, 1850, in Cette, France. He was probably a very good student, as implied by the prize he received for high scholastic ability while attending the Lycée in Marseilles. His medical degree was obtained from the École de Médicine in the same town. He stayed in Marseilles throughout his life, serving first as substitute professor of medicine at the University of Marseilles, later taking charge of the course in pathologic anatomy, and finally serving as professor of hygiene and legal medicine until his death.

Fallot was renowned as an excellent clinician who was painfully accurate in the physical examination of the patient and who was apparently well respected for his diagnostic

FIG. 1   Etienne-Louis Fallot, 1850–1911. Courtesy of New York Academy of Medicine.

skills. In addition to his description of the tetralogy, Fallot also reported a case of congenital pectoral dysplasia, a case of hysterical hemiplegia, the incidence of encephalitis among Corsicans, and his observations during a local cholera epidemic. Strangely enough, he did not publish any medical articles during the last 10 years of his life. The only publication during this time was his description of a Neolitt cave in Reillane. Mattei reported that he died in May 1911 "after a period of purifying loneliness."[9] Other sources place the time of his death on April 30, 1911.

Probably the most interesting individual to have had the tetralogy of Fallot was the patient described by White and Sprague in 1929.[8] That individual was Henry F. Gilbert, who, despite being born with this malady, managed to overcome his handicap and carry on a very active life as a talented composer of music. Gilbert managed to live to the age of 60 just shy a few months. The oldest patient in Fallot's original series was 36 years of age at the time of his death. Unable to exert

himself even in the slightest without marked discomfort, plagued by cyanosis, clubbing, dyspnea, weakness, and fainting episodes, Gilbert even managed to survive a successful European tour, only to die from apoplexy a year later. He left a legacy of native American musical compositions, which included "Comedy Overtures on Negro Themes," "Negro Rhapsody," and "Indian Sketches."[8]

Merely discovering or being the first to describe a disease should not mandate that the disease be identified eponymously with the discoverer's name. In actuality, there are many instances and cogent reasons when such has not been the case. Duke aptly points this out, when he quotes Hans Selye, who wrote in his book *From Dreams to Discovery* that "it is not to see something first, but to establish solid connections between the previously known and the hitherto unknown that constitutes the essence of scientific discovery."[10]

Fallot's role in this regard can be easily justified and thus allows us to continue honoring his memory by retaining "tetralogy of Fallot" as the eponymous designation for *morbus caeruleus*.

References

1. Acierno LJ: *History of Cardiology*, p. 160–161. London, New York: Parthenon Publishing Group (1994)
2. Duke M: Whose Tetralogy is it? A short history of the tetralogy of Fallot. *Connecticut Med* 1984;48(2):103–104
3. Fallot EA: Contribution à l'anatomie pathologique de la maladie bleue (cyanose cardiaque). *Marseilles Med* 1888;25:77–82
4. Birmingham A: Extreme anomaly of the heart and great vessels. *Trans Roy Acad Ire* 1892;10:430–445
5. Steno N: Anatomicus regij Hafniensis Embryo Monstro affinis Parisiis dissectus. Acta Med *Et Philosophiâ, Hafminsiâ* 1671;I: 200–205
6. Sandifort E: *Observations Anatomico-Pathologicae*, Ch. 1, translated by Bennett LR: Sandifort's *Observations*, Ch. 1, concerning a very rare disease of the heart. *Bull Hist Med* 1946;20:539–547
7. Hunter W: Medical observations and inquiries. 1784;6:291–309, 417–419 (private publication)
8. White, PD: The tetralogy of Fallot. Report of a case in a noted musician who lived to his sixtieth year. *J Am Med Assoc* 1929; 92, 10:787–791
9. Mattei C: Savoir et humilité a l'école de médecine de Marseilles, p. 21. Paris: Masson et Cie
10. Selye H: *From Dreams to Discovery*, p. 89, 92. New York: McGraw-Hill, 1964

Graham Steell

BARRY D. SILVERMAN, M.D.

Department of Cardiology, Northside Hospital, Atlanta, Georgia, USA

Graham Steell (Fig. 1) was the exemplary Victorian physician and was among those 19th century physicians who excelled at correlating physiology and physical signs through careful bedside observation. He was described by F.A. Mahmed at his testimonial for advancement to assistant physician at the Manchester Royal Infirmary as follows: "His modest, retiring and courteous disposition must gain the highest esteem of all who have the privilege of knowing him well."[1] He was dedicated, industrious, loved to teach at the bedside, and contributed numerous papers and a textbook of cardiology. His philosophy of medicine is expressed in the quote of Trousseau, which he used in his article *On the Art of Diagnosis* in the *Medical Chronicle of Manchester* in 1885: "De grace, un peu moins de science, un peu plus d'art, Messieurs."[2]

At the end of his life there were many new technologies in medicine and he stated, I suspect somewhat wistfully, that "Clinical medicine seems to me at the present moment to be in danger of losing something of its old charm, and in the future of losing much more."[1] It is notable that during his practice he used a monaural stethoscope made of light boxwood and of unusual length. There was no laboratory at the Manchester infirmary until 20 years after his arrival. X-rays were only possible after 1904, 5 years later, and the electrocardiographic machine was not available until 1909, just 2 years before his retirement.[2] Dr. Steell was that exceptional practicing clinician with a bedside acumen which seems to have been lost with our present technology in medicine.

Graham Steell was born in Edinburgh in 1851, the son of John Steell, a famous sculptor. His uncle was the curator of the National Gallery of Scotland and his grandfather was a woodcarver. He expressed a desire to pursue the military, but was persuaded by his brother to enter medicine. He graduated from Edinburgh University in 1872 and spent the next 10 years as a resident medical officer, an unusually long period at that time.[3] He first went to Berlin for a course of study during the winter, then returned to study and practice under Dr. George Balfour in the Royal Infirmary of Edinburgh. He credits Balfour with developing his life-long interest in cardiology. From Edinburgh he traveled to the Stirling Infirmary and Dispensary, where he remained for several months, then practiced at fever hospitals in Edinburgh, London, and Leeds. He became ill during this period with both typhoid fever and typhus. He had, however, completed his thesis, a compendium of 66 handwritten pages, with clinical material on four patients with scarlet fever and on others with enteric and typhus fevers. The thesis, *On scarlatina,*

was awarded the gold medal from the University of Edinburgh in 1877.[1]

In 1878, he left his position as assistant to Professor Thomas Fraser in the Department of Materia Medica and Therapeuties at Edinburgh University to become a resident medical officer at the Manchester Royal Infirmary. The Manchester area was a textile center where workers experienced deleterious and brutal working conditions. Illness was common, and the in-patient mortality at the infirmary exceeded 10 percent. Steell lived in the hospital, was constantly on call, and had an almost nonexistent social life.[2] In 1883, he was appointed to the staff. He certainly had acquired extensive training, but at a considerable price. A man of slight build and below average height, he was described as a "very delicate skeleton of a man;" he became thinner, pale, with an appearance that was "alarmingly ill." This culminated in his protracting tuberculosis in 1888, requiring leave to recuperate.[2]

Graham Steell had been an athlete as a student, a champion boxer, and was an early advocate of exercise.[4] He often recommended horseriding for his patients. Later in his life he commented that "the importance of exercise in the treatment of heart troubles has been more and more borne in upon me and, in my own case, I have more and more made appreciation of it."[1] He returned from leave 20 pounds heavier and sporting a beard. Except for chronic bronchitis, he remained active to the end of his life.

His practice was slow to develop, but he eventually became the leading cardiologist in the North of England. He had a kind and gentle bedside manner, but was very reserved and painfully shy. He spoke curtly with a nasal twang and could be difficult to understand. The junior staff often had to defend him for his inelegant style, especially with female patients.[2]

As a teacher, he was an ardent bedside instructor and as a medical resident he wrote two monographs on physical exam for medical students. He enjoyed exposing physical signs and discussing their clinical significance. He felt one should never trust only a single physical sign.

As a lecturer he was boring and unenthusiastic.[4] The Manchester Medical Student's Gazette of 1902 depicted Steell in the lecture hall addressing an audience of just three students. He read verbatim from crumpled pieces of paper in a stilted, discursive style. When he had difficulty reading his own writing he would skip to the next sentence without comment, and once, when interrupted by the bell, he finished a lecture abruptly without completing his sentence.

FIG. 1 Graham Steell (1851–1942). (Photograph supplied by W. Bruce Fye, M.D.)

Steell married Agnes McKie, the matron of the Manchester Royal Infirmary, in 1886.[2] They had one son, who became a doctor. He left the Royal Infirmary in 1911 after 33 years, required by statutory law to retire at the age of 60. He continued a private practice for some years. After his wife's death, he lived with his son.[4] True to his nature, he refused a retirement banquet in 1911 and would not grant permission for a biographical sketch when Willius and Keys published his paper, "On the Murmur of High-Pressure in the Pulmonary Artery," in their 1941 text, *Classics of Cardiology*. He died at Streatham at the age of 90 in January 1942.[2]

Dr. Steell's name is associated with the murmur of pulmonic regurgitation secondary to rheumatic mitral stenosis. He first described the finding in a paper to the Manchester Medical Society and subsequently published it in the *Manchester Chronicle* in 1888. He notes that his mentor Dr. G.W. Balfour noted the finding but ascribed the condition an auricular diastolic murmur. Steel, however, states:

> I wish to plead for the admission among the recognized auscultatory signs of disease of a murmur due to pulmonary regurgitation, such regurgitation occurring independently of disease or deformity of the valves, and as the result of long-continued excess of blood pressure in the pulmonary artery.[5]

He describes the finding as follows:

> In cases of mitral obstruction there is occasionally heard over the pulmonary area (the sternal extremity of the third left costal cartilage), and below this region, for the distance of an inch or two along the left border of the sternum, and rarely over the lowest part of the bone itself,

a soft blowing diastolic murmur immediately following, or more exactly running off from the accentuated second sound, while the usual indications of aortic regurgitation afforded by the pulse, etc. are absent. The maximum intensity of the murmur may be regarded as situated at the sternal end of the third and fourth intercostal spaces. When the second sound is reduplicated, the murmur proceeds from its latter part… The murmur of high pressure in the pulmonary artery is not peculiar to mitral stenosis, although it is most commonly met with as a consequence of this lesion. Any long-continued obstruction in the pulmonary circulation may produce it.[5]

Steell published the textbook *Diseases of the Heart* in 1906. Mackenzie wrote,

> Many congratulations on your excellent handbook, and many thanks for the copy. I have been eagerly devouring it, and I have no hesitation in saying it is by far the best book on the heart on the market. Your remarks are so pungent and pithy that it is a delight to read.[4]

Mackenzie was a friend of Dr. Steell and occasionally rounded on his ward from his nearby practice at Burnley. They shared an interest in the sphygmograph, a subject on which Steell wrote a monograph in 1889.

An interesting paper, published by Alan Fraser and Clive Weston in the *Journal of the Royal College of Physicians of London* in 1991,[2] chronicles the history of clinical descriptions of the pulmonary regurgitant murmur of pulmonary hypertension, suggesting the Graham Steell eponym was a serendipitous naming. They comment on earlier descriptions of functional pulmonic regurgitation by James Hope and John Hunter and note a case report by Dyce Duckworth describing the finding published before Steell's article appeared. They suggest the eponym resulted from the use of Steell's description of the finding in Osler's *Principles and Practice of Medicine* in 1898. Knowing Steell's character, they feel that he certainly would not have encouraged the use.

Steell has a certain immortality. If this reminds us of that age when the physician was both a good listener and an astute observer, then we are so much better off.

References

1. Bramwell C: Graham Steell. *Br Heart J* 4, 115–119 (1942)
2. Fraser AG, Weston CFM: The Graham Steell murmur: Eponymous serendipity? *J Roy Coll Phys London* 25, 66–70 (1991)
3. Obituary. *Br Med J* (1941)
4. Brockbank W: Professor Graham Steell. The Honorary Medical Staff of the Manchester Royal Infirmary. 1830–1948
5. Steell G: On the murmur of high-pressure in the pulmonary artery. *Classics of Cardiology* (Eds. Willius FA, Keys TE). Dover Publications, New York (1941)

William Murrell

W. Bruce Fye, m.d., m.a.

Department of Cardiology, Marshfield Clinic, Marshfield, Wisconsin, USA

William Murrell (Fig. 1) is remembered because he first advocated nitroglycerin as a remedy for angina pectoris.[1] Born in London in 1853, Murrell received his medical training at University College Hospital, London.[2] That institution was then home to some of Great Britain's leading medical scientists, including John Burdon-Sanderson, a physiologist who made classic observations on cardiovascular function, and Sydney Ringer, a pioneering pharmacologist. Murrell served as Burdon-Sanderson's assistant and collaborated with Ringer in a series of studies on the physiologic effects of various substances on the nervous system and the heart.

In 1877, Murrell was appointed to the staff of the Westminster Hospital where he served as a medical registrar and lectured on practical physiology. Two years later Murrell published his classic paper in the *Lancet* in which he described the physiologic effects of nitroglycerin and recommended it as a treatment for angina pectoris.[3] Although he was the first to advocate nitroglycerin for angina, Murrell did not introduce the drug into medical therapy. It was first used by American homeopath Constantin Hering in 1849.[4]

The peculiar doctrine of homeopathy is the reason that an explosive got into the pharmacopeia. A fundamental tenet of homeopathy is "like cure like." Homeopaths believe that a drug which causes specific side effects is useful in treating diseases with symptoms similar to those side effects. The Italian chemist Ascanio Sobrero, who first synthesized nitroglycerin, cautioned that tasting it predictably caused a severe headache. Reading this warning, Hering thought nitroglycerin might be effective in the treatment of headache because it caused this side effect in individuals who tasted it.

Initially, the regular medical profession showed little interest in nitroglycerin, which Hering termed Glonoine. This is not surprising because they were skeptical of homeopathic dogma. Moreover, regular doctors worried that they were losing patients to a sect whose practitioners promised cures without using traditional heroic therapies like bleeding and purging. A few regular physicians and medical scientists studied the homeopathic remedy nitroglycerin, however.

A British homeopath urged regular physician Alfred Field to try nitroglycerin in 1858. His 1858 paper on the drug prompted Henry Fuller and George Harley of University College London to administer nitroglycerin to animals and themselves. Although Fuller developed tachycardia when he ingested the drug, he thought this reaction was caused by some contaminant. German physician Johann Albers published a study of the physiologic effects of nitroglycerin in 1864. He was especially interested in the effects of the substance on the heart and circulation. Albers's studies led him to conclude that nitroglycerin caused paralysis of the vasomotor nerves.

Although scattered reports on the use of nitroglycerin in the treatment of neuralgia and other conditions began to appear in the 1870s, no one (including the homeopaths) prescribed it for angina pectoris. This suggestion was first put forth by Murrell in 1879. Murrell opened his article on nitroglycerin with a review of the debate over its efficacy and mode of action. Aware of Harley and Fuller's experiments performed at his alma mater 20 years earlier, Murrell explained, "being quite at a loss to reconcile the conflicting statements of the different observers, or arrive at any conclusions respecting the properties of the drug, I determined to try its action on myself."[5]

Murrell explained that he had unwittingly touched the moist cork stopper of a vial of nitroglycerin solution to his tongue while seeing outpatients. This caused a severe, pounding headache associated with tachycardia and a dramatic increase in the force of his heartbeat. Aware of the variable responses to nitroglycerin reported by Harley and Fuller, Murrell decided to test the substance on others. Each of 35 individuals (12 males and 23 females, ages 12 to 58) who took the substance experienced symptoms similar to those described by Murrell.

It was obvious to Murrell that nitroglycerin produced impressive side effects, but why did he think the drug might be useful in treating patients with angina? His interest in organic nitrates can be traced to the observations of the Scottish physician and pharmacologist T. Lauder Brunton.[6] A pioneer of cardiovascular pharmacology, Brunton was the first to propose a vasodilator as a treatment for angina. He advocated amyl nitrate for the treatment of the complaint in 1867.[7] Earlier experiments had led medical scientists to classify this substance as a vasodilator that acted on the vasomotor nerves.

Brunton knew that some patients with angina seemed to improve with phlebotomy, and he thought that amyl nitrite might accomplish the same result without causing anemia. Soon after Brunton published his findings in the *Lancet,* other physicians confirmed his observations and amyl nitrate became a standard remedy for angina. Although Brunton studied nitroglycerin before Murrell experimented with it, he did not administer it to humans because it gave him such a severe headache he thought patients would not tolerate it.[8]

Murrell was not deterred. He thought nitroglycerin might be useful in angina because the two drugs seemed to have the

FIG. 1 William Murrell (1853–1912). Photograph provided by the National Library of Medicine, Bethesda, Maryland.

The special role of nitroglycerin in the treatment of angina pectoris was acknowledged rapidly. British physician William Green claimed in 1882, "I am not overstating [nitroglycerin's] merits when I say it deserves to rank only second to digitalis in the treatment of disease of the heart."[9] The liquid nitroglycerin preparation Murrell prescribed was inconvenient, however. Within a year the drug was available in tablet form in a variety of strengths. Anticipating the logical concern about the explosive potential of nitroglycerin, British chemist William Martindale explained that it was stable and "perfectly inexplosive—it cannot be detonated."[10]

In addition to his classic work on nitroglycerin, which was reprinted in book form in 1882, Murrell published monographs on several other subjects including the treatment of bronchitis, the medical value of massage, and toxicology. He died in 1912.

References

1. Fye WB: Nitroglycerin: A homeopathic remedy. *Circulation* 73, 21–29 (1986)

2. Smith E, Hart FD: William Murrell, physician and practical therapist. *Br Med J* 3, 632–633 (1971)

3. Murrell W: Nitro-glycerine as a remedy for angina pectoris. *Lancet* 1, 80–81, 113–115, 151–152, 225–227 (1879)

4. Fye WB: Vasodilator therapy for angina pectoris: The intersection of homeopathy and scientific medicine. *J Hist Med Allied Sci* 45, 317–340 (1990)

5. Murrell W: *Nitro-glycerine.* (1879) 81

6. Fye WB: T. Lauder Brunton and amyl nitrite: A Victorian vasodilator. *Circulation* 74, 222–229 (1986)

7. Brunton TL: On the use of nitrite of amyl in angina pectoris. *Lancet* 2, 97–98 (1867)

8. Brunton TL, Tait ES: Preliminary notes on the physiological action of nitroglycerin [1876]. In *Collected Papers on Circulation and Respiration. First Series.* Macmillan & Co., London (1907) 220–339

9. Green WG: Notes on the use of nitro-glycerine in the treatment of heart disease. *Ther Gaz* 6, 304–306 (1882) 304

10. Martindale W: Nitroglycerin in pharmacy. *Practitioner* 24, 35–39 (1880) 37

same effect on the circulation. Murrell's theory was supported by his early experience with the drug. He began administering nitroglycerin to patients with angina in the summer of 1878. His first patient was a 64-year-old heavy smoker with symptoms consistent with angina. After ingesting a 1% solution of nitroglycerin three times a day for a week, the patient reported that the anginal attacks occurred less frequently and were less severe. Murrell did not depend solely on his patient's subjective impressions. He used the sphygmograph, an instrument recently invented for graphically recording the pulse, to document the drug's effects on the heart rate and pulse wave form.

Robert Tigerstedt—Scientist, Educator, Social Activist, Humanitarian

BARRY D. SILVERMAN, M.D.

Northside Cardiology, Atlanta, Georgia, USA

Robert Tigerstedt (Fig. 1) was a Scandinavian physiologist who is famous as the discoverer of renin, the active hormonal system that originates in the kidney and controls blood pressure. Robert Tigerstedt was born in Finland in 1853, into a family prominent for its academic and civil service. His father was a historian of considerable reputation and Robert was the eldest of his three children. As a student, he was both accomplished and productive; his interests extended beyond the classroom and he developed a pattern of community involvement that extended throughout his life.

Education

Tigerstedt's family had immigrated to western Finland in the seventeenth century, when Finland was governed by Sweden. His education and graduate work was completed at the University of Helsinki, Finland, where he graduated from college at the age of 20 and completed his medical studies and Ph.D. thesis at the age of 27. The thesis resulted in a disagreement with his professor of physiology, Hallsten, and the conflict was the cause of his departure from Helsinki for Stockholm in 1881. He joined the Karlinska Institute in 1886, and there, at the age of 33, he was promoted to full professor of physiology. Tigerstedt's initial interest was in the area of neurophysiology. His Ph.D. thesis concerned nerve stimulation. In studies completed from 1880 to 1885, Tigerstedt determined the latency of muscle contraction after nerve stimulation, an important discovery that was instrumental in his appointment to the chair of physiology in Stockholm.

Karlinska Institute in Stockholm

While in Stockholm, Tigerstedt traveled to Leipzig to study with the great physiology professor Carl Ludwig. In Ludwig's laboratory, he developed an interest in the circulation and instrumentation. In 1901, at the age of 48, he returned home to accept the chair of physiology in Helsinki. Finland at that time was a part of the Russian empire and his appointment was hailed as a torchbearer for Finland's freedom. At the university, he built a new physiology laboratory, devel-oped studies in energy metabolism, wrote a number of textbooks of physiology, published papers on the history of medicine, and became increasingly involved in university administration.

Discovery of Renin

Among Tigerstedt's many achievements and considered his greatest was the discovery, in 1897, of the hormone renin as the active hormonal system originating in the kidney and controlling blood pressure. The studies were unique in Tigerstedt's work, and he completed nothing similar before or after this discovery. Experiments conducted from 1856 to 1858 by Brown-Sequard in Paris, had discovered the adrenal hormone. His studies launched investigations in a number of important physiology laboratories to identify new hormones. Tigerstedt, who was interested in the circulation and blood flow, had considered the kidney a likely source for control of the blood pressure. Between November 1896 and May 1897, he conducted 50 experiments. In 1897, Tigerstedt was elected president of the International Congress of Medicine in Moscow, Russia. He presented the renin studies as a long abstract with a paper that followed in the *Scandinavian Archives of Physiology* in 1898. His paper *Niere und Kreislauf* demonstrated the actions of the extract and tried to clarify the mechanism of action. He concludes the paper with the statement "We would like to point out, however, that we do not put forward a new hypothesis concerning renal diseases and hypertrophy of the heart because that would require many more experiments. We would only suggest a role for this pressure-elevating substance from the kidneys." The discovery was widely applauded but could not be duplicated by other laboratories so that after a time it was forgotten. Mattias Aurell suggests that Tigerstedt was an elegant investigator with an outstanding reputation for his skill in the laboratory and that his contemporaries simply could not match his technique. Although Tigerstedt never doubted his discovery of renin and included references to the hormone in his textbooks, including the last edition in 1923, it was not until the 1930s and Goldblatt's studies that the hormone was rediscovered and Tigerstedt's study was validated.

Fig. 1   Robert Tigerstedt, 1853–1923. Photograph provided by the National Library of Medicine.

Teacher and Humanitarian

Robert Tigerstedt was not only a gifted and brilliant scientist, but also a preceptor to students, a mentor for fellows, and a communicator to the general public. He has been described as a charming, open, and lively individual who enjoyed working with medical students, nurses, and paramedical hospital employees. He was interested in many social and medical issues. He disseminated his views directly to the public, and his lectures were regularly covered and discussed in the newspapers. Tigerstedt was instrumental in instituting new teaching methods and modernizing medical training in both Stockholm and Helsinki. He constructed new research laboratories in Stockholm and Helsinki, graduated more than 30 Ph.D. students, and taught students throughout his entire 40-year career.

He is the author of three important textbooks. His textbook of physiology, *Lehrbuch der Physiologie des Menschens*, appeared in 10 editions between 1897 and 1923. It was translated into English, Italian, and Russian. The book was popular and dominated physiology teaching through the decades of its publication. The *Handbuch der Physiologischen Methodik* was published between 1911 and 1914 in three volumes. The handbook was an important contribution to physiology and confirmed Tigerstedt's reputation as a world leader in this area. The third book was *Physiologie des Kreislaufes*. Published in four volumes between 1921 and 1923, the books were an encyclopedic collection of knowledge on the circulation. They are a comprehensive compendium of what was known about the central and peripheral circulation.

Social Activist

Tigerstedt was active in improving nutrition and the quality of food for working people, advocating tirelessly for the temperance movement, promoting international cooperation among scientists, and campaigning for the rights of prisoners of war.

In 1920, he carried out scientific investigations in nutrition and described an illness that may have been scurvy. The drinking habits in Scandinavia were very liberal at the time and Tigerstedt, a teetotaler, advocated a strong antiliquor program. His activity in the temperance movement resulted in books and pamphlets that were printed in editions of over 100,000 copies, an enormous number for the time. In 1919, Finland became an independent state and suffered a difficult civil war. Tigerstedt accepted a position as chief physician for the prison camps, the only clinical position he ever held in his life. He was active in a program to improve the prisoners' conditions and promote their rights.

Additional Interests and Achievements

Robert Tigerstedt was a bibliophile who collected a large library of physiologic literature. The large and famous library was located in the Department of Physiology at Helsinki; unfortunately, the collection was largely destroyed by fire in 1923. When the industrialist Alfred Nobel died, Tigerstedt was chosen to help with the execution of the will. Tigerstedt was a key contributor on the committee that promoted and established the Nobel Prizes. He was a man of the world who was active in many academic and scientific societies in Europe. He spoke fluent German, French, and Russian. He did not speak English and apparently had very few connections with England or the United States. A man of strong convictions, he had been elected President of the International Congress of Physiology in 1916. The Congress was cancelled due to World War I and, after the war, when the congress convened in Paris in 1920, Tigerstedt resigned the presidency and did not attend when Germany was excluded from participation. He died in 1923 and was honored by The American Society of Hypertension under the leadership of John Laragh with the establishment of the "The Robert Tigerstedt Award."

Robert Tigerstedt's achievements are best characterized by his motto "truth will be revealed only to those who doubt." A scientist, teacher, humanitarian, and social activist, Robert Tigerstedt was a man who never ceased the search for the truth.

Selected Reading

1.   Aurell M: Robert Tigerstedt—scientist, teacher and critic. In *Renin —Angiotensin* Wenner-Gren International Series, Vol. 74 (Eds. Ulfendahl HR, Aurell M), p. 1–12. London: Portland Press, 1997
2.   Marks LS, Maxwell MH: Tigerstedt and the discovery of renin, a historical note. *Hypertension* 1979;1:384–388
3.   Hirvonen L: Robert Tigerstedt and physiology in Finland. In *The Roots of Modern Physiology*, p. 75–89. Oulu: Societas Physiologica Finlandiae, 1990
4.   Tigerstedt R: *A Text-Book of Human Physiology* (Ed. and trans. Murlin JR). New York & London: D. Appleton and Company, 1906

Sir James Mackenzie

D. M. KRIKLER, M.D., F.R.C.P.

Royal Postgraduate Medical School, Hammersmith Hospital, London, England

James Mackenzie (Fig. 1) represents an extraordinary paradox in British medicine. Looking back from this vantage point he can clearly be identified as the first pure cardiologist in the country, yet most of his professional life was spent as a general practitioner in a modest provincial town. He worked as a consultant cardiologist in London for only a decade but his achievements had previously brought him world renown.

Mackenzie was born in Scone, Scotland, on April 12, 1853, the second son of a farmer (Mair, 1973). At the age of 15, after four years at Perth Grammar School, he was apprenticed to a pharmacist for four years and worked in this field for another two years before entering the medical school of the University of Edinburgh at the age of 21. After graduating in 1878, he was an assistant in general practice for six months and spent another six months in a resident appointment at the Edinburgh Royal Infirmary. This was followed by a visit to Vienna, then in its heyday as a magnet for postgraduate students. This was the sum total of his postgraduate training; he had decided to enter general practice in the cotton manufacturing town of Burnley in Lancashire, where he clearly had congenial partners, whom he joined in 1880. The unexpected death of a patient from puerperal heart failure focused his attention on cardiology and in the next decade he spent much time developing instruments for pulse recordings. Mackenzie worked along very similar lines to those of Potain in Paris, but instead of a smoked drum he used continuous rolls of paper for longer recording, and obtained simultaneous tracings from several pulses with the ink polygraph that he developed (Fig. 2) with Mr. S. Shaw, a watchmaker from a neighboring town. With this device Mackenzie was able to make a number of observations subsequently confirmed and amplified when the electrocardiograph was developed. As early as 1890, he identified extrasystoles and distinguished their origin. Although his terminology was inexact, he also recognized for the first time the clinical entity of total irregularity of the pulse in which he could see, from venous tracings, that the characteristics of the pulse wave acquired what he called the ventricular form; he later called this nodal rhythm—it was, of course, atrial fibrillation.

These technical developments reflect only one aspect of Mackenzie's life. He found abnormalities on the pulse tracings in individuals who were, to all intents and purposes, well. He made the same observation with auscultation of murmurs, and learned and taught how important myocardial function was as a determinant of prognosis.

Mackenzie, the busy general practitioner in Burnley, soon became the best known British cardiac physician among the leaders of the profession on the European continent. He paid visits to continental centers and received in return academicians as distinguished as Karl Frederik Wenckebach, who, when he came to Burnley in 1904, bypassed the London physicians. Mackenzie now seriously wondered whether to continue in general practice and considered moving to Edinburgh, Manchester, or London, but even before he left Burnley, he had the distinction of being elected to the Association of Physicians of Great Britain and Ireland when it was formed by Sir William Osler in 1907: not only this, but he was invited to open the discussion on the heart. Later that year he moved from Burnley to London. As a general practitioner arriving there at the age of 54, Mackenzie did not find a ready welcome from his contemporaries, and it was two years before he was appointed to the visiting staff of the Mount Vernon Hospital for Diseases of the Chest in Hampstead. The previous year, while working in consultant practice, he had completed his textbook (Mackenzie, 1908). In 1910 a post was created for him as lecturer on cardiac research at the London Hospital, where he was given few clinical facilities until 1913 when he was put in charge of the cardiac department.

His influence in his early years in London was clearly profound. Thomas Lewis was embarking on his vigorous research career. The Mackenzie polygraph was already in use in most of the hospitals including University College Hospital. With the advent of the Einthoven string galvanometer, Mackenzie encouraged Lewis to explore its value as a clinical and research tool, even though the lessons that it taught were sometimes painful, as in the clarification of atrial fibrillation; the polygraph remained his favored intrument.

During World War I Mackenzie and Lewis worked intensively on functional cardiac disorders, rediscovering what previous generations had learned—and forgotten—including the fundamental observations made by Da Costa during the American Civil War. In 1915, Mackenzie was honored with a knighthood, but though he continued to observe and write, he was unhappy with life in London and in 1918 moved to St. Andrews in Scotland to establish an institute for clinical research. This proved a difficult task. He developed angina pectoris, and returned to London in 1924. He died there on January 25, 1925, at the age of 71.

In his later years, his relations with Lewis were marred by the inflexibility of the latter as editor (and proprietor) of the

FIG. 1 Portrait of Sir James Mackenzie by Herbert Sedcole, after D. Mackenzie. Reproduced with permission of the Wellcome Institute Library, London.

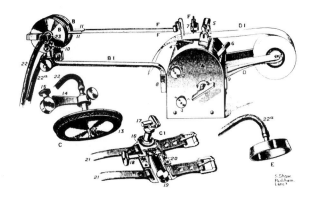

FIG. 2 The ink polygraph, as designed by Sir James Mackenzie and made by Mr. S. Shaw.

of digitalis which had been neglected in the century after Withering's seminal observations (Krikler, 1985).

It is difficult to think of another physician who rose in the same way, from the obscurity of general practice, through his talents, ingenuity, and sound clinical observations, to breach the fortress of conservative medicine in London and establish himself as head of the cardiac department of a leading teaching hospital: this achievement is one measure of Mackenzie's qualities, which had been recognized abroad long beforehand.

only journal devoted to cardiology in Great Britain, *Heart*. He had encouraged Lewis to establish this in 1909 and was mortified when his contribution on the vagal component of the action of digitalis on the heart was summarily rejected (McMichael, 1981). This was a bitter pill for Mackenzie who had, above all other physicians, rescued digitalis from near oblivion. In Burnley he reviewed the response of patients with atrial fibrillation ("nodal rhythm") and rediscovered the efficacy

References

Krikler DM: The foxglove, "The Old Woman from Shropshire" and William Withering. *J Am Coll Cardiol* 5, 3A (1985)

Mair A: *Sir James Mackenzie, M.D. 1853–1925, General Practitioner*. Churchill Livingstone, Edinburgh and London, 1973

Mackenzie J: *Diseases of the Heart*. London, Henry Frowde, 1908

McMichael J: Sir James Mackenzie and atrial fibrillation. A new perspective. *J R Coll Gen Prac* 31, 402 (1981)

Augustus Desiré Waller

LOUIS J. ACIERNO, M.D., FACC

Cardiopulmonary Sciences, Department of Health Professions and Physical Therapy, University of Central Florida, Orlando, Florida, USA

The name of Einthoven has figured most prominently throughout the history of electrocardiography; however, the name of Waller should also be recalled as that of an important pioneer in the development and clinical implementation of the first technological innovation for the diagnosis and management of cardiac disturbances.

Augustus Desiré Waller (Fig. 1) was born in Paris in 1856, the scion of an eminent scientist, Augustus Volney Waller, who was noted for his work on nerve degeneration, now eponymously known to us as Wallerian degeneration. Young Waller lost his father and role model in 1870, when the boy was only 14 years old. Even at that tender age, Augustus Desiré wanted to emulate his father. The boy's upbringing now rested on the shoulders of his mother who, for personal reasons, moved with her son to Scotland, where eventually he studied medicine at Aberdeen and Edinburgh. Immediately upon graduation, Waller began his lifelong career in physiology, contributing a great deal to this discipline in due course. His textbook *An Introduction to Human Physiology*, published in 1891, was at that time a comprehensive treatise on the subject.[1, 2]

His first academic appointment was as lecturer at the School of Medicine for Women in London in 1883. The following year, he was also appointed lecturer in physiology at St. Mary's Hospital in Paddington. Waller remained at St. Mary's until 1903, when he was appointed professor of the newly established physiologic laboratory at the University of London. This was followed very shortly by his appointment as consulting cardiologist to the National Heart Hospital in London where he continued his clinical investigations in electrocardiography.[3]

Waller also maintained a private physiologic laboratory at his spacious home in St. John's Wood, London.[4] He was helped here by his wife who had qualified in medicine but never practiced her profession. He had three sons and a daughter, none of whom married. His children were often the subject of his electrocardiographic studies, but his best known subject was his bulldog, Jimmy.[5] There are many photographs of Jimmy either by his side or standing in a tray of saline having an electrocardiogram taken.[3, 6]

Perhaps the biggest supporter of Waller in his role as a pioneering force of electrocardiography was Edwin Besterman and his colleagues of the Waller cardiopulmonary unit at St. Mary's Hospital in London.[3] Waller's initial work on electro-cardiography was conducted at St. Mary's Hospital, and it was there that he gave the first public demonstration of his recording device. Waller's original apparatus and some of the tracings obtained with it are still housed in this unit.[6–8]

It is true that Alexander Muirhead may have been the first to record a human electrocardiogram, but Waller was the first to do so in a combined clinico-physiologic setting, the first to publish a report on his findings, and a pioneer in acquiring extensive experience with this new diagnostic modality. Muirhead conducted his investigations with a Thompson siphon recorder at St. Bartholomew's Hospital in 1869 or 1870. The device had been designed by William Thompson to record signals passing through the newly laid transatlantic cable.[9] Prior to this, electric potentials of the heart were obtained from exposed animal hearts.[10]

Initially, Waller had said "I do not imagine that electrocardiography is likely to find any very extensive use in the hospital. It can at most be of rare and occasional use to afford a record of some rare anomaly of cardiac action."[11] No doubt, his continued usage of the modality caused him to change his mind because in 1917, just six years after expressing this sentiment, Waller presented before the Physiological Society of London a paper entitled "A Preliminary Survey of 2,000 Electrocardiograms."[12] This was also the first time that he used the word "electrocardiogram" in an official manner; prior to this he had referred to the tracings as "electrograms." This raises the question as to who really coined the word "electrocardiogram." Einthoven attributed it to Waller,[13] as did Waller's daughter, herself a lecturer in physics. Sykes, however, found no evidence of this, advancing the proposition that Einthoven really coined the term but attributed it to Waller as a token of respect and generosity toward his colleague.[14]

The groundwork for Waller's presentation to the Physiological Society began in 1887 and 1888 when he published his findings, first, on electric potentials obtained from intact living animals, and then from the limbs and chest of humans.[10, 15] He used the Lippmann capillary electrometer to deflect a light beam from the recording of these electrical forces. The Lippmann capillary electrometer was a far better device than the siphon recorder for measuring the electrical activity of the heart.

Besterman relates an interesting anecdote that illustrates Waller's gentle personality, that of a man who could appreciate without umbrage a greeting from his students after his

FIG. 1 Augustus Desiré Waller, 1856–1922. Waller and his famous dog Jimmy. Source: *Brit Heart J* 1979;42:61–64 (Ref. No. 3). Reproduced with permission from the BMJ Publishing Group.

marriage to one of them. The student he married was Alice Mary Palmer, the daughter of Sir George Palmer (of Huntley & Palmer biscuit fame). The blackboard bore the inscription "Waller takes the biscuit." Waller, in good humor, and not the least offended, added the words "and the tin as well."[3]

Another interesting facet of his personality can be appreciated by the recollection of Robert Marshall wherein Waller is portrayed as possessing a "certain unconventionality":

Waller presented a very different appearance from that of our physicians, who were always soberly garbed in frock coats or morning coats and silk hats. He was a short, stocky man, very light on his feet. His gray beard and double breasted blue jacket made him look exactly like a skipper in the merchant navy. Like Sir Winston, he seemed to be habitually smoking cigars, and was invariably followed by his bulldog, Jimmy, who also had a Churchillian quality and had the distinction of having had a question asked about him in the House of Commons.

Q. 'At a converzaione [*sic*] of the Royal Society at Burlington House on May 12th last, a bulldog was cruelly treated when a leather strap with sharp nails was wound around his neck and his feet were immersed in glass jars containing salts in solution, and the jars in turn were connected with wires to galvanometers. Such a cruel procedure should surely be dealt with under the "Cruelty to Animals Act" of 1876?'

A. 'The dog in question wore a leather collar ornamented with brass studs, and he was placed to stand in water to which some sodium chloride had been added, or in other words, common salt. If my honourable friend had

ever paddled in the sea, he will appreciate fully the sensation obtained thereby from this simple pleasurable experience!'[3]

Throughout his career, Waller received many awards in Britain and abroad. A notable one was election as a fellow of the Royal Society at the young age of 35, the same age his father had been at election.[14] Waller's one consuming pastime was dashing about with the newly invented motor car. He was somewhat of a showman and enjoyed giving popular lectures. His spacious home was often the seat of entertainment for visiting scientists.

Waller died in 1922 after suffering two strokes. That same year a summary of his electrocardiographic investigations and viewpoints was published in a monograph edited by his son.[16]

Waller and Einthoven should stand side by side in the historical annals of electrocardiography. Burchell pointed out quite rightly that although the two men were alike in their manifold contributions to the new science, they were quite different in so many ways. Einthoven was formal while Waller was quite informal and folksy. Einthoven was methodical and demanding of technical perfection whereas Waller was not too keen on overcoming technical mediocrity. Einthoven was much more inclined toward application of this modality in the clinical arena. Waller, on the other hand, although working in a hospital-based school, was apparently not greatly interested in exploring its utility in the management of the sick.[7]

References

1. Acierno LJ: *The History of Cardiology*, p. 520–521. London, New York: Parthenon Publishing Group, 1994
2. Waller AD: *An Introduction to Human Physiology.* London: Longmans, Green & Co. 1891
3. Besterman E, Creese RL: Waller—pioneer of electrocardiography. *Br Heart J* 1979;42:61–64
4. Krikler DM: Historical aspects of electrocardiography. *Cardiol Clin* 1987;5, No. 3:349–354
5. Sykes AH: A biographical note. *St. Mary's Gazette* 1985;91:19–20
6. Burchell HB: A centennial note on Waller and the first human electrocardiogram. *Am J Cardiol* 1987;59:979–983
7. Besterman E: Waller before Einthoven in the clinical development of noninvasive ECG. *Am Heart J* 1982;103:572–575
8. Cope Z: Augustus Desiré Waller (1856–1922). *Med Hist* 1973;17:380–384
9. Burnett J: The origins of the electrocardiogram as a clinical instrument. *Med Hist* 1985;(suppl)5:60
10. Burch GE, De Pasquale NP: *A History of Electrocardiography.* Chicago: Year Book Medical Publishers, Inc., 1964
11. Barker LF: Electrocardiography and phonocardiography: A collective review. *Bull Johns Hopkins Hosp* 1910;21:358–359
12. Waller AD: A preliminary survey of 2000 electrocardiograms. *J Physiol* 1917;51:18–24 (*Proc Physiol. Soc* July 28)
13. Einthoven W: The different forms of the human electrocardiogram and their significance. *Lancet* 1912;1:853–860
14. Sykes AH: A. D. Waller and the electrocardiogram. *Br Heart J* 1987;294:1396–1398
15. Waller AD: A demonstration on man of electromotive changes accompanying the heart beat. *J Physiol* 1887;8:229–233
16. Waller AD: Ed.: *The Electrical Action of the Human Heart.* London: University of London Press, 1922

Dr. Friedrich Maass: 100th Anniversary of "New" CPR

RICHARD L. TAW, JR., M.D., FACC

Pacific Heart Institute, Santa Monica, California, USA

In science the credit goes to the man who convinces the world, not the man to whom the idea first occurred.[1]

William Osler

Medical historians credit an obscure German surgeon, Friedrich Maass, with the first successful use of external cardiac massage a century ago.[2] Maass was a surgical assistant to Professor Franz Koenig of Göttingen and tried a modification of Koenig's previous method which proved successful on October 26, 1891. His subsequent report of two cases was the first to document in man the successful use of chest compression to create an arterial pulse and his simple observation regarding the most effective rate of compression has proven to be remarkably prescient. Following his report, he became the first proponent of chest compression as an effective means of assisting circulation rather than ventilation alone.

Nineteenth century efforts at resuscitation were directed at mechanical techniques to stimulate breathing. Leroy-d'Etiolles is credited with the first attempts to manipulate the body and extremities to ventilate the lungs in 1827.[3] In 1858 Silvester introduced a method of artificial ventilation which was used with various modifications for over a century.[4] The arms of the supine patient were pulled above the head to force inspiration and then folded onto the chest where pressure was applied to force expiration. Subsequently, airway obstruction was recognized as a limiting factor with this technique and the tongue was pulled forward to open the airway.

In 1858 a Hungarian surgeon, Janos Balassa, reported the revival from death of a young woman with pharyngeal obstruction via tracheostomy and a "bellows-like rhythmic pressure to the front of her chest imitating breathing."[5] This has been viewed by some as the first use of external heart massage,[6] but was clearly viewed by the author as ventilatory assistance similar to the successful method reported by Silvester in the same year.

As of 1891 little progress had been made in improving surgical survival in instances of "chloroform syncope." This anesthetic caused sudden circulatory collapse which was usually irreversible. In his 1883 textbook of surgery, Professor Koenig had proposed compression of the "heart region" as an alternative to the ventilatory procedures used in the operating room at the time.[7] This method involved compressing the xiphoid area and costal margins at the rate of spontaneous respiration and was undoubtedly a form of assisted ventilation. It usually worked in a few minutes or not at all.

Maass discovered his new technique in a desperate attempt to save a young life. Heinrich A., a 9-year-old boy, was admitted to the Surgical Clinic in Göttingen for repair of a cleft palate. He had been operated upon twice previously for a double harelip. There was some difficulty in obtaining adequate anesthesia with chloroform and two or three extra applications on the mask were required. He then became cyanotic and dilated his pupils. No pulse could be detected but he still had "shallow breathing." Koenig's method of xiphoid compression was applied at the rate of respiration, 30 to 40 times per minute. Although cyanosis disappeared and the pupils constricted, no pulse could be found. A tracheostomy was performed. After 30 minutes of effort, the boy was moved to an adjoining room to free up the operating room for another case. Usually resuscitative efforts were stopped at this point. Maass wrote:

> I now had to consider the patient dead. Nevertheless, I went to direct compression of the heart region and, in my excitement, I worked very fast and vigorously. The pupils quickly constricted and when I continued at great speed, they were soon smaller and during pauses, the slow, gasping respiration started up again.

After 30 minutes of this new approach and a full hour from the start, cyanosis disappeared and a carotid pulse was felt. The patient made a gradual recovery, manifesting slow return of mental function and was discharged December 1, 1981.

A second case is described occurring December 4, 1891 in Georg F., an 18-year-old boy operated on for tubercular coxitis of the right hip. Koenig's method was tried again, but abandoned earlier in favor of the new approach. Maass described using "the faster tempo of 120 and more compressions per minute." He noted a pulse in the carotid with each compression and a return of spontaneous pulse within 25 minutes. After a suitable recovery the patient was reoperated and the surgical procedure completed successfully.

Maass felt that his major clinical observation was the success encountered with a more rapid rate of chest compression.

> So long as compression is applied at the speed of the patient's breathing, slow deterioration. When compression

is speeded up, gradual improvement follows… At this point it becomes clear that, first of all, forceful pressure on the heart region with its relatively small effect on respiration has accomplished more than the very extensive artificial respiration according to Silvester; second, that compressions at the speed of a fast pulse were more effective than those that were executed at the speed of respiration.

This central feature of Maass' method also represents the first application of one of the modern cardiopulmonary resuscitation (CPR) variants termed "New" CPR. These variations on standard technique first appeared in the 1970s. Many have been discarded after more clinical experience or animal experimentation has proven them either useless or in some cases harmful.[8] However, those that increase coronary perfusion pressure are still of clinical interest: Interposed abdominal compression—CPR and high-impulse CPR (120 compressions/min).[9] The latter was first described by Maass.

Although the new method involved compression over the "heart region," it was not sternal compression. Maass described the technique as follows:

Stand at the patient's left, facing his head, and with quick, energetic motions, deeply compress the heart region with the ball of the right thumb placed between the point of apical impulse and the left sternal rim. Compressions are executed at a speed of 120 or more a minute. At this speed it is usually more important to apply enough pressure than to worry about pressing too hard.

It helps to simultaneously grasp the patient's right thorax side with the left hand in order to hold the body in place. The efficacy of the treatment can be gauged by the artificially produced carotid pulse and constriction of the pupils. Speed and strength of pressure have to be measured accordingly. In order to control the effect and at the same time keep the respiratory passages open, another person should stand at the patient's head. As long as the patient's condition has not noticeably improved, it is necessary to pause as infrequently and as briefly as possible. Later it is permissible, whenever pupils have constricted completely, to pause as long as they remain small and spontaneous breathing continues.

It is unfortunate that medical science made such slow and halting progress toward the use of effective cardiopulmonary resuscitative methods. As Safar has observed, much of the knowledge on which modern CPR is based was known by 1900 but lay dormant until laboratory researchers, clinicians and prehospital rescuers addressed the problem together in the 1950s.[10] Why was the method of Maass not adopted before the turn of the century?

Perhaps the world was not ready to be convinced. In 1891 the physiologic basis of cardiopulmonary arrest was not understood. Although sudden cardiac death had been recognized for centuries, its mechanism remained obscure. Elec-

trocardiography to document arrhythmias evolved after Einthoven's invention of the string galvanometer in 1901. The clinical syndrome of myocardial infarction was not described until 1912. Before 1900 circulatory collapse was encountered by clinicians primarily in the operating room and thus was viewed as a surgical problem. A surgical solution was provided by Ingelsrud in 1901 when he successfully employed thoracotomy and direct cardiac compression.[11] Thereafter attention was focused on this method for in-hospital collapse.

Experimental support for external chest compression existed at the time but clinicians were not convinced of the relevance of animal data. Boehrn had restored circulation in cats by chest compression in 1878.[12] Gottlieb combined closed chest cardiac massage and the use of adrenaline with success in 1896.[13] However, there was little communication between physiologists and clinicians in the nineteenth century. Neither group referenced the work of the other in their publications and the clinical figures of the day scorned the work of basic scientists.[14]

Finally, the use of chest compression for circulatory support may have seemed misdirected. Collapse outside the hospital was focused on accidental drowning and viewed as a ventilatory issue. Various "Humane Societies" sprang up in many countries to promote ventilatory resuscitation in these instances.[15] Collapse in the hospital was usually only observed in the operating room as an anesthetic complication, and was thus also viewed as a ventilatory problem. Chest pressure had become a standard means of assisting ventilation, not circulation. A rate of compression suitable for respiration was much slower than that proposed by Maass and 120 per minute seemed most inappropriate for breathing.

Little is known of Friedrich Maass and further efforts to promulgate his resuscitative method after 1892. He published his two cases in the German and French literature and he and Koenig went on to demonstrate their technique at the Surgical Congress in Berlin.[16] He came to America and practiced as a surgeon in Detroit and New York between 1897 and 1914, thereafter returning to Bremen.[17] Green's review of reported cases of successful internal and external heart massage as of 1906 fails to reference Dr. Maass' cases or his method.[18] It appears that the discovery was never adopted outside of Germany and was put aside as attention focused on internal cardiac compression to restore circulation

Maass' observations were unknown to William Kouwenhoven when he "rediscovered" external chest compression for heart massage.[10] His publication, 69 years after that of Maass, convinced the world of the efficacy of this method for cardiac arrest.[19] Now, 100 years later, Dr. Maass' discovery of clinical benefit using a rapid compression rate of 120 has been repeated, and others attempt to convince the world of the efficacy of this "new" modification of standard practice.

Acknowledgments

My thanks to Maria Pelikan for her translation of Dr. Maass' 1892 paper in its entirety as well as W. Bruce Fye,

M.D., and J. Willis Hurst, M.D., for their gracious review and suggestions for additional historical references.

References

1. Osler W: *The Evolution of Modern Medicine: Lecture Series of April 1913.* New Haven: Yale University Press, 1921
2. Maass F: Die Methode der Wiederbelebung bei Herzten nach Chloroformeinathmung. *Berlin Klin Wochenschr* 1892;29:265
3. Leroy-d'Etiolles J: Recherches sur l'asphyxie. *J Physiol Exp Path* 1827;7:45
4. Silvester HR: A new method of resuscitating still-born children and of restoring persons drowned or dead. *Br Med J* 1858;2:576
5. Balassa J: Jelvenyes gogvízdag fekelyes gogporckorilob koveckezteben; tetszhalal, megmentes gogmetazes altal (oedema glottides symptomaticum ex perichondrite laryngeali ulcerexa-asphixia-laryngotomia um exitura fausto). *Orvost Hetilap* 1858;2:653
6. Robiscek F, Littman L: The first reported case of external heart massage. *Clin Cardiol* 1983;569–571
7. Koenig F: Lehrbuch der allgemeinen Chirugie. G*öttingen,* 1883
8. Swenson RD, Weaver WD, Niskamen RA, Martin J, Dahlberg S: Hemodynamics in humans during conventional and experimental methods of cardiopulmonary resuscitation. *Circulation* 1988; 28:630
9. Maier GW, Newton JR, Wolfe SA, Tyson GS, Olsen CO, Glower DD, Sprait JA, Davis JW, Feneky MP, Rankin JS: The influence of manual chest compression rate on hemodynamic support during cardiac arrest: High-impulse cardiopulmonary resuscitation. *Circulation* 1986;74(suppl IV):IV–51
10. Safar P: History of cardiopulmonary cerebral resuscitation. In *Cardiopulmonary Resuscitation* (Eds. Kaye W, Bircher N). Churchill Livingstone, New York, 1989
11. Keen WW: A case of total laryngectomy (unsuccessful) and a case of abdominal hysterectomy (successful), in both of which massage of the heart for chloroform collapse was employed, with notes of 25 other cases of cardiac massage. *Therap Gaz* 1904;28:217
12. Biehm R: Ueber Wiederbelebung nach Vergiftungen und Asphyxie. *Arch Exp Pasthel Pharmakol* 1896;8:68
13. Gottlieb R: Ueber die Wirkung der Nebennierenextracte auf Herz und Blutdruck. *Arch F. Exper Path Pharmakol* 1986:38:96
14. Pearson JW: *Historical and Experimental Approaches to Modern Resuscitation.* Springfield: Charles C Thomas, 1965
15. Keith A: Three Hunterian lectures on the mechanism underlying the various methods of artificial respiration practiced since the foundation of the Royal Humane Society in 1774. *Lancet* 1909; I:745
16. Overbeck W, Susskind-Schwendt G: Historical considerations on cardiac arrest and resuscitation. *Thoraxchir Vask Chir* 1909;17(2): 177–184
17. Fischer I: *Biographisches Lexikon der hervorragenden Ärzte der letzien fünfzig Jahre.* Berlin: Urban und Schwarzenberg, 1933
18. Green TA: Heart massage as a means of restoration in cases of apparent sudden death, with a synopsis of 40 cases. *Lancet* 1906;II:1708
19. Jude JR, Kouwenhoven WB, Knickerbocker GG: Cardiac arrest: Report of application of external cardiac massage in 1818 patients. *J Am Med Assoc* 1961;178:1063

Willem Einthoven—The Father of Electrocardiography

MARK E. SILVERMAN, M.D.

Emory University School of Medicine and Piedmont Hospital, Atlanta, Georgia, USA

The truth is all that matters, what you or I may think is inconsequential.
—Willem Einthoven to Carl Wiggers, 1926[1]

In 1856 von Kölliker and Muller were the first to discover that the heart generated electricity.[2] Sixty-eight years later the Nobel Prize was awarded to Willem Einthoven, the Dutch investigator who transformed this curious physiologic phenomenon into an indispensable clinical recording.[3]

Einthoven was born May 21, 1860, in Semarang, Java, in the Dutch East Indies (now Indonesia), the son of a military physician and the descendant of Spanish Jews who had fled to Holland at the time of the Spanish Inquisition. His father died when he was only six, and four years later his mother moved her six children to Utrecht. Einthoven attended the University of Utrecht Medical School where he was greatly influenced by Frans Donders, a physiologist studying action currents of the heart, and Herman Snellen, the ophthalmologist of optical chart fame. He was awarded his medical degree magna cum laude for his thesis, "The Influence of Color Differences in the Production of Stereoscopic Effects." Initially, Einthoven intended a career in ophthalmology in the East Indies to repay a government grant; however, with the support of Donders, he was appointed in 1885 to the recently vacated chair of professor of physiology at Leiden where he remained the rest of his life.[2–5] His research interests were extensive; his 127 papers included the study of bronchial musculature, the physiology of the eye, the function of the cervical sympathetic nerve, radiotelemetry, and his fundamental work on the electrocardiogram.

In 1887 Einthoven attended an International Congress of Physiology in London where he observed Augustus D. Waller demonstrate the use of the capillary electrometer to record an "electrogram" of the heart using pan electrode limb leads.[5–7] The capillary electrometer, invented in 1873 by Gabriel Lippmann (who won the Nobel Price in 1908 for the principle of color photography), consisted of a glass capillary tube partially filled with mercury and placed vertically into a bath of sulfuric acid.[2,8] Electrical potentials flowing through the glass tube would cause the mercury meniscus to fluctuate sluggishly. The surface movements were recorded by magnifying the shadow onto a moving photograph, a technique devised by Marey in 1876.[5] Using this method, Marey, Burdon-Sanderson, Page, Gotch, Burch, Englemann, Bayliss, and Starling had recorded the electrical activity of an exposed animal heart.[2,5]

Waller was the first to record an "electrogram" from a dog and human (himself initially) using a lead system that did not require opening the chest.

> … so I dipped my right hand and left foot into a couple of basins of salt solution, which were connected with the two poles of the electrometer and at once had the pleasure of seeing the mercury column pulsate with the pulsation of the heart … this first demonstration was made in St. Mary's laboratory in May 1887 and demonstrated there to many physiologists and among others, to my friend Professor Einthoven of Leiden…[6]

Waller's contributions also included the variability of the electrogram, the dipole concept that led to isopotential mapping and the vector concept, the angle of the manifest vector in the frontal plane, a comprehensive textbook of physiology published in 1891, and the measurements of chloroform and other anesthetic gases.[5] He is also remembered because of his "famous bulldog, Jimmy"—so-called because a concern was raised in the House of Commons that Waller's experiments, in which Jimmy's feet were immersed in salt solutions, might constitute a cruelty to animals offense.[5] Waller failed to see any clinical value in his experiments, commenting later, "I certainly had no idea that the electrical signs of the heart's actions could ever be utilized for clinical investigation."[6] In part, this was due to the aggravation related to using the capillary electrometer—poor frequency response due to inertia, viscous drag through the capillary tubes, sensitivity to vibration, and hours required to obtain a decent tracing.[4]

In the early 1890s Einthoven turned his attention to recording electricity from the heart using the capillary electrometer of Lippmann.[2,3] Because of vibration produced by horse drawn vehicles rumbling over the cobblestone street in front of his wood frame laboratory, Einthoven constructed a platform of rocks in a hole cut into the floor of his laboratory to provide stability for his experiments.[4] By improving the frequency response and correcting for distortion mathematically, Einthoven enhanced the fidelity of the instrument and, in 1895, was able to report recognizable waves that he labeled "P, Q, R, S, and T," a notation disliked by Waller.[2,3,5,6] The origin of this nomenclature is uncertain; it probably was from

FIG. 1   Willem Einthoven, 1860–1927. Published with permission from the National Library of Medicine.

the geometric convention of Descartes that straight lines are labelled beginning with A and curved lines starting with P.[8]

Frustrated by the inherent technical problems of the capillary electrometer, Einthoven began to work on a different type of galvanometer, a string galvanometer, developed independently in 1897 by Clement Ader, a French electrical engineer.[3, 4] The string galvanometer, which would be the basis of future electrocardiography, consisted of a silver-coated quartz thread suspended within the magnetic field of two poles of a large, water-cooled electromagnet. The electrical current flowing from the subject through the silverized thread would cause the thread to move at right angles to the line of the magnetic field in proportion to the strength of the current. This fluctuating movement could be magnified by a lens and its shadow projected by a carbon arc lamp onto a photographic plate moving at 25 mm/s. The quartz thread was created by a unique form of archery in which the quartz was attached to the tail of an arrow and heated until it released the arrow from a drawn bow.[2] As it shot across the lab, the thread would be drawn into a fine filament so light that it would float and be captured by his able assistant, Van der Woerd. The original equipment, all developed by Einthoven, was very large, weighing 270 kg, occupying two rooms, and requiring five

people to operate it. It was the most elaborate and ingenious diagnostic instrument as well as electrical measuring device invented up to that time.[9] In addition to laboratory experiments the equipment was connected from the laboratory to patients in the hospital by a 1.5 km cable, a telecardiogram, in order to gain clinical information. With this technique, originally suggested by Bosscha[8] and reported by Einthoven in 1901, he standardized the tracing and described extra systoles, complete heart block, auricular and ventricular hypertrophy, atrial fibrillation and flutter, the U wave, the effects of heart rate and respiration, and examples of various heart diseases in his important papers published in 1903, 1906, and 1908.[2, 3] The first commercial machine was made by Edelmann and Sons in Munich. Apparently, Einthoven was to receive a royalty of $25.00 for each machine; however, Edelmann claimed to develop a superior machine and refused further payment of any royalties.[2]

In 1908, Thomas Lewis, on the urging of James Mackenzie, visited Einthoven's laboratory to see if the string galvanometer might advance the study of arrhythmias.[5] Through Horace Darwin, the son of the great biologist and founder of Cambridge Scientific Instrument Company, Einthoven arranged for Cambridge to manufacture electrocardiographic equipment. Using this equipment, Lewis began his pioneering work that would establish the electrocardiogram as a useful clinical test.[5, 10] In 1911, Einthoven, in a letter to Lewis, showed his appreciation: "An instrument takes its value not so much from the work that it possibly might do, but from the work that it really does. So your discoveries in the field of pathology of the heart increase the value of the string galvanometer greatly..." With the help of physicists and mathematicians at Leiden, Einthoven studied the spread of action potentials through tissues, introduced the three standard limb leads, and formulated the concept of the equilateral triangle by mathematically relating the three leads (Lead III = Lead II – Lead I).[3] For his monumental contribution in developing the string galvanometer to be used as an electrocardiographic machine, Einthoven received the Nobel Prize in 1924. In characteristic manner, he felt that half of the $40,000 prize should be shared with Van der Woerd, his invaluable laboratory assistant, who had retired years before. When Einthoven learned that Van der Woerd was deceased and had two sisters living in poverty, he gave them the $20,000 instead.[4] In his Nobel address he credited the many investigators who had preceded him:

A new chapter has been opened in the study of heart diseases, not by the work of a single investigator, but by that of many talented men, who have not been influenced in their work by political boundaries and, distributed over the whole surface of the earth, have devoted their powers to an ideal purpose, the advance of knowledge by which, finally, suffering mankind is helped.[3]

Einthoven was considered a modest genius with a sense of humor, a natural curiosity, a zeal for work, and a devotion to search for the truth.[2-4] He would ride his bicycle to his laboratory each day, remove his coat, tie, and collar, put on slippers, and work methodically and tirelessly, having to be reminded repeatedly by his assistant, on Mrs. Einthoven's instructions, when it was time to go home. Einthoven would acknowledge him but continue working, often until as late as 8:00 p.m. He was known for prolonged deep thinking. One time he lapsed into such deep thought that he told an assistant at the last minute to deliver his lecture so that he could continue his thinking. In the laboratory he applied his knowledge of physics to solve problems in physiology. His friend and colleague, Samojiloff, wrote "His mind was like an instrument of precision. He worked only on what could be measured and his measurements reached the limit of precision possible under the circumstances."[3] Though clumsy with his hands, he was graceful in his mannerisms and speech and fluent in three languages. His warm hospitality and generosity to younger colleagues and visitors were remarked upon and he enjoyed international respect and admiration.[1] The "father of electro-cardiography" died from cancer on September 28, 1927, at the age of 67.

In his lifetime, his quest for an improved electrical recording led to the single most important advance in the diagnosis of heart disease—the electrocardiogram. It would eventually make possible coronary care units, ambulatory monitors, pacemakers, exercise testing, intracardiac and fetal record-ings, ablation, automatic implanted defibrillators, signal averaging, and other tests and treatments essential to the modern diagnosis and treatment of heart disease.

References

1. Wiggers CJ: Willem Einthoven (1860-1927): Some facets of his life and work. *Circ Res* 1961;9:225–234
2. Burch GE, DePasquale NP: *A History of Electrocardiography*. Chicago: Year Book Medical Publishers, 1964
3. Snellen HA: *Selected Papers on Electrocardiography*. Leiden University Press, 1977
4. Erschler I: Willem Einthoven—the man. *Arch Int Med* 1988;148: 453–455
5. Rantaharju PM: A hundred years of progress in electrocardiography. I: Early contributions from Waller to Wilson. *Canad J Cardiol* 1987;3:362–374
6. Burchell HB: A centennial note on Waller and the first human electrocardiogram. *Am J Cardiol* 1987;59:979–983
7. Besterman E, Crease R: Waller—pioneer of electrocardiography. *Br Heart J* 1979;42:61–64
8. Cooper J: Electrocardiography 100 years ago: Origins, pioneers and contributions. *N Engl J Med* 1986;315:461–464
9. Burnett J: The origins of the electrocardiograph as a clinical instrument. *Med Hist* 1985;5:53–76
10. Barron SL: The development of the electrocardiograph in Great Britain. *Br Med J* 1950;1:720–725

James Bryan Herrick

Louis J. Acierno, m.d., and L. Timothy Worrell, m.p.h.

Department of Health Professions and Physical Therapy, University of Central Florida, College of Health and Public Affairs, Orlando, Florida, USA

Physician par excellence, scientist and humanist, James Bryan Herrick (Fig. 1) was born in Oak Park, Illinois, on August 11, 1861, the son of Origen White Herrick and Dora E. Kettlestrings. His mother's father, an immigrant from England, had arrived in that area in a covered wagon and settled on a homestead which was later to be the site of the village known as Oak Park. The subsequent birth of Herrick's mother in Oak Park gave her the distinction of being the oldest native daughter of that village.[1]

Herrick's early education was confined to the local Oak Park High School and the Rock River Seminary at Mount Morris, Illinois. He then earned his Bachelor of Arts degree in 1882 from the University of Michigan, which imbued him with a firm background in the humanities. Apparently, Herrick had a penchant for literature even as a youngster, an interest that was nurtured during his stay at Michigan by Moises Coit Tyler, a professor of English literature. Above all, Tyler instilled in young Herrick an enduring fascination with Chaucer. Herrick was to reveal the extent of this fascination in an article he wrote on Chaucer more than five decades later, the article being the published version of an after-dinner speech that he had given at an annual meeting of the Association of American Physicians.[2] It was quite evident from this long discourse that Herrick had read everything that Chaucer ever wrote. This fact was brought out many years later by J. Willis Hurst in his article, *The Canterbury Tales and Cardiology*.[3]

Throughout his life, Herrick always found time to pursue and cultivate all of his literary interests. However, rather than focusing primarily on the humanities, Herrick, fortunately for us, chose medicine as his major field of endeavor. He enrolled at Rush Medical College sometime after receiving his Bachelor's degree from Michigan and graduated just two years later as a Doctor of Medicine. After an internship of one year at Cook County Hospital, he married Zellah P. Davis, also of Oak Park, Illinois. The first year of his marriage saw the publication of three articles initiating a life-long contribution to the medical literature of 135 papers in all. The very first article was inadvertently ascribed to a James B. Henrick due to a typographical error.

Herrick became such a contributor to the medical literature that there were probably no more than five individual years during which he was not represented. Indeed, in 1896, his output for that year totaled 11 articles, three of which dealt with cardiovascular disease.[1]

As the maturity of his professional career evolved, it became apparent that Herrick adhered to a dual role in his practice. However, it was not until his eightieth year that he summarized this dualism with the statement that "the true physician must possess a dual personality, the scientific towards disease, the human and humane toward the patient."[4] The humanistic side manifested itself in the careful attention he paid to patients, listening to them, and stressing the personal relationship between patient and doctor despite the technological encroachments ap-pearing on the horizon during the first half of the twentieth cen-tury. And yet, the dualism of his philosophy became even more evident despite the rigors of an active practice and the demands of his academic obligations. At the age of 43, sorely cognizant of his deficiency in chemistry and realizing the increasing importance of this discipline in the clinical arena, Herrick matriculated at the University of Chicago for courses in biologic, physical, and organic chemistry. He pursued this interest in chemistry even further when he temporarily left his practice to study in Germany with the famous organic chemist, Emil Fischer.[5]

Although time has bestowed upon him the image of an astute observer of cardiovascular phenomena, Herrick's interests in medicine covered a wide range of topics. In 1910 he published an account of "peculiar, elongated and sickle-shaped red corpuscles in a case of severe anemia." The case report was based on original observations made 6 years earlier in a "Negro patient that came under his care with a sore on his ankle and evidence of previous scarring."[6] Thus, Herrick bears the distinction of being the first to describe the hematologic markers of sickle cell anemia. Incidentally, in that same year, 1910, Herrick's first article on angina pectoris also appeared.

James B. Herrick is remembered today primarily because of his lucid descriptions of angina pectoris that rival those of Heberden, and for his thrombogenic theory in the causation of myocardial infarction. In addition, he is also remembered for the implementation of the electrocardiogram in the diagnosis and surveillance of myocardial infarction.

Early in 1912, when he approached the podium to read his paper at a meeting of the Association of American Physicians, James B. Herrick did so with the conviction that he was outlining to his peers a scenario of astounding proportions. To his utter disappointment and frustration this was not to be. His paper, formulating, for the first time on American soil, the relationship between coronary thrombosis and myocardial infarction did not engender any form of enthusiasm on the part of the audience. In fact, it was critiqued by only one man, namely, Dr. Libman of New York's Mt. Sinai Hospital.[7] Herrick's disappointment was expressed by the following remarks:

FIG. 1 James Bryan Herrick, 1861–1954. Photograph from the collection of W. Bruce Fye, M.D.

'You know I've never understood it. In 1912 when I arose to read my paper at the Association I was elated for I knew I had a substantial contribution to present. I read it, and it fell flat as a pancake. No one discussed it except Emanuel Libman, and he discussed every paper read there that day. I was sunk in disapppointment.'[8]

Later on in the same year 1912, this same paper, duly revised and fine tuned, was published in the *Journal of the American Medical Association*, the official organ of the American Medical Association.[9] It is of interest to note that the Association of American Physicians was formed in 1886 as a protest against the manner in which the Section on Medicine of the American Medical Association was run and that Dr. Herrick considered the AMA a reactionary organization run by "a wire pulling, narrow-minded clique of old fogies."[10]

Undaunted by the initial cold reception, Herrick presented six years later an updated version of his calamitous presentation before the very same Association of American Physicians. This time he offered rather concrete electrocardiographic documentation in support of his conclusions. In a brilliant presentation, he announced to his peers the ability of the electrocardiogram to diagnose the presence of an acute myocardial infarction in a living patient.[11] This was a revelation to the medical profession because it was the conventional wisdom of the time that an acute myocardial infarction was incompatible with life. Much of the documentation was based on experimental work done by his colleague and friend, Fred Smith, demonstrating the serial electrocardiographic changes in the dog following ligation of the coronary arteries, and fortified by his own observations of the patients who came under his care.[12]

Although primarily a practitioner of medicine, Herrick was also fully immersed in the academic aspects of his profession. He began as an instructor of medicine at his alma mater just two years after his graduation. In 10 years he rose through the academic ranks to become a full professor, a post he held from 1900 to 1926. Starting also in 1900, he was, though briefly,

Professor of the Theory and Practice of Medicine and Professor of Materia Medica and Therapy at the old Northwestern University Women's Medical School before it became extinct in 1902.[1]

Among his many honors and awards we must mention that in 1907 the University of Michigan recognized him with the honorary degree of Master of Arts, and again in 1932 with the honorary degree of Doctor of Laws; that he was an honorary fellow of the New York Academy of Medicine; that in 1931 he delivered a lecture before the Harvey Society of that institution; and that in 1939 he received at the 90th annual meeting of the American Medical Association the second distinguished service medal awarded by the association. Apparently, the officers of the society at that time had forgotten Herrick's castigation of them as "old fogies" many years before. He also received the Gold Heart award from the American Heart Association. Finally, the Council on Clinical Cardiology of the American Heart Association paid homage to his status as a great clinician by establishing the James B. Herrick award. This is presented on an annual basis to any living physician who has advanced scientific knowledge, either basic or clinical research, that relates directly to clinical cardiology. Our own editor of this section of *Clinical Cardiology* was a recipient of this award.[10(a)]

Herrick also served as president of various medical organizations. Among them were the Chicago Pathological Society, the Chicago Society of Internal Medicine, the Institute of Medicine of Chicago, the Association of American Physicians, and the American Heart Association. As late as 1940, in his 79th year, he was president of the Congress of American Physicians and Surgeons.[1(a)]

Dr. Herrick died on March 7, 1954, at the ripe old age of 93. In a fitting tribute, Richard S. Ross, of Johns Hopkins University, eulogized him as a leader in clinical science but "unwilling to let the human values of the family doctor vanish."[10(a)]

His dualistic philosophy of life persisted to the end, a fitting testament to a life well spent.

References

1. Willius FA, Keys TE: *Cardiac Classics*, p. 815. C. V. Mosby Company, St. Louis, 1941; (a) p. 816
2. Herrick JB: Why I read Chaucer at 70. *Ann Med Hist* 1933;5:62–72
3. Hurst JW: The Canterbury Tales and cardiology. *Circulation* 1982; 65:4–6
4. Herrick JB: *Memoirs of Eighty Years*. Chicago: University of Chicago Press, 1949
5. Acierno LJ: *History of Cardiology*, p. 300. U.K. and New York: The Parthenon Group, 1994
6. Herrick JB: Peculiar elongated and sickle shaped red blood corpuscles in a case of severe anemia. *Arch Intern Med* 1910;6:517–521
7. Herrick JB: Certain clinical features of sudden obstruction of the coronary arteries. *Trans Assoc Am Phys* 1912;27:100–105
8. Means JH: *The Association of American Physicians. Its First Seventy-five Years*, p.108. New York: McGraw-Hill, 1961
9. Herrick JB: Clinical features of sudden obstruction of the coronary arteries. *J Am Med Assoc* 1912;59:2010–2015
10. Ross RS: A parlous state of storm and stress. The life and times of James B. Herrick. *Circulation* 1983;67:955–959; (a) p. 958
11. Herrick JB: Concerning thrombosis of the coronary arteries. *Trans Assoc Am Phys* 1918;33:408–415
12. Smith FM: The ligation of coronary arteries with electrocardiographic study. *Arch Intern Med* 1918;22:8–27

Harris H. Branham

J. W. HURST, M.D.

Department of Medicine, Emory University School of Medicine, Atlanta, Georgia, USA

"Branham's sign" is known by every serious student of cardiovascular medicine. The name is usually listed in association with arteriovenous fistula, but the sentence containing his name is rarely referenced. The reason for the omission is that the reference is difficult to locate. Accordingly, the reference and the entire article have been reproduced below.

Dr. Branham (Fig. 1) was born in 1862 in Fort Valley, Georgia. He died in 1938. There is very little known about him. He made his observation when he was 28 years old. He published the case report of his patient in the *International Journal of Surgery* in January 1890 (Branham, 1890). It is reproduced below.*

W.B., aged twenty-four years, on the 12th of April, 1890, accidentally shot himself with a 32 calibre pistol. The ball entered the antero-internal aspect of the left thigh about 4½ inches below Poupart's ligament, and ranged downwards, backwards and outwards, lodging under the integument of the postero-external surface of the limb, 6 inches above the knee.

Profuse haemorrhage occurred until checked by syncope; and it did not recur when reaction set in. Examination of the wound fifteen minutes after the accident, revealed nothing of note, other than an enfeebled circulation in the injured limb.

The wound was covered with an antiseptic dressing, and healed in a short time without suppuration. The temperature ranged between 99° and 101°, with a slightly quickened pulse beat for two weeks, after which time both remained normal. Retention of urine occurred during the first twenty-four hours following the injury, and was relieved by catheterization.

Three days after the accident, a slight thrill could be felt over the wound, and a decided bruit heard upon auscultating. A diagnosis of traumatic aneurism of the superficial femoral was made by myself and several prominent members of the Georgia State Medical Association, which was in session here at that time.

An operation was decided upon, but for several reasons had to be postponed for a time. The thrill and bruit increased in intensity, and a slight swelling was

FIG. 1   This hardline drawing of Dr. Harris H. Branham (1862–1938) was done by Dr. Carl Askren from a photograph supplied by Dr. Calhoun Witham.

revealed by palpation. The most mysterious phenomenon connected with the case, one which I have not been able to explain myself, or to obtain a satisfactory reason for from others, was slowing of the heart's beat, when compression of the common femoral was employed. This began to be noticeable after the wound had entirely healed. The patient was apparently well, with exception of the injured vessel, which necessitated his confinement to bed. This symptom became more marked until pressure of the artery above the wound caused the heart's beat to fall from 80 to 35 or 40 per minute, and so to remain until the pressure was relieved. Compression of the artery of the sound limb would produce no such effect. Examination of the heart showed it to be free from any valvular trouble. Attending the slowing of the heart beat was a slight dizziness and some dyspnea.

Two months after the injury was inflicted, the patient was anaesthetized, and an incision made over the seat of trouble in the line of the artery. Upon careful dissection of the vessel it was found that the artery and vein were adherent at the point where the thrill was most perceptible, and that the arterial blood was being pumped into the vein, as shown by the pulsation of that vessel below the wound, and an almost entire absence of pulsation in the distal portion of the artery. The vein was considerably distended opposite the opening, and upon pressing the artery above, appeared to be in danger of rupturing.

A silk ligature was passed around the artery above and below the varix, tied and cut short. The wound was irrigated with a weak solution of bichloride, and closed with silk sutures, a bundle of prepared horsehair being used for drainage.

In two hours after the operation the circulation in the limb was better than it had been at any time subsequent to the injury. Considerable pain was experienced for a week or two, but the wound healed by first intention, and the patient is now enabled by the use of a crutch to go where he wills.

I report this case because of its unique character, in that the varix was caused by the passage of the ball between the vein and artery; and also to elicit some information as to the correct cause of the retarded heart action.

The name of Branham did not become a household word. His case report did not stir worldwide attention. Dr. Rudolf Matas of New Orleans became aware of Branham's discovery and, being a famous vascular surgeon, was able to successfully attach Branham's name to the sign. Dr. D.C. Elkin, also a well-known vascular surgeon at Emory University, believed that the sign had been observed by Nicoladoni. Dr. Matas persisted in calling the sign "Branham's sign," and owing to his effort, the name became attached to the slowing of the heart rate when an arteriovenous fistula is obliterated.

Acknowledgment

Dr. Calhoun Witham provided the source material and stimulus for me to write this "Profile". Dr. Calhoun Witham is Professor of Medicine (Cardiology), Medical College of Georgia, Augusta, Georgia. He also furnished the photograph from which the hardline drawing by Dr. Carl Askren was constructed.

Reference

Branham HH: Aneurismal varix of the femoral artery and vein following a gunshot wound. *Intern J Surg* 3, 250 (1890)

William Townsend Porter*

W. Bruce Fye, m.d.

Cardiology Department, Marshfield Clinic, Marshfield, Wisconsin, USA

William Townsend Porter (Fig. 1) made major contributions to our understanding of the physiology of the coronary circulation. The scope and sophistication of his experiments on acute coronary occlusion, performed nearly a century ago, would surprise present-day clinicians and investigators in the field. These studies had a significant impact on clinical medicine: James Herrick's recognition of the clinical syndrome of acute myocardial infarction with survival in man can be traced, in part, to Porter's observations.

Porter was born in 1862 in Plymouth, Ohio.[1-3] The son of a physician, he entered St. Louis Medical College in 1882. His interest in physiology can be traced to Gustav Baumgarten, a native of Germany, who was Porter's professor of physiology. Baumgarten encouraged Porter to study physiology in Europe after he graduated from medical school. The young medical graduate followed the advice of his mentor and spent the summer of 1887 abroad. Upon his return to St. Louis that fall, Porter was appointed assistant professor of physiology at his alma mater. The following year he succeeded Baumgarten as professor of physiology.

In the spring of 1889, Porter traveled abroad once again, this time to visit several prestigious medical and scientific institutions in Europe. Full-time positions in physiology were available in fewer than a dozen American medical schools in this era—most physiology professors were active medical practitioners who spent a few hours a week lecturing pupils and performing routine demonstrations.[4] Porter was inspired by the scientific productivity of German full-time medical scientists, and hoped to follow their example. He wrote to Baumgarten,

> There can be no question that I can be more useful in St. Louis as a physiologist than as a practitioner. The making of a physiological institute in our community is worth living for. It is not possible to succeed in such an undertaking and to succeed in practice at the same time. To practice medicine and experimental physiology is to be an amateur in two things. I must make a choice . . . Physiology means absolute poverty for some years, comparative poverty during life. Practice means giving up the best thing in sight for the sake of

material comforts. These are the horns of the dilemma. I believe that I have chosen wisely.[5]

Porter returned to Europe in the summers of 1891 and 1892 to work with Karl Hürthle at the Physiological Institute at Breslau and Johannes Gad at the University of Berlin. The origin of Porter's classic experiments on ligation of the coronary arteries can be traced directly to Gad. Porter began these experiments in 1892 in Berlin under Gad's direction and continued them in St. Louis the following year. He published the results of this research in 1893.[6]

Porter studied the effect of coronary artery ligation on left ventricular function and on the incidence of fatal cardiac arrhythmias in dogs. Using sophisticated physiologic apparatus he had brought from Europe, he made the first accurate measurements of the effects of coronary ligation on intracardiac and intra-aortic pressures. He observed that ligation was followed almost immediately by a gradual but continuous decrease in peak intraventricular pressure. Porter reached the important conclusion that ligation of the coronary arteries was not uniformly fatal. This claim contradicted the widely held belief that sudden coronary occlusion was invariably fatal and served as a stimulus for continued investigation by Porter and others into the effects of abrupt coronary occlusion.

In a separate series of experiments performed in early 1893, Porter investigated the pathology of myocardial infarctions produced by ligating the left anterior descending coronary artery in the dog.[7] These were among the earliest pathologic and histologic descriptions of myocardial infarction, which had first been reported by Weigert in 1880.

Porter was elected assistant professor of physiology in Henry Bowditch's department at Harvard Medical School in the fall of 1893.[8] This appointment allowed Porter to devote himself exclusively to physiology, something that had not been possible in St. Louis. Moreover, several members of the Harvard faculty shared his interest in the pathophysiology of the cardiovascular system. Henry Bowditch had a sound knowledge of cardiac physiology, which dated from his studies with Carl Ludwig at the Leipzig Physiological Institute two decades earlier.[9] Porter's coronary artery experiments initiated in Germany and continued in St. Louis were resumed in Boston. In addition to ligating the coronary arteries, he occluded them by embolization with lycopodium spores and de-

---

*This paper is adapted from an essay prepared for the Preludes and Progress Series of *Circulation*.

FIG. 1 William Townsend Porter: 1862–1949. (Portrait supplied by and reproduced with the permission of Countway Medical Library, Harvard Medical School, Boston, Massachusetts.)

veloped an innovative technique for obstructing them with a solid glass rod inserted through a small incision in the innominate artery. This remarkable technique, performed before the discovery of x-rays, preceded clinical catheterization techniques by several decades.[10]

In other experiments reported in 1896, Porter inserted a hollow glass tube into a coronary artery through which he infused warm, defibrinated, oxygenated ox blood to perfuse the myocardium. Using techniques he had learned in Germany and state-of-the-art equipment, Porter studied the effects of coronary ligation on cardiac output in dogs. He noted the association of decreased cardiac output and the likelihood of fatal arrhythmias after ligation of the coronary arteries and implied that the extent of myocardial ischemia was a major factor in determining these consequences of acute coronary occlusion. He reported that several of the dogs survived for up to 2 weeks following ligation of the left anterior descending coronary artery. Postmortem examinations of these animals revealed "characteristic anemic infarcts . . . occupying the anterior part of the septum and that part of the anterior wall of the left ventricle which adjoins the interventricular furrow." From his experiments, Porter concluded that "The rapid closure of a coronary artery is followed by the death of the part which it supplies."[11]

Before 1900, using advanced techniques and sophisticated apparatus, Porter had studied many of the major physiologic and pathologic consequences of acute obstruction of the coronary arteries. He collaborated with Walter Baumgarten in research that led to the publication, in 1899, of the most comprehensive and most insightful article on myocardial infarction written by an American in the nineteenth century. Within several months of the discovery of x-rays, they performed experiments in which roentgenograms were made after the injection of radiopaque substances into the coronary arteries of hearts excised from experimental animals.

Porter and Baumgarten were also interested in the relationship of ischemia and myocardial contractility and raised issues that are currently of great clinical interest with the introduction of thrombolytic therapy for acute myocardial infarction. Baumgarten declared, "The discovery that portions of the mammalian ventricle will resume their contractions if fed with defibrinated blood enables us to determine how long an ischaemic area in the heart remains contractile."[12] With Porter he observed that loss of contractility after experimentally induced ischemia was reversible. They found that contractility persisted for a time after acute coronary occlusion, but even if it ceased, the potential for the return of contractility after reperfusion of the coronary circulation existed for several hours. They also observed that contractility was most impaired in the central zone of an infarction and least impaired at the periphery. Today, the clinical relevance of these important observations is obvious. Porter's experiments, and those of his assistants, were of significance in the slow but steady recognition of the clinical syndromes of ischemic heart disease by contemporary clinicians.[13]

In addition to his important research, Porter made significant contributions to the professionalization of physiology in the United States. He was instrumental in founding the *American Journal of Physiology* and was a strong advocate for meaningful student participation in sophisticated physiologic experiments as part of the physiology curriculum in American medical schools.[14] In an effort to make high-quality physiologic apparatus more readily available and at a reasonable cost, Porter established the Harvard Apparatus Company.

Personality and political issues led to the appointment of Walter B. Cannon as Henry Bowditch's successor as chairman of the Harvard physiology department. Although Porter was promoted to professor of comparative physiology, he was deeply disappointed by his failure to win the Harvard chair. Porter remained active in teaching and research, but his greatest accomplishments in research were already behind him. At his death in 1949, the experiments Porter preformed more than half a century earlier had been extended by many workers, and a sophisticated understanding of the relationship of coronary artery disease, angina pectoris, and acute myocardial infarction was evolving. The critical role Porter's experiments played in the growing understanding of the pathophysiology of coronary artery disease is a poignant example of the ultimate clinical significance of fundamental scientific observations.

References

1. Fye WB: Acute coronary occlusion always results in death—or does it? The observations of William T. Porter. *Circulation* 71, 4 (1985)

2. Barger AC: The meteoric rise and fall of William Townsend Porter, one of Carl J. Wiggers' "old guard." *Physiologist* 25, 407 (1982)

3. Carlson AJ: William Townsend Porter: 1862-1949. *Science* 110, 111 (1949)

4. Fye WB: *The Development of American Physiology: Scientific Medicine in the Nineteenth Century*. Johns Hopkins University Press, Baltimore (1987)

5. Porter to Baumgarten, 12 August 1891, Baumgarten papers, Archives. Washington University School of Medicine

6. Porter WT: On the results of ligation of the coronary arteries. *J Physiol* 15, 121 (1893)

7. Porter WT: Ueber die Frage eines Coordinationscentrum im Herzventrikel. *Arch Ges Physiol (Bonn)* 55, 366 (1893)

8. Fye WB: Why a physiologist? The case of Henry P. Bowditch. *Bull Hist Med* 56, 19 (1982)

9. Fye WB: Carl Ludwig and the Leipzig Physiological Institute: "A factory of new knowledge." *Circulation* 74, 920 (1986)

10. Fye WB: Coronary arteriography: It took a long time! *Circulation* 70, 781 (1984)

11. Porter WT: Further researches on the closure of the coronary arteries. *J Exp Med* 1, 46 (1896)

12. Baumgarten W: Infarction in the heart. *Am J Physiol* 2, 243 (1899)

13. Fye WB: The delayed diagnosis of myocardial infarction: It took half a century! *Circulation* 72, 262 (1985)

14. Porter WT: The teaching of physiology in medical schools. *Boston Med Surg J* 139, 647 (1898)

Scipione Riva-Rocci

G. MANCIA, M.D.

University of Milan, Department of Internal Medicine, S. Gerardo Hospital, Monza, Italy

The year 1996 marked a century since the publication of the paper by Scipione Riva-Rocci on the sphygmomanometer that bears his name in the *Gazzetta Medica di Torino*.[1] It therefore seems appropriate first to outline briefly the most important moments of the professional life of a man who made such an important contribution to medicine, and then to remember what this has meant for modern cardiovascular research and clinical practice.

Scipione Riva-Rocci (Fig. 1)[2] was born in Almese (a small town east of Turin) in 1863. He graduated in medicine at the University of Turin in 1888 and spent his first postgraduate years in the Institute of Clinica Medica directed by Professor Forlanini. He soon showed a creative and critical mind and was one of the major contributors to Forlanini's studies on artificial pneumothorax. These studies were the basis for one of the leading therapeutic procedures used for many years in the battle against tuberculosis. Probably because of the expertise he gained studying air filling of the pleural cavity at controlled pressures, he became interested in the problem of noninvasive measurements of blood pressure, which had exercised the ingenuity of many investigators for decades. His studies on this issue were finalized in two presentations at the Accademia Medica Reale di Torino and were reported in two publications in the *Gazzetta Medica di Torino*, the first, "Un nuovo sfigmomanometro" in 1896,[1] and the second in 1897.[2]

Scipione Riva-Rocci left the University of Torino in 1898 to follow Professor Forlanini who had become the Director of the Institute of Patologia Medica at the University of Pavia. In 1890, he became Head of the Division of Internal Medicine at the Varese Hospital, although he kept close contact with the academic environment of Pavia where he continued to teach pediatrics, which was then still part of internal medicine. He retired from his position in Varese in 1928 because of a neurological disease which he probably had contracted in the laboratory. He spent the last years of his life troubled by failing health problems and died in 1937 in Rapallo at the age of 74.

The importance of Riva-Rocci's work in blood pressure measurement area cannot be emphasized enough. Although several investigators had already looked into the possibility of using sphygmomanometry for the noninvasive assessment of blood pressure, his contribution was fundamental for three reasons. First, he proposed the use of the brachial rather than the radial artery to measure blood pressure, as he had a clear understanding of the advantage of a larger arterial size and of

FIG. 1 Scipione Riva-Rocci, 1863–1937. Reproduced from Ref. 3 with permission.

a more direct continuity with aortic blood pressure. Second, the pneumatic cuff he devised allowed exertion of an even circumferential pressure around the artery. This avoided the eccentric compression of the more peripheral arteries which had led previous devices to overestimate blood pressure and made their readings unreliable. Third, he assembled an instrument so simple to use and so small that it was possible to measure blood pressure outside the laboratory and at the bedside, which was unthinkable with the heavy and bulky machines formerly devised for this purpose. Perhaps no better acknowledgment can be made of Riva-Rocci's work than to point out that his sphygmomanometer has lasted across the century and, with few and marginal changes, is the same as those we use today.

Several other aspects of Riva-Rocci's work make it outstanding. One is the clear analytic description he makes, on one hand, of the sources of errors inherent in the use of sphygmomanometry and, on the other hand, of the rules for avoiding them. The guidelines for the correct use of the sphygmomanometer (and also of manometers based on an aneroid capsule), issued by the World Health Organization Committees in recent years, reflect almost entirely those mentioned in Riva-Rocci's papers.

Another aspect is Riva-Rocci's deep insight into the hemodynamic phenomena associated with and responsible for blood pressure values. Cardiac output, systemic vascular resistance, arterial compliance, side and tip pressures were by no means extraneous to his thinking, which went as far as conceiving the possibility of also measuring diastolic blood pressure, as would become possible a decade later through the contribution of Korotkow and Yablonski.

A third aspect is the discovery of the white-coat effect and blood pressure variability, which he described so accurately that his assessment is valid today, even though much more sophisticated methods of measuring blood pressure are employed.

Scipione Riva-Rocci is clearly one of the greatest scientists in the history of medicine. He combined technical expertise with the cultural background of a clinician, which allowed him a clear perception of the implications his work could have for practical medicine. He also realized the potential of number-based information compared with the more vague clinical assessment of the patient available at most medical institutions, thereby becoming a precursor of cardiovascular epidemiology. Finally, he was also a man of scientific integrity who did not feel diminished by mentioning the important contributions of his colleagues and by acknowledging how much he owed conceptually and practically to their work. It is interesting, however, that his work would have remained confined to a limited number of laboratories if it had not been for the American neurosurgeon Harvey Cushing who visited him in Pavia in 1901, took a drawing of his sphygmomanometer, used it in his surgical interventions, and thus determined its worldwide success. We may cite this as one of the first intercontinental cooperative works in science.

References

1. Riva-Rocci S: Un nuovo sfigmomanometro. *Gazz Med Torino* 1896;50–51:1001–1007
2. Riva-Rocci S: La tecnica sfigmomanometrica. *Gazz Med Torino* 1897;9–10:161–172
3. Zanchetti A, Mancia G: The centenary of blood pressure measurement: A tribute to Scipione Riva-Rocci. *J Hypertens* 1996;14(1):1

Karel Frederik Wenckebach, 1864–1940*

W. B. FYE, M.D.

Cardiology Department, Marshfield Clinic, Marshfield, Wisconsin, USA

Karel Frederik Wenckebach (Fig. 1) was born on March 24, 1864, in The Hague, The Netherlands.[1,2] He began his medical studies at the University of Utrecht in 1881, where his professors included the eminent physiologists Frans Cornelis Donders and Theodor Wilhelm Engelmann.[3] While a medical student, Wenckebach's main interest was morphology rather than clinical medicine. His inaugural dissertation was a study of the development and comparative anatomy of the bursa of Fabricius.

After Wenckebach received his medical degree, he remained at Utrecht as an assistant in the Zoological Institute. Soon, he received appointments in the department of pathology and anatomy at Utrecht and began to work with his former teacher Theodor Engelmann. At this time Engelmann was particularly interested in the heartbeat.[4] Through Engelmann, Wenckebach gained familiarity with the most sophisticated apparatus and the newest techniques for studying cardiac physiology.

Although economic circumstances made it necessary for Wenckebach to leave the university to enter practice in the small rural village of Heerlen in 1891, Wenckebach's interest in cardiac physiology persisted. As physician to the local old age home, Wenckebach frequently noted irregularities of the pulse when he was examining the elderly patients there. One case especially interested Wenckebach. While he was auscultating an elderly woman's heart, he noted that there was a periodicity to the irregularity. During prolonged auscultation, he appreciated the similarity between the irregularity of his patient's heartbeat and the abnormal rhythm that had been induced in a frog heart while he was working in Engelmann's laboratory. Specifically, Wenckebach was reminded of the experiments he had witnessed with Engelmann where electrically induced extrasystoles were followed by a compensatory pause. Now, Wenckebach recognized a similar phenomenon in a human—and it occurred spontaneously. This experience led him to seek an opportunity to investigate the phenomenon of extrasystoles in the laboratory once again.

In 1896, Wenckebach returned to Utrecht to practice medicine and serve as attending physician to Barthlomeus Gasthuis. He also resumed his scientific work in the Utrecht physiology laboratory now headed by Engelmann's succes-

sor Hendrik Zwaardemaker. During the next five years, Wenckebach published several papers on the heartbeat and pulse. One of Wenckebach's greatest contributions was to point out that extrasystoles, which had been induced in experimental animals, could occur spontaneously in man.[5]

Wenckebach was selected to fill the chair of medicine at the University of Gröningen in northeast Holland in 1900. There, he continued his clinical and experimental studies and published several papers on disorders of cardiac rhythm and conduction defects. It is important to note that these early experiments were performed without the aid of the electrocardiograph. Although Augustus D. Waller first recorded an electrocardiogram in man in 1887, this technique was not used in the laboratory or clinic until the early twentieth century when Willem Einthoven refined the string galvanometer.

At Gröningen, Wenckebach prepared the manuscript of his monograph on cardiac arrhythmias. The original edition of this classic work was published in 1903 in German and was translated into English the following year.[6] The Scottish general practitioner James Mackenzie, who had already written a pioneering monograph on arrhythmias, arranged to have Wenckebach's monograph translated. Their common interest in cardiac arrhythmias and pulse tracings drew Wenckebach into contact with Mackenzie, and the two became good friends and frequent collaborators.[7]

In the introduction to his book on arrhythmias, Wenckebach informed the reader that he sought to provide new insight into cardiac irregularity in man. His analysis was based on observations made in the laboratory and at the bedside using new physiologic instruments that made it possible to record the mechanical phenomena of the heart and circulation. Wenckebach's analysis of heart rhythms was based on his acceptance of the "myogenic" theory of heart action: that cardiac contraction originated in the heart muscle cells themselves, it was not conducted from the nervous system to the muscle cells.[8]

An important concept that Wenckebach promoted in his book was that of the extrasystole, a subject that had interested him for several years. A discovery that was of significance in Wenckebach's conceptualization of the mechanism and significance of extrasystoles was Étienne Jules Marey's description of the refractory period of heart muscle. In the course of his discussion of the scientific basis and clinical features of extrasystoles and the associated phenomenon of the compen-

*This paper is adapted from an essay prepared for the Classics of Cardiology Library, Gryphon Edition, Birmingham.

FIG. 1 Karel Frederik Wenckebach, 1864–1940. Dutch physician who made classic observations on cardiac arrhythmias. (From Ref. 1, reprinted with permission.)

satory pause, Wenckebach included important new observations. He popularized Engelmann's observation that atrial extrasystoles were not accompanied by a compensatory pause, whereas ventricular extrasystoles were.

Although physiologists were familiar with many of the principles outlined by Wenckebach in his monograph on cardiac arrhythmias, contemporary clinicians were not used to thinking of concepts like extrasystoles, compensatory pauses, and periodic dropped beats due to abnormalities of conduction. Wenckebach attempted to make it easier for physicians to understand the mechanisms he was proposing for cardiac arrhythmias by incorporating ladder diagrams that showed how the electrical impulse traveled through the heart and where it might be blocked.

While most contemporary physicians believed that irregularity of the pulse signified serious cardiac disease, Wenckebach emphasized that the presence of an irregular pulse did not necessarily imply a significant heart disorder. He thought it unwise to draw conclusions regarding the existence or type of heart disease in patients simply because extrasystoles were present, because he had discovered extrasystoles in healthy individuals as well as patients of all ages with various cardiac problems.

Numerous important observations had been made on the anatomical, pathologic, physiologic, and pharmacologic aspects of cardiac conduction between 1893 when Wilhelm His, Jr. described the auriculoventricular bundle and 1906 when Arthur Keith and Martin Flack discovered the sinoatrial node and Sunao Tawara described the auriculoventricular node. It was in this context that Wenckebach extended his

studies of cardiac conduction. For some time, he had observed cases in which he believed that the irregularity of the pulse was caused by "regular falling out of a beat." Although he acknowledged that this phenomenon could also be caused by extrasystoles, Wenckebach believed that abnormalities in conduction probably accounted for "the formation of groups of contractions." Wenckebach had showed in 1899 that conduction disorders could lead to this form of group beating.

Using sophisticated mathematical formulas in addition to detailed and precise measurement of pulse tracings, Wenckebach was able to elucidate the mechanism of these periodic dropped beats. He believed most instances were due to the failure of an atrial systole to lead to a ventricular systole: "in other words, the conduction is arrested at the auriculoventricular groove." In order to explain this phenomenon, he referred to the work of Engelmann, Gaskell, and others who had produced delay in transmission of the electrical impulse through the auriculoventricular bundle and eventual "heart-block" in experimental animals.[9]

Wenckebach believed that many factors could contribute to the development of conduction abnormalities. These included myocardial ischemia, abnormalities of the blood, toxic conditions, infectious diseases, degeneration of the cardiac muscle (particularly in the region of the auriculoventricular groove), and chronic fibrous myocarditis—we now recognize this as the result of myocardial infarction. He was also among the first to stress the increased frequency of extrasystoles and heart block in cases of digitalis intoxication.

In 1906, Wenckebach reported the periodic prolongation of the P-R interval that was occasionally accompanied by a dropped ventricular beat. He termed this phenomenon a "Luciani" period because a similar event had been described more than a quarter of a century earlier by the Italian physiologist Luigi Luciani while he was working with the pioneering physiologist Carl Ludwig in Leipzig.

As his fame as a consultant and his reputation as a scientist grew, Wenckebach grew increasingly busy. He told James Mackenzie in 1905: "I am very, very much occupied; my laboratory is now going full speed, so does my clinic and my teaching and I have taken so many tracings of high interest in these last weeks, that I have scarcely time for breathing!"[10]

From 1911 to 1914, Wenckebach held the chair of medicine at the University of Strasbourg. While there, he reported the value of quinine in the treatment of patients with atrial fibrillation. The French physician Jean Baptiste Senac had written of the value of quinine in patients who had "rebellious palpitation" in 1749. Wenckebach reported the case of a merchant with atrial fibrillation who took quinine while he was in the Dutch East Indies and noted that he had fewer palpitations while taking this medicine. This led Wenckebach to try quinine in other patients who were in atrial fibrillation. In his series of cases Wenckebach noted that while only a few patients converted to sinus rhythm, many felt better.

At the outbreak of World War I, Wenckebach accepted the chair of medicine at the University of Vienna. There, he initiated a study of cardiac function and pathology in soldiers. During the 1920s, Wenckebach's clinic in Vienna became a popular center for visiting foreign physicians who sought to enhance their understanding of cardiac arrhythmias. Moreover, many patients sought Wenckebach's services, as his reputation as a leading specialist in heart disease grew on an international scale. Wenckebach held the chair of medicine at Vienna until 1929. He died in Vienna 11 years later.

References

1. Lindeboom GA: *Karel Frederik Wenckebach (1864–1940), een korte schets van zijn leven en werken*. De Erven F. Bohn NV, Haarlem (1965)
2. Obituary: Prof. K. F. Wenckebach, M.D. *Br Med J* 1, 219 (1941)
3. Lindeboom GA: *Dutch Medical Biography: A Biographical Dictionary of Dutch Physicians and Surgeons, 1475-1975*. Editions Rodopi BV, Amsterdam (1984)
4. *Th. W. Engelmann, Professor of Physiology, Utrecht (1889–1897), Some Papers and his Bibliography with an Introduction by Dr. Frits L. Meijler and a Foreward [in Dutch] by Dr. Dirk Durrer*. Editions Rodopi BV, Amsterdam (1984)
5. Scherf D, Schott A: Historical remarks. In *Extrasystoles and Allied Arrhythmias*. William Heinemann, London (1953) 1
6. Wenckebach KF: *Arhythmia [sic] of the Heart: A Physiological and Clinical Study*. (Translated by Thomas Snowball). William Green, Edinburgh (1904)
7. Mair A: *Sir James Mackenzie, M.D., 1853–1925. General Practitioner*. Churchill Livingstone, Edinburgh (1973)
8. Fye WB: The origin of the heart beat: A tale of frogs, jellyfish, and turtles. *Circulation* 76, 493 (1987)
9. Ref. 6, p 86
10. Wenckebach to Mackenzie, 12 February 1905. Published in Ref. 7, p 172

Louis Faugères Bishop

W. Bruce Fye, M.D., M.A.

Department of Cardiology, Marshfield Clinic, Marshfield, Wisconsin, USA

Louis Faugères Bishop of New York City was the first American physician to limit his practice to cardiovascular disease and to proclaim himself a "cardiologist." He transformed himself from an internist into a cardiologist at a time when heart disease was not viewed as a distinct specialty in the United States. Born in New Brunswick, New Jersey, in 1864, Bishop graduated from Rutgers College in 1885 and the College of Physicians and Surgeons of New York four years later.[1] In 1892, after a two-year internship at St. Luke's Hospital, he entered private practice in Manhattan. The following year he was appointed assistant physician in the outpatient department of the new Vanderbilt Clinic of the College of Physicians and Surgeons. Few New York City doctors had hospital privileges when Bishop was appointed attending physician to the Colored Home and Hospital on East 65th Street in 1898.

Bishop began to limit his practice to internal medicine shortly after he completed his internship. During the first decade of the twentieth century, he progressively narrowed his focus to cardiology. Bishop's identity as a heart specialist was affirmed in 1907 when he was appointed "clinical professor of diseases of the heart and circulation" at the Fordham University School of Medicine. This part-time appointment reflected Bishop's special interest in heart disease and the fact that he had lectured and written clinical papers on the subject. There were no opportunities for cardiology training in America before the First World War. For decades, ambitious American doctors had traveled abroad to supplement the meager opportunities for clinical training available in the United States.[2] Following this custom, Bishop spent the summers of 1908 and 1910 at Bad Nauheim, Germany, a world center for the treatment of cardiac patients.[3] His experiences at Bad Nauheim shaped his views of the diagnosis and treatment of patients with heart disease.[4] During his visit to Bad Nauheim, Bishop was very impressed by doctor Isidor Groedel and his physician-sons Theo and Franz (who immigrated to America in 1933). These prominent Bad Nauheim physicians helped to popularize the saline bath and exercise approach for treating heart patients.[5]

Another experience that molded Bishop's vision of cardiology was a brief meeting (in 1908) with James Mackenzie, who was just being recognized as a leader of contemporary cardiology thought and practice.[6] From Mackenzie, Bishop gained an appreciation of how pulse tracings could be used to help correlate heart patients' symptoms with their physical findings. When he returned home, Bishop began to use a Mackenzie polygraph in his routine evaluation of heart patients.[7] Aware of the novelty of his career choice, Bishop told a friend in 1910 that he was the only doctor in New York City "*frankly* devoting himself to this line of work as a specialty"[1] (quote p. 127).

Bishop entered medical practice just as several technological innovations were transforming cardiac diagnosis: the discovery of x-rays in 1895, the invention of the electrocardiograph in 1901, and the advent of practical and reliable sphygmomanometers.[8, 9] He was among the first to use a sphygmomanometer routinely and to describe the clinical manifestations and adverse consequences of abnormal (high or low) blood pressure.[10] By 1915, Bishop had incorporated fluoroscopy and electrocardiography into his office practice.[11, 12]

Bishop was one of approximately 50 physicians present in 1922 at the organizational meeting of the American Heart Association (AHA), originally named the "National Association for the Prevention and Relief of Heart Disease."[13] An office-based private practitioner, Bishop became frustrated with the AHA's focus on public health, however. He and a few other clinical cardiologists from New York City and the Northeast created a new society in 1926. They sought a forum where practitioners could discuss diagnostic techniques and clinical problems they encountered in their practices. These clinicians named their new organization the "Sir James Mackenzie Cardiological Society" in honor of the influential British cardiologist who had died one year earlier.[14]

The Mackenzie Society was mainly a local association for physicians in the New York metropolitan region. In 1927, Bishop publicly revealed his vision for a new national cardiology society. Without mentioning the American Heart Association or the Mackenzie Society, he told an audience of physicians: "There are some signs that make me believe that very soon there will be a group of men devoted to cardiology, large enough to form their own national society where they can confer with each other on their intimate problems."[15] The following year the members of the Mackenzie Society changed the name of their organization to the New York Cardiological Society (NYCS). In 1949, the American College of Cardiology (ACC) evolved out of the NYCS because of the efforts of Bishop's friend Franz Groedel.[16]

Bishop shared his experiences and expressed his opinions about advances in the diagnosis and treatment of heart disease through lectures and publications. He published nine books and more than 100 papers on cardiovascular disease between

Fig. 1 Louis Faugère Bishop, 1864–1941. (From the collection of the author.)

1896 and 1940. When Bishop died in 1941, the specialty he helped to create was on the threshold of a period of extraordinary growth, fueled by the advent of cardiac surgery and passage (in 1948) of the National Heart Act which created the National Heart Institute. Bishop's son, Louis Jr., carried on his practice and eventually became a president of the ACC. At the beginning of the century, Louis Bishop sensed that cardiology could be a viable clinical specialty. He was correct—there are now approximately 17,000 cardiologists in the United States.

Acknowledgment

The author thanks Arthur Hollman and Paul Kligfield for Reference 14 and related material about the Mackenzie Society.

References

1. Bennett RV: *Hope in Heart Disease: The Story of Louis Faugères Bishop.* Dorrance and Co., Philadelphia (1948)
2. Bonner TN: *American Doctors and German Universities: A Chapter in International Intellectual Relations, 1870–1914.* University of Nebraska Press, Lincoln, Neb (1963)
3. Pierach CA, Wangensteen SD, Burchell HB: Spa therapy for heart disease, Bad Nauheim (circa 1900). *Am J Cardiol* 72, 336–342 (1993)
4. Bishop LF: The Nauheim methods in the management of cardiac disease. *Med Rec* 79, 531–532 (1911)
5. Groedel J, Groedel T: *Bad-Nauheim: Its Springs and Their Uses with Useful Local Information and a Guide to the Environs.* 5th ed. Carl Bindernagel, Friedberg and Bad-Nauheim (1909)
6. Mair A: *Sir James Mackenzie, M.D. 1853–1925, General Practitioner.* Churchill Livingstone, Edinburgh (1973)
7. Reichert P, Bishop LF Jr.: Sir James Mackenzie and his polygraph: The contribution of Louis Faugères Bishop, Sr. *Am J Cardiol* 24, 401–403 (1969)
8. Howell JD: Diagnostic technologies: X-rays, electrocardiograms, and CAT scans. *S Calif Law Rev* 65, 529–564 (1991)
9. Davis AB: *Medicine and its Technology: An Introduction to the History of Medical Instrumentation.* Greenwood Press, Westport, Conn. (1981)
10. Bishop LF: *Heart Disease and Blood Pressure.* 2nd ed. E. B. Treat, New York (1907)
11. Bishop LF: The fluoroscope in modern cardiology. *N Y State J Med* 23, 205–208 (1923)
12. Bishop LF: The practice of cardiology. *Ann Intern Med* 2, 352–366 (1928)
13. Moore WM: *Fighting for Life: The Story of the American Heart Association 1911–1975.* American Heart Association, Dallas (1983)
14. Minutes, Sir James Mackenzie Cardiological Society, 28 October 1926, xerox copy in possession of the author.
15. Bishop LF: History of cardiology. *N Y State J Med* 28, 140–141 (1928)
16. Schlepper M, Dack S: Franz Groedel, Bruno Kisch and the founding of the American College of Cardiology. *Am J Cardiol* 12, 577–580 (1988)

Arthur Cushny

W. BRUCE FYE, M.D., M.A.

Department of Cardiology, Marshfield Clinic, Marshfield, Wisconsin, USA

Arthur R. Cushny (Fig. 1) made several important contributions to cardiovascular pharmacology and was the first to claim that atrial fibrillation occurred in humans. He was born on March 6, 1866, in Fochabers, Morayshire, Scotland, and received his undergraduate and medical degrees from the University of Aberdeen.[1] John T. Cash, professor of materia medica at Aberdeen, stimulated Cushny's interest in experimental physiology and the new field of pharmacology.[2] After graduating from Aberdeen, Cushny traveled to Switzerland to study physiology with Hugo Kronecker at the University of Berne. Kronecker's sophisticated approach to experimental physiology reflected his experience as assistant to Carl Ludwig, the foremost physiologist of the late 19th century.[3]

After a year with Kronecker, Cushny moved to Strasbourg to work with Oswald Schmiedeberg, Europe's leading pharmacologist. Schmiedeberg's new pharmacologic institute at the University of Strasbourg was unsurpassed in the world. John Jacob Abel, America's foremost pharmacologist a century ago, claimed that Schmiedeberg "more than any other one man … turned the age-old Materia Medica and Therapeutics of our medical schools into the modern and fundamental science of Pharmacology."[4]

Cushny came to America in 1893 to replace John Abel as chair of pharmacology at the University of Michigan when Abel accepted a similar position at the new Johns Hopkins Medical School in Baltimore. Abel recruited Cushny to Michigan, having first met him in Berne in 1889. The position in Ann Arbor provided Cushny with the chance to devote himself to physiologic and pharmacologic research and teaching. He was not forced to practice medicine to support himself, as was the case with practically all medical scientists in America and Great Britain at the time.[5]

Just 27 when he arrived in America, Cushny lost no time in establishing a productive program of research at Michigan. The focus of this effort was on the physiology and pharmacology of the cardiovascular system. Cushny was especially interested in digitalis and published several papers on the subject. In a 1925 book on digitalis he reviewed its early history, summarized recent pharmacologic investigations of the drug, and presented the results of his own research.[6] The book was warmly received and today is regarded as a classic.

Cushny published an authoritative textbook of pharmacology in 1899. Abel characterized it as "the first severely critical, rigorously scientific and hence really authoritative general textbook to be written in English by an experimental pharmacologist."[4a] The book, which went through several editions, reflected Cushny's conviction that the medical sciences, and pharmacology in particular, were relevant to medical practice.

Clinical research was in its infancy at the turn of the century when Cushny emphasized the importance of correlating bedside observations with experimental findings.[7] This philosophy led Cushny to undertake a study that resulted in his recognition that atrial fibrillation occurred in humans. He noticed that arterial pulse tracings recorded from patients with extreme cardiac irregularity, then termed delirium cordis, were essentially the same as those recorded from dogs known to be in atrial fibrillation. Although Cushny was reluctant to conclude that the arrhythmias were identical, he claimed in an 1899 paper that the resemblance was "striking."[8]

By 1906, Cushny was sure that atrial fibrillation occurred in humans. That year he and Charles Edmunds published a case report in which they concluded that the dramatic variation in their patient's pulse was "due to irregular discharge of impulses [from the atrium] and not to defects in the contraction of the ventricle, which appears to respond to the impulses received."[9] Prior to this paper doctors did not realize that atrial fibrillation occurred in humans. Still, the article attracted little attention until Thomas Lewis published an electrocardiographic tracing of the arrhythmia in 1910.[10]

Another Scotsman, James Mackenzie, made important contributions to the understanding of atrial fibrillation and acknowledged Cushny's critical role in his own appreciation of the clinical significance of the arrhythmia. Mackenzie credited Cushny with first appreciating its importance and claimed that "the recognition of this condition and the symptoms associated with its presence is the most important discovery yet made in the domain of the functional pathology of the heart."[11]

In 1905, Cushny was selected to fill the new chair of pharmacology at University College, London. There he joined several men with a special interest in heart disease, including pharmacologist Sydney Ringer, physiologist Ernest Starling, and clinical scientist Thomas Lewis. Cushny contributed several papers on arrhythmias and digitalis to the early volumes of Thomas Lewis's pioneering journal *Heart* inaugurated in 1909.

In addition to his classic work on digitalis, Cushny made major contributions to two other areas. His studies on renal physiology greatly advanced understanding of the mechanism of urinary secretion. These investigations culminated in the publication, in 1917, of *The Secretion of the Urine.*[12] Cushny also clarified the role of optical isomerism as it related to the

Fig. 1   Arthur Cushny, M.D. (1866–1926).

that was, in some ways, unique … He was at home in several countries, and known and respected by every pharmacologist in the world."[15]

References

1. Geison GL: Arthur Robinson Cushny. In *Dictionary of Scientific Biography*, Vol. XV (suppl I) (Ed. Gillispie CC). Charles Scribner's Sons, New York (1978) 99–104
2. MacGillivray H: A personal biography of Arthur Robertson Cushny, 1866–1926. *Ann Rev Pharm* 8, 1–24 (1968)
3. Fye WB: Carl Ludwig and the Leipzig Physiological Institute: A factory of new knowledge. *Circulation* 74, 920–928 (1986)
4. Abel JJ: Arthur Robinson Cushny and pharmacology. *J Pharm Exp Ther* 27, 265–286 (1926); (a) p. 268
5. Fye WB: *The Development of American Physiology: Scientific Medicine in the Nineteenth Century*. The Johns Hopkins University Press, Baltimore (1987)
6. Cushny AR: *The Action and Uses in Medicine of Digitalis*. Longmans, Green & Co., London (1925)
7. Harvey AM: *Science at the Bedside: Clinical Research in American Medicine, 1905-1945* The Johns Hopkins University Press, Baltimore (1981)
8. Cushny AR: On the interpretation of pulse tracings. *J Exp Med* 4, 327–347 (1981)
9. Cushny AR, Edmunds CW: Paroxysmal irregularity of the heart and auricular fibrillation. In *Studies in Pathology* (Ed. Bulloch W). University of Aberdeen, Aberdeen, Scotland (1906) 95–110
10. Lewis T: Auricular fibrillation and its relationship to clinical irregularity of the heart. *Heart* 1, 306–372 (1910)
11. Mackenzie J: *Diseases of the Heart*. Oxford University Press, London (1913)
12. Cushny AR: *The Secretion of the Urine*. Longmans, Green & Co., London (1917)
13. Parascandola J: Arthur Cushny, optical isomerism, and the mechanism of drug action. *J Hist Biol* 8, 145–165 (1975)
14. Cushny AR: *Biological Relations of Optically Isomeric Substances*. Williams & Wilkins Co., Baltimore (1926)
15. Dale HH: Obituary. A.R. Cushny. *Br Med J* 1, 456 (1926)

mechanism of drug action.[13] His long series of experiments on the subject resulted in the publication of a monograph *Biological Relations of Optically Isomeric Substances* in 1926.[14]

    Cushny returned to his native Scotland in 1918 to hold the chair of materia medica and pharmacology at the University of Edinburgh. His career was cut short in 1926 at the age of 59 when he suffered a cerebral hemorrhage—he died the following day. Henry Dale, a leading British pharmacologist, claimed "Cushny held a place in the medical science of this country

Ludwig Aschoff

W. BRUCE FYE, M.D., M.A.

Department of Cardiology, Marshfield Clinic, Marshfield, Wisconsin, USA

Ludwig Aschoff (Fig. 1) made important contributions to cardiac pathology. He was part of an influential research tradition in pathology that Rudolf Virchow, Julius Cohnheim, and other Europeans cultivated so successfully during the second half of the nineteenth century.[1] The son of a prominent physician, Aschoff was born in Berlin, Germany, on January 10, 1866. After completing his preliminary education in Berlin, he received his medical degree from the University of Bonn in 1889. Thereafter, he studied with several prominent German medical scientists, including Robert Koch and Rudolf von Kölliker. Typical of aspiring academics in this era, Aschoff worked and studied at several universities as a young man. After spending two years at Strasburg, a decade at Göttingen, and three years at Marburg, he joined the faculty of the University of Freiburg in 1906. He spent the rest of his career at that institution.[2]

Aschoff's most productive years as an investigator were from 1904 and 1914, when, like so many other Europeans, his work was disrupted by the First World War. Two contributions from his laboratory were especially significant in the history of cardiology: the discovery of the atrioventricular node (remembered eponymically as "Aschoff's node," the "Aschoff-Tawara node," or "Tawara's node") and the description of "Aschoff bodies." These discoveries resulted from the detailed histologic studies of the heart undertaken by Sunao Tawara, a recent Japanese medical graduate who worked in Aschoff's laboratory at Marburg for three years. Between 1870 and World War I, Germany was a magnet for ambitious clinicians and medical scientists from around the world and many foreign postdoctoral students worked with Aschoff in Marburg and Freiburg.[3]

Tawara acknowledged his debt to Aschoff in the introduction to his classic 1906 monograph on the cardiac conduction system.[4] Tawara's research projects were inspired by Aschoff's interest in the pathophysiology of heart failure. The young Japanese medical scientist explained that since "the cause of heart failure was not ascribed to histological changes in ordinary muscle fibers, Professor Aschoff suggested that I perform an anatomical study of the atrioventricular bundle, to which experimental physiologists, but not anatomists, had given attention."[5]

During two years of intense research, Tawara identified a network of specialized muscular fibers that he termed "Knoten des Verbindungsbeutels." He argued that the bundle

of His originated in this specialized structure and terminated in the Purkinje network in the ventricular musculature.[6] This discovery stimulated British pathologist Arthur Keith to renew his studies of the cardiac conduction system, research that resulted in his description (with Martin Flack) of the sinus node in 1907.[7]

Like most of his contemporaries, Aschoff embraced the myogenic theory of the heartbeat. The research that led to the acceptance of this theory during the closing years of the nineteenth century focused attention on the myocardium. In this context, a few researchers became interested in the pathophysiology of heart failure. Ludolf Krehl and Ernst Romberg of the University of Leipzig were impressed by the histologic changes in the myocardium that accompanied heart failure in some protracted cases of diphtheria, scarlet fever, and typhoid fever. They speculated that interstitial inflammation (myocarditis), rather than some disorder of cardiac innervation, caused heart failure.[8] Hoping to help prove the myocarditis theory of heart failure, Aschoff asked Tawara to examine several hearts under the microscope.[5] Although their research did not support Krehl and Romberg's theory, it led to the discovery of "Aschoff bodies," the small nodules present in the myocardium in some cases of rheumatic fever.[9, 10]

For decades, pathologists and clinicians had focused on the pathology and dysfunction of the cardiac valves in patients with rheumatic fever. Although some workers including Krehl had reported that myocardial changes were sometimes present in rheumatic fever, Aschoff was the first person to describe a specific pathologic finding in this disease. He explained that the "peculiar nodules" were "regularly situated in the vicinity of the small or medium blood vessels and often show an intimate relation to the adventitia. Or there may be a lesion of all the vessel coats such as is described in arteritis nodosa. The actual nodules are very small, submiliary, and consist of the approximation of strikingly large cells with one or more abnormally large, slightly indented or polymorphous nuclei."[11]

Renewing friendships after the war, Aschoff toured the United States in 1924 and lectured in New York, Philadelphia, Pittsburgh, Chicago, Los Angeles, San Francisco, and other cities. His lecture on atherosclerosis, delivered at the Stanford Medical School, was a perceptive overview of the pathophysiology of this common condition as it was then understood. He supported the new theory, based on animal ex-

FIG. 1 Ludwig Aschoff, 1866–1942. Photograph from the private collection of the author.

periments, that atherosclerosis was due, in part, to a "general disturbance of the lipoid metabolism." Aschoff declared, "There is no doubt in my mind that the lipoid concentration of the plasma is essentially influenced by the nature of the diet determined both by the richness and character of its lipoid content." He acknowledged that "wear-and-tear" on the vascular intima resulting from mechanical stresses was another important factor that determined the location of atherosclerotic lesions and their rate of progression.[12]

A prolific author, Aschoff published several books and more than 200 papers. He was a leading teacher of his generation and a founder of the German Pathological Society.

One of Aschoff's last American pupils, F. Tremaine Billings, characterized him as "the last of the great Austro-German descriptive anatomic pathologists."[13] Aschoff died in Freiburg on June 24, 1942.

References

1. Long ER: A *History of Pathology*. New York: Dover Publications, Inc. 1965
2. Büchner F: Ludwig Aschoff zum Gedenken an seinen 100. Geburtstag. *Verhandlungen der Deutschen Gesellschaft für Pathologie* 1966;50:475–488
3. Bonner TN: *American Doctors and German Universities: A Chapter in International Intellectual Relations, 1870–1914.* Lincoln, Ne.: University of Nebraska Press, 1963
4. Tawara S: *Das Reizleitungssystem des Säugetierherzens.* Jena: Gustav Fischer, 1906
5. Selections from Tawara's Monograph, *The Conduction System of the Mammalian Heart*, p. 1. (English translation) (Tokyo, Japan). The Organizing Committee of the 5th Asian-Pacific Symposium on Cardiac Pacing and Electrophysiology and the 8th Annual Meeting of the Japanese Society of Cardiac Pacing and Electrophysiology, 1993
6. James TN: The development of ideas concerning the conduction system of the heart. *Ulster Med J* 1982;51:81–97
7. Fye WB: The origin of the heart beat: A tale of frogs, jellyfish and turtles. *Circulation* 1987;76:493–500
8. Krehl L: Diseases of the myocardium and nervous diseases of the heart. In *Diseases of the Heart* (Ed. Dock G), p. 421–763. Philadelphia: W.B. Saunders & Co., 1908
9. Aschoff L: Zur Myocarditisfrage. *Verh Dtsch Pathol Ges* 1904; 8:46–53
10. Aschoff L: Concerning the question of myocarditis, in *Cardiac Classics* (Eds. Willius FA, Keys TE), p. 733–739. St. Louis: C.V. Mosby Co., 1941
11. Bloomfield AL: *A Bibliography of Internal Medicine, Communicable Diseases*, p. 151–152. Chicago: University of Chicago Press, 1958
12. Aschoff L: Atherosclerosis. In *Lectures on Pathology*, p. 131–153 (quotes from p. 150, 151). New York: Paul B. Hoeber, Inc., 1924
13. Billings FT Jr: Ludwig Aschoff (1866-1942): Reminiscences. *Pharos* 1988;51:35–36

Sir Leonard Erskine Hill

CLYDE PARTIN, M.D.

Emory University School of Medicine, Atlanta, Georgia, USA

Sir Leonard Erskine Hill (Fig. 1) was born in Tottenham, England, on June 2,1866. Of the numerous eponyms associated with the physical findings of aortic insufficiency, it is enigmatic that Hill's sign, one of the most reliable, is the least known. Sir Leonard Hill first described his "reversed brachiopedal systolic gradient sign" in 1909[1] and further embellished it in 1911.[2] Hill had already found that in young healthy men in the horizontal position there was no difference in the arm and leg blood pressures. However, it was a colleague of Hill's, Dr. W. Holtzmann at the London Hospital Medical School, who first noted the arm-leg blood pressure differential in cases of aortic regurgitation. Holtzmann, at Dr. Hill's behest, was making some independent blood pressure measurements. He ascertained the pressures in several cases of aortic regurgitation and "found a noticeable difference between arm and leg readings in such."[1] After further study, Hill and Holtzmann confidently concluded, "a difference between arm and leg readings is most marked in all cases of aortic regurgitation, and when such patients are lying quiet in bed this difference is a diagnostic sign of aortic regurgitation."[1] Frank compared the measured popliteal-brachial systolic gradient with the degree of aortic regurgitation found at catheterization and surmised that Hill's "neglected bedside sign proved the most useful clinical index to the severity of aortic regurgitation."[3]

While Hill's sign may be his legacy, it was a bit player nestled among a multitude of more heralded contributions to physiology. These were made all the more magnificent in view of the fact that he had no formal training in physiology, limited training in the sciences and "never took his M.D., and it was not until the University of Aberdeen made him an honorary LLD in 1931 that he was strictly entitled to call himself 'doctor.'"[4]

Education was highly valued in the Hill family. Leonard Hill's great-grandfather, Thomas Wright Hill, became a schoolmaster by simply purchasing a school in Birmingham, England. With family involvement, the Hazelwood School "developed on lines which anticipated the most advanced schools of today and in the 1820s it reaped an international fame."[4] In 1833, the school was moved to Bruce Castle, England, where Leonard was born in 1866. There, Leonard conducted his first scientific experiment, "dropping the family cat out of the window to see if it would really fall on its feet."[4] Hill's father, George Birkbeck, presided over the

school until 1877, when it was sold. Birkbeck went on to literary fame, "known for his scholarly and accurate editing of Boswell's *Life of Johnson* and of other eighteenth century works."[4] Leonard aspired to be a farmer. However, Birkbeck was in the habit of telling his three sons what profession they would enter. The oldest, Maurice was allotted the Bar and subsequently knighted for his work as a judge. Norman, the middle son, became a solicitor and was made a baron for his success and "influence in directing British shipping policy in the first world war."[4] Leonard was directed toward medicine. Curiously, Birkbeck, despite his background in education, seemed unaware that medicine required any special educational background. Leonard was sent to Haileybury College and in his own words was "given an ordinary classical education and no scientific, and unfortunately, very poor mathematical training."[4] He never did practical work at the laboratory, received not even the "remotest knowledge of science and if he excelled at anything, it was, in his own judgement, as a forward on the Rugby football field."[4]

Entering medical school at University College, London, in 1885, he had a rocky start when a professor of zoology laughed at his first attempt to draw a diagram of a frog dissection. Nonetheless, he began to excel in his studies, winning the Bruce gold medal for surgery and medals in anatomy and physiology. (He sold the medals and purchased a painting with the proceeds.) He then gained experience as house surgeon at University Hospital College and qualified for his London M.B. in 1890. Shortly thereafter, he was inspired by a lecture delivered by a visiting professor from Oxford, Sir John Burdon Sanderson. So captivated was he by this presentation that he wrote a letter to his future wife delineating three avenues for his professional career. The choices were those of a traditional medical consulting practice, to set up an office in a poorer part of London, or to devote his life to medical research—"the path which saves the millions when found."[4] He chose the latter, received the Sharpey Scholarship at University College and began to study under the famous physiologist Edward Schafer, finally getting some directed experience in physiology. He completed his studies, then briefly taught at Oxford and returned to University College in 1891 as assistant professor. In 1895, he was appointed lecturer in physiology at London Hospital.

His initial research concerned the circulation, primarily the cerebral circulation. He published his first book in 1896, enti

FIG. 1 Sir Leonard Erskine Hill (1866–1952). (*Source:* Obituary notices of Fellows of the Royal Society of London 1952–53;21:8.)

tled *The Physiology and Pathology of the Cerebral Circulation*. He then directed his research toward influences on the blood pressure. In collaboration with H.L. Barnard, they developed the armlet method of blood pressure measurement. This paper, initially rejected for publication by the Royal Society since it was "only an account of an instrument,"[4] was later published in the *British Medical Journal*. This delay cost them some recognition, for in the interim in 1896 the Italian Scipione Riva-Rocci reported on his sphygmomanometer. Hill and Barnard did refine Riva-Rocci's model in 1897 by the addition of a needle pressure gauge.[5]

Following his election to the Royal Society in 1900, he began to investigate caisson disease. He felt that with slow uniform decompression the bends could be prevented. Using themselves as subjects, Hill and his partner underwent successful decompression after exposure to six atmospheres. Their method was eventually replaced by Haldane's more efficient and safer staged decompression. In 1912, Hill published his second book, *Caisson Sickness and the Physiology of Work in Compressed Air*. He followed this work with many studies on the regulation of breathing and the effects of oxygen and is credited with being the first to design a bedside tent for the administration of oxygen. The intriguing finding that inhaling oxygen allowed a vocalist to sustain a note or trill led him to comment "that music, different in form from the usual, could be written for a singer who breathed oxygen first."[4]

Leaving London Hospital in 1914 to become Director of the Department of Applied Physiology in the National Institute of Medical Research, Hill began the most influential phase of his career, investigating the health of workers and the environment. His work was interrupted in 1916 by a second bout of tuberculosis (the first infection was in 1904), again re-

quiring a lengthy convalescence. His research interests covered a wide spectrum of issues such as the health of munitions workers, the diet of the population, ozone, the ventilation of dug-outs, the medical aspects of gas warfare, and the influence of temperature, humidity and air movement on human comfort and health and work capacity.[4] To study the latter, he developed the kata thermometer, a device with which he "endeavoured to get in a single figure the cooling power of the environment from convection, radiation and evaporation."[4] He did extensive fieldwork and published prolifically in the arena of what we today might call occupational health. His magnum opus, *The Science of Ventilation and Open Air Treatment* was published in three parts in 1919, 1920, and 1923. In an effort to make his research more accessible to the public, he wrote *Health and Environment* in 1925, "emphasizing the benefit that would result to national health from closer attention to ventilation indoors, the prevention of smoke pollution out of doors and, more generally, from an open air life and proper food."[4] He resigned from the National Institute in 1930, the same year he was made a Knight. He finished out his scientific career as director of research at the St. John Clinic and Institute of Physical Medicine, examining the effects of ultraviolet and infrared rays, actually refuting some of the extravagant claims as to their therapeutic efficacy.

If there were a cloud over his career, it would have cast its shadow upon some of his early work on the cerebral circulation. Since 1783, the Monro-Kellie doctrine had held sway, stating that due to the incompressibility of the cranium, the volume of blood in the brain was always constant although blood flow may vary. In 1890, Roy and Sherrington, through experimental demonstration coupled with brilliant and perceptive reasoning, concluded, "the blood supply of the brain varies directly with the blood pressure in the systemic arteries."[6] They also reported, "the brain possesses an intrinsic mechanism by which its vascular supply can be varied locally in correspondence with local variations of functional activity."[6] Recall that Hill published his book on cerebral circulation 6 years later in 1896, which "rejected all previous work as being based on fallacious methods."[6] It was felt that Hill had failed to evaluate his own methods critically, failed to indicate clearly how he reached his conclusions, and was using techniques "peculiarly unsuited to discovering evidence for intrinsic circulatory control of the brain. . . and rebuked those who, with better methods or more sagacious reasoning, found evidence for its presence."[6] Others were even less benevolent in their denigration of Hill's studies with such remarks as, "Occasionally while tracing the development of ideas one must take into account work that retarded rather than contributed to their progress."[7] Hill's studies, "propounded with force and authority," overshadowed the work of Roy and Sherrington and dominated the field for some 20 years before being refuted in the late 1920s.

A proper description of Hill's sign is in order. His method was to place an armlet (blood pressure cuff) around the upper arm and another just below the knee. The cuff was then inflated and maximum systolic pressure was deemed to be the point of palpable disappearance of the radial pulse. For the leg, the obliteration of the stronger of the dorsalis pedis or posterior tibialis pulse was the index for the systolic pressure. These measurements taken in healthy young men while standing "differ by the hydrostatic pressure of the column of blood, which separates the points of measurements."[2] In the supine position, there is little or no difference in the values. While lying down, if the leg pressure is 20 mm of mercury greater than the arm pressure, aortic regurgitation should be suspected. Hill's sign is highly sensitive, but other conditions that are associated with decreased systemic vascular resistance such as thyrotoxicosis, sepsis, arteriovenous fistulas, beriberi, pregnancy, and strenuous muscle exertion may create false positives.[8,9] Aortic stenosis and occlusive peripheral vascular disease may cause false negative results. Patients with mild (1+) aortic insufficiency may have gradients less than 20 mm of mercury.[10] Those with atrial fibrillation and irregular R-R intervals may give erroneous results.[9] The pathophysiology of the sign is not well understood. The summation of the rebound wave returning from the periphery and the aortic pressure pulse may in part explain the phenomena since it is only noted with indirect blood pressure measurements.[9] Sapira *et al.* reported that 84% of the standard textbooks of medicine and cardiology they consulted did not mention Hill's sign.[10]

Despite the breadth of his research interests, Hill led an active and imaginative life beyond the scientific realm. He was a practitioner of his own advice regarding the benefits of fresh air and living a healthy life. Each morning at six he would bike through the Epping Forest to swim in a forest pool.[4] He was an accomplished artist and founded the Medical Art Society in 1935. After he befriended a Japanese artist, many Japanese sought him when they visited London. This resulted in three successful exhibitions of his paintings in Japan, where his painting of a turkey created quite a sensation.[11] The *Dictionary of British Artists* noted that he exhibited eight pieces of art with the International Society, three with the London Salon, two with the Royal Society of British Artists, one with the Royal Institute of Painters in Water Colours, and two with the Royal Institute of Oil Painters (Nelson M: Personal communication. Letter from Oxford, England, August 13, 1999). After the death of his eldest daughter in 1929, their grandchild came to live with them, which inspired him to write a collection of stories published as *The Monkey Moo Book*. He had previously penned and illustrated a collection of fairy tales entitled *The Scarecrow and Other Fairy Tales*. *Philosophy of a Biologist*, the last of 10 medical books he published, was a "small book of somewhat disjointed reflections on what his life and scientific studies had taught him."[4] His obituary in the *British Medical Journal* mentions this book as a "work which would not please the orthodox

Christian, nor, indeed, the upholders of any religious dogma, but he declared that modern science had brought us to the conception of a power, eternal, infinite, unknowable."[13]

Vigorous until the end, Hill died suddenly of a cerebral thrombosis at age 86 on March 30, 1952, survived by his wife and four of his five children. "Though his speech was incisive and he was inclined to be dogmatic, and in his laboratory and lecture theatre he could be rather forbidding," his friends remembered him fondly, remarking that "his broad and genial humanity soon became perceptible, illuminated by the warm affection of his colleagues and assistants."[13] In an era of high technology medicine, it is fitting then that we should pay homage to a "great-hearted gentleman who loved in equal measure science and humanity,"[13] who also described a simple bedside test for aortic regurgitation that is the only "known reliable predictor of the degree of the murmur."[9]

Acknowledgments

The author expresses special thanks to Ms. Mae Nelson for her research assistance.

References

1. Hill L: The measurement of systolic blood pressure in man. *Heart* 1909;1:73–82
2. Hill L, Rowlands RA: Systolic blood pressure, (1) in change of posture, (2) in cases of aortic regurgitation. *Heart* 1911;3:219–232
3. Frank MJ, Casanegra P, Migliori AJ, Levinson GE: The clinical evaluation of aortic regurgitation. With special reference to a neglected sign: The popliteal-brachial pressure gradient. *Arch Intern Med* 1965;116:357–365
4. Hill AB, Hill B: The life of Sir Leonard Erskine Hill FRS (1866–1952). *Proc Roy Soc Med* 1968;61:307–316
5. Acierno LJ: *The History of Cardiology.* Pearl River, N.Y.: Parthenon Publishing Group, 1994
6. Fishman AP, Richards DW (Eds.): *Circulation of the Blood: Men and Ideas.* New York: Oxford University Press, 1964
7. Clarke E, O'Malley CD: *The Human Brain and Spinal Cord: A Historical Study Illustrated by Writings from Antiquity to the Twentieth Century,* p. 788–817. Berkeley: University of California Press (1968)
8. Talley JD: The correlation of clinical findings and severity of aortic insufficiency: Hill's sign. *Heart Dis Stroke* 1993;2:468–470
9. Sapira JD: *The Art and Science of Bedside Diagnosis,* p. 311. Baltimore: Urban & Schwarzenberg, 1990
10. Sapira JD: Quincke, de Musset, Duoroziez, and Hill: Some aortic regurgitations. *South Med J* 1981;74:459–467
11. Douglas CG: Leonard Erskine Hill. *Obituary Notices: Fellows of the Royal Society of London* 1952, 3;8:431–443
12. Obituary: Sir Leonard Erskine Hill, LLD, MB, FRS. *Br Med J* 1952;1:767–768

Maude Abbott

A. R. C. DOBELL, M.D.

Division of Cardiovascular and Thoracic Surgery, McGill University, Montreal, Quebec, Canada

Maude Elizabeth Seymour Abbott (Fig.1) was born in 1869 in the town of St. Andrews about 40 miles northwest of Montreal.[1–4] Her mother died of tuberculosis when Maude was seven months old and so Maude was raised by her maternal grandmother. In fact, all nine of her grandmother's children died at a young age, eight of tuberculosis and one accidentally while on a surveying trip.

Maude was educated at home until she was 15 years old, but had already confided to her diary her strong desire to attend school with other young women, and in 1884 she entered a private school in Montreal. She won a scholarship to McGill University the following year but was obliged to delay her studies for a year because of a smallpox epidemic. She finally began her Arts course in 1886 and graduated in 1890. The university, founded in 1829, had first accepted women into the class of 1887 and, in 1890, of the five medals awarded, three went to women, Maude being awarded the medal in Classics. During her undergraduate years, she had organized a women's debating society and had been an editor of the college's only publication.

She set her mind on studying medicine at McGill which had not yet accepted a woman into the medical faculty (and would not until 1918). She petitioned the faculty, first privately and then publicly in open meetings and in the press, but the medical school authorities were adamant, regarding the introduction of women as "nothing short of a calamity." The professor of surgery announced he would resign if women were allowed into the medical school.

Fortunately, a second medical faculty (affiliated with the University of Bishop's College) opened its doors to her and she was able to undertake clinical training at The Montreal General Hospital in company with the McGill students. She graduated in 1894, winning two of the major prizes, and promptly sailed for Europe where, after visiting centers in London, Heidelberg, Berne, and Zurich, she settled in Vienna for two years, studying a range of clinical disciplines and a good deal of pathology.

She returned to Montreal in September 1897 at the age of 28, with "a sense of utter loneliness" according to the then Dean of the medical faculty. She never seriously engaged in medical practice and gratefully accepted an offer to work in the wards of the Royal Victoria Hospital.

Her first paper entitled "On So-Called Functional Heart Murmurs" was published in the *Montreal Medical Journal* in 1899. She analyzed 2,780 case records from 1895 to 1898 and found 466 systolic murmurs without other evidence of heart disease. She documented a number of functional diastolic murmurs, a controversial issue at the time. The paper was characterized by time-consuming data analysis, logical presentation, and a refreshing ability to draw conclusions from the data, qualities which Dr. Abbott demonstrated throughout her professional career.

She had been appointed to the staff of the Medical Museum and became responsible for cataloging the entire pathological collection which played an immense role in medical teaching at the turn of the century. One of the largest contributors to the museum was William Osler during his term as pathologist to The Montreal General Hospital (1876–1884). In preparation for the cataloging, Dr. Abbott visited a number of important centers in the vicinity of Washington. So it was that she visited Hopkins, met Osler, and came under his magnetic influence. He told her that she had a marvellous opportunity in the museum, that it should be the focal point of medical teaching, and suggested how she might learn more of museum organization.

Returning to Montreal, she gave herself up almost entirely to the museum collection. As she came to know the specimens intimately, medical students began dropping in and questioning her about them. Soon her demonstrations became integrated into the formal medical curriculum.

Her sixth paper reviewed the anatomy and pathophysiology of the famous Holmes heart, first described in 1824 by A. F. Holmes and well known to Osler. She arranged for excellent diagrammatic sketches to illustrate the blood circulation and interpreted the anomaly as a single left ventricle with a right ventricular outflow tract, an interpretation that would be entirely compatible with modern concepts. The preparation of this paper involved further correspondence with Osler.

In 1905, Osler invited her to write a chapter on congenital heart disease for Osler and McCrae's *Modern Medicine*. She wrote in her autobiography: "I asked him how to treat it and he said 'statistically.'" She collected the records of 412 cases with their autopsy reports and tabulated the findings in large charts prepared for her by a local newspaper. These tabulated data allowed her to draw the conclusions on symptomatology, pathophysiology, and prognosis that were salient features of her 22-page chapter published in 1908. (The work expanded steadily; the chapter for the second edition in 1915 was 125

FIG. 1 This portrait was painted in 1940 by Mrs. Eastlake, one of Dr. Abbott's close friends, on commission from the McGill medical faculty.

pages and for the third, in 1927, it was 200 pages.) The original chapter drew warm praise from Osler who commented on its "extraordinary merit" adding, "It is by far and away the very best thing ever written on the subject in English—possibly in any language."

The extension of this work comprised Maude Abbott's remarkable professional accomplishment. She organized and systematized knowledge on congenital heart disease and produced 41 papers, case reports, and book chapters on the subject including her *Atlas of Congenital Cardiac Disease*, published in 1936. She classified the anomalies pathologically and clinically, considered the embryology of the maldevelopments, and made contributions to physiologic diagnosis (using arterial and venous CO_2 tensions). Single-handedly she laid the foundation of knowledge on which Helen Taussig and

others would continue to build. During the first 40 years of this century, she was the world authority on congenital heart disease.

She was given an honorary MDCM from McGill in 1910, still eight years before women were admitted to the medical school. After her retirement, she was granted an honorary Doctor of Laws, the highest honor the university could bestow. She claimed to have been well treated and wrote of the support she had received from medical leaders in Montreal, but the fact is that she was poorly remunerated and poorly recognized as far as university rank was concerned, rising to the position of Assistant Professor in 1923. She moved to the Women's Medical College of Philadelphia in 1923, where she acted as Professor of Pathology and Bacteriology until 1925. She then returned to McGill at her former rank but never advanced beyond it.

Dr. Abbott was a workaholic. "She had the faculty of being able to entirely immerse herself in a problem with complete disregard for time or other engagements." Her museum office always seemed in confusion because she had so many projects underway simultaneously. She had tremendous enthusiasm which was passed on in all her demonstrations to medical students. She was constantly behind on publication deadlines, in part because she wanted each paper to be complete and authoritative, but mainly because she took on too much. In addition to congenital heart disease, she wrote extensively about history, medical museums, and women in medicine. In all she wrote 102 papers, an immense output for this era.

In addition to her outstanding academic qualities, which included profound curiosity and an ability to think and write clearly, Dr. Abbott loved people. She loved to travel, to entertain, to go to parties. She had a complete life as a woman married to her work.

References

1.   MacDermott HE: *Maude Abbott—A Memoir*. MacMillan Company of Canada Limited, Toronto (1941)

2.   Martin CF: Maude Abbott—an appreciation. *J Pathol Bacteriol* 41, 390 (1941)

3.   Scriver JB: Maude Abbott. In *The Clear Spirit: Twenty Canadian Women and Their Times*. (ed. MQ Innis). University of Toronto Press, Toronto (1966) pp 142–157

4.   Abbott MES: Autobiographical sketch. *McGill Med J* 28, 127 (1959)

The Scientific Contributions of Alexis Carrel

G. M. LAWRIE, M.D.

Baylor College of Medicine, The Methodist Hospital, Houston, Texas, USA

Alexis Carrel was born near Lyons, France on June 28, 1873 and died in Paris on November 5, 1944 at the age of 71. During his long and active career as a surgical scientist, Carrel made many important contributions to vascular, thoracic, and cardiac surgery, transplantation, surgery of war wounds, tissue culture, and organ preservation.

Carrel was educated in Lyons and there studied under Jabouley, who in 1886 had reported an improved technique of vascular anastomosis. Carrel subsequently spent considerable time refining these techniques. In 1902 he published in the French literature his first manuscript on vascular surgery.

In May of 1903, Carrel attended a pilgrimage to Lourdes. He believed he witnessed the spontaneous cure of terminal tuberculous peritonitis in a young woman. His accounts of this experience which reached the lay press had a damaging effect on his reputation and his surgical career, which already had lost momentum in Lyons. This controversy was a factor in his decision to leave Lyons on May 6, 1904 for Montreal.

Carrel was welcomed into the medical community in Montreal, but in July of 1904 his presentation of a paper in Montreal on vascular anastomosis lead to an invitation to move to Chicago. He began work at the Howell Physiology Laboratory of the University of Chicago with Dr. Charles Guthrie. Together with Guthrie he wrote 21 scientific papers in a 22-month period.

The initial efforts of this team were directed toward the perfection of vascular anastomotic techniques. The triangulation method of stabilizing the ends of two vessels while the anastomosis was performed was devised. Carrel continued his work on the anastomosis of veins to arteries. He was the first to recognize that veins placed in the arterial bed developed thickened walls. Carrel described his continous suturing techniques in 1905, and continued reporting on the results of various methods of preservation of arterial and venous grafts.

Following the development of vascular anastomosis to a point where it could be routinely performed with success, Carrel, with Guthrie, resumed organ transplantation. Experiments were performed with amputation and reattachment of the hind limb of a dog. As early as 1902, while in Lyons, Carrel had transplanted the kidney of a dog from the retroperitoneum to the neck. This work continued now in Chicago to evaluate the function of such transplants. Carrel observed hyperemia of these kidneys and hypersecretion of urine. He recognized the difficulty of successful transplantation from one species to another but did not appreciate the fact that homografts could undergo rejection. Further experiments in 1905 involved the thyroid and suprarenal glands, the ovaries, spleen, and intestines. Carrel performed cardiac transplantation from the chest of one dog to the neck of another dog. The heart was observed to beat strongly for about two hours before the experiment was ended.

Carrel was offered the post of Director of the newly formed Experimental Surgery Department at the Rockefeller Institute in New York under Dr. Simon Flexner and began work there in September 1906. Initially he continued his experiments on preservation of vascular heterografts and reported them in the paper "Latent Life of Arteries" published in the *Journal of Experimental Medicine* in 1910.

It was about this time that Meltzer and Auer developed the technique of endotracheal respiration at the Rockefeller Institute. Carrel became the first to apply it to experimental surgery within the thorax in 1909. In January 1910 he reported in the *Journal of the American Medical Association* that he had performed pulmonary lobectomy, partial esophagectomy with reanastomosis, replacement of segments of the superior vena cava, and experimental resections of the descending thoracic aorta. In the course of these experiments he observed for the first time the phenomenon of paraplegia secondary to descending thoracic aortic occlusion and resection. One of his dogs who had had a 17 minute occlusion awoke with paralysis of the hind limbs.

In 1910 a landmark paper was published in the *American Journal of Surgery* entitled "On the Experimental Surgery of the Thoracic Aorta and the Heart." He described experiments directed toward treatment of aneurysms of the thoracic aorta. He also discussed efforts "to find out some method for the treatment of valvular diseases and localized sclerosis of the coronarian arteries" (sic). He stated that "in certain cases of angina pectoris, when the mouth of the coronary arteries is calcified, it would be useful to establish a complementary circulation for the lower part of the arteries." He described an attempt to perform an anastomosis between the descending thoracic aorta and the left coronary artery using a cryopreserved carotid artery. The animal died and Carrel, a superb surgical technician, was impressed by the difficulty of achieving a successful coronary anastomosis on the beating heart. This led him to observe that the heart would have to be stopped to do this type of surgery and that the brain would be

FIG. 1   Alexis Carrel, in characteristic garb, at the Rockefeller Institute after World War I. From *Surgery and Life,* copyright © 1979 by Theodore I. Malinin. Reproduced by permission of Harcourt Brace Jovanovich, Inc.

the organ most severely affected by ischemic arrest. He foresaw the need for some form of support for the rest of the body, especially the brain, while the heart was arrested.

Carrel was fascinated by the fate of tissues deprived of their circulation. He observed that organs deprived of circulating blood could lose their function but still maintain viability for variable periods of time. This along with his long-standing interest in mechanisms of wound healing led him to the subject of tissue culture which Harrison, at Yale University, had first achieved in 1908. Soon a variety of tissues had undergone culture at the Rockefeller Institute. These experiments fired the imagination of the lay press at that time. His most famous culture was that from an embryonic chick heart which was maintained for 34 years.

Throughout this period at the Rockefeller Institute his work received considerable attention from the foremost leaders of the surgical profession and was widely reported in pres-

tigious journals. The award of the Nobel Prize in 1912 was acclaimed internationally. Why then did this enormous impetus to progress in cardiovascular surgery lead to so little subsequent clinical application? Michael E. DeBakey (personal communication) feels that vascular surgery did not develop at that time because of lack of safe general anesthesia, blood transfusion, and antibiotic therapy. Furthermore, arteriography was not sufficiently refined for safe clinical use.

On August 1, 1914, Carrel, still a French citizen, was called up for service in World War I. He established a research hospital at Compiegne where he developed the Carrel system of wound care and the Carrel-Dakin wound irrigating solution for the grossly infected traumatic wounds sustained in trench warfare. As the war ended, Carrel completed studies on shock and fluid and electrolyte balance and returned to New York in January of 1919 and began investigations of dietary, genetic, and environmental influences on the development of cancer. He tried to develop techniques for the preservation and culture of whole organs. Attempts at long-term organ perfusion were complicated by infection. Charles A. Lindbergh expressed interest in this problem and developed an apparatus which was able to provide sterile, long-term organ perfusion.

In 1935 Carrel published *Man, the Unknown,* a book which became an international bestseller. In it he expressed his scientific, philosophical, and mystical views. His advocacy of sexual inequality, eugenics, and the liberal use of capital punishment created controversy, but his primary goal in writing the book was to express his desire for unified scientific study of the problems of man and society.

Carrel was forced to retire from the Rockefeller Institute on his 65th birthday in 1939 despite his bitter protests. He closed his laboratory and returned to France in July 1939.

Following mobilization in France in response to the German invasion of Poland, Carrel tried unsuccessfully to establish a research laboratory. He then returned to the United States to organize a mobile field hospital for French casualties. Following the fall of France on March 22, 1940, Carrel returned to Vichy, France. He finally established the "Fondation Française pour l'Etude des Problèmes Humains," fulfilling his long held dream of a unified "Institute of Man." However, following the liberation of France in 1944, Carrel was hounded by the new government with allegations, never proven, of collaboration. Severely demoralized, he died of heart failure on November 5, 1944, his reputation still compromised and his beloved institute disbanded.

Acknowledgments

In addition to the scientific papers of Carrel, important sources for this brief review have been W. S. Edwards *Alexis Carrel: Visionary Surgeon,* published by Charles C Thomas, Springfield, Ill., in 1974, and T. I. Marlinin, *Surgery and Life: The Extraordinary Career of Alexis Carrel,* published by Harcourt Brace, Jovanovich, New York, 1979.

Sunao Tawara

Kozo Suma, M.D.

Department of Cardiovascular Surgery, Tokyo Women's Medical College, Tokyo, Japan

Sunao Tawara (Fig. 1), the son of Sadao Nakajima, was born in Ooita Prefecture, Kyushu, Japan in 1873. Early in his childhood he was adopted by Shunto Tawara, his uncle and a physician. In 1901, Tawara graduated from the Faculty of Medicine, the University of Tokyo, and in 1903 he went to Marbury to work with Ludwig Aschoff, one of Europe's young leading pathologists.

At first, Tawara was asked to define an anatomical-pathologic basis for the feebleness of the hypertrophied heart muscle, a frequent observation in patients suffering from rheumatic heart diseases, arteriosclerosis, and nephritis. He thoroughly examined more than 100 hearts systematically and concluded that only in a very small percentage of cases was any pathologic change to be found, and even if present, it was seldom extensive enough to account for the weakness of the heart observed during life. However, during this tedious work, he found a peculiar body, which is now called Aschoff's body. Aschoff[1] reported Tawara's finding at the Congress of the German Pathological Society, ascribing the finding to Tawara's work.

As the causes for weakness of the heart were not found in the heart muscle itself, attempts were made to examine the pathologic changes in the connecting bundle described by Wilhelm His, Jr. in 1893. While Tawara was unable to find any significant abnormality in the connecting bundle, he did observe that the statements hitherto made with regard to the pathway of the bundle of His were not exhaustive.

Tawara's investigation followed another direction. His study focused on elucidating the nature of the connecting pathway between the bundle and the cardiac chambers in various mammalian hearts. In 1906, Tawara's[2] results were reported in his monograph titled *Das Reizleitungssystem des Säugetierherzens: Eine anatomisch-histologische Studie über das Atrioventrikularbündel und die Purkinjeschen Fäden*. It was concluded from these results that the bundle originated from a complicated network of small muscle fibers which he named "Knoten des Verbindungsbündels"; moreover, the results demonstrated how the bundle was divided into twigs, encased in a connective tissue sheath, and how the bundle ultimately interconnected directly with a network of Purkinje fibers. Prior to this it had been thought that the connecting bundle fused with myocardial fibers of the ventricular septum, and that the Purkinje fibers had no special role in the conduction system. Tawara dubbed the entire network bundle "Reizleitungssystem (the conduction system)." This work was a strenuous endeavor, as Aschoff stated in the foreword of the monograph.

In 1906 Tawara returned to Japan and became Professor of Pathology at Kyushu University, where he continued until his retirement in 1933. The Imperial Prize of the Japan Academy was conferred on him for his work on the conduction system in 1914. He died in 1952 at Fukuoka.

FIG. 1 Sunao Tawara (1873–1952).

References

1. Aschoff L: Zur Myocarditisfrage. *Verhand Deutsch Path Gesellschaft* 8, 46 (1904)
2. Tawara S: *Das Reizleitungssystem des Säugetierherzens. Eine anatomisch-histologische Studie über das Atrioventrikularbündel und die Purkinjeschen Fäden*. Jena, Gustav Fischer (1906)

John Hay: Discoverer of Type II Atrioventricular Block

CHARLES B. UPSHAW, JR., M.D., AND MARK E. SILVERMAN, M.D.

Department of Internal Medicine, Section of Cardiology, Piedmont Hospital, and the Emory University School of Medicine, Atlanta, Georgia, USA

John Hay, a highly respected physician of Liverpool, England, (Fig. 1) and a disciple of Sir James Mackenzie, was the first to discover a form of second degree atrioventricular (AV) block that is now known as Mobitz type II AV block.[1] Hay was born near Liverpool on November 25, 1873, the eldest son of Scottish parents; his father was a notable architect.[2, 3] He studied medicine at the University College of Liverpool, a division of Victoria University of Manchester, where he was considered a brilliant student, gaining a diploma in 1895. The next year he obtained the Manchester degrees of Bachelor of Medicine and Bachelor of Surgery with honors, and in 1901 the M.D. degree from Victoria University. His postgraduate training included studies in physiology, anatomy, and pathology. From 1900 to 1903, he was house physician at the Liverpool Royal Infirmary. In 1904, he was granted an additional M.D. degree from the University of Liverpool, and the next year was appointed to the staff of the Stanley Hospital of Liverpool. He soon became a friend and admirer of James Mackenzie, the pioneer of British cardiology, who was the first to use the sphygmogram, a small kymographic pulse wave recorder of the venous and arterial pulses, to study unexplained disturbances of cardiac rhythm in a large series of patients. Hay frequently visited Mackenzie in Burnley, learning how to apply Mackenzie's technique to study his own patients and discussing the interpretation of the findings. In 1909, Hay published an excellent text of his experience, *Graphic Methods in Heart Disease*, crediting James Mackenzie with stimulating him to write the book.[4]

The Discovery of Type II Atrioventricular Block

On October 19, 1905, in the Stanley Hospital, Hay examined a 65-year-old man who had been aware of a slow pulse rate for 8 years and of dyspnea on exertion for 2½ years. At cardiac fluoroscopy that day, he noted a heart rate of 80 beats per minute (beats/min) that suddenly decreased to 40 beats/min. "During the long pauses which now occurred, the ventricles were seen to remain motionless."[1] From the simultaneous radial arterial sphygmogram and jugular phlebogram recorded the same day (Fig. 2), Hay noted that the a waves and radial arterial pulse remained stable initially, but after six

consecutive normal cycles, the seventh, ninth, and eleventh a waves were not followed by c wave or radial pulse, and the ventricular rate declined from 80 to 40 beats/min. The a–c jugular wave interval, that is, the time between the atrial wave and the carotid pulse, an indirect measurement of atrioventricular (AV) conduction time, did not change after a pause, and each pause was equal to two atrial pulse wave intervals.[1]

Hay believed that the heart block demonstrated in Figure 2 was not due to depression of conductivity since the a–c intervals remained normal. He reasoned that the pauses were due to the failure of the ventricle to respond to a stimulus. He explained:

> We are compelled, therefore, to conclude that the . . . function of excitability is the one impaired. Depression of excitability exists in the patient . . . in the musculature of the ventricle; the consequence is that a stimulus normally produced and normally conducted fails under certain conditions to obtain a response

from the ventricle.[1] Following repeated seizures and syncopal attacks, the patient died May 16, 1906. At autopsy, there was significant coronary artery disease, patchy inflammation of the central fibrous body and the a–v bundle, and fibrosis of the surrounding cardiac musculature.[5]

In 1899, Karel Frederik Wenckebach had published his classic paper, "*On the Analysis of Irregular Pulses*," in which he analyzed atrial and ventricular pulse kymographic recordings from a frog experiment and related his findings on progressive impairment of AV conduction to his patient with a similar pulse irregularity.[6, 7] Writing in 1906, Wenckebach acknowledged the earlier report that year by Hay and suggested that the pauses found in Hay's patient were the result of both abnormal AV conduction and abnormal ventricular excitability.[8] The same year Tawara discovered the AV node. Einthoven's electrocardiogram would not be introduced into England until 1909 by Thomas Lewis.[9] In 1924, Woldemar Mobitz reported the electrocardiographic correlations of the abnormal jugular wave findings as originally described by Wenckebach and Hay, and classified AV block into two types.[10] Since then, the type of second degree AV block described by Hay in 1906 has been referred to as Mobitz type II AV block.[11]

FIG. 1 John Hay, 1873–1959. Photograph supplied and used with the permission of the Royal College of Physicians, London, England.

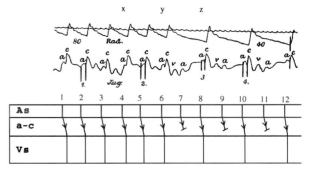

FIG. 2 Selected segment of simultaneous radial arterial sphygmogram and jugular phlebogram of the patient recorded by John Hay on October 19, 1905 with our laddergram added. The following phenomena are observed: (1) The first six consecutive atrial systoles (a waves) are followed by c waves and radial arterial pulse waves indicating atrial conduction to the ventricle. The a–c intervals are constant and normal (0.2 s); (2) the 7th, 9th, and 11th atrial systoles are not followed by c wave or radial pulse wave; (3) the pause (y–z), which includes a blocked atrial systolic wave, equals two atrial pulse wave intervals (x–y); and (4) the a–c interval does not change after a pause. These findings indicate the presence of Mobitz type II atrioventricular block. Rad = radial arterial sphygmogram; Jug = jugular phlebogram; 80 and 40 = ventricular pulse rates in beats/min; a = right atrial systolic wave; c = wave from presumed impact of the carotid pulse; v = wave resulting from filling of the right atrium while the tricuspid valve is closed; numbers 1, 2, 3, and 4 are under the a–c intervals. On the laddergram, As = atrial systole; a–c = interval between atrial systole and the carotid pulse; Vs = ventricular systole. Numbers 1 through 12 above the top line of the laddergram refer to sequential right atrial systolic waves. Arrows point in the direction of impulse propagation. Time marker running through the upstroke of the radial pulse waves has notches at 0.2 s. Paper speed by our measurement is 10 mm/s. The figure has been lightly retouched for clarity.

Later Career

Hay's subsequent career was distinguished.[2, 3, 12] He was the author of 45 medical papers, 28 dealing with various cardiovascular topics, and 17 concerning the broad field of internal medicine. Between 1906 and 1913, he served as editor of the Liverpool Medico-Chirurgical Journal. He was elected a member of the Royal College of Physicians of London in 1903, advancing to Fellow in 1915. In 1914, he started the heart clinic of The Liverpool Royal Infirmary, the first of its kind in northern England. During World War I, he served in the Royal Army Medical Corps of the British Army and was the commanding officer of the Medical section of the 57th General Hospital in France. In 1922, Hay was a founding member of the Cardiac Club, later becoming the British Cardiac Society, serving as chairman in 1928, 1932, and 1948.[2, 3, 12, 13] This group exerted a far-reaching influence on the organization and development of twentieth century British cardiology. In addition, he was an original member and later president of the Association of Physicians. In 1924, he became Professor and Chairman of the Department of Medicine of Liverpool University, influencing many junior associates by his example, and continuing in this position until his retirement in 1934 when he became an emeritus professor. His major research interests were related to cardiac pain, arrhythmias, and heart failure.[14–25] In addition, his studies on the health and welfare of children in Liverpool, and the effect of malnutrition and poverty on their education, contributed to the start of the school health service. He was a distinguished lecturer throughout his career, delivering several major addresses, including the Bradshaw lecture in 1923, the St. Cyres lecture in 1933, and the Strickland Goodall lecture in 1936. His "felicity of speech and wealth of reminiscence" brought him great demand as an after dinner speaker.[13] A modest and vigorous man of high ideals with a fine sense of humor,

known for his tolerance of all views and his skill at the art of medicine, Hay was referred to as "The Compleat Physician."[12] It was said "From him patients drew strength and courage. His serenity and confidence, and his lively personality, charm, and wit radiated an irrepressible optimism."[2]

In 1906, he married Agnes Margaret Duncan, the daughter of a physician. They had four children, three of whom became physicians, and the fourth was married to a physician. His interests were not confined to medicine. In his personal life he was proficient with water colors and oil paintings, sending his friends distinctively painted Christmas cards and becoming president of the Liverpool Sketching Club. He loved music and played the violin and viola with skill. His hobbies included hiking, camping, golf, photography, beekeeping, and gardening. Though he lost his vision late in life and was a widower for his last 12 years, his cheerful disposition and courage were never diminished, and he enjoyed a wide circle of devoted friends and colleagues. He died April 21, 1959, at the age of 85, leaving behind a legacy as a beloved early leader of British cardiology, an influential member in the medical and cultural life in Liverpool for 50 years, and a man who deserves to be remembered as the first to describe a new form of AV block.

Acknowledgments

The authors desire to record their thanks to Arthur Hollman, M.D. of London, England, for review of the manuscript and helpful suggestions; and to Nicole Lannon and Terri Barnard, librarians at the Sauls Memorial Library of Piedmont Hospital, for assistance during the study.

References

1. Hay J: Bradycardia and cardiac arrhythmia produced by depression of certain of the functions of the heart. *Lancet* 1906;1:139–143
2. Hay J: Obituary. *Br Med J* 1959;1:1190–1191
3. Hay J: Obituary. *Lancet* 1959;1:946–947
4. Hay J: *Graphic Methods in Heart Disease.* London: Oxford Medical Publications (1909)
5. Hay J, Moore SA: Stokes-Adams disease and cardiac arrhythmia. *Lancet* 1906;2:1271–1276
6. Upshaw CB Jr, Silverman ME: The Wenckebach phenomenon: A salute and comment on the centennial of its original description. *Ann Intern Med* 1999;130:58–63
7. Cooper J, Marriott HJL: To Wenckebach: A centenary salute. *Tex Heart Inst J* 1999;26:8–11
8. Wenckebach KF: Beiträge zur Kenntnis der menschlichen Herztätigkeit. (Contributions to the knowledge of human cardiac activity). *Arch Anat Physiol* 1906;297–354 (in German)
9. Hollman A: *Sir Thomas Lewis: Pioneer Cardiologist and Clinical Scientist.* London: Springer-Verlag (1997)
10. Mobitz W: Über die unvollständige Störung der Erregungsüberleitung zwischen Vorhof und Kammer des menschlichen Herzens. (Concerning partial block of conduction between the atria and ventricles of the human heart). *Z Ges Exp Med* 1924;41:180–237 (in German)
11. Langendorf R, Pick A: Atrioventricular block, type II (Mobitz)—its nature and clinical significance. *Circulation* 1968;38:819–821
12. Bramwell C: John Hay and the founders of the Cardiac Club. *Br Heart J* 1965;27:849–855
13. Campbell M: The British Cardiac Society and the Cardiac Club: 1922–1961. *Br Heart J* 1962;24:673–695
14. Hay J: Remarks on the pathology of bradycardia. *Br Med J* 1905;2:1034–1036
15. Hay J: Paroxysmal tachycardia. *Edinburgh Med J* 1907;n.s. 21:40–58
16. Hay J: The heart in pulmonary tuberculosis. *Liverpool Med-Chir J* 1910;30:86–95
17. Hay J: The senile heart: Prognosis and treatment. *Liverpool Med-Chir J* 1911;31:46–53
18. Hay J: The treatment of cardiac arrhythmia. *Liverpool Med-Chir J* 1911;31:329–345
19. Hay J: The vagaries of the auricles. *Liverpool Med-Chir J* 1913;33:88–100
20. Hay J: Two cases of auricular flutter. *Lancet* 1913;2:986–989
21. Hay J: Acute cardiac failure: Treatment by intravenous injection of strophanthin. *Liverpool Med-Chir J* 1916;36:71–81
22. Hay J: Prognosis in patients presenting rapid action of the heart. *Lancet* 1921;2:750–753
23. Hay J: A British Medical Association Lecture on cardiac failure. *Br Med J* 1922;2:899–902
24. Hay J: The Bradshaw Lecture on angina pectoris: Some points in prognosis. *Br Med J* 1923;2:957–962
25. Hay J: The action of quinidine in the treatment of heart disease. Based on the experiences of certain members of the Cardiac Club. *Lancet* 1924;2:543–545

Nicolai S. Korotkoff (1874–1920)

J. D. Cantwell, m.d.

Preventive Medicine Center, Georgia Baptist Medical Center, Atlanta, Georgia, USA

It is easy to see why Nicolai S. Korotkoff (Fig. 1) has been largely ignored by medical historians despite his important discovery of recording blood pressure by listening to sounds over the brachial artery. [1–5] Little is known about his life. Valiant searches by Segall that began nearly 50 years ago produced little information.[5] The first published photo of him appeared in 1970. A biographical manuscript written by Korotkoff's physician son (now deceased) is said to exist, but remains elusive. Perhaps it will surface in this new era of glasnost. At present, we do possess at least a few pieces of the profile puzzle.

Early Years

The son of a merchant, Korotkoff was born at 40 Milenskaya (now Sovetskaya) St. in Kursk on either February 13 or 26, 1874. His early schooling and college work was in Kursk, where he received good marks in behavior and diligence but not in "divine law." After one semester of medical school at the University of Kharkov he transferred to Moscow University and graduated with distinction in 1898.

From 1898 to 1900 he worked without pay as an intern in the surgical clinic of Professor A. A. Bobrov at Moscow University. He supported himself by moonlighting in a private practice. In 1900, he translated (from German) Albert's book on *Surgical Diagnosis*. That same year, his academic work was interrupted by his service with the Russian forces in the Far East during China's Boxer Rebellion. Korotkoff travelled via the Trans-Siberian railway, eventually to Vladivostok. He worked with the Nurses Order of the Red Cross, under Dr. Aleksinskii (who had also previously worked under Dr. Bobrov in Moscow). Korotkoff received the Order of Saint Anna for his "outstanding zealous labours in helping the sick and wounded soldiers."[4] After visiting Japan, Singapore, and Ceylon, he returned to Moscow via the Red Sea, Suez Canal, the Mediterranean, and the Black Seas.

February 1901 until 1903 found Korotkoff again at work in Bobrov's clinic as "chief ordinator." Then, in 1903, he accepted a position in the Military Medical Academy of St. Petersburg (now Leningrad), helping to organize the surgical clinic.

In 1904, after Japan's declaration of war against Russia in an attempt to increase Japanese power in eastern Asia, Korotkoff returned to active military duty, stationed in the Manchurian city of Harbin. He was initially designated as surgeon in charge of the second St. George's Unit and then surgeon in the First General Hospital. He organized the care of those wounded in the war and had a special interest in arterial injuries, noting that the results of vascular surgery depended upon the adequacy of the collateral arteries.

A number of the vascular war wounds resulted in arteriovenous (AV) fistulae formation. Korotkoff recalled the teachings of the surgeon, Nikolai I. Pirogoff (1810–1881), who had described murmurs over vascular tumors and AV fistulae during auscultation. These murmurs disappeared if one occluded the arterial flow to the affected limb by using the Riva-Rocci blood pressure cuff. In experiments with the cuff and the stethoscope, Korotkoff discovered sounds with each heartbeat when the pressure was gradually lowered below the palpated systolic level. The sounds disappeared at levels corresponding to presumed diastolic blood pressure levels (based on published data from cannulated arteries in animals).

When the Russo-Japanese War ended in 1905, Korotkoff returned to St. Petersburg, and began work on his doctoral thesis ("Experiments for Determining the Strength of Arterial Collaterals"), based primarily on 41 vascular cases he had treated during the war. In preparing the dissertation topic, he wrote:[5]

> The unpredictable results of operations are unpleasant for the physician and even more unpleasant for the patient. Therefore it would be advisable to seek the basic signs by which it is possible to know whether after the ligation of the artery the patient would be alive or dead.

Discovery of Korotkoff Sounds

In a staff meeting in St. Petersburg on November 8, 1905, Korotkoff gave a brief report on the measurement of blood pressure by using both the cuff and the stethoscope. The published account took up less than a page of the *Reports of the Imperial Military Medical Academy*:[2]

> The cuff of Riva-Rocci is placed on the middle third of the upper arm; the pressure within the cuff is quickly raised up to complete cessation of circulation below the

FIG. 1 Nicolai S. Korotkoff, M.D. (1874–1920) discovered a method of recording blood pressure. (From Ref. 6. Reproduced with permission from the publisher and author).

cuff. Then, letting the mercury of the manometer fall one listens to the artery just below the cuff with a children's stethoscope. At first no sounds are heard. With the falling of the mercury in the manometer down to a certain height, the first short tones appear; their appearance indicates the passage of part of the pulse wave under the cuff. It follows that the manometric figure at which the first tone appears corresponds to the maximal pressure. With the further fall of the mercury in the manometer, one hears the systolic compression murmurs, which pass again into tones (second). Finally, all sounds disappear. The time of the cessation of sounds indicates the free passage of the pulse-wave; in other words, at the moment of the disappearance of the sounds the minimal blood pressure within the artery predominates over the pressure in the cuff. It follows that the manometric figures at this time correspond to the minimal blood pressure.

The report stimulated lively discussion and critical comments. Some contended that the sounds Korotkoff described were transmitted from the heart rather than originating from the area of arterial compression. A month later Korotkoff pre-

sented additional data, based on animal experimental studies, to support his original contentions. An early supporter of the new method was Professor M. V. Yanovski, who stated that "Korotkoff has noticed and intelligently utilized a phenomenon which many observers have overlooked.[4] If not for Yanovski's follow-up studies to verify the accuracy of this new technique, it "might have languished in obscurity,"[4] for Korotkoff apparently said and wrote very little about it subsequently.

Korotkoff's doctoral thesis was published in 1910. The 150-page manuscript contains brief mention of the new technique of blood pressure measurement:[3]

I pointed out in my reports of November 8th and December 13th, 1905 that immediately below a fully compressed artery (with complete occlusion of the lumen), no sounds are heard. As soon as the first drops of blood escape from under the compressed site, we hear a clapping sound, very distinctly."

Later Years

While working on his thesis, in 1908–1909, Korotkoff also served as a research physician in the Siberian mining district of Vitimsko-Olekminsky.

After getting his doctorate in 1910, he served as surgeon to the workers in the gold mines in Lensk, where he witnessed some atrocities of the tsarist regime, including the murder of unarmed striking miners. Accordingly, he was supportive of the October 1917 revolution. He returned to St. Petersburg and, during World War I, was surgeon to the Charitable House for Disabled Soldiers in Tsarskoeselo.

Little information is available about his life thereafter, except that he became physician-in-chief of the Metchnikov Hospital in Leningrad. Korotkoff died of tuberculosis in 1920, at age 46. His wife, a nurse, survived for an additional 20 years, dying during the siege of Leningrad. A son, Sergei N. Korotkoff, followed in his father's medical footsteps and practiced sportsmedicine and rehabilitation in Leningrad. In correspondence with Dr. H. N. Segall, the son wrote about how his father came to discover the blood pressure sounds:[5]

The surgeon (N. S. Korotkoff) noticed during the examination of the aneurysm the change of the swelling when the main artery was pressed central (proximal) from the aneurysm. He had to investigate the pulse in the peripheral vessel, to auscultate the aneurysm murmurs, and the change of their intensity and pattern.

Sergei Korotkoff died around 1978. His wife may still be living in Riga. No trace has been found of his biographical manuscript which, if found, would shed additional light on his father's life. Perhaps it could tell us more about his personal traits beyond the fact that he was tall, slender, studious, modest, and rigidly self-disciplined (once foolishly jumping into a freezing river to test his determination). It also might help explain why he turned away from academic life after such a promising beginning. Was he turned off by the initial criticism or skepticism of his auscultation discovery, or did he prefer to focus his talents elsewhere, such as surgical alleviation of suffering among both soldiers and miners? The final chapter has yet to be written.

Summary

As a 31-year-old surgeon, with special interest in vascular disease, Korotkoff discovered the sounds of the blood pressure in 1905 while working on his doctoral thesis. After publication of the latter, he wrote nothing further about his remarkable discovery. As is often the case, others picked up on it, however, and the technique of measuring arterial blood pressure changed from one of touch to one of hearing. If not for Nicolai Korotkoff's astute observation, writes Dock, "we might still be unable to estimate diastolic pressure without trauma or use of complex devices."[1]

References

1. Dock W: Korotkoff's sounds. *N Engl J Med* 302, 1264 (1980)

2. Korotkoff NC: To the question of methods of determining the blood pressure (from the clinic of Professor CP Federoff). *Reports of the Imperial Military Academy* 11, 365 (1905)

3. Korotkoff NC: Experiments for determining the efficiency of arterial collaterals (Doctoral dissertation). PP Soykine's Press, St. Petersburg (1910)

4. Lacher M, O'Brien E: In search of Korotkoff. *Br Med J* 285, 1796 (1982)

5. Segall HN: Quest for Korotkoff (editorial review). *J Hypert* 3, 317 (1985)

6. Segall HN: N.C. Korotkoff—1874–1920—pioneer vascular surgeon. *Am Heart J* 91, 816 (1976)

Albion Walter Hewlett

W. BRUCE FYE, M.D., M.A.

Cardiology Department, Marshfield Clinic, Marshfield, and University of Wisconsin, Madison, Wisconsin, USA

An American pioneer of clinical investigation of the cardiovascular system, Albion Walter Hewlett made important contributions to our understanding of cardiac arrhythmias and their pharmacological treatment.[1–3] He also was one of the first in the United States to encourage the study of pathologic physiology. Hewlett was born on November 27, 1874, in Petaluma, California, near San Francisco. He attended the San Francisco Boys' High School and the University of California at Berkeley. After two years at the Cooper Medical College in San Francisco, Hewlett transferred to Johns Hopkins in 1895. There, medical students had unprecedented opportunities for participation in research, and the Hopkins environment stimulated Hewlett's lifelong interest in clinical investigation.[4] Following his graduation from Hopkins in 1900, he spent two years as an intern and resident on the medical service of New York Hospital.

An experience that shaped Hewlett's career was 18 months of study in Tübingen with Ludolf Krehl, a leading German medical scientist and physician. Krehl was one of the first to encourage the study of abnormal function—pathologic physiology—in contrast to abnormal structure—pathologic anatomy—which was emphasized by Rudolph Virchow and his pupils.[5] Upon his return from Germany in 1903, Hewlett was appointed assistant in the medical clinic at Cooper Medical College. Reflecting his enthusiasm for the new field of pathologic physiology, he translated Krehl's pioneering monograph on the subject.[6] Krehl sought to integrate clinical skills learned at the bedside with newer scientific approaches to the diagnosis of disease that relied on laboratory techniques. Hewlett embraced his mentor's philosophy and methods and succeeded in encouraging their adoption in the United States.

The main focus of Hewlett's research throughout his career was the cardiovascular system. This interest owed much to Krehl's influence on Hewlett. The German physician had published several papers on the heart and circulation as well as an important monograph on diseases of the myocardium. In 1906, Hewlett published a paper on paroxysmal tachycardia, the first of many he wrote on cardiac arrhythmias. In this era before the introduction of the electrocardiograph, James Mackenzie of Great Britain and Karel Wenckebach of Germany had made important observations on cardiac arrhythmias using a sphygmograph, and Hewlett used this approach in his early investigations of disorders of the heartbeat.[7] During the five years Hewlett was on the Cooper faculty, he published several other papers on cardiac arrhythmias and conduction disturbances as well as a study of the effect of amyl nitrite on blood pressure.

It was already apparent that Hewlett was destined to be a leader in the new area of internal medicine, where the scientific physician trained in the laboratory as well as at the bedside would be the academic model and, according to the reformers of medical education, the most successful practitioner. Despite his youth, Hewlett's scientific contributions were acknowledged by other Americans who also hoped to encourage clinical research and scientific medicine. In 1907, he was invited to join eight other physicians in establishing a society for clinical investigators. Samuel J. Meltzer, a New York physician with a strong background in experimental physiology, sought to form an organization for young physicians interested in research. Thus, Hewlett became a founding member of the American Society for the Advancement of Clinical Investigation, a group known familiarly as the "Young Turks."[8]

Hewlett left California to assume the chair of medicine at the University of Michigan in 1908. Of Hewlett's selection, his colleague Frank Wilson recalled, "Hewlett was one of the first men appointed to the chair of medicine in an important medical school whose chief interest lay in the functional rather than in the structural aspects of disease—in pathologic physiology rather than in pathologic anatomy. He had a strong instinct for research, and his reputation rested more upon his attainments in the field of productive scholarship than upon his renown as a clinician."[9]

Hewlett sought to make medical practice more scientific by teaching physiological principles and techniques which could be employed in the evaluation of patients. When electrocardiography was introduced into clinical practice in Europe, he immediately realized the potential of this technique. In 1909, he published a review on the new instrument—four years before he would acquire one for the University of Michigan. Hewlett was excited about the potential value of the electrocardiograph and observed, rather prophetically, "It is not improbable that the electrocardiogram will ultimately permit of an early diagnosis of disease of the heart muscle."[10, 11]

Hewlett's sophistication in, and contributions to, cardiovascular physiology led British cardiologist Thomas Lewis to select him as one of six co-editors of his new journal *Heart* when it first appeared in 1909. Three years later at Michigan,

Fɪɢ. 1   Albion Walter Hewlett (1874–1925). (Reproduced from the Roy Craig Barlow Collection, Bentley Historical Library, University Michigan, with permission of the Bentley Historical Library.)

Stanford. A condition that greatly interested Hewlett was atrial fibrillation, and he was among the first to study the value of quinidine in this arrhythmia. Hewlett also undertook a series of pioneering investigations into the pathophysiology of dyspnea.

Active in professional and scientific societies throughout his career, Hewlett was elected president of the American Society for Clinical Investigation in 1925. He became ill during the summer of 1925 and died later that year of a malignant brain tumor. His premature death at the age of 50 took from the United States a pioneer of clinical investigation who catalyzed the shift from pathological to physiological thinking among the nation's medical teachers and practitioners. Stanford's president, Ray Wilbur, characterized Hewlett as "a trained physiologist who developed into a skilled practitioner ... Throughout his life he was orderly, thorough, scientific and analytical and he became a brilliant teacher and man of medicine ... His heart was in the clinic and the laboratory. To bring them closer together was his ideal."[12]

References

1. Harvey AM: Albion Walter Hewlett: Pioneer clinical physiologist. *Johns Hopkins Med J* 1979;144:202–214
2. Erlanger J: A physiologist reminisces. *Ann Rev Physiol* 1964;26: 1–14
3. Additional biographical information was kindly provided by William Hewlett, Palo Alto, California
4. Chesney AM: *The Johns Hopkins Hospital and the Johns Hopkins School of Medicine, A Chronicle. Volume II, 1893–1905*. Baltimore: The Johns Hopkins Press, 1958
5. Maulitz RC: Pathologists, clinicians, and the role of pathophysiology. In: *Physiology in the American Context, 1850–1940* (Ed. Geison GL), p. 209–235. Bethesda: American Physiological Society, 1987
6. Krehl L: *The Principles of Clinical Pathology, A Text-Book for Students and Physicians*, trans. Albion Walter Hewlett, p.3. Philadelphia: J.B. Lippincott, 1905
7. Hewlett AW: Doubling of the cardiac rhythm and its relation to paroxysmal tachycardia. *J Am Med Assoc* 1906;46:941–944
8. Brainard AR: History of the American Society for Clinical Investigation, 1909–1959. *Clin Invest* 1959;38:1784–1864
9. Wilson F: The Department of Internal Medicine. I. The period ending in 1908. In *The University of Michigan: An Encyclopedic Survey* (Ed. Shaw W), v. 2, p. 833–842. Ann Arbor: University of Michigan, 1951
11. Hewlett AW: The clinical value of the electrocardiogram. *Physician and Surgeon* 1909;31:322–323
12. Fye WB: The delayed diagnosis of myocardial infarction: It took half a century! *Circulation* 1985;72:262–271
13. Wilbur RL: Appreciation. In A.W. Hewlett, *Pathological Physiology of Internal Diseases, Functional Pathology. Revised in Memoriam by his Colleagues*. New York: D. Appleton & Co., 1928

Hewlett offered a course in the clinical physiology of the circulation. This popular elective dealt with cardiac arrhythmias, the consequences of valvular lesions, the causes and consequences of hypertension, pulmonary edema, and other subjects of clinical relevance. During his tenure at Michigan, Hewlett published several papers on cardiac arrhythmias and disorders of cardiac conduction as well as papers that reflected his interest in the peripheral circulation and endocrine disorders.

In 1916, Hewlett returned to California to assume the chair of medicine at Stanford Medical School, which had recently taken over Cooper Medical College where his medical career had begun two decades earlier. He continued his investigations of cardiac arrhythmias and conduction disturbances at

Louis Gallavardin

LOUIS J. ACIERNO, M.D.

Department of Health Professions and Physical Therapy, Cardiopulmonary Sciences Program, University of Central Florida, College of Health and Public Affairs, Orlando, Florida, USA

Master without rival, a great French doctor, and one of the premier European cardiologists of our time; these were the opening remarks describing Louis Gallavardin (Fig. 1) when he was eulogized by R. Froment in the December 1969 issue of the *Lyon Medical Journal*.[1] Another peer, A. Gonin, also eulogized him, and together they painted a portrait of a man who was not only an outstanding cardiologist but an aesthete and humanist as well.[2] Endowed with a keen intelligence and a prodigious memory, Gallavardin was the consummate clinical diagnostician in an era when bedside physical diagnosis was "de rigeur." And yet, despite all the honors bestowed upon him and amid the grateful acknowledgments of his contributions by his peers, Gallavardin still maintained throughout his life a modest appraisal of himself, fortifying even more the respect and admiration of all those who came into contact with him. His modesty was such that he even refused to accept the special chair at the Lyonnaise hospital created especially in his honor.

Louis Gallavardin was born on August 20, 1875 in Lyon, the son of a homeopathic physician. He was soon attracted to medicine, pursuing all his educational requirements in his hometown, and finally receiving his doctorate in medicine from the University of Lyon.

He began his professional career in an auspicious capacity, having been appointed *hospitalier* at the Lyons hospital at the tender age of 26. A legislative statute limited the duration of this post so that by the time he was 56 he had to relinquish it. Despite this, he continued to practice and conduct research on numerous clinical matters, amplifying a previously established and well-earned reputation as an outstanding clinical cardiologist.[2] Among his earliest contributions was the classic paper he published in 1900 on fatty degeneration of the heart.[3] His observations and conclusions helped remove the fatty degeneration seen at postmortem from the pathologic changes produced by coronary occlusion and myocardial infarction. By so doing, he was able to put the morbid anatomy of the "fatty heart" into its own proper niche. Gallavardin recognized two forms of fatty degeneration based on their detection with the naked eye or with a microscope. The microscopic variety was a diffuse process while the grossly visible type was characterized by an endothelial speckling with islets of fatty changes.[3]

Gallavardin first impressed his Parisian colleagues with his clinical acumen when, from his home base in Lyon, he published an essay on diastolic hypertension in 1910. Twelve years later he expanded the essay into a treatise. His French peers were further impressed with a series of articles on myocardial infarction and angina pectoris. He was one of the first to describe the multiple forms of myocardial infarction. Based on clinical observations alone, he antedated Attilio Maseri's description of vasospasm as one of the causes of myocardial infarction. Spasm of the coronary arteries as one of the precipitating mechanisms of angina has been widely accepted since Henri Houchard suggested in 1889 that paroxysmal spontaneous episodes of angina could be explained on the basis of spasm superimposed on fixed obstructive lesions.[10] Gallavardin first described his opinions on this matter in 1925.[11] Several of his cases, however, had normal coronary arteries at autopsy. The anginal episodes appeared on effort as well as at rest. He compared the transient episodes of spasm with those seen in Raynaud's disease since so many seemed to be induced by cold and emotions.

Gallavardin was one of the earliest commentators on the origin of the midsystolic click, so characteristic of mitral valve prolapse. Although in error when he ascribed the auscultatory phenomenon to pleuropericardial lesions, Gallavardin's prestige at this time was such as to override all other opinions.[4, 5] Three decades were to elapse before the true nature of the midsystolic click was delineated by Reid.[6]

There is a painless equivalent variant of angina pectoris called blockpnea. It was first described by Gallavardin as early as 1924.[7] It is characterized by an increasingly agonizing feeling of blocked respiration or suffocation while walking. The patient must stop and stand still to ward off what he feels is impending death. The respiratory blockade and apnea gradually subside so that the patient can resume walking. There is no wheezing or cough with resumption of thoracic movements.[7] The word "blockpnea" was coined by Gallavardin in 1933.[9]

Turning his attention to the valvulopathies, Gallavardin described in detail the clinical picture of pulmonary edema secondary to mitral stenosis. It is now called the "reticissimente de Gallavardin." Gallavardin also left his mark on a special element of aortic stenosis during auscultation which is

FIG. 1 Louis Gallavardin, 1875–1957. Courtesy of New York Academy of Medicine.

now eponymously referred to as Gallavardin's phenomenon. It concerns the transformation of the harsh murmur of aortic valvular stenosis as heard at the aortic area to one with a high-pitched musical quality when elicited at the apex. Gallavardin described it in 1925.[12] He attributed the change to a preferential transmission of the musical components of the murmur from its location at the aortic area through solid tissue to the apex. More recently, Burch instead attributed the mechanism to the development of an associated papillary muscle dysfunction with resultant mitral regurgitation.[13]

These then are the highlights of an outstanding physician. However, his eulogy described him as an aesthete and a universal humanist. These should not merely be accepted as empty words spouted at a funeral, but a true appraisal of Galla-vardin's personality. Aside from his accomplishments at the bedside, he was respected as an individual whose tastes were highly refined, rivaling those of any sophisticated Parisian gentleman. Moreover, he had an impressive knowledge of art objects and rare books. Gonin recounts how, even in his twilight years, when one's memory begins to fade, Gallavardin was still able to point out from memory and with precision the subtle nuances of an El Greco painting at the Seville museum.[2]

Louis Gallavardin died at the age of 82, having lived an intellectually and emotionally satisfying life. He is deservedly well respected and admired for his brilliant career in clinical cardiology. However, he should also be inscribed in the annals of medicine as the personification of William Osler's "compleat physician."

References

1. Froment R: Louis Gallavardin (1875–1957). *Lyon Med* (Dec.) 1969;118–119
2. Gonin A: *Presse Med* 1958;66, no. 42:967–970
3. Gallavardin L: *La Degénerscence Grasseuse du Myocarde.* Paris: J. B. Ballière, 1990
4. Gallavardin, L: Pseudodoublement du duxième bruit de coeur simulant le redoublement mitral par bruit extracardiaque télésystolique surajouté. *Lyon Med* 1915;121:409
5. Gallavardin L: Nouvelle observation avec autopsie d'un pseudo-doublement du bruit de coeur simulant le redoublement mitral. *Prat Med Fr* 1932;13:19–21
6. Reid JVO: Mid-systolic clicks. *S Afr Med J* 1961;35:353–355
7. Chevalier H: Blockpnea on effort in emphysematous patients: A diagnostic challenge. *Amer Heart J* 1961;73, no. 5:579–581
8. Gallavardin L: Y a-t-il un equivalent non-douloureux de l'angine de poitrine d'effort? *Lyon Med* 1924;2:345–349
9. Gallavardin L: Les syndromes d'effort dans les affections cardioaortiques. *J méd Lyon* 1933;14:539–542
10. Huchard H: *Traité des Maladies du Coeur et des Vaisseaux, Arteriosclérose, Aortities, Cardiopathies Arterielles, Angines de Poitrine.* Paris: 466, 1889
11. Gallavardin L: *Les Angines de Poitrine.* Paris, 1925
12. Gallavardin L, Ravault P: Le souffle de rétrécissement aortique peut changer de timbre et devenir musical dans sa propagation apexienne. *J méd Lyon* 1925;135:523–529
13. Giles DT, Martinez EC, Burch GE: Gallavardin phenomenon in aortic stenosis. A possible mechanism. *Arch Intern Med* 1974;134:747–749

Jean George Bachmann

J. WILLIS HURST, M.D.

Department of Medicine (Cardiology), Emory University School of Medicine, Atlanta, Georgia, USA

Jean George Bachmann (Fig. 1), Professor and Chairman, Department of Physiology at Emory University School of Medicine from 1910 to 1947, was among the first to do medical research in Atlanta, Georgia. He reported his observations on *"The Inter-auricular Time Interval"* in the *American Journal of Physiology* in 1916. French and Austrian scientists duplicated his work and named the newly discovered connection "Bachmann's Bundle." The summary of his article is reproduced below with permission from the publisher. (See reference with asterisk).

The time of onset of right and left auricular contraction, contrary to general belief, is not synchronous.

The excitatory wave originating in the sino-auricular node reaches the right auricle sooner than the left; hence the right auricle contracts an appreciable time before the left. The time difference averages 0.013 second.

The most important path of conduction between the two auricles appears to be the inter-auricular band. This special importance is demonstrated by the effects of crushing the band, the conduction being delayed 3 to 4.6 times the normal average.

The inter-auricular band has not the same importance relatively to the auricles that is possessed by the auriculo-ventricular band, as crushing does not cause a complete block. Its importance lies in the circumstance that its fibers form the most direct inter-auricular path and that the rate of conduction is highest along this path.

Jean George Bachmann was born in Mulhouse, Alsace Province, on July 18, 1877, and was raised in Nancy, France. He ran away from home at the age of 20 and joined the merchant marines. He made more than 20 trips across the Pacific Ocean in this service. Obviously, he was an individualist.

He finally settled in the United States in 1902 and taught French and German in the Pennsylvania school system before entering Jefferson Medical College in Philadelphia. He graduated from Jefferson at the top of his class in 1907. He won the Phillips Award as the "most worthy student." Following graduation he became an intern and then resident physiologist and demonstrator at Jefferson Medical School. He moved to Atlanta in 1910 to become Professor and Chairman of the Department of Physiology in the Atlanta College of Physicians and Surgeons. This was five years before that school became a part of Emory University School of Medicine. He continued in that role until 1947.

He wrote many articles on the electrophysiology of the heart (see References). The textbook he coauthored with A. Richard Bliss, Jr., *Essentials of Physiology and Pharmacodynamics,* was widely used in the United States and Europe. He was a medical officer in the U.S. Army during 1917–1918.

Dr. Bachmann had many interests. He was an accomplished artist. He painted landscapes and drew scientific charts and illustrations. He was a linguist, speaking French, German, Spanish, and perfect English. He was a culinary expert. He revealed that his ambition during his youth was to manage a grand hotel. He occasionally worked as a chef in French, Swiss, British, and Irish hotels. He actually paid his tuition at Jefferson Medical College by working in Eastern hotels. Dinner in his home was, by reputation, a great delight.

FIG. 1 Jean George Bachmann, 1877–1959.

He was witty and possessed a great sense of humor. He was called "George" by his students and a "great physiologist" by medical men on two continents. He owned a copy of Dr. Paul White's first book *Heart Disease* (1931); I have it with his (Bachmann's) signature on the first page.

He retired from Emory in 1947 at the age of 70, but continued to practice medicine for a number of years. He died at Emory University Hospital in November 1959.

Acknowledgments

The sources of the material used to write this article are: The Emory Alumnus, November 1947; *The Atlanta Journal*, September 11, 1947; and Dr. Byron Hoffman of Atlanta, Georgia, who was Dr. Bachmann's friend and associate.

References

Bachmann G: The interpretation of the venous pulse. *Am J Med Sci* November (1908)

Bachmann G: Complete auriculoventricular dissociation without syncopal or epileptiform attacks. *Am J Med Sci* 137, 342 (1909)

Bachmann G: Sphygmographic study of a case of complete heart-block. *Arch Intern Med* 4, 238 (1909)

Bachmann G: The measurement of arterial pressure in man. *New York Med J* 93, 212 (1911)

Bachmann G: A physiologico-pathological study of a case of heart-block occurring in a dog as a result of natural causes. *J Exper Med* XVI, 1 (1912)

Bachmann G: An automatic spinning device for the Harvard kymograph. *JAMA* LXVI, 188 (1916)

*Bachmann G: The inter-auricular time interval. *Am J Physiol* XLI, 309 (1916)

Bachmann G: The distribution of the vagus nerves to the sino-auricular junction of the mammalian heart. *Am J Physiol* LXIII, 2 (1923)

Bachmann G: *A Course in Experimental Physiology*. Privately printed by author with illustrations by author (1924), 94

Bachmann G: The significance of splitting of the P-wave in the electrocardiogram. *Ann Intern Med* 9, 14 (1941)

Bachmann G, Haldi J: A comparative study of the respiratory quotient following the ingestion of glucose and of fructose as affected by the lactic acid and carbon dioxide changes in the blood. *J Nutri* 2, 13 (1937)

Bachmann G, Haldi J, Ensor C, Wynn W: The effects of the ingestion of glucose and of fructose on the rate or excretion of urine and various constituents. *Am J Physiol* 1, 12 (1938)

Bachmann G, Haldi J, Ensor C, Wynn W: Creatinuria in man following the oral administration of caffeine. *Am J Physiol* 1, 138 (1942)

Bachmann G, Haldi J, Wynn W, Ensor C: The respiratory quotient and carbohydate metabolism following the ingestion of glucose and of fructose, as affected by exercise taken immediately and 30 minutes after ingestion. *Am J Physiol* 3, 120 (1937)

Bachmann G, Haldi J, Wynn W, Ensor C: The effects produced by decreasing the calcium and phosphorus intake on calcium and phosphorus absorption and disposition and on various body constituents of the rat. *J Nutri* 2, 20 (1940)

Haldi J, Bachmann G, Ensor C, Wynn W: Muscular efficiency in relation to the taking of food and to the height of the respiratory quotient immediately before exercise. *Am J Physiol* 1, 12 (1938)

Haldi J, Bachmann G, Ensor C, Wynn W: Comparative effects of a high glucose and a high fructose diet on activity, body weight and various constituents of the liver and body of the albino rat exercising at will. *J Nutri* 3, 16 (1938)

Haldi J, Bachmann G, Ensor C, Wynn W: The effects on respiratory metabolism produced by equal amounts of caffeine in the form of coffee, tea, and the pure alkaloid. *J Nutri* 4, 27 (1944)

Carey F. Coombs

W. Bruce Fye, m.d., m.a.

Department of Cardiology, Marshfield Clinic, Marshfield, Wisconsin, USA

British physician Carey Coombs is remembered eponymically for his description of the diastolic murmur of early rheumatic mitral valvulitis. He published, in 1924, the first comprehensive monograph in English on rheumatic heart disease.[1] The son of a physician, Carey Franklin Coombs was born in 1879 at Castle Cary in Frome in Southwest England.[2] After preliminary education at University College, Bristol, he entered St. Mary's Hospital Medical School in London in 1897. A superior student, Coombs graduated four years later with prizes in medicine, surgery, and pathology. After three years of additional training at St. Mary's, he returned to Bristol to enter medical practice.

Coombs's interest in rheumatic fever and its cardiac manifestations was stimulated by John Poynton. With Alexander Paine, Poynton had shown that rheumatic fever was the result of infection with streptococcus. Poynton and Payne's masterful summary of their extensive investigations on rheumatic fever, *Researches on Rheumatism*, appeared in 1913.[3] Poynton contributed an introduction to Coombs's book on rheumatic heart disease in which he observed,

> Dr. Coombs' volume has been published at a most opportune time, for in this country and abroad there has been a rapidly growing realization of the gravity of rheumatic diseases... Acute rheumatism is the most important and frequent cause of organic heart disease, and if it can be prevented or minimized there will result the most promising advance in cardiac therapeutics of modern times.[4]

Coombs identified four principal manifestations of rheumatic infection: carditis, polyarthritis, chorea, and subcutaneous nodules. Of 100 consecutive cases of rheumatic fever he saw in the outpatient department of Bristol General Hospital, 59 had signs of carditis at the time of the first visit. Many of the remaining patients subsequently developed evidence of cardiac disease. Based on his experience Coombs concluded that at least three quarters of all patients with rheumatic fever would eventually show evidence of cardiac involvement.

During one year, Coombs saw in his outpatient clinic 196 patients suffering "from the various phenomena of rheumatic infection." More than half of these patients were younger than sixteen. He was deeply concerned that the rheumatic fever often went unrecognized. On the basis of his experience and his familiarity with the literature, Coombs concluded, "The foundations of a number of these [rheumatic] lesions must have been laid during childhood, in attacks of cardiac infection that escaped attention, or were at all events forgotten by the time adult life had been reached."[1a]

Like many of his contemporaries, Coombs was interested in the pathological correlation of clinical problems. Careful histological studies led Coombs to conclude that the involved tissues—whether heart valves, myocardium, pericardium, synovial membranes, periarticular tissues, subcutaneous tissues, or the meninges—shared common histological features. His book on rheumatic heart disease included a number of photomicrographs of subcutaneous nodules, cardiac valve tissues, and joint tissues to illustrate this point.

The etiology of rheumatic infection had long been a subject of speculation and controversy. Coombs concluded without equivocation that "the specific cause of rheumatic carditis was [the] diplostreptococcus of Poynton and Paine."[1a] He pointed out that in various patients with rheumatic fever this organism had been cultured from pericardial fluid, cardiac valve vegetations, cerebrospinal fluid, subcutaneous nodules, and joint fluids.

In summarizing the etiology of rheumatic heart disease Coombs observed that it

> ...begins as a rule during childhood or adolescence; that it is a little commoner in girls than in boys; and that there is a family predisposition to it. It appears to be a disease of the temperate climates and of urban communities. Probably it bears some relation to the level of the subsoil water, and almost certainly to poverty; but the precise nature of these relations is unknown. The infective agent is a streptococcus, probably a modification of that type commonly found in the human alimentary tract. In a number of instances it enters the circulation through the tonsils.

He cautioned, "Very much remains to be proved, however."[1c]

On the basis of his clinical experience and knowledge of the literature, Coombs recognized that patients with a history of previous rheumatic infection were predisposed to infective endocarditis. He confirmed earlier reports that the left-sided valves were more likely to be affected in cases of rheumatic fever. In 97 cases of rheumatic endocarditis that underwent autopsy at the Bristol General Hospital, abnormalities of the valves were found with the following frequency: mitral 97, aortic 57, tricuspid 35, and pulmonary 2. Coombs believed that virtually all cases of mitral stenosis in the adult were the result of prior rheumatic fever. He claimed, "It is as correct to regard mitral stenosis as being always rheumatic as it is to speak of tabes dorsalis as being without exception due to syphilis."[1d]

Auscultation, introduced by the French physician René Laennec a century earlier, was quite advanced by the time Coombs's monograph appeared. Coombs detailed the characteristic auscultatory findings of mitral stenosis and presented a sophisticated interpretation of their origin and significance. He is remembered eponymically for his description of the Carey Coombs murmur: a mid-diastolic rumble often heard in children during their first attack of rheumatic carditis. He emphasized that this murmur did not result from true stenosis of the mitral valve. Rather, Coombs believed that inflammation of the mitral valve tissue led to irregularities and stiffening of the leaflets that produced the turbulence that resulted in a murmur. Typically, the Carey Coombs murmur diminishes and disappears as the acute inflammation of the heart resolves and cardiac size decreases.

One chapter of Coombs's classic monograph on rheumatic heart disease was devoted to diagnosis. He emphasized that in cases where chorea, arthritic pains, and subcutaneous nodes were present with symptoms of an active infection there was no excuse for missing the signs and symptoms of cardiac involvement that would suggest acute rheumatic carditis. Persistence on the part of the physician was required, however: "Everyone with an elementary knowledge of medicine will realize the need for examination of the heart in such a case. When the first examination is negative, the child must be examined again and again, even after all obvious signs of active infection have disappeared."[1e]

One of the most interesting chapters of his book dealt with the course and prognosis of rheumatic heart disease. Following World War I, Coombs tracked down patients with rheumatic heart disease that he had followed at the Bristol General Hospital prior to the war. His follow-up study of nearly 700 cases revealed excessive mortality in the first year following the diagnosis of rheumatic carditis. Both the short and intermediate term mortality due to rheumatic heart disease were striking in his series.

With respect to treatment Coombs emphasized bed rest and the use of sodium salicylate. Thomas Maclagan first introduced salicylates for the treatment of acute rheumatism half a center earlier.[5] Coombs also discussed the merits of tonsillectomy in preventing further streptococcal infections. It is interesting that he anticipated the debate about this procedure that persists to this day. Coombs claimed that the removal of the tonsils "should do something to prevent further escape of streptococci into the circulation." But he cautioned, "On the other hand, even if the tonsils are removed, streptococci remain in the pharynx, and perhaps they will get through into the body the more readily if there is less lymphoid tissue to guard the pharyngeal portal."[1f]

Coombs's monograph appeared the year after Eliot Cutler and Samuel Levine of Boston published their report of a surgical approach to the treatment of mitral stenosis.[6] Regarding their case report Coombs observed: "It is not long enough since this was done to judge of results, but it is safe to say that the operation can never become a general method of treatment for a disease of which the mitral lesion is only one feature—to say nothing of the technical difficulties attending surgical approach to such a structure."[1g]

Coombs would not live to see the impact that the introduction of antibiotics would have on the incidence and consequences of streptococcal infections or the dramatic developments that would permit the safe repair or replacement of valves damaged by rheumatic fever. He died in 1932 shortly after becoming the first director of the University Center of Cardiac Research in Bristol. His efforts at describing the pathophysiology and natural history of rheumatic heart disease are notable.

References

1. Coombs CF: *Rheumatic Heart Disease.* Bristol, England: John Wright & Sons Ltd., 1924 (a) 8; (b) 9; (c) 27; (d) 65; (e) 233; (t) 325; (g) 330
2. Brown GH: *Lives of the Fellows of the Royal College of Physicians of London 1826–1925*, Royal College of Physicians, London (1955) 55 1–552
3. Poynton Fl, Paine A: *Researches on Rheumatism.* London: J. & A. Churchill, 1913
4. Poynton FJ: Introduction. In Coombs CF. *Rheumatic Heart Disease*, p. xiii–xiv. Bristol, England: John Wright & Sons Ltd., 1924
5. Maclagan T: The treatment of acute rheumatic by salicylates. *Lancet* 1876;1:342
6. Cutler EC, Levine SA: Cardiotomy and valvulotomy for mitral stenosis. Experimental observations and clinical notes concerning an operated case with recovery. *Boston Med Surg J* 1923;188:1023

Thomas Lewis: Physiologist, Cardiologist, and Clinical Scientist*

A. HOLLMAN, M.D., F.R.C.P., F.L.S.

Cardiac Department, University College Hospital, London, England

Thomas Lewis was born in Cardiff, Wales on December 26, 1881. His father was a mining engineer who was awarded the Albert Medal for bravery during rescue work in underground mines. His mother was also an outstanding person in many respects—for example, she taught herself Latin in order to be able to teach it to her sons.

Lewis' formal attendance at school lasted only two years. For the most part, he was educated almost entirely by his mother and a hired tutor. We are told that he took little heed of book learning, rather spending every spare moment in the countryside fishing and watching the animals and birds. He was in his teens when he decided to become a doctor, for the curious reason that conjuring fascinated him, and the family doctor being an expert conjurer, young Tom linked sleight of hand with medical practice! So it was not the impress of a formal education that led to him being singled out of the first year class in physiology at Cardiff University by Professor Swale Vincent with the request to undertake research onto the proteins of unstriated muscle. This was the subject of his first scientific paper. Another written in the same year, when Lewis was 19, on the menolymph glands became the standard work on this subject. Altogether a group of six papers gained him the degree of Doctor of Science at the age of 23.

By now he had moved to University College Hospital in London for his clinical training and while still an undergraduate he became a member of the Physiological Society, where he met the outstanding physiologists of the day, including Starling, Bayliss, Cushny, and also Henry Dale who wrote, "Lewis had a precocious maturity of outlook and scientific judgment which made it natural for him to associate with older men, and although I was six years his senior it never occurred to me to think of Lewis as other than a contemporary in scientific development and experience."

After qualifying he became house surgeon to Sir Victor Horsley, the pioneer neurosurgeon. Horsley was a Royal Medalist of the Royal Society and it was he, together with Vincent and Starling who first interested Lewis in research. When he was house physician to Sir Thomas Barlow he did his first clinical research work on the arterial pulse and blood pressure. He had written seven papers in less than a year. The most important one was on the dicrotic pulse, when he first

used that combination of clinical observation and laboratory experiment which he later said—in defining clinical science—was the integration that is of so much consequence to the vitality of medical research. He showed that a dicrotic pulse occurred with venesection and he constructed a model of the circulation with an artificial pulse to demonstrate that rapid output from the periphery was a chief factor in dicrotism. He must have learned much from E. H. Starling—the arch experimenter as his European friends called him—because a 42-page paper written at the age of 26 shows him to be a first class animal physiologist. He recorded simultaneously the arterial pericardial and tracheal pressures in 44 closed chest cats and showed how they varied in relation to each other. He also pointed out that the term *pulsus paradoxus* was a misnomer.

In 1908 Lewis first met James Mackenzie, the authority on cardiac arrhythmias, and in spite of the 28-year age gap they soon became close friends. Mackenzie urged Lewis to become editor of a new journal for cardiovascular papers to be called *Heart* and he took up this post at the age of 28. *Heart* ran to 16 volumes between 1909 and 1933. It contained, all told, 340 papers and Lewis was author or part author of one quarter of these with an average length of 25 pages each.

He became a diligent and exacting editor and few papers went to press unaltered. Many were beneficially rewritten and putative contributors might have the ordeal of a long and sometimes painful interview with the editor. At this time Mackenzie's influence led Lewis to take up the study of cardiac irregularities. Fortunately, unlike Mackenzie he did not have to rely solely on the polygraph.

In 1902 the string galvanometer had been invented by Willem Einthoven of Leyden, The Netherlands. It was a massive piece of apparatus occupying two rooms and taking five assistants to work it. Lewis visited Leyden and became good friends with Einthoven who was 20 years his senior. A compact modification of the Einthoven apparatus was made by Engelmann in Munich and by 1910 it was installed in such institutions as the Heart Station at The Johns Hopkins Hospital where Llelewys Barker described the simplicity of its operation. The recording was on continuous paper, which was excellent for arrhythmia analysis. However, Lewis' first paper with an electrocardiogram was in fact an Einthoven recording, and had a simultaneous arterial tracing. It was recorded for him by Waller, and puzzlingly, was recorded from right to

*The Fitzpatrick Lecture of the Royal College of Physicians of London delivered on October 6, 1982.

FIG. 1   Sir Thomas Lewis (1881–1945)

left with the electrocardiogram not only upside down but also labelled with the polygraph notation. At the same time he first published his famous ladder diagram as a convenient summary of the spread of the excitation wave through the heart. Lewis then obtained his own Engelmann apparatus and a flood of papers on arrhythmias, 21 between 1909 and 1910 alone, came from his laboratory at University College Hospital. They included a study of arrhythmias produced by coronary artery ligation in dogs. Soon afterwards atria fibrillation was defined in a totally comprehensive paper of 66 pages in a 1910 issue of *Heart*. Previously Mackenzie had concluded that this arrhythmia, the irregular irregularity of the heart, was due to nodal rhythm so there was a need to show what nodal rhythm really was. Fortunately for Lewis a patient came along at about the same time with paroxysmal nodal tachycardia, and using the polygraph to record the giant "a" waves he was able to delineate this rhythm and to show its difference from atrial fibrillation.

His monograph on the *Mechanism of the Heartbeat*, published in 1911, was a truly magnificent summary on the state of the art at that time. It covered all aspects of normal and abnormal heartbeat with a full description of all the methods then in use. No wonder the Americans described it as the "bible of electrocardiography."

The title page significantly contained the phrase "Clinical Pathology." Clinical pathology "by which I mean" he said "the study of disease in the living man" was a phrase he was fond of using and 22 years later when he founded the school of clinical science, he was sad that this title had become "too narrowly fenced off by test tube and needle" to allow its continued use by him in that context.

In 1912 Lewis proudly welcomed Einthoven to a special meeting of the clinical section of the Royal Society of Medicine at University College Hospital Medical School. Considering that his work on arrhythmias had been proceeding for only four years, it is breathtaking to read his remark made at that meeting that "the chapter of the analysis of cardiac irregularities is fast closing." This, however, was in fact the truth, so intensive had his application been to the problems in hand. He had distilled his now great knowledge of the heartbeat into two small books for the practitioner. He did so from a sense of duty to the profession and not from any desire for personal gain. He had more than enough research work on hand to wish to dissipate his energies in other directions. The books were *Clinical Disorders of the Heartbeat* and *Clinical Electrocardiography*. This latter work contains a remarkable example of the resolution of the physiological right ventricular hypertrophy in a normal baby between birth and three months of age.

In 1911 the Cambridge modification of the Einthoven apparatus was received. This was superbly designed by W. Duddell, F.R.S. and beautifully machined by the Cambridge Instrument Company. He requested that a twin string galvanometer be created and he even used two of these side by side, thus permitting four-channel recording. The Cambridge Company also made, at his request, a carbon microphone which allowed recording of excellent quality phonocardiograms.

However, after the initial work on this subject he undertook no further research work on cardiac murmurs. Similarly, Lewis made very good photographic tracings of the jugular venous pulse, but again he pursued this research no further—although he notably did so on the venous pressure.

Lewis next turned his attention to extensive animal work designed to map out the way in which the heart is electrically activated, and in 1914 published the first of three papers on the "Excitatory Process in the Dog's Heart." All three papers appeared in the *Proceedings of the Royal Society*. They represented totally original and technically very demanding scientific work of the highest order. He was fortunate in this work to be assisted by B. A. Robinson of the Cambridge Instrument Company. This work involved using six or more electrodes simultaneously, and it is doubtful whether Lewis could have accomplished this without Robinson's important technical advice. Later in his life, Robinson said "during the three years I was associated with him so closely I never once saw him ruffled. Always quietly speaking he had infinite patience, even when things went wrong."

A second edition of the *Mechanism of the Heartbeat* appeared in 1920, and the preface, for the first time, contained the famous statement on his scientific credo. "Inexact method of observation, as I believe, is one flaw in clinical pathology today. Prematurity of conclusion is another, and in part follows from the first; but in chief part an unusual craving and veneration for hypothesis, which besets the mind of most medical men is responsible. The purity of a science is to be judged by the paucity of its recorded hypothesis. Hypothesis has its right place, it forms a working basis; but it is an acknowledged makeshift, and, as a final expression of opinion, an open confession of failure, or, at the best, of purpose unaccomplished. Hypothesis is the heart which no man of right purpose wears willingly upon his sleeve. He who vaunts his lady love, ere yet she is won, is apt to display himself as frivolous or his lady a wanton." The third edition in 1925 was a truly magnificent volume. It had 529 pages, 400 figures, and 1003 references—with exact page references—and the whole, including the illustrations, done by Lewis alone.

Willem Einthoven was awarded the Nobel prize in 1924 and in his Nobel lecture he paid tribute to the work of Lewis. He also showed an ECG tracing of bundle-branch block and labeled it incorrectly. Lewis had also made the same error in confusing right and left bundle-branch block, and the work which led him to this erroneous conclusion was, in fact, his meticulously carried out experimental work on the dog heart. This involved the difficult operation of dividing the right and the left branches of the bundle of His in the intact beating heart, and also stimulating the epicardium of the two ventricles to produce appropriate extrasystoles. In the preface to the *Mechanism of the Heartbeat* he said that the work "emphasised the value of reproducing in animal experiments changes witnessed during the progress of human maladies." This approach however sadly failed him in this particular case. George Fahr pointed out the proper nomenclature in 1920, but it was not until 1945 that Lewis printed the correct version.

We must now go back to 1914 and the First World War. The problem of "soldiers' heart" was first noted during the retreat from Mons in 1914 when soldiers, sleepless and exhausted, complained of chest pains, palpitation, dyspnea and giddiness on effort, incidentally providing a powerful hint as to its etiology. The problem worsened and action was urgently required. Early in 1916 the former Mount Vernon Hospital was selected for the investigation and treatment of soldiers' heart. Lewis was placed in charge and he displayed his capacity for organization and unrelenting hard work to the full; only one year later he had written a report based on the study of 1000 soldiers and dealing especially with 600 who displayed "a particular group of symptoms which may be termed for purposes of convenience the effort syndrome." He highlighted the value of a system of graded exercises in judging unfitness and happily these turned out also to be the "chief therapeutic measure." By the end of the war 70,000 sick soldiers had been classified as cardiovascular, but at least one man had been retained in service for every man discharged. The Army was grateful and Lewis was knighted in 1921. During the war, in 1916, the Medical Research Committee gave him a full-time appointment—the first full-time appointment ever in this country in clinical research.

Toward the end of the war the Heart Hospital moved to Colchester and with the pace of work slackening Lewis was able to indulge in his hobby of birdwatching and bird photography. This led to his only nonmedical paper which was on the breeding habits of the lesser tern, in *British Birds*, and which was superbly illustrated by his own photographs.

He then returned to University College Hospital to his newly funded MRC Department and, between 1920 and 1924, with Drury and others he wrote 33 papers on arrhythmia and formulated the famous concept of the circus movement in atrial flutter which is still valid today. Lewis then switched abruptly to a series of researches on the vascular reactions of the skin. Krogh of Copenhagen had just been awarded the Nobel prize for his work on the capillaries, but Lewis' work was much more than just an extension of Krogh's. He showed the similarity of the skin's reaction to different forms of injury, delineated the triple response of red line, flare, and wheal, and formed the hypothesis of a histamine-like compound, H substance, being liberated into the skin in response to injury. He also showed how skin reacted to ischemia with his experiments on reactive hyperemia. In 1927, after 21 published papers, he summarized his work in the monograph *Blood Vessels of the Human Skin and Their Responses*—just as he had brought together his arrhythmia work in the *Mechanism of the Heart Beat*. But this time there was a difference, because he said that "the chief motive which led me to write this book was a desire to stimulate a wider study and teaching of physiology." In 1928, at the time of the tercentenary of William Harvey's immortal work *De motu cordis*, Lewis and Henry Dale made an imaginative recreation on cine film of Harvey's experiments.

In the same year George Pickering, then a student at Thomas' Hospital, came on a ward round of Lewis' at University College Hospital. "It was," he said, "sparsely attended as his ward rounds always were. The patient he chose to teach on that day had chronic bronchitis, a theme that few teachers select. He gave a masterly survey of the genesis of physical signs in the chest, I had never heard clinical teaching like it." Pickering joined the Department of Clinical Research soon after qualifying and ascribing his early work he wrote "using no apparatus more complicated than a blood pressure cuff and a tuning fork, the phenomena of pain from exercising muscles and of nerve paralysis during ischaemia were analysed and the results described in two papers of thirty pages each in a period of six months. This was Lewis at his best, the Lewis who gave up electrocardiography because he grew tired of answering the kind of questions the instrument could answer and who longed for the adventures suggested by his own mind."

It is only fair to add that there is another view, from William Evans, then at the London Hospital. He said "Lewis turned his back on Electrocardiography and in so doing he absconded from exploration of the important and expansive field provided by affections of the myocardium. He would have gleaned even a richer harvest in the field of cardiology had he not deviated from the path he had traversed so profitably." Another worker in the department in Pickering's time was the South African W. H. Craib. Craib had ideas on the genesis of the electrocardiogram which were at variance with Lewis' and according to contemporary accounts there were constant arguments between the two men. Eventually Craib was forced to undertake his work solely in the evenings after the chief had gone home. However, in spite of this personal clash Lewis wrote a generous appreciation of Craib's work in the Annual Report of his department in 1930.

His work on the physiology of blood vessels led naturally to a study of vascular disease and especially Raynaud's disease. Raynaud, he said, had given a good observational account but there was no more progress because the various hypotheses such as spasm and vasomotor irritability were not tested. It did seem clear, he said, that these problems could be attacked successfully by the experimental method, by clinical pathology which Lewis renamed "clinical science." He employed the full range of this method, studying the blood vessels in normal, living patients, dead patients and in animals. The work was summarized in his book *Vascular Disorders of the Limbs*, which is to this day an excellent and comprehensive account of the subject. Fortunately this manuscript has survived and is so replete with alterations that it makes one realize that Drury must have been describing Lewis writing up papers and not books when he said "He so schooled himself to see clearly what to say before putting pen to paper that he could write swiftly and often almost without erasure."

When his book *Diseases of the Heart* was published in 1933, it was welcomed by doctors and students alike. The directness of its teaching and the clarity of its writing made a strong and immediate impact. The prose was of superb quality. Many still remember his remarks on the murmur of mitral stenosis. "Much labour is lost through persisting in the effort to time instead of learning to know it as one learns to know a dog's bark." This book might never have been written had he not had an attack of brachial neuritis. He consulted the neurologist, F.M.R. Walshe for advice on this, and later Walshe said that with some apprehension he told Sir Thomas that it would be necessary for the treatment to consist of six weeks in bed. Walshe said that Lewis immediately agreed to this, much to his surprise, and with his painful left arm propped on pillows wrote the famous textbook. The preface contained a statement emphasizing the importance of assessing the function of the heart and not relying on the structure.

The *Lancet* reviewed the book enthusiastically and went on to publish a fulsome annotation on "The New Cardiology." However, what was not new was his position regarding valvular heart disease. Of mitral stenosis he wrote "there are no symptoms that can be ascribed to this deformity of the valve." This was a repetition of Mackenzie's viewpoint "In chronic valvular affections the subjective symptoms of heart failure only arise when exhaustion of the heart muscle sets in." Even Richard Cabot, founder of the C.P.C., who had studied over a thousand cases of cardiac disease at autopsy had the same opinion. This apparently superior attitude of physicians in denying the importance of the anatomical lesion led the pioneer cardiac surgeon Russell Brock to declare "I can only conclude it is something in the very nature or atmosphere of the Royal College of Physicians—perhaps a cloud of some special canonizing dust falls upon the habituees." Nevertheless the chief message of the book, that of gauging function of

the heart was a great and enduring one and the importance of measuring the jugular venous pressure was the subject of an excellent film also made by Lewis.

In 1933, Lewis changed the title of his journal from *Heart* to *Clinical Science* and intensified his campaign for the recognition of clinical science as a university-based discipline. His thoughts on the subject may be summarized thus: Noting the high scientific standing of physiology, but rejecting emphatically the belief that medicine is only applied physiology, it became his conviction that a science of medicine should develop with a similarly high standard. He believed the way to do this was by establishing permanent full-time posts in medical research—which before his own appointment in 1916 were nonexistent in Britain—linked with an appropriately structured department headed by a professor of clinical science.

In his Harveian Oration in 1933 he showed how Harvey's experimental approach and scientific reasoning was as important, if not more so, than his conclusion on the circulation of the blood. In fact, Harvey's work, with its pioneering observations on living man, dead man, and animals, was almost identical with Lewis's concept of clinical science. In 1934 he wrote an excellent book on ". . .Clinical science, illustrated by personal experiences," and it contained a very interesting chapter entitled "Testing the Curative Properties of Remedies." In it he says, "To ascertain if a remedy succeeds or fails and the measure of its success or failure two groups of cases should be selected, being composed as similarly as possible. They are then treated in exactly the same way and simultaneously except that in one group they receive the remedy and in the other they do not. Comparison between treatment of a series of cases under an earlier regime with later treatment of a second series under a new regime, is not satisfactory." This must have been one of the earliest statements about controlled trials. There is no doubt that Lewis' untiring efforts to encourage the Medical Research Council to attract men and women of ability to clinical research was a most important factor in the development of scientific medicine in Britain. However, it may be that he made an equally great contribution by his founding in 1930 of the Medical Research Society. Only full-time research workers were admitted to membership, and the society provided a unique opportunity for young research workers to meet and argue their views. Sir Harold Himsworth said "they used to fight like tigers." His last phase of sustained research work was on pain, and as before he gathered together all the material in a monograph. It lacks the sparkle of his earlier writings and one suspects that the difficulties of the subject taxed even his great experimental powers. However, much was accomplished. With Pochin he demonstrated the meaning of the double response of pain nerves in the skin. With Kelgren he investigated referred pain and produced maps of the segmental areas for deep pain by injecting 6% saline into interspinous ligaments. He emphasized the value in clinical practice of making time-intensity curves of pain. With Pickering he had studied pain in ischemic muscle and postulated a metabolite, Factor P, as the cause of the pain.

In the hospital he was meticulous in attendance at his out-patient clinics, at his ward work, and his teaching visits. A former student wrote "I remember him as having a personal, friendly and quite classless approach which put most patients completely at ease and made them trust him absolutely. He was closely concerned with the details of their lives and the exact history of their illness." Another wrote "he was a humane and understanding doctor." Undoubtedly his students were to some extent intimidated by him. "He had the reputation," said one "of being a rather fierce teacher but he had a true humility and I have known him spend several minutes checking the absence of a murmur which an unskilled student claimed to have heard. He taught us hard but I never remember him being sarcastic." His formal teaching was done in the medical school and his lectures, like all else in his life, were carefully organized. The main details were on typed sheets and all slides were contact-printed mounted in volumes, and appropriately numbered. The UCH students magazine, no doubt like others, assiduously collected remarks made by their teachers, but there are very few recorded of Lewis, though there were two cartoons. However, at the age of 48 he did have a comment printed. "At age 45 a change takes place in the cerebral vessels. They become more rigid and perhaps as a consequence our ideas become more fixed. You will find it very difficult to get a man over 45 to listen to a new idea. That is why the writers of textbooks are always behind the time." This, interestingly, was three years before he wrote his book on diseases of the heart.

The last of his 12 books was entitled *Exercises in Human Physiology*, and it reflected his life-long concern about the difficulties facing a student in the transition period between preclinical and clinical work. Almost the last of his 230 papers was one on Caleb Hiller Parry, an early writer on thyrotoxicosis and angina pectoris. It was a tribute from one great Welsh scientist and doctor to another. In 1941, Lewis was awarded the Copley medal—the highest recognition in the gifts of the Royal Society. Previously in its long history only one clinician, Lord Lister, had been awarded the medal, and since Lewis' time no other clinician has gained it.

Sir Thomas Lewis died on March 17, 1945 in a third attack of myocardial infarction. After the second he had said "another arrow from the same quiver and one will get me in the end." He was buried in Llangasty Churchyard by Llangorse Lake near Brecon in Wales, an area which he had grown to love as a boy and his grave has an imaginatively created headstone depicting birds and animals with the family motto, "Ar Dduw I Gyd"—To God the Honour.

Franz M. Groedel

W. Bruce Fye, M.D., M.A.

Department of Cardiology, Marshfield Clinic, Marshfield, Wisconsin, USA

Franz M. Groedel (Fig. 1) was born on May 23, 1881, in Bad Nauheim, Germany.[1,2] He was a pioneer of cardiac radiology, electrocardiography, and scientific hydrotherapy, and was the founder of the American College of Cardiology. His father, Isidore Maximilian Groedel, was a physician who helped develop Bad Nauheim as a spa that specialized in the treatment of cardiac patients.[3] As a high school student, Groedel was especially interested in physics. It is not surprising, therefore, that he became interested in the new field of radiology that developed rapidly after Wilhelm Röntgen discovered x-rays in 1895.

Groedel studied medicine at the universities in Munich, Giessen, and Leipzig. In 1904, he received his medical degree from the University of Leipzig, home of the world's leading physiologic institute during the second half of the nineteenth century.[4] He then served as assistant to Friedrich von Müller in his renowned medical clinic in Munich. Müller was a role model for several first-generation clinical scientists in the United States, including Lewellys Barker of Johns Hopkins Hospital and Rufus Cole of the Rockefeller Institute Hospital. In Munich, Groedel also worked with Hermann Rieder, a pioneer in radiology, and helped expand the use of x-rays for diagnosis in Müller's clinic.[5]

Cardiac diagnosis was entering a new era when Groedel joined his father in practice at Bad Nauheim around 1906. Several of his earliest publications dealt with the utility of x-rays in evaluating the size and function of the heart.[6] In 1909, Groedel invented the first machine for taking serial-x-rays; his *Fallkasettenapparat* exposed 25 film cassettes in 5 s.[7] Three years later, Groedel reported a study in which he combined electrocardiography and x-ray cinematography to evaluate the motion of the heart. He also invented an improved orthodiagraph, an x-ray apparatus that facilitated the accurate measurement of heart size. After his book on x-ray examination of the heart was published in 1912, Groedel was viewed as a world authority on cardiac radiology. A decade later he was named president of the German Radiological Society.

A leading proponent of physiologic pathology—a paradigm that attributed the signs and symptoms of illness to disordered function rather than structural abnormalities—Groedel encouraged the use of pulse tracings and electrocardiography as clinical and research tools. One of the first clinical scientists to use the electrocardiograph, Groedel's first paper on the technique appeared in 1912. Independent of Frank Wilson's group at the University of Michigan, he developed the concept of the unipolar chest lead or precordial electrode in the early 1930s.[8] Groedel summarized two decades of electrocardiographic research in a 1934 book that included his theory that each cardiac ventricle generated an independent or "partial" electrocardiogram.[9] Although this theory was disproved, Groedel's later work on the technique included pioneering studies on the direct recording of the electrocardiogram from the surface of the heart during surgery in humans. His 1948 book on the subject reported the results of electrocardiograms recorded directly from the surface of the atria and ventricles.[10]

Groedel was also deeply interested in hydrotherapy as a treatment modality for cardiac patients. Bad Nauheim, long a health resort because of its hot mineral springs, had become a world center for cardiac patients by the turn of the century. Like his father and other Nauheim physicians, Groedel advocated hydrotherapy as an adjunctive treatment for cardiovascular disease. There was no consensus on the value of hydrotherapy in the treatment of heart disease during the first decades of the century; however, William Osler, the English-speaking world's leading internist, and Harvard physician Joseph Pratt, among others, felt the technique was useful in chronic heart disease. The influential British physician James Mackenzie was, however, very skeptical of the approach.

Groedel succeeded his father as head of a popular private hospital and spa at Bad Nauheim following World War I. As post-war tensions eased, the facility once again became a magnet for wealthy and socially prominent patients from America, Great Britain, and the continent. In 1929, a German American industrialist, William Kerckhoff, bequeathed $4 million to create a research institute at Bad Nauheim for the scientific study of hydrotherapy. Groedel spared no expense in designing and equipping the facility. It included clinical and research units as well as departments of experimental pathology, statistics, and education. The result was a cardiovascular research institute unmatched by anything in Europe or the United States.[11]

By 1932, Groedel had published nearly 300 papers, was a full professor at the University of Frankfurt, had a thriving practice at Bad Nauheim, and was viewed as a world leader in cardiac radiology and hydrotherapy. Then suddenly everything changed for Groedel because his mother was Jewish. Although he had converted to Christianity two decades earlier, Groedel was classified by the Nazis as a "non-Aryan," and he knew that his career was at risk. He took advantage of his rep-

FIG. 1 Franz M. Groedel, 1881–1951. Photograph from the private collection of the author.

utation in the United States and his friendship with financier Bernard Baruch to emigrate to the United States in 1933.

Groedel was on the crest of the huge wave of German immigrants that came to the United States in the 1930s. Arriving in the midst of the Great Depression, Groedel was no longer seen as a leading cardiac radiologist and clinician—many struggling physicians saw him and the thousands of other immigrant physicians as competitors. Excluded from New York City's medical elite, Groedel accepted an offer to be chief of staff of the Beth David Hospital, a small hospital on West 90th Street. He used his wealth and influence to establish a practice on Park Avenue. After moving to the United States, Groedel's focus shifted from radiology and hydrotherapy to clinical cardiology and electrocardiography.[12]

An active participant in several medical societies in Germany, Groedel had cofounded the German Society for Heart and Circulatory Research in 1928. Societies held a certain fascination for Groedel, and he gravitated to the top of two local medical societies in New York City that catered to practitioners, many of whom were immigrants. Groedel served as pres-

ident of the Rudolf Virchow Medical Society of New York between 1943 and 1945 and was elected president of the New York Cardiological Society in 1949. From this local society of practitioners, he inaugurated a new national organization for cardiologists. The American College of Cardiology was chartered in December 1949, and Groedel launched a membership campaign 13 months later. The college held its first scientific meeting in New York on October 6, 1951, but Groedel was too ill to participate. He died a week later. During a career that spanned almost half a century, Franz Groedel published almost 400 papers and several books. His main legacy, however, is the American College of Cardiology, a professional society with almost 25,000 members.

References

1. Schlepper M: Franz Maximilian Groedel: Ein deutsches Schicksal von internationaler kardiologischer Bedeutung. *Z Kardiol* 1988;77 (suppl 5):155–177

2. Kisch B (ed.): *Franz M. Groedel Anniversary Volume on the Occasion of his Seventieth Birthday.* New York: Brooklyn Medical Press, 1951

3. Pierach CA, Wangensteen SD, Burchell HB: Spa therapy for heart disease, Bad Nauheim (circa 1900). *Am J Cardiol* 1993;72: 336–342

4. Fye WB: Carl Ludwig and the Leipzig Physiological Institute: A factory of new knowledge. *Circulation* 1986;74:920–928

5. Grigg ERN: *The Trail of the Invisible Light.* Springfield, Ill.: Charles C Thomas, 1965

6. Groedel FM: *Die Röntgendiagnostik der Herz- und Gefässerkrankungen.* Berlin: Hermann Meusser, 1912

7. Groedel FM: Roentgen cinematography and its importance in medicine. *Br Med J* 1909;1:1–3

8. Kossmann CE, Johnston FD: The precordial electrocardiogram. *Am Heart J* 1935;10:925–941

9. Groedel FM: *Das Extremitäten-, Thorax- und Partial- Elektrokardiogramm des Menschen.* Leipzig: Theodor Steinkopff, 1934

10. Groedel FM, Borchardt PR: *Direct Electrocardiography of the Human Heart and Intrathoracic Electrocardiography.* New York: Brooklyn Medical Press, 1948

11. O'Farrell PT: Cardiological research at Bad-Nauheim. *Irish J Med Sci* 1933;ser. 6, vol. 94:579–586

12. Fye WB: *American Cardiology: The History of a Specialty and its College.* Baltimore: Johns Hopkins University Press, 1996

Sir Alexander Fleming, 1881–1955

H. BERGER, M.D.

Department of Medicine, New York Medical College, New York, New York, USA

"In the field of scientific observation, chance only favors the mind prepared," so wrote Louis Pasteur. This truism was demonstrated in St. Mary's Hospital Medical School in the Wright Institute of Microbiology where Alexander Fleming was studying staphylococcus bacteria, which were being grown on agar plates. It was necessary for Dr. Fleming to examine them repeatedly under the microscope. When the cover of the petri dish containing the bacteria was removed for this study, an airborne mold fell on the plate. The next day, as a result of unintended incubation, there was a large growth of mold. In most instances such contamination would have rendered further experimentation with this dish useless. Many years later, Fleming said, "you know I'm Scotch and I don't throw anything away." He noted that the staphylococci grew very well at a distance from the mold, but near to it, the colonies had disappeared.

Immediately this strange occurrence recalled to his astute mind a previous experience. Once, while suffering from a cold, he had smeared his own nasal secretions on a culture plate. While examining it, a tear from his eye fell on the plate. After incubation, he noted that the tear prevented organisms from growing. Fleming believed this substance, which seemed to kill bacteria, to be an enzyme, and dubbed it lysozyme. This occurrence interested him particularly. During World War I, he and his mentor, Dr. Almroth Wright, had become convinced that all the antiseptics being used in the sterilization of wounds were useless. Indeed, they noted that these chemicals destroyed the leukocytes to a greater extent than they killed the microbes. Therefore, they arrived at the conclusion that the ultimate killers of any organisms in the body were its own immune responses. Therefore, Fleming strongly advised against the continued use of antiseptic irrigations and suggested that they instead be washed with a strong salt solution which would tend to draw the body's own protective serum into the wound area and thus permit the white cells to accumulate in sufficient numbers to destroy any organisms present. Further study with lysozymes proved that while they did not kill every organism, they did destroy many and that the lethal effect was shortlived. For this reason it was looked upon as impractical.

Alexander Fleming's friends seemed certain that this man was destined for greatness. He was born on August 6, 1881 at Lockfield Farms in Ayrshire, Scotland, near the town of Darvel. His father was a farmer who had four sons by each of two wives. Alexander was the youngest. He attended a single room school on Loudoun Moor and later an upper school at Darvel, walking four miles each way to attend classes. At the age of 12 he went to Kilmarnock Academy, a distance of 16 miles from his home. All of these were excellent schools; two famous alumni were Robert Louis Stevenson and Robert Burns. In 1895, at the age of 14, he matriculated at London's Polytechnic School on Regent Street, where he boarded with an older brother who was an ophthalmologist. On graduation, he obtained work in a shipping company.

When war broke out, he joined the Scottish volunteers. Some years later, his senior officer, Colonel Lyle Grant, said of Fleming, "He couldn't play the pipes, so he did the next best thing and discovered penicillin." In 1901 he inherited a small legacy, and at his brother's insistence, entered medical school. He chose St. Mary's only because he had played water polo there. He was an expert swimmer, having mastered this ability in the streams of his native Scotland.

At St. Mary's he came under the influence of Dr. Almroth Wright through his interest in bacteriology. After graduation he expected to be a surgeon, and accordingly joined the Royal College. But on the very next day, he entered Dr. Wright's laboratory where he worked for the rest of his life. He had won practically every award as a student without having to work very hard. Wright fostered his interest in the body's normal protection against invasion by organisms, and instead of concentrating on the few patients in the hospital, Fleming wondered at the vast majority of the populace who did not become infected. There had to be something in the body that protected human beings from the myriad infections to which we are exposed. While studying leukocytes with Wright, they discovered opsonins. This chemical makes the germs more palatable to the leukocytes and they are therefore destroyed more rapidly. This material was put to use in the management of several infections, particularly pneumonia. During the 1918 influenza epidemic, Fleming proved that the Pfeiffer bacillus, which was thought to be the causative organism, was not indeed so, but rather that the condition was due to a filterable virus. Unfortunately, the electron microscope had yet to be invented, and study of these viruses was not possible.

Continuing his studies on lysozyme, he presented a paper in 1922 before the Royal Society on "A remarkable bacteriolytic element found in tissues and secretions" that destroyed bacteria in only 30 seconds. He noted that in a 1:100 dilution,

FIG. 1 Sir Alexander Fleming, 1881–1955. (Photograph provided by the National Library of Medicine.)

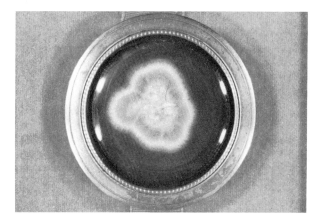

FIG. 2 The original petri dish contaminated with *Penicillum notatum*. (Photograph courtesy of the New York Academy of Medicine Library.)

tears could prevent many microbes from growing, and that the lysozyme was also to be found in white blood cells and in mothers' milk, but not in bottled milk, explaining why breast-fed children were more resistant to infection. Professor Charles Pennet, his classmate and fellow worker, stated, "with lysozyme, the first step in the discovery of penicillin had been accomplished."

Fleming was not a bookworm; he had many interests, played a good game of darts, was accomplished at pool, swam, gardened, and was an amateur photographer. He often planted bulbs in his garden in Suffolk spelling out his various friends' names. In 1921, at the age of 40, he wed Sarah Marian McElroy, who happened to be the twin sister of his brother's wife. He possessed all of the characteristics which Chapman Pincher once described as indicative of true genius: curiosity, ingenuity, persistence, and insight. Samuel Johnson once said that true genius is found in a mind of large general powers which is accidentally determined in some particular direction.

His fine sense of humor was illustrated when on a visit to an immaculate, beautifully appointed stainless steel and tiled laboratory in the United States, he said, "Isn't it fortunate that I never had the opportunity to work in such a fine laboratory. It is so clean that a spore or a mold could have never found its way onto my petri dish." He discovered that the mold on his petri dish was one of the general class of penicilliums, but knew too little about fungi to classify it accurately. It was only after the spore was examined in the United States that its correct name and type was identified as *Penicillum notatum*. The

spore killed many organisms, but not all. It was extremely efficient against gonorrheal, staphylococcic, and streptococcic organisms, but not against *Escherichia coli*. He recognized that it was not the mold itself that produced the destruction of bacteria, but rather something that the mold itself produced. Filtered broth in which the mold had grown was bacteriolytic. The material was extremely sensitive to both acid and alkali, and like his lysozyme, seemed to have a rather short life. These observations were published in the *British Journal of Experimental Pathology* in 1929 under the title of "The Acute Bacteriocidal Action of Culture of a Penicillium."

Several biochemists attempted to isolate the active substance during the next two years. Foremost among these was Dr. Raistrich, who had been succeeding quite well when his assistant was killed in a bus accident, and he discontinued the experiments. There ensued a tragic 10 years during which the world was denied this life-saving drug. The puzzle of the culture never left Fleming's mind. He experimented with it now and then, but he never reached a point where it could be used successfully in the management of infections in humans.

In 1939, at Oxford, Dr. Howard Flory and E. B. Chain began the study of bacterial antagonists. In searching the literature on any instances of this feature, they came upon Fleming's papers—the first on lysozyme, the second on penicillin. They debated which of the two they should investigate, and decided on the latter. As biochemists, rather than bacteriologists, they had access to the facilities necessary for extracting the pure chemical. Twenty-five mice were given large doses of streptococci, enough to be fatal, and were then given penicillin. A similar group of 25 mice were not given the drug. Of the 25 treated mice, 24 survived. All 25 of the untreated mice died. This discovery was looked upon as the dawn of a miracle.

Efforts were made to produce the substance in large quantities, but this was impossible for war-time England, when almost every piece of equipment that would be needed for mass production was in scarce supply. However, its efficacy in humans was proved at that time when a policeman dying of generalized septicemia was admitted to Radcliffe Infirmary at Oxford. The constable's case was looked upon as being hopeless. Dr. Flory injected what penicillin he had available and the patient improved remarkably. He was given the drug every day with continued constant improvement, when tragedy struck. On the 10th day their supply of penicillin was depleted; there was no way treatment could be continued, and the constable died.

These investigators had previously been aided in their studies by the Rockefeller Foundation to which they now turned for help. Dr. R. D. Cogill of the U. S. Department of Agriculture asked U.S. pharmaceutical manufacturers to attempt to manufacture penicillin in large quantities. The ingenuity of these manufacturers quickly solved one of the most significant problems. In Britain, the serum had been made on the surface of broths, in bottles. In the United States it was placed in large tanks and air was bubbled through it, so that there was always a quantity of penicillin in contact with air, and large quantities of this material were able to be produced.

Flory had believed that the penicillin he had made was quite pure, but on comparative analysis with the U.S. product, it was found to be only 1% pure, while ours was 99–100% pure. The first American patient treated was a woman dying of puerperal fever due to a streptococcus infection. Penicillin was given after treatment with sulfa drugs had failed. Here again, the same story was repeated as with the British constable. She improved remarkably and was overcoming the infection when her physician ran out of penicillin. This time, however, the manufacturers were able to tap into a new batch being manufactured and this was administered to her with considerable success. By D-Day in 1944, there was sufficient penicillin available to treat every soldier in need of it. Other molds were quickly discovered; some were found to be even more potent than the original. The drug was first used intrathecally on a friend of Fleming's who was admitted to St.

Mary's Hospital. The gentleman was suffering from spinal meningitis and he was dying despite the administration of penicillin. In a bold move, it was injected directly into the spinal canal, and he recovered. Later, sufficient penicillin was available so that it could be given prophylactically to injured soldiers. The first patient treated in the United States was Patricia Malone, a child at the Lutheran Hospital in Brooklyn, in August 1943. After a request was made to the Surgeon General, Dr. Richards, who was supervising the use of penicillin in the United States, he reached Chester Kiefer in Boston who authorized Scribbs in New Brunswick to release some of the precious drug. It was carried by police escort from the factory to Brooklyn where it is credited with saving the life of this young child.

Recognition without end began to be heaped on the shoulders of Dr. Fleming. He was knighted and was granted innumerable honorary degrees from scientific institutions and universities the world over. On December 11, 1945 he was awarded the Nobel Prize along with Drs. Flory and Chain and he was most pleased to learn that he had been created a burgh of Darvel in Scotland.

Despite all of these honors, he continued working in the same laboratory at St. Mary's. The only sign on the door of his laboratory was a handwritten note to the effect that a cat was in residence there. Not even his name was lettered on the door.

On March 11, 1955, he succumbed suddenly to a heart attack. We in the field of cardiology, as well as millions of patients through the years, have a particular reason to thank Sir Alexander Fleming: prior to the use of penicillin, bacterial endocarditis was uniformly fatal; while some dispute it, the widespread use of penicillin in the management of upper respiratory infections had all but eliminated the incidence of rheumatic fever in this country; and its use to treat syphilitic heart disease has been very successful.

At his funeral, at St. Paul's Cathedral, Dr. Charles Pennet said, "He has saved more lives and relieved more suffering than any other human."

Carl J. Wiggers—the Inventive Physiologist, 1883–1963

B. Silverman, m.d.

Department of Cardiology, Northside Hospital, Atlanta, Georgia, USA

No one who pauses to reflect can fail to admire the masterminds of medicine who, by simple signs and statistics, not only interpreted many disease processes correctly, but upon them built an admirable system of diagnosis. Nothing can be substituted for the power of accurate observation, either at the bedside or in the laboratory. Nevertheless, it happens that many phenomena of the circulation, normal and abnormal, remain undetected by our unaided senses. Consequently various instrumental methods have been introduced which supplement our direct observations, either by recording the functions of the circulation graphically or by translating them into numerical terms which the mind can more definitively grasp.[1]

This statement of Carl Wiggers (Fig. 1) reflects the philosophy of one of America's wisest and most productive physiologists.

Carl Wiggers was born May 24, 1883, the son of immigrants from the Duchy of Holstein and Schleswig. These provinces were part of the Danish domain and later the consolidated German State. Wiggers' father was of peasant origin and immigrated to the United States to escape the limited opportunities at home. He settled in Davenport, Iowa, a Mississippi River town with an agricultural economy and strong German traditions. It was there that his parents met and married. Carl was a long, lanky, underweight young man, who was not good in athletics. He considered himself introverted and expressed himself by studious behavior. His upbringing was characterized by strong doses of philosophy on frugality, economy, and thrift. His parents discouraged laziness and required that assigned tasks be performed well and expeditiously. The primary school education he received encompassed reading, writing, arithmetic, spelling, grammar, geography, and history. There was little exposure to physical education, music, or the fine arts. School training was designed to inculcate the principles of punctuality, cooperation, obedience, and conformity. This was a time of "immigrant America," and the German language was taught daily throughout the first eight grades.

In 1895, when Carl was 12 years old, the family organized an extended trip to Europe because of his mother's poor health. During their return, his sister Helen developed appendicitis in the mid-Atlantic, and died. His mother's grief and her prolonged mourning continued over the next two years, and were the dark years of his early childhood. Wiggers comments that his dedication to schoolwork increased considerably because of the depressing home atmosphere. His excellent performance at this time convinced his father that he was fitted for a profession and brought about in his mother a change from grief over her lost daughter to dedication to the success of her surviving son. In the 1890s, high school education was ranked as equivalent to college education today, and students aspired to enter high school only if they were considering a profession or high industrial position. In Carl Wiggers' school, only he and one other pupil advanced from primary school to high school. Only Carl completed high school. Prior to entering high school he chose pharmacy as his profession; his interest in medicine developed later with exposure to zoology and biology and to the works of Darwin and Huxley. This resulted in a decision to change from pharmacy to medicine. Many medical schools in 1900 were considered diploma mills where a degree could be purchased after a mere semblance of medical education. The most respected and renowned medical school at the time was Johns Hopkins University which had been organized in 1893. Hopkins, however, required an academic degree for admission. One of Wiggers' teachers suggested the medical school of the University of Michigan, which accepted high school graduates. Its organization was similar to that of the Johns Hopkins School of Medicine, and it was known to have a fine tradition, good faculty, excellent laboratories, and generally low fees.[2]

Wiggers entered the University of Michigan in 1901. He describes the school as having three floors with narrow, rickety wooden stairways; poorly lit rooms; and toilet facilities limited to an area adjacent to the dog kennels in a dark basement. The medical curriculum embodied the concept that clinical work must rest on a sound scientific foundation. The aim was to teach basic courses and look exclusively to their application in medicine and surgery. The professor of physiology, Warren P. Lombard, believed that students should be trained to analyze and think, as well as memorize. Wiggers' principal interest in entering medical school was pharmacology, but through an error in the registrar's office, he was assigned to physiology laboratory instead of pharmacology. In those days, laboratory experience was largely elective and not required. To his astonishment, experimental physiology was not drill, but proved very intriguing. It was his exposure to this

FIG. 1   Carl J. Wiggers, 1883–1963—the inventive cardiac physiologist.

course that stimulated his interest in physiologic research. During this period he had an opportunity to work closely with Lombard, who taught him many of the workshop tricks necessary for the assemblage of apparatus so important to his later investigations. But Wiggers' subsequent involvement in experimental physiology was related more to the need to earn additional income than to a primary interest in academic work. In 1903, he was offered a two-year appointment as an assistant in physiology. This was of interest to Wiggers because the annual stipend of $300 allowed him to afford additional clinical work at the Rush Medical College in Chicago during his summer recess. It was this work that he hoped would improve his clinical skills for a private practice.

In 1903, laboratory work became compulsory at Michigan and there was a need to increase the number of instructors. The laboratory course was designed to give students an inkling of experimental techniques which were being utilized to understand physiology and appreciate clinical problems such as blood pressure and heart rate. Because of Wiggers' knowledge of German, he was exposed during this period to the work of the German physiologists Bodwitch, Englemann, and H. E. Hering. Physiology was just being applied to clinical assessment by McKenzie, McWilliams, Wenkebach, and Rihl. Wiggers comments that research had generally been considered asking a question and finding an answer. But he defined research more precisely as "asking a reasonable and pertinent question and through unbiased approach and use of adequate methods, obtaining a correct answer."[2] It was through his investigations during this period as an assistant in

physiology that he began to appreciate the thrill of achievement in investigation and the satisfaction associated with this work. He became acquainted with well-known American investigators of the time, including Brodie, Erlanger, and Y. Henderson.

In June, 1906, Wiggers received his Doctorate of Medicine. It had been his plan to return to Iowa to enter private practice, but he was offered a position as instructor in physiology at the University of Michigan. His interest was too great to leave the physiology department. At that time, fellowships for development of research did not exist, and research was regarded more as a hobby than as a requirement for faculty whose main function was teaching. Faculty salary was supplemented by medical practice. However, Wiggers had several particularly exasperating experiences in medical practice that resulted in his desire to avoid practice and concentrate on teaching and laboratory research. He comments that his decision not to practice was related to several souring incidents. These include an episode in which a patient came to him stating that her son had refractured an arm that had been set by a eminent surgeon in town the previous year. On examination, Wiggers found no evidence of deformity or fracture and suggested an x-ray. The patient considered this an unnecessary expense at a cost of five dollars; however, she did agree to the procedure with great reluctance. The x-ray showed no fracture, and Wiggers recommended against a cast. The patient was quite upset and again took her son to the prominent surgeon, who promptly placed the arm in a cast. The patient was indignant that Wiggers had not appreciated the "fracture." His second experience involved a child who had choked on popcorn and was near death. He urged the family to call an expert laryngologist—one of the few individuals in town who had an automobile. He arrived in about 15 minutes, quickly opened the trachea, and extracted the obstruction. However, by this time, the child was clinically dead and a prolonged attempt at resuscitation failed. The sad family was appreciative of Wiggers' efforts until the specialist thoughtlessly indicated that it was too bad he had not been called sooner—he could certainly have saved the child's life. This thoughtless remark so soured Wiggers, who felt it reflected on his competence, that he lost any enthusiasm for regular medical practice.

From 1907 to 1911, during his last years at Michigan, Wiggers devoted himself to teaching and research. During this time the medical school was developing clinical research activities, and Wiggers prospered under the department that encouraged and developed laboratory science. He was well enough thought of at this time to have been offered a chair in physiology at several second-rate medical schools; however, he felt he was too young and unprepared. He was more interested in extending his laboratory experience and sought a position with Otto Frank, the world-renowned physiologist. Frank had developed a laboratory that particularly excelled in developing devices for quantitative readings of systolic and diastolic pressures. Wiggers resigned his position as instructor at the University of Michigan to travel to Frank's laboratory in Munich, only to find that his position at the Munich Institute of Physiology had not been secured.

At this time, with no position at Michigan, he was offered an instructorship at Cornell University. This position was offered by Graham Lusk who directed a department in which research was regarded as a duty rather than a hobby for the medical school instructor. Lusk encouraged Wiggers' work in circulation research and assisted him in establishing a laboratory shop to develop the necessary equipment for his specialized studies. Good machine shops were necessary for research, and close coordination between the physiology laboratory and the machine shop was critical in developing experimentation. Lusk arranged an appointment to Otto Frank's Physiology Institute for Wiggers, and provided the financing. In the summer of 1912, Wiggers went to Europe. His work in Frank's laboratory was extremely helpful in developing the methodology and measuring equipment that were important to many of his later studies. His first book, *Circulation in Health and Disease*, is dedicated to Otto Frank for his appreciation of Frank's contribution to his training.

Wiggers worked at Cornell from 1911 until 1918. He directed the department when Lusk was on leave to work on a commission during World War I. In 1918 he received an offer to direct the Physiology Department at Western Reserve University in Cleveland, Ohio. The University had been founded in 1826 by relocated residents from Connecticut in the hope of establishing a school equivalent to their own Yale University. Here Wiggers developed an extensive clinical research program and an excellent postgraduate training program. Wiggers began his program during World War I and developed his laboratory in the prosperous post-war years. Western Reserve was committed to a research-oriented program with space for extensive laboratories and funds for equipment. The Depression had a profound effect on the University, which nearly faced bankruptcy, and on Wiggers' department, which lost over half its funding. However, both perservered and were, in fact, productive. It was during this time that a number of America's most outstanding physiologists spent time training with Wiggers. These include D. Rapport, G. Ray, L.N. Katz, H. Feil, J. P. Quigley, D. E. Gregg, and H. D. Green.

Wiggers' principal areas of physiologic research involved vascular control of cerebral coronary and pulmonary circulation; study of internal hemorrhage; registration of heart sounds and murmurs; interpretations of electrocardiographic, excitatory, and dynamic events during the cardiac cycle; abnormal ventricular rhythms; the dynamics of valvular lesions; the coronary circulation; and experimental shock. At the end of his career in research, he was invited to edit *Circulation Research*, a new journal of the American Heart Association. He accepted the task and established this journal as preeminent in the area of circulation research until he relinquished the editorship in 1957.

An example of Wiggers' hemodynamic studies is found in his study of heart sounds and murmurs. Until 1911 a number of devices had been used for recording the time relationships between heart sounds and murmurs, but they lacked sufficient fidelity to be of clinical or experimental value.

Otto Frank developed segment capsules for direct registration of heart sounds. Frank had analyzed the vibrating mechanics of the typanum and attached ossicles of the middle ear, and had found a way to duplicate their physical characteristics in the segment capsule. He called this instrument "Herztoncapsel" and used it to record sounds from the dog at the Physiology Institute in Munich. Wiggers studied this instrument during his sojourn to Munich and developed a similar capsule on his return to Cornell. The capsule required considerable modification since the Frank capsule was developed for studies in dogs and the Wiggers-Dean capsule had to be adjusted for changes in the human chest, pendulous female breasts, and obesity. A critical problem related to finding a thinner and more sensitive membrane that had an appropriate natural frequency response. Initially, condoms were used, but the thinner, delicate condom found in Europe was not available in the United States and it was against the law at that time to import contraceptive devices. Therefore, Wiggers, assisted by a medical student, A. Dean, developed a membrane made up of commercially available rubber cement. Thus, in 1918, he began to publish records of presystolic, systolic, and diastolic murmurs of various valvular lesions. Their instrument permitted simultaneous recordings to correlate heart sounds and murmurs with left ventricular and left atrial pressure changes, as well as with the electrocardiographic information. Wiggers followed up these studies in Cleveland after World War I. The frequency response of the capsule was significantly improved and the technique was critical in developing an understanding of the cause of the heart sounds, gallop sounds, and the physiologic significance of murmurs. This is a typical example of Wiggers' work, in which he developed an instrument to record a physiologic function and used that instrument to correlate hemodynamic changes for a better understanding of the circulation. It was Wiggers' and his associates' brilliant use of mechanical devices that permitted comprehensive exploration of the circulation and the relationship of the various phenomena occurring in the heart.

Carl Wiggers was one the first of the outstanding American physiologists at the beginning of this century. Their work established U.S. universities as preeminent medical scientific institutions of the world. In commenting on Dr. Wiggers' 20 years as a professor of physiology at Western Reserve in 1938, J. P. Quigley states:

This learned eye from the shadow of a tree that to and fro did sway upon the wall—our shadow-selves, are influenced, may fall where we can never be.[2]

References

1. Wiggers CJ: *Circulation in Health and Disease*. Lea and Febiger Philadelphia and New York (1915)
2. Wiggers CJ: *Reminiscences and Adventures in Circulation Research*. Grune and Stratton, New York and London (1958)

Sir John Parkinson—A Leader in Cardiology

Lawson McDonald, m.d.

National Heart Hospital, London, England

A friend had said "you will enjoy listening to John Parkinson in his clinic at the National Heart Hospital." After telephoning his secretary I went to the clinic and was much inspired by this man. A long friendship began at that time. Immediately his distinctive character was apparent; it was delightfully coupled with a direct and pragmatic approach to life, as well as an innate courteousness.

In the clinic the case history of the patient under study was presented by a senior assistant. It was carefully appraised and points of particular importance explored, as might have been done by a sympathetic and skilled barrister. Then clinical examination of the patient was meticulously performed and the electrocardiogram analyzed. After a discussion of the patient's problems so far, we all went to the x-ray room, where Parkinson very carefully examined the heart by fluoroscopy, with a unique commentary of all that he saw and encouraged us to observe—"Yes, the left atrium is certainly somewhat enlarged, look!—there—do you see it?" Subsequently all the findings were correlated in an accurate diagnosis, on which treatment was based.

Fig. 1 John Parkinson in 1934, from a drawing by Schwabe, kindly lent by his daughter, Mrs. Elva Carey.

John Parkinson certainly founded modern British cardiology, and it is significant that Paul Wood dedicated his classical work *Diseases of the Heart and Circulation* to him.

At a time when John Parkinson was very likely to be asked to join the staff of the London Hospital, it is said that he was asked by Dr. (later Sir James) Mackenzie if he would care to join him in his cardiac department at the hospital. This was probably the first special cardiac department in a general hospital in the world, and had been started by Mackenzie in 1911. It consisted of a small building in the garden of the hospital, where Mackenzie was continuing his study of the venous pulse, particularly in patients with rheumatic heart disease. Because of resentment of cardiology by consultant physicians of the hospital, Mackenzie's invitation threatened Parkinson's chance of being elected one of them. It is a measure of his loyalty and integrity that he unhesitatingly joined Mackenzie, and because of his character and excellence in his profession became one of the outstanding members of the staff of the London Hospital. His work on cardiac infarction and angina pectoris and various aspects of congenital and valvar heart disease is well-recognized. His greatest contribution probably lay in exploring and making known the importance of radiology in the diagnosis of heart disease.

He established in the Cardiac Department of the London Hospital what became the training ground over many years of future consultant cardiologists in the United Kingdom and what was then the British Empire, and in their future lives very many of those whom he trained paid him the considerable compliment of endeavoring to emulate him.

Parkinson was certainly the friend of the young, and would always find time for discussion of their research work and of any problem in their careers. To those who worked well with him he gave his continuing and firm support. When the Junior Cardiac Club was founded in 1947 the author, with the other founders, discussed the project with Parkinson, who gave it his blessing and encouragement, likening it to a group known as the "Young Turks" (American Society for Clinical Investigation) in the United States.

The National Heart Hospital had for many years been somewhat separate from the then great undergraduate teaching hospitals which were held in high regard. Parkinson was farseeing in his recognition of the important place of a specialist hospital concentrating on all aspects of heart disease, and he joined the staff of the National Heart Hospital. This

FIG. 2 Members of the Junior Cardiac Club with Parkinson at his home in 1950. Key to names: (1) Arnold Woods, (2) Jack Shillingford, (3) Peter Wilson, (4) Edward Holling, (5) Aubrey Leatham, (6) Lawson McDonald, (7) John Parkinson, (8) James Lowe, (9) Raymond Daley, (10) Michael Matthews, (11) Max Zoob, (12) Richard Bayliss, (13) Kenneth Allenby, (14) Bertram Wells, (15) John Goodwin, (16) Walter Somerville, (17) Patrick Mounsey.

was a turning point in the sure foundation and future of that institution, and led to its worldwide recognition as a center for graduate training and research as well as the care of patients.

Naturally, Parkinson soon acquired a large private consulting practice, with patients referred to him from all parts of the world. Nevertheless, he maintained a steady output of meticulously prepared writings and was a regular and most popular teacher and lecturer at home and abroad. It was his custom to have his medical texts edited by an expert in English prose, who was not a doctor of medicine. National and international recognition of his abilities came in the form of honorary memberships of many societies, invited lecturerships, and the award of honorary degrees.

He had the enthusiastic support of a wonderful wife and kept a most gracious home in Devonshire Place and later in Hampstead, where a happy family grew up. It was a great sadness that his only son was killed early in World War II while serving with the Fleet Air Arm of the Royal Navy.

He was meticulous about punctuality, which helped him to fit so much into his life, and showed greatness in his meticulous attention to small details as well as larger issues: A comment must always be written in the notes after seeing patients; the writing must be clear and the comment not take too much space. Electrocardiograms, which were photographic in his early years of practice, had to be black and white and with a steady baseline. He never failed to emphasize the importance of telling the patients good news: "If the electrocardiogram is normal, tell the patient, do not keep the information to yourself. He wants to know!"

There were many aspects of Parkinson's life. He was a man who lived in style, although never ostentatiously, and drove or was driven to and from the London Hospital in his Bentley motor car, a make that was considered of the best, but slightly more sporting than Rolls Royce. He was a connoisseur of good food and good wine, and among his many card index systems was one for good restaurants that he had enjoyed. His hospitality was unfailing and he particularly made a point of entertaining young cardiologists in his home, often so that they might meet some well-known cardiologists visiting from another country. A number of us met, early in our careers, both Samuel Levine and Paul White for the first time this way. Parkinson, together with his friend Paul White, was instrumental in initiating a spirit of international friendship and collaboration in the specialty of cardiology, and this has become a happy feature of cardiology today. In those days transatlantic friendship was less common, but out of this came the first description of the Wolff-Parkinson-White syndrome [*Am Heart J* 5, 685 (1930)]. Parkinson spoke both French and German well.

Deeply interested in painting, he spent time with the English artist, John Nash, and was an accomplished painter himself. The painters Paul Nash and Stanley Spencer were also friends. Parkinson had a real appreciation of art and of form. On one occasion he commented, in a straightforward fashion, that the contour of a certain shape had the beauty of a woman's breast. He was a frequent visitor to the Whitechapel Art Gallery, which is situated close to the London Hospital. He was, as well, an enthusiastic gardener but somewhat intolerant of plants which did not do well. They were quickly removed from his garden.

John Parkinson was born in 1885 in Lancashire; his father John Parkinson was a Justice of the Peace. He was educated at University College, London, the London Hospital, and the University of Freiburg. He was Chief Assistant to Sir James Mackenzie in the Cardiac Department of the London Hospital 1913–1914, and served with distinction in the Royal Army Medical Corps during the 1914–1918 war. He was appointed Consultant Physician to the Cardiac Department at the London Hospital and to the National Heart Hospital in 1920. In 1948 he was knighted by King George VI for his services to cardiology.

John Parkinson was a pioneer in establishing cardiology as a specialty independent of general or internal medicine. In 1989 it is easy to forget how recent this history is. He was a man of great wisdom with a ready smile, and one who was very well liked and respected throughout his career by all his colleagues, young and old. He died in 1976 at the age of 91.

A close colleague and pupil, the distinguished cardiologist Evan Bedford, who was described by Charles Laubry of France as Parkinson's "grand élève," wrote (*Br Med J* 19th June 1976):

I first encountered John Parkinson in 1923 at the Ministry Pensions Hospital, Orpington, where he visited the cardiac wards once weekly. I kept in close touch with him ever since, first as Paterson research scholar in the cardiac department at the London Hospital and later as a colleague at the Heart Hospital. Like Osler, he was the young man's friend, and many of us have reasons to be grateful to him for help and encouragement at the start of our careers. To have been trained by Parkinson was a hallmark to be proud of and a passport to the best cardiological centres in other countries. Though he could be brusque in manner and speech on occasion, he was full of kindness to his assistants, who regarded him with affection. At the age of 74 he retired from practice and lived in a flat near Baker Street, where old students and colleagues were always welcomed, though he became sad and lonely after Lady Parkinson's death two years ago. His passing, 50 years after the death of Mackenzie, will mark the end of an era in British cardiology, and his many disciples, however saddened, will look back with pride at his achievements.

An obituary of Sir John Parkinson appeared in the *British Heart Journal* 38, 1105–1107 (1976).

George Ralph Mines: Victim of Self-Experimentation?

Louis J. Acierno, M.D., facc, and L. Timothy Worrell, M.P.H., r.r.t.

Cardiopulmonary Sciences, Department of Health Professions, University of Central Florida, Orlando, Florida, USA

A life unfulfilled is lamentable; a life unfulfilled of its potentiality is a tragedy. Such was the life of George Ralph Mines (Fig. 1), an enigma in the annals of cardiology. Struck down at the age of 29, Mines left this earth with the key to important electrophysiologic data, but with the door unopened for further exploration. His life, though short, could best be described as an explosively vibrant one characterized by brilliant intellectual achievements and human enjoyment. Why, then, should he have died so young without evidence of a lethal disease?

George Ralph Mines was born in Bath, England, on May 13, 1886. His parents were H. P. Mines and Alice G. Ward. He began his early formal education at Bath College and the Grammar School in Kings Lynn. He matriculated at Sydney Sussex College, Cambridge University, when he was 19 years old and graduated from there in 1908. The years from 1908 to 1909 were important in George Mines's life. During this time period, he received a scholarship at the Allen University, a fellowship at Sidney Sussex, and he married Marjorie Rolfe of Newnham College, an aspiring poet.[1] For the next few years, Mines taught at Needham College and conducted research in the physiological laboratory at Cambridge. His rise in academic circles was rapid and astounding for one so young. At the age of 24, he was elected to the Physiological Society. A year later, he was awarded the Gedge Prize and soon thereafter became Assistant Demonstrator in the physiological laboratory at Cambridge. During his brief tenure at Cambridge, Mines was very productive.[1] He seemed to have boundless energy. With the assistance of a second-year student at Needham named Dorothy Dale, a number of manuscripts were published in the *Journal of Physiology*. The focus of these experiments centered on the various effects of nerve stimulation on the in vitro frog heart and the influence of electrolytic solutions on in vitro frog cardiac muscle function.[2, 3]

Mines's life as a researcher from 1912 to 1914 can only be described as peripatetic and frenzied. His work took him from Plymouth to Naples and then, in 1913, to Roscoff, France, where his continued research at the Biological Station led him to the concept of the vulnerable period of the ventricle, the period where the cardiac muscle he was studying was prone to fibrillate during electrical diastole. This work would remain unpublished until after his death in 1914. His travels also took him to various university laboratories, including that of Brodie at Toronto and McGill in Montreal. At the University of Toronto, Mines was appointed assistant to Professor Brodie, a position he held for only a few months. During this time, an academic search for the position of Professor of Physiology at McGill University was underway, and he was recruited to lecture to the McGill faculty. His depth of knowledge in the area of physiology coupled with his research productivity so impressed them that he was offered the position of Professor and Chair of the Department of Physiology. It was now 1914. Unfortunately, he was to die within months of his appointment.[1]

In the laboratory, Mines proved himself a master of ingenuity and mechanical expertise as exemplified by his construction of the various types of apparatus used in his research protocols. He was truly in his element in the physiology laboratory, much as a conductor is at home in front of a symphonic orchestra. Incidentally, he also had a great interest in the piano: so much so, that before turning to physiology, he seriously considered a career in music. This gift for music was transmitted to his daughter Anatole who became a professional viola player.[1]

Mines's investigations into cardiac muscle physiology led to two seminal contributions in electrophysiology. The first of these contributions was his work in the area of reentrant rhythms in cardiac muscle. In his paper, "On Dynamic Equilibrium in the Heart," Mines, utilizing frog, tortoise, and electric ray muscle, described a phenomenon that he aptly named "reciprocating rhythm."[4] He attributed this rhythm to a circulating excitation of conduction tissues in the cardiac muscle of his experimental models, which he determined to be unidirectional in nature; one path conducting in an antegrade direction (atrium to ventricle), the other conducting in a retrograde direction (ventricle to atrium). In addition, Mines noted that this reciprocating rhythm could either be terminated or triggered by an extrasystolic beat and that this might be a possible cause of some of the clinical paroxysmal tachycardias. In this experiment, Mines noted that the motion of the tissues caused by this reciprocating rhythm resembled that of fibrillating mammalian hearts, and that this mechanism might serve as the explanation for this lethal dysrhythmia.[4]

His other major contribution to electrophysiology was his work that eventually led to the posthumous publication in 1914 of a paper entitled "On Circulating Excitations in Heart Muscles and Their Possible Relation to Tachycardia and Fibrillation." In this study, Mines modified the usual method

FIG. 1   George Ralph Mines (1886–1914). (*Source*: Physiological Laboratory, Downing Street, Cambridge, U.K. Used with permission.)

of inducing ventricular fibrillation in animal hearts that utilized repeated shocks from an induction coil. His method involved the application of single shocks timed to occur at specific periods during the cardiac cycle. The rabbit served as the mammalian heart model. Mines developed an apparatus that allowed for the administration of the electrical impulse to the rabbit heart via a Morse key. He found that in a number of experiments, only a single activation of the Morse key was required to trigger fibrillation depending on the timing of the impulse delivery, and that this timing appeared to be crucial in determining whether fibrillation would occur. He further determined that this point in time, when fibrillation occurred, was immediately after the refractory period. This was the first time this zone of vulnerability to fibrillation had been identified.[5] In 1923, DeBoer described the reentry phenomenon and also demonstrated how an electrical shock applied to the heart of the frog could result in ventricular fibrillation if applied late in systole.[6, 9] Louis Katz reported in 1928 that premature ventricular contractions could produce life-threatening dysrhythmias if they occurred on the T wave.[7, 9] It was not until 1940 that Wiggers and Wegria reported their findings in the *American Journal of Physiology* in a paper entitled "Ventricular Fibrillation Due to Single Localized Induction and Condenser Shocks Applied during the Vulnerable Phase of Ventricular Systole."[8, 9] This was the first time the term "vulnerable phase" had been used in the literature, 26 years after Mines's posthumous paper.

Mines's death occurred under a shroud of mystery and speculation. He was discovered in an unconscious state in his laboratory at McGill University on November 7, 1914, still attached to his physiologic monitoring equipment. He was transported to the Royal Victoria Hospital for further management. After a transient period of consciousness late that night, he suddenly died before midnight. A complete postmortem examination led to no conclusive diagnosis of the cause of death. In fact, the autopsy failed to reveal any evidence of structural alteration of his vital organs. It has been speculated that Mines may have been a victim of self-experimentation. In retrospect, this speculation was fueled by Mines's own words in his October 6, 1914, Founder's Day address to the faculty of McGill University one month before his death. In his address, Mines spoke of two other researchers who had become well known for their self-experimentation. One was Head, who had severed his own arm nerves in his quest to understand the origin of skin sensations, and the other was Washburn, who reportedly swallowed a stomach tube in order to study the physiology of digestion in his work with his partner, Cannon. The inclusion of these two researchers' names in his address may have been a veiled reference to his own intense desire for knowledge obtainable through self-experimentation.[1]

In the light of the autopsy findings and the circumstances under which he was found in his laboratory, the possibility arose that a fatal ventricular dysrhythmia was the precipitating cause of his demise. Also, since the events leading to his death occurred in his laboratory, the further possibility arose that the dysrhythmia may have been self-induced. There is no definite proof of this, but despite all attempts to the contrary the nagging question still remains: Did George Ralph Mines die of a lethal ventricular dysrhythmia and could this have been self-induced?

References

1. De Silva R: George Ralph Mines, ventricular fibrillation and the discovery of the vulnerable period. *J Am Coll Cardiol* 1997;29: 1397–1402
2. Dale D, Mines GR: The influence of nerve stimulation on the electrocardiogram. *J Physiol* 1913;46:319–336
3. Mines GR: On functional analysis by the action of electrolytes. *J Physiol* 1913;46:188–235
4. Mines GR: On dynamic equilibrium in the heart. *J Physiol* 1913; 46:349–383
5. Mines GR: On circulating excitations in heart muscle and their possible relation to tachycardia and fibrillation. *Trans Roy Soc Can* 1914;8:43–52
6. De Boer S: Die Physiologie und Pharmakologie des Flimmers. *Ergeb Physiol* 1923;21:1–4
7. Katz LN: The significance of the T wave in the electrogram and the electrocardiogram. *Physiol Rev* 1928;8:447
8. Wiggers CJ, Wegria R: Ventricular fibrillation due to single localized induction and condenser shocks applied during the vulnerable phase of ventricular systole. *Am J Physiol* 1940;128:500–503
9. Acierno LJ: *The History of Cardiology*, p.357. U.K. and New York: The Parthenon Group, 1994

Paul Dudley White: The Father of American Cardiology*

J. WILLIS HURST, M.D.

Department of Medicine (Cardiology), Emory University School of Medicine, Atlanta, Georgia, USA

Paul Dudley White is widely acclaimed as the father of American cardiology (Fig. 1). What did he do? When did he do it? How did he do it? Why did he do it?

Paul White, the son of a family practitioner who taught medicine at Tufts, was born in Roxbury, Massachusetts, on June 6, 1886.[1] As a boy he went on house calls with his father in their horse-drawn buggy.[1] The father undoubtedly influenced the boy in many ways. I expect young Paul heard something like the words his father later wrote in his "journal."[1] Listen—

> . . . I have lived long enough to see that eventually right and truth do survive, that the real scientific practice of medicine is only just begun and that there must be some startling and most wonderful victorious discoveries just ahead. . .

His father died of coronary artery disease at the age of 71 (having consumed daily bowls of cream advised because of old tuberculosis).[1]

Dr. White's mother, who died of pneumonia at age 88,[1] was active in volunteer work in a home for the sick and in missionary work.[1] These activities must have influenced young Paul's social conscience.

His younger sister, Dorothy, died of rheumatic heart disease,[1] an event which he stated influenced him profoundly toward the study of heart disease. Warren White, his younger brother, became an orthopedic surgeon. He also had an older sister, Miriam.[1]

His early schooling influenced his life greatly. He studied science, mathematics, history, English, Greek, Latin, French, and German.[1] This set the stage for him to become an expert grammarian and scholar of the classics.

When he was 18 years old Paul entered Harvard College. He enjoyed history, but was influenced by Theodore Roosevelt to become a forester.[1] He changed his course, however, and decided to become a physician.[1] He needed additional courses to qualify for admission to medical school, and undertook summer studies at the Massachusetts Institute of Technology. He entered Harvard Medical School in 1907 at the age of 21.[1] He received his Harvard College degree cum laude,[1] in 1908 and graduated from medical school in 1911.

Dr. White enjoyed his contact with patients, but the lectures given by medical school faculty did not please him.[1] This experience influenced his approach to bedside teaching, making the patient the center of his teaching exercises.

He became the first pediatric intern at Massachusetts General Hospital in 1911,[1] which may well have spurred his interest in congenital heart disease. During 1912 and 1913, he obtained additional house staff training as an intern on the general medical service. It was during this period that he worked with Dr. Roger I. Lee to develop the Lee-White method of measuring the coagulation time of the blood.[1]

Dr. White, apparently still interested in pediatrics, had agreed to become the assistant to Dr. Richard Smith.[1] Dr. David Edsall, Chief of Medicine at Massachusetts General, recommended him for a Harvard Traveling Fellowship to study electrocardiography and cardiac physiology with Thomas Lewis in London. The plan was for White to study with Lewis and return to Massachusetts General to develop an electrocardiographic laboratory. Dr. Smith agreed with the new plan and his work with Lewis began in October 1913.[1]

Lewis was difficult to work with and initially he ignored White. Eventually White won the confidence and friendship of Lewis and they engaged in endless night and day research that resulted in the publication of a number of scientific papers.[1] They were engaged in what would now be called electrophysiologic work dealing with cardiac arrhythmias. While in London, Dr. White also visited the cardiac clinics of James Mackenzie and John Parkinson.[1]

In July 1914, as the clouds of World War I were hovering above Europe, Paul White returned to Boston. He developed the electrocardiographic laboratory in the "basement of the Skin Ward" of Massachusetts General Hospital[1] and was determined to pursue his study of the heart and circulation, disregarding friends' advice that it was too narrow a field.

Dr. White organized cardiac clinics, taught every one in sight, and soon was asked to see patients in consultation. It was during this time that his friendship developed with Dr.

*The words on these few pages are not adequate to describe Paul Dudley White. I urge all those who are interested to read Dr. White's autobiography, *My Life and Medicine*, published in 1971, and Dr. White's biography, *Take Heart*, written by Oglesby Paul in 1986.[2] These two books, plus previous articles of my own,[3,4] served as the original sources for most of the information used in the preparation of this document.

FIG. 1 Paul Dudley White, M.D. (1886–1973). (Photograph courtesy of National Library of Medicine, Bethesda, MD.)

Sam Levine, who was destined to pioneer cardiology research at Peter Bent Brigham Hospital.*

Dr. White spent 25 months in the armed forces and returned home in August 1919. I believe his war experience profoundly influenced Dr. White's interest in encouraging world leaders to pursue peace.

I have written previously of six reasons why Dr. White is recognized as the father of cardiology in the United States.[3] These reasons are, of course, in addition to the fact he was brilliant, kind, gentle, devoted to the cause, hardworking, optimistic, and retained the precious quality of childlike enthusiasm and naivete.

The six reasons are abstracted with the permission of the publisher:[3]

He married Ina Reid on June 18, 1924. She worked in the Social Service Department of Massachusetts General Hospital and became Dr. White's lifelong partner adapting to his life of consultations, teaching throughout the world, writing, and offering instant hospitality to visitors. She now lives near Boston and is revered by all who know her.

In 1920 he organized a training program in cardiology at Massachusetts General Hospital for students, house staff, fellows, and graduate students. Trainees flocked to him from

*Their friendship was such that Dr. Levine, along with others, initiated the drive to have Paul White nominated for the Nobel Peace Prize. Dr. White did not win the prize but there was a worldwide ground swell in favor of it.

this and virtually every other country in the world. He stimulated all of them to return to their homes—here and abroad—to teach and write about heart disease. Many of them became world leaders.

He was one of the physicians who urged the New England Association for the Prevention and Relief of Heart Disease to join several other organizations to form the American Heart Association. He was elected its treasurer with a budget of $2,500. He did not become president of the American Heart Association until 1940. He once remarked to me that he regretted that the name, The American Heart Association, did not retain the word *prevention* because prevention is so important. Throughout his life, he traveled far and wide on behalf of the American Heart Association and encouraged many nations to create heart associations.

Dr. White was awarded a traveling fellowship in 1928 to write a book on heart disease. The book was undertaken after he had collected data on 12,000 patients (4,000 of these patients were seen by him in private practice). Accordingly, his own meticulously kept records served as a unique source of information. He went from library to library here and in Europe. He also talked with numerous friends in Europe and finally he and Ina settled in on the Isle of Capri where he wrote most of the book. *Heart Disease* was published in 1931. It was a scholarly document that represented the most complete work on the heart ever produced in the United States. Quotations from our predecessors were found throughout the book and there were abundant references. Dr. White had translated most of them from their original sources. He emphasized the need to establish the etiology, anatomy, and functional status of each patient—a discipline later recommended by the New York Heart Association. The book did it; he became the leader of American cardiology and was recognized throughout the world.

Dr. White was a major force in the development of the National Heart Institute. He became its executive director and spent one third of his time in Washington. He saw the opportunity to increase the funds for heart research, which he felt was needed throughout the country. So, as the 1949 academic year came to a close, he resigned his position as chief of cardiology at Massachusetts General Hospital and moved his office to Beacon Street. The very capable Ed Bland became chief of cardiology at Massachusetts General Hospital. I, along with Dr. Lee Messer of St. Petersburg, was Dr. White's cardiac fellow at the time and we watched the transition—he was sad about making the change but was convinced the National Heart Institute would play a major role in spearheading cardiac research throughout the world. He spent more than eight years as its executive director. Now, of course, the National Heart, Lung, and Blood Institute is recognized throughout the world as the major cardiovascular research institute as well as the major source of funding for cardiovascular research throughout the United States.

Dr. White, along with Dr. Louis Katz, created the International Cardiology Foundation in 1957 in order to raise public funds for the support of the International Society of Cardiology. Dr. White by then was extremely concerned about world peace and saw this organization as a vehicle for his stand against violence and war.

These are the major reasons why Paul White is recognized as the father of American cardiology. These acts do not, however, dwarf the importance of the personality of the man in his day to day work. He listened to his peers and wrote down the essence of conversations he had with them in his little black memo book. He literally gave himself to medicine and cardiology. He never raised his voice in anger; he could soothe an angry group simply by entering the conversation because he was so respected.

It was my privilege to attend Lyndon Johnson at the time of his myocardial infarction in July 1955. Because of my work under Dr. White, who emphasized total rehabilitation, I urged Johnson to return to his vigorous life as majority leader in the Senate of the United States.

Dr. White gained national prominence with nonphysicians when he was asked to consult with the physicians attending President Eisenhower at the time of his myocardial infarction in September 1955. Dr. White advised Eisenhower to return to the presidency, as I later advised Johnson that he could seek the vice presidency and then the presidency. Dr. White had made his point to the world at large; most people with myocardial infarction can return to work.

Dr. White rarely told jokes but he chuckled at humorous situations. Here is one:[5] I had seen Lyndon Johnson at Emory University Hospital in Atlanta in late 1955 and was pleased to find him doing exceptionally well. Johnson asked me to report the result of my examination to the press, so, along with other statements, I reported that Johnson's electrocardiogram had returned to normal. Accordingly, this point was mentioned in the newspapers. The next day I received a call from Dr. White who asked, "Willis, is Johnson's electrocardiogram normal?"

I responded, "Yes sir, it is slightly different to his pre-infarction tracing but it is now within normal range. Why do you ask?"

He said, "Eisenhower wants me to tell him why his electrocardiogram has not returned to normal too!" I then heard a little Paul White chuckle and could mentally see the twinkle in his eyes. What he did not know was that I promptly got in my car and went to Emory University Hospital to double check my interpretation!

He was an adventurer. He recorded the electrocardiogram of an elephant in 1938[6] and also examined the heart of an elephant. He went on expeditions and tried to record the electrocardiogram of a large whale and actually succeeded in recording the electrocardiogram of a Beluga whale.[7] While this made him happy, he still wanted to record the electrocardiogram of the large grey whale. Was this a foolish whim? Of course not. He wanted to dissect the heart of earth's largest mammal because, he reasoned, the cardiac structures were larger than those of the human and he would be able to examine them more easily. Remember, the electron microscope had not, at that time, been invented.

He wrote four editions of *Heart Disease*[8] and several books on electrocardiography.[9] His book on *Hearts—Their Long Follow-Up*[10] was symbolic of his optimism. A most important book, written with Manard Gertler, entitled *Coronary Heart Disease in Young Adults, a Multidisciplinary Study*[11] emphasized that coronary disease was not simply due to aging alone but represented a disease demanding investigation. In addition to the books, he published more than 700 articles.

As we go about our daily work we might remember who guides our actions:

Dr. White's hand is with us when we recommend a low-fat, low-cholesterol diet, the abstinence from smoking, the maintenance of normal blood pressure, normal body weight, normal blood sugar, and an exercise program in our efforts to prevent coronary atherosclerosis. He taught and emphasized this in the late 1940s and stimulated interest and support of the classic Framingham Heart Study.

Dr. White's hand is with us when we marvel at the molecular biology that is determined by genes. He said more than 40 years ago that if one's parents lived into their eighties the child was likely to do so. He felt that the basic cause of coronary atherosclerosis was inherited and that modifying factors were the level of serum cholesterol, diet, smoking, exercise (or lack of it), hypertension, and so forth.

Dr. White's hand is with us when we urge our patients to return to work after a myocardial infarction and when we recommend rehabilitation programs. He spearheaded this approach more than 40 years ago.

Dr. White's hand is with us when we see a patient with atrial tachycardia or atrial fibrillation who, when there is normal rhythm, exhibits a short P-R interval and an abnormally long QRS duration. This, of course, is the Wolff-Parkinson-White syndrome.[12, 13]

Dr. White's hand is with us when we identify any disease of the pulmonary arteries.[14] We especially should think of him when we think of pulmonary embolism and deep venous thrombosis of the leg veins.[2]

Dr. White's hand is with us when we diagnose constrictive pericarditis and recommend the removal of the pericardium.[15]

Dr. White's hand is with us when we classify heart disease according to etiology, anatomy, physiology, and functional status, for this originated with Dr. White.[16] The New York Heart Association deserves the credit for popularizing this discipline. The New York Heart Association changed the Functional Category to Cardiac Status in 1973.[17]

Dr. White's hand is with us when we try to determine the range of normal of the heart and circulation.[18]

Dr. White's hand is with us when we try to establish the cause of chest discomfort.[19]

Dr. White's hand is with us when we identify a congenital anomaly of the coronary arteries.[20]

Dr. White's hand is with us when we order a coagulation time on our patients.[1]

Dr. White's hand is with us when we ponder the effect of digitalis on the electrocardiogram.[21]

Dr. White's hand is with us when we talk with patients and especially when we encourage them. He often said, "In most instances, heart disease is not as bad as the patient thinks it is."

Dr. White's hand is with us when we support research in the prevention of heart disease (including the Framingham program).

Dr. White's hand is with us when we recognize the enormous impact that the National Heart, Lung, and Blood Institute has had on the progress made in cardiology, and when we apply to the National Heart, Lung, and Blood Institute for a research grant.

Dr. White's hand is with us when we apply to the American Heart Association for a research grant, or recognize an American Heart Association-sponsored community educational program. Dr. White was not only one of the founding fathers of the American Heart Association but had encouraged the organization to allow nonphysicians to join it. This action created a source of research money and enabled physicians to extend their educational efforts into the community at large.

Dr. White's hand is with us when we think of and welcome the future. He always did that. For example, he wrote the following paragraph in 1957. It is reproduced here with permission of the American Heart Association.[22]

We know from our clinical experience in the practice of medicine that in diagnosis, prognosis, and treatment, the individual and his background of heredity are just as important, if not more so, as the disease itself. Far too little attention has been paid to research on the host, i.e., on human genetics, while much study has been done and is projected for the future on the agent, that is, on the effect of the various ways of life. It is timely that we should begin concentrated efforts to determine the candidates for whose sake we should apply in particular the prevention measures that we may discover in the future.

A short time before his last series of illnesses, Dr. White asked me, during dinner, to auscultate his heart and listen for mild aortic regurgitation, which had been discovered in 1964. I declined because we were in the midst of the wonderful meal prepared by Mrs. White in their home.

He developed angina pectoris in April 1967 at the age of 81.[2] The angina occurred while he was running so he could witness the end of the Boston marathon. The angina, always produced by effort, continued; he used about five tablets of nitroglycerin each week.

On December 20, 1970, at the age of 84, he developed chest pain that lasted 3½ hours; it was accompanied by nausea and sweating.[2] His physician, Dr. Allan Friedlich, saw him quickly and, at his insistence, transported him in his automobile to Massachusetts General Hospital. On the way to the hospital Dr. White was determined to stop at his office for a suitcase full of papers because he wished to continue to work while in the hospital.[2] During the 10-day hospitalization he taught the residents and nurses the nuances of coronary disease. He was eager to have the media stress his proper actions when pain occurred as an opportunity for effective public education.

I recall that years earlier he had said to me, "Small heart attacks are so common they are almost within the normal range." He, as recorded by Oglesby Paul, referred to his own attack as "a smidgen of coronary trouble."[2] He addressed the Mexican Heart Foundation on January 21, 1971, one month after his small myocardial infarction.[2]

He developed a stroke, presumed to be embolic in origin, on May 29, 1973, but recovered sufficiently to talk at a cardiac conference on coronary spasm on June 12, 1973.[2] He later developed a subdural hematoma that was evacuated at surgery.[2] Atrial fibrillation became persistent.[2] He then developed pulmonary emboli and was restarted on coumadin, which had been discontinued because of the subdural hematoma.[2] He left the hospital on September 18, 1973, but was admitted for the last time October 15, 1973, due to another stroke.[2] He died on October 31, 1973, at the age of 87.[2]

Mrs. White asked me to speak at his memorial service at the Harvard Memorial Chapel in Cambridge on November 13, 1973. My eulogy was later published in *Circulation*.[4] A portion of the speech which, in my view, sums up his personality is reproduced here with permission of the American Heart Association.

A few years ago Dr. White came to Emory University to present a lecture entitled "The Evolution of Cardiology." The lecture room was filled with people. Excitement filled the air. The audience clearly sensed the talent of a master artist at work on one of his finest pieces. The applause, which was rendered on three separate occasions, was thunderous. Dr. White discussed the men who had contributed to our knowledge over the centuries. He pointed out how he and Alfred Boursey would labor for an hour over one word in their efforts to accurately translate into English Lancisi's book on sudden death (the book was published in 1971). He then came to the contributions that were made in the twentieth century. He started with Sir James MacKenzie, then went on to Sir Thomas Lewis, with whom he had worked, and John Parkinson and on and on. The story he unfolded could only be told by a man who knew them all. He pleaded that the names of various organizations should contain the words 'for the prevention and relief of heart disease.' He discussed the contributions of his friends in numerous countries who were working for international cardiology which to him was virtually the same as working for world peace. He did all this without mentioning his own contributions. A very special incident occurred near the end of the lecture. He apparently did not wish to take more than his allotted time and to be certain he did not do so he set his alarm wrist watch to signal him. He was in the middle of an important statement when the alarm went off with a startling buzz. He glanced at his wrist watch and turned off the alarm with a quick slap and said, 'I'm not through yet.' He then went on to quote from poet-physician Oliver Wendell Holmes's 'For the Meeting of the National Sanitary Association.' He read the first and last stanzas but placed more emphasis on the last.

And lo! the starry folds reveal
The blazoned truth we hold so dear:
To guard is better than to heal,—
The shield is nobler than the spear!

Acknowledgment

The material used from *My Life and Medicine* is reprinted with the permission from the Harvard University Press. Copyright © 1971 Paul Dudley White, M.D.;[1] I thank Dr. Oglesby Paul and the Harvard University Press for permission to use material from the book *Take Heart;*[2] I thank the *American Journal of Cardiology* for permission to quote from the article "Paul Dudley White: To Know Him Better";[3] I thank the American Heart Association for permission to quote from "I'm Not Through Yet"[4] and "The Evolution of Our Knowledge About the Heart and Its Diseases Since 1628."[22] I thank Dr. Allan Friedlich and Dr. Oglesby Paul for reviewing the manuscript.

References

1. White PD: *My Life and Medicine. An Autobiographical Memoir.* Gambit Inc., Boston (1971) 1, 4–6, 10-18, 20, 43
2. Paul O: *Take Heart.* Harvard University Press, Boston (1986)
3. Hurst JW: Paul Dudley White: To know him better. *Am J Cardiol* 56, 169–177 (1985)
4. Hurst JW: I'm not through yet. *Circulation* 49, 199–204 (1974)
5. Hurst JW, Cain JC: *LBJ: To know him better.* Lyndon Baines Johnson School of Public Health, Austin, Tx (1995)
6. White PD, Jenks JL Jr, Benedict FG: The electrocardiogram of the elephant. *Am Heart J* 16, 744–750 (1938)
7. King RL, Jenks JL Jr, White PD: The electrocardiogram of a Beluga whale. *Circulation* 8, 387–393 (1953)
8. White PD: *Heart Disease,* 3rd Ed. Macmillan, New York (1931), (1937), (1946), (1951)
9. Graybiel A, White PD, Wheeler L, Williams C: In *Electrocardiography in Practice,* 3rd Ed. WB Saunders, Philadelphia (1951) 186
10. White PD, Donovan H: *Hearts—Their Long Follow-Up.* WB Saunders, Philadelphia (1967)
11. Gertler MM, White PD: *Coronary Heart Disease in Young Adults.* Harvard University Press, Cambridge (1954)
12. Wolff L, Parkinson J, White PD: Bundle-branch block with short P-R interval in healthy young people prone to paroxysmal tachycardia. *Am Heart J* 5, 685–704 (1930)
13. Wolff L, Parkinson J, White PD: An undescribed cardiac mechanism: "Intraventricular block" with short P-R interval in healthy young people prone to paroxysmal tachycardia. *J Clin Invest* 9, 28 (1930)
14. White PD, Brenner O: Pathological and clinical aspects of the pulmonary circulation. *N Engl J Med* 209, 1261–1265 (1933)
15. White PD, Churchill ED: The relief of obstruction of the circulation in a case of chronic constrictive pericarditis (concretio cordis). *N Engl J Med* 202, 165–168 (1930)
16. White PD, Myers MM: The classification of cardiac diagnosis. *J Am Med Assoc* 77, 1414–1415 (1921)
17. Criteria Committee of the New York Heart Association: *Nomenclature and Criteria for Diagnosis of Diseases of the Heart and Great Vessels.* Little, Brown & Company, Boston (1973)
18. White PD: The range of the normal heart rate. *Am Scholar* 22, 315–322 (1953)
19. White PD: Neurocirculatory asthenia (Da Costa's syndrome, effort syndrome, irritable heart of soldiers). *Army Med Bull* 65, 196–202 (1943)
20. Bland EF, White PD, Garland J: Congenital anomalies of the coronary arteries: Report of an unusual case associated with cardiac hypertrophy. *Am Heart J* 8, 787–801 (1933)
21. White PD, Sattler RR: The effect of digitalis on the normal heart electrocardiogram, with special reference to A-V conduction. *J Exp Med* 23, 613–629 (1916)
22. White PD: The evolution of our knowledge about the heart and its diseases since 1628. *Circulation* 15, 915–923 (1957)

Frederick A. Willius

W. Bruce Fye, M.D., M.A.

Cardiovascular Division, Mayo Clinic, Rochester, Minnesota, USA

Fredrick A. Willius (Fig. 1), one of America's first academic cardiologists, was born in Saint Paul, Minnesota, on November 24, 1888. He received a B.S. degree from the University of Minnesota in 1912 and an M.D. from the same institution 2 years later. After an internship at University Hospital in 1915, Willius began a 3-year fellowship at the Mayo Clinic in Rochester, Minnesota.[1,2] At the time, the staff of the Mayo Clinic consisted of 42 physicians and surgeons, and the Mayo Foundation for Medical Education and Research had just been established (in affiliation with the Graduate School of the University of Minnesota).[3]

When he arrived in Rochester, Willius was assigned to work with Henry S. Plummer, an internist with a special interest in disorders of the esophagus, the thyroid, and the cardiovascular system. Willius admired Plummer and later characterized him as "an outstanding clinician and teacher [who] had very advanced concepts of medicine."[4] Plummer was instrumental in establishing the electrocardiography (ECG) laboratory at the Mayo Clinic in 1914, just 5 years after Alfred Cohn installed the first ECG machine in the United States at Mount Sinai Hospital in New York City.[5] When the Mayo Clinic's original ECG, a Cambridge model constructed in England, arrived in 1914, Plummer asked internist John M. Blackford to help launch the new laboratory. The following year Plummer assigned Willius to assist Blackford.

Willius was a prolific author whose special interest in the ECG as a clinical and research tool was evident in his earliest publications. Because the instrument provided direct graphic evidence of the electrical activity of the heart in health and disease, it was a powerful tool for delineating cardiac arrhythmias—far superior to the pulse tracings that James Mackenzie and Karel Wenckebach used around the turn of the century to study disorders of the heartbeat.[6] Willius's first paper, published in 1917, dealt with chronic heart block.[7] That year, he was appointed head of the ECG laboratory when Blackford moved to Seattle. Like other first generation cardiologists, Willius proclaimed the value of technology as an adjunct to traditional clinical and research methods. In 1919, he declared that "much recent knowledge of heart disease has been attained by the use of such methods as electrocardiography."[8] During the next few years, Willius published papers on atrial flutter, paroxysmal ventricular tachycardia, arborization block, chronic bradycardia, and atrial fibrillation. He also published an important ECG book with 368 illustrations.[9]

Willius was promoted to associate in medicine at the Mayo Clinic in 1920. By this time he had decided to become a cardiologist. His medical and surgical colleagues acknowledged Willius's special interest in cardiac disorders and began to ask him to evaluate their patients with known or suspected heart disease. Cardiology was just emerging as a specialty in the United States, and Willius was part of that dynamic process.[10] As one of the nation's first academic cardiologists, he not only focused his practice on heart patients, he was also committed to teaching and research.

Plummer asked Willius to organize a cardiology section at the Mayo Clinic early in 1922. There was demand for the specialty services that Willius provided. During that year, patients from 16 states were admitted to the cardiology inpatient service at Rochester's Kahler Hospital.[11] To help Willius cope with the increasing demands, Arlie R. Barnes was appointed assistant in the newly created section. In 1927, Willius published an illustrated description of Mayo Clinic's cardiology section.[12] It included three units: a diagnostic and consultative service, a hospital service, and a laboratory service dedicated to electrocardiography. The academic atmosphere of the Mayo Clinic was reflected in the personnel of the cardiology section. Several other physicians and trainees helped Willius: an associate, a first assistant, three to five assistants, and one or more fellows who spent three to six months in the section.

Mayo Clinic's commitment to integrating postgraduate medical education with care was reflected in the way patients were evaluated in the cardiology section. Willius explained,

> The patient is first received by one of the examining physicians, who is a graduate student in the Mayo Foundation for Medical Education and Research. He records the patient's history, makes a complete physical examination, and writes a tentative diagnosis and opinion. The patient is then seen by the head of the section or by his associate or first assistant, who indicates the special investigations that are to be undertaken. On completion of the special examinations the patient is seen by the head of the section or his associate, who carefully reviews the history and the records of the physical examination, and correlates laboratory records and other data. A diagnosis is made and the treatment outlined.[12]

Willius and the other members of the cardiology section taught in the clinic, the hospital, and in the laboratory. The

FIG. 1 Frederick A. Willius (1888–1972). (Source: Mayo Clinic Archives).

hospital service admitted only patients with cardiovascular disease. Basic research was undertaken at the Institute of Experimental Surgery and Pathology, which included laboratories for animal experimentation. Fellows in medicine were encouraged to participate in clinical investigation or laboratory research under the supervision of Willius and his staff. He boasted in 1927 that "all the members of the permanent staff of the section are engaged in clinical investigation. The results of the work carried on by the . . . staff of the section during the last five years have been published in nearly fifty articles."[12]

Willius revealed his sophisticated knowledge of cardiology and his familiarity with the recent literature of the field in a comprehensive literature review published in 1925. He explained, "In this age of scientific progress, in which the cogs of clinical and laboratory investigations grind ceaselessly, it seems appropriate to record the achievements in diseases of the heart and circulation."[13] Willius emphasized the importance of cardiovascular research and explained that heart disease was not only responsible for the largest number of deaths annually in the United States but it was also the greatest single cause of disability. This same year, Willius told members of the newly founded Minnesota Heart Association (of which he was president) that they must devote more energy to the "great cause of preventive cardiology."[14]

During the 1940s Willius became America's leading historian of cardiology. In addition to writing several historical and biographical articles dealing with the circulation, he published *Cardiac Classics: A Collection of Classic Works on the Heart and Circulation* with Mayo librarian Thomas E. Keys in 1941,[15] and *A History of the Heart and Circulation* with fellow Mayo cardiologist Thomas J. Dry in 1948.[16] Willius retired in 1953 and died in Rochester in 1972.

References

1. Physicians of the Mayo Clinic and the Mayo Foundation. Minneapolis: University of Minnesota Press, 1937
2. Willius FA: *As I Lived It.* Unpublished manuscript (1953). Mayo biographical file. *Mayo Archives*, Plummer 3, Mayo Clinic, Rochester, Minn.
3. Nelson CW: *Mayo Roots: Profiling the Origins of Mayo Clinic.* Rochester: Mayo Foundation for Medical Education and Research, 1990
4. Willius FA: *Henry Stanley Plummer: A Diversified Genius.* Springfield: Charles C Thomas, 1960
5. Fye WB: A history of the origin, evolution, and impact of electrocardiography. *Am J Cardiol* 1994;73:937–949
6. Fye WB: Disorders of the heartbeat: A historical overview from antiquity to the mid-20th century. *Am J Cardiol* 1993;72:1055–1070
7. Blackford JM, Willius FA: Chronic heart-block. *Am J Med Sci* 1917;154:585–592
8. Willius FA: Myocardial disease with reference to the subendocardial myocardium. *Med Clin North Am* 1919;3:653–659
9. Willius FA: *Clinical Electrocardiograms: Their Interpretation and Significance.* Philadelphia: W. B. Saunders Co., 1929
10. Fye WB: *American Cardiology: The History of a Specialty and its College.* Baltimore: Johns Hopkins University Press, 1996
11. *Section of Cardiology and the Laboratories of Electrocardiography.* Report of Dr. F. A. Willius to the Mayo Clinic Board of Governors. Unpublished manuscript (1924) Willius 1924–1944 folder, Box BAR-4, Mayo Archives
12. Willius FA: Cardiology in the Mayo Clinic and the Mayo Foundation for Medical Education and Research. In *Methods and Problems of Medical Education* (Eighth series), p 193–197. New York: Rockefeller Foundation, 1927
13. Willius FA: The progress of cardiology during 1924: A review of the works of clinicians and investigators in the United States. *Minnesota Med* 1925;8:165–170, 230–236, 293–297
14. Willius FA: A plan for the organization of preventive cardiology in Minnesota. *Collected Papers of the Mayo Clinic* 925; 17: 1020–1024
15. Willius FA, Keys TE: *Cardiac Classics: A Collection of Classic Works on the Heart and Circulation.* St. Louis: C. V. Mosby, 1941
16. Willius FA, Dry TJ: A *History of the Heart and Circulation.* Philadelphia: W. B. Saunders Co., 1948

Frank Norman Wilson

J. K. KAHN, M.D., J. D. HOWELL, M.D.

Department of Medicine, University of Michigan, Ann Arbor, Michigan, USA

Electrocardiography has now become an integral part of clinical medicine. Our modern understanding of the electrocardiogram comes, in large part, from the lifelong research and teaching of Frank Norman Wilson (Fig. 1). In his prime, Wilson dominated use of the electrocardiogram as only two men, Thomas Lewis and Willem Einthoven, had done before him, and as none has done since.

Wilson was born in Livonia Township, outside of Detroit, Michigan, on November 19, 1890 (Johnston and Lipeschkin, 1954). He was the only child of Norman Orlando Wilson, a farmer, and Mary Holtz Wilson. In 1907, Wilson graduated from Western High School in Detroit and began undergraduate studies at the University of Michigan in Ann Arbor. In 1911, he graduated with a Bachelor of Science degree and was accepted into the university's medical school. Wilson was nominated to Alpha Omega Alpha and graduated from medical school in 1913, the same year he married Juel A. Mahoney, a music student.

Wilson remained in the Department of Medicine in Ann Arbor as an assistant. In 1914, Wilson's only child, Julia Anne, was born. Also in 1914, the hospital purchased a Cambridge string galvanometer, one of only about 12 in the United States. Albion Walter Hewlett, Chief of Medicine at Michigan, put Wilson in charge of assembling and using the machine. In 1915 Wilson published his first paper, an investigation with the electrocardiogram, in the British journal *Heart*, a journal founded only 6 years earlier by the young electrocardiograph expert Thomas Lewis (Wilson, 1915).

Wilson moved to Washington University in St. Louis in 1916. However, World War I broke out, and from 1917 to 1919 Wilson served in the U.S. Army Medical Corps. He was the youngest of a group of American physicians sent to Colchester, England, to study soldiers suffering from a poorly understood disease initially called "soldiers' heart." There Wilson met Thomas Lewis, who had become the world's leading expert on the electrocardiogram. Lewis and Wilson initiated what was to be a close friendship. They discussed not only electrocardiography, but also a hobby they both shared —bird photography. The two electrocardiographic experts spent many days together photographing unusual birds, developing the photographs at night.

At the end of the war, Wilson returned to St. Louis and teamed with George Herrmann to study electrocardiographic manifestations of hypertrophy and bundle-branch blocks. In 1921, Wilson returned to Ann Arbor as Associate Professor in charge of the Cardiology Service and remained at the University of Michigan for the rest of his career. Wilson drew several noted foreign visitors to Ann Arbor. In 1922, Thomas Lewis and his wife, now Sir Thomas and Lady Lewis, visited Wilson in Ann Arbor. Sir Thomas received an honorary Doctor of Science from the University, althought some suspected that one reason for his visit was to share photographs of the black tern with Wilson. In 1924, Willem Einthoven, the inventor of the electrocardiogram, stopped in Ann Arbor with his wife and sister-in-law.

In 1925, Wilson recruited Paul Barker and A. Garrard MacLeod to Ann Arbor to assist him in his electrocardiographic research. When Cyris Sturgis was appointed Chairman of Medicine in 1927, he freed Wilson from most clinical responsibilities in order that Wilson might pursue his research interests. That same year a double-string galvanometer specially built for Wilson arrived from Leyden, The Netherlands. Also in 1927, Wilson became ill, underwent a cholecystectomy, and required 2 years convalescence on his farm in Stockbridge, Michigan. Wilson used this prolonged recuperation to master higher mathematics and physics.

On his return to work in 1929, Wilson entered his most productive period. Whereas Lewis had concentrated on using the electrocardiogram to study arrhythmic disorders of the heart, Wilson led research into a new area, the study of the form of the electrocardiographic complex. As Wilson had put it in 1920:

> For the first few years after the introduction of the string galvanometer into clinical medicine, electrocardiographers devoted most of their attention to the analysis of the cardiac irregularities. This field has been so extensively cultivated that it is approaching exhaustion and there is an increasing tendency to turn to the significance of abnormalities of the form of the electrocardiographic deflections as a subject of research (Wilson, 1920).

During the early 1930s, Wilson performed seminal studies on surface precordial electrodes, observing that the tracings thus produced were "in many respects similar to those obtained by placing one electrode upon the exposed heart" (Wilson, 1930). He described chest lead placement using five leads. Because he recognized that recordings from the bipolar chest leads were distorted by interference from the "indiffer-

FIG. 1 Frank N. Wilson.

ent" electrode placed on the leg, he developed a method to record precordial deflections free of interference. Connecting the three extremities through equal 5000 ohm resistors, Wilson demonstrated that the central point, or terminal, would act as an indifferent electrode, allowing true unipolar precordial recordings (Wilson, 1934). The Central Terminal of Wilson has since been incorporated in almost all electrocardiographic equipment, and unipolar leads have greatly increased the accuracy of electrocardiographic diagnosis. Wilson also corrected misconceptions about the electrocardiographic manifestations of right and left bundle-branch block (Wilson, 1932).

Wilson used his knowledge of mathematics and physics to great effect in a highly theoretical monograph on the electrical properties of the heartbeat, a subject previously poorly understood (Wilson et al., 1933). He proposed a dipole theory to explain the electrical basis of the ventricular complex and the injury currents recognized in patients with myocardial injury.

Wilson's swiftness and accuracy of intellect were recognized by his friends, who called him "Snake Wilson." Only a few weeks after he was introduced to chess in Colchester, Wilson was regularly defeating those who had taught him. He appreciated that his work was too complex and theoretical for some and often discouraged his noncardiology colleagues at the University from picking up reprints of his research, aware that they would not comprehend them. It is this complexity which was the reason that some of Wilson's finest work was rejected by leading medical journals, and why his scientific presentations at the yearly meetings of the Association of American Physicians were often poorly attended due to their technical nature. However, Wilson's expertise in clinical electrocardiography was widely recognized. In the 1930s, he initiated a yearly postgraduate course in Ann Arbor, which drew physicians from the United States, Europe, and Central and South America, many of whom remained in Ann Arbor for further training.

In 1940, Wilson was selected to give the Henry Russel Lecture at the University of Michigan, the highest award bestowed on a faculty member. That year, Samuel Levine, Paul Barker, and others also initiated a lectureship in Wilson's name. Early lecturers included Samuel Levine, William Dock, and Emmanuel Libman, but the series was later interrupted by World War II.

In 1943, Wilson summarized his work to date in a delivery to the Association of Life Insurance Medical Directors of America (Wilson, 1944). He received over 2500 reprint requests for the article, and it was later translated into Spanish and reproduced in journals in Argentina and Uruguay.

Wilson lectured extensively throughout South America on electrocardiography. In the summer of 1943, he suffered a mild myocardial infarction. Again, in 1946, while in Mexico City at a cardiology conference, he experienced chest pain. He spurned requests by Paul Dudley White and Samuel Levine that he be hospitalized, and returned to Ann Arbor by airplane to recuperate on his farm.

In 1948, Wilson was found to have pulmonary tuberculosis, forcing him to limit his clinical activities. The following year, his daughter married Eugene Lepeschkin, a cardiologist from New Orleans. In 1950, the July edition of *Circulation* was dedicated to Wilson, and in November 1950, the *American Heart Journal* published an appreciation written by George Herrmann. The American Heart Association presented him the Gold Heart Award in June 1951. Wilson's health declined and in the spring of 1952, during surgery to resect a tuberculous lesion, he suffered a cardiac arrest from which he was revived. However, on September 11, 1952, he died suddenly. At the time of his death, he was the author of over 120 scientific articles and on the editorial boards of the *Journal of Clinical Investigation,* the *American Heart Journal, Circulation, Cardiologia,* and *Experimental Medicine and Surgery.* His passing was recognized in over ten journals in several languages. With the assistance of Franklin D. Johnson, a display of Wilson's work and original equipment was established on permanent display in the Museum of American History in the Smithsonian Institution, Washington, D.C.

References

Johnston FD, Lipeschkin E: *Selected Papers of Dr. Frank N. Wilson.* Edwards Brothers, Ann Arbor (1954)

Wilson FN: Report of a case showing premature beats arising in the junctional tissues. *Heart* 6, 17 (1915)

Wilson FN: The distribution of potential differences produced by the heartbeat within the body and at its surface. *Am Heart J* 5, 599 (1930)

Wilson FN, Herrmann GR: Bundle branch block and arborization block. *Arch Int Med* 26, 153 (1920)

Wilson FN, MacLeod AG, Barker PS: The order of ventricular excitation in bundle branch block. *Am Heart J* 7, 305 (1932)

Wilson FN, Johnston FD, MacLeod AG, Barker PS: Electrocardiograms that represent the potential variations of a single electrode. *Am Heart J* 9, 447 (1934)

Wilson FN, MacLeod AG, Barker PS: The interpretation of the initial deflection of the ventricular complex of the electrocardiogram. *Am Heart J* 6, 637 (1931)

Wilson FN, MacLeod AG, Barker PS: *The Distribution of the Currents of Action and Injury Displayed by Heart Muscle and Other Excitable Tissues.* University of Michigan Studies, Scientific Series, Vol. 18; 58, University of Michigan Press, Ann Arbor (1933)

Wilson FN, Johnston FD, Rosenbaum FF, Erlanger H, Kossmann CE, Hecht HH, Cotrim N, Mehezes de Oliveira R, Scavsi R, Barker PS: The precordial electrocardiogram. *Am Heart J* 27, 19 (1944)

Samuel A. Levine (1891–1966)

HERBERT J. LEVINE, M.D.

Department of Medicine, Cardiology Division, New England Medical Center Hospitals, Boston, Massachusetts, USA

Samuel A. Levine (Fig. 1) was born in Lomza, Poland, on January 1, 1891. The seventh of eight sons and the eighth of ten children, he was brought to this country at the age of three and grew up in Boston's North End, moving to the West End when he was ten. His early life was marked by scholastic brilliance, a goal-oriented work ethic, and a struggle to support himself and his family. By the time he was eight, he entered the eighth grade and began to sell newspapers. His "corner," the intersection of Tremont and Boylston Streets, although envied by his peers, was one of the coldest in Boston. Earning five dollars a week, he always gave three dollars to his mother and put two in the bank. No job was too menial for him—he worked as a street car conductor, elevator operator, tutor—but he continued his job as a newsboy until he started college. Indeed, following graduation from English High School, he became the second recipient of the Newsboy Union Scholarship to Harvard College. Initially, he planned to become an engineer, but after hearing a medical career lecture by Dr. Richard C. Cabot, he altered his curriculum to prepare for medical school.

Sam graduated Harvard College at age 20, and Harvard Medical School three years later in the class of 1914. While a medical student, he became interested in heart disease, in large part due to his contact with Dr. Joseph H. Pratt, founder of what later was to become the New England Medical Center. He was the first medical student to work at the newly opened Peter Bent Brigham Hospital and did so during the summer of 1913 under the tutelage of Dr. Reginald Fitz. During his internship at that hospital he began a lifelong friendship with his mentor and Physician-in-Chief, Dr. Henry A. Christian. "Uncle Henry," as he was known to many, shepherded Sam Levine through his house officer training at the Brigham and made arrangements for him to spend a year at the Hospital of the Rockefeller Institute in New York under Dr. Alfred E. Cohn. Dr. Cohn was an authority on the electrocardiograph and Sam had worked with this new apparatus briefly as a medical student.

Sam had planned to continue his studies abroad on a Moseley Traveling Scholarship, but these plans were cancelled when World War I broke out in Europe. The United States declared war in April 1917 and soon thereafter a British commission asked Washington to provide 2,000 medical men. Sam volunteered, and at 26 years became one of the youngest officers in the British medical corps. By a stroke of luck he was assigned to the British Heart Hospital in Colchester, where he had the good fortune to meet regularly with four celebrated and outstanding clinicians: Sir Clifford Allbutt, Sir William Osler, Sir James McKenzie, and the Medical Director of the hospital, Sir Thomas Lewis. Sam savored these associations with the four "British giants of cardiology" and in particular enjoyed a rich friendship with Sir Thomas Lewis that continued for years following the war. It is interesting that both Lewis and Levine separately contributed to the evolution of the syndrome that was to become mitral valve prolapse—Lewis by his detailed writings about "soldier's heart" and "the effort syndrome" and Levine by his report[1] on neurocirculatory asthenia (together with others working at the British Heart Hospital) and his publication with W. P. Thompson 17 years later entitled "Systolic gallop rhythm."[2]

Among seven to eight other American and Canadian medical officers assigned to the British Heart Hospital was Frank N. Wilson of St. Louis. Although Wilson's major interests involved physical science and basic principles of medicine and Sam was primarily concerned with clinical aspects of medicine, they became very close friends in England and remained so for the rest of their lives. Years later, it would become a custom for Sam Levine, Frank Wilson, Tinsley Harrison, and William Dock to share a suite at the annual ASCI/AFCR/AAP meetings each May in Atlantic City.

By April of 1918, Sam was transferred to Vittel, France. The war was going poorly and the influenza epidemic was causing almost as many deaths as the battle itself. Sam escaped the flu—and convinced his colleagues that he did so by washing his hands before each meal and constantly smoking strong Fatima cigarettes. He remained overseas for two years and after repeated requests for leave had been denied, in disgust he went AWOL to Algiers for a holiday and upon return was promptly given an overdue promotion from lieutenant to captain.

He finally returned home in July 1919 and joined the staff of the Peter Bent Brigham Hospital in Boston (now Brigham and Women's Hospital). He had, however, already made quite an impact upon that institution. In 1916, as a 25-year-old house officer he made an antemortem diagnosis of acute coronary thrombosis, which he and his colleagues thought at the time to be a medical first.[3] It was learned later that Dr. James D. Herrick of Chicago had made a similar diagnosis four years earlier. Sam Levine's teaching about heart attacks

Fig. 1   Dr. Samuel A. Levine (1891–1966).

was widely disseminated in this country and abroad, aided by a comprehensive monograph on the subject in 1929 that reviewed his experience with 145 cases of acute coronary thrombosis.[4]

Although Dr. Levine gained a reputation as one of the world's finest cardiologists, he prided himself on being an astute and experienced internist. Of his more than 250 publications, one of his favorites was a monograph on pernicious anemia,[5] which was the first to describe gastric achlorhydria as an integral part of that disease. He also considered himself to be an expert in poliomyelitis, having been involved in a good number of epidemics of this disease. Indeed, it was he who first made the diagnosis of polio in President Franklin D. Roosevelt, who initially had been treated for a cerebrovascular accident.

In 1923, Dr. Levine and Dr. Elliott Cutler reported the first successful mitral valvulotomy in a 12-year-old girl who survived for four and a half years following operation.[6] It is of interest that the procedure was done through a median sternotomy using a valvulotome (similar to a curved tonsil knife) passed between two mattress sutures in the left ventricular apex. The knife was advanced blindly through the stenotic mitral valve and cuts made medially and at 180 degrees "...the resistance encountered being very considerable." Despite this initial successful experience, the next three patients succumbed postoperatively and enthusiasm for the procedure waned and lay dormant until 1948 when mitral valvulotomy was revived by Dr. Dwight E. Harken and by Dr. Charles P. Bailey.

On June 20, 1926, Sam married Rosalind Weinberg and within four years, they had three children, Carol, Herbert, and Joan, all of whom still live in the Boston area. After a long honeymoon in Europe and the Middle East, Sam returned to Boston and initiated a routine that changed very little over the

next forty years. Mornings until about 1:00–2:00 P.M., he spent at the Brigham Hospital making rounds, holding clinics, attending conferences, and teaching house staff and students. By 2:00 each afternoon, he was in his office on Commonwealth Avenue in Boston where he would remain until 6:00–6:30 P.M. Saturdays he would work with his graduate students reviewing scientific data and writing manuscripts. Nights and weekdays were constantly interrupted by trips to nearby hospitals or to a patient's home. As his reputation grew, it was not unusual for him to drive to Rutland, Vermont, or Hartford, Connecticut, or to fly to California or Caracas, Venezuela, to see a patient in consultation. He vacationed with his family every August, initially in Georgetown, Massachusetts, and later in Falmouth on Cape Cod. Mornings of these vacations were spent writing, or working on his text *Clinical Heart Disease*, the first edition of which was published in 1936. Although he enjoyed an occasional day's fishing and played tennis until he was about 50, he was not particularly athletic—the only sporting event he ever won was a 25-mile walking race when he was a medical house officer. He greatly enjoyed theater, particularly musicals. As an impecunious youth, he purchased "standing room" tickets to all performances, but with financial success, his one extravagance was to obtain the best seats to a Cole Porter musical or to Shakespeare's *Hamlet*. Once, while at home dressing for first night at the opera, he received a call from the Brigham emergency ward about a woman with paroxysmal atrial tachycardia who had not responded to the usual measures. Wearing his tuxedo and top hat, he rushed to the hospital, ran to the patient's bedside, deftly terminated the arrhythmia with carotid sinus pressure and quickly proceeded to the opera. The next day the patient was asked to relate the events of the previous evening. "Well," she said, "the doctors tried everything to stop my palpitation, but couldn't—so they called in this magician! He tickled my neck and it stopped—you know, this hospital is not a very Christian place."

Dr. Levine gave a summer postgraduate course in cardiology for 36 years (1921–1956)—the longest course in the history of Harvard Medical School. These lectures in the Brigham amphitheater every July were full of personal anecdotes and delivered with a minimum of slides, interrupted by the frequent lighting of his Chesterfield cigarettes. Sam loved to teach. Whatever he discovered or learned, he felt the need to impart to others. Like many good teachers, he was a bit of a ham. His performances at the hospital parties—a song, a dance routine, or a poem—often with Dr. Merrill Sosman (Radiologist-in-Chief at the Brigham Hospital) were legendary.

Dr. Levine's greatest talent was his ability to make clinical observations and to share these observations with others. Many of the postgraduate students and house staff who trained with him became the leaders of American academic cardiology in the 1950s and 1960s. In 1949, Dr. W. Proctor Harvey collaborated with Dr. Levine on a text devoted entirely to bedside cardiac diagnosis, entitled *Clinical Auscultation of the Heart*. Since that time, Dr. Harvey has championed the importance and value of bedside examination, extending the lessons taught by Dr. Levine. Another of his students, Dr. Bernard Lown, developed a unique and lasting professional relationship with Dr. Levine that fueled a long period of productive collaborative research. Dr. Lown recalled, "By the time I had become one of Dr. Levine's fellows, he had already seen about 30,000 patients in his career. I had the impression that he remembered all of them!"

In the early 1950s Levine startled the medical community by recommending that heart attack victims be gotten out of bed and into a chair within the first couple of days following their acute attack.[7] Conventional therapy in those days mandated four to six weeks of bedrest following acute coronary thrombosis and, despite Levine's convincing litany of the harmful effects of recumbency, it took years for the "armchair" treatment of heart attack patients to evolve. Another of his important contributions was to teach physicians how to recognize "masked" thyrocardiac disease, emphasizing the role of thyrotoxicosis in the genesis of congestive heart failure in these patients. Dr. Levine constantly admonished his students always to look for curable disease no matter how rare a condition might be. "I would rather miss ten cases of amyotrophic lateral sclerosis than a single case of pheochromocytoma," he would say.

Dr. Levine effectively combined good science and good sense. He once wrote a paper on the art of medicine, concluding that the art of medicine in reality is the science of medicine. He was always alert to iatrogenic disease and was strongly critical of polypharmacy. Once after examining a depressed, anorexic heart failure patient taking thirteen different medications, he told the house officer to stop all but two of the medicines, and walked away. The intern called after him, "Dr. Levine, which two?" "Any two!" he replied.

One of the highpoints of his career came in 1954 when the New York investment banker, Charles E. Merrell, endowed the Samuel A. Levine Professorship at Harvard Medical School. At that time this was the largest endowment for any single chair in the history of the school. Sam remained a loyal member of the Harvard Medical faculty for more than forty-five years.

Dr. Levine enjoyed excellent health throughout his life. An episode of acute bronchitis requiring a bronchoscopy at age 60 induced him to give up smoking, and except for a brief hospitalization for prostate surgery, he almost never missed a day of work for illness. However, on January 1, 1966, while celebrating his 75th birthday with his wife, Rosalind, and his three children and their spouses, he first noticed some midepigastric discomfort. Two weeks later he underwent a total gastrectomy for gastric carcinoma. The surgery was not curative and on March 31, 1966, two and a half months following surgery, he died at his home in Newton Centre, Massachusetts.

Dr. Levine will be remembered as one of the great clinical cardiologists of his time. To the medical community, perhaps his signal contribution was his unique capacity to share with others an intuitive and trained power of clinical observation and to do so with great flair and a masterful sense of timing. Tinsley R. Harrison wrote in a tribute to Dr. Levine, "I have not known a keener bedside clinician, a more inspiring teacher, a kindlier physician, a more loyal friend, a nobler gentleman nor a sweeter human spirit."[8] To his family, he will be remembered for his profound love and devotion and for demonstrating a way of life that espoused honor and integrity. Written on his gravestone is the phrase: "Above all else, the crown of a good name."

References

1. Oppenheimer BS, Levine SA, Morison RA, Rothschild MA, St. Lawrence W, Wilson FA: Report on neurocirculatory asthenia and its management. *Military Surgeon* (April–June 1918)
2. Thompson WP, Levine SA: Systolic gallop rhythm: A clinical study. *N Engl J Med* 213, 1021–1025 (1935)
3. Levine SA, Tranter CL: Infarction of the heart simulating acute surgical abdominal conditions. *Am J Med Sci* 155, 57 (1918)
4. Levine SA: *Coronary Thrombosis: Its Various Clinical Features*. Williams and Wilkins Co., Baltimore (1929)
5. Levine SA, Ladd WS: Pernicious anemia: A clinical study of one hundred and fifty consecutive cases with special reference to gastric anacidity. *Johns Hopkins Bull* 32, 1–32 (1921)
6. Cutler EC, Levine SA: Cardiotomy and valvulotomy for mitral stenosis: Experimental observations and clinical notes concerning an operated case with recovery. *Boston Med Surg J* 188, 1023–1027 (1923)
7. Levine SA, Lown B: The "chair" treatment for acute coronary thrombosis. *Trans Assoc Am Phys* 64, 316–327 (1951)
8. Harrison TR: Tribute to Dr. Levine. *N Engl J Med* 275, 222–223 (1966)

William Hamilton, 1893–1964

A. C. WITHAM, M.D.

Medical College of Georgia, Augusta, Georgia, USA

A golden era in cardiovascular physiology existed in America for three decades after 1930. The stage was the meetings of the Circulation Group of American Physiological Society. The most famous actors in a distinguished group were probably Carl Wiggers, Hiram Essex, Louis Katz, and William Hamilton. European visitors were always shocked at the sharp comments, frank skepticism, and brutal questions, all politely labeled "discussion" in the program, that these famous scientists hurled at each other. They were much relieved to discover that warm personal friendships, bonded by a shared zeal for truth, existed outside the debating arena. The fiery crucible of criticism through which this research passed may account for the viability of so much of it today.

William Hamilton, the gentle professor, had a surprisingly turbulent childhood. He was born in 1893 in Tombstone, Arizona Territory, not long after Wyatt Earp's departure and the surrender of Geronimo's Apaches. His family wandered about the Southwest and northern Mexico, which was loosely controlled by Pancho Villa and others of his ilk. His father was an itinerant physician to a succession of remote ranches and mining camps. Unfortunately, opportunities for speculation abounded and he rarely resisted (Hamilton, unpublished notes). Family finances were predictably volatile, but Hamilton managed to finish high school in Tucson and then worked his way through Pomona College in Claremont, California. He developed a life-long interest in biology at that institution and received the A.B. degree in 1917. After a stint in the army he entered the University of California, Berkeley, and received the Ph.D. in Zoology in 1921. He married Helen Dula in 1918. They produced a close-knit family of four children and seven grandchildren.

Before he finally settled in at the Medical College of Georgia in 1934 as Chairman of the combined Department of Physiology and Pharmacology, he had ascended the academic ladder in physiology departments at the University of Texas (1920–1921), Yale (1921–1923), Louisville (1923–1931), and Washington University in St. Louis (1932–1934).

Hamilton's avidity for research awakened early; while still at Pomona he authored four publications in the field of marine biology, an interest which lasted a decade (Hamilton, 1922). Color vision also caught his early attention. Studies in this field, still considered basic, punctuate his bibliography between 1922 and 1944.

He is, of course, more widely known for his contributions to hemodynamics. These studies began about 1929 and continued until his death in 1964. While basically a theorist, he often had to devise unique instruments to test his hypotheses. For example, his interest in arterial pulse-wave velocity and the effect of standing and reflected waves on pulse contour demanded high-fidelity manometry (Hamilton *et al.,* 1934). Thus was born the membrane manometer. Its impact was immediate. Its accuracy and availability stimulated wide-ranging research both in his own laboratory and in many others.

The fortuitous choice of beryllium copper for the sensitive membranes, a material whose properties proved to be ideal, was apparently intuitive, since he had neither metallurgical training nor consultants. It seems probable that accurate blood pressures in humans were measured for the first time with this device since it had no peer in fidelity. The results were reported in 1936 in a study detailing the relationships between intrathoracic, intraspinal, and arterial pressures (Hamilton *et al.,* 1936). Simultaneous recordings were possible utilizing a battery of manometers. With his clinical co-investigators, relationships between pressures in almost every reachable human body space and vessel were also explored—uterus, fetus, abdomen, lungs, arteries, and veins, for example—and during various interventions such as anesthesia, surgery, shock, drugs, electroconvulsive therapy, and labor (Woodbury *et al.,* 1938). Strain gauges and electronics eventually displaced membrane manometers and photographic records, but by improving convenience, not fidelity.

His broad curiosity led him to direct his attention briefly to a variety of problems. He needed a rapid method of measuring the specific gravity of blood and, as he frequently did, devised one himself. This was the "falling drop" technique which became, for many years, the standard in clinical laboratories for estimating serum protein concentration (Barbour and Hamilton, 1926). He focused on the electrocardiogram just long enough to point out that the ST "shift" attributed to injury was erroneous terminology (Nahum *et al.,* 1943). This segment, he reasoned, could not actively respond to injury because the ventricles were electrically inert after depolarization; injury potentials actually occurred during the diastolic (T-P) interval and the baseline shift created the illusion of movement of the ST segment.

His mathematical description, with his colleagues, of the sequenced arterial concentration of foreign dye injected into

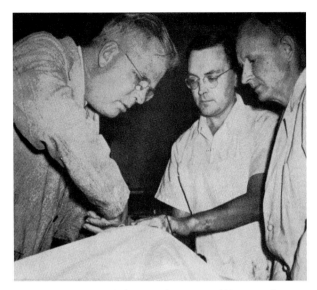

FIG. 1   Hamilton (left), Remington, and Dow—a famous research trio working at the Medical College of Georgia, Augusta, Georgia.

the venous circulation ('Stewart-Hamilton" equations) must rank with his greatest gifts to contemporary cardiologists (Hamilton *et al.,* 1932; Moore *et al.,* 1929). Fortunately, black boxes, storing Hamilton's formulations, now compute dye or thermodilution outputs almost instantaneously instead of requiring laborious sampling, color-metric analysis, and calculations.

Considering the cost and logistics of quality research today, it is sobering to review Hamilton's budget in the 12 years 1934–1946 as extracted by Dr. Carlton Baker from the Medical College of Georgia records (Baker *et al.,* 1984). There were no grants. About $2,000 per year was allocated for "teaching and research" supplies. Sixty-five research reports, almost all attacking fundamental cardiovascular problems, were generated in this period (perhaps $200/study). The experiments were performed entirely by Hamilton and his tiny faculty (usually Woodbury, Dow, and Remington) or with the help of his clinical collaborators (particularly Torpin, Volpitto, Cleckley, and Harper). Equipment was modified student apparatus or, like the manometer, built in his own machine shop. Technicians, if any, were secretaries dragooned, often under protest, from their typewriters. There were no fellows or graduate students then. Hamilton, because he felt the undergraduate teaching obligation keenly, compartmentalized the academic year. Physiology was taught almost daily for three months, research frozen. Then for nine months he managed a vigorous mini-research institute.

A scientist's place in history is often evident by the stamp of excellence he places on those whom he touches. Many of those around him became prominent in their own right— Phillip Dow and John Remington, his most frequent co-authors, and his clinician volunteers consisting of thoracic sur-

geons, cardiologists, internists, and even psychiatrists, who were inspired to donate their talents to fundamental research. He brought Raymond Ahlquist to Georgia to spin off pharmacology as a separate department. Hamilton, almost alone, recognized Ahlquist's theory of adrenergic receptors as a milestone and sponsored its publication in spite of a stack of rejections. Finally in his later years, under the auspices of the National Institutes of Health and the American Heart Association, he trained 32 young investigators from all over the world in investigative techniques. A modest and unassuming man, he would probably have insisted that the inspirational virus passed to him from his collaborators rather than the other way around.

He was not unappreciated in his own lifetime. He received many honors including the Connor Lectureship and Gold Heart Award of the American Heart Association. He was a founder and first chairman of the AHA Basic Science Council and President of the American Physiological Society. Andre Cournand, in his Nobel address of 1956, singles Hamilton out with generous praise, considering his concepts, technology, and "kindly criticisms" as fundamental to his own success.

Hamilton had a low regard for the writing of texts. He dismissed this activity as appropriate for scientists only when totally bereft of research ideas. But he eventually felt compelled to write one anyway, a short book of general physiology, as a companion to his own undergraduate course. It served its purpose and was, in fact, adopted by many other universities.

References

Baker CH, Davis DL, Ellison LT, Schoenborn CEH, Little RC, Waugh WH: Twenty-Eighth APS President. William F. Hamilton. *Physiologist* 27, 64 (1984)

Barbour HG, Hamilton WF: The falling drop method for determining specific gravity. *J Bio Chem* 69, 625 (1926)

Hamilton WF: Unpublished autobiographical notes in the Department of Physiology, Medical College of Georgia

Hamilton WF: A direct method of testing color vision in lower animals. *Proc Nat Acad Sci* 8, 350 (1922)

Hamilton WF, Brewer G, Brotman I: Pressure pulse contours in the intact animals. I. Analytical description of a new high-frequency hypodermic manometer with illustrative curves of simultaneous arterial and intracardiac pressures. *Am J Physiol* 107, 427 (1934)

Hamilton WF, Moore JW, Kinsman JM, Spurling RG: Studies on the circulation. IV. Further analysis of the injection method, and of changes in hemodynamics under physiological and pathological conditions. *Am J Physiol* 99, 534 (1932)

Hamilton WF, Woodbury RA, Harper HT, Jr: Physiological relationships between intrathoracic, intraspinal and arterial pressures. *JAMA* 107, 853 (1936)

Moore JW, Kinsman JM, Hamilton WF, Spurling RG: Studies on the circulation. II. Cardiac output determinations; comparison of the injection method with the direct Fick procedure. *Am J Physiol* 89, 331 (1929)

Nahurn LH, Hamilton WF, Hoff HE: The injury current in the electrocardiogram. *Am J Physiol* 139, 202 (1943)

Woodbury RA, Hamilton WF, Torpin R: The relationship between abdominal, uterine and arterial pressures during labor. *Am J Physiol* 121, 640 (1938)

The Synthesis of Humanism and Medical Science: Herrman Ludwig Blumgart, 1895–1977—Teacher, Physician, Administrator, Scientist

Nanette K. Wenger, m.d.

Department of Medicine, Division of Cardiology, Emory University School of Medicine, Cardiac Clinics, Grady Memorial Hospital, Atlanta, Georgia, USA

Without scientific knowledge, a compassionate wish to serve mankind's health is meaningless and it should be possible to acknowledge the triumphs of medicine without denigrating the art.

—Herrman Ludwig Blumgart

Teacher

Several decades of Harvard medical students vividly and with great pleasure recall Dr. Herrman Blumgart's orientation-day clinic, an exercise that rapidly became a tradition for the entering class at the Harvard Medical School. Initially begun as an elective clinic for first-year medical students, this session was soon viewed as an elegant introduction to the Medical School. Conversing with a patient in a case presentation format, Dr. Blumgart would skillfully and effectively define the highlights of the clinical history and the features of the physical examination evident on observation, emphasizing first the importance of learning to perform these clinical skills but rapidly thereafter depicting the reliance of clinical medicine on data derived from the several basic sciences: physiology, biochemistry, pharmacology, and so forth. Some 40 years later, I can clearly see the slender woman with thyrotoxicosis, her obvious proptosis, the enlarged thyroid gland, the demonstrable fine tremor; and can remember the subsequent facile discussion of the interrelationships between thyroid and cardiac function. Other students might relate the presentation of a patient with complete heart block, treated with a newly available implanted cardiac pacemaker; or a cyanotic patient with congenital heart disease. In one short afternoon, Dr. Blumgart memorably reinforced for the entering medical class the rationale for and applicability to clinical care of their next two years of study of the basic health sciences. His course "Application of Physiologic Principles to Medicine" remains a model for contemporary curriculum committees.

Dr. Blumgart's lifelong interest in medical education involved not only the content and implementation of academic training for the medical students, interns, and residents, but a personal interest in each trainee as an individual, evident in his concern for both the scientific and the personal development of each. As Dr. A. Stone Freedberg wrote, "He selfless-ly created an environment within which productive scholarship could thrive. He was a superb teacher and lecturer and a model physician, wise and compassionate, skillfully blending the art and science of medicine."

After attaining Emeritus status in 1962, he became the Consultant Physician to the Harvard Medical Area, where he enjoyed thoroughly delivering primary care to patients, concomitantly teaching this discipline to medical students.

Although a cerebrovascular accident in 1973 with resulting expressive and receptive aphasia ended his active medical and teaching career, he laboriously relearned both to speak and to comprehend spoken language, facilitated by the constant support of his devoted wife Margaret and their daughter Ann.

Physician

Seated on the edge of a patient's bed to chat in the course of formal teaching ward rounds, Dr. Blumgart regularly astonished the medical students, who were accustomed to formal pronouncements and discussions by most professors made from the foot of the bed. But to Herrman Blumgart, the patient was part of the teaching equation; he regularly cited the need to know about the person as well as about the disease and to appreciate their interactions and interrelationships. He thoroughly enjoyed bedside teaching, noting that he continued to learn when addressing fascinating patient problems, both in the United States and during a visiting professorship in Lucknow, India.

This daily emphasis, by example, on the care of a patient rather than of a disease, profoundly influenced most of the 300 physicians who trained either totally or in part under his supervision at the Beth Israel Hospital (and it equally guided the later teaching styles of many of them who subsequently became professors in a number of medical schools and universities). Acknowledging Dr. Francis Peabody as the major single influence in the shaping of his career, Dr. Blumgart noted that Peabody was his mentor in clinical training, in research, and in the philosophy of medical care. The title of Dr. Blumgart's Gay Lecture on Medical Ethics, presented at the Harvard Medical School in 1963, was "Caring for the Patient," derived from Peabody's credo that "the secret of the

FIG. 1   Herrman Ludwig Blumgart, 1895–1977.

care of the patient is in caring for the patient." Dr. Blumgart si-multaneously emphasized "excellence and compassion in the care of the sick."

Blumgart was a meticulous observer, and many of his published papers detailed the characteristics of the many uncommon medical problems he encountered in his patients: right-sided infective endocarditis, parasystolic rhythms, and March hemoglobinuria, among others.

His clarity in the synthesis of clinical observations and resulting recommendations for care rendered these patient-based discussions memorable. During the then characteristic protracted hospital stay of patients following myocardial infarction, he found the precipitation of angina pectoris by their initial very gradual resumption of physical activities at seemingly inconsequential intensities very puzzling. The scene to be visualized includes male patients who sharpened their straight razors for shaving against a leather strap, and post-infarction women who painstakingly and slowly placed multiple rollers in their hair to achieve the popular pompadour style hairdo. Both of these activities commonly induced angina. Again and again, Dr. Blumgart would observe during ward rounds:

We do not yet appreciate the mechanism for the precipi-tation of chest pain, but one day we will—however, let your patients only very late in their recovery from my-ocardial infarction undertake either shaving or rolling their hair, for these activities will more likely provoke chest pain than will slow walking or bathing.

So clear was this recollection that, several years later, when the increased myocardial oxygen demand of these isometric activities was demonstrated, the reason for precipitation of angina pectoris at seemingly low intensity activity now ac-quired a scientific basis. I immediately telephoned Dr. Blum-gart to tell him of the presentation at a scientific meeting and the subsequent reports in the medical literature. Apparently my telephone call to him was only the first of many; in our subsequent conversations, with characteristic humility, he ex-pressed amazement at the number of former students and house officers who had remembered his precise observations and who were gratified that, as promised, a rational mecha-nism had been delineated.

Administrator

In 1928, both financial support and research space were al-located by the Beth Israel Hospital, which had been relocated close to the Harvard Medical School; at age 33, Dr. Herrman Blumgart was appointed Director of Medical Research at Beth Israel and Assistant Professor of Medicine at Harvard, as well as Head of the newly established Harvard Teaching Service of Medicine at the Beth Israel Hospital. (Dr. A. Stone Freedberg noted that a total of $20,000 constituted the annual support for the salaries of Dr. Blumgart, two physician assis-tants, and a laboratory technician.)

Dr. Blumgart methodically developed the Beth Israel Hos-pital to be a fully university-affiliated hospital. This involved the recruitment and development of a clinical staff whose training, competence, and standards of performance equalled that of the older units of the Harvard Medical system. Major changes in the requirements for hospital staff appointment, supported by the Board of Trustees, assured the level of ex-cellence required for full academic affiliation. This was ac-complished concomitantly with Dr. Blumgart's recruitment of colleagues and trainees to full-time positions in the Clinical Research Department of the hospital, which helped to meet the level of accomplishment in teaching and research required by the Harvard Medical School. This Beth Israel Hospital model was subsequently used by many community hospitals throughout the United States in their affiliation with medical schools; and it also served as a guide for the affiliation of Vet-erans' Administration Hospitals with medical schools and universities.

Taking advantage of the skills of the full-time research physicians, as well as the part-time clinical hospital staff, Blumgart rapidly expanded the two-month senior clerkship into a full medical teaching service. He included the medical students as members of the patient care team and skillfully adjudicated the roles of the house officer and the patient's pri-vate physician in the newly created "teaching services." A highlight, and evidence of his creative programming, was the combination of the teaching of patient care with the reitera-tion of pertinent and often new information from the sciences of physiology, biochemistry, and pharmacology.

In 1946, Dr. Blumgart succeeded Dr. Harry Linenthal as Physician-in-Chief and Professor of Medicine at the Beth Is-rael Hospital, where he remained until his retirement in 1962. Because the hospital by that time had active teaching programs in general surgery, pathology, and psychiatry, as well as in medicine, Dr. Blumgart was able to obtain full professor appointments at the Harvard Medical School for the newly selected chairmen of the Departments of Surgery and Psychiatry.

He recruited Dr. Grete Bibring as Head of the Department of Psychiatry (and the first woman professor at Harvard), and fostered the integration of the teaching of psychiatry with that of clinical medicine, emphasizing the need to understand the psychologic problems complicating medical illness and to employ the skills taught by that department in the management of patients with medical illness. He viewed this complex process as a means of improving the quality of the teaching of patient care; years later, terms in common usage such as "affirmative action in the hiring of women faculty" and "interdisciplinary or interdepartmental teaching" could describe the process, but would fail to identify the all-important goal.

At the time of World War II, the advent of large-scale federal funding for research increased the interest in research in the general community. In Boston, guided by Dr. Blumgart, this community involvement resulted in the formation of Patrons of Research, often patients or families of patients, who continued to support the Research Departments at the Beth Israel Hospital.

To honor Dr. Blumgart when he attained Emeritus status, the Herrman Ludwig Blumgart Professorship of Medicine at the Harvard Medical School was established by his friends, patients, colleagues, and other members of the Beth Israel family, and he was awarded an honorary Doctor of Science degree by Harvard University. The citation for the latter read "Distinguished Physician, Harvard Teacher, Imaginative Experimentalist; his ear is ever attuned to the heartbeat of mankind." For the next decade, he served as a Special Consultant to the Dean of the Harvard Medical School, primarily functioning as a member of the Admissions Committee, where he emphasized the cultivation of a relaxed interview atmosphere that permitted the attributes of each applicant to be readily assessed.

Scientist

Dr. Blumgart's initial research studies began while a third year medical student at Harvard; he worked with Cecil Drinker and Francis Peabody in Dr. Walter Cannon's laboratory to study the effects of pulmonary congestion on lung function. During an internship at the Peter Bent Brigham Hospital, on the service of Dr. Henry Christian, he demonstrated the absorption of pituitary extract via the nasal mucosa; publication of results of these experiments was followed by successful treatment of diabetes insipidus using this technique.

After completing his clinical training at Harvard, Dr. Blumgart was awarded a Moseley Traveling Fellowship. This was spent with Sir Thomas Lewis and Professor Henry Dale in London, where he studied the relationship of digitalis dosage to the exercise heart rate response of patients with atri-

al fibrillation; he determined that full-dose digitalis was required to block the exercise inhibition of vagal effect on the heart rate.

On returning to Boston, he joined the Harvard Medical Service and the Thorndike Memorial Laboratory at the Boston City Hospital, led by Drs. George Minot and Francis Peabody, and resumed his investigations of the velocity of blood flow. Radium C (no longer useful for therapy) was available at the Huntington Memorial Laboratory and Dr. Blumgart used this natural radioactive tracer 10 years before the advent of artificially produced radioactivity. He was among the first research scientists to use a radioactive isotope to study blood flow. Collaborating with Otto Yens, a physicist, he developed a small ionization chamber as well as a tube counter to produce the radiopharmaceutical radium C to measure the velocity of blood flow in both normal and disease states. His monograph "The Velocity of Blood Flow in Health and Disease," published in *Medicine* in 1931, summarized the 20 papers that documented his 5 years of clinical studies. For this work, the Society of Nuclear Medicine named him in 1969 to the Honor Roll of Nuclear Pioneers as the first physician pioneer in nuclear medicine and awarded him honorary fellowship in the Society of Nuclear Medicine.

When he moved his research base to the Beth Israel Hospital, his prior studies on the velocity of blood flow in hyperthyroid and hypothyroid patients fostered an interest in the beneficial effects of thyroid ablation on cardiac disease. His research provided the initial documentation of improvement of angina pectoris, congestive heart failure, and intractable supraventricular arrhythmias, first as a result of surgical thyroidectomy and subsequently due to ^{131}I thyroidectomy. Many of the elderly elevator operators at the Beth Israel Hospital (who often became self-appointed caretakers of the medical students and house officers) were coronary patients with previously intractable angina. They were enabled to return to work because the induced hypothyroidism controlled their chest pain, and their reemployment was facilitated by Dr. Blumgart.

Precise observation of the clinicopathologic correlations in patients with coronary heart disease led to another major research contribution: definition of the anatomy of the coronary circulation and demonstration of development of a coronary collateral circulation in response to coronary arterial obstruction. The technique for injection and dissection of the coronary arteries developed by Dr. Monroe Schlesinger led Blumgart, Schlesinger, and their associates to explain the disparities between the clinical manifestations of coronary disease and the morphologic abnormalities of coronary occlusion and myocardial infarction, substantially based on the contribution of the coronary collateral circulation to the preservation of myocardial viability. These pathoanatomic delineations have subsequently been validated by the contemporary techniques of coronary arteriography and formed the conceptual basis for the application of myocardial revascularization procedures, coronary artery bypass surgery, and coronary angioplasty.

And More...

Among Dr. Blumgart's additional contributions to medicine, medical care, and medical education were his service as Editor-in-Chief of *Circulation* for 10 years, and membership on the Editorial Boards of many prestigious journals, including the *New England Journal of Medicine*. He served as President of the Harvard Medical School Alumni Association, the Massachusetts Heart Association, and the New England Cardiovascular Society, among others. He was the recipient of the first James D. Herrick Award of the American Heart Association for his contributions to cardiology, and the recipient of the Gold Heart Award of the American Heart Association as well. He was a Master of the American College of Physicians and was in the Founders Group of the American Board of Internal Medicine and Cardiology.

He was a member of the American Academy of Arts and Sciences, the American Physiological Society, the Association of American Physicians, and the American Society of Clinical Investigation.

His nonmedical interests were diverse: fishing, both at his summer home in Maine and in the Florida Everglades; music, particularly chamber music; and art, to name a few. But it was his passion for people—for patients, for medical students and clinical and research trainees, for colleagues, for family, and for friends—that served as the catalyst to fuse his multiple and effective roles; and that added a special dimension to his view of the tasks of a doctor (docere=to teach) in his over half of century of service as a physician to the Harvard Medical School.

Acknowledgment

Most of the quotes are from the Archives of the Beth Israel Hospital and were supplied to the author by Ruth Freiman, Archivist. The quotation attributed to Dr. A. Stone Freedberg is from the *Harvard Medical Alumni Bulletin* May/June 1977. The quotation from Dr. Francis Peabody is from his paper entitled "The Care of the Patient," *J Am Med Assoc* 88, 877-882 (1927).

André F. Cournand: Father of Clinical Cardiopulmonary Physiology

ROBERT H. FRANCH, M.D.

Department of Medicine, Division of Cardiology, Emory University School of Medicine and Emory University Hospital, Atlanta, Georgia, USA

André Frédéric Cournand (Fig. 1) was born in Paris, France, on September 24, 1895, the son of an inventive and prominent dentist. From his father he learned the value of applied sciences; his mother's love of reading led him to a lifelong interest in literature. He studied the humanities and sciences at the Sorbonne and received the B.A. degree from the University of Paris in 1913 and the *certificat d'études physiques, chimiques, et biologiques* in 1914. However, his medical studies were interrupted by World War I. He served from 1915 to 1919, receiving the Croix de Guerre with bronze stars. During medical school and from 1924 to 1930, as an *interne des hôpitaux de Paris*, he coauthored papers reflecting broad patient interest: variations in blood sugar after Novarsin injection (1922); resuscitative use of intracardiac adrenalin in the dying infant (1924); and pulmonary edema associated with infection in the infant (1926). Four papers regarding (1) bronchiectasis, (2) surgery in progressive tuberculosis, (3) disseminated nodular tuberculosis, and (4) chronaxie of the facial nerve in patients with Chvostek's sign were coauthored in 1928, and in 1929 he reported on blood transfusion for bleeding secondary to typhoid fever. The subject of his M.D. thesis in 1930 was disseminated sclerosing encephalomyelitis.

In 1930 he came to New York to take up a position as a first-year resident on the chest and tuberculosis service under the direction of Dr. James A. Miller at Bellevue Hospital, the Columbia division. Prior to beginning these duties Dr. Miller placed him, for four months, on the Trudeau Sanatorium service at Saranac Lake, where a few years later he was to present his first scientific paper at a national meeting. Dr. Cournand states: "I was greeted by distinguished physicians, introduced to American ways and customs and helped by many to acquire more fluent usage of English" (Cournand, 1971).

In 1932 Dr. Miller asked Cournand, then chief resident of the chest service, to develop a laboratory at Bellevue Hospital. "I was to create in this service a small unit for the study of pulmonary function . . . A young French clinician totally untrained in physiological research" was placed "under the expert and enlightening tutelage" (Cournand, 1970) of Dickinson W. Richards, whose own laboratory at that time was uptown at Columbia Presbyterian Hospital. This initial mandate began a relationship that would span 41 years:

For all his affability, even temper and friendliness Dick was a hard taskmaster and a demanding teacher . . . He expected from his associates, if not the perfection, at least the acceptance of the work pace that he set for himself. Indeed I recall my mixed feelings when confronted by a deluge of books, manuscripts and reprints fed to me in our early meeting and during my initiation into the many techniques which I was supposed to rapidly master (Cournand, 1970).

Doctor Cournand also recalls relaxing at summer visits at the Richards' family home on Lake Sunapee in New Hampshire.

A lonely foreigner sitting around the table discovered and enjoyed the comforting and warm spirit of a closely knit American family. In this setting and roughing it along the trails of the White Mountains grew and ripened a friendship (Cournand, 1970).

Dr. Richards states,

The first three years were frustrating, our methods being faulty . . . Above the struggle with clumsy techniques, there was our continuing exchange of suggestions, ideas and opinions . . . This led us to look at problems from many sides and sometimes to move in a new direction (Richards, 1970).

Their research object was to study cardiopulmonary function in normal humans and in patients with pulmonary disease. As Lawrence J. Henderson had proposed in concept, in the laboratory they would treat the lung, heart, and circulation as a single system for gas exchange. Some methods were available, but many needed to be devised. Attempts to estimate the CO_2 and O_2 tension in mixed venous blood using rebreathing techniques in order to calculate pulmonary blood flow by the indirect Fick method in patients with pulmonary emphysema were unsatisfactory. Much was learned, however, about the inhomogeneous mixing and distribution of respiratory gases in a closed breathing circuit in normal subjects and in patients with pulmonary fibrosis and emphysema. Pulmonary function was studied before and after various

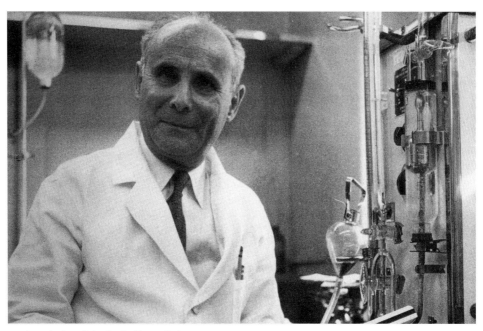

FIG. 1 André F. Cournand, at the bench in the Bellevue Laboratory.

forms of collapse therapy, including thoracoplasty. Circulatory failure in bilateral pneumothorax with elevated intrapleural CO_2 was described. Accurate spirometric methods and rebreathing as well as open circuit method of measuring residual air in the lung were developed in the Bellevue Laboratory, and a quantitative description of lung washout of N_2 during high oxygen breathing was made with R. C. Darling in 1940 (Darling *et al.,* 1940). These methods were to lead to the clinical and physiologic classification of various forms of pulmonary disease.

Dr. Cournand states:

In one of our early planning sessions, during which we were discussing methods for securing mixed venous blood for direct analysis of O_2 and CO_2 as an alternative to the rebreathing method, Dick Richards produced an issue of the 1929 *Klinische Wochenschrift* describing Forssmann's self experiment (Forssmann, 1929).

In 1936, together with Richards and Darling, and following a visit to a former teacher in Paris who had introduced catheters into the right atrium in order to perform pulmonary angiography, Dr. Cournand, convinced of the safety of the technique, began experiments, placing catheters in the right atrium of human cadavers, dogs, and in a chimpanzee—and then, in 1940, in a human in association with brachial or femoral artery cannulation (Cournand, 1975). The seed had fallen on prepared soil. It was now possible to measure blood flow, lung ventilation, and gas exchange over several hours without harm. A decade of working on methods was about to yield a harvest. Dr. Richard L. Riley, speaking of the early days, states: "I vividly recall Dr. Cournand struggling in the

dark to place the catheter in the right atrium, then calling 'now' and expecting instant arterial blood to match his mixed venous sample" (Riley, 1971). In their 1941 report, Cournand and Ranges showed that right atrial blood samples provided a reproducible measurement of cardiac output by the Fick method (Cournand and Ranges, 1941). Subsequently, pressure recordings were obtained from the right atrium in normals and in patients with heart failure using the Hamilton manometer, and blood volume studies were done utilizing dye techniques. The Riley-Cournand, three-part, arterial needle permitted chronic cannulation of an artery. A double-lumen catheter was also designed in order to permit simultaneous pressure recording from adjacent chambers. Right ventricular catheterization and pulmonary artery catheterization were done by Cournand in 1942 and in 1944, respectively (Cournand, 1975).

As World War II began, these methods found urgent use in a 3½-year physiologic study on traumatic shock headed by Dr. Richards and Dr. Cournand and sponsored by the Office of Scientific Research and Development. Studies on hemodynamic changes, effects on oxygen transport, and some cases of renal blood flow were made (Cournand *et al.,* 1943). A physiologic basis for treatment was derived. The clinical use of concentrated human serum albumin in shock was compared with whole blood and with rapid saline infusion.

R. L. Riley spoke of Cournand and Richards as follows:

They were the right men in the right place at the right time. They guided the destinies of the Bellevue Laboratory with scientific imagination and ethical sensitivity, with balance between intellectual curiosity and respect for the patient, with appreciation of the many to be helped by new knowledge and the one who might be injured by overenthusiastic investigation, with the desire to exploit techniques never before applied to human subjects without giving offense to the conservative standards of the medical community. In the public image Dick Richards stood for caution and André Cournand for daring. The reality was far more complex but together these men struck an unbelievable balance (Riley, 1971).

After World War II, Dr. Cournand became director of the cardiopulmonary laboratory at Bellevue Hospital and Dr. Richards was appointed chief of the Columbia Medical Service. Their collaboration continued unabated. The Columbia Presbyterian Medical Center laboratory was headed successively by Eleanor Baldwin, John R. West, and Alfred Fishman, and a common interest over the next eight years united these investigators. Dr. Cournand and co-workers put to statistical analysis the physiologic studies on 122 patients with pulmonary emphysema, 39 patients with pulmonary fibrosis, and 16 patients with bullous pulmonary disease. A classic series of three papers followed, coauthored with Eleanor Baldwin (Baldwin et al., 1949a, b, 1950). An initial paper had dealt with clinical methods of analysis and normal values for pulmonary function measurements as well as physiologic classification of pulmonary insufficiency (Baldwin et al., 1948). Diffusion insufficiency secondary to disseminated fibrosis was recognized. Patients with emphysema were classified physiologically on the basis of ventilatory insufficiency, alveolorespiratory insufficiency, and combined cardiac and pulmonary insufficiency.

In 1945, the study of atrial septal defect by Brannon, Warren, and Weens at Emory University in Atlanta was reported (Brannon et al., 1945), and a demonstration of ventricular septal defect by catheterization was noted by Baldwin (Baldwin et al., 1946). Dr. Cournand's textbook, *Cardiac Catheterization in Congenital Heart Disease*, coauthored with Janet Baldwin, a pediatrician, and Aaron Himmelstein, a thoracic surgeon, was published in March 1949 and dedicated to the memory of his son Pierre Birel Rosset-Cournand (Cournand et al., 1949). The techniques of right heart catheterization, arterial puncture, and collection of blood and expired air were described and catheter positions on spot films, pressure curve contours, and formulae for blood flow and shunt calculations were outlined. Seventeen illustrative cases were then presented with complete clinical and hemodynamic data in a box diagram format. The desire was to correlate clinical and physiologic data. In the introduction, appropriate and meticulous credit was given to all other investigators, characteristic of Dr. Cournand's sense of proper primacy in the community of his peers. He stressed the need for a well-trained team and a well-organized laboratory. Safety and reliability of results were uppermost in his mind. Zoll's paper on termination of ventricular fibrillation in man by externally applied electric countershock did not appear until 1956. Cournand chaired a national committee whose report in 1953 dealt with the risk of catheterization and ways to minimize them based on the experience of 5,700 right heart catheterizations (four deaths) from eight laboratories and 1325 venous angiograms from two laboratories (no deaths) (Cournand et al., 1953).

In a 1948 joint report, Dr. W. F. Hamilton and Cournand found close agreement comparing the Fick and dye injection (Stewart-Hamilton) methods of measuring cardiac output in man (Hamilton et al., 1948). Several physiologic studies of the effects of intermittent positive pressure breathing on the cardiac output in man were completed in the late 1940s (Cournand et al., 1948; Motley et al., 1947). In 1951, the effect of cortisone and adrenocortiotrophic hormone (ACTH) on patients with chronic pulmonary disease and impaired diffusion was assessed and the term *alveolar capillary block syndrome* was introduced (West et al., 1951).

The hemodynamics spectrum of circulatory changes secondary to chronic lung disease and rheumatic valve disease was described in serial reports with Irene Ferrer and Rejanne Harvey, together with studies on the circulatory and cardiac effects of quinidine (Ferrer et al., 1948); the effect of digoxin in chronic cor pulmonale (Ferrer et al., 1950); and in left ventricular failure (Harvey et al., 1949); the relationship between electrical and mechanical events of the cardiac cycle (Coblentz et al., 1949); hemodynamic studies in rheumatic tricuspid stenosis (Ferrer et al., 1953) and mitral stenosis (Harvey et al., 1955); mechanical and myocardial factors in chronic constrictive pericarditis (Harvey et al., 1953); effects of mitral commissurotomy with reference to selection of patients for surgery (Ferrer et al., 1955); and cardiocirculatory studies in pulsus alternans of the systemic and pulmonary circulation (Ferrer et al., 1956) and in atrial flutter (Harvey et al., 1955b).

The Columbia cardiopulmonary laboratories became a spawning ground for important work carefully performed, and, as important, for young investigators who went out to set up similar laboratories in other medical centers.

Dr. Cournand's own special field was the physiology of the pulmonary circulation and cor pulmonale pursued from 1944 to 1960. The Fourth Walter Wile Hamburger Memorial lecture, "Some Aspects of the Pulmonary Circulation in Normal Man and in Chronic Cardiopulmonary Diseases," was presented to the American Heart Association by Dr. Cournand in 1950 and remains a benchmark in the study of the pulmonary circulation (Cournand, 1950).

He shared the Nobel prize for medicine and physiology on December 11, 1956, with Werner Forssmann and Dickinson W. Richards "for their discoveries concerning heart catheterization and pathological changes in the circulatory system" (Sourkes, 1966). Dr. Forssmann presented his Nobel lecture first, stating that the late development of his method was from "a lack of a technical hypothesis and the lack of understanding that followed therefrom but also from weighty ethical considerations" (Sourkes, 1966). Dr. Richards followed, describing the decade of work required to assemble a group of methods for testing cardiopulmonary function that could be applied to normal humans and to patients with safety. He pointed out the urgent need for data on traumatic shock during World War II as a proving ground for methods, and finally the advances in the surgery of congenital heart disease that made cardiac catheterization important in this area. Dr. Cournand gave the concluding lecture. He modestly acknowledged that we had acquired some understanding of the relationship between pressure and flow in the pulmonary bed but that we poorly understood the mechanism of action of hypoxia on the pulmonary bed (even to this date) and he expressed concern on "how to extrapolate into indefinite time the results from a very short observation during catheterization" (Sourkes, 1966).

Shortly after the Nobel award to Dr. Cournand was announced, he visited us at the invitation of Dr. Noble Fowler who was then Director of the Cardiovascular Laboratory in the Department of Medicine at Emory University. We sat at a table in the Grady Hospital-Steiner Building catheterization laboratory previously used by Drs. Stead and Warren. He spoke of evaluating the myocardial component as well as the mechanical (valvular) factor in patients with pulmonary artery hypertension and clinical heart failure secondary to rheumatic heart disease. Interventions with exercise and intravenous digoxin were used to assess these factors. We were struck by his keen planning, meticulous attention to detail, and the great effort expended in achieving a steady state during cardiac output measurements in these patients. We asked a youthful question: "What was he to do with his Nobel Prize money?" He replied that "he might acquire a small cabin where he could read and enjoy the outdoors he had learned to love." In the years that followed he continued to work with young colleagues on ventilation perfusion relations, the oxygen consumption of tissue in the human lung, the quantitative anatomy of the lung, and the control of respiration.

Speaking of Dr. Cournand, Richards states:

As a leader he is infinitely generous of his sympathy, time and interest, equally strict in his critique of data and the logic of their interpretation. For myself I have marveled always to find what a spirited and pleasing interchange there can be between the adventurous flights of the French philosopher and the dogged interrogation of the New England puritan. We have moved quite independently at times, very closely in others; not always in agreement, but with a continuing trust that has held the scheme of things together (Richards, 1970).

In 1964, after 250 scientific publications and numerous honorary degrees and awards, Cournand retired as Professor Emeritus of Medicine. He also assumed the position of faculty associate of the Institute for the Study of Science in Human Affairs of Columbia University. In his 1970 essay "The Code of Science," written with Harriet Zuckerman, he outlines a functional guide for the scientist, his research activity, and his association with colleagues and the community (Cournand and Zuckerman, 1970). Moral and ethical overtones and the spirit of self-correction are present in his thoughts: investigators are to be continuously skeptical of scientific truths since the latter are capable of disproof but not validation, that is, "More truth can be known than can be proved." Discoveries may occur when the investigator "believes more deeply than others in the correctness of an idea" or if he has an "equally deep doubt of the validity of a commonly accepted idea" (Cournand and Zuckerman, 1970).

Cournand agreed with Polanyi that even though an occasional important work is overlooked, or rarely, a person deprived of an honor, serious evaluation in assessing scientific promise of publication is important to avoid "the entry of error into the system of communication" (Cournand and Zuckerman, 1970).

Regarding the tolerance for new ideas: "Novelties should not be rejected precipitously . . . dissent should be tentative rather than unyielding" (Cournand and Zuckerman, 1970).

Difficult as it may be to see one's work overturned he thinks it necessary for the scientist to declare his error publicly. "The point of such confessions is not the parading of one's humility but the reaffirmation of the values of reason and experience" (Cournand and Zuckerman, 1970).

Though science is a communal enterprise, he is concerned that restriction of information may occur in the conflict between early disclosure of research findings and the protection of priority. He notes that scientific research has moral and ethical consequences resulting in both admiration and hostility for its powers. Isolation of research from the economic, social, and national interest is likely a thing of the past, thus the propriety of personal gain for the scientist may soon be accepted and his work may shift from the scientifically significant to the socially and economically prudent.

Dr. Richards died in 1973 (Cournand, 1974); Dr. Forssmann in 1979. Dr. Cournand continues to lead an active life in his home in New York City. In addition to a philosophical bent, he has had a lifelong interest in contemporary painting and music, enriched by tutelage and friendship with renowned artists.

Finally, it is fitting that the importance of his great contribution, right heart catheterization, has been underscored by its use at the bedside to help the clinician with day-to-day hemodynamic problems.

Acknowledgment

Permission for direct quotations from references through the courtesy of the publisher and author (when available).

References

Baldwin E de F, Harden KA, Greene DG, Cournand A, Richards DW Jr: Pulmonary insufficiency IV. A study of 16 cases of large pulmonary air cysts or bullae. *Medicine* 29, 169 (1950)

Baldwin E de F, Cournand A, Richards DW Jr: Pulmonary insufficiency II. A study of 122 cases of chronic pulmonary emphysema. *Medicine* 28, 201 (1949a)

Baldwin E de F, Cournand A, Richards DW Jr: Pulmonary insufficiency III. A study of 39 cases of pulmonary fibrosis. *Medicine* 28, 1 (1949b)

Baldwin E de F, Cournand A, Richards DW Jr: Pulmonary insufficiency I. Physiological classification, clinical methods of analysis. Standard values in normal subjects. *Medicine* 27, 243 (1948)

Baldwin E de F, Moore LV, Noble RP: The demonstration of ventricular septal defect by means of right heart catheterization. *Am Heart J* 32, 152 (1946)

Brannon ES, Weens HS, Warren JV: Atrial septal defect. Study of hemodynamics by the technique of right heart catheterization. *Am J Med Sci* 210, 480 (1945)

Coblentz B, Harvey RM, Ferrer MI, Cournand A, Richards DW Jr: The relationship between electrical and mechanical events in the cardiac cycle. *Br Heart J* 11, 1 (1949)

Cournand A: Cardiac catheterization: Development of the technique, its contributions to experimental medicine, and its initial applications in man. *Acta Med Scand* 579 (suppl.), 7 (1975)

Cournand AF: Dickinson Woodruff Richards: 1895-1973, a survey of his contributions to the physiology and physiopathology of respiration in man. *Am J Med* 57, 312 (1974)

Cournand AF: Acceptance of the Trudeau Medal for 1971. *Am Rev Resp Dis* 104, 616 (1971)

Cournand AF: Presentation of the Kober Medal for 1970 to Dickinson W. Richards. *Trans Assoc Am Phys* 83, 36 (1970)

Cournand A: Some aspects of the pulmonary circulation in normal man and in chronic cardiopulmonary diseases. *Circulation* 2, 641 (1950)

Cournand A, Ranges HA: Catheterization of the right auricle in man. *Proc Soc Exp Biol Med* 46, 462 (1941)

Cournand AF, Zuckerman H: The code of science. Analysis and some reflections on its future. *Studium Generale* 23, 941 (1970)

Cournand A, Bing RJ, Dexter L, Dotter C, Katz LN, Warren JV, Wood E: Report of the Committee on Cardiac Catheterization and Angiocardiography of the American Heart Association. *Circulation* 7, 769 (1953)

Cournand A, Baldwin JS, Himmelstein A: Cardiac *Catheterization in Congenital Heart Disease*. The Commonwealth Fund, New York (1949)

Cournand A, Motley HL, Werko L, Richards DW Jr: The physiological studies of the effects of intermittent positive pressure breathing on cardiac output in man. *Am J Physiol* 152, 162 (1948)

Cournand A, Riley RL, Bradley SE, Breed ES, Noble RP, Lauson HD, Gregersen MI, Richards DW Jr: Studies of the circulation in clinical shock. *Surgery* 13, 964 (1943)

Darling RC, Cournand A, Mansfield JS, Richards DW Jr: Studies on the intrapulmonary mixture of gases I. Nitrogen elimination from blood and body tissues during high oxygen breathing. *J Clin Invest* 19, 591 (1940)

Ferrer MI, Harvey RM, Cournand A, Richards DW: Cardiocirculatory studies in pulsus alternans of the systemic and pulmonary circulations. *Circulation* 14, 163 (1956)

Ferrer MI, Harvey RM, Wylie RH, Himmelstein A, Lambert A, Kuschner M, Cournand A, Richards DW: Circulatory effects of mitral commissurotomy with particular reference to selection of patients for surgery. *Circulation* 12, 7 (1955)

Ferrer MI, Harvey RM, Kuschner M, Richards DW Jr, Cournand A: Hemodynamic studies in tricuspid stenosis of rheumatic origin. *Circ Res* 1, 49 (1953)

Ferrer MI, Harvey RM, Cathcart RT, Webster CA, Richards DW Jr, Cournand A: Some effects of digoxin upon the heart and circulation in man. Digoxin in chronic cor pulmonale. *Circulation* 1, 161 (1950)

Ferrer MI, Harvey RM, Werko L, Dresdale DT, Cournand A, Richards DW Jr: Some effects of quinidine sulfate on the heart and circulation in man. *Am Heart J* 36, 816 (1948)

Forssmann W: Die Sondierung des Rechten Herzens. *Klin Wohnschr* 8, 2085 (1929)

Hamilton WF, Riley RL, Attyah AM, Cournand A, Fowell AM, Himmelstein A, Noble RP, Remington JW, Richards DW Jr, Wheeler NC, Witham AC: Comparison of the Fick and dye injection methods of measuring the cardiac output in man. *Am J Physiol* 153, 309 (1948)

Harvey RM, Ferrer MI, Samet P, Bader RA, Bader ME, Cournand A, Richards DW: Mechanical and myocardial factors in rheumatic heart disease with mitral stenosis. *Circulation* 11, 531 (1955a)

Harvey RM, Ferrer, MI, Richards DW, Cournand A: Cardiocirculatory performance in atrial flutter. *Circulation* 12, 507 (1955b)

Harvey RM, Ferrer MI, Cathcart RT, Richards DW, Cournand A: Mechanical and myocardial factors in chronic constrictive pericarditis. *Circulation* 8, 695 (1953)

Harvey RM, Ferrer MI, Cathcart RT, Richards DW Jr, Cournand A: Some effects of digoxin upon the heart and circulation in man. Digoxin in left ventricular failure. Am J Med 7, 439 (1949)

Motley HL, Werko L, Cournand A, Richards DW Jr: Observations on the clinical use of intermittent positive pressure. *J Aviat Med* 18, 417 (1947)

Richards DW: Acceptance of the Kober Medal for 1970. *Trans Assoc Am Phys* 83, 43 (1970)

Riley RL: The Award of the Trudeau Medal for 1971 to Andre F. Cournand. *Am Rev Resp Dis* 104, 615 (1971)

Sourkes TL: *Nobel Prize Winners in Medicine and Physiology*. 1901-1965. Abelard-Schuman, New York (1966)

West JR, McClement JH, Carroll D, Bliss HA, Kuschner M, Richards DW Jr, Cournand A: Effects of cortisone and ACTH in cases of chronic pulmonary disease with impairment of alveolarcapillary diffusion. *Am J Med* 10, 156 (1951)

William Evans

DAVID MENDEL, FRCP, AND MARK E. SILVERMAN, M.D., FRCP, MACP, FACC

Department of Medicine, Emory University School of Medicine, and the Fuqua Heart Center of Piedmont Hospital, Atlanta, Georgia, USA

"No patient should be the worse for seeing the doctor."
—William Evans

William Evans (Fig. 1) was a greatly loved and highly respected physician, teacher, and personality in Great Britain during the middle years of the twentieth century.[1, 2] As a youth, he wanted to be a preacher and would recite sermons written from a pulpit of straw in a barn at his father's farm. After his father dissuaded him from the ministry, he became a clerk in Lloyds Bank in 1914. Evans served as an officer in the British Expeditionary Force in France in World War I, survived the decimation of his regiment at Passchendaele, and then decided to take up medicine.

In 1925, at the age of 29, he graduated from the London Hospital Medical College. He returned to the London Hospital in 1927 as house physician to John Parkinson, where he was not allowed to give any drugs without Parkinson's permission. At the time, he felt that this meant that Parkinson had no faith in him, but he later realized that patients often improved with bed rest and nursing care alone. In 1930, he was appointed the Paterson Research Scholar, and in 1938 Assistant Physician to the Cardiac Department at the London Hospital. In 1948, when Parkinson retired, Evans succeeded him as Physician in Charge of the Cardiac Department. He became consultant to the National Heart Hospital in 1944, continuing to practice and teach at both hospitals, and to maintain a private practice until his retirement in 1960.[1, 2]

His writings and research were influential, especially in the areas of electrocardiography, cardiac radiology, alcohol and the heart, pulmonary hypertension, atrial fibrillation, the diagnosis of coronary disease, the treatment of angina pectoris and heart failure, and neuromuscular diseases affecting the heart. He was one of the first to utilize phonocardiography to study systolic murmurs, and in this regard he greatly influenced Aubrey Leatham to pursue a career that would use phonocardiography as an essential method of advancing the art of auscultation. Perhaps his most important contribution to the science of medicine was that he and Clifford Hoyle pioneered the controlled trial in 1933, coining the term "placebo effect," long before the role of statistics in medicine was appreciated. Evans wrote over 100 articles and five books on cardiology as well as an autobiography, *Journey to Harley Street*, in which he recounted many of his colorful experiences in medicine. As a leading cardiologist, he also played his part in the founding of the British Cardiac Society and the British Heart Foundation. He was instrumental in the creation of the Society of Cardiological Technicians and served as its first President.

Evans was a magnificent performer with a gift for oratory in the consulting room, the ward, or the lecture theater. At the National Heart Hospital, he also taught international postgraduate doctors, extending his influence worldwide. His flavorful teachings were full of wise and witty one-liners which he often embedded indelibly by insisting that his students write down his clinical comments: "To correct one's error is insurance against committing another. . . ." "Never act on first impressions, but don't discard them; keep them aside but safe; they often proved to be the true diagnosis. . . ." "Among the medicaments which doctors carry in their bags, there can be none more precious than the pill 'Reassurance,' precious in that it is the one he has to use most frequently. . . ." "Assiduity is what pays in the end. . . ." And "Man is being preferred to the rat for investigation because he doesn't bite and has better veins."

A keen observer, he was regarded as an astute clinician with great common sense. His thinking was intuitive and empirical rather than deductive and rational. In this regard, he remained locked in the prevailing unscientific mold of the prewar doctor. Although his lectures had great appeal for the majority, his rigid certainty, his tendency to reject the rational, and the meager scientific basis of his teachings annoyed his more scientific listeners. He was known for his impressive and dogmatic statements which sometimes ran counter to prevailing opinion and to which he held long after convincing proof was available. For example, he maintained that in the absence of rheumatic heart disease, mitral incompetence did not exist. "Incompetence, yes," he would say, "but not mitral." He strongly opposed anticoagulation, regarding warfarin as rat poison, and insisted that the diagnosis of angina could be excluded if the electrocardiogram were normal. To a friend diagnosed with hypertension, he wrote:

I cannot but pour contempt on any who worry about a complaint which is but a figment of the imagination, and entertains a belief which holds no truth. You have hypertonia (if indeed your blood pressure has been raised

FIG. 1 William Evans, 1895–1988. Reproduced from Ref. No. 2 with permission.

from time to time to values like 230/130) which is a normal physiological state, and one which does not in time change into the pathological state of hypertension. So for goodness sake cease to worry about something which cannot but make you unhappy, as well as the lady at your side. Above all, take no tablets, and keep away from doctors! In no other fields do these two agents create greater unwarranted invalidism than in this, where the blood pressure in health is mistaken for that in disease. I am never the carrier of false reassurance, nor can I bear to see healthy subjects made to suffer from the mendations of medical meddlers.

Whether or not you agreed with his teachings, you never forgot them or him.

Always talked about by others as "Willie," "Sir" was the usual form in which he was addressed. Of yeoman stock, he was one of nature's gentlemen, and this, with his Welsh accent—which he made no attempt to eradicate—gave him the common touch. He did not talk a lot, nor did he show off to the patients. This combination made it easy to confide in him, and his humanity made the patient, rather than the doctor, the center of the consultation. He was a master of the doctor–patient relationship a quarter century before this became fashionable, and he treated his private patients exactly as he treated his nonpaying patients. He was very aware of the harm that doctors can do and emphasized in his teaching that "the patient should never be the worse for seeing the doctor." The Fates had combined to make him a complete doctor—skilled, well loved by the patients, and a hero to his assistants and students.

Willie enjoyed diagnosing bypassers in the streets, or when waiting for trains, a practice he called "Wayside Diagnosis." His favorite Wayside Diagnosis was thyroid disease. He would hand the selected person his card, and tell them to show it to their own doctor. On the back were the words, "Your patient is suffering from thyroid disease." He once saw a woman in the street sniffing amyl nitrite; he gave her a peppermint and told her that she had flatulent dyspepsia, not angina. The patients were delighted, but their own doctors probably had mixed feelings about Willie's clinical acumen.

In 1936, the King's physician called for him in his car, followed by a second car to transport the electrocardiograph machine and a technician under hush-hush conditions.[2] They were off to consult on Stanley Baldwin, the Prime Minister, during the difficult political period of the German menace and the King's desire to marry the American, Wallis Simpson. Questions had been raised as to whether Baldwin was fit enough to continue in office; these were not entirely laid to rest by his letter to *The Times* stating "I shall retire when I think fit." The three-lead electrocardiogram showed a deep Q wave and inverted T wave in lead III. Willie interpreted this as being within normal limits and reassured Baldwin, saying that he would use his ECG as a frontispiece of a book to illustrate a normal electrocardiogram. In so doing, he not only exercised his usual criterion—the well-being of the patient—but also the well-being of the British people, for Baldwin was a firm hand on the tiller in dangerous seas. Baldwin lived for another eleven years, symptom free, surviving a bomb on his house and dying in his sleep at age 81.

In 1954, he made his first visit to the USA at the age of 59. On the airplane, an air hostess said that he might be interested to know that Errol Flynn was seated behind him. Willie answered: "Tell him that Dr. William Evans is seated in front of him." He had a good reception in America and liked what he found. Hubert Humphrey quoted Willie when he addressed the Senate on corruption in the drug trade. A large number of American postgraduates listened to him at the National Heart Hospital, and some of the most surprising admirers were among the more avant garde and scientific visitors. One American postgraduate said "If that guy ever came to America, we would make him President of the United States."

One of us (DM) was his registrar at the National Heart Hospital when he was due to retire, and arranged for his former registrars to attend a surprise party planned to follow his last outpatients clinic. The timing was perfect. Willie started teaching his two or three students in his usual way without any mention of the significance of the day. After about fifteen minutes, Walter Somerville arrived. "Hello Walter," said Willie. "What are you doing here?" "Just passing, so I thought I'd drop in." Willie looked a bit stunned, but left it at that. Over the next hour, an additional thirty-five or forty cardiologists from as far afield as Wales and Australia dropped in as if for no reason. Willie had the greatest difficulty holding back the tears. The showman in him, ever on the qui vive, soon took over and the audience was treated to a spectacular exhibition of verbal fireworks, both from him and from the assembled cardiologists. This was followed by tea with cakes from one of the best shops in London, and an iced birthday cake. His thanks were heartfelt and heartwarming. DM took Willie home in his Morris Minor, not the easiest car for him to enter, sit in, or extricate himself from. He commented, "I'll need an obstetrician to get me into and out of that thing, Mendel."

How did Willie gain such a place in the hearts of so many? He was portly and nondescript, with an embonpoint befitting an alderman. Although uniformly pleasant, he typified the British prewar caricature of reserve, unusually combined in his case with showmanship. He rarely talked about anything except cardiology, nor did he entertain the students with new ideas and observations as Paul Wood did. He was never a member of the establishment in his hospitals or in the British Cardiac Society. A most endearing quality was his wit; he was the only cardiologist who made you laugh. This too was reserved for his performances; an audience seemed to switch him on, and you could feel him expanding with the role. His ability to inspire affection in his colleagues was extraordinary. He exuded integrity, humanity, intelligence, and wit—all in unusually high dosage, and a trustworthiness that made you feel that he was a just man. It was obvious, for no obvious reason, that he was lovely. He had something that made hordes of people love him. Exactly what it was remains a mystery.

He retired in 1965 at age 70. His wife died in 1968, and he returned to live alone on the farm where he was born and would die, enjoying his final years gardening, fishing—"taking the rod to its bank" as he would say—and keeping in touch with his many friends. In his eighties, he wrote amusing vignettes in *The Lancet* and a heartwarming article on the joys of aging.

When Willie was 90, a celebration was held for him at Cardiff Arms Park, the Mecca of Welsh rugby football. The invitation was accompanied by a note which advised early booking because the 80th birthday celebration had been a sellout. So was the 90th. The first 150 applicants for tickets dragged through the winter gloom to distant Wales and filled the clubhouse to capacity. Although he had been retired for 25 years, admiration and affection for him brought almost all his surviving assistants down to Cardiff in mid-November. Willie, wearing the tie of his old regiment, the Lancashire Fusiliers, made a sprightly speech and the applause raised the roof.

Though he died in 1988 at the age of 92, long removed from the clinical scene that was his cherished stage, he is still frequently recalled by former colleagues who tell "Willie Evans stories" with relish and remember him fondly, saying "There is a tendency to laugh when you think about him." On his deathbed, he counseled one of his in-laws with the last words of Walter Scott; "Be a good man, nothing else will give you comfort when you lie here." As Willie himself has said, "Immortality depends on other people's memories."

Acknowledgments

The authors thank Wallace Brigden, Malcolm Towers, Aubrey Leatham, and Walter Somerville for advice, and Buddug Owen, author of *A Rare Hero: Dr. William Evans*.

References

1.   Obituary of William Evans. *Br Med J* 1988;297:1040
2.   Owen B: *A Rare Hero: Dr. William Evans*. Denbigh, N. Wales: Gee & Son Limited, 1999

Arthur M. Master, 1895–1973

N. K. Wenger, M.D.

Emory University School of Medicine, Cardiac Clinics, Grady Memorial Hospital, Atlanta, Georgia, USA

He used electrocardiography machines, and x-ray equipment, and his famous two wooden steps. But beyond that, his most important resources were a pencil and paper, a large number of patients to observe, and a rather unusual mind with which to observe them.

With these words Arthur M. Master, Jr., described his father at the 1975 dedication of the Arthur and Hilda Master Chair of Cardiology, a memorial to his parents at the Mount Sinai Medical Center in New York City. Dr. Arthur M. Master had been associated with the Mount Sinai Hospital for over half a century, from his internship in 1921, through his appointment as Chief of the Cardiac Clinics and of the Electrocardiography Department (at age 38) in 1933, to his appointment as Attending and then Consulting Cardiologist, and (with the establishment of the Medical School) Clinical Professor Emeritus of Medicine in 1968. His career of teaching students, young physicians, and associates; his busy consultative private practice of cardiology; and his passion for research in cardiology—for discovery, clarification, and confirmation—are documented in the more than 400 scientific articles and five textbooks that delineate the saga of twentieth century cardiology at the Mount Sinai Hospital—pioneered by his inquisitive mind, astute observations, and encouragement and support of his trainees and colleagues.

Born in New York City, he worked, primarily by teaching, to support his education in high school, at the College of the City of New York, and subsequently at Cornell University Medical College from which he graduated first in his class in 1921; this pattern of diligence was to continue for a lifetime. He had become interested in the emerging specialty of cardiology while still a medical student and volunteered to work for two afternoons a week during his senior year in medical school with Dr. B. S. Oppenheimer in the cardiographic department at the Mount Sinai Hospital, learning the use of this developing technique in the evaluation of cardiac patients. His first two papers, published within two years of graduation, undoubtedly contributed to his being awarded the Cornell Travelling Fellowship that permitted postgraduate study with Sir Thomas Lewis at the London University College Hospital and furthered his interest in the electrical activity of the heart.

The Two-Step Exercise Test

Despite a multitude of original clinical and research contributions to cardiology, the name of Arthur Master is virtually synonymous with the two-step exercise test[1,2]—and its evolution reflects his ever-present concerns for standardization, accuracy, and safety. Originally designed as a test of cardiac function, a purpose for which exercise testing is once again increasingly employed today, it reflected the belief of Dr. Master and the British physiologist E. T. Oppenheimer[1] that a standardized exercise test was needed to evaluate the heart rate and blood pressure responses as measures of cardiac function; they painstakingly formulated a protocol that considered the patients' age, sex, weight, and height, enabling the application of a standardized workload. Although the two 9″ steps that the patients walked for one and a half minutes readily enabled the calculation of foot-pounds of work per minute, the time was changed to three minutes in the late 1930s because of the increased precision of results; interestingly, a three-minute exercise stage, using far more sophisticated equipment, would subsequently be shown to be the time required to attain a near steady state.

They showed that cardiac efficiency declined with age, and as early as 1929 delineated the deleterious effect of obesity on cardiac function; he further demonstrated that weight reduction improved the exercise tolerance of the patient. These observations were extended to document the decrease in cardiac work associated with weight reduction—oxygen consumption was shown to decrease, arteriovenous oxygen difference to increase, and cardiac output to fall.

In the late 1930s, the postexercise electrocardiogram was substituted for heart rate and blood pressure responses; although exercise ECGs had previously been recorded by Einthoven, Scherf, Katz, and others, the Master standardized exercise protocol represented a major advance. Dr. Master emphasized its role as a safe, simple, and reliable office procedure. Long a proponent of the importance of detecting "silent" or latent coronary disease, Master emphasized that even patients with severe coronary disease could have normal resting ECGs and, in later years, advocated a two-step test for everyone over age 35. The abnormal two-step ECG demonstrated the frequency of occurrence of activity-induced my-

FIG. 1 Arthur M. Master, M.D. (Photograph courtesy of Dr. Isadore Rosenfeld.)

ocardial ischemia in asymptomatic people and enabled the serial elucidation of the consequences of latent coronary disease by the meticulous follow-up of patients with abnormal test responses. Indeed, Master had suggested that as many as 30% of myocardial infarctions were "silent," an incidence comparable to that subsequently documented in a number of epidemiologic studies. The two-step test also permitted the preventive interventions advocated by Dr. Master for these "potential" coronary patients: weight reduction; blood pressure control; cessation of cigarette smoking; control of diabetes, hypercholesterolemia, hypertriglyceridemia, and hyperuricemia; and moderate exercise. Especially important, a normal two-step test response was used to "de-label" patients previously invalided by an incorrect diagnosis of coronary disease. Master had often emphasized the inability of any single characteristic feature of anginal pain—response to nitroglycerin, precipitation by exercise, etc.—to differentiate a coronary from a noncoronary etiology of the chest pain. He frequently cited instances where a negative two-step test prompted a successful search for a noncardiac cause of the chest pain.

Tragically, it was "silent" coronary disease that would claim the life of Arthur Master's beloved wife Hilda, who accepted, supported, and encouraged his total commitment to cardiology and to the care of his patients, both as his vocation and his avocation. Dr. Master's son described their vacation home in Harrison, New York, as "practically a summer cam-

pus of the cardiology department." His constant medical work—always with patients, with clinical observations and their recording, with writing, and with editing (his work and that of his colleagues, as well as participation on the editorial boards of a number of respected journals)—inspired his colleagues and students alike, because of his obvious delight with and dedication to whatever aspect of medicine was currently of foremost interest to him. He remained in active clinical practice and research until his death at age 77.

There was constant attention, over the years, to improving the safety and accuracy of the two-step test technique. Concerns for the safety of testing were repeatedly addressed by stopping the two-step test at the onset of chest discomfort and never testing patients with "impending" infarction or with severe prolonged chest pain within a week or two prior to the test.

During World War II, the 12-lead ECG came into standard use and was also soon applied to postexercise electrocardiography. In 1964, Master and Rosenfeld[3] described the recording of the ECG *during* exercise by radiotelemetry or direct recording, and emphasized its importance in detecting arrhythmias not present at rest or following exercise (a clinical observation Master first reported in 1942—without ECG confirmation). Further modifications such as the "augmented" or "double" two-step test improved the diagnostic accuracy.[4]

Myocardial Infarction

Careful observation of many patients with myocardial infarction, with attention to the details of their clinical presentation, the abnormalities of the physical examination, and subsequent outcomes encouraged Arthur Master to challenge the characteristically pessimistic accepted precepts of his day concerning acute myocardial infarction. His meticulous review of patient histories showed that transmural myocardial infarction (coronary thrombosis) was not typically precipitated by physical or emotional stress or "strain," but rather occurred as an unrelated event; this observation was to profoundly affect industrial compensation determinations, as well as to stimulate the American Heart Association's consensus conference and statements on Stress, Strain, and Heart Disease.

Confirming his auscultatory findings with phonocardiographic recordings, Master established that a fourth heart sound, an S_4, was characteristic in patients with acute myocardial infarction, both with and without heart failure; but that a third heart sound, an S_3, was virtually always associated with congestive cardiac failure. He described the soft S_1 as common both with acute infarction and on a chronic basis after infarction as well.

He challenged the practice of high caloric feedings for patients with acute infarction (based on the rationale that since cardiac conduction tissue contained glycogen, glucose was good for the heart), but rather advocated caloric restriction to reduce basal metabolic rate and cardiac work. He recommended the prophylactic use of nitroglycerin, rather than reserving it (as was the practice) for severe anginal pain.

Prior to the advent of coronary care units and continuous ECG monitoring of patients with acute infarction, he identified that abnormalities of conduction occurred frequently in this setting and advocated the recording of daily ECGs for their detection, despite the cumbersome procedures involved in the recording of an ECG in the early years of this technology. He further documented that the development of intraventricular conduction defects worsened the prognosis; and first described the occurrence of P-wave abnormalities in acute myocardial infarction in 1933. He was the first to describe abnormalities of ventricular wall motion in man, paradoxical pulsations in the absence of aneurysm formation; these abnormalities, detected by cardiac fluoroscopy and roentgenkymography, have been confirmed in recent years by a variety of ventriculographic techniques and their importance has been reemphasized.

Most important, he promulgated the favorable prognosis for patients who survived one year after infarction and used these data as a basis to advocate, in the 1920s and 1930s, what today is considered coronary rehabilitation: resumption of a normal lifestyle, return to sexual activity, and return to work.

Acute Coronary Insufficiency/"Subendocardial" Infarction

Acute myocardial ischemia in the absence of acute coronary occlusion was another area of continuing interest and multifaceted active investigation for Arthur Master.

With Drs. Dack, Jaffe, Field, Horn, Grishman, and Donoso[5–11] he reported, in the 1940s and 1950s, differences in the physiology, precipitating factors, pathology, and clinical and electrocardiographic features, as well as the therapy and prognosis, between this entity and transmural myocardial infarction (coronary occlusion); these observations often paralleled data collected only in recent years, using a variety of high technology procedures.

He emphasized that subendocardial ischemia or necrosis could occur, even with minimal or absent coronary disease, as a result of severely reduced coronary flow or increased cardiac work, as occurred with hemorrhage, shock, hypertensive crisis, and the like. He erred, however, in ascribing a more favorable prognosis to patients with severe coronary disease without Q waves on the ECG, advocating earlier ambulation because only the subendocardium was involved and heart failure and arrhythmia were unusual. Again, though, only in recent years has the high risk status for a recurrent ischemic event been defined for patients with non-Q-wave infarction.

Hypertension

Over the years, by meticulous observation of large numbers of patients, with data carefully recorded and collated (with the assistance of the American Medical Association and the Metropolitan Life Insurance Company) he defined normal levels of blood pressure by age and sex (even in the elderly) and advocated treatment of hypertension, even if asymptomatic.

This recommendation, based on documentation of the long-term clinical course of his hypertensive patients, would be validated in subsequent years by controlled clinical trials.

Community and National Service

Arthur Master also found time to participate in leadership roles in professional societies, particularly the American College of Chest Physicians, the New York and American Heart Associations, the New York County Medical Society, the New York Academy of Medicine, and the American College of Cardiology.

He actively served his country in the U.S. Navy during World War I, and rejoined the Navy in World War II after Pearl Harbor, relinquishing a post at the Naval Medical Center in Bethesda, Maryland for active duty in the Solomon Islands. He was a Navy Captain at the time of his return to civilian life.

His honors were many: he was President of the New York County Medical Society and of the American College of Chest Physicians. He was a member of the Editorial Boards of *Chest* and *The New York State Journal of Medicine*. Ever the patient's doctor, he valued most his title of Attending Cardiologist of the Mount Sinai Hospital.[12,13]

References

1. Master AM, Oppenheimer ET: A simple exercise tolerance test for circulatory efficiency with standard tables for normal individuals. *Am J Med Sci* 177, 223 (1929)
2. Master AM: The two-step test of myocardial function. *Am Heart J* 10, 495 (1935)
3. Rosenfeld I, Master AM, Rosenfeld C: Recording the electrocardiogram during the performance of the Master two-step test. *Circulation* 29, 204 (1964)
4. Master AM, Rosenfeld I: Two-step exercise test: Current status after twenty-five years. *Mod Concepts Cardiovasc Dis* 4, 19 (1967)
5. Master AM: Treatment of coronary thrombosis and angina pectoris. *Med Clin N Am* 19, 873 (1935)
6. Master AM, Dack S, Jaffe HL: Premonitory symptoms of acute coronary occlusion. A study of 260 cases. *Ann Intern Med* 14, 1115 (1941)
7. Master AM, Friedman R, Dack S: The electrocardiogram after standard exercise as a functional test of the heart. *Am Heart J* 24, 777 (1942)
8. Master AM, Dack S, Grishman A, Field LE, Horn H: Acute coronary insufficiency: An entity. Shock, hemorrhage and pulmonary embolism as factors in its production. *J M Sinai Hosp* 14, 8 (1947)
9. Horn H, Field LE, Dack S, Master AM: Acute coronary insufficiency: Pathological and physiological aspects. *Am Heart J* 40, 63 (1950)
10. Master AM, Jaffe HL: Coronary occlusion and coronary insufficiency. *Postgrad Med* 9, 279 (1951)
11. Master AM, Jaffe HL, Field LE, Donoso E: Acute coronary insufficiency: Its differential diagnosis and treatment. *Ann Intern Med* 45, 561 (1956)
12. Master AM: Reminiscences of fifty years in cardiology at Mount Sinai with special reference to the two-step test. *Mt Sinai J Med NY* 39, 486 (1972)
13. Kuhn L: *Cardiology in the 20th Century. The Contributions of Arthur M. Master, M.D.* A publication of the American College of Chest Physicians (1973)

Wilhelm Raab

BORYS SURAWICZ, M.D.

Nasser, Smith & Pinkerton Cardiology, Inc., Indianapolis, Indiana, USA

> *Lack of physical exercise, resulting from motorization, automation, television sitting, and from the nearly universal availability of a multitude of labor saving devices, has become one of the most conspicuous characteristics of 20th Century Western civilization.*
>
> —*Wilhelm Raab*

Dr. Wilhelm Raab, born in Vienna, Austria on January 14, l895, is a descendant of an aristocratic family with a long medical and artistic tradition (Fig. 1). His grandfather was Dean of Medical Faculty and editor of Pharmacopeia Austriaca, and his grandmother Isabella, the daughter of the famous graphic artist Doré who tutored the emperor Franz-Joseph in French, was the niece of Schubert's friend Franz von Schober.[1] Dr. Raab's proficiency in drawing, playing the violin, composing poetry, and his multilingual fluency might have been inherited from the artistic, musical, literary, and linguistic tradition of his progenitors. His mother died when he was 4 years old, and to this tragic event of his childhood he attributed his resolution to become a physician.[1]

Dr. Raab received his M.D. degree in Vienna in 1920, and immediately plunged into the field of experimental physiology and pathology in Vienna and Berlin. In 1921 he became an assistant of Professor Biedl (Lawrence-Moon-Biedl syndrome) in Prague. In one of Raab's publications during this time he described the clinical picture of a patient with a basophilic adenoma of the pituitary gland. Cushing cited this case as one of the three cases originating the eponym of Cushing syndrome, which could have been more properly named Cushing-Raab syndrome.[1] Later, while exploring the effect of hypophysis on lipid metabolism, he isolated the substance lipoitrin. In 1926, Dr. Raab became a Privatdozent in the Department of Professor Karl Wenckebach in Vienna.

His scientific curiosity and scarcity of research funds led him occasionally to perform experiments on himself. One such experiment had a particularly profound effect on his career. While studying the effects of catecholamines on lipid metabolism, he injected himself with a large dose of adrenaline. The initial surge of hypertension was followed by a circulatory collapse and an excruciatingly painful attack of angina pectoris with typical electrocardiographic changes of ischemia and prolonged arrhythmia. His deduction, and the central theme of his future investigations that myocardial ischemia resulted from an imbalance between oxygen supply and demand rather than from pure mechanical obstruction, received confirmation during his lifetime when beta-adrenergic blockade became the cornerstone of antianginal therapy.

In 1929, Dr. Raab was awarded a fellowship by the Rockefeller Foundation in New York in the Physiology Department of Professor Walter B. Cannon at the Harvard Medical School in Boston. There he met his wife, Olga Palmborg, with whom he returned to Vienna. Most of his publications during the subsequent 10 years dealt with various endocrine and autonomic nervous system aspects of hypertension in humans. In 1933, he made an epidemiologic survey of the association between fat, cholesterol-rich diet, and atherosclerosis, and formulated a set of dietary guidelines not unlike those recommended by epidemiologists today. In 1936 Dr. Raab became Chief of Medicine in one of Vienna's teaching hospitals, enjoying the opportunity to combine clinical and experimental work on hypertension and atherosclerosis, but after the Anschluss in 1938, his outspoken hostility to the Nazis and his marriage to an American citizen created difficulties with the Gestapo, forcing him to leave Austria.

In December of 1939, he arrived in the U.S., and was offered the chairmanship of the newly created Division of Experimental Medicine at the University of Vermont where he remained as Professor of Medicine until his retirement at the age of 70. In 1942, he discovered the presence of catecholamines in the brain, and in a series of pioneering publications about the toxic vascular and myocardial effects of catecholamines he combined his hypothesis of oxygen wasting by excess of catecholamines with emphasis on the protective role of vagal stimulation. At the same time, less than 100 miles away from Burlington, Vermont, Dr. Hans Selye in Montreal was collecting evidence of the harmful effects of stress. The ideas of these two visionaries interacted, but in Raab's scheme the chief culprit was excessive sympathetic stimulation evidenced by an increased catecholamine release during angina pectoris.

In 1959, Raab organized an international symposium about the effect of catecholamines on the heart and circulation, (several years before the discovery of beta-adrenergic blocking drugs) and in 1964 he organized the first international conference on preventive cardiology.[1] At that time he was engaged in a world-wide campaign aimed at exposing the consequences of physical inactivity (he coined the term loafer's heart) combined with the effects of fat-rich diet, emotional stress, and

Fig. 1 Wilhelm Raab, M.D., 1895–1970.

cigarette smoking. To practice what he preached he walked to and from work, did not use elevators, and exercised half an hour each day. To this he attributed his outliving all of his ancestors by many years. In his autobiographical sketch written in German, Dr. Raab expressed hope that his attempts to formulate the theory of degenerative (ischemic) heart disease would be acknowledged posthumously. He also credited his own tenacity in pursuing his work in spite of the opposition and active resistance of numerous influential critics of his missionary zeal. While focusing on those who opposed his ideas, he characteristically underestimated his own considerable influence and acclaim, which was apparent from the invitations to lecture in many medical centers on several continents, his ability to attract many research associates, and frequent visits by scientists from European and American countries and from Japan to his laboratory.

After the death of his wife, which occurred while he was retiring, he suffered temporarily from depression, but apparently made a recovery and resumed lecturing. He remarried and accepted a consulting position in Bavaria. On the 22nd of September, 1970, a few days before his scheduled move to Europe, Dr. Wilhelm Raab took his own life at the age of 75 years. His tangible scientific legacy consists of hundreds of articles in the many languages mastered by him as well as of several books. The most important of these are *Hormonal and Neurogenic Cardiovascular Disorders* (1963), *Prevention of Ischemic Heart Disease* (1966), and *Preventive Myocardiology* (1970). From his bibliography I have selected a few references[2–5] to point out the chronology of his main ideas and emphasize his pioneering role in the development of concepts fundamental to the prevention of atherosclerosis.

I was a member of Dr. Raab's Division for several years, thanks to my association with Dr. Eugene Lepeschkin, whom he had invited to join the faculty in 1949. Not having participated in the experimental work of Dr. Raab's team, I was not directly exposed to the intellectual power of his creative genius but was captivated by his erudition, wisdom, sense of humor, and personal charm. As time goes by and few of Raab's contemporaries are alive today, it appears appropriate to reaffirm his place in the history of preventive cardiology and to commemorate him as a prophetic visionary of today's elementary public health measures.

References

1. Halhuber MJ: Wilhelm Raab. *Med Klin* 1971;66:1318–1320
   Raab W, Alimentaere Faktoren in der Entstehung von Arteriosklerose und Hypertonie. *Med Klin* 1932;28:487–494

2. Raab W: The pathogenic significance of adrenaline and related substances in the heart muscle. *Exper Med Surg* 1943;1:188–202

3. Raab W, Gigee W: Norepinephrine and epinephrine content of normal and diseased human hearts. *Circulation* 1955;11:9,593–604

4. Raab W, De Paula E, Silva P, Marchet H, Kimura E, Starcheska YK: Cardiac adrenergic preponderance due to lack of physical exercise and its pathogenic implications. *Am J Cardiol* 1960;5:309–320

5. Raab W, Chaplin JP, Bajusz E: Myocardial necroses produced in domesticated rats and in wild rats by sensory and emotional stresses. *Proc Soc Exper Biol Med* 1964;116:665–668

Howard B. Sprague, M.D. (1895–1970)

E. F. BLAND, M.D.

Harvard Medical School, Honorary Physician, Massachusetts General Hospital, Boston, Massachusetts

Howard B. Sprague (Fig. 1) was born in the conservative North Shore community of Swampscott, Massachusetts, and educated in the public schools of that town. At a relatively early age he was exposed to scientific thought from a greatly admired neighbor, Professor Elihu Thompson of the Massachusetts Institute of Technology and the General Electric Company.

Sprague graduated Phi Beta Kappa from Harvard in 1918 and from the Harvard Medical School in 1922, with a fine scholastic record. This was followed by a 21-month internship at the Massachusetts General Hospital. After completing his internship, he spent another year there as a Dalton Scholar and, for the rest of his life, served that institution as a member of its medical staff, becoming Physician in 1953, Consultant in 1956, and Honorary Physician in 1967. He was also Chief of Staff of the House of the Good Samaritan Hospital from 1943 to 1957. During World War II, he served with distinction in the Medical Corps of the Navy, mostly on a hospital ship in the Southwest Pacific, and achieved the rank of Captain. After the war, he became Chief of Cardiology for the New England area with the Veterans Administration.

At the Harvard Medical School, his first appointment was Assistant in Medicine in 1927. He later became Instructor, Clinical Associate in 1950, and Lecturer in 1956. He was a lucid speaker and teacher and an active organizer and participant in the courses in cardiology at the MGH.

Howard Sprague's close association with Dr. Paul White began in 1924, with his appointment as Dr. White's Senior Associate. It was an association that lasted for the rest of his life. Among his pupils were T. Duckett Jones, Robert S. Palmer, Edward F. Bland, Ashton Graybiel, Sylvester McGinn, and James E. Currans. These names appear as coauthors on many of Sprague's numerous contributions to medical literature. Eight of his first nine papers were published with Dr. White, the first being "Progress in the Study and Treatment of Heart Disease."[1]

His native interest in "gadgetry" was often applied to his medical specialty. The development of a combined stethoscope chest piece in 1926 led to a careful analysis of the physiologic and physical laws concerned with auscultation. These studies, conducted with his electrical engineer collaborator, M. B. Rappaport, were documented in several publications[2–4] and eventually in a book.[5]

In the early days of cardiology, there was little interest in congenital defects, which were considered too infrequent and too hopeless to excite special study. However, among those who thought otherwise was Howard Sprague. His early interest in this neglected field was enhanced by his friendship and association with Dr. Maude Abbott of Montreal where, at Osler's suggestion, she had established an outstanding collection of pathologic specimens and had organized a special society (The Association of Medical Museums), in which Dr. Sprague was an active member, and to which he contributed a number of clinical reports. Notably, in 1933, with Carl Ernland and Fuller Albright, he described two cases of dysphagia lusoria (Latin "lusor" = a deceiver), in which the esophagus was constricted by a vascular ring: namely, a persistence of the right fourth aortic root, passing behind the trachea and esophagus.[6] In this report, he predicted that, before long, this special condition should be readily amenable to surgical relief, as indeed it was some years later.[7]

As a corollary of this study, he designed and produced, in wax, a set of models depicting the development and evolution of the embryonic aortic arches, together with some of the anomalies resulting therefrom. These models served for many years as standard references in the Cardiac Laboratory at the MGH.

In addition to his hospital work, Dr. Sprague carried on an active consulting practice. He was elected to the Association of the American Physicians and he served for two years as President of the American Heart Association. In 1965, he received the Gold Medal of the American College of Cardiology and, at the time of his death, he was Treasurer of the International Cardiology Foundation.

Throughout his life, he maintained a lively interest in medical history, sometimes tending to the macabre, as in his scholarly research concerning the Parkman murder. His wide reading and love of books were further expressed by a long and active fellowship in the Boston Medical Library, where he served for 21 years, including 9 years as President. Indeed, it was principally due to his statesmanlike vision, and the respect in which he was held by the medical community, that

---

In this profile of Howard B. Sprague, I have referred frequently, and often literally, to the memorial minutes prepared by a committee of which Dr. William B. Castle was chairman and principal author, and of which I was a member. These minutes were presented to the medical faculty of Harvard in March 1972.

F<small>IG</small>. 1 Howard B. Sprague, M.D. (1894–1970).

the proposal for bringing together the Boston Medical Library and the Harvard Medical Library to form the Countway Library of Medicine became a reality in 1965. It was largely Howard's powers of persuasion that finally allayed the apprehensions of those who feared for the identity of the two existing libraries. In this major event resides Howard Sprague's great and lasting contribution to our medical community and it is indeed fitting that his portrait now hangs in the entrance foyer of the Countway. Incidentally, I recall the delight of the audience at this presentation ceremony, when Howard, in his inimitable manner, congratulated the artist for "having captured the true likeness of the grape just before it turned into a raisin." Likewise, his friends will always remember his role as a charming after-dinner speaker; his subtle wit and humor never failed to end the evening on a happy note. For example, in his President's address at a meeting of the Fellows of the Medical Library in 1967, he said, "I read recently about a small girl who had to submit an essay at school, which she entitled 'Advice—Subtitle Socrates.' Her essay consisted of this: 'Socrates was a very wise man. He went around giving advice to people. They poisoned him.'"

Howard was an avid sailor. Strangely enough, although born within sight and sound of the sea, it remained an unfamiliar element to him until his internship; then followed a summer on the island of North Haven, Maine, as the "locum tenens."

He learned much about small boats from his own experience and from the local dockside experts. A few years later,

he acquired a lovely ketch that he, understandably, named the *Diastole* and, in sailing her, he became a prudent and skillful navigator of the New England coast.

Howard Sprague died November 4, 1970, in his 76th year. It was at a meeting of the P.D.W. Society where, at lunch, he was sitting between Ogelsby Paul and myself; Willis Hurst sat across the table; abruptly, Howard's animated conversation became unintelligible. It was apparent immediately that he was having a stroke, and one from which he succombed a few days later.) Postmortem examination revealed the cause of death to be a cerebral embolus. (The heart chambers were free of thrombi.) In recent years, Howard had had occasional spells of atrial fibrillation, controlled with quinidine. He had considered anticoagulation, but, in the absence of valvular disease, had elected to forego this alternative.

At the memorial service, the words of Dr. Paul White, spoken with deep feeling and emotion, seemed quite appropriate. I quote in part:

> I am grateful for this brief moment to pay tribute to a remarkable person who meant so much to so many of us, and even so much more to medical science and the care of the sick in his own community, in the state, in this nation, and to the whole world. He was a superb realist and helped to keep my own feet on the ground even while tolerating some of my excursions into flights of fancy, of excessive optimism, and undue faith in human nature. Fortunately for me, he did this with gentle humor, but on occasion his wit could be sharp and caustic. He was a gratefully appreciated advisor for many of us here today. For me personally he was a tower of strength for more than 45 years.

And so, Howard B. Sprague takes his rightful place among the eminent cardiologists of our times.

References

1. Sprague HB, White PD: Progress in the study and treatment of heart disease. *Boston Med Surg J* 192, 799 (1925)
2. Rappaport MB, Sprague HB: Physiologic and physical laws that govern auscultation, and their clinical application. *Am Heart J* 21, 257 (1941)
3. Rappaport MB, Sprague HB: The graphic registration of the normal heart sounds. *Am Heart J* 23, 591 (1942)
4. Sprague HB, Ongley PA: The clinical value of phonocardiography. *Circulation* 11, 127-134 (1954)
5. Ongley PA, Sprague HB, Rappaport MB, Nadas AS: *Heart Sounds and Murmurs.* Grune and Stratton, New York (1960)
6. Sprague HB, Ernlund CH, Albright F: Clinical aspects of persistent right aortic root. *N Engl J Med* 209, 679 (1933)
7. Gross RE, Ware PF: Surgical significance of aortic arch anomalies. *Surg Gynecol Obstet* 5303, 435 (1946)

Homer W. Smith and His Contribution to Cardiovascular Medicine

RICHARD J. BING, M.D.

Experimental Cardiology, Huntington Medical Research Institutes, Pasadena, California, USA

Homer W. Smith was born in Denver, Colorado, in January 1895, the youngest of six children. When he was four years of age, his family moved to the mining town of Cripple Creek, Colorado, at the foot of Pike's Peak. After graduation from the University of Denver he joined the Army during the first World War to work with the Chemical Warfare Division. There he met Dr. E.K. Marshall, a renowned pharmacologist, Chairman of the Department of Pharmacology at the Johns Hopkins University School of Medicine. Smith collaborated with him for several years, and it was Marshall who arranged graduate studies under Dr. William Howell at the Johns Hopkins University School of Hygiene and Public Health, where he received his D.Sc. in 1921. After a short period with the Eli Lilly Company in Indianapolis, Smith became a Fellow of the National Research Council at Harvard with Dr. Walter Cannon. He left Harvard for the University of Virginia as Head of the Department of Physiology in 1925. In 1928 he was appointed Professor of Physiology and Director of the Physiological Laboratories, New York University College of Medicine, where he remained until his retirement in 1961. He died in March 1962 of a cerebral hemorrhage.

His death brought to a close what his colleague, Robert F. Pitts, called the "Smithian Era of Renal Physiology."[1] Much of Smith's work in renal physiology was based on the concept of renal clearances, first formulated by Van Slyke and by Rehberg, who had introduced the creatinine clearance to measure glomerular filtration rate in humans. His work on the kidney was distinguished by careful analyses; but what made Homer Smith so unusual was the projection of physiology into the fields of philosophy. Those of us who worked with him often joked that he saw the world through glomeruli and tubules. The architecture of the kidney exists, so he wrote,

. . . not to design or foresight or to any plan, but to the fact that the earth is an unstable sphere with a fragile crust, to the geologic revolutions that for six hundred million years have raised and lowered continents and seas, to the predacious enemies, and heat and cold, and storm and droughts; to the unending succession of vicissitudes that have driven the mutant vertebrates from seas into fresh water, into desiccated swamps, out upon the dry land, from one habitation to another, perpetually in search of the free and independent life, perpetually failing, for one reason or another, to find it.[1]

This quotation gives the flavor of both Smith's style and his ability to project his scientific thoughts into the fields of evolution.

Smith became interested in circulation via his work in renal physiology. He was the nucleus of a group of physicians interested in essential hypertension. The ensuing cooperation resulted in a series of outstanding publications on the role of the kidney in hypertension, summarized by Smith in 1943.[2] He defined his position as an intermediary between exploratory investigation and practical medicine, "sandwiched between theory and practice." The question, which occupied Smith and some of his clinical co-workers, was the role of the kidney in hypertension. He came to the conclusion that as far as essential hypertension is concerned, "the kidney appears to be the victim rather than the culprit".[2] Smith admitted that the kidney may play an intermediary role in essential hypertension. He concluded by stating that the origin of essential hypertension is unknown. This statement is still valid today despite the fact that we have a better understanding of the renin-angiotensin mechanism and have learned to treat hypertension with beta blockers, ACE inhibitors, and with centrally acting agents. This variety is the result of the kaleidoscopic nature of hypertension due to increased nervous system activity; inappropriate renin secretion; deficiency of vasodilator factor, for instance, EDRF; or prostaglandins.

Smith's other contributions to cardiovascular medicine are concerned with glomerular dynamics and the effect of pyrogenic reactions in hypertension.[3] He found that pyrogenic material reduces blood pressure without a rise in body temperature and is the result of "asthenic action on the cardiovascular system" rather than a correction of the fundamental disturbances underlying the hypertensive process. We now know that pyrogen is a lipopolysaccharide, which produces cytokines, thus activating nitric oxide synthase.

Smith's influence on cardiovascular medicine was testimony of his cooperation between clinician and experimental physiologists. Dickinson Richards and André Cournard worked side by side with Smith on respiratory physiology and circulatory shock at Columbia University in its Bellevue Division. Both Cournand and Smith were members of the Cardiovascular Study Section of Bethesda, Maryland, from 1954 to 1958.

Many scientists are completely focused on their work. Not Homer W. Smith. I would do this great man an injustice if I

FIG. 1 Homer W. Smith (1895–1962). (Photograph from Dr. Richard J. Bing's collection.)

were to confine my remarks entirely to his physiologic studies. What added to his stature are his literary style and his poetic insight into evolution. Like other great writers, Smith's style conveys personal involvement expressing both his scientific and romantic nature. This duality made him a great writer who produced such works as *Man and his Gods* and especially *Kamongo*, a philosophical dialogue dealing with evolution as viewed by a theologian and a biologist.[4,5] It is a literary masterpiece! To quote one passage from *Kamongo*: "Life is like a whirlpool in many ways … When once set a-going, it spins on and on. It is not self-sustained because its energy is but borrowed from the river, being constantly renewed upstream and discharged below. If you deprive it of that energy it dies. In its tendency to spin on forever there is life's purpose—to go on living." And he continues, "With good luck, the battle may be drawn out endlessly, while the whirlpool cries 'Won't die!' And environment cries 'Must die'."

Many books on evolution have been written since Smith published *Kamongo*. The whirlpool has been replaced with the spiral of the DNA. But the mystery remains, never more beautifully expressed than in Homer Smith's book.

References

1. Chasis H, Goldring W (Eds.): *Homer William Smith, Sc.D., His Scientific and Literary Achievements.* New York University Press (1965) 11–21
2. Smith HW, Goldring WM, Chasis, H: Role of the kidney in the genesis of hypertension. *Bull N Y Acad Med* 19, 449–460 (1943)
3. Bradley SE, Chasis H, Goldring W, Smith H: Hemodynamic alterations in normotensive and hypertensive subjects during the pyrogenic reaction. *J Clin Invest* 24, 749–758 (1945).
4. Chasis H, Goldring W (Eds.): *Homer William Smith, Sc.D., His Scientific and Literary Achievements.* New York University Press (1965) 217–220
5. Smith HW: *Kamongo.* The Viking Press, New York (1932), revised edition (1949)

Louis Nelson Katz (1897–1973): An Appreciative Profile

H. K. HELLERSTEIN, M.D.

Department of Medicine, School of Medicine, Case Western Reserve University, and the University Hospitals of Cleveland, Cleveland, Ohio, USA

With the death of Louis Nelson Katz on April 13, 1973, physiology lost one of the most productive scientists and educators, and cardiology lost one of its greatest pioneers and teachers. He contributed in many ways to the affairs of the American Physiological Society, the American Heart Association, the Inter-American Congress, and International Society of Cardiology.

This dynamic, rugged individualist produced an unbroken torrent of original research and more than 500 disciples in cardiovascular physiology and medicine. His vision, inexhaustible energy, forceful personality, and unusual administrative ability helped to shape the course of national and international communication and science (Fishman, 1973).

Louis Nelson Katz and his accomplishments can be considered in terms of the dimensions of the man, the time, and the place, and their interactions.

The Cleveland-Western Reserve University (WRU) Era (1900–1930)

The first of these three dimensions begins in Pinsk, Poland, where Doctor Katz was born in 1897. From here, he was brought by his parents to Cleveland in 1900. Learning was in the air he breathed. In Europe his father had been an Orthodox Hassidic Talmudist teacher. The boy Louis was an excellent student and graduated at the top of his class at Central High School. Even in high school, he knew that he wanted to be a physician. While in Adelbert College, WRU, he excelled in mathematics. He was elected to the Phi Beta Kappa honorary society in his third year. At times he worked as an elevator operator in an apartment building, and would study while waiting for passengers. He obtained the A.B. degree in 1918, and medical degree in 1921 from WRU.

While a second-year medical student, he volunteered to assist in experimental work in the Physiology Department of Professor Carl J. Wiggers, where he completed a project on Factors Modifying the Duration of Ventricular Systole. Work stimulated by this experiment resulted in a thesis for which he received an Alpha Omega Alpha award.

While serving as a clinical clerk at Cleveland City Hospital, he developed what would be a life-time friendship with Dr. Roy Scott, Chief of Cardiology. His clinical training as an intern and assistant resident in medicine with Scott from 1921

to 1923 contributed to his orientation in physiology. It was here that he first met Dr. Harold S. Feil, with whom he collaborated on the dynamics of auricular and ventricular systole. While at City Hospital in association with H.W. Gauchat, he published a clinical and experimental study on the paradoxical pulse which won commendation from the renowned physiologist E.H. Starling. Scott was impressed by the bright, energetic, often irritating inquiring young physician, and facilitated Katz's appointment in the subsequent year as a Demonstrator in Physiology in Wiggers' Department.

In 1924 he was awarded a National Research Council Fellowship to work with Starling. However, Starling suggested that, since Katz had already a good knowledge of mammalian technique, he would probably get more benefit by working along the lines of Professor Archibald V. Hill, later a Nobel Laureate. In the year 1924 to 1925, he worked in Hill's Department of Physiology in the University of London, England. His main research was on lactic acid metabolism in mammalian cardiac muscle. Later Katz smilingly acknowledged that he was one of a few people who ever worked with Hill who did not continue in research on skeletal muscle. As a result of his fellowship abroad, Katz felt he was "hooked" by research for life. Despite the two months he also spent in clinical medicine with Sir Thomas Lewis, the work with Hill so converted Katz to the value of basic physiologic research, that he became its champion later in the affairs of the American Heart Association.

He returned to Cleveland to the Department of Physiology at Western Reserve University in 1925 as a Senior Instructor, and in 1927 was appointed Assistant Professor of Physiology. He served as Consultant in Cardiology to the St. Luke's Hospital in Cleveland from 1928 to 1930. This exposure to physiology and clinical medicine undoubtedly accounted for the clinical overtones and implications of his subsequent research (Fishman, 1973).

Notes on the Scientific Era of 1925–1930 and the Place: Western Reserve University

This was an exciting era for cardiology. Numerous institutes of physiology flourished in Europe. Technology was rapidly developing. On the international scene, Einthoven's string galvanometer, for which he was awarded the Nobel

Fig. 1   Louis Nelson Katz, M.D.

Prize in 1924, was being rapidly applied to clinical medicine by Lewis, Rothberger, Wenckebach, and others. Electrocardiographic knowledge was considered to be so advanced that Lewis, one of its great pioneers, abandoned the study of electrocardiography because he believed that the "cream had been skimmed off."

Optical manometers were then available to obtain ventricular pressure curves with instruments of high-frequency responses. Starling had described the Law of the Heart in 1918 and his heart-lung preparation was being widely used for studies of cardiodynamics. Equipment had been developed by Katz in 1921 to record excellent volume curves of the ventricles in association with pressure curves. The clinical entity of coronary thrombosis, described by Herrick in 1912, was beginning to be appreciated and studied.

Others may call the 1920s the jazz era; for cardiologists, this was the heyday of physiology! Wiggers had just moved his Department of Physiology into the new Medical Building in the spring of 1924. The era of prosperity from 1924 to 1929–1930 was characterized by availability of space, modern equipment, a large Hindle galvanometer, optical records of the Frank type, and so forth. Feil who had returned in 1920 from a period of training with Lewis brought the latest knowledge of electrocardiology. It was in this scientific ferment that the productivity of Katz expressed itself. His research interests at that time were devoted mainly to the characterization of the pressure pulses of the atria and ventricles, and to the dynamics of ventricular and atrial contraction.

His first experiments involving the electrocardiogram were performed in 1927. He showed a lack of correlation between the terminus of the T wave and mechanical event of ventricular systole. As a result of this paper, Donald R. Hooker, editor

of *Physiological Reviews*, invited Katz to write a review concerning the origin and significance of the T wave. This stimulated Katz's interest in electrocardiography and undoubtedly contributed to his eminence in this field in later years. In collaboration with Scott and Feil, he characterized the electrocardiogram in pericardial effusion. Katz and Feil were the first to record optically human subclavian arterial pulses in aortic stenosis simultaneously with radial pulses. The dynamics of all types of valve abnormalities were also systematically investigated by them 30 years later to be valuable in the clinical evaluation of pressure curves obtained by right and left heart catheterization.

The Michael Reese Chicago Era

In July 1929, Katz was invited by Doctors Sidney Strauss and Walter Hamburger to discuss the possibilities of his coming to the Michael Reese Hospital in Chicago. In October 1929, Katz signified his interest and submitted a budget for a department. Two weeks later, the economic elevator dropped and the stock market crashed. On April 30, 1930, Katz left Western Reserve University to become the Director of the Cardiovascular Department of the newly established Michael Reese Institute and Assistant Professor of Physiology at the University of Chicago. At this time there were no other research institutes in a nonuniversity private community hospital devoted to cardiovascular research. The research institute was a confederation of intellectual giants who pursued separate paths which often overlapped. These giants included Samuel Soskin, Rachmiel Levine, Otto Saphir, Henry Necheles, and Katz.

You may ask: Why did Katz leave the academic establishment—the protective environment of a flourishing university department of physiology, whose intellectual neighbors included Harry Goldblatt, Howard T. Karsner, Roy Scott, Feil, and Claude Beck, all outstanding in the cardiovascular field? Why go to a private community hospital, a nonuniversity medical environment? After all, Katz had been extremely productive and happy in Wiggers' laboratory. Why then did Katz leave the establishment? The nonuniversity institute at Michael Reese offered him intellectual elbowroom: an opportunity to build his own department, to express himself, and to pursue his own efforts.

Another advantage was that Michael Reese became the mecca for bright young Jewish physicians who were interested in research and who were not welcomed *in those days* by many university departments.

If he seemed a live wire in Cleveland, in Chicago he became a dynamo. A dynamo converts mechanical energy to electrical energy, paralleling Katz's own shift of interest from hemodynamics to electrophysiology. Katz's dynamism was not due to hyperthyroidism alone since it flowered, prevailed, and indeed persisted, even though thyroidectomy was performed in 1931. After his arrival in Chicago, he expeditiously organized his research laboratory and an unusual electrocardiographic station that combined research with service. He attracted generous benefactors for financial aid, and thus developed a center of excellence (Fishman, 1973). As Director of the Michael Reese Cardiovascular Institute, he had freedom of action and the responsibility of raising private funds to support his research. In the first decade at Michael Reese (1930–1940), Katz and his research program flourished despite the fact that there was an economic depression. Accompanying the dynamism and abundance of energy was an insatiable curiosity.

Doctor Frank Wilson at Ann Arbor emerged as the head of one school of electrocardiography, and Katz of another. Particularly tempestuous but fruitful were their vigorous interactions finally to clarify the validity of the central terminal as an indifferent electrode, the meaning of the intrinsicoid deflection, the clinical interpretation of records using unipolar leads, and later, in 1947, the vector analysis of the effects of myocardial injury.

Katz welcomed to his laboratory scientists who fled from Hitler's Europe. With the arrival of Richard Langendorf in 1939, and of Alfred Pick in 1949, Katz formed a renowned triumvirate in clinical research on electrocardiology, physiology, and cardiology. His textbook on electrocardiography, published in 1946, rapidly became a standard reference.

In the three Chicago decades, the encyclopedic magnitude of Katz's productivity can be assessed *tangibly* in terms of his research and participation in learned societies and public activities, and *intangibly* in his impact on the men he had trained.

Katz and his associates contributed significantly to a broad spectrum of subjects involving the cardiovascular system. His interests were catholic. He did not pour himself into a mold of convention. He probed deeply into the problems of hemodynamics and cardiovascular metabolism, electrophysiology, pharmacodynamics, respiration, cardiovascular anatomy and pathology, hypertension, atherosclerosis, and psychosomatic and epidemiologic aspects of heart disease. To have so many outlooks and to be active in so many fields is now and was not then fashionable. He belonged to the group of scientists who were thinkers more than counters, unique individuals who in their keen scanning of many fields saw new and untried areas for exploration.

In Cleveland, he was preoccupied with the hemodynamics of myocardial contraction in the decade of 1930–1940. The majority of his efforts were devoted to electrophysiology and to the hemodynamic effects of valvular disease deformity, arrhythmias, and electrophysiologic effects of coronary artery occlusion, and of myocardial injury. In the subsequent decade, two additional major interests developed viz., experimental hypertension (stimulated in big part by Goldblatt's production of renal hypertension) and the experimental production of atherosclerosis, the most important cause of coronary disease—a logical sequitur for Dr. Katz's interests. In seeking for a more suitable experimental animal than the rabbit for the study of atherosclerosis, Drs. Deborah Dauber and Katz selected the chicken after a careful survey of the existing literature. In this decade, an experimental model of atherosclerosis was produced in collaboration with Dauber and lat-

er Louis Horlick, Simon Rodbard, and, most extensively, with Ruth Pick and Jeremiah Stamler. They developed effective interventions, and in the following decade embarked on clinical trials. Katz's concept that atherosclerosis was a disease, not the immutable outcome of aging, was supported by his and other studies which indicated that the lesions of atherosclerosis could be prevented and even reversed.

Katz was the author of over 600 communications in national and international journals, and more than 400 other communications were published by his colleagues and associates. He authored seven textbooks and numerous reviews and editorials.

He belonged to the generation with global interests. He was involved in genesis and leadership of cardiologic societies, local, national, and international. He served as president or held other major offices in the Chicago Heart Association, in the American Heart Association (1942), American Society for the Study of Arteriosclerosis (1954), American Physiological Society (1957), Inter-American Society of Cardiology (1948), in addition to the International Society of Cardiology (1962). He served on the editorial boards of 14 important cardiovascular journals. He was the recipient of many honorary degrees and awards including national and international memberships, Albert Lasker Award of the American Heart Association for Distinguished Achievement in Cardiovascular Research (1953), and lectureships, including the Carl J. Wiggers Award of the American Physiologic Society (1967), the Lewis A. Connor (1960), Lymann Duff (1970), the third W. Einthoven Memorial Lectureships, and honorary Degrees of Doctor of Science, of his own alma mater of Western Reserve University (1965), and the Chicago Medical School (1966).

All this occurred while happily married to a devoted and understanding wife, Aline, and while nurturing a brilliant son, Arnold.

Katz, the Teacher and Molder of Men

Throughout his career, Katz remained a superb teacher and molder of men. From 1930 to 1965, over 500 trainee physicians enjoyed the contacts with Katz in the Cardiovascular Institute of Michael Reese. His teaching perpetuated the noble tradition of his own mentor and "intellectual" father, Professor Wiggers, who in turn frequently and proudly acclaimed "Doctor Katz as one of his outstanding students." The wisdom and guidance of Katz has had a life-long influence. Each of us students and colleagues have felt that we have taken a part of the laboratory and a part of Katz with us, his indomitable spirit, his attitude, his integrity, and hopefully, some part of his ability to attain and accomplish. Katz attracted talented young people and young ideas. He recognized that in the young it was easy to kindle enthusiasm and to set afire the drive and force of imagination so essential for discovery.

He had wonderful business and organization skills. He provided opportunities for many young people to work independently in his laboratory on projects of their own design. Each trainee was encouraged to participate in a research program, to share in the excitement of discovery, even of the recognition of false leads; to be exposed to the challenge and discipline of defining a worthwhile problem; the strategy of its clarification; and ultimately the organization of its data for presentation to peers in the department and eventually as a scientific publication.

A mere recitation of the number of his pupils was not the only measure of his accomplishments. They were widely scattered geographically. In the survey I made in February 1966, when he was honored by the American College of Cardiology, he had attracted 38 associates from 21 different countries as well as 246 native-born Americans then located in 28 states in the United States. He had reason to take pride in his intellectual progeny: 1 was a dean, 13 full professors, 25 associate professors, 30 assistant professors, 27 instructors, 12 directors of Research Departments in nonuniversity establishments, 109 practicing cardiologists (of whom 60 had affiliations with a teaching hospital, 23 pursued other medical specialties, and 4 were engaged in nonmedical vocations [1 was a businessman, and 3 had become housewives!]); 28 were still in training, 10 had died, and information was not available on 8!

Katz helped to forge a new concept of research and teaching in the nonmedical school environment. He stated that research does not necessarily have to be done in the laboratory. "It may be conducted at the bedside, in the operating room, and in the field of public health and epidemiology. It is not the place that counts. It is the perspective. It is the original mind asking a question and designing an experiment to find the answer. It should not be pebble picking, it should be building of magnificent castles. . ."(Katz, 1956). Research should advance a fundamental concept or it should have an obvious practical value. Research is not gadgeteering, it is the pursuit of capital ideas.

Attitudes Toward Research

Katz encouraged the need to examine the old and the new with an open mind. Like the ancient Talmudist Maimonides, he emphasized that men can be close personally, yet philosophically be in great disagreement. He long applied Roger Bacon's method of acquiring knowledge by experiment and (in a scientific connotation) by argument. To many of us who first came in his laboratory, it was shocking to be subjected to this attitude and bombardment. Initially some of us veterans of World War II, indoctrinated by military discipline, timidly would "sir" him in the course of an argument; with flashing eyes he would warn "Don't sir me, unless you see a red glint in my eye. If so, say 'Yes Sir!' and the following day I will apologize to you."

Out of his range, he was called "Louie the lion." The tag was appropriate. He had a shaggy mane, especially when a haircut was overdue, despite the gentle urging of Aline, his helpmate. His book-lined office was the lion's den where his fellows and associates presented their work-in-progress, to be engulfed by the Boss's verbal artillery, challenge, scrutiny, counsel, and occasional approval.

Katz's attitude toward his students and associates had been more like that of a warrior-father-tutor or a fellow-warrior-colleague rather than of father-to-son or indeed of grandfather-to-son. This intellectual warrior had girded himself willingly and ably for battle and had set the example for his associates as well as for his own talented son, Arnold. He was a formidable figure with scintillating personality, mental agility, encyclopedic knowledge and memory, bounding energy, high personal and scientific standards, and outspoken intolerance and scorn of sloppy thinking and work.

Katz once explained that brusque bombarding was his way to get to the core of business at hand. It saves time. His gruff exterior masked a compassionate interior. All of his associates at one time or other in their training had been browbeaten, but "their worship of their chief, 'The Boss' remained akin to cultism." They recognized that "the art of research starts with finding oneself *un bon patron*—a good boss" (Judson, 1980). It was remarkable that for only a few of his fellows, the boisterous, enthusiastic, and competitive environment of Katz's laboratory was overwhelming and was less than ideal for their particular pace. His attitude exemplified a strong feeling that kowtowing to authority was incompatible with clear thinking and that continuous questioning was the most distinctive feature of the real investigator.

The willingness to question *in camera* extended to the public arena: to seek the fact, to strip data of sham and pretext was not and is not common in the medical world. "He spurned the rule of public reticence beyond the circle that most scientists observe, that all enforce upon each other, that none violates, without hazarding his reputation" (Judson, 1980). He abhorred dogma, defied tradition and the unquestioning acceptance of authority. Customarily he would sit in the front row at the national meetings, and quietly chew gum as he was engrossed in the details of each presentation. Often he was the first to arise to his feet during the discussion period, to quiz, challenge, support, and occasionally, even to praise the investigator who later treasured this interaction. While questioning the inexperienced presenter in a scientific meeting, Katz was careful not to traumatize, and he made it clear that the attack on ideas was not personal. The audience appreciated his ability to extract the essence, to clarify its impact, to pinpoint the uncertainties, all done with vigor but without malice. His questioning showed that he cared. He respected and loved people who "fought back" and supported their arguments with clear thinking and hard facts.

Katz frequently pointed out that one of his greatest personal accomplishments had been to attract bright people from whom he could learn as well as whom he could teach. He treasured his position as a symbol of intellectual honesty and discipline in science and medicine and as a teacher and catalyst for young investigators.

He also savored with great pride that he had been able to further research in the American Physiologic Society, to facilitate the establishment of the American Heart Association's Established and Career Investigatorships, the Young Investigators Award, and the transformation of the association from an elitist society for professionals into a national voluntary agency. In collaboration with his friends, Professors Ignacio Chavez of Mexico City and Paul Dudley White of Boston, he helped to formulate plans for international cooperation in cardiology, ultimately resulting in the birth of the Inter-American and International Congresses. Thus his interest was not only individual but also global.

Following retirement from the Directorship of the Michael Reese Cardiovascular Institute in 1967, he withdrew from the hurly-burly of research and administration, but remained intellectually active and accessible to students and colleagues. He was able to devote even more time to his wife, Aline, his equally vigorous son, Arnold, and his four grandchildren until he became incapacitated by a painful terminal illness.

He continued to be a visionary. All his life he had wanted to be not on the frontier but years ahead of the frontier. Still forward looking, he opined that biochemistry of the brain would be the next frontier—to explain "Why are people always fighting, when there are so many exciting ideas to pursue? That's the question we have to answer." Genius is inborn and one so endowed knows intuitively how to discover. He cannot be held back. The high morale of the discovering questioning laboratory spreads from individual to individual. Once kindled, the need to discover persists lifelong and science becomes a way of life.

Louis N. Katz exemplified this as well as any man in the past or living today.

References

Fishman AP: Louis N. Katz, MD (1897-1973). An Appreciation. *Physiologist* 16(4), 691 (1973)

Katz LN: Harvey and medical research. *JAMA* 160, 1137 (1956)

Judson HF: *The Eighth Day of Creation*. Simon Schuster, New York, 1980, 352

Professor Ignacio Chávez

MARCO A. MARTINEZ-RÍOS, M.D.

Instituto Nacional de Cardiologia "Ignacio Chávez," Tlalpan, Mexico

Professor Ignacio Chávez, founder of the National Institute of Cardiology in Mexico City, Mexico, was born in Zirandaro (which at present bears his name), Guerrero, on January 31, 1897. He began his study of medicine at the University of Michoacán but later transferred to the National University in Mexico City from which he obtained his M.D. degree. He did his postgraduate training in Paris, France, with Professors Henri Vazquez and Charles Laubry, and when he returned to Mexico was appointed Dean of the School of Medicine at the National Autonomous University. In 1933, Professor Chávez was elected President of the National Academy of Medicine in Mexico.

In 1935, he founded the Mexican Society of Cardiology and became the Society's first president. In 1936, he was appointed Director of the General Hospital in Mexico City. He then began to work on plans for the creation of a National Institute of Cardiology, which was inaugurated in 1944. The National Institute of Cardiology was the first institution of its kind in the world and would turn out to be Dr. Chávez's most important accomplishment; the institute now bears his name.

In 1946, in an effort to improve international cooperation and collaboration, Professor Chávez founded the Inter-American Society of Cardiology and, in 1950, co-founded the International Society of Cardiology, in Paris, with Professor Laubry as its first President. The International Society of Cardiology would have as its second president Professor Paul D. White from the United States and Professor Chávez as its third president, from 1958 to 1961.

In 1961, Professor Chávez stepped down as Director of the National Institute of Cardiology when he was elected President of the National Autonomous University of Mexico. However, he would return to finish a new building of the National Institute of Cardiology as its Director from 1975 to 1978. Professor Chávez died on July 12, 1979. Today, his remains are located in the "Rotunda of Illustrious Men" in Mexico City, Mexico.

Professor Chávez's intellectual, scientific, and academic capabilities were unique and have been recognized by scientific and political leaders both in Mexico and abroad. He was an outstanding physician, scientist, humanist, educator, and leader. In addition, he had a great capacity for recognizing and planning for future needs, which undoubtedly helped him create the National Institute of Cardiology, a highly special-

FIG. 1   Professor Ignacio Chávez (1897–1979)

ized institution at a time when general hospitals were the norm. Many things have been said about Professor Chávez; among them, that he was a "renowned scientist, outstanding educator, lucid philosopher, privileged writer, man of probity, and devoted Mexican."

Professor Chávez was honorary member of 17 societies of cardiology in the Americas and Europe, including the American College of Cardiology (1957) and the American Heart Association (1941). He was also honorary member of 33 other scientific societies around the world: 17 in Mexico, 5 in the United States, as well as societies in Guatemala, France, Costa Rica, Chile, Korea, Poland, and Argentina. In addition, he was made honorary professor of 15 universities in the Americas and honorary member of 14 academies of medicine.

Professor Chávez received honorary degrees (Doctor Honoris Causa) from 21 universities, including, among many others, the Sorbonne in Paris, Oxford University in England, and the University of Salamanca in Spain. He received 31 decorations and awards from abroad and was the recipient of eight important decorations and awards from Mexico.

Finally, the Executive Committee of the World Heart Federation decided in 1996 that during each world congress the inaugural conference would be known as the "Ignacio Chávez Lecture."

Harold Nathan Segall (1897–1990)

ROBERT E. BEAMISH, M.D.

Division of Cardiovascular Sciences, St. Boniface Hospital Research Centre, Winnipeg, Manitoba, Canada

Cardiology has been fortunate in attracting its full share of disciples blessed with generosity of spirit, global vision, and bounteous talent. Hemispheric examples are Paul Dudley White in the United States and Ignacio Chavez in Mexico. Their Canadian counterpart was Harold Nathan Segall of Montreal (Fig. 1). Like White and Chavez, both of whom he knew and admired, he pioneered cardiology as a clinician but also as the founder of organizations which ensured its acceptance and growth as a specialty. This century has seen cardiology flourish as never before and it is men such as these that made it happen. As clinician, teacher, scholar, historian, physiologist, researcher, and a benevolent human being, Segall liberally manifested the tenets of the Oslerian tradition in Canadian medicine.

It did not come easily. Born Chaim Nissan Segall in Romania in 1897 he came to Canada in 1900 with his mother and his 6-year-old brother to join the father who had come ahead of the family to find work and a place to live, and to escape the severe anti-Semitic pogroms of the time. Their first home was above a Chinese laundry in a poor area of Montreal where his playmates were French Canadian. They taught him French and renamed him Anatole, a convenient translation of Nathan, the name used in the family. The family fortunes gradually improved, and at the age of seven he was able to enter the Protestant English school system. Nathan's intellectual capacities were soon apparent and he won scholarships to high school where his name again changed—to Harold. He subsequently entered McGill Medical School and graduated in 1920.

Medical graduation was followed by six years of postgraduate training, two in pathology at McGill, the first with Dr. Maude Abbott and the second with Professor Horst Oertel, then two further years in Boston at Massachusetts General Hospital. Holding the H.P. Walcott Scholarship of Harvard University, he spent a year on thyroid studies with Dr. J.H. Means followed by a residency in cardiology with Dr. P.D. White; this initiated a life-long friendship. In October 1924, financed by the Libman Scholarship Fund, Segall went to London where he researched the coronary circulation, working with G. von Anrep in Professor Starling's laboratory. Further studies in Vienna, Munich, and Paris preceded his return to Montreal in 1926. From this experience he learned, and never forgot, the European heritage that so influenced North American cardiology.

In Montreal he found that cardiology was practiced by general internists and that there was resistance to it as a specialty. Despite the lowly rank of Junior Assistant Physician at Montreal General Hospital and Assistant Demonstrator, McGill University, he persuaded colleagues to let him establish a cardiac clinic. In the next eight years he founded three more, the last at the Jewish General Hospital where most of his work was done from 1934 on. A year after his return he bought a Cambridge electrocardiograph (the first in Montreal and possibly in Canada) which he took with him on visits to patients too ill to come to the office. After 34 years he retired from Montreal General Hospital as Associate Physician and from McGill as Assistant Professor; by then one of his clinics engaged a dozen cardiologists. Among other "firsts" he held the first postgraduate courses in cardiology in Canada in 1938; these flourished for 25 years in English and French for Canadians and Americans. Generations of undergraduate students remember him as a stimulating and provocative teacher.

Although exposed to more physiology than most physicians of his time (he attended physiological congresses into his eighties), Segall was primarily a bedside physician. Of his over a hundred publications, the most frequent deal with auscultation and the graphic registration of heart sounds and murmurs. His system and its diagrams became known as "Segallograms" or "L'Auscultogrammes Segall". They were first published in the American Heart Journal in 1933 but later appeared in the Encyclopedia of Cardiology and in British, Japanese, and numerous Canadian papers. Of this interest came the first translation into English of N.S. Korotkoff's work on the auscultatory measurement of blood pressure.

As early as 1926 Segall tried to establish a Canadian Heart Association, but this was not to occur until 1947 when an organization was formed in Winnipeg with Segall as the first secretary; he served as its President from 1953–1955. He was also a founder of the Montreal Cardiac Society (1946) and of the Quebec Association of Cardiologists (1951). The need for funds to support cardiovascular research became increasingly apparent and here again Segall was in the forefront—he was a founding member of the Canadian Heart Foundation (1956) and of the Quebec Heart Foundation (1957), serving as President of the latter from 1960–1967. In recognition of his large contributions, the Canadian Heart Foundation awarded him the Distinguished Service Award (1967) and the

F<small>IG</small>. 1   Harold Nathan Segall (1897–1990).

Award of Merit (1971)—he was one of the few physicians ever to receive both awards.

After the tragic death of his role model and mentor, Dr. Louis Gross, in an airplane crash in 1937, Segall founded the Louis Gross Memorial Lecture at the Jewish General Hospital. This became an annual event sponsored by the Montreal Clinical Society and featured internationally famed speakers. In 1986 his colleagues changed the name to the Louis Gross-Harold Segall Lecture. Following Segall's death, the Canadian Cardiovascular Society established the Harold N. Segall award recognizing contributions to cardiovascular health.

The first bestowal was to Air Canada for its initiative in prohibiting smoking on its planes.

Segall was an enthusiastic bibliophile. He amassed a library of several thousand volumes which in later life he gave to the Osler library of McGill University and to the Jewish Public Library. From 1974 on he was on the Board of Curators of the Osler library and spent much time there. In 1989 the library produced a "Festschrift" containing contributions from his friends and students in Canada and abroad. It was titled "It is Good to Know"—one of the mottos governing his life. It was the message on his library bookplate and was surrounded by spokes representing the concepts of relativity and infinity. McGill University honored him and itself by an honorary D.Sc. in 1983. The breadth of his interest and concern was again shown by his convocation address entitled "Education for World Citizenship."

Medical history was his principal avocation. He was President of the Jewish Historical Society (1977–1979) and twice was Honorary President of the Osler Society of McGill. The Hannah Institute for History of Medicine chose him as one of the two recipients of the Neilson Award in 1984. He was Archivist of the Canadian Cardiovascular Society for many years and published a book entitled *Pioneers of Cardiology in Canada: 1820–1970*. This book appeared in 1988 when he was 90 years of age!

A chronology of achievements and events, no matter how many or how important, may fail to reveal the authentic man. Harold Segall was of small stature but of noble nature. His wife of nearly 50 years was confined to hospital for 15 years; he visited her every day and when away he telephoned her more than once daily. He drove a convertible until he was 90 and gave it up only because it was stolen and destroyed. He was animated and tireless to the end—he died suddenly on his way home from a meeting in support of Hebrew University—in his 93rd year.

References

1. Segall, HN: *Curriculum vitae and publications* (1982)
2. Roland, CG: Obituary—Harold Nathan Segall. *Can Bull Med History* 8, 133–134 (1991)
3. Segall, HN: *Brief Biography* (1990)
4. David, PP, Segall, S: Harold N. Segall, 1897–1990. *Can J Cardiol* 6, VI–VII (1990)

Louis Wolff: 1898–1972

G. S. KURLAND, M.D.

The Dana Farber Research Institute and the Harvard-Thorndike Laboratory of Beth Israel Hospital, Department of Medicine, Beth Israel Hospital and Harvard Medical School, Boston, Massachusetts, USA

In many ways, the life of Dr. Louis Wolff (Fig. 1) is the story of the strength that America derived from those who immigrated at the turn of the century. He was born in Boston on April 14, 1898, to a family recently arrived from Lithuania. An older sister had been born in London and a brother was born in Peru before the family finally settled in Boston. He prepared at Boston English High School for the Massachusetts Institute of Technology where he majored in biology and public health. He worked his way through college by playing the violin in a well-known dance orchestra, which he occasionally conducted. He graduated from MIT in 1918 and from the Harvard Medical School in 1922. He interned at the Massachusetts General Hospital from 1922 to 1924 and stayed on there to work with Paul Dudley White. In 1928, he was appointed Chief of the Electrocardiographic Laboratory at Beth Israel Hospital, Boston, where he remained for the rest of his professional career. He stepped down from that post in 1964 but continued his consulting practice. He died on January 28, 1972, of Parkinson's disease. The tradition of a Wolff in cardiology is carried on by his son Richard.

On April 2, 1928, a young man was referred to Paul Dudley White because his physician was perplexed by the occurrence of paroxysmal atrial fibrillation in a healthy individual. The knowledge that began with that case has expanded to include the entire concept of re-entry mechanism and its role in the pathogenesis of arrhythmias, and is a triumph of clinical investigation. In the original report, the authors described the typical electrocardiogram, the apparently normal hearts, the response to exercise and to vagal stimulation, and its release and the occurrence of paroxysmal tachycardia, paroxysmal fibrillation or perhaps flutter.[1]

The varied reception of the new syndrome as recounted by Dr. Wolff makes fascinating reading.[2] "It so happened that Dr. White started out on a visit of foreign medical centers at this time and he took with him the electrocardiograms that were our great concern." The reaction to them in two cities is worth recording. In Vienna, the opinion was expressed that the tracing did not represent anything more unusual than bundle-branch block and atrioventricular (AV) nodal rhythm. In London, Sir Thomas Lewis was not interested. However, Dr. Parkinson's interest was aroused. He found seven cases in London that, added to the four from Boston, made a total of eleven recorded in one joint article, "Bundle Branch Block with Short P-R Interval in Healthy Young People Prone to Paroxysmal Tachycardia."[1] Dr. Wolff did not actually meet Dr. Parkinson until many years later at the Second World Congress of Cardiology in 1954. In the original report, the authors noted similar cases described by F. N. Wilson in 1915 and by A. M. Wedd in 1921, but the article by Wolff, Parkinson, and White was the first to recognize the constellation. They offered no explanation of the etiology. However, as Paul White recalled, "even at that time, Louis was very uncertain about designating the rhythm as bundle-branch block even though he agreed to the title pro-tem." Dr. Wolff later noted that "the idea of a muscular bypass occurred to us; it seemed fanciful and unsupported by the facts available. Again we turned to the literature for help but found none." By 1960 it was clear that a single mechanism was responsible for the abnormal electrocardiogram and paroxysmal tachycardia. Premature activation via an accessory conducting neuromuscular tract of a small fraction of ventricular musculature shortens the P-R interval and lengthens the QRS interval, thus accounting for the electrocardiographic peculiarities of the syndrome.

Although Louis Wolff's name will always be best remembered in association with the Wolff-Parkinson-White syndrome, his contributions to cardiology extended well beyond that. His first publication with Dr. White reported 23 autopsied cases of acute coronary occlusion.[3] His interest in coronary artery disease continued throughout his career and included an early, perhaps the first, description of unstable angina. He was particularly interested in the electrocardiographic and vectorcardiographic diagnosis of myocardial infarction and the influence of bypass tracts on the diagnosis. He had a long-standing interest in paroxysmal rapid heart action and reported the effect of quinidine on atrial fibrillation.[4] He early recognized the good prognosis in uncomplicated atrial fibrillation now called "lone" atrial fibrillation and of the familial occurrence of atrial fibrillation. The breadth of his interest is also shown by his descriptions of pulmonary embolism and pericarditis. In the 1950s, when cardiology intensively explored the merits of spatial vectorcardiography, Louis Wolff was one of the major contributors to knowledge in this area.[5]

Dr. Louis Wolff was not only an astute clinician and an inquiring investigator, but he took particular pride in his post-

Fig. 1 Dr. Louis Wolff, 1898–1972.

graduate teaching. At a time when memorizing patterns was the standard way of learning electrocardiography, he recognized that, lacking basic knowledge, students retained little of what they learned. He was determined to remedy this discouraging situation by teaching the principles of electrocardiography without referring to patterns, but rather through basic electrophysiology. Any misgivings that he may have had

were unfounded; his students responded with enthusiasm. He subsequently published his experience in the textbook *Electrocardiography: Fundamentals and Clinical Application.*[6]

To speak only of his extensive contributions to cardiology is to slight other aspects of his life. His love of music and the arts was evident everywhere. His home was said to have three household gods: Jascha Heifetz, Sigmund Freud, and Frank Wilson. From his early student years, music was an important part of his life. Sunday morning quartets with well-known musicians provided a major diversion. It is fascinating to speculate on what direction his career might have taken: when he graduated from MIT in 1918, there was some indecision whether he should go to Europe and study music. However, World War I was still in progress, and he decided to pursue medicine instead. Music's loss was cardiology's gain. He became a disciple of Frank Wilson and not of Jascha Heifetz. Thus, the genesis of the Wolff-Parkinson-White syndrome.

References

1. Wolff L, Parkinson J, White PD: Bundle-branch block with short P-R interval in healthy young people prone to paroxysmal tachycardia. *Am Heart J* 5, 685 (1930)

2. Wolff L: Wolff-Parkinson-White syndrome: Historical and clinical features. *Progr Cardiovasc Dis* 2, 677 (1960)

3. Wolff L, White PD: Acute coronary occlusion: Report of 23 autopsied cases. *Boston Med Surg J* 195, 13 (1926)

4. Wolff L: Angina pectoris (or status anginosus) and cardiac asthma induced by paroxysmal atrial fibrillation and paroxysmal tachycardia; value of quinidine sulfate in treatment of these conditions. *N Engl J Med* 208, 1194 (1933)

5. Wolff L, Wolff R, Samartzis M, Soffe AM, Reiner L, Matsuoka S: Vectorcardiographic diagnosis—a correlation with autopsy findings in 167 cases. *Circulation* 23, 861 (1961)

6. Wolff L: Electrocardiography. In *Fundamentals and Clinical Application*. WB Saunders, Philadelphia (1950)

George C. Griffith

P. R. MANNING, M.D.

University of Southern California School of Medicine, Los Angeles, California, USA

George C. Griffith was an outstanding teacher, a superior clinician, superb consultant, and a truly remarkable human being. Born in 1898 in the Amish community of Myersdale, Sommerset County, Pennsylvania, he received his A.B. degree in 1921 from Juniata College and his M.D. from Jefferson Medical College in 1926.

George at one time was a lay minister. He frequently told his colleagues that once after hearing George's sermon, the then Governor of Pennsylvania said, "Son, you would make a better doctor than a preacher." Whether this incident really influenced George's decision to enter medicine, I do not know. But medicine gained a truly great disciple.

He interned and was chief resident at the Presbyterian Hospital in Philadelphia. He trained under Professor James E. Talley of the Graduate School of Medicine in Philadelphia and was much influenced by two short-term courses under Paul Dudley White at the Harvard Postgraduate School of Medicine.

During World War I, George was a seaman in the U.S. Naval Reserve, and in World War II, he served as a Lieutenant Commander in the Rheumatic Fever Unit of the Corona Naval Hospital. He joined the faculty of the University of Southern California School of Medicine in 1946 and made major contributions to the school until his death in 1975.

George was active in all cardiovascular circles, serving as President of the American College of Cardiology and as an Associate Editor of the *American Journal of Cardiology*. He contributed 231 articles in medical journals. He was Governor of the American College of Physicians of Southern California and served on the Executive Committee of the Board of Regents.

When George joined the USC faculty, he established an outstanding clinical training program, attracting physicians from around the world, who became excellent cardiologists. As a teacher, George was a magnificent example to students, interns, residents, and practicing physicians. He radiated warmth to patients that is seldom equaled and never exceeded. He performed careful and accurate examinations of the patient. One might say that, in Los Angeles at the time, he was the leading exponent of a superior cardiovascular examination at the bedside.

His students will remember George's attention to details in auscultation—details that at the time were not emphasized by many cardiologists. These details have, of course, now become part of the armamentarium of all good clinicians. Thus, in southern California, George was a major trail blazer of relating pathophysiology to the physical examination. In his lectures, George had an ususual knack for discussing information at all levels of sophistication. He was at home with medical students, residents, and senior cardiologists. His lectures to medical students on very basic material always had a freshness and showed no trace of boredom, even though he had discussed the same material with literally hundreds of students previously. Every time George spoke, the audience heard a very dedicated individual who was truly interested in his subject.

FIG. 1 Dr. George C. Griffith.

George was a consultant's consultant. After World War II, when he settled in Los Angeles, most patients with difficult cardiovascular diagnostic problems were ultimately seen in George Griffith's office. His intensity as a listener and skill in physical diagnosis, as well as his ability to interpret the diagnostic studies of those days, always sent the patient away in awe. George was careful to support the referring physician so that the patient maintained confidence in his own physician, but never compromised on any change of therapy that he felt was indicated.

He performed the first cardiac catheterization and first angiocardiogram at the Los Angeles County/USC Medical Center. He shared his research activities, which were fundamentally clinical, with colleagues and fellows. He studied a wide range of clinical topics with emphasis on rheumatic heart disease and diet in the treatment of atherosclerosis. He wrote early articles on surgery in cardiovascular disease. He had interest in arrhythmias, infective endocarditis, and anticoagulation.

From 1946 to 1949, George ran the Postgraduate Division of the University of Southern California School of Medicine and through this experience developed a great interest in continuing education. Personally, George was my teacher in cardiology, my teacher in continuing education, and my teacher in the doctor-patient relationship.

The academic accomplishments of George Griffith would, by themselves, have made him an outstanding contributor to medicine. However, George's sense of humanity, especially his compassion for the sick and his compassion and respect for student physicians and colleagues, permitted him to make major contributions both in direct patient care and by fostering the best in all physicians with whom he came in contact. His spirit remains a major force in cardiovascular circles in southern California.

The George C. and Lee Griffith Library located in Heart House at the Headquarters of the American College of Cardiology in Bethesda, Maryland, assures that the spirit of George C. Griffith in medical education will be preserved. The George C. Griffith Chair of Cardiology at the University of Southern California School of Medicine fosters and rewards outstanding teachers. The Chair is now filled by Shahbudin Rahimtoola, who received the 1986 Gifted Teacher Award of the American College of Cardiology. Thus Dr. Rahimtoola follows in the Griffith footsteps, as George was awarded the American College of Cardiology's Gifted Teacher Award in 1967 and the Distinguished Teacher Award of the American College of Physicians in 1971. The tradition George established lives on. Those of us who studied with him studied with the best.

D. Evan Bedford: Master Cardiologist and Bibliophile

MARK E. SILVERMAN, M.D., MACP, FRCP, FACC, AND *EDWIN BESTERMAN, M.A., M.D., FRCP, FACC

Department of Medicine, Emory University School of Medicine and The Fuqua Heart Center, Piedmont Hospital, Atlanta, Georgia, USA; *University Hospital, University of West Indies, Jamaica, and St. Mary's Hospital and Royal Postgraduate Medical School, Hammersmith, London, U.K.

Evan Bedford (Fig. 1) was an eminent twentieth century British cardiologist regarded as an international authority on the post World War II advances in cardiology.[1-3] Born on August 21, 1898, in Boston, Lincolnshire, where his grandfather had been mayor and his father a flour miller, he was educated at Epsom College and trained in medicine at the Middlesex Hospital, qualifying as a doctor in 1921, and as M.D. in 1925, after he patriotically interrupted his schooling to enlist during World War I. Following junior positions at Middlesex Hospital and Orpington, Bedford went to France in 1926 to study under the famed Charles Laubry and Louis Gallavardin. A year later, he returned to England to become a Paterson Research Scholar at the London Hospital working under John Parkinson. From then on his name was linked closely with Parkinson, who would greatly influence his future directions. From 1926 onward, except for a month in Vienna in 1929 to study cardiac radiology, and the period of World War II, he was a consultant and then physician in charge of cardiology at the Middlesex Hospital and, beginning in 1933, an honorary consultant at the National Heart Hospital. His practice was described as the largest and most distinguished in his specialty. His fee for a patient was established on the first visit and never varied thereafter. He married in 1935 and was the father of two sons.

During World War II, Bedford was a Brigadier in the Royal Army Medical Corps and consulting physician to the Middle East Forces, where his reputation as a leading cardiologist was further enhanced by his care of then Prime Minister Winston Churchill.[1, 3] While in Tunis in December 1943, Churchill contracted pneumonia complicated by atrial fibrillation and congestive heart failure. Lord Moran, Churchill's personal physician, sent for Bedford, commenting, "His presence will keep the people at home quiet." They prescribed digitalis and sulphadiazine. The latter, marketed by May and Baker, was known as "M & B," and Churchill would say afterward that he was cured by "M and B"—Moran and Bedford.[4] When Churchill refused Bedford's advice to rest, Bedford withdrew, leaving Moran to deal with his difficult patient. Bedford received a mention in despatches in 1944 for his distinguished military service.

From his French experience, Bedford had learned the importance of documenting the findings on his patients and personally conducting autopsies to make clinical correlations.

Bedford was once informed by a colleague that one of his patients had died the night before. Bedford replied, "Thank you, I know. I have his heart in my bag." Bedford was one of the first in England to study myocardial infarction, which had been thought to be infrequent and fatal. His 1928 papers on myocardial infarction, written with John Parkinson, were landmark contributions that delineated the presentation, clinical features, pathology, laboratory testing, serial electrocardiographic findings, and prognosis of 100 cases of coronary thrombosis.[4, 5] They also described electrocardiographic findings during angina and with cardiac aneurysm. After his return from World War II, he was quick to ride the wave of advances in diagnosis provided by cardiac catheterization and to see the potential for cardiac surgery. He worked closely with surgeons Thomas Holmes Sellors and Russell Brock, spending many hours in the surgical theater, and he co-authored a paper on a series of patients operated upon for mitral stenosis and also repair of atrial septal defect under hypothermia.[6, 7] His comprehensive 1941 publication on atrial septal defects improved the understanding of that disorder.[8] In 1946, he provided the first description of endomyocardial fibrosis in Africans based on his wartime observations. His careful analysis of 154 patients with left ventricular failure, delivered as the Strickland Goodall lecture in 1939, provided convincing evidence that the cause of pulmonary congestion was "backward failure," not "forward failure," as had been championed by James Mackenzie, Thomas Lewis, and others.[9]

Bedford was an acknowledged leader in British cardiology—a founding member and President of the British Cardiac Society, Chairman of the Council of the British Heart Foundation, and original joint editor of the *British Heart Journal*. His reputation was international, and he was President of the European Society of Cardiology and Vice President of the International Society of Cardiology. His accomplishments were rewarded by a Commander of the British Empire (C.B.E.) in 1963, honorary membership in nine international cardiological societies, and the prestige of delivering a number of named lectures, including the Harveian Oration on the historical aspects of the coronary arteries which he presented to the Royal College of Physicians in 1968.[1, 2, 10]

Blunt, honest, possessing a deadpan humor, Bedford was a highly literate man who wore tortoiseshell glasses and spoke

Fig. 1   D. Evan Bedford (1898–1978). Photograph courtesy of the Royal College of Physicians, London.

while a cigarette stub dangled from his lower lip.[2] Bedford was known for his great store of clinical information, instinctive understanding of his patients' problems, and fastidious attention to what was certain and essential. His innate shyness was well concealed behind a frosty and forbidding exterior. He was often short with others, and colleagues and junior staff were careful to handle him with great tact. Hospital noise, traffic congestion, and hospital administrators were well known to set him off. He held several strong prejudices and was highly intolerant of those patients whom he felt had psychologic problems—neurotic ill health ("NIH") as he would label them. He was often frank and unsparing in his comments, and this could be unsettling for the patient to hear, requiring consoling by the nursing staff. One man asked Bedford whether his heart attack could be cured. Bedford responded, "Cured? If you lose your foot under a bus you don't ask to be cured. You've lost the foot of your 'eart." At the Middlesex Hospital, he was referred to as "the old top," a nickname stemming from his comment at billiards—"Give it a bit of the old top (spin)."[11] He was respected and liked by his junior staff who regarded him as a master cardiologist and appreciated his dedication to his large practice, love for his work, his bedside teaching, and his encyclopedic knowledge. His teaching was spiced by his special knowledge of medical history and quotations from French and Irish cardiology, and his carefully prepared lectures were regarded as classics. His wide range of interests also included art, history, French culture, travel, food, wine, and collecting rare books. In his younger days, he excelled at cricket, hockey, golf, and billiards.

Bedford had a keen interest in the history of cardiology and authored many important articles on the subject, including a masterly review on the ancient art of feeling the pulse in which he said, "If, in looking back, we remember that the state of affairs today is the consequence of that which existed yesterday, then in feeling the pulse we shall not forget that we still owe something to Galen."[12] Beginning in 1926 as a registrar (resident), he would search bookshops for classic papers and books on heart disease and other subjects. His bibliophilic desires ultimately resulted in the acquisition of 1,112 items. In 1971, this magnificent collection, greatly enhanced by his catalogue and valuable annotations, was donated to the Royal College of Physicians in London where it is kept separately as "The Evan Bedford Library of Cardiology."[13, 14] This comprehensive collection, including almost every important book in cardiology as well as original offprints, bound volumes of journals, biographies, and secondary source material, will remain his enduring legacy to the field that he loved and practiced so well.

Acknowledgment

The authors appreciate the contributions and review by John Evan Bedford, Peter Fleming, Arthur Hollman, Wallace Portal, Alex Sakula, Walter Somerville, and Charles Upshaw.

References

1.   Obituary: D. Evan Bedford. *Br Heart J* 1978;40:820–822
2.   Obituary: D. Evan Bedford. *Br Med J* 1978;I:308, 515
3.   Sakula A: Churchill in Carthage, 1943: Dr Evan Bedford's war diary. *J Med Bio* 2000;8:241–243
4.   Parkinson J, Bedford DE: Cardiac infarction and coronary thrombosis. *Lancet* 1928;I:4–11
5.   Parkinson J, Bedford, DE: Successive changes in the electrocardiogram after cardiac infarction (coronary thrombosis). *Heart* 1928; 14:195–239
6.   Holmes Sellors T, Bedford DE, Somerville W: Valvotomy in the treatment of mitral stenosis. *Br Med* J 1953;2:1059–1067
7.   Bedford DE, Holmes Sellors TH, Somerville W, Belcher JR: Atrial septal defect and its surgical management. *Lancet* 1957;I:1255–1261
8.   Bedford DE, Papp C, Parkinson J: Atrial septal defect. *Br Heart J* 1941;3:37–68
9.   Bedford DE: Left ventricular failure. *Lancet* 1939;1:1303–1309
10. Bedford DE: Harvey's third circulation. De circulo sanguinis in corde. *Br Med J* 1968;4:273–277
11. Hollman A: Societies, journals, and books. In *British Cardiology in the 20th Century* (Eds. Silverman ME, Fleming PR, Hollman A, Julian DG, Krikler DM), p. 73. London: Springer-Verlag, 2000
12. Bedford DE: The ancient art of feeling the pulse. *Br Heart J* 1951; 13:423–437
13. Bedford E: The Evan Bedford Library of Cardiology. London: Royal College of Physicians, 1977
14. Besterman E: The Evan Bedford Library of Cardiology and its catalogue. *Br Heart J* 1978;40:707–708

Dr. Helen Brooke Taussig, Living Legend in Cardiology

M. A. ENGLE, M.D.

Division of Pediatric Cardiology, Department of Pediatrics, The New York Hospital-Cornell Medical Center, New York, New York, USA

The mother of pediatric cardiology, the first lady of cardiology, the world's most famous woman physician—all of these titles fit Dr. Helen Brooke Taussig, and she came to merit them the old-fashioned way. She earned them.

It was not easy. Helen had to overcome an early childhood handicap of dyslexia, an early adult handicap of losing her hearing as she was pursuing her goal of becoming a cardiologist, and often the handicap of society's views of a woman in pursuit of a career in medicine.

She did have help along the way. In addition to her strong character, her intellect, purposefulness, and determination, she had the benefit of wise guidance and counsel from two important people in her life: first her father, Frank William Taussig, the eminent Professor of Economics at Harvard; and later, her mentor, Edwards A. Park, Professor of Pediatrics at The Johns Hopkins University.

Born May 24, 1898, in Cambridge, Massachusetts, she felt it a great privilege to grow up in a university atmosphere. Her mother, ill for several years, died when Helen was 11 years old. It was her father who worked patiently with her as she struggled to learn to read, to spell, to get numbers straight. She improved in time, but reading was never to be a pleasure for her. Summers were spent on Cape Cod. She loved the village and she has remained a "Cape Codder" all her life. Her father would spend his mornings at the Cape writing, and then he would join the family for lunch and an afternoon of fun at the beach. Later, when she built her own house on the Taussig land, Helen followed the same practice, spending her mornings writing and enjoying her beach and the beauty of the Cape the rest of the day. Her famous book, *Congenital Malformations of the Heart*, took shape there over a period of 10 years. Her family and neighbors were pressed into duty to help with the index. When it was published in 1947, it was the right book at the right time. It immediately became the bible for those all over the world caught up in the excitement of helping blue babies.

Enroute to that great moment of the first blue baby operation, Helen Taussig had first to secure entry to medical school. She entered Radcliffe College and then transferred to the University of California at Berkeley, where she obtained her A.B. degree in 1921 and began to think about a career in medicine. Harvard was adamant against admitting women to its medical school, and even against awarding her a degree, should she study in its new School of Public Health. She was permitted, however, to study histology under Dr. Brennar at Harvard Medical School. She was given a seat in a remote corner during lectures and a room to herself when she looked at slides, "so as not to contaminate the Harvard students," she said.

Dr. Brennar advised her to study anatomy at Boston University for credit. Dr. Alexander Begg, Dean and Professor of Anatomy at BU, unknowingly started her on the path to cardiology when he handed her an ox heart and advised her to learn about the muscle bundles. This she did with interest and industry. Next she began the study of the physiology of the heart, and published her first paper, "Rhythmic Contractions in Isolated Strips of Cardiac Muscle." Dr. Begg encouraged her to apply to The Johns Hopkins University School of Medicine, which accepted women on the same basis as men. Fortunately, for her and for Hopkins, she was accepted. Thus began a long and distinguished career at Hopkins.

Throughout medical school, she worked in the heart station on electrocardiograms, and continued doing so for a year of research after she received her M.D. degree in 1927. The next year she interned in pediatrics and came under the influence of Dr. Park, the new chairman of that department. Dr. Park had recognized that acutely ill children received good care in the hospital, but that those with chronic illness who attended the out-patient clinic often did not. He developed the idea of specialty clinics and, despite strong protest, he set them up in four areas; cardiology, pulmonary disease (tuberculosis), epilepsy, and psychiatry.

He appointed Helen Taussig chief of the Cardiac Clinic. He provided a fluoroscope and urged her to use it, to look at the heart from different views. He instructed her not only to learn about rheumatic fever, which was the main cardiac problem in those days before penicillin and the establishment of the link to streptococcal sore throat, but also to learn about congenital malformations. At first, Helen saw little purpose in that assignment, but soon congenital malformations came to fascinate her. She thrilled to the discovery that certain anomalies presented patterns that repeated and could be recognized: tetralogy of Fallot, tricuspid atresia with rudimentary right ventricle, and others of the cyanotic and acyanotic groups. Her tools were careful history and examination with measurement of blood pressure, three-lead electrocardiogram, fluoroscopy, and chest x-ray with barium swallow in frontal, both right and left anterior oblique, and lateral views. She correlat-

Fig.   Helen Brooke Taussing, M.D. (Reproduced with permission of the *American Journal of Cardiology.*)

ed her observations with postmortem specimens and began to arrive at remarkably accurate function diagnoses.

As her clinical skills were being honed, Helen began to lose one of the major tools of any cardiologist, her hearing. This did not stop her. She obtained a hearing aid, which hung like a necklace around her neck and which she would aim toward the person speaking to her. She also obtained an amplifying stethoscope, which she carried around in its box. Perhaps she also compensated for her hearing loss by intensifying her other powers of observation and clear-thinking analysis. The hearing impairment made lecturing difficult because she could not judge her voice level or adjust it easily for her audience; so she would ask a friend to be in the rear of the audience to signal her and to let her know if her words were coming through at the right levels. It was about 10 years after her blue baby work had made her world famous that hearing aids were miniaturized and placed in the external ear inconspicuously as an extension of the temple pieces of eyeglasses. She happily proclaimed how nice it was to have her "ears" back where they belonged. Not until her official retirement did she have first one and then the other stapes operation, both successful. Imagine her great joy when she found she could hear through a regular stethoscope!

Believing that in an academic setting, one should teach what one has learned, she set about writing her observations, analyses, and differential diagnoses in the chapters that 10 years later in 1947 appeared as the book, *Congenital Malformations of the Heart*. She provided circulatory diagrams in color and B. J. Browning's beautiful anatomic drawings of specimens, together with x-rays, illustrative case reports, and a lucid, easy-to-read text. The book that started simply as a

scholar's desire to share knowledge, without any dream at the outset of the practical application, had a tremendous impact owing to the concept of the newly acquired reality of surgical treatment and the importance of accurate diagnosis and management.

In 1939 Dr. Robert Gross of Harvard opened the door of cardiac surgery when he ligated a child's patent ductus arteriosus. Dr. Taussig had realized that some of her patients with cyanotic congenital heart disease and diminished pulmonary blood flow died when the ductus closed and that those who had a continuous murmur of flow from the aorta through collateral circulation to the pulmonary circuit did better than those who did not. She reasoned that they might benefit from surgical creation of a patent ductus, and thought that if surgeons could tie off such a vessel, perhaps they could also build one. She approached Dr. Gross with this idea but he was not interested.

She had to wait until Dr. Alfred Blalock was appointed Chairman of Surgery at Johns Hopkins in 1941. At Vanderbilt University, he had experience in ligating the ductus in three children and in surgical attempts to establish a subclavian pulmonary arterial shunt as a model to study pulmonary hypertension. He thought about the idea, said he would take it to the laboratory, and in 1944 he told Dr. Taussig that he was ready. On November 29, 1944, he performed the first Blalock-Taussig operation successfully on Eileen Saxon, a desperately ill cyanotic baby, who prior to the operation had suffered many hypercyanotic spells each day. A second operation was performed two months later, and the next several followed that spring. Dr. Taussig and Dr. Blalock presented these children and described their work at a very exciting meeting of the medical and surgical staff and of medical students at Hopkins. When they reported their results in the *Journal of the American Medical Association* in 1945, the wonder that children with pulmonary stenosis or atresia could be changed from blue to pink by surgical creation of an artificial ductus became known the world over. Doctors came to observe and learn from this pair, and patients and parents arrived from all parts of the globe. Drs. Taussig and Blalock unselfishly gave their time to lecture, consult, and present their experiences at medical gatherings and in publication.

Helen Taussig and Alfred Blalock divided responsibilities in a way that led to the establishment of two cooperating subspecialties: pediatric cardiology and cardiothoracic surgery. Referrals came to Dr. Taussig for scheduling appointments for examination and diagnosis. Those considered suitable for surgery were then referred to Dr. Blalock by Dr. Taussig, who attended all of the early operations and many of the difficult ones afterward. Both combined their expertise for postoperative care, and Dr. Taussig began the long-term follow-up, with analysis of successes and failures, that she continued even after her official "retirement."

The influx of patients needing care called for assistants, and thus led to the appointment of fellows and, in turn, to the establishment of training programs in the new specialties. I consider myself fortunate to have been one of the first of Dr. Taussig's fellows.

Without giving it that name, she established an ongoing program of continuing education by inviting her former fellows back in the spring to meet the current trainees and to present a 2-day scientific program by and for both groups. Sharing problems, new insights, and discoveries advanced knowledge and knit together a close group of fellows, dubbed the "Knights of Taussig." The highlight of each gathering was a lawn party at Dr. Taussig's, with broad expanse of lawn terminating in a rock garden full of May-blooming flowers and a view of Lake Roland.

At these meetings and at national meetings, she encouraged us to present our work, patiently taught us to write abstracts, and organize our material for publication. She even shared her precious time on the Cape in the summers in going over manuscripts.

On completion of training, her fellows fanned out to medical centers in this country and abroad, to emulate and continue her precepts of learning, teaching, and caring. It soon became evident that the new specialty needed a forum for presentation and discussion and that high standards needed to be set for pediatric cardiologists. The Council on Cardiovascular Disease in the Young became the focus in the American Heart Association, while in the American Academy of Pediatrics, the Cardiology section was established and then the Sub-Board of Pediatric Cardiology as a certifying body was created with Dr. Taussig one of the founding members.

In 1962, at the peak of her career, Dr. Taussig made another major contribution by pursuing a lead mentioned on a visit from Germany by one of her former fellows. He related that many babies had recently been born with absent or malformed limbs like flippers and that some doctors suspected the deformities might result from a sleeping pill taken by the mothers. She traveled to Germany, visiting clinics, examining the babies with phocomelia, talking with the mothers and doctors. Accumulated evidence was overwhelming that thalidomide taken even as a single tablet early in pregnancy was the offender. The drug was taken off the market in Europe, ending the dreadful epidemic. Her reports to the medical profession in the Unites States and to Congress prevented a repetition of the disaster here, for the Food and Drug Administration refused to approve the drug. Not only did her actions stop the serious damage to unborn infants but they also established the principle that drugs need to be tested carefully before they are given, especially to pregnant women.

Dr. Helen Taussig has been honored many times in her career, and she graciously accepts each honor with modesty and genuine pleasure. Beginning with Phi Beta Kappa and elec-

tion to Alpha Omega Alpha in medical school, the awards escalated after the blue baby operation in 1944; among them are the Chevalier Legion d'Honneur, Passano Award, Albert Lasker Award, Gold Heart Award, and the Herrick Award of the American Heart Association, the Howland Award of the American Pediatric Society, the Milton S. Eisenhower Award in 1976 from Johns Hopkins (the highest honor the University confers), and our nation's highest civilian award, the Medal of Freedom in 1964. She was elected to the National Academy of Sciences, and she became the first woman to be President of the American Heart Association, 1965–1966. Since 1963, she has been Professor Emeritus of Pediatrics at Hopkins. In December 1983, she was present for the dedication of the Helen B. Taussig Children's Cardiac Center at Johns Hopkins. Included in her honors list are honorary Doctor of Science degrees from over 20 universities, among them Duke, Dartmouth, and Harvard.

This great lady is retired, but she continues to do research on congenital heart disease. She recently reported on a survey of congenital anomalies in mammals and found that common malformations were common in humans and animals. She is now examining hearts of birds, seeking gross defects. She was honorary chairman of the Second World Congress of Pediatric Cardiology, held in 1985 in New York City.

She continues to do each summer what she has always loved to do on Cape Cod: swim twice a day, boil lobsters, make beach plum jelly, bake bread, entertain her friends, and go for long walks with her dachshund. In the winter, she lives in a retirement village in a lovely section of Pennsylvania near the magnificent Longwood Gardens, which she loves to visit. There she has many friends and visitors who share her intellectual interests and her enthusiasms.

Helen Taussig has won the love of her patients and her students, and the admiration and respect of the medical profession throughout the world. She has done it simply by being herself, using her gifts, overcoming her handicaps, persevering despite adversity, setting high standards and worthy goals, modestly receiving acclaim, and always sharing what she has learned.

In 1982 she wrote: "One of the great satisfactions of medicine is being able to help those in need. I thank all my colleagues who have improved the lives of children, bringing happiness to them and their families. The never-ending challenge of medicine is that there is always more to learn. I extend my best wishes to all who will continue to advance our knowledge and help the future generation."

She has set a fine example, and our world is the better for it.

The Legacy of William Dock, A Giant of American Cardiology

Samuel Zoneraich, M.D.,

Albert Einstein College of Medicine, Research Division, Cardiology and Hypertensive Center, Flushing Medical Center, Flushing, New York, USA

William Dock (Fig. 1), the son of Dr. George Dock, was born in 1898 in Ann Arbor Michigan. His father was one of the first full-time professors of medicine at the University of Michigan until 1908, and at Washington University in St. Louis until 1922. In the same year, he retired from his position of head of the department to a distant town where he continued to practice medicine until he was 86 years old. Bill felt a lifelong profound love for his father, who educated him in a puritan atmosphere.

William Dock earned his medical degree at Rush, from which he graduated in 1923. He completed his internship and residency at the Peter Bent Brigham Hospital in Boston and continued his training at Stanford. He was a pupil of Merrick, Fred Smith, and Sam Levine. During his training he witnessed the great progress in cardiology following the introduction of the 12-lead electrocardiogram by his master Frank Wilson, who was also an astronomer (he had his own observatory) and a splendid ornithologist. Bill's father felt that his son needed additional postgraduate training and sent him to Vienna, where he studied with K. F. Wenkenbach, the head of the First Medical Clinic. By coincidence, my first teacher, who taught me cardiology, was also a pupil of Wenkenbach. The "Wenkenbach Periods" were part and parcel of all cardiology seminars.

The First Meeting with Dock

At the Sorbonne in Paris, in the winter of 1962, I attended Jean Lenégre's morning rounds. A close associate of Lenégre stated during the rounds that an American, William Dock, was the first to describe the origin of the first heart sound.[1] This statement was somehow unexpected. The French cardiologists were considered the best in the field. In the afternoon, in the laboratory at Boucicaut where I watched Lenégre performing histopathologic studies of the blocks, the discussion about Dock came up again. At that time I decided to leave France for the United States to try to work with Dock. In a brief period of time I read and became familiar with some of his writings.[1–7] Their erudition, and a style that excelled in clarity and concision, made an extraordinary impression on me. In New York, following a lengthy interview, I was accepted to work with him.

Dock was an unassuming man of medium stature, who exuded a feeling of self-confidence. His office, which also served as his laboratory, contained his voluminous multichannel recording including the 3-plane ballistocardiogram built to his specifications, a narrow ballistocardiographic table with springs, and many other laboratory instruments. During the interview he showed a special interest in France. Bill had received the "Croix de Guerre" for his participation as a volunteer in the French army in World War I and then in World War II. His sons also fought in Europe during World War II. "History," he said, "may not repeat itself exactly, but it keeps trying."

Dock's Morning Rounds

In the intensive care unit and on the floors during rounds Dock displayed unsurpassed skill in bedside physical examination. No one of the master clinicians I observed on rounds, including Jean Lenégre and Charles Debray in Paris, Isadore Snapper and William Dressler in New York, and Sodi-Pallares in Mexico City, came close to him—would make a diagnosis from inspection palpation and auscultation. We learned at his rounds how one can make a bedside clinical diagnosis from palpating the heaves and from listening to the characteristics of the first and second heart sounds, the clicks, and the gallops.[8] Recently, S_3 gallop—described 100 years ago by Portain—was found to be more reliable than the ejection fraction[9] in patients with congestive heart failure.

During rounds, Bill made use of his solid background in chemistry, histopathology, physiology, and radiology. He was Professor of Pathology for six years at Stanford and Cornell. He always embellished his rounds with the beauty of art, fiction, philosophy, and social behavior. In the afternoon he recorded the tracings and then he gave them to me for writing the interpretation. We both signed the reports and placed them in the charts. For three years, I studied the tracings daily between 6 and 11 P.M. The medical students loved Dock not for his leniency—lenient he was not— but they considered him their hero because he was a symbol of perseverance, steadfastness, and honesty, always ready to take on a new challenge. Irving Page once wrote that Bill Dock was a genius, and the students knew it.

FIG. 1 William Dock, M.D., (1898–1990)

The Scientist

Bill published extensively, but his concepts were ahead of his time. Therefore, his original ideas were never easily accepted by his peers. For instance, as a pathologist in 1936 at Stanford, he was aware of the thromboembolic complications caused by prolonged bed rest, and he recommended early ambulation.[10] At a symposium at Cornell he presented the topic "The Abuse of Bed Rest," which appeared at that time to be a simple hypothesis. But it was not until 1944, after the publication of his paper in the *Journal of the American Medical Association* that his idea was accepted. During the war the shortage of beds for the wounded could not be solved by building new hospitals, as the funds were lacking. Finally, physicians all over the world—surgeons, obstetricians, and cardiologists caring for their patients with heart attacks who were kept in bed for a minimum period of three weeks—accepted Bill's idea. His photograph appeared on the cover of *Time* magazine.

Bill never believed in his own original work unless it was confirmed by other researchers employing independent techniques. He constantly challenged his own astute sense of observation, inventiveness, and originality in thinking.

The diastolic murmur of a stenosed coronary artery which I detected for the first time was published only after I could record the murmur and after the stenosis and poststenotic dilatation was confirmed by complex histopathologic studies. Such finding was later confirmed by others.[11]

It was Bill Dock who introduced the three-plane ballistocardiography[12] and we proposed for this technique the term "seismicardiography,"[13] to reflect the complex multiplan movement. When he retired, Bill was very unhappy that this technique, which he considered useful in the noninvasive detection of ventricular filling pressures at rest and during phar-

macologic interventions, was of no interest to physicians. He could not predict at that time that after 20 years newer added technical improvements would bring back the ballistocardiogram.[14]

Famous scientists and teachers came to see Bill Dock, to gain his friendship and to ask advice and criticism for their ongoing research. Such meetings, one on one, which took place in his office were preceded by lengthy discussions and detailed preparations.

Once, I had the privilege of attending such a meeting with the well-known geneticist and cardiologist, Victor McKusick from Johns Hopkins, the author of *Human Genetics*.[15] Dr. McKusick's presentation was simple, well documented, and eloquent, but the discussion which followed was extremely complex. There was a constant effort to overcome the apparent lack of unity in the state of the art in genetics and at the end of the meeting, emphasis was placed on future trends.

Dock's Legacy

In August 1985, when he was approaching ninety, I visited Bill in his apartment in Paris located behind the magnificent building of the French Pantheon. He showed me a photograph of his grandson displayed on the mantelpiece. Every week Bill received newspaper clippings, magazines, and medical journals from New York, and his mind was fast and sharp, as always. At that time his vision of the future progress of medicine was more optimistic than in the 1950s when he wrote that the investigator in heart disease faces a fertile territory that has barely been scratched by the crude tools of the pioneers.[7]

He said that real progress in diagnostic techniques and treatment have changed the basic aspects of medicine, "But progress has its disappointments, too. We are losing our clinical skills which are replaced by columns of figures supplied by machines." Dock felt that we are gradually losing our self-confidence and our deep sense of criticism, and that ordering unnecessary tests reflects our lack of self-confidence. He believed that technicians and medical instruments could not replace clinical experience and sound medical judgement, that we must master the latest techniques judiciously, and think twice before employing new drugs.

His conviction about academic freedom was as strong as ever.[16]

He held that the prospective medical student should be given the widest possible latitude in selecting his premedical curriculum. Again he quoted his preferred popular proverb: "Leading horses to water is futile when they are not thirsty; thirsty horses will seek it out." He felt that both science and humanities must play a decisive role in creating the proper academic atmosphere in medical schools and hospitals and that the concept of medical robots whose entire interest lies in the practical phases of diagnosis, therapy, and operative procedures is unrealistic.

Dock said that in order to improve daily practice, the student and the house staff require training and retraining in bedside cardiology, and he felt that an entire generation was at loss for having not paid attention to the fundamentals in clinical teaching. On the other hand, he felt that education of the medical student requires good training in cellular, biochemical, and molecular genetics in cardiology and that we can not escape the contemporary realities. From his retirement, he again summarized his lifelong credo concerning coronary artery disease.[17] In a letter published in the *New England Journal of Medicine* he wrote: "Physicians can reassure patients, nearly all heart attacks are the result of overeating, lack of exercise, and smoking too many cigarettes."[18]

Bill suffered his first two episodes of gout at age 32. At age 59 he was stricken by a heart attack. He felt that his longevity—he lived to 91 years of age—was definitely influenced by his lifestyle (severe diet and good medical treatment). Before I left him in Paris, Bill said, while showing me to the door, "I really envy the newer generation for having at its disposal so many new techniques which supplement, complete, and confirm clinical data. In my time," he said, "we had to rely on our clinical experience and on some graphic techniques. You should consider yourself a lucky generation."

Acknowledgement

The author wishes to thank Carole Marko for her help with the typing of the manuscript.

References

1. Dock W: Mode of production of the first heart sound. *Arch Intern Med* 51, 737–746 (1933)

2. Harrison RT, Dock W, Holman E: Experimental studies in arteriovenous fistulae: Cardiac output. *Heart* 11, 337–341(1924)

3. Dock W: Presbycardia, or aging of the myocardium. *NY State J Med* 45, 983–986 (1945)

4. French AJ, Dock W: Fatal coronary arteriosclerosis in young soldiers. *J Am Med Assoc* 124, 1233–1237 (1944)

5. Railsbach DC, Dock W: Erosion of the ribs due to stenosis of the isthmus (coarctation) of the aorta. *Radiology* 12, 58–61 (1929)

6. Dock W: The capacity of the coronary bed in cardiac hypertrophy. *J Exp Med* 74, 177–186 (1941)

7. Dock W: Physiological problems in the treatment of heart disease. *J Mount Sinai Hosp* 13, 310–317 (1947)

8. Dock W: What can auscultation of the heart tell us about diagnosis, prognosis and therapeutic effects. Postgrad Med 35, 155–158 (1964)

9. Zoneraich S: Editorial evaluation of century-old physical signs, S3 and S4 by modern technology. *J Am Coll of Cardiol* 458–459 (1992)

10. Dock W: The evil sequelae of complete bed rest. *J Am Med Assoc* 125, 1983–1985 (1944)

11. Dock W: , Zoneraich S. A diastolic murmur arising in a stenosed coronary artery. *Am J Med.*742, 617–619 (1967)

12. Dock W: *Ballistocardiography: The Application of the Direct Ballistocardiograph to Clinical Medicine.* Mosby, St Louis, (1953) 293

13. Zoneraich S: Seismocardiography is not a new term. *Am J Card* 69, 573–574 (1992)

14. Salerno DM, Zanetti JM, Green LA, Mooney MR, Madison JD, VanTassel RA: Seismocardiographic changes associated with obstruction of coronary blood flow during balloon angioplasty. *Am J Cardiol* 68, 201–207 (1991)

15. McKusick, VA: *Human Genetics.* Prentice-Hall, Englewood Cliffs (1964)148

16. Dock W: Training and cultural background of the physician. *J Am Med Coll* 15, 381–384(1940)

17. Dock W: Hypercholesteremia: Its Clinical Significance and Management. *Med Clin North Am* 36, 865–874 (1952)

18. Dock W: Myocytes, macrophages, and "Atheromas." *N Engl J Med* 305(18) 1096–1097 (1981)

T. Duckett Jones and His Association with Paul Dudley White

O. Paul, m.d., E. F. Bland, m.d., B. F. Massell, m.d.

Countway Library of Medicine, Boston, Massachusetts, USA

Dr. T. Duckett Jones (Fig. 1) was one physician whose professional life was essentially devoted to the problems associated with a single disease: rheumatic fever.

Duckett, as he was called by all who knew him, was born in 1899 into a medical family in Petersburg, Virginia. His father, John Boiling Jones, was a distinguished doctor, a brother was a surgeon, one sister was a physician, and two other sisters married doctors. He graduated from Virginia Military Institute in 1919, and received his M.D. from the University of Virginia in 1923, where he then served as intern and resident. A fellow Virginian, J. Edwin Wood, Jr., had spent the year 1922–1923 at the Massachusetts General Hospital as cardiac resident under Dr. Paul Dudley White, and doubtless influenced by his example, Duckett Jones followed him in 1925–1926. During and after this 12-month residency, Jones and White authored six scientific papers (one of which was coauthored with Dr. Howard Sprague) on a variety of clinical topics including "Heart Disease and Disorders in New England," "Paroxysmal Ventricular Tachycardia—Report of an Unusual Case," "Atrioventricular Nodal Rhythm," and "The Heart in Severe Diphtheria." After serving as an instructor in medicine for one more year at the University of Virginia School of Medicine, Jones went to London as National Research Council Fellow, training at the University College Hospital under Paul White's former mentor, Sir Thomas Lewis, and his associate Ronald T. Grant.[1]

The next 19 years of his life were to be devoted to work in Boston at the House of the Good Samaritan. The House of the Good Samaritan had been founded in 1861, and in recent years prior to Jones's association had been a small high caliber institution caring especially for patients with tuberculosis, cancer, and rheumatic fever. In 1921, the Hospital Board decided that enough beds were available within the community hospitals to serve patients with tuberculosis; the Board resolved to concentrate the resources of the House of the Good Samaritan on meeting the long-term needs of young people with rheumatic fever and rheumatic heart disease, then the number one cause of death in the age group 5 to 15 years.[2] By 1924, the hospital had 53 beds devoted solely to such patients, most of whom had been referred after initial diagnosis and treatment at Massachusetts General Hospital (although some cases were referred from the Boston City and other hospitals).

On October 1, 1928, Duckett Jones became the first resident physician at the "Good Sam" while also serving as assistant in medicine at the Harvard Medical School. The Annual Report of the House of the Good Samaritan for the year 1928 mentions that "Dr. Jones also holds a Dalton scholarship at the Massachusetts General Hospital, dividing his time between the two institutions but living at our hospital."[3] Dr. Paul White had been visiting the wards of the House of the Good Samaritan since 1920, and he and others, including Dr. Howard Sprague, had established a close working relation between the two hospitals. Duckett Jones fitted easily into this cooperative arrangement. In 1929, he was appointed Research Director, in large measure due to the influence of Dr. Howard Sprague who had described to the Hospital Board "the urgent need of the study of this disease which, in its chronic form, is responsible, more than any other, for the suffering and economic crippling of young people."[4] Also at this time, a distinguished Research Advisory Committee was appointed which included Kenneth Blackfan, Cecil Drinker, Paul White, John R. Paul, Homer F. Swift, and Hans Zinsser. With the encouragement of Paul White, Duckett Jones had meanwhile established a Rheumatic Fever Clinic at the Massachusetts General Hospital which he attended on a regular basis, in addition to the out- and inpatient facilities at the House of the Good Samaritan.

Duckett Jones began a research program almost at once. One undertaking was that of assessing the role of climate; and for six years, small groups of patients with rheumatic fever were transferred for the winter months from the House of the Good Samaritan to St. Francis Hospital in Miami Beach—with salutary consequences. In addition, after Alvin Coburn, in 1931,[5] emphasized the role of the hemolytic streptococcus in the genesis of rheumatic fever, Duckett Jones conducted his own throat culture and serological studies, but felt that the data did not support this hypothesis. Even as late as 1937,[6] he wrote "infection with the hemolytic streptococcus is closely associated with rheumatic fever, especially with the onset of the disease, but this association may be secondary, and does not satisfy the usual postulates necessary to accept such infection as the actual cause of the disease." Frustrated, he also investigated the possibility of a primary viral infection but with negative findings. Beginning in 1941, he undertook a major study of an hemolytic streptococcal epidemic at the U.S. Naval Training Station at Newport, Rhode Island, which had

Fig. 1   Thomas Duckett Jones, 1899–1954.

been followed by an epidemic of acute rheumatic fever. Probably his most important research contribution was the creation of a detailed record system at the House of the Good Samaritan, permitting documentation of the long-term course of rheumatic fever and rheumatic heart disease. With Edward F. Bland, he completed 10 years of follow-up of 1,000 patients with rheumatic fever, a unique and rewarding project, the results of which were published in 1942.[7] Later (1951), a 20-year follow-up was also completed.[8] The group at the "Good Sam" was also active in the investigation of the role of penicillin in treating hemolytic streptococcal infections in rheumatic subjects, and in 1948 Massell, Dow, and Jones presented the first report of the use of oral penicillin in eradicating such infection from the throat, thereby preventing rheumatic fever.[9]

Not a research activity, but signally important in clinical medicine and public health, was a statement entitled "The Diagnosis of Rheumatic Fever" written by Duckett Jones and published in *The Journal of the American Medical Association* in 1944.[10] This landmark report set forth five major manifestations of rheumatic fever, and seven minor ones, with the recommendation that a diagnosis of rheumatic fever was justified with any combination of the major manifestations, or with at least one major and two minor ones. The "Jones criteria" filled a pressing need and were quickly and widely adopted. It is significant that in keeping with his prior restraint, the criteria did not include supporting evidence of a preceding streptococcal infection.

In 1947, Duckett Jones left Boston to assume the position of Medical Director of the new Helen Hay Whitney Foundation in New York City. Established by Mrs. Charles S. Payson with a grant of $5,000,000, the Foundation was created "to promote basic research in rheumatic fever and rheumatic heart disease." From this ideal base Jones could continue to extend his influence to the end that research in rheumatic fever, and indeed all biologic science, might begin to receive more appropriate financial support. Further, it gave him an opportunity to continue his active role in professional education and various scientific committees and societies. Over the years, he had assumed a role of expanding leadership in several organizations concerned with the rheumatic fever problem. He served as a member of the Advisory Committee of the Services for Crippled Children of the Children's Bureau of the U.S. Department of Labor, and was a leader in the first National Rheumatic Fever Council held under the auspices of the Bureau in 1943. In January 1944, he was an organizer of the 2-day Rheumatic Fever Conference of the American Heart Association held in New York City, and subsequently was Chairman of the Rheumatic Fever Council of the Association. Later, he was President of the American Rheumatism Association, and of the Protein Foundation. At the time of his death, he was President-Elect of the National Health Council.

A particular challenge to his active mind came at the end of World War II, when the first moves were made to create a National Heart Institute. In March 1948, Duckett Jones was one of 79 prominent citizens who signed a telegram to Senator James E. Murray of Montana calling for an immediate hearing on pending legislation to create a federally funded National Heart Institute. The most influential individual in this and subsequent lobbying was Mrs. Mary Lasker, who mobilized and goaded scientists into waging an aggressive and effective campaign. In June 1948, Duckett Jones testified before the Subcommittee on Health of the Senate Labor and Public Welfare Committee in favor of such legislation, and was instrumental in promoting its passage. President Truman signed Public Law 655, which was the National Heart Act, on June 16, 1948. Duckett Jones was thereupon intent on seeing that this golden opportunity to obtain and use wisely funds for cardiovascular research was not dissipated. He promptly enlisted his mentor, Paul White, to meet forthwith with the Surgeon General of the U.S. Public Health Service. The result was that early in July 1948, Paul White was appointed Executive Director of the National Advisory Heart Council of the new National Heart Institute.[11] Not surprisingly, Duckett Jones became one of the 12 members of this Council.

When the Second World Congress of Cardiology met in Washington, D.C., in September 1954 under the chairmanship of Paul White, Duckett Jones was in charge of an international panel on rheumatic fever. During these sessions it became apparent that he was ill; persuaded by friends to seek medical advice he was diagnosed with malignant hypertension. He lived only 2 months, dying on November 22, 1954, at the age of 55.

In retrospect, the achievements of Duckett Jones and his associates in searching for solutions to the problem of rheumatic fever have stood the test of time and have done so well. True, the credit for establishing the critical etiologic role of the hemolytic streptococcus belongs to others; however, Duckett Jones transformed the small, previously insignificant House of the Good Samaritan into a beacon in the recognition, treatment, and investigation of rheumatic fever. His role was not restricted to the research laboratory, but took in the wards, the clinics, and the community, as well as private and governmental bodies. His "Jones criteria" set a practical standard for diagnosis which proved durable with minor modifications over the decades. His vigorous efforts in conjunction with others helped to create an effective National Heart Institute. As Dr. Floyd N. Denney has written, Duckett Jones was "the father of modern-day acute rheumatic fever in that he did more than any other one person to advance knowledge about its nature and diagnosis, and about care and prognosis of patients with this dread disease."[12] A colleague wrote at the time of his death that there remained in Boston alone "3,000 patients who recall with gratitude and affection his careful and kindly guidance through their childhood rheumatism."[1]

References

1. *Ninety-fourth Annual Report.* House of the Good Samaritan, Boston (1954) 7-8
2. *Sixty-First Annual Report.* House of the Good Samaritan for the year 1921. Boston (1922) 14-15
3. *Sixty-Eighth Annual Report.* House of the Good Samaritan for the year 1928. Boston (1929) 7, 17, 23
4. *Sixty-Ninth Annual Report.* House of the Good Samaritan for the year 1929. Boston (1930) 6, 14, 17-18
5. Coburn AF: *The Factor of Infection in the Rheumatic State.* Williams and Wilkins, Baltimore (1931)
6. *Seventy-Seventh Annual Report.* House of the Good Samaritan for the year 1937. Boston (1938) 15
7. Jones TD, Bland EF: Rheumatic fever and heart disease, completed 10-year observations on 1000 patients. *Tr A Am Phys* 57, 265 (1942)
8. Bland EF, Jones TD: Rheumatic fever and rheumatic heart disease; a twenty year report on 1000 patients followed since childhood. *Circulation* 4, 836 (1951)
9. Massell BF, Dow JW, Jones TD: Orally administered penicillin in patients with rheumatic fever. *J Am Med Assoc* 138, 1030 (1948)
10. Jones TD: The diagnosis of rheumatic fever. *J Am Med Assoc* 126, 481 (1944)
11. Paul O: *Take Heart. The Life and Prescription for Living of Paul Dudley White.* Harvard University Press for Countway Library of Medicine. Boston (1986) 137
12. Denny FW: T. Duckett Jones and rheumatic fever in 1986. *Circulation* 76, 963 (1987)

Alfred Blalock

C. R. HATCHER, JR., M.D.

Department of Cardiothoracic Surgery, Robert W. Woodruff Health Sciences Center, Emory University School of Medicine, Atlanta, Georgia, USA

Alfred Blalock (Fig. 1) was born on April 5, 1899 in Culloden, Georgia, and reared in Jonesboro, Georgia, a small town near Atlanta. As a boy he attended Georgia Military College, Milledgeville, Georgia, where his performance was average. After serving in the United States Army during World War I, he received the Bachelor of Arts degree from the University of Georgia in 1918. At the University, Alfred Blalock was an active member of the Sigma Chi Fraternity and led a very active social life. Although he was not a varsity athlete, he was involved in athletics as a team manager. He obtained his M.D. degree from The Johns Hopkins University School of Medicine. In 1922 he completed his surgical internship and a year of residency at Johns Hopkins before entering the surgical program of Dr. Barney Brooks at Vanderbilt University in Nashville, Tennessee.

In 1925 Blalock became the resident surgeon at Vanderbilt. Upon completion of residency he became a member of the faculty in surgery, rising to the rank of full professor in 1938. It was at Vanderbilt that Professor Blalock first achieved national prominence. His work there established the fact that shock results from loss of blood and/or body fluids, a radical concept at the time and one disputed by the leading physiologists of the day. Through his experiments on hemorrhagic and traumatic shock, Dr. Blalock recognized the need for volume replacement with colloids and crystalloids, and he was the first to suggest massive application of blood and plasma transfusions for war wounds. Dr. Mark Ravitch and many others feel that this work was Dr. Blalock's greatest scientific contribution (Blalock, 1966).

In 1941, Dr. Blalock was named Professor of Surgery at The Johns Hopkins University and Surgeon in Chief of The Johns Hopkins Hospital. His appointment represented somewhat of a compromise. A previous search committee had become stalemated, unable to decide between two outstanding local candidates for the surgical chairmanship. Officials at Johns Hopkins subsequently appointed a second search committee headed by the late Dr. Alan Woods, Professor of Ophthalmology and Director of the Wilmer Eye Institute at Johns Hopkins. In later years, Dr. Woods remarked that when handed a list of nine candidates by the chairman of the first search committee, he looked over the list and immediately supported Dr. Alfred Blalock, the only person on the list whom he did not know personally!

Dr. Blalock's early period at Johns Hopkins resulted in the systemic pulmonary shunt on cyanotic heart disease. Working in the Hunterian Laboratory, Dr. Blalock and his associates developed an operation in which the subclavian artery was divided and attached end to side to the descending thoracic aorta, a technique they considered quite applicable to the treatment of coarctation of the aorta. Dr. Helen Brook Taussig, the pediatric cardiologist at Johns Hopkins, noted that her infants with tetralogy of Fallot characteristically deteriorated with closure of their patent ductus arteriosus. She consulted Dr. Blalock about the plausibility of creating an artifical ductus. The idea intrigued Dr. Blalock, and he felt that with modification, his subclavian to aorta anastomosis could be converted to a subclavian pulmonary artery anastomosis.

This type of thinking was quite revolutionary and ushered in an era of physiologic surgery. Prior to the development of these concepts, surgery predominantly involved correctional anatomical procedures, such as the removal of tumors, relief of obstructions, drainage of abscesses, and so forth. Dr. Blalock and Dr. Taussig attacked the physiologic cause of a number of anatomical abnormalities. In the case of tetralogy of Fallot, the basic physiologic problem was inadequate pulmonary blood flow. Therefore, a systemic to pulmonary artery shunt would add significant physiologic correction at the expense of an additional anatomical defect.

Dr. Blalock encountered great difficulty in having these patients managed by members of the faculty in anesthesiology who were concerned about the hazards of anesthesia in a deeply cyanotic infant. Finally, he prevailed upon Miss Olive Berger, nurse anesthetist at Johns Hopkins who worked with him on this project. Dr. Blalock and Miss Berger maintained a close working relationship during the years that followed. Miss Berger came to be known affectionately as "Lady Olive" by members of the house staff in surgery. At that time the anesthesia service was under the Department of Surgery, and these early problems and interpersonal relationships possibly delayed the development of a strong and independent Department of Anesthesiology at Johns Hopkins.

The Blalock-Taussig or "blue baby" operation electrified the surgical world. His scientific presentations on the subject produced standing ovations, and Dr. Blalock and his residents demonstrated the operation in the major medical centers of Europe. A steady stream of distinguished national and

To
Charles Hatcher,
with all good wishes
from
Alfred Blalock

FIG. 1   Dr. Alfred Blalock.

international guests visited Dr. Blalock's operative theatre at Hopkins. As a result of these contributions, Dr. Blalock was recipient of numerous awards and honors. He was elected a member of the National Academy of Sciences and Surgeon-in-Chief of the National Research Council. He became a member of the Editorial Board of *Archives of Surgery, Southern Surgical Association, Surgery,* and *Gynecology and Obstetrics.* He was elected to and an officer of all of the major national and international societies. His honorary degrees include: Sc.M., (Hon.), Yale University, 1946; M.D., Honoris Causa, University of Turin, 1951; Sc.D., (Hon.), University of Rochester, 1951; Sc.D., (Hon.), University of Chicago, 1951; Sc.D., (Hon.), Lehigh University 1953; LL.D., (Hon.), Hampden-Sydney College, 1954; Sc.D., (Hon.), Emory University, 1954; Sc.D., (Hon.), Georgetown University, 1959; LL.D., (Hon.), University of Saskatchewan, 1963. His numerous awards include the Research Medal of the Southern Medical Association, 1940; the Gorden Wilson Medal, 1941; the Distinguished Service Award of the American Medical Association, 1953; the International Feltrinelli Prize for Medicine, 1954: and the Modern Medicine Award for Distinguished Achievement, 1960. Dr. Blalock's close associate and biographer, Dr. Mark Ravitch, has conjectured that "he was perhaps most proud of the two awards least commonly awarded to surgeons, membership in the National Academy of Sciences and in the American Philosophical Society" (Blalock, 1966).

During the Vanderbilt years, Alfred Blalock married Mary Chambers O'Bryan, and this union produced two sons and a daughter, William Rice, Alfred Dandy, and Mary Elizabeth. Although a devoted family man, Dr. Blalock maintained a fierce commitment to his work. Mary Blalock was once asked how her husband liked to spend his summers, and she re-

sponded "Why, he spends them the way he spends his winters—working" (Rothe, 1947). After many years of failing health she died in December 1958 at The Johns Hopkins Hospital. Dr. Blalock's ensuing melancholy and depression found solace in the friendship of his long-time acquaintance, the charming widow, Alice Seney Waters. This relationship culminated in marriage on November 12, 1959. They remained devoted to one another during the final five years of Dr. Blalock's life.

Much has been written about Dr. Blalock's unique relationship to his resident staff. Certainly it is true that Dr. Blalock demonstrated an amazing knack for the proper selection and motivation of his surgical trainees. The training program in surgery under Alfred Blalock was a refined and modified version of the program of William Halsted. The program was sharply pyramidal with up to 18 surgical interns selected for a prolonged course of study and work (normally seven years) which would result in two Halsted residents. A single Halsted resident was preferable, but the sheer size of the service and volume of work made it impossible for a single individual to accept such responsibilities. Accordingly, Dr. Rollo Hanlon was the last single Halsted resident. His year terminated in such profound exhaustion that Dr. Blalock thereafter and reluctantly appointed two Halsted residents per year.

In spite of the years of grueling work for residents, the program was popular, and applicants were always numerous and well qualified. In spite of the intense competition, the *esprit de corps* of the residents was excellent. I never witnessed any event or overheard any comment in which a resident attempted to downgrade a colleague. The residency program was like a golf tournament: you played the course with rather than against individual competitors. Doing the very best you could would be sufficient. For those outstanding young men who could not be retained as Halsted residents at Hopkins, superb training programs were available in distinguished programs around the United States where departments of surgery were then headed by former Halsted residents.

Dr. Blalock was intensely admired and respected by his residents. From that relationship he brought out the best in an individual, and this he attempted to do at every occasion. He shared credit for every success, and he never passed responsibility for failure to another. Dr. Blalock sought the advice and recommendations of his residents and acted upon that advice. This, of course, placed greatly increased responsibility on the resident staff.

Always a gentleman outside the operating room, Dr. Blalock could become testy on occasion within it, if the operation in progress was not going well. Trained in the era before blood transfusion was common, Dr. Blalock was never completely comfortable with massive hemorrhaging. Knowing this, his residents sought and achieved an amazing degree of hemostasis and did everything possible to prevent any type of surgical misadventure. He recognized and rewarded such performance. In discussing an operation with a family after the completion of surgery, Dr. Blalock almost invariably explained that the operation would have been difficult or impossible without the inspired work of his assistants.

In the complex world of the pyramidal type of postgraduate program in surgery, communication from the Chief's Office could produce intense interactions. Dr. Blalock was anxious to assist the development of the careers of his trainees in any possible way. Lengthy discussions with him, however, often indicated he had not yet made his final recommendations for a specific case. No verbal discussion of the future, on the other hand, generally meant that a candidate had been selected to complete the residency program. For many, the only official indication of annual promotion was the notification that one's new white uniforms were available at the hospital sewing room. Once asked how he made selections among so many talented young men, Dr. Blalock stated that he tried to select those individuals who would have the greatest beneficial impact on the field of surgery in the decade following completion of their training.

At reunions and certain social occasions, Dr. Blalock would be inclined to discuss how and when he selected a particular individual to complete the residency program. These discussions could be quite candid. It was somewhat surprising how early Dr. Blalock made most of these decisions. Characteristically, he met with the interns individually after six months, and at that time offered a position as Assistant Resident, suggested a period of laboratory work, suggested training in a surgical subspeciality at Johns Hopkins, or indicated the availability of an excellent resident position at another major university.

In my case, Dr. Blalock indicated that he would require anyone advancing in the residency program first to complete his two-year obligation for military service. He had therefore arranged an appointment for me in the Cardiovascular Laboratories at the National Institutes of Health. With some trepidation, I suggested that I would prefer working with Dr. Francis Moore at the Peter Bent Brigham Hospital for such a period. For a long time, Dr. Blalock was silent, then he smiled and said "that appeals to me." The conversation was terminated. I left for Brigham in July and the following Christmas received a note from Dr. Blalock which was to be of great importance to me. In the note, Dr. Blalock stated, in addition to his holiday greetings, that "there would always be a position for me at The Johns Hopkins when I wished to return." After working at Brigham and two years of military service at the Walter Reed Army Medical Center in Washington, I was in position to re-enter the residency program at Hopkins. I drove over from Washington for a very pleasant visit with Dr. Blalock. He welcomed me back to the house staff for the next July, and we shook hands. That was the last time we discussed my personal situation until I was the Halsted resident. In August of my final year, Dr. Blalock offered me a faculty position as an Assistant Professor of Surgery in his department. I was flattered but stated that I would prefer to return home to Georgia. This he understood quite well. He immediately suggested Emory University as the opportunity of choice and that very day undertook discussions with Dr. J. D. Martin, Chairman of the Department of Surgery at Emory. That led to my career at Emory.

My personal relationship to Dr. Blalock's medical history is perhaps worthy of a brief comment. One day, when I was the Halsted resident, I received a call to Dr. Blalock's office. Upon arrival I noted a barium enema illuminated on the x-ray view boxes. He asked my opinion of the films, and I spoke of an obvious rectal mass. Dr. Blalock informed me that he was the patient and that unfortunately, my interpretation of a rectal tumor was correct. We discussed his options, and he decided to ask Dr. Edward Stafford to attend his case. Arrangements were made for a hospitalization over the weekend, and he asked me to discuss the case with only the health professionals directly involved. Almost as an afterthought, Dr. Blalock asked that I check an inguinal hernia which he had developed, and he stated that if the rectal lesion was benign, he would like to have the hernia repaired. I started to mention concerns about following a rectal procedure with a hernia repair, when I was sternly interrupted and told that he understood quite well what I was saying but that he wanted the hernia repair. I, of course, assured him that a herniorrhaphy would indeed take place. A local excision of the villous adenoma and inguinal herniorrhaphy were performed without difficulty. A later recurrence of the villous adenoma was successfully managed by Dr. Mark Ravitch.

As Dr. Blalock's retirement approached, much discussion centered upon his successor and Dr. Blalock's subsequent role, if any, in the department. During this period, Dr. Blalock became rather depressed and also began to complain of back pain. A spinal fusion was necessary for relief of this pain and subsequently took place. However, shortly after emerging from anesthesia, Dr. Blalock commented that the pain was still present, and he made no further concessions to achieve a satisfactory fusion. His condition deteriorated until a needle biopsy of the liver confirmed an increasing jaundice due to metastatic carcinoma. Ultimately, the site of the tumor proved to be the ureter on the site of a nephrectomy performed for tuberculosis years earlier. Dr. Alfred Blalock died on September 15, 1964. Halsted residents served as his honorary pallbearers. He was 65 years of age and less than three months past retirement. Thus ended the career of a unique medical scientist, surgeon, and teacher. In the hearts and minds of all who worked and trained at The Johns Hopkins Hospital during the Blalock era, he will forever be known as "the Professor."

References

Blalock A; *The Papers of Alfred Blalock*. (Ed. Ravitch MM). John Hopkins University Press, Baltimore (1966) pp iv, xxv

Rothe A (Ed.): *Current Biography: Who's Who and Why*, Vol. 1946. H. W. Wilson Company, New York (1947)

David Scherf

PAUL SCHWEITZER, M.D.

Heart Institute, Beth Israel Medical Center, New York, New York, USA

David Scherf (1899–1977) (Fig. 1) was born in an eastern province of the Austro-Hungarian Empire, in a small town which, during World War I, was temporarily occupied by the Russian Army. As soon as the Austrians liberated the town, Scherf's mother took her two children for a long trip over the Carpathian Mountains through Hungary into Vienna. After finishing high school, Scherf studied medicine at the Medical Faculty of Vienna from which he graduated in 1922.[1] As a young physician, he joined the Department of Medicine headed by Wenckebach. The rise of fascism in Germany and Austria forced Scherf to leave Wenkebach's Department of Medicine, and for a short period he worked in the Department of Medicine at the Rothschild Hospital in Vienna. Because of worsening of the political tension, Scherf immigrated to the United States and settled in New York. Here he was offered a position as Chief of Cardiology at the New York Medical College were he stayed for almost 30 years until his retirement.

Before and after World War I, the Medical School of Vienna was one of the leading institutions in Europe. According to Cohen[2] who became Scherf's co-worker in New York: "Patients from all over the world came to have the diagnosis made by Skoda and to have it proved correct by Rokytansky at autopsy."[2] In addition to Wenckebach, other early pioneers of the Viennese School of cardiology were Rothberger, Winterberg, Eppinger, and Kaufman, whose classic studies of the intraventricular conduction system, extrasystoles, and parasystole are well known and quoted.[3]

Scherf is best known for his clinical and experimental research of electrocardiography (ECG) and arrhythmias. Among his early work were studies of atrioventricular (AV) junctional rhythm after clamping off the sinus node, and the documentation of AV junctional reentry following atrial and ventricular premature beats, which led to the concept of longitudinal dissociation of the AV junction.[4] Scherf and his co-workers were the first to describe Wenckebach periodicity within the bundle branches. In 1932, shortly after the Wolff-Parkinson-White syndrome was reported, Holzman and Scherf[5] suggested that the short PR interval and the delta wave were most likely due to conduction through the Kent bundle. Because information regarding the existence of the accessory pathways in humans was lacking, Holzman and Scherf urged others to look for accessory connections in humans. Eleven years later, Wood and co-workers[6] confirmed a right accessory pathway in a patient with preexcitation syndrome. While still in Vienna, Goldhammer and Scherf[7] were among the first who reported the effect of exercise on the ST segment in patients with angina pectoris. After immigrating to the United States, Scherf continued his clinical and experimental research. Among his research interests were ECG changes during hyperventilation, orthostasis, and severe hemorrhage.[1] Furthermore, using aconitine, he suggested that atrial fibrillation could be due to an ectopic focus. Early in his career, Scherf became interested in parasystole, which remained one of his favored subjects throughout his whole life.[8] In the 1920s, Scherf studied barium-induced parasystolic rhythms and later he and his co-workers were among the first to describe intermittent parasystole. Scherf retired before introduction of invasive clinical electrophysiology, which confirmed some of his experimental observations, particularly longitudinal AV junctional dissociation and ectopic origin of atrial fibrillation in some patients.

In addition to numerous publications, Scherf is also author and co-author of several monographs. In Vienna and in the United States he published the *Textbook of Cardiology and Electrocardiography*. The early German edition of this book was translated into several languages. In 1964, in cooperation with Cohen, *The Atrioventricular Node and Selected Arrhythmias* was published.[9] This monograph deals with normal and abnormal function of the AV junction and its role in various arrhythmias. In the chapter on preexcitation syndrome, Scherf and Cohen took issue with the term "delta wave" recommended by Segers *et al.*,[10] writing: "We can not understand why the Greek letter delta was used to denote this wave which resembles the Greek letter lambda." In 1972, in cooperation with Schott, the second edition of *Extrasystoles and Allied Arrhythmias* was published.[8] In this book, the authors summarized their life-long experimental and clinical experiences together with a comprehensive review of the literature until 1970. Both monographs include well-written historical notes.

Scherf was one of the leading cardiologists of his time, and made everlasting contributions to the field of arrhythmias and electrocardiography. Even after his retirement, he regularly visited the New York Medical College library to keep up with advances in cardiology. Among Sherf's most important attributes was his highly critical approach to research, his unyielding devotion to principles, and his modesty which is best

F<small>IG</small>. 1   David Scherf, M.D., 1899–1977. Photograph courtesy of the National Library of Medicine.

expressed in the first sentence of a short autobiographic note written in 1968. "Why Scherf? Others who contributed more to cardiology might better preempt this page than I."[1]

References

1. Scherf D: A cardiologist remembers. *Perspective Biol Med* 1968; 11:615–630

2. Cohen J: In memoriam: David Scherf M.D. 1899–1977. *J Electrocardiol* 1978;11:101–102

3. Fisch C: *Electrocardiography of Arrhythmias*. Philadelphia: Lea & Febiger, 1990

4. Scherf D, Shookhoff C: Experimentale Untersuchungen ueber die "Umkehr-Extrasystole" (reciprocating beat). *Wien Arch Inn Med* 1926;12:501–514

5. Holzman M, Scherf D: Ueber Elektrocardiogramme mit verkürzter Vorhof-Kammerdistanz und positiven P-Zacken. *Ztschr Klin Med* 1932;121:404–423

6. Wood F, Wolferth C, Geckeler G: Histologic demonstration of accessory muscular connection between auricle and ventricle in a case of short P-R interval and prolonged QRS complex. *Am Heart J* 1943;25:454–462

7. Goldhammer S, Scherf D: Electrokardiographische Untersuchungen bei Kranken mit Angina Pectoris ("ambulatorischer") Typus. *Ztschr Klin Med* 1932;22:134–151

8. Scherf D, Schott A: *Extrasystoles and Allied Arrhythmias*. Chicago: Year Book Medical Publisher, 1973

9. Scherf D, Cohen J: *The Atrioventricular Node and Selected Cardiac Arrhythmias*. New York: Grune & Stratton, 1964

10. Segers P, Lequime J, Denolin H: L'activation ventriculaire précoce de certains coeurs hyperexcitables: Atude de l'onde Δ de l'electrocardiogramme. *Cardiologia* 1944;6:113–167

Tinsley Randolph Harrison: Medical Investigator, Physician, and Educator (1900–1978)

E. E. EDDLEMAN, JR., M.D.

University of Alabama at Birmingham, School of Medicine, Birmingham, Alabama, USA

I had the very fortunate experience of being associated with Dr. Tinsley Harrison for a number of years. They began when I was a resident in Medicine at Southwestern Medical School in Dallas in 1949. Two years later I again joined Dr. Harrison (who had moved to become Chairman of the Department of Medicine at the University of Alabama School of Medicine in Birmingham) and was associated with him from that time until he died in 1978. It is with great respect and a sense of pride in this long association with Dr. Harrison that I have written this tribute to him.

Dr. Tinsley R. Harrison has been honored with words and presentations, including an unusual dinner in his honor in Atlantic City. Many of his friends and associates gathered to honor him at the time he voluntarily gave up the chairmanship of the Department of Medicine at the University of Alabama. The dinner coincided with the American Society for Clinical Investigation and the American College of Physicians meetings. Tribute was paid to Dr. Harrison both as a person and as a friend by many of the outstanding leaders of medicine in the world. My purpose is not to repeat and list all of his outstanding accomplishments. Instead, I will try to point out some of the aspects of his life which are not commonly known, those traits I have personally witnessed, and to emphasize Dr. Harrison as an outstanding physician, educator, and investigator.

The Investigator

Dr. Harrison graduated from The Johns Hopkins University School of Medicine and subsequently trained at the University of Michigan Medical School, Ann Arbor, Michigan, and at the Peter Bent Brigham Hospital in Boston, Massachusetts. His career really began while he was a junior faculty member at Vanderbilt University School of Medicine in Nashville, Tennessee. Those years were probably the most productive of his life as an investigator, although he continued some research up to the time of his death. He was never able to get away from the fact that there were unanswered questions in medicine which deserved answering, and his inquisitive mind was active throughout his entire career. During his tenure at Vanderbilt, Dr. Harrison spent many long hours in investigation, primarily concerning heart failure. It was there he did most of the fundamental physiopathologic

work of congestive heart failure. Many of these studies were performed in animals, and he was one of the first to use the Fick principle to measure cardiac output in dogs. In addition, he was observant and made many critical physiological measurements in his treatment of patients with heart failure. Much of his work pioneered a quantitative approach rather than descriptive methodology in the study of human disease. Various aspects of heart failure were studied, including the mechanisms of dyspnea, change in cardiac output, fluid balance problems, and electrolyte abnormalities. It was from all of these basic investigations that he wrote one of the most classic books on the subject of heart failure, *Failure of the Circulation*, published in 1935.[1] Most of its data are still as reliable today as when first published. There were two editions of this book and it is a collector's item. Even now it should be read by all those who are interested in heart failure and cardiovascular disease. It was an unusual volume in that it was one of the few texts that included only the author's original investigations, and it serves as a fundamental collection of data and concepts by one man that has not been surpassed. After publication of the second edition, the publishers wanted it to be revised, but Dr. Harrison refused primarily because he had no new personal investigation to add to the contents. This book expounded the concept of backward heart failure.* He did not realize that this would be the impetus for considerable investigation into heart failure, which subsequently led to a controversy as to whether the heart failed backward or forward. This controversy really began after cardiac catheterization data in heart failure in humans was obtained by Dr. Eugene Stead and Dr. Arthur Merrill. Dr. Harrison and Dr. Stead would stage debates on whether the heart failed backward or forward. These discussions further stimulated investigation, particularly from up-and-coming

---

*Specifically, this concept proposes that, being unable to empty properly, the blood backs up behind either the left or the right ventricle of the heart, producing the symptoms associated with congestive heart failure. If the right ventricle is involved it produces increased venous pressure which subsequently leads to enlarged liver and edema. If the left ventricle fails, the blood backs up behind it, resulting in dyspnea, etc.

In forward failure, decreased cardiac output leads to a decreased renal perfusion, decreased sodium excretion, and secondary retention of water, resulting in the symptomatology of heart failure, as later proposed by Eugene Stead, Arthur Merrill, and others.

FIG. 1   Tinsley Randolph Harrison (1900–1978).

young investigators who were anxious to add their contribution to the field as well.

These presentations were exciting and stimulating affairs, thanks to the eloquence of both speakers who deliberately exaggerated their own positions in order to "turn on" the minds and thoughts of young people. Modern medicine has probably not witnessed such debates since these, which occurred in the early 1950s. As the consequence of these (more or less staged) debates, the stimulation to the young investigators was enormous, and much of the work that was subsequently done in the 1950s and early 1960s by other people clarified many of the questionable points raised in the debates. It soon became irrelevant to argue whether the heart failed forward or backward, since the understanding of the various physiologic mechanisms which take place in heart failure were largely explained. This whole sequence is being emphasized to give insight into the character of the man who stimulated considerably more investigative work than he could have ever accomplished himself.

Another important aspect of Dr. Harrison's research work at Vanderbilt was his interest in biochemistry arid cellular metabolism. This work is seldom remembered. Dr. Harrison began studying the role of sodium and potassium metabolism and their transport across the cell membrane as far back as 1931.[2] In fact, he became so interested in this that he (using the old gravametric method for measuring sodium and potassium) demonstrated that digitalis resulted in a shift of potassium out through the membrane from the myocardial cells.

This has been rediscovered several times since its original publication and presentation. It is interesting that this work was presented at one of the meetings of the American Society for Clinical Investigation and at that time, older experts such as Van Slyke and others so severely criticized Dr. Harrison for this work that he became discouraged and essentially discontinued investigations along these lines. This probably set back the study of cellular metabolism in heart disease several years.

After his Vanderbilt years, Dr. Harrison's investigation was primarily in the field of noninvasive study of heart disease. Many of the methods which he initially became involved in, such as a ballistocardiogram and the kinetocardiogram, have now outlived their usefulness and have been supplanted by more accurate techniques such as the echocardiogram.

Even though he published in these areas throughout most of his lifetime, his investigative and inquisitive mind prevailed from a mechanistic standpoint which was constantly implanted into the minds of his students and fellows. In addition, he constantly displayed an array of original ideas and concepts. I remember, as a fellow of Dr. Harrison in Birmingham in 1953, when he first found nitroglycerin to be a useful adjunct as an ointment to be applied to the skin for treatment of angina pectoris. He was seeing a patient who was experiencing intermittent claudication, and persuaded a drug company to make up an ointment that could be rubbed on the legs of the patient to relieve discomfort the patient felt during walking. Because the patient also had angina, Harrison soon observed that instead of relieving the intermittent claudication, the ointment was therapeutically beneficial in treating the angina pectoris. Consequently, we were using the ointment regularly to alleviate the pain of angina pectoris by 1953, long before this therapy gained the popularity it has known over the past 10 years.

Space does not permit the presentation of all his accomplishments, but a few will illustrate the extraordinary talents of the man.

The Physician

Tinsley Harrison was an unusually astute physician at the bedside. This was well recognized by anyone who ever had contact with him. His general philosophy was that one should look at the entire patient and spectrum of problems and not concentrate on one organ system such as the heart. Although he was well recognized as a cardiologist, he actually disliked being called a cardiologist, but much preferred to be called an internist who was capable of handling almost any type of problem that would arise in the field. In fact, this was the general approach that he always used in caring for patients.

The second most important aspect which set Dr. Harrison apart as a truly outstanding physician was his keen interest in history taking. This is an art that often seems lacking now. In history taking, he paid acute attention to every minute detail, and often quizzed patients to great length about each facet, some of which might seem unimportant. It was astonishing how often this approach led to correct diagnoses. He was truly a medical Sherlock Holmes. His keen interest in the detailed analysis of symptoms actually led to the publication of the *Principles of Internal Medicine*.[3] He felt that standard textbooks available at that time really never addressed the approach to the patient and, consequently, in the design of the *Principles of Internal Medicine*, the first half of the book was concerned with the manifestations of disease. This was one reason this work has become such an outstanding textbook; it not only includes descriptions of diseases, but gives invaluable advice on what approach to take with a patient with a given set of symptoms.

Another type of analysis of the history Dr. Harrison used was the "reproduction of symptoms." If one can reproduce and observe symptoms at the time they are happening, one could achieve insight into their mechanism and origins.* A good example is the symptom complex associated with hyperventilation. He would regularly hyperventilate patients who were suspected of having the disorder. It was important to observe and be sure that the patients experienced the *exact* manifestations of which they complained. If the symptoms were not precisely the same, then the diagnosis was suspect. If reproduction resulted in exactly the same symptom complex, then the diagnosis was generally confirmed. This approach could be applied to a number of problems. For example, one could distend the stomach with air to reproduce pain or discomfort in the epigastric area or distend the splenic flexure of the large colon to reproduce the symptoms associated with a "splenic flexure syndrome." The procedures were useful in distinguishing mid and left upper abdominal pain that can be confused with angina pectoris. These procedures take time, but often are beneficial in sorting out a difficult problem. Another example of the usefulness of reproducing the symptoms occurred in one instance when a patient gave a history of chest pain resembling angina that occurred only on cold days when the patient was walking uphill. All studies were negative for angina and the cause of the pain was not understood until the patient was exercised by climbing stairs carrying ice in both hands. The diagnosis of angina pectoris was then confirmed.

Thus a careful history, the reproduction of symptoms, and astute bedside observations were qualities which made Dr. Harrison one of the most outstanding physicians of his time.

The Educator

Dr. Harrison had a distinguished career in the overall field of medical education. He is one of the few individuals ever to make a major contribution in the development of three of our outstanding medical schools. His tenure as Chairman of the Department of Medicine at Bowman Gray School of Medicine at Wake Forest University, Winston Salem, North Carolina; as Chairman of the Department of Medicine at University of Texas Southwestern Medical School at Dallas, Texas; and at the University of Alabama at Birmingham School of Medicine were all outstanding. In fact, he has been given considerable credit for making major contributions in developing these schools into first-class medical institutions. This has been well recognized and there is no need to discuss this further other than to point out a few personal observations which I feel are interesting, and no doubt account for why he was able to accomplish as much as he did.

He believed strongly that to educate both students and house staff properly, considerable time had to be devoted by the faculty, and that a full-time faculty staff had to be established in medical schools so that this could be accomplished. In the early days of many institutions, a majority of the faculty was often comprised of physicians in practice rather than full-time medical school staff. This was not to say that he did not have an appreciation for physicians who were in practice, but he realized the limitations which were dictated by available time. He believed in establishing a full-time staff dedicated to teaching, patient care, and medical investigation. Thus, he attempted to recruit types of individuals whom he called "triple threaters." These were young physicians who not only were good physicians and good teachers, but also investigators. He compared them with a three-legged stool. The stool, in order to be stable, needs to have three legs, but each leg need not be of equal length. It is obvious that people who are highly qualified and productive in all of these aspects of medicine are rare but, nevertheless, he attempted to seek out as many of them as possible for staff. Fortunately, he was quite successful in all three institutions in whose development he played a major role. This, above all other things, probably led to the fact that all three institutions are now considered outstanding medical schools. It is obvious how this plays an important role in the development of a school. Quality people attract quality people. After a critical mass of these individuals was reached, they themselves would attract people of comparable stature. This was brought out eloquently when, as President of the Society of Clinical Investigation, he was discussing the selection of junior staff members for a department of medicine. His presentation ended with the statement "every corporal should be selected as though he had in his hand the baton of a Marshall."

Outstanding though they were, his contributions in establishing three excellent medical schools in this country were surpassed by his greatest contribution, that of being a teacher. Dr. Harrison was very sensitive to the philosophy of Hippocrates in that he believed that "one to one" teaching was the ideal way to inspire and teach a young scholar, and in this he was exceedingly competent. He attempted this not only with the resident staff, which at this time was small enough that it could easily be handled almost on a one-to-one basis, but even more so with his fellows who were more closely associated with him. I remember that once a week we would go to his home, sit around enjoying refreshments, and listen to him discuss various medical research problems and even philosophical problems about medicine or the "art of medicine," as

---

*This is particularly important in the diagnosis of "spells." He had particular delight in seeing patients with "spells" and faced the problem as though solving a mystery.

he used to call it. These made wonderful memories for all of us who had the opportunity to be with him, and will never be forgotten. Their inspirational value and stimulation to further learning imparted a desire to be the best physicians that we could possibly be.

As you can see, Dr. Harrison had all the qualities which made him a giant in the field of modern medicine. In addition, he was a kind, humble, and compassionate man. He was broadminded and his interests were not limited to medicine. For example, he was a scholar on the Bible, Shakespeare, and Greek mythology, and quoted from them frequently. He also liked sports; he was a champion tennis player and water skier, even after he suffered a heart attack. All these traits were really appreciated by those who were trained by Dr. Harrison as well as those who knew him. I am sure I can speak for all of us: that we see him as truly a great man, a physician, educator, and friend. He is missed by all of us, for such a great man rarely comes along in a lifetime.

References

1. Harrison TR: *Failure of the Circulation*, 1st ed. The Williams and Wilkins Company, Baltimore (1935)
2. Calhoun JA, Harrison TR: Studies on congestive heart failure: IX The effect of digitalis on potassium content of the cardiac muscle of the dog. *J Clin Invest* 10, 1 (1931)
3. Harrison TR (Ed.): *Principles of Internal Medicine*. 1st ed. Mc-Graw-Hill, New York (1958)

Robert Ritchie Linton

THOMAS F. DODSON, M.D.

Section of Vascular Surgery, The Emory Clinic, Atlanta, Georgia, USA

The year 1900 was not only the first year of a new century, but it was also a time of significant achievements: the publication of Conrad's Lord Jim, the birth of Thomas Wolfe and the death of Oscar Wilde, the opening of the opera "Tosca" by Puccini in Rome, the transmission of human speech by radio waves, and Planck's formulation of "quantum theory." William McKinley was reelected the 25th President of the United States, World War I waited in the wings, and vascular surgery's infancy was signaled that year by the attempt of Matas at Tulane to treat an abdominal aortic aneurysm by the introduction of wire and electrical current into the aneurysm. Into this changing world Robert Ritchie Linton was born on May 20, 1900, in Grangemouth, Scotland. His father was a physician, and after being injured in the Boer war, he took Robert and his brother, James, to the Puget Sound area of Washington State for a fresh start in life.[1]

Robert went to college at the University of Washington and graduated summa cum laude in 1921. He was an ambitious student, and he chose Harvard for medical school. Again showing his strong native intelligence, he was elected to Alpha Omega Alpha while at Harvard. In 1925, he was selected for an internship in medicine at Johns Hopkins Hospital, and a year later he went to Boston for a surgical residency at Massachusetts General Hospital. Vascular surgery was not much further along, but three years earlier, in 1923, Matas had carried out the first successful complete ligation of the aorta.[2]

In 1928 Robert Linton was listed as one of six surgical house officers at Massachusetts General Hospital, and the Vascular Clinic was first organized as a surgical group in the hospital.[3] Two years later, in 1930, Dr. Edward Churchill was named Johns Homans Professor of Surgery at Harvard Medical School. One of his young faculty members, Bob Linton, began to take an interest in the new work being performed in vascular surgery, and he began to work in the animal laboratory in this and other fields. At about the same time, John Homans' *Textbook of Surgery*, published in 1932 and covering the entire field of surgery in over 1000 pages, had only 25 pages devoted to the "blood vessels."[4]

It is interesting and ironic that, in a *New England Journal of Medicine* clinicopathologic conference in 1945, Bob Linton was presented with the case of "a seventy-five-year-old business executive (who) was brought to the hospital after he had collapsed in the street." The patient was noted to have a "slight tenderness" in the right lower quadrant and an "easily felt pulsation" in the left abdomen. The patient died suddenly the next day, and Linton was able to make the correct diagnosis of a ruptured abdominal aortic aneurysm as the cause of the man's death.[5]

World War II provided a fertile though tragic ground for improvements in vascular surgery, but DeBakey and Simeone noted in a subsequent article in 1946 that of 2,471 acute arterial injuries during the war, there were only forty cases of repair with vein grafts and an amputation rate of approximately sixty percent.[6] That same year, a group of prominent surgeons met at the Fairmont Hotel in San Francisco to discuss the formation of a new society of physicians interested in vascular surgery. One year later, on June 8, 1947, at the Dennis Hotel in Atlantic City, New Jersey, the first meeting of The Society for Vascular Surgery was held. Bob Linton joined Arthur Allen and Robert Gross of Boston, Alfred Blalock of Baltimore, Michael DeBakey and Rudolph Matas of New Orleans, and twenty-five other individuals as the charter members of this society. He was on the Program Committee and gave one of the nine papers at the meeting on "Post-thrombophlebitic states of the lower extremity. Treatment by superficial femoral vein interruption and ligation and stripping of long and short saphenous veins."[7]

Three years later, in 1949, Kunlin from France revolutionized this emerging field with the publication of his paper on the utilization of a "greffe veineuse," a segment of saphenous vein to bridge the obstructed artery in a patient with severe peripheral vascular disease.[8] In the years that followed, other small series of cases began to appear, and in 1962, Bob Linton and Clem Darling were able to report seventy-six consecutive saphenous vein bypass grafts.[9] Coming out of slow-to-change and conservative Boston, this paper was an early indication of the acceptability of this new technique.

Linton was also interested in portal hypertension, and he made one of the early contributions to the literature on the selection of patients for portacaval shunts.[10] At the sixth annual meeting of the Society for Vascular Surgery, which he had helped to found, he presented his data on the emergency treatment of massive bleeding from esophageal varices by a transthoracic approach to the esophagus. In that paper he also described a balloon with only an intragastric component which he had utilized to stop bleeding in this series of patients. That device later became known as the "Linton balloon." In his report of eleven patients operated upon over the

Fig. 1   Robert Ritchie Linton (1900–1979).

previous two years, Linton had only one immediate postoperative death, a mortality consistent with his insistence on perfection and his unwillingness to accept anything less.[11] As Bob Linton was often heard to say at meetings and conferences, there was only one way to do things, "the right way."

With his technical capabilities and his enormous energies came increasing responsibilities in surgical organizations: He became president of the Society for Vascular Surgery in 1955 and of the Boston Surgical Society in 1960. Ed Churchill retired in 1962 as Chief of Surgery at Massachusetts General Hospital, and he was succeeded by Paul Russell for six years and then, in 1969, W. Gerald Austen became the new chief of the department. With Linton, Darling, and Abbott in the vascular division, this was one area about which Austen did not have to worry.

Four years later, in 1973, the career of Robert Ritchie Linton knew both triumph and tragedy. In that year he helped found the New England Society for Vascular Surgery, and he published his monumental work, *Atlas of Vascular Surgery*, which, with 220 plates, was the distillate and culmination of his life's work in the field.[12] Tragedy struck in September of that year when Bob and Emma Linton were in a terrible car accident on the way home from their cottage in Maine. They

were both transferred to Massachusetts General Hospital and, for a time, were side by side in the intensive care unit. They both recovered, but Bob Linton was by now frail and infirm. He would come to the operating room to help an associate or advise a friend, but the man who would work "until it was right" was not able to meet his own standards. The Lintons celebrated their fiftieth wedding anniversary in 1978, and with health gradually fading, Bob Linton quietly passed away on July 21, 1979. He had seen vascular surgery in its infancy and, like a proud parent, he could admire its growth and development over three quarters of a century.

When I recently asked Jerry Austen about Bob Linton, he wrote that, "He was an absolutely outstanding technical surgeon with fine judgment. I was always impressed with his dogged pursuit of a perfect result." In 1975, as the vascular senior resident on the vascular service at Massachusetts General Hospital, I asked Dr. Linton to sign my copy of his atlas. He wrote that he was sure I would find the field of vascular surgery "interesting, challenging and rewarding." With quiet understatement, he would probably have said the same thing about his own life.

Acknowledgment

The author acknowledges with appreciation the advice and comments of W. Gerald Austen and R. Clement Darling in the preparation of this manuscript.

References

1. Darling RC: Robert Ritchie Linton In: *The Massachusetts General Hospital, 1955-1981*, p. 217. Boston: Little, Brown and Company, 1983
2. Friedman SG: Rudolph Matas. In: *A History of Vascular Surgery*, p. 63. New York: Futura Publishing, Inc., 1989
3. Washburn FA: *The Massachusetts General Hospital, 1900-1935*, p. 624. Boston: Houghton Mifflin Company, 1939
4. Homans J: The Blood Vessels. In: *A Textbook of Surgery*, 2nd Ed, p. 221. Springfield, Illinois: Charles C Thomas, Springfield, Illinois, 1932
5. Linton RR: Case Presentation 31172. *N Engl J Med* 1945;232:484
6. DeBakey ME, Simeone FA: Battle injuries of the arteries in WWII: An analysis of 2471 cases. *Ann Surg* 1946;123:534
7. Thompson JE: The founding fathers. S*urgery* 1977;82:801
8. Kunlin J: Le traitement de l'arterite obliterante par la greffe veineuse. *Arch Mal Coeur* 1949;42:371
9. Linton RR, Darling RC: Autogenous saphenous vein bypass grafts in femoropopliteal obliterative arterial disease. *Surgery* 1962;51:62
10. Linton RR: The selection of patients for portacaval shunts with a summary of the results in 61 cases. *Ann Surg* 1951;134:433
11. Linton RR, Warren R: The emergency treatment of massive bleeding from esophageal varices by transesophageal suture of these vessels at the time of acute hemorrhage. *Surgery* 1953;3:243
12. Linton RR: *Atlas of Vascular Surgery*. W.B. Saunders Co., 1973

Irvine H. Page

R. GIFFORD, M.D.

Department of Hypertension and Nephrology, Cleveland Clinic Foundation, Cleveland, Ohio, USA

By any criteria, Irvine H. Page is one of the most respected physicians of the 20th century—a legend in his own time. He is not only a world-renowned physician and scientist, he is also a philosopher, editor, critic, author, and humanitarian.

Born in Indianapolis 85 years ago, his illustrious career spanned most of this century. He became a physician almost by accident. His desire was to become a chemist—a biochemist which was almost unheard of when Irv started his studies at Cornell. In fact, while taking a biochemistry course in the medical school, he was persuaded by the Dean of Medicine to enroll in Medical School. He never regretted that decision.

But his interest in chemistry remained, and after his internship at Presbyterian and Bellevue Hospitals in New York he became involved in research in physical chemistry at Woods Hole and then New York. In 1928 he was invited to join the Kaiser Wilhelm Institute in Munich to start a new department of brain chemistry. No similar department existed anywhere in the world. While in Munich he met and married Beatrice ("Bea") Allen, a professional dancer.

The Pages were happy in Munich and might have been there yet if not for the ominous threat of Hitler's rise to power. Irv's secret desire was to work with Donald Van Slyke, Ph.D. at The Rockefeller Institute in New York City, and by a quirk of fate his wish was granted when Dr. Van Slyke, visiting Germany with his family, called Dr. Page in the middle of the night to treat his daughter's infected finger.

He worked with Dr. Van Slyke at The Rockefeller Institute from 1931 to 1937. It was there that he first became interested in hypertension, at a time when no one else was. Using Van Slyke's recently developed clearance method for measuring renal function, he showed that blood pressure could be reduced without reducing renal blood flow—a revolutionary concept which was largely ignored at the time.

In 1937 Dr. Page moved back to Indianapolis to take up a post as Director of the Laboratory for Clinical Research at Eli Lilly Company's research unit at City Hospital. It was there, working with Drs. Ken Kohlstaedt and Oscar Helmer, that he discovered angiotensin. It was also there that the Pages' two sons, Nick and Chris, were born.

In 1945, Dr. Page was invited to organize a new research division at the Cleveland Clinic. Within a few years he had recruited a now famous group of colleagues whose contributions to research in hypertension and later atherosclerosis are legendary. The cast included Taylor and Corcoran who came from Indianapolis with him, McCubbin, Bumpus, Masson, Dustan, Lewis, Brown, and more recently Tarazi and Ferrario. Serotonin was discovered, angiotensin and angiotensin inhibitors were synthesized, nitroprusside was first used in humans, the interaction of the sympathetic nervous system and angiotensin was described, and the diagnosis and treatment of renovascular hypertension were developed, to mention a few of the contributions which this talented group made under Dr. Page's leadership. Early in this period Dr. Page first described the now famous "mosiac theory" of hypertension.

The Research Division at the Cleveland Clinic now has 60 staff members and, in addition to the Cardiovascular Department, there are also departments of Artificial Organs, Biostatistics and Epidemiology, Molecular and Cellular Biology, and Musculoskeletal Research.

Dr. Page was not satisfied to stay in the laboratory—he wanted to apply the fruits of his research to the patient. He made rounds regularly in the clinical research unit of the Cleveland Clinic Hospital. He was the first to deplore and to debunk the widely held concept that atherosclerosis was the inevitable result of aging and that hypertension was necessary to perfuse vital organs supplied by atherosclerotic arteries. He headed up the diet-heart study of the NHLBI which demonstrated that it was possible to reduce serum cholesterol on a mass scale by an achievable diet. He was one of the first to advocate preventive measures to control atherosclerosis, and he addressed this subject repeatedly in his popular, pithy, poignant, and sometimes prickly editorials in *Modern Medicine*. He was an exercise enthusiast and became famous for the admonition to "get off your fatty acids."

Irvine Page was also an organizer. Shortly after he moved to Cleveland in 1945 he organized the American Foundation for High Blood Pressure which included not only researchers in hypertension throughout the country but also executives and industrialists whom Dr. Page charmed like a pied piper. This later became the Council of High Blood Pressure Research of the American Heart Association. Every fall for the last 38 years, the leaders in hypertension research from all over the world meet in Cleveland for two days to present papers in what is recognized as the most elite scientific meeting on hypertension in the world.

After he had his myocardial infarction in 1967, Dr. Page organized the Coronary Club, Inc., a nonprofit organization to

FIG. 1   Dr. Irvine Page (1901–1991).

provide camaraderie and to encourage not only victims of coronary disease but also their families and friends who would like to follow Dr. Page's advice on "moderation in everything." This is now a nationwide organization with 21 chapters in 10 states and headquarters in Cleveland.

He was also a prime mover and founding member of the Institute of Medicine which had its origin at the Cleveland Clinic Foundation.

Dr. Page has authored 13 books, the first in 1937 and the most recent *Mechanisms of Hypertension* in 1985. He has lost track of how many scientific publications he has had, but it is safe to say that he holds the all-time record.

His genius and foresight have been recognized by his peers. He has been awarded 10 honorary degrees. He has been president of the American Heart Association, the American Society for Clinical Pharmacology and Therapeutics, and the Society for Experimental Biology and Medicine. He has received the Gold Heart Award and the Distinguished Achievement Award of the American Heart Association, the Distinguished Service Award and the Sheen Award of the AMA and is an Honorary Fellow and former Trustee of the American College of Cardiology. He received the Lasker Award in 1958 and the Stouffer Prize in 1970.

Although he relinquished the chairmanship of the Division of Research in 1966, Irv continued to serve as Senior Consultant and Emeritus Consultant to the Division of Research at the Cleveland Clinic until 1978 when he and Bea moved to Hyannis Port. Notice that I didn't say "retired." He is now Director Emeritus of the Division of Research and is still revered and respected by his colleagues at the Cleveland Clinic, both within and without the Research Division, who each spring honor him with the Page Lecture and a dinner. Such distinguished physicians as Julius Comroe, Jacques Genest, Ed Haber, James Wyngaarden, Norman Shumway, and Eugene Braunwald have been lecturers at these events. When the search was going on for a new director, Dr. Page's opinion was sought and he made trips to Cleveland to confer with the Board and the Search Committee. He still appears at national meetings including the fall meeting of the Council for High Blood Pressure Research, which he founded.

Just last week the phone rang: "Giff," said the crisp voice sounding just like it did 25 years ago, "I just heard that Otis Bowen is going to be named secretary of HHS. Now about that new society———." No, Irv Page is not retired. He never will be. The word is not in his vocabulary.

Edward F. Bland

A. L. FRIEDLICH, M.D.

Harvard Medical School, Massachusetts General Hospital, Boston, Massachusetts, USA

Edward F. Bland was born in 1901 at West Point in Tidewater, Virginia. His family had lived there since 1640, well before the founding of Williamsburg. His forebear Richard Bland published a pamphlet entitled *An Inquiry into the Rights of British Colonies*, which influenced Thomas Jefferson's thinking about the need for a Bill of Rights in our Constitution. Dr. Bland attended the University of Virginia as an undergraduate and also received his M.D. there as did his grandfather before him. One of his medical school professors was Edwin Wood, Jr., who had trained in medicine and cardiology at the Massachusetts General Hospital. With his encouragement, Dr. Bland also interned at the MGH.

There he describes himself as "hooked" by the skill and the thoughtfulness of Dr. Paul D. White. He became Cardiac Resident (1929–1930) and Dalton Fellow which enabled him to study in England. Even in those years he published clinical articles. These included a review of progress in the study of cardiovascular disease,[1] the use of Southey tubes for the relief of obstinate edema,[2] and the prognosis of angina pectoris and coronary thrombosis.[3] The next year he was a research fellow in the laboratory of Sir Thomas Lewis. He also worked with Dr. Ronald Grant at the University College Hospital, London. Sir George Pickering and Sir Horace Smirk were engaged in research in the same laboratory during this time.

In 1931 he returned to join the staff of the Massachusetts General Hospital. He maintained wide interests in cardiology. This included the first clinical description of the anomalous origin of the left coronary artery from the pulmonary artery, which he reported with Doctors Paul White and Joseph Garland.[4] He also served as Secretary of the New England Heart Association for twenty years "because nobody else would do it." But he became particularly involved in the problems of rheumatic fever. In this pursuit, he worked with Dr. T. Duckett Jones at the House of the Good Samaritan, a rheumatic fever hospital in Boston. There he made important contributions in describing the significance of chorea,[5] early clues to events preceding rheumatic fever,[6] and both the subsidence of valve disease,[7] and its delayed appearance.[8] His studies of the natural history of 1,000 patients with rheumatic fever followed for 10[9] and for 20 years[10] are classics of the cardiac literature.

During World War II, Dr. Bland served as Lieutenant Colonel in the Army of the United States becoming Chief of Medicine of the MGH Unit, the Sixth General Hospital, in North Africa and Italy. During those years he published studies of the cardiac effects of typhus,[11] foreign bodies in and about the heart,[12] later with a 20-year follow-up,[13] and studies of rheumatic fever and heart disease[14] in the theater of operation in which he served for nearly three years. For these and other services he was awarded the Bronze Star Medal. Later, at the request of the Surgeon General of the Army, he prepared the section on heart disease for the official *History of Medicine in World War II*.[15]

On his return to the Massachusetts General Hospital, in addition to heavy teaching and practice responsibilities, he investigated multiple emboli as a cause of pulmonary hypertension[16] and early experiences with the penicillin treatment of bacterial endocarditis.[17] With Dr. Richard Sweet, he developed an ingenious pulmonary venous to azygos vein shunt (the Bland-Sweet operation)[18] for the relief of recurrent pulmonary edema in severe mitral stenosis. This was superseded by the development of mitral valvotomy. Doctors Gordon Scannell, William Brewster, and he described the first successful removal in this country of a left atrial myxoma[19] utilizing hypothermia and cardiac inflow occlusion. Important 25-year follow-up studies involved 200 patients with myocardial infarction[20] and 456 patients with angina pectoris.[21] These early studies of the natural history of coronary disease are well worth rereading. With Dr. Edwin Wheeler he described the prognosis and place of the Hufnagel ball valve prosthesis[22] inserted in the descending aorta of young people with severe aortic regurgitation. This was before cardiopulmonary bypass made intracardiac valve replacement possible.

In 1949, when Dr. Paul D. White moved to direct the beginnings of the National Heart Institute of the National Institutes of Health, Dr. Bland became Chief of Cardiology at the Massachusetts General Hospital. He accepted this post reluctantly, but having done so was highly effective. His first action was to insist that good patient care required that an electrocardiogram with a typed report be in a patient's record the day the tracing was taken. And he made it stick! Under his leadership, the clinical training program for cardiac fellows included six months at the House of the Good Samaritan followed by 12 months of training and clinical experience at the Massachusetts General Hospital. Following World War II he organized the annual 9-month Cardiac Postgraduate Course which helped train a remarkable international group of physicians. Later he appointed Dr. Charles Sanders the first full-

FIG. 1 Edward F. Bland, M.D.

time head of the Cardiac Catheter Laboratory. Subsequently, he was instrumental in his becoming General Director of the Hospital.

Dr. Bland was a superb chief, a quiet gentleman, not given to overstatement, intensely loyal to his patients, his colleagues, and the MGH. The hospitality of his home, where we came to know his family and his nonmedical friends, meant more than he can know to his fellows and his staff. Dr. Bland was first and foremost a master clinician. His notes are concise marvels of clear thinking and expression. Yet despite their brevity, all the important facts are included. He encouraged similar traits in his trainees. If a fellow presented a complex clinical problem, his focus was apt to be sharpened by Ed Bland's gentle unnerving question, "What's the problem?".

Ernest Hemingway defined guts as "grace under pressure." We saw and admired that characteristic in Dr. Bland. But he was also a warm person. No one can really know Ed Bland who has not seen the affection and tenderness so apparent as he examines a child with rheumatic fever. His lectures were beautifully organized and illustrated, as were his publications. But his special contribution was by personal example. He taught the niceties of history taking and physical examination. His clinical wisdom and ethical standards guided the development of generations of physicians.

Following his retirement as Chief of Cardiology in 1961 he was promoted to Clinical Professor of Medicine at the Harvard Medical School. He remained a strong and respected influence in the Hospital and in active clinical practice another

25 years. In this role he continued to demonstrate the firm commitment to excellence which characterized his career. In 1987, as if to mock any hint of age, he left us another gem of cardiac literature entitled "Rheumatic Fever: The Way It Was."[23] Don't miss it.

References

1. Bland EF, Sprague HB: Progress in the study of cardiovascular disease in 1929. *N Engl J Med* 203, 574 (1930)
2. Bland EF, White PD: The use of mechanical measures in the treatment of obstinate edema. *J Am Med Assoc* 95, 1489 (1930)
3. White PD, Bland EF: A further report on the prognosis of angina pectoris and of coronary thrombosis. *Am Heart J* 7, 3 (1931)
4. Bland EF, White PD, Garland J: Congenital anomalies of the coronary arteries: Report of an unusual case associated with cardiac hypertrophy. *Am Heart J* 8. 787 (1933)
5. Jones TD, Bland EF: Clinical significance of chorea as a manifestation rheumatic fever. *J Am Med Assoc* 105, 571 (1935)
6. Bland EF, Jones TD: Clinical observations on the events preceding the appearance of rheumatic fever. *J Clin Invest* 14, 633 (1935)
7. Bland EF, Jones TD, White PD: Disappearance of the physical signs of rheumatic heart disease. *J Am Med Assoc* 107, 569 (1936)
8. Bland EF, Jones TD: The delayed appearance of heart disease after rheumatic fever. *J Am Med Assoc* 113, 1380 (1939)
9. Jones TD, Bland EF: Rheumatic fever and heart disease: Completed 10 year observations on 1000 patients. *Tr Assoc Am Phys* 57, 267 (1942)
10. Bland EF, Jones TD: Rheumatic fever and rheumatic heart disease: A twenty-year report on 1000 patients followed since childhood. *Circulation* 4, 836 (1951)
11. Woodward TE, Bland EF: Clinical observations in typhus fever. With special reference to the cardiovascular system. *J Am Med Assoc* 126, 287 (1944)
12. Bland EF: Foreign bodies in and about the heart. *Am Heart J* 27, 588 (1944)
13. Bland EF, Beebe GW: Missiles in the heart. A twenty-year follow-up report of World War II cases. *N Engl J Med* 274, 1039 (1966)
14. Bland EF: Rheumatic fever and rheumatic heart disease in the North African and Mediterranean Theater of operations, United States Army. *Am Heart J* 32, 545 (1946)
15. Bland EF: *Internal Medicine in World War II*, Vol. 3. Office of the Surgeon General of the Army, Washington DC (1968) 419
16. Castleman B, Bland EF: Organized emboli of the tertiary pulmonary arteries. An unusual cause of cor pulmonale. *Arch Pathol* 42, 531 (1946)
17. Paul O, Bland EF, White PD: Bacterial endocarditis. Experiences with penicillin therapy at the Massachusetts General Hospital, 1944-1946. *N Engl J Med* 237, 349 (1947)
18. Bland EF, Sweet RH: A venous shunt for advanced mitral stenosis. *J Am Med Assoc* 140, 1259 (1948)
19. Scannell JG, Brewster WR Jr, Bland EF: Successful removal of a myxoma from the left atrium. *N Engl J Med* 254, 601 (1956)
20. Richards DW, Bland EF, White PD: A completed twenty-five year follow-up study of 200 patients with myocardial infarction. *J Chron Dis* 4, 415 (1956)
21. Richards DW, Bland EF, White PD: A completed twenty-five year follow-up study of 456 patients with angina pectoris. *J Chron Dis* 4, 423 (1956)
22. Bland EF, Wheeler EO: Severe aortic regurgitation in young people. A long-term perspective with reference to prognosis and prosthesis. *N Engl J Med* 256, 667 (1957)
23. Bland EF: Rheumatic fever: The way it was. *Circulation* 76, 1190 (1987)

Irving S. Wright—Innovator in Cardiovascular Medicine

RICHARD L. MUELLER, M.D.

Division of Cardiology, The New York Hospital-Cornell Medical Center, New York, New York, USA

Irving Sherwood Wright personifies the adage "living legend." At age 92, he is a treasured emeritus scholar at Cornell University Medical College and its sister institution, The New York Hospital; he has served the Cornell medical community during eight remarkable decades in the evolution of cardiovascular medicine. Indeed, one of Dr. Wright's most important legacies remains his role, along with others, in wedding vascular medicine and circulatory physiology to classical, heart-centered cardiology. The integrated product, cardiovascular medicine, emphasizes the critical interdependence of the heart and vascular tree central to modern concepts in today's cardiology. Before the efforts of Dr. Wright and colleagues to view the heart in the context of an integrated circulatory system, cardiologists were concerned exclusively with the heart; many fundamental advances in cardiology occurred only after this subtle, yet profound change in viewing the heart was ushered in by visionaries such as Irving Wright.

Excelling in each of Osler's triad of patient care, research, and teaching, Wright has made indelible marks in this century as a caring clinician; as an innovative investigator in fields as diverse as thrombosis, vascular biology, ischemic heart disease, stroke, and the cellular bases of aging; as a beloved mentor to physicians and researchers the world over; and as a leader in organized medicine. In the current era of subspecialization, Dr. Wright examplifies the versatile physician distinguished in all aspects of his field, who set lofty standards in the process.

Irving Wright was born in New York City on October 27, 1901, to parents with deep American roots. His Dutch maternal ancestors settled in New Amsterdam (later to be New York) around 1630, while his English paternal ancestors settled in Massachusetts in 1749. Several ancestors fought the British in the Revolutionary War, and a paternal ancestor, Silas Wright, was a governor of New York State. His father was an inventor who instilled a deep sense of curiosity and interest in books and history in young Wright. Moving to Bloomfield, New Jersey, at age eight, Wright attended high school there before embarking on a lifelong association with Cornell University by starting a 7-year medical program in 1919.

After spending three undergraduate years in Ithaca, Wright returned for good in 1922 to Manhattan, home of Cornell's Medical College, and received his M.D. degree there in 1926. He worked summers as a kind of caretaker-companion for patients of a psychiatry professor, capping this off with a four-month auto tour with one of the patients throughout much of Europe.

He briefly left the Cornell fold by moving a few blocks to the Post Graduate Medical School of Columbia University's College of Physicians and Surgeons for a residency in internal medicine. Upon completion in 1929, Wright joined Dr. Arthur Chase, the chairman of the medical board of Post Graduate Hospital, in private practice for several years before starting his own practice. He also began decades of clinical research and teaching at that time, splitting his days between his laboratory in the hospital and his private practice office. He undertook research on the vascular system, and in his practice endeavored to integrate vascular medicine with classical cardiology, as did colleagues such as Lewis Conner, a medical school professor and the first president of the American Heart Association. At the time, it was the norm for all researchers to support themselves with private practices, and Wright split his time between academic laboratory and private office for nearly 40 years.

In 1931, he returned to Cornell via his clinical activities at the Cornell division of Bellevue Hospital through 1937. He chaired the Department of Medicine of the Cornell division of the Welfare Hospital for Chronic Disease (now Goldwater Hospital on Roosevelt Island, New York City) from 1937 to 1942. He also joined the voluntary staff of Doctor's Hospital in 1934, from which he retired at the age of 75 years. By 1938, he became the Chairman of the Department of Medicine and Professor of Clinical Medicine at the Post Graduate Medical School and Hospital. In addition to ongoing research, he ran a busy practice in cardiovascular medicine, taking in a series of young associates. In the milieu of this busy schedule, serendipity and Wright's clinical acumen intervened that same year to change his career and American medicine forever.

Wright underwent an appendectomy that year and developed postoperative thrombophlebitis. He was gravely ill for months due to the lack of effective treatment at the time. The experience was unforgettable and unexpectedly led to historic innovation. Shortly after recovering, Wright was referred a 30-year-old patient, Arthur Schulte, who was dying of migratory thrombophlebitis. Recalling an acquaintance from a series of Josiah Macy conferences in New York, Wright contacted Charles Best of the University of Toronto (Fig. 1). Better known for his work with Banting on purifying insulin, Best and a group in Stockholm had recently been the first to purify heparin and administer it to humans. Wright convinced Best to bring the novel agent personally to New York in a desperate attempt to help Schulte. The rest is history, best summarized by Wright himself:

Fig. 1   Pioneers of anticoagulant therapy in 1958: (left to right) Charles Best, Irving Wright, Armand Quick, and Karl Paul Link. Reproduced with permission of Irving Wright, M.D.

Dr. Best came down from Toronto with a vial containing much of the world's supply of heparin, and in 15 or 16 days the phlebitis subsided. It was the first success of anticoagulant therapy in this country, and today, 56 years later, the patient is still going strong, and is still on anticoagulant therapy since thromboembolism ensues whenever anticoagulants have been discontinued. He has been on anticoagulant therapy longer than any person in the world, and he was presented at grand rounds in 1991.

With this dramatic effort, Wright went on to pioneer anticoagulant therapy in the U.S. He was chairman of the American Medical Association's section on experimental medications and therapeutics and of the American Heart Association's section on peripheral circulation from 1939 to 1940. From 1940 to 1949 he was a member of the advisory board of the American Board of Internal Medicine. By 1940, he had obtained the new oral anticoagulant dicoumarol from Karl Paul Link (Fig. 1), who had isolated it from spoiled sweet clover hay. Dicoumarol was first used in human volunteers by Meyer at the University of Wisconsin and by Allen at the Mayo Clinic. Beginning in 1940, Wright was among the first to administer it to volunteers on the East Coast (first at Welfare Hospital) and was likely the first to use it therapeutically, again in Arthur Schulte.[1]

The second world war supervened and Wright was commissioned as a colonel in the Army. He served as Chief of the Medical Service at the Army and Navy General Hospital in Hot Springs, Arkansas, from 1942 to 1943, and as a consultant in medicine for the Army's 6th Service Command from 1944 to 1945, and for the 9th Service Command from 1945 to 1946. Through the latter, he was the Coordinator of the health survey of U.S. prisoners of war from the Far East in 1945. In 1946 and 1947, Secretary of Defense Forrestal appointed Wright co-chairman of a special commission to help rehabilitate German and Austrian medical schools devastated by bombings and the deaths of Jewish and German staff. His service to the nation began before the war as a lieutenant commander in the Navy Reserve, and continued after the war on a civilian advisory committee to the Secretary of the Navy from 1946 to 1947 and as a civilian consultant in medicine to the Surgeon General of the Army.

At several military hospitals during the war, Wright treated a number of patients with acute myocardial infarction and rheumatic heart disease with dicoumarol, with great clinical yet anecdotal success.[2] This represented the first use of anticoagulants for myocardial infarction and led to the American Heart Association's appointment of Wright in 1946 as chairman of a landmark multicenter, randomized, prospective trial of dicoumarol for myocardial infarction. By then he had returned to Post Graduate Hospital after the war, but moved uptown in 1946 to Cornell and The New York Hospital as Associate Professor of Medicine and head of a new division of vascular medicine. With over 1,000 patients, the trial was the largest clinical trial of any kind to date; reports in 1948[3] and 1954[4] found a highly significant mortality advantage with dicoumarol therapy.

In 1948, Wright became Professor of Clinical Medicine at Cornell. His work on the clinical use of anticoagulants, thrombosis, and vascular biology continued, as did his mentorship of research fellows from around the globe, many now renowned researchers in vascular biology and thrombosis. Of note, he took no salary upon joining the faculty at The New York Hospital in 1946 in exchange for the freedom to pursue private practice; by his choice, he was never paid for his research and teaching work in his 22 years there. From 1947 to 1952, Wright chaired the Josiah Macy, Jr., Foundation's Conferences on Blood Clotting, where he had met Best in the 1930s. Over a number of years, he has also served as a consulting physician to four suburban hospitals in the area. Wright lectured tirelessly around the globe for decades as interest in his work expanded. He and his wife Lois visited 71 countries, where they also indulged their passion for history, archaeology, and ancient civilizations.

In 1952, Wright was elected president of the American Heart Association—it's first "non-classical" cardiologist reflecting acceptance of the concept of cardiovascular medicine. He served on that group's executive committee and board of directors from 1935 to 1957. He was one of Lewis Conner's associate editors of the *American Heart Journal* in the 1930s when it was the organization's official journal. When the Association decided to publish a new official journal of its own in 1950, it was Wright who convinced the editors to name it *Circulation*. From 1954 to 1963, he chaired the International Committee on Blood Clotting Factors and, during its 1960 conference in Rome, convinced all workers in the field to "do in Rome as the Romans do" by adopting the Roman numeral system of clotting factor nomenclature. From these early conferences grew the International Society on Thrombosis and Hemostasis. Wright organized the first American Heart Association conference on cerebrovascular disease. That organization honored him with its Gold Heart Award in 1958.

Perhaps the most prestigious honor came in 1960, when Wright and fellow dicoumarol pioneers K.P. Link and Edgar Allen were awarded the Albert and Mary Lasker Award for Clinical Medical Research. Again Wright was recognized for his anticoagulant work as well as his efforts to view the heart in the context of the entire circulation. From 1961 to 1965, Wright chaired the National Institutes of Health's committee on cerebrovascular diseases. In 1965, he was elected president of the American College of Physicians, and from 1966 to 1968 he served on the President's Committee on Heart Disease, Cancer, and Stroke.

In 1968, Wright retired from his laboratory work at The New York Hospital and became Emeritus Professor of Clinical Medicine at Cornell. However, he continued his busy private practice until the age of 78, in 1979. Despite advancing years, Wright was by no means finished with his life's work. Beginning to turn his attention to the study of aging, Wright was distressed at the relative lack of basic science research in the fundamental mechanisms of aging. He became a vigorous advocate for geriatrics research, becoming the president of the American Geriatrics Society from 1971 to 1972 and receiving its Henderson Award in 1970 and its Thewlis Award in 1974. In 1976, he was again honored by the American Heart Association with its Distinguished Service Award. The same year, Cornell University Medical College established the Irving Sherwood Wright Professorship in Geriatrics. Undaunted by his own age, Wright went on to found the American Federation for Aging Research (best known as AFAR) in 1980 and served as its president through 1986; AFAR has provided funding for over 500 young investigators beginning research careers in geriatrics.

Wright has authored hundreds of scientific papers, but emphasizes that most of his work has involved collaboration with many co-workers and junior investigators who, as a matter of principle, have always been acknowledged fully in these papers. A modest man, Wright is ever vigilant in his desire to credit all those who came before him or worked with him at any level. He was editor-in-chief of *Modern Medical Monographs* and is a Fellow of the Royal College of Physicians (London). He is also a member of the Association of American Physicians, the New York Academy of Medicine, the American Society for Clinical Investigation, the Society for Experimental Biology and Medicine, the New York Academy of Sciences, the Harvey Society, Sigma Xi, Alpha Omega Alpha, and an honorary member of several foreign medical societies, including the Royal Society of Medicine of London.

Wright's diverse interests, not only within medicine but in life in general, are exemplified by his extensive travels, his position as physician for New York's Metropolitan Opera from 1935 to 1962, and his ongoing rigorous tape reading schedule (undeterred by his near blindness from macular degeneration, Wright listens to books dictated onto audiotapes).

Father of two daughters and now a widower, Wright lives in Manhattan. He reads via tapes for the blind, attends Medical Grand Rounds at The New York Hospital, and continues a correspondence with friends and colleagues. He continues to advocate the integration of the study of the heart within the context of a dynamic vascular system, the pursuit of basic research in aging mechanisms, and the primacy of the physician–patient interaction over high technology. Wright himself writes:

> My aim in life has been to improve the quality of medical care in the fields of internal medicine, geriatric cardiovascular diseases by research, teaching at undergraduate, graduate, and international levels, the development of standards and guidelines, and the application of the best of modern knowledge to the care of patients. In light of the technology of recent years, I have placed particular emphasis on the role of a primary physician for the patient, who will apply his scientific knowledge with compassion and an understanding of the total illness— including the social and emotional aspects of the patient's problems rather than his disease alone. This, as I see it, is the challenge of the modern physician. [5]

It is a challenge he has mastered for eight decades by excelling as a scientist, teacher, clinician, and leader in medicine.[*]

References

1. Mueller RL, Scheidt S: History of drugs for thrombotic disease. Discovery, development, and directions for the future. *Circulation* 89, 432–449 (1994)

2. Wright IS: Experience with dicoumarol (3,3'-methylene-bis-[4-hydroxycoumarin]) in the treatment of coronary thrombosis with myocardial infarction. *Am Heart J* 32, 20–31 (1946)

3. Wright IS, Marple CD, Beck DF: Report of the committee for the evaluation of anticoagulants in the treatment of coronary thrombosis with myocardial infarction. *Am Heart J* 36, 801–815 (1948)

4. *Myocardial Infarction—Report of the Committee on Anticoagulants of the American Heart Association* (Eds. Wright IS, Marple CM, Beck DF). Grune & Stratton, Inc., New York (1954)

5. *Who's Who in America* (48th ed.). Reed Reference Publishing Co., New Providence, N.J. (1994), vol. 2, 3737

_____

[*]Irving Wright died in 1997.

The "Lone Eagle's" Contribution to Cardiology

Richard J. Bing, M.D.

Experimental Cardiology, Huntington Medical Research Institutes, Pasadena, California, USA

Practically everyone knows that Charles Lindbergh (Fig. 1) made the famous solo flight to Paris in 1929; he was born in Detroit on February 4, 1902, spent some of his youth in Little Falls, Minnesota, and was involved in the unsuccessful campaign for U.S. Senate by his father. Many are also aware of his barnstorming days, his self-imposed exile, his controversial participation in political movements, and finally his interest in environmental causes.[1,2] Many also remember that he married Ann Morrow, the daughter of the American ambassador to Mexico and partner of J.P. Morgan. He died in Hawaii in 1974. For his aviation exploits, Charles Lindbergh was called the "Lone Eagle." His life, however, was not one of continuing triumphs. It was darkened by the horrible experience of the kidnapping and murder of his infant son.

These facts are known to the general public. Few people, however, know that Lindbergh was also involved in medical research. This is why I met him and worked with him at the Rockefeller Institute in New York in 1936. I was a young physician, 27 years old, working at Carlsberg Biological Institute in Copenhagen, Denmark, to learn cell culture methods. There, I met both Lindbergh and Alexis Carrel, the surgeon. Both attended an international meeting of biology to demonstrate their new perfusion system. In setting up this apparatus, they needed someone who spoke both Danish and English, and luckily I was assigned the job. Carrel and Lindbergh planned to establish their perfusion system in Denmark, and I was chosen to learn their method in New York and return to Copenhagen where the perfusion system was to be installed. After several attempts, Carrel was able to obtain a Rockefeller stipend for me, and after some painful interviews with the Rockefeller people in Paris (the personnel at the Paris Headquarters of the Foundation had no concept of the Nazi menace), I traveled to New York, stopping in England to visit the Lindberghs in Seven Oaks, Kent.

In America, working at the Rockefeller Institute (now Rockefeller University) in New York City, I had frequent contact with Charles Lindbergh. For him these frequent visits to Carrel's department at the Rockefeller Institute constituted an escape from the memory of the kidnapping and murder of his son.

What brought Charles Lindbergh into biological research? The motivation was personal. Lindbergh's sister-in-law had rheumatic fever as a child and developed mitral stenosis. It was a protracted illness accompanied by hemoptysis, pulmonary edema, shortness of breath, fatigue. Apparently she was a vibrant, vital person, enjoying life, and fighting the illness that finally killed her.[1–3] Few of us today realize the tremendous advances that medicine has made in the last 50 years. In the field of cardiology, cardiopulmonary bypass has made possible surgery on the open, virtually bloodless heart. But at the time of Lindbergh's sister-in-law's illness, only inadequate medical therapy was available. Lindbergh, who had an inquisitive mind, trying to apply mechanical solutions to technical problems, asked the question why surgery on the bloodless heart might not be possible. This idea was 20 years ahead of its time. He posed the question to his wife's anesthesiologist, who then directed him to Alexis Carrel, the Director of the Department of Experimental Surgery at the Rockefeller Institute in New York. Carrel was known for his surgical technique. He was a Nobel Prize winner for his work on transplantation of organs, made possible by his technique of blood vessel suture. At the same time, Carrel was a seasoned research worker, who was not apt to indulge in fly-by-night projects. When Lindbergh approached him with his idea of operating on the bloodless heart to rescue his sister-in-law from certain death, Carrel was not overly enthusiastic, knowing that these techniques were still in the future. Instead, he suggested that Lindbergh participate with him in a study that was more to Carrel's taste, the culture of whole organs, a system to maintain an organ outside the body by circulating nutrient fluid through its artery; this would enable Carrel and Lindbergh to study the interplay between the circulating fluid and the perfused organ, using the latter as an indicator. Lindbergh's perfusion system was, in principle, a sterile glass container consisting of three chambers: organ, equalization, and pressure chambers. A flask filled with mineral oil under pulsatile pressure acted like the piston of a pump. Lindbergh's contribution was a perfusion system, which combined sterility with perfusion of a small organ at variable systolic and diastolic pressures and heart rate (frequency). Sterility was of major importance, since both Carrel and Lindbergh wanted to perfuse organs for several weeks, making possible the study of different perfusion fluids on the organ. Lindbergh accomplished this by his system of floating valves, making the whole apparatus a closed system by sealing it appropriately with airplane glue. The disadvantage in this system was the disproportionate volume of the perfusion fluid to the weight of the organ, frequently the cat's thyroid gland, and the lack of

Fig. 1 Charles Lindbergh (1902–1974) at the age of 70. The
inscription reads as follows:

Dr. Richard J. Bing   Charles A. Lindbergh
Professor of Medicine
Huntington Memorial Hospital, Pasadena, California
(Photograph from the personal file of the author.)

respiratory pigment, which would have carried oxygen to the
perfused organ and made possible the use of larger organs. I
tried to accomplish these goals later when I worked in the
Department of Surgery at Columbia University, New York.
Since hemoglobin in these perfusion systems is rapidly oxidized to nonoxygen-carrying pigments, I tried the respiratory
pigment of the horseshoe crab, hemocyanin: when oxidized,
it is a beautiful marine blue, and when reduced a pale white.

If Carrel had followed Lindbergh's suggestion to develop
bypassing the heart during cardiac surgery, he could have
advanced the future of cardiac surgery by many years. More
than 20 years later, in 1954, thanks to the imagination and
tenacity of another surgeon, Charles Gibbon, open heart
surgery became a reality.[4]

Carrel's interest in the culture of whole organs was a natural extension of his work on cell cultures. The perfusion of
whole organs was in line with Carrel's conceptual research.
He saw it as a method of studying the interplay between the
internal environment (the perfusion fluid) and the single organ, using the latter as an indicator.

Because Carrel left the Institute soon afterward to begin
his ill-fated and ill-advised journey to France during the Nazi
occupation, neither he nor Lindbergh ever saw the fulfillment
of the potentials of this technique. The method may become
of considerable value in the study of the cultivation of viruses.

The last time I saw Lindbergh was when he visited me at
the Huntington Memorial Hospital and Huntington Medical
Research Institutes in Pasadena in 1970. He stayed at my
house in La Canada. I am reprinting a letter he wrote me in
1970 after this visit, that shows how nostalgic he was at the
memory of our joint stay at the Rockefeller Institute. It also
shows that his excursion into the field of biomedical (cardiac)
research was an experience he treasured all his life as a quiet
period in a turbulent and disturbing past.

This is his letter:

Switzerland
Dec. 12, 1970

Dear Richard:

I thoroughly enjoyed my visit with you at Pasadena—seeing your research projects, inspecting the
hospital, meeting your associates, the pleasant hour at
your home, etc. You were most considerate to drive me
back to the airport that night.

How time collapses under the circumstances of our
visit—the thirty years between Carrel's laboratory and
your own. There are moments when it seems to me that
the time-gap disappears, and that you, Carrel, and I are
still together—without the separation that we think so
obvious in death. Maybe if man had deeper awareness,
life and death would make less difference. I am inclined
to think so.

Again, thanks for your hospitality and friendship.
I hope your experimental projects meet with the utmost
success.

Best wishes to you always,
Charles A. Lindbergh

References

1. Ross WS: *The Last Hero: Charles A. Lindbergh*. New York: Harper
    & Row, 1968
2. Bing RJ: Recollections of an eyewitness. *Perspectives in Biology
    and Medicine* 1996;39(2):227–238
3. Berg AS: *Lindbergh*. New York: Penguin Putnam, Inc., 1998
4. Bing RJ: John H. Gibbon, Jr.: Cardiopulmonary bypass—triumph
    of perseverance and character. *Clin Cardiol* 1994;17:456–457

Agustin W. Castellanos

A. Castellanos, M.D., A. M. Castellanos, M.D.

Division of Cardiology, Department of Medicine, University of Miami School of Medicine, Miami, Florida; Department of Neuro-Oncology, M.D. Anderson Hospital and Tumor Institute, Houston, Texas, USA

Presumably the reasons which Dr. J. Willis Hurst had for inviting us to write this article are related to the conspicuous circumstances which, by an accident of birth, have placed us close to the source. It has been implied that the highest requisite which must be possessed by anyone writing about the life of another person, whatever his motives–whether to justify or to defend the individual, to hold up a certain ideal of conduct, to apply a new writing approach (as done here), or to simply present facts–is the equipment or knowledge which the writer himself brings to the task (Scammell, 1984). In addition, some sympathy must be shown toward the person. "To know the poet you must love him," wrote William Wordsworth and this holds true for teachers as well (Bond, 1968).

Also there must be sincerity which should be interpreted as being as objective as one can be. In our case complete objectivity is, of course, not possible. As in physics, where the very act of measuring influences the measurement, in biography the writer himself influences history. This influence is usually greater in an autobiography than in a classic biography. In other words, there can be more bias in writing the former than the latter. The degree of bias of anyone writing a "filobiography" (which is what this article is) falls somewhere between. For us, sincerity means not only presenting facts as they are said to have been, but interpreting the corresponding events through our own eyes. Indeed, this article is not a panegyric which must be all praise, but the write-up is about a person's life and the events which surrounded it, which great and good as they were, must not be supposed to have been entirely perfect.

Neither are they at first glance clearly comprehensible, since some of these events may appear somewhat alien to most physicians born and raised in the United States (Straight, 1977). Foremost among these is the incontrovertible fact that the life of every Cuban physician, in fact of every person born in Cuba in the last half century, has been shaped or predestined by nondemocratic political events (Fernandez-Conde, 1959; Hoffmann, 1968). An entire issue, including 21 articles of the Journal of the Florida Medical Association,

Fig 1 Agustin W. Castellanos, M.D. (1902-2000)

(64[8], 1977) dealt with this subject. Suffice it to say that in the 57 years which the senior author has roamed this earth, the "Pearl of the Antillas" (as Christopher Columbus called this Island) has been ruled directly or indirectly, with a brief interlude of eight years during which democracy prevailed, by three dictators, two from the right and one from the left (Hoffmann, 1968). Many of the events described here are made more significant because they occurred while the "bullets were flying and the bombs exploding," during periods of revolutionary or counterrevolutionary activities or of political oppression or dictatorial repression (Castellanos, 1977).

The preceding introduction, though lengthy, is necessary to understand the life of Agustin Walfredo Castellanos. This physician, best known for his work in pediatric cardiology, was born in Havana, Cuba, on September 12, 1902. In a century during which most "voluntary" immigrants went to Cuba from Spain or the other Caribbean Islands, his ancestors had emigrated from Central Asia and Mexico, respectively. Because of the limited economic resources of his Cuban-born father, he had to pay high school, college, and medical school tuitions by performing odd activities such as playing professional "lawn-tennis" and giving private violin lessons, both activities having been learned as a child.

Castellanos (Fig. 1) obtained his M.D. degree from the University of Havana School of Medicine in 1925. During his

---

*To avoid confusion it should be stated that prior to becoming a naturalized American citizen, Agustin W. Castellanos was referred to as simply Agustin Castellanos. On the other hand, prior to 1967 this article's first author appears in the *Index Medicus* as Agustin Castellanos, Jr. The other coauthor has always been listed as Agustin M. Castellanos.

training he caught the eye of the "Father of Cuban Pediatrics," Professor Angel Arturo Aballi, who encouraged him to go into academic medicine. In 1932, Castellanos won, not by appointment but by "public competition," the position of Assistant Professor of Pediatrics at the University of Havana School of Medicine. At this early date he became interested in the study of congenital heart disease. According to him, the publications of several authors, Forsmann (1929), Moniz and co-workers (1931), Dos Santos (1931), and Ameuille (1936) led many to believe that the appropriate contrast substance could indeed be used for the *in vivo* visualization of the cardiac chambers (Castellanos AW, 1981). After considerable work in dogs and cadavers, Castellanos, Pereira, and Garcia-Lopez published the first important paper on the clinical applications of "intravenous (peripheral) angiocardiography." The article, which appeared in the *Archivos de la Sociedad de Estudios Clinicos* in 1937, dealt with the normal patterns and those in ventricular septal defect and pulmonic stenosis (Doby, 1976). A scene showing the primitive equipment used at the time is depicted in Figure 2. An expanded version of this work was published one year later in *La Presse Medicale* (1938). Subsequently, they introduced the method of retrograde (countercurrent) injection of dye into the aorta (aortography) mainly to diagnose patent ductus arteriosus (Castellanos and Pereira, 1938). For this purpose they used an automatic apparatus for rapid injection of the dye (Perabrodil) which was constructed by a co-worker, A. V. Pausa (Castellanos *et al.*, 1938).

In 1938, Robb and Steinberg visualized the cardiac chambers of adults, also by injecting in a peripheral vein. This led to the discussion on priority in a field which, at different times, was claimed by pediatricians, internists, radiologists, and cardiologists. The controversy, once initiated, lasted for many years. It was shaped by world events in the early 1940s. During this time Cuba, though afflicted by an internal dictatorship, was less affected by World War II than was the United States. Therefore, for a change, life in general and work on congenital heart disease in particular, was able to proceed at a more steady, relatively continuous and less interrupted pace than in the United States.

It should be remembered that today cardiac catheterization and contrast visualization of the cardiac structures are considered as a single procedure. This was not so in the late 1930s. Even when cardiac catheterization was introduced as a regular clinical method by Cournand and Ranges in 1941, cardiac catheterization and angiocardiography were considered as distinct procedures for another eight years, until the work of Jonson *et al.*, in 1949 (Snellen, 1984)

Castellanos' work on the subject was expanded to the study of the various congenital malformations of the heart. He also was involved in the procedure known as *pneumomediastinum* (used to differentiate between hypertrophy of the thymus gland and cardiac hypertrophy) and in multiple investigations involving parasitology, hematology, and infectious diseases (Castellanos AW, 1981).

From the beginning, Castellanos was not only a researcher, but a practitioner and a teacher as well. These activities really

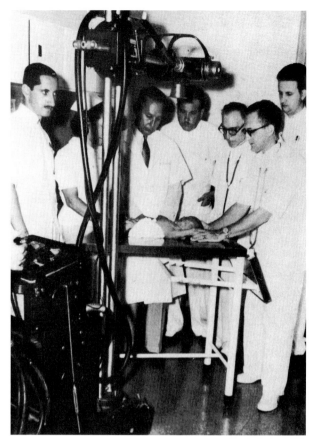

Fig 2 Unpublished photograph of Castellanos (fifth from right), at the Hospital Municipal de Infancia, Havana, Cuba (1937) a few minutes before obtaining one of the first peripheral angiocardiograms ever performed. (Courtesy of Dr. R. Montero, fourth from right.)

began in 1935 when he was appointed Medical Director of the newly created Children's Hospital of Havana. Interestingly, his appointment was not based on scientific merit. As a revolutionary leader opposed to the current ruler of Cuba, he was given the option of living as a scientist or going to jail. That time he made the decision pragmatically.

In one of the short interludes where democracy, though frail, nevertheless existed in Cuba, a substantial donation from one of his patients, a duly elected senator, made possible the creation of the Agustin W. Castellanos Foundation for Cardiovascular Research which occupied a floor at the Children's Hospital. This allowed for a greater recognition of his work especially by physicians from Spanish-speaking countries. Mexico honored Castellanos by including him in Diego Rivera's mural on "Great Men of Cardiology" which still stands in the Instituto Nacional de Cardiologia de Mexico. Ecuador and Colombia nominated him for the Nobel Prize in Medicine and Physiology in 1959 and 1960 respectively.

In 1960, when Marxist Leninism was becoming entrenched in Cuba, Castellanos was given another important lifetime choice: Either give up his ideals or keep them and accept exile. This time he made the decision philosophically. Therefore, in the grand tradition of his compatriots (Juan Carlos Finlay the "patron saint" of Cuban doctors had emigrated to Trinidad around a century before, also for political reasons) he settled in the second largest Cuban city in the world, Miami.

Following his arrival in Miami, he held different academic and institutional positions: Visiting (and later Clinical) Professor of Pediatrics at the University of Miami School of Medicine, Senior Scientist at the National Children's Cardiac Hospital, Acting Chief of Pediatric Cardiology at Variety Children's Hospital, and Professor of Pediatrics at the federally sponsored International School of Medicine's Postgraduate Courses for Foreign Medical Graduates (ECFMG).

Castellanos is an Honorary Member of more than 25 national and international societies of pediatrics, pediatric cardiology, radiology, and adult cardiology. He has authored or coauthored 327 articles, the two most recent published in 1984. Foremost among the multiple awards received and unique for its strangeness is the "Pedro Cossio Award" given by the VII International Congress of Cardiology in Buenos Aires, Argentina, in 1974. Similarly to what Bean did when describing Finlay as a "Scottish-French physician in Havana" (Bean, 1983), Castellanos received this award as a "Cuban physician in Miami" in spite of the fact that he had become a naturalized American citizen seven years before.

In 1967, after having passed the examination given by the Florida Board of Medical Examiners, Castellanos restarted private practice of pediatrics and pediatric cardiology in Coral Gables, Florida. He was then 65 years old, an age when most physicians tend to retire.

Acknowledgments

We are greatly indebted to Drs. R. Montero, R. Pereira, A. Garcia, and A.V. Pausa for their versions of the events in which they participated during the years 1936–1944. Mr. Rafael Mena, Editor of *Prensa Medica,* also supplied valuable information. Data obtained from the Calder Memorial Library of the University of Miami School of Medicine also was most helpful.

References

Bean WB: Walter Reed and yellow fever. *J Am Med Assoc* 1983;250:659

Bond DF: Biography. *Encyclopedia Britannica*, p. 636–640. Chicago: William Benton, 1968

Castellanos A, Pereira R: Counter-current aortography. *Rev Cub Cardiol* 1939;2:187

Castellanos A, Pereira R, Garcia L: L'Angiocardiographie chez l'enfant. *Presse Med* 1938;46:1474

Castellanos A, Pereira R, Garcia-Lopez A: La angio-cardiografia radioopaca. Arch Soc Est Clin (Havana) 1937;523:31

Castellanos A, Pereira R, Pausa AV: On a special automatic device for angiocardiography. *Bol Soc Cub Pediatr* 1938;10:209

Castellanos AW: Personal memories of angiography of cardiac malformations. In *History and perspectives of Cardiology. Catheterization, Angiography, Surgery and Concepts of Circular Control* (Eds. Snellen HA, Dunning AJ, and Arntzenius AC), p. 59–63. The Hague: Leiden University Press, 1981

Castellanos AW: Resume of the history of Cuban medical research. *J Fl Med Assoc* 1977;64:558

Cournand AF, Ranges HS: Catheterization of the right aurical in man. *Proc Soc Exper Biol Med* 1941;46:462

Doby T: *Development of Angiography and Cardiovascular Catheterization*, p. 150–158. Littleton: Publishing Sciences Group, Inc., 1976

Fernandez-Conde A: Los Medicos y la revolucion. *Rev Soc Cub Hist Med* 1959;32:11

Robb GP, Steinberg I: A practical method of visualizing the heart, the pulmonary circulation and the great blood vessels in man. *J Clin Invest* 1938;17:507

Scammel M: Preface, *Solzhenitsyn: A Biography*, p. 11–19. New York, W.W. Norton & Company, 1984

Snellen HA: *History of Cardiology*, p. 126. Rotterdam: Donker Academic Publications, 1984

Straight WM: Medicine and the Cuban physician. Introduction. *J Fl Med Assoc* 1977;64:533

Dr. Castellanos died in 2000, after this profile was written.

John H. Gibbon, Jr.
Cardiopulmonary Bypass —Triumph of Perseverance and Character

RICHARD BING, M.D.

Huntington Medical Research Institutes, Pasadena, California, USA

As environmental factors shape a landscape, thus a life's events alter a person's inherited characteristics. In the case of John H. Gibbon, Jr. (Fig. 1), his family background reveals much that is pertinent to his career. Gibbon was the son of a Philadelphian surgeon and one of four generations of physicians. He was born in 1904, educated at Princeton, and attended medical school at the Jefferson Medical College in Philadelphia. After a research fellowship in Boston with Dr. E.D. Churchill he returned to Philadelphia, again returning to Boston for a fellowship. In 1931 he began to practice surgery in Philadelphia and remained there for the rest of his life. In 1956 Dr. Gibbon became head of the department and Samuel D. Gross Professor of Surgery at his medical alma mater, Jefferson Medical College, until his retirement in 1967. He died in 1973 from an apparent heart attack.[1]

Gibbon contributed to medicine and surgery by developing and using the first successful cardiopulmonary bypass. In 1953, he and his co-workers performed the first surgical repair of an intra-atrial septal defect, using total cardiopulmonary bypass for 45 minutes.[2]

These are the dry facts. How much do they conceal! Greatness can appear in different forms: as imagination, inspiration, depth of emotion, strength of conviction. John H. Gibbon's greatness was his absolute dedication to a definite goal, unperturbed by rejection and ridicule by his fellow physicians. His career was not very different from that of other pioneers, but he was a scientific neophyte who progressed painfully, step by step and inch by inch. He was not a Ph.D., nor was he trained in mechanical engineering; he had no degree in physiology or in biophysics, and he was not schooled in sophisticated laboratory methods. He was primarily a surgeon who was scientifically self-trained. There are many other examples of self-trained men of genius, such as Gregor Mendel in biology, or Arnold Schoenberg in music. In the last analysis everyone is self-trained to some extent. But to a scientist, initial training is considered essential, since he is dependent upon acquisition of technology which must be learned by studying and following preceptors. John H. Gibbon, Jr., had no such preceptors; there was no one who could possibly have taught him how to build a heart–lung machine. Many years after he had already made big inroads, he finally received financial and technical help from trained engineers at IBM; by that time the main problems had been recognized and had been at least partially overcome.

Gibbon wanted to combine research with surgery. Therefore, after surgical training, he applied to Edward D. Churchill at Harvard Medical School where a research fellowship was available. He wanted to see whether he "liked or was capable of carrying out the work and the research disciplines involved in becoming an academic surgeon."[2] While working with Churchill, he also met his future wife, Mary Hopkinson, then Churchill's surgical research technician. There are examples of husband-and-wife teams who accomplish great things professionally. Some examples are Carl and Gerti Cori, who pioneered knowledge on carbohydrate metabolism, or Pierre and Marie Curie with their pathfinding work on radioisotopes. Meeting and marrying Mary Hopkinson was one of the most fortunate things Gibbon ever did. Mrs. Gibbon came to surgery and medicine via contact with a young cousin who was married to a physician. She made the decision then and there to get herself into the world of medicine. It is remarkable that she had no college degree, nor had she studied any of the basic sciences. Nothing daunted her and she applied for a job at the Harvard Medical School Placement Bureau and was fortunate to secure immediate employment with Dr. Edward D. Churchill. The Gibbons jointly started work on the heart–lung preparation on October 3, 1930.

As is often the case, an encounter with a patient furnished the stimulus. A female patient was admitted to Massachusetts General Hospital suffering a postoperative massive pulmonary embolism. The story from then on is well known: Dr. Gibbon watched the patient's deterioration helplessly during the night until Churchill was willing to perform a Trendelenburg operation (an operation for pulmonary embolectomy) which carries with it a forbidding mortality. Dr. Gibbon's patient died during the operation.

From that day on the idea of cardiopulmonary bypass became an obsession. Three months later Gibbon and Mary were married and went to tell Dr. Churchill that they had an idea for a new experiment which would result in maintenance of the circulation during occlusion of the pulmonary artery. When Gibbon talked to a number of people of his idea of artificially oxygenating blood and devising an artificial pulmonary circuit, no one was interested or encouraging. Churchill was anything but enthusiastic, but he provided funds for a research fellowship at Harvard, a laboratory space, and a technician's salary which went to Mrs. Gibbon. Churchill was not the only one who dis-

FIG. 1 John H. Gibbon, Jr., 1904–1973.

couraged Gibbon. The professor of medicine at Massachusetts General Hospital advised against attempting to build an extracorporeal circulation because "if one wants to pursue an academic career in surgery, one should undertake a number of smaller and less ambitious projects that could be reported in the medical literature regardless of the results." This does not sound too unfamiliar because it is indeed risky to start a new venture in research—some granting agencies refer to it as "a fishing expedition"—without preliminary positive results. Therefore the professor of medicine was quite right; when an important project in which the investigator invested time and money does not succeed, the hapless scientist has lost time and has nothing to report, thus jeopardizing his career.

Gibbon was undeterred. He had to overcome a number of difficulties which appeared insurmountable, such as what fluid to use in the extracorporeal circuit (gum acacia, which produced severe anemia, was finally used), how to connect the blood vessels to the extracorporeal circuit, and what type of anesthesia to use. Particularly important and difficult was the problem of oxygenation of the blood. He mentions that the real breakthrough in increasing oxygenation of the blood was the development of the screen oxygenator, which could be conveniently adapted to any size subject.

It would be strange if Gibbon did not have contemporaries interested in developing a cardiopulmonary bypass. Two surgeons, Clarence Dennis and James A. Helmsworth, attempted to develop cardiopulmonary bypass. But they started later than Gibbon (after the end of the war) and they did not succeed in a clinical application of their model.

The first success came in 1934 when the Gibbons demonstrated for the first time that it was possible to keep an animal alive and in a relatively normal physiological state with their heart–lung apparatus, while no blood at all was passing through the animal's own heart and lungs. As Gibbon described it,

> I will never forget the day when we were able to screw the clamp down all the way, completely occluding the pulmonary artery, with the extracorporeal blood circuit in operation and with no change in the animal's blood pressure. My wife and I threw our arms around each other and danced around the laboratory laughing and shouting hooray … although it gives great satisfaction to me and others to know that the operations are being performed daily now all over the world, nothing in my life has duplicated the ecstacy and joy of that dance with Mary around the laboratory of the old Bulfinch building in the Massachusetts General Hospital 28 years ago.[3]

When he finally successfully closed an atrial-septal defect on a patient on May 6, 1953, Dr. Gibbon was unable to write or dictate the operating procedures himself (although this was, of course, done by one of this assistants). He wrote, "I suppose that I did not want to relive the tension, emotional excitement by again recalling the details."[2] Several years later when heart–lung machines were in general use throughout the world, he disliked opening a surgical journal and finding it full of articles about bypass surgery, thinking that he had opened some kind of Pandora's box. This reluctance to describe the operation probably extended also to his reluctance to continue with this work. He was emotionally drained following this historic operation. In 1967, Dr. Gibbon retired at the age of 64. He died of an apparent heart attack while playing tennis at the age of 69.

Gibbon's life can be compared with that of the great explorers of the 15th and 16th century. Like them, he strove mightily to discover new lands. The discovery was the ultimate goal. Exploitation of this discovery he left to others. One cannot help but wonder why a man whose lifework saved hundreds of thousands of lives, who worked for years with tenacity and imagination, was not honored by the highest award medicine and science can bestow.

References

1. Gibbon JH Jr, Shumacher HB: Transaction American Surgical Association, 41–45 (1973)
2. Gibbon JH Jr: Application of a mechanical heart and lung apparatus to cardiac surgery. *Minnesota Medicine* 37, 171 (1954)
3. Gibbon JH Jr: Medicine's living history. *Medical World News* 13, 47 (1972)

Werner Forssmann: A German Problem with the Nobel Prize

H. W. Heiss, m.d.

Medical University Clinic, Department of Internal Medicine III, University of Freiburg, Freiburg, Germany

Imagine a cardiologist considering a ureteric catheter to perform a cardiac catheterization. Unbelievable, impossible. However, it took all the courage and determination of a young surgical resident to use exactly that means in order to achieve one of clinical cardiology's greatest advances. The name of that resident was Werner Forssmann and he did it in 1929.

Werner Forssmann (Fig. 1) was born on August 29, 1904 in Berlin. His father, a lawyer, was killed in action during World War I in 1916. At the time, Werner was a student at the humanistic Askanische Gymnasium, following a family tradition for this profound and highly esteemed education. Unable to provide for her family on her small pension, his mother had to work as an office clerk. Therefore, his grandmother supervised his education and the household. Werner often visited the office of his uncle Walter, a general practitioner living outside Berlin. From there came his resolve to become a physician. This intention was encouraged by a family gift—a beautiful Leitz microscope—on the occasion of his confirmation. He used this gift for studies of protozoa which he took from his aquarium. Shortly before graduation in 1922 his teacher, Semiller, asked him what profession he would pursue. Werner had changed his mind and said "Tradesman." The teacher responded, "Forssmann, when you become a tradesman everybody will earn money but you. You must study medicine. This is your great talent." And so it was.

Forssmann entered Medical School at the Friedrich-Wilhelm-University in Berlin in 1922. Two of his most remarkable academic teachers were Prof. R. Fick, son of the great physiologist Adolf Fick, well-known to every cardiologist, and Prof. Dr. F. Kopsch, who planted the idea in Forssmann's mind to reach the heart "atraumatically via the vasculature." Passing the state examination in February 1928, Forssmann prepared his doctoral thesis, which was concerned with the influence of liver extract on blood chemistry. He also began his first self-experiment by taking daily one liter of that extract. After early futile attempts to obtain a residency in internal medicine, he was accepted at the Second Division of Surgery at the Auguste-Victoria-Heim in Eberswalde. The chief of this small department was Sanitätsrat Dr. Richard Schneider, whose youngest sister, Margarete Lüdes, had recommended Forssmann. She happened to be a dear friend of his mother. Dr. Schneider was well versed not only in general surgery but also in obstetrics and gynecology and well experienced in internal medicine. Through painful experience,

Forssmann came to realize the divergence between clinical diagnoses and postmortem findings. He was particularly interested in the development of pulmonary sclerosis in the course of mitral stenosis and the intriguing clinical question of whether a mitral valvular defect should be operated upon or not. Forssmann was convinced that the solution to the problem was to find a safe path to the heart without general anesthesia and without disturbing intrathoracic pressures or provoking vegetative reflexes. He was particularly fascinated by an old print published in the work of Marey which illustrated a man passing a tube via the jugular vein into the heart of a horse for measurement of ventricular pressure changes. Forssmann rejected the idea of jugular vein cannulation. Instead, he decided to try an approach via the cubital vein to pass a ureteric catheter toward the heart with the arm elevated. However, local anesthesia for incision was necessary.

He discussed his well-prepared plan in detail with his chief. Permission was refused mainly because his chief could not permit experiments at his small department. He advised him to try animal experiments first. Forssmann suggested a self-experiment which also was refused because of Dr. Schneider's apprehension for Forssmann's safety. Forssmann then discussed his venture with Gerda Ditzen, the OR nurse, weighing all details and consequences of the procedure. Her approval was mandatory because she supervised the surgical instruments required for the procedure. A fortnight later she was convinced and offered her full support. She even volunteered to become the first subject for a cardiac catheterization.

On a day early in the summer of 1929, Forssmann pretended to do the incision on Gerda Ditzen's left arm. She wanted to sit on a chair, but he explained that it would be better to lie on the OR table because of the possible side effects of local anesthesia. As she positioned herself on the OR table, Forssmann strapped her legs and hands firmly in place. Unnoticed by her, he locally anesthetized his own left cubital region. To gain the time needed for the anesthesia to become effective, he continued to prepare her left arm for incision. Feeling the effect of the local anesthesia, Forssmann made the incision on his own left arm, introduced the ureteric catheter for 30 cm and covered the wound with sterile tissues. He then released the right hand of the nurse and asked her to call the x-ray nurse. Only then did Gerda Ditzen notice that it was not her arm to which the catheter was attached. She cried and grumbled her dismay. He then released her completely and both

FIG. 1   Werner Forssmann, 1904–1979. Reproduced with permission of Droste Verlag GmbH, Düsseldorf.

went to the x-ray room, one story below. Both were received by nurse Eva who placed Forssmann behind the fluoroscope. At the same time, his friend, Peter Romeis, rushed into the room and tried to pull the catheter out of Forssmann's vein. However, Forssmann overcame him. With Eva holding a mirror, he was able to see the fluoroscopic image of his chest and left arm. He noticed that the catheter had reached the area of the shoulder joint. He advanced the catheter up to the 60 cm mark and was able to see its tip in his right ventricular cavity, exactly as he had imagined. The position of the catheter was documented on chest x-ray film.

Barely recovered from the excitement, Forssmann was summoned before his very annoyed chief. Forssmann, however, convinced him of his achievement by showing the film to him. After due congratulation, Forssmann was granted permission to do a second cardiac catheterization, this time on a terminally ill female patient. Forssmann used the catheter to apply medication directly into the right ventricle which proved in this case more effective than by the routine i.v. route. The catheter was advanced in the patient without fluoroscopic guidance merely by measuring the distance at the body's surface. Postmortem examination revealed the exact position of the catheter in the right ventricle and proved the catheters could safely be advanced to the heart without fluoroscopic control. A report prepared and submitted to Klinische Wochenschrift was accepted in a short time.

Encouraged by his chief, Forssmann continued his surgical residency through October 1929 at the Charité in Berlin. A few weeks later, on November 5, 1929, his report "Über die Sondierung des rechten Herzens" was published. It caused some turbulence at this great institution due to the attention being paid to it by the media. Forssmann was forced to withdraw because he had not asked his new chief, Prof. Dr. F. Sauerbruch, for permission to proceed. At least that was the formal reason given for his dismissal without notice. Fortunately, he was allowed to return to Eberswalde. There, he started animal experiments in rabbits and dogs to visualize the cardiac chamber by contrast media (Thorotrast) and he continued his self-experiments, altogether nine cardiac catheterizations. He had achieved incredible feats making him one of the great fathers of cardiology: cardiac catheterization, with and without fluoroscopic control, and interventional cardiac catheter therapy.

Because of the attention his work attracted, Sauerbruch asked him in 1931 to return to the Charité. He agreed and stayed there until the end of July 1932. He was discharged at that time, because he did not meet the scientific expectations of his chief. However, his surgical skills were acknowledged and he was recommended to the Städtisches Krankenhaus in Mainz where he arrived on July 31, 1932. This date was of particular personal importance because shortly after arrival he met a female resident in internal medicine, Dr. Elsbet Engel. They were soon engaged and were married in 1933. Because husband and wife were not allowed to work together, both had to leave the hospital. The couple went to Berlin where Forssmann started his career as a urologist at Rudolf-Virchow-Krankenhaus. During World War II Forssmann served as a military surgeon mainly in the east and the north. As a postwar POW for a short time, he learned that his family had survived the war in the Black Forest village of Wambach. He rejoined his family there and worked as a general practitioner for almost three years. Because he could not gain a surgical position at a hospital, he applied as a urologist and so succeeded in Bad Kreuznach where he had an office and could operate at the Diakonie-Anstalten.

During all those years he had given up hope that his idea to further develop cardiac catheterization and cardiac angiography could succeed. To his great surprise he learned soon after the war that a cardiac catheter lab was operating at the Paediatric Department in Basel. On entering such a lab for the first time, he was stunned. At the invitation of Professor Dr. John McMichael he visited London and participated in the making of a scientific film concerning heart catheterization. He also was invited by Prof. Dr. Wollheim, at that time President of the German Society for Cardiovascular Research, to present the opening lecture of the Annual Convention of that Society. In 1951 he also had his first meeting with André Cournand at the invitation of Prof. Dr. F. Eichholtz. It was in 1954 that he was awarded the highly esteemed Leibniz Medaille by the German Academy of Science in Berlin. He considered this period of his life "my comeback." However, his efforts to receive a professorship at the University of Mainz, though supported by many of his friends, such as Profs. Knipping and

Fassbender as well as the German Bundespräsident, were rejected because he had failed to complete a Ph.D. thesis and his position as an outsider was considered detrimental to the reputation of a German faculty.

Then on October 11, 1956, while meeting with members of the Vereinte Aquarienfreunde in a local pub, his wife told him to return home immediately because a woman with a foreign accent would call again from Bonn at 10 p.m. She had mentioned the Nobel Prize. The call indeed returned and an interview was requested for the next day. Forssmann refused. However, the next morning he received a letter from the Karolinska Institute asking him for a 13×18 cm photograph. He was informed by a reporter that he and two Americans had been elected Nobel laureates. On Thursday, October 18, 1956, he had operated upon three patients with kidney disease in the morning and had just finished when the Medical Director of the hospital entered the OR and announced in a low and touched voice: "Mr. Forssmann, I would like to be the first to congratulate you and your wife. You have received, with two Americans, this year's Nobel prize." This event changed the Forssmann family's life completely. He did not consider himself to be a man of world renown, only a practicing physician as were many thousand others who had been awarded that outstanding honor. The ceremonies in Stockholm took place at the time of the Hungarian uprising. One of the many benefits derived from his award was that the Medical Faculty of the University of Mainz granted Forssmann the position of honorary Professor. Upon his return from the ceremonies in Stockholm, he tried again to obtain a better position. Although he was elected chief of the Surgical Department of the Evangelisches Krankenhaus in Düsseldorf in 1957, again local forces were against him.

After retirement he returned to the Black Forest. He was particularly pleased by an invitation from Prof. F. Loogen to visit his department of cardiology, where everything he could have dreamed of was accomplished to Forssmann's full satisfaction. Considering the life and fate of Prof. Werner Forssmann, one must pay tribute to a great character, gifted surgeon, and pioneer in cardiology.

Werner Forssmann died on June 1, 1979, following two myocardial infarctions.

Reference

Forssmann W: Selbstversuch. Erinnerungen eines Chirurgen. Droste-Verlag, Düsseldorf (1972)

Sir John McMichael

JOHN F. GOODWIN, M.D., F.R.C.P., F.A.C.P., (HON.), F.E.S.C.

Royal Postgraduate Medical School and St. George's Hospital, London, England.

John McMichael was born in 1904 in Gatehouse of Fleet, Kirkcudbrightshire, Scotland, and was educated at Kirkcudbright Academy, Edinburgh. It was clear early on that he was of exceptional intelligence and clarity of mind. He studied medicine in Edinburgh and rapidly emerged as one of the brightest students of his time, winning many medals and scholarships. After graduation, he soon became intrigued with the challenge and excitement of the unknown in medicine. He perceived an urgent need to attack the problems that his questing imagination detected all around him. His approach was the epitome of John Hunter's advice to Jenner, "…but why think, why not try to experiment?"

At the age of 29 McMichael won the Gold Medal for his M.D. thesis during the tenure of a Beit Memorial Fellowship under Sir Stanley Davidson in Aberdeen and Sir Thomas Lewis in London. From 1937 to 1931 he was a Royal Society Research Fellow and Assistant Physician in Edinburgh. His early research had been in respiratory disease, but after he moved to London he became interested in the heart and was quick to appreciate the enormous possibilities for research offered by cardiac catheterization. He joined the staff of the Royal Postgraduate Medical School (then the British Postgraduate Medical School) as Reader in Medicine and succeeded the Director, Sir Francis Fraser, in 1946. He introduced cardiac catheterization to Great Britain along the lines of the pioneering work of Cournand and Richards in New York. He faced great opposition from the moguls of the London County Council who controlled Hammersmith Hospital to which the British Postgraduate Medical School was attached. Grave predictions rained down upon him: the intravenous catheters would become clogged with thrombus, strings of clots would block the veins, discharge into the lungs, and mayhem would ensue; as a result, his career would be shattered and he would certainly be dismissed from his post. Useless to say that Werner Forsmann, the first man to pass a catheter into the heart (on himself) had not had these complications, though he was indeed dismissed from his hospital post in pre-war Germany. Even McMichael's chief, Sir Francis Fraser, discouraged him—but withdrew his objections when tactfully reminded that he (Sir Francis) had once suggested plunging a needle into the right ventricle through the anterior chest wall to measure the right ventricular pressure!

With great courage and complete selflessness McMichael pressed ahead. None of the ghastly predictions were fulfilled and he was brilliantly successful, but there were other difficulties to be faced.

Manometry was in its infancy, delicate catheter tip transducers were unknown, instrument firms were cautious in giving support or funds, and money for research was severely restricted. In the best tradition of British science (as exemplified by the Cavendish Laboratory at Cambridge) of personally designed equipment, McMichael and his colleagues Sharpey, Schafer, and Howarth published the first paper on transvenous catheterization of the right atrium in cases of congenital heart disease in 1946.[1] This work confounded the critics and showed that the heart could indeed be explored successfully and studied in life. His efforts shone a spotlight on the dark places of the heart and illuminated with precision what had previously only been suspected. Cardiac catheterization made cardiac surgery possible and opened the way for later advances such as open heart surgery, pacemakers, and ultimately cardiac transplantation. It was sad that the rules of the Nobel Prize did not allow him to share it with Richards and Cournand.

If John McMichael had made no more contributions than these, he would have secured a firm niche in the Hall of Fame for his achievements in advancing medical science—but he achieved much more.

When the British Postgraduate Medical School had first been established in 1935, the intention had been to provide series of courses for physicians and surgeons pursuing further education. However, Sir Francis Fraser, himself a man of great vision, saw a more important role for the school as a center for research and training in research methods, providing a force of highly skilled young doctors who would give their full time to patient care, research, and teaching. Fraser studied the system at Columbia-Presbyterian Medical Center in New York and concluded that the way to achieve his ideals was to appoint young people of exciting potential to relatively senior positions and give them a free hand. In John McMichael he found an ideal supporter to carry forward his plans. During World War II the school and hospital operated with a skeleton staff but, even so, notable research emerged from John McMichael's department, especially on the "crush syndrome" and on liver disease. When the war ended, the supply of talented research workers expanded and over the next five years key appointments were made to ensure the preeminence of the school. Not surprisingly, this policy provoked criticism which

Fig. 1   Sir John McMichael (1904–1993).

descended on McMichael after Fraser had retired. Waving their gold-headed canes enthusiastically, the leaders of the medical profession pointed out that only disaster could come of this policy: these young people were being given responsibilities far beyond their capabilities, would burn themselves out rapidly or make dangerous mistakes—possibly both. Furthermore, they would miss the essential exposure to the real world given by the hurly burly of personal private practice. There was a germ of truth in both these allegations, but McMichael was unperturbed and the policy was outstandingly successful. This policy was, however, not always without problems; talented individuals were lost to the school when they requested the opportunity to go into private practice and still stay on the school staff—requests McMichael firmly resisted. "By all means do personal private practice if you wish to, but you won't do it here" summed up his attitude. He believed that private practice would dilute the single-minded thrust of research. Times have changed and the rigid exclusion of private practice that McMichael insisted on then would not be appropriate now. The policy of selecting young staff, giving them their freedom, and encouraging cooperation between departments made Hammersmith a model for research and postgraduate education in the 1950s and 1960s.

McMichael placed the patient in the center of the stage; to him, research was a means of detecting problems and attempting to solve them in the interest of the patient who should be studied in detail, with every scientific test result being carefully correlated with the clinical data. Every means available through all departments of the school should be concentrated in a team effort. Such an approach, of course, was not only helpful to the patient, but also provided data of incalculable value to the advance of medicine. It did not, however,

necessarily encourage the development of basic science to underpin applied medicine, nor was the policy of studying a small number of patients in great detail always appropriate when the spectrum of medical investigation became wider and large numbers of patients were needed to solve urgent problems of method, diagnosis, and treatment.

McMichael was quick to appreciate the importance of linking physician cardiologists with their cardiac surgical colleagues and, as heart surgery developed, he assigned junior consultants and registrars in medicine to work closely with the cardiac surgeons. This plan was of great value, particularly when open heart surgery was introduced at Hammersmith. Cardiologists would join surgical colleagues in the operating theater, monitor physiological events, assist with postoperative care, and even help with animal research on occasion.

Having established cardiac catheterization and encouraged angiocardiography at the Royal Postgraduate Medical School, McMichael withdrew personally from this field of investigation and stimulated by his wife's hypertension, turned his attention to the problems of high blood pressure. These were the early days of effective hypotensive agents such as hexamethonium, which had fearsome side effects and required great courage and perseverance on the part of the patients; however, for the first time the prognosis of severe complicated and malignant hypertension was significantly improved by pharmacological means, opening the way for even more effective and safer drugs.

McMichael's interest in hypotensive therapy had an interesting and important spinoff in the development of clinical pharmacology as an important aspect of academic and hospital medicine. Even before research into effective hypotensive therapy began, McMichael had been keenly interested in digitalis. He realized early on that Sir Thomas Lewis' contention that digitalis was of value only in atrial fibrillation and had no place in the treatment of heart failure contained more than a germ of truth, and that his (McMichael's) work showed that digitalis in so-called "high output failure" was of little value. This research added important knowledge to the treatment of congestive heart failure, as his classical monograph "The Pharmacology of the Failing Human Heart."[2]

The school staff increased notably during McMichael's time at the school as Professor of Medicine and Director of the Department of Medicine. He was largely responsible for expanding the school premises and for developing two new large buildings—the Wolfson Institute and later the Commonwealth building. In his tireless efforts he was greatly assisted by Professor Earl King, Professor Lord Stamp, and many others. For many years he played a leading role in the development of the British Heart Foundation.

John McMichael has sterling qualities as a leader. He inspires confidence and has always shown deep interest in his staff, imparting to them his own enthusiasm and his ideals of medical research. He has an instinctive knack of collecting the right people to work with and of giving opportunities to gifted research workers. Occasionally he could make misjudgments and fail to accord support to a deserving colleague or be initially intolerant of what eventually emerged as good ideas. He had no time for administrative red tape—a request to supply in detail the exact proportion of time spent by staff on each of their teaching, research, and clinical responsibilities met with a predictably brusque response. His judgments on medical fashions and published work were acute and perceptive. For example, he never accepted the fashion for the widespread use of anticoagulants in coronary heart disease in the 1950s. He detected flaws in the arguments at a time when accurate statistical trials had not yet been developed. Nevertheless, he respected honest contrary views and did not attempt to obstruct them. His suspicions of enthusiastic and apparently uncritical approaches to problems may have had something to do with his initial reluctance to accept epidemiology as a respectable branch of science, and he resented the lead taken by epidemiologists in promoting methods, usually dietary, to reduce the risk of coronary heart disease. In this he was supported by many cardiologists, which was unfortunate for it probably set preventive cardiology back by a decade.

Apart from cardiology, John McMichael was interested in all facets of medicine and was quick to exploit new talent and advances. He set up one of the first pulmonary function laboratories at Hammersmith Hospital in the late 1940s. As would be expected, honors came thick and fast upon him. He became a Fellow of the Royal College of Physicians of Edinburgh in 1940 (honorary in 1981). He was awarded an honorary M.D. degree by the University of Melbourne in 1965 and was elected a member of many national cardiac societies, notably the American Medical Association, the National Academy of Washington, the Finnish Academy of Sciences, the Académie Royale de Med Belgique, and many others. He delivered a number of keynote lectures at the Royal College of Physicians of London, including the Oliver Sharpey in 1952, Croonian in 1951, and he was Harveian orator in 1975.

He was awarded the Cullen Prize of the Royal College of Physicians Edinburgh in 1953. The distinction of which he was probably most proud, however, was the Fellowship of the Royal Society to which he was elected in 1957—a rare honor for the practicing physician that he remained, during his entire career, at Hammersmith. He was knighted in 1965 and was President of the British Cardiac Society from 1968 to 1972 and President of the Fifth World Congress of Cardiology held in London in 1970.

He was a member of the Medical Research Council, a Wellcome Trustee and Vice President of the Royal Society. By this time he had already left the Royal Postgraduate Medical School to become Director of the British Postgraduate Medical Federation in succession to Sir James Patterson Ross.

The sight of his upright figure and smiling face striding down the main corridor at Hammersmith was sadly missed, for he had the ability to inspire great loyalty and affection. He had a notable talent for making his junior colleagues feel appreciated, even though he could occasionally be a shade intimidating.

The moving finger writes and having writ, moves on. The name of John McMichael is writ large in the annals of medical teaching and scientific advances. Generations of patients and doctors past and to come owe him a great debt.

References

1. Howarth S, McMichael J, Sharpey, Schafer EP: Cardiac catheterization in cases of patient interauricular septum, primary pulmonary hypertension, Fallot's tetrology and pulmonary stenosis. *Br Heart J* 9, 292 (1947)
2. McMichael J: *Pharmacology of the Failing Human Heart*. Blackwell Scientific Publications, Oxford (1950)

Robert E. Gross

ALDO CASTANEDA, M.D., PH.D.

Department of Surgery, The Children's Hospital, Boston, Massachusetts, USA

Dr. Robert E. Gross was born on July 2, 1905, in Baltimore, Maryland. He graduated Phi Beta Kappa from Carleton College in 1927 and from Harvard Medical School (Alpha Omega Alpha) in 1931. He first came in contact with congenital malformations during a pathology rotation at Children's Hospital, Boston. This experience captured his imagination and he subsequently applied for a position in pediatric surgery under Dr. William E. Ladd, then the Surgeon-in-Chief at Children's Hospital. His decision to become a surgeon was reinforced by Dr. Elliot C. Cutler, Harvey Cushing's successor as Surgeon-in-Chief at the Peter Bent Brigham Hospital. In 1935 Robert Gross was selected for a six-month Peter Bent Brigham Traveling Fellowship, which permitted him to visit prominent European surgical clinics. Included in these travels was a short research experience at the University of Edinburgh. After his return from Europe he served as chief resident in surgery at both the Children's Hospital and the Peter Bent Brigham Hospital. It was during his chief residency at the Children's Hospital that on August 26, 1938, he first successfully ligated a patent ductus arteriosus. Clearly, this epoch-making procedure, carefully planned and first practiced on animals, inaugurated the era of pediatric cardiovascular surgery. In 1945, with Charles A. Hufnagle, Dr. Gross reported on aortic resections and re-anastomosis in animals with the intent ultimately to repair coarctation of the aorta in humans. Appended to this report were the case histories of two recently operated children with coarctation, one of whom survived (June 1945). This publication appeared shortly after Clarence Crafoord's first successful repair of coarctation of the aorta performed in Stockholm in October of 1944. During the early experience with coarctation surgery, Dr. Gross encountered patients with long segment coarctation in whom resection and end-to-end anastomosis proved impossible. He therefore began to search for a method that would allow him to interpose a conduit to re-establish aortic continuity. Subsequently, Dr. Gross was the first to preserve human aortic homografts successfully, and, in fact, used such a graft for the first time (1946) in a patient after resection of a coarctation. In 1945, he also reported the first successful repair of a double aortic arch in an infant. In his characteristic thorough and scholarly fashion, he began to study this problem with Dr. E. B. D. Neuhauser, Radiologist-in-Chief at Children's Hospital. Their description of the various forms of this anomaly and the surgical methods recommended for repair has withstood the test of time.

As a surgical educator, Dr. Gross was a strong believer in stimulating his trainees to spend time in the research laboratory, to pursue academic work, and to publish their findings and results. His own multifaceted interests are well documented in more than 250 publications, covering subjects in general pediatric and urologic surgery and also cardiovascular surgery. His first book, coauthored with William E. Ladd, *Abdominal Surgery of Infants and Childhood,* was first published in 1941. *The Surgery of Infancy and Childhood* followed in 1953. This volume encompassed all of pediatric surgery, and still is considered a classic. Without question, it was the most widely read book on pediatric surgery of its time. In 1970, Dr. Gross published his third and last book, *An Atlas of Children's Surgery,* which included a wide range of pediatric cardiac surgical procedures.

In 1947, Dr. Gross was appointed the first William E. Ladd Professor of Child Surgery at the Harvard Medical School and Surgeon-in-Chief at Children's Hospital. After 20 years, this very large unit was divided into a general and a cardiovascular surgical department. Dr. Gross remained as the Cardiovascular Surgeon-in-Chief until he retired in September 1972.

In addition to his many personal contributions to both experimental and clinical pediatric surgery (general and cardiovascular), Dr. Gross was the most influential force in establishing pediatric surgery as a specialty and also is distinguished for training the largest number of qualified pediatric surgeons. His impact upon the specialty is still strong. Of the 25 pediatric surgical training programs in this country today, 7 are headed by surgeons trained by Dr. Gross and 13 by second-generation Gross trainees. What a remarkable academic legacy; 20 of 25 pediatric surgical training programs today still are influenced, either directly or indirectly, by this remarkable surgeon.

In 1964, Dr. Gross became President of the American Association of Thoracic Surgery. In addition, he was the first President of the American Pediatric Surgical Association founded in 1970; in fact, 10 of the next 17 presidents of the Association were his trainees. Both Carleton College and Harvard University bestowed upon him honorary degrees. He also received honorary degrees from Louvain University, the University of Turin, and the University of Sheffield. He was awarded 26 medals in recognition of his many salient contri-

FIG. 1 Dr. Robert E. Gross (1905–1988). (Photograph by Bradford F. Herzog.)

After his retirement in October 1972, we continued to place residents, an operating room, and a perfusion team at his disposal; however, he advised me in no uncertain terms that he had completed his tour of duty, and that he did not plan to continue to operate or see patients. In fact, he returned only once, to attend the inauguration of our new Robert E. Gross Cardiac Intensive Care unit.

Dr. Gross retired to Brattleboro, Vermont. He liked working outdoors and he also enjoyed the scenery. It was not a surprise that he kept up with the surgical literature. On several occasions I received a short "well done" note after one of our reports appeared in print. On the occasion of Dr. Gross's eightieth birthday in 1985, and in the presence of Dr. Gross and many of his pupils, Dean Daniel C. Tosteson of Harvard Medical School announced the establishment of the Robert E. Gross Chair in Surgery at Harvard Medical School. The first incumbent of this chair is Dr. W. Hardy Hendren, a distinguished alumnus of Dr. Gross and the present Chief of General Pediatric Surgery at Children's Hospital, Boston.

Robert Gross died in his sleep on October 11, 1988, at age 83 years. This inspiring leader, innovative thinker, lucid writer, and gifted surgeon was surely the most influential pediatric surgeon of this century. Children everywhere continue to benefit from the many lasting contributions of this surgical giant.

butions to surgery. Among them was the American Surgical Association Medallion for Scientific Achievement in 1973 and, most unusual, he received the Albert Lasker Award twice, in 1954 and 1959. Other honors included the Dennis Brown Medal of the British Association of Pediatric Surgeons, the William E. Ladd Medal of the American Academy of Pediatrics, the Bigelow Medal of the Boston Surgical Society, and the Sheen Award of the American Medical Association. Despite these many honors, Dr. Gross remained a very unassuming, private and indeed shy person. He disliked speaking about himself or his accomplishments. During some of my conversations with him, he never failed to mention his good fortune to have been afforded the opportunity to work at Harvard Medical School and Children's Hospital.

References

1. Craford C, Nylin G: Congenital coarctation of the aorta and its surgical treatment. *J Thorac Surg* 14, 347 (1945)
2. Gross RE: *The Surgery of Infancy and Childhood*. WB Saunders, Philadelphia (1953)
3. Gross RE: *An Atlas of Children's Surgery*. WB Saunders Co., Philadelphia (1970)
4. Gross RE, Hubbard JP: Surgical ligation of a patent ductus arteriosus. Report of first successful case. *J Am Med Assoc* 112, 729 (1939)
5. Gross RE, Hufnagel CA: Coarctation of the aorta. Experimental studies regarding its surgical correction. *N Engl J Med* 233, 287 (1945)
6. Ladd WD, Gross RE: *Abdominal Surgery of Infancy and Childhood*. WB Saunders, Philadelphia (1941)

Robert Hebard Bayley: 1906–1969

C. S. LEWIS, JR., M.D.

Department of Medicine, University of Oklahoma College of Medicine—Tulsa, Tulsa, Oklahoma, USA

Doctor Robert Hebard Bayley was born in 1907 in Paterson, New Jersey. He received his Bachelor of Science and Doctor of Medicine degrees from Emory University and served his internship and residency training at the University Hospital, Ann Arbor, Michigan. During his four years at Ann Arbor he became a lifelong friend and collaborator of Frank N. Wilson. After four years at Ann Arbor, he was appointed as a Resident Physician at the Leahy Home Tuberculosis Sanitarium in Honolulu, at which time he began his self-training in mathematics. In 1936 he began a productive 8-year period as an instructor in medicine at Louisiana State University, during which time he advanced to Associate Professorship.

In 1944, Dr. Bayley joined the faculty of the University of Oklahoma as Professor of Medicine and Director of the Heart Station. He later served as the George L. Cross Research Professor of Medicine and Director of the BioPhysics Section of the Department of Medicine.

Although his first published papers concerned "Right Aortic Arch" (1932),[1] "Dynamic Dilatation of the Thoracic Aorta" (1933),[2] and "Thyroid Crisis" (1934),[3] the majority of his large bibliography was devoted to the application of mathematical principles to electrocardiography. His publications produced at Louisiana State University included "The Significance of the Duration of Q3 with Respect to Coronary Artery Disease,"[4] "The Potential Produced by Cardiac Muscle,"[5] "Acute, Local, Ventricular Ischemia, or Impending Infarction, Caused by Dissecting Aneurysm,"[6] "The Normal Human Ventricular Gradient,"[7] and "On Certain Applications of Modern Electrocardiographic Theory to the Interpretation of Electrocardiograms Which Indicate Myocardial Disease."[8] The latter article, which was published in the *American Heart Journal* in 1943, has become a classic. In 1950, Dr. Bayley wrote "Peri-Infarction Block."[9] Some of his articles during the 1950s and 1960s dealt with "The Zero of Potential of the Electric Field Produced by the Heart Beat,"[10, 11] "The Problem of Adjusting the Wilson Central Terminal to a Zero of Potential in the Living Human Subject,"[12] "Exploratory Lead Systems and 'Zero Potentials.'"[13] A number of writings concerned "The Electrical Field Produced by the Eccentric Current Dipole in the Nonhomogeneous Conductor,"[14] and various alterations and problems of nonhomogeneity.[15, 16] He published 16 reports between 1950 and 1969 on these biophysical problems.

Dr. Bayley was a member of the original Research Committee of the American Heart Association and was instrumental in establishing many of its present policies. He was one of the first Established Investigators of the American Heart Association. In 1959 he received a citation for Distinguished Service to Research from that organization. He was an honorary Fellow of the American College of Cardiology and a Founding Member of the Southern Society for Clinical Investigation.

In his obituary, written by two of his associates and friends, L. L. Conrad, M.D., and J. M. Kalbfleisch, M.D.,[17] Dr. Bayley was described as "a person of superb clinical acumen, modesty, enthusiasm, and genius." He was a gifted teacher with an uncanny ability for analysis and synthesis which served as a constant stimulus to his students.

FIG. 1 Robert Hebard Bayley, M.D., 1906–1969.

Ironically, he suffered from the same diseases for which he had strived to bring about better understanding. In his final years he suffered two episodes of myocardial infarction and severe intermittent claudication. Up to his death following vascular surgery on April 11, 1969, Dr. Bayley served as Professor of Medicine at the University of Oklahoma Medical Center and was a cardiologist of international reputation and renown.

References

1. Blackford LM, Davenport TF, Bayley RH: Right aortic arch. *Am J Dis Child* 44, 823–844 (1932)
2. Bayley RH: Dynamic dilatation of the thoracic aorta. *Am Heart J* 585–594 (1933)
3. Bayley RH: Thyroid crisis. *Surg Gynecol Obstet* 59, 41–47 (1934)
4. Bayley RH: The significance of the duration of Q3 with respect to coronary disease. *Am Heart J* 18, 308–311 (1939)
5. Bayley RH: The potential produced by cardiac muscle. *Proc Soc Exp Biol Med* 42, 699–702 (1939)
6. Bayley RH: Monte LA: Acute, local ventricular ischemia, or impending infarction, caused by dissecting aneurysm. *Am Heart J* 25, 262–270 (1943)
7. Bayley RH, The normal human ventricular gradient. *Am Heart J* 25, 16–35 (1943)
8. Bayley RH: On certain applications of modem electrocardiographic theory to the interpretation of electrocardiograms which indicate myocardial disease. *Am Heart J* 26, 769–831 (1943)
9. Bayley RH, Bedford DR, First SR: Peri-infarction block. *Circ Res* 2, 31–36 (1950)
10. Bayley RH, Head JF, Kinard CL, Reynolds EW: The zero of potential of the electric field produced by the heart beat. *Circ Res* 2, 4–12 (1954)
11. Bayley RH, Kinard CL: The zero of potential of the electric field produced by the heart beat. *Circ Res* 2, 104–111 (1954)
12. Bayley RH, Schmidt AE: The problem of adjusting the Wilson central terminal to a zero of potential in the living human subject. *Circ Res* 3, 94–102 (1955)
13. Bayley RH: Exploratory lead systems and "Zero Potentials." *Ann NY Acad Sci* 65, 1110–1126 (1957)
14. Bayley RH, Berry PM: The electrical field produced by the eccentric current dipole in the nonhomogeneous conductor. *Am Heart J* 63, 808–820 (1952)
15. Bayley RH, Berry PM: Body surface potentials produced by the eccentric dipole in the heart wall of the nonhomogeneous volume conductor. *Am Heart J* 65, 200–207 (1963)
16. Bayley RH, Berry PM, Kalbfeisch JM: Changes in the body's QRS surface potentials produced by alterations in certain compartments of the nonhomogeneous conducting model. *Am Heart J* 77, 517–528 (1969)
17. Conrad LL, Kalbfleisch JM: Obituary. *Am Heart J* 78, 846–847 (1969)

Howard Burchell

R. Brandenburg, m.d.

Section of Cardiology, University of Arizona Health Sciences Center, Tucson, Arizona, USA

The American College of Cardiology bestowed the Gifted Teacher Award on Dr. Howard Burchell at its annual convocation in 1984 (Fig. 1). The opening paragraph of this citation was as follows—

The career of Dr. Burchell has been characterized by insatiable curiosity, dedication to scholarship, and a continued pursuit of the truth. His quiet, gentle manner and subtle humor belie his intense and tenacious devotion to the acquisition of knowledge from the laboratory and its application to the patient.

These comments continue to be an appropriate salutation to this learned physician. Howard Burchell was born November 28, 1907, in Athens, Ontario, Canada. His postgraduate education was at the University of Toronto, where he received the M.D. degree in 1932. Following a rotating internship at Toronto General Hospital, he served an additional year as intern in pathology at the same hospital. During his career, he acquired an outstanding array of accomplishments and credentials. From 1934 to 1936 he was Mellon Scholar at Mercy Hospital, Pittsburgh, Pennsylvania, and Instructor in Medicine at the University of Pittsburgh. He was a Fellow in Medicine in the Mayo Foundation, Rochester, Minnesota, for the next three years (1936–1939). Next came a one-year term as Special Student at the London Hospital Medical School and Heart Hospital in London, England. In 1940 he was appointed to the staff of the Mayo Clinic, where he served as Consultant in Medicine and Cardiology until 1968 (except for the period 1942–1946 when he was a Consultant to the U.S. Airforce in England, Germany, and Randolph Field, Texas). He rose rapidly through academic ranks to become Professor of Medicine in the Mayo Foundation, University of Minnesota (now the Mayo Graduate School of Medicine) in 1952. In 1968, he took early retirement from the Mayo Clinic and Mayo Foundation to become Professor of Medicine and Chief of Cardiology at the University of Minnesota Hospitals. In 1975 he retired from the University of Minnesota and became Senior Consultant in Cardiology, University Unit, Northwestern Hospital. During each winter quarter from 1976 to 1981, he also was Visiting Professor at Stanford University, and served in a similar capacity 1978 to 1981 at the University of Arizona.

Dr. Burchell was certified by the American Board of Internal Medicine (Cardiovascular Disease) in 1941 and the American Board of Preventive Medicine in 1954. He is numbered among the members of Alpha Omega Alpha, Sigma Xi, the American Physiologic Society, American Heart Association, Central Society for Clinical Research, Association of American Physicians, American Medical Association, and Aerospace Medical Association. Other prestigious appointments include service as Chairman of the Research Committee of the American Heart Association from 1955 to 1956 and a term (1952–1956) as a Member of the Aeromedical Panel of the Scientific Advisory Board of the Airforce. He was a Member, National Heart Council (NIH) from 1958 to 1962. Dr. Burchell served as Editor-in Chief of *Circulation* from 1965 to 1970. He received the James B. Herrick Award of the American Heart Association in 1972.

Fig. 1 Dr. Howard Burchell.

His clinical and investigative interests have been diverse, extensive, and continuous, resulting in almost 400 published articles. It is noteworthy that 15 of these discourses have been produced since 1983, the most recent still in press! Areas of particular interest to Dr. Burchell have been electrocardiography—the excitation process, rhythm abnormalities and their mechanisms, and alterations in body potassium and its effect on repolarization and depolarization; pulmonary vascular disease; the role of dye dilution curves in cardiac catheterization; therapeutic and ill effects of quinidine and digitalis; uncommon manifestations of common heart disease as well as the recognition of uncommon heart disease; the spectrum of pericardial disease and selected areas of valvular and coronary disease.

A review of his bibliography attests to the numerous residents, trainees, fellows, and consultants who have been encouraged and stimulated to pursue investigations with him. Cardiovascular conferences at the Mayo Clinic in the 1950s and early 1960s are remembered by all who attended because the presiding team of Drs. Burchell, Jesse Edwards, Raymond Pruitt, and Earl Wood invariably provided a stimulating and quality educational experience.

Over the span of his career Howard Burchell has maintained a special interest in the historical background of cardiovascular disease, and presented and written informative and interesting reports on the subject. His precise, creative, and accurate use of scientific terms and data became well known to associates and contributors to *Circulation* during his years as Editor-in-Chief of that journal. A recent editorial review, "Thoughts on Eponyms," is recommended.[1]

Dr. Burchell and his wife, the former Margaret Helmholz, are the parents of four daughters. Mrs. Burchell is an enthusiastic sportswoman, particularly adept at swimming and tennis, in addition to her other interests. Dr. Burchell is almost tireless in his use of medical libraries. In addition, he reads widely in nonmedical literature. Hiking and swimming are his main athletic interests.

It is seldom that a clinical cardiologist can be so productive in such diverse areas of clinical and basic science. Perhaps even more remarkable is for one to continue this activity up to the ninth decade (and probably beyond!). His quiet, scholarly, and ethical personal qualities added to his productivity and intelligence account for the admiration and respect felt for him by his colleagues.

References

1. Burchell H: Thoughts on eponyms. *Intern J Cardiol* 8, 229 (1985)

The Meteoric Career of Paul Wood

E. Grey Dimond, m.d.

University of Missouri-Kansas City, Kansas City, Missouri, USA

Soon after the death of Paul Wood at age 54 on July 13, 1962, I was given several items from his consulting room. Among these was the tape from the dictation he had been doing just up to the moment before he was stopped by chest pain. And the other was a folder in which he had, in his own hand, summarized his career and noted those professional efforts that he had considered his best achievements.

The tape, in essence his last professional act, displays his skill as he carefully constructed for the referring physician a report of his findings.

The tape also gives hints of the very vital human inside the consultant's robe, as he remonstrates with a London automobile dealer over the terms for the purchase of a quite fancy sports car. And it is this interplay of remarkable clinician and gay-spirited human that made Paul Wood such a delight, challenge, stimulus, and, yes a painful experience. Among my collection of friends, he was the quickest witted, the most opinionated, the best informed, the most sensitive, the most vain, the most skilled, the most energetic, the most mercurial, the most charming, the most dogmatic, the most provocative, the most stimulating. An afternoon in his clinic at the National Heart Hospital demonstrated all these qualities, with his disciples alternating between quaking fear of his riposte and awe over his dazzling diagnostic skill.

And the same evening, a guest at his home would see all of these same facets at play, but somehow the thermostat turned down on the abrasive ones and revealed a charming, outreaching host, presiding, pouring, carving, toasting, tugging one and all on a tour of his garden with a joyful moment before his spritely fountain.

His life, laid out in statistics has a hint of the full man. He was born in Conoor, India in 1907. His father was in Indian Civil Service. In that spartan British way, Paul, at age 3 ½ years, was sent to a boarding school in Kent, England, where he remained until age 13. His father had taken up fruit farming in Australia and Paul was further educated at Launceston Grammar School in Tasmania and then Trinity College, Melbourne University. He graduated, M.B., B.S. in 1931. He did his house officership at Christchurch General Hospital, New Zealand. It was there he met Elizabeth Guthrie, and they were married in England in December 1934.

These are the data, but there is also that extra dimension that was special. He was on Melbourne University's rugby team and he made the All Australian Universities' team and

played against the Japanese and New Zealand universities. In 1931 he won the 12-mile Langlauf cross-country ski event from the top of the Tasman Glacier to Ball Hut, Mount Cork, New Zealand.

Among the listings of the milestones he felt worth recording, there is this cryptic comment: "Crimes (detected), successfully impersonated the Queen when she visited Melbourne as the Duchess of York in 1927." In those wonderful days of less concern for security, the Duchess was to be driven in an open car around the running track inside the stadium to be seen, to wave, to smile. At about the expected time, an open car, complete with liveried attendance entered the stadium and a splendidly attired female, with the large hat enjoyed by English noblewomen, waved grandly, regally, during the slow circumnavigation of the track. Quite an impish prank by a 20-year-old college man.

In London, at age 27 (1934), he was Resident Medical Officer at the National Heart Hospital. In 1935, the University of London organized a postgraduate insititution and the Hammersmith Hospital was selected as the clinical facility for this new school. The key professorship in medicine was given to Francis Fraser. He brought in young Wood, age 27, to found the section of cardiology, and in January 1938, at age 33, Wood was appointed Physician to the Outpatient Department of the National Heart Hospital.

The war years came and he was in service from 1942 to 1947. Upon his return to England in 1947, Fraser asked him to set up the Institute of Cardiology and the next year he became Dean and Director of the Institute and the National Heart Hospital, and Physician-in-Charge, Cardiac Department, Brompton Hospital; remarkable recognition by the London establishment of the young colonial. With five years out for war service he was still but 42 when these major appointments came.

This began the energetic and fruitful years in which he combined his remarkable skills at the bedside with the data he was obtaining in the cardiac catheter laboratory. His main contribution to medicine was in the refinement and perfection of clinical bedside diagnosis. His technique was based on simple deductive reasoning, simple but multiplied by his remarkable acuity of observation of the precordial movement, the venous pulse, the tactile sensation, and the stethoscope. No one perhaps will ever again have an equal skill, because Wood spanned the era of supremacy of the bedside to the present supremacy of the machine.

FIG. 1   Paul Wood. (From Dimond EG: Paul Wood Revisited. *Am J Cardiol* 30. 121 (1972). Reproduced with permission of the publisher.

In 1950 he published his landmark book, *Diseases of the Heart and Circulation* and in his preface he made clear his

awareness of the changes bearing down to alter the role of the clinician,

> . . . yet there is already plenty of evidence to show that we are in danger of losing our clinical heritage and of pinning too much faith in figures thrown up by machines.

Paul Wood's influence on cardiology was vast and it was based in the main on his book and on his personal teachings at the National Heart Hospital. In the 1950s, the National Heart Hospital was Paul Wood. Graduate students from throughout the world came there to study under him. The clinical performance of Wood was just that. A master at work, enjoying the game, sparring, testing, teasing, hammering. Paul Wood's rate of thinking, his almost painful sensitivity, his high good humor punctuated by flashed smiles, quick jibes, were all part of the show, but the essence of the experience remained with one: the absolute mastery of bedside diagnosis.

Readers who want to capture, to relive a hint of what was Paul Wood (and be made aware of what is meant by true bedside skill), should try to view Wood's film, "The Jugular Venous Pulse." There one can hear his voice, see his hands, understand his analysis, and synthesize what it was like to be in the outpatient clinic on the day when Paul Wood attended.

He suffered a myocardial infarction while in his office one day, was hospitalized, and instructed his physician that if the event arose, no resuscitation was to be attempted, "or I'll come back and haunt you." Two days later, on July 13, 1962, he arrested.

Eugene A. Stead, Jr.*

JAMES V. WARREN, M.D.

The Ohio State University, College of Medicine, Columbus, Ohio, USA

Eugene Stead has done so much for the advancement of cardiology that some look on him as a cardiologist, but he really is not the card-carrying type. I don't think that he ever was responsible for an electrocardiographic reading service nor ever passed a cardiac catheter. He certainly is not a conventional cardiologist, but Dr. Stead is not a conventional anything. Nevertheless he is responsible for the development of important concepts which influence today's practice of medicine and cardiology. He has been responsible for the evolution of our ideas about circulatory failure, for development of diagnostic cardiac catheterization, and possibly most important of all, spawning a generation of academicians and inquisitive practicing physicians (Table I). He helped bring the new science of medicine to the bedside, but always coupled with demonstrations of his function as a caring thoughtful physician. He operated in the search mode, always asking questions, not the sponge mode just sopping up facts (Fig. 1). Though past 70, he still practices what he preaches, has an active interest in medicine and its questions, and remains a consummate physician.

Eugene Stead was born in Atlanta, Georgia. He attended Emory University and when a friend bet him that he couldn't get straight A's in anatomy, he decided to go to Emory University Medical School where he did get straight A's in anatomy. On completion of his training there he went to Boston to serve as a surgical house officer at the Peter Bent Brigham Hospital. He then did the unusual—a Stead hallmark—he took a second appointment as a medical house officer. He next went to Cincinnati as chief resident physician under Dr. Blankenhorn, and later returned to Boston to take up a fellowship at the Thorndike Memorial Laboratory, then a Harvard-supported research effort at the Boston City Hospital. There he fell under the influence of Dr. Soma Weiss. Dr. Weiss, a young charismatic physician from Hungary, was the classic example of the teacher and clinical investigator of the early part of the twentieth century. He studied a variety of subjects such as carotid sinus syncope, beriberi heart disease, and others and made them well known; on the other hand, he never became a slave to the laboratory bench and always remained a clinician. Dr. Stead followed the same pattern. When Dr. Weiss, at the age of 39, was asked to become Har-

vard's Hersey Professor of the Theory and Practice of Physik and Chief of the medical service at the Peter Bent Brigham Hospital, Dr. Stead went along as one of his lieutenants. Unfortunately, Dr. Weiss died in early 1942 at the peak of his career, but Dr. Stead had already arranged to return to Atlanta as Professor of Medicine and Chairman of the department at Emory University. He brought a group of young investigators with him, laboratories were set up in the basement of Grady Hospital and a never-to-be-forgotten era of medicine in that hospital was instituted. Dr. Stead ran the show, set the pace, and emphasized being a good doctor along with scientific theory and investigation. The youngsters worked diligently in their laboratories and at the bedside. There were notable contributions. The first diagnostic cardiac catheterization was carried out. The first demonstration that the kidney completely extracts substances such as sodium para-aminohippurate was demonstrated. The role of the kidney in congestive heart failure was demonstrated. Perhaps most notable of all was a conceptual presentation called "Fluid Dynamics in Congestive Heart Failure" which revolutionized contemporary thinking about the formation of edema in congestive heart failure. The five-year period (1942–1947) at Grady Hospital was remarkable.

Moving to Duke University as Professor and Chairman of the Department of Medicine, the stage was somewhat larger, the numbers were greater, and his role in producing the academicians of the next generation continued to expand. He really became the Pied Piper of academic medicine. Table I shows some of the people trained under Dr. Stead who subsequently came either to chair departments or became officials at a wide range of medical schools. He did not get his hands very dirty from then on in the laboratory, but he was very close to it and his young colleagues were there morning, noon, and night.

Dr. Stead has been recognized as one of the leaders in American medicine and has received many awards and accolades. He is a broadly based internist with a particular interest in cardiovascular disease, but never was so restricted to be able to call himself a cardiologist. He did become the Editor of the journal, *Circulation*, a post he held for five years. His impact on cardiovascular medicine has been great, not only in the development of concepts and techniques, but particularly in the matter of developing cardiologists as exemplary physicians.

Eugene Stead's personal involvement in research began soon after his arrival in Boston. He did some early work on

---

*Much of this article was previously published in the *Transactions of the Association of American Physicians*, vol. xciii, 1980. It is reproduced here with permission.

TABLE I   Department chairmen and academic officers trained by Eugene Stead, M.D.

Paul B. Beeson	William H. Knisely
Ivan L. Bennett	Peter O. Kohler
Morton D. Bogdonoff	James J. Leonard
Stuart Bondurant	Samuel P. Martin
Philip Bondy	Henry D. McIntosh
Rubin Bressler	Charles E. Mengel
C. Hilmon Castle	A. Donald Merritt
Leighton Cluff	Earl N. Metz
William P. Deiss	H. Victor Murdaugh
Richard V. Ebert	Jack D. Myers
E. Harvey Estes	Bert W. O'Malley
Abner Golden	Roscoe R. Robinson
Sidney Grossberg	Joseph C. Ross
John B. Hickam	Peritz Scheinberg
Bernard C. Holland	Theodore B. Schwartz
J. William Hollingsworth	J. Graham Smith
Wallace R. Jensen	Jarnes V. Wanen
David Kipnes	Arnold M. Weissler
	James V. Wyngaarden

the then new and powerful mercurial diuretics, and a new compound known as T-1824, or Evans blue dye, later to figure so importantly in blood volume and circulatory dynamic measurements. He worked with Richard Ebert and others on studying reactions of the peripheral circulation. He did one of the few animal studies of his career there by observing how, under the conditions of shock, the liver could not produce plasma albumin in adequate amounts. He learned to be a critical and inventive clinical investigator. After moving back to Atlanta, the investigative program turned to wartime subjects such as the treatment of shock with human serum albumin. I well remember the first case. The patient was brought to the Grady Hospital emergency room on a busy Saturday night with multiple stab wounds over his body. He had bled profusely. Sophisticated measurements were made in the emergency room as replacement therapy was given. It was the beginning of many studies of hemodynamics which had never before been possible in humans.

While sitting around the emergency room on those Saturday nights waiting for patients presenting with shock, the conversations turned to other subjects. A prime topic was the questions that Dr. Stead had about the then accepted mechanisms for the development of edema in congestive heart failure. An article was developed which eventually became a, perhaps *the*, milestone in the Stead bibliography. It was published in the *Archives of Internal Medicine* in 1944 under the title "Fluid Dynamics in Congestive Heart Failure." It aroused great conversation, forward failure versus backward failure, especially at the Atlantic City meetings with such people as Homer Smith, Isaac Starr, and Tinsley Harrison. Interestingly enough, the paper, predominantly an interpretive manuscript, was turned down for publication by the *Journal of Clinical Investigation* because it did not have enough numbers in it!

At about this time, a distinguished delegation lead by Dr. Alfred Blalock from the Office of Scientific Research and

Development, a wartime medical research agency, arrived in Atlanta. They proposed to Dr. Stead that a program involving the recently introduced technique of cardiac catheterization be set up in Atlanta to study the problems of shock, then still a desperate medical need of this country at war. Such a program was rapidly undertaken. Atlanta, along with New York and London, became one of the pioneer centers in the world in the development of a totally new understanding of human cardiovascular physiology. The Atlanta group set up normal standards of cardiac output, and its variations under physiologic and pathologic conditions. They were the first to diagnose congenital heart disease with a catheter, the first to demonstrate the role of the liver in the clearance of bacteria from the blood stream, and the first to demonstrate alterations of renin content of renal venous blood. I mention all of these dividends to point out another characteristic of Gene Stead. He sponsored and, indeed, made it possible for this program to be carried out by his younger associates. In most of the papers that were published, the name of Stead does not appear. He wanted the younger people to get the credit. I think this is key to the understanding of Gene Stead.

Development at Emory was truly astonishing for five years, but the increasing enmeshment of Dr. Stead in the operation of the school, and his eventual appointment as Dean for a short period of time, took its toll. The offer of a fresh new field of development at Duke presented a new challenge for him. The phenomenal pace of development at Duke is well known.

Dr. Stead was personally involved less in the laboratory at Duke, but he sent many of his youngsters scurrying off to solve a wide diversity of clinical problems. His thinking went in other directions. While at Duke, along with his colleague, Philip Handler, he began working on a new medical school curriculum. Again, it was a typical Stead production: a remarkably different curriculum departing from usual standards, starting clinical clerkships in the second year. It has already seen the test of time. He developed new ideas about controlling food intake, low fat cooking, and about physician's assistants. His name became synonymous with programs of that sort. He retired as Chairman in 1967, yet Gene Stead has remained an effective stimulating member of the Duke family. Today, he is still a prominent figure of forward thinking in medicine. He has developed a computer-based "textbook" of medicine and new ideas about nursing and geriatrics.

Whether it is a matter of developing a department of medicine, setting up a program in the laboratory, or dealing with people, Gene has always gone about things with a direct vigor and with a lack of concern about how others might do it. He would do it the best way he knew how. If one were to present ten medical educators with a situation to solve, nine would probably do it in a similar conventional way, Gene would be different. It is not that his methods are different, but that they are done with a difference that is inventive and stimulating. Books about Gene have already been written. One, interestingly enough, was co-authored by his secretary of many years, Bess Cebe. Even though he is officially retired at Duke,

FIG. 1   Eugene Stead in the "teaching mode." (From Warren JE: Presentation of the George M. Kober Medal to Eugene A. Stead. *Transactions of the Association of American Physicians*, vol. xciii, 1980. Reproduced with permission from the author and publisher.)

he is still going strong. For the last several years he has served as a "distinguished physician" of the Veterans Administration at the Durham VA hospital. He still makes ward rounds, teaches, and consults in his own provocative way. Evelyn, his wife, is a graduate of Mount Holyoke, was Soma Weiss' secretary when they met. She has done many things including writing a book with Gloria K. Warren, *Low Fat Cookery* which has sold over 100,000 copies. Evelyn and Gene collect

ancient lighting devices and are actually licensed antique dealers.

A group of academicians have been produced, dedicated to teaching who have never gotten too far from the bedside, never been totally immersed in the laboratory. At the same time they have maintained a questioning and scientific air. They were all devoted to the Stead "search mode." Being in the "sponge mode," just sopping up medical facts, was not enough. I can summarize no better than one of his pupils who said, "People respect, admire and love Dr. Stead because within the turmoil of this life he seems to have a simplicity, directness and detachment which makes him able to be calm and helpful. Furthermore, his character is virtuous. At times when most men are selfish, his qualities of selflessness and dedication loom large."

Selected References

Ebert RV, Stead EA, Warren JV, Watts WS: Plasma protein replacement after hemorrhage in dogs with and without shock. *Am J Physiol* 136, 299 (1942)

Stead EA, Warren JV, Brannon ES: Effect of lanatoside C on the circulation of patients with congestive heart failure. *Arch Intern Med* 81, 282 (1948)

Stead EA, Warren, Merrill AJ, Brannon ES: The cardiac output in male subjects as measured by the technique of right atrial catheterization. *J Clin Invest* 44, 326 (1945)

Wagner GS, Cebe B, Rozear MP: E. A. Stead, Jr.: *What This Patient Needs is a Doctor*. Carolina Academic Press, Durham (1978)

Warren JV: Presentation of the George M. Kober Medal to Eugene A. Stead. *Trans Assoc Am Phys* 93, 28 (1980)

Warren JV, Stead EA: Fluid dynamics in chronic congestive heart failure. *Arch Intern Med* 73, 138 (1944)

Warren JV, Brannon ES, Stead EA, Merrill AJ: The effect of venesection and the pooling of blood in the extremities on the atrial pressure and cardiac output in normal subjects with observations on acute circulatory collapse in three instances. *J Clin Invest* 44, 337 (1945)

Weiss S, Stead EA, Warren JV, Bailey OT: Scleroderma heart disease. *Arch Intern Med* 71, 749 (1943)

Michael E. DeBakey

ANTONIO M. GOTTO, JR., M.D., D. PHIL.

Department of Medicine, Baylor College of Medicine, Houston, Texas, USA

Michael E. DeBakey, M.D., is internationally recognized as a medical innovator, a dedicated teacher, a premier surgeon, and a distinguished medical statesman. Dr. DeBakey currently serves as Chancellor of Baylor College of Medicine, where he is also Olga Keith Wiess Professor and Chairman of the Department of Surgery and Distinguished Service Professor. He is Director of The DeBakey Heart Center, which was established in Houston in 1985 by Baylor College of Medicine for research and public education in the prevention and treatment of heart disease.

Student and Physician

Michael Ellis DeBakey (Fig. 1), born September 7, 1908, in Lake Charles, Louisiana, attended university in his home state, receiving his bachelor's degree from Tulane University in New Orleans in 1930. He continued at Tulane for his medical degree, awarded in 1932. He completed his internship at Charity Hospital in New Orleans and residencies in surgery at Charity Hospital; at the University of Strasbourg under Professor René Leriche, whose field was circulation; and at the University of Heidelberg under Professor Martin Kirschner. His mentor in New Orleans was Alton Ochsner.

In 1937, Dr. DeBakey joined the faculty of Tulane University. He volunteered for military service during World War II, and in 1942 was named Director of the Surgical Consultants' Division in the Surgeon General's Office. He received the Legion of Merit Award in 1945. Today, he holds the rank of Colonel in the United States Army (Reserve).

When the war ended, Dr. DeBakey returned to Tulane as Associate Professor of Surgery. In 1948, he accepted the chairmanship of the Department of Surgery at Baylor University College of Medicine in Houston. He initiated the school's 1969 separation from Baylor University and was appointed President of the newly formed Baylor College of Medicine. He has been Chancellor since 1979.

Scientist

Michael DeBakey is best known for his innovative and landmark contributions in the surgical treatment of cardiovascular diseases. When he entered medical school, heart surgery did not exist: he was part of the development of heart surgery. In a career spanning more than six decades he has developed many new operations, devices, and surgical instruments for the improvement of patient care.

1930s–1940s

In 1932, as a young medical student, Michael DeBakey invented the roller pump that became a major component of the heart-lung machine and thus helped usher in the era of open heart surgery.

1950s

Through angiographic studies of patients with cardiovascular disease, Dr. DeBakey recognized the segmental nature of vascular disease. This observation allowed effective treatment to be undertaken even while the various causes of disease remained obscure. Dr. DeBakey classified arterial occlusive disease on the basis of its recognized anatomicopathologic characteristics into atherosclerotic lesions affecting (1) the coronary arteries, (2) the major branches of the aortic arch, (3) the visceral branches of the abdominal aorta, and (4) the terminal abdominal aorta and its major branches. He described and classified its patterns in these major arterial beds as proximal, midproximal, and distal—with the first two patterns amenable and the last usually not amenable to surgical treatment.

Between 1950 and 1953, Dr. DeBakey developed the Dacron and Dacron-velour artificial grafts for replacement of diseased arteries. He sewed the first Dacron graft on his wife's sewing machine, using sewing skills he had learned as a child from his mother. Later, the grafts were made using a knitting machine he, along with a research associate from the Philadelphia College of Textiles and Science, had developed. On January 5, 1953, Dr. DeBakey performed the first successful resection and graft replacement of a fusiform aneurysm of the thoracic aorta. His Dacron artificial arteries are now used throughout the world in the treatment of diseased vessels.

In 1953, Dr. DeBakey performed the first successful carotid endarterectomy. This procedure showed that a major cause of strokes could be treated effectively. His other surgical firsts in the 1950s included the resection and graft replacement of an aneurysm of the distal aortic arch and upper de-

FIG. 1   Dr. Michael E. DeBakey.

scending thoracic aorta, the resection of a dissecting aortic aneurysm, the resection and graft replacement of an aneurysm of the ascending aorta (all 1954), the resection and graft replacement of an aneurysm of the thoracoabdominal aorta (1955), and patch-graft angioplasty in conjunction with endarterectomy (1958).

1960s–1970s

In 1963, Dr. DeBakey described a fundamental concept of therapy in arterial disease, namely, that surgical treatment could be effective in many forms of aortic and arterial disease because of the localization of the pathologic process and the patent and relatively normal proximal and distal arterial beds. For this contribution, Dr. DeBakey received the Albert Lasker Award for Clinical Research.

In 1964, Drs. DeBakey and Edward Garrett performed the first successful aortocoronary artery bypass using a vein from the leg. Dr. DeBakey and his associates did not publish the case until late 1972, several years after René Favaloro described successful coronary bypass surgery at the Cleveland Clinic.

In the early 1960s, Dr. DeBakey began testing artificial heart models to sustain the lives of calves. Although some of the animals lived for months, test results to date have not warranted permanent implantation in humans.

In 1966, Dr. DeBakey was the first to use a partial artificial heart successfully. The device was a left ventricular bypass pump. He conceived the idea of lining a bypass pump and its connections with Dacron-velour, a concept he later applied to the Dacron arterial grafts he had developed. Dr. DeBakey's early research on artificial hearts and his testimony before Congress led to federal support of the artificial heart program. Since its inception, Dr. DeBakey has chaired the US-USSR artificial heart program of the National Heart, Lung, and Blood Institute.

Over an 18-month period beginning in 1968, Dr. DeBakey performed 12 heart transplantations. In a historic multiple-transplantation procedure, also performed in 1968, he led a team of surgeons in transplanting the heart, kidneys, and one lung of a donor into four recipients. Because of organ rejection problems, the transplantation program was discontinued in 1970; however, it was resumed in 1984 when the advent of cyclosporine and other advances made the procedure more feasible.

1980s–1990s

In recent years Dr. DeBakey has continued to expand the frontiers of cardiovascular research. In 1983, Dr. Joseph Melnick, Dr. DeBakey, and colleagues reported evidence of cytomegalovirus involvement in the arterial walls of some patients with atherosclerosis. Since replicating virus was not detected, the study suggested that the occurrence of cytomegalovirus early in life may initiate the lesions that later cause atherosclerosis. Extending this line of investigation, Dr. DeBakey and colleagues in 1987 reported that patients with heart disease have higher-than-normal levels of antibodies to cytomegalovirus.

Architect

Michael DeBakey has been instrumental in shaping some of the leading medical institutions of this century. As a member of the Task Force on Medical Services of the Hoover Commissions on Organization of the Executive Branch of the Government in 1949 and 1954, Dr. DeBakey led the movement to establish the National Library of Medicine, which is now the world's largest and most prestigious depository of medical archives. He served on the first board of regents of the library and has since been a consultant on many occasions. In 1964, President Johnson appointed Dr. DeBakey Chairman of The President's Commission on Heart Disease, Cancer, and Stroke. As a result of the commission's recommendations, regional medical libraries were established at strategic geographic sites throughout the country to expedite the dissemination of medical information.

Dr. DeBakey's work in the Surgeon General's Office during World War II led to the development of mobile army surgical hospitals (MASH units). He later helped establish a specialized medical and surgical centers system for treating military personnel returning from the war, which eventually became the Veterans Administration Medical Center System. Dr. DeBakey's suggestion that veterans with certain medical histories be followed up in a systematic way led to the establishment of the Committee on Veterans Medical Problems of the National Research Council and an extensive medical research program administered by the Veterans Administration.

It occurred to Dr. DeBakey that the center concept could be extended usefully to civilian medicine. In the late 1950s, Dr. DeBakey testified before Congress to recommend the establishment of multidisciplinary centers for the study of a given disease. He believed that researchers studying a particular disease would be more productive working as a group in geographic proximity. This concept is represented by the establishment of program project grants and categorical centers, such as cancer, cardiovascular, and diabetes centers. The Cardiovascular Research and Training Center, which Dr. DeBakey established and directed in the Texas Medical Center, became one of the first embodiments of this concept. This center, supported initially by a program project grant, was unique in its multidisciplinary approach to cardiovascular research and therapy. Under Dr. DeBakey's leadership, several investigators were recruited to work in the center, including Drs. Mark Entman, Henry McIntosh, and Arnold Schwartz, as well as myself.

In the early 1970s, Baylor College of Medicine competed successfully for a Specialized Center of Research (SCOR) grant in arteriosclerosis. The SCOR and the Cardiovascular Research and Training Center were combined in 1974 as Baylor competed successfully to become the only National Research and Demonstration Center (NRDC) in Heart and Blood Vessel Disease. Dr. DeBakey served as Director and I served as Scientific Director of the NRDC. The NRDC combined, within one center, groups of investigators studying basic and clinical aspects of cardiovascular disease and groups carrying out educational projects geared toward physicians and the public. The demonstration projects allowed us to study the translation of cardiovascular knowledge into community applications. When funding for the NRDC expired, we secured endowment from private sources to continue community education activities and to support care laboratories and pilot projects through the establishment of The DeBakey Heart Center. The DeBakey Heart Center now includes a multidisciplinary transplantation center, of which Dr. James Young is the medical director. Recently, The DeBakey Heart Center became a joint activity of Baylor College of Medicine and The Methodist Hospital and began publication of the *DeBakey Heart Center Health Letter*.

Thus, with Dr. DeBakey's support and leadership, Baylor-Methodist in the 1970s became a national and international center for preventive medicine activities. In 1981, The Methodist Hospital inaugurated the Sid W. Richardson Institute for Preventive Medicine.

Statesman

Because of his extraordinary ability to bring his professional knowledge to bear on public policy, Michael DeBakey has earned an enviable reputation as a medical statesman. He has served as adviser to almost every president of the United States in the past half-century.

Dr. DeBakey has worked tirelessly in numerous capacities to improve standards of health and medical care. As an influential figure in national government, he continues to devote considerable time to advisory health committees. He has numerous consultative appointments, having served an unprecedented three terms on the National Heart, Lung, and Blood Advisory Council of the National Institutes of Health.

He has not, however, limited his work as a medical statesman to the United States. He has served as consultant in Europe, the Eastern bloc, and the Middle and Far East, and has helped establish health care systems, including cardiovascular surgery programs, throughout the world: in England, Belgium, Germany, Spain, Italy, Greece, Turkey, Yugoslavia, the USSR, Saudi Arabia, Egypt, the United Arab Emirates, Jordan, Morocco, Indonesia, Thailand, China, Japan, Australia, New Zealand, and Central and South American countries. He has also served as medical adviser to heads of state throughout the world.

Author

Michael DeBakey's lifelong scholarship is reflected in the more than 1,200 articles, chapters, and books he has published on various aspects of surgery, medicine, health, medical research, and medical education, as well as ethical, socioeconomic, and philosophic discussions in these fields. Many of these are considered classics. The books he has authored or edited include *The Blood Bank and the Technique and Therapeutics of Transfusions, Battle Casualties, Vascular Surgery in World War II, Christopher's Minor Surgery, Cold Injury, Buerger's Disease, Advances in Cardiac Valves,* and *Factors Influencing the Course of Myocardial Ischemia.*

Dr. DeBakey helped found and became the first editor of the *Journal of Vascular Surgery*. He was editor of *Year Book of General Surgery* for 14 years, and has served on the editorial boards of numerous eminent medical and surgical journals, including *Annals of Surgery, Surgery, Journal of Cardiovascular Surgery, Postgraduate Medicine, Contemporary Surgery, Comprehensive Therapy, Hippocrates,* and *Evaluation in the Health Professions.*

Dr. DeBakey and I coauthored *The Living Heart*, first published in 1977, to inform the general public about heart disease and strategies for its prevention. We subsequently collaborated with Ms. Lynne Scott and Dr. John Foreyt on *The Living Heart Diet*, which appeared in 1984 and became a *New York Times* best-seller.

Honoree

Michael DeBakey has received 36 honorary degrees from colleges and universities, including his alma mater, Tulane University, as well as hundreds of awards from educational institutions, professional and civic organizations, and governments worldwide. In 1969, President Johnson bestowed on him the Medal of Freedom with Distinction. In 1987, President Reagan awarded him the National Medal of Science. These and other major awards are listed in Table I.

Dr. DeBakey is a member of numerous distinguished medical societies, having served as president of many of these. He has been named an honorary member of many foreign medical societies, including the Royal Societies of England, Ireland, and Scotland.

Guide

Michael DeBakey has been an extremely active practicing surgeon and teacher and is legendary for his nonstop working days. He has performed more than 50,000 cardiovascular procedures and has trained some 1,000 surgeons. He takes a personal interest in his patients and their families and conducts a voluminous correspondence with former patients, students, and others who write to him. In 1976, in recognition of his dedication to the training of young physicians, his students from throughout the world founded the Michael E. DeBakey International Cardiovascular Surgical Society, later recast as the Michael E. DeBakey International Surgical Society to include more of his surgical residents and trainees. The organization conducts international medical symposia and confers the Michael E. DeBakey Award biennially. In 1978, in appreciation of Dr. DeBakey's untiring pedagogical and investigative efforts, the Trustees of Baylor College of Medicine established the Michael E. DeBakey Center for Biomedical Education and Research.

These many honors and medical and scientific achievements portray a man dedicated over a lifetime to the highest standards of excellence. But a description of accomplishments cannot convey a true picture of Michael DeBakey: a warm, caring humanitarian, a devoted husband and father, a comforter to thousands of patients, and a wise counselor and supporter of many, many colleagues.

From my vantage point, I have seen Dr. DeBakey's incalculable impact on Baylor College of Medicine and The Methodist Hospital. He has been responsible for bringing those institutions to international prominence. But I have also witnessed the warmth and hope he has brought to individual

TABLE I   Major awards received by Michael E. DeBakey

Legion of Merit, United States Army (1945)

American Medical Association Hektoen Gold Medal (1954)

Rudolph Matas Award in Vascular Surgery (1954, 1970)

International Society of Surgery Distinguished Service Award (1958)

American Medical Association Distinguished Service Award (1959)

International Society of Surgery Leriche Award (1959)

Albert Lasker Award for Clinical Research (1963)

St. Vincent Prize for Medical Sciences (1965)

Prix International Dag Hammarskjöld Great Collar with Golden Medal (1967)

American Heart Association Gold Heart Award (1968)

Medal of Freedom with Distinction (1969)

Eleanor Roosevelt Humanitarian Award (1969)

Yugoslavian Presidential Banner and Sash (1971)

Union of Soviet Socialist Republics Academy of Sciences Jubilee Medal (1973)

Independence of Jordan Medal (1980)

American Surgical Association Distinguished Service Award (1981)

National Medal of Science (1987)

Merit Order of the Republic of Egypt (1980)

International Society of Surgery Distinguished Service Award (1981)

National Medal of Science (1987)

Theodore E. Cummings Memorial Prize for Outstanding Contributions in Cardiovascular Disease (1987)

International Platform Association George Crile Award as The Trailblazer in Open Heart Surgery (1988)

Thomas Alva Edison Foundation Award (1988)

patients and their families, and the help he has given to countless colleagues and worthy causes. I have experienced his humanity and his sharing of suffering as he daily visited my daughter and wife during many months of my daughter's serious illness. I have seen Dr. DeBakey's fortitude as he faced illness himself. I feel truly blessed to have been one of the many to whom Michael DeBakey has been friend, counselor, confidant, and superb example of what a true physician should be.

Charles K. Friedberg

N. K. WENGER, M.D.

Emory University School of Medicine, Grady Memorial Hospital, Atlanta, Georgia, USA

With the untimely death of Dr. Charles K. Friedberg in 1972, the world cardiology community lost a master clinician and scholar, and a distinguished teacher, author, editor, and clinical research scientist. As Editor-in-Chief of *Circulation*, the Founding Editor of *Progress in Cardiovascular Disease*, Chief of the cardiology laboratories and the clinical cardiology services (1956–1969) at the Mount Sinai Hospital in New York City, and Director of the Annual Postgraduate Course in Cardiology for the American College of Physicians at that institution, he had exerted a profound influence on the clinical practice of cardiology, the training of clinical cardiologists, and the direction of cardiovascular research. The latter was reinforced by his appointment to key advisory committees of the National Heart and Lung Institute, the American Heart Association, and so forth. He was Clinical Professor of Medicine at the Mount Sinai School of Medicine as well.

Author of the classic textbook of cardiology, *Diseases of the Heart*, his knowledge was encyclopedic; and his eloquence in describing and his skills in analyzing, organizing, and categorizing clinical cardiac problems remain unparalleled. Several examples are offered.

The serial progression of mitral stenosis, as described in the first edition of the book in 1949, emphasizes its intrusion on the patient's ability to function (Friedberg, 1949, p. 571). The *stage of complete compensation* with "mitral obstruction of slight or moderate degree," characterizes an asymptomatic patient without activity limitation. But caution is given that "bacterial endocarditis, auricular fibrillation, embolization, pulmonary infection and acute pulmonary edema may suddenly abbreviate a previously uneventful course" . . . The *stage of left atrial failure*, . . . "in which compensation is imperfect and there are evidences of pulmonary congestion," because the left atrium "although dilated and hypertrophied, is no longer able to eject or accommodate the excess of blood dammed up behind the mitral obstruction." For this stage he defines the presence of exertional dyspnea and cyanosis, identifying shortness of breath as "the commonest complaint . . . and the one most disturbing to the patient," but notes that "palpitation and precordial distress . . . occur almost as frequently as dyspnea." And finally the *stage of right heart failure*, the "common termination of mitral stenosis" wherein the "longstanding increase of pressure in the pulmonary circulation . . . leads to dilatation and hypertrophy of the right ventricle . . . when right-sided failure is well developed, the dyspnea and orthopnea are alleviated due to the diminished right ventricular output." Interestingly, Mrs. Charles Friedberg (Gertrude), an author in her own right, would subsequently incorporate this pattern of progression into a short story ("Where Moth and Rust," *Atlantic Monthly*, September 1957).

An acknowledged expert in the recognition and management of subacute bacterial endocarditis, and coauthor with Emanuel Libman of the classic monograph on the topic in 1941, his diagnostic dictum has helped guide several generations of physicians: "The diagnosis of subacute bacterial endocarditis should be assumed as most probable whenever a patient with an organic cardiac murmur experiences fever, without apparent cause, for more than one week" (Friedberg, 1949, p. 793). Ever striving to limit the morbidity of cardiovascular disease, he stressed that "treatment should begin as early as possible before fatal or irremediable complications occur," appropriately noting that "early treatment demands early diagnosis." Citing at that time the need for ligation and interruption of an infected persistent ductus arteriosus or resection of an infected arteriovenous aneurysm, he could be expected, today, to champion early surgical intervention for infective endocarditis, designed to remove or correct infected valvular lesions.

But his favorite clinical problem was heart failure, and many of his research endeavors were designed to help elucidate (1) the pathoanatomic changes in the failing heart, (2) the chemical changes in the heart, and (3) (still of major interest today) the relationship of cardiac hypertrophy to cardiac failure (Friedberg, 1949, p. 45). In the first edition of *Diseases of the Heart*, published in 1949, he taught that

. . . cardiac enlargement (dilatation and hypertrophy) predisposes to heart failure because (1) it encroaches on cardiac reserve, which is limited by the ability of muscle fibers to elongate and to become thicker . . . (2) the enlarged heart . . . consumes a greater quantity of oxygen, although it performs the same amount of useful work (3) the thickened fibers do not permit . . . diffusion of oxygen, nutriments, and metabolites . . . in moderately hypertrophied fibers, anoxia occurs readily during exertion or with any arrhythmia or disease which increases the heart rate or reduces the diastolic period of recovery, and (4) the blood supply of the hypertrophied heart does not increase pari pasu with its enlargement . . . this deficiency becomes greatly intensified in the course of years if the coronary vessels become narrowed by arteriosclerosis.

FIG. 1   Snapshot of Dr. Charles Friedberg.

A number of years later he would emphasize the prevention of heart failure by "(1) prevention of heart disease; (2) prevention of heart failure in patients with compensated heart disease; and (3) prevention of recurrence of heart failure" (Friedberg, 1968).

A further valuable clinical approach was his classification of the presentations of illness according to their distinctive features. For example, he divided the clinical presentation of acute myocardial infarction into:

(1) cases dominated by pain, (2) cases dominated by shock, (3) cases dominated by pulmonary edema or other evidence of acute left ventricular failure, (4) cases characterized by the more gradual development or aggravation of congestive heart failure, and (5) cases dominated by complications (Friedberg, 1949, p. 426).

Again, in the category of classification and listing, is his description of the difficulty in recognition of the high output cardiac failure associated with hyperthyroidism:

A greater problem arises in those cases in which the predominant manifestations are cardiac and the presence and importance of the hyperthyroidism are discovered only secondarily. Such discovery will occur if the possibility of hyperthyroidism is considered in all cases in which auricular fibrillation, cardiac enlargement, or heart failure of uncertain etiology is encountered. Often in thyrocardiac patients, the thyroid gland is small and there is no exophthalmos, but there are usually a slight stare, warm moist skin, tachycardia, a high pulse pressure, and a history of weight loss. A search for an associated hyperthyroidism should be considered under the following circumstances: (1) paroxysmal or persistent auricular fibrillation of undetermined etiology, (2) heart failure without apparent cause or heart failure which does not respond to digitalis and other appropriate treat-

ment, (3) heart disease with unexplained tachycardia, (4) presence of congestive heart failure without significant fever, anemia, or serious vitamin B_1 deficiency, in which the circulation time is within the normal range (Friedberg, 1949, p. 924).

An extension of this approach was his interest (1970) in computers in cardiology (Friedberg, 1970). He emphasized that

. . . a primary deficiency is the lack of the fundamental information to provide appropriate matrices of such data as the incidence of disease and frequency of symptoms, signs and laboratory abnormalities as a basis for the program logic . . . An understanding of computer methods may thus improve our technique of handling symptoms and signs to make a clinical diagnosis and of teaching clinical diagnoses. It teaches us how to distribute emphasis in history taking and physical and laboratory examination in order to improve diagnostic accuracy by attaching major significance to items which are diagnostically important and omitting items which are not of value.

Surgical procedures performed on patients with cardiac disease, then, as now, were a topic of great interest. Dr. Friedberg believed that a cardiac consultation should involve a complete assessment of the patient, rather than simply a review of the cardiac status:

The cardiologist must give consideration to the surgical condition as well as to the cardiac status, for occasionally he will discover that the so-called 'surgical condition' is actually a 'medical' manifestation of the diseased heart, e.g., abdominal manifestations of myocardial infarction, rheumatic fever or subacute bacterial endocarditis . . . In general it may be stated that the cogency of the surgical indication is usually more important than the cardiac status in determining whether an operation should be performed.

In reference to the patient with atherosclerotic coronary heart disease, he commented that

The surgical risk is higher with coronary artery disease than with other cardiac diseases. Therefore it is especially important that the surgical indication be unequivocal...Frank heart failure increases surgical risk in patients with coronary disease as it does in rheumatic patients, but the close correlation with the degree of functional impairment is absent . . . Surgical risk is greatly enhanced if operation is performed in the course of a recent myocardial infarction. Unless there is an acute emergency demanding immediate operation, surgical procedures should be delayed at least three months following the acute myocardial infarction. If there is a history of increasing frequency of angina pectoris or of its occurrence with less and less provocation, an impending coronary occlusion is probable and operation should be avoided or delayed if possible. The association of Adams-Stokes syndrome also adds to the risk of operation and the latter should be performed only for urgent emergencies (Friedberg, 1949, p. 1030).

Diseases of the Heart, translated into half a dozen languages, was often referred to as the "bible of cardiology." The following, published in the *JAMA* just three days after his death, best characterizes this comprehensive monograph. "For cardiology, Dr. Friedberg's conspicuous success in maintaining uniform excellence while covering the entire field provides the stratospheric standard against which other single-authored texts can continue to be judged" (Spodick, 1972).

Dr. Richard Ross described well the attributes of Dr. Charles Friedberg as a teacher. "He knew what physicians needed to know, and he could tell it in language which was clear, forceful, and to the point" (Ross, 1972). With the explosion of information about cardiovascular diseases and their management, his unique talent was the ability to distinguish the essential from the extraneous. A Master of the American College of Physicians, his clinical teaching, as well as his editorship of *Circulation*, emphasized the interdependent elements of the basic triad in medicine—education, patient care, and research—all needed for the continued learning of the clinical cardiologist. His expansion of the Symposia in *Circulation* were designed to attain these objectives.

He was compiling a Symposium on Angina Pectoris at the time of his death; the Introduction, already completed, reads like a crystal ball view of the next decade (Friedberg, 1972). "Rather suddenly angina pectoris has become a glamour subject, intellectually and clinically exciting in almost every aspect—pathology, pathophysiology, diagnosis, treatment." Previously, it

> . . . was regarded as dull and drab. The physical examination was . . . unrevealing, . . . the electrocardiogram at rest was . . . normal, . . . treatment was simplistic . . . More than any other development, selective cinecoronary angiography is responsible for most of the exciting advances in our knowledge and management of angina pectoris . . .
>
> When angina pectoris occurs, even if it is relatively mild and stable, it represents not early and moderate, but advanced and very severe occlusive atherosclerosis of the coronary arteries . . . These conclusions are amply supported by the classic studies of Schlesinger, Blumgart, and their associates . . . There is a great need for a method to determine regional myocardial perfusion in angina pectoris, since regional ischemia is the essential physiologic basis of the disease . . .
>
> The heart of the problem of management of angina pectoris is now to do or not to do coronary bypass surgery . . . If coronary bypass surgery is now the heart of the problem of management of angina pectoris, then the appropriate surgical indication is the heart of the prob-

lem of coronary surgery. Appropriate indications cannot yet be formulated because of the inadequacy of data. Decisions must still be made on an individual basis with due regard for (1) anticipated natural history of the disease in a particular patient, (2) his satisfaction with his quality of life (tolerability of symptoms, capacity for useful work, and other activity), (3) the risk of the surgical procedure (in relation to the risk without operation), and (4) his willingness to assume this risk . . .

The relative outlook with medical and surgical treatment should be determined by prospective studies and by randomization of control and operated patients.

His views on cardiac transplantation (1969) were likewise prophetic (Friedberg, 1969):

> Despite the relatively poor outlook for prolonged survival at the present time, there are cogent reasons for continuing cardiac transplantation in the human: (1) By analogy with the experience in renal transplantation, one may anticipate, with increased experience, continued improvement in rate and duration of survival. At the present time, the majority of cadaveric renal grafts are functioning for more than a year. (2) A postoperative duration of more than a year in 2 patients and of more than 8 months in perhaps another 10 of the surviving patients suggests that survival for more than a year is an attainable objective for many recipients in the near future. (3) It is probable that the high incidence of early graft rejection and death of recipient were due to poor matching, even though there are occasional examples of relatively favorable survival despite relatively poor histocompatibility. There is reason, therefore, to hope that with the research efforts listed earlier, this problem will be overcome. (4) Although animal experimentation should predominate in any further studies of cardiac transplantation and the immunology of rejection, some human cardiac transplantation must also be performed, since it is doubtful that observations from animal experimentation can be consistently applied to the human, or that the necessary information for controlling rejection can be obtained from animal experimentation alone. The knowledge already obtained from human cardiac transplantation supports this viewpoint. (5) Human cardiac transplanation has been demonstrated to be a feasible surgical procedure with an acceptably low surgical mortality, considering the early stage of its development, and with a satisfactory functional result.

Born in New York City, Dr. Friedberg worked his way through undergraduate school and medical school by teaching mathematics at night school. At Columbia University, attesting to the breadth of his interests and his scholarship, he was awarded the Chandler Prize in history and the Einstein Prize in American Diplomacy. Following graduation from the College of Physicians and Surgeons of Columbia University in 1929, he was an intern at the Mount Sinai Hospital, continuing his career at that prestigious institution until his death almost half a century later.

From 1929 through 1932, he continued his postgraduate studies in physiology and pharmacology, as an Emanuel Libman Fellow, in Amsterdam and Vienna. A plaque in the Einthoven Laboratory in Leyden, The Netherlands, marks the desk area where Dr. Charles Friedberg studied and worked. Returning to the Mount Sinai Hospital, all the while maintaining a clinical practice, he continued his investigative pursuits. He worked with Dr. Louis Gross to define the cardiac pathoanatomy of rheumatic fever and lupus erythematosus; and his investigations with Emanuel Libman on bacterial endocarditis continued for many years.

But his greatest legacy was his unwavering pursuit of excellence in clinical care. He taught the value of meticulous observation; of seeking to understand the mechanisms underlying a clinical problem; of defining the expectations of therapy and determining if they were met; and of the role of true caring, of compassion, in the therapeutic equation. Continuing an extensive consultation practice throughout his career, he was often characterized as a "physician's physician." Dr. Charles Friedberg was the victim of an automobile collision while returning from an out-of-town consultation. For me, he was a beloved mentor and a cherished friend; he remains as a role model of the "compleat physician."

References

Friedberg CK: *Diseases of the Heart*, 1st ed. W. B. Saunders Co., Philadelphia (1949) 45, 426, 571, 793, 924, 1030

Friedberg CK: Computers in cardiology. *Prog Cardiovasc Dis* 13, 86 (1970)

Friedberg CK: Introduction. Some comments and reflections on changing interests and new developments in angina pectoris. *Circulation* 46, 1037 (1972)

Friedberg CK: Prevention of heart failure. *Am J Cardiol* 22, 190 (1968)

Friedberg CK: Selection of recipients for cardiac transplantation. *Prog Cardiovasc Dis* 12, 164 (1969)

Ross RS: Preface. *Circulation* 46, 1035 (1972)

Spodick DH: Book Forum. *JAMA* 221, 306 (1972)

Myron Prinzmetal

CLARENCE M. AGRESS, M.D.
Cedars-Sinai Medical Center, Los Angeles, California, USA

Myron Prinzmetal (Fig. 1) was born in Buffalo, New York, on February 8, 1908, the second son of Anna and Harry Prinzmetal. The family moved to Los Angeles where the death of Prinzmetal's invalid father forced his impoverished mother to run a boarding house for subsistence. Despite these hard beginnings, his brother, Isadore, became an outstanding lawyer, while Myron would leave his name in the annals of medical science.

Myron attended Roosevelt High School in Los Angeles and received a B.A. degree from U.C.L.A. in the year of the great depression. He won an M.A. degree in pharmacy at the University of California in San Francisco and, in 1933, his M.D. degree. While still a student he was a co-author of a paper on the effect of broncho-constricting drugs on intrapleural pressure, the first of over 165 medical publications during his brilliant career.

Following Dr. Prinzmetal's internship in San Francisco, he went to Barnes Hospital at Washington University in St. Louis for his residency. By the time he had finished a fellowship from the National Research Council at Harvard, he had already published 20 more articles on pulmonary disease, ventricular tachycardia, emphysema, and his first papers on electrocardiography. He worked with W.B. Kountz and H.L. Alexander in a joint publication on emphysema.

He became Sutro Fellow at Mt. Sinai Hospital in New York City in 1935. Eleven more studies, including his first publication on hypertension, led to his appointment as Fellow of the American College of Physicians at University College, London. There he worked with Dr. G.W. Pickering on renin. After one year, he became Fellow of the Dazian Foundation, returning to California at U.S.C. where he continued his studies on hypertension. By 1939 he was working in his laboratory at Cedars of Lebanon Hospital and beginning private practice.

With his first wife (later divorced) Blanche Keiler he had four children, Byron, Anita, William, and Cynthia.

He did not serve in the U.S. Armed Forces during the second World War because of loss of sight of one eye, but he continued to publish papers on hypertension, some with the noted pathologist and his dear friend, the late Dr. John L. Tragerman. For the war effort he turned to the study of shock due to muscle trauma and burns. A total of 23 publications came of this effort. At the end of the war, he began his first studies on the coronary circulation. With Dr. Clarence Agress, he was the first on the West Coast to use Chapman

FIG. 1 Myron Prinzmetal (1908–1987).

and Evans' discovery of the efficacy of radioactive iodine in the treatment of Graves disease. In 1950 he began his work on the auricular arrhythmias, making use of high-speed cine-electrocardiography. Paper after paper on atrial and ventricular arrhythmias saw publication during this period. These included the confirmation of the circus movement in atrial flutter, first suggested by Sir Thomas Lewis; the mechanism of ventricular activity; the origin of the RS-T segment changes in acute myocardial infarction; and the nature of spontaneous atrial fibrillation.

In 1959, with Dr. Rexford Kennamer and others, he published their first observations on the variant form of angina pectoris, a landmark report that was to ensure him a place in the annals of medicine. This type of angina became known as "Prinzmetal's angina." Many other articles and several books were to follow until illness forced him to retire from research and practice.

Dr. Prinzmetal published 165 articles or more. His interest ranged from disease of the lung, kidneys, and peripheral vascular disease to cardiac arrhythmias, circulatory shock, hypertension, and coronary syndromes. (I am listing only four of his articles in the references to this paper).

In addition to belonging to many leading medical societies, Dr. Prinzmetal was on the editorial board of the *American Heart Journal* and the *American Journal of Cardiology*. He was a prime moving force in the formation of the American College of Cardiology and the development of cardiology on the West Coast. He was the recipient of numerous awards and was a guest lecturer in many foreign countries, especially England, where he gave the Sir Thomas Lewis Memorial Lecture.

Dr. Prinzmetal died on January 8, 1987. He will be remembered also for his rare book collections which include all four folio editions of Shakespeare and a first edition of Harvey's De Motu Cordis—the only one not owned by a museum. He restored to the Royal College of Physicians in London the only known portrait of Harvey. Most outstanding was his collection of the memorabilia of his idol, Sir William Osler. His knowledge and love of classical music should not be forgotten.

His spirit will live on in his inspiration of the young men who had the privilege of working with him in the laboratory and in private practice to make important contributions to research and the advancement of cardiology.

Acknowledgments

A portion of this article appeared in the Cedars-Sinai Medical Center Medical Staff News. It is reproduced here with permission.

References

1. Prinzmetal M, Corday E, Spritzler RJ, Flieg W: Radiocardiography and its clinical applications. *J Am Med Assoc* 139, 617–622 (1949)
2. Prinzmetal M, Corday E, Oblath RW, Kruger HE, Brill IC, Fields J, Kennamer SR, Osborne JA, Smith LA, Sellers AL, Flieg W, Finston E: Auricular flutter. *Am J Med* 146, 1275–1281 (1951)
3. Prinzmetal M, Kennamer R, Merliss R, Wada T, Bor N: Angina pectoris. I. A variant form of angina pectoris. (Preliminary report). *Am J Med* 27, 375–388 (1959)
4. Prinzmetal M, Ekmekci A, Kennamer R, Kwoczynski JK, Shubin H, Toyoshima H: Variant form of angina pectoris, previously undelineated syndrome. *J Am Med Assoc.* 174, 1794–1800 (1960)

Richard J. Bing: Point and Counterpoint in Medicine and Music

H. Taegtmeyer, M.D., D.PHIL.

Department of Medicine, Division of Cardiology, University of Texas Medical School at Houston, Houston, Texas, USA

Cardiovascular scientists are fortunate to have in their midst men and women of many talents, backgrounds, and personalities. One of those who has widely contributed to the colorful picture of contemporary cardiology is Richard J. Bing (Fig. 1). Half a century ago, Richard Bing had been at the forefront of physiology and the diagnosis of congenital heart disease by cardiac catheterization. Today he is considered by many the "father of cardiac metabolism." He was the first to demonstrate the noninvasive assessment of coronary flow by radioactive tracers. Now living in his ninth decade, he is still in charge of a busy research lab, serves as Editor-in-Chief of the *Journal of Applied Cardiology*, and carries out a full schedule of activities that keep him at his desk until late at night and often on weekends as well. He even makes the occasional house call on one of his homebound patients. In short, he lives true to his words that "the love for the patient does not preclude the love for science."

More than that, Richard is also endowed with a well-developed musical talent. He has played and composed music from his early childhood up to the present day. He has lived through times that have seen upheaval, uncertainty, and displacement of many (including himself); in the midst of such turbulence he, according to his own words, "has had the good fortune to cling to life rafts that made it possible for me to survive: the science of medicine and the art of music."

Childhood and Studies in Germany

Who is this colorful scientist whom J. Willis Hurst recently called "a true Renaissance man if there ever was one"?[1] Richard J. Bing was born in Nuremberg, Germany, on October 12, 1909. The strong musical talent is on his mother's side. He learned to play the piano early and, when a teenager, was accepted into the Master Class of the Conservatory in Nuremberg. Richard wrote his first compositions at the age of eight.

High school did little to prepare him for a career in science, yet upon graduation he found himself faced with the decision: music or medicine? He opted for medicine, not the least because he considered himself a poor sight-reader and therefore not eligible for a career as player of chamber music. What attracted him to medicine and science was in some way identical to what attracted him to music: a search for the unknown.

Richard entered medical school at the University of Frankfurt in 1928. During his first semester he also joined the Hoch'sche Conservatory in the same city. Medical training in Germany at that time, and to some extent still today, allowed students much freedom in the arrangement of their courses. Students were also permitted, even encouraged, to attend more than one medical school. All that was required was to pass two examinations, one at the end of the second year, the other at the end of the fourth year. Although the exams were in general of a high standard, the students were between times at liberty to pursue their own inclinations. Most students availed themselves of the opportunities offered at other universities and moved to a different medical school at least once, if not more often, in the course of their studies.

It was as a second year medical student in Berlin that Richard first became interested in research, especially in tissue culture and cell biology work. He later continued this line of research with Albert Fischer in Copenhagen, where he met (and was strongly influenced by) Alexis Carrel and Charles Lindbergh. Through them he later came to the Rockefeller Institute. Music got somewhat the short end, and the piano lessons Richard took in Berlin were the last formal musical education he was to receive for more than 20 years. Although clinical studies took most of his time and interest, he still continued to compose and wrote a cello sonata and several string quartets.

Most of Richard's clinical training took place in Munich with the exception of one semester each in Berlin and in Vienna. He remembers his Viennese sojourn with sorrow and disappointment. Political storm clouds had already gathered over Austria, and the flower of Viennese medicine—once considered the most beautiful in the Aesculapian garden—had begun to wither. Likewise, he found the cultural scene ultraconservative and stifling. There was one exception: Richard was introduced to the music of Franz Schubert. He has confided to his friends that his love for the melancholic joy of Schubert's compositions has never abated and only grown on him with the years.

Wanderer Between Two Worlds

His studies in Munich gave Richard the opportunity on weekends to engage in another much loved activity: moun-

FIG. 1   Richard J. Bing, M.D.

taineering and skiing. His happiness would not last for very long as he wrote to me:

> The day it all changed was a beautiful winter's day in January 1933. I was skiing with friends in the mountains and after a lovely day we retreated to the local inn, where we were greeted with the announcement that Hitler had been appointed chancellor of Germany. From that moment on I had only one wish: to get out of Germany as fast as possible, although personally I was threatened less than others. Of necessity I had to hold out until I had finished my studies in Munich and completed a year of internship. Only then was I able to obtain a license in Germany, which would then enable me to repeat a licensing examination elsewhere.

And so it happened: Richard took his finals and after completing his internship in 1934 he left for Switzerland, where he spent almost a year, completing a thesis on the role of platelets in thrombosis, and requalifying at the University of Bern in 1935. Since it was impossible for him to continue his professional career in Switzerland, he accepted a position at the Carlsberg Biological Institute in Copenhagen. Workers at the Carlsberg Institute at that time were a motley crew, among them Fritz Lipman (who in 1953 shared the Nobel Prize with Hans Krebs for his discovery of acetyl-CoA), Alexis Carell, and Charles Lindbergh. Carell, the pioneer of cardiovascular surgery, was instrumental in bringing Bing to America, first by arranging a brief fellowship with him at the Rockefeller Institute and then by writing a letter of recommendation for a position in surgery at the Presbyterian Hospital in New York with Allen O. Whipple.

A New Beginning in America

During his year as a surgical intern Richard was able to spend time in research. He continued work on perfusion of isolated organs, a technique he had acquired under Carell, and published his first paper in no lesser a journal than *Science*.[2] Richard soon left surgery for an instructorship in the Physiology Department at Columbia College of Physicians and Surgeons. This was a turning point in his life. He likes to refer to it as "the beginning of my serious apprenticeship in science," which was in turn followed by a fellowship in the laboratory of Homer W. Smith of New York University. During his time at Columbia University, Richard for the first time heard his own music performed in America—the New York City radio station WNYC played his 2nd Violin Sonata. Many people would have turned such a success into a career in composing, yet Richard was realistic about his limited chances to earn a living as a composer. Other important factors were that he had found in Homer Smith a role model, and that he had never encountered such scientific fervor as at New York University. Bing recalls that in New York it was always possible to get advice on any project and to meet with someone who was willing to listen. His work in Homer Smith's laboratory was directed toward clinical applications of renal physiology, and among other things, he demonstrated that renal failure was a nonspecific response to a variety of interventions including hemorrhage and hypotension.

From New York to Baltimore

Although very successful in his work at the bench and in the classroom, Richard never intended to become a straight-laced physiologist, but rather a physician with a thorough background in the pathophysiology of disease. So, in 1942, he applied for, and obtained, a position in the Department of Medicine at Johns Hopkins. He recalls with pride his paper on the treatment of hypertension with antiadrenergic agents, which is today an almost forgotten milestone in pharmacotherapy.[3]

Blalock and Cardiac Catheterization

In 1943 Richard enlisted in the Army Medical Corps. Two years later he was hired by Alfred Blalock, Chairman of the Department of Surgery at Hopkins. Blalock gave him the task of organizing a physiology laboratory for the investigation and diagnosis of congenital heart disease. Richard accepted the offer on the spot.

Blalock had at that time already established a close collaboration with Helen Taussig on the preoperative diagnosis of congenital heart disease by physical examination and fluoroscopy. At Hopkins, in 1945, Bing began to organize a catheterization laboratory, although he had never performed a cardiac catheterization himself (he had visited and observed Cournand and Richardson at the Bellevue Hospital in New

York before his arrival in Baltimore, though). His early papers on the subject described formulas for the study of the circulation of patients with congenital heart disease. Critics would call it a period of easy pickings, since everything was new. Dan McNamara has recently published a masterly review of Bing's contributions to the elucidation of congenital heart disease.[4] The early papers were published in the now defunct *John Hopkins Bulletin*, since Bing did not want to fight the editors of the *Journal of Clinical Investigation* (to this day he has retained a sympathetic heart for the victims of editorial decisions founded on petty arguments). Although the papers dealt with physiologic questions such as the adaptation to hypoxia, and the development of pulmonary hypertension and diagnosis was often only a byproduct, the chips came down in the operating room when Blalock had to have a diagnosis. At that time only the tetralogy of Fallot, patent ductus arteriosus, and coarctation of the aorta were operable malformations; a preoperative misdiagnosis could have had fatal consequences.

Richard, in charge of the invasive physiology laboratory, felt he had been thrown into a lion's den. Although his efforts in the early days of cardiac catheterization were richly rewarded by new insights into the physiology of congenital heart disease, he himself has likened his position to a Daniel, between Blalock and Taussig. While much of the credit for the pioneer work in congenital heart disease went to Blalock and to Taussig, Bing delineated in short succession the hemodynamic features of twenty different forms of congenital heart disease.[4] But Blalock was generous with his praise. He was proud of having in his department a lab entirely devoted to the study of the physiology of congenital heart disease.

In 1947, while at Hopkins, Bing was sent to Germany with the army for four weeks as consultant to the Surgeon General. He tried to locate (in vain) Werner Forssmann, who in 1929 had performed on himself the first cardiac catheterization in a human.[5] Bing met Forssmann later on in 1964, and described him as a tenacious and imaginative man whose life was made continuously difficult by misunderstandings (most famous is the incident when he was denied a fellowship position with the chairman's remark: "You can show off with your tricks in a circus, but not in my department"). So it was Bing who, in 1947, performed the first heart catheterization in Germany after Forssmann. He recalls: "When I turned on the fluoroscope I could not believe my eyes: the catheter tip had entered the heart and in the right chamber it had made contact with a bullet acquired during the war!"

The Coronary Sinus and Adventures in Cardiac Metabolism

Just when Bing felt that his work was becoming rather routine and purely diagnostic as he had investigated one congenital heart defect after the other, a new field of research suddenly opened up for him. While catheterizing patients he had frequently noticed that the catheter tip entered

a region of the heart where the pressures were lower than in the ventricles and where the blood was very dark. It took a few simple experiments to ascertain that the catheter had entered the coronary sinus.[6] This discovery coincided with the reading of an article by C. Lovatt Evans, physiologist and collaborator of Ernest Starling at University College in London, who had measured substrate usage by an isolated heart-lung preparation. Bing immediately recognized the importance of his observation for measuring arteriovenous differences for O_2 and substrates across the heart—a new branch of the tree of cardiovascular physiology began to sprout. In a series of papers, reviewed in the famous Harvey Lectures,[7] Bing and his co-workers established that the human heart extracts almost all O_2 delivered on the arterial side, that an increase in O_2 supply can only be achieved through an increase in coronary blood flow, and that human heart muscle is able to meet its energy needs through the oxidation of a variety of substrates such as glucose, fatty acids, ketone bodies, and amino acids. In his work he characterized the conditions which determine substrate preferences and looked at disease states such as the failing and the diabetic heart. The initial observations quickly led to more detailed biochemical studies in isolated hearts and tissue preparations, that is, from the physiologic to the molecular levels—research that has preoccupied Bing for the last 40 years. The importance of the work Bing has set into motion is perhaps best illustrated by the founding of the International Society for Heart Research by him and his colleagues 25 years ago, together with the Society's journal, the *Journal of Molecular and Cellular Cardiology*.

From Baltimore to Alabama

Bing was not spoiled by success, and he realized that Blalock had not hired him to study cardiac metabolism and the nutrition of the heart. Thus, in 1951, when Tinsley Harrison, Professor of Medicine at the University of Alabama in Birmingham, offered him a position as Professor of Medicine and Director of the Cardiac Clinic, he accepted immediately. Harrison was, among other things, interested in Bing's skills in cardiac catheterization, which at the time was still a relatively new technique. Bing remembers that once, when delivering a lecture on catheterization, an older physician let him know that he had practiced catheterization for the last 30 years—he was a urologist!

At Birmingham, Bing and his co-workers discovered that the human heart prefers fatty acids over other substrates and may even oxidize amino acids. He investigated cardiac metabolism in myocardial infarction in hypothermia and cardiac arrhythmias. Bing was much aware of the limitations of his work. He frequently used the analogy of watching the stage doors during the performance of a Shakespearian drama: observing the actors entering and leaving gives little indication of what happens on the stage. Hence, he commenced a new line of work which focused on cellular elements of the heart starting with contractile proteins—

an obvious choice for a cardiac physiologist. Although Bing considered the time at Birmingham the most productive time in his scientific career, he remained there for only three years.

Interludes at St. Louis and Detroit

In 1954 Bing accepted the position of Professor of Medicine and Director of the Washington University Service at the Veterans Administration Hospital. The professional climate of Washington University was most supportive of his research activities, and a number of excellent collaborators were attracted by the reputation of the institution.

Still, when in 1959 the position of chairman of the department of medicine at Wayne State University was offered to him, Bing moved to Detroit, where he spent the next ten years. He privately considers this period as the most difficult of his professional life, mainly because of administrative quandaries. Richard's research productivity was, however, little affected by the environment. He again attracted a good number of young scientists, many of them also from foreign countries, and began the collaboration with other researchers, among them Dr. George Clark, a physicist and cousin of his wife. On Clark's advice he used positively charged electrons (positrons) for measurement of coronary flow. Although he did not follow up on the fundamental observation,[8] he can rightfully lay claim to originating this technique, which is now, in the form of positron emission tomography (PET), widely used for the noninvasive assessment of regional myocardial blood flow and metabolism.

During his Detroit period, Richard once again began to write music, and he even began to take lessons in instrumentation. He wrote the first of several string quartets, many of which have been publicly performed, as have his larger orchestral works of recent years. In conversation, Richard is drawn to compare creativity in music and in science. Inspiration is the absolute *sine qua non* of musical composition, whether it comes as a gentle breeze or as a hurricane. Intelligence and industry will never substitute for it. In contrast, the writing of a scientific paper is always a painstakingly slow effort in which every sentence has to be scrutinized, every result has to be documented. Here the inspiration, if any, is a single event, the formation of a concept. As a man who continues to add to the 420 scientific publications bearing his name and who continues to produce four musical compositions in a year, he is quick to point out that musical and scientific creations often share a common tale: lack of acceptance by peers and difficulty in having them published.

On to California

After ten years in Detroit, Richard made the next big move in his life—to the Huntington Memorial Hospital and Research Institutes in Pasadena, California, where he began, in 1969, his work as director of clinical cardiology, of the residency program, and of experimental cardiology. He eventually retired from the first two jobs. However, he has never retired from research, and in 1990 he continues his work with undiminished vigor, supported by three postdoctoral fellows and two technicians. As always, he has chosen to work on a problem of clinical relevance: the endothelium-derived relaxing factor (EDRF). Even more important, he has been the driving force behind the development of a first-rate nuclear magnetic resonance (NMR) spectroscopy laboratory which in a short period of time has become one of the leading facilities of its kind in the country. But his interests extend even further. In 1986 he founded the *Journal of Applied Cardiology*, as he felt an increasing need to bring basic research from the bench to the bedside. He continues to serve as its Editor-in-Chief. Bing also recently completed a book on the history of cardiology.

Richard has never lived longer at one place than in California. Although removed from the intrigues of academia, he cherishes the intellectual environment and the stimulation provided to him by friends and colleagues both at the Huntington Memorial Institute and at neighboring Caltech. And cardiologists around the world seek him out at meetings. He is hard to overlook: a towering man, slightly stooped, with a mane of white hair. Once engaged in conversation, his face lights up with a glow of excitement and the expression of forgiving kindness.

Honors, Family, and Friends

It is not surprising that Richard Bing has been honored by many professional and civic awards, among them honorary degrees from the Universities of Bologna, Düsseldorf, and Würzburg. Many of Bing's scientific accomplishments and their impact on contemporary research in cardiovascular physiology are collected in a festschrift written by a group of his friends on the occasion of his eightieth birthday in 1989.[9]

Anyone who knows Richard Bing also knows of his fondness of his family and friends. He met his wife Mary Whipple in 1938. They were married in the same year after only a brief courtship. Richard played the piano at his own wedding. The Bings have four children—two sons and two daughters—and six grandchildren. Richard values in particular his friendship, since early childhood, with Ernst Gombrich (now Sir Ernst Gombrich), the Austrian-born British art historian, known to the public for his popular work *The Story of Art* and in academic circles for his study of the psychology of perception ("most people tend to see what they expect to see"). He also enjoyed a close friendship with Max Delbrück, the physicist-turned-biologist and father of molecular biology, whom he met at Caltech. Richard admired in him an aristocrat in the field of science with a broad interest in natural sciences, as well as philosophy, mathematics, and physics. In addition to these close personal friends, Richard has earned the love and affection of countless trainees, fellows, and colleagues in the United States and around the world.

Summa Summarum

The author may be permitted to quote from a letter he received from Richard Bing dated April 9, 1990:

If you want to sum up what my interests in life are I would rate them as my family, which has assumed ever greater importance the less I go hunting on the trails of academic success, medicine, and science. You see, I make little distinction between the latter. The little success I had, I had primarily in the application of scientific principles to medicine, such as metabolism of the heart. And finally, Music. It should be spelled with a capital "M", because it has played a very important role in my life. At some time I thought it would be the only role in my life, but the situation in Europe being what it was I felt at risk having to emigrate and having to make my living solely on the basis of music." And he continues: "I have been blessed with friends, people who overlook my weaknesses, and I must honestly say I have been blessed with enemies in my professional life. Blessed, because they have prevented me from developing a swelled head. Thus, I have been forced to keep my feet on the ground and face the vicissitudes of professional life even in my old age.

References

1. Hurst JW: Personal communication.
2. Bing RJ: The perfusion of whole organs in the Lindbergh apparatus with fluids containing hemocyanin as respiratory pigment. *Science* 87, 554 (1933)
3. Bing RJ, Thomas CB: Effect of two diazone derivations, 883 and 933 F on normal dogs and on animals with neurogenic and renal hypertension. *J Pharm Exper Ther* 85, 21 (1945)
4. McNamara DG: Contributions of Richard Bing to the field of congenital heart disease. *J Appl Cardiol* 4, 351 (1989)
5. Forssmann W: *Experiments on Myself.* Saint Martin's Press, New York (1974), 352
6. Bing RJ, Hammond MM, Handelsmann JL: The measurement of coronary blood flow, oxygen consumption and efficiency of the left ventricle in man. *Am Heart J* 38, 1 (1949)
7. Bing RJ: Metabolism of the heart. *Harvey Lect* 50, 27 (1955)
8. Bing RJ, Bennisch A, Bluemchen G, Cohen A, Galagher JP, Faleski EJ: The determination of coronary flow equivalent with coincidence counting technique. *Circulation* 29, 833 (1964)
9. Taegtmeyer H, Ross BD (Ed): Half a century in cardiovascular research: A tribute to Richard J. Bing on his 80th birthday (festschrift). *J Appl Cardiol* 4, 399 (1989)

Lewis Dexter

R. C. SCHLANT, M.D.

Department of Medicine, Division of Cardiology, Emory University School of Medicine, Atlanta, Georgia, USA

Lewis Dexter was born March 1, 1910, in Concord, Massachusetts. His father was an Episcopal minister who subsequently became Curate of Grace Episcopal Church in New Bedford. The first Dexter to arrive in North America was the Reverend Gregory Dexter, a Baptist minister and printer who arrived in 1644, and who was a friend and admirer of Roger Williams. Subsequent generations of Dexters have mainly been businessmen in Rhode Island with some being active in diplomacy and the legal profession.

Lewis ("Lew") Dexter went to Concord High School and then to Choate School prior to attending Harvard College, where he graduated cum laude in 1932. He then entered Harvard Medical School and graduated in the famous class of 1936, also cum laude. After two years of residency in New York City at Presbyterian Hospital, he became a research fellow at Boston City Hospital, studying with Dr. Soma Weiss and concentrating on the toxemia of pregnancy. This experience resulted in a book on the subject, which he and Dr. Weiss co-authored.[1]

Dr. Dexter's father died of cancer in 1936, and in 1939 his mother succumbed to the same disease. That same year his older brother, Smith Owen Dexter (also a physician at the Rockefeller Institute) died suddenly from an occlusion of the left anterior descending coronary artery. In 1940, Lew went to the Institute of Physiology in Buenos Aires, Argentina, for a year of research on the rennin-angiotensin system under Noble Laureate Bernardo A. Houssay and Dr. Eduardo Braun-Menendez.

The following year Lew returned to the Peter Bent Brigham, where Dr. Soma Weiss had been appointed physician-in-chief. After Dr. Weiss' death just a few months later in early 1942, Lew teamed with Dr. Florence Haynes to set up a plasma renin assay. They found renin to be elevated in some, but not all, patients with hypertension. In order to increase the sensitivity of his assay method, Dr. Dexter visited Dr. Stan Bradley, who taught him how to manipulate the tip of a catheter into the renal vein to sample renal venous blood. Using this technique, Drs. Dexter and Haynes still found elevated plasma renin levels in some patients with hypertension but normal levels in other patients.

Just five days after Pearl Harbor in 1941, Lew married Cassandra ("Sandy") Kinsman and after a one-week skiing honeymoon, he returned to the "Brigham" Hospital, where he was the only full-time staff member when Dr. George Thorn

came on as the successor to Dr. Soma Weiss in 1942. Dr. Dexter remained at "the Brigham" (originally Peter Bent Brigham and more recently Brigham and Women's Hospital) for the rest of his career.

Lew and Sandy adopted two boys and a girl, Lewis, Jr.; Smith Owen III; and Sandra B. Short. Their two sons now live in Westport, Massachusetts, while Sandra lives with her husband in Santa Barbara, California. The Dexters have three grandchildren.

On December 7, 1944, Lew catheterized a renal vein and then explored the heart with the catheter. He noted that the catheter suddenly appeared in the lung field and initially he was concerned that the catheter had perforated the heart. Later that day he happened to have lunch with Dr. C. Sidney Burwell, at that time Dean of Harvard Medical School. Burwell, who a few years previously with Dr. Eugene Eppinger had studied patent ductus arteriosus shunts in patients during surgery performed by Dr. Robert Gross, pointed out how this technique could be used as a tool to elucidate congenital heart disease. In some ways, this single episode in 1944 helped to change Lewis Dexter from a hypertensionist-nephrologist into a cardiologist.

The first problem Dr. Dexter investigated with the catheter was the recognition and pathophysiology of congenital heart disease. This soon resulted in a series of classic articles that described techniques for the recognition and quantification of left-to-right and bidirectional shunts in many of the common forms of congenital heart disease.[2–6] In 1956 Lew wrote the classic article describing the pathophysiology and natural history of atrial septal defect.[7] It is interesting that during the early phase of this research it was necessary for Dr. Dexter to construct his own pressure transducers, since these did not become commercially available until about 1948. In those days, Richard Bing was also very active in cardiac catheterization of congenital heart disease, particularly in patients with cyanosis from tetralogy of Fallot. In Atlanta, Dr. James Warren was also actively developing the diagnostic value of cardiac catheterization.

On a second fateful day, November 15, 1945, Lew withdrew a completely oxygenated blood sample from a catheter positioned in the pulmonary artery. Eventually, it was established that blood so obtained comes from the pulmonary capillaries when an end-hole catheter is wedged into a branch of the pulmonary artery. Lewis Dexter's early studies also established

FIG. 1 Copy of the portrait of Dr. Dexter in the amphitheatre of the Brigham and Women's Hospital in Boston.

FIG. 2 At the helm: Lew and Sandy Dexter, July 13, 1957.

that the pressure recorded from this "wedge" position was virtually identical with that of the left atrium.[8] It is significant that, for a number of years, not all physiologists or cardiologists were initially willing to accept these findings or conclusions. Dr. Dexter has always noted that Lars Werko in Sweden discovered this same phenomenon almost simultaneously.

In the mid-1940s, exercise with a catheter in the heart was considered dangerous to a large degree, because most previous studies had been performed with the catheter in the right ventricle. One day, Dr. Dexter decided to prove that exercise could be safely performed with the tip of the catheter in the pulmonary artery. He did this by having his first research fellow, Dr. Harper Hellems (currently Professor and Chairman of the Department of Medicine at the University of Mississippi) pass a catheter into his (Dexter's) pulmonary artery, following which Lew stood up, walked a bit, and ran in place sufficiently to increase his heart rate to about 150. No premature beats occurred and he came home for supper, much to the relief of Sandy, his wife. For a number of years, right heart catheterization was performed via an antecubital venous cutdown on most of his cardiology fellows. He found, however, that their anxiety level was often so high that the hemodynamic measurements were not useful as normal controls, and eventually he gave up this routine when one cardiac fellow developed ventricular bigeminy with the catheter tip advanced only as far as the high superior vena cava. Subsequent Dexter trainees were relieved that this routine was no longer a standard part of the training program.

Academically, Dr. Dexter rose through the ranks at Harvard Medical School, beginning as Assistant in Medicine and rising to Professor of Medicine. He is currently Professor of Medicine Emeritus at both Harvard and the University of Massachusetts Medical School. Dr. Dexter has been honored as a recipient of the James B. Herrick Award and the Research Achievement Award of the American Heart Association as well as by the Paul Dudley White Award of the Massachusetts Heart Association.

Although Dr. Dexter is a superb lecturer, he appears to enjoy bedside teaching even more, with the logical analysis of symptoms and physical findings, along with the electrocardiogram and chest films, to predict what will be found at cardiac catheterization or surgery. Conversely, the detailed analysis of the hemodynamics of valvular or congenital heart disease at cardiac catheterization provides both fellows and students a vivid impression of the importance of the basic determinants of cardiac performance in different disease states (such as the influence of tachycardia or the loss of atrial contraction upon flow across a stenotic mitral valve).

In his younger days, Lew was very active in hockey and skiing, baseball and track (high jump and pole vault) and, in the summertime, swimming, fishing, and sailing. For many years one of his major hobbies was sailing his 38-foot yawl up and down the New England coast with Sandy and his children. Residents, students, and cardiology trainees were frequent guests at the Dexter summer home and on their yacht. Although the morbidity from seasickness and other hazards on such occasions was occasionally rather high, there were no known fatalities. For many years the Dexters traditionally ended a teaching rotation with dinner at their home, inviting the entire teaching or attending team. In anticipation of such occasions, he has for many years kept superb martinis in the freezer and olives in the refrigerator. This tradition continues to this day with University of Massachusetts Medical School third-year clinical clerks, with whom Lew meets for several hours each week.

In 1969 at the age of 59, Dr. Dexter waded into the warm water in Antigua. He noted that when the water reached the level of his apex impulse, he developed distressing substernal pressure. He returned to shore and the discomfort disappeared. He repeated it and the discomfort recurred. He took a few brief steps of light running and the discomfort reappeared. After he returned to Boston it was noted that his electrocardiogram and exercise tolerance test were normal; however, for the next 10 years he had stable angina on effort. Although he continued smoking cigarettes, he remained moderately active chopping wood, raking leaves, digging in the garden, swimming, and sailing. In 1972 he underwent elective resection of an asymptomatic abdominal aneurysm without incident.

After about 10 years of stable angina, however, the discomfort began to appear with less and less activity. Despite the apparent change in his symptoms from stable to unstable angina, he went on trips to medical meetings in Bermuda and Holland. Eventually, however, while walking up the entrance to the Peter Bent Brigham Hospital, he became very short of breath and his chest film revealed acute pulmonary edema for which he was admitted to the Samuel A. Levine Coronary Care Unit. There, his electrocardiogram showed changes suggestive of apical infarction. Coronary arteriography was postponed in the hope that his condition would become more stable. Unfortunately, the angina did not quiet down and after about a week of recurrent pain, occurring both with mild exertion and without provocation, and on awakening at night, he suddenly developed acute electrical mechanical dissociation. CPR was started promptly. Luckily this happened during morning rounds. The chief cardiac surgeon (Dr. John Collins), who happened to be nearby, was immediately contacted and he agreed to operate. Dr. Dexter was given continuous CPR for about 40 minutes while being transferred from the Coronary Care Unit to the operating room, where, fortunately, surgical and extra-corporeal pump teams were awaiting the arrival of another patient for elective coronary bypass surgery. Dr. Dexter was put on bypass without anesthesia and Dr. Collins inserted two bypass grafts, one to the left anterior descending artery and one to the circumflex, despite the fact that no preoperative coronary angiogram had been obtained. Lew required intra-aortic balloon assist for a short time post-operatively. He had amnesia for 10 days, but then his memory and other mental functions returned and his main problem was the considerable pleuritic pain from a number of broken ribs. Finally, after this remarkable episode, he discontinued smoking cigarettes.

Four months later, he had serum hepatitis from a blood transfusion during his surgery. In 1980 Lew developed systemic hypertension and a new murmur of aortic stenosis. His blood pressure was well controlled with a calcium-channel blocker. In 1983 he perforated a peptic ulcer, likely due to daily aspirin taken for his bypass grafts. In 1986, however, he became dyspenic rather suddenly and had his aortic valve replaced by Dr. Collins. Since that time he has enjoyed generally good health except for some additional bleeding from his

peptic ulcer. It is noteworthy that Lew returned to teaching with great enthusiasm following each illness.

In addition to being responsible for many early classic studies on hypertension, cardiac catheterization, congenital heart disease, and pulmonary capillary pressure, Lew and his fellows made major contributions to many other areas of cardiology including mitral and aortic valve disease, the hemodynamics of normal subjects and of subjects with heart failure both at rest and during exercise, important studies on pulmonary embolism, primary pulmonary hypertension, chronic cor pulmonale, pulmonary blood volume, and right ventricular function. Lew played a major collaborative role in the classic paper by Gorlin and Gorlin delineating the formula for calculation of valve area.[9] Dr. Richard Gorlin was a fellow in Dr. Dexter's laboratory when Gorlin and his father developed the valve area formula. It is a typical example of Dr. Dexter's humility and sense of fairness that he removed his name from the original valve area manuscript prior to its submission for publication. In addition to being responsible for many advances in cardiology, Lew Dexter is responsible for the training of many physicians in his laboratory. Many of these physicians today occupy important positions of leadership in academic medicine and continue the Dexter tradition.

Lew Dexter's life has had three great medical loves: his research, his teaching, and his training of young cardiology trainees and fellows. In each of these endeavors he has had the unfailing support and assistance of his partner and loving companion, Sandy Dexter.

References

1. Dexter L, Weiss S: *Preeclamptic and Eclamptic Toxemia of Pregnancy*. Little, Brown and Co., Boston (1941)
2. Dexter L, Burwell CS, Haynes FW, Seibel RE: Venous catheterization for the diagnosis of congenital heart disease. *Bull New Engl Med Cen*, 8, 113 (1946)
3. Dexter L, Haynes FW, Burwell CS, Eppinger EC, Seibel RE, Evans JM: Studies of congenital heart disease. I. Technique of venous catheterization as a diagnostic procedure. *J Clin Invest* 26, 547 (1947)
4. Dexter L, Haynes FW, Burwell CS, Eppinger EC, Sagerson RP, Evans JM: Studies of congenital heart disease. III. Venous catheterization as a diagnostic aid in patent ductus arteriosus, tetralogy of Fallot, ventricular septal defect, and auricular septal defect. *J Clin Invest* 26, 561 (1947)
5. Dow JW, Levine HD, Elkin M, Haynes FW, Hellems HK, Whittenberger JW, Ferris BG, Goodale WT, Harvey WP, Eppinger EC, Dexter L: Studies in congenital heart disease. IV. Uncomplicated pulmonic stenosis. *Circulation* 1, 267 (1950)
6. Dexter L: Cardiac catheterization in the diagnosis of congenital heart disease. *Bull New York Acad Med* 26, 93 (1950)
7. Dexter L: Atrial septal defect. *Brit Heart J* 18, 209 (1956)
8. Hellems HK, Haynes FW, Dexter L, Kinney TD: Pulmonary capillary pressure in animals estimated by venous and arterial catheterization. *Am J Physiol* 155, 98 (1948)
9. Gorlin R, Gorlin SG: Hydraulic formula for calculation of stenotic mitral valve, other cardiac valves and central circulatory shunts. *Am Heart J* 41, 1 (1951)

In Memoriam: George Burch, 1910–1986

C. THORPE RAY, M.D.

Department of Medicine, Tulane University School of Medicine, New Orleans, Louisiana, USA

Writing a memorial to George is both a sad task and an opportunity to direct attention to some of his characteristics observed over many years of working in close association with him. His interests and activities in medicine and cardiology were very broad and remained so throughout his life. His scientific productivity covered many areas of research and clinical observations.

His extreme dedication to research was sincere. He always had more ideas than time allowed to be investigated. On his return from one of his many trips he would scribble ideas and projects to be discussed via telephone that night. By the next morning he would have added to the list.

While associates required several minutes to get organized and get it "in gear," George stayed in high gear all the time. When concentrating on a problem he was not distracted by things that bothered the rest of us, and was therefore able to make every minute count. He would dash into his office between classes, conferences, and so forth, add a few sentences to a manuscript, and then be off in another direction.

In research data George insisted on absolute accuracy. He had no interest in "factoring" or "salvaging" data. If it needed "factoring" it wasn't worth filing or analysis. Some of us can recall the sad day when data we had been compiling for over a year were discarded when they could easily have been corrected by a proper factor. This was but one indication of his insistence on absolute accuracy and reliability of research data.

Dr. Burch possessed a unique analytic ability for both basic science and clinical data. He was incisive and physiologic in this ability, and fundamental principles were immediately evident to him. In his opinion, catch phrases or nicknames such as "preload" and "afterload" were not necessary to scientific writing. These principles were clearly described in 1951 and 1952 and George scrupulously followed them in his clinical studies.

George felt strongly about research funding, particularly about the support of imaginative researchers rather than specific projects. He often commented that no really great discovery could have been anticipated to the point that it would have been approved as a formal research grant application. This view was often repeated throughout his career in research, and a scientific presentation of these ideas formed the basis of the Fellows Program of the MacArthur Foundation (specific funding for promising imaginative research people).

FIG. 1   George Burch, 1910–1986.

George worked hard, spending many long hours in an organized and effective fashion, wasting no time getting the job done, and he expected the same from his associates although he did not always get it. At times he could be a bit difficult and on some occasions seemingly impossible until we understood what he had in mind and then it made good sense.

Honest self-criticism was a strong and readily apparent trait in George Burch. Reservations and limitations regarding scientific data were always clearly stated and I know of no instance where he "overinterpreted" the data. He was never tempted to waste time on polemics and arguments through the mail. His answer was always that time would prove who was right.

George was as interested in clinical medicine and teaching as he was in research. This continued broad base of interests was the platform from which he saw medicine in perspective. He had an unusual ability to recognize the basic principles and clinical relevance of research data.

His dedication to the clinical service at Charity Hospital in New Orleans and to the teaching of students and house officers will not be forgotten. An equal interest in the academic development of members of the Department of Medicine cannot be overlooked. His influence and success are reflected in the 35 members of the faculty who became chairmen, deans, or chancellors in other institutions.

Space does not permit a listing of all the memberships in societies or honors Dr. Burch has received. He was recognized and respected locally, regionally, nationally, and internationally. He published over 860 scientific articles, about 200 of which were published after he "retired." He published 12 books, and served as Editor and on Editorial Boards of numerous journals. His far-ranging and continuous contributions to medicine are well known to all and have been praised in other memorials. I have chosen to present something of the man and not his works. Our association was long, stimulating, and productive. However, there were a few things for which no reason was ever apparent—why he wore his scrub suit shirt backwards was never understood. Nor was it clear why he always carried such a vast array of "things" in his coat pocket, but was never seen to use any of them. I am sure that there were reasons, for there was a reason for all that he did. For George things did not happen by accident. He was true to his convictions and his philosophy.

With full appreciation for his contributions in medicine and with appreciation of the strong characteristics of the man, it is clear that he is missed, completely respected, and remembered with a smile.

Lewis E. January

FRANÇOIS M. ABBOUD, M.D.

Department of Medicine, University of Iowa College of Medicine, Iowa City, Iowa, USA

One of the distinct privileges of being chairman for 17 years of an illustrious department of medicine is that one is often asked to write about the giants who made it so. I was asked to write about Lewis E. January for the "Profiles in Cardiology" series. I am honored.

Lew January's character and career symbolize the Department of Medicine at Iowa during the second half of the twentieth century: goodness and loyalty, professionalism and excellence, hard work and commitment to an academic life of scholarship and teaching, and simple yet honorable values.

He is a pioneer, a role model, a super teacher, a master clinician, a champion of beauty expressed in flowers or in art, and a "Hawkeye" to the core.

As you approach him to shake his hand, you are attracted to that magnetic smile of the "silver fox," as he is affectionately called by his junior colleagues. You feel the warmth of his kindness, the eagerness of his caring, the stirring of his enthusiasm, and the bustle of his love of life. He is our Iowa phenomenon.

Born in Colorado in 1910, he received his education in the public schools, Colorado College, and the University of Colorado. When he graduated from the University of Colorado School of Medicine in 1937, medical schools traded prospective interns the way major league teams trade players. The dean of one school would exchange a bright young prospect with the dean of another for an equally bright prospect. Lew's dean told him he was going to Iowa and not, as Lew had planned, to Ohio. It was Iowa's gain.

Beginning with this internship, during which he and his colleagues were on call 24 hours a day, 365 days a year, in exchange for room and board, six uniforms, and $100, Lewis January has contributed enormously to the growth of the University of Iowa and the Iowa City community.

There was an interruption of his career at Iowa from 1942–1946 when he served in the United States Army Air Force Medical Corps, rising in rank from first lieutenant to lieutenant colonel. Upon his return to the Department of Medicine at the end of World War II, his appointment to the faculty as assistant professor was announced with reference to his distinguished military service as chief of medical service at an Army Air Force regional hospital in Texas and his authorship of "Subacute Bacterial Endocarditis Treated with Penicillin," which was published in the *Air Surgeon's Bulletin* in 1945 and which was one of the earliest reports on the subject. He received the Army Commendation Ribbon in 1945.

Dr. January organized and began the supervision of the Heart Station in the Department of Medicine at the University of Iowa. He had a special fellowship to train in electrocardiography with Frank Wilson and Franklin Johnston at the University of Michigan in 1947. For years he taught electrocardiography and, from its early days, vectorcardiography to medicine residents and cardiology fellows. Senior medical students also took the "elective" course in electrocardiography under his supervision.

Now, nearly 50 years later, even in his "retirement," Lew January can still be found reading electrocardiograms in a much expanded and improved station with state-of-the-art equipment and a staff who have been trained in the program he began.

Lew has been admired and respected by his students, trainees, and colleagues, and has been sought after by many leaders in the medical center. He received a Clinical Cardiology Training Grant (one of the first) from the National Institutes of Health. At a time of special recognition for Dr. January in 1981, a former dean wrote: "I developed a special interest in internal medicine as a result of your influence. You may not recall, but your conversations, advice, and example during my junior year in medical school were important in my decision to seek a residency in internal medicine. And again, your influence was important in my decision to remain in academic medicine."[1]

A former president of the university commented: "Lew is not a person of muted tones. His intensity of feelings ranges from the Republicans, on the one hand, to the Joffrey Ballet, on the other hand. He cares and cares intensely. He is able in talent, cosmopolitan in interest, steadfast in purpose, and devoted in friendship."

A professor in the Department of Internal Medicine remembered his days as a medical student:

> I recall standing in the old Metabolic Unit on the third floor of the Medical Research Center as John Glenn was launched into space. You [Dr. January] and I were standing side by side; I at the time was a rather inconspicuous medical student and you were one of the most distinguished professors in the college. As the rocket was going up there was great excitement and everyone in the room was consumed by the event. I distinctly remember your looking at me and saying, "Here we are, watching one of the really outstanding moments of history, seeing one of man's truly miraculous accomplishments, and some people around this place aren't even watching!"[1]

Fig. 1   Lewis E. January, M.D. (1910–2002)

And a grateful patient wrote:

My lucky day was a football Saturday afternoon in
Kinnick Stadium in October 1955, when Iowa tied
Purdue in a thrilling game. But I never saw the finish of
that game, for at half-time an ambulance took me to
Emergency at University Hospital for what you later
called a heart attack. *I* call it my *lucky day*, for it was at the
hospital later that afternoon that I first met you. From that
day on when you took over my care for the next forty
years, I have felt that I have been most fortunate and
highly privileged to have had you as a dutiful, kind, unyielding, and devoted doctor.[1]

Outside the University of Iowa, a great many accomplishments should be noted, chiefly in the service he has given the
American Heart Association. Lew January joined the AHA in
1948 and became a founding member of the Iowa Heart
Association the same year. He served as medical editor of Heart
Page in "Topics" from 1948–1950; as secretary in 1950 and
1951; as president in 1952 and 1953; and served on the Board
of Directors from 1948–1962.

At the national level, Lew went to work first on the Committee on Cardiovascular Clinics (1950–1951), then the Board
of Directors (1955–1958, 1960–1971), and the Executive Committee of the Board (1961–1963, 1965–1968), moving from
vice president to president-elect and then serving as president
(1966–1967). He did not rest on his laurels. Immediately after
completing his presidency, he served on the Central Committee
for Medical and Community Programs, the Editorial Board of
Circulation, and continued to participate in all the functions of
the Council on Clinical Cardiology. He holds Certificate Number One as a fellow of this council.

From 1969 to 1972, he was on the Advisory and Executive
Committee of the Inter-Society Commission for Heart Disease
Resources, and from 1972 to 1976, he was on the National Heart
and Lung Institute's Cardiovascular Training Committee. Then

he served on the Editorial Board of the *American Heart Journal*
from 1974 to 1979, all the while serving as vice president of the
International Federation of Cardiology and later on the Executive Board of the International Society and Federation of Cardiology. Paul Dudley White credited him with being a major
contributor to achieving the merger of the International Cardiology Society and the International Cardiology Federation.

In medicine, education, and the arts, Lew has been a constant
source of new ideas and generous support. Countless organizations and committees are thankful for his talents, leadership,
and strong sense of direction which he has given as president,
vice president, chairman, advisor, delegate, fellow, founding
member, editor, author, director, and in many other capacities.

What he has accomplished is second only to the *way* in which
he has gone about it. Loyalty and devotion are his most distinctive character traits. Beginning with loyalty and devotion to his
wife, Eloise, and their family, Lew January has expanded his
care and concerns to medical education, patient care, the department, college, and university he has served so diligently, and
to the leaders and directors who have relied on his advice.
He has received honors and recognitions from every organization to which he has given himself. The list is long, but a few
should be mentioned. Colorado College conferred upon him an
honorary doctor of science degree in 1966. From the American
Heart Association he received the Gold Heart Award in 1969;
the Silver and Gold Award (Distinguished Alumni Award) from
the University of Colorado School of Medicine in 1971; the
Distinguished Service Citation from the Inter-Society Commission for Heart Disease Research in 1971; the Helen B. Taussig
Award from the Central Maryland Heart Association in 1972;
the International Achievement Citation from the American
Heart Association in 1977; a Special Citation for Distinguished
Service to International Cardiology from the American Heart
Association in 1978; and Master of the American College of
Physicians in 1978. He is author or co-author of 83 scientific
papers or chapters.

In addition to his impressive array of achievements, Lewis
January is credited for introducing the Joffrey Ballet to Iowa
City and for starting a love affair between the two that is now
in its third decade. He has been a member of the National Committee of the Foundation for the Joffrey Ballet and has served
on the Board of Directors since 1979.

As his colleague and friend, I pay tribute to him with a compelling sense of admiration, respect, and love.

I would like to end by quoting from my favorite poet, Kahlil
Gibran, who was asked by a rich man to speak of giving: "You
give but little when you give of your possessions. It is when you
give of yourself that you truly give."[2] Lew, we thank you for
giving yourself to cardiology and Iowa.

References

1.   Abboud FM: Retirement tribute to Lewis E. January. Given at the
     University of Iowa, June 23, 1981.
2.   Gibran K: *The Prophet*. Alfred A. Knopf, Inc., New York (1975) 19
3.   Bierring WL: *A History of the Department of Internal Medicine, State
     University of Iowa College of Medicine 1870–1958*. State University of
     Iowa, Iowa City (1958)

Dr. January died in 2002, after this profile was written.

George William Manning

ROBERT E. BEAMISH, M.D.

Division of Cardiovascular Sciences, St. Boniface Hospital Research Centre, Winnipeg, Manitoba, Canada

One of the hazards of having an ardor for research is that it may lead to areas on the periphery of the central focus of a lifetime of work. This happened to George W. Manning (Fig. 1) whose career began in biology and physiology, moved to medicine and thence to aviation medicine, but ended in four decades of outstanding contributions to practice, teaching, and research in cardiology. It all began in the heady milieu of Sir Frederick Banting's laboratory where attention had turned from diabetes to coronary artery disease, silicosis, asphyxia, and other conditions needing illumination. The prescient Banting had begun research in the problems of aviation before World War II, but advent of the war drastically increased it and it was to envelop Manning for the next five years.

Born in Toronto in 1911, the only child of a railway man who later went into the hat business, Manning decided in high school that he would be a doctor. He enrolled in the University of Toronto in 1931, taking the honors course in biological and medical sciences. He graduated B.A. in 1935 and was appointed research assistant in the Banting Institute, completing his M.A. there in 1937. This period was spent in research on coronary artery disease which was published with G.E. Hall and F.G. Banting under the title "*Vagus Stimulation and the Production of Myocardial Damage*" in the Canadian Medical Association Journal, (1937). He then proceeded to study medicine and received his M.D. in 1940.

Manning interned for three months at St. Michael's Hospital and then requested release to return to the Banting Institute which was now fully engaged in aviation research associated with the war. He registered for Ph.D. but completion of this was to be deferred until 1948. The Banting group was studying urgent problems such as motion sickness and the effect of altitude on peripheral and night vision; in 1940, Manning joined the R.C.A.F. and was placed in charge of No. 2 Clinical Investigation Unit in Regina. In 1943 he was transferred to a British research station in England, working on pressure breathing jackets and oxygen masks. Later he was sent to Belfast to work with (later Sir) Henry Barcroft on anoxic collapse. Nearly 40 full reports were authored or co-authored by Manning during his years with the air force. At the end of hostilities in 1945 he returned to Canada and was offered appointment in the faculty of medicine at the University of Western Ontario (London) subject to further studies in cardiology. There followed a year as a senior intern at Toronto General Hospital and then an additional year or more as a Nuffield Fellow in Britain.

In civilian Britain, Manning became a member of the Heart Unit of London Hospital in Whitechapel which, as the world's first, was founded by Sir James Mackenzie (1853–1925) who was followed by Sir John Parkinson and Dr. William Evans. This was a period when bedside cardiology was at its peak and new developments such as cardiac catheterization and phonocardiography were beginning to be introduced. Parkinson and Evans and their Heart Unit had a profound effect on Manning and were to determine the creation of his own Heart Unit when he returned to Canada in 1947. He then completed his Ph.D. at the University of Toronto and moved to his new post at the University of Western Ontario.

FIG. 1 George William Manning (1911–1992).

As agreed when he was still in the air force, Manning became the second full-time faculty member at U.W.O. and continued full time for 25 years at Victoria Hospital and after that for an additional 16 years when a University Hospital was built. During the earlier years he rose from Fellow to full Professor and to Chief of Cardiology in both hospitals and acquired fellowship in the Canadian Royal College and the American Colleges of Physicians and Cardiology. In 1948 he established the first specialized cardiac care unit in Canada and saw it grow from one tiny basement room with a staff of two to one of the largest and best equipped in Canada with a large staff of cardiologists and technicians. Among other achievements the unit has become Canada's leading center for cardiac transplantation and for the surgical and medical treatment of arrhythmias.

Dr. Manning's consuming interest has been electrocardiography. During the years 1947–1986, he received all the electrocardiograms from R.C.A.F. stations in Canada and overseas. His Heart Unit served as the ECG laboratory for the R.C.A.F. and by 1986 had received over 350,000 tracings; this was of great value to the Air Force but, in addition, was the source of numerous papers of significance to clinical cardiologists. In 1965 he developed a vectorcardiograph capable of recording three spatial loops from the same cardiac cycle. Although shown at several scientific meetings, it was eventually abandoned when other diagnostic procedures in cardiology rendered it less useful.

In addition to dozens of unpublished reports and addresses, Manning has published over a hundred papers and edited three books—one on electrical activity of the heart, one on atherosclerosis, and a privately printed two-volume book entitled *Banting, Insulin and Aviation Medical Research*. Keenly interested in medical history, he has also written *A Forty Year History of the Department of Medicine, 1945–1985*, published by the University of Western Ontario and a *History of the Royal Canadian Air Force Electrocardiographic Program, 1939–1986*, published by The Queen's Printer, Ottawa, for the Defense and Civilian Institute of Environmental Medicine, Downsview, Ontario.

Like so many talented leaders in medicine, Manning has spread his mantle widely. He has served innumerable organizations and has been honored by many. He was a founding member of the Ontario and Canadian Heart Foundations and has received its Distinguished Service Award; the Civil Aviation Medical Association made him an Honorary Life Member and gave him the Award of Service in 1982, while the Institute of Aviation Medicine conferred the Award of Merit in 1979. He was also awarded the W.R. Frank's Merit of Service to Aviation Medicine Medal in 1984. He is a Life Member of the American College of Cardiology and is the only Canadian to have served as its Vice President. His university made him Professor Emeritus on his retirement.

Science, cardiology and aviation have not consumed him entirely. During the "Dirty Thirties" he helped put himself through school by teaching the piano and he also formed an orchestra through which he met his wife. Married in 1940, they now enjoy three children and four grandchildren.

References:

1.   Manning, GW: *A Forty Year History of the Department of Medicine, 1945–1985*. Published by University of Western Ontario (1987)
2.   Gray, Charlotte: Profile—George William Manning. *Can Med Assoc J* 15, 744 (1982)
3.   Segall, HN: *Pioneers of Cardiology in Canada 1820–1970*. Willowdale Hounslow Press (1988) 191–197
4.   Manning, GA: *History of the Royal Canadian Air Force. Electrocardiographic Program, 1939–1986*. Defence and Civil Institute of Environmental Medicine (1987)

Paul M. Zoll and Electrical Stimulation of the Human Heart

W. H. ABELMANN, M.D.

The Charles A. Dana Research Institute and the Harvard-Thorndike Laboratory of Beth Israel Hospital, Department of Medicine, Beth Israel Hospital and Harvard Medical School, Boston, Massachusetts, USA

In 1952, Paul M. Zoll demonstrated that a single electrical stimulus to the surface of the chest could produce a heart beat in patients with heart block due to Stokes-Adams disease, and found that in the presence of complete cardiac arrest, repeated stimuli could maintain an effective cardiac rhythm for long periods of time. Subsequently, he showed that external electrical stimulation effectively resuscitated patients with cardiac standstill secondary to vagal stimulation, drugs, or anesthetics. This discovery led to the development of temporary internal and permanent implanted pacemakers, used widely in the treatment of patients with disturbances of cardiac conduction to prevent sudden death and to permit rehabilitation. The advent of pacemakers has also led to many clinical investigations in cardiac physiology and pharmacology not possible previously.

Also in 1952, Paul M. Zoll suggested and later introduced the use of external countershock as an effective method of resuscitation from ventricular fibrillation. Subsequently, he also applied this method to terminate other arrhythmias such as supraventricular tachycardia, ventricular tachycardia, and atrial fibrillation. Electrical cardioversion has become a well-established treatment of arrhythmias.

These discoveries of the beneficial application of controlled electrical energy to the human heart led to the development of cardiac monitors to permit instant recognition of cardiac arrest, still a mainstay of intensive care units. The discovery of the beneficial effects of controlled application of electrical energy to the human heart, both directly and indirectly, has contributed significantly to the prolongation of life and to the reduction of mortality from heart disease.

Paul Zoll, The Man

Paul Maurice Zoll (Fig. 1) was born on July 15, 1911, in Boston, the son of a merchant. After graduating from the scholastically demanding Boston Latin School, he entered Harvard College, where he became interested in philosophy and psychology and came under the influence of Professor Edwin G. Boring, who introduced him to the experimental method. Under his guidance, the young Zoll carried out psychophysical studies, addressing the "volume aspects of sound" (Zoll, 1934) and also explored the multidimensionality of consciousness under John Beebe-Center (Zoll, 1934).

These were the depression years, and although Paul had an inclination toward academics, it was at the insistence of his mother that he took premedical courses in summer school. The experience of his older brother, who after graduating from Harvard College in English literature could not find a job, played a role in the family's attitude toward career planning. Accordingly, after receiving the A.B. degree *summa cum laude* in 1936, Paul turned down a postgraduate research fellowship offered to him by Professors Boring and Gordon Allport, and went on to Harvard Medical School (Class of 1936). In his last year, instead of clinical elective courses, he chose six months of research with Soma Weiss, then the Associate Director of the Thorndike Memorial Laboratory at Boston City Hospital and Professor of Medicine at the Harvard Medical School. Paul was assigned to study the relationship of alcoholism to heart disease: a retrospective search through the files of the Mallory Institute of Pathology revealed four cases of "alcoholic heart disease" with questionable beriberi. He also attempted to produce beriberi in mice (Weiss *et al.,* 1938; Zoll and Weiss, 1936). He gave serious thought to going into pathology, still unsure about his ability to handle patients. "The clinical giants of the day overawed me." However, he accepted a clinical internship at Beth Israel Hospital, followed by a year of residency at Bellevue Hospital in New York City, under Dr. Norman Joliffe (New York University Service). In 1939, Zoll returned to Boston's Beth Israel hospital, as a Research Fellow of the Josiah Macy Foundation, to work with H. L. Blumgart and M. J. Schlesinger on the clinicopathologic correlations of coronary artery disease (Blumgart *et al.,* 1941; Schlesinger and Zoll, 1941).

In World War II, Zoll served in the U.S. Army Medical Corps, first in Georgia, Texas, and the Aleutians, and then at the 160th U.S. Army Station Hospital in the United Kingdom, dedicated to thoracic problems, where he was cardiologist and Chief of Medicine. Here he met up with his classmate Dwight Harken, whom he supported in pioneering the successful removal of foreign bodies from the heart (Harken and Zoll, 1946). Observing the behavior of the heart during surgical manipulations, he was impressed by its irritability as well as by the close relationship of the heart to the esophagus.

In 1945, Zoll returned to Boston, entered private practice, but also assumed his research activities with Blumgart and Schlesinger, focusing upon the pathophysiology of angina pectoris (Freedberg *et al.,* 1948; Zoll *et al.,* 1951a, 1951b). In

FIG. 1   Paul M. Zoll, M.D. (1911–1999)

the late 1940s, he recalls seeing a 60-year-old lady with Stokes-Adams disease, who had been well until three weeks prior to hospitalization with seizures. He called all the experts he could think of, but no useful advice on the treatment of heart block was forthcoming. The patient died, and the post-mortem examination was negative. Zoll was deeply upset: "this should not happen to a heart perfectly normal except for a block of conduction. It should be possible to stimulate the heart." He was aware of earlier work in the 1930s which had demonstrated that rabbit atria could be stimulated electrically to contract (Hyman 1930), and later of successful stimulation of the sinoauricular node in dogs by Callaghan and Bigelow (1951). He thought of using the esophageal approach. In 1950, Zoll borrowed Professor Otto Krayer's stimulator and, using an esophageal wire, was able to produce ventricular extrasystoles in a dog. Later, he found that he could elicit the same response with stimuli applied externally to the chest. It was not until 1952, however, that he had the opportunity to apply this treatment to a patient. He was able to maintain a regular rhythm for 25 minutes in a 75-year-old patient with complete heart block and intermittent ventricular standstill, but the patient did not survive. In a second patient, a 65-year-old man with end-stage coronary disease, complete heart block, and recurrent cardiac arrest, external stimulation was successful for 52 hours, and the patient survived for six months. Although these clinical experiments were published by a prestigious medical journal (Zoll, 1952) and were praised in an accompanying editorial (Editorial, 1952), they were not well received by many of his colleagues, who considered this work "against the will of God."

Undaunted, albeit not unaffected, by criticism and resistance, Zoll proceeded with his investigations (detailed be-

low), while continuing an active clinical practice and teaching in pharmacology and pathophysiology courses, as well as physical diagnosis and clinical medicine.

He rose from Research Fellow and Assistant in Medicine to Clinical Professor at the Harvard Medical School and Physician at the Beth Israel Hospital. From 1947 to 1958, he was Chief of the Cardiac Clinic at Beth Israel Hospital. In 1977, he became Clinical Professor of Medicine, Emeritus, at Harvard Medical School.

Paul Zoll received the U.S. Army Legion of Merit Award in 1944, the John Scott Award of the City of Philadelphia in 1967, the Eugene Drake Memorial Award of the Maine Heart Association in 1968, the Albert Lasker Award for Clinical Medical Research in 1973, the Award for Merit of the American Heart Association in 1974, the first Polytechnic/ Wunsch Award from the Polytechnic Institute in New York in 1981, the Texas Heart Institute Medal and Ray C. Fish Award in 1981, and the Paul Dudley White Award from the American Heart Association, Massachusetts affiliate, in 1985.

He is a member of the Harvard Chapter of Phi Beta Kappa, of Sigma XI, the American Federation for Clinical Research, the American Heart Association, the Association of American Physicians, and the Massachusetts Medical Society.

Zoll served as Associate Editor of *Circulation* from 1956 to 1965, as well as on the Scientific Review Board of the *Journal of Medical Electronics*, the International Board of Editors of the Excerpta Medical Foundation, and the Editorial Board of the *Journal of Electrocardiology*.

Paul Zoll has made over 50 original contributions to the scientific literature.

In 1939, Paul Zoll married Janet Jones. His physicist son Ross is now completing his medical studies. His daughter Mary, who has a doctorate in biochemistry, is a science editor. Janet died in 1978, after a long illness. In 1981, Paul married Ann Blumgart Gurewich. Always a very private individual, Paul has been closest to his family and a few long standing friends, among whom are his close collaborators Arthur J. Linenthal, Howard A. Frank, and Alan H. Belgard. Early interests included football and basketball; later he became very fond of water-skiing. Tennis has remained his principal sport.

Paul Zoll's Major Scientific Contributions (Fig. 2)

Resuscitation from Ventricular Standstill by External Electrical Pacing

The external electrical stimulation of the heart for resuscitation from ventricular standstill was Paul Zoll's fundamental discovery in 1952 (Zoll, 1952; Zoll *et al.*, 1953). He found that a single electrical stimulus to the surface of the chest could produce a heart beat in patients with heart block due to Stokes-Adams disease. Repeated stimuli enabled him to maintain an effective cardiac rhythm for long periods of time when there were no intrinsic ventricular beats. Previously, cardiac standstill had been a serious and usually terminal event that rarely responded to therapeutic measures. Now, for the first time, it became possible to keep such a patient alive during stand-still lasting for hours or days. Subsequently, external electrical stimulation was also shown to be effective in resuscitating patients with cardiac standstill resulting from vagal stimulation, drugs, or anesthetics. External electrical stimulation is still in use for emergency resuscitation prior to more invasive procedures for direct electrical stimulation of the heart by means of surface electrodes, a percutaneous needle electrode, or a transvenous catheter electrode.

Resuscitation from Ventricular Fibrillation by External Electrical Countershock

External electrical countershock was introduced by Zoll as a basic method of resuscitation from cardiac arrest due to ventricular fibrillation. In his 1952 paper on external electrical stimulation, Zoll suggested that it should be possible to interrupt ventricular fibrillation and resuscitate a patient from cardiac arrest by applying a strong countershock externally (Zoll, 1952). Later a safe and clinically practicable technique for this purpose was developed and applied successfully in man (Zoll et al., 1956, 1960). Previously, emergency surgical thoracotomy and manual compression of the heart was the only available approach. External countershock is presently in routine use in numerous clinical situations in which cardiac arrest due to ventricular fibrillation requires emergency resuscitation.

Electrical Cardioversion of Other Cardiac Arrhythmias

Although external electrical countershock was originally developed for the termination of ventricular fibrillation, it was soon found to be effective in terminating supraventricular tachycardia, ventricular tachycardia, and atrial fibrillation (Zoll et al., 1960). This immediately effective procedure is now used widely in the treatment of these arrhythmias and is considered safer than the administration of large doses of antiarrhythmic drugs.

Control of Irregular Ventricular Rhythms by Electrical Acceleration of the Ventricular Rate

Acceleration of the ventricular rate by external electrical stimulation or by sympathomimetic drugs was found to prevent recurrent Stokes-Adams attacks due to ventricular tachycardia or fibrillation. Zoll noted that the spontaneous ventricular rhythm was regular above a certain rate, whereas below that rate multifocal ectopic ventricular activity or ventricular tachycardia-fibrillation recurred (Linenthal et al., 1963; Zoll et al., 1960). These observations are the basis for electrical "overdrive," now widely used to control both supraventricular and ventricular arrhythmias.

The Cardiac Monitor

Optimal use of the newly developed electrical techniques for emergency resuscitation (external stimulation and countershock) required instantaneous recognition of cardiac arrest in the hospitalized patient. For this purpose, a practical monitoring device was proposed by Zoll and was developed by his technical collaborators to display the electrical activity of the heart on an oscilloscopic screen, to register each heart beat with an audible signal, and to sound an alarm upon the onset of cardiac arrest (Zoll et al., 1956). Cardiac monitors and pro-

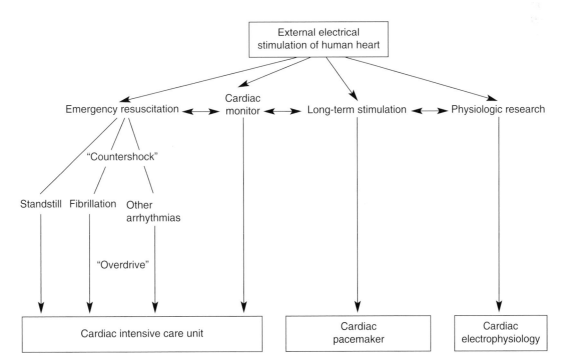

FIG. 1   Impact of Zoll's discovery of external electrical stimulation of the heart upon cardiology.

grams for the management of cardiac arrest form the foundation of modern coronary care units.

Physiologic and Pharmacologic Research Facilitated by Electrical Pacing

In addition to its therapeutic importance, electrical stimulation of heart, both external and direct, permitted fundamental studies of the physiologic and pharmacologic behavior of the human heart, not previously possible in humans. These provided significant insights into quantitative aspects of ventricular refractory and supernormal periods (Linenthal *et al.*, 1962), fusion beats and measurements of myocardial conduction times (Linenthal *et al.*, 1965), the response curve of ventricular excitability (Linenthal *et al.*, 1965), effects of sympathomimetic amines on ventricular rhythmicity and atrioventricular conduction (Zoll *et al.*, 1958), depression of idioventricular pacemakers by rapid stimulation, and features of antegrade and retrograde atrioventricular conduction.

The Implanted Pacemaker

After the development of the external emergency resuscitation technique, the therapeutic focus in Stokes-Adams disease became the prevention of recurrent seizures. Since drug therapy was usually inadequate, the complete prevention of seizures, whether due to ventricular standstill or ventricular fibrillation, could be expected only if the ventricles could be driven electrically for an indefinite period of time. A method was developed by Zoll and his colleagues for such long-term direct electrical stimulation of the heart by an implanted pacemaker (Zoll *et al.*, 1961, 1964). This pacemaker was also used to improve congestive heart failure in patients with a slow ventricular rate. Implanted cardiac pacemakers derived from this basic technological breakthrough have become a major form of cardiac therapy, both in the temporary and permanent mode. Cardiac pacemakers have played a significant role in the prevention of sudden death and in the rehabilitation of cardiac patients. It has been estimated that more than 500,000 patients in the United States are presently being kept alive by implanted pacemakers.

Recent Contributions

In the quest for a rapid, easily applied, safe, and well-tolerated noninvasive method of temporary cardiac stimulation, Zoll and associates re-examined external mechanical stimulation of the heart and developed a mechanical pacemaker (Falk *et al.* 1983; Zoll *et al.*, 1976, 1981, 1985). This device was shown to be an effective substitute for temporary transvenous pacing. This method of cardiac stimulation also lent itself to the induction of ventricular extrasystoles for physiologic and clinical studies of postextrasystolic potentiation (Angoff *et al.*, 1978; Cohn *et al.* 1977).

Conclusion

Paul Zoll's discovery of the feasibility and effectiveness of external electrical stimulation of the human heart in 1952 and his subsequent research initiated a remarkable era of advances in understanding and treatment of important aspects of heart diseases of many different causes (e.g., ischemic, rheumatic, congenital heart disease, cardiomyopathy). This discovery has contributed significantly to the documented decrease in mortality from heart disease in the United States.

Acknowledgment

The author is indebted to Arthur J. Linenthal, M.D. for his significant contributions to this report.

References

Angoff GH, Wistran D, Sloss LJ, Markis JE, Come PC, Zoll PM, Cohn PF: Value of noninvasively induced ventricular extrasystole during echocardiographic and phonocardiographic assessment of patients with idiopathic hypertrophic subaortic stenosis. *Am J Cardiol* 42, 919 (1978)

Blumgart HL, Schlesinger MJ, Zoll PM: Angina pectoris, coronary failure and acute myocardial infarction. The role of coronary occlusions and collateral circulation. *JAMA* 116, 91 (1941)

Callaghan JC, Bigelow WG: Electrical artificial pacemaker for standstill of heart. *Ann Surg* 134, 8 (1951)

Cohn PF, Angoff GH, Zoll PM, Sloss LJ, Markis JE, Graboys TB, Green LH, Braunwald E: A new, noninvasive technique for inducing postextrasystolic potentiation during echocardiography. *Circulation* 56, 598 (1977)

Editorial: Electrical stimulation in cardiac arrest. *N Engl J Med* 247, 781 (1952)

Falk RH, Zoll PM, Zoll RH: Safety and efficacy of noninvasive cardiac pacing. *N Engl J Med* 309, 1166 (1983)

Freedberg AS, Blumgart HL, Zoll PM, Schlesinger MJ: The clinical syndrome of cardiac pain intermediate between angina pectoris and acute myocardial infarction. I. Coronary failure. *JAMA* 138, 107 (1948)

Harken DR, Zoll PM: Foreign bodies in and in relation to the thoracic blood vessels and heart. III. Indications for the removal of intracardiac foreign bodies and the behavior of the heart during manipulation. *Am Heart J* 32, 1 (1946)

Hyman AS: Resuscitation of the stopped heart by intracardiac therapy. *Arch Intern Med* 46, 553 (1930)

Linenthal AJ, Zoll PM: Prevention of ventricular tachycardia and fibrillation by intravenous isoproterenol and epinephrine. *Circulation* 27, 5 (1963)

Linenthal AJ, Zoll PM: Quantitive studies of ventricular refractory and supernormal periods in man. *Trans Assoc Am Phys* 75, 285 (1962)

Linenthal AJ, Zoll PM: Ventricular fusion beats during electric stimulation in man; application to conduction velocity and anomalous A-V excitation. *Circulation* 31, 651 (1965)

Linenthal AJ, Zoll PM: A new curve of cardiac excitability in man. Its bearing on the mechanism of A-V block. *Trans Assoc Am Phys* 78, 269 (1965)

Schlesinger MH, Zoll PM: The incidence and localization of coronary artery occlusions. *Arch Pathol* 32, 198 (1941)

Weiss S, Haynes FW, Zoll PM: Electrocardiographic manifestations and the cardiac effects of drugs in vitamin B$_1$ deficiency in rats. *Am Heart J* 15, 206 (1938)

Zoll PM: The relaxation of tonal volume, intensity and pitch. *Am J Phychol* 46, 99 (1934a)

Zoll PM: The pluridimensionality of consciousness. *Am J Psychol* 46, 621 (1934b)

Zoll PM: Resuscitation of the heart in ventricular standstill by external electric stimulation. *N Engl J Med* 247, 768 (1952)

Zoll PM, Linenthal AJ: Termination of refractory tachycardia by external countershock. *Circulation* 25, 596 (1962)

Zoll PM, Weiss S: Electrocardiographic changes in rats deficient in vitamin B$_1$. *Proc Soc Exper Biol Med* 35, 259 (1936)

Zoll PM, Wessler S, Blumgart HL: The pathogenesis of angina pectoris: A clinical and pathologic correlation. *Am J Med* 11, 331 (1951a)

Zoll PM, Wessler S, Schlesinger MJ: Interarterial coronary anastomoses in the human heart with particular reference to anemia and relative cardiac anoxia. *Circulation* 4, 797 (1951b)

Zoll PM, Norman LR, Linenthal AJ: Control of cardiac rhythm by an external electric pacemaker (abstr.). *J Clin Invest* 32, 614 (1953)

Zoll PM, Linenthal AJ, Gibson W, Paul MH, Norman LR: Termination of ventricular fibrillation in man by externally applied electric countershock. *N Engl J Med* 254, 727 (1956)

Zoll PM, Linenthal AJ, Norman LR, Paul MH, Gibson W: Treatment of unexpected cardiac arrest by external electric stimulation of the heart. *N Engl J Med* 254, 541 (1956)

Zoll PM, Linenthal AJ, Gibson W, Paul MH, Norman LR: Intravenous drug therapy of Stokes-Adams disease. Effects of sympathomimetic amines on ventricular rhythmicity and atrioventricular conduction. *Circulation* 17, 325 (1958)

Zoll PM, Linenthal AJ, Zarsky LRN: Ventricular fibrillation. Treatment and prevention by external electric currents. *N Engl J Med* 262, 105 (1960)

Zoll PM, Frank HA, Zarsky LRN, Linenthal AJ, Belgard AH: Long-term electric stimulation of the heart for Stokes-Adams disease. *Ann Surg* 154, 330 (1961)

Zoll PM, Frank HA, Linenthal AJ: Four-year experience with an implanted cardiac pacemaker. *Ann Surg* 160, 351, (1964)

Zoll PM, Belgard AH, Weintraub MD, Frank HA: External mechanical cardiac stimulation. *N Engl J Med* 294, 1274 (1976)

Zoll PM, Zoll RH, Belgard AH; External noninvasive electric stimulation of the heart. *Crit Care Med* 9, 393 (1981)

Zoll PM, Zoll RH, Falk RH, Clinton JE, Eitel DR, Antman EM: External noninvasive temporary cardiac pacing: Clinical trials. *Circulation* 71, 937 (1985)

Dr. Zoll died in 1999, after this profile was written.

Inge Edler: Father of Echocardiography

LOUIS J. ACIERNO, M.D., FACC, AND L. TIMOTHY WORRELL, M.P.H., R.R.T.

Cardiopulmonary Sciences, Department of Health Professions, University of Central Florida, Orlando, Florida, USA

Echocardiography has come a long way since its introduction as a clinical tool by Inge Edler (Fig. 1). As head of the Department of Cardiology at the University Hospital, Lund, Sweden, it was his responsibility to evaluate the cardiac patients prior to surgical correction of their cardiac abnormality. In particular, the surgical repair of mitral stenosis mandated a precise delineation of the severity of the valvulopathy. This was in 1953, at which time cardiac catheterization and contrast imaging were still in their infancy and failed to provide enough data for an accurate appraisal of the status of the mitral valve. At the same time, Carl Helmuth Hertz was working as a graduate student in the nuclear physics department at the University of Lund. Young Hertz was the son of famous Nobel laureate Gustav Hertz. During this era, the University of Lund was small enough to accommodate the entire faculty in the lunchroom. This provided the necessary intimacy for an unregulated interplay of ideas and research results among the various disciplines. This, no doubt, provided the ambience for the fortuitous interchange of objectives and research results between the young graduate student and Professor Edler. Thus, a merger was formed between the physicist Hertz and the cardiologist Edler.[1]

It so happened that Carl Hertz had a marked interest in ultrasound and was already acquainted with the ultrasonic reflectoscope developed for nondestructive materials testing. Work leading to the development of the reflectoscope began in the 1930s. A device was needed to test the construction of metal ship hulls and battle tank armor. This was first suggested in 1928 by a Soviet scientist, Sergei Y. Sokolov, at the Electrotechnical Institute of Leningrad. Other researchers in this area of interest included Floyd A. Firestone at the University of Michigan and Donald Sproule in England. Firestone's work led to the development of the supersonic reflectoscope in 1941. Other similar devices were developed in England and Germany.[2] The version which Carl Hertz would ultimately use was developed by the Siemens Corporation of Germany. Carl Hertz had a connection with the Techniska Rontgencentralen section of Siemens and was able to borrow an ultrasonic reflectoscope from the company, which was located in the nearby town of Malmö.[1] The first person to be examined with this device was himself. At that time, he identified a signal that moved with cardiac action using the time-motion or M-mode approach. On the basis of this initial attempt, both he and Edler immediately began a series of observations on patients with mitral stenosis.[3] In a short span of time, World War II became

history, and again Carl Hertz was able to borrow an improved reflectoscope manufactured by Siemens. Hertz's father was the director of the Siemens Research Laboratory before the end of the war and it was through this connection that young Carl was able to borrow the instrument. The scope was delivered in October 1953, and the young researchers immediately expanded on their previous studies with the improved version.[1]

The first publication appeared in 1954; it was entitled "The Use of Ultrasonic Reflectoscope for the Continuous Recording of the Movements of the Heart Wall."[4] Although the equipment was somewhat primitive, Edler and Hertz were able to register well-defined echoes on the cathode ray tube screen that moved synchronously with the heartbeat. Further observations clarified that the echoes were originating from the mitral valve as well as from the wall of the left atrium, in contrast to their original belief that they were emanating only from the wall of the left atrium.[5] Many of these examinations were conducted on dying patients. Upon completion of the exam, Edler marked the direction of the ultrasound beam on the patient's chest. After the patient died, he would pass an ice pick into the chest in the same direction the beam had been directed during the exam. On postmortem examination of the patient, he found that the anterior leaflet of the mitral valve had been transected by the ice pick and not necessarily the posterior wall of the left atrium.[3] All of this work was demonstrated in a scientific film shown at the Third European Congress of Cardiology in Rome in 1960[6] and published in 1961.[7,8] The remainder of the observations was presented at a symposium on ultrasound held at the University of Illinois in June 1962.[9] Seven years later Edler, in collaboration with Lindström, introduced the combined use of Doppler and echocardiography at the First World Congress on Ultrasonic Diagnostics in Medicine in Vienna. At that time, they demonstrated the importance of this approach in the diagnosis of aortic and mitral valve regurgitation.[10,11]

Inge Edler was a very private man, so much so that it has been virtually impossible to obtain adequate biographical material regarding the personal details of his life. Most of the information outlined here was obtained from a personal communication with his colleague, Dr. Jan Eskilsson, and from the curriculum vitae of Dr. Edler in his possession. In addition, we were fortunate to receive more personal details of his life from his son, Professor Lars Edler.

These sources provided us with the date of Edler's birth on March 17, 1911, in Burlöv, Malmöhus County, Sweden. His

FIG. 1 Inge Edler (1911–2001). Photograph courtesy of the Albert and Mary Lasker Foundation Archives and The National Library of Medicine.

parents were Carl and Sophia who were teachers in the primary school in that vicinity. He graduated from the local high school, Högre Allmänna Läroverket, in 1930. Young Edler wanted to continue with University studies in physics, particularly micronics, but he was convinced by his sister to go for dentistry instead. As it was too late to enroll in the faculty of dentistry, he was able to be accepted by the faculty of medicine at Lunds University. This was supposed to be a stop gap measure. However, medicine intrigued him so that he continued his studies at the university, receiving his medical degree in 1943. While there, he met another medical student, Karin Jungbeck. They married in 1939. Karin later became an ophthalmologist and had her own practice until she retired. Their marriage was blessed with four children. Lars, the youngest and the one who supplied the information, is now Professor of Biological Oceanography. Dr. Edler's professional career was initiated in the field of general medical practice, but was soon restricted to his employment in the Department of Internal Medicine at the University Hospital of Lund, and in the space of several years revolved primarily around cardiology. He was appointed director of the Laboratory for Heart Catheterization (again at the University Hospital) in 1948 and functioned in this capacity until 1950. At that time, he was appointed director of the Department of Internal Medicine and the Cardiovascular Laboratory. He remained in this capacity until 1960, assuming additional administrative duties in 1953 as Head of the Department of Cardiology until his retirement in 1977 (curriculum vitae of Inge Edler and personal communication from Dr. Jan Eskilsson and Prof. Lars Edler).

Edler was quite active as a member of many societies devoted, in whole or in part, to the advancement of ultrasound. Among them were the American Institute of Ultrasound in Medicine, Deutsche Gesellschaft für Ultraschall Diagnostik in der Medizin, the Swedish Society of Medical Ultrasound, the Yugoslav Association of Societies for Ultrasound in Medicine and Biology, the Swedish Society of Cardiology, and the American College of Cardiology (curriculum vitae of Inge Edler and personal communication from Dr. Jan Eskilsson and Prof. Lars Edler).

Throughout his professional career, Dr. Edler was awarded many honors. The Albert and Mary Lasker Foundation awarded him and Helmuth Hertz the Clinical Medicine Research Prize in 1977 for pioneering the clinical application of ultrasound in the medical diagnosis of abnormalities of the heart. This was followed in 1983 by the Rotterdam Echocardiography Award for his most outstanding and pioneering work applying ultrasound as a diagnostic tool in cardiology. In December 1984, he received the Lund Award for "scientific work of extraordinary significance" from the Royal Physiologic Society. In 1987, Lund University bestowed upon him the title of Professor H. C. One year later he was again honored with the Münchener and Aachener Preis für Technik und angewandte Naturwissenschaft, and finally in 1991, he was awarded the Eric K. Fernströms Stora Nordiska Pris (curriculum vitae of Inge Edler and personal communication from Dr. Jan Eskilsson and Prof. Lars Edler).

Typical of his quiet academic life, Inge Edler died in his sleep on March 7, 2001, just 10 days short of his 90th birtday.

References

1. Lunds University: Available at http:\\www.ob-ultrasound.net\inge-hertz.html. Accessed April 13, 2001
2. *History of Ultrasound and Gynecology.* Available at http:\\www.ob-ultrasound.net\history.html. Accessed April 13, 2001
3. Feigenbaum H: Evolution of echocardiography. *Circulation* 1996; 3:1321–1327
4. Edler I, Hertz CH: The use of ultrasonic reflectoscope for the continuous recording of the movements of heart walls. Kungl. Fysiografiska sällskapets i Lund förhandlingar 1954;24.5:1–19
5. Edler I, Hertz CH: The early work on ultrasound in medicine at the University of Lund. *J Clin Ultrasound* 1977;5:352–356
6. Edler I, Gustafson A, Karlefors T, Christensson B: *The Movements of Aortic and Mitral Valves Recorded with Ultrasonic Echo Techniques.* Scientific film at 3rd European Congress of Cardiology, Rome, Italy, September 1960
7. Edler I, Gustafson A, Karlefors T, Christensson B: Mitral and aortic valve movements recorded by an ultrasonic echo-method. An experimental study. *Acta Med Scand* 1961;370(suppl):67–82
8. Edler I: Ultrasoundcardiography, Part III: Atrioventricular valve motility in the living human heart recorded by ultrasound. *Acta Med Scand* 1961;370(suppl):83–124
9. Edler I: The diagnostic use of ultrasound in heart disease. Proceedings of the symposium held at the University of Illinois, Urbana 1962. In *Ultrasonic Energy* (Ed. E. Kelly), p. 303–321. Urbana: University of Illinois Press, 1965
10. Lindström K, Edler I: Ultrasonic Doppler technique used in heart disease. An experimental study. *Ultrasono Graphia Medica,* Proceedings of the 1st World Congress on Ultrasound on Ultrasonic Diagnostics in Medicine, Vienna, Austria, June 1969. Vol. III: 447–454, 1971
11. Edler I, Lindström K: Ultrasonic Doppler technique used in heart disease. Clinical application. *Ultrasono Graphia Medica.* Proceedings of the 1st World Congress on Ultrasonic Diagnostics in Medicine, Vienna, Austria, June 1969. Vol. III: 455–461, 1971

Jesse Edwards

R. O. Brandenburg, M.D.

Section of Cardiology, The University of Arizona, Tucson, Arizona, USA

Jesse Edwards professional career has been as a pathologic anatomist and teacher (Fig. 1). His expertise in both areas has earned him a well-deserved international reputation. At the age of 75 years, he maintains his zest and enthusiasm for medical challenges. This is evidenced by his current position as Senior Consultant in Anatomic Pathology at United Hospitals, St. Paul, Minnesota, which has an active program of cardiology and cardiac surgery. In addition, he conducts cardiovascular pathology conferences on a monthly basis at Abbott-Northwestern Hospital and the University of Minnesota. These conferences have been ongoing since 1960. He also attends and conducts conferences at a number of other Twin City hospitals. Another activity is his program of research and training in cardiovascular pathology for students and physicians, mainly from Minnesota, but also other states and a number of foreign countries. His program now houses 9,000 specimens of cardiovascular disease; 40,000 lantern slides with photographic negatives; and 4,000 line drawings to illustrate many of the disease states.

Jesse Edwards was born in Hyde Park, Massachusetts, July 14, 1911. He graduated from Tufts College with a B. S. degree in 1932, and he received the M. D. degree from Tufts College Medical School in 1935.

Postgraduate training included a term as Resident in Pathology at the Mallory Institute, Boston (1935–1936); a mixed clinical internship, Albany Hospital, Albany (1936–1937); a return to Mallory Institute of Pathology, Boston City Hospital as assistant to the pathologist (1937–1940); and a research fellowship at the National Cancer Institute, U. S. Public Health Service, Bethesda (1940–1942).

From 1942 to 1946, Jesse Edwards served in the U. S. Army Medical Corps, progressing from Captain to Lt. Colonel. From 1942 to 1945 he was Chief of General Hospital Laboratories in the United States and European theater. During 1945–1946 he was Commanding Officer, Central Laboratory for the U. S. Army in Europe, and concurrently, Laboratory Consultant to the Chief Surgeon, European theater. He is now Colonel in the Medical Corps, U. S. Army Reserve (Ret.). From 1947 to 1967, he was Civilian Consultant to the Surgeon General, U. S. Army.

Dr. Edwards' civilian practice began in 1946 when he was named a consultant, Section Pathologic Anatomy, Mayo Clinic, a post he held until 1960. He progressed rapidly through academic ranks, in 1954 becoming Professor of

Pathology at the Mayo Foundation Graduate School of the University of Minnesota. It was during this period that his weekly cardiovascular pathology conferences became an educational highlight for residents, fellows, and staff. Interfaces involving Dr. Edwards with Howard Burchell, Earl Wood, Raymond Pruitt, and John Kirklin were particularly stimulating and rewarding during much of this period since this was the era of burgeoning development in cardiac catheterization and cardiac surgery.

In 1960, Dr. Edwards resigned from the Mayo Clinic to become Director of Laboratories, United Hospitals-Miller Division, St. Paul, Minnesota, and in 1978 he became Senior Consultant at that institution, where he remains to date. Since 1966 he has been Consultant to the Departments of Pathology of Hennepin County Medical Center and the Veterans Administration Medical Center, both of which are in Minneapolis, Minnesota. Since 1968 he has, in addition, been Consultant in Pathology to the St. Paul-Ramsey Medical Center, and, since 1960, he has served as Clinical Professor of Pathology at the University of Minnesota School of Medicine and Professor of Pathology at the University of Minnesota Graduate School.

Dr. Edwards' professional activities have included many distinguished positions, memberships, and editorial boards. He is currently on the editorial boards of *Pediatric Cardiology* and the *American Journal of Cardiovascular Pathology*. In the past he has been on the editorial boards of *Laboratory Investigation, Circulation, American Journal of Cardiology, American Heart Journal*, and *Geriatrics*. He is currently on the Mortality Review Committee of the Multicenter Diltiazem Post-Infarction Trial (MDPIT), University of Rochester, N.Y.

He was President of the International Academy of Pathology (1955–1956); President of the Minnesota Heart Association (1962–1963); President of the American Heart Association (1967–1968); and President of the World Congress of Pediatric Cardiology (1980).

Dr. Edwards is a member of Alpha Omega Alpha and Sigma Xi Honorary Scientific Societies. His memberships include the College of American Pathologists, the International Academy of Pathology, American Association of Pathology, American Heart Association, American Medical Association, Minnesota Heart Association, Minnesota Society of Clinical Pathologists, American Society of Clinical Patholo-

FIG. 1   Dr. Jesse E. Edwards.

gists, Scientific Board of the American Longevity Association, the Serbian Academy of Sciences and Arts, and a Founding Member, Council on Geriatric Cardiology.

He is a Diplomate of the National Board of Medical Examiners and is certified by the American Board of Pathology (Pathologic Anatomy).

One of the most striking and remarkable aspects of Dr. Edwards' career has been his productivity which includes 677 papers (the majority in the field of cardiovascular pathology), 12 books, and 53 book chapters! It is of interest that starting with the first volume of *Circulation*, he had at least one paper in each volume until 1965 and numerous ones after that time.

Dr. Edwards is married to the former Marjorie Helen Brooks and they have a son and a daughter. His son, Brooks, has earned a special Clinical-Investigative Fellowship at the Mayo Clinc.

To his colleagues Dr. Edwards has always had an inquisitive and receptive mind, willing to listen, but then probing, challenging, and stimulating in his friendly, personable, open manner. This method has made him an exemplary teacher and a motivating factor in persuading so many of his students to pursue studies with him.

Dr. Edwards' early training and interest was in cancer. His diversion to the cardiovascular field was our good fortune in the light of his extensive and notable contributions to all areas of cardiovascular disease, but particularly to congenital heart disease. Noteworthy in all his teaching and writings has been his effort to correlate pathologic anatomy with clinical findings—"a clinician's pathologist."

R. Bruce Logue, M.D.

J. WILLIS HURST, M.D.

Division of Cardiology, Emory University School of Medicine, Atlanta, Georgia, USA

R. Bruce Logue (Fig. 1) was born in Augusta, Georgia, on October 9, 1911. He was graduated from Landon High School in 1930, received a Bachelor of Science degree from Emory University in 1934, and completed medical school at Emory University in 1937. He married Carolyne Clements in 1938. He spent a year on the house staff at Royal Victoria Hospital in Montreal, Canada, in 1938 and completed his residency in internal medicine at Grady Memorial Hospital in Atlanta, Georgia, in 1940. World War II was raging and Logue spent five years (1941–1946) in the medical corps of the Army of the United States. He was assigned to Lawson General Hospital for three years where he served as Chief of Cardiology. He served one year at Fort Bragg General Hospital and completed his army duty at the 248th General Hospital in the Philippines where he served as Chief of Medicine. He achieved the rank of Lieutenant Colonel. Even during those troubled times his reputation as an excellent cardiologist was emerging and his contributions to the medical literature were beginning.

Following discharge from the army in 1946 he became an Instructor in the Department of Medicine at Emory University School of Medicine. At that time Eugene Stead was Chairman of the Department of Medicine at Emory. He had assembled a group of excellent young men, many of whom were destined to be chairmen of departments of medicine at other medical schools. They were Paul Beeson, James Warren, Jack Myers, and John Hickam. Robert Grant, who later became Director of the National Heart Institute, was among them. Gene Stead appointed Bruce Logue to join the staff and later said "appointing Bruce was one of the smartest things I ever did." That is a real compliment because Gene Stead did many smart things. Gene wrote the following two paragraphs in July 1992.

When I came to Emory and Grady in May of 1942 Bruce Logue was stationed at Lawson General on the outskirts of Atlanta. He had completed training at Grady Hospital where his colleagues predicted a bright future. His clinical skills were put to good use and the legends attached to his name began to grow. Arthur Merrill insisted that we schedule our major medical conference on Sunday at 10 a.m. Arthur spent half-time in the research lab and half-time in private practice. Sunday morning was the only free time to advance his knowledge of general medicine. In time "my Sunday School" became well known in Atlanta and Durham. Sunday was also

"free time" at Lawson General and Fort McPherson. Bruce brought his army associates who came from many states to our Sunday conference. This gave our young department great visibility on the national scene.

Gene Stead, Willis Hurst, many professors of medicine and cardiology, numerous students and residents, many fellows and thousands of patients are in debt to Bruce Logue. His friends watched with interest as he became a legend in his own time.

Logue spent most of his time at Emory University Hospital where he established a first-rate medical service and became a world class consultant in cardiology. He was a major mover in establishing the Private Diagnostic Clinic in 1950, which was the forerunner of the Emory Clinic. He continued his weekly ward rounds at Grady Memorial Hospital and held a weekly teaching conference at the Atlanta Veterans Administration Hospital. Eager house officers and colleagues flocked to his informative, exciting, and entertaining conferences.

Bruce's influence at Emory and in the world of cardiology continued to grow. He rose to the rank of Professor of Medicine, served as Chief of Medicine at Emory University Hospital from 1957 to 1980 and as Chief of the Medical Section of the Emory Clinic from 1955 until 1980. He played a major role in the creation of the Emory Clinic which grew out of the Private Diagnostic Clinic. The Emory Clinic, under his influence, grew steadily and it is now one of the largest private clinics in the nation and one of a few that is intimately entwined with a medical school.

In 1980, Logue moved his office to Emory-owned Crawford Long Hospital where he became Director of the Carlyle Fraser Heart Center. He held that position until 1986. His contribution to the development and growth of cardiology at Crawford Long Hospital is another monument to his ability.

Accomplishments and Honors

- Bruce Logue became certified by the American Board of Internal Medicine in 1940 and became a Fellow in the American College of Physicians in 1946. He was certified by the Subspecialty Board of Cardiovascular Disease in 1947.
- He was the first full-time member of the medical service at Emory University Hospital (1946).

Fig. 1   R. Bruce Logue, M.D.

- He was a major mover in the creation of the Private Diagnostic Clinic at Emory University Hospital in 1949.
- He established the first cardiology fellowship program at Grady Memorial Hospital.
- He was founding President of the Georgia Heart Association.
- He was Vice President of the American Heart Association and for a number of years was a member of the Executive Committee.
- He was President of the American Federation for Clinical Research.
- He was Chairman of the Subspecialty Board of Cardiovascular Disease.
- He won the Master Teacher Award of the American College of Cardiology in 1969.
- He is the author of 90 scientific papers dealing with heart disease. He contributed greatly to the development of the book *The Heart*. We met for several hours each Thursday morning for almost the entire year of 1964 in order to critique and edit each sentence of every page of the first edition of *The Heart*. He contributed significantly to the book's next seven editions and deserves much credit for its success.

Logue was always a much sought-after speaker at postgraduate courses and received numerous honors and awards. He was presented the Award of Honor by the Emory Medical Alumni in 1970, and the Board of Trustees of Emory University established the R. Bruce Logue Chair of Cardiovascular Disease in 1981; the Chair is now held by Wayne Alexander.

The Persona of R. Bruce Logue

The preceding comments are true enough but they are dwarfed by the person who is named R. Bruce Logue. As I write this portion of his profile I am confident I speak for hundreds of students, house officers, cardiac fellows, and patients when I try to portray a mental picture of this charismatic man. He is highly intelligent and his mental and physical actions were (and are) quicker than anyone around him. In a flash he could snatch his stethoscope from the pocket of his white coat and listen to one heart cycle of a patient and then give a learned discourse on the details of the auscultatory events including the physiologic derangement associated with the abnormal heart sounds and murmurs. Many exhausted cardiology fellows lay prostrate with fatigue as Bruce made his rounds. He could read, write, and talk with ease. His memory was (and still is) unexcelled. He was a superb observer and built an enormous personal experience in cardiology. The famous Samuel Levine once told me, "That fellow can observe—he is a great clinician." Levine was impressed with Bruce's description of the pulsation of the right sternoclavicular joint that occurs in some patients with dissection of the aorta. Bruce made many important observations, most of which he never published. They were not lost, however, because he discussed them with numerous trainees and colleagues. He shunned administrative positions but accepted his share of administrative posts. He was an excellent administrator but preferred to spend his time with patients and trainees. With all of this he was (and is) a superb chef, cabinet maker, dancer, and golfer. Everyone respected and admired Bruce. He was comfortable with his patients, trainees, and colleagues and so they were comfortable with him. Had this not been the case, the influence of his intellect would have been stifled. Everyone enjoyed Bruce (and we still do). His method of expressing himself not only marked him as being different from others, but also made what he said memorable. He is one individual of whom I can say, without being challenged by anyone who knew him, that he has made a great difference for the good of this world that is full of problems.

Carolyne, his wife, has made a great contribution as well. There is no more gracious hostess in the world. Now both Bruce and Carolyne spend a lot of time on the golf course. They are good at that, too!

A Personal Note

In 1950, R. Bruce Logue and Paul Beeson, then Chairman of the Department of Medicine at Emory University, asked me to join the department of medicine at that institution. I did so and was privileged to work by Bruce's side. I owe my professional career to him—I thank him with all the words I possess.

In Memoriam: William Likoff, 1912–1987

J. R. DiPalma, M.D.

Department of Pharmacology and Medicine, Hahnemann University School of Medicine, Philadelphia, Pennsylvania, USA

To know William Likoff (Billy to his friends) and especially to be his colleague was a rare privilege. As a second-generation cardiologist, his life was intimately interwoven with the development of this field in Philadelphia and especially with his alma mater, the Hahnemann Medical College and Hospital, now the Hahnemann University School of Medicine. Granted that he attained national and even international recognition because of his work, the main structure of his career was woven in the fabric of a group of aggressive and energetic men who, in the prime of this century, advanced the field of cardiology to its present eminence.

Billy's father was a successful businessman in the wholesale food supply industry. There were hard times during the great depression, but the essentials such as education were not denied to him. He was brought up in the strict Jewish tradition and had a very thorough grounding in religion and ethics which plainly showed to his advantage in later life.

His early education in the then very excellent primary and secondary schools in Philadelphia strengthened his natural abilities in language and cultural expression. He chose Dartmouth as his college and there he became one of the very rare premeds who majored in English rather than science. After graduation from Dartmouth, he was accepted at Hahnemann where he graduated in 1938, receiving not only a regular medical diploma but also one in homeopathy (which discipline he never exercised). His internship and residency in internal medicine, as well as a year in pathology, were done at the old Mt. Sinai Hospital in Philadelphia (later to become the Albert Einstein Medical Center, Southern Division). In those days, Mt. Sinai was akin to a city hospital and extensive clinical experience was to be gained there. In addition, it had a fine attending staff. Not satisfied with this rather extensive training (for that time), he sought and obtained a Cardiac Fellowship at the Peter Bent Brigham Hospital in Boston.

The year was 1942, the United States was at war, and those who remained behind on hospital house staffs were busy indeed. Billy came under the spell of Samuel Levine, then at the acme of his career as one of America's most eminent cardiologists. Sam Levine's daily teaching rounds were famous and were attended by many visiting physicians. Also, at Harvard at that time was a very distinguished group of scientists and clinicians developing new approaches to treatment of heart, renal, and vascular disease. To Billy, this was heaven, and he became like a sponge, absorbing, listening, learning.

The Armed Services claimed Billy in 1943 and he served his tour of duty in New Guinea and the Philippines as a major and Head, Cardiovascular Section '51 General Hospital. After the war, he was undecided as to where to locate, and toyed for a period with the idea of settling in California as so many of his colleagues had done. He could not, however, escape the Philadelphia tradition and came back to the staff of Hahnemann Hospital and to establish a private practice.

At Hahnemann this was the era of development of cardiac surgery, mostly due to the foresight and drive of the thoracic surgeon Charles P. Bailey. The Division of Cardiology was then headed by George Geckeler, an experienced and conservative clinician who was much opposed to Bailey's new and highly controversial heart operations. He strictly forbade any medical staff from collaborating in any way with Bailey. Billy, however, managed not only a collaboration with Bailey but also served as the medical component of the surgical team. To Geckeler's credit, he came to recognize the value of the work but only after some very successful demonstrations and the acceptance of the techniques by outside peers.

Thus, with the leadership of Bailey and Likoff and a group of interested scientists and clinicians, the idea of establishing an institute of cardiology which would consist of a cooperative of various disciplines working to develop new and advanced techniques, came to fruition. The idea was new in the United States, antedated only by the Institute of Cardiology in Mexico City. Private money was raised, mostly through the efforts of Bailey and Likoff, to buy an old one-story automobile showroom on Broad Street adjacent to Hahnemann. Soon some dozen principal investigators and their staffs were busy at work. Eventually, substantial money was also obtained from the National Institute of Health, although they never really approved the idea of an institute. From the beginning the institute was called the Mary Bailey Institute for Cardiovascular Research in memory of Bailey's young daughter who had died of hepatitis.

This was a very productive period, and undoubtedly the seminal ideas and experimental approaches for open heart surgery, cardiac physiology and pharmacology, radiology techniques, electrophysiology, pump techniques, hypothermia, and transplantation of organs were developed at this time. Some of the firsts were at least originated and partially developed at the institute.

FIG. 1   William Likoff, M.D. (1912–1987)

In all of this Billy was the supporter, the observer, the recorder, the stabilizing influence. Never a bench researcher, Billy concentrated on what he could do best—be a clinician and make pertinent observations, but most important, publish these in the best journals in his own lucid style. The Likoff papers which cover the overall results of Bailey's many operative series represent some of the most reliable documentation of this period.

Meanwhile, as a clinician and a teacher he developed an excellence and maturity which emulated and perhaps even surpassed that of his mentor, Samuel Levine. These talents made Billy one of the most honored and remembered clinical teachers by the alumni of Hahnemann, and indeed, by the numerous house staff, fellows of the CVI, as well as his colleagues. So avid was his dedication to teaching that his own myocardial infarction, acquired while playing tennis, served to demonstrate to students the abnormal pulsation of the heart when a portion of the wall of the left ventricle was damaged.

On the national scene, Billy was most active in the affairs of the American College of Cardiology, becoming its president in 1967. Locally, he was a staunch supporter of the Heart Association of Southeastern Pennsylvania. Honors and lectureships are too numerous to list here.

In 1977, Hahnemann was in financial difficulty and its CEO had just resigned. Billy was asked to assume the vacant presidency. It was a difficult decision as he was in the prime of his professional career with a large and faithful retinue of patients and referring doctors. He would also have to give up his first love, the directorship of the cardiovascular institute, which was now named after him in honor of his many contributions. (Charles Bailey had left for New York some years before.) The institute had grown in size and facilities and had a much greater research and educational potential. Today, the institute is one of the largest cardiovascular programs in the United States, with over 55 faculty, 15 trainees, and over 100 support personnel encompassing all areas of cardiac medicine and surgery.

Characteristically, Billy decided to take on this onerous task and for five years he struggled and toiled successfully to put Hahnemann back into a stable position. He did not give up his practice completely, retaining his older patients and taking on only important consultations. Yet he continued to teach and still many papers flowed from his pen.

In 1982, Billy retired, becoming Emeritus Professor of Medicine and Cardiology. Despite his retirement, his optimism and good nature did not leave him. He still attended many social functions which provided some outlet for the still pent-up energy in this remarkable man.

Sadly, on July 3, 1987, Dr. Likoff died. This was received with great sadness by his family, friends, colleagues, and patients. But, contrary to the career of many other greats, William Likoff was loved and esteemed by all. His generosity, his open character, his conscientiousness, his gift of repartee, and his unfailing sense of humor put him in a separate category. Naturally, only "his deeds can praise him," and were certainly so numerous that they have placed him among the truly outstanding cardiologists which this country has produced in this century. He will be sorely missed.

Raymond Pruitt

R. O. Brandenburg, M.D.

Section of Cardiology, The University of Arizona, Tucson, Arizona, USA

Raymond Pruitt has had a distinguished career as a cardiologist, investigator, administrator, and educator (Fig. 1).

He was born February 6, 1912, in Wheaton, Minnesota. He attended Baker University in Kansas where he received the B.S. degree in 1933. He then was appointed a Rhodes Scholar, and went on to Oxford University in England where he received a B.A. degree. Returning to Kansas for his undergraduate medical education, he earned an M.D. degree in 1939. Following an internship at the University of Kansas Hospitals (1939-1940), Raymond Pruitt was a Fellow in Medicine at the Mayo Graduate School of Medicine in Rochester, Minnesota (1940-1943).

Dr. Pruitt was appointed to the staff of the Mayo Clinic in 1943 as a consultant in internal medicine and cardiology. In 1945, he was appointed to the faculty of the Mayo Graduate School of Medicine and rose rapidly through academic positions to become Professor of Medicine in 1954. From 1954 to 1959 he was Associate Director of the Mayo Graduate School of Medicine and Head of Medicine for Medical Education.

In 1959, he left the Mayo Institution to become Professor and Chairman of the Department of Medicine of Baylor University College of Medicine in Houston, Texas, serving in this capacity until 1967, and simultaneously during 1966–1967, he was also Vice-President for Medical Affairs.

Dr. Pruitt returned to Rochester, Minnesota, in 1968 as Director for Education of the Mayo Foundation and Director of the Mayo Graduate School of Medicine. Prolonged discussions of the advantages and disadvantages of an undergraduate medical school in the Mayo setting were ongoing at this time. The decision was finally made that it was prudent for many reasons to have both undergraduate and postgraduate education in the Mayo setting. Dr. Pruitt was named the first dean of the school in 1970 and he served in this position until his "retirement" in 1977. He then requested a return to the Division of Cardiology where he was welcomed back for additional years of service until his second "retirement" in January 1981. Since then he has been a consultant in cardiology at the Veterans Hospital in Memphis, Tennessee, which is home to some of his children.

Raymond Pruitt received numerous honors and awards in addition to his memberships and offices in many prestigious organizations. He received the Outstanding Alumnus Award of the University of Minnesota and an honorary doctorate from Baker University. He has served as president of the As-sociation of University Cardiologists (1966–1967), secretary of the American Board of Cardiovascular Disease (1955–1960), and also president of the American Osler Society. In addition, Pruitt has been an editorial board member of the journals *American Heart Journal* (1960–1968), *Circulation* (1963–1967, 1969–1973). From 1973-1975 he was chairman of the Council of Clinical Cardiology of the American Heart Association. Because of his expertise and knowledge, he was invited to become a member of the President's Panel on Heart Disease and has served on several national advisory councils and committees. In addition, he was on the Rhodes Scholarship Selection Committee and holds innumerable memberships in professional societies.

Dr. Pruitt's investigative interest was primarily that of the excitation process through the A-V conduction system and

FIG. 1   Raymond D. Pruitt, M.D. (1912–1993).

the myocardium. An early effort was noting the effects of physical stress and hypoxia on the electrocardiogram. Later he spent 6 months with Dr. Frank Wilson at the University of Michigan, who further stimulated him to pursue additional investigative efforts on the mysteries of the excitation process. Pruitt, with his associates, produced almost 100 papers related mainly to the electrocardiogram.

Dr. Pruitt is remembered as a teacher for many reasons, but for the graduate student, residents, and fellows, his course in electrocardiography was noteworthy. He diligently pursued the premise that we should understand the reasons for electrocardiographic abnormalities and not simply rely on pattern recognition. Years later, his students can attest to the value of this approach to the interpretation of the electrocardiogram.

The election of Dr. Pruitt as the first dean of the Mayo Medical School was an important event for both the medical school and the Mayo Institution. He was intimately familiar with the workings of the Mayo Clinic and its similarities to, and especially, differences from other medical school centers.

His experience at Baylor University College of Medicine acquainted him with the traditional medical school operation. Consequently, he was ideally suited to become the first dean of the Mayo School of Medicine. His Oxford, Mayo, and Baylor experiences had developed some views about the traditional educational process for physicians that warranted change. His tenure as dean was remarkable for its different approach to the educational process. He had a remarkable rapport with both students and teachers, and, in a day of deficit spending in most areas of education, he maintained a strict adherence to the carefully designed budget for the first years of the school.

Dr. Pruitt was a devoted husband to his wife Lillian (recently deceased) and a proud father of his two daughters and two sons. His professional life has been that of an intelligent, dedicated, quiet, unassuming scholar. These traits were recognized by his patients, his colleagues, and his students. His personal and professional life exemplify the finest qualities of dedication and service.

Earl H. Wood: Outstanding Twentieth Century Investigator of the Heart and Circulation

H. B. BURCHELL, M.D.

Cardiovascular Division, University of Minnesota, Minneapolis, Minnesota, USA

On New Year's Day in 1912, a fourth son was born to William and Inez Wood in Mankato, Minnesota. I expect that within a few days he was evidencing signs of "taking charge," showing leadership qualities. The closely knit Wood family eventually consisted of five boys and one girl, all of whom were imbued with ambition to excel and to pursue an advanced education. All were successful in doing so. One brother, Harland, became a biochemist, now well known for his work in intermediary metabolism, and he has outlined the early period of the Wood family in memoirs published last year in Annals of Biochemistry (Wood H, 1985). All the Wood brothers, in turn, were captains of their high school and college football teams and were good athletes generally, indeed their educations were aided by athletic scholarships. Chester became a teacher and a university administrator; Delbert was, in turn, a lawyer, an agent for the Federal Bureau of Investigation, and a railway executive; Wilbur, a physician and a founder of a medical clinic: and Louise became the overseas director of the American Red Cross during World War II, and then Executive Director of the Girl Scouts of America. It was fitting that in 1950 their mother was awarded the title "Minnesota Mother of the Year."

Coming from a pioneer farming background, both parents had been school teachers. Mr. Wood later went into the real estate business which, while generally successful, had its "ups and downs," with critical financial times during the depression years, a time when the children were going off to college. Each autumn, the Wood brothers assembled with indomitable spirit at a deer hunt camp, where Earl gradually emerged as the field marshal, in charge of field strategies and the tactics of the hunt. The enclave had corporate and academic guests who became infected with the communal enthusiasm. On the 40th anniversary of the group's (Deer Slayers, Inc.) hunting campaign (1984), Governor Perpich of the State of Minnesota sent a "Certification of Commendation" for the hunts as exemplary and a credit to Minnesota sportsmen. Earl is also an avid bird hunter and fisherman. At times, I have shared in these activities with great enjoyment. In 1984 also, he was honored during the phantasies of the St. Paul Winter Carnival by being appointed "Huntsman Supreme" by the reigning Boreas Rex XLVIII.

Earl Wood's formal education includes a B.A. from Macalester College, and B.S., M.S., Ph.D., and M.D. degrees from the University of Minnesota. Macalester College is a highly respected liberal arts college in St. Paul, having a Presbyterian lineage, and a certain pride in a Scottish pipe band and a losing football team.

The title of Earl's Ph.D. thesis at the University of Minnesota was "The Distribution of Water and Electrolytes Between Cardiac Muscle and Blood Serum with Special Reference to the Effects of Digitalis." I would perceive the highlights of Earl's University of Minnesota connection to be the lasting friendship and mutual respect that developed with his mentor, Maurice Visscher, and with a fellow trainee, Gordon Moe. At that time, both Earl and Gordon worked on the isolated heart preparations and the pharmacologic effects of digitalis. The reader will recognize Dr. Moe's name in relation to his major contributions over the past three decades to the understanding of the mechanism of arrhythmias. The M.D. degree at Minnesota was made possible by a special arrangement fostered by Dr. Visscher, whereby a student, while working for a Ph.D. in his laboratory could attend medical school classes and fulfill the requirements for the M.D. degree.

In 1941, Dr. Wood was awarded a National Research Fellowship and went to work at the University of Pennsylvania under Professor A.N. Richards. The following year he received an appointment as Instructor in Pharmacology at Harvard under Professor Krayer. From Boston, he came to the Mayo Clinic and immediately became active in the aeromedical unit and the development of the human centrifuge. With such notable colleagues as Charles Code, Edward Lambert, and E.J. Baldes, he played an outstanding role in the design and implementation of investigations which clarified the problems related to the transient increased G forces observed in airforce pilots. With David Clark, an anti-G suit for pilots was developed. This became standard equipment in the U.S. Air Force in World War II, and basically it has changed little since. He also developed and taught certain respiratory maneuvers which mitigated against the occurrence of blackout or unconsciousness in pilots exposed to transient high positive G forces. For this work, which had contributed so greatly to the success of American fighter pilots in combat, he was awarded the Certificate of Merit signed by President Truman in 1947.

In 1945, Dr. Wood visited Germany, as a consultant to the Air Force and helped greatly in the collection and analysis of

FIG. 1   Earl H. Wood working on a pleural pressure research project in the Universitaets-Kinderklinik, Kiel, West Germany, August 1985. The experimental animal was an anesthetized young pig. Dr. Wood was a Humboldt Foundation awardee for senior United States scientists.

the research in aviation medicine which had been done during the war years by scientists of the Luftwaffe. In this year also, fortunately for the Mayo Clinic, he became interested in the clinical importance of cardiac catheterization and organized a superb laboratory for the study of human circulation in health and disease. His research and teaching attracted many graduate students both from within the Mayo Clinic and from centers all over the world. An account of the first 15 years of this experience and the resulting philosophy in graduate training at Mayo has been published (Wood, 1961). Two early outstanding developments in the laboratory were an oximeter from which immediate readings of the oxygen saturation of a catheter sample of blood were possible, and of a strain-gauge pressure transducer. Also, in rapid sequence, he adapted the oximeter equipment to the indicator dilution technique for the measurement of blood flow and the detection and quantitation of intracardiac shunts. With these techniques perfected, Dr. Wood could espouse the philosophy that after a cardiac catheterization was initiated, it could be "tailored" during the procedure in accord with the accruing data, and a definitive diagnosis reached at the termination of the procedure.

Dr. Wood also made important contributions to the development of the artificial heart-lung machine, opening the new era of open heart surgery. About 1965, Earl Wood conceived of a new variety of computer-generated three-dimensional imaging from multiple roentgen planigrams. Over subsequent years, aided by colleagues (particularly by the electronics genius of Ralph Sturm), the machine was constructed.

This is described in an editorial (Wood E, 1985) in a recent special issue of *Herz*.

In 1962, Earl was the tenth scientist to be named "Career Investigator," of the American Heart Association. This distinction and the accompanying financial support afforded him an increased independence in his research and the opportunities for working sabbaticals in distant laboratories. One period was spent with Silvio Weidemann in Switzerland in 1968 and the report of the work (Wood *et al.*, 1969) written with Drs. Heppner and Weidman has become one of the most frequently cited papers in that area of science. Many honors have come to Dr. Wood from the cardiological community—that of the Research Achievement Award of the American Heart Association merits special mention. He has been a constant worker for the American Heart Association, though perhaps I suspect his first love, naturally, might be the American Physiological Society, of which he became 53rd president in 1980 (Wood, 1980).

He has served on many committees and been a member of visiting delegations from the American Physiological Society to Russia and China. Not unexpectedly, he has been a longtime consultant to the National Space Program. He has been a respected defender of the ethical propriety of animal research and headed committees which have reviewed complaints regarding the care of dogs and the lower primates. He has been candid in his criticisms if the facts warranted them. In 1982, at a symposium to honor him at his official retirement from the Mayo Clinic, I pointed out that he could be cited as a role model in human subject research (Burchell, 1982).

Over the years, the Earl Wood bibliography and the number of citations listed in the *Index*, published by the Institute for Scientific Information, has shown a consistent and impressive growth. The last figure for published papers which I have seen is 688. Dr. Wood's own selection of the eleven most favorite publications in which he was involved are listed in the references at the end of this biographical essay and marked with an asterisk.

In years past, the Mayo Clinic had a mandatory retirement age of 65, a policy which has been modified in the past decade. However, when Dr. Wood's retirement at age 70 from the active clinic staff was decreed (1982), he felt that he was not yet ready to close a career in investigation and has since had awards and opportunities to work in various laboratories around the world. His energy seemingly continues undiminished. I know he misses the directorship of his old laboratory and the developments occurring in his "dream child," the dynamic spatial reconstructor (DSR). Now under indictment as being outdated, in competition with other techniques, it is a research behemoth miracle. Nevertheless on the basis of technological advances now in the wings, Dr. Wood remains convinced that the dream of noninvasive vivisection of structural-functional dynamics of the heart, lungs, and circulation in health and disease will before 2000 AD become a reality in major biomedical centers around this globe (Wood, 1977, 1978, 1985a).

Dr. Wood married a Macalester graduate in 1936, and she has given him loyal support for these many years; a Golden

Wedding Anniversary was celebrated in 1987. Their four children continue an exemplary tradition of a dedication to work and to earned play: Phoebe, a teacher; Mark, an ophthalmologist; Guy, a professor of foreign languages; and Andrew, a physical therapy teacher.

The accompanying picture was submitted by Dr. Wood as a possible alternative to a formal portrait. It does, I believe, symbolize Earl's dedication to physiologic investigation. Here is a man of purpose, energy, and integrity. Cardiology as well as physiology may claim him as one of "its" own. The American Heart Association may also point to him as an example of its vision and wisdom in establishing the career research program.

References

*Avasthey P, Wood EH: Intrathoracic and venous pressure relationships during responses to changes in body position. *J Appl Physiol* 37, 166 (1974)

Burchell HB: The investigator as a volunteer subject. *Mayo Clinic Proc* 57, 28 (1982)

*Groom D, Wood EH, Burchell HB, Parker RL: The application of an oximeter for whole blood to diagnostic cardiac catheterization. *Proc Staff Meet Mayo Clin* 23 (26), 601 (1948)

*Pollack AA, Wood EH: Venous pressure in the saphenous vein at the ankle in man during exercise and changes in posture. *J Appl Physiol* 9 (1), 649 (1949)

Wood EH: Editorial. The dream of a dynamic high fidelity, synchronous, Volumetric imaging system and the Road to its utilization. *Herz* 10 (4), 183 (1985b)

Wood EH: Editorial. Fifty-third president of A.P.S. *Physiologist* 23, June (1980)

*Wood EH: Evolution of instrumentation techniques for studies of cardiovascular dynamics from the thirties to 1980. *Ann Biomed Eng* 6, 250 (1978)

*Wood EH: New vistas for the study of structural and functional dynamics of the heart, lungs, and circulation by non-invasive numerical tomographic vivisection. *Circulation* 56, 506 (1977)

Wood EH: Graduate training in cardiovascular physiology at a clinical center. An analysis of 15 year's experience. *Proc Staff Meet Mayo Clin* 36, 567 (1961)

*Wood EH, Hoffman EA: Interoserosal forces, the pressure environment of the central circulations and nature's internal "G suit." *Physiologist* 26, S20 (1963)

*Wood EH, Moe GK: Blood electrolyte changes in the heart-lung preparation with special reference to the effects of cardiac glycosides. *Am J Phys* 137 (1), 6 (1942)

*Wood EH, Heppner RL, Weidemann S: Inotropic effects of electric currents: I. Positive and negative effects of constant electric currents or current pulses applied during cardiac action potentials. II. Hypothesis: Calcium movement, excitation-contraction coupling and inotropic effects. *Circ Res* 24, 409 (1969)

*Wood EH, Swan HJC, Marshall HW: Techniques and diagnostic applications of dilution curves recorded simultaneously from the right side of the heart and from the arterial circulation. *Proc Staff Meet Mayo Clin* 33 (22), 536 (1958)

*Wood EH, Nolan AC, Donald DE, Cronin L: Influence of acceleration on pulmonary physiology. *Fed Proc* 22 (4), 1024 (1963)

*Wood EH, Lambert EH, Baldes EJ, Code CF: Effects of acceleration in relation to aviation. *Fed Proc* 3 (5), 327 (1946)

Wood H: Then and now. *Ann Rev Biochem* 54, 1 (1985)

Wilfred Gordon Bigelow

R. E. BEAMISH, M.D.

Division of Cardiovascular Sciences, St. Boniface Hospital, Research Centre, Winnipeg, Manitoba, Canada

The years between 1950 and 1990 were the golden age of cardiology.[1] The intellectual ferment in North America in the decades following World War II induced phenomenal advances in the diagnosis and treatment of disease, but none more spectacular than the development of cardiac surgery. Canadians were in the forefront, led by Dr. Wilfred G. Bigelow (Fig. 1), an innovative surgeon-scientist at the Toronto General Hospital. He contributed extensively to the advances of the time by his role in developing hypothermia and the cardiac pacemaker. He recorded his work in more than 120 publications, some in Russian, and capped his career with two elegant accounts of the medical and surgical progress of his day.[2, 3]

Inevitably, when countries are as close as the United States and Canada, there will be instances when greatness in one country has its roots in the other. For instance, the American Wilder Penfield achieved international fame in Canada as the founder of the Montreal Neurological Institute. In contrast is Wilfred G. Bigelow, Canada's preeminent heart surgeon, whose ancestry is tenth generation American and seventh generation Canadian. While it is not easy to determine how far the career of an individual is a prolongation of those of his predecessors, the records of his family members in surgery, invention, and literature may have presaged the achievements of Wilfred G. Bigelow. His Boston origins began with John Biglo who arrived in Watertown (present site of Harvard University) in 1634, 14 years after the Mayflower. By 1691 the name had become Bigelow, a name made famous in surgery by Henry Jacob Bigelow, M.D.,[4] Professor of Surgery at Harvard (1849–1882) and a surgeon to the Massachusetts General Hospital. He is commemorated by the Bigelow Medal awarded by the Boston Surgical Society for new and valuable work in surgery (presented to many famous surgeons beginning with W.J. Mayo in 1921) and by the Bigelow Amphitheatre (The Ether Dome) in the Massachusetts General Hospital. There were others, including his father, Dr. Wilfred Abram Bigelow, pioneer surgeon in Brandon, Manitoba, and founder of the first medical clinic in Canada.

"Bill" Bigelow was born in Brandon in 1913. Early education was in Brandon and Victoria, B.C., and he graduated B.A. (1935) and M.D. (1938) from the University of Toronto. As a resident in surgery at the Toronto General Hospital, he developed an interest in hypothermia initiated by the experience of having to amputate the frost-bitten fingers of a young man. He joined the Canadian army in 1941 and served as a front-line surgeon in northwest Europe during the most intense battles of the allied invasion. He again thought of hypothermia as a way to save limbs in which the main artery had been severed, but the war ended before this could be tried. On his return to civilian practice in 1945, he became a research fellow at Johns Hopkins University and Hospital in Baltimore where he was influenced by Alfred Blalock and Richard Bing. While watching operations performed with the heart beating forcefully, he realized that surgeons would never be able to cure most heart conditions unless they could stop the heart, open it, and operate in a bloodless field under direct vision. At that time the heart-lung pump was not yet practical. Then the inspiration came: "One night I woke with a simple solution to the problem, and one that did not require pumps and tubes—cool the whole body, reduce the oxygen requirements, interrupt the circulation, and open the heart."[2a] Returning to Toronto, he acquired a basement room in the Banting Institute, attracted a group of co-workers, and studied the effects of hypothermia on body and heart metabolism. After 5 years of basic research, the technique was applied successfully to human patients and made possible the first open heart operation in humans (1953). It was soon widely used throughout the world in both heart and brain surgery and is still used today in modified forms.

Another crucial observation arose from these studies. One morning in 1949, during an experiment on hypothermia, the heart stopped and did not respond to cardiac massage. "Out of interest and desperation,"[2] Bigelow gave it a poke with a metal probe to which the heart responded with an effective contraction. Rhythmic poking evoked satisfactory circulation. It was then found that an electrical impulse had the same effect; the concept of an electrical pacemaker was born. Electrical engineer Jack Hopps of the National Research Council of Canada, working with Bigelow and Callaghan, carefully designed a circuit that provided electrical stimulation, duplicating the physiologic currents, with no muscle damage. In 1950, a pacemaker used in animals was presented before an American surgical meeting[5] and inquiries were received from many centers. Among these was one from Dr. Paul Zoll of Boston. Dr. Zoll was given full information about the device and two years later reported successful use of a pacemaker in two humans with heart block. Medtronic of Canada Ltd. recognized Bigelow's contribution to the pacemaker by estab-

FIG. 1   Wilfred Gordon Bigelow.

lishing the Bigelow Travelling Fellowship in Cardiac Pacing
and Electrophysiology.

Not all of his vigor and creativity was confined to the research laboratory. A gifted clinical surgeon, an enthusiastic
teacher with a deep concern for people, it was inevitable that
he became the father of cardiovascular surgery in Canada. He
formed the first cardiovascular training program in Canada,
headed it for over 20 years, trained scores of cardiac surgeons,
and operated on hundreds of patients. He saw himself as a
member of a team and by example taught colleagues and students compassion and caring for patients. Admired and respected, he served as President of the Canadian Cardiovascular Society, the Society for Vascular Surgery, and the
American Association for Thoracic Surgery. A popular
speaker, he has given lectures around the world.

Such significant contributions have not gone unnoticed.
Among many awards are the first Gairdner Award (1959),
first medal of the International Society of Surgery (1955), the
highest award of the Canadian Medical Association (F.N.G.
Starr award) (1992), and honorary degrees from the
Universities of Toronto, Hamburg, and Brandon. He received
the Order of Canada in 1981.

Dr. Bigelow and his wife, Ruth Jennings, have four children and are celebrating 54 years of marriage. A keen out-
doorsman, he has enjoyed duck hunting and fishing throughout his life. Despite worldwide recognition, he remains a
friendly and unassuming man devoted to human values, nature conservation, and family life.

References

1. Braunwald G: The Golden Age of Cardiology. In *An Era in
   Cardiovascular Medicine* (Eds. Knoebel SB, Dack S). New York:
   Elsevier, 1991
2. Bigelow WG: *Cold Hearts. The Story of Hypothermia and the
   Pacemaker in Heart Surgery*. Toronto: McClelland and Stewart,
   1984; (a) 40
3. Bigelow WG: *Mysterious Heparin. The Key to Open Heart
   Surgery*. Toronto: McGraw-Hill, Ryerson, 1990
4. Holmes OW, Fetz RH, Cabot AT, *et al.*: *Henry Jacob Bigelow—A
   Memoir*. Boston: Little, Brown & Co., 1900
5. Callaghan JC, Bigelow WG: An electrical artificial pacemaker for
   standstill of the heart. *Ann Surg* 1951;134:8–17

Demetrio Sodi-Pallares: The Man and His Thought

A. CASTELLANOS, M.D.

Division of Cardiology, Department of Medicine, University of Miami School of Medicine, Miami, Florida, USA

The life of a person is more than a record of undisputed facts. Even when such facts are plentiful, the writer's real business is how to present them, since he must penetrate behind mere ideas to the purpose and character they disclose. This can only be done by an effort of constructive imagination based on as much information, obtained from as many sources, as can be gathered.[1]

Demetrio Sodi-Pallares, a living legend of international renown in the field of cardiology, was born in Mexico City, or more correctly, Mexico, DF (Distrito Federal), in 1913. A complex educational background is capable of explaining parts of the personality of this multifaceted individual. Elementary instruction took place in a French institution and high school instruction in a greco-roman atmosphere. The appropriate Mexican environment was provided by the city where he grew up, and where he attended and graduated from the Medical School at the Universidad Nacional de Mexico in 1929. After training in internal medicine in the latter institution, he specialized in cardiology at Case Western Reserve University (1941), where he witnessed the social and cultural repercussions of World War II on the United States.

Thereafter came what can be considered the beginning of his journey on the road to glory in the area of electrocardiography: two years spent, respectively, with Carl J. Wiggers in Cleveland and Frank N. Wilson in Ann Arbor, who at the time were the leaders in mechanical and electrical functions of the heart. This experience was extremely valuable in opening to him the doors of the, then, recently inaugurated Instituto Nacional de Cardiologia de Mexico where he was appointed Chief of the Department of Electrocardiography (1944). Much of the above occurred with the counsel and advice of his mentor, the late Professor Ignacio Chavez, who for many years was to be Mexico's most powerful and influential physician. Henceforward, both Sodi-Pallares and the Instituto Nacional de Cardiologia became part of medical history at a time when electrocardiography played a much more important role in our subspecialty than it does today.

Sodi-Pallares has authored, or coauthored, around 250 articles and 11 books, some translated from English or Spanish to other languages. A member of 35 medical societies in North and South America, Mexico, and India, he has received special awards for Humanitarian Services given by the Republics of Italy, Brazil, Colombia, and Spain and has been granted honorary degrees from three universities.

Many physicians acknowledge Sodi-Pallares' unique abilities in electrocardiographic interpretation.[2] However, less known today, especially by the younger generation, is that he can be rightly considered one of the (if not the) greatest teachers of electrocardiography that ever lived. Practically a reincarnation of Socrates (even in physical appearance), he is always at his best with smaller groups. It is this setting that allows the use of the classical dialectic debate or dialogue, wherein some premise taken as a starting point leads to a conclusion almost always accepted by convinced listeners as the incontrovertible truth (at least for the moment).[1] Nor was it surprising that he was a recipient of the Master Teacher Award from the American College of Cardiology and the Sir William Osler Award, with a bust presented to him by the University of Miami School of Medicine. These qualities made him, in North America, South America, and European countries, the most popular "imported" guest speaker in cardiology during three decades (1950s, 1960s, and 1970s).

In contrast to his teaching consistency, his lines of thinking occurred, as usually happens, in several stages. First, they were oriented toward "deductive electrocardiography"[3,4]—the genesis of normal and abnormal electrocardiographic morphologies could be reasoned by extrapolating from experimental studies interpreted according to Wilson's "dipole" concept and Craib's "doublet" theory. Such a method attempted to analyze the sequence of cardiac activation by integrating Wilson's scalar concept of unipolar leads with current vectorial methods of precordial lead interpretation. Thus considered, it was not exactly like Grant's concept of "vectorial electrocardiography" or the more well-known "spatial vectorcardiography." The validity of Sodi-Pallares' method rested on the possibility of verifying the deduction made by clinical, radiological, and postmortem studies.[3]

But after 27 years of applying this method, Sodi-Pallares changed his thinking by attempting to correlate electrocardiographic changes with other nonelectrical parameters such as cellular metabolism and ultrastructure, ionic pump mechanisms, and ventricular contractility. Thus emerged the concept of polyparametric electrocardiography.[5] Space does not allow a full description of the underlying theory, which considered that certain "etiological" factors (poor insulin activity, harmful catecholamine effects, thyroid deficiency, and excessive sodium intake) provoked thermodynamic abnormalities manifested by decreased energetic function, reduction of stored energy, unavailability of energy for construction, and

FIG. 1 Demetrio Sodi-Pallares (ca. 1983) before answering a complex question about the polarizing diet.

increased entropy. Moreover, a generalized state of metabolic disturbance supposedly produced metabolic abnormalities of the heart capable of leading even to the so-called "ischemic" cardiomyopathy. With this premise, it followed that a specific therapy could correct the underlying metabolic and thermodynamic abnormalities. The latter was the much-debated polarizing solutions and polarizing diets, later complemented by beta blockers, thyroglobuline, and controlled exercise.[5,6] Sodi-Pallares has used this treatment for cardiac and certain systemic diseases for more than two decades.

The previously mentioned approach constituted "a thermodynamic model of causality."[6] Unfortunately, the latter statement introduced the problem of interpreting the meaning of the terms "thermodynamic" and "causation" as applied to medicine, since both are alien to most cardiologists (including myself) and subject to diverse interpretations.[7,8] For instance, I have inferred that Sodi-Pallares did not use the laws of thermodynamics in a restricted sense applied to a closed system, but rather applied them, consciously or subconsciously, in a generalized fashion. In such a context, the laws of thermodynamics probably constitute the most fundamental generalization made by physicists and the one they seem to be more reluctant to discard.[7] Such a view holds through all the departures of the real universe from the ideal models set up by scientists; it holds for living systems as well as for nonliving ones, and from the tiny world of the subatomic realm to the cosmic world of the galaxies.[7]

Similarly, "causality" can be interpreted as referring to the "first cause," a term applied outside "pure" science.[8,9] It appears that Sodi-Pallares integrated biology with physics and metaphysics, utilizing some sort of neo-Thomism.[10] To do this he had, first and foremost, to become a single entity, in

whom the thinking of the scientist was one with the thinking of the man. Using his own words, "my scientific personality is not different than my everyday self."[6] What he has expressed in actions, as well as in oral and written presentations, suggests that by then he was attempting to proclaim the unity between man, science, and universe.[6] This need is not exceptional in scientists working in diverse fields, especially physics, who by different means and in various ways act as gallant knights in pursuit of a visionary grail.[11] In physics, the quest is for an elusive theory of everything (TOE) capable of explaining the fundamental unity of things.[11]

Persons imbued with this ideal feel compelled to express or reaffirm it even against overwhelming odds. Einstein was not deterred when, at the Solvay debate with Niels Bohr, he was not capable of disproving Heisenberg's indeterminacy law. "It hardly brings us closer to the secret of the Older one," he said.[12] Similarly, Sodi-Pallares has responded to his many critics with statements of proclamation and confirmation of beliefs such as the ones appearing in the masterpiece entitled "Ischemic Heart Disease and Polarizing Treatment," which was presented in 1976.

There is no doubt that Sodi-Pallares is a committed person with a complex scientific reasoning process. But no one can deny that it is rather unique (to say the least).

Acknowledgments

I am indebted to Dr. Ana E. Leurinda and Dr. Antonio Gomez-Hernandez for their valuable assistance.

References

1. Taylor AE: *Socrates. The Man and His Thought.* Doubleday and Anchor, Inc., New York, 1953, 11, 12, 147–149
2. Lipman BS, Massie E, Kleiger RE: *Clinical Scalar Electrocardiography*, sixth edition. Year Book Medical Publishers, Chicago, 1973, IX–XI
3. Sodi-Pallares D: *New Bases of Electrocardiography.* Mosby, St. Louis, 1956, 3, 4
4. Sodi-Pallares D, Bisteni A, Medrano GA: *Electrocardiografia y Vectorcardiografia Deductivas.* La Prensa Medica Mexicana, Mexico, DF, 1964, 188
5. Sodi-Pallares D, Medrano GA, Bisteni A, Ponce de Leon J: *Deductive and Polyparametric Electrocardiography.* Instituto Nacional de Cardiologia de Mexico, Mexico, DF, 1970, VII, VIII
6. Sodi-Pallares D, Ponce de Leon J: *Cardiopatia Isquemica y Tratamiento Polarizante.* Editorial Parmenides, Mexico, DF, 1975, IX–IV
7. Asimov I: *Understanding Physics: Motion, Sound and Heart.* New American Library, New York, 1966, 100
8. Jancar B: *The Philosophy of Aristotle.* Simon and Schuster, New York, 1966, 55, 56, 137, 138
9. Maritan J: *A Preface to Metaphysics.* Mentor Omega Publishers, New York, 1961, 128–129
10. Collins JD: Thomism. *Encyclopaedia Britannica.* William Benton Publisher, Chicago, 1968, 1066–1067
11. Angier N: Hanging the universe on strings. A bizarre new theory may unite the forces of nature. *Time* 127, 56 (1986)
12. Cline BL: *Men Who Made a New Physics. Physicists and the Quantum Theory.* The New American Library, New York, 1965, 195–198

Walter Somerville

SYLVAN LEE WEINBERG, M.D., MACC, FESC

The Dayton Heart Hospital and the Wright State School of Medicine, Dayton, Ohio, USA

Lives of great men, all remind us
We too can make our lives sublime,
And, departing, leave behind us
Footprints on the sands of time.

—Henry Wadsworth Longfellow

In Dublin, on October 2, 1913, a son, Walter, was born to Patrick and Kate Somerville in an Ireland largely oblivious to the darkening clouds of war that were soon to engulf Europe and most of the world. Nevertheless, Walter and his sister Eileen enjoyed a happy and healthy childhood. In due course Walter was enrolled in the prestigious Belvedere College located in historic Belvedere House in Dublin where he maintained honors in his classes throughout his school career.

At age 23, Dr. Walter Somerville (Fig. 1) qualified with honors in medicine, surgery, and obstetrics at University College, Dublin. On graduating, he was appointed house physician at Dublin's The Martyr Misericordie Hospital where he was awarded the Doctor of Medicine Degree.

Realizing that advancement in clinical medicine could be best achieved in London teaching hospitals, Walter applied for and was granted an honorary appointment in the outpatient department of St. Mary's Hospital. He was scheduled to work under the famed London consultant in chest medicine, Dr. D.W.D Brookes. But as fate would have it, World War II was declared on the very day of his appointment, and the exigencies of war mandated the closure of the St. Mary's Out Patient Department. Preferring to serve as a pilot rather than as a military doctor, the young Somerville volunteered for the Royal Airforce, not knowing that qualified doctors of medicine were not accepted for flight training. Turning then to the Royal Army Medical Corps, Somerville served aboard troop ships with duty in Egypt, the Middle East, and in India. Still hankering for a military role he perceived more useful, Walter was sent to Porton Down for training in chemical and biological warfare. In the course of this training he was seconded to the Canadian Department of Defence at Suffield, Alberta, Canada. After two years in Canada, Somerville was assigned to the United States War Department Chemical Warfare Unit at the Edgewood Arsenal in Maryland, and later for similar training at Bushnel, Florida. Ultimately his unit was incorporated into the U.S. Forces in the Southwest Pacific. There he participated in highly classified preparations for the invasion of Japan, where extensive casualties on both sides were anticipated. Fortunately, for reasons now well known to us all, this invasion did not occur and Somerville never had to use the dire instruments of war for which he had been trained. During the four and a half years that he was attached to the U.S. Army, Somerville attained the rank of Lt. Colonel and was awarded the Legion of Merit.

During his service with the American military, Dr. Somerville became friends with one George Merck, whose father was an executive with the burgeoning pharmaceutical company that bore his name. George suggested to Walter that there might be a great opportunity for someone with his talents and experience; but somehow the prospect of manufacturing pills did not appeal to the youthful Somerville. Shortly thereafter, while in a Boston pub, Somerville was accosted by a Metro-Goldwyn-Mayer talent scout who, observing the handsome young doctor and hearing his elegant English accent, believed that he had discovered another "Ronald Coleman" and offered him a screen test and a potentially lucrative Hollywood contract. Happily, Somerville again declined in favor of postgraduate training in cardiology at the Massachusetts General Hospital. One can only speculate on what Walter Somerville's career might have been had he accepted either of these glamorous propositions.

In 1947, now back in London, Somerville was attending a refresher lecture for doctors returning from military service given by the legendary Paul Wood. After the lecture, having heard a question from Somerville, Paul Wood came up to him and asked if he were an American. Walter answered that he was not, but that his several years with the American forces had probably modified his speech to give the impression of being an American. Those of us who have known Walter for many years, and never noting even the merest vestige of American speech, can only wonder at Paul Wood's question. But American accent or not, Wood forthwith asked Walter to join his unit as a registrar at the Hammersmith Postgraduate School. Thus began a relationship that would endure until Paul Wood's untimely death in 1962. Paul Wood would become Walter Somerville's teacher, colleague, and friend in a relationship of deep mutual respect. Walter, in turn, became imbued with Wood's philosophy of the practice of medicine, teaching, and research.

Dr. Somerville's post-war medical education was not limited to the United Kingdom. On a fellowship, he worked in Paris and Sweden and also had extensive experience with American cardiology. He studied under Dr. Paul Dudley White at the

FIG. 1   Walter Somerville, M.D., FRCP, FACC, CBE.

Massachusetts General Hospital, with Dr. Frank Wilson in Ann Arbor, and with Dr. Samuel Levine at the Peter Bent Brigham. At the Brigham, he did fundamental research on the effects of potassium on the heart with Dr. John Merrill, with whom he formed a close bond.

In 1954, Dr. Somerville was appointed Consultant Cardiologist to the Middlesex Hospital and the Harefield Hospital, where cardiac surgery was established with great success by Sir Thomas Holmes Sellars. Later, a fruitful cooperation and friendship developed with the young Magdi Yacoub, who was to become one of the world's premier cardiac surgeons. Walter held this position with great distinction until his retirement in accordance with the policies of the British National Health Service. He continued in the private practice of cardiology, enjoying a wide following in Britain and overseas until he was forced to retire from practice following a street assault outside his home in London which caused a drastic and progressive loss of his vision. In spite of this, with characteristic grit and grace, Walter continues his interests in medicine and world affairs. He is today as stimulating, challenging, and informed a conversationalist as always.

Dr. Somerville was elected President of the British Cardiac Society and became Editor of the *British Heart Journal*. As President, he changed the fortunes of the British Cardiac Society and broadened the vistas of British cardiologists. He also initiated scientific and collegial exchanges with the French Cardiac Society. During these meetings in Paris, he enunciated only one irrevocable rule: that each British member must speak only French, and each French member must speak only English. Later the German, Dutch, Czech, Swedish, and Finnish societies became involved. Joint meetings were held in the capitals of each country. These relationships pioneered by Dr. Somerville were the historic and philosophic forerunners of the now flourishing European Society of Cardiology.

One of the most dramatic, poignant and personally devastating events in Dr. Somerville's clinical experience occurred in July of 1962. He recalled the events of that distant summer

when I visited with him in his study in London on the afternoon of December 6, 2001.

On the Sunday before Paul Wood was admitted to hospital, he was using a long pole to scrape the bottom of his garden pool to remove weeds. He then extracted the pole from the lake water and separated the weeds which were clinging to it. Preparing for a second try at extracting weeds, he turned to his assistant, Liz Turner and said, 'Will you give me two of those headache pills that you use because I've got an indigestion pain in the center of my chest?' Liz Turner, heeding his request, presented him with two or three pills, which he took with relief. On the following Wednesday evening, Paul Wood was examining a patient with coronary disease in his consulting rooms when chest pain came on again. An electrocardiogram was taken by Liz Turner who recorded ECGs in Woods' office. She showed it to Dr. Wood who said the ECG was abnormal, showing ischemic changes. He then called me. I joined Wood in his consulting room and directed him to be admitted to the Middlesex Hospital. He was given sublingual nitroglycerin and reported to have lost the pain in one and a half minutes.

Dr. Somerville had asked Paul Wood if he wanted to see any other doctor specializing in heart disease. He answered: "No, I want no one but you."

It must be remembered that this was 1962, when the prospects and alternatives for a patient with even a modest myocardial infarction were drastically different from today. The first coronary care unit dates from that time. External cardiac defibrillation was in its infancy and not yet available at the Middlesex Hospital. Cardiac resuscitation meant open chest cardiac massage. I asked Dr. Somerville if he had discussed this with Dr. Wood should an emergency occur. He said that he had, and Paul Wood had answered: "Please remember that if the course of this sickness is not as we hope it will be, and the pain will not go away and remain away, I want no interference such as an incision made into my chest and cardiac massage. I do not want that. And if anyone attempts to do that, I will come back and sue him." I said, "Yes, Paul, I know that. There will be no incisions made in your chest and no attempt made to do cardiac massage manually." He said, "Yes, you know it, but does the house physician know it?" I said, "Yes, he does." Sadly, as Walter Somerville recounted to me, two days later, on Friday, Paul Wood's wife Betty saw that his breathing became "irregular and shallow." His sleep appeared to be unusually deep. Walter, doing ward rounds nearby, was summoned and found Wood to be unresponsive and deduced quite correctly that "a terminal arrhythmia" was present. As Wood had wanted, and as his friend Walter had promised, there was no attempt at resuscitation. With the inevitable murmuring of colleagues about inappropriate treatment, Somerville, against their advice, sought permission for necropsy from Betty Wood. Necropsy showed a single lesion of the anterior descending coronary artery. Only a few years later such an episode would have ended so differently. Ironically, Paul Wood's death stands as a marker of subsequent progress in cardiology to which, in his time, he had contributed so much, and also to the steadfastness and integrity of his friend Walter Somerville.

Dr. Somerville's commitment to global medicine has been constant throughout his career. He was appointed Consultant Cardiologist to the British Army and to the Royal Airforce, which led to extensive travel and contacts in Europe and Asia. He has a deep interest in the medical and sociological aspects of alcohol and for more than a decade was a member of the National Committee in Britain concerned with these matters. He played a major role in developing laws designed to control alcohol abuse in many countries, including the United States, Canada, and Australia. For many years he has been concerned with the law, particularly as it related to medical affairs; he served as President of the British Academy for Forensic Sciences. Dr. Somerville's interests are eclectic. He did extensive research on the effect of catecholamines on the electrocardiogram and performance of public speakers, racing drivers, sky divers, and others under physical and emotional stress. He was one of the founders of the British Performing Arts Medical Association and advisor for medical and ex-service charities. He is a devotee of the arts and especially the theater, and an avid and astute observer of governments and politics worldwide, with a special and penetrating interest in the American scene.

Although, considering the scope of his professional activities one might suspect that Walter's personal life might have been neglected, nothing could be farther from the truth. More than four decades ago, he married Jane Platnauer whose career in pediatric cardiology rivals his own in international stature. She is responsible for the term "GUCH" which stands for "grown up congenital heart disease." Jane is perhaps the world's premier advocate for proper care for adult patients with congenital heart disease and for the creation of centers of excellence around the world. Walter and Jane have three sons and a daughter. Their home in London is a place where leaders in the professions and in the arts often gather, where conversation and repartee sparkle, and where ideas, humor, and wit abound.

In 1982, Dr. Somerville was decorated by Her Majesty, the Queen, with the insignia of Commander of the British Empire. Many find it inexplicable that he was not knighted.

Early in his career, Dr. Somerville became a fellow of the American College of Cardiology. He presented papers frequently and often rose to make cogent comments at its annual meetings. In his editorial capacity, he forged links between the *British Heart Journal* and the *Journal of the American College of Cardiology*. A close friend of the late Dr. Simon Dack, founder and long-time editor-in-chief of the *Journal of the American College of Cardiology*, Walter was a regular and incisive participant at the editorial board meetings of the Journal.

When the meetings of the American College of Cardiology were not so large and were perhaps less formal than they are now, Dr. Somerville served as unofficial spokesman for the overseas cardiologists in attendance. Often at the postconvocation banquet, after enjoying the dancing, he would rise, take the microphone and, on behalf of his overseas colleagues, express appreciation for the hospitality and collegiality accorded them by the ACC. The warmth and sincerity of his remarks and his impeccable and elegant use of the language are not to be forgotten.

Walter Somerville, as a man and as a doctor of medicine, and in every aspect of his career, epitomizes not only the synthesis of scientific and clinical cardiology, but also the humane and universal essence of medicine. He has advocated to generations of cardiologists in Britain, America, Europe, and around the world commitment and responsibility not only for the technical and scientific aspects of patient care, but also compassion for patients and for the dignity and integrity which should be the defining elements of our profession.

In a career in cardiology conducted on the highest moral, intellectual, and clinical plane, it is his consummate style and elegance that best characterize Walter Somerville. In reality, he became the face of British cardiology, which he has represented so well throughout the world. In this, as in every facet of his career, he has set a standard we all might well strive to emulate.

Raymond P. Ahlquist (1914–1983)

R. C. LITTLE, M.D.

Medical College of Georgia, Augusta, Georgia, USA

Modern adrenergic pharmacology began in 1948 with publication of Raymond Ahlquist's seminal study on adrenotropic receptors. In that landmark paper he reported that the excitatory or inhibitory response to a series of adrenergic agonists could be explained by the relative number of two different postganglionic receptors in the organ system under study. He named these receptors alpha and beta. This fundamental proposal provided the key that permitted a rational explanation for adrenergic action, a subject which up to that point had eluded solution. Appropriate alpha- and beta-blocking drugs were soon developed. These compounds, in turn, opened the door to an important new chapter of medical therapy.

Dr. Ahlquist, or Ray as he was known to his friends and associates, was born in Missoula, Montana, in 1914 where his father was stationed as traveling auditor for the Northern Pacific Railroad. Both his parents had come from Sweden as young children and Ray grew up in a home environment that emphasized education, art, and languages. His boyhood was spent in Everett, Washington. Dr. Ahlquist received his B.S. degree in pharmacy (magna cum laude) in 1935, M.S. degree in pharmacology in 1937, and the Ph.D. degree in pharmacology in 1940, all from the University of Washington. He was the first person to be awarded the Ph.D. degree in pharmacology at that institution.

Dr. Ahlquist met his wife, Dorotha Duff Ahlquist, when they were both graduate students in Seattle. With her scientific training she was later to be of considerable help to her husband in his research activities. Following his graduate work, Dr. Ahlquist was appointed to the faculty of South Dakota State College. After four years in Brookings, South Dakota, Dr. and Mrs. Ahlquist moved to Augusta, Georgia where he became Assistant Professor of Pharmacology at the Medical College of Georgia. He was promoted to Associate Professor in 1946 and became Professor and Chairman of the Department of Pharmacology in 1948. From 1963 to 1970 he served as Associate Dean of the School of Medicine and Research Coordinator for the medical college. He returned to the Chairmanship of Pharmacology in 1970 and served until 1977 when he was appointed Charbonnier Professor of Pharmacology. Dr. Ahlquist died in April 1983. He is survived by his wife.

Raymond Ahlquist's interest in adrenergic function began in South Dakota with his study of the pharmacology of aliphatic amines. At that time, the mechanism of action of

FIG. 1 Raymond P. Ahlquist (1914–1983).

adrenergic agonists was undergoing intense study. A few years earlier, the neurotransmitter at sympathetic nerve endings had been identified by W. B. Cannon and A. Rosenbleuth[1] as being chemically similar to epinephrine. While unsure of its precise composition, they named the transmitter sympathin. However, these investigators, as did others before them, had difficulties in explaining how a single transmitter was able to produce both the excitatory and inhibitory results of sympathetic stimulation. Cannon and Rosenbleuth proposed that the single neurotransmitter, combined with some unidentified tissue intermediary present in the target organ could form either sympathin E, an excitatory neurohormone, or sympathin I, an inhibitory substance. This theory provided a nice answer to the problem and at that time was generally accepted although, as pointed out by Dr. Ahlquist in his 1948[2] paper, no known adrenergic amine fulfilled the requirement for either sympathin E or I.

Dr. Ahlquist's proposal that the inhibitory or excitatory response to sympathetic stimulation was due to the varying density of two different types of adrenergic receptors was based on a well-designed and carefully analyzed series of experiments. However, his conclusion was contrary to the established view and initially was not favorably accepted. For example, the 1948[2] manuscript was rejected for publication by the *Journal of Pharmacology and Experimental Therapeutics*. The paper was, however, published in the *American Journal of Physiology* because Dr. William Hamilton, Chairman of the Department of Physiology at the Medical College of Georgia and a member of that journal's editorial board, recognized its importance. Dr. Ahlquist continued his interest in adrenergic receptors and subsequently published several important papers on the action of beta-blocking drugs.

Dr. Ahlquist received many honors. His awards include the Oscar B. Hunter Memorial Award in Therapeutics, the Ciba Award for Hypertension Research, and the Albert Lasker Medical Research Award. He served on the Editorial Board of the *Journal of Clinical Pharmacology, Proceedings of the Society for Experimental Biology and Medicine, Journal of Cardiovascular Pharmacology, American Heart Journal, and Journal of Autonomic Pharmacology*. Dr. Ahlquist served on various committees for the National Heart Institute, the U.S. Pharmacological Convention and the American College of Clinical Pharmacology. He served as president of the latter organization and as chairman of the American Pharmaceutical Association. In addition to his teaching, research, and administrative duties at the Medical College of Georgia, he served as consultant to a number of pharmaceutical companies and as an expert witness in state and federal courts.

Ray was a very private individual. He had a rough exterior and a low tolerance for sham or pretense; however, underneath was a warm and friendly individual who was well liked by his close associates and students. The disciplines of pharmacology and clinical medicine owe a large debt to this outstanding individual.

References

1. Cannon WB, Rosenbleuth A: *Autonomic Neuro-Effector Systems.* New York, Macmillan Co. (1937)
2. Ahlquist RP: A study of the adrenotropic receptor. *Am J Physiol* 153, 586 (1948)

Robert Purves Grant*

J. Willis Hurst, M.D.

Department of Medicine, Emory University School of Medicine, Atlanta, Georgia, USA

Robert Purves Grant, M.D., was born in Orillia, Ontario, Canada, September 17, 1915. He graduated from Cornell University in 1937 and received his medical degree from the same institution in 1940. Following his internship and first-year medical residency at the Peter Bent Brigham Hospital in Boston, Grant served four years in the Army Medical Corps. He then served as a resident in Medicine at the New York Hospital. During 1947 he worked as a research associate at Tulane Medical School in New Orleans and then joined the Departments of Medicine and Physiology at Emory University School of Medicine, where he remained until 1950.

Grant was a very creative individual who could have mastered any subject, but his time and talents were devoted to electrocardiography (Fig. 1). His ability to visualize the spatial characteristics of any item was astonishing. This ability was reflected in his sculpturing. Robert Purves Grant would not paint on a flat surface. He was an artist who had to sculpture. Perhaps this is why he was so successful in visualizing the electrical forces of the heart in three-dimensional space. While he was at Emory University, this creative scientist with an ability to visualize items in space tackled electrocardiography. He developed the vector method of analyzing and teaching electrocardiography. Day after day, and night after night, he plotted vectors and tested his method. His first book, which he used to teach medical students and physicians, was published privately by Emory in 1949. A more detailed book, with Dr. Harvey Estes as co-author, was published in 1951 (Grant and Estes, 1951). The following passage has been reproduced from the preface with permission from the publisher. This passage will convey Grant's ability to write clearly and succinctly.

In the spatial vector method of interpretation each of the conventional leads used in clinical electrocardiography is considered to represent a measurement of the electrical forces of the heart along a specific axis through the electrical field of the heart. In other words, the various deflections recorded in the conventional leads simply represent so many different points of vantage in examining a single electrical field. When compared with other methods of interpretation, then, the vector method represents a different 'point of view,' for the same electrode positions and the same deflections are used in this method as in other methods.

The vector method of interpretation has several advantages over empirical methods which base their interpretation on the 'pattern' or contour of the deflections on individual leads: (1) It greatly simplifies clinical interpretation of the ECG because it eliminates the need to memorize deflection patterns. With the introduction of unipolar limb leads and multiple precordial leads into clinical electrocardiography, the interpretation of the ECG from deflection contours has become more and more arbitrary, and the memorizing of the contours on each lead for the various normal and abnormal syndromes has become nearly impossible for the average physician. (2) It is more accurate and objective than empirical methods, for the deflections than to a few relatively simple quantitative and objective measurements of the electrical field in the given subject. Thus, some of the intuitive and arbitrary aspects of 'pattern' interpretation are eliminated. (3) Changes in wave forms due to a change in the position of the heart are easily separated from changes due to intrinsic myocardial abnormalities by using the vector method. There is no way to make this differentiation with certainty in empirical methods of interpretation. (4) The criteria for the normal and abnormal tracing become simple, rational, and relatively precise, which makes the evaluation of marginally normal and follow-up tracings much easier and more accurate.

It is not meant, however, that the spatial vector method should supplant 'pattern' methods of interpretation. Rather, it should supplement these methods. When the beginner has become familiar with the use of the vector method, he will unconsciously find himself recognizing contour deformities which represent one or another abnormality of electrical forces, and will soon find it unnecessary actually to determine the characteristics of the vectors in a given case. He is now interpreting the ECG from 'patterns.' However, he will have several advantages over the physician who has learned to read the ECG from the 'patterns' alone. He will know 'why' a given pattern is abnormal. He will know how to approach the tracing which does not present a typical pattern abnormality or is marginally normal. He will know

---

*From the Department of Medicine (Cardiology), Emory University School of Medicine.

FIG. 1   Dr. Robert P. Grant—teaching. These photographs of Dr. Robert P. Grant were made at Emory University in 1954 by Dr. Leslie French of Hyattsville, Maryland. (From JW Hurst and R Myerburg, *Introduction to Electrocardiography*, McGraw-Hill Book Co., New York (1968), v. Reproduced with permission from the publisher).

how to interpret leads taken from regions of the body which may be unfamiliar to him—such as esophageal or ensiform of intracardiac leads. And, finally, he will have a better understanding of the limitations and the sources of error in the ECG, for he will understand some of the ways in which intracardiac and extracardiac factors can influence body surface recordings.

So, his method became recognized as an exciting new approach to electrocardiography. He then joined, to his own embarrassment, the ranks of Einthoven, Lewis, Wilson, Bayley, and others as a contributor to the understanding of the electrical forces of the heart.

After he joined the staff of the National Institutes of Health, I would ask him to return to Emory to participate in postgraduate courses in electrocardiography. He did so initially, but then graciously declined because he said, "It is time to earn my spurs in other fields."

He became Assistant Chief of the Grants and Training Branch of the National Heart Institute in 1959 and for two years guided the Institute's program of training grants and fellowships. In 1961 he lectured and carried out research in three European universities and in 1962 joined the NIH Office of International Research with emphasis in Europe and the Middle East. During this period he became recognized as one who had the ability to select research projects that were likely to yield results. This was possible for him, I believe, because of his innate ability to identify excellent researchers. He became Director of the National Heart Insititue on March 8, 1966, and died in August 1966.

This gentle, kind, creative person should not be forgotten. He contributed unselfishly to the field of cardiology and, indeed, "earned his spurs" in all that he did.

Reference

Grant RP, Estes EH Jr: *Spatial Vector Electrocardiography. Clinical Electrocardiographic Interpretation*. The Blakiston Company, Philadelphia (1951) vii

James V. Warren: A Tribute

A. M. WEISSLER, M.D.

Department of Medicine, Rose Medical Center, and Department of Medicine, University of Colorado Health Sciences Center, Denver, Colorado, USA

In the annals of cardiovascular medicine, the mid-twentieth century will long be recognized as the period when the concept and practice of human cardiac catheterization were first introduced. The contribution that this innovation made to our understanding of the pathophysiology, diagnosis, and treatment of human cardiovascular disease will remain a tribute to those clinical investigators who pioneered the technique. It is with keen sense of humility and great personal gratification as his former student, long-term colleague, and devoted friend that I present this tribute to one of those pioneers, James Vaughn Warren, M.D.

Born in Columbus, Ohio, James V. Warren was the only child of Dr. James Halford and Lucile Vaughn Warren. His father, Hal Warren, as his friends knew him, was among the first clinical practitioners to be distinguished as a consultant in the specialty of internal medicine in Ohio. As a renowned and busy practitioner one might have expected that father and son would have little time to grow together. Such was not the case in the Warren family where Lucile Warren engendered a warm and affectionate ambiance ensuring time for mother, father, and son to share their many interests in science, music, the arts, travel, and the exploits of their local football team, the Buckeyes of Ohio State.

Young James attended public school in Columbus. He enrolled at the Ohio State University in 1931 as a premedical student. One can only imagine the delight that he brought to his parents when four years later he was admitted to the Harvard Medical School. After receiving his M.D. degree in 1939, he joined the postgraduate program at the Peter Bent Brigham Hospital. After a two-year internship he entered assistant residency and won a special research fellowship in medicine.

Those of us who have known Dr. Warren closely recognize his unfailing gratitude to his early mentors at the Peter Bent Brigham Hospital. Dr. Soma Weiss who headed the medical family had a special influence on Jim Warren. In a commentary on Dr. Weiss entitled "The Legacy of Soma Weiss," Dr. Warren focused attention on his former professor and chief:

> Clinical learning with Dr. Weiss was an exciting experience. It was not that he was such a brilliant clinician, but he asked probing and stimulating questions. Even more importantly, he brought the medical student from the

back row in ward rounds to the front where he became the key figure. If the student did not know the answer, the intern or the resident, or Dr. Weiss himself would try. The questions often dealt with mechanisms and with what was not known, but he never lost sight of the patient. What resulted was a stimulating discussion that sent all charging off to seek the answer. By sheer force of his personal investment and enthusiasm he thus attracted eager young men by employing the case method to its ultimate.

What James V. Warren revered most in his academic parent, he emulated and built upon in his own brilliant career. His experience on the Harvard teaching service brought him in daily contact with some of the most powerful clinical investigative minds of the period. In addition to Soma Weiss there were Eugene A. Stead, Jr., Charles Janeway, John Romano, Samuel Levine, Sidney Burwell, Sibley Hoobler, and Joseph Aub. His colleagues on the house staff included several of his lifelong academic associates, Jack Myers, Robert Grant, Max Michael, Richard Ebert, John Hickam, Louis Hempelmann, and Paul Beeson.

The years at the Brigham Hospital served as a great stimulus to Dr. Warren's career in internal medicine and cardiovascular research. In 1942 he was invited by Eugene A. Stead, Jr. to join the faculty at Emory University in Atlanta as instructor in medicne. At the same time he was appointed medical investigator for the Office of Scientific Research and Development on problems of shock in vascular injuries. There followed four highly productive years of research which established Dr. Warren's special expertise in circulatory dynamics. After a brief stint as Assistant Professor of Medicine at Yale, he returned to Emory in 1947 as Professor and Chairman of the Department of Physiology and Associate Professor of Medicine. Soon thereafter, he was promoted to full Professor of Medicine. In 1952 he joined the Department of Medicine at Duke University, where Dr. Stead was then Chairman. With his appointment as Chief of Medicine at the newly constructed Durham VA Hospital, Dr. Warren initiated the now well established tradition of excellence in the Duke VA medical service. In 1958 Dr. Warren accepted the appointment of Professor and Chairman of the Department of Medicine at the University of Texas Medical Branch

FIG. 1 James V. Warren.

in Galveston. Three years later he returned to his native Columbus to assume the Chair of Medicine at Ohio State University School of Medicine, a position he held for 18 years. In 1976 he relinquished his administrative duties at the University to devote full time to continuing his scholarly pursuits in medicine.

James V. Warren had done many things first and all things well. His publications began to enrich the scientific literature as early as 1941 and his brilliant investigations have continued to make an important impact to the present day. At a time when cardiac catheterization was at its inception, he was among the first to perceive its potential in the investigation of normal and abnormal circulatory responses. His early investigations on the acute hemodynamic alterations accompanying head-up tilt, venesection, the application of venous occlusive tourniquets, and the opening and closing of arterial fistulae led him to a conceptualization of circulatory regulation in humans in which peripheral resistance, as opposed to venous inflow, was the dominant determinant of ventricular output. During this productive period he described the method of hepatic and renal vein catheterization and was among the first to document the hemodynamic spectrum of clinical shock

and pericardial tamponade. Among his most celebrated innovations was the first use of the cardiac catheter in the definitive diagnosis of congenital heart disease. The day on which Dr. Warren, in collaboration with Drs. E.S. Brannon and H.S. Weens passed the catheter through an atrial septal defect is now commemorated in a plaque erected at the laboratory site in Grady Memorial Hospital. His early studies on human cardiac output, in particular those relating to congestive heart failure, are now classical investigations and he was among the originators of the technique of cineangiography.

Among Dr. Warren's most notable contributions was his observation, in collaboration with Dr. Eugene A. Stead, Jr., that the development of edema and the increase in plasma volume in congestive heart failure occurred prior to the development of an elevation in venous pressure. This led to their concept of forward heart failure in which renal sodium retention was determined to be the critical factor in the development of the congestive state. These unique observations served as a stimulus for innumerable later investigations on the mechanisms underlying the renal retention of sodium and water by the kidney. Among other investigations which attained notoriety were Dr. Warren's studies on the salutary circulatory effects of concentrated human serum albumin in the treatment of shock, his studies on the circulation of such animals as the giraffe, the cow, and the ox, his observations on the acute circulatory consequence of emotional arousal, and his early description of scleroderma heart disease. His expeditions to Africa to study the circulation of the giraffe resulted in unique contributions to the field of comparative physiology. As his career in cardiovascular research unfolded, Dr. Warren turned to the problems of the management of patients with acute myocardial infarction. He was one of the original advocates of the efficacy of the coronary care unit and he was among the earliest to conceive mobile coronary care, establishing the first such system in this country in Columbus. The report of the NIH Ad Hoc Task Force on Cardiac Replacement, of which Dr. Warren was Chairman, was the first comprehensive assessment of the ethical, psychological, and economic implications in human cardiac transplantation. He was a leader of one of the earliest collaborative controlled studies on the long-term effectiveness of anticoagulant therapy after acute myocardial infarction; a study which first demonstrated the feasibility of conducting well-controlled clinical trials through the cooperative efforts of several institutions at a multinational level.

Dr. Warren's contributions to medicine are only partially portrayed in a description of his vast reasearch efforts. Through a distinctive style of teaching, he has illuminated the paths of students and trainees, many of whom rank among today's leaders in internal medicine and cardiology. The lineage of eight chairmen of university departments of medicine can be traced through his years of leadership at Ohio State University. The field of cardiovascular medicine is indebted to Dr. Warren for molding the career of scores of distinguished academic cardiologists.

Dr. Warren's contributions to science, research, and education have been well recognized in the past. He was National

President of the American Federation for Clinical Research (1952), National President of the American Heart Association (1962), and President of the Association of Professors of Medicine (1968). The American Heart Association has honored Dr. Warren through its Gold Heart Award (1966), the James B. Herrick Award (1976), the Outstanding Achievement Award (1985), and the Blakeslee Award (1985). He has been recognized as a Distinguished Alumnus of Duke University and he has received the Medical Alumni Merit Award from Ohio State University. He has received Honorary Degrees of Doctor of Science from Emory University and the Medical College of Ohio at Toledo. The City of Columbus has recognized him as one of its most notable citizens through the Mayor's Award for Voluntary Service.

The years 1952–1958 were exceptionally productive ones for James V. Warren. During this period he not only gained international eminence for his pioneering research, served as Chairman of the American Federation for Clinical Research, and launched his first expedition to Africa, but attained a crowning achievement of his lifetime in his marriage to the charming and brilliant Gloria Kicklighter, who was then Chief of Therapeutic Dietetics at Duke Hospital. Gloria Warren, a graduate of the University of Georgia, served her internship in dietetics at the Medical College of Virginia. She was a therapeutic dietician at University Hospital in Augusta, Georgia, and participated in innovative research on sodium metabolism at Tulane University with Dr. Thorpe Ray and the late Dr. George Birch, before she joined the staff at Duke. The partnership between Gloria and James has flourished since its inception. The productive collaboration between the Warren and Stead families took on a new image in 1956 when Mrs. Gloria Warren and Mrs. Evelyn Stead collaborated to produce the first edition of their now famous *Low-Fat Cookery*, a publication which remains a classic reference in clinical nutrition.

No biography of James V. Warren could be completed without an appreciation of James V. Warren the man—his charm, his grace, his humility, and his humane spirit. To be his student is to feel a spirit of enthusiasm and optimism, a sense of well being, a confidence in oneself, and to gain an understanding that the pursuit of scientific knowledge enhances all human experience. It is not unexpected that a mind so fertile and imaginative would turn to many interests beyond the science of his profession. Throughout his life Dr. Warren has kept a camera close at hand. His skill as a photographer is evidenced in several lay and scientific publications. Gloria Warren, too, is a photographer of extraordinary skill. Throughout their many world travels, the cameras of Gloria and James Warren have captured the essence of exotic islands, majestic landscapes, beautiful flora, and a host of artistic portraits.

Dr. Warren has harbored an irrepressible love for music throughout his life. An avid collector of records and tapes, he enraptures any who would care to listen to his scintillating stereo system, frequently projected at a level of decibels which only less delicate tympanic membranes can tolerate. One can add to photography and music a ubiquitous interest and taste in the arts and architecture. Together with Gloria Warren's culinary skills, an evening with the Warrens is a memorable experience of enduring pleasure, accentuated by delectable details of the most recent performances at Salzburg, Vienna, Bayreuth, and Glynebourne or of the latest exhibits of art and sculpture on the Continent.

The career of James V. Warren epitomizes what can be accomplished when human energy and enthusiasm are coupled to an inquiring mind. Each decade of his life brought new horizons, new visions, and new directions. He retains in his senior years optimism, youthful vigor, the desire to achieve, and a refreshing zest for living. When others might well be winding down, James V. Warren is leading the pack as President of the Association of Former Chairmen of Medicine, President of the Clinical and Climatological Association, Chairman of the Medical Humanities Committee at his University, and visiting professor at several universities. He remains today a model academician for all to emulate.

Herman Hellerstein Remembered

SYLVAN LEE WEINBERG, M.D., F.A.C.C.

The Weinberg Marcus Cardiovascular Group, Inc., Dayton, Ohio, USA

My earliest and most indelible memory of Herman Hellerstein dates back to the Michael Reese Hospital in the late 1940s (Fig. 1). At the time, he was a Fellow in Cardiology with the late Dr. Louis Nelson Katz. I was a senior medical clerk from Northwestern, and several months later an intern. I can still see Herman, clipboard in hand, stalking the 40- and 50-bed wards studying post myocardial infarction patients randomized to warfarin or placebo as part of Irving S. Wright's landmark study. It proved the effectiveness of anticoagulation after myocardial infarction and was one of the first great double-blind multicentered trials.

To the housestaff, Herman Hellerstein epitomized everything we wanted to be as doctors, but saw little chance of attaining. How could we ever hope to quote the literature, know cardiac physiology, read electrocardiograms, and examine and understand patients as well as Herman Hellerstein?

So large does Herman loom in my memory that only recently did I realize that he and I had spent less than one year together at Michael Reese. Somehow it seemed to me that he was at Michael Reese all the time that I was there—internship, residency, and fellowship in cardiology.

Herman graduated from Western Reserve University in 1937 and received his medical degree from that institution in 1941. He interned at Philadelphia General Hospital and had a residency in pathology at University Hospitals in Cleveland. He then served in the United States Army from 1942 to 1945 as a battalion surgeon with the 40th Tank Battalion in General Patton's famed 7th Armored Division as it swept across Europe, and he reached the rank of Major. None of us at Michael Reese in the late 1940s had any idea of his military accomplishments until one day, at the interns' library, we happened upon a book of citations and decorations given to medical officers in combat during World War II. There we learned that Herman received the Silver Star for gallantry in action with his tank battalion and, in addition, the Bronze Star with Oak Leaf Cluster and the Verdun Medal. He fought five major campaigns. Characteristic of his style, Herman never spoke about his military career or what it took for a tank battalion surgeon to earn a Silver Star. Later he told me that one of his proudest and most painful moments was helping to liberate many of his fellow Jews from the Nazi concentration camp at Bergen-Belsen.

After Michael Reese, Hellerstein returned to Cleveland and his alma mater where he distinguished himself in teaching, practice, and research for more than four decades until his death on August 17, 1993, at age 77.

This man was one of the giants of American cardiology. Although his knowledge of hemodynamics and electrophysiology was deep and sophisticated, his monumental contributions to cardiology were related to patients. He was a pioneer in exercise physiology and in cardiac rehabilitation. His laboratory was not just an ivory tower, but was a work place where he took electrocardiograms and measured oxygen consumption and work capacity. He established the Cleveland Work Classification Clinic in 1950, and he was among the first to show that patients with heart disease could return to productive life and work. This research reversed previous dogma about heart attack victims.

A little known facet of Herman Hellerstein's contribution to American cardiology is that he and his good friend, E. Grey Dimond, in a hotel room during a medical meeting in Boston, played a key role in bringing Bill Nelligan to the American College of Cardiology. As the years have shown, this was a pivotal event in the history of the College.

In 1990 he authored a book titled *Healing Your Heart* that emphasized the reversibility of heart disease through exercise, diet, and the control of lipids, blood pressure, and use of tobacco. His book reflected the optimism with which Herman approached heart disease.

By participating in national and international organizations, he carried his message of hope for cardiac patients throughout the world. He consulted in many capacities for the United States government. The American Heart Association awarded him its Gold Heart for distinguished service. He was a member of the Medical Commission for the International Olympic Committee and of the Scientific Committee of the International Federation of Sports Medicine. In 1963 Hellerstein was appointed Consultant in Cardiovascular Disease to the World Health Organization and represented the United States in Geneva on eight occasions. The North American Association of Pacing and Electrophysiology recognized him as its 1993 pioneer in cardiac pacing and electrophysiology.

But a mere catalog of Herman Hellerstein's honors, awards, and citations can in no way do him justice. He was a prodigious worker and a prolific author. He published more than 400 papers and was the author of or contributor to some 20 books. His career spanned the introduction of cardiac catheterization and surgery. One of Herman's characteristics was to

FIG. 1   Herman K. Hellerstein, M.D., 1916–1993.

change with the times. In the early days of bypass surgery, Herman was a skeptic but soon became an enthusiast.

If I had but one word with which to describe Herman it would be "integrity." This pervaded everything he did—in research, practice, writing, and in his relations with organizations, students, peers, and patients. He was always upfront. No one ever had to wonder where he stood on any issue. What he said was what he believed. For Herman, integrity took precedence over diplomacy.

Although I knew him for more than four decades, my first impression of Herman is unchanged—a physician whose devotion to his patients was backed by profound knowledge of the science and psychology of medicine. He was a doctor in the most humane sense of the word.

His preeminence in science and medicine never detracted from his devotion to his family. He and his wife Mary, a pediatrician, raised six children: four physicians, an English professor, and an environmental scientist, all distinguished in their fields.

A few months after he died, his autobiography, *A Matter of Heart*,[1] was published. In the introduction, Hellerstein said that he considered himself to be "a human ecologist … that is why I have often entered the field to study the cardiovascular systems of people at work, in the factory, jumping out of airplanes, arguing, exercising, and even during sexual intercourse."

The essence of Hellerstein's philosophy is expressed in the last few lines of his autobiography: "As far as I am concerned, the key thing is not that the past was glorious, but that the future is better … probably the next advances will concern the brain, the last terra incognito—unknown land. The heart was once like that."

It was difficult to get Herman on the telephone during the day and he was not prompt at answering mail. But it was easy to reach him at home in the evening, and we would often talk for an hour or more. These conversations over the years were stimulating because of Herman's brilliant intellect and incisive grasp of significant trends in medicine and society. It is rare for one so gifted and accomplished to be an attentive listener with so great an interest in others. As a man and as a friend, his like will not soon be seen again.

Whoever knew and exchanged ideas with Herman Hellerstein was privileged. Those who sought to emulate him chose a difficult goal. To have tried and failed is no disgrace.

Reference

1.   Hellerstein HK: *A Matter of Heart*. Caldwell, Ida.: Griffith Publishing, 1994

John J. Osborn

CLYDE PARTIN, M.D.

Emory University School of Medicine, Atlanta, Georgia, USA

The curious but distinct terminal aberration of the QRS complex often noted on the electrocardiogram (ECG) of hypothermic patients is now commonly known as the Osborn wave. It is fitting that Dr. Osborn's (Fig. 1) name should be held in perpetuity in association with hypothermia. His contributions to medical science were part of the pioneering effort in cardiothoracic surgery to provide surgeons with a bloodless and nonbeating heart by iatrogenically inducing hypothermia. History will reflect that he left an indelible fingerprint on the pulse of modern medical progress and technology.

While working as an Assistant Professor of Pediatrics at New York University College of Medicine in 1953, Dr. Osborn published a paper entitled *Experimental Hypothermia: Respiratory and Blood pH Changes in Relation to Cardiac Function*. In this article he describes the ECG as showing

> a secondary wave closely following the S-wave, so closely that it appears to be part of the QRS complex. Evidence from leads V_1 and V_6 indicates that this abnormal wave following S represents a current of injury, rather than a widening of the ventricular complex due to a conduction defect. This wave, which we interpret as a current of injury, is so closely associated with the QRS complex as to prevent accurate measurement of the actual duration of the QRS wave.[1]

The debate lingers as to whether this current of injury is truly part of the QRS complex and what actually causes it. What is not disputed is that the use of the term "Osborn wave" became commonplace by the 1980s, finding its way into many standard textbooks of medicine and cardiology. Exactly when the eponym stood on its own is uncertain. In 1959, D. Emslie-Smith, writing in the *British Heart Journal*, noted, "The characteristic deflection of hypothermia has sometimes been named after Osborn who discussed it in 1953."[2] In *The Lancet* in 1961, Helen Duguid remarks, "The electrocardiogram may show the distinctive 'J' or 'Osborn' waves."[3] To be sure, others had previously described similar afflictions of the QRS complex in association with low body temperature, yet it is Osborn's portrayal that seems to have captured posterity's imagination. Osborn noted some other ECG manifestations of hypothermia and, indeed, ECG changes ascribed to hypothermia can be found in the literature as far back as 1920.[4]

I recently interviewed Dr. Osborn, and he reminisced about his research. He became interested in the medical applications of hypothermia while in medical school at Johns Hopkins. Challenging the accepted notion that warm-blooded mammals could not survive deep hypothermia, he cooled anesthetized dogs to 5° C, left them without circulation for an hour and then rewarmed them. He restored heartbeat with open cardiac massage and a defibrillator consisting of two spoons with insulated handles, connected directly through a knife-switch to an electrical wall outlet. Although none of the animals survived, he was able to demonstrate brain activity after rewarming.[5] In 1943, he submitted a paper on his findings. He then graduated and embarked on a 9-month whirlwind pediatric residency and entered the U.S. Army. "I received a letter from a very nice man, Dr. Blalock (of the Blalock-Taussig Procedure) asking for revisions on my paper," Dr. Osborn recalls, "but I was lying in a tent in the rain in the Philippine Islands and revising the paper did not seem like a viable project at the time." He spent two years in the Army as a medical officer for a field artillery battalion, "waiting for the invasion of the islands that never took place because of the atomic bomb, thus probably saving my life."

Following the war, Dr. Osborn made his way to New York University College of Medicine and studied under the widely respected pediatrician Emmett Holt. However, his interest in hypothermia never cooled. Utilizing laboratory space given to him by the nephrologist Homer Smith, he resumed his research. Clinically, he was working with premature babies, most of whom died. "My thoughts turned toward an artificial placenta and perfusion techniques. We never were successful with the artificial placenta but realized our perfusion techniques might be useful for open-heart surgery. I fashioned my own rotating oxygenator, a wonderful 'Rube-Goldberg' apparatus," Dr. Osborn fondly recalled. In a modern day acquiescence to Horace Greeley, Dr. Osborn migrated west in 1954 to Stanford University to continue his efforts in the pioneering days of cardiothoracic surgery. There he turned his talents toward taming the temperamental heart-lung machine. His undergraduate degree in biology from Princeton did not provide him with any formal engineering training, yet this did not prevent him from contributing significantly to solving the operational problems of the heart-lung machine. In his scholarly lecture on the history of cardiac surgery, Dr. Dwight

FIG. 1   John J. Osborn, M.D. (photo taken ca. 1956).

Harken refers to Era III, namely, "open heart surgery involving hypothermia, mechanical bypass or both."[6] Having already laid the groundwork with his study of hypothermia, Dr. Osborn began to perfect his heart-lung machine with the rotating disc oxygenator.[7] (Fig. 2). Teaming up with the gifted cardiac surgeon Frank Gerbode, they performed the first successful heart-lung bypass procedure west of the Mississippi in 1956 when they repaired a ventricular septal defect, thus securing an integral position in the history of cardiac surgery.

The success of the cardiothoracic surgery program at Stanford University hinged on several issues. As part of the team headed by Dr. Gerbode, Dr. Osborn was instrumental in introducing continuous hemodynamic computer monitoring of postoperative cardiac patients. They were the first to show that sudden cardiac death was not due to stray electrical currents travelling down the monitoring devices, but rather due to failure to recognize subtle changes in acid-base status, fluid

balance, and other seemingly minor deviations that could lead to sudden decompensation. On his early encounters with the heart-lung machine, Dr. Osborn took great care to make two points. First was cognizance of the need to make sure that any part of the bypass machine that came in contact with the patient's blood had to be absolutely biologically and chemically clean.* As he wrote in 1960, "As a minimum, every part which can possibly touch blood should be scrubbed individually with appropriate detergent, then rinsed long and hard. All parts should be dried and coated with baked silicone before each use."[7] His second point stressed the need for a good blood filter. Using the Swank filter developed by Dr. Roy Swank at Oregon, the team prevented the postsurgical encephalopathy related to central nervous system emboli from clumped cells. Several weeks of postoperative delirium and fevers were not unusual. Dr. Osborn's group was the first to publish the benefits of utilizing the Swank filter, describing a patient who discussed home finances with his wife the morning after open-heart surgery. Application of these principles, the meticulous attention to details, and the introduction of continuous postoperative computer monitoring culminated in an internationally famous advanced cardiac surgery unit[8] and ushered in the dawn of the intensive care unit.

The remainder of Dr. Osborn's career was spent as an intensivist at Stanford. He was a founding member of the Society for Critical Care Medicine. He published over 130 papers although he "considered only three or four of these to

---

*The first successful use of the heart-lung machine in a human is credited to John Gibbon in Philadelphia in 1953, when he repaired an atrial septal defect. Many thought the procedure so radical that they refused to send their patients to Dr. Gibbon. With Dr. Gibbon's permission, Dr. J. W. Kirklin took the machine to the Mayo Clinic and established a successful open-heart surgical program. Dr. Kirklin had figured out what Osborn and colleagues at Stanford had learned—the heart-lung machine had to be meticulously cleaned and rinsed in order to minimize postoperative fevers, emboli, and other complications. Dr. Kirklin kept in his employ two exceptionally fastidious ladies to sanitize the machines, whose contribution to the success of the program at the Mayo Clinic may have been underappreciated.[5]

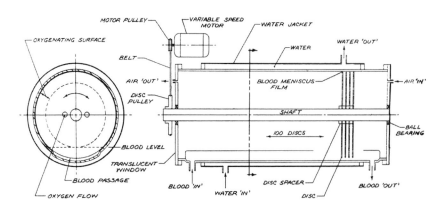

FIG. 2   Sectional diagrammatic sketch of 21 cm disc oxygenator. Reproduced from Ref. No. 7 with permission.

be of any importance." With a trace of chagrin in his voice he admitted that the article in which he described the Osborn wave had erroneous blood pH calculations because he utilized the wrong temperature corrections. His miscalculations were discovered by John Severinghaus, known for developing the Severinghaus electrode. They subsequently developed a friendship that has persevered for nearly 50 years.

Although IBM and the National Institutes of Health supplied much of the initial research funding in the incipient years of hemodynamic computer monitoring, their support eventually dwindled. Undaunted, Dr. Osborn, using venture capital, founded a business developing and manufacturing intensive care unit monitoring devices. The business flourished and in 1978, declaring intensive care medicine a "young man's game," he retired from active practice to devote his energies to the company. He eventually sold his enterprise, Research Development Corporation, to Johnson & Johnson and retired to Tiburon, California, with his wife Anne. They are the parents of seven children and grandparents of sixteen, which leaves "precious little time to pursue our love of sailing." It should be noted that the soon-to-be Mrs. Osborn, serving in the dual capacity of girlfriend and research assistant during Dr. Osborn's experiments at Johns Hopkins in the early 1940s, assiduously remarked, "If we are going to do such nasty and messy experiments, let us at least keep decent notes on what happens." And she did.[5] One of Dr. Osborn's sons, Oliver, practices medicine near San Francisco. Growing up, Oliver remembers being vaguely aware that his father was helping develop the heart-lung machine, but that his father "was very modest and never gave the impression that he was working on anything important. He seemed to enjoy what he was doing and projected that at home."[9]

Born in Detroit, Michigan, on November 5, 1917, Dr. Osborn was one of two sons and four daughters of Frederick Henry Osborn. His father was a businessman who served as a U. S. Army General of Information and Education during World War II. His career was noteworthy for helping create and introducing the G.I. Bill.

I informally polled 16 of my internal medicine colleagues, half of whom were able to tell me that an Osborn wave suggested hypothermia. Eleven of 12 cardiologists were able to answer the same query correctly. Dr. Osborn seemed truly amazed to learn that present day physicians knew anything at all about his "current of injury" as he prefers to call it. Moreover, he had no inkling that his name was being invoked in medical wards across the globe in association with the enigmatic J point deflection. "It is," he stated, simply and elegantly in his articulate fashion, "nice to be remembered."

References

1. Osborn JJ: Experimental hypothermia: Respiratory and blood pH changes in relation to cardiac function. *Am J Physiol* 1953;175: 389–398

2. Emslie-Smith D: The significance of changes in the electrocardiogram in hypothermia. *Br Heart J* 1959;21:343–351

3. Duguid H, Simpson RG, Stowers JM: Accidental hypothermia. *Lancet* 1961;2:1213–1219

4. Bazett HC: An analysis of the time-relations of electrocardiograms. *Heart* 1920;7:353–370

5. Osborn JJ: Personal communication (letter and telephone). May 1997

6. Harken DW: Heart surgery—legend and a long look. *Am J Cardiol* 1967;19:393–401

7. Osborn JJ, Bramson ML, Gerbode F: A rotating disc oxygenator of improved inherent efficiency. *J Thorac Cardiovasc Surg* 1960;39: 427–437

8. Hurt R: *The History of Cardiothoracic Surgery*, p. 468. New York: The Parthenon Publishing Group, 1996

9. Osborn O: Personal communication (telephone) May 26, 1997

Donald Arthur McDonald

MICHAEL F. O'ROURKE, M.D., MICHAEL G. TAYLOR, M.D., PH.D., D.SC.*

University of New South Wales St. Vincent's Hospital; *University of Sydney, Sydney, Australia

Donald Arthur McDonald was a British physiologist of colorful personality who established the modern approach to the study of arterial hemodynamics over a 20-year period from 1953–1973. His career epitomized on the positive side the value of interdisciplinary research and on the negative side the trials and frustrations encountered by one who dares to be different.

Donald McDonald was born of English parents in Katni, India, in 1917. His father was an officer in the British Army. He was educated at Christ's Hospital School and won an open scholarship in Natural Science to Oriel College, Oxford, in 1936. He graduated B.A. in physiology in 1939, then completed his medical course at the Radcliffe Infirmary and Oxford University in 1942 when Britain was immersed in war. After an attenuated residency in Oxford and Leicester, he joined the Royal Army Medical Corps and worked predominantly in neurosurgery from 1943–1947. Even in war he maintained his intellectual curiosity and scholarship. He compiled a treatise on brain injuries and their neurological sequelae, which was successfully submitted as a thesis for the Doctorate of Medicine at Oxford University in 1951. In 1948 he was appointed Senior Lecturer in Physiology at St Bartholomew's Hospital, London, and was promoted to Reader in 1953. His early research was in neurophysiology and he established collaboration with Rudolph Hess and others in Europe. He became intrigued with blood flow in the Circle of Willis and established high-speed cinematographic techniques for flow measurement.[1] Blood flow became more interesting to him than neurophysiology, and he described himself in the preface of his classic book[2] as "slipping down the vertebral arteries into the systemic circulation." Flow recordings, primitive as they were, created problems of interpretation and McDonald sought appropriate analytic methods and looked to the physical sciences for guidance. He was fortunate to strike up a relationship with John Womersley, then a most accomplished applied mathematician who also was looking for a new challenge. This part of McDonald's life is elegantly described in the preface to his 1960 monograph. He stressed how interdisciplinary research can only advance on the basis of mutual respect, with all parties taking the time and effort to become familiar with their colleagues, and with none regarding any other as an instrument to success. McDonald was pressed to formulate his problems in a way that was subject to rigorous mathematical analysis. He had to be more precise than ever before. Womersley in turn was surprised at the imprecision of biological measurement and learned that a different approach was required of him than had been before. The two worked most productively with each other over a 3-year period. In this time, Womersley tackled the Navier-Stokes equations as they apply to the motion of blood in arteries and showed that nonlinearities were sufficiently small to be neglected to a first approximation. This was the basis for Womersley's method for determining pulsatile flow from the pulsatile pressure gradient,[3] and for validation of longitudinal impedance by McDonald and Womersley.[4, 5] This work established the logic of using Fourier analysis to break down pressure and flow waves and for the general concept of vascular impedance which was developed further by McDonald and one of us (MGT) in the late 1950s.[6] After Womersley's departure for the Wright Air Development Centre in Columbus, Ohio, McDonald continued his studies on arterial hemodynamics at St. Bartholomew's Hospital. This period was crowned with publication of his classic book *Blood Flow in Arteries* in 1960.[2] This summarized work of the previous eight years and presented it in a way that was easily digested. But the exercise had taken McDonald way ahead of his contemporaries. His work was well accepted in parts of the United States of America, but not at all in Britain. He was passed over for the Chair of Physiology at St. Bartholomew's Hospital when this was vacated by K. J. Franklin. Frustrated and demoralized, he sought a position in the New World.

In 1962, Donald McDonald was appointed to a position in Philadelphia at the University of Pennsylvania, with Ernst Attinger. He had come under the very strong influence of Sam Talbot, who was the first Chief of the Bioengineering Department at Johns Hopkins, and who had helped to create the Philadelphia position with Attinger. At this time, the University of Alabama was recruiting for its rejuvenated medical campus in Birmingham. John Kirklin had been appointed Chief of Surgery, leaving the Mayo Clinic at the peak of his career in cardiac surgery; Talbot himself accepted appointment as Chief of Bioengineering, securing at the same time a position for McDonald as Professor of Physiology and Biophysics. McDonald moved to Birmingham in 1966, but sadly, Talbot was stricken with cancer and died in Baltimore.

Donald McDonald worked as Professor of Physiology and Bioengineering at U.A.B. until the time of his death. He directed work into the clinical sphere while continuing in basic

FIG. 1 Donald Arthur McDonald (1917–1973)

physiology and hemodynamics. He influenced many young physicians and physiologists, including Wilmer Nichols, Karl Weber, and Joe Janicki. His own work never rose to the heights that it had reached in London. Even in the United States of America, arterial hemodynamics was not a fashionable subject, especially in the field of cardiology. Frustrations continued. McDonald died on May 24, 1973, while working on the drafts of the second edition of his book. This eventually appeared in 1974,[7] with the editorial assistance of his friends and colleagues, Wilmer Nichols and Bill Milnor.

Donald McDonald suffered all the problems of a true pioneer. He was supported throughout his productive life by his family and his devoted and charming wife Renée who contin-ues to live in Birmingham and who acts as a link for his former colleagues and students. His son Robin and daughters Penny and Allison are married and live with their families in the United States.

Donald McDonald had a great influence on his profession. He established the value of Fourier analysis and the validity of analyzing the arterial pulse in the frequency domain. He linked with engineers and with physicians, and he encouraged his students and colleagues to do likewise. He had very high standards. He was vocal in presenting his views at meetings and conferences and was persistent in his criticism of work he considered poor or indifferent. Speakers at conventions feared his presence in the audience and all the more his move to the microphone at question time. But his own work was based on approximations and on compromise. He was fair in his criticism and this enhanced the science he pursued. He was a warm and humorous human being and a highly intelligent and cultured man. He had a phenomenal memory. Few bettered him in queries on passages from the Bible, from literary classics, or from Italian opera. His influence remains. A third edition of his textbook was published in 1990 and prepared by Wilmer Nichols and one of us (MFO'R), with segments from old pupils and colleagues.[8] The challenge in writing this book was to have it as factual, as lucid, as balanced, and as entertaining as the first edition. Large segments of the third edition were completely unchanged from the first—because they could not be improved. Probably they never will.

References

1. McDonald DA: The velocity of blood flow in the rabbit aorta studied with high-speed cinematography. *J Physiol* 118, 328–339 (1952)
2. McDonald DA: *Blood Flow in Arteries*. Arnold 1960
3. Womersley JR: Method for the calculation of velocity, rate of flow, and viscous drag in arteries when the pressure gradient is known. *J. Physiol* 127, 553–563 (1955)
4. McDonald DA: The relation of pulsatile pressure to flow in arteries. *J Physiol* 27, 533–552 (1955)
5. Womersley JR: The mathematical analysis of the arterial circulation in the state of oscillatory motion. Wright Air Development Centre Technical Report. WADC-TR 56–614
6. McDonald DA, Taylor MG: The hydrodynamics of the arterial circulation. *Progress in Biophysics* 9, 107–173 (1959)
7. McDonald DA: *Blood Flow in Arteries*. 2nd ed. Arnold, London (1974)
8. Nichols WW, O'Rourke MF: *McDonald's Blood Flow in Arteries*. 3rd ed. Arnold, London (1990)

Herbert N. Hultgren

E. WILLIAM HANCOCK, M.D.

Stanford University Medical Center, Stanford, California, USA

Herbert N. Hultgren, M.D., Professor of Medicine (Cardiovascular) Emeritus at Stanford University School of Medicine died on October 18, 1997, at his home on the Stanford University campus. His career epitomized the growth and development of academic cardiology during the last half of the twentieth century that saw a remarkable development of cardiology and cardiac surgery.

Herbert Nils Hultgren was born on August 29, 1917, in Santa Rosa, California, a small city in the northern part of the San Francisco Bay area. His parents were of Swedish origin. He attended Santa Rosa Junior College for two years and then transferred to Stanford University, from which he was graduated in 1939. He then attended Stanford University School of Medicine, whose clinical facilities were located in San Francisco, with the preclinical years on the main university campus 38 miles south in Palo Alto. He received the M.D. degree in 1943, stayed at Stanford for a residency in internal medicine, and then served in the U.S. Army in Europe from 1944 to 1945. His period of military service was notable for his experience at the end of the war with starved prisoners in German concentration camps. He later published careful and systematic observations on severe starvation, using simple methodology; the account displayed a scientific style that remained characteristic throughout his career.[1]

He returned to San Francisco in 1946 for a year of residency in pathology, and then went to Boston for a year of training in cardiology at the Thorndike Memorial Laboratory of the Harvard Medical School at Boston City Hospital, under the direction of Dr. Laurence B. Ellis. He arrived in the midst of the beginnings of a new era in cardiology, in which cardiac catheterization was being introduced into clinical practice and the surgical treatment of mitral stenosis was beginning.

Dr. Hultgren joined the faculty of the Stanford University School of Medicine in San Francisco in 1948, founding the Division of Cardiology and establishing the first cardiac catheterization laboratory in northern California. Over the next eleven years he teamed with the cardiac surgeon, Dr. Frank Gerbode, in guiding Stanford to a place among the world's leading institutions in the new fields of hemodynamically oriented cardiology and cardiac surgery. Pathophysiologic and diagnostic aspects of valvular and congenital heart disease comprised his central research interests in this period, as they did for many of the young leaders of academic cardiology during the 1950s. Memorable contributions from this period included the description of the respiratory variation in the systolic ejection click of pulmonary valve stenosis,[2] the venous pistol shot sound in severe tricuspid regurgitation,[3] the clinical and physiologic picture of patent ductus arteriosus with severe pulmonary hypertension,[4] and the syndrome of reopened ventricular septal defect after attempted total correction of tetralogy of Fallot.[5] He continued his interest in this area throughout his career, continuing to employ simple clinical and hemodynamic methods even as ever more elaborate and technological methods of study developed. Thirty years later, in the 1980s, he explored the assessment of left bundle-branch block and of aortic stenosis by means of phonocardiograms and indirect carotid arterial pulse recordings, techniques long since abandoned by the cardiological mainstream.[6, 7]

An outgrowth of his interest in the pathophysiology of congenital heart disease in the 1950s was a focus on the problem of arterial hypoxemia and its relation to the physiology of the pulmonary circulation. He linked this academic interest to his lifelong interest in mountain climbing. On a trip to Peru in 1959 he encountered the entity of high altitude pulmonary edema, previously known to relatively few and not described in the U. S. medical literature. An account published in the Stanford Medical Bulletin in 1960 noted 41 cases from the Chulec General Hospital, located at an altitude of 12,000 feet in the Peruvian Andes mountains.[8] In 1961, with several colleagues, he described these cases in detail, along with 15 cases in U.S. mountaineers, in the first definitive U. S. presentation of this entity.[9]

High altitude medicine in general, and high altitude pulmonary edema in particular, remained his most avid academic interests for the rest of his career. His many subsequent studies documented increased reactivity of the pulmonary vascular bed to hypoxia in high altitude residents and the frequent occurrence of pulmonary hypertension, particularly in those subject to high altitude pulmonary edema. He developed a theory of the mechanism of this condition, holding that pulmonary vasoconstriction in response to acute hypoxia may be nonuniform in the lung, resulting in diversion of the blood flow to less constricted areas, overperfusion of these areas, and extravasation of fluid through the capillary walls of overperfused areas. An analogy was made with the pulmonary edema occasionally seen in acute pulmonary embolism in humans. Experimental work supported this theory, which remains viable although controversial. Dr. Hultgren collected his many years of work on hypoxemia and high altitude medicine into a comprehensive book, published a few months before his death.[10]

FIG. 1 Herbert N. Hultgren, M.D., 1917–1997.

In 1959, the Stanford University School of Medicine reorganized, moving all its activities from San Francisco to the main campus in Palo Alto, where a new comprehensive academic medical center was built. Only a small nucleus of full-time faculty members in the clinical departments made the move, since most of the clinical faculty were primarily based in practice in San Francisco. The new school featured a true full-time faculty and a redirection toward research. As the head of the Division of Cardiology, working with a young and relatively unknown cardiac surgeon, Dr. Norman E. Shumway, Dr. Hultgren faced a major rebuilding program. The program was brilliantly successful, greatly supported by Dr. Hultgren's widely recognized excellence in the field of valvular and congenital heart disease. Dr. Shumway quickly demonstrated excellence in the new field of open heart surgery, and the program blossomed, culminating in a signal event—the first adult human heart transplant in the U. S. in 1968.

In 1967, Dr. Hultgren moved across the campus to the Palo Alto Veterans Administration Medical Center, where he remained the head of the Cardiology Division for the next two decades. Here he developed a third area of research interest— the clinical results of coronary artery bypass graft surgery. In the early 1960s, he had already shifted his primary cardiological interest to coronary artery disease. The Veterans Administration Cooperative Study of Coronary Artery Surgery, in which he played a leadership role for many years, was a pacesetter in the use of large, randomized, controlled clinical trials of the type that later assumed vast influence with the advent of thrombolytic therapy for acute myocardial infarction. Dr. Hultgren brought his clinical acumen and his analytic abilities to bear on this field, becoming the chief spokesman for the study. He ably defended the study against the critics who found its conclusions not always to their liking. The superiority of surgical over medical therapy in left main coronary artery disease was shown, but for other patients the differences in mortality were not striking. His summary after many years of follow-up has stood the test of time:

Patients who have high-risk left main disease should have prompt surgery irrespective of the severity of symptoms . . . Survival is improved by surgery in the subgroup of patients with three-vessel disease and impaired LV function. However, it should be pointed out that the most significant improvement . . . was had only in the presence of multiple clinical risk factors such as resting ST depression, history of MI, and history of hypertension . . . There is no evidence that survival is significantly improved by surgery in subgroups of patients without left main disease who have a good prognosis on medical therapy, i.e., patients with single- or double-vessel disease, those without multiple clinical risk factors, and those with normal LV function.[11]

Dr. Hultgren was one of a small group of founding members of the Association of University Cardiologists in the early 1960s. He was active in the Association, becoming its President later in the 1960s and arranging for the move of its annual meeting from January in Chicago to Arizona and later to other sunbelt sites. He was a member of the Cardiovascular Subspecialty Board of the American Board of Internal Medicine, becoming its Chairman in the 1970s, and overseeing the conversion of its examination from the oral to the written format. He was an active and respected voice at the national level in policy statements regarding training and manpower in cardiology. As in his research, his thoroughness, balanced approach, and emphasis on proven fundamentals won him respect in the policy area.

Dr. Hultgren continued his research and teaching after his retirement in the late 1980s. He also continued his avid outdoorsmanship and mountaineering until the last year of his life.

References

1. Hultgren HN: Clinical and laboratory observations in severe starvation. *Stanford Med Bull* 1951;9:175–191
2. Hultgren HN, Reeve R, Cohn K, McLeod R: The ejection click of valvular pulmonic stenosis. *Circulation* 1969;40:631–640
3. Hultgren HN: Venous pistol shot sounds. *Am J Cardiol* 1962;10: 667–672
4. Hultgren HN, Selzer A, Purdy A, Holman E, Gerbode F: The syndrome of patent ductus arteriosus with pulmonary hypertension. *Circulation* 1953;8:15–35
5. March H, Gerbode F, Hultgren HN: The reopened ventricular septal defect. *Circulation* 1961;24:250–262
6. Nitta M, Nakamura T, Hultgren HN, Bilisoly J, Marquess B: Noninvasive evaluation of the severity of aortic stenosis in adults. *Chest* 1987;81:682–687
7. Hultgren HN, Craige E, Fujii J, Bilisoly J: Left bundle branch block and mechanical events of the cardiac cycle. *Am J Cardiol* 1983;52: 755–762
8. Hultgren HN, Spickard W: Medical experiences in Peru. *Stanford Med Bull* 1960;18:76–95
9. Hultgren HN, Spickard W, Hellriegel K, Houston C: High altitude pulmonary edema. *Medicine* 1961;40:289–313
10. Hultgren HN: *High Altitude Medicine.* Stanford, Calif.: Hultgren Publications, 1997
11. Hultgren H, Takaro T, Kroncke G, Fowles R: Veterans Administration Cooperative Study of Medical versus Surgical Treatment for Stable Angina - Progress Report, Section 15. Summary and clinical applications. *Progr Cardiovasc Dis* 1986;28:397–401

John F. Goodwin, M.D.

Celia M. Oakley, M.D.

Royal Postgraduate Medical School, Hammersmith Hospital, London, England

John Forrest Goodwin (Fig. 1) is Emeritus Professor of Clinical Cardiology at the Royal Postgraduate Medical School, Honorary Consultant Physician at Hammersmith Hospital, and also Honorary Consulting Cardiologist to St. George's Hospital, London.

Dr. Goodwin was born on December 1, 1918, in Ealing, West London, and was educated at Cheltenham College. He comes from a family with a strong and distinguished army background; his father, uncle, and two brothers are professional soldiers, two of them having reached the rank of Lieutenant-General and all having been decorated. John Goodwin, however, went to medical school, qualifying M.B.B.S. in 1942 from St. Mary's Hospital, University of London, at the top of his year. After gaining membership in the Royal College of Physicians in 1944 and earning his M.D. two years later, his academic career began with his appointment in 1946 as Medical First Assistant at the Royal Infirmary in Sheffield and Research Fellow in Pharmacology and Therapeutics under Edward Wayne. Three years later he was spotted by John McMichael, then Head of Medicine, and brought to Hammersmith as Lecturer in Medicine at the Postgraduate Medical School, with consultant status. In 1949 McMichael was investigating the failing (and normal) human heart by the new technique of right heart catheterization, and these new developments attracted John Goodwin to cardiology.

Dr. Goodwin's first papers in the early years of investigational cardiology were all written in collaboration with his long-standing friend and colleague, Robert Steiner, later Professor of Radiology and one of the first invasive cardiac radiologists. He performed some of the earliest angiocardiograms using the "shove halfpenny board" which required a strong registrar assistant to put the plates through with maximum speed. When Dennis Melrose, with the Hammersmith team, developed the first successful pump oxygenator in the U.K., John Goodwin was heavily involved. In those early days of open heart surgery, selection of patients was difficult though all- important. In 1958 the team wrote up the results of surgical treatment of ventricular septal defect. At that time it was their custom to place a specimen rose plucked from the garden that morning on top of the machine to bring good luck.

John's growing international reputation in cardiology blossomed with his work in cardiomyopathy. The surviving siblings of the brother and sister described in Pearce's classic pa-

FIG. 1   John F. Goodwin, M.D.

per on asymmetrical hypertrophy were John's patients, and so was the first patient in the world to be operated upon for this condition by Bill Cleland in 1960. By then the condition had been named "obstructive cardiomyopathy," soon to be called "hypertrophic obstructive cardiomyopathy" in the U.K. and "idiopathic hypertrophic sub-aortic stenosis" across the water. This preceded international agreement that the condition should be known as "hypertrophic cardiomyopathy" in view of the fact that obstruction often is absent or transient. Patients with every type of heart muscle disease were referred to John not only from within the U.K. but from all over the world. Budding cardiologists flocked to Hammersmith to work with him in elucidating the hemodynamics and researching the best management.

Despite his national and international roles, John always took a full part in the clinical assessment of patients. He wrote his notes neatly, although sometimes illegibly, and was somewhat put out when one day a "translation" was subtended after a consultation on a noncardiac ward. Some of us can remember the early days in the lower medical corridor at Hammersmith when the notice "changing" would suddenly appear on John's door and he would subsequently emerge dressed in greens for the catheter laboratory. A metamorphosis was remarked upon in the *Lancet* when he "changed" into Professor of Clinical Cardiology.

John became Treasurer of the British Cardiac Society in 1958 and its President in 1972, and subsequently Chairman of the Cardiology and Specialist Advisory Committee on Cardiovascular Disease at the Royal College of Physicians and Adviser in Cardiology to the Chief Medical Officer at the Department of Health. John championed the development of cardiology as a career specialty as he had done right from its early days when it was still claimed by general physicians as part of their repertoire. He strived to improve numbers and status of cardiologists and carried this into the world arena in 1978 when he successfully amalgamated the International Society of Cardiology with the International Cardiology Federation creating the International Society and Federation of Cardiology and becoming its first President.

In recent years he has focused his attention on preventive cardiology, becoming Chairman of the National Forum for Coronary Heart Disease Prevention and Vice President of the Coronary Prevention Group. He was made first President of the Hypertrophic Cardiomyopathy Association, which was started at Hammersmith Hospital to provide information and advice to patients and their families.

John has been awarded many distinctions and is Honorary Member of numerous overseas cardiac societies. Among these, John especially values the Gifted Teacher Award of the American College of Cardiology conferred in 1985.

John's extensive bibliography indicates the numbers of now distinguished and internationally known cardiologists from all over the world who have passed through his hands. All would testify to his insistence on the clinical approach and on the importance of linking technology with clinical expertise. This message still remains as important today as it was in the past.

W. Proctor Harvey

J. J. Leonard, M.D.

Department of Medicine, Uniformed Services, University of the Health Sciences, F. Edward Hébert School of Medicine, Bethesda, Maryland, USA

Proctor Harvey (Fig. 1) may be one of a vanishing breed—an endangered species—that is, the master clinician cardiologist who is able to extract a meaningful cardiac history with a minimum of time and effort and then obtain critical, accurate, and detailed information from bedside physical examination, especially auscultation of the heart. One hopes that the 200 or more cardiac trainees who have graduated from his program at Georgetown University over the last 35 years will successfully keep this knowledge, skill, and tradition alive and flourishing.

Dr. Harvey has always espoused a balanced approach to the patient, that is, the "five finger approach" (Fig. 2). It is obvious from the diagram that the history and physical examination are the important thumb and index fingers, but accurate clinical diagnosis uses all five digits. Dr. Harvey has pointed out clearly that the recent introduction of powerful new diagnostic instruments complement and supplement, rather than replace, the skills of the master clinician.

Dr. Harvey finds that the thirst for more knowledge and skill in bedside auscultation has, in many places, not abated but actually increased as clinicians, including cardiologists, recognize their deficiencies in this area. The result is that Dr. Harvey is in greater demand than ever. More and more graduate and continuing medical educational programs sponsored by local, regional, and national organizations, are requesting that he hold clinics at their institutions. Since Dr. Harvey retired as Director of the Division of Cardiology at Georgetown a few years ago, he now has more time to honor these many requests.

W. Proctor Harvey is a graduate of Lynchburg College, Class of 1939, and Duke Medical School, Class of 1943. Well into his senior year at Duke, Dr. Harvey had not yet made a decision on where to apply for internship. He worked nights and on weekends at the Duke Medical School Library to help support himself through medical school. One Saturday night when the library was quiet and practically deserted, he set about the task of selecting potential internship positions. There was a family living in his home town of Lynchburg, Virginia, who was known to have an illustrious member, a Professor of Medicine. This man's name was Dr. Henry A. Christian. Proctor Harvey found Henry Christian's name in a then current textbook of medicine and learned that Christian had been Chief of Medicine at the Peter Bent Brigham Hospi-

tal in Boston. He immediately applied to the Brigham despite the fact that his peers and mentors discouraged him, stating that Brigham had never selected a Duke medical student for internship. Harvey was undaunted. His persistence paid; he was successful in his venture and accepted as an intern at the Peter Bent Brigham Hospital on the service of Dr. George Thorn, who recently had become Chief of Medicine, having arrived from Johns Hopkins.

At the completion of his internship, his training was interrupted by World War II, and he spent the next several years in the service of the U. S. Army. He was shipped overseas and assigned to the 154th General Hospital in England, where he stayed for approximately 18 months. At the end of this time he was reassigned to Germany, serving as an Army Tank Battalion Medical Officer until after the end of the war.

Upon returning from Germany, Dr. Harvey found that, for the first time, formal subspecialty fellowships were being awarded at the Brigham Hospital. He successfully applied for a fellowship position under Dr. Samuel A. Levine—the first such fellowship in cardiology offered at that institution.

This was the beginning of a long and close friendship between mentor and student. After completing his fellowship, Dr. Harvey continued in the field of cardiology with Dr. Levine and returned to the internal medicine training program at Brigham as a second- and third-year resident followed by the chief residency in medicine, a prestigious position in the Harvard medical system.

He maintained a close relationship with Dr. Levine through the years, as they embarked upon preparing the first edition of *Clinical Auscultation of the Heart*. Each Saturday afternoon was spent reviewing phonocardiograms which Dr. Harvey had recorded during the previous week. Examples of the sounds and murmurs to be illustrated in the volume were selected during these working sessions. In the division of labor for the first edition, Dr. Harvey prepared the phonocardiographic illustrations and Dr. Levine prepared the text.

Some years later these two teachers again collaborated on the second edition, with Proctor Harvey writing the text material. In the meantime, many new concepts had emerged. Harvey recalls his effort to convince Samuel Levine of the importance of splitting of the second heart sound in clinical auscultation. Levine was not at all certain that such splitting could be readily appreciated on auscultation. Harvey con-

FIG. 1   W. Proctor Harvey, M.D., master clinician.

recordings of actual patients representing heart sounds and murmurs exemplifying hundreds of different cardiovascular auscultatory findings. This modern textbook is actually a set of video cassettes with accompanying written text.

At the end of his chief residency, Protor Harvey was successfully recruited to the position of Director of the Division of Cardiology at Georgetown University Hospital. This position was offered to him by Harold Jeghers, then Chairman of the Department of Medicine at that institution. Dr. Jeghers had walked the halls and wards of the Harvard medical teaching services in various Boston hospitals and found that Dr. Harvey was the most popular and respected teacher of cardiology among Harvard medical students and houseofficers. They frequently attended Dr. Harvey's rounds at the Brigham although they were assigned to Massachusetts General or other Harvard teaching units.

During his time at Georgetown, Dr. Harvey established the Thursday night cardiology conference. This conference rapidly became an established institution in the Washington, D.C., area. There were well over 100 regular attendees, not only from nearby hospitals, but also from the surrounding area such as the National Institutes of Health and Bethesda Naval Hospital. Military physicians stationed at Walter Reed Army Hospital, Quantico, Virginia, and Fort Meade, Maryland, attended regularly. Practicing physicians, former houseofficers, and fellows at Georgetown frequently attended these sessions whenever they were in the Washington area for national medical meetings or on holiday visits. Shortly after his retirement, the Thursday evening conference was scaled back, but it is still scheduled at Georgetown each Wednesday morning at 11:15.

During his 35 years as Chief of Cardiology at Georgetown, the Cardiac Fellowship Program under his tutelage had been highly sought after by young houseofficers from all over the world. Now, it is their turn and their responsibility to carry on this tradition. As previously stated, more than 200 such fellows have graduated from this program. More than half of these are in positions in academic medicine today. Many are

vinced him by rapping his knuckles against the table in the manner we all have seen him display on the podium, on the conference table, or against the wall on ward rounds. Dr. Harvey striking the first two knuckles of his right hand either synchronously or asynchronously proved to Dr. Levine that the resultant sound was readily heard as a single or reduplicated sound: the significance of splitting of heart sounds became a major component of the second edition.

Harvey's most recent textbook just off the press, *Clinical Auscultation of the Cardiovascular System,* is authored with David Canfield. Phonographic tracings to illustrate heart sounds have all but been replaced by high-fidelity tape

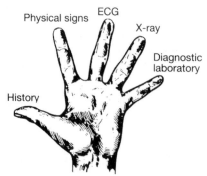

The five fingers of clinical diagnosis

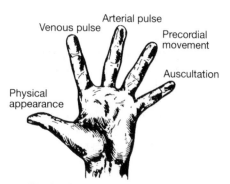

The five fingers of physical signs

FIG. 2   The five-finger approach to the examination of the patient. [From Gordon MS: Technology and modem bedside diagnosis. *Med Times* III(4), 74 (1983). Reproduced with permission from the publisher and author.]

chiefs of the divisions of cardiology and medicine at the various medical schools and hospital centers.

These former fellows have already responded to this call. Some 30 years ago the W. Proctor Harvey Foundation was formed. Money raised by and from these fellows, and especially from grateful patients, was used to support the teaching program, teaching rooms, and teaching equipment at Georgetown. This year, through the Foundation's continuing energy, generosity, and loyalty, an endowed teaching Chair, "The W. Proctor Harvey Professorship of Clinical Cardiology," has been established. The Foundation membership is adamant that the occupant of the endowed Chair be a renowned cardiologist who has established his or her reputation as a consummate teacher of clinical cardiology.

The value of Dr. Harvey's contribution to teaching, especially teaching the skill of auscultation, has not gone unrecog-

nized. He has received many prestigious awards. To name only a few, these include the Golden Heart Award and the Herrick Award of the American Heart Association and the Gifted Teacher Award of the American College of Cardiology, as well as Mastership in the American College of Physicians. But surely Dr. Harvey's greatest reward is the love and respect of thousands of medical students, houseofficers, and fellows who have learned so much from this kind and gentle man who taught them much more than auscultation.

Dr. Harvey frequently offers a seminar or clinic which is entitled "Cardiac Pearls." A cardiac pearl, according to W. Proctor Harvey, is a finding which is a clue leading to a diagnosis. "A finding which has not changed with the times. It is just as helpful today as it was 40 years ago." Dr. Harvey's students and fellows realize that Dr. Harvey himself *is* that cardiac pearl.

Dirk Durrer: The Scientist and the Man

LOUIS J. ACIERNO, M.D., FACC

Department of Health Professions and Physical Therapy, University of Central Florida, College of Health & Public Affairs, Orlando, Florida, USA

Labeled the godfather of Dutch cardiology, Dirk Durrer (Fig. 1) should be considered as one of the major founders of modern electrocardiology. His enormous output, contagious zest, and intense enthusiasm were the essential elements that fueled the emergence of Amsterdam as a mecca of study and research in cardiology. These ingredients continued to foster a favorable academic climate. Durrer also created the soon to be acclaimed Netherlands Inter-University Institute of Cardiology[1] that opened with great promise in 1972. By uniting the departments of cardiology of all eight medical schools in the Netherlands, the country was now able to garner the full benefits of its researchers and scholars through the efficient utilization of their combined efforts. It was a sorrowful day for Durrer when the institute closed the year before his death.

By far, however, it was his own laboratory at the University of Amsterdam that, under his stewardship and unflagging discipline, contributed so much to our knowledge of the electrophysiology of the heart. In an atmosphere of camaraderie, amiability, and teamwork, the laboratory he founded became an institute that proudly bore the label "Wihelmina Gasthuis." Under Durrer's guidance, and in a relatively short span of time, studies were conducted on total excitation of the human heart, excitability of the myocardium, the calcium paradox, postextrasystolic potentiation, experimental programmed electrical stimulation, epicardial and intramural excitation in acute and chronic myocardial infarctions, and reentrant tachycardias in the Wolff-Parkinson-White (WPW) syndrome.

Dirk Durrer was born in the Netherlands in 1918. His early medical studies began at Leiden, fittingly enough, the seat of Einthoven's activities. He then transferred to the University of Utrecht from whence he received his medical degree. In 1943, the young medical graduate began the practice of medicine in wartorn Rotterdam. Even at that time, he had an intense interest in electrocardiography. During these formative years his mentor and supporter was Professor van Ruyven. Even at this early stage of his career, and despite his extensive readings on the subject, Durrer realized the lack of definitive experimental observations for many of the electrocardiographic findings. In fact, he looked upon electrocardiography as a "stamp collection rather than a scientific discipline."[3] It was this perception that provided the impetus for his entry into the experimental laboratory where, in the course of just several years, he transformed "the empirical electrocardiography of those days into a quantitative and predictive clinical discipline."[3] The opportunity came in 1947, when he was invited by Professor Formijne to join the faculty of medicine at the University of Amsterdam. Young Dirk Durrer had found his niche. He was to remain on the faculty at Amsterdam until his death in 1984, serving for many years as Professor of Cardiology and Clinical Physiology.

Durrer's original work at Amsterdam led to his truly inspired multielectrode needle, described in detail in his Ph.D. thesis. The degree was granted *summa cum laude* in 1952.

Brimming over with ideas that were described by Meijler, one of his pupils, as "unexpected and full of brand-new logic and beauty,"[2] and activated by a seemingly boundless energy, his career at Amsterdam was characterized by an amazingly productive output. Among his lasting contributions was his introduction of programmed electrical stimulation. This was a significant breakthrough in the development of the methodology that could verify the concepts of automaticity and reentry while establishing at the same time the basis for the management of several types of rhythm disturbances.

His quest for leaving no stone unturned may have been the reason for surrounding himself with the best collaborators possible, specialists from such diverse disciplines as surgery, pathology, physics, engineering, and cell biologists. Janse, another of his pupils, described him as following the dictum "If you don't have the brains yourselves, hire them."[3] Durrer's closest collaborator among the Amsterdam faculty was Professor L. H. van der Tweel, a medical physicist, with whom Durrer established a very close working relationship early in his career, and one that was to prove fruitful over a span of more than 18 years.[4-6]

In 1953, Durrer published a collaborative study with van der Tweel on the spread of activation in the left ventricular wall of the dog.[4] This was accomplished with his newly devised and innovative multi-terminal intramural needle that had two small electrodes in close proximity to each other. The electrical signal resulting from insertion of the electrodes into the epicardial or intramural portion of the ventricle provided proof that the intrinsic deflection in unipolar leads is due to the passage of the excitation front under that particular lead. Eighteen years of experimental observations

FIG. 1 Dirk Durrer, M.D. (1918–1984). Reprinted from *Int J Cardiol* 1984;6:750 with permission from Elsevier Science.

with this needle provided the data necessary for mapping the pathway in the total excitation of the isolated revived human heart. The classic paper describing this appeared in *Circulation* in 1970.[6]

The Durrer needle, as it came to be called, served in yet another role—a stimulating device that helped unravel the sequential elements of conduction, velocity, and duration of the refractory period in the initiation and perpetuation of reentry.[7,8]

Durrer's group developed a unique technique for the study of reentry and ventricular arrhythmias in local ischemia and infarction in the intact dog heart.[9] They were able to record multiple sites of stimulation simultaneously (as many as 128) that led to the conclusion that reentry was, indeed, the perpetuating mechanism for ventricular tachycardia and fibrillation, occurring spontaneously during the first 10 minutes of myocardial ischemia.[9] These observations were published in 1980. Along the way, Durrer, continuing his collaboration with the medical physics faculty and in unison with Leo Schoo, helped in building an apparatus capable of delivering three electrical impulses, separately or combined, and varying in strength and duration. The characteristics of this apparatus enabled Durrer and his group to prove in 1966 that reentry was also the basic mechanism for the recurrent tachyarrhythmias in the WPW syndrome. The anatomical groundwork for this mechanism was later spelled out in collaboration with two outstanding pathologists, Anton Becker and R. H. Anderson, another example of Durrer's interdisciplinary approach.[10]

The calcium paradox, which is of increasing importance for the understanding of reperfusion damage in the ischemic myocardium and for the preservation of the myocardium during cardiac surgery, was also identified in his laboratory.[11]

Throughout his life, Dirk Durrer presented himself as a model physician, teacher, and investigator. He published nearly 500 articles while delivering a great number of prestigious lectures. His extraordinary output earned him many scientific prizes and awards. In America, his peers designated him a master teacher of the American College of Cardiology. Notwithstanding his intensive personal involvement in the ongoing experiments in the laboratory, he still found time to serve on the editorial boards of numerous cardiology journals. The same indefatigable energy caused him to be a member of many prestigious national and international societies. Among his awards was knighthood in the order of the Netherlands Lion and commander in the order of the Finnish Lion.[5] The year before his death, the American College of Cardiology bestowed upon him the Distinguished Scientist Award.

As with all men of his caliber, Durrer's standards were quite high, although marred at times by an imperious and caustic attitude when these standards were not met. The high standards he demanded caused him the loss of some friends in the scientific community. This was Durrer, the scientist. However, Durrer, the man had several human qualities that endeared him to all who knew him. His patients, especially, held him in high regard for his warmth and keen interest in their welfare. As a matter of fact, much of the excellent facilities of the "Gasthuis" were donations by grateful patients.

Durrer's life came to an end on March 3, 1984. He was eulogized that same year by now famous former pupils with an entire issue of the *International Journal of Cardiology*. It was a fitting tribute to a great man, appropriately recorded in the very journal that saw light from its progenitor, the *European Journal of Cardiology*, which was founded by Durrer himself. An unabashed eulogy was rendered by Frits Meijler when he described his mentor as "a diamond sparkling from whatever angle you looked at him, and . . . that it was impossible to be in a room with Durrer without literally feeling his vibrant presence."

References

1. Acierno LJ: *History of Cardiology*, p. 337–338. London, New York: Parthenon Publishing Group, 1994
2. Meijler FL: Prof. Dirk Durrer, godfather of Dutch cardiology. A personal note. *Int J Cardiol* 1984;6:750–753
3. Janse MJ: Dirk Durrer and experimental cardiology. *Int J Cardiol* 1984;6:763–766
4. Durrer D, van der Tweel LH: Spread of activation in the left ventricular wall of the dog. (I). *Am Heart J* 1953;46:683–691
5. Meijler FL: Historical notes on Prof. Dirk Durrer. *Eur Heart J* 1984;5:607
6. Durrer D, van Dam RTH, Freud GE, Janse MJ, Meijler FS, Arzbaecker RC: Total excitation of the isolated human heart. *Circulation* 1970;41:895–912
7. Van Dam RTH, Durrer D, Strackee J, van der Tweel LH: The excitability for cathodal and anodal stimulation of the dog's ventricle during the cardiac cycle. *Proc K Ned Akad Wet Ser* 1955;C58 No. 4:412–427
8. Van Dam RTH, Durrer D, Strackee J, van der Tweel LH: The excitability cycle of the dog's left ventricle, determined by anodal, cathodal and bipolar stimulation. *Circ Res* 1956;4:196–204
9. Durrer D, van Dam RTH, Freud GE, Janse MJ: Reentry and ventricular arrhythmias in local ischemia and infarction of the intact dog heart. *Proc K Ned Akad Wet Ser* 1971; C74 No. 4:321–334
10. Becker AE, Anderson RH, Durrer D, Wellens HJJ: The anatomic substrates of Wolff-Parkinson-White syndrome: A clinico-pathologic correlation in seven patients. *Circulation* 1978;57:870–879
11. Durrer D, Meijler FL: Past and future of the calcium paradox. *Eur Heart J* 1983;4(suppl H):1–2

F. Mason Sones, Jr.—Stormy Petrel of Cardiology

WILLIAM C. SHELDON, M.D.

Department of Cardiology, The Cleveland Foundation, Cleveland, Ohio, USA

When I first met Dr. Sones (Fig. 1) it was clear that this was an unusual man. One could not help but be awed by his intense concentration and his fervent pursuit of perfection. I visited Cleveland in 1959 to be interviewed for a fellowship position in cardiology. About to begin a catheterization procedure, he took me into his small windowless office, reviewed my file, and asked a few probing questions. He told me about coronary angiography. At that time he had performed about one hundred procedures, and I had only heard rumors about the procedure and this maverick from Cleveland. Abruptly he grabbed an armful of 16 mm movie films and ordered me to follow him. We went to a third floor conference room where one by one he showed me coronary angiograms, normal and abnormal, variations of the anatomy, collaterals, coronary spasm, and so on. After about an hour he suddenly remembered the patient awaiting him in the catheterization lab. He sent me on my way and hurried downstairs.

Frank Mason Sones Jr. was born in Noxapater, Mississippi, in 1918, the son of a mechanic. His undergraduate degree was from the Western Maryland College in Westminster, Maryland in 1940, and he graduated from the University of Maryland Medical School in 1943. After an internship at the University of Maryland Hospital and 2 years in the U.S. Army Air Force, in 1946 he began training in internal medicine at the Henry Ford Hospital where he became interested in congenital heart disease and cardiac catheterization under the mentorship of Dr. Robert Ziegler. Cardiac catheterization had been introduced in the United States in 1941, and surgery for congenital heart disease was emerging. In 1950 he was invited to establish a cardiac catheterization laboratory at the Cleveland Clinic by Dr. A. Carlton Ernstene, who predicted that cardiac catheterization would have a limited future in cardiac diagnosis.

Dr. Sones began work in a small room on the third floor of the Clinic. He did everything himself, delegating little to a few admiring but frustrated fellows who struggled to keep up with him as he worked day and night. He could not be constrained by a schedule and regularly kept patients and families waiting for hours in the outpatient department while making rounds or performing catheterizations.

In 1956 he was given a larger area in the basement of the Clinic, later heading the separate department. He began to develop a new, state-of-the-art catheterization laboratory. Convinced that smaller image amplifiers would be inadequate for adults, he installed an 11" image amplifier. The equipment was so large that it could not be accommodated in the available space and a pit had to be excavated in the basement floor. It was with this apparatus, in October 1958, that he accidentally photographed the injection of 40 ml of contrast media into the right coronary artery of a 26-year-old man with rheumatic mitral and aortic valvular disease.

The following account is from a letter he wrote to J. Willis Hurst on August 9, 1982. He prepared to perform an aortogram:

> When the injection began I was horrified to see the right coronary artery become heavily opacified and realized that the catheter tip was actually inside the orifice of the dominant right coronary artery...At that time we did not have direct current defibrillators and knew nothing about closed chest massage. I climbed out of the hole and ran around the table looking for a scalpel to open his chest in order to defibrillate him by direct application of the paddles of an alternating current defibrillator. I looked at the oscilloscope tracing of his electrocardiogram and it was evident that he was in asystole rather than ventricular fibrillation. I knew that explosive cough could produce very effective pressure pulse in the aorta and hoped this might push the contrast media through his myocardial capillary bed. Fortunately he was still conscious and responded to my demand that he cough repeatedly. After three or four explosive coughs his heart began to beat again with initially a sinus bradycardia which accelerated to a sinus tachycardia within 15–20 seconds.

> Initially, I could feel only unbelievable relief and gratitude that we had been fortunate enough to avert a grievous disaster. During the ensuing days I began to think that this accident might point the way for the development of a technique which was exactly what we had been seeking. If a human could tolerate such a massive injection of contrast media directly into a coronary artery it might be possible to accomplish this type of opacification with small doses of more dilute contrast agent. With considerable fear and trepidation we embarked on a program to accomplish this objective.[1]

(Reprinted with permission)

F. Mason Sones, Jr., 1918–1985.

He devised a special catheter and proceeded to perfect the technique. Improved image amplifiers and x-ray tubes, faster cine film, direct current cardiac defibrillators, and closed chest massage all contributed to making coronary arteriography safer, simpler, and more effective. His most definitive report of his early experience, in more than 1,020 patients, was not published until 1962.[2] At this time many still considered the technique experimental. More accurate diagnosis was a hollow objective in the absence of a definitive therapeutic approach. However, coronary arteriography provided a unique opportunity to correlate clinical signs and symptoms with anatomy. Follow-up studies of the clinical course of patients with angiographically detailed coronary artery disease began.

In 1962 Sones studied two patients who had been operated upon by Vineberg's method of internal mammary artery implantation and showed conclusively that myocardial perfusion could be achieved. Experience at the Cleveland Clinic confirmed that this was a metabolically useful perfusion that could improve angina and protect myocardium. However, the benefit of the operation was not only delayed until new channels developed, but uncertain, limited mainly to patients with the most severe obstructive lesions. During these years direct coronary artery surgery—coronary endarterectomy—was also explored. Coronary arteriography was beginning to have a rational objective: to identify candidates for revascularization surgery. Increasingly, as more patients were referred for evaluation nationally as well as in Cleveland, new cardiac catheterization laboratories were launched, more cardiologists sought training in cardiac catheterization and angiography, and the number of procedures began to grow. Surgeons became interested in revascularization techniques, but controversy flourished over their benefits.

Dr. René Favaloro joined the Clinic as a surgical fellow in 1962. He became intrigued by revascularization surgery and the role of coronary arteriography in evaluating its results. He spent hours reviewing the teaching files of 16 mm cines that Sones had compiled, learning coronary anatomy and picking Sones' brain. In 1967, he performed an interposition saphenous vein graft to the right coronary artery of a 57-year-old woman. Vein grafts had been used sporadically as early as 1962, but had not been reported nor systematically studied. Favaloro's first report in 1968 stimulated great interest. The safety and efficacy of the technique were readily confirmed in several centers. Sones' predictions for coronary arteriography were realized and the naysayers were silenced.

Coronary arteriography was performed by both cardiologists and radiologists and a rivalry developed between the two disciplines. In 1967, Judkins, a radiologist, introduced the percutaneous technique for coronary arteriography and advocated cut film rather than motion picture photography. It seemed very simple, even for those without formal training in cardiac catheterization. In 1967, after completing his one-hundredth procedure, Judkins called Sones and invited him to visit Loma Linda to see for himself. Sones replied that Judkins should wait until he had done six hundred cases, as he had done, then he would visit Judkins' lab. A few months later Judkins reached the goal and Sones accepted his invitation. He was impressed with the ease of the technique and the quality of the films obtained, but believed that the brachial approach, a single catheter, and cine photography were more advantageous. However, he respected Judkins' innovation and commitment to quality and safety.

In 1976, during a meeting of the American Heart Association, Judkins and Sones met to discuss mutual concerns regarding the utilization of cardiac angiography, lack of standards for training, variable performance among laboratories, and the threat of federal regulation. The major cardiology and radiology societies had failed to address these issues. Continued inaction would jeopardize responsible application of the techniques they had fostered, as well as the orderly evolution of new methods. They resolved to convene a forum to which leading cardiologists and radiologists would be invited. This was held in Las Vegas in March 1977, and in January 1978 the Society for Cardiac Angiography was launched with Sones as its first president and Judkins its second. Both men continued to guide this organization until their deaths in 1985.

In 1977, at a meeting of the American Heart Association, Sones heard Andreas Gruentzig's electrifying report of the first successful percutaneous transluminal coronary angioplasty. In 1964 Sones had attempted unsuccessfully to dilate a stenosed right coronary artery with a catheter and a guidewire, and with Lowell Edwards he had devised a catheter with a rotating tip ("rotorooter"). (He also had attempted unsuccessfully to abort an acute inferior myocardial infarction with intracoronary streptokinase in 1959.) After Gruentzig finished his presentation Sones hurried toward the podium, tears streaming down both cheeks and warmly greeted Gruentzig in a congratulatory embrace. From that moment the two became close friends.

His early career at the Cleveland Clinic was fraught with stress for both Sones and his family. As his reputation spread, increasing numbers of visitors came to visit his laboratory. A gregarious man, he enjoyed companionship, often talking with visitors into the early morning hours. He loved to talk but hated to write, fearing that writing required more care to avoid misinterpretation than he was inclined to provide. He especially enjoyed people who were innovators. Because of his laboratory schedule, the many visitors, and his penchant for accepting practically all speaking invitations, family events were often sacrificed. Sones was divorced in 1963. He dove into his work. He became more irascible.

Consumed by his need for new facilities to support the increasing numbers of referrals, he badgered the Clinic administration until it finally acquiesced in 1968 and planning began for a new hospital wing. In 1974 the two separate cardiology departments moved into the new facility and conjoined into a single department. Sones stepped down to make way for new leadership. Despite a brush with lung cancer in 1981 he continued to practice and travel extensively until he retired in 1983. A recurrence of lung cancer was discovered a year later. In the meanwhile, after a second marriage and divorce, he remarried his first wife.

He received hundreds of honors and awards. Among the more auspicious were the Albert Lasker Clinical Research Award in 1983 and, in 1985, the Galen Medal of the Historic Worshipful Society of Apothecaries of London. His health did not permit him to go to London to receive the Galen Medal, so it was presented in Cleveland at a ceremony in his home attended by close friends and colleagues.

His final months were agonizing, but he faced death without resentment or sentimentality. One day, while in the radiation therapy department, another patient asked him why he was there. Sones, appearing aged, gaunt, and bald, looked askance at the questioner and replied, "I have AIDS!" There were no more questions. During his last weeks dozens of friends and colleagues visited him. Contemplating the afterlife, he confessed his uncertainty, but his eternal curiosity assured him that he would soon find out!

At a symposium honoring Sones' career his friend and colleague William Proudfit summarized Sones' Laws as he had observed them:[3]

1. Be honest
2. Nothing is good enough
3. Find an expert
4. Don't read (or write). If you must write don't use semicolons.
5. Don't calculate
6. Don't rely on gadgets
7. Don't watch the clock
8. Don't repeat experiments indefinitely
9. Concentrate on the problem
10. Simplify the problem
11. Make a decision
12. Communicate

In reflecting on his experiences in 1982, Sones stated that "for me this has been the best time in medical history to have been alive, and I am deeply grateful for the privilege." Indeed, Sones helped to make medical history in his time great, the privilege of his association was ours, and it is our patients who benefited from his genius.

References

1. Hurst JW: History of cardiac catheterization. In *Coronary Arteriography and Angioplasty* (Eds. King SB III, Douglas JS Jr). McGraw-Hill, New York (1985) 6
2. Sones FM Jr, Shirey EK: Cine coronary arteriography. *Mod Concepts Cardiovasc Dis* 31, 735–738 (1962)
3. Proudfit WL: Personal communication.

Jeremiah Stamler

JOHN D. CANTWELL, M.D.

Preventive Medicine, Cardiac Rehabilitation, and the Internal Medicine Residency Program, Georgia Baptist Medical Center, Atlanta, Georgia, USA

I first read of Jeremiah Stamler in a cover story on preventive cardiology in *Time* magazine around 1960. I subsequently read his classic, *Your Heart Has Nine Lives*,[1] and was stimulated by his lecture to my Northwestern University Medical School class on coronary risk factors. In 1972, I was fortunate to attend the 4th annual seminar on cardiovascular epidemiology and prevention in Skovde, Sweden, where Dr. Stamler and his colleagues convinced me to become a preventive cardiologist. I wonder how many other lives this New York native has influenced through his scholarly research and dynamic lectures?

Dr. Stamler was born in New York City on October 27, 1919 (Fig. 1). At Columbia University, he won Phi Beta Kappa honors, and he was a member of AOA at Long Island College of Medicine. After an internship at Kings County Hospital (Long Island College Division), he served two years in the army toward the end of World War II. He then served a fellowship in pathology with Dr. Jean Oliver at Long Island College of Medicine and, in 1948, became a research fellow with Dr. Louis N. Katz at Michael Reese Hospital in Chicago. Over the next decade at Michael Reese, Stamler, Katz, and colleagues conducted pioneering experimental research on atherosclerosis and hypertension. Their accomplishments were significant as described below.

Results of Experimental Research on Atherosclerosis and Hypertension

1. They showed that adding small amounts of cholesterol and fat to diets of chickens induces atherosclerosis despite little or no rise in serum cholesterol levels.
2. The group compiled evidence that both exogenous and endogenous estrogens protect chickens against coronary atherosclerosis usually resulting from cholesterol feeding and that estrogens reverse cholesterol-induced plaques despite continued cholesterol feeding.
3. Finally, they demonstrated that salt depletion of renal hypertensive dogs induces falls in blood pressure to normal levels.

Epidemiologic Studies and Clinical Trials

In the mid-1950s, convinced of the likelihood that key animal experimental findings were relevant for the human species, Dr. Stamler focused on epidemiologic studies and clinical trials. He played a leading role in conducting (a) the Chicago Peoples Gas Company long-term prospective study (73,000 men); (b) the Chicago Heart Association's Detection Project in Industry (almost 40,000 young adult and middle-aged men and women, both white and black); (c) the Western Electric Study (2,100 middle-aged men); (d) the U.S. National Cooperative Pooling Project (eight long-term prospective population studies); (e) the International Collaborative Group (15 prospective studies of middle-aged men in 10 countries, totaling more than 38,000 men); (f) the 5-year follow-up study of the Gubbio population in Italy, involving etiology and pathogenesis of hypertension in more than 5,000 persons age 5 years and older; (g) the Intersalt Study, codirected with Dr. Geoffrey Rose and involving over 10,000 persons in 32 countries of every inhabited continent. He was also Vice Chairman of the Hypertension Detection and Follow-up Program, and a leading member of the Multiple Risk Factor Intervention Trial (MRFIT). The latter involved major responsibilities for epidemiologic studies on the 361,662 primary screenees and on the 12,866 men randomized into that trial. Dr. Stamler heads MRFIT's editorial committee.

Some of the key findings from these various studies included the following:[2]

1. Relationship of serum cholesterol, systolic and diastolic blood pressure, and cardiovascular risks are continuous, graded, curvilinear, independent, and etiologically significant. The optimal serum cholesterol level is <180 mg/dl. Optimal blood pressure is <120/80 mmHg.
2. Cigarette use is strongly related to coronary and cardiovascular risks, as well as cancer risks, independent of other risk factors.
3. Clinical diabetes is strongly related to coronary and cardiovascular risks in men and women, both black and white. Dietary lipid, particularly cholesterol, is significantly related to cardiovascular and all-cause mortality, independent of other risk factors. Hypertension is the strongest risk factor for strokes.
4. The various coronary risk factors synergize with each other to yield compounded high risks. Improved lifestyles have a substantial potential for reducing current high epidemic rates of cardiovascular diseases and for increasing longevity.

Fig. 1 Jeremiah Stamler, M.D.

5. The Coronary Drug Project showed the ability to achieve long-term secondary prevention of coronary heart disease by lowering serum lipids with high-dose nicotinic acid.

6. The Hypertension Detection and Follow-Up Program for the first time demonstrated significant efficacy of sustained stepped care antihypertensive drug therapy in reducing long-term all-cause mortality of men and women, black and white, with mild hypertension.

7. The MRFIT Study, in a recent 10-year follow-up report, showed significant reduction in coronary and all-cause mortality in coronary-prone men (without resting ECG abnormalities) in its special intervention group. The latter were counselled long-term on nutritional modifications to lower serum cholesterol, weight and blood pressure, along with smoking cessation. They were also given antihypertensive medication when indicated.

Personality Traits

Dr. Stamler has two guiding principles, which he tells newcomers in his department: (1) Be impeccably honest with data and (2) health care is a service. If you can't be nice to people you don't belong in the field.[3]

As a mentor, he had been likened to "riding the tail of a comet."[3] To colleagues, such as Geoffrey Rose in England, he is simply the world's best cardiovascular epidemiologist, with an awesome energy level:[4]

He packs into one week an amount of activity which would occupy most of us for a month. We have known each other, as friends and collaborators, for 23 years; and during the whole of that acquaintance I have never seen him doing nothing, nor even proceeding at half-speed. Relaxation for him simply means doing something different, but with undiminished commitment. In fact, his energy is only exceeded by his warmth of character: he has left a trail of goodwill behind him in cardiovascular medicine all around the world.

Dr. Rose also considers him a man of moral courage:

A House of Representatives committee attacked him for what in those far-off days were called 'un-American activities,' and they would have had him inside prison if they could. Not content with self-defense, Jerry characteristically went over to the attack. 'Stamler vs. U.S. Congress' was a famous victory—for Stamler, and the right to hold one's own opinions. Lately he has shown equal courage and determination in his commitment to nuclear disarmament. In all these endeavors—scientific, international and political—his closest and most effective colleague has been his wife, Rose.

Dr. Robert Levy, President of Sandoz Research Institute and a friend of Dr. Stamler's for over 25 years, considers him "a phenomenon—a giant of a man in spirit, intellect and enthusiasm. Though small in stature and limited by some physical disabilities, Jerry has contributed immeasurably to our current understanding and control of cardiovascular disease."[5] He recalls a program the two appeared on in the 1970s, in a church renovated as a lecture hall: "Hearing his talk from the pulpit made his first calling clear... We in cardiovascular disease research should feel pleased that it was in our field that he chose to preach the gospel."[5]

Academic Activities, Publications, Awards, and Honors

In 1972, Dr. Stamler became the first chairman of the newly established Department of Community Health and Preventive Medicine at Northwestern University Medical School, and the Dingman Professor of Cardiology. Under his spirited leadership, the department has achieved international recognition.

He has been or is currently a member of 44 scientific societies, and is a member or past member of four editorial boards. He is currently a member of 22 committees and served as President of the Organizing Committee for the 2nd International Conference on Preventive Cardiology, held in Washington, DC, in 1989.

His list of honors covers three typewritten pages and includes the Distinguished Service Award from the American College of Cardiology and the Distinguished Achievement Award from the American Heart Association. In 1989 he was the first recipient of the Achievement Award in Preventive Medicine, given by the American College of Advancement in

Medicine, and of the Distinguished Alumnus Award from Michael Reese Hospital and Medical Center. In March 1990, he received the John Jay award, honoring distinguished alumni of Columbia College.

Family

Dr. Stamler's wife, Rose, began collaborating with him at Michael Reese Hospital in the late 1940s. Herself a professor of community health and preventive medicine, Mrs. Stamler has contributed to numerous of her husband's scientific endeavors and is devoted to and loved by all of us who have attended the international workshop in cardiovascular epidemiology. Their son, Paul, lives in St. Louis and pursues interests in folk music and photography. The Stamlers spend several months each year at their winter home in the south of Italy, where they continue to keep up with their international research endeavors.

Summary

Jeremiah Stamler has had a major impact on the primary and secondary prevention of cardiovascular disease. His work began in the animal experimental laboratory and shifted to large-scale epidemiologic studies and clinical trials, resulting in nearly 800 contributions to the world medical literature. His influence is felt, not only through these publications and his innumerable lectures, but also

. . .through the hundreds of young people he has helped train (in the U.S. and abroad), and through the leadership role he has played locally, nationally, and internationally in preventive cardiology. . . . The spirit imbuing the work of Dr. Stamler is a deep concern for human welfare, for the prevention of unnecessary disease, and for the prolongation of healthy life. This same spirit has made his name synonymous also with preservation of civil liberties, international cooperation among scientists of all countries, and efforts to avoid the catastrophe of nuclear holocaust.[6]

According to Dr. Geoffrey Rose, Dr. Stamler

. . . confronted the most devastating health problem of Western Society, cardiovascular disease. He espoused the belief that diet holds the key to its control at a time when that belief was widely considered to be false and its proponents a little crazy. That is now accepted wisdom, and the fact that in many countries at last the problem is in decline is due to this man more than to any other.[4]

References

1.   Blakeslee A, Stamler J: *Your Heart Has Nine Lives*. Prentice-Hall, Inc., Englewood Cliffs, NJ (1963)

2.   Peterson F: Biographical information from Northwestern University Medical School files

3.   Hoo ES: Jerry Stamler: Promoting healthy lifestyles with data, data and more data. *Ward Rounds* 3, 13–19 (1986)

4.   Rose G: Personal communication, 1990.

5.   Levy R: Personal communication, 1990.

6.   Beaty H: Nomination form for Albert Lasker Medal Research Award (1986)

Noble O. Fowler: The Complete Cardiologist

ROBERT J. ADOLPH, M.D.

Division of Cardiology, University of Cincinnati, College of Medicine, Cincinnati, Ohio, USA

Noble Fowler was born in Mississippi and raised and educated in Memphis, where he received his M.D. degree in 1941 from the University of Tennessee. His postgraduate training in medicine was at the Cincinnati General Hospital and Peter Bent Brigham Hospital. He returned to Cincinnati in 1947 as Senior Assistant Medical Resident and then Chief Medical Resident. From 1948 to 1952, Dr. Fowler was a Fellow in Cardiology where he honed his skills in clinical cardiology and served as a Research Fellow of the American Heart Association. During that period, his publications document his early interest and investigations in pulmonary hemodynamics, pulmonary hypertension, right heart cardiac catheterization, vectorcardiography, and electrocardiography. His work was clearly influenced by his association with Robert A. Helm, a pioneer in vectorcardiography, and Ralph C. Scott, in electrocardiography.

After one year as Assistant Professor of Medicine, Noble Fowler moved to the State University of New York where he was Assistant Professor of Medicine from 1952 to 1954. His interest in pulmonary hypertension was pursued in conjunction with William J. Noble. In 1955, he was recruited to Emory University School of Medicine where he was promoted to Associate Professor and was awarded the Georgia State Heart Association Chair of Cardiac Research. While at Emory, he worked with scientists such as Walter Bloom, Joseph Greenfield, Eugene B. Ferris, J. Willis Hurst, and Robert H. Franch, who was his first Fellow in Cardiology. His publications from that period reflect a continuing interest in cardiac catheterization in congenital and acquired heart disease as well as newfound interests in anemia and other high output states, pharmacologic effects of cardiovascular drugs, and diastolic properties of the isolated rat heart, that is, apparent suction in the beating heart.

Dr. Fowler was induced to return to Cincinnati in 1957 and was appointed Director of the Cardiac Research Laboratory. His interest in the pericardium began in 1962 following a casual question by the then Director of Cardiology, Johnson McGuire, namely, what Noble thought was the physiologic basis of pulsus paradoxus? This began an important redirection of Dr. Fowler's research interest and a productive research association and long-time friendship with Ralph Shabetai who was then a Fellow in the Cardiac Laboratory. I joined the staff in 1962 and recall the brainstorming that led to a series of brilliantly designed experiments that elucidated the physiologic mechanisms underlying pulsus paradoxus and eliminated many previous misconceptions.[1] Dr. Fowler became Director of the Division of Cardiology in 1970 and held his position until 1986 when he was appointed Professor Emeritus of Medicine.

Dr. Fowler's research interests encompass 40 years of accomplishment. He is perhaps best known for his investigations in pericardial disease, pathophysiology, and management of cardiac tamponade, pulsus paradoxus, constrictive pericarditis, pulmonary hypertension, high cardiac output states, and cardiomyopathies. Many of these basic studies were made possible by a National Heart, Lung, and Blood Institute program project grant awarded in 1962. He was equally well known for his clinical publications in congenital and valvular heart disease, bedside clues to cardiac diagnosis, and clinical pharmacology of cardiovascular drugs. He has written or edited 13 textbooks, written 52 textbook chapters, and published more than 150 major articles in peer-reviewed journals. His best known textbooks are *Diagnosis of Heart Disease* (1991), *Cardiac Diagnosis and Treatment* (3rd edition), and *The Pericardium in Health and Disease* (1985).

His publications and teachings have strongly influenced the field of cardiology. Not widely appreciated is that he coined the term "unstable angina" in 1971 in an effort to debunk the implied dire consequences implied by the term "preinfarction angina," which led to more rational management of patients.[2] A landmark paper published with Shabetai and Guntheroth in 1970 characterized the pressure waveforms obtained at right heart catheterization, which differentiated cardiac tamponade caused by effusive pericarditis from constrictive pericarditis.[3]

Dr. Fowler's accomplishments can be found in the wider cardiology area. Many of his trainees and associates have achieved prominence in clinical and academic cardiology. They attest to the demanding quality of his training program over a 25-year period. He served on the editorial boards of all the leading clinical cardiology journals. Special awards and notable positions include member of the Cardiovascular and Renal Drug Advisory Committee of the F.D.A., 1970–1973 and Chairman, 1974–1978; founding member of the Association of University Cardiologists and President, 1976; Chairman of the Subspecialty Board of Cardiovascular Disease of the American Board of Internal Medicine; and Chairman of the Operations Committee of the V.A. Coronary Cooperative Study, 1973–1984, which represents the first controlled and randomized longitudinal study to define the efficacy of coronary artery bypass grafting.

FIG. 1   Noble O. Fowler, M.D.

unique in an era of largely multiauthored clinical cardiology texts in that it is written largely by one man who compares critically his vast personal experience with the world's literature. Recent history has proved him right in most controversial issues; he never fails to take a critical and constructive stand. No one better exemplifies the complete cardiologist than does Dr. Fowler, at least by standards existent prior to the introduction of molecular biology. He is a master internist, superb clinical cardiologist, respected teacher, prolific writer of unusual clarity, established investigator, experienced administrator, and a gentleman. Three qualities stand out but do not appear in Dr. Fowler's curriculum vitae: intellectual honesty, integrity, and rare wisdom in patient management. A few of his aphorisms help explain the man: "When you examine a patient, you should first know what you expect to find." "Do not send this manuscript for publication unless you would be proud of it five years later." "If you have published 50 manuscripts in your career of which you are truly proud, you have had a worthwhile research career." "Perfection is the enemy of good."

Noble Fowler has been my friend and colleague for 36 years. He is still going strong. As Emeriti, we have adjoining offices and codirect the University of Cincinnati Hospital outpatient Cardiac Clinic. We teach bedside skills and the art of consultative cardiology to young trainees and students. In addition, Noble teaches electrocardiographic interpretation of difficult tracings and complex arrhythmias to our fellows. He is currently writing another textbook on bedside diagnosis by observation—a lifelong collection of photographic (in color) clues to diagnosis.

He was given the Master Teacher Award of the American College of Cardiology in 1974 and a special award for his contributions to cardiology by Georgetown University in 1978. In 1994, he received the Laennec Society Special Recognition Award given by the Council on Clinical Cardiology of the American Heart Association.

In my judgment, Noble Fowler personifies a cardiologist of international reputation whose scientific and scholarly achievements have contributed greatly to the practice and advancement of clinical cardiology. He is a master internist who gives his cardiac patients total primary care. His clinical judgment is documented in his writings and contributions at conferences. His textbook *Cardiac Diagnosis and Treatment* is

References

1. Shabetai R, Fowler NO, Fenton JC, Masangkay M: Pulsus paradoxus. *J Clin Invest* 1965;44:1882–1898
2. Fowler NO: "Preinfarctional" angina. A need for an objective definition and for a controlled clinical trial of its management. *Circulation* 1971;44:755–758
3. Shabetai R, Fowler NO, Guntheroth WG: The hemodynamics of cardiac tamponade and constrictive pericarditis. *Am J Cardiol* 1970;26:480–489

William Ganz

H. J. C. SWAN, M.D., PH.D., M.A.C.P.

U.C.L.A. School of Medicine (Cardiology), and Cedars-Sinai Medical Center, Los Angeles, California, USA

William Ganz (Fig. 1) was born in 1919 in Kosice in the eastern part of what is now the newly separated Republic of Slovakia. A leader in his high school studies and in soccer, he entered the Charles University School of Medicine, Prague in 1937. With the occupation of the Sudetanland in 1939 and subsequently all of Czechoslovakia by the Nazis, the students were dispersed to their regions of origin. Fortunately, Kosice was but a few miles from the Hungarian border and Willi was interned in a Hungarian labor camp for the "duration." In 1944, invited for a short vacation at Auschwitz, Willi responded, "I refused the offer and instead went underground." He survived, met and married his wife Magda, and returned to Charles University in 1945. He graduated with the M.D. degree at the top of his class in 1947. In 1951 he was appointed director of Coronary Research at the newly founded Cardiovascular Research Institute in Prague under the leadership of Jan Brod. It was during this time that he was influenced by Fegler in the thermodilution principle for the measurement of blood flow in blood vessels and together with Fronek, published original papers from Czechoslovakia. In 1960 he received the C.Sc. (Ph.D.) degree from the Czechoslovak Academy of Sciences. Despite positions of relative privilege within the scientific medical community in the Eastern Block, Willi was disillusioned with Communist orthodoxy and decided that he would not wish his sons to grow up in that environment. Accordingly, in 1966, he crossed the Czech-Austrian border with Magda and his sons, Tomas and Peter, ostensibly to vacation in Italy, a privilege reserved for but a few. Instead, when he reached Vienna, he applied for an entry visa to the United States. Fortunately, he had relatives in the Los Angeles area and a friend, Simon Rodbard, a respected research cardiologist at the City of Hope Medical Center in Duarte, California. Apparently, Rodbard suggested he see Max Harry Weil, then Chief of the Shock Unit at the Hollywood Presbyterian Hospital, and from there a call directed him to the Cedars of Lebanon Hospital where he joined the fledgling Division of Cardiology at the newly amalgamated Cedars-Sinai Medical Center. My personal recollection of this particular event will follow.

Willi Ganz was and is a medical scientist in the true meaning of the term. He addresses important issues and avoids the trivial. He requires facts to support hypotheses. He devises experimental protocols and procedures which are as simple as possible, yet allow a definitive answer to the hypothesis under question. He is equally familiar with the experimental laboratory and with bedside research. He is always present. He personally analyzes each piece of data and satisfies himself to its validity and relevance. He reviews the pertinent medical literature critically and in detail and depth. He writes each of his manuscripts in longhand until he is satisfied with every word.

The highlights of his scientific contribution include the original method developed in Czechoslovakia for measurement of blood flow by thermodilutions in single vessels including the coronary sinus, the femoral vein, and the jugular system.[1] He has been my own close collaborator in the development and application of the balloon flotation catheter[2,3] and in bedside hemodynamics. By simple experiments, he demonstrated that pharmacological interventions purported to preserve myocardium in experimental myocardial infarction were so dependent on administration before or at the time of occlusion that, from a practical standpoint, they had little or no direct effect on clinical myocardial salvage. First in an animal model, and then in careful clinical studies, he demonstrated the efficacy of intracoronary thrombolysis in myocardial salvage[4,5] and confirmed the significance of thrombus in myocardial infarction. Willi Ganz never necessarily adopted the fashion of the times. In 1990, he presented incontrovertible data that reperfusion does not cause immediate death in otherwise viable myocardium—which has major implications as to the relevance of "reperfusion injury" in actual practice.[6] A continuing interest in the regulation of coronary blood flow.[7] In the early 1970s, he demonstrated that reduction in myocardial oxygen demand is the primary mechanism by which nitroglycerin relieves demand-induced angina,[8] and has examined the influences of collateral blood flow and "steal" conditions, as well as pharmacological interventions.

What are the basic characteristics of this unusual physician, awarded the 1992 Distinguished Scientist Award of the American College of Cardiology? I believe it is his absolute commitment to—perhaps obsession with—cardiovascular research. To him this is all-important. He is a true searcher for truth. He looks at the larger rather than the smaller picture. While his name is associated with my own in the development of the pulmonary artery balloon flotation catheter, it is clear that he has also been a major force in the rational application of thrombolysis and in the clinical management of the acute coronary syndromes.[9]

FIG. 1   William Ganz, M.D., C.Sc.

remember the time that I first met him. My own background in dilution theory with Dr. Earl Wood at Mayo had defined several of my research interests, including the measurement of flow and volumes utilizing the dilution principle. Max Harry Weil called me in September of 1966 and told me that there was a relatively senior scientist who, he thought, could make a major contribution to a physiologically oriented program in cardiology. When Willi came to my office the same day, I recall his firm handshake and my sense of his integrity, dedication, and honesty. I had no resources other than a small grant that I had been able to bring with me the year before from the Mayo Clinic. At that time, building a department of cardiology at Cedars-Sinai Medical Center was more or less "catch as catch can." I, therefore, used the total available funds from that particular grant to support Willie Ganz for as long as it would last, so as to allow me time to identify other resources. I didn't quite know how I was going to do that —but I knew a good bet is on a winner. That decision—not possible today in any institution— was probably one of the best, if not *the* best decision that I ever made in my medical career. Willi Ganz came to Cedars-Sinai Medical Center in 1966. His contribution to that institution and to cardiology are now history. His place is assured.

References

1. Fronek A, Ganz W: Measurement of flow in single blood vessels including cardiac output by local thermodilution. *Circ Res* 1960; 8,:175–182

2. Swan HJC, Ganz W, Forrester JS, Marcus H, Diamond G, Chonette D: Catherization of the heart in man with the use of a flow-directed balloon-tipped catheter. *New Engl J Med* 1970; 283:447–451

3. Ganz W, Donose R. Marcus H, Forrester JS, Swan HJC: A new technique for measurement of cardiac output by thermodilution in man. *Am J Cardiol* 1971;27:392–396

4. Ganz W, Buchbinder N, Marcus H, Mondkar A, Maddahi J, Charuzi Y, O'Connor L, Shell W, Fishbein MC, Kass R, Miyamoto A, Swan HJC: Intracoronary thrombolysis in evolving myocardial infarction. *Am Heart J* 1981;101:4–10

5. Ganz W, Geft I, Shah PK, Lew A, Rodriguez L, Weiss T, Maddahi J, Berman D, Charuzi Y, Swan HJC: Intravenous streptokinase in evolving acute myocardial infarction. *Am J Cardiol* 1984;53: 1209–1216

6. Ganz W, Watanabe I, Kanamasa K, Yano J, Han DS, Fishbein MC: Does reperfusion extend necrosis? A study in a single territory of myocardial ischemia, half reperfused, half not reperfused. *Circulation* 1990;82:1020–1033

7. Ganz W, Tamura K, Marcus H, Donoso R, Yoshida S, Swan HJC: Measurement of coronary sinus blood flow by thermodilution in man. *Circulation* 1971;44:181–195

8. Ganz W, Marcus H: Failure of intracoronary nitroglycerin to alleviate pacing-induced angina. *Circulation* 1972;46:880–889

9. Shah PK, Cercek B, Lew A, Ganz W: Angiographic validation of bedside markers of reperfusion. *J Am Coll Cardiol* 1993;21:55–61

Politically, Willi Ganz would describe himself as a conservative. His experience with communism, "socialism," and free enterprise has drawn him strongly to the latter. For those in the early 1970s who proposed the merit of the former two political philosophies, he would snort: "Let them go there and they'll change their opinions in a very short time." He is a true American in the spirit of the pioneers. However, I suspect he still thinks in Czech— "Thanks, God" he says, when something good but unexpected happens.

Willi takes enormous pride in his two sons. Tomas received a Ph.D. degree in low temperature physics from CalTech. He then found that there were not very many people in the world who had an abiding interest in the behavior of molecules at –272°C. He entered medicine and is now a Professor of Medicine (pulmonary diseases) at UCLA and is following in the steps of his distinguished father. Peter is an Associate Professor of Medicine at Harvard Medical School (Brigham and Woman's Hospital), a leader in invasive cardiology, and a world authority on endothelial function and dysfunction. Willi speaks with pride of a brilliant grandson, at Harvard College with a career of leadership in who knows what, as yet.

Willi and Magda and my wife and I have been firm friends for close to 27 years. She has been the backbone of his support at home and during their many overseas visits. I well

Harriet P. Dustan

EDWARD D. FROHLICH, M.D.

Alton Ochsner Medical Foundation, New Orleans, Louisiana, USA

Cardiovascular medicine and the world hypertension research community sadly lost one of its major forces on June 27, 1999, with the death of Dr. Harriet Pearson Dustan (Fig. 1). A long and tireless leader of the American Heart Association, Dr. Dustan personally contributed to its vitality and strength and to the role of voluntary health organizations in healthcare research.

Born in Craftsbury Common, Vermont, she received her early education at the Craftsbury Academy and then attended the University of Vermont for her undergraduate and medical degrees. After her postgraduate training in internal medicine at the Mary Fletcher Hospital and at the Royal Victoria Hospital in Montreal, she returned to the University of Vermont's Bishop DeGrasbriand Hospital to help establish a medical student teaching program. She came to the Research Division of the Cleveland Clinic in 1948 to begin a productive and illustrious career in hypertension with Drs. Irvine H. Page and Arthur C. Corcoran. Dr. Dustan's research work began at the Cleveland Clinic with the early antihypertensive drugs. Some of these agents are now only of importance to pharmacologic history. All were very vital stepping stones in the development of the broad armamentarium of agents that we now have to prevent and reverse the tremendous morbidity and mortality associated with hypertension and other cardiovascular diseases. Hers was one of the first reports to demonstrate reversal of the course of malignant hypertension. Working with a remarkable team of radiological, renal, cardiovascular, and pathology specialists, she participated in the development and demonstration of selective renal arteriography as the standard of reference for the demonstration of renal arterial disease as the major remediable form of hypertension. Their longitudinal studies of patients with renal arterial disease in the 1960s identified the various forms of atherosclerotic and fibrosing renal arterial lesions; and their careful studies permitted an arteriographic and pathologic correlation and the elucidation of the natural history of these various diseases. Her studies, in the early days of plasma renin activity measurement, permitted a correlation of the relationship between the plasma concentration of this enzyme and the role of intravascular volume and other factors in various clinical forms of hypertensive diseases. Personally, I believe her recent reports hypothesizing the relationship between keloid formation and hypertensive renal arteriolar lesions in black patients will be shown to be of great fundamental importance.

After many productive years in Cleveland, she moved to Birmingham, Alabama, in 1977 to direct the Cardiovascular Research and Training Center of the University of Alabama School of Medicine. It was there that she directed the research activities of the Specialized Center of Hypertension and, later, became inaugural editor of *Hypertension*. She was named Distinguished Faculty Lecturer of the University of Alabama in Birmingham in 1984 and, in 1987, University Distinguished Professor. She was also appointed Distinguished Physician of the Veterans Administration at the Birmingham VA Medical Center in 1987.

Dr. Dustan returned to her home in Vermont in 1990 where she continued to serve her alma mater. She had been a member earlier of the University of Vermont's Board of Trustees, and on her retirement continued to participate actively in the University's Departments of Medicine, Pharmacology, and Physiology. For service to her University she received the honorary degree of Doctor of Science, and was so honored by Cleveland State University and the Medical College of Pennsylvania. She also received the Doctor of Humane Letters from St. Michael's College in Vermont. For her long-standing work in the hypertensive field, Dr. Dustan was invited to serve on the Advisory Panel of the National Heart, Lung, and Blood Institute of the National Institutes of Health. During this tenure she was Co-Chairman of the Hypertension Research Task Force. Later, she chaired the Joint National Committee's Third Report on the Detection, Evaluation, and Treatment of Hypertension.

Throughout her long career, Dr. Dustan was a tireless leader and advocate of the American Heart Association. She worked for many years on its research committee, finally chairing this important activity. Other important responsibilities were with its first ethics committee and the administrative restructuring of the organization. She was President of the American Heart Association from 1976 to 1977. Following her tenure with the Association, she agreed to establish the journal *Hypertension* and served as its first editor. She was a strong advocate for the role of its pharmaceutical roundtable for donation of therapeutic agents to the nation's underserved population. For her long-standing service to the American Heart Association and to the Council for High Blood Pressure Research, she received the Gold Heart Award of the Association, the Lifetime Achievement Award of the Council, and the President's Award of the Northeast Ohio Affiliate. Harriet

FIG. 1   Harriet P. Dustan, M.D. (1920–1999).

Dustan worked tirelessly on behalf of most professional and other organizations to which she belonged. She was the first woman to be named to the board of the American Board of Internal Medicine and the Board of Regents of the American College of Physicians, chairing the Residency Review committee. For her service to these organizations and for her contributions in establishing the principles that underlie the successful treatment of hypertension that led to the decrease in the death rates and improved health for the millions of hypertensive Americans, she was awarded the Scientific Achievement Award of the American Medical Association in 1988, the John Phillips Memorial Award from the American College of Physicians in 1994, and the Distinguished Service Award of the American College of Cardiology in 1998.

All of us who have known and worked with Dr. Dustan and enjoyed her warm personality, keen intellect, delightful sense of humor, and unusual style will miss her friendship and her continued contributions. For those who never had the privilege of knowing Dusty personally, they and those who will follow on in their footsteps will be the beneficiaries of her major service to her fellow man. We shall all miss you!

Henry T. Bahnson

DAVID C. SABISTON, JR., M.D.

Department of Surgery, Duke University Medical Center, Durham, North Carolina, USA

Henry T. Bahnson is a native of Winston-Salem, North Carolina, and a summa cum laude graduate of Davidson College (B.S. 1941). He was elected to Phi Beta Kappa and Omicron Delta Kappa during his junior year and served as president of the student body. In addition, he was president of his fraternity, a member of the varsity football team, and he graduated third in his class scholastically. He was later elected Permanent President of the Class of 1941.

Following graduation he entered Harvard Medical School where he was an outstanding student and graduated cum laude (M.D. 1944). In his second year at Harvard, he did research on blood coagulation at the Thorndike Laboratory at Boston City Hospital under Dr. George Maynard and Dr. Charles Davidson, and in his senior year he worked with Dr. Lewis Dexter at the Peter Bent Brigham Hospital. He was one of six third-year students elected to Alpha Omega Alpha and one of three to be awarded a John Harvard Fellowship. He was also the student head of the Boylston Medical Society.

Dr. Bahnson spent the summer following his second year in medical school working with Dr. Tinsley R. Harrison, the noted professor of medicine and editor of the well-known text *Principles of Internal Medicine*. In October 1943, Dr. Harrison wrote to Dr. Alfred Blalock, Professor and Director of the Department of Surgery at Johns Hopkins, a letter recommending Dr. Bahnson for internship in which he said,

> The purpose of my letter is to tell you something about Mr. Henry T. Bahnson who is a third year student at Harvard, and writes me that he is going to apply to you for an internship. . . . Last summer when he was on his vacation from Harvard, he bobbed up in the labs here the day he got home and said he wanted to do some research. I laughed at him when he told me he had only three weeks vacation and told him to go and have a good time. His answer was that he could have a good time and do research, too. . . . When the three weeks were up, the boy came and brought me some beautiful data which demonstrated quite conclusively that removal of the kidneys made the rats more susceptible to hemorrhage. . . . It was the best research performance I have ever seen in a lad who has had only two years of medical school.

This work was published in the *American Journal of Physiology*, and following that experience Henry Bahnson began a remarkable career in scientific surgery and was to make many basic and clinical contributions in the years ahead.

After entering the Surgical Residency Training Program at Johns Hopkins under the direction of Alfred Blalock, he rapidly recognized his mentor's many outstanding traits and especially his dedication to research and teaching. Stimulated by these factors, he decided to do basic work on the pulmonary circulation and arranged to spend a year at the University of Rochester in the laboratory of two great pulmonary physiologists, Dr. Wallace O. Fenn and Dr. Herman Rahn. While there he held a National Science Foundation Fellowship and made fundamental observations on the effect of unilateral hypoxia on gas exchange and calculated pulmonary blood flow in each lung. In addition, he studied adaptation to high altitudes including changes in breath-holding time and a study on blood and tissue cases of animals exposed to one and seven atmospheres of oxygen or air. These observations were published in the *American Journal of Physiology*. After Henry Bahnson returned to continue surgical training at Johns Hopkins, Dr. Fenn wrote Dr. Blalock stating,

> I want to tell you how much we appreciated having Dr. Henry Bahnson this year. We all became very much attached to him personally, and we also valued his professional ability and industry very highly indeed. I am sure that we shall hear from him in the years to come. His surgical skill was a very great asset to our group and he gave a big boost to the work of the laboratory. We consider it a great privilege to have had him here for a year and we want you to know what a fine impression he left upon us.

While Henry Bahnson was in residency training Dr. Blalock became very impressed with his brilliance and hard work. Together they exchanged ideas and performed studies which led to the publication of a number of outstanding papers. By the time he finished the residency program, Bahnson had published works on angiocardiography in congenital heart disease, coarctation of the aorta at unusual sites, causes of death following operation for congenital heart disease of the cyanotic type, aortic vascular rings encountered in the surgical treatment of congenital pulmonic stenosis, observations on tricuspid stenosis or atresia with hypoplasia of the right

FIG. 1 Henry T. Bahnson (1920 –), an outstanding surgeon and investigator. (Reproduced from Ref. 2 with permission.)

ventricle, and evidence for a renal factor in the hypertension of experimental coarctation of the aorta.

In retrospect it is clear Dr. Blalock recognized very early that Henry Bahnson was quite exceptional. In fact, while he was a junior resident he wrote Admiral Lamont Pugh saying, "Bahnson is a very outstanding young man who will go far in academic work. I have never known a young man with more ability along these lines!" It soon became recognized nationwide that Alfred Blalock had a unique ability to select individuals who were destined to have successful careers in the field for his training program.

In a letter nominating Henry Bahnson for a Markle Scholarship, Dr. Blalock said,

Probably the most significant statement that can be made about Dr. Bahnson is that he is an excellent clinical surgeon, having performed a great variety of major operations successfully, that he is a successful teacher, and he still finds time to carry on problems in the laboratory. It is of interest that he performed the first successful closure of a patent ductus arteriosus in France while visiting the Hospital Broussais in Paris in 1947 [while still a young resident].

He then proceeded to laud his fundamental studies on the pulmonary circulation, on oxygen poisoning with special reference to pulmonary edema, climatic studies at an altitude of 14,000 feet, the role of the kidney in hypertension associated with coarctation of the aorta, and his commitment to academic surgery. Later, Dr. Blalock emphasized his pioneering role in the excision of thoracic aortic aneurysms, and he cited his first pioneering procedure, performed in 1952, as a milestone in the surgical treatment of this condition.

In 1957, Henry Bahnson and Frank Spencer were invited to Australia to initiate open heart surgery at the Royal Prince Albert Hospital in Sydney. Following that visit, Sir Herbert Schlink wrote to Dr. Blalock,

Dr. Henry T. Bahnson left the hospital yesterday to return home. He has been with us for the past month and I am writing to tell you how much we have enjoyed having him with us. Dr. Bahnson has proven himself to be a most competent surgeon, a congenial and inspiring colleague and a worthy ambassador of your great Country. All patients operated on have done well and his advice and practical example has been of immense help in initiating open heart surgery in this Country.

The noted Australian cardiac surgeon, Rowan Nicks wrote, saying,

We have had a most stirring visit from Henry Bahnson and Frank Spencer. The results of their work here had a profound effect on Australian Surgery. We found them both fine companions who took us up, cemented us together to their own world, and left us with their 'Know how' and their stamp to carry on with some confidence. Myself, I think that this gesture of theirs, in coming on such an assignment revealed great depths of moral courage.

On the faculty at Johns Hopkins, Henry Bahnson was very creative and established the open heart program, training a number of residents in this field, including the author who remains deeply indebted to him. He was also devoted to the experimental laboratory, and he and his co-workers continued outstanding research. In 1961 he was promoted to the rank of Professor of Surgery and the following year was invited to spend three months at the University of Vienna to assist Professor Fritz Helmer in establishing a new cardiovascular surgical service. On return from Vienna he was appointed the George V. Foster Professor of Surgery and Chairman of the Department of Surgery at the University of Pittsburgh. There he built an unusually strong surgical residency training program combined with basic surgical research. He initiated a highly successful cardiac transplantation program which was further extended to other organs, especially the liver, when he successfully attracted the brilliant and exceedingly productive pioneering academic surgeon, Thomas E. Starzl, to lead this effort. In a short time Pittsburgh became and has remained the leading transplant center in the world.

In his recently published biography, Tom Starzl said, "If there ever was a person in whom character and superlative professional performance combined to a perfect blend, it was Bahnson." In his recently published autobiography, Tom Starzl said in reflecting back on the founding of the Pittsburgh transplant program,

To understand how all of this could have happened without a systematic administrative plan, it is necessary to understand Hank Bahnson, chair of the surgical department, who already had passed his sixtieth year by the time Iwatsuki and I arrived in Pittsburgh. Bahnson's greatest assets and human qualities were fairness and integrity. When he was a child, he was an innocent bystander in an accident which became a linchpin of his character. While he was nearby, his mother fell down a steep flight of stairs in a church near their home in Winston-Salem, North Carolina. To his horror, he realized that she thought that she had been pushed—by him. He told me this in June 1985, while we walked down a quiet street in Vienna. We were there for his induction as an honorary member of the Austrian Surgical Society. The week before, one of the Pittsburgh newspapers had published a sensational report about alleged improprieties in the transplant program. I heard in his voice the pain that the unfair childhood accusation and now the recent ones had caused.

Who was responsible for the distorted information that had been leaked as ammunition in the intramural turf war? There would be no rush to judgement in Bahnson's life. This trait paralyzed him in his executive functions, but it created a protective buffer for those who were in the fusion of the old and new in the transplant world. No complaint, however minor, went unattended by him personally. The paper trail—notes of meetings, letters sent and unsent, answers to complaints, summaries of testimony—showed, without intending to, the purity and purpose of the new program and destroyed the web woven over it by those intent upon its destruction or fractionation.

This was the old-fashioned way of management. When Bahnson retired from surgery in 1987, the turf wars were over. If they were to recur, it would have to be through the councils and oversight committees that were designed to prevent them.

Transplantation had been institutionalized in Pittsburgh, setting the stage for the next harvest of ideas and new technologies. These already were simmering on the back burner.[1]

A remarkable contributor across the broad field of clinical and investigative surgery, Henry T. Bahnson remains quite active and holds one of only several of the highly prestigious appointments as a Distinguished Physician of the Veterans Administration. His achievements have been of monumental proportions, and he has clearly achieved a well-deserved place in the history of surgery.

References

1. Starzl TE: Politics. In: *The Puzzle People*. University of Pittsburgh Press, Pittsburgh, Pennsylvania (1992) 279–280.

2. A Note about the Surgeon. In *Surgical Procedures: The Pictorial Preview of Significant Developments in Surgery*. Morris Hill, NJ, Warner-Chilcott Laboratories 2:7 (1965) 1

Denton A. Cooley

ROBERT J. HALL, M.D.

Texas Heart Institute; Department of Adult Cardiology, St. Luke's Episcopal Hospital; Department of Medicine, Baylor College of Medicine, and University of Texas Health Science Center, Houston, Texas, USA

Denton Arthur Cooley, M.D. (Fig. 1), Surgeon-in-Chief of the Texas Heart Institute, has been described as the world's most productive cardiac surgeon as well as one of the most skilled technicians in his field. Even more important, he is an innovator in the field of cardiovascular surgery—constantly revising and improving existing procedures as well as developing new surgical techniques.

Following perfection of the heart-lung machine in 1955, Dr. Cooley specialized in open-heart surgery, including surgery on infants with congenital heart defects. In 1956, he used temporary cardiopulmonary bypass to perform the first open-heart operation in the southern United States, repair of a postinfarction ventricular septal defect. Also in 1956, he performed the first successful carotid endarterectomy in the world. In less than 5 years, he had performed more than 1,000 open-heart operations, and by 1990, Cooley with his team had performed over 75,000 open-heart operations—more than any other heart center in the world.

In the 1960s, Cooley introduced "bloodless" heart surgery, using a nonblood solution of 5% dextrose and diluted saline to prime the heart-lung machine. At the time, 4–10 units of freshly drawn, matched blood were needed for each open-heart procedure. Using nonblood prime increased the availability and reduced the risk of open-heart surgery for patients with all types of heart disease, including patients of the Jehovah's Witness faith. In 1961, Cooley succeeded in establishing a procedure of pulmonary embolectomy to combat pulmonary embolism, for which medical science had tried in vain to find a remedy. In May 1968, Cooley performed the first "successful" heart transplantation in the United States, 5 months after Christiaan Barnard's historic operation in Cape Town, South Africa, and several months after attempts by Kantrowitz and Shumway in the United States. Approximately one year later, in 1969, he implanted the first total artificial heart in a human. The total artificial heart sustained life for some 64 hours while a donor was sought for heart transplantation.

Dr. Cooley has contributed to the development of techniques for repair and replacement of diseased heart valves and is widely known for operations to correct congenital heart anomalies in infants and to repair aneurysms of the aorta. Cooley has long been a leading practitioner of the coronary bypass operation. In 1963, he performed a bypass procedure to reconstruct the coronary system in a patient with a congenital defect of the coronary arteries. Christiaan Barnard wrote in his book, *One Life,* about Cooley's surgical skill:

> It was the most beautiful surgery I had ever seen. . . . Every movement had a purpose and achieved its aim. Where most surgeons would take three hours, he could do the same operation in one hour. It went forward like a broad river—never obvious in haste, yet never going back. . . . No one in the world, I knew, could equal it.

One of Dr. Cooley's most significant contributions to the field of cardiac surgery and cardiology was founding the Texas Heart Institute in the Texas Medical Center in Houston. In the 29 years since its founding in 1962, the Institute has become world renowned for its leadership in patient care, education, and research in the field of cardiovascular diseases. Through its history, Cooley has unselfishly opened the Institute's doors to physicians from all parts of the United States and other countries to train under him as fellows in cardiovascular surgery, cardiovascular research, and cardiology.

A native of Houston, Denton Arthur Cooley was born on August 22, 1920. His grandfather, Daniel Denton Cooley, was a founder in 1890 of Houston Heights, then a major suburb of the city. His father, Ralph Clarkson Cooley, was a prominent dentist. Cooley majored in Zoology at the University of Texas and graduated in 1941 with highest honors. While at the University, he lettered in varsity basketball for three years.

After two years of medical studies at the University of Texas Medical Branch in Galveston, Texas, Dr. Cooley entered the Johns Hopkins University School of Medicine, graduating in 1944 at the head of his class. As a medical student, he practiced his manual skill by tying surgical knots inside a match box. As an intern and resident under Dr. Alfred Blalock, he participated in the early development of the famous Blalock "blue baby" operation for the correction of tetralogy of Fallot. Cooley revealed later that it was that revolutionary operation, as well as Dr. Blalock's inspiration, that led him to make heart surgery his specialty.

His military service between 1946 and 1948 was as Captain in the Medical Corps and Chief of Surgery at the 124th Station Hospital in Linz, Austria. After completing his surgical training at Johns Hopkins in 1950, he spent a year with Lord Russell Brock in London. At that time, mitral valvoto-

Fig. 1 Denton A. Cooley, M.D.

my by the closed technique was being developed by this great English surgeon.

Dr. Cooley joined the full-time faculty of Baylor University College of Medicine in 1951 and was Professor of Surgery from 1962 to 1969. He is now Surgeon-in-Chief of the Texas Heart Institute, Director of Cardiovascular Surgery at St. Luke's Episcopal Hospital, Consultant in Cardiovascular Surgery at Texas Children's Hospital, and Clinical Professor of Surgery at the University of Texas Medical School in Houston.

Dr. Cooley is a member or honorary member of more than 50 professional societies around the world. He is the author or coauthor of more than 2,000 scientific articles and several texts. Cooley began work on his first text in 1962 with Dr. Grady Hallman. *Surgical Treatment of Congenital Heart Disease*, published in 1965, was the first major comprehensive book on pediatric cardiovascular surgery. Cooley had embarked on the project out of a desire to share experiences and to help other cardiac surgeons, all of whom were struggling to learn the new techniques that could be used to treat congenital heart disease.

Among his 59 honors and awards are the Medal of Freedom, the nation's highest civilian award, presented by President Reagan; the Gifted Teacher Award bestowed by the American College of Cardiology; the Theodore Roosevelt Award, the highest honor awarded by the National Collegiate Athletic Association to a varsity athlete who has achieved national recognition in his profession; and the René Leriche Prize, the highest honor of the International Surgical Society.

Dr. Cooley has been named Distinguished Alumnus at both the University of Texas and the Johns Hopkins University and has received honorary degrees from the University of Turin, Hellenic College, and Holy Cross Greek Orthodox School of Theology, Houston Baptist University, College of William and Mary, and the United States Sports Academy. He has been decorated by the governments of Argentina, Ecuador, Italy, Jordan, Panama, Peru, the Philippines, Spain, Venezuela, The Netherlands, and Greece. Cooley has been named a fellow of the Royal College of Physicians and Surgeons of Glasgow, the Royal College of Surgeons of Ireland, the Royal Australian College of Surgeons, and the Royal College of Surgeons of England.

In 1972, the Denton A. Cooley Cardiovascular Surgical Society was founded as a tribute to Dr. Cooley's contributions to cardiovascular surgery and physician education throughout the world, with goals of continuing education, professional growth, and progress. Included in the Society membership are residents and fellows who have received surgical training under Cooley at the Texas Heart Institute, along with other physicians prominent in the advancement of cardiovascular medicine. The society's motto, which is Cooley's personal philosophy, is "Modify, Simplify, Apply." This philosophy of simple, expeditious, and efficient performance has helped Cooley achieve his goals. Hard work is another key to his success. According to Cooley, "A few achieve success through luck, but I believe that the harder one works, the luckier he becomes."

As was said recently by Arthur Hailey, celebrated author and surgical patient at the Texas Heart Institute,

> What happens in the Texas Heart Institute reflects not only the exceptional skills of Denton Cooley, which are world famous and acknowledged, but also his warm humanity, and the rarest of human qualities—inspired leadership which leaves its hallmark everywhere.

> Each of us who has been privileged to know Dr. Cooley will long appreciate the fruits of the association. The rewards of learning are inestimable.

Dr. Cooley has truly been one of the pioneers in the treatment of cardiovascular disease. The care and treatment of thousands of patients with cardiovascular diseases and the education and training of numerous students and physicians have been influenced directly or indirectly by his vision, intuition, innovation, dedication, continuing basic and applied investigations, and pursuit of excellence.

The following stanzas from "A Bag of Tools" by the American poet R.L. Sharpe are inscribed in the foyer of the Texas Heart Institute:

> *Isn't it strange*
> *That princes and kings*
> *And clowns that caper*
> *In sawdust rings,*
> *And common people*
> *Like you and me*
> *Are builders for eternity?*
> *Each is given a bag of tools,*
> *A shapeless mass*
> *A book of rules;*
> *And each must make*
> *Ere life has flown*
> *A stumbling block*
> *Or a stepping stone.*

J. Willis Hurst—a Man of Achievement

MARK E. SILVERMAN, M.D.

Division of Cardiology, Emory University School of Medicine, and Piedmont Hospital, Atlanta, Georgia, USA

"A true teacher is a teacher who has the ability to stimulate his or her students to learn. True teachers know their goal has been accomplished when they feel the overpowering joy—ecstasy—that occurs when a student grasps a new concept."

—*J. Willis Hurst, M.D.*[1]

Gifted teacher, master clinician, prolific author, and esteemed leader—these are the words often used to describe J. Willis Hurst, whose ongoing career now spans almost 50 years (Fig. 1). He was born October 21, 1920, in Cooper, Kentucky (later part of Monticello), the only child of John and Verna Bell Hurst. When he was eleven months old, his family moved to Carroll County, Georgia, where his father became principal of a small school. The family lived in a large house that also boarded an aunt and another woman who were his grade school teachers. In this concentrated atmosphere of schooling, the young Hurst was disciplined to read extensively, especially from the *World Book Encyclopedia*, and to memorize quotes and poems. He was profoundly influenced by the Socratic teaching method of his father, whose style was to lead a student to discover an answer through a series of leading questions and assigned reading. He also observed his father's compassionate efforts to teach illiterate older people to read and write.

By age 10, he knew he wanted to become a physician. At age 16, he entered West Georgia College in Carrollton where he met Nelie Wiley, his future wife, to whom he would later dedicate many of his books ("No Nelie, no book"), and was active in sports and drama. After two years at this small college, he followed Nelie to the University of Georgia where he graduated with a B.Sc. in chemistry and zoology. He entered the University of Georgia Medical School (now Medical College of Georgia) in 1941 and married Nelie in 1942. He soon realized that he admired the teachers who taught him how to learn as opposed to those who required rote memorization. In medical school, he began his lifelong habit of beginning the day at 4 A.M. to think about and solve problems. He credits this early jump on the day as contributing in large measure to his success. He was influenced by V.P. Sydenstricker, Chairman of the Department of Medicine and a keen diagnostician; William Hamilton, the famous cardiovascular physiologist; and Perry Volpitto, the respected head of the Department of Anesthesia. During this period, he developed his interest in cardiology and was impressed by the pioneering catheterization work of André Cournand, the Nobelist, whom he met when Cournand was a visiting professor. He was junior A.O.A., president of A.O.A., and graduated first in his class in 1944 at the age of 23. In medical school, he began teaching sessions with his classmates, some of whom predicted he would be a future chief of medicine.

His internship and residency training took place at the University Hospital in Augusta. During this time, the first of the Hurst's three sons was born. After two years of military service, from 1946–1948 at Fitzsimmons General Hospital in Denver, Willis Hurst became a graduate student and then a cardiac fellow at the Massachusetts General Hospital starting July 1948. Paul Dudley White, the foremost cardiologist in America, was his mentor and role model of bedside observation, teaching, writing clearly and succinctly, and reporting clinical research. At the Massachusetts General Hospital, he developed important relationships with leading cardiologists and started lifelong friendships with future leaders in medicine, including Lloyd Smith, James Wyngarden, Ernest Craige, and E. Grey Dimond. During his two years in Boston, he co-authored his first five articles. In July 1949 he left Boston for Atlanta where he entered private practice. In his spare time, he developed a local reputation by speaking to medical groups, starting a Heart Station at Georgia Baptist Hospital, and teaching at Grady Memorial Hospital. It became apparent to him that his teaching, writing, and clinical research could be best accomplished in a university setting. So when an offer was made by Paul Beeson, the Chairman of Medicine, to join the Emory faculty in July 1950 to work closely with R. Bruce Logue in a newly developed private diagnostic clinic, he eagerly accepted. Over the next four years, he worked closely with Dr. Logue in developing the reputation of the Emory Clinic as a referral center. He gave talks throughout the state and worked with trainees and students. His interest in teaching electrocardiography was abetted by Robert Grant, a leader in the vectorial approach to interpreting the scalar electrocardiogram. With Gratten Woodson, a cardiac fellow, Hurst wrote his first book, *An Atlas of Vector Electrocardiography*. It became obvious to him that his writing interacted with his teaching—writing could distill his ideas into the clearest form of communication; teaching communicated ideas, not facts, making each concept as vivid and as exact as possible. He would write as if he were discussing matters with the listener.[2]

Fig.1   J. Willis Hurst.

Just as his academic career began to flourish, it was abruptly interrupted by the Korean conflict. Because of a serious family illness requiring his presence, he had been allowed to leave the military early in 1947, before fully completing his two-year obligation. He was recalled into military service in 1954 and assigned to the Bethesda Naval Hospital where he started a cardiac catheterization laboratory and later became Chief of Cardiology. When Lyndon Johnson, then majority leader of the Senate, suffered a heart attack July 2, 1955, Hurst became his cardiologist.[3] This led to an enduring relationship as physician and friend, including travel together to 15 foreign countries. The day of Kennedy's assassination, Hurst was rushed to Washington to be with Lyndon Johnson and participate in the transition process. An offer to become the White House physician was tactfully declined by Hurst who told the 36th president, "A patient doing well does not need a physician every day and a physician needs more than one patient to retain his skills. I can best serve you as a consultant." Johnson reluctantly agreed. From Johnson, he learned two important lessons: "The best fertilizer for any man's ranch is the footprints of the owner" and "An excellent idea is no good unless implemented at the right time."[2]

In November 1955, he returned to Emory where he resumed teaching bedside skills and electrocardiography and practicing consultative cardiology. This was a turbulent period of discord between the medical school administration and the chiefs of the various departments. Meanwhile, Hurst entertained an opportunity to join the Mayo Clinic. As he was considering the offer, the Chiefs of Medicine, Surgery, and Obstetrics (and later Pathology) resigned, leaving Emory rudderless. Hurst was asked to be the new Chief of Medicine. Before accepting, he visited Gene Stead at Duke and Paul Beeson at

Yale to seek their advice. Dr. Stead offered him the same counsel that Soma Weiss, Chief of Medicine at Peter Bent Brigham, had given him when Stead was asked to come to Emory in 1942: "So far you have proved to be a man of promise; if you succeed at Emory, you will also be a man of achievement." In February 1957, at the youthful age of 36, he assumed the mantle of Chairman of Medicine at Emory. His daunting task was to rebuild a depleted department that in the 1940s had been one of the finest in the country. Like Weiss and Stead, Hurst selected a young faculty with great promise who had not yet achieved national recognition. From this nucleus, the faculty grew over the next 30 years to 144 full time and many volunteers, and the medical housestaff and research fellows expanded to over 250 per year. The teaching program for students, housestaff, and fellows became recognized as among the best, and research capabilities were enlarged. Patient-care and town-gown relationships were greatly strengthened and a full-time faculty position was established at several community hospitals. On September 1, 1986, after a 30-year tenure, he stepped down as Chief of Medicine—a time span, as he pointed out, that was 14.3% of the time the United States had been a nation. Since 1986, he has continued his energetic schedule, still arising at 4 A.M. to think and write, and beginning his teaching activities at 7 A.M. at Emory and Grady Hospitals. Afterwards, he works on his books and articles at his office over the Emory Medical Library and continues to mentor students and housestaff.

During his remarkably productive career, he has (so far) written over 300 articles and essays, authored or edited 57 books, including three books on teaching and education, seven editions of *The Heart*, and four editions of *Medicine for the Practicing Physician*. He has served on the editorial boards of 21 journals, and was President of the American Heart Association (1971–1972), President of the Association of Professors of Medicine (1984–1985), Chairman of the Subspecialty Board of Cardiovascular Disease (1967–1970), and a member of the President's Commission on Heart Disease, Cancer, and Stroke (1964-1965), and the National Advisory Heart, Lung, and Blood Council (1971–1981). A selected list of his numerous awards includes Master Teacher of the American College of Cardiology (1974); the Gold Heart of the American Heart Association (1974); Master of the American College of Physicians (1978); the Herrick Award of the American Heart Association (1980); Candler Professorship of Emory University (1980); Distinguished Alumnus, Medical College of Georgia (1984); Distinguished Teacher, American College of Physicians (1985); the Williams Award of the Association of Professors of Medicine (1986); the Cumming Award presented by President Reagan (1989); the Bedside Teacher Award of the Georgia Chapter of the American College of Physicians (1992); and the Evangeline T. Papageorge Teaching Award of Emory University (1995). The J. Willis Hurst Chair of Cardiology was established in his honor in 1992.

Although his major textbooks and accomplishments as a chairman and leader of medicine are national legend, he will always be thought of first as a teacher. Teaching, to Willis Hurst, means to instill principles, ethics, and lifelong habits of learning. In his writings, he makes a clear distinction between a teacher as someone who just announces facts and a "true teacher" as one who takes the time to ascertain whether the trainee is using the facts in a thought process.[2] Throughout his career, he has taught that low-tech data collection and analysis often negate the need for more expensive technology. His emphasis on the importance of history taking, physical examination, the electrocardiogram, and the chest x-ray is the most consistent theme of his teaching and writing.[4] He is particularly adroit in analyzing the 12-lead electrocardiogram by a vectorial approach, and former cardiac fellows remember that he could easily spend an hour each Saturday morning conference interpreting just one or two electrocardiographic tracings. Medical records as a form of communication and education have always been a matter of great concern to him. He championed the Problem-Oriented Record, developed by Lawrence Weed in the 1970s, as the best method to teach, communicate, and deliver excellent patient care.[1,5] Its lack of widespread application has been one of his few disappointments. In the 1960s, when valvular disease and surgery captured the most interest, Hurst was the golden standard of auscultation and diagnosis that all the cardiac fellows aspired to reach. He was always supreme at teaching at the bedside, where he was able to demonstrate subtle findings from the history and examination that would allow him to reach a precise diagnosis that would correlate closely with the findings at cardiac catheterization. When coronary disease pushed into the limelight, he patiently waited until national trials showed the benefit of bypass surgery for certain conditions, then he became a leading advocate in this area.[2] After angioplasty was introduced by Andreas Gruentzig, he used his enormous persuasive powers to convince Gruentzig to come to Emory where large-scale trials and major teaching symposia that established angioplasty as one of the major advances in medicine were held. He was instrumental in developing the Professional Assistants (P.A.) Program at Emory, one of the first and largest in the nation, and he also helped to establish one of the first closed-circuit medical television networks in the country. Throughout his career, Hurst has always been a vigorous advocate for nurses, patient education, the importance of medical history, and has always been farsighted in his anticipation of the direction of academic medicine.[2,6]

Willis Hurst is a tall and imposing man with a room-filling presence. His expressive face often beams with warmth, energy, and pleasure. He easily breaks into a deep chuckle that can become a convulsive whoop when he enjoys a story immensely. He likes to shake a person's hand with both his hands brought together, a mannerism that he learned from Lyndon Johnson and that he uses effectively to build friendships. When he knows you or wants to make a point, he will often clasp his large right hand on your shoulder and say, "Now look here"— a technique that conveys his strength and has an effect on people similar to kryptonite on Superman. Like Osler, to whom he often refers with reverence, Hurst believes that the "masterword of medicine is work." By beginning his day at 4:00 A.M. and working productively and indefatigably seven days a week, he is able to accomplish far more than most and satisfy his inner drive to communicate his ideas and teachings.

His boundless enthusiasm for teaching everyone in his vicinity; his ready enjoyment for discussing medicine, ethics, and professionalism from the start to the finish of each day; and his availability beginning with coffee at 7 A.M. in the old Grady cafeteria are fondly recalled by the many students, housestaff, and fellows who sat at his side. His trainees will always regard him as a man of high principle who preached and practiced only one style of medicine—what is best for the patient—and whose goal was to boost each of them up to that level. He judged himself by his ability to inspire each person to learn and enjoy medicine as much as he does and chided himself when he failed. The ultimate tribute to him is the remark that many students and housestaff invariably make when asked about Hurst's effect on their careers: "I practice as if Dr. Hurst is looking over my shoulder." Through his commitment to high personal standards of intellectual honesty, his dedication to patient care and education, his consummate skills as a bedside clinician, and his enthusiasm for medicine, he has served as the role model for a generation of students, housestaff, and practicing physicians. In many ways, and continuing unabated today, Willis Hurst has fulfilled the challenge that Gene Stead passed on from Soma Weiss to him in 1956—to be a "man of achievement."

References

1. Hurst JW: *The Bench and Me: Teaching and Learning Medicine*. New York: Igaku-Shoin, 1992

2. Silverman ME: An Interview with J. Willis Hurst, M.D. *Am J Cardiol* 1998; 81:478–489

3. Hurst JW, Cain JC: *LBJ—To Know Him Better*. Austin: LBJ Foundation, 1995

4. Hurst JW: *Cardiovascular Diagnosis: The Initial Examination*. St. Louis: Mosby, 1993

5. Walker HK, Hurst JW, Woody MF: *Applying the Problem-Oriented System*. New York: Medcom Press, 1973

6. Hurst JW: *Four Hats: On Teaching Medicine and Other Essays*. Chicago: Year Book Medical Publishers, 1970

Aubrey Leatham: Twentieth Century Pioneer in Auscultation

MARK E. SILVERMAN, M.D.

Division of Cardiology, Emory University School of Medicine and Piedmont Hospital, Atlanta, Georgia, USA

Widely regarded as a leading figure in twentieth century cardiology, Aubrey Leatham (Fig. 1) has elevated the art of auscultation to a science through innovative studies with phono- and echocardiology. Born in 1920 near London, England, he was educated at Charterhouse, Cambridge, and St. Thomas Medical School. After further training at St. Thomas and the Queen's Square Neurological Unit, he directed his career toward cardiology as a resident medical officer at the National Heart Hospital in 1945, where he devised a recording device by connecting a telephone earpiece to a string galvanometer and studied the retinal vessels in hypertension.[1] A Sherbrook Research Fellowship followed at the London Hospital from 1948 to 1950, where he was greatly influenced by the eminent John Parkinson, the successor to the heritage of James Mackenzie, and also by the keen clinician and teacher, William Evans. During this period, with help from Malcolm Towers and William Dicks, he devised a phonocardiogram with the unique capability of multiple precordial site recordings with a simultaneous carotid arterial pulse and electrocardiogram.

Following World War II, a renaissance in British cardiology sparked by Peter Sharpey-Schaffer and John McMichael using the new technique of cardiac catheterization to study cardiac physiology, and by the dynamic clinician-investigator Paul Wood, began at the Hammersmith Hospital. In 1947, the British Postgraduate Medical Federation appointed Wood to be the Director of the newly formed Institute of Cardiology at the National Heart Hospital. The purpose of the Institute was to provide short refresher courses and more extensive specialty training in cardiology for the many physicians whose careers had been interrupted by World War II. Young physicians from Great Britain, North America, Australia, New Zealand, and elsewhere flocked to London to study under the charismatic Wood whose flair for teaching and applied logic elevated the bedside cardiac examination to a new and exciting level.

In 1951, Aubrey Leatham left the London Hospital to become the first Assistant Director of the Institute of Cardiology under Paul Wood. His role was to oversee the care of patients and perform research on auscultation and other aspects of cardiac examination using graphic methods. Continuing his phonocardiographic work started at the London Hospital, Leatham pursued his original studies of heart sounds and murmurs with the technical assistance of John Norman.[2] By using more sophisticated equipment with low-frequency fil-

ters to simulate auscultation, he was able to identify the high-frequency mitral and tricuspid components of the first heart sound and the aortic and pulmonic contributions to the second heart sound. This led to a detailed analysis of the effect of inspiration and expiration on the second heart sound under various abnormal conditions, the temporal relation of systolic murmurs to the two components of the second heart sound, and eventually to the elucidation of the aortic and pulmonic ejection sounds (his terminology).[3] His studies also showed that the widely split second heart sound in atrial septal defect was fixed due to an equal inspiratory delay of the aortic and pulmonic components, provided a graphic delineation between the murmurs of aortic stenosis and mitral regurgitation, allowed valvular pulmonic stenosis with intact ventricular septum to be separated from tetralogy of Fallot, and extended observations on the mitral opening snap. By comparing the splitting interval of the second heart sound in various causes of the Eisenmenger complex, Wood and Leatham were able to indicate how the exact location of the shunt could be diagnosed from auscultation even though the murmur was altered or absent. Later, at St. George's Hospital, with the assistance of Graham Leech, he would be the first to use combined echo-phonocardiography to record further proof of his correlation of heart sounds with valvular motion as well as the tricuspid explanation of the early systolic sound in Ebstein's anomaly.[4] Because of his influential teaching, the second heart sound became known as "the key to the auscultation of the heart."

His 1958 *Lancet* article, *Auscultation of the Heart*, based on his Goulstonian Lecture to the Royal College of Physicians, provided a comprehensive update of his views on auscultation that remains a landmark and needs little updating today.[5] Most important, this article provided a new classification for murmur analysis. Prior to Leatham's work, systolic murmurs were seldom differentiated by their configuration or timing; cardiac surgery was only just beginning and there was little impetus to make such fine distinctions. Leatham's new classification of mid-systolic ejection murmurs versus pansystolic regurgitant murmurs, based on his graphic analysis, changed the way clinicians approached the bedside diagnosis of valvular disease and contributed to decision making for cardiac surgery.[4] Leatham and Wallace Brigden reported the first long-term follow-up of mitral regurgitation in 1953 and, in 1980, called attention to the excessive diagnosis of mitral valve prolapse and the exaggerated fear of sudden death in

FIG. 1   Aubrey Leatham, M.D.

this syndrome.[6, 7] A natural history study of the nonstenotic bicuspid aortic valve was published in 1978.[8] He designed an improved stethoscope, introduced in 1958, that became widely favored throughout the world. His many lectures and publications on auscultation brought his views on auscultation to the attention of a worldwide audience.[9]

In 1954, he was appointed consulting cardiologist to St. George's Hospital, London. When he arrived, there was no cardiac department and cardiology was represented by one electrocardiographic machine. He recalls that his first lecture as a new consultant received a great ovation when he left by the wrong door and entered a cupboard! Leatham organized the first cardiac department at St. George's and remained in charge until 1985. He became interested in coronary disease after visiting Montreal and Cleveland in 1956 to see the internal mammary artery implants by Arthur Vineberg, the external pericardial anastomoses by Claude Beck, and the technique of selective angiography by Mason Sones. Together with Keith Jefferson, who spent several months with Sones, he set up the first selective coronary arteriographic laboratory in Great Britain and probably Europe in 1962. His St. Cyre's Lecture in 1963 was on "The Value of Coronary Arteriography."

In 1962, following Paul Wood's death at age 54, Leatham became Dean of the Institute of Cardiology, holding that important position until 1969 while continuing his work at St. George's Hospital. As Dean, he helped Peter Harris develop a myocardial metabolism laboratory; suggested the integration of the National Heart Hospital with the Brompton Hospital; and, with Wallace Brigden, stimulated the Royal College of Physicians and the Royal College of Surgeons to establish criteria to improve outcome for cardiac surgery patients.

In addition to his lifelong interest in elevating auscultation to a science, he became deeply involved in developing new pacemaker technology, working at St. George's Hospital with his technician Geoffrey Davies and others. The first studies on the use of external pacing for cardiac standstill had just been reported by Paul Zoll in Boston; however, Zoll's pacemaker was a fixed system without a demand capability and could cause an "R on T"-induced ventricular fibrillation. At St. George's, Leatham asked Davies to develop the first demand circuit device with resultant publication in 1956.[10] He became interested in chronic pacing for complete heart block and, in collaboration with Geoffrey Davies, Michael Davies, Edgar Sowton, and Harold Siddons, a permanent endocardial pacing system was designed which was superior to the epicardial approach then in common use. Important byproducts of their work included reports on the pathology of the diseased conducting tissue by Michael Davies, the low endocardial potentials after acute myocardial infarction, heart block following acute myocardial infarction, the suppression of arrhythmias by rapid pacing, the prognosis of patients with pacemakers, and the association of systemic emboli with sinoatrial disease.[11]

In 1975, he convinced John Parker, surgeon at the National Heart Hospital, to come to St. George's where they developed one of the most productive cardiovascular medicine and surgical programs in Europe. The British Heart Foundation acknowledged his leadership by establishing the first Chair in Academic Cardiology at an undergraduate teaching hospital at St. George's. For his many contributions to clinical cardiology, the American College of Cardiology awarded him an honorary fellowship in 1986.

Aubrey Leatham is a tall, trim man, quick to laugh, who favors braces, bow ties, and blunt, honest talk. A youthful age 78, he lives in Chichester, 75 miles south of London, and continues to see patients weekly in his London Wimpole Street office overlooking his former phonocardiography laboratory at the National Heart Hospital. In his semi-retirement, he has had an opportunity to indulge his many avid interests, including grass court tennis, gardening, sailing, skiing, mountain walking (one of his favorite memories is trekking in the Himalaya Mountains with his children on royal yaks with his friend and patient, the King of Bhutan), and photography together with Judith, his wife of 42 years and accomplished in her own right as a bilingual guide and a former tennis coach. The Leathams have four children, all excellent tennis players. Following in the tradition of their grandfather, a British and U.S. racquets and court tennis champion, two children were nationally ranked, including a daughter, Charlotte, winner of junior doubles at Wimbledon. His son, Edward, is a rising cardiologist; daughter Julia is a general practitioner; and Louise is a teacher and mother of three.

Leatham has enjoyed his life to the fullest while pioneering our current understanding of auscultation; making important contributions to pacemaker technology; and advancing our knowledge of congenital, valvular, and coronary disease. He is described as an approachable man who does not turn away from a question he cannot answer but rather responds, "Why don't we look into that?" This dedication to solving problems with the best techniques he can devise has brought him high esteem as a leader in the world of cardiology.

References

1. Leatham A: The retinal vessels in hypertension. *Quart J Med* 1949:18:203–216
2. Leatham A: Phonocardiography. *Br Med Bull* 1951:4;333–342
3. Leech G, Mills P, Leatham A: The diagnosis of a non-stenotic bicuspid aortic valve. *Br Heart J* 1978;9:941–950
4. Crews TL, Pridie RB, Benham R, Leatham A: Auscultatory and phonocardiographic findings in Ebstein's anomaly. Correlation of first heart sound with ultrasonic records of tricuspid valve movement. *Br Heart J* 1972;34:681–687.
5. Leatham A: Auscultation of the heart. *Lancet* 1958;II:702–708, 757–765
6. Brigden W, Leatham A: Mitral incompetence. *Br Heart J* 1953;15:55–73
7. Leatham A, Brigden W: Mild mitral regurgitation and the mitral prolapse fiasco. *Am Heart J* 1980;99:659–664
8. Mills P, Leech G, Davies M, Leatham A: The natural history of a non-stenotic bicuspid aortic valve. *Br Heart J* 1978;9:951–957
9. Leatham A: *Auscultation of the Heart and Phonocardiography, 2nd Ed*. New York: Churchill Livingstone (1975)
10. Leatham A, Cook P, Davies JG: External electric stimulator for treatment of ventricular standstill. *Lancet* 1956;II:1185–1189
11. Fairfax AJ, Lambert CD, Leatham A: Systemic embolism in chronic sinoatrial disorder. *N Engl J Med* 1976;295:190–192

William R. Milnor: Teacher, Scientist, Administrator, Friend

WILMER W. NICHOLS, PH.D.

Department of Medicine, Division of Cardiology, University of Florida College of Medicine, Gainesville, Florida, USA

Those having torches will pass them on to others…

—Plato

Dr. William R. Milnor (Fig. 1) was born May 4, 1920, in Wilmington, Delaware. After graduating from the Tower Hill School inWilmington, he entered Princeton University in 1937 to lay the foundation for his entrance into medical school. His major was biology, and for his senior research thesis he studied the newly discovered virus that causes myomatosis. Dr. Milnor graduated from Princeton and entered Johns Hopkins Medical School in September 1941 to pursue a career in medicine.

At this time in history, Hitler was rampaging in Europe and it was inevitable that the U.S. would soon enter the war. Early Sunday morning, December 7, 1941, the news of the bombing of Pearl Harbor came over the radio while Dr. Milnor was in his room reading from *Gray's Textbook of Anatomy*. With the U.S. at war in Europe and the Pacific, most medical students were enrolled in the military service and placed on inactive duty until they completed medical school and internship. In order to accelerate the production of physicians, the medical school curriculum was compacted and completed in 3 years instead of 4, with only a few days between terms. Dr. Milnor, therefore, graduated from Johns Hopkins School of Medicine in 1944 (and married Gabriella Mahaffy on graduation day). His internship and residency at Hopkins ran through 1944 and into 1946. Many of the senior staff had been called to military service and the medical house staff was small compared to today's numbers. He did, however, find time for one small research project—the measurement of renal blood flow in hypertensive patients using a new method that had just been published. He found that renal blood flow in these patients was normal. Even though the war had ended, Dr. Milnor was called to active military service and assigned to the U.S. Army Air Force in the Pacific. This duty led to a 1-year assignment in Japan where he served as Medical Chief of a small hospital and as Flight Surgeon for various fighter and bomber wings.

After military service, Dr. Milnor returned to Johns Hopkins as a postdoctoral research fellow under the direction of a brilliant clinician and scientist, Dr. Elliot Newman, who inspired the devotion to research that has stayed with him ever since. When Dr. Newman moved to Vanderbilt in 1951, Dr. Milnor was appointed to the faculty and asked to direct the Hopkins Hospital Heart Station, the unit responsible for recording and interpreting electrocardiograms throughout the hospital. It was in this environment that his cardiovascular research career blossomed, and he published his first scientific paper with Drs. Genecin, Talbot, and Newman as co-authors. His research during this period was concerned with electrocardiography and spatial vectorcardiography. The latter, he concluded, was a valuable approach to understanding and teaching electrocardiography, but was of limited clinical value. He was particularly interested in the electrocardiographic signs of right ventricular hypertrophy, because many of his patients with valvular or congenital heart disease suffered from pulmonary hypertension.

During that same year (1951), Dr. Milnor joined Dr. E. Cowles Andrus as Associate Director of the Adult Cardiac Clinic. Cardiac surgery was developing rapidly at the time, especially at Johns Hopkins under the leadership of Drs. Alfred Blalock and Helen Taussig. The adult cardiologists were deeply involved with Dr. Blalock and his colleagues in selecting patients for surgical correction of valvular abnormalities, while Dr. Taussig and her colleagues in pediatrics were doing the same for "blue babies." Dr. Milnor's research work at this time was directed primarily at studies involving measurement of cardiac output and pulmonary blood volume, in such cases using indicator dilution methods that had been refined by Drs. Hamilton, Dow, and Wood at The Medical College of Georgia and by Dr. Milnor's group at Hopkins. This research continued until the early 1960s.

A particularly exciting opportunity came Dr. Milnor's way in 1954, when he was invited to collaborate with Dr. William Kouwenhoven in his pursuit of the idea that ventricular fibrillation could be stopped and myocardial contraction restored by an appropriate countershock, without performing a thoracotomy. This basic research, which was published in November 1954 in the *Journal of Applied Physiology*, together with subsequent investigations by Drs. Kouwenhoven, Knickerbocker, and Jude, led to the modern technique of cardiopulmonary resuscitation.

In 1962, Dr. Milnor made the very difficult decision to leave clinical practice so that he could devote full time to research and teaching. He moved from the Department of Medicine to the Department of Physiology, then directed by Dr. Philip Bard, where he had already been involved in teaching cardiovascular physiology (from 1980 to 1985, he

F‍IG. 1   William R. Milnor.

took over as Acting Director of the department after Dr. Vernon Mountcastle retired as Director).

Coincident with Dr. Milnor's move to the Department of Physiology was the commercial availability of the electromagnetic flowmeter, which could be used to measure accurately the pulsations of blood flow in the arterial system and not just the average flow per unit time. This was an extremely important step in the investigation of pulsatile pulmonary hemodynamics, which had become Dr. Milnor's major research focus. His experiments were first performed in dogs, anesthetized or conscious, and later in human subjects. An important aspect of these studies, which would continue for the next 16 years, was the measurement of vascular impedance, a concept introduced by Dr. Donald McDonald and his associates, Drs. John Womersley and Michael Taylor, in England. Results from these studies included the definition of aorta and pulmonary artery input impedance as ventricular afterload and the recognition that the smooth muscle of large conduit arteries, like that of the small resistive arterioles, is also involved in physiological responses. Another important aspect of these studies was the measurement of total ventricular external hydraulic power and the observation that a large portion of the power is associated with pulsatile blood flow. During these 16 years, several researchers including Dr. Derek Bergel from Oxford, Dr. Michael O'Rourke from Sydney, and myself from Dr. Donald McDonald's laboratory in Birmingham, Alabama, worked under Dr. Milnor's direction.

The next large series of experiments undertaken by Dr. Milnor explored the relation of membrane receptors and neurotransmitters of smooth muscle cells to vasomotor function. These experiments were made possible when Dr. Antonio Sastre, who had worked extensively with radioligand methods of measuring receptor properties, joined the Johns Hopkins Department of Physiology in 1982. This collaborative investigation would continue for the next eight years and would produce some very interesting results. The fundamental properties of a given class of receptors were found to be essentially the same wherever they were located in the circulation. For example, alpha-one receptors in the aorta, pulmonary artery, femoral vein—and for that matter in the brain—all had the same affinity for norepinephrine. The number of such receptors per cell, however, was different in each of these tissues, which probably accounts in part for the observed regional differences in response to the neurotransmitters. The same was also found to be true for vascular cholinergic and serotonergic receptors.

Dr. Milnor officially retired in 1990, but continues to write, teach in the student laboratories at Johns Hopkins, and carry on a modest research project on the mechanical properties of muscle cross-bridges, combining his interests in vasomotion and biomechanics.

During his active years in academia, Dr. Milnor and his wife traveled frequently. They were particularly fond of England, where they had many friends. Occasionally, work and travel could be happily mixed, as in a 1968 sabbatical at St. Catherine's College, Oxford, and an exchange professorship at Guy's Hospital Medical School in London in 1974. During these visits to England, writing of a book on hemodynamics was begun and the first edition appeared in print in early 1980. For part of each summer, the Milnor family would escape to their camp called "Talisman" on Great Pond in Belgrade Lakes, Maine, to enjoy the out-of-doors life—sailing, fishing, tennis, and so on.

Dr. Milnor has truly been one of the pioneers in cardiovascular research. His major contributions have been in the area of hemodynamics, especially pulsatile hemodynamics of the pulmonary circulation. His expertise in these areas becomes apparent upon reading his textbooks on hemodynamics and cardiovascular physiology.

Dr. Milnor's sincere devotion to the medical students and his excellence in teaching them basic cardiovascular physiology has earned him praise from both faculty and students. Those of us who were fortunate enough to work under his guidance have been influenced tremendously by his stimulating ideas and insights into basic research and his dedication to medical teaching.

Charles Fisch

SUZANNE B. KNOEBEL, M.D.

Department of Medicine, Krannert Institute of Cardiology, Indianapolis, Indiana, USA

After 30 years as Director of the Krannert Institute of Cardiology and the Division of Cardiology at Indiana University School of Medicine, Charles Fisch has turned over his administrative duties. He will continue to be active in the School of Medicine as a Distinguished Professor, in divisional affairs as a teacher extraordinary of electrocardiography, and a role model for the complete academic cardiologist. He will continue to direct the heart station at the Indiana University Hospital, to stimulate medical students, housestaff, fellows, and faculty to ask questions about mechanisms and therapy of cardiac arrhythmias and the nuances of electrocardiographic interpretation, and, most important, he will continue his open door policy for those who "just want to toss some ideas around."

Dr. Fisch was born May 11, 1921, and although his birthplace was Zolkiew City, Poland, he received his elementary education in Indiana, his family having established its permanent residence in Indianapolis. He returned to Europe to complete his high school education where, he says, he majored in skiing although he remembers his Latin teacher with some vividness.

Dr. Fisch entered Indiana University as a freshman in the fall of 1939. He received an A.B. degree in 1942 and an M.D. in 1944 from that university. During these war years, medical education was accelerated to assure that enough physicians would be available to provide for the needs of wounded servicemen. Following graduation, he served an internship at St. Vincent Hospital in Indianapolis. Dr. Fisch became Captain Fisch in 1946, assigned to the Veterans Administration Hospital in Indianapolis, and it was here that his interest in cardiology and, in particular, electrocardiography, was stimulated. Following discharge from the Army he completed a residency in internal medicine at the Veterans Administration Hospital followed by a fellowship in cardiology at the Marion County General Hospital.

Upon completion of his cardiology training in 1953, Dr. Fisch entered the private practice of cardiology; however, he was not satisfied. He missed teaching; both the intellectual stimulation of the teaching and research environment, and the opportunity to ask questions and seek answers. It did not take him long to decide that his heart was in academia. He closed his office and became a full-time faculty member in 1955.

Because of Dr. Fisch's enthusiasm, patience, and diagnostic skills, cardiology clinics at the Medical Center hospitals expanded, teaching rounds "with Fisch" became the place to be and his reputation grew. Mr. and Mrs. Herman C. Krannert, prominent philanthropists with an interest in heart disease, pleased with the progress they were seeing in some of the early programs they had funded, began to plan for a heart institute dedicated to research into the causes and treatment of cardiovascular diseases. Dr. Fisch was their choice for its leadership. They established a laboratory for him, and studies on the effect of potassium on conduction and cardiac repolarization began to be reported from the Krannert Heart Research Institute, later to be renamed the Krannert Institute of Cardiology.

It was approximately at this same time that Dr. John B. Hickam arrived at Indiana University to serve as Chairman of the Department of Medicine. He began hearing about Dr. Fisch from students and housestaff. Wanting to see this "paragon" in action, Dr. Hickam paid Charles a visit at the General Hospital and recruited him on the spot, so the story goes, as Chief of Cardiology. Even in the midst of the rapid growth of both the School and the Department of Medicine that occurred in the 1960s, it was not long before positions on the cardiology rotations were coveted by students and housestaff alike. Dr. Fisch's classes on electrocardiography were faithfully attended and all cardiology clinics at the University Hospital became teaching clinics. Fellows began applying to work with him in the laboratory. Charles Fisch began to be known around the world as a teacher and electrocardiologist with a special interest in arrhythmias and the effect of potassium on the heart.

The Krannert Institute of Cardiology grew parallel with the advances in cardiovascular medicine. From a faculty of 3 in 1963, it currently has approximately 40 faculty members and 20 to 25 fellows and graduate scientists. The success of the Krannert Institute in the performance of medical research and its application in the clinic is evidence of the effectiveness of Dr. Fisch as a leader and administrator. Over 150 fellows in cardiology have trained at the Krannert Institute, and students from 30 states and 9 countries have worked in the Institute's laboratories. Many of Dr. Fisch's former students are themselves teachers now, providing academic leadership at a number of prominent institutions throughout the United States, Europe, and the Orient. His style has been to ask questions intended to guide and stimulate rather than criticize, to correct without discouraging, and to praise excellence. His philosophy has been simple-make it possible to achieve.

FIG. 1 Charles Fisch, M.D., Director of Krannert Institute of Cardiology at Indiana University. (Photograph from Archives of Indiana University.)

Dr. Fisch's own achievements have been many. He served as President of the American College of Cardiology for two terms (1975–1977) and received its Distinguished Fellow Award in 1978. He was awarded the Distinguished Alumni Award by Indiana University School of Medicine in 1979. The American Heart Association honored him by asking him to deliver the Lewis A. Conner Memorial Lecture in 1980, and with its prestigious James B. Herrick Award in 1983. The State of Indiana has made him a Sagamore of the Wabash, its highest award for service to the State. He received an Honorary Doctor of Medicine Degree from the University of Utrecht, The Netherlands, in 1984. He is listed in *Who's Who in America and the World* and has authored more than 250 scientific publications. In 1990, his book *The Electrocardiography of Arrhythmias* received enthusiastic reviews.

What of the man behind the achievements? Most of those who know him well would say, "He is reserved and purposeful." He sees his primary mission to be that of furthering traditional academic goals of excellence in teaching, research and patient care. Knowing where he wants to go, he plans carefully as to how to get there. His philosophy has always been to recruit persons "smarter than he and give them a stable environment and resources to work with." Above all, he is modest and still "fascinated by the heart."

Dr. Fisch's career has been remarkable. As a gifted teacher, a caring physician, scholarly researcher and author, visionary administrator, and eminent leader of our professional associations, he has established a distinguished record of extraordinary contributions to the State of Indiana, Indiana University, and to our profession throughout the world. From 1939, when he began his undergraduate studies at Indiana University, to his graduation from the School of Medicine in 1944, through his military service, residency, and fellowship, up to the present, Dr. Charles Fisch has been a tireless student, always seeking answers and methods to search out those answers. This one trait probably is the essence of the man.

Peter C. Gazes: Physician, Teacher, Scholar

MICHAEL R. ZILE, M.D.

Division of Cardiology, Department of Medicine, the Gazes Cardiac Research Institute, the Medical University of South Carolina and Ralph H. Johnson Veterans Affairs Medical Center, Charleston, South Carolina, USA

No one in South Carolina, perhaps no one in the Southeast, has done more to promote the advancement of cardiac care, to educate those who provide this care, and to open the frontier of investigation into cardiac disease than Peter C. Gazes. For more than forty years, Dr. Gazes has led the field of cardiology at the Medical University of South Carolina. We, who are his students, his colleagues, and his patients gratefully salute him for his leadership, boundless enthusiasm, and his friendship.

Peter C. Gazes, M.D. (Fig. 1), was born in rural Matthews, South Carolina, in 1921. He received his primary and secondary education in Charleston and earned his Bachelor of Science degree at the College of Charleston. He was the first honor graduate at the Medical University of South Carolina in 1944. After a year in the Navy as a Lieutenant JG, he completed a residency in internal medicine and a fellowship in cardiology at the Philadelphia General Hospital. He returned to the Medical University of South Carolina, was rapidly promoted from Assistant to Associate to full Professor, and then for eighteen years was the Director of the Division of Adult Cardiology in the Department of Medicine at the Medical University of South Carolina. Under his leadership, cardiology at the Medical University grew to become recognized and respected both for its excellence in clinical care and its innovation in cardiovascular research. During this period of time, he trained more than 50 cardiologists, many of whom currently practice in South Carolina, Charleston, and the Medical University. He taught countless medical students, residents, nurses, and attending physicians here at the Medical University. He continues to maintain an active role in these educational endeavors. In 1982, he was named Distinguished University Professor and Assistant Dean for Alumni Affairs. Today, while he insists he is reducing the pace of his practice, he continues to be sought out for his superb clinical care and singular teaching through didactic lectures, small group seminars, and his many publications. He continues to provide state and national education as Program Director for a three-day cardiology seminar sponsored by the American College of Cardiology, which this year held its Twenty-Fifth Annual Update: Cardiology for the Primary Physician, Managing the Cardiovascular Patient.

Dr. Peter C. Gazes has been recognized for his seminal skills in teaching, clinical care, research, and leadership through the many awards and citations he has received over the years. He is an active member of a number of local, state, and national organizations. He has been a member of a number of editorial boards for prestigious scientific publications. His accomplishments include:

National Heart, Lung and Blood Advisory Council membership

The Association of University Cardiologists

Executive Committee of Council on Clinical Cardiology of the American Heart Association

American College of Cardiology, Governor of South Carolina

South Carolina Heart Association, President

Alpha Omega Alpha, Medical University of South Carolina

Excellence in Teaching, multiple Golden Apple Awards

National Gifted Teacher Award, American College of Cardiology

MUSC Health Sciences Foundation, Teaching Excellence Award (Educator-Mentor)

Ellis Island Medal of Honor Award

Distinguished Alumni Award, College of Charleston

Distinguished Faculty Service Award, MUSC

Honorary Doctorate Degree from The College of Charleston and The Citadel

The Order of the Palmetto (Highest State of South Carolina Honor)

The Order of the Silver Crescent (State of South Carolina Honor)

Dr. Gazes' scientific career has spanned more than 40 years. His first publication appeared in 1945[1] and his most recent publication in 2001.[2] He has authored more than 300 full-length articles, abstracts, book chapters, and books. Perhaps the book that has had the largest educational input is *Clinical Cardiology*.[3–6] Its first three editions focused on "A Bedside Approach;"[3–5] his most recent edition, "A Cost Effective Approach,"[6] has focused on the changing realities in the practice of medicine. His research efforts have focused on the most important disease process in cardiology, that of ischemic heart disease, its causes, its consequences, methods to assess risk, methods of active prevention, detection, diagnosis, and prognosis.[7] He has been an active contributor to both the Charleston Heart Study and the Coronary Drug Project. These nationally funded studies examined risk factors for the development of cardiac disease, the effects of race on these

FIG. 1   Peter C. Gazes, M.D. A portrait similar to this picture of Peter C. Gazes, M.D., painted by Ray Goodbred, hangs in the lobby of the Gazes Cardiac Research Building at the Medical University of South Carolina.

risk factors, and the effect of strategies to treat and prevent cardiac disease that are consequent to these risk factors. Publications that have resulted from this work have been published in the most prestigious cardiac and general medical journals.[8–10] In addition to these studies, he was an active contributor to a number of randomized clinical trials including the Beta Blocker Heart Attack Trial Research Group (BHAT).

Dr. Gazes has been a fervent advocate for cardiac prevention, including nutrition, exercise, and a balance between work and relaxation. He is a man who practices what he preaches. At age 80 he chooses a balance between working 3 to 4 days a week and playing golf 2 to 3 times per week. While his long game has become shorter with age, it is more accurate and his short game is legend. He has rightfully earned his nickname as "Pete the Putter." Always the teacher, he frequently plays with, instructs, and encourages both his grandchildren and the cardiology fellows in lessons of life and the fairway. He carries an aspirin in his pocket. He exercises regularly and never strays from a heart healthy diet.

I first met Dr. Gazes when I joined the Medical University faculty as an associate professor. He welcomed me into the division, supported my efforts, and always provided a source of insightful advice regarding patient care. I often discuss my most difficult cases with him. He always has new insight, allowing me to add to the quality of the care of my patients. He remains unquenchably curious, frequently asking me what I have learned and what I can teach him about the research that my collaborators and I in the Gazes Cardiac Research Institute have performed (examination of cardiovascular pathophysiology and molecular and genetic control of disease based on changes in cardiovascular pathophysiology): How could he use this new knowledge to improve the care of his patients?

His portrait hangs in the lobby of the building and the research institute that bears his name. While his contributions will be remembered and have been acknowledged in this honor, his real legacy will live on in the men and women whom he has educated, the patients whose health he has improved, and in the practice of cardiology he helped to advance.

References

1. Pratt-Thomas HR, Kelley WH, Gazes PC: Fulminating meningococcemia (The Waterhouse-Friderichsen syndrome). *Int Med Digest* 1945;47:92–96
2. Carabello BA, Gazes PC (Eds.): *Cardiology Pearls.* Philadelphia: Hanley and Belfus, 2001
3. Gazes PC (Ed.): *Clinical Cardiology: A Bedside Approach.* Chicago: Year Book Medical Publishers, 1975
4. Gazes PC (Ed.): *Clinical Cardiology: A Bedside Approach,* 2nd Edition. Chicago: Year Book Medical Publishers, 1983
5. Gazes PC (Ed.): *Clinical Cardiology: A Bedside Approach,* 3rd Edition. Philadelphia: Lea and Febiger, 1990
6. Gazes PC (Ed.): *Clinical Cardiology: A Cost Effective Approach,* 4th Edition. New York: Chapman and Hall, 1997 (sold to Lippincott, 1998)
7. Gazes PC, Mobley EM Jr, Faris HM, Duncan RC, Humpries GB: Preinfarction (unstable) angina—a prospective study—ten year follow-up. *Circulation* 1973;48:331–337
8. Keil JE, Sutherland SE, Knapp RG, Lack DT, Gazes PC, Tyroler HA: Mortality rates and risk factors for coronary disease in black as compared to white men and women. *N Engl J Med* 1993;329: 73–78
9. Sutherland SE, Gazes PC, Keil JE, Gilbert GE, Knapp RB: Electrocardiographic abnormalities and 30 year mortality among white and black men of the Charleston Heart Study. *Circulation* 1993;88: 2685–2692
10. Keil JE, Sutherland SE, Hames CG, Lackland DT, Gazes PC, Knapp RG, Tyroler HA: Coronary disease mortality and risk factors in black and white men. Results from the combined Charleston, South Carolina, and Evans County, Georgia, heart studies. *Arch Intern Med* 1995;155:1521–1527

Reginald E. B. Hudson

E. G. J. OLSEN, M.D., F.R.C. PATH., F.A.C.C.

National Heart Hospital, London, England

Until his retirement in 1971, Dr. Reginald E. B. Hudson was Professor and Director of Pathology at the Institute of Cardiology (now the Cardiothoracic Institute) and National Heart Hospital. He is one of the outstanding pioneers of modern cardiac pathology and through his ability has been instrumental in bringing this speciality to the forefront of the field. He was uniquely qualified to undertake this task so successfully.

Reginald Hudson was born in Chatham in Kent, England, and in 1922, after completing his elementary school education at the age of 11, won a scholarship to Sir Joseph Williamson's Mathematic School in Rochester, Kent where he took first place in all terminal examinations. He matriculated with honors in the University of London in 1925 at the early age of 15. Financial restraints prevented him from pursuing his academic career and so he became an apprentice in pharmacy. His tenacity, dedication, and quest for academic achievement had become established at this early stage of his life, and during his apprenticeship he attended night school and, by unstinting private study, gained an inter B.Sc. degree of the University of London in 1930. He subsequently worked as an assistant in pharmacology, and at the age of 22 years, won the Jacob Bell Scholarship, competing with some 60 candidates from the entire United Kingdom for this coveted award. This enabled Dr. Hudson to enter the School of Pharmacology at the University of London, where he gained the Bachelor of Pharmacology degree and the Diploma of Pharmaceutical Chemistry in 1935 as well as winning silver medals in pharmacy and chemistry.

Having gained the highest honors pharmacology could offer, Reginald Hudson did not rest on his laurels but went on to win an entrance scholarship to St. Mary's Medical School in London and subsequently qualified as MB BS in 1940, with several prizes to his credit. On qualifying, the world-renowned Sir Alexander Fleming, recognizing his outstanding potential, offered him a research post in the Inoculation Department in what is now the Wright-Fleming Institute. He accepted the post and concentrated his researches on the production of tetanus and diphtheria toxoids. During this period he also gained training in bacteriology.

In 1941, he joined the Royal Army Medical Corps, attaining the rank of Major, and until demobilization in 1946 gained experience in all branches of pathology including morbid anatomy and hematology in the temperate as well as subtropical regions (Iraq and Egypt) of the world.

In 1946, he entered the Department of Pathology at St. Mary's Hospital in the capacity of an Ex-Service Registrar for six months. In 1947, he became the first holder of the Boot Research Fellowship in the Wright-Fleming Institute and during this year he also gained his Doctorate of Medicine by thesis on the manufacture of tentanus toxoid and by examination. Determined to gain clinical experience, he relinquished the Boot Fellowship after one year and joined Professor Pickering's Medical Unit. During this time he visited the National Heart Hospital where the eminent cardiologist, Paul Wood, recognizing his outstanding ability, asked him to apply for the post of pathologist to that hospital, a post for which he was uniquely qualified, having experience in pharmacology, bacteriology, hematology, and morbid anatomy as well as clinical experience. Establishing a new department of pathology was too great a challenge for Dr. Hudson to resist and so he applied for the job and was duly appointed. He began at once to design new laboratories with facilities for all branches of pathology, his planning and foresight resulting in laboratories that have remained up to date. While building was in progress he continued his clinical studies, and when the laboratories opened in July 1949 he became a full-time pathologist at the Institute of Cardiology, National Heart Hospital. In 1951 he gained consultant status. In 1959 he became a Fellow of the Pharmaceutical Society and in the same year received recognition as a teacher of the University of London. In 1963, the Fellowship of the Royal College of Pathologists followed and the University of London conferred the title of Professor of Pathology in 1966.

On commencing his work at the National Heart Hospital he was assisted by one senior technician and much of the work load had to be shouldered by himself. Under his guidance and vision, the various disciplines of pathology grew progressively so that within a relatively short period the department could count among its staff a consultant clinical pathologist, a registrar, a senior house officer, 11 technical staff, a medical photographer, 2 laboratory assistants, a mortuary attendant, and 2 secretaries, covering all disciplines in pathology. He developed a stereographic photographic technique and established a museum that ranks foremost in the world in content and layout. With the advent of cardiac surgery, the Department of Hematology was greatly expanded and consultant hematologist was appointed.

F<small>IG</small>. 1 Photograph of Dr. Reginald E.B. Hudson by B.W. Richards.

With his outstanding ability and broad-based experience he was a constant inspiration and a highly respected colleague to all members of staff at the Institute and the Hospital. His studies and contributions to the medical literature are immense and include many classic papers on congenital and acquired heart diseases. Special mention must be made of his studies on the conduction system and human aortic valve homograft. He did not only confine himself to morbid anatomy and histopathology but, in addition, published work on cholesterol and arterial diseases and participated in a Medical Research Council trial on long-term anticoagulation. He has also published on the stereographic photography technique and a new museum of cardiac pathology, which established guidelines for the planning of modern museums. His monograph, *Cardiovascular Pathology*, Volumes 1 and 2, published in 1965 and Volume 3, published in 1970, totals some 3300 pages and contains the most comprehensive contribution to that topic ever published. It is difficult to conceive that such detailed information could flow from the pen of one person. It is an outstanding textbook and it is doubtful whether it will ever be equaled.

From the beginning, his work attracted national and international acclaim and invitations soon flooded in for him to attend congresses and to lecture at various centers in Britain and abroad, including Holland, Italy, the United States, and Canada. He also was chosen to deliver many titled lectures including the St. Cyres Lecture (1959), the Dr. Sir Lakshmanaswami Mudaliar Lecture in Madras, India (1966), the Emmet Bay Lecture at Chicago University (1971), the Graugnard Lecture, Tulane Medical School, New Orleans (1971), the Edgar Mannheimer Memorial Lecture, Dublin, Ireland (1971), and the International Lecture of the American Heart Association in Dallas (1972).

He was a member of many learned societies and he became an Honorary Fellow of the Council on Clinical Cardiology of the American Heart Association in 1972.

To complete the profile of this eminent pathologist, his teaching deserves special mention. From his undergraduate teaching at St. Mary's Hospital Medical School to his postgraduate teaching at the Institute of Cardiology, National Heart Hospital and in various schools at home and abroad, his close association with Emory University and Grady Memorial Hospital in Atlanta, which began in 1970 and continued until 1976, reflects his outstanding ability and popularity as a teacher. His clear thinking and expert, simple delivery, sprinkled with a dry humor, made his lectures, even when the most complex and, perhaps, at times dull subjects were discussed, a joy to hear. His teaching has inspired many a young medical person throughout the world.

He retired in 1971 and in the same year the Emeritus status was conferred on him. His many return visits to Atlanta testify to the fact that, though retired, he has continued to remain in harness. In 1976, Emory University honored him with the well-deserved honorary Doctorate of Science. He has continued to write and contribute chapters to a variety of textbooks.

What of the man? His formative years were fraught with many difficulties which he overcame by dedicated application to work. These early years have no doubt been instrumental in forming his character, which is one that we all know and love. His tolerance, forebearance, and understanding of human nature has made him into the man that we all remember. His marvelous sense of humor, which he cannot surpress even on the most official occasions, bubbles over privately so that it is always a pleasure to be in his company. In his teaching and instruction of young doctors he showed great patience and had the ability to nurture talent when he saw it.

He married his wife, Dorothy, in 1939 and both of them are enjoying life in a beautiful house right on the edge of the sea on the south coast of England. Their two children, a son and a daughter, are now grown, and his daughter has taken up the practice of medicine. May Reginald and Dorothy Hudson enjoy many, many years of a happy retirement.

Christiaan Neethling Barnard

DAVID K.C. COOPER, M.D., PH.D., FRCS

Transplantation Biology Research Center, Massachusetts General Hospital/Harvard Medical School, Boston, Massachusetts, USA

"Simply the most unforgettable character
of the second generation of cardiac surgeons."
—Robert Frater[1]

Christiaan (Chris) Barnard (Fig. 1) literally gained overnight fame on the night of December 2 to 3, 1967, when he led the team that performed the first human-to-human heart transplant.[2] The dramatic nature of this surgical procedure, which took the world by surprise, and his youthful good looks and charismatic personality ensured not only his place in medical history but worldwide public recognition. Indeed, it is unlikely that any physician or surgeon before or since has been so widely recognized by the man in the street.

Today, heart transplantation is commonplace, but the confidence and courage it took to undertake the first heart transplant should not be underestimated. Although Barnard had practiced the Stanford (Lower/Shumway) surgical technique in dogs and was aware of this group's experimental studies, he was entering a largely unknown world. The first patient, Louis Washkansky, did well for a couple of weeks but then, probably due to over-immunosuppression, developed pneumonia of which he died on Day 18 post transplant. Barnard almost immediately went ahead with a second transplant. The patient, Philip Blaiberg, was the first heart transplant patient to leave hospital and lead an active life before he developed the hitherto unknown complication of graft atherosclerosis (chronic rejection), of which he died after 19 months. The relative success of this second patient, when most patients undergoing this procedure at other centers were dying at an early stage, did much to sustain some optimism that heart transplantation would eventually become a reliable therapeutic option for patients with end-stage cardiac failure.

The initial results from Barnard's group were quite remarkable, due in part to his innate ability to make the correct clinical decisions and, in part, to the outstanding team of physicians supporting him. Two of his first four patients survived for more than a year, and the fifth and sixth patients survived for nearly 13 and 24 years, respectively.

Chris Barnard was born in 1922 in Beaufort West, a small town about a six-hour drive inland from Cape Town. As a pastor to the mixed-race population of the town, Barnard's father was poor and could provide his four sons with no luxuries. After attending the local school, Barnard won a place at the University of Cape Town to study medicine, where he qualified in the middle of his class. He initially went into family practice in a small rural community near Cape Town, but, after 18 months, personal difficulties with his partner led him to return to the city. After some time spent at the city's infectious disease hospital, during which time he made a special study of the treatment of patients with tuberculous meningitis, he was accepted as a registrar (resident) at Groote Schuur Hospital. While training in general surgery, he found time to carry out some highly ingenious research on the etiology of congenital intestinal atresia in neonates.

In 1956, the opportunity arose for him to take up a scholarship at the University of Minnesota to work under the tutelage of two of the great pioneers of heart surgery, Richard Varco and C. Walton Lillehei. Barnard worked immensely hard, learning the fundamentals of open heart surgery and developing an aortic valve prosthesis in the laboratory.

On his return to Cape Town, the U.S. Government generously provided him with a heart-lung machine, which he put to good use. He rapidly developed one of the best heart surgery units in the world, despite the disadvantage of his geographic isolation from any other group performing this type of work. In particular, he had outstanding results for the correction of congenital cardiac defects in children and for valve surgery. In the operating room he proved to be somewhat temperamental, but invariably obtained the surgical result he desired.

By 1965, even though the results of kidney transplantation were generally poor, his thoughts turned to transplanting the heart. During 1967, he spent three months in the USA, where he learned the fundamentals of immunosuppressive therapy from transplant pioneers David Hume and Thomas Starzl. On his return to Cape Town, he performed one kidney transplant in a patient who was destined to survive for more than 20 years. With this minimal experience, he transferred his attention to heart transplantation.

After performing only 10 orthotopic heart transplants between 1967 and 1973, he decided to give up this approach after being faced by a donor heart that did not function after implantation. He reasoned that, if the donor heart were anastomosed as an accessory heart, then, if the donor heart failed, the native heart might provide support until donor heart function recovered. With this aim, he and his colleague, Jacques Losman, developed a technique for heterotopic heart transplantation, where the donor heart was placed in the right

FIG. 1   Christiaan Barnard at the time of his retirement in 1983.

side of the chest and provided support for both the native right and left ventricles.[3]

Forty-nine consecutive heterotopic heart transplants were performed in Cape Town between 1975 and 1984, with approximate 1- and 5-year survivals of 50 and 20%, respectively. Several of these patients, however, lived for more than 10 years. Barnard's group reported cases in which the native heart had maintained life during a severe rejection episode until recovery or until a second donor heart could be obtained. One notable patient with dilated cardiomyopathy recovered sufficient native heart function to allow excision of the accessory donor heart. In desperate attempts to maintain life, Barnard used the heterotopic technique to transplant chimpanzee and baboon hearts into patients who could not be weaned from cardiopulmonary bypass after routine cardiac surgery. With the introduction of cyclosporine and the accompanying greatly reduced incidence of severe life-threatening rejection, Barnard's group resumed orthotopic heart transplantation.

Throughout these years, Barnard ran an active surgical research laboratory. A system of storage of the heart by hypothermic perfusion was developed, largely by biochemist Winston Wicomb, and was used clinically in a number of patients, the earliest in 1981.[4] A period of hypothermic perfusion of up to 13 h was demonstrated to be successful and allowed transportation of hearts from other cities in South Africa, which had hitherto been impossible. This work remains unique in clinical heart transplantation practice and was an ambitious step at that time. Seminal experimental and

clinical studies were made on the effects of brain death, which it was found could be damaging to the donor heart, both structurally and functionally.[5] Rapid declines in the plasma levels of certain hormones, particularly triiodothyronine, were recorded after brain death, leading to the concept of hormonal replacement therapy in potential donors. These studies, led largely by Dimitri Novitzky, remain classics. Experimental studies were also performed on immunosuppressive agents and on xenotransplantation.

During the 1970s, Barnard developed an interest in writing for the public. He wrote or edited several books on health matters, but also authored or coauthored several novels, which were largely based on his experience in medicine.[1] Although his name probably helped in getting them published, they are as good as many that are on the market. For many years, he also contributed a weekly newspaper column to the *Cape Times*, which was invariably readable and stimulating. Earlier, he had penned his autobiography, *One Life*, which sold worldwide. He generously donated his royalties to the Chris Barnard Fund, which has since supported research into heart disease and organ transplantation in Cape Town. Twenty years later, he traced his subsequent life in *The Second Life*.

In late 1983, at the age of 61, Barnard took early retirement from his post at the University of Cape Town. His interest in clinical surgery had diminished, in part due to painful rheumatoid arthritis which made it difficult for him to operate to his satisfaction. In his retirement, he spent time as a research advisor to the Clinique la Prairie in Switzerland, where the controversial "rejuvenation therapy" was practiced. He became embroiled in publicity over a skin cream, Glycel, that harmed his reputation. He advised on the development of a successful new heart transplantation program in Oklahoma City. In 1988, he returned to live in South Africa, where he has been occupying himself with developing a small game reserve and with lecturing and writing for the public.

References

1. Cooper DKC: *Chris Barnard—By Those Who Know Him*, pp. 1–362. Cape Town, Vlaeberg, 1992

2. Barnard CN: A human cardiac transplant: An interim report of a successful operation performed at Groote Schuur Hospital, Cape Town. *S Afr Med J* 1967;47:1271–1274

3. Barnard CN, Losman JG: Left ventricular bypass. *S Afr Med J* 1975;49:303–312

4. Cooper DKC, Wicomb WN, Barnard CN: Storage of the donor heart by a portable hypothermic perfusion system: Experimental development and clinical experience. *J Heart Transplant* 1983;2:104–110

5. Novitzky D, Wicomb WN, Cooper DKC, Rose AG, Fraser RC, Barnard CN: Electrocardiographic, hemodynamic and endocrine changes occurring during experimental brain death in the Chacma baboon. *J Heart Transplant* 1984;4:63–69

Dr. Barnard died in 2001, after this profile was written.

Robert S. Fraser

ROBERT E. BEAMISH, M.D.

Institute of Cardiovascular Sciences, University of Manitoba, Winnipeg, Manitoba, Canada

It is not unusual that unexpected creativity and accomplishment arise in unexpected places. When they do, it is always due to extraordinary individuals or small groups of them. This happened in Edmonton, Alberta, following World War II, when Robert Fraser, a youthful cardiologist, and John Callaghan, recently trained in cardiac surgery in Toronto, London (England), and San Francisco, found themselves at the University of Alberta. The university was recovering from the effects of the Great Depression and the restrictions imposed by the recent war. However, like some other Canadian institutions, it was poised to progress to a world-class medical center. The important contributions of Callaghan have been documented elsewhere.[1] Those of Fraser (Fig. 1) are briefly cited here—it is another story of the evolution of today's sophisticated cardiology from its primitive beginnings.

Born in Nelson, British Columbia, in 1922, Fraser graduated with an M.D. degree from the University of Alberta in 1946. As an aid in choosing a career, he spent a year in family practice, an experience that prompted him to specialize. On the advice of Dean John Scott, he elected to study biochemistry as a prelude to internal medicine. Awarded a National Research Council fellowship, he spent 1949 to 1950 conducting a clinical study of ergothionine on normal subjects and patients. This was followed by 3 years in the training program at the University of Minnesota, which determined his future career. While the distinguished Professor Cecil J. Watson offered an opportunity to participate in his important studies of the porphyrins, it was the newly opened Variety Heart Hospital that lured the young physician into the fledgling field of cardiology.

With the stimulating mentors Dr. Richard Ebert and Dr. Carleton Chapman, Fraser enjoyed an exciting entrée to cardiovascular research, and his interest in cardiac surgery was aroused by the nearby surgical work of Dr. John Lewis, Dr. Walton Lillihei, Dr. Richard Varcoe, and others who were working on ways to operate within the heart: cross circulation, hypothermia, and the pump oxygenator. It was a heady time and set the course for his professional future.

Another event further determined his destiny. Back in Edmonton on vacation in 1952, he encountered Dean John Scott outside the medical buildings. Scott had been persuaded (by Dr. Joseph Dvorkin, recently returned from working with Dr. Arthur Master in New York), that it was necessary to attract someone to start invasive studies in Edmonton. He proposed that the University of Alberta nominate Fraser for a Markle Scholarship and that Fraser return to Edmonton and establish the necessary laboratory. The "Markle" provided an income of $6,000.00 per year for 5 years with the expectation that the recipient university have plans for a continuing full-time appointment. After interviews in New York and at the Seignery Club at Montebello, the scholarship was granted. At that time, cardiac catheterization was not part of Fraser's activities, so he arranged to participate in a catheterization team in Minneapolis; he later found that most of the essential skills were learned on the job.

Returning to Edmonton in 1953, Fraser found that the specialty of internal medicine recognized only two subspecialities: dermatology and neurology. After all, invasive studies using cardiac catheterization were less than 10 years old. Added to the original objectives of Cournand, which were to measure intracardiac pressures and cardiac output, was the need to identify left-to-right shunts by measuring oxygen saturation and right-to-left shunts by intracardiac injection of radio-opaque material or by intracardiac dye curves. Resolutely, Fraser set about securing the space, equipment, assistants, and cooperative colleagues to comprise an effective diagnostic laboratory and eventually a fully pledged Division of Cardiology in the Department of Medicine of the University of Alberta. He was the pivotal figure in bringing the "golden age of cardiology" to Alberta. He has documented the trials and triumphs of these years in an important and delightful book, *Cardiology at the University of Alberta, 1922–1969.*[2]

Professional skill, commitment, and integrity brought their rewards. By 1958, nearly 250 catheterizations in children and adults had been performed and a pediatric cardiac clinic had been established. Academic promotions progressed to a full professorship awarded in 1964. Joined by cardiac surgeons John Callaghan (1956), Cecil Couves (1957), and Larry Sterns (1966), the group eventually reached approximately 1,000 open heart surgeries by June 1967. A rather unusual feature of the group was the informal but very close liaison, cooperation, and friendship of surgeons, cardiologists, anesthetists, and nurses—an ingredient of their remarkable success.

Despite heavy obligations in patient care, research, and teaching, Fraser became an expert in computer applications to data storage and to interpretation of electrocardiograms. He

FIG. 1   Robert S. Fraser, M.D.

participated in several conferences in the United States and Canada, particularly with Dr. Cesar Caceres in Washington, D.C., and Dr. Ralph Smith at the Mayo clinic. By 1976, a computer system for ECG interpretation was operational at the University Hospital. Along the way he acquired MSc, FRCP(C), FACP, and FACC.

In the United States, the need to involve citizens and governments in the provision of money for heart research was recognized in 1947 when the American Heart Association became a voluntary health agency. Canada followed in 1956, when a meeting of leading cardiologists with the Minister of Health, the Honorable Paul Martin, was held in Ottawa. Representing Dean Scott, Fraser attended the meeting at which it was decided to form the National Heart Foundation—now the Heart and Stroke Foundation of Canada. On reporting back to Dean Scott, Fraser was asked to organize an Alberta Heart Foundation and, because of default by a lay director, Fraser found himself the first president of the new organization. He remained a director for 22 years; in recognition of his contribution, the offices of the Foundation have been named "Fraser Centre."

The Canadian Heart Association was founded in Winnipeg in 1947 with Dr. John Keith of Toronto as Secretary-Treasurer. Ten years later he resigned in order to assume similar responsibilities with the International Society of Cardiology. Fraser was appointed to replace him. This led to a long and fruitful role in an organization that later became the Canadian Cardiovascular Society. After four years as Secretary-Treasurer, he proceeded through offices to become the 11th president, serving from 1965 to 1966. During his years on the Council, significant decisions were made that have guided the Society ever since. Among these were the decision to hold the annual meeting along with the National Heart Foundation rather than with the Canadian Medical Association or the Royal College of Physicians and Surgeons of Canada, and also to press for recognition of cardiology by the RCP&S as a specialty, which was achieved in 1970. Through these activities, he became well known and respected across Canada and was instrumental in forging links with the Interamerican Society of Cardiology. These were times of much different expectations, and he recalls being so economically driven that he told the guest lecturer from England that the two of them would be sharing a hotel room during the annual meeting in Halifax in 1958!

Aldous Huxley wrote "There is no substitute for talent"— which is true. Fraser's success in developing cardiology led to his appointment as Professor and Head, Department of Medicine, a position he held from 1969 to 1974. Abilities honed in cardiology stood him in good stead as his responsibilities and influence spread. His successful achievements are recorded in a book of 176 pages.[3] Among its charms is the correlation of departmental activities with what was happening in the wider world. Not surprisingly, his academic career ended as Associate Dean, followed by Acting Dean from 1983 to 1984.

His principal hobby is genealogy, which he has pursued diligently in Scotland, Utah, and Canada. He likens it to internal medicine where one works from soft and hard evidence, dealing with possibilities and probabilities. Having accumulated over 2,000 names, he has completed a draft of the Frasers. One of the frustrations has been to find that a third great grandfather, married in 1786, appears never to have been born. If he is like his father, now over 100 years of age, Fraser will have time to complete the search.

Cardiology has been successful in attracting its share of great men, combining the talents of physicians, scientists, teachers, diplomats, and humanists. It is fitting that Robert Stewart Fraser found himself in their midst.

References

1. Callaghan JC: *Thirty Years of Open Heart Surgery at the University of Alberta Hospital*. University of Alberta Hospitals, Edmonton, 1986
2. Fraser RS: *Cardiology at the University of Alberta 1922–1969*. Edmonton: University of Alberta Printing Services, 1992
3. Fraser RS: *University of Alberta, Department of Medicine, a Personal View, 1969–1974*. The University of Alberta, 1986

H. J. C. Swan

J. WILLIS HURST, M.D.

Department of Medicine (Cardiology), Emory University School of Medicine; Department of Cardiology, Emory University Hospital and Emory Clinic, Atlanta, Georgia, USA

H. J. C. Swan, M.D., Ph.D., F.A.C.C., M.A.C.P. (Fig. 1) known as Jeremy to his friends, was born June 1, 1922 in Sligo on the west coast of Ireland, now known as Yeats Country. He has been an "American Treasure" since he became a naturalized U. S. citizen in 1956.

Jeremy was graduated from St. Vincent's College in Dublin in 1939 and received his M.B. from the University of London, St. Thomas's Hospital, in 1945. He was an intern and junior resident in medicine at St. Thomas's Hospital from 1945 to 1946. He obtained the Membership of the Royal College of Physicians of London in 1946 and served in the Royal Air Force medical service from 1946 to 1948. From 1948 to 1951 he was Research Fellow in Physiology, University of London, being awarded his Ph.D. in 1951. Jeremy Swan immigrated to the United States to become a Research Associate from 1951 to 1953 at the Mayo Clinic in Rochester, Minnesota. After a Fellowship term at the Minnesota Heart Association in 1954, he became a consulting physician at the Mayo Clinic in 1956. Following training with Bengt Jonsson and Ulf Rhude in Stockholm in 1959, he became Director of the Cardiac Catheterization Laboratory, St. Mary's Hospital, Mayo Clinic from 1959 to 1965. From 1960 to 1965 he served as Professor of Physiology at the University of Minnesota Graduate School. In 1965, moving from Rochester to Los Angeles, Dr. Swan was appointed Director of the Division of Cardiology at the Cedars-Sinai Medical Center, and Professor of Medicine, University of California.

Dr. Swan has always been a hardworking participant in the activities of the American College of Cardiology, serving as President in 1973, and was selected as a Distinguished Fellow in 1985. He was elected a Master of the American College of Physicians in 1985. He has also been active in the American Heart Association, and was a member of the Board of Directors of the Los Angeles County Heart Association from 1966 to 1972, serving as Chairman of the Research Committee from 1967 to 1969. The American Heart Association awarded him the coveted James B. Herrick Award for outstanding achievement in clinical cardiology in 1985.

Jeremy has received many honors for his contributions to cardiology. He has given his time and energy to the editorial boards of all of the major cardiology journals. He is an active member of many professional societies in the United States and abroad. He has traveled to 16 countries as a teacher for the American College of Cardiology Circuit Courses. He has participated in many of the activities of the National Heart, Lung and Blood Institute.

He has written chapters for about 105 books and by 1986 had written 289 articles.

Jeremy recalls some of the highlights of his life as follows. He is proud of his family's relationship to medicine. Both of his parents were physicians and about 50 percent of his parents' familial relatives are physicians. His father occasionally administered his services to W. B. Yeats during the 1930s. Jeremy has seven children and eight grandchildren. His youngest daughter is a third-year resident in medicine at the Beth Israel Hospital in Boston and another daughter is a physical therapist.

Influential to his professional life were Henry Barcroft and Sir Henry Dale. They stimulated the young Jeremy and many others by their selfless interest in seeking biologic truths. They believed it was a wondrous privilege to do so and led Jeremy to believe the same. Earl H. Wood of the Mayo Clinic was also a powerful and frequently decisive influence. Earl demanded intellectual honesty and technical excellence and lived by the rule that—you should never ask anybody to do something that you won't do yourself. He instilled in Jeremy the fundamental principle that diagnosis and treatment of cardiological problems must be sufficiently related to the basic biological sciences. Being the perfect blend of a scientific cardiologist and compassionate physician, it is proper for Jeremy to relate a statement the Chairman of the Board of Mayo Clinic made to him when he, Jeremy, joined the staff in Rochester. The then Chairman of the Board, the courteous and kindly Dr. Samuel Haynes, pointed out of his office window, commenting that the most important person at the Mayo Clinic was the patient. He then added, "The day you forget that, you can leave." Jeremy has always remembered that incident but did not need to be reminded of it because he was born with that view and has influenced numerous trainees and colleagues to feel the same.

During his tenure at Cedars-Sinai Medical Center and UCLA School of Medicine, Jeremy demonstrated that excellent clinical investigation could be carried out in a private community hospital by the cooperative relationship with private physicians and private patients. He proved that such activity could influence the quality and standard of patient care,

FIG. 1   Dr. H. J. C. Swan.

and the prestige of the institution and of the physicians associated with it.

Jeremy is a scholar and a superb teacher and consummate lecturer. His brilliance linked to common sense, his seriousness studded with flashes of wit, and his pathophysiologic insights linked to practical problems have made him one of the few lecturers who can teach.

So, whenever you float a Swan-Ganz catheter into a patient in order to gain new knowledge about the patient's hemodynamics preliminary to more precise therapy, you should think of Jeremy and Willie Ganz and what they have done for our patients.

Bibliography

Bibliography in which an important concept is emphasized:

Rastelli GC, Hallermann FJ, Fellows JL, Swan HJC: Cardiac performance during exercise in dogs with constricted artery. *Circ Res* 13, 410 (1963)

Swan HJC: Effect of noradrenalin on the human circulation. *Lancet* (II) 508 (1949)

Swan HJC: Observations on a central dilator action of adrenalin in man. *J Physiol* 112, 426 (1951)

Swan HJC, Zapata-Diaz J, Burchell HB, Wood EH: Pulmonary hypertension in congenital heart disease. *Am J Med* 16, 12 (1954)

Swan HJC, Wood EH: Diagnostic applications of indicator dilution technics in congenital and acquired heart disease. *Circulation* 16, 943 (1957)

Swan HJC: Indicator dilution methods in the diagnosis of congenital heart disease. *Progr Cardiovasc Dis* 2, 143 (1959)

Swan HJC, Forrester JS, Diamond GA, Chatterjee K, Parmley WW: Hemodynamic spectrum of myocardial infarction and cardiogenic shock: A conceptual model. *Circulation* 45, 1097 (1972)

Swan HJC: Mechanical function of the heart and its alteration during myocardial ischemia and infarction with specific reference to coronary atherosclerosis. *Circulation* 60, 1587 (1979)

Swan HJC, Shah PK, Rubin S: Role of vasodilators in the changing phases of acute myocardial infarction. *Am Heart J* 103, 707 (1982)

Swan HJC, Ganz W: Hemodynamic measurements in clinical practice: A decade in review. *J Am Coll Cardiol* 1, 103 (1983)

Selected Bibliography

Diamond GS, Forrester JS, Hargis J, Parmley WW, Danzig R, Swan HJC: Diastolic pressure-volume relationship of the canine left ventricle. *Circ Res* 29, 267 (1971)

Forrester JS, Diamond GA, McHugh TJ, Swan HJC: Filling pressures in the right and left sides of the heart in acute myocardial infarction. *N Engl J Med* 285, 190 (1971)

Forrester JS, Diamond GA, Parmley WW, Swan HJC: Early increase in left ventricular compliance following myocardial infarction. *J Clin Invest* 51, 598 (1972)

Ganz W, Tamura K, Marcus HS, Donoso R, Yoshida S, Swan HJC: Measurement of coronary sinus blood flow by continuous thermodilution in man. *Circulation* 44, 181 (1971)

Geha AS, Swan HJC: Catecholamines and right ventricular response to outflow obstruction in unanesthetized dogs. *Am J Physiol* 217, 1565 (1969)

Kivowitz C, Parmley WW, Donoso R, Marcus HS, Ganz W, Swan HJC: Effects of isometric exercise on cardiac performance: The grip test. *Circulation* 44, 994 (1971)

Laks MM, Morady F, Swan HJC: Canine right and left ventricular cell and sarcomere lengths after banding the pulmonary artery. *Circ Res* 24, 705 (1969)

Laks MM, Morady R, Adomian GE, Swan HJC: Presence of widened and multiple intercalated discs in the hypertrophied canine heart. *Circ Res* 27, 391 (1970)

Laks MM, Callis G, Swan HJC: Hemodynamic effects of low doses of norepinephrine in the conscious dog. *Am J Physiol* 220, 171 (1971)

*Swan HJC, Ganz W, Forrester JS, Marcus HS, Diamond GA, Chonette D: Catheterization of the heart in man with the use of a flow-directed balloon-tipped catheter. *N Engl J Med* 283, 447 (1970)

Swan HJC, Forrester JS, Danzig R, Allen HN: Power failure in acute myocardial infarction. *Progr Cardiovasc Dis* 12, 568 (1970)

Swan HJC, Forrester JS, Diamond GA, Chatterjee K, Parmley WW: Hemodynamic spectrum of myocardial infarction and cardiogenic shock: A conceptual model. *Circulation* 45, 1097 (1972)

Tamura K, Laks MM, Garner D, Swan HJC: Distribution rates of coronary inflow in the postmortem canine heart. *Cardiovasc Res* 3, 324 (1969)

This paper is a benchmark contribution. Dr. Swan and his colleagues describe the use of the Swan-Ganz catheter.

Dr. René G. Favaloro: A Biographical Note

RICARDO H. PICHEL, M.D., F.A.C.C.

Department of Research and Teaching, Buenos Aires, Argentina

Dr. René G. Favaloro (Fig. 1) was born on the 14th of July 1923 in the city of La Plata, capital of the province of Buenos Aires, located about 30 miles to the south of Buenos Aires City, the federal capital of the Argentine Republic. He is the grandson of Italian immigrants, Sicilian on his father's side and Tuscan on his mother's. His father was a carpenter and his mother a dressmaker. His maternal grandmother taught him an enduring love for the land and nature. The other great influence in his early years was an uncle who was a general medical practitioner. The young Favaloro accompanied his uncle on his daily rounds, and it was this exposure to the reality of a doctor's life which decided him to pursue a medical career.

He received his secondary education in the famous Colegio Nacional of La Plata, which in those days was staffed by some of the most brilliant minds in Latin America. The warm relationship between student and teacher which existed at that time allowed this generation of students to develop esthetic sensibility and sound scientific knowledge. It was an unforgettable period which Dr. Favaloro always refers to with pride and great pleasure. He graduated as a Bachelor in the upper third of his class and then began his studies in the Medical Science Faculty of La Plata University. His immediate attraction was to surgery, and he voluntarily attended the classes and rounds of the great surgeons of the time long before the requisite of his scheduled study program. He presented his thesis and graduated at the top of his class in 1949 with the title of Doctor in Medicine.

By this time Favaloro was the fervent disciple of two great Argentinian masters of surgery, professors Federico Christmann and José María Mainetti, and had developed a deep interest in thoracic surgery. This led him to travel to Buenos Aires every week in order to participate in the postgraduate course on pulmonary and esophageal surgery taught by Ricardo and Enrique Finochietto in the Rawson Hospital.

The time was ripe for Favaloro to develop a career as a distinguished thoracic surgeon, but this seemingly natural order of events was altered by the political climate of the time. He resigned his hospital post rather than sacrifice his principles of ethical and academic liberty. Circumstances led him to assume the task of filling in for a country doctor whose practice was located in a small town called Jacinto Aráuz, southeast of the province of La Pampa. His original intent was to stand in for his country colleague only until that gentleman had recovered his health, but the primitive conditions of life which he encountered in his daily work awakened his social conscience; he decided to stay and try to improve the quality of health care in the zone.

Dr. Favaloro was immersed in this endeavor for more than a decade. As a country doctor he branched out into other fields, experimenting with preventive medicine at the most basic level, teaching his patients the basic rules of hygiene, or undertaking more sophisticated projects. For example, the first group of blood donors in the locality was established through his effort (this was in fact a "mobile" blood bank; he knew where each donor of a required group was living and called donors in as needed). He also developed his own operating room and trained general and surgical nurses. In all of these tasks he was aided by his brother, Juan José, who came to join him in La Pampa upon graduating from medical school.

Yet again, the seemingly natural order of events, which would have predicted Favaloro's future to be that of an increasingly influential local practitioner, was altered. On this occasion, as on another important one later in his career, it was his own decision to change his course radically. His interest in thoracic surgery, still as keen as it was when he first met the Finochietto brothers, coupled with the latest news about the new technique of open heart surgery, inspired him to consult his old master Dr. Mainetti, who recommended that he further his studies by traveling to the Cleveland Clinic. Here, Dr. Donald Effler invited him to observe the work of the Department of Thoracic and Cardiovascular Surgery. Soon afterward, Effler allowed him to scrub up and participate as second assistant; subsequently, he became Effler's and Groves's permanent assistant. This entailed helping the anesthetist and the extra-corporeal pump operator, as well as removing drains postoperatively. In short, he undertook a wide variety of supplementary tasks with the same degree of enthusiasm and sheer physical stamina which he applies even today to all his activities.

He developed a lasting friendship with Mason Sones, the father of coronary cineangiography, who taught him to read and interpret coronary and ventricular images.

At that time, myocardial revascularization was limited to the indirect technique of Vineberg and patch reconstruction of occluded coronary arteries. This latter technique often suffered the complication of postoperative thrombosis, but Favaloro was attracted to it and reasoned that an alternative

FIG. 1   Dr. René G. Favaloro (1925–2000).

method of reconstruction would be to utilize the patient's own saphenous vein to unite the unoccluded proximal and distal sections of the vessel, thus bypassing the obstruction. In May 1967 he bypassed a total obstruction of the right coronary artery of a 51-year-old patient, and eight days later Sones confirmed that the bypass was still patent. Direct revascularization was soon replaced by that of the aortocoronary bridge. The early operations were performed only on the right coronary; however, in 1968, the first revascularization of the left anterior descending artery was performed as an emergency intervention. The same year saw the development of adequate criteria for patient selection, the combination of bypass surgery with other procedures such as valve replacement and aneurysmectomy, and emergency bypass surgery in impending infarction and acute infarction. By the end of 1969, the Cleveland Clinic team had operated on 570 patients, and by June 1970 this figure had increased to 1,086 with a mortality of 4.2%. The success of revascularization surgery was such that the surgical mortality rate was less than that for patients awaiting surgery, which led the Cleveland Clinic to expand the Cardiovascular Surgery department in order to satisfy the overwhelming patient demand.

Over the next few years, the Cleveland Clinic became the world center for cardiac surgery, attracting patients, cardiologists, and surgeons to Favaloro's operating table. His prestige soon exceeded the limits of the United States, and he was nominated as an honorary member of many foreign societies of cardiology and cardiac surgery. On one memorable occasion in London during the 6th World Cardiological Congress, a discussion between Favaloro and Friedberg attracted such a large audience that many were unable to enter the conference

room and demanded that the (spontaneous) interchange be repeated. Nowadays, no one is in doubt that Favaloro's coronary bypass procedure has changed the natural history of coronary disease. Indeed, Mason Sones once said that twentieth century cardiology can be divided into the pre-Favaloro and the post-Favaloro era.

The United States offered both economic and academic progress to Favaloro, but his love for Argentina was so strong that he decided to return there in 1971. Dwight Harken, commenting on this decision, referred to Favaloro as: "René, whose love and patriotism to his fatherland made the United States lose one of the world's finest surgeons."

Favaloro took with him to Argentina not only his fame, his prestige, and his knowledge, but also his dream of developing a center of excellence similar to the Cleveland Clinic. There, he had learned that clinical excellence cannot exist in the absence of research and of an efficient educational system for the transfer of research findings to the clinical setting. It was for these reasons that Favaloro decided to develop a center based on research, teaching, and clinical activities, all carried out at the highest possible level. He quickly established Argentina's most important center for cardiovascular surgery, and developed an intense teaching schedule which encompassed not only the training of surgeons and cardiologists who came from all over Latin America, but also disseminated his ideas and experiences in courses, conferences, and congresses. Five years after his return to Argentina, the first of the "new generation" of cardiovascular surgeons graduated and began to occupy key positions in countries as varied as Peru, Ecuador, Venezuela, Mexico, Colombia, Chile, Uruguay, Costa Rica, Honduras, Brazil, Spain, and Italy. Some of the Latin American countries simply did not possess cardiovascular surgery facilities until the first crop of graduates from Favaloro's school began to emigrate to these areas. The human impact was therefore all the more important at the local level, where patients could now be given a new lease on life. At the time of this writing, more than 300 cardiologists and cardiovascular surgeons have been trained by Favaloro. He himself has often stated that he wishes to be remembered more as a teacher than as a surgeon, and those in close contact with him know that one of his greatest satisfactions is that no matter where he goes in Latin America he is bound to meet up with at least one of his graduates.

His fame continues to increase in his own country, where he is known not only as the great cardiovascular surgeon but also as a compassionate human being whose publicly expressed views on the reality of Argentina more than once raised the displeasure of the dictatorships in office.

By 1980, Favaloro had realized two of his three desires—those of the establishment of a medical center and a teaching unit, both located in the Güemes private hospital. The desire to develop a research department was made possible by the Society of Distributors of Newspapers and Magazines, who donated an eight-story building, immediately designated as the research building, to the Favaloro Foundation.

That a surgeon has established and personally financed a basic research department in a country like Argentina is probably a unique event even in world terms. That he has encouraged the activities of the department to develop along the lines suggested by the researchers without interference from above is little short of a miracle, much appreciated by those of us who have the privilege of working in the research department.

With this gesture, Favaloro has clearly distinguished himself from his contemporaries in public life in this part of the world by displaying a remarkable degree of coherence between what he thinks, what he says. and what he does.

The culmination of Favaloro's plan is to take place shortly with the opening, on a site adjacent to the research building, of the Institute for Cardiology, Cardiothoracic Surgery, and Organ Transplantation. This Institute, like the Cleveland Clinic, is a nonprofit organization with no owner other than the community at large to which it is dedicated without any form of discrimination, and in which clinical activities will be totally integrated with teaching and research.

A fundamental objective of the Institute is to expand upon the international connections already established by the research department. Every month, an important foreign specialist will be invited to work as a group leader within his own field so that the clinicians and surgeons of the Institute together with visitors from all over Latin America can maintain both the theoretical and practical aspects of cardiology at a state-of-the-art level.

At the present time, Favaloro is an active member of 23 learned societies, a corresponding member of 3, an honorary member of 28, and he has received 23 significant international awards. This brief biography of Favaloro cannot, however, end without some comment on his personality and his personal qualities. He is a passionate student of history, especially Latin American history, which is in accordance with his concern for the problems of this region and his admiration of San Martin who won freedom for Argentina, Chile, and Peru. Indeed, Favaloro has written two books on San Martín: *Do You Know San Martín* and *The Guayaquil Memoir.* He also wrote *Memories of a Country Doctor* which is an eminently readable account of his years in Jacinto Aráuz. We who have worked with him over many difficult years have come to know him as an immensely warm, sensitive, loyal, and indeed simple man. His Sicilian blood boils in the face of injustice, and yet he can be moved to tears when confronted by human suffering.

One great unknown remains. His period as a country doctor lasted for 10 years and was followed by his unexpected move to Cleveland. This period also lasted for 10 years and also ended with an unexpected decision: to return to Argentina. After his first 10 years of work back in his own country, he could easily have retired on his laurels, to relax in the knowledge that he had truly done good for his fellow man. Instead, he embarked on the Herculean task of developing an Institute whose characteristics are not readily understood by minds trained in the old European tradition, and whose planning and construction took place during times of dramatic social and economic upheavals. After 10 years, the Institute is a reality. The question we now ask ourselves is "What is the new challenge that Favaloro will be presenting to us for development over the next 10 years?"

Dr. Favaloro died in 2000, after this profile was published.

Arthur Hollman

DENNIS M. KRIKLER, M.D., FACC

Hammersmith Hospital and Royal Postgraduate Medical School, London, England, U.K.

Arthur Hollman (Fig. 1) epitomizes the broad-based British cardiologist, although he is unique in the diversity of his interests. Born in 1923, he qualified from University College Hospital Medical School in 1946 and was a clinical student under Sir Thomas Lewis. As a senior student he was awarded the McGrath Scholarship in Medicine. Having qualified with the British degree of Bachelor of Medicine and Surgery (MB, BS), he proceeded to the degree of M.D. in 1950, and became a Member of the Royal College of Physicians of London in 1947 and, in 1967, a Fellow (FRCP).

In his early postgraduate days he was exposed to the leading post-war British cardiologist Paul Wood, first as his registrar at the special unit for juvenile rheumatism at Taplow, where, in 1949, Wood instructed him in cardiac catheterization. Later he was Wood's clinical assistant at the National Heart Hospital in London. During the period 1952–1957 he was Medical Registrar at University College Hospital, and from 1957 to 1962 Senior Registrar at the Hammersmith Hospital and Royal Postgraduate Medical School, under Professor John Goodwin. This work involved him closely with the pioneering development of open heart surgery at the Hammersmith Hospital, where D. G. Melrose had invented a heart-lung machine. He worked closely with the surgical team in the operating room (see Fig. 2), where, on one occasion, he urged the surgeon Bill Cleland to proceed with surgery on a patient with hypertrophic cardiomyopathy even though the known outflow tract gradient was no longer present. This was one of the earliest operations of its type, if not the first. He was the cardiologist of the Hammersmith team that went to Moscow in 1959 to instruct Russian surgeons in open heart surgery with the Melrose machine. He assisted Goodwin with his study of cardiomyopathy, and together they made a study of ventricular septal defect and delineated the features of double outlet right ventricle.

In 1962, Arthur became Consultant Cardiologist at University College Hospital, and his consultant role was expanded to include Great Ormond Street Childrens' Hospital in 1971; he filled both posts until he retired in 1987. His paper on phenindione sensitivity, in 1964, helped change anticoagulant therapy to the use of warfarin; he also wrote chapters on congenital heart disease.

In 1971, the then European Economic Community (EEC) directed that blood pressure should be measured in kilopascals, and not in millimeters of mercury. This directive was blindly accepted by a number of official British medical institutions and journals, but they were forced to recant when, in 1975, Arthur founded "the Committee for the Protection of the mmHg." He persuaded other European countries, including the Soviet Union, to get the EEC to reverse its decision and persuaded the World Health Organization to state in 1980 that the "mmHg would be retained for the time being." Arthur felt very strongly that the actual measurement unit, visible to the eyes of the doctor making the recording, should be retained, and he succeeded in reaching his target. He has said that he would liked to be remembered as the man who saved the millimeter of mercury.

Hollman's influence was widely felt at the personal level, as he had early training in pediatric cardiology in Toronto and was appointed Visiting Cardiologist to the governments of Mauritius and the Seychelles.

His interest in plants in medicine led him to represent the Royal College of Physicians of London on the Advisory Committee of the Chelsea Physic Garden for 26 years. He is now the curator of the ancient herb garden founded in 1550 in the heart of the City of London and a livery member of the Worshipful Company of Barbers. He is also livery member of the Society of Apothecaries, to whom he gave the Hans Sloane Lecture entitled "Plants in Medicine." As editor of the *British Heart Journal*, I was able to enlist Arthur's services to provide a series of fillers on plants in cardiology, which culminated in the publication of a book with this title in 1991. He has subsequently provided *Heart* with a series of about 40 fillers on stamps in cardiology.

His wide interests in the history of medicine and cardiology have developed an important focus on the contribution of Sir Thomas Lewis. In 1981, he gave the Thomas Lewis Lecture to the British Cardiac Society, of which he had been secretary in 1974–1975, and of which he has subsequently been archivist since 1992. His biography of Sir Thomas Lewis, published by Springer in 1997, brought him the Society of Authors prize for the best book on medical history for 1998.

Arthur's associated interest in plants and medicine brought him the Fellowship of the Linnean Society (FLS) in 1985. In that same year he published an article entitled "The History of Bundle Branch Block" in *Medical History*, supplement 5, which thoroughly explained the different views on right and left bundle-branch block and the reason Thomas Lewis and other early workers who relied on studies in dogs initially con-

FIG. 1   Arthur Hollman, M.D., FRCP, FLS

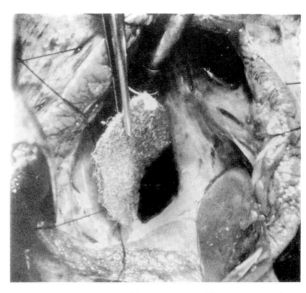

FIG. 2   Photograph taken by Arthur Hollman at open heart surgery showing a teflon patch being sewn onto a large ventricular septal defect. View via the right ventricle. (Reproduced from Hollman A, Stinton P: Open heart photography. *Med Biol Illus* 1963;13:15).

fused the laterality of block in man. In this article he gives full credit to the American workers who rectified our knowledge of bundle-branch block.

Arthur is married to Dr. Catharine Hollman, herself formerly a consultant in community pediatrics. One daughter, an eminent radiologist, died recently; his other three daughters are all at the forefront in their respective occupations of teacher of English, general practitioner, and senior railway manager. In characteristic intrepid fashion, Arthur continues his extensive travels, focusing more closely in recent years on India. The final word must lie with his important contributions as editor and author of chapters in *British Cardiology in the Twentieth Century* published by Springer in 2000. In that book one will see the depth of his knowledge of cardiology as well as his contribution to a diverse range of items about the specialty.

Norman E. Shumway

ROBERT C. ROBBINS, M.D.

Falk Cardiovascular Research Center, Department of Cardiothoracic Surgery, Stanford University School of Medicine, Stanford, California, USA

Early Background, Education, and Research

Norman E. Shumway was born on February 9, 1923, in Kalamazoo, Michigan. He completed one year of pre-law studies at the University of Michigan before being drafted into the Army in 1943. He completed basic training at Camp Wolters in Mineral Wells, Texas. He was sent to the John Tarleton Agriculture Junior College in Stephenville, Texas, for engineering training. At the end of six months, Dr. Shumway was given a medical aptitude test. The final question of the examination asked: "If you were to pass this test would you prefer a career in medicine or dentistry?" He marked the box after "medicine," and the rest is history.

Dr. Shumway was enrolled in the Army Specialized Training program which consisted of a nine-month pre-medicine course at Baylor University in Waco, Texas. Following completion of this program he entered medical school and received his medical degree from Vanderbilt University in 1949. He completed an internship and one year of residency training in surgery at the University of Minnesota with Dr. Owen Wangensteen before being drafted into the Air Force in 1951. He served as a flight surgeon for two years in Lake Charles, Louisiana, after which he returned to the University of Minnesota for the final four years of his residency training. During his time at Minnesota, Dr. Shumway began his research career first as a postdoctoral research fellow, then as a special trainee of the National Heart Institute from 1954 to 1957. He received a surgical Ph.D. in 1956. His studies included the use of total body hypothermia for direct vision intracardiac surgery, prosthetic grafts for blood vessel replacement, investigation of coronary circulation and ventricular fibrillation, and the design and development of an effective pump oxygenator for open heart surgery.

Dr. Shumway developed an intense interest in cardiac surgery during these years of mentorship by Dr. C. Walton Lillehei and Dr. F. John Lewis. During his residency at the University of Minnesota, he participated in the first open-heart operations for the correction of congenital malformations. A parent or volunteer was used to provide circulatory support for the children undergoing these pioneering operations, which were performed prior to the refinement of the pump oxygenator machine.

Following completion of his surgical residency in 1957, Dr. Shumway began a private surgical practice at the Cottage Hospital in Santa Barbara, California. He was recruited by Dr. Vic Richards to the Stanford University faculty on February 1, 1958. The Stanford University Hospital was located in San Francisco at that time, and Dr. Frank Gerbode was the chief of cardiac surgery. A new Stanford University Hospital was built on the main campus in Palo Alto, and Dr. Shumway started the cardiac surgery program in January 1960. Dr. Gerbode continued a private surgical practice in San Francisco and continued his friendship with Dr. Shumway until his death in 1984.

The Revolutionization of Cardiac Surgery

Shortly after his arrival at Stanford in 1958, Dr. Shumway began his studies on cardiac transplantation. Building on the total body hypothermia research begun while a trainee at Minnesota, he devised a method of cooling only the heart, thereby revolutionizing cardiac surgery. As Dr. Shumway has stated, "[t]his method of elective cardiac arrest provided plenty of time for any procedure we cared to do. From then on we were only limited by our imagination, rather than by the fear that the heart would not beat again."[1]

Applying this imagination to the problem of transposition of the great vessels in pediatric patients, Dr. Shumway and Dr. Richard Lower began research of a technique, using elective cardiac arrest, whereby the heart could be completely severed and replaced with viability. The less radical arterial switch operation was developed at about the same time to correct transposition, but Dr. Shumway's success with this early bi-atrial technique of cardiac replacement in animal studies set the stage for human cardiac transplantation. Over a 10-year period of animal experimentation, Dr. Shumway and his colleagues perfected the technical details and systematically investigated and documented the clinical, physiologic, and pathologic events following orthotopic cardiac transplantation with both homograft and autografts. This information was critical to the successes achieved later with immunosuppressed hosts, a crucial step before this new form of treatment for end-stage heart disease could be applied to humans.

The Stanford laboratory team had refined the surgical technique, established adequate methods of myocardial preservation, and achieved 1-year survival of animals following orthotopic cardiac allograft transplantation. On November 20, 1967, Dr. Shumway proclaimed that the time was right to pro-

FIG. 1   Norman E. Shumway, M.D., Ph.D.

ceed with human cardiac transplantation. On January 6, 1968, Dr. Shumway performed the world's fourth human heart transplant. By 1970, a moratorium had been placed on cardiac transplantation because of the poor results realized by the many cardiac centers that attempted the operation without the foundation of a strong team to deal with the comprehensive care these patients required. Dr. Shumway refused to observe the moratorium and continued the Stanford program in the early 1970s at a time when most programs had abandoned the procedure. This was a period during which the diagnosis and treatment of rejection and infection was refined. Based on the knowledge acquired from the persistence of the Stanford program led by Dr. Edward Stinson and supported by Dr. Shumway, today almost 50,000 cardiac transplants have been performed at over 300 centers world-wide. In addition, the clinical application of combined heart-lung transplantation was introduced by Dr. Shumway and his colleague, Dr. Bruce Reitz, current chairman of the Department of Cardiothoracic Surgery at Stanford, in 1981. Single- and double-lung transplantation, and living-related lung transplants followed. Dr. Shumway is credited with making Stanford University's transplantation program one of the largest and most respected in the world.

Dr. Shumway's contributions to cardiac surgery do not end with transplantation. His animal research resulted in the use of homograft and autograft valves for the replacement of diseased valves and provided the foundation for the pulmonary autotransplantation operation for the replacement of the aortic valve. He achieved remarkable success with the correction of congenital heart defects and made major contributions in the surgical treatment of tetralogy of Fallot and atrioventricular canal defects. Dr. Shumway has made significant advancements in the treatment of aortic dissections and aneurysms in addition to the use of bioprostheses for the treatment of valvular heart disease.

Leadership

Dr. Shumway came to Stanford in 1958 as an Instructor in Surgery. He became an Assistant Professor in 1959, an Associate Professor in 1961, and a full Professor in 1965. In 1964, he was made Chief of the Division of Cardiac Surgery, and in 1974 the Chairman of the Department of Cardiovascular Surgery. Dr. Shumway served as chairman until 1992. He remains the Frances and Charles D. Field Professor in Cardiothoracic Surgery. He served as president of the Western Thoracic Surgical Association in 1979 and as president of the American Association for Thoracic Surgery, 1986–1987. He was elected as Honorary President for Life by the International Society of Heart and Lung Transplantation in 1980.

Honors and Awards

Dr. Shumway has been recognized worldwide for his endeavors. A member of many national and international medical societies, Dr. Shumway is the recipient of numerous awards. A selected list of his awards is found in Table I.

Teaching and Patient Care

Dr. Shumway has always been held in high regard by his trainees as a mentor and friend. A testament to his teaching and leadership abilities lies in the number of distinguished cardiac surgeons he has trained (Table II). In addition, there are many other internationally recognized cardiothoracic surgeons who credit Dr. Shumway with their success. Of all of his accomplishments, the training of an entire generation of cardiac surgeons may be his most important. He always strived to maintain an environment that was "friendly to learning." Dr. Shumway surrounded himself with bright, young individuals and constantly supported their efforts and careers. He used the Stanford training program to provide opportunities for others while using the knowledge he gained from each resident's contributions to provide incremental refinements to the program. Dr. Shumway provided a relaxed, fun atmosphere in the operating room that allowed each member of the team to perform at maximum capacity. During operations he would frequently say, "Isn't this fun? Isn't this easy? What could be better? Nothing could be better!" He has been known to say that "I might not be the best surgeon in the world, but I am the best first assistant." Many of his colleagues will always remember standard lines such as "Air rises; the pump is your friend; just keeping operating; and, he needs the usual three."

TABLE I   Honors and awards

The Rene Leriche Prize, International Society of Surgery, 1971
First recipient, Texas Heart Institute Medal, 1972
Docteur honoris causa, Nancy University, France, 1975
Cameron Prize in Practical Therapeutics, University of Edinburgh, Scotland, 1976
Honorary Degree of Doctor of Science, University of Chicago. 1977
Honorary Degree of Doctor of Science, Pomona College, 1979
Honorary Degree of Doctor of Science, Wittenburg University, 1979
President, Western Thoracic Surgical Association, 1979
Honorary Fellowship, The Royal College of Surgeons of England, 1980
Honorary President for Life, International Society of Heart and Lung Transplantation, 1980
Alumnis Honoris Causa Distinguished Achievement Award, Baylor University, 1981
International Recognition Award, Heart Research Foundation, 1982
Gold Heart Award, American Heart Association, 1982
Dottore Honoris Causa, University of Turino, Italy, 1983
Honorary Fellowship, The Royal College of Surgeons and Physicians of Glasgow,1983
Distinguished Alumnus Award, Vanderbilt University, 1983
Outstanding Achievement Award, University of Minnesota, 1985
Michael E. DeBakey Award,Michael E. DeBakey International Surgical Society, 1986
Honorary Fellowship, The Royal College of Surgeons of Edinburgh, 1986
Rudolph Matas Award in Cardiovascular Surgery, Tulane University, 1986
Ellen Browning Scripps Society Award, 1986
Trustees Medal for Distinguished Achievement, Massachusetts General Hospital, 1986
President, American Association for Thoracic Surgery, 1986–87
American Medical Association Scientific Achievement Award, 1987
La Medaille Internationale Lannelongue, Academie de Chirurgie, France, 1988
Albion Walter Hewlett Award, Stanford University School of Medicine, 1988
Bayer Cardiovascular Research Mentor Award, 1988
Honorary Degree of Doctor of Science, Mount Sinai School of Medicine, 1989
Theodore E. Cummings Prize, Cedars-Sinai Medical Center, 1990
Albion O. Bernstein, M.D. Award, Medical Society of the State of New York, 1990
Medal of the City of Paris, 1991
Medawar Prize, The Transplantation Society, 1992
Medallion for Scientific Achievement, American Surgical Association, 1993
Research Achievement Award, American Heart Association, 1993
Honorary Fellowship, Royal College of Surgeons of Ireland, 1993
Lister Medallist, The Royal College of Surgeons of England, 1994
Congressional Award, Philippine Government, 1995
Glenn Lectureship, American Heart Association, "The Future of Organ Transplantation," 1993
Scientific Achievement Award, American Association for Thoracic Surgery, 1998
First recipient, Lifetime Achievement Award, International Society of Heart and Lung Transplantation, 1998
Flance-Karl Award, American Surgical Association, 1999

Dr. Shumway has always been known for his dedication to and compassion for his patients. His dedication to his patients was probably best described, unwittingly, in the statement he made after his first human heart transplant: "It's going to be a very long vigil—I hope."[1]

Personal

Dr. Shumway is the father of three daughters: Lisa, a business development manager for a computer company; Amy, a retail manager; and Sarah, who is Professor of Cardiothoracic Surgery at the University of Minnesota and co-author with her father of *Thoracic Transplantation*,[3] the definitive textbook of cardiothoracic transplantation. In addition, Dr. Shumway has one son, Michael, a CPA and controller for a law firm. He has two grandchildren, Siena and Sander. Dr. Shumway was introduced to the game of golf by his father at the age of 15 and continues to be an avid golfer.

Summary

Dr. Norman E. Shumway has had the privilege to live through the entire evolution of cardiac surgery. He is an intelligent, imaginative individual who possesses a true pioneer-

TABLE II Distinguished Trainees

Richard R. Lower (1961), Chief, Division of Cardiothoracic Surgery, Medical College of Virginia
Edward B. Stinson (1968), Professor, Department of Cardiothroacic Surgery, Director, Cardiac Transplantation, Stanford University School of Medicine
Thomas J. Fogarty (1970), Professor, Department of Surgery, Stanford University School of Medicine
Lawrence H. Cohn (1971), Chief, Division of Cardiothoracic Surgery, Brigham and Women's Hospital, Harvard University School of Medicine
Randall B. Griepp (1972), Chief, Division of Cardiothoracic Surgery, Mount Sinai School of Medicine
Philip E. Oyer (1974), Professor, Department of Cardiothroacic Surgery, Stanford University School of Medicine
Jack G. Copeland (1975), Chief, Division of Cardiothoracic Surgery, University of Arizona School of Medicine
Bruce A. Reitz (1976), Chairman, Department of Cardiothoracic Surgery, Stanford University School of Medicine
D. Craig Miller (1977), Professor, Department of Cardiothroacic Surgery, Stanford University School of Medicine
William A. Baumgartner (1978), Chief, Division of Cardiothoracic Surgery, Johns Hopkins School of Medicine
Donald C. Watson (1979), Chief, Division of Cardiothoracic Surgery, University of Tennessee School of Medicine
Stuart W. Jamieson (1980), Chief, Division of Cardiothoracic Surgery, University of California San Diego School of Medicine
John Wallwork (1981), Chief, Division of Cardiothoracic Surgery, Cambridge University School of Medicine
R. Scott Mitchell (1982), Professor, Department of Cardiothoracic Surgery, Stanford University School of Medicine
John C. Baldwin (1983), Dean, Dartmouth University School of Medicine
Vaughn A. Starnes (1986), Chairman, Department of Cardiothoracic Surgery, University of Southern California
William H. Frist (1986), United States Senator, Tennessee

Dates are those of completion of residency programs.

ing spirit. He has been blessed with the fundamental qualities of leadership and continues to be capable of inspiring greatness from his associates. Through his skill, perseverance, and courage he was able to affect the course of cardiac surgery. Despite the enormous accomplishments that he has achieved, he retains the qualities of humility, humor, and generosity. Dr. Shumway possesses a keen sense of intuition and charming quick wit that he uses to place everyone he meets at ease.

References

1. Shumway NE: Contemporaries. *Mod Med* 1969;37:20–31
2. Shumway SJ, Shumway NE: *Thoracic Transplantation*. 1st edition. Cambridge, Mass.: Blackwell Science, 1995

Appendix

Dr. Shumway and associates have published over 500 peer-reviewed scientific articles. A selected list of publications is found below:

1. Lower RR, Shumway NE: Studies on orthotopic homotransplantation of the canine heart. *Surg Forum* 1960;11:18–21
2. Lower RR, Stofer RC, Shumway NE: A study of pulmonary valve autotransplantation. *Surgery* 1960;48:1090–1100
3. Lower RR, Stofer RC, Shumway NE: Homovital transplantation of the heart. *J Thorac Cardiovasc Surg* 1961;41:196–204
4. Shumway NE, Lower RR, Hurley EJ, Dong E Jr, Stofer RC: Total surgical correction of Fallot's anomaly. *Am J Surg* 1963; 106:267–272
5. Hurley EJ, Lower RR, Dong E Jr, Pillsbury RC, Shumway NE: Clinical experience with local hypothermia in elective cardiac arrest. *J Thorac Cardiovasc Surg* 1964;47:50–65
6. Dong E Jr, Hurley EJ, Lower, Shumway NE: Performance of the heart two years after autotransplantation. *Surgery* 1964;56:270–274

7. Shumway NE, Lower RR, Hurley EJ, Pillsbury RC: Results of total surgical correction for Fallot's tetralogy. *Circulation* 1965; 31:57–60
8. Lower RR, Dong E Jr, Shumway NE: Long-term survival of cardiac homografts. *Surgery* 1965;58;110–119
9. Iben AB, Hurley EJ, Shumway NE: Surgery for combined lesions of the aortic and mitral valves. *Am J Surg* 1965;110:262–269
10. Pillsbury RC, Shumway NE: Replacement of the aortic valve with the autologous pulmonic valve. *Surg Forum* 1966;XVII:176–177
11. Stinson EB, Angell WW, Shumway NE: Triple valve replacement with aortic homografts. *J Am Med Assoc* 1968;204:67–69
12. Stinson EB, Dong E Jr, Schroeder JS, Harrison DC, Shumway NE: Initial clinical experience with cardiac transplantation. *Am J Cardiol* 1968;22:791–803
13. Stinson EB, Dong E Jr, Bieber CP, Schroeder JS, Shumway NE: Cardiac transplantation in man: I. Early rejection. *J Am Med Assoc* 1969;207:2233–2247
14. Stinson EB, Dong E Jr, Bieber CP, Popp RL, Shumway NE: Cardiac transplantation in man: II. Immunosuppressive therapy. *J Thorac Cardiovasc Surg* 1969;58:326–337
15. Daily PO, Trueblood HW, Stinson EB, Wuerflein RD, Shumway NE: Management of acute aortic dissections. *Ann Thorac Surg* 1970;10:237–247
16. Stinson EB, Griepp RB, Schroeder JS, Dong E Jr, Shumway NE: Hemodynamic observations one and two years after cardiac transplantation in man. *Circulation* 1972;45:1183–1194
17. Caves PK, Stinson EB, Graham AF, Billingham ME, Grehl TM, Shumway NE: Percutaneous transvenous endomyocardial biopsy. *J Am Med Assoc* 1973;225:288–291
18. Stinson EB, Griepp RB, Shumway NE: Clinical experience with a porcine aortic valve xenograft for mitral valve replacement. *Ann Thorac Surg* 1974;18:391–401
19. Stinson EB, Griepp RB, Oyer PE, Shumway NE: Long-term experience with porcine aortic valve xenografts. *J Thorac Cardiovasc Surg* 1977;73:54–63
20. Copeland JG, Griepp RB, Stinson EB, Shumway NE: Isolated aortic valve replacement in patients over the age of 65. *J Am Med Assoc* 1977;237:1578–1581
21. Miller DC, Stinson EB, Oyer PE, Rossiter SJ, Reitz BA, Griepp RB, Shumway NE: The operative treatment of aortic dissections:

Experience with 125 patients over a 16-year period. *J Thorac Cardiovasc Surg* 1979;78:365–382

22. Billingham ME, Baumgartner WA, Watson DC, Reitz BA, Masek MA, Raney AA, Oyer PE, Stinson EB, Shumway NE: Distant heart procurement for human transplantation. *Circulation* 1980;62:11–19

23. Oyer PE, Stinson EB, Jamieson SW, Hunt SA, Reitz BA, Bieber CP, Schroeder JS, Billingham ME, Shumway NE: One year experience with cyclosporin A in clinical heart transplantation. *Heart Transplant* 1982;1:285–290

24. Reitz BA, Wallwork J, Hunt SA, Pennock JL, Billingham ME, Oyer PE, Stinson EB, Shumway NE: Heart-lung transplantation: Successful therapy for patients with pulmonary vascular disease. *N Engl J Med* 1982;306:557–564

25. Miller DC, Oyer PE, Mitchell RS, Stinson EB, Jamieson SW, Shumway NE: Independent determinants of operative mortality for patients with aortic dissections. *Circulation* 1984;70:(suppl 1) 153–164

26. Zhao H, Miller DC, Reitz BA, Shumway NE: Surgical repair of tetralogy of Fallot—long-term follow-up with particular emphasis on late death and reoperation. *J Thorac Cardiovasc Surg* 1985;89:204–220

27. Starnes VA, Oyer PE, Portner PM, Ramasamy N, Miller PJ, Stinson EB, Baldwin JC, Ream AK, Wyner J, Shumway NE: Isolated left ventricular assist as bridge to cardiac transplantation. *J Thorac Cardiovasc Surg* 1988;96:62–71

28. Starnes VA, Berstein D, Oyer PE, Gamberg PL, Miller JL, Baum D, Shumway NE: Heart transplantation in children. *J Heart Transplant* 1989;8:20–26

29. Starnes VA, Lewiston NJ, Luikart H, Theodore J, Stinson EB, Shumway NE: Current trends in lung transplantation. Lobar transplantation and expanded use of single lungs. *J Thorac Cardiovasc Surg* 1992;104:1060–1066

30. Sarris GE, Smith JA, Shumway NE, Stinson EB, Oyer PE, Robbins RC, Billingham ME, Theodore J, Moore KA, Reitz BA: Long-term results of combined heart-lung transplantation: The Stanford experience. *J Heart Lung Transplant* 1994;13:940–949

31. Robbins RC, Barlow CW, Oyer PE, Hunt SA, Miller JL, Reitz BA, Stinson EB, Shumway NE: Thirty years of cardiac transplantation at Stanford University. *J Thorac Cardiovasc Surg* 1999;117:939–951

Earl E. Bakken

WILLIAM H. SPENCER III, M.D.

Baylor Heart Clinic, Smith Tower, Houston, Texas, USA

Earl E. Bakken (Fig. 1) was born in 1924 in Minneapolis, Minnesota, and grew up there with a strong Norwegian heritage. For all intents and purposes, he was raised as an "only child" since his sister was 18 years his junior. As he had no siblings, he had the run of the house as a boy and a young man, and he used this freedom to great advantage. Even as a very small boy he appeared to be interested in the electrical wiring of the house and the porcelain insulators. He was constantly tinkering with electrical equipment, experimenting with batteries, electrically activated bells and buzzers, and, finally, robots that would puff cigarettes and wield knives. Finally, it was his mother who encouraged his scientific interest and provided him with the freedom for developing these interests at his own rapid rate.

As a student in secondary school, he was assured by his teachers that it was perfectly all right to be what today is called a "nerd." Bakken then became the nerd who took care of the public address system, the movie projector, and other electrical equipment at school. To his credit, he did have athletic interests and earned a varsity letter in track. During these formative years, he developed the habits that made him an inveterate reader which has stood him in good stead to the present day. Despite excellent formal instruction, he recognized that the most important lessons learned were those that were self taught. Since he estimates that the "half life of an engineer's education is three years," his life has been one of constant quest and investigation. It is of particular interest that in these early years his favorite science fiction film was *Frankenstein*, a fateful choice in view of his later endeavors with pacemakers. Through it all, he has faithfully followed his pastor's advice that it was his responsibility, if he pursued a scientific career, to use it for the benefit of humankind and not for destructive purposes.

Earl Bakken spent three years in World War II in the Army Signal Corps, serving as a radar instructor. He returned to Minneapolis and earned a B.S. degree, then a Masters Degree in electrical engineering from the University of Minnesota. His first wife, Connie Olson, was a medical technologist at Northwestern Hospital in South Minneapolis. As a graduate student, Earl Bakken visited her frequently in the hospital and finally began spending more and more time conversing with housestaff, attending physicians, and medical students in the hospital. As he became acquainted with the hospital staff, he slowly began providing, at their request, ad hoc medical equipment repairs. Soon it became obvious to him that these hospitals were in need of a person or company dedicated to medical equipment repair.

On April 29, 1949, Earl Bakken and Palmer Hermundslie, his brother-in-law, founded Medtronic, Inc., and set up shop in a garage in Northeast Minneapolis for the purpose of repairing medical equipment. Medtronic's earnings for its first month of operation were $8.00. By contrast, Medtronic's gross earnings for January 2000 were approximately one half billion dollars.

Eventually, the company also began selling equipment to hospitals and physicians. The company barely made ends meet for eight years until October 1957, when Dr. C. Walton Lillehei approached Mr. Bakken and asked him to make a better pacemaker than the alternating current pacemakers then in use in the intensive care units. Within four weeks, Bakken produced a small, self-contained, transistorized, battery-powered pacemaker that could be taped to the patient's chest. The very next day, the pacemaker was used in the hospital on the first patient. Soon thereafter, Dr. Samuel Hunter and Norman Roth, a Medtronic engineer, developed a bipolar pacing lead which was more efficient than anything in existence. Following the development of the lead, Medtronic contracted with Dr. William Chardack and Wilson Greatbatch of Buffalo, N.Y., to manufacture and market an implantable pacemaker utilizing the Hunter-Roth lead. Following these early developments, Medtronic has encountered a few notable failures and many more outstanding successes to become the world's most prominent medical device manufacturer. In 1984, the National Society of Professional Engineers named the cardiac pacemaker one of the 10 outstanding engineering achievements of the last half of the twentieth century.

The development of Medtronic, Inc., into the industry leader to whose example all others aspire can be attributed to much more than Earl Bakken's engineering genius. His insightful leadership of the company is summed up in the three words he uses as one of his mottos "*ready, fire, aim!*" That is, a given need is identified; a product is produced or a task is performed, and later refinements are made while the long-term possibilities of the product are debated. He believes one should act on one's intuition, not overanalyze, and correct the aim later. To quote Mr. Bakken, he believes that "failure is closer to success than inaction."

FIG. 1 Earl E. Bakken, Medtronic, Inc.

Since his "retirement" from Medtronic, Earl Bakken has made some of his greatest contributions to mankind. Specifically, he founded and developed the Bakken Library and Museum which emphasizes the role of electricity in medicine and life. He has helped develop Medical Alley, a consortium of various manufacturers in Minnesota to develop and promote the area as a hotbed of medical innovation. Earl Bakken is most proud of his endeavors to develop the big island of Hawaii as a "healing island." He has been instrumental in the development of the North Hawaii Community Hospital, the Five Mountain Medical Community, and the Archeaus Project. The goal of the Archeaus Project is to devise a system that would provide optimum health care for the North Hawaii community by the year 2010. This health care is envisioned as being very different from the care ordinarily delivered today. Mr. Bakken recognized very early that there was more to medicine and medical practice than simply double-blind studies and statistical significance. He noted that patients fared much better with certain treatments or devices when they were administered by caring and loving physicians. Similarly, the Archeaus Project is based on our knowledge of phenomena such as the difference between the relief of symptoms and true care, the interdependence of the body as well as the mind, the innate ability of the body to heal itself, and the curative effect of a positive relationship between patient and healthcare professionals.

Earl Bakken has followed his early pastor's advice very closely and spent a lifetime serving his fellow man. He created a company that is the envy of the industry and based it on a goal that helps humanity with instruments and appliances that alleviate pain, restore health, and extend life. Representatives and employees of Medtronic, Inc., have the reputation of going anywhere at any expense to satisfy a given customer's needs. Leading by example, Earl Bakken has made the values expressed in the Medtronic Mission Statement "to be recognized as a company of dedication, honesty, integrity and service"—his own values throughout his daily life.

John B. Barlow: Master Clinician and Compleat Cardiologist

Tsung O. Cheng, M.D.

Division of Cardiology, Department of Medicine, The George Washington University Medical Center, Washington, DC, USA

John Brereton Barlow (Fig. 1) was born in Cape Town, South Africa, in 1924 and was educated in Johannesburg. He was well known as a rugby player and obtained his "letters" at the university as a lock forward (equivalent to a guard or tackle in American football). Because he elected to go into the army during World War II, his medical school career was interrupted temporarily. After the end of the war, he returned to Johannesburg and graduated from medical school in 1951. He trained in medicine, surgery, and pediatrics at Baragwanath Hospital in Soweto (an acronym which stands for South West Township, a city situated southwest of Johannesburg) for three years and then spent three years of postgraduate training in London, mainly at the Postgraduate School of Medicine at Hammersmith Hospital with Sir John McMichael. Under McMichael he was exposed to the view that current dogma must always be carefully examined, and he has done so throughout his productive years with valuable results. He had so much respect for McMichael that, in 1961, when he became Chief of Cardiology at the University of the Witwatersrand (literally "white water reef" under which the gold lies), he named his cardiac catheterization laboratory at Johannesburg Hospital the McMichael Cardiac Catheterization Laboratory.

The following story, which illustrates how Barlow followed McMichael's doctrine, was told to me recently by his schoolmate Dr. Bernard Tabatznik, who was working with Barlow at Baragwanath Hospital in the mid 1950s and later moved to Sinai Hospital, Baltimore, in the late 1950s. A robust black man was admitted to the hospital with pulmonary edema. Because his electrocardiogram was normal and he had a fever and eosinophilia, the differential diagnosis was left heart failure versus an unusual form of bronchopneumonia. A detailed history revealed that several family members and friends of the patient had been admitted to area hospitals with similar complaints. So Barlow and Tabatznik went around to all the hospitals, tracking them down, and also to the area from which these patients came, so as to interview other family members. The latter were quite cooperative except when they saw Barlow, because they were all convinced that Barlow was a policeman and thus would not talk in his presence. Barlow and Tabatznik with Pocock (a long-time colleague of Barlow's) eventually wrote a paper together on this epidemic of acute eosinophilic pneumonia.[1]

Barlow entered the international cardiology scene in 1963 with publication of his landmark paper on the midsystolic click and late systolic murmur,[2] subsequently known as the Barlow syndrome. It was Barlow who demonstrated that the midsystolic click(s) and late systolic murmur were in fact associated with billowing of the mitral valve leaflets and mitral regurgitation, respectively. Previously, the click(s) and the murmur had been considered extracardiac in origin.[3] Barlow's discovery was so controversial at the time that it did not win acceptance easily. In fact, Barlow's paper was not accepted for publication in the journal Circulation to which it was first submitted. Tabatznik had the foresight to convince Barlow to publish a short version in the *Maryland State Medical Journal* in February 1963.[4] Barlow's full article was later published in the October 1963 issue of the *American Heart Journal*.[2] When Barlow visited Baltimore the following year, Victor McKusick, who was the "Heart Sounds" editor of *Circulation* during the time when Barlow's original article was rejected, could not have been more gracious. He offered Barlow the Conjoint Clinic forum at the Johns Hopkins Hospital and subsequently published Barlow's presentation in the *Journal of Chronic Disease*.[5] Also, it was during Barlow's visit to the Johns Hopkins Hospital in April 1964 that he met John Michael Criley who introduced the term "prolapse" of the mitral valve.[6] Although Barlow never liked using the term prolapse and preferred the term "billowing" mitral leaflet,[7] he had the highest respect for Criley. As a matter of fact, Barlow originally interpreted the left ventricular cineangiograms of his patients with midsystolic click and late systolic murmur as showing a subvalvular ventricular aneurysm until Criley pointed out that the protrusion occurred during ventricular systole and emptied completely during diastole. Then Barlow readily accepted that it was the posterior leaflet of the mitral valve that billowed into the left atrium and not a subvalvular ventricular aneurysm which filled. Barlow always gave Criley credit for this observation.[5, 8]

Although Barlow confirmed the diagnosis of mitral regurgitation in the first seven of his patients with midsystolic click(s) and late systolic murmur by cineangiography after retrograde catheterization of the left ventricle, he subsequently was able to confirm his findings in a much larger series of patients noninvasively by observing the effect on the click(s) and murmur of alteration in the hemodynamic state brought

FIG. 1 John Brereton Barlow.

about by either vasoactive drugs or various maneuvers including the Valsalva maneuver.[7] Once the Barlow syndrome was recognized and accepted as a definitive entity, it gained worldwide attention. It has now become the most common valve disorder in the world.[9]

In practice in Johannesburg for over 35 years, Barlow has patients from all walks of life, ranging from the underprivileged black children from Soweto to the South African President Mandela to whom Barlow is personal physician. He utilized the opportunity to practice cardiology in an environment where the broad spectrum of clinical material combined with the sophisticated means of investigation and treatment is unique. Thus, he has been able to take advantage of this unique situation to expand his research and publish on many topics, including rheumatic carditis,[10] submitral left ventricular aneurysm,[11] restriction-dilatation syndrome,[12] and so forth, in addition to the Barlow syndrome. Barlow has maintained a keen interest in cardiac auscultation and emphasized the importance of history and physical examination throughout his professional life. As he so aptly put it in the Dedication of his textbook *Perspectives on the Mitral Valve*,[13] "To all students of medicine who listen, look, touch, and reflect; may they hear, see, feel, and comprehend." This is why I chose to call Barlow a master clinician and compleat cardiologist.

Barlow and I have been close friends for many years. We share a common interest in mitral valve prolapse, although I started with my work on midsystolic click and late systolic murmur in papillary muscle dysfunction[14] and coronary

artery disease.[15] We collaborated on a chapter on mitral valve billowing and prolapse in my book *The International Textbook of Cardiology*[7] and also on an article on the worldwide prevalence of mitral valve prolapse.[9] We do not always agree on everything. Barlow would never let me forget what he thought of balloon valvuloplasty for tricuspid stenosis,[12] which I discussed in my book *Percutaneous Balloon Valvuloplasty*.[16] However, we are never afraid of speaking out on those things we believe in. Thus, we have become very close friends, as have our families. One can tell the kind of man Barlow is from a few of his iconoclastic aphorisms, which can be seen on a plaque on the wall of the Duroziez Conference Room in the Johannesburg Hospital which I visited not long ago (Fig. 1).

References

1. Barlow JB, Pocock WA, Tabatznik BA: An epidemic of 'acute eosinophilic pneumonia' following 'beer drinking' and probably due to infestation with *Ascaris lumbricoides*. *S Afr Med J* 1961;35: 390–394
2. Barlow JB, Pocock WA, Marchand P, Denny M: The significance of late systolic murmurs. *Am Heart J* 1963;66:443–452
3. Humphries JO, McKusick VA: The differentiation of organic and "innocent" systolic murmurs. *Prog Cardiovasc Dis* 1962;5: 152–171
4. Barlow JB, Pocock WA: The significance of late systolic murmurs and mid-late systolic clicks. *Maryland State Med J* 1963;12:76–77
5. Barlow JB: Conjoint Clinic on the clinical significance of late systolic murmurs and non-ejection systolic clicks. *J Chron Dis* 1965; 18:665–673
6. Criley JM, Lewis KB, Humphries JO, Ross RS: Prolapse of the mitral valve: Clinical and cine-angiographic findings. *Br Heart J* 1966;28:488–496
7. Barlow JB, Cheng TO: Mitral valve billowing and prolapse. In *The International Textbook of Cardiology* (Ed. Cheng TO), pp. 497–524. New York: Pergamon Press, 1987
8. Barlow JB, Bosman CK: Aneurysmal protrusion of the posterior leaflet of the mitral valve: An auscultatory-electrocardiographic syndrome. *Am Heart J* 1966;71:166–178
9. Cheng TO, Barlow JB: Mitral leaflet billowing and prolapse: Its prevalence around the world. *Angiology* 1989;40:77–87
10. Barlow JB, Marcus RH, Pocock WA, Barlow CW, Essop R, Sareli P: Mechanisms and management of heart failure in active rheumatic carditis. *S Afr Med J* 1990;78:181–186
11. Barlow JB, Antunes MJ, Sareli P, Pocock WA: Submitral left ventricular aneurysm. In *Perspectives on the Mitral Valve* (Ed. Barlow JB), pp. 183–197. Philadelphia: FA Davis, 1987
12. Barlow JB: Mitral valve disease: A cardiologic-surgical interaction. *Isr J Med Sc* 1996;32:831–842
13. Barlow JB: *Perspective on the Mitral Valve*. Philadelphia: FA Davis, 1987
14. Cheng TO: Some new observations on the syndrome of papillary muscle dysfunction. *Am J Med* 1969;47:924–945
15. Cheng TO: Late systolic murmur in coronary artery disease. *Chest* 1972;61:346–356
16. Cheng TO: *Percutaneous Balloon Valvuloplasty*. New York: Igaku-Shoin, 1992

Sir Brian Barratt-Boyes

Bruce C. Paton, m.d.

Health Sciences Center, University of Colorado, Denver, Colorado, USA

Thirty years ago, in September 1962, a young surgeon in New Zealand replaced an aortic valve destroyed by bacterial endocarditis with a fresh, unstented allograft. The patient was a 14-year-old girl who is alive today, and married, with three children. Twenty-five years after the first operation; severe calcification required that the first valve be replaced by a second allograft.

The surgeon was Brian Barratt-Boyes (Fig. 1), and allograft replacement of the aortic valve has proved to have better long-term results than any similar procedure.

Brian Barratt-Boyes was born in Wellington, New Zealand in 1924. His premedical education was in the same city and his medical education at the University of Otago, then the only medical school in New Zealand.

After graduation in 1946, he trained in orthopedic, general, and thoracic surgery, and spent a year in pathology. A surgeon with whom he worked was a friend of O. Theron Clagett of the Mayo Clinic and, through him, Barratt-Boyes received a two-year surgical fellowship at the Mayo Clinic.

During these years he met and worked with John Kirklin who was on the staff of the clinic and was starting his pioneering work on the surgical treatment of congenital heart disease. The two young surgeons became fast friends.

At the end of his fellowship, Barratt-Boyes was invited to join the staff of the clinic, but declined in order to study in Bristol, England. There he developed an extracorporeal perfusion system for the Department of Surgery where clinical open heart surgery had not yet been implemented. At the end of the year he wrote to John Kirklin to ask if the job at the Mayo Clinic was still open and received a reply that said, "Sorry, we have given the job to a young surgeon from Johns Hopkins called Dwight McGoon."

His chief, Professor Milnes-Walker, drew his attention to an advertisement in the *British Medical Journal* for a thoracic surgeon to work in Auckland, New Zealand. Barratt-Boyes applied and was chosen for the position of Senior Thoracic Surgeon at the Green Lane Hospital.

The Government wanted to make Green Lane Hospital a showplace in the health system. Within a short time, Barratt-Boyes was sent around the world to look at cardiac units and returned with a mandate to design and build what has since become a magnet institution both for cardiac surgeons and patients from around the world.

Inspired by the remarkable long-term results obtained by Gordon Murray of Toronto with aortic valve allografts implanted in the descending aorta, Barratt-Boyes believed that the best substitute for a diseased aortic valve would be an allograft rather than a mechanical prosthesis. (Harken and Starr implanted the first mechanical valves in 1960). He developed a technique for sewing an unstented allograft into the subcoronary position and performed the first operation in September 1962. He was unaware that Donald Ross in London had been working on the same solution and had preceded him with the first allograft implantation.

There have now been nearly 3000 aortic valve allograft operations performed at the Green Lane Hospital. The results, which have been meticulously compiled, demonstrate that over a period of 15 years 85% of patients have not needed a second operation, and 75% remain totally free of complications—results equaled only by other series of aortic valve allografts.

The first small group of patients received fresh valves, kept outside the body for the shortest possible time. The supply and demand logistics of the operation made it imperative to develop methods for preserving the valves until they could be used. Several techniques were tried. Valves are now soaked in antibiotic solution for 48 hours, then stored at 4°C until used. Valves preserved in this way are not viable but, in spite of this, have stood the test of time. Research continues to find better methods of long-term preservation.

After a decade of work, Barratt-Boyes found that the small salary he received in his full-time government position was insufficient to support a growing family and, as is allowable in the system, he took a part-time appointment that enabled him to operate on private patients one day per week. He was still able to retain his position as Surgeon-in-Chief at Green Lane until his retirement in 1989.

While the use of aortic valve allografts may have brought him the greatest fame, he regards his work in perfecting techniques for deep hypothermia and cardio-respiratory arrest for the surgery of congenital cardiac defects to be equally important. In the late 1960s, Dr. Hitoshi Mori of Japan began a "deep freeze" technique on small children. The child was cooled to about 15°C and circulation and respiration stopped for 45–60 minutes while the intracardiac procedure was performed. Barratt-Boyes invited Mori to New Zealand where

Fig. 1 Sir Brian Barratt-Boyes (1924 –).

they cooperated in perfecting a technique which almost instantly became the method of choice for repairing complicated congenital lesions. This method, which made possible the primary repair of congenital heart defects at an early age, is, arguably, Barratt-Boyes' greatest contribution to cardiac surgery.

During these years Barratt-Boyes led a hectic life operating, carrying out research, traveling to meetings around the world, and visiting and lecturing at centers where he might learn more. He smoked a pack of cigarettes a day although he tried to stop many times by changing to a pipe or cigars. One night, while visiting Bangkok he had severe pain in the chest that he thought was esophageal spasm. Nocturnal pain continued intermittently for several years, but he never experienced pain with exertion. When he discovered that the pain was relieved by one of the early calcium channel blockers he realized that he might have angina. He was studied and found

to have coronary disease. Although given the chance to go to any surgical center in the world to be operated on Barratt-Boyes chose to have the operation performed by an associate whom he had trained and knew to be an excellent surgeon. Seven years later a second operation (at which an internal mammary artery was used in an era when this was not common) became necessary. Now, nine years after reoperation, he has normal left ventricular function and no pain. The sight of him waterskiing is proof positive, if proof were needed.

On Barratt-Boyes' frequent visits to the United States, his steps lead to the doorway of John Kirklin, early on at the Mayo Clinic and later in Birmingham, Alabama. Kirklin suggested to him that they write the definitive text on cardiac surgery.

At first, Barratt-Boyes was hesitant, believing that their friendship might be strained beyond recovery. Both men are focused perfectionists, with strong opinions, content with nothing but the best in patient care, surgical technique, and reporting of results. They labored for eight years and their friendship survived. "But only just," says his wife Sara, an attorney, and as charismatic as her husband. The book set a new standard for cardiac surgical texts, providing detailed statistics that cast a bright, critical light on the analysis of surgical results and the making of surgical decisions. A second edition—"much better than the first" according to Barratt-Boyes—was at the printer at this writing.

Over the years Barratt-Boyes has received many honors, including 14 honorary degrees and fellowships. In 1971 he was knighted by Queen Elizabeth of England, but the title "Sir Brian" lies lightly on his shoulders. He is still active in research, directing a laboratory for the study of tissue valves. His lecture and travel schedule would intimidate someone half his age. When he is at home he tends his crops of table grapes grown for export. He is as much a perfectionist in these endeavors as he was in the operating room.

As a boy he seriously considered only three professions—medicine, the Episcopal Church, and concert pianist. Inclination steered him away from the second and logic from the third. Now, as he sits smiling in the sun, tanned and healthy, with a rim of snow-white hair, it would not be hard to imagine him as a slim, trim bishop; but, come to think of it, he would probably not have settled for anything less than archbishop.

Joseph K. Perloff

DAVID J. SKORTON, M.D.

The University of Iowa, Iowa City, Iowa, USA

The care of patients with congenital heart disease has become an important aspect of modern clinical cardiology, not only for pediatric cardiologists but increasingly for internist-cardiologists and for many other physicians and health care providers. The astonishing success of surgical and medical management of infants and children with congenital heart disease has permitted most of these patients to survive to adulthood. Improved survival has necessitated a new area of practice concentrating on the adolescent and adult with congenital heart disease. Perhaps no single individual can be credited more clearly for the dissemination of information on adults with congenital heart disease and the encouragement of their thoughtful care than Dr. Joseph K. Perloff (Fig. 1).

Joseph Perloff was born in New Orleans, Louisiana, USA, on December 21, 1924. Many practitioners who have had the privilege of learning from Dr. Perloff's spoken and written words have commented on the linguistic elegance with which his erudition is conveyed in textbooks, journal articles, and lectures. A brief review of the extraordinary career path Dr. Perloff followed sheds light on his unusually well-developed communicative skills. Joseph Perloff initially pursued education in the humanities, earning a bachelor's degree in English from Tulane University. After military service as an ensign in the U.S. Navy in the Pacific theater and in China, Dr. Perloff obtained his scientific education and premedical credentials at the University of Chicago in the heady intellectual atmosphere of that institution under the leadership of Chancellor Robert Maynard Hutchins immediately after World War II. It was at the University of Chicago that Joseph Perloff steeped himself in studies of philosophy and learned the value of rigorous inquiry that has been the hallmark of his subsequent clinical practice, research, and teaching.

Dr. Perloff earned his M.D. at Louisiana State University School of Medicine in 1951. His postgraduate training at Mt. Sinai Hospital in New York included an internship, a year of residency in pathology, and a year of residency in medicine.

In the 1954–1955 academic year, Dr. Perloff was the recipient of a Fulbright fellowship at the Institute of Cardiology in London, England, where he worked with Paul Hamilton Wood. It was during that year that Dr. Perloff was exposed to Wood's syllogistic clinical reasoning. Dr. Perloff credits Dr. Wood with the application of syllogistic reasoning to clinical cardiac diagnosis. Dr. Perloff uses the term *syllogistic* in this context to indicate a deductive, logical approach to clinical di-

agnosis, reasoning from general principles and knowledge to the specific patient under evaluation. It is also significant that Dr. Perloff was exposed to a broad age range of cardiac patients while in London, since the British system was not then subspecialized into age groupings representing pediatric versus internal medicine cardiology. This exposure contributed to Dr. Perloff's view of congenital heart disease as a continuum from birth to adulthood.

Following the year spent with Dr. Wood, Dr. Perloff returned to the United States where he completed his residency in medicine and a fellowship in cardiology at Georgetown University Hospital in Washington, D.C. He was appointed Clinical Instructor in Medicine at Georgetown in 1957 and rose through the ranks to become Professor of Medicine, Chief Consultant in Pediatric Cardiology, and Lecturer in Physiology and Biophysics at Georgetown, where he also served as Director of the Cardiac Diagnostic Laboratory and Assistant Director of the Division of Cardiology. In 1972, he accepted an appointment as Professor of Medicine and Pediatrics and Chief of the Cardiovascular Section at the University of Pennsylvania School of Medicine, a position he held for 5 years. He then moved to UCLA and, in 1980, he began what soon evolved into the UCLA Adult Congenital Heart Disease Center, of which he remains founder and director. Dr. Perloff also holds the Streisand/American Heart Association Professorship of Medicine and Pediatrics at UCLA. Under Dr. Perloff's leadership, the UCLA center became one of the premier patient care, teaching, and research centers in this field. The center has garnered widespread recognition and support, including a major endowment from the Ahmanson Foundation.

Dr. Perloff's bibliography is impressive testimony to his prolific career, containing approximately 300 investigative and review papers, a large number of book chapters and, perhaps of greatest pedagogical importance, several major books. Two of these books, *Physical Examination of the Heart and Circulation*[1] and *The Clinical Recognition of Congenital Heart Disease*,[2] have had enormous impact on trainees and practitioners in cardiology throughout the world. The book on physical examination has been translated into Spanish, Portuguese, Japanese, and Chinese, and *The Clinical Recognition of Congenital Heart Disease* has been translated into Spanish and Portuguese. The recently published second edition of *Congenital Heart Disease in Adults*,[3]

FIG. 1. Joseph K. Perloff, M.D.

called a classic textbook in a recent review,[4] reflects the experience of Dr. Perloff and his colleagues at the UCLA Adult Congenital Heart Disease Center.

Dr. Perloff's interest in congenital heart disease should not eclipse another interest—the heart in systemic neuromuscular disease.[5–9] This arcane field is at the interface between neurology and cardiology; Dr. Perloff has greatly assisted those clinicians negotiating this interface.

Dr. Perloff has garnered many honors. A particularly noteworthy recent recognition for his many contributions is a Commemorative Medal from the Czech Republic on the occasion of the 650th anniversary of the founding of Charles University in Prague.

As impressive as these accomplishments may be, no dry recitation of the details of Dr. Perloff's curriculum vitae and bibliography can convey the magnetism of this superb clinician, scholar, and teacher, nor the impact he has had on my career and on that of many of my contemporaries. No other individual in my estimation has had a similar influence on several generations of clinicians choosing to care for the challenging adult patient with congenital heart disease. What are the attributes and characteristics that have so distinguished Joseph Perloff and his scholarship and teaching? First, Dr. Perloff has always shown an abiding reverence for and mastery of the bedside physical examination.[1, 10] This reverence is expressed both for the enormous utility of carefully considered physical signs—even in this day of sophisticated diagnostic technology—and for the artistry of the physical examination. Second, Dr. Perloff has produced clear and compelling works dealing with the state of the field of con-

genital heart disease, works that are of great value both to the newly initiated and the expert.[2, 11] Third, Dr. Perloff has not been content to practice and teach based on conventional knowledge. Instead, he has generated and inspired a large body of clinical investigation directed at delineating mechanisms of the pathophysiologic accompaniments of congenital heart disease.[12–15]

Perhaps the orientation of this master cardiologist's influence can best be summarized in his own words, taken from the preface to the third edition of *The Clinical Recognition of Congenital Heart Disease*: ". . . an understanding of anatomy and physiology makes the clinical manifestations of congenital heart disease intelligible, and . . . comprehension of these manifestations sets the stage for refined clinical recognition of the anatomic and physiologic derangements." This emphasis on deductive diagnosis derived from a clear understanding of first principles of anatomy and physiology supports effective clinical care that is based on bedside evaluation first, no matter how complex the disorder and no matter how tempting the diagnostic laboratory possibilities.

Perhaps a vignette relating one of my first experiences with Dr. Perloff will provide a finer focus on his approach to teaching the art and science of logical diagnosis. My fellowship in cardiology began coincident with Dr. Perloff's appointment at the UCLA Medical Center. I was asked by our chief to present an unknown case to Dr. Perloff as grist for his diagnostic mill. I was entreated not to share much information with Dr. Perloff, since he was (and is) legendary for his ability to discern important clinical clues that would lead to a diagnosis even when given incomplete data. The case was that of a 27-year-old man with coarctation of the aorta, bicuspid aortic valve, and significant aortic insufficiency. The piece of data I thought least likely to reveal the diagnosis was the electrocardiogram, which to my eyes revealed only impressive left ventricular voltage. Dr. Perloff looked at the electrocardiogram and asked me if I would state the patient's age and gender. I did so. Dr. Perloff commented—talking as much to himself as to the audience—that young males are in the appropriate demographic category for aortic disease, noted that the pattern of left ventricular hypertrophy suggested both volume and pressure overload, and concluded that a likely scenario was that the young man had coarctation of the aorta, bicuspid aortic valve, and significant aortic insufficiency! I retired from the encounter with an abiding respect for the man and his approach to clinical diagnosis. This respect has only grown with the years.

References

1. Perloff JK: *Physical Examination of the Heart and Circulation.* Philadelphia: WB Saunders Co (3rd edition, 2000)
2. Perloff JK: *The Clinical Recognition of Congenital Heart Disease*, 4th edition. Philadelphia: WB Saunders Co., 1994
3. Perloff JK, Child JS: *Congenital Heart Disease in Adults*, 2nd edition. Philadelphia: WB Saunders Co., 1998
4. Marelli A: *Congenital Heart Disease in Adults* (book review). *Circulation* 1998;98:1039

5. Perloff JK, Henze E, Schelbert HR: Alterations in regional myocardial metabolism, perfusion and wall motion in Duchenne muscular dystrophy. Studies by radionuclide imaging. *Circulation* 1984;69:33–42

6. Perloff JK, Stevenson WG, Roberts NK, Cabeen W, Weiss J: Cardiac involvement in myotonic muscular dystrophy (Steinert's disease). *Am J Cardiol* 1984;54:1074–1081

7. Child JS, Perloff JK, Bache PM: Cardiac involvement in Friediech's ataxia. *J Am Coll Cardiol* 1986;7:1370–1378

8. Stevenson WG, Perloff JK, Weiss JN, Anderson TL: Facioscapulohumeral muscular dystrophy: Evidence for selective, genetic electrophysiologic cardiac involvement. *J Am Coll Cardiol* 1990;15:292–299

9. Perloff JK: Neurologic Disorders and Heart Disease. In *Heart Disease*, 5th edition (Ed. Braunwald E), p. 15–52. Philadelphia: WB Saunders Co., 1997

10. Perloff JK, Braunwald E: Physical examination of the heart and circulation. In *Heart Disease*, 5th edition (Ed. Braunwald E), 1865–1886. Philadelphia: WB Saunders Co., 1997

11. Engle MA, Perloff JK (eds.): *Congenital Heart Disease after Surgery*. New York: Yorke Medical Books, 1983

12. Ross EA, Perloff JK, Danovitch GM, Child JS: Renal function and urate metabolism in late survivors with cyanotic congenital heart disease. *Circulation* 1986;73:396–400

13. Perloff JK, Marelli AJ, Miner PD: Risk of stroke in adults with cyanotic congenital heart disease. *Circulation* 1993;87:1954–1959

14. Perloff JK: Systemic complications of cyanosis in adults with congenital heart disease. *Cardiol Clin* 1993;11:689–699

15. Territo MC, Perloff JK, Rosove MH, Moake J: Acquired von Willebrand factor abnormalities in adults with congenital heart disease. *Clin Appl Thromb/Hemost* 1998;4:257–261

Richard Starr Ross

C. RICHARD CONTI, M.D.

University of Florida, College of Medicine, Gainesville, Florida, USA

Richard Starr Ross (Fig. 1) was born in Richmond, Indiana, in 1924. He received his M.D. degree cum laude from Harvard Medical School in June 1947 and served his medical internship and residency on the Osler Medical Service at the Johns Hopkins Hospital. He obtained further training as a Research Fellow in physiology at Harvard Medical School and returned to Johns Hopkins in 1953 where he directed the Cardiovascular Division of the Department of Medicine from 1961 to 1975. From that Division came many of the current leaders in cardiovascular medicine throughout the world. These include, in the USA, Gottlieb C. Freisinger, J. Michael Criley, J. O'Neal Humphries, Bertram Pitt, Myron Weisfeldt, Bernadine Healy, Bruce Fye; in Australia, Aubrey Pitt, Lew Bernstein, David Kelly; in Germany, Paul Lichtlen; in Japan Yasuro Sugishita, and many others. I had the great good fortune to train and work as a faculty member in this division so that I got to know Dr. Ross up close and personal.

Dr. Ross's scientific contributions are many, but he is particularly proud of his role in the development of a method for measuring myocardial blood flow with radioactive xenon injected selectively into the coronary arteries.[1] This method was used to study the effects of myocardial ischemia on myocardial blood flow and the action of antiangina agents such as nitroglycerin. Dr. Ross was instrumental in organizing one of the earliest multicenter randomized trials to evaluate the use of coronary bypass surgery in the emergency management of unstable angina.[2]

O'Neal Humphries writes that "I well remember his preparation for a major lecture or research site visit. Make an outline, prepare the presentation, rehearse the presentation, rewrite the plan and presentation, rehearse again, rewrite again, again—and again—and again, until it is right. He taught us all not to use slides that could not be read at the back of the room by someone with 20/40 vision" (J. O. Humphries, personal communication).

Michael Criley wrote the following about Dr. Ross:

If restricted to the use of one descriptive term to characterize Richard Ross it would be mentor. The dictionary defines a mentor as "wise and trusted counselor." These qualities have been evident in over four decades of memorable encounters that began when I was a medical student interviewing for a position on the house staff and continue to this day when we exchange e-mail over 3,000 miles of cyberspace. As a physician, he cares *about* in addition to caring *for* his patients, and the same can be said for his devotion to this profession and his trainees. As an intern, resident, fellow, and member of his cardiology faculty, I benefited greatly from his wisdom and counsel. He was then and is now eminently approachable. His thoughtful and thorough evaluations of my manuscripts and scientific presentations were humbling at the time, but in every instance clarified, focused, and greatly improved the final product. He was able to impart many of his qualities to a legion of trainees. I will be the first to admit that his consistently high standards are difficult to emulate and impossible to exceed (J. M. Criley, personal communication).

I would add to Criley's comments: Those of us who worked with him were always humbled by the way he could identify the crucial aspects of our research and simplify the presentations of our data so that everyone interested in the subject could fully understand it. He was a master at this.

As a cardiovascular clinician, Dr. Ross had no peer. He had the unique ability to analyze complex data obtained from patients and diagnostic studies and arrive at a sensible solution to the patient's problems.

When asked about what he was most proud of as Chief of the Cardiovascular Division at Johns Hopkins he responded, "I love seeing and hearing about my former fellows' and associates' accomplishments. You have to be able to get your kicks out of what your students do. Because that's all there is." (Interview with W. B. Fye, June 11, 1993, Baltimore, Md.)

Dr. Ross was active in the American Heart Association, serving as Chairman of the Scientific Sessions Program Committee, the Publications Committee, and as President of the Association 1973–1974. He was a recipient of the Gold Heart Award in 1976 and delivered the Conner Lecture at the American Heart Association in 1979. In 1982, the Heart Association honored Dr. Ross by presenting him with the James B. Herrick Award.

In 1975, Dr. Ross left the Cardiovascular Division and became Dean of the Medical Faculty and Vice President for Medicine. As Dean, he considered his primary responsibility to be the maintenance of quality of medical education, research, and patient care in a large private medical school and hospital, that is, Johns Hopkins. In that position, he expressed

FIG. 1   Richard Starr Ross, M.D.

physicians to enter careers in research and teaching so that the progress of biomedical research that had characterized the last 40 years would continue. Through Dr. Ross's efforts, a fund was established to support young investigators during their early years at Johns Hopkins. These internal grants provide start-up funds that will enable a new generation of Hopkins faculty to compete successfully for outside funds such as NIH, American Heart, and so forth. Dr. Ross thought this program was an important investment in the academic leadership of tomorrow.

Prior to his retirement as Dean and Vice President, Johns Hopkins honored him again, dedicating a $98 million research building as the Ross Research Building.

Dr. Ross retired from Johns Hopkins as Vice President for Medicine and Dean of the Medical Faculty in 1990. Since that time he and his wife Elizabeth (Boo) have been enjoying their retirement in Baltimore and Florida.

concern about the shrinking pool of medical investigators, a trend that he believed would have a profound undesirable consequence on the practice of medicine in the future. Obviously Dr. Ross had vision. Throughout his tenure as Dean and Vice President he continued to see a need to encourage young

References

1.   Ross RS, Ueda K, Lichtlen PR, Rees JR: The measurement of myocardial blood flow in animals and man by selective injection of radioactive inert gas into the coronary arteries. *Circ Res* 1964;15:28–41

2.   Unstable angina pectoris: National Cooperative Study Group to compare medical and surgical therapy. I. Report of protocol and patient population. *Am J Cardiol* 1976;37:896–902

David Coston Sabiston, Jr.: Surgeon, Scientist, Teacher, and Leader

SAMUEL A. WELLS, JR., M.D.

Department of Surgery, Duke University Medical Center, Durham, North Carolina, USA

David C. Sabiston, Jr. (Fig. 1) was born in Jacksonville, North Carolina, on October 4, 1924. He was valedictorian of his high school class and was graduated with honors from the University of North Carolina (Phi Beta Kappa) and the Johns Hopkins University School of Medicine (Alpha Omega Alpha). He completed the surgical residency at the Johns Hopkins Hospital during the time that the Chairman, Dr. Alfred Blalock, was developing a school of gifted academic surgeons, several of whom became leaders in American surgery. Following his Chief Residency, he served 2 years in the U.S. Army Medical Corps in the Department of Cardiovascular Research at the Walter Reed Medical Center. He worked with Dr. Donald E. Gregg, a leading cardiovascular scientist, and began a life-long interest in the physiology and pathophysiology of the coronary arteries.

Upon completion of military service, Dr. Sabiston returned to Johns Hopkins as an Assistant Professor of Surgery and an Investigator in the Howard Hughes Medical Institute. In 1961, he received a Fulbright Research Scholarship to study at two prestigious British Institutions: the Hospital for Sick Children (Great Ormond Street) of the University of London and the Nuffield Department of Surgery at Oxford University. Within 10 years of joining the faculty at Johns Hopkins, he was promoted to Professor of Surgery.

In 1964, he returned to his native North Carolina as the James B. Duke Professor and Chairman of the Department of Surgery at the Duke University School of Medicine, a position that he held with great distinction for 32 years.

The Clinical Investigator

While a medical student working with Dr. Mark Ravitch, Dr. Sabiston published his first scientific paper, *Anal Ileostomy with Preservation of Sphincter: A Proposed Operation in Patients Requiring Total Colectomy for Benign Lesions.*[1] This work is widely quoted today, since the experimental procedure described was the forerunner of the definitive operation for children with Hirschsprung's disease.[2] However, most of Dr. Sabiston's research concerned the field of cardiothoracic surgery. He made significant contributions to the understanding of coronary artery blood flow, many of which led to innovative clinical therapies. He also conducted important studies on pulmonary embolism and defined many of the

mechanisms associated with thrombus formation and lysis, and pulmonary injury.

While funded from his first research grant from the National Institutes of Health, a Research Career Development Award, he became the Principal Investigator of a National Heart Institute (HL 09315) grant that was funded continuously for 35 years. During his tenure at Duke, he was the Principal Investigator of a National Institutes of Health Grant supporting an Academic Surgical Research Training Program, which supported the Duke Teaching Scholar in Academic Surgery program.

The Clinician

Dr. Sabiston was a gifted clinical surgeon, with a broad interest in cardiothoracic, vascular, and general surgery. During his early years as chairman at Duke, he was heavily involved in clinical practice; however, as he recruited younger faculty and as his administrative burdens increased, he devoted less time to patient care. He was an excellent clinical surgeon, whose keen insight into clinical medicine was evident not only to medical students and house officers but to his colleagues on the faculty. Many sought his clinical advice and often asked that he care for them or their families.

The Educator

Dr. Sabiston's teaching skills were legendary and he always seemed able to focus on the essence of a complicated clinical problem. His teaching rounds, whether at the bedside or in the classroom, were heavily attended. His abilities as a teacher were especially appreciated by the medical students, who awarded him the Golden Apple Award for excellence in teaching on four separate occasions. Also, in four separate years he received the Teacher of the Year Award, given by the graduating senior medical students to the most outstanding educator on the medical faculty.

His energies were clearly devoted to the Duke surgical house officers and the junior faculty, who recognized him as a highly effective teacher, an excellent clinical surgeon, and an outstanding administrator. His work ethic and attention to detail were apparent to everyone associated with him, and he was

FIG. 1 David Coston Sabiston, Jr., M.D.

an excellent role model for those aspiring to careers in academic surgery.

He was committed to the education of surgical house officers and emphasized their being soundly prepared as clinical surgeons and as clinical investigators. Almost all of the residents at Duke spent two or three years in basic laboratory investigation. He developed excellent relations with the Chairs of other clinical and basic science departments and encour-

aged house officers to explore research opportunities with them. It was not unusual in any given year for more surgical house officers to be studying in basic science departments than in clinical departments. During his tenure many of the surgical residents obtained Ph.D. degrees.

The residency at Duke was noted for its rigor and discipline, and residents who finished the Duke program were extremely well prepared to pursue careers as academic surgeons. Dr. Sabiston was very supportive of medical students, residents, and faculty, and was eager to see them succeed in their careers. It was uncanny how much he remembered about each resident's family life and background, even years after they had graduated from medical school or the surgical residency. His generosity and warmth for them and their families was appreciated by the Duke academic community, few of whom will forget the wonderful Christmas parties held in the Sabiston home that were graced by his and his wife Aggie's presence. This relationship extended beyond one's departure from Duke, as he supported his graduates throughout their careers. The majority of his graduating chief residents pursued careers in academic surgery. Of those who completed their training at Duke during his tenure as Chairman, 10 became departmental chairs at other medical schools and 29 either became chiefs of divisions or professors of surgery in university departments.

His educational abilities were also expressed as an editor of learned surgical publications. From 1966 to 1996 he was the editor of the *Annals of Surgery*, the most highly cited surgical journal. In addition, he was the editor of two of the leading textbooks in surgery, *The Biological Basis of Modern Surgical*

TABLE I

Distinguished Alumnus Award. University of North Carolina, 1978
North Carolina Award in Science Gold Medal (Presented by the Governor of North Carolina), 1978
American Heart Association Scientific Councils' Distinguished Achievement Award, 1983
Michael E. DeBakey Award for Outstanding Achievement, 1984
College Medalist, American College of Chest Physicians, 1987
Honorary Degree, University of Madrid, 1994
Gimbernet Prize, Societat Catalana de Cirurgia, 1994
Honorary Fellowship, European Surgical Association, 1995
The Johns Hopkins University Distinguished Alumnus Award, 1995
Bigelow Medal, Boston Surgical Society, 1996
The Society Prize, the International Surgical Society, 1999
Honorary Member of the Royal College of Surgeons of England
Honorary Member of the Royal College of Surgeons of Edinburgh
Honorary Member of the Royal College of Physicians and Surgeons of Canada
Honorary Member of the German Society of Surgery
Honorary Member of the Royal College of Surgeons of Ireland
Honorary Member of the Royal Australian College of Surgeons
Honorary Member of the Japanese College of Surgeons
Honorary Member of the French Surgical Association
Honorary Member of the Philippine College of Surgeons
Asociacion de Cirugia del Litoral (Argentina)
Brazilian College of Surgeons
Spanish Association of Surgeons
Columbia Surgical Society

Practice, which he edited through 14 editions, and *Surgery of the Chest*, which he co-edited with Dr. Frank Spencer through five editions. He also served on the editorial boards of other surgical journals both in the United States and abroad.

Leadership

Dr. Sabiston was the President of all the most important surgical organizations, including the American Surgical Association, the Society of University Surgeons, the American Association for Thoracic Surgery, the Southern Surgical Association, the Society of Surgical Chairmen, and the American College of Surgeons. He was Chairman of the National Institutes of Health, Surgery Study Section, and Chairman of the Research Committee of the American Heart Association. He is one of the few surgeon members of the Institute of Medicine of the National Academy of Sciences.

David Sabiston was a true leader in American surgery, and for three decades led the dominant academic residency program in surgery. During his tenure, the Department of Surgery at Duke rose to become the academic department with the largest yearly funding from the National Institutes of Health. There are few academic surgeons who have excelled in so many areas. He was an excellent clinical surgeon, a gifted investigator, an excellent teacher, and a skilled administrator.

Honors and Awards

Dr. Sabiston received numerous national and international awards and delivered many prestigious named lectureships. He was also inducted as an honorary member of many international surgical colleges. These are listed in Table I.

References

1. Ravitch MM, Sabiston DC Jr: Anal ileostomy with preservation of sphincter: A proposed operation in patients requiring total colectomy for benign lesions. *Surg Gynecol Obstet* 1947;84:1095–1099
2. Soave F: A new original technique for treating Hirschsprung's disease. *Surgery* 1964;56:1007–1014

Richard Gorlin

EDMUND H. SONNENBLICK, M.D.

Division of Cardiology, Montefiore Medical Center, Bronx, New York, USA

On October 16, 1997, Dr. Richard Gorlin died from pancreatic cancer. At the time of his death, Dr. Gorlin, a highly distinguished and productive cardiologist as well as the former Head of the Department of Medicine at Mt. Sinai Medical Center, was the George Baehr Professor of Clinical Medicine and Senior Vice President of the institution with the broad responsibilities for expanding its regional health center program.

Dr. Gorlin (Fig. 1) had a brilliant career as a creative clinical investigator as well as an innovative cardiologist whose contributions covered the critical years when cardiovascular medicine progressed from passive observation to active intervention, resulting in major improvements in the quality of cardiological care and the prolongation of life for countless patients. Richard Gorlin's brilliant mind, with his incisive and critical approach to complex cardiological problems, brought science to clinical cardiology and helped to revolutionize this central field to the great benefit of physicians, cardiologists, and patients throughout the world.

Dr. Richard Gorlin was born in 1926 in Jersey City, New Jersey, and by the age of 22 had already received his Bachelor and Medical Degrees from Harvard University. After serving as a house officer at the Peter Bent Brigham Hospital and studying cardiology at St. Thomas Hospital in London, he served his military time by creating the Cardiac Service at the United States Naval Hospital in Portsmouth, Virginia. In 1953, he returned to the Brigham where he began his remarkably productive investigative and clinical career in cardiology. Initially, he joined Dr. Lewis Dexter at a time when cardiac catheterization was in its infancy, and in this laboratory he rapidly realized the need for quantification of cardiological studies. A vexing problem in the evolution of cardiovascular surgery had been the evaluation of valvular obstruction, especially mitral stenosis. Working with his father who was a hydraulic engineer, Dr. Gorlin developed the "Gorlin Formula" which allowed one to determine the size of the mitral valve orifice from determined hemodynamic data. Ultimately, Dr. Gorlin created the cardiovascular division and diagnostic laboratories at the Brigham and became one of the very early pioneers in the use of coronary angiography to evaluate coronary disease. Here again, he brought innovation and imagination to this important field, helping to define not only coronary obstructive disease, but also the impact of this process on ventricular function. In the process, he created an entire vocabulary that is still used to this day.

FIG. 1   Richard Gorlin, M.D. (1926-1997).

While Richard Gorlin was pursuing his clinical investigative studies and fostering the advancements of not only clinical cardiology but of cardiovascular surgery as well, he readily recognized the need to combine basic cardiovascular research with clinical endeavors. Because of this consideration, I was "drafted" from the National Heart Institute to join Richard Gorlin in directing the cardiovascular unit and creating basic research laboratories. This was done in 1968, and a close and productive collaboration was established that was not only remarkably productive in terms of cardiovascular research, but also served as a focal point of training for many young investigators in both basic cardiovascular physiology and clinical cardiology. This was a truly happy and productive partnership.

In 1974, Dr. Richard Gorlin left the Brigham to become Chairman of the Department of Medicine at the Mt. Sinai School of Medicine and the Murray M. Rosenberg Professor of Medicine. In this role as Chief of Medicine, he fostered creative and vigorous growth at the institution and excellent clinical care, as well as a dynamic base for clinical and basic research. With his retirement from the role as Chief of Medicine in 1994, he became Medical Director of the Mt. Sinai Health Center and Senior Vice President of the Medical Center, where he expanded the medical network of the Mt. Sinai Hospital into the next century. Although he had major clinical and administrative responsibilities, Dr. Richard Gorlin remained an active and creative cardiologist as well as a leader in clinical investigation in his later years. In his dynamic career, he published over 700 papers of the highest quality. He was always open to new ideas and fostered imagination and growth in his peers, fellows, and students. Above all, Richard Gorlin was always a gracious and generous gentleman. He loved his family dearly as they did him in return. His former fellows and associates have always respected him as a leader, a teacher, and a good friend. "R.G.," as he was always known to his fellows, set a very high standard both professionally and personally, and these pristine qualities will be greatly missed and long remembered.

Selected References

1. Gorlin R, Gorlin SG: Hydraulic formula for calculation of area of stenotic mitral valve, other cardiac valves and central circulatory shunts. I. *Am Heart J* 1951;41:1–29
2. Krasnow N, Neill WA, Messer JV, Gorlin R: Myocardial lactate and pyruvate metabolism. *J Clin Invest* 1962;41:2075–2085
3. Cohen LS, Elliott WC, Klein MD, Gorlin R: Coronary heart disease: Clinical cinearteriographic and metabolic correlations. *Am J Cardiol* 1966:17:154–168
4. Herman MV, Heinle RA, Klein MD, Gorlin R: Localized disorders in myocardial contraction. Asynergy and its role in congestive heart failure. *N Engl J Med* 1967;277(5):222–232
5. Gorlin R, Sonnenblick EH: Regulation of performance of the heart. *Am J Cardiol* 1968;22:16–23
6. Sonnenblick EH, Gorlin R: Reversible and irreversible depression of ischemic myocardium. *N Engl J Med* 1972;286:1154–1155
7. Popio K, Gorlin R, Bechtel D, Levine JA: Postextrasystolic potentiation as a predictor of potential myocardial viability: Preoperative analyses compared with studies after coronary bypass surgery. *Am J Cardiol* 1977;39:944–953.

Desmond Gareth Julian: Pioneer in Coronary Care

MARK E. SILVERMAN, M.D., FACC, MACP, FRCP

Departments of Medicine, Emory University School of Medicine and Piedmont Hospital, Atlanta, Georgia, USA

Desmond Julian (Fig. 1) is an admired leader in European cardiology, whose many accomplishments include the introduction of the concept of coronary care, the publication of many articles and textbooks, and an important influence on the practice of modern cardiology. Born in Liverpool, England, in 1926, he graduated with honors from St. John's College, Cambridge, in 1946, and the Middlesex Hospital Medical School in London in 1948. After house officer positions in Liverpool and the Central Middlesex Hospital, and a registrar position at the National Heart Hospital in London, he was a research fellow in Boston at the Peter Bent Brigham Hospital from 1957 to 1958, returning to the Royal Infirmary, Edinburgh, as a senior registrar from 1958 to 1961.[1] He considers his early influences to include his father, who was an internist, Evan Bedford, Paul Wood, and Sidney Burwell. He obtained the M.R.C.P. (London) in 1952, the M.A. in 1953, the M.D. in 1954, and was elected F.R.C.P. in 1970.

At the Royal Infirmary, Edinburgh, in 1959, Julian administered open chest cardiac massage on several patients with myocardial infarction who had suffered a cardiac arrest. This dramatic experience led to a lasting research interest in coronary disease and sudden coronary death. From a patient who was successfully resuscitated, he learned about the work of Kouwenhoven at Johns Hopkins, who proposed closed chest massage in 1960. It seemed logical to Julian that patients at risk for arrest should be grouped together in a monitored area so rescue resuscitation could be instituted immediately. This pioneering approach, published in *Lancet* in 1961, after an earlier rejection by the *British Medical Journal*, included the comment:

> All wards admitting patients with acute myocardial infarction should have a system capable of sounding an alarm at the onset of an important rhythm change and of recording the rhythm automatically on an ECG. . .the provision of the appropriate apparatus would not be prohibitively expensive if these patients were admitted to special intensive-care units. Such units should be staffed by suitably experienced people throughout the 24 hours.[2]

Julian's article was the first to advocate a specialized coronary care unit. In 1962, after moving to Sydney, he initiated a coronary care unit. About the same time, similar units were also started in Kansas City, Philadelphia, and Toronto.[3]

Because no consultant vacancies were available at desirable institutions in the U.K., Julian moved to Australia in 1961 to become staff cardiologist at Sydney Hospital. There he organized a cardiac catheterization laboratory, continued his research into the monitoring and treatment of acute myocardial infarction, and traveled widely to report his results. He returned to Edinburgh in 1964 as a consultant cardiologist at the Royal Infirmary, where his research focused on reducing the time lag between the onset of symptoms and admission, the use of antiarryhythmic drugs to prevent sudden death, and a mobile coronary care concept. He and Michael Oliver organized the first international conference on coronary care in 1967.

In 1969, Julian became an adviser on coronary care to the World Health Organization (WHO), later serving as a consultant to the WHO from 1980 to 1999. His growing reputation led to an appointment from 1975 to 1986 as the British Heart Foundation Professor of Cardiology at the University of Newcastle-upon-Tyne, where he developed a cardiac center of importance. Along the way, he was a mentor to Valentin Fuster, Ronnie Campbell, and others who would become leading figures in cardiology. His trainees especially valued his careful approach to the examination of the patient, his common sense and judgment, his admonition to avoid dogmatism and arrogance, and his love of clinical cardiology. In 1986, Julian left active involvement with clinical medicine to become the medical director of the British Heart Foundation (1986–1993). In that important post, he was influential in raising funds and developing research and community programs throughout Britain. In addition, he accepted organizational responsibilities as President of the British Cardiac Society (1985–1987) and Second Vice-President of the Royal College of Physicians (London) (1991–1992). He was also Chairman of the British Action on Smoking and Health (1993–1996) and the National Heart Forum (1993–1999).

While he was at Edinburgh, his colleague Michael Oliver introduced him to the new concept of multicenter randomized clinical trials. From this stimulating experience, Julian learned about the power of large clinical studies in deciding the value of a cardiac therapy. This led to an increasing involvement in many large clinical trials, including the ISIS (International Study of Infarct Survival) trial, an acronym which he coined. His great experience, keen intelligence, and understanding of the complexities of these trials made him a

F<small>IG</small>. 1   Desmond Gareth Julian

leading international expert in this area and has kept him extraordinarily busy after a so-called retirement. He has now participated in more than 40 studies, often chairing the Data and Safety Monitoring Board. He also initiated an invaluable Clinical Trials website (http://www.cardiosource.com) to maintain a comprehensive listing and update of trials and abstracts of presented papers. Currently, Julian continues to lecture around the world and to write about well-conducted clinical trials which, he contends, should form the basis for our clinical practice. At the same time, he notes a lamentable failure to implement the findings of clinical trials into everyday practice.

Desmond Julian is widely admired for his intelligence, warm and charming personality, modesty, broad cultural and historical interests, and the great enthusiasm that he brings to everything that he undertakes. It is well known that he finishes whatever he starts and that the results are always first class. His seemingly inexhaustible energy and editorial skills have led to the publication of more than 20 books. His single author book *Cardiology*, now in its seventh edition since 1970, remains in great demand by medical students and postgraduates.[4] He is co-editor of *Diseases of the Heart*, a highly respected, major reference source in cardiology, now in its second edition.[5] Some of his coedited books include *Angina Pectoris, Management of Heart Failure, Management of Myocardial Infarction, Women and Heart Disease, Clinical Trials in Cardiology*, and *British Cardiology in the Twentieth Century*.[6–11] From 1979 to 1988, Julian was the Foundation Editor of the *European Heart Journal*. The American Heart

Association chose him to give its prestigious International Lecture in 1975. In 1993, Julian was awarded the honor of Commander of the British Empire (C.B.E.), and in 1998 he was the Gold Medallist of the European Society of Cardiology. In addition, he has received a number of honorary degrees from universities as well as honorary fellowships from the American Heart Association and the Australian Cardiac Society. Despite the many demands of an international professional life, he finds time for his many friends, is an avid reader of fiction, and enjoys theater, entertaining, and the pleasure of walking holidays with his wife Claire.

While working at the National Heart Hospital in London in 1956, his former medical school professor advised him not to pursue a career in cardiology stating that "all the mitrals had been operated upon."[12] Julian tells this story to explain why he is not pessimistic about the field of cardiology as an exciting place for an aspiring potential cardiologist. The world of cardiology can be thankful that Julian did not follow the advice of his professor.

Acknowledgments

The author greatly appreciates Gaston Bauer, David Mendel, Arthur Hollman, Douglas Chamberlain, Phillip C. Adams, and Valentin Fuster for their review and suggestions.

References

1. Bauer G: Desmond Julian: A pioneer in cardiac care. *On the Pulse* 1998;10:12–13
2. Julian DG: Treatment of cardiac arrest in acute myocardial ischemia and infarction. *Lancet* 1961;ii:840–844
3. Day HW: History of coronary care units. *Am J Cardiol* 1972;30: 405–407
4. Julian DG: *Cardiology*, 2nd edition. London: Balliere, Tindall, and Cassell, 1977
5. Julian DG, Camm AJ, Fox KM, Hall RJC, Poole-Wilson PA (Eds.): *Diseases of the Heart*, 2nd edition. London: Saunders, 1996
6. Julian DG (Ed.): *Angina pectoris*, 2nd edition. Edinburgh: Churchill Livingstone, 1986
7. Julian DG, Wenger NK: *Management of Heart Failure*. London: Butterworths, 1986
8. Julian DG, Braunwald E (Eds.): *Management of Acute Myocardial Infarction*. London: Saunders, 1994
9. Julian DG, Wenger NK (Eds.): *Women and Heart Disease*. London: Martin Dunitz, 1997
10. Pitt B, Julian D, Pocock S: *Clinical Trials in Cardiology*. London: Saunders, 1997
11. Silverman ME, Fleming PR, Hollman A, Julian DG, Krikler DM (Eds.): *British Cardiology in the 20th Century*. London: Springer-Verlag, 2000
12. Julian DG: The forgotten past: The practice of cardiology in the 1950s and now. *Eur Heart J* 2000;21:1277–1280

Chuichi Kawai

MARIO R. GARCIA-PALMIERI, M.D., M.A.C.P., F.A.C.C., F.A.C.C.P., F.E.S.C.

Department of Medicine and Adult Cardiology Section, University of Puerto Rico, School of Medicine and University Hospital, San Juan, Puerto Rico

Dr. Chuichi Kawai was born in Japan on March 31, 1928. He graduated in 1953 as a Doctor of Medicine at the Faculty of Medicine of Kyoto University and subsequently received training in internal medicine and cardiology at the same institution, receiving a Doctorate in Medical Sciences in 1950.

From 1962 to 1964 he was appointed a Fulbright Research Scholar and during the period of 1962-1963 he was a Research Fellow in Cardiology at Stanford University School of Medicine in California. From 1963 to 1964 he served as a Cardiology Research Fellow at the Heart Station of Boston City Hospital under the aegis of Harvard Medical School.

Upon return to his country Dr. Kawai was appointed Instructor in Medicine at Osaka Medical College in 1965 and stayed at that institution until 1974. That year he moved to the Faculty of Medicine at Kyoto University where he was Professor of Medicine and served as Director of the 3rd Division, Department of Medicine, at Kyoto University Hospital from 1974 to 1991 and as the hospital's Director from 1989 to 1991. He held the professorship and directorship at Kyoto University until his retirement in 1991. At present he is Professor Emeritus at Kyoto University and Chief Director of the Japanese Circulation Society.

During his professorship of medicine, Dr. Kawai was one of the leading academicians in his native Japan and the mentor of many hundreds of medical students and residents in internal medicine and cardiology.

He has held, with excellence, some of the most prestigious positions in internal medicine and cardiology in Japan, such as President of the Japanese Circulation Society, Chief Director of the Board of Directors of the Japanese Circulation Society, Councillor of the Japanese Society of Internal Medicine, Director of the Japanese Society of Nephrology, and Councillor of the Japanese Society of Geriatric Medicine. He was Chairman of the Research Committee on Cardiomyopathy of the Ministry of Health and Welfare of Japan (1974–1980), and Chairman of the Committee on Cardiomyopathy of the Japanese Circulation Society. He is a Fellow of the American College of Cardiology and of the American College of Chest Physicians. The World Health Organization appointed him as a member of the Expert Committee on Cardiomyopathy.

Dr. Kawai has been a leader in the International Society and Federation of Cardiology. He served as President-Elect from 1985 to 1986, as President from 1987 to 1988, and as Past President from 1989 to l990. He is one of the most prolific medical writers, being the author or co-author of more than 1,350 scientific articles, reviews, books, and chapters including 447 publications in English.

He has served on the editorial boards of a number of publications, including the *Japanese Circulation Journal*, the *Japanese Heart Journal*, the *International Journal of Cardiology*, *Cardiology*, *Coronary Artery Disease*, and *Clinical Cardiology*.

Dr. Kawai was invited as guest speaker for a number of lectures, such as the "Antonio Samia Lecture" during the X Asian-Pacific Congress of Cardiology in Taiwan and the "Sackler Distinguished Lecture" at Tel Aviv University in Israel. He also delivered the "International Lecture" during the 59th Scientific Sessions of the American Heart Association in Dallas, Texas, in 1986, the "International Lecture" during the 13th Interamerican Congress of Cardiology in Rio de Janeiro, Brazil, the "ISFC Lecture" during the XI World Congress of Cardiology in Manila, Philippines, the "Hammersmith Lecture" at the Royal Postgraduate Medical School in London, and the "R. T. Hall Lecture" in Australia. He has also delivered special lectures at Würzburg University in Germany; at

FIG. 1   Chuichi Kawai, M.D., D.Med.Sc., 1928–.

Harvard Medical School in Boston; in Jakarta, Indonesia; at the Favaloro Foundation in Buenos Aires, Argentina; at the Republic of China Society of Cardiology in Taipei, Taiwan; at an International Symposium in Munich, Federal Republic of Germany; at the International Symposium of Cardiology in San Juan, Puerto Rico; at the International Symposium on Cardiovascular Pharmacotherapy in Geneva, Switzerland; at the Xth Asian-Pacific Congress of Cardiology in Seoul, Korea; and at the Second International Symposium on Heart Failure in Melbourne, Australia.

Dr. Kawai's publications have contributed new knowledge, both in basic research with experimental animals and in clinical research with patients. His main contributions have been in the areas of cardiomyopathies, myocarditis, and related subjects in which he is one of the leading world experts, as well as research concerning renal diseases, primarily pathophysiological studies concerning renin. Additional cardiovascular subjects to which he has contributed include congestive heart failure, sudden death, acute myocardial infarction, left ventricular hypertrophy and contractility, stress thallium, myocardial emission tomography, use of drugs in congestive heart failure and cardiomyopathy, cardiac arrhythmias, cardiac immunology, prostaglandin and thrombocyte research, cardiovascular pharmacology, ischemic heart disease, thrombolysis, nuclear cardiology, atherosclerosis and viral diseases of the heart.

Dr. Chuichi Kawai and his lovely wife Toshi have four children, Hiroko, Ken, Junko and Makoto, and live in Kyoto, Japan. He has earned the respect of his undergraduate and postgraduate students, as well as of his peers in Japan and worldwide for his accomplishments in teaching, research, service and administration. He has served as a model to a new generation of cardiologists in Japan. His smooth and cordial personality and his distinguished career have allowed him to maintain not only friendships but respect and admiration all over the world. This soft-spoken, elegant, articulate, and humble person will long be remembered by the world of cardiology not only for his contributions to science and clinical cardiology but also for his tremendous talent as a consensus builder at the international level.

Dennis Michael Krikler

ARTHUR HOLLMAN, M.D.

Pett, East Sussex, England, U.K.

Dennis Krikler (Fig. 1) has an enviable range of talents and interests that encompass skills as a clinician, mastery of electrophysiology and arrhythmias, expertise as an editor, and enthusiasm for the history of cardiology. He was born in 1928 in Cape Town, where his father was a general practitioner with an interest in cardiology. His father had qualified in Liverpool, where he was a student of the renowned cardiologist Dr. John Hay. He also had his own electrocardiograph, which was unusual for the 1930s. Dennis graduated in 1951, and his early professional career was first in Cape Town and then in Rhodesia (now Zimbabwe). In 1966, he came to Britain, where he soon gained a consultant appointment.

It was mainly the influence of Dr. Velva Schrire in Cape Town that led Dennis to a career in cardiology with a special interest in arrhythmias that Sir John McMichael in London encouraged him to pursue. At the Prince of Wales's Hospital in London, it was he who was the first to discover the effect of verapamil on supraventricular arrhythmias and, with Leo Schamroth in Johannesburg, on atrial fibrillation.[1] He proposed that the drug worked through its calcium antagonistic action on the atrioventricular node, and this led to his friendship and collaboration with Albrecht Fleckenstein in Germany. McMichael's influence enabled him to join the staff of Hammersmith Hospital and the Royal Postgraduate Medical School in 1973. There he established an electrophysiology unit, having earlier been fascinated by the new techniques of intracardiac electrophysiology introduced in France and Holland by Paul Puech, Phillipe Coumel, and Dirk Durrer. His studies showed that verapamil and diltiazem, but not nifedipine, had electrophysiologic properties that acted on the atrioventricular node. He became an international expert on the pharmacology of arrhythmias, and one aspect of this was his Hideo Ueda lecture in Japan in 1990 on "preexcitation syndrome." Indeed, the Wolff-Parkinson-White syndrome has followed him right through his career, for it was the title of his M.D. thesis in Cape Town in 1973. In 1974, he edited an excellent book on the modern electrophysiologic approach to cardiac arrhythmias; this book was translated into French and Italian.

Dennis is an acclaimed teacher. His visiting professorships and major lectureships are numerous—notably the William Osler Lectureship of the University of Miami in 1981 and the Paul Dudley White Award of the American Heart Association in 1984. He must have been especially pleased to give the Howard B. Burchell inaugural lecture in Minneapolis because

he has great admiration for Dr. Burchell and treasures his friendship. Also in the United States, he was a member for 22 years of the editorial board of ACCEL, the distant learning medium of the American College of Cardiology of which he became a fellow in 1971. At Hammersmith, he inaugurated annual courses in arrhythmias and electrophysiology.

One can readily accept the attraction of arrhythmias and teaching, but it is less easy to understand why Dennis was drawn to the task of being an editor. Walter Somerville wrote, "Successful editors obey a vocational call to office and so willingly forego many professional and material deserts. Krikler had no option but to listen to this summons."[2] He was on the editorial board of the *British Heart Journal* for six years before being appointed its editor in 1981 and in that capacity serving until 1991. The journal flourished under his leadership, and with his scholarly approach he put a special stamp on it, providing guidance and encouragement without restricting the individual style of authors. For over 20 years he has been a member of the Comité Scientifique of the *Archives des Maladies du Coeur* and had been an associate editor of the *European Journal of Cardiology*.

Dennis is not one of those who let others do the hard work of running professional societies. He was the treasurer of the British Cardiac Society for five years, being on their council for 11 years, and has been a council member of the British Heart Foundation and the council on clinical cardiology of the American Heart Foundation.

Dennis is certainly a European. Having learned French in order to give lectures in that language, he became a corresponding member of the Société Française de Cardiologie in 1982, and in 1999 he had the great distinction of receiving the honor of Chevalier dans l'Ordre National de la Legion d'Honneur. He has been a member of the advisory committee of the Einthoven Foundation in the Netherlands since 1983, and a Dutch physician has said, "Dr. Krikler is one of Britain's best cardiological ambassadors. Many cardiologists outside Britain regard Dr. Krikler as the personification of the best of traditional British cardiology."[3] This was emphasized by his selection as the George Burch Memorial Lecturer in the U.S. when he spoke on "the roots of modern British cardiology."

He is one the small band of doctors with a keen interest in the history of medicine, an interest that he shares with his friend, the American medical historian Dr. Bruce Fye. He has written several articles on the history of electrocardiography.

FIG. 1   Dennis Michael Krikler, M.D., F.A.C.C., F.E.S.C.

While still a junior doctor in Cape Town, he read by chance an article by the Russian physiologist A. F. Samojloff, who had written the first book on electrocardiography in 1909. This led him to detailed research about Samojloff, including the tracing of his son and his links with Paul White and Sir Thomas Lewis. Without this inquiry, much information about the life and work of Samojloff could well have been lost, and his study demonstrates the gifts that Dennis has for careful research and pursuit of detail. Recently, he has been a co-editor and author of the book *British Cardiology in the 20th Century*.

Dennis is rightly proud of his Jewish ancestry, and one of his earliest papers was entitled "The Pioneering Jews of Rhodesia."[4] In it, he told of the significant part that Jewish settlers played in the development of Rhodesia and of Cecil Rhodes's appreciation of their importance in forming that country. He gave the Paul Wahler memorial lecture before the London Jewish Medical Society in 1991.

In 1955 he married Anne Winterstein who had been a nurse at Groote Schuur Hospital. They have a daughter who is a cardiac technician at Hammersmith Hospital and a son who is an investment banker in New York. His hobbies include the study of French art, English art of the twentieth century, photography, and contemporary history.

References

1. Schamroth L, Krikler DM, Garrett C: The immediate effects of intravenous verapamil in the treatment of cardiac arrhythmias. *Br Med J* 1972;I:660–662
2. Somerville W: Envoi. *Br Heart J* 1992;67:14–15
3. Meijler FL: Continental connections. *Br Heart J* 1992;67:12–13
4. Krikler DM: The pioneering Jews of Rhodesia. *The Wiener Library Bulletin* 1968;13:19–24

Frank I. Marcus

J. Willis Hurst, m.d.

Division of Cardiology, Department of Medicine, Emory University School of Medicine, Atlanta, Georgia, USA

The Early Years

Frank Marcus (Fig. 1) was born in Haverstraw, New York, on March 23, 1928. He entered Columbia University at the young age of 16 and graduated in 1948 at the age of 20. He then spent a year in research in endocrinology at the Worcester Foundation in Shrewsbury, Massachusetts. He entered Boston University School of Medicine in 1949 and received a masters degree in physiology from Tufts University in Massachusetts in 1951. (The work-research had been done previously at Tufts. He wrote his thesis while attending medical school.) He graduated cum laude in 1953 from Boston University School of Medicine. Marcus completed a medical internship at the Peter Bent Brigham Hospital in Boston in 1954 and entered the United States Air Force where he spent two years in Japan as a medical officer. He returned to the Brigham as an assistant resident in medicine in 1956 and became a research fellow in cardiology at the same institution in 1957 under the tutelage of Drs. Samuel Levine and Bernard Lown. In 1958, he moved to Washington, D.C., where he was a cardiology fellow at Georgetown University Hospital and then became chief resident in medicine at the same institution in 1959. His work at Georgetown University Hospital brought him in contact with the master cardiologist, Dr. Proctor Harvey, who wrote the following note to me on November 22, 1997:

> Frank Marcus was one of our cardiac fellows here at Georgetown. After arriving, it was not long before we became aware of his personality and talents: a kind, dedicated, sincere, intelligent physician who had true empathy for his patients as well as his fellow men and women. He was just the type of fellow that we wanted in our program. His performance was outstanding and he was able to continue the clinical as well as the research aspects of cardiology.
>
> As a 'twist of fate,' it happened that Dr. Gordon Ewy, at that time, also became one of our fellows. A lifelong bonding and friendship quickly took place. Frank Marcus, several years older, was subsequently appointed chief of cardiology at Georgetown's Division of Cardiology at the District of Columbia General Hospital. He took Gordon Ewy with him as his associate there. The rest has been history. They wanted to stay together as a pair and when the new medical center at the University of Arizona opened several decades ago, they, along with Dr. Robert O'Rourke, also from Georgetown, were wisely selected to develop the division of cardiology there at Tucson. Immediately, the cardiology division 'took off like a jet airplane' to become, as present, one of the best in the country.

Frank initially was chief of cardiology and in 1982 was honored by being appointed as the first Distinguished Professor of Cardiology thereby affording opportunity for his research activities. Gordon Ewy then became a professor of medicine and chief of cardiology.

I know I speak for all who have known Frank and Gordon, to thank them for their outstanding contributions to medical education and research in the field of cardiovascular diseases.

Dr. Frank Marcus is a role model. We at Georgetown are justly proud of him.

Leadership Positions

Marcus was chief of cardiology at the Georgetown University Service at the D.C. General Hospital from 1960 to 1968. He was promoted in a timely and orderly manner and became associate professor of medicine at Georgetown in 1968. His reputation for excellence became nationally known, and he became professor of medicine and chief of the cardiology section at the University of Arizona College of Medicine in Tucson, Arizona, in 1969.

Honors and Awards

Dr. Marcus's honors and awards include the following: member of Alpha Omega Alpha (Boston University School of Medicine), research fellowship from the Massachusetts Heart Association, John and Mary Marble Scholar, Career Development Award from National Institutes of Health, "Golden Apple Award" for excellence in teaching at Georgetown University College of Medicine, award of excellence from the Cardiology

FIG. 1 Frank I. Marcus, M.D.

Section of the University of Arizona College of Medicine, Laureate Award from the Arizona chapter of the American College of Physicians, and Outstanding Reviewer Award of the American College of Cardiology.

Over the years, Marcus has served on the editorial boards of 12 journals. He was a member of 20 organizations where he was an active participant in numerous committees.

Sabbatical Leaves

Marcus has taken two sabbaticals during his career. The first of these, from July 1979 to June 1980, was spent at Hospital Jean Rostand in Ivry, France. He worked with Professor Yves Grogogeat and Guy Fontaine who further stimulated his intense interest in electrophysiology.

The second sabbatical lasted from January 1994 to June 1994. Marcus worked with Dr. Michael Haissaguerre in Pessac, France. The purpose of these 6 months of study was to learn the techniques of electrophysiologic diagnosis of supraventricular tachycardia and radiofrequency ablation of these arrhythmias.

Research Contribution

When Marcus was chief of cardiology at the Georgetown Division of Cardiology of the D.C. General Hospital, he began studies to elucidate the metabolism of digoxin and other cardiac glycosides using radioisotope techniques learned from the pharmacologist, Dr. George Okita, at the University of Chicago. He and his colleagues investigated the metabolism of digoxin in normal subjects,[1] in patients with renal insufficiency,[2] in obese people,[3] in the elderly,[4] and in patients with jejuno ileo bypass.[5]

He was among the first to describe the phenomenon of the post extrasystolic decrease in pulse pressure in patients with idiopathic hypertrophic cardiomyopathy.[6, 7]

After moving to Arizona, Dr. Marcus investigated important drug interactions in conjunction with Dr. Paul Nolan, Pharm. D. Their group of investigators studied the interactions of digoxin and digitoxin with quinidine,[8, 9] digoxin with amiodarone, and digoxin and propafenone amiodarone with phenytoin.[10–12]

In 1979, Marcus became intrigued with cardiac arrhythmias and spent a year on sabbatical leave working with the brilliant electrophysiologist, Dr. Guy Fontaine, in Paris, France. He predicted that electrophysiology would develop into an important subspecialty of cardiology. Dr. Fontaine had recognized some patients who had sustained ventricular tachycardia that was due to heterogeneous infiltration of fat in the right ventricle, a condition called right ventricular dysplasia. Fontaine was also the first to observe and name the epsilon waves in the electrocardiogram. Marcus, along with Dr. Fontaine and Dr. Frank, as well as with other associates in France, decided to study this entity, which had been barely discussed in the English literature. Marcus, Fontaine and colleagues published a landmark paper on this subject in *Circulation* in 1982.[13] Marcus has continued to study this unusual condition with Dr. Fontaine and recently established an international registry for the disease which accounts for unexplained sudden death in a small percentage of athletes and young individuals.

Dr. Marcus learned the techniques of catheter ablation of arrhythmias using DC energy during his sabbatical leave in France and began to use the technique at the Medical College of Arizona. He then sought a safer energy source for catheter ablation. Working with Dr. Steve Huang, they introduced radiofrequency energy for cardiac ablation in 1986.[14–16] As time passed, catheter ablation using radiofrequency energy has replaced DC energy for this purpose. With this safer energy source, the technique of catheter ablation has profoundly changed the treatment of supraventricular arrhythmias.

Dr. Marcus has been an active participant in a number of multicenter trials.[17–25] He urged the creation of the study that compared Holter monitoring with electrophysiologic testing to determine the efficacy of antiarrhythmic drugs for the treatment of patients with sustained ventricular arrhythmias, the Electrophysiologic Study Versus Electrocardiographic Monitoring (ESVEM) trial. He also participated in the following trials: the Multicenter Post-Infarction Trial (MPIT) that helped characterize patients at risk after myocardial infarction; the Multicenter Diltiazem Post-Infarction Trial (MDPIT) that evaluated the use of diltiazem after myocardial infarction; and the Autonomic Reflexes after Myocardial Infarction (ATRA-MI) trial that demonstrated that decreased baroreceptor receptivity is an additional risk factor after a myocardial infarction.

Teaching and Patient Care

Dr. Marcus has always been highly regarded by trainees for his teaching skills, as well as by patients for his compassionate and devoted care. These attributes were honed during his own training by Levine, Lown, and Harvey.

Home and Other Activities

Dr. Marcus has recently celebrated his 40th wedding anniversary with Janet, who is an elected member of the Tucson City Council. They are the proud parents of three children, Steve, Anne, and Lynn, as well as grandparents to Rachel, Nicco, and Daniel.

Dr. Marcus continues to pursue his hobbies of bicycling and photography.

References

Dr. Marcus and associates have published 46 book chapters. He has published 216 scientific articles with an additional 13 in press or in preparation. The references listed below are only those that are germane to this article.

1. Marcus FI, Kapadia GJ, Kapadia GG: The metabolism of digoxin in normal subjects. *J Pharmacol Exp Ther* 1964;145:203–209
2. Marcus FI, Peterson A, Salel A, Scully J, Kapadia GG: The metabolism of tritiated digoxin in renal insufficiency in dogs and man. *J Pharmacol Exp Ther* 1966;152:372–382
3. Ewy GA, Groves BM, Ball MF, Nimmo L, Jackson B, Marcus FI: Digoxin metabolism in obesity. *Circulation* 1971;44:810–814
4. Ewy GA, Kapadia GG, Yao L, Lullin M, Marcus FI: Digoxin metabolism in the elderly. *Circulation* 1969;39:449–453
5. Marcus FI, Quinn EJ, Horton H, Jacobs S, Pippin S, Stafford M, Zukoski C: The effect of jejunoileal bypass on the pharmacokinetics of digoxin in man. *Circulation* 1977;33:537–541
6. Marcus FI, Westura EE, Summa J: The hemodynamic effect of the Valsalva maneuver in muscular stenosis. *Am Heart J* 1964;67:324–333
7. Marcus FI, Perloff JK, DeLeon AC: The use of amyl nitrate in the hemodynamic assessment of aortic valvular and muscular subaortic stenosis. *Am Heart J* 1964;68:468–475
8. Hager WD, Fenster P, Mayersohn M, Perrier D, Graves P, Marcus FI, Goldman S: Digoxin-quinidine interaction: Pharmacokinetic evaluation. *N Engl J Med* 1979;300(22):1238–1241
9. Fenster PE, Powell JR, Graves PE, Conrad KA, Hager WD, Goldman S, Marcus FI: Digitoxin-quinidine interaction: Pharmacokinetic evaluation. *Ann Intern Med* 1980;93(5):698–701
10. Nolan PE Jr, Marcus FI, Erstad BL, Hoyer GL, Furman C, Kirsten EB: Effects of coadministration of proafenone on the pharmacoki-

11. netics of digoxin in healthy volunteer subjects. *J Clin Pharmacol* 1989;29:46–52
12. Nolan PE Jr, Marcus FI, Hoyer GL, Bliss M, Gear K: Pharmacokinetic interaction between intravenous phenytoin and amiodarone. *Clin Pharmacol Ther* 1989;46:43–50
13. Nolan PE, Erstad BL, Hoyer GL, Bliss M, Gear K, Marcus FI: Steady-state interaction between phenytoin and amiodarone in normal subjects. *Am J Cardiol* 1990;65:1252–1257
14. Marcus FI, Fontaine GH, Guiraudon G, Frank R, Laurenceau J, Malergue C, Grosgogeat Y: Right ventricular dysplasia: A report of 24 adult cases. *Circulation* 1982;65:384–398
15. Hoyt RH, Huang SK, Marcus FI, Odell RS: Factors influencing transcatheter radiofrequency ablation of the myocardium. *J Appl Cardiol* 1986;1:469–486
16. Huang SK, Bharati S, Graham AR, Lev M, Odell RC, Marcus FI: Closed-chest catheter desiccation of the atrioventricular junction using radiofrequency energy—A new method of catheter ablation. *J Am Coll Cardiol* 1987;9:349–458
17. Huang SK, Bharati S, Lev M, Marcus FI: Electrophysiologic and histologic observations of chronic atrioventricular block induced by closed-chest catheter desiccation with radiofrequency energy. *PACE* 1987;10(4):805–816
18. The Multicenter Post-Infarction Research Group: Arthur J. Moss, Principal Investigator. Risk stratification and survival after myocardial infarction. *N Engl J Med* 1983;309:331–336
19. The Multicenter Diltiazem Post-Infarction Trial Research Group. The effect of diltiazem on mortality and reinfarction after myocardial infarction. *N Engl J Med* 1988;319:385–392
20. Marcus FI, Bigger JT Jr, and the Multicenter Post-Infarction Research Group: Mechanism of death after acute myocardial infarction. *Cardiol Board Review* 1989;6(1):37–43
21. Marcus FI, Friday K, McCans J, Moon T, Hahn E, Cobb L, Edwards J, Kuller L: Age related prognosis following myocardial infarction. Experience from the Multicenter Diltiazem Postinfarction Trial. *Am J Cardiol* 1990;65:559–566
22. Benhorin J, Moss AJ, Oakes D, Marcus FI, Greenberg H, Dwyer EM Jr, Algeo S, Hahn E, and the Multicenter Diltiazem Post-Infarction Research Group: The prognostic significance of first myocardial infarction type (Q-wave vs. non-Q-wave) and Q wave location. *J Am Coll Cardiol* 1990;15:1201–1207
23. Narahara KA and the Western Enoximone Study Group: Oral enoximone therapy in chronic heart failure: A placebo-controlled randomized trial. *Am Heart J* 1991;121:1471–1479
24. Moss AJ, Goldstein RE, Hall WJ, Bigger JT, Fleiss JL, Greenberg H, Bodenheimer M, Krone RJ, Marcus FI, Wackers FJ, Benhorin J, Brown MW, Case R, Coromilas J, Dwyer EM, Gillespie JA, Gregory JJ, Kleiger R, Lichstein E, Parker JO, Raubertas RF, Stern S, Tzivoni D, Voorhees LV, for the Multicenter Myocardial Ischemia Research Group: Detection and significance of myocardial ischemia in stable patients after recovery from an acute coronary event. *J Am Med Assoc* 1993;269(18):2379–2385
25. Mason JW for the ESVEM Investigators: A comparison of electrophysiologic testing with Holter monitoring to predict antiarrhythmic-drug efficacy for ventricular tachyarrhythmias. *N Engl J Med* 1993;329:445–451
26. Mason JW for the ESVEM Investigators: A comparison of seven antiarrhythmic drugs in patients with ventricular tachyarrhythmias. *N Engl J Med* 1993;329:452–458

Robert C. Schlant

J. WILLIS HURST, M.D.

Division of Cardiology, Emory University School of Medicine, Atlanta, Georgia, USA

Dr. Robert Carl Schlant (Fig. 1), the son of Edward and Elaine Schlant, was born in El Paso, Texas, on April 16, 1929. His father was an attorney in the Judge Advocate General's Department in the U.S. Army. As commonly occurs, army personnel move every few years. Accordingly, Schlant's early schooling was in several different towns and cities. His family eventually moved to Atlanta, Georgia, where he attended and graduated valedictorian from Boys High School in 1945. Boys High was famous because it was tough and had the reputation of developing leaders.

Schlant attended Vanderbilt University in Nashville, Tennessee, and graduated Phi Beta Kappa in 1948. At Vanderbilt, he may have been the youngest quarterback ever to start in the Southeastern Conference. In 1951, he graduated from Vanderbilt University School of Medicine where he was a member of Alpha Omega Alpha Honorary Society.

Schlant served his internship and assistant residency in medicine from 1951 to 1953 at the Peter Bent Brigham Hospital in Boston. He joined the army and was stationed in Brooklyn, Korea, and Japan from 1953 to 1955. He returned to the Peter Bent Brigham Hospital for his senior residency in medicine, which he completed in 1956. From 1956 to 1958 he was a research fellow in cardiology under Dr. Lewis Dexter, who was one of the leaders in cardiac catheterization.

Schlant joined the faculty at Emory University in Atlanta, Georgia, in 1958 as an Assistant Professor in the Department of Medicine. He became Associate Professor of Medicine at Emory in 1962 and Professor of Medicine in 1967. He was appointed Director of the Division of Cardiology in 1962 and retained that position until 1988 (see personal note below).

During Schlant's career he has been an active member of more than 20 medical organizations. He has played a major role in the American Heart Association where he was chairman of many committees and task forces. He was chairman of the Council on Clinical Cardiology of the American Heart Association from 1985 to 1987.

He is an active member of the American College of Cardiology and was Governor of the College in Georgia from 1960 to 1962 and again from 1968 to 1971. He has been chairman of many committees of the College, including four Bethesda conferences, and was a member of the Board of Trustees from 1983 to 1988.

He served on many important committees of the American College of Physicians.

He became a member of the Association of University Cardiologists in 1967. He served as the organization's secretary-treasurer from 1978 to 1981, vice president from 1981 to 1982, and its president 1982 to 1983.

Schlant is active in many international societies including the International Cardiology Foundation in which he served as vice president from 1983 to 1987.

Schlant was a member of the Subspecialty Board of Cardiovascular Diseases from 1971 to 1978. During that time he was chairman of the Oral Exam Committee from 1975 to 1978 and served on several other committees dealing with the written exam and cardiovascular graphics.

During his productive career, Schlant has served on the editorial board of more than 30 journals including *Circulation*, *The Journal of the American College of Cardiology*, *The American Journal of Cardiology*, the *American Heart Journal*, and *Clinical Cardiology*.

Schlant has served on numerous diverse committees of Emory University School of Medicine. His wide range of interest and competence led to his appointment to many research committees and to the medical school diploma ceremony committee.

Schlant was recognized and honored when he received an USPHS Research Career Development Award from 1961 to 1971. He was then awarded the Georgia Heart Chair of Cardiovascular Research from 1972 to 1982. He received the Distinguished Achievement Award from the Council on Clinical Cardiology of the American Heart Association in 1990 and the James B. Herrick Award of the American Heart Association in 1994. In 1983, along with Hurst, Gruentzig, and King, he received the cum laude diploma and Golden Eagle Award at the International Film Festival held in Parma, Italy, for the film "Can We Arrest an Impending Myocardial Infarction?"

He was chosen as the honorary chairman of the Atlanta Heart Ball in 1995. The purpose of the event is to raise money for the research effort of the American Heart Association.

Schlant has written more than 240 scientific articles, numerous book chapters, 10 book reviews, was one of the editors of 19 books, and, as discussed at the end of this essay, helped me develop the book *The Heart*.

Schlant's rise to national and international prominence is described in the paragraphs that follow. This passage was written by Dr. Robert O'Rourke, who is Professor of Medicine at the University of Texas in San Antonio.

Dr. Robert Schlant's contributions to American and international cardiology have been extraordinary. He has been secretary, vice-chairman, and chairman of the

FIG. 1   Robert C. Schlant, M.D. (1929–2002).

International Society and Federation of Cardiology, now known as the World Federation of Cardiology.

Bob Schlant has participated in many postgraduate education courses for the American College of Cardiology and the American Heart Association, and has designed, implemented, and chaired many cardiology courses for third world countries.

He is a dedicated clinician and educator whose contributions to world-wide cardiology have been immense.

A Personal Note

Bob Schlant has remained at Emory University School of Medicine during his entire academic career. Here is the story. I was appointed Professor and Chairman of the Department of Medicine in 1957. I was looking for a physiologically oriented physician to be the director of the cardiovascular laboratory at Grady Hospital because my friend Dr. Noble Fowler, who was director of the laboratory, had accepted a position at the University of Cincinnati. The laboratory had been made famous by Drs. Eugene A. Stead, Jr., and James V. Warren during the 1940s. Bob Schlant applied for the position. He was completing his fellowship at the Brigham Hospital under the direction of the famous Dr. Lewis Dexter. Dexter called me and said, "Schlant is one of the best trainees we have ever had." I always thought it was wise to appoint physicians to my department who were smarter than me. Bob was clearly the man for the job. So, Bob and I sealed the agreement with a handshake and he joined the Department of Medicine at Emory in 1958. It was immediately apparent that Schlant was one of a handful of physicians who, after World War II, was interested in the scientific explanations for the abnormalities found on the routine ex-

amination of patients with heart disease. He was a meticulous observer and influenced others to be the same. He saw the potential value of using the drug nitroprusside and reported on its pharmacologic actions.[1] He participated in one of the early studies on the use of direct current countershock for atrial fibrillation.[2] He performed the first selective coronary arteriogram in Georgia in 1966-1967.

Paul Wood visited us at Emory University in 1962. His diagnostic brilliance was evident but he was frustrated. He felt he could no longer write his famous book because, as he said, "By the time I write the last chapter the first one is out of date." He died in London two weeks later. His comments during his visit led me to conceive of the idea of a well organized multiauthored textbook of cardiology. This led to the birth of *The Heart* in 1966.

My long-time associate, Bruce Logue, and I began to work on the book. Bob Schlant and Nanette Wenger were assistant editors of the book. Schlant contributed the text dealing with physiologic matters throughout the book. His competence and enormous talent were also evident when he, along with Wenger, who also contributed to the text, created the index for the first edition of the book. Such an act by each of them not only requires keen intellect and an extraordinary memory but also demonstrates an intense loyalty to the cause. Schlant contributed heavily to the subsequent nine editions of *The Heart* serving as assistant and associate editor. I stepped aside when the 8th edition of *The Heart* was to be produced and Schlant and Wayne Alexander became co-editors of the 8th edition of Hurst's *The Heart*. Schlant joined Alexander and Valentin Fuster as coeditors of the 9th edition of the book.

Schlant reviews many of my manuscripts before I send them to the publisher. He never lets our friendship interfere with his use of a pen with green ink. I know when I give him a manuscript that he will fill it with green editorial marks. I have learned to appreciate his comments and corrections because he is always right. I recently gave him a manuscript to check and, being accustomed to his penchant for green ink, I included a pen with green ink in the envelope that carried the message, "Help me." He did.

His excellent research and writing are matched by his teaching. He participates in ward rounds and teaching conferences. His lectures are carefully prepared and well received, but he realizes, as I do, that the best teaching takes place on ward rounds and in small teaching sessions.

By 1962 Dr. Schlant had become nationally recognized and I appointed him Director of the Division of Cardiology in the Department of Medicine. The program thrived and about 10 new fellows were appointed each year to a 3-year program which made Emory's program one of the largest in the nation. Schlant was a superb organizer and created a first-rate teaching program for 30 fellows who were located at our four teaching hospitals, which included Grady Memorial Hospital, Emory University Hospital, Crawford W. Long Hospital, and the Atlanta Veterans Administration Hospital. He retained his position as Director of the Division of Cardiology until 1988, when Wayne Alexander became the Director. Schlant continued his role as chief of cardiology at Grady Memorial Hospital until 1998. He continues to teach and write as a productive and respected member of the Division of Cardiology of the Department of Medicine at Emory University.

Schlant has shown us all that a person can be a clinical scientist and think in a cold logical manner, but can, at the same time, be a warm and compassionate doctor. Everyone cannot do that but he excels at it because he is devoted to excellent patient care. With it all he has been loyal to Emory University and to the Department of Medicine and has influenced two generations of students, house officers, and fellows to be better physicians.

At this point in time I have known Bob Schlant for 41 years. Dexter's original appraisal was correct—he is smart but there are a lot of smart people. Schlant is also kind and compassionate and his middle name is integrity.

References

1. Schlant RC, Tsagaris TJ, Robertson RJ Jr: Studies on the acute cardiovascular effects of intravenous sodium nitroprusside. *Am J Cardiol* 1962;9:51–59

2. Hurst JW, Paulk EA Jr, Proctor HD, Schlant RC: The management of patients with atrial fibrillation. *Am J Med* 1964;37:728–742

Additional Important References:

Schlant RC, Novack P, Kraus WL, Moore CB, Haynes FW, Dexter L: Determination of central blood volume. Comparison of Stewart-Hamilton method with direct measurements in dogs. *Am J Physiol* 1959;196:499–501

Hurst JW, Schlant RC: Coronary atherosclerosis and its management, p. 1–47. Disease-a-Month, Chicago: Year Book Medical Publishers, January 1960

Schlant RC, Tsagaris TJ, Robertson RJ Jr, Winter TS III, Edwards FK: The effect of acetylcholine upon arterial saturation. *Am Heart J* 1962;64:512–524

Schlant RC, Galambos JT, Shuford WH, Winter TS III, Edwards FK, Rawls WJ: The clinical usefulness of wedge hepatic venography. *Am J Med* 1963;35:343–349

Schlant RC, Galambos JT: Autoradiographic demonstration of ingested cholesterol-4-C14 in the normal and atheromatous aorta. *Am J Pathol* 1964;44:877–887

Hurst JW, Paulk EA Jr, Proctor HD, Schlant RC: The management of patients with atrial fibrillation. *Am J Med* 1964;37:728–742

Hurst JW, Schlant RC: *Examination of the Heart. Part 3: Inspection and Palpation of the Anterior Chest*. New York: American Heart Association, 1965, 24 pp (2nd edition 1970, 28 pp; 3rd edition 1972, 28 pp)

Krayenbuhl HP, Crosthwait JL, Schlant RC: Einfluss der paarigen elektrischen Stimulation auf die Dynamik des linken Hundeherzens. *Schweiz Med Wschr* 1966;96:1035–1044

The Coronary Drug Project, Publication 1695. National Institute, Public Health Service, 1968

Symbas PN, Schlant RC, Gravanis MB, Shepherd RL: Pathologic and functional effects on the heart following interruption of the cardiac lymph drainage. *J Thorac Cardiovasc Surg* 1969;57:577–584

The Coronary Drug Project Research Group: Initial findings leading to modifications of the initial protocol. *J Am Med Assoc* 1970;214:1303–1313

Schlant RC, Nutter DO: Heart failure in valvular heart disease. *Medicine* 1971;50:421–451

Siegel W, Gilbert CA, Nutter DO, Schlant RC, Hurst JW: Use of isometric handgrip for the indirect assessment of left ventricular function in patients with coronary atherosclerotic heart disease. *Am J Cardiol* 1972;30:48–54

Nutter DO, Schlant RC, Hurst JW: Isometric exercise and the cardiovascular system. *Mod Con Cardiovasc Dis* 1972;41:11–15

The Coronary Drug Project Research Group: Findings leading to further modifications of its protocol with respect to dextrothyroxine. *J Am Med Assoc* 1972;220:996–1008

Schlant RC, Hurst JW (Eds): *Advances in Electrocardiography*. New York: Grune & Stratton, 1972

Felner JM, Schlant RC: *Echocardiography, A Teaching Atlas*. New York: Grune & Stratton, 1976

Schlant RC, Hurst JW (Eds): *Advances in Electrocardiography*, volume 2. New York: Grune & Stratton, 1976

Schlant RC: Metabolism of the heart. In *The Heart*, 4th edition (Eds. Hurst JW, Logue RB, Schlant RC, Wenger NK), p. 107–118. New York: McGraw-Hill, 1978

Barolsky SM, Gilbert CA, Faruqui A, Nutter DO, Schlant RC: Differences in electrocardiographic responses to exercise of women and men: A non-bayesian factor. *Circulation* 1979;60:1021–1027

Schlant RC, Felner JM, Lutz J, Miklozek C, Hurst JW: Mitral valve prolapse, XXVI (No. 10), p. 1–51. Disease-a-Month. Chicago: Year Book Publishers, 1980

The Beta-Blocker Heart Attack Study Group: The beta-blocker heart attack trial. *J Am Med Assoc* 1981;246:2073–2074

The Coronary Drug Project Research Group: Implications of findings in the coronary drug project for secondary prevention trials in coronary heart disease. *Circulation* 1981;63:1342–1350

Schlant RC, Felner JM, Blumenstein BA, Wollam GL, Hall WD, Shulman NB, Heymsfield SB, Gilbert CA, Tuttle EP Jr: Echocardiographic documentation of regression of left ventricular hypertrophy in treatment for essential hypertension. *Eur Heart J* 1982;3(suppl A):171–175

Schlant RC: Physiology of exercise. In *Exercise and the Practice of Medicine* (Ed. Fletcher GF), p. 1–43. Mt. Kisco, New York: Futura Publishing, 1982

Libow M, Schlant RC: Smoking and diet after myocardial infarction. *Physician and Patient* 1982;11:131–161

Schlant RC: Aortic stenosis. In *Cardiology* (Eds. Parmley WM, Chatterjee K), p. 1–13. Philadelphia: JB Lippincott, 1987

Schlant RC: Prevention of sudden cardiac death: Lessons from the cardiac arrhythmia suppression trial (CAST). *J Med Assoc Georgia* 1990;79(4):245–247

Schlant RC: Pharmacologic therapy and secondary prevention in the postinfarct patient. In *Acute Myocardial Infarction* (Ed. McCall D), p. 159–179. New York: Churchill Livingston, 1991

Capone RJ, Pawitan Y, El-Sherif N, Geraci TS, Handshaw K, Morganroth J, Schlant RC, Waldo AL, and the CAST investigators: Events in the cardiac arrhythmia suppression trial. Baseline predictors of mortality in placebo-treated patients. *J Am Coll Cardiol* 18:1434–14381991;

Schlant RC: The current management of the patient with uncomplicated myocardial infarction. In *Advances in Internal Medicine* (Eds. Stollerman GH, Lamont JT, Leonard JJ, Siperstein MD), p. 1–19. Chicago: Mosby-Year Book, 1992

Schlant RC, Adolph RJ, DiMarco JP, Dreifus LS, Dunn MI, Fisch C, Garson A, Haywood J, Levine HJ, Murray JA, Noble RJ, Ronan JA: Guidelines for Electrocardiography: A report of the American College of Cardiology/American Heart Association Task Force on Assessment of Diastolic and Therapeutic Cardiovascular Procedures (Committee on Electrocardiography). *J Am Coll Cardiol* 1992;19:473–481

Schlant RC, Collins JJ Jr, Engle MA, Gersh BJ, Kaplan NM, Waldo AL: *The 1993 Year Book of Cardiology*. Chicago: Year Book Medical Publisher, Inc., 1993

Schlant RC, Alexander RW (Eds), O'Rourke RA, Roberts R, Sonnenblick EH (Assoc Eds): *The Heart*, 8th edition. New York: McGraw-Hill, 1994

Schlant RC: Mitral stenosis. In *Current Therapy in Cardiovascular Disease*, 4th edition (Ed. Hurst JW), p. 209–214. St. Louis: Mosby-Year Book, Inc., 1994

Schlant RC, Alexander RW: Diagnosis and management of chronic ischemic heart disease. In *The Heart*, 8th edition (Eds. Schlant RC, Alexander RW, O'Rourke RA, Roberts R, Sonnenblick EH), p. 1055–1082. New York: McGraw-Hill, 1994

Schlant RC: Perioperative evaluation and management of patients with known or suspected cardiovascular disease who undergo noncardiac surgery. In *The Heart*, 8th edition (Eds. Schlant RC, Alexander RW, O'Rourke RA, Roberts R, Sonnenblick EH), p. 2421–2431. New York: McGraw-Hill, 1994

Schlant RC: Cardiac manifestations of pulmonary embolism. In *Pulmonary Embolism* (Ed. Morpurgo M), p. 67–78. New York: Marcel Dekker, 1994

Dr. Schlant died in 2002, after this profile was written.

Eugene Braunwald

JOHN ROSS, JR., M.D.

Department of Medicine, University of California, San Diego, La Jolla, California, USA

Eugene Braunwald's (Fig. 1) remarkable journey began in pre-World War II Vienna on August 15, 1929. Among his earliest memories is his mother's declaration that he was to become a professor of medicine. These years were marked by a pleasant Viennese social life and immersion in the opera, which instilled in him a lifelong love of music. In 1938, as did many others, his family left for political asylum, first in Switzerland, and then in England where they spent more than a year before moving to New York City.

The Early Scholar

A period of scholastic achievement followed, which culminated in Eugene Braunwald graduating as the youngest and first in his medical school class at New York University in 1952. His interest in cardiology was sparked as a fourth-year medical student during an elective course with Ludwig Eichna; the excitement concerned congestive heart failure which was then being defined, a search which has continued. House staff training in medicine and cardiology followed at the Mount Sinai Hospital in New York (a residency later completed at the Johns Hopkins Hospital), with subsequent service as a research fellow in André Cournand's laboratory.

The Scientist and Statesman

Following important research in Stanley Sarnoff's laboratory from 1955 to 1957, Dr. Braunwald then became the first Chief of the newly established Cardiology Branch at the National Institutes of Health in Bethesda, where he remained until 1968 when he left to become Chairman of the Department of Medicine at the new medical school at the University of California, San Diego.

As one who participated in that 10-year period at the NIH (which some have called a scientific "Camelot"), I can confirm that it was indeed a remarkable coalescence of technologies, people and ideas, constantly stimulated by Eugene Braunwald's extraordinary intelligence, perception and insatiable scientific curiosity. The publication of the first edition of *Mechanisms of Contraction of the Normal and Failing Heart* in 1967 epitomized the productivity of those years.

In 1972, after creating a distinguished Department of Medicine at UCSD, he assumed his present position as the Hersey Professor of Medicine and Chairman of the Department of Medicine of Harvard Medical School at the Peter Bent Brigham Hospital (now Brigham & Women's Hospital). Between 1980 and 1989 he simultaneously served as the Herman Blumgart Professor of Medicine and Physician-in-Chief at the Beth Israel Hospital.

Among Dr. Braunwald's numerous honors he most readily cites the Carl J. Wiggers Award of the American Physiological Society, the Abel Award of the American Society for Pharmacology and Experimental Therapeutics, the James B. Herrick Award of the American Heart Association, the Distinguished Scientist Award of the American College of Cardiology, election to the National Academy of Sciences (the only cardiologist in that society), and fellowship in the American Academy of Arts and Sciences. He holds five honorary degrees, and his international honors include the Ferrari Prize and membership in the Royal Society of Medicine (England) and Honorary Fellowship in the Royal College of Physicians.

He is one of the few individuals invited to serve more than one term as a member of the National Heart, Lung, and Blood Advisory Council.

Scientific Legacy

The Braunwald legacy in research is wide and long, although several clear themes can be identified, including a number of contributions on congenital heart disease early in his career. One major line of investigation on factors influencing cardiac contraction began with early studies on intracardiac pressures in New York, continued at the NIH with analyses of ventricular and atrial function in animals and in humans, including a body of research on Starling's law of the heart in which he brilliantly documented the significance of diastolic fiber length as a major determinant of cardiac function. His interest in heart failure as a medical student later flowered in a still-cited series of studies with Chidsey, Gaffney, and others on the physiology and pharmacology of the failing heart, including its adrenergic control, and the first demonstration that myocardial catecholamine stores were decreased in experimental and human heart failure.

Another important research trajectory began with work in Sarnoff's laboratory on myocardial oxygen consumption, with development of the tension-time index and other correlations with the mechanics of contraction. The.se studies culmi-

Fig. 1   Eugene Braunwald, M.D.

giotensin converting enzyme inhibition to limit left ventricular dilation and to reduce mortality in experimental animals following acute myocardial infarction. Recently, this discovery was extended to humans in an important clinical trial showing that captopril administered to patients with left ventricular dysfunction after acute myocardial infarction reduces morbidity and mortality.

The Person

Eugene Braunwald's prodigious capacity for work is legendary. In addition to his many outstanding personal research accomplishments, which include nearly 900 publications, he has also produced *Heart Disease; A Textbook of Cardiovascular Medicine* which has received worldwide acclaim and is now in its fourth edition. Endowed with unusual organizational skills, ranging from the organization of an academic department of medicine to the design of a superb clinical trial, he also knows how to find and appreciate talent. As an editor, I have had many occasions to note his uncanny ability to immediately spot the major flaw or the key observation in a scientific argument. Those who know him intimately appreciate and enjoy his keen flashing wit; if at times acerbic, it is always insightful, colorful, and profoundly amusing. With an extraordinary insight into human motivation and behavior, he knows the human "heart" metaphorically as well as physiologically.

His wife of 40 years, Nina H. Starr Braunwald, died in 1992. She was a pioneer, the first woman to be boarded in cardiovascular and thoracic surgery, who made important contributions to heart valve replacement. It is characteristic of Eugene Braunwald's strength and resilience that despite his grief he has continued with his enormous responsibilities. His three daughters live in the Boston area and he takes great pride in these professionally accomplished and personally gifted young women.

Eugene Braunwald, probably the most famous academic cardiologist of his generation, thinks of himself mainly as the chairman of a department of medicine, yet he continues to leave his primary mark with truly remarkable contributions to cardiovascular science and education. His story yet remains only half-told.

nated in 1969 in the oft-quoted Bowditch Lecture of the American Physiological Society. Among his most outstanding clinical contributions has been work on hypertrophic cardiomyopathy, work which has continued at the NIH long after his departure. His first paper on idiopathic hypertrophic subaortic stenosis appeared in 1960, followed by a series of papers, including demonstration of the beneficial effects of beta blockade and a classic monograph describing the disorder in 1964.

The research idea which I believe has had the greatest scientific impact was the concept that the extent of myocardial infarction following coronary occlusion is not static, but rather can be modified by intervention. The concept grew out of earlier investigations on interrelations between myocardial oxygen supply and demand. This seminal idea led to a large body of research in his laboratory in experimental animals, indicating that myocardial infarct size could be reduced by pharmacological intervention to diminish oxygen consumption (such as beta blockade) or to increase coronary blood flow, as well as by anti-inflammatory agents. With the advent of coronary reperfusion by thrombolysis in the clinical setting, he was principal investigator in the TIMI trials documenting its effectiveness in producing coronary artery patency, limiting ischemic damage, and improving clinical outcome. He was also responsible for the idea that even late reperfusion of an occluded artery can lead to clinical benefit.

Braunwald's investigations have continued actively with exciting work (with Pfeffer and others) on the effects of an-

A Few Key Scientific Publications and Reviews (from a total of 895)

Braunwald E, Sarnoff SJ, Case RB, Stainsby WN, Welch GH, Jr.: Hemodynamic determinants of coronary flow: Effect of changes in aortic pressure and cardiac output on the relationship between myocardial oxygen consumption and coronary flow. *Am J Physiol* 192, 157–163 (1958)

Braunwald E, Frye RL, Ross J Jr.: Studies on Starling's law of the heart: Determinants of the relationship between left ventricular end-diastolic pressure and circumference. *Circ Res* 8, 1254–1263 (1960)

Braunwald E: The control of ventricular function in man. *Br Heart J* 27, 1–16 (1965)

Braunwald E, Lambrew CT, Rickoff SD, Ross J Jr., Morrow AG: Idiopathic hypertrophic subaortic stenosis. I. A description of the disease based upon an analysis of 64 patients. *Circulation* 30 (suppl 4) 3–119 (1964)

Chidsey CA, Braunwald E, Morrow AG: Catecholamine excretion and cardiac stores of norepinephrine in congestive heart failure. *Am J Med* 39, 442–451 (1965)

Braunwald E, Chidsey CA: The adrenergic nervous system in the control of the normal and failing heart. *Proc Roy Soc Med* 58, 1063–1066 (1965)

Braunwald E: 13th Bowditch Lecture. The determinants of myocardial oxygen consumption. *The Physiologist* 12, 65–93 (1969)

Maroko PR, Kjekshus JK, Sobel EB, Watanabe T, Covell JW, Ross J Jr., Braunwald E: Factors influencing infarct size following experimental coronary artery occlusion. *Circulation* 43, 67–82 (1971)

Braunwald E, Maroko PR: The reduction of infarct size—an idea whose time (for testing) has come. *Circulation* 50, 206–209 (1974)

Braunwald E: Protection of ischemic myocardium. *Harvey Lecture Series* 71, 247–282 (1978)

The TIMI Study Group: The thrombolysis in myocardial infarction (TIMI) trial. *N Engl J Med* 312, 932–936 (1985)

Pfeffer JM, Pfeffer MA, Braunwald E: Influence of chronic captopril therapy on the infarcted left ventricle of the rat. *Circ Res* 57, 84–95 (1985)

Braunwald E: Myocardial reperfusion, limitation of infarct size, reduction of left ventricular dysfunction, and improved survival. Should the paradigm be expanded? *Circulation* 79, 441–444 (1989)

Pfeffer MA, Braunwald E, Moye LA, Basta L, Brown EJ Jr., Cuddy TE, Davis BR, Geltman EM, Goldman S, Flaker GC, Klein M, Lamas GA, Packer M, Rouleau J, Rouleau JL, Rutherford J, Wertheimer JH, Hawkins CM, on behalf of the SAVE Investigators: Effect of captopril on mortality and morbidity in patients with left ventricular dysfunction after myocardial infarction. Results of the Survival and Ventricular Enlargement Trial. *N Engl J Med* 327, 669–677 (1992)

William C. Roberts

J. WILLIS HURST, M.D.

Department of Medicine (Cardiology), Emory University School of Medicine, Atlanta, Georgia, USA

I first met Bill Roberts (Fig. 1) when he was assigned to the medical service of Emory University School of Medicine. I was Chairman of the Department of Medicine and he was a junior student. He stood out as an attentive and interested student. He was obviously interested in identifying all of the abnormalities that occurred in his patients but was equally interested in *why* the abnormalities occurred. He seemed to focus his thoughts and language so that he talked clearly and simply. I supported his later efforts to become a straight medical intern at Boston City Hospital. All this took place in 1957–1958. Since then, as one of Bill's former teachers, I have watched his spectacular work with pleasure and admiration.

Birth and Family

William C. Roberts was born in Atlanta, Georgia, on September 11, 1932. His father, Stewart R. Roberts, M.D., a famous physician, was Clinical Professor of Medicine at Emory University School of Medicine. He also became President of the Southern Medical Association in 1925 and, having grown up among notable pioneers in the burgeoning science of cardiology, he became President of the American Heart Association in 1933. He wrote 94 scientific papers and wrote a book on pellegra in 1912 at the age of 34. He was on the first editorial board of the *American Heart Journal*. Bill's mother, Ruby Holbrook Roberts, was born in 1903 and currently lives in Atlanta. She recognized a need for and became founder, owner, and director of the Medical Placement and Mailing Service in Atlanta (1947–1966). Bill's brother, Stewart R. Roberts, Jr., is Associate Professor of Radiology at Emory University School of Medicine. Another brother died in 1966.

During my 30-year tenure as Chairman of Medicine at Emory, I consider it my good fortune to have had the sons and daughters of former students as students in their turn. Charles S. Roberts, second of four of Bill's children (he also has three grandchildren), is among them.

A Brief Biography

Curriculum Vitae and Bibliography

To prepare this short biography of William C. Roberts, I asked him to supply me with his curriculum vitae and bibliography. He sent it; the document, as of June 1991, is 220 pages long—single spaced! I have reviewed hundreds of similar documents during my career, but never one that is better organized and more complete than this one. The arrangement and details of his curriculum vitae and bibliography tell us much about the man. He is organized, strives for accuracy and perfection, and works efficiently.

Schooling and Appointments

Roberts was graduated from public high school in Atlanta, Georgia, in 1950 and received an A.B. degree from Southern Methodist University in Dallas, Texas, in 1954. He graduated from Emory University School of Medicine in Atlanta in 1958.

He served a straight medicine internship at the Boston City Hospital from 1958 to 1959 and then served as a resident in anatomical pathology at the National Cancer Institute in Bethesda, Maryland, from 1959 to 1962. He pursued further training in internal medicine by serving as an assistant resident on the Osler service at The Johns Hopkins Hospital in Baltimore, Maryland.

Roberts gained additional experience in surgery (6 months) and cardiology (6 months) at the National Heart Institute. He then began his productive career as the cardiovascular pathologist at the National Heart, Lung, and Blood Institute, a position which offers him a chance to work closely with the Institute's excellent cardiologists. In return, Roberts has given the Institute an inquiring mind and excellent spokesman.

Roberts holds clinical faculty positions at Georgetown, George Washington, Howard, and Hahnemann Universities. He gives his time and talent to other medical institutions in the Washington area, including the Washington Hospital Center, VA Hospital, National Children's Medical Center, DC General Hospital, DC Medical Examiner's Office, National Naval Medical Center, and Suburban Hospital in Bethesda.

Honors

The College of Cardiology awarded Roberts its Gifted Teacher Award in 1978. The American Heart Association awarded him the Richard and Hinda Rosenthal Foundation Award for his contributions to cardiology in 1984. He has been honored by the Emory Medical Alumni Association and was elected to Alpha Omega Alpha at Georgetown. He has received numerous additional honors including the Public

FIG. 1   Dr. William C. Roberts.

Health Service Commendation Medal in 1979 for the distinction he had brought to the National Institutes of Health and the Public Health Service.

Writing and Editing

Books

During each of the last 10 years Dr. Roberts has edited an annual book on cardiology. He also edited *Congenital Heart Disease in Adults* in 1979.

Journals

As of June 30, 1991, William Roberts has published 920 articles; his name is listed as the sole author, or the first author in 402 (44%) of the 920 articles. This number includes his 105 From-the-Editor Columns in *The American Journal of Cardiology*. He and his colleagues have also published 219 abstracts in major scientific journals.

Major Presentations

Roberts is a sought-after lecturer. From October 1960 through June 1991 he gave 1,942 lectures in 1,180 cities in the United States and abroad. In a 25-year period (July 1966–June 1991) he gave an average of 1.5 major lectures a week. These numbers must be a record.

Editor in Chief of *The American Journal of Cardiology*

He was appointed Editor in Chief of *The American Journal of Cardiology* in June 1982. After almost 10 years he continues to receive a high grade for his leadership since the journal is often quoted and is very popular. Roberts has demonstrated that he has a keen eye for the trends in cardiology and has the ability to push forward an idea he believes in. His prepared talk on the responsibilities of editorship is fascinating.

Persona

Roberts is tall, lean, forceful, but gentle and kind. He has the ability to state his views simply and clearly. For example, he states that the time has come for everyone to "know your numbers," by which he means weight, blood pressure, and blood lipid "numbers." This simple statement implies his strong support for modifying risk factors to prevent atherosclerotic coronary heart disease.

What He Does

Roberts is a correlator. His skill in correlating pathologic data with clinical data creates a bridge between pathology and medicine. He has made pathology live for the cardiologist and internist. Relatively few individuals have had the impact Roberts has had in this important endeavor. He has studied many aspects of congenital heart disease, hypertensive heart disease, coronary heart disease, cardiomyopathy, valvular heart disease, including ruptured chordae tendineae, prosthetic valvular heart disease, infective endocarditis, pericardial disease, carcinoid heart disease, neoplastic heart disease, and sarcoid heart disease. He has correlated electrocardiographic and hemodynamic abnormalities with the pathologic findings.

Selected Publications

I reviewed the titles of his 920 publications with the idea that I would select several references that I could list in this manuscript to emphasize Roberts' contribution to our daily behavior. As I finished the review I had assigned myself, I gave up. There were too many references to list! So, I will leave this aspect of Roberts' contributions with this admonition: if you have questions about the heart and its diseases find out what Roberts has written on the subject.

A Tribute to Dr. Edgar Haber

MARSCHALL S. RUNGE, M.D., PH.D., CHRISTOPH BODE, M.D.,* CAM PATTERSON, M.D.

Department of Internal Medicine, Division of Cardiology, The University of Texas Medical Branch, Galveston, Texas, USA, and
*Kardiologie, Medizinische Klinik III der Universität Heidelberg, Heidelberg, Germany

Several elegant reviews of Dr. Edgar Haber's career and contributions have been published since his death from multiple myeloma on October 13, 1997 (Fig. 1). There is no doubt that cardiovascular medicine and science have lost a most influential leader of his time in these areas. Prior reviews[1, 2] have succinctly summarized his countless awards, academic honors, and achievements, and although some of these are mentioned here, our hope is to capture the essence of that which made him such a very special mentor for his many trainees.

Ed Haber was much like the fine wine and works of art that he studied and so enjoyed. As one came to know Ed, each successive layer offered insight into his intelligence, humanity, and personality. And just as with a fine wine or work of art, different individuals appreciated different aspects of the whole. As the three authors of this paper discussed our many fond memories of Ed, we came to the conclusion that each of us had a unique relationship with him, as we know many of his hundreds of trainees and professional colleagues and friends did as well.

The relationships that Edgar Haber fostered with his trainees, and the pleasure that he took in serving as their mentor, supporter, and confidant is truly distinctive. Of the many legacies he leaves, a very important one is the tradition of having Haber-trained fellows occupy many prestigious positions in cardiovascular medicine in the U.S. and abroad. During the past 30 years, more than 45 of his trainees became chairs, deans, and directors at many of the premier institutions in the U.S. and in eight countries on three different continents. Beginning in the late 1960s, the directors of cardiology divisions and departments of medicine at many of the nation's leading institutions trained at the Massachusetts General Hospital with Edgar Haber. To name only a few, this list includes leadership positions at Brigham and Women's Hospital; the Johns Hopkins Hospital; Massachusetts General Hospital; Stanford University; Texas Heart Institute; University of California Medical Schools at San Francisco and Los Angeles; University of Texas Medical Schools in Dallas (Southwestern), Houston, and Galveston; University of Virginia; and Vanderbilt University. In addition, there are approximately 65 full professors among the list of Haber trainees, many of whom occupy endowed chairs and have made major contributions to cardiovascular research. At least 60 associate and assistant professors count Edgar Haber as their mentor. A testament to the genuine affection that his trainees from more than 30 years of academic training felt toward him was evident on the occasion of his 65th birthday in February 1997. More than 150 former trainees, friends, and colleagues traveled to Boston for a scientific session, wrote and spoke from their hearts about their respect, admiration, and appreciation toward him and, together, contributed over $85,000 to establish the Edgar Haber Award of the American Heart Association.

So how did one person impact so many people in such a positive way? Clearly, Edgar Haber was an absolutely brilliant man, and a master at establishing truly novel directions in research and clinical medicine. He was equally able to put together talented groups of individuals to accomplish these tasks. However, it was his unique interest in continually pushing forward his own work and that of others in a highly supportive manner that distinguished Edgar Haber from others.

Because he was a private and reserved man who did not relish self-promotion, many of his trainees never knew of the scope of his intellectual accomplishments. These included pure intellectual ability—the fact that he made the highest scores possible on the Board examinations in Internal Medicine, for example. His creativity in basic science was embodied by the sentinel experiments that he conducted and that became the foundation for work leading to the award of the Nobel Prize in Chemistry to his mentor at the National Institutes of Health, Professor Christian Anfinsen. He had an unending drive to apply creatively the principles of basic science to the practice of medicine. For example, together with his wife, Carol, he developed the first versions of telemetry monitoring and he held 24 patents on commonly used diagnostic and therapeutic approaches for patients with cardiovascular diseases.

His administrative acumen and skills came close to equaling his scientific talents. He leaves many legacies in this regard. No single person was more important in integrating basic research with the study and treatment of cardiovascular diseases. His organization of the Cardiac Unit at the Massachusetts General Hospital into autonomously functioning units, including the cardiac catherization laboratory, the echocardiography laboratory, the heart station, and the electrophysiology laboratory, is a model that has stood the test of time and has been embraced by most U.S. medical insti-

FIG. 1 Edgar Haber, M.D., 1932–1997.

tutions. Indeed, even in today's world of evolving roles for physicians, administrators, and businessmen, his model persists. During his career, the treatment of cardiovascular diseases passed through infancy and adolescence. Edgar Haber can truly be considered one of the founding fathers of modern cardiovascular medicine.

While we have focused on addressing Edgar Haber as the scientist and cardiologist, his personal side is equally compelling. He was always careful to separate work from personal matters, and he would not infrequently remind us to do the same in our conversations when talk of science crept into occasions where it did not belong. Ed pursued his interests outside of medicine—art, music, travel, friends, and wine—with a passion that equaled his love of science, but the interest to which he gave his highest priority was his family. He was intensely proud of the accomplishments of his wife, Carol, and his sons Eben, Graham, and Justin. Whereas we infrequently

saw Ed in his role as family man and father, it is obvious from looking at the professional accomplishments of his children—and remembering Ed's enthusiasm in recounting these accomplishments—that this was a role he filled with his typical single-minded gusto and adeptness.

We have not yet examined precisely how Edgar Haber built the legacy that his trainees will now carry forward. There have been and will continue to be other brilliant men, but few who have had an impact on so many trainees. To paraphrase Dr. James T. Willerson's elegant description,[1] Edgar Haber's own very high standards, his encouragement and his style "made others do their best to emulate him."

His ability to motivate was due, in essence, to the way he made others feel about their work and themselves, which was somewhat different for each person. For the driven, it was to be more creative: for the creative, it was to be more driven. He influenced all to practice with integrity and excellence everything they did. He was always there, during and after training, whether by telephone or personal visit, or by answering his e-mail in the middle of the night. With all of his responsibilities and interests, and his hectic lifestyle, he made the effort to keep in touch with his trainees over the years, perhaps better than any of us did with him. If there are others who can combine keen intelligence with an innate ability to understand and motivate with warm compassion, these individuals are few indeed.

Each of us really misses being able to speak with Ed, or send him e-mail—usually overly long and complicated—only to receive his prompt reply, which not only distilled the critical components and solutions to our questions, but also gave a clear and thoughtful direction. He touched many as he touched each of us. He was unique. Although it is doubtful that any single person today will be able to recreate the influence of Edgar Haber on training cardiovascular scientists as this field enters middle age, we can, collectively, try to begin to fill his most elegant shoes.

References

1. Willerson JT, Edgar Haber MD: Innovative scientist, mentor, and leader in cardiovascular medicine. *Circulation* 1998;97:713–714
2. Dzau VJ, Re RN: In Memoriam: Edgar E. Haber, 1932–1997. *Hypertension* 1998;31:1–2

Charles Richard Conti

JAMIE BETH CONTI, M.D.

Division of Cardiology, University of Florida, Gainesville, Florida, USA

Life and Medical Career

Charles Richard Conti (Fig. 1) was born on October 26, 1934, in Bethlehem, Pennsylvania. He is a distinguished 1952 graduate from Central Catholic High School in Allentown, Pennsylvania, a Phi Beta Kappa graduate of Lehigh University in Pennsylvania, and a 1960 AOA graduate of The Johns Hopkins University School of Medicine. In 1957, he married his high school sweetheart, Ruth Ellen Wursta, with whom he subsequently had four children, Jill Ann, Jamie Beth, Jennifer Charle, and Charles Richard III.

Dr. Conti was an intern and assistant resident from 1960 to 1962 at Hopkins, and then served as a captain in the medical corps in the United States Army, including paratrooper training in 1963. The rigors of military training promoted a lifelong commitment to physical fitness and strenuous exercise. Dr. Conti then returned to Hopkins to complete his internal medicine residency and his fellowship in the Cardiovascular Division from 1965 to 1967. His achievements as an outstanding house officer and leader were recognized when he was asked to be Chief Resident of the Osler Medical Service in 1967.

It was at Hopkins that Dr. Conti developed his interest in coronary artery disease. His clinical, investigative, and teaching interests have remained primarily in the area of ischemic heart disease, for example, chronic and acute ischemia, coronary spasm, and silent myocardial ischemia. Coronary angiography was in its infancy during his training, allowing him and others of his generation to pioneer this field. He assumed responsibility as Medical Director of the Cardiovascular Diagnostic Laboratory and Wellcome Research Laboratory from 1968 to 1974. He remained on faculty until 1974, when he was recruited to the University of Florida as Chief of the Division of Cardiology.

At the age of 39, Dr. Conti became Professor of Medicine and Chief of Cardiology at the University of Florida. The weather in Florida allowed him to pursue his passion for physical fitness year round. He and his wife both became marathon runners, doing well in many local marathons in their age category. Dr. Conti completed both the Boston and New York Marathons more than once. He was commonly seen running on Florida backroads, either with Ruth or his longtime friends and colleagues, Richard Panush and Carl J. Pepine.

When Dr. Conti arrived in Florida, the program consisted of five other attending physicians and four fellows. Under his leadership, the University of Florida Division of Cardiovascular Medicine grew to be a nationally and internationally recognized center of excellence in research and training. Throughout his career, Dr. Conti has influenced more cardiovascular fellows, medical residents, and medical students than can be counted. His insistence upon excellence in teaching, caring for patients, professional responsibility and deportment is well known. No male fellow, resident, or medical student rounded with Dr. Conti more than once without a tie; the stories of those who showed up for rounds shabbily dressed or with running shoes are legendary.

Dr. Conti's mission has always been one of teaching and effective communication. "If it's not written down, it didn't happen" aptly describes his view of patient care as well as scholarly endeavor. He was a stickler for documentation long before Medicare became involved in medical chart reviews. His encouragement to "write it down" has led to untold publications by colleagues and fellows. Dr. Conti's own career as a writer can only be described as prolific. He is the author or coauthor of over 600 scientific papers, book chapters, and abstracts, has edited five books and written two. His accomplishments include physiologic research in myocardial ischemia; organizing the National Heart Lung and Blood Institutes (NHLBI) National Cooperative Randomized Trial of Medical versus Surgical Therapy for Unstable Angina; monthly editorials in *Clinical Cardiology*, of which he has been Editor-in-Chief since 1988; and his own textbook of basic cardiology for housestaff.[1]

He is extraordinarily active at the national and international levels in organized cardiology. His service to the American College of Cardiology (ACC) is extensive, including a year as the President. He has served as chair on many of the ACC's committees, including the Education Committee for Extramural Programs, the Educational Program Committee, the Grant Review Committee, the Board of Trustees, and the Executive Committee. As chairman of the Self Study Education Materials Committee, he was responsible for the development of the ACC Self Assessment Program (ACCSAP). Most recently, he successfully completed a national search and is now Editor-in-Chief of *ACCEL*, the continuing medical education audio journal of the ACC.

Fig. 1   Charles Richard Conti, M.D.

His national service included time spent as the Chairman of the first national randomized prospective trial of medical versus surgical intervention in patients with unstable angina pectoris in 1972 (NHLBI), and as Chairman for ACIP (Asymptomatic Ischemia Pilot) (NHLBI), a trial comparing medical therapy with revascularization in patients with stable angina. He has served on the Subspecialty Board of Cardiovascular Diseases of the American Board of Internal Medicine (ABIM) as well as on the Cardiology Advisory Committee of the National Heart Lung and Blood Institutes. He has been or is currently on multiple editorial boards, including the *American Journal of Cardiology*, the *American Heart Journal*, *Circulation*, *Journal of the American College of Cardiology*, the *European Heart Journal*, and many other national and international journals.

Dr. Conti's participation in professional societies is equally impressive. He is a member of Phi Beta Kappa, the Johns Hopkins Medical and Surgical Society, Alpha Omega Alpha, the American Heart Association, the Southern Society of Clinical Investigation, and a Master of the American College of Cardiology, to name only a few. His career excellence has been honored by elected membership to many other societies, including the Association of University Cardiologists, the Association of Professors of Cardiology, the British Cardiac Society, the American Clinical and Climatological Association, the French Cardiac Society, The Interamerican Society of Cardiology, the European Society of Cardiology as a Founding Fellow, the Dominican Society of Cardiology, the Southern Africa Cardiac Society, the South African College of Physicians, the Johns Hopkins University Society of Scholars, the Venezuelan Cardiac Society, and finally as Docteur Honoris Causa from the Université de Marseilles in June 2000.

His advocacy for interaction with European and other international colleagues was honored by the American College of Cardiology when he was named the first Liaison to the European Society of Cardiology. Dr. Conti has always as-

pired to include these international colleagues in his writing, committee work, research, and friendships. His ongoing friendships with many of the most distinguished European and other international cardiologists has led to a sense of community in the international cardiovascular world and has lent itself to important collaboration on issues such as myocardial infarction, silent ischemia, and so forth. His friendship with these cardiologists extends beyond the professional arena. Many have been to his home as often as he has been to theirs.

Perhaps the greatest legacy Dr. Conti provides his many students is pride in being the best one can be in whatever endeavor one chooses. He is a perfectionist, but emphasizes to those around him that all he expects is their best effort. His natural charm and humor encourages each individual with whom he has contact to excel at what he or she does. To be fair, fear is also a great motivator. Those who have experienced his disapproval can vouch that it is not a position they want to be in again anytime soon!

In 1998, Dr. Conti stepped down as Chief of Cardiology at the University of Florida after serving as Chief for 24 years, one of the longest tenures of any acting Chief of Cardiology in the United States. Although no longer the administrative chief, he remains a leader of the division, providing direction to many of the faculty and fellows that came to the University of Florida specifically to work and train with him. He remains incredibly active, attending approximately 10 months/year on either inpatient or consultative services and continuously in the Ambulatory Cardiology Section that he directs. He remains very active in the American College of Cardiology and served as Editor-in-Chief of Educational Highlights; Editor-in-Chief of the American College of Cardiology Self Assessment Program (ACCSAP 2000); and is currently Editor-in-Chief of the international journal, *Clinical Cardiology,* and of the ACC Audio Journal *ACCEL.* He holds an endowed chair entitled "Palm Beach Heart Association Eminent Scholar" (Clinical Cardiology), Professor of Medicine, Adjunct Professor of Physiology at the University of Florida.

Despite these responsibilities, he finds time to pursue activities that he enjoys, which include teaching, taking care of patients, spending time with his family, and golf, definitely not in that order! He still jogs thirty minutes each day, and he golfs, lifts weights, and fast walks with his family. His five grandchildren require an inordinate amount of his attention. Four of them are currently under five years old and keep him and Ruth quite busy on evenings, weekends, and holidays.

On a personal note, my father has guided me through life with unerring good sense and sound advice. He has always been available to me for the smallest of problems, be they patient related, administrative, or personal. He is a father of whom I am extraordinarily proud. Very few people are blessed with the unique opportunity to train under and then work as a colleague with their father. He has been my mentor, my teacher, and my role model. Knowing he is just down the hall makes work a pleasure. People ask me daily if I'm "following in my father's footsteps." I hope so.

The following quotation from Dr. Conti's high school annual says it all:

They wondered and wondered and still
The wonder grew
How one small head could carry
All it knew.
                              —Oliver Goldsmith

This aptly describes Dick Conti whose seriousness in study is reflected in his position as president of the National Honor Society. Popular and ambitious, CCHS's school treasurer takes active part in the Science, French, and Key clubs, and plays shortstop on the baseball team. Lehigh's Pre-Med course beckons to Dick.

His wide circle of friends testifies that Dick's genial manner will carry him far along on the way of success.*

Reference

1.   Conti CR: *Introduction to Clinical Cardiology*, pp. 1–288. New York: Raven Press, 1991

---

*Source: *The Seneschal*, May 28, 1952, vol. 13, no. 8, p. 2; Central Catholic High School, Allentown, Penna.

Pavlos K. Toutouzas

MICHAEL B. GRAVANIS, M.D.

Department of Pathology and Cardiology, Emory University School of Medicine, Atlanta, Georgia, USA

Pavlos K. Toutouzas (Fig. 1) was born in Thebes, Greece, in 1935. Thebes, which is located about 80 km northwest of Athens, was a major city and power of ancient Greece. In those times it was the seat of the legendary King Oedipus and the locale of most of the ancient Greek tragedies, notably Aeschylus' *Seven Against Thebes*, and Sophocles' *Oedipus the King* and *Antigone*.

Pavlos grew up in a traditional large, rural Greek family that included seven children. Both his primary and secondary education were completed in the city of Thebes. Although he showed an interest in music from early childhood, he chose to pursue a medical career after graduation from high school. After successful entrance exams in 1952, he enrolled in the Medical School of the University of Athens, from which he graduated in 1959.

His combined training in internal medicine and subsequently cardiology took place at the University's Hippokration Hospital from 1959 to 1964. He remained in the hospital beyond 1964 and, until 1966, as a fellow in cardiology. In 1966, Pavlos traveled to Great Britain where he spent one year at the National Heart Hospital and two years at Hammersmith Hospital for postgraduate studies in cardiology as a research fellow. There his research activities were centered on apex impulse recording and vectorcardiographic studies, and the results of these studies were published in the *British Heart Journal* in 1969. Pavlos' mentor in England was Professor John Shillingford who, in Pavlos' own words, influenced his career in cardiology during those formative years.

Returning to Greece, Pavlos became a registrar in cardiology at Hippokration Hospital in 1969, assistant professor in 1972, and associate professor in 1976. In 1984, he was appointed Director of the Department of Cardiology at Hippokration Hospital in Athens, and on April 1989 was elected Professor and Chairman of the Department of Cardiology of the University of Athens.

He inherited a good but rather small department and, in a short time, made it into an excellent one, comparable with most western European cardiology departments. Along with capable associates, he organized nine divisions including interventional cardiology, echocardiography, hypertension, lipids laboratories, electrophysiology, biochemical laboratories, stress testing, an experimental laboratory, and a sophisticated computerized patient data bank. The latter became an extremely valuable tool for clinical research.

Since 1984, when Pavlos Toutouzas became director of the Cardiology Service at Hippokration Hospital, 133 fellows have received their cardiology training at Hippokration; this constitutes the largest cardiology training program in Greece. Pavlos' appointment to the chair of cardiology came at the most opportune time, a time when the academic department needed revitalization and new impetus. The young faculty he recruited needed direction in the application of their scientific skills to achieve a healthy balance among the eagerness of discovery, intellectual curiosity, and respect for patients' rights. Thus, new technological avenues could be explored without violating medical ethical standards. Pavlos Toutouzas indeed guided this group closely over the years, and he must be proud that some are independent investigators today.

Pavlos Toutouzas' curriculum vitae lists 282 publications in peer-reviewed journals, along with at least 124 additional contributions to the literature. He has edited, either alone or with others, eight textbooks ranging in scope from classic cardiology topics to more esoteric subjects such as *Functional Abnormalities of the Aorta*. Toutouzas' group has participated in 11 international cardiology trials since 1993.

Dr. Toutouzas is a member of the editorial board of several international cardiology journals, including the *European Heart Journal*, *Clinical Cardiology*, *Heart*, *The Non-invasive Heart Journal*, *Journal of International Cardiology*, and *Dialogues on Cardiovascular Medicine*. He is chief editor of the *Hellenic Cardiovascular Review*, the official journal of the Hellenic Cardiological Society, and chief editor of *Heart and Vessels*, the official publication of the Hellenic Heart Foundation. Pavlos has also served as president of the Hellenic Cardiological Society, the Antihypertension Society, and the Hellenic Echocardiographic Society.

Pavlos Toutouzas has been honored with many civic and professional awards, including the Commander of the Order of Honor by the President of the Hellenic Republic (1997), received an award from the Athenian Academy of Arts and Sciences (1987), an award from his native city of Thebes, and numerous other awards. In addition, he has been elected corresponding member of the Serbian Academy of Arts and Sciences.

Cardiology has been fortunate to have in its midst men and women of many talents, backgrounds, and personalities. I can say without hesitation that Pavlos Toutouzas has demonstrated over the last two decades that he is multitalented. Besides be-

FIG. 1   Pavlos K. Toutouzas.

ing an excellent clinician, he has revealed exceptional leadership and organizational skills, and the ability to motivate young physicians to excel and philanthropists to support the humanitarian goal of improving public health. In this regard, Pavlos has made, in the opinion of many, his major contribution through the Hellenic Heart Foundation (HHF).

The Foundation was created in 1991 and Pavlos was a founding member. Since its inception he has been its Vice-President and General Director.

The cardinal purpose of the HHF has been to inform the public about heart disease and, most important, its prevention. In this regard, the HHF publishes five popularized journals, some of which have been adopted by the Ministry of Education for high school students. In a number of these publications the risks of smoking, so prevalent in Greek society, are particularly stressed.

The Foundation is a member of the European Heart Network. In conjunction with the Network, it has successfully synchronized its educational activities throughout Europe in order to reach greater segments of the public.

HHF has established "Fidipides," a program named after the soldier who ran from Marathon in 490 B.C. to announce to the Athenians the victory against the Persians. This program addresses issues of congenital heart disease and the risk of sudden death in young athletes.

Through the electronic or printed media, the HHF has organized educational programs, published pamphlets, or scheduled lectures by the 300 medical advisors of the Foundation in public schools, municipalities, the Army, churches, and other organizations. These activities have provided invaluable public service by heightening awareness of the risks associated with heart disease.

Furthermore, since its inception, the HHF has funded over 30 scholarships for fellows in cardiology to enable them to continue their studies either in Greece or abroad.

A current ambitious goal of the HHF is to establish a research center for cardiovascular disease in a location near the city of Athens. The funds for such a worthy endeavor have been primarily donated by public-minded individuals. It will not be an overstatement to say that the heart and the driving force of all the activities of the HHF, since its inception, has been Pavlos Toutouzas, who has dedicated an enormous amount of time and effort to the success of the institution.

Anyone who knows Pavlos Toutouzas appreciates his pride in and dedication to his family. He met Eleni, his wife, at a social event in 1969, and after a relatively short courtship they were married in 1970. Eleni is a constant source of support for Pavlos, giving credence to the proverbial saying that "behind every successful man there is a woman." The Toutouzas have three children, two sons and a daughter. One of the sons, Constantine, is a physician. He has followed in his father's footsteps, pursuing cardiology training.

In contrast to what happened to Pindar, the greatest lyric poet of ancient Greece (522 B.C.), who was fined 1,000 drachmas by the authorities of his native Thebes for praising the rival city of Athens ("Thou famous Athens, divine city; shining, violet-wreathed, song inspiring pillar of Greece"), Pavlos Toutouzas has been honored by his native city of Thebes in spite of his lifelong service and dedication to Athenian institutions such as the University of Athens, the Hippokration Hospital and, above all, the Hellenic Heart Foundation.

Guy Fontaine: A Pioneer in Electrophysiology

FRANK I. MARCUS, M.D.

Section of Cardiology, The University of Arizona, University Heart Center, Tucson, Arizona, USA

Guy Fontaine (Fig. 1) was born in the city of Corbeil Essonnes, a suburb of Paris. He is the son of a bank worker who was responsible for the department of international affairs. His primary school was in the city of Bordeaux, in a Loyola institution, and he moved to the secondary school at the Lycée Montesquieu in Bordeaux and then moved to Paris. During World War II he lived in the city of Orleans at the time his father was a prisoner of war. After the end of World War II he entered secondary school in Paris.

Dr. Fontaine is the epitome of the international scientist. When one tries to locate him, it is as likely that he is lecturing in Japan, Brazil, Greece, or in the United States, as it is to find him working at his office at the Hôpital Jean Rostand, Ivry, France, where he is co-director of the University Department of Clinical Electrophysiology.

For the past 30 years he has continuously been expanding the frontiers of electrophysiology. His training in electrical engineering, together with his medical degree, was the perfect background to enable him to contribute to this field when he first started his career in the 1960s, a time of rapid development in pacemaker technology. In 1966, he received his doctoral degree for his work entitled "Contributions of Electrical Stimulation to the Human Heart." He then used his knowledge of electrical phenomena to make significant advances in pacemaker technology. He was among the first to implant permanent pacemakers using intracardiac leads in Paris in May 1967. His expertise in this area resulted in his receiving referrals of patients with difficult arrhythmia problems from Europe and abroad. In 1968, he joined the cardiology staff at the Hôpital de la Salpetrière in Paris in the service of Professor Jean Facquet. In 1976, he published *The Essentials of Cardiac Pacing*, co-authored by his mentors and colleagues, Professors Y. Grosgogeat and J.J. Welti. This work was translated from French into English, German, and Spanish. Together with his talented and thoughtful surgical colleague, Dr. G. Guiraudon, Dr. Fontaine and colleagues were the first Europeans to perform successful surgical treatment of an accessory pathway. Patients with difficult arrhythmia problems, both supraventricular and ventricular, were referred to the group at La Salpetrière hospital, and later to Hôpital Jean Rostand where Dr. Fontaine relocated. Often these patients were unresponsive to or intolerant of antiarrhythmic drugs. Dr. Fontaine and his associate, Dr. Robert Frank, then perfected the technique of epicardial mapping, which permitted them

to obtain the first recordings of epicardial delayed potentials in humans. Using hand-held probes, Drs. Fontaine, Frank, and Guiraudon began to map the reentrant circuits in patients with ventricular tachycardia during surgery with the aim of interrupting the reentrant arrhythmia by a "simple ventriculotomy." It was during this experience that they discovered that some patients with sustained ventricular tachycardia had a peculiar condition characterized by fatty replacement of the free wall of the right ventricle, which was the site of origin of the tachycardia, whereas the left ventricle generally appeared normal. This led to the discovery of "arrhythmogenic right ventricular dysplasia," (ARVD) which resulted in the publication of some of the first clinical descriptions of this condition. Dr. Fontaine has continued to enhance our knowledge of this condition by many astute observations, including his discovery of delayed epicardial potentials on the surface electrocardiogram. Together with Dr. Fontaliran, these physicians found that patients with right ventricular dysplasia appear to be prone to an inflammatory process of unknown etiology involving the right and sometimes the left ventricular myocardium superimposed on the genetic background of ARVD. Recently, Dr. Fontaine made the important clinical observation that patients with right ventricular dysplasia have a parietal block which results in a QRS complex that has a longer duration in lead V_1, V_2, or V_3 compared with that in V_6. This should be of clinical value for screening or for assisting in verification of this condition. An exciting discovery by Dr. Fontaine in conjunction with Dr. Mallat and other colleagues is that there is evidence of apoptosis in right ventricular dysplasia that may provide insight into the pathogenesis of this inherited condition. He was instrumental in organizing and was President of the First International Symposium devoted to right ventricular dysplasia held in Paris in 1996. Since it is now known that this is a genetic disease, the problem of how to define the risk of sudden death or identification of this condition in family members has come to the forefront. This and other considerations have brought Dr. Fontaine to initiate a registry of right ventricular dysplasia with the International Society and Federation of Cardiology (ISFC) and the working group of the European Society of Cardiology including Drs. McKenna in London, Wichter in Germany, and Corrado in Italy, as well as Dr. Marcus of the United States.

Dr. Fontaine also did extensive research to help understand ablation using direct current energy. This culminated in his

Fig. 1   Guy Fontaine, M.D.

being awarded a doctoral degree in science from the 11th faculty in Paris in 1991. The title of his thesis was "Physical, Biophysical and Electrophysiological Effects of Fulguration: Application to the Treatment of Cardiac Arrhythmias."

Dr. Fontaine has always stressed international cooperation in medicine. He realized that the traditional French policy of insisting that congresses in France had to be conducted in French impeded this goal. In 1985, he organized an international symposium in Paris on the topic of fulguration and lasers in cardiac arrhythmias. This was one of the first medical scientific meetings in Paris conducted entirely in English—a revolutionary development at that time.

He is frequently sought for his expertise in catheter ablation of arrhythmias, especially for ventricular tachycardia, and has participated as a consultant on this procedure in a number of laboratories in the United States and elsewhere. He is also sought after as a lecturer and is a prodigious worker. When he is at home in Paris, it is routine for him to be working on a manuscript or at his desktop computer until 11:00 P.M. daily or on weekends. He is the author of 739 scientific articles and abstracts, of which 364 have been published in English. He is the author of five books on different subjects in electrophysiology. The world of technology has not left Dr. Fontaine behind. He is seldom seen without his laptop computer. He has learned dBase programming language and is currently using his computer skills for statistical analysis of his data.

Dr. Fontaine is fortunate to have a devoted wife, Ilfat, who is a practicing psychiatrist in Paris, and four children who are accomplished in their own ways. His eldest daughter has a degree in business management; another daughter is a medical student in Paris. His youngest daughter is applying to medical school. His son, who is a computer expert, is assisting his father in developing computer programs for the right ventricular dysplasia registry.

Dr. Fontaine truly exemplifies the scientist who has an international view and scope. His contributions continue because he is always looking ahead and applying whatever technology is needed to answer difficult questions.

Thomas Woodward Smith

ROMAN W. DESANCTIS, M.D.

Cardiac Unit, Massachusetts General Hospital, and Harvard Medical School, Boston, Massachusetts, USA

The cardiological world lost one of its giants with the death of Dr. Thomas W. Smith on March 23, 1997. He was 61 years old.

A native of Akron, Ohio, Dr. Smith obtained his undergraduate education at Harvard University, graduating cum laude in 1958. After college he served for three years as a line officer in the United States Navy. He was stationed on a destroyer, and it was during this time that he was exposed to asbestos, which in later years caused the mesothelioma that ultimately claimed his life.

He returned from the Navy to enter Harvard Medical School, graduating magna cum laude in 1965. He completed his internship, residency, and fellowship training at the Massachusetts General Hospital (MGH), joining the staff of that institution in 1969. In 1974 he was selected by Dr. Eugene Braunwald to become Chief of the Cardiovascular Division at the Peter Bent Brigham Hospital (now Brigham and Women's Hospital), a position that he held until his death. He was also Professor of Medicine, jointly at Harvard Medical School and in the combined Harvard-MIT Division of Health Sciences and Technology.

In 1967, Dr. Smith joined the laboratory of Dr. Edgar Haber at the MGH, initiating a distinguished career in basic and clinical investigation that continued throughout his lifetime. It was there that he developed an enduring love affair with the digitalis glycosides. He was undoubtedly the leading investigator in the field of digitalis in the last half of this century. He even possessed an original edition of William Withering's historic treatise on the foxglove!

In a medical classic, Dr. Smith reported in 1970 with Haber and Butler the determination of serum digoxin concentrations using a radioimmunoassay.[1] This measurement is now used worldwide in common clinical practice and has been largely responsible for a marked reduction in the incidence of digitalis toxicity, as well as helping enormously in the day-to-day management of patients taking digoxin.

This seminal work led to the development of binding antibodies to the digitalis glycosides for use in life-threatening digitalis toxicity. In 1976, he and his colleagues reported the reversal of nearly fatal digitalis toxicity using the Fab fragment of the antibodies against digitalis.[2] This compound (Digibind®) is now available for clinical use and has been responsible for reversing many cases of severe, potentially lethal glycoside toxicity.

From these investigations, Dr. Smith moved on with his colleagues to a study of the cellular mechanisms of the action of digitalis, using cultured chick myocytes.[3] In recent years, Dr. Smith was involved in basic molecular studies involving adrenergic and cholinergic signaling within the heart, and mechanisms of excitation-contraction coupling. He had recently turned his attention to the action of endothelial compounds—especially endothelin and nitric oxide—on cardiac cells.[4]

Dr. Smith was also one of the principal investigators of the "DIG" (Digitalis Investigation Group) study, which clarified the role of digoxin in congestive heart failure. This study, published one month before his death, showed that although digoxin did not improve overall survival, it reduced the rate of hospitalization in patients with heart failure.[5]

In all, Dr. Smith was the author or co-author of approximately 240 original papers and 150 symposia, book chapters, and editorials. He also wrote and edited several books, including the modern classic on digitalis.[6]

Dr. Smith was a true academic triple threat. He was a superb teacher, and took pride—perhaps above all other of his professional accomplishments—in nurturing and mentoring scores of brilliant young trainees, many of whom now occupy major positions of leadership in cardiology throughout the world. In addition, he was a gifted clinician.

Dr. Smith was very much interested in medical education. He served as Chairman of the Curriculum Committee at Harvard Medical School and was one of the driving forces behind the so-called "New Pathway" curriculum, which has set the direction of medical education for the next century. He served as President of the Association of University Cardiologists and was very active in the American Heart Association, for which he chaired many important committees through the years, particularly those related to publications, research, and training.

He was widely sought after as a lecturer and visiting professor and received numerous prestigious awards, including a Merit award from the National Institutes of Health for his research achievements. He was a member of the Association of American Physicians and a Master of the American College of Physicians.

But Dr. Smith was also a worldly man, with many interests outside of medicine. He had a keen wit and a fine sense of humor and was a scintillating conversationalist because of his wide range of knowledge stemming from an insatiable

FIG. 1 Thomas Woodward Smith, M.D. (1936-1997). Photograph provided by Mrs. Smith.

curiosity about anything and everything. He loved literature, music, sports, good food, and good wine. And he had a special love for golf, spending as much time as his busy schedule would allow at the country club in pursuit of the little white ball.

I cannot end this profile on Dr. Smith without commenting on the dignity and courage with which he conducted himself during his illness. Despite the fact that he became steadily more frail and weak, both from his underlying disease and its treatment, he never complained or indulged in self-pity, nor did he allow anyone else to feel sorry for him. He was firmly in control of his department right up to the time of his death, living every day to its maximum, meeting every commitment. He was inspirational beyond expression.

One of Dr. Smith's great good fortunes in life was his marriage to his wife, Sherley, who was not only a wonderful mate and a pillar of strength during this illness, but also has pursued her own successful career as an educator. The Smiths have three children, Julie, Geoffrey, and Allison, and four grandchildren.

Shortly before his death, a special symposium in Dr. Smith's honor was held at the Brigham and Women's Hospital. At that time, The Thomas Smith Fellowship in Cardiovascular Research was established, which will honor appropriately and in perpetuity this great man who was taken from us much too soon.

References

1. Smith TW, Butler VP Jr, Haber E: Determination of therapeutic and toxic serum digoxin concentrations by radioimmunoassay. *N Engl J Med* 1969;281:1212–1216

2. Smith TW, Haber E, Yeatman L, Butler VP Jr: Reversal of advanced digoxin intoxication with Fab fragments of digoxin-specific antibodies. *N Engl J Med* 1976;294:797–800

3. Barry WH, Biedert S, Miura DS, Smith TW: Changes in cellular Na, K, and Ca contents, monovalent cation transport rate, and contractile state during washout of cardiac glycosides from cultured chick heart cells. *Circ Res* 1981;49:141–149

4. Gross WL, Bak MI, Ingwall JS, Arstall MA, Smith TW, Balligand J-L, Kelly RA: Nitric oxide inhibits creatine kinase and regulates rat heart contractile reserve. *Proc Natl Acad Sci USA* 1996;98: 5604–5609

5. The Dititalis Investigation Group: The effect of digoxin on mortality and morbidity in patients with heart failure. *N Engl J Med* 1997; 336:525–533

6. Smith TW (Ed.): Digitalis glycosides. Orlando: Greene & Stratton, Inc., 1986

D. John Parker

AUBREY LEATHAM, M.D.

The Heart Hospital, London, U.K.

The death of John Parker (Fig. 1), Consultant Cardiac Surgeon at St. George's Hospital London, at the age of 60 from a cerebral tumor, was a sad loss to British cardiology. His career demonstrated some important general principles that should be widely appreciated. Although aiming at cardiac surgery early on in his career, he completed his higher medical degrees before his surgical degrees and was President of the British Cardiac Society before he was elected President of the Cardiothoracic Surgeons. Even when practicing surgery he made a point of attending a weekly medical round and, when at St. George's, he seldom missed the weekly cardiac conference. Thus, knowledge of cardiac medicine not only gave him enormous insight into the natural history of cardiovascular problems so that his judgment on a course of action was greatly respected, but also enabled him to see ahead much more clearly than most physicians or surgeons and more than most administrators. Indeed, his wisdom and skill in planning for the future of cardiovascular services in the United Kingdom was as great a contribution to medicine as his skill in cardiac surgery.

John Parker was born in Harrow on February 1, 1938, and spent the first 10 years of his youth in Zimbabwe where he demonstrated his ability to combine academic excellence with leadership, becoming school captain, captain of the rugby team, and winning a scholarship to study medicine at the University of St. Andrew's (1956–1962). While there, he won prizes in almost every scientific subject, still finding time to become President of the Scottish Union of Students.

Parker's giant intellectual capacity, organizational ability, and energy were evident from the beginning. What made him unique was the combination of these qualities of natural leadership with kindness, fairness, intellectual honesty, and thoughtfulness for others.

Although he was interested in every aspect of medicine, Parker was naturally inclined to surgery. After an academic appointment at St. Andrew's and general surgical appointments in Dundee and six months of cardiology at the Victoria Infirmary in Glasgow, he settled on cardiothoracic surgery. He became Registrar and later Senior Registrar at the Brompton Hospital, National Heart and London Chest Hospitals (1968–1972). This included a very stimulating year at the University of Alabama with John Kirklin, generally regarded as the world's foremost cardiac surgeon at that time. The two Johns developed great mutual respect while sharing their main interest in research and developing safe intracardiac surgery and, in particular at that time, valve replacement. The writer first met John and Niki Parker while visiting John Kirklin.

When John Parker returned to the National Heart Hospital as Senior Lecturer he immediately demonstrated his excellent preoperative assessment and postoperative care: his surgical results equaled those of his more experienced colleagues. He had a broad view of medicine and believed in the integration of the cardiologists with the cardiac surgeons, which included undertaking ward rounds with his cardiologist colleagues. In 1975, a surgical vacancy was advertised at St. George's, soon to move from Hyde Park Corner to Tooting and to become the only teaching hospital in the South West Region. Those aware of Parker's ability persuaded him to apply to St. George's Hospital, where he was appointed Consultant Cardiothoracic Surgeon. With its expansion after the move to Tooting, St. George's became one of the leading centers for cardiac surgery in Europe.

One main reason for the success of St. George's was the remarkable symbiosis that Parker helped to establish between medicine and cardiac surgery. A unique feature of John Parker's prowess was his interest in cardiac medicine as well as surgery. This started with his obtaining the MRCP in 1966 (before his FRCS), and his FRCP came in 1984. It was no surprise when he was elected President of the British Cardiac Society in 1993, the first surgeon to head this medical group. His performance for the physicians was outstanding, including suggesting, planning, and acquiring the Society's home in Fitzroy Square. He was appointed President of the Society of Cardiothoracic Surgeons in 1998.

John Parker's interest in basic research in the early days (e.g., changes in the lungs during coronary bypass surgery) was superceded by his awareness of the practical importance of assessing the values of various medical and surgical procedures, and of long-term planning. Not only was he in the Chair or a valued member of every important long-term planning committee at St. George's Hospital, but at the national level he was concerned with the Randomised Intervention Treatment of Angina (RITA) trials, comparing angioplasty with surgical and medical treatment of coronary disease, the Read Centre on coding and terms for cardiology and cardiothoracic surgery, the National Health Service Casemix Office for assessing health resources and group developments for

FIG. 1   D. John Parker (1938–1997).

cardiology and cardiothoracic surgery, and the Clinical Standards Advisory Group, producing a report on access to and availability of coronary artery bypass graft and coronary angioplasty.

Parker was much sought after for independent reviews, such as the introduction of the external market and its effect on the organization and management of cardiology at Guy's Hospital, the report on the utilization of resources for cardiac surgery at the Freeman Hospital, Newcastle, and the review of adult cardiac and cardiothoracic services in the North West Region for the NHS Executive North West. He was Chairman of the Working Group on Cardiovascular Surgery for the European Society of Cardiology and President of the Cardiothoracic Section of the Royal Society of Medicine from 1993 to 1995.

His awards were many and included his appointment as Hunterian Professor of the Royal College of Surgeons in 1972 and the Clement Price Thomas Award for recognition of outstanding contributions to cardiac surgery in 1992. Finally, his CBE in 1997 was enthusiastically welcomed by his colleagues as a just recognition of a lifetime of prodigious and outstandingly successful service to medicine.

John Parker was a shy and modest man and never sought recognition for his professional efforts. He recognized the value of the contribution of every member of his team and sought to involve each of them. He was almost continuously available and always invaluable for surgical emergencies. It is amazing that he found time to indulge his passion for sailing. This was a challenging leisure activity, planned and organized to visit interesting places with good restaurants as well as enjoying the variety of sailing on the way—always safely because of careful forethought. On no occasion did he have to make use of the Royal National Lifeboat Institution, of which he was a valued member of their Medical and Survival Committee.

His family was very important to him, and this was most evident in the last year of his life. His stoical and realistic acceptance of a bad prognosis and his capacity to undertake advisory and organizational work was quite incredible and, in the writer's opinion, nobody could have given a better example. The life and work of John Parker have inspired his colleagues and will always be remembered.

Dennis V. Cokkinos

MICHAEL B. GRAVANIS, M.D.

Department Pathology and Cardiology, Emory University School of Medicine, Atlanta, Georgia, USA

Dennis Cokkinos (Fig. 1) was born in Thessaloniki, Greece, on November 18, 1938, where his father, a high-ranking cavalry officer in the Greek army, was assigned at the time. Dennis proudly says that although he was born in Northern Greece, his parents registered the newborn son in Athens and thus he is a full-fledged Athenian! Who said that the wars between the Greek states are over?

Dennis's primary and secondary education was completed at the "Athens College," a very reputable private institution. After graduation in 1957, in selecting a professional career, Dennis was not influenced by his father, then a General in the Greek army. However, his mother's brother, Dr. Gardikas, a physician who later became a distinguished professor of internal medicine at the University of Athens, had more influence and encouraged young Dennis to pursue a medical career.

After successful entrance exams in 1957, Dennis enrolled in the Medical School of the University of Athens and graduated summa cum laude in 1963. After graduation, from 1965 to 1967, he had one year of internship and two years of internal medicine residency at Evangelismos Hospital in Athens. This period also coincided with his service to the Greek army as second lieutenant.

In 1966, Dennis married Vana Christodulou, also a physician, who later specialized in laboratory hematology. In spite of the couple's busy professional lives, they managed to raise three bright sons, all of whom followed in their parents' footsteps, one becoming a cardiologist, another a radiologist, and the youngest pursuing a career in internal medicine. Vana comes from a long line of physicians (grandfather, father, and sister). When you sit at the dinner table with the Cokkinos family and relatives, you have the distinct feeling that you are participating in a multispecialty symposium. However, the conversation very often is centered on the arts, including painting, theater, and music. Vana is an accomplished essayist and novelist. Dennis writes a poem or two during his limited spare time.

Dennis reaffirmed his desire to become a cardiologist after a short cardiology course at the British Heart Institute in London in June 1967. From then on, cardiology became a calling and a commitment that has lasted throughout his professional career.

The newly wedded couple came to Houston, Texas, for additional postgraduate training where Dennis took an additional year of internal medicine (1967–1968) at Baylor University, and subsequently two years of cardiology fellowship at St. Luke's Hospital and Texas Heart Institute from 1968 to 1970. He is a diplomat of the American Boards of Internal Medicine and Cardiovascular Medicine.

Dennis's affiliation with the Texas Heart Institute has remained strong over the years with extended visits to the Institute as a Special Scholar in 1981, 1982, and 1983, and short annual visits since then. During his training at St. Luke's Hospital, he began a special friendship with his mentor, Robert Leachman, which lasted until Leachman's untimely death.

Returning to Greece, Dennis served as attending physician and cardiology registrar in three hospitals, namely, King Paul Hospital, Corinth State Hospital, and Evangelismos Medical Center in Athens. However, the position that gave him the chance to demonstrate his organizational skills and unquestionable leadership was his appointment in 1978 as Chief of Cardiology at Tzanio Hospital in Piraeus, Greece, where he remained until 1993. Before 1978, this hospital had had no training program in cardiology, and by 1993 it was ranked among the best three in Greece. While still at Tzanio Hospital, Dennis was elected Associate Professor of Cardiology at the University of Athens in 1990 and was promoted to full professor in 1998.

A new challenge arose when he was asked to get involved in the planning of the Onassis Cardiac Surgery Center. Later he was offered the directorship of one of the two Departments of Cardiology at the center. The legacy of the late Aristotle Onassis was to establish a center that would provide quality cardiology and cardiac surgery care to Greek patients at home rather than requiring travel abroad. Eight years later one can safely state that indeed the original goal of the Onassis Center has been accomplished to a significant degree. Apart from a very heavy load of cardiologic interventions, the Onassis Center ranks among the first 10 in scientific output annually in Europe.

Dennis Cokkinos has been very active at the national and international levels of organized cardiology. He was elected President of the Hellenic Cardiological Society (1989–1990), Vice President of the European Society of Cardiology (1989–1990), and member of the Executive Scientific Council of the same society. He is also a member, by invitation, of the British Cardiac Society and corresponding member of the French Cardiac Society, fellow of the American College of Cardiology, member of the American Heart Association (Hypertension Council), Chairman of the Working Group of the

FIG. 1 Dennis V. Cokkinos.

European Society of Cardiology on Exercise Physiology, and numerous other international and Hellenic societies. Dennis has been a visiting professor in many European and U.S. medical schools.

In the year 2000 he was appointed Clinical Professor of Cardiology at Emory University School of Medicine where he lectures a number of times during the academic year. Dennis has been a participant and often a member of the steering committee in several clinical trials under the auspices of the European Society of Cardiology.

In Dennis's curriculum vitae are listed over 125 articles in peer-reviewed journals, approximately 350 abstracts, and 17 chapters in cardiology books. His first book, *Cardiology Problems*, was published in 1975 in Athens; the second, *Cardiological Therapy*, in 1980; and the third, *Acute Myocardial Infarction*, in 1987. The first volume of the second edition of *Cardiological Therapy* was published in 2000, while the second volume appeared in 2001.

The main thrust of Dennis's research activities, in collaboration with scientists from the Department of Pharmacology of the University of Athens, has been the study of preconditioning in diseased hearts. This study is conducted on isolated rat hearts in a Langendorff preparation. Specifically, preconditioning is studied in cardiac hypertrophy, hyper- and hypothyroidism, and a number of other cardiac disorders. This laboratory has gathered a number of dedicated young scientists, resulting in numerous publications and four Ph.D. theses.

In the teaching arena, Dennis is superb. Regardless of whether it is a short lecture in a cardiology meeting or a formal lecture in a medical school classroom, or whether the lecture is given in Greek or English, he completely satisfies even the most demanding audience. His speech is incisive without being dogmatic, clear without repetition, and appropriately interlaced with subtle humor.

Dennis's clinical skills are very well known beyond the city of Athens, in fact, throughout Greece. High-ranking political figures, former prime ministers, and many personalities in the arts and sciences have sought his medical advice. Yet, over the years he generously donated his time to the least fortunate, the indigent patient.

However, Dennis's accomplishments extend beyond his contributions to medical literature, teaching, clinical research, and practice of cardiology. He is one star in the small constellation of cardiology stars of whom Greece can be proud.

From the mid to late 1980s, a small, select group of cardiologists, Dennis among them, were responsible for Greek cardiology catching up with the rest of the western world. These vintage cardiologists, all of whom trained at reputable cardiology centers around the world, returned to Greece and eventually were elevated to positions of leadership that enabled them to recruit junior associates, also trained in well-known centers abroad, who were eager to advance the frontiers of medicine.

This new cadre of cardiologists, regardless of whether they were in university centers or institutions such as the Onassis Center, began to participate in international meetings, as well as to invite experts in cardiology from abroad to participate in Greek cardiology congresses. This interplay stimulated small-scale research activities that grew larger over the years.

A strong testimony for the significant progress in Greek cardiology is that the number of abstracts submitted to meetings such as the European Society of Cardiology, American College of Cardiology, and American Heart Association by Greek cardiologists has increased exponentially in the last 10 years. At a recent meeting of the American College of Cardiology in Orlando, Florida (Spring 2001), Greece, a rather small country, was ninth in the number of accepted abstracts.

Although compared with other western societies the means for basic research in cardiology are relatively meager in Greece, the collaboration of cardiologists with basic scientists facilitated the advancement of diagnostic and therapeutic modalities. Thus, in an era of high technology medicine, institutions such as the Onassis Center, in which Dennis has a position of leadership, can take pride in the delivery of excellent medical care, research activities, and training programs, thanks to the high quality of its faculty.

Dennis has always recognized the value of the contributions of every member of his team and sought to involve each one of them. In his position, he has influenced many cardiology fellows and in more recent years numerous medical students. Dennis's natural leadership abilities, combined with his kindness, fairness, and thoughtfulness, have gained him respect and warm affection from his colleagues.

Andreas Roland Gruentzig, M.D.: The Teaching Genius*

J. WILLIS HURST, M.D.

Department of Medicine, Emory University School of Medicine, Atlanta, Georgia, USA

Andreas Gruentzig's name will forever be linked to the procedure he invented, percutaneous transluminal coronary angioplasty (PTCA) (Fig. 1). I, and many others, will write about his creativeness, courage, integrity, and scientific achievements. The purpose of this communication is to highlight his great teaching ability. The popularity of coronary angioplasty occurred because its inventor, Andreas Gruentzig, cared deeply for his patients and was obsessed with teaching the technique to those who wished to learn it.

Andreas Gruentzig joined the Department of Medicine of Emory University School of Medicine in 1980. I gave him one half of my office suite at Emory University Hospital so, because of his proximity, I observed him in his daily activities. I wish to report on some of my observations.

Physicians from the world at large flocked to talk with him. They often met in his office and walked with him to the cardiac catheterization laboratories which are located nearby. While in the catheterization laboratory, some of them would stand by his side near the patient and others would observe from the booth. They observed his remarkable skill, his kindness to patients, and witnessed, first-hand, his teaching ability.

He met with us at "morning report" at Emory University Hospital where about 20 people gathered. The group consisted of cardiology faculty, cardiology trainees, medical residents, and senior medical students. He breezed into the room with a smile. He listened. He usually waited to hear the opinions of others, but then would rise and walk to the "white board" where he would take a black magic marker and diagram the coronary arteries in such a way that his point was obvious. I suppose every cardiologist can diagram the coronary arteries, but no one can do it as he could. His diagrams were works of art. The lines, which were drawn with lightning speed, seemed extensions of his fingers. He was like Picasso drawing a single line as no one else could draw it. But more than that—the lines he drew, plus the words he said, led the viewer to understand.

Each year he organized two large postgraduate courses in an effort to teach angioplasty to anyone who wished to learn it. The courses began when he was in Zurich and were contin-

ued twice a year at Emory University in Atlanta. In all, he gave 14 courses, four in Zurich and ten at Emory. The courses grew increasingly popular until 300–500 people came to see him work. Almost all who attended were already skilled at performing coronary arteriography. But they saw him perform, innovator that he was. They witnessed his skill at dilating the coronary arteries. This was possible because he developed the television system that made it possible to transmit his performance in the catheterization laboratory in Emory University Hospital to the Woodruff Administration Building, where the audience was sitting. They viewed a huge television screen. During the course, he would often perform coronary angioplasties on 20–25 patients and, when a coronary obstruction was difficult to pass and relieve, the audience, which was a block away, groaned, but when the obstruction was eliminated the audience cheered. He, of course, was constantly talking to the patient and the remote audience. He, as usual, was in complete control of the moment. He, Dr. Spencer King, Dr. John Douglas, and invited speakers, such as Dr. Richard Myler and Dr. Simon Stertzer, often participated in the courses and took their turns at the live teaching of the procedure. When the course was over, Andreas would have a photograph made of the entire audience. This photograph was always made on the steps of the Woodruff Administration Building. Andreas directed the action like a motion picture director, often peering into the photographer's camera to be certain the scene was to his liking. There were no stragglers for this photograph; everyone wanted to be in it (Fig. 2).

His most important teaching was directly related to patients. He taught cardiology trainees as he performed coronary angioplasty (Fig. 1). The trainees who worked with him completed two to three years of cardiology fellowship and then worked a full year or more with him. The patient was always placed at ease with his comforting words and, in this setting, Gruentzig taught continuously.

He always insisted that the cardiology fellows assigned to him become involved in research. He believed that there were many unanswered questions that needed answers. He wanted the fellows he trained to be more than skilled technicians. So they prepared for and presented new data at the annual meetings of the American Heart Association and American College of Cardiology.

He lectured all over the world. He could not accept all of the invitations issued to him, even though he was mentally and physically able to arrive home from a trip during the ear-

---

Andreas Roland Gruentzig and his wife, Margaret Ann Thornton Gruentzig, died in a plane crash in Monroe County, Georgia, on October 27, 1985.

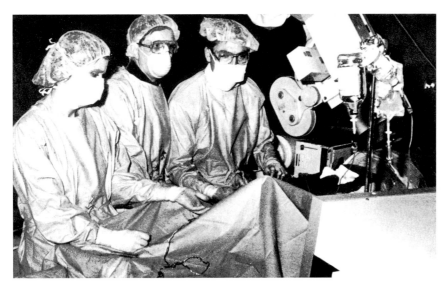

FIG. 1 Teaching, always teaching. Andreas Gruentzig, M.D. (right), Jay Hollman, M.D. (center), and Sally Deneen, R.T. (left).

ly morning and go to the hospital for work by 7:30 A.M. At the podium he was in charge. Even the largest room became quiet as the fascination of the audience grew. Each person in the room became intrigued by the "story" that the speaker unfolded. They were spellbound by his honesty and demeanor. He came through as creative but humble. He would emphasize the complications, which were few in number, as much as he emphasized the success of the procedure. He stated how much additional work had to be done. The paradox was that he was simultaneously coming through as being aggressive in what he believed in, but conservative in his approach to achieving it. The audience invariably detected his integrity and honesty. Therefore, they listened and remembered. He qualifies, I believe, as being a great lecturer.

FIG. 2 Photograph of the participants in the August 1981 course on Percutaneous Transluminal Coronary Angioplasty given at Emory University in Atlanta.

Panel discussions were his delight. They seemed to quicken his thought processes and enabled him to express himself in response to questions. For example, a nationally known expert who was participating with him on a panel discussion indicated that he preferred bypass surgery and not balloon dilatation for a tight lesion in the left anterior descending coronary artery. The nationally known expert later changed his mind because his own experience showed that Gruentzig's points were correct. He later told me that one of his regrets was that he never had a chance to tell Dr. Gruentzig that he had changed his mind, because the plane crash prevented him from doing so.

What a role model he was. The greatest stimulus to learning is the behavior of another person who exhibits noble attributes. Everyone who knew him realized he was unique. As each individual discovered his great attributes, he or she became a better person. This, I believe, was his greatest teaching achievement.

Auf wiedersehen, Andreas and Margaret Ann.

A. John Camm

BERNDT LÜDERITZ, M.D.

Department of Medicine/Cardiology, University of Bonn, Bonn, Germany

John Camm (Fig. 1) is an Englishman born in Lincolnshire in the north of England on January 11, 1947. At the age of eighteen he entered London University, where he obtained his baccalaureate degree with a physiology major. He went on to study medicine at Guy's Hospital Medical School, receiving his M.D. in 1971. Afterwards, he worked at Guy's Hospital for three years under the tutelage of cardiologist Edgar Sowton, one of the greats of the early days of pacing. Dr. Camm was his hands in 1973 and did several hundred pacemakers by himself with the help of a radiographer and a nurse. After leaving Guy's Hospital, Dr. Camm spent a year in Burlington, Vermont. In the U.S., Dr. Camm worked with cardiologist Art Levy in the field of electrophysiology and with E. Lepeschkin, a famous electrocardiologist who had worked with Frank Wilson and had married his daughter, Julie Wilson.

After his time in Vermont, Dr. Camm returned to London in 1975 to work at St. Bartholomew's Hospital, the oldest of the London hospitals, founded in 1123. At that time, Dr. R.A.E. Spurrell was in charge of St. Bartholomew's relatively small cardiac department. Dr. Spurrell had worked with Dr. Dirk Durrer and Dr. Hein J.J. Wellens as well as with several other pioneers in electrophysiology. Dr. Camm quickly rose in the ranks at St. Bartholomew's, eventually implementing electrophysiology services at the hospital. He assembled a team of very accomplished young physicians, including electrophysiologists David Ward and Antony Nathan. One of their research projects was the definition of the anatomical basis of Mahaim fibers; they were also one of the first groups involved in antitachycardia pacing.

Dr. Camm's doctoral thesis entitled "The Application of Pacemakers to Tachycardia Termination," was accepted by the University of London in 1981. He spent 12 years at the university, first as a Junior, then as a Wellcome Senior Lecturer, and finally as the Sir Ronald Bodley Scott Professor of Cardiovascular Medicine. In 1986, Professor Camm moved to London's St. George's Hospital Medical School as Professor of Clinical Cardiology. He was elected Chairman of Medicine in October 1990, a post rotated from in 1995.

Professor Camm has a broad range of professional interests. His speciality is cardiac arrhythmias, but he is also involved in clinical cardiac electrophysiology, cardiac pacemakers, and risk stratification, as well as postmyocardial infarction, heart failure, and patients with cardiomyopathy. He has also been involved in the development of large clinical trials. For example, he played an important role in the EMIAT (European Myocardial Infarction Amiodarone Trial) study and in the ill-fated SWORD (Survival With Oral D-Sotalol) study. Professor Camm has given over 1,000 lectures to international audiences, written more than 820 peer-reviewed papers, 181 book chapters, and appears on almost 1,200 abstracts (as of November 2002). He is a Fellow of The Royal College of Physicians, the American Heart Association, the American College of Cardiology, and the European Society of Cardiology (Founding Fellow). He is a member of the British Cardiac Society, the British Pacing and Electrophysiology Group, the North American Society of Pacing and Electrophysiology, and the Council of Geriatric Cardiology. Professor Camm is past Chairman of the European Working Group of Cardiac Arrhythmias, past President of the British Pacing and Electrophysiology Group, and past Council Member of the Royal College of Physicians of London. He is a former—and the first international—member of the Board of Trustees of the North American Society of Pacing and Electrophysiology and the International Cardiac Pacing and Electrophysiology Society (ICPES), and is President of the British Cardiac Society.

Professor Camm holds five editorships, including *Clinical Cardiology* (editor), *Cardiology in the Elderly* (founding editor), and *PACE* (senior editor); he also serves on a total of 26 editorial boards. In addition to editorial board duties, Professor Camm serves as journal reviewer for more than 15 leading journals of medicine and cardiology, including *Lancet* and *The New England Journal of Medicine*. He has been an abstract reviewer for many years.

Professor Camm is widely recognized for his research and teaching roles at the national and international levels. In 2001, the North American Society of Pacing and Electrophysiology (NASPE) awarded him the Distinguished Teacher Award.

Beginning in 1968, Professor Camm has received various prizes and honors, including the Honorary Fellowship of the Hong Kong College of Cardiology in 2000. Furthermore, he holds international honorary memberships of cardiac and pacing societies in Spain, Greece, Argentina, and Portugal. Professor Camm's resume includes nine visiting professorships in Canada, the U.S., and Hong Kong, and a remarkable number of named lectures, including the Norman Holter Lecture (International Society of Holter and Non-invasive

FIG. 1   Prof. A. John Camm.

Electrocardiography) in 1998, the Edgar Sowton Memorial Lecture (King's College Hospital), the Ronald W.F. Campbell Memorial Lecture (British Cardiac Society), and the Inaugural Lecture of the South African Heart Association "Antiarrhythmic Therapy in the Next Millennium" in 1999.

Professor Camm's brilliant career is marked by several national health service appointments since 1986; various honorary academic appointments from 1986 on; distinguished society memberships; membership in three guilds; 11 advisorships, including the Royal Automobile Club Medical Advisory Panel; a wide range of committee memberships, including the Ethics Committee and Grand Committees; and medical directorships and patronage in England and overseas.

Professor Camm is a trustee of six scientific organizations and a member of 23 task forces appointed by NASPE, ESC, AHA, ACC, and other scientific societies. Furthermore, he holds 10 positions in various Working Groups at the national and international levels.

Professor Camm is a worldwide renowned trialist and holds memberships in 18 multicenter study committees, including DIAMOND (Danish Investigation of Arrhythmias and Mortality on Dofetilide), ATRAMI (Autonomic Tone and Reflexes After Myocardial Infarction), ELITE II (Effects of Losartan in the Elderly), ALIVE (Azimilide Post-Infarct Survival Evaluation), and DAPHNE (Dronedarone Atrial Fibrillation Post Conversion Evaluation).

Steering committee positions in three registries, membership in four exclusive clubs, and four academic appointments as honorary lecturer, senior lecturer, and recognized teacher are among Professor Camm's achievements.

Professor Camm is involved in a multitude of professional activities. Among them are examiner in the United Kingdom and Canada; opponent at the public defense of a thesis in Sweden, the Netherlands, and Belgium; project reviewer and assessor for national and international councils; university promotions advisor; and a member of various professorial appointments committees.

Professor Camm's first paper as principal author, "The Irregular Heart Beat" (The *Chest, Heart and Stroke Journal* 1:14–23), was published in 1976. His most recent article, published in 2002, is entitled "The Design and Conduct of Human Studies to Detect and Quantify QT Interval Prolongation Induced by New Chemical Entities" (*Fundam Clin Pharmacol* 2002;16:141–145).

Professor Camm is recognized as one of the most accomplished exponents of teaching, scholarship, and research in cardiovascular medicine. During his illustrious career, he has trained undergraduate and graduate students all over the world. He has been instrumental in the training of postdoctoral fellows, clinical cardiologists, electrophysiologists, and investigators from Australia to North America. His legacy in cardiac arrhythmias is best seen in his students, who have established electrophysiology programs in a multitude of countries and medical centers worldwide. He is an indefatigable investigator and teacher, and is well known for his global interest in continuing clinical research in cardiac arrhythmias. He has been Visiting Professor and Examiner at major universities in the United Kingdom, the Middle East, and Asia, particularly Hong Kong. He is a highly sought-after speaker for his articulate and thoughtful analyses of complex subjects. In his scientific lectures, he has the flair for bringing together classical foundations with current concepts in a distinctive and witty oratorical style. Despite many administrative and organizational demands, he remains a committed educator and investigator; he is currently editing a major textbook entitled *Electrophysiological Disorders of the Heart*.

Last but not least, Dr. Camm's unique reputation becomes obvious at the annual congresses of the European Society of Cardiology: he is the only one permitted to give more than two lectures and to chair more than two scientific sessions at the same meeting.

Professor Camm lives in the south of London. His major hobbies are gemstones and British watercolors of the eighteenth and early nineteenth centuries. He is a member of the Royal Society of Medicine, the Oriental Club, and the Athenaeum.

AJC's 20 most important peer-reviewed publications selected by the author (from 822)

Camm AJ, Ward DE, Cory-Pearce R, Rees G, Spurrell RAJ: The successful cryosurgical treatment of paroxysmal ventricular tachycardia. *Chest* 1979;75:621–624

Camm AJ, Ward DE, Spurrell RAJ: Cryothermal mapping and cryoablation in the treatment of refractory cardiac arrhythmias. *Circulation* 1980;62:67–74

Camm AJ, Ward DE, Cory-Pearce R, Rees GM, Spurrell RAJ: Surgery for ventricular tachycardia. *Lancet* 1980;i: 579–579

Camm AJ, Evans KE, Ward DE, Martin A: The rhythm of the heart in active elderly subjects. *Am Heart J* 1980;99: 598–603

Camm AJ, Ward DE, Whitmarsh V: The acute cardiac electro-physiological effects of intravenous metoprolol. *Clin Cardiol* 1982;5:327–331

Saksena S, Camm AJ, Bilitch M, *et al.*: Clinical investigation of implantable antitachycardia devices: Report of the policy conference of the North American Society of Pacing and Electrophysiology. *J Am Coll Cardiol* 1987;10:225–229

Malik M, Camm AJ: Mechanism of Wenckebach periods—a hypothesis based on computer modelling experiments. *Am J Physiol* 1989;257:H1263–H1274

Malik M, Camm AJ: Heart rate variability. *Clin Cardiol* 1990;13:570–576

Camm AJ, Garratt CJ: Drug therapy: Adenosine and supra-ventricular tachycardia. *N Engl J Med* 1991;325:1621–1629

Saksena S, Camm AJ: Implantable defibrillators for preven-tion of sudden death. Technology at a medical and econom-ic crossroad. *Circulation* 1992;85 (6):2316–2321

Levy S, Camm AJ: An implantable atrial defibrillator. An im-possible dream? *Circulation* 1993;87:1769–1772

Murgatroyd FD, Camm AJ: Atrial arrhythmias. *Lancet* 1993;341:1317–1322

Waldo AL, Camm AJ, deRuyter H, *et al.*: Effect of d-sotalol on mortality in patients with left ventricular dysfunction af-ter recent and remote myocardial infarction. The SWORD Investigators. Survival With Oral d-Sotalol. *Lancet* 1996; 348:7–12

Grace AA, Camm AJ: Drug therapy: Quinidine. *N Engl J Med* 1998;338:35–45

Wellens HJJ, Lau CP, Lüderitz B, Akhtar M, Waldo AL, Camm AJ, Timmermans C, Tse HF, Jung W, Jordaens L, Ayers G, for the Metrix investigators: Atrioverter: An im-plantable device for the treatment of atrial fibrillation. *Circulation* 1998;98:1651–1656

Camm AJ, Janse MJ, Roden DM, Rosen MR, Cinca J, Cobbe SM: Congenital and acquired long QT syndrome. *Eur Heart J* 2000;21:1232–1237

Malik M, Camm AJ, Janse G, Julian DG, Frangin G, Schwartz PJ: Depressed heart rate variability identifies postinfarction patients who might benefit from prophylactic treatment with amiodarone: A substudy of EMIAT (The European Myocardial Infarct Amiodarone Trial). *J Amer Coll Cardiol* 2000;35:1263–1275

Camm AJ, and Members of the Sicilian Gambit: New ap-proaches to antiarrhythmic therapy, Part I. *Circulation* 2001;104:2865–2873

Camm AJ, and Members of the Sicilian Gambit: New ap-proaches to antiarrhythmic therapy, Part II. *Circulation* 2001;104:2994

Savelieva I, Paquette M, Dorian P, Lüderitz B, Camm AJ: Quality of life in patients with silent atrial fibrillation. *Heart* 2001;356:2052–2058

INDEX